American Slavery, American Imperialism

Slavery casts a long shadow over American history; despite the cataclysmic changes of the Civil War and emancipation, the United States carried antebellum notions of slavery into its imperial expansion at the turn of the twentieth century. African American, Chinese and other immigrant labourers were exploited in the name of domestic economic development, and overseas, local populations were made into colonial subjects of America. How did the United States deal with the paradox of presenting itself as a global power which abhorred slavery, while at the same time failing to deal with forced labour at home? Catherine Armstrong argues that this was done with rhetorical manoeuvres around the definition of slavery. Drawing primarily on representations of slavery in American print culture, this study charts how definitions and depictions of slavery both changed and stayed the same as the nation became a prominent actor on the world stage. In doing so, Armstrong challenges the idea that slavery is a merely historical problem, and shows its relevance in the contemporary world.

Catherine Armstrong is Senior Lecturer in American History at Loughborough University.

Slaveries since Emancipation

General Editors

Randall Miller, *St. Joseph's University*
Zoe Trodd, *University of Nottingham*

Slaveries since Emancipation publishes scholarship that links slavery's past to its present, consciously scanning history for lessons of relevance to contemporary abolitionism and that directly engages current issues of interest to activists by contextualizing them historically.

Also in this series:

Elizabeth Swanson and James Brewer Stewart, eds., *Human Bondage and Abolition: New Histories of Past and Present Slaveries*

R. J. M. Blackett, *The Captive's Quest for Freedom: Fugitive Slaves, the 1850 Fugitive Slave Law, and the Politics of Slavery*

Anna Mae Duane, ed., *Child Slavery before and after Emancipation: An Argument for Child-Centered Slavery Studies*

American Slavery, American Imperialism

US Perceptions of Global Servitude, 1870–1914

CATHERINE ARMSTRONG
Loughborough University

CAMBRIDGE
UNIVERSITY PRESS

CAMBRIDGE
UNIVERSITY PRESS

University Printing House, Cambridge CB2 8BS, United Kingdom

One Liberty Plaza, 20th Floor, New York, NY 10006, USA

477 Williamstown Road, Port Melbourne, VIC 3207, Australia

314–321, 3rd Floor, Plot 3, Splendor Forum, Jasola District Centre, New Delhi – 110025, India

79 Anson Road, #06–04/06, Singapore 079906

Cambridge University Press is part of the University of Cambridge.

It furthers the University's mission by disseminating knowledge in the pursuit of education, learning, and research at the highest international levels of excellence.

www.cambridge.org
Information on this title: www.cambridge.org/9781108477093
DOI: 10.1017/9781108663908

First published 2020

A catalogue record for this publication is available from the British Library.

ISBN 978-1-108-47709-3 Hardback

Contents

List of Figures — *page* vi
Acknowledgements — vii

Introduction — 1
1 A Rhetorical Continuum? How Representations of Antebellum Slavery Endure in Post-War Culture — 28
2 Global Contexts: How External Factors Drive US Perceptions of Slavery — 67
3 Othering the Slave Owner — 107
4 Othering the Enslaved — 147
5 Gender and the Rhetoric of Slavery — 185
6 Resistance and the Slavery Counter-Narrative — 225
Conclusion — 269

Bibliography — 276
Index — 286

Figures

1 'Slavery as it exists in England, Slavery as it exists in America', lithographic print by John Haven, printed Boston 1850. Library of Congress. *page* 38
2 'Couple at fireside: Possum am Sweet', photograph by Huestis Cook, 1900. © The Valentine, Richmond. 50
3 'The duty of great nations', chromolithographic print by Udo Keppler, 1899. Library of Congress. 71
4 'What the United States has fought for', cartoon by John T. McCutcheon, 1914. © Wisconsin Historical Society. 97
5 'Tibo Tip's fresh captives being sent into bondage', reproduction of wood engraving by James W. Buel, 1891. Library of Congress. 114
6 '*Uncle Tom's Cabin* – As it will be played if Johnson wins', front cover illustration in *Puck*, by Louis Glackens, 1910. Library of Congress. 209
7 'Nsala of Wala with remains of daughter', photograph by Alice Harris, 1904. © Anti-Slavery International. 234
8 'Slavery is dead?' print from wood engraving by Thomas Nast, illustration in *Harper's Weekly*, 1867. Library of Congress. 249
9 'Evolution of the African race', print, artist & publisher unknown. Nashville, c. 1910. Library of Congress. 262

Acknowledgements

Researching and writing this book was supported by many colleagues at Loughborough University, and beyond. During the early stages of this project, librarians and historians at the Rothermere American Institute and its Vere Harmsworth Library in Oxford were invaluable in their inspiration and reassurance. The Slaveries since Emancipation series editors, Professors Zoe Trodd and Randall M. Miller, have been extremely supportive and encouraging throughout the process, as have the editorial team at Cambridge University Press. As always, the greatest debt of gratitude must be paid to my parents, Maureen and Michael Armstrong, whose tireless enthusiasm for my writing, and comments on my strange turns of phrase, have made this a much better book. And to my husband, Michael Batchelor, without whose support none of this would have been possible, thank you.

Introduction

This book will examine the interplay of various factors that influenced American perceptions of slavery and other forms of unfree, coerced or forced labour in the period after the emancipation of slaves within its own borders. It argues that while, undoubtedly, the shadow of antebellum chattel slavery loomed large in the American imagination, as influential was the model of imperial antislavery practised by European powers, especially after the United States itself developed an overseas empire in the 1890s. However, representations of slavery were not only a battleground on a geopolitical level. They were also used to work out the significance of competing scientific racial ideas, and also became a way for more radical thinkers to express their distaste for such ideas, while proposing new and more broad approaches to labour problems. Abolitionists were far from simplistic humanitarians and often their approach to the problem of slavery was a pragmatic one, designed as much to maintain control and hegemonic order as to give equal rights and opportunities to the world's poorest. This was especially the case when imagining the sexual enslavement of women, as gender and race intersected to provide a potent rhetoric intended to reinforce patriarchal dominance. This period, and especially the early twentieth century, does provide a significant evolution in the ways that slaves and slavery were described and the United States' participation in international efforts to stop the phenomenon of slavery, and also increased endeavours to stamp out coercive labour practices within its own borders, reflected a foregrounding of more radical voices of resistance to the imperial standard.

Four themes are crucial to understanding slavery in this period: how global and local American concerns intersected; how the definition of slavery evolved; how the United States used slavery to mould its post-Civil War identity; how popular culture provides the historian with a unique vision of the American imagination.

GLOBAL AND LOCAL CONCERNS

For the United States, conceptualising slavery in the late nineteenth century almost always included a reference to their own antebellum chattel slave past. The nature of slavery framed and offered a point of comparison to discussion about slavery and forced labour in all other contexts, whether in the post-emancipation US itself, in American colonies or in the world more broadly. Since 1865, the transatlantic slave system and especially the role of English-speaking North America has also been foregrounded by scholars of slavery, leaving many non-experts with the impression that it was the only form of slavery. School and university curriculums also reinforce the notion that transatlantic slavery is the foremost, if not only, example of its kind. Partly this is due to the important self-expression in recent years of the African diaspora, and also to the availability of resources to study this era. The visible legacy and scars left by the slave era on United States society and culture are also crucial here. In the period immediately after emancipation, the United States struggled, and partially failed, to take account of its slave past. By negating its horrors with the mythologizing and romanticising of the Jim Crow era, the pre-war abolitionist narrative of the importance and power of free labour was minimised, and the opportunity was lost to make more sweeping labour reforms. This manipulation of the story of domestic slavery naturally impacted on the ways that the United States acted in the world in regards to slavery encountered elsewhere.

A transatlantic abolitionist alliance existed in the early part of the nineteenth century and this affected the ways that people on both sides of the Atlantic conceptualised slavery. Britain came to define itself as an abolitionist nation in this period, with its values and self-perception underpinned by religious and economic motives for ending slavery, and thus defining itself as a modern nation. Once the transatlantic slave trade had been legally abolished in 1807, and slavery abolished in British territories in 1834, British abolitionists turned their attention elsewhere within the Atlantic world. As Maurice Bric has argued, the World's Anti-Slavery convention of 1840, held in London, had universal, international aims, although almost all of the discussion focused on slavery in the Atlantic world.[1] Bric's work demonstrates that, although the fight against slavery was conceived as a global endeavour, it was US chattel slavery that drew the world's attention. Slavery in many locales was on the agenda at the World Convention, but it is the US context that dominated discussions then and so perhaps it is natural that scholars have since followed this lead and that the US itself found it so challenging to objectively consider slavery elsewhere. American abolitionists always had a problematic relationship with their Anglophone brothers and sisters, but shared the all-consuming goal of ending slavery within the United States. Other types of forced labour and coercive practices, wherever they existed, were rarely considered during this period, rather the chattel slavery of people of African descent was an all-consuming evil for abolitionists. When slavery was abolished after the American Civil War, the American abolition movement had little drive to reconvene and turn globally, as the British one did. Despite an interest in slavery and forced labour around the world, it was the transatlantic context which continued to draw British attention even after it had affected its own abolition in its colonial holdings. Richard Huzzey has shown that while *Uncle Tom's Cabin* created abolition fever among British readers, concerns over the aftermath of slavery in the Caribbean continued to occupy many in Britain. He sees the British and American conceptions of slavery and possibilities for its abolition as being distinct during the middle years of the nineteenth century.[2] I argue that this trend continued in the later period, with two separate traditions that are nonetheless of mutual influence.

As well as an ongoing concern with the Atlantic world, those thinking about slavery in the later nineteenth century also became increasingly focused on Africa and the diversity of its slavery. This had an important conceptual function because in the minds of both British and American readers, 'slavery' as a concept became something more than the chattel slavery found in the New World, and the 'slave trade' something more than the Atlantic Ocean crossing. The concept of Africans as protagonists and not merely victims of slavery was recognised by contemporaries and also grappled with by modern scholars and political leaders who

[1] Maurice Bric, 'Debating Slavery and Empire', in William Mulligan and Maurice Bric, eds., *A Global History of Anti-Slavery Politics in the Nineteenth Century* (Palgrave, 2013), p. 61.

[2] Richard Huzzey, *Freedom Burning: Anti-Slavery and Empire in Victorian Britain* (Cornell University Press, 2012), p. 22.

acknowledge that reparations are a thorny issue when it is impossible to differentiate between the heirs of perpetrators and the heirs of victims. Patrick Manning's work has shown that slavery within Africa in this period was incredibly diverse and that outsiders struggled to grasp its complexity. He sees two separate systems at work with two very different demographic drivers: the East African and West African slave systems.[3] This goes some way to explaining the early confusion and misunderstanding on the part of Americans about the East African slave system, and the desire of conservative American commentators to use global slavery to deflect attention from America's recent history of slavery.

British and American attention when examining slavery was not solely focused on the African continent. The British were increasingly becoming interested in the Ottoman Empire and their reporting of conditions of enslavement found there also caught the imagination of the American public. Yusuf Hakan Erdem has explored the ambivalence of British and American audiences who, on the one hand, railed against such backwards and cruel forms of oppression, but at the same time felt powerless to intervene because slavery was thought to be so embedded within Ottoman culture.[4] The nature of slavery, especially its distinctive features such as the military slaves of the *devshirme* and the female slavery of the Harem fascinated Western readers, who deployed the Orientalist gaze in their assessment of the perpetrators and victims of the system. The plight of female slaves in the Ottoman Empire, prominent in American newspapers in the 1870s, prefigured, by a generation, the later 'white slavery' panic which operated on both sides of the Atlantic, in which campaigners, often with a conservative agenda to reinforce the patriarchy by restricting the movement and freedoms of single women, especially in urban areas, highlighted or over exaggerated the plight of white women trafficked to or within the United States for use as prostitutes. Therefore, slavery and forced labour was a fact of life for many people around the globe – the Americas, Africa and the Middle East and elsewhere – but it was also a global phenomenon in another way. Matthew Hopper argues that slavery in the Indian Ocean world, as well as the Atlantic world, cannot be considered closed systems; both were influenced by global economic trends and developments. To imagine that Indian Ocean slavery was isolated and unique, timeless and static or of a peculiar nature due to the

[3] Patrick Manning, *Slavery and African Life: Occidental, Oriental and African Slave Trades* (Cambridge University Press, 1990), pp. 45, 175.

[4] Yusuf Hakan Erdem, *Slavery in the Ottoman Empire and Its Demise 1800–1909* (Macmillan, 1996), p. 72.

ethnic and religious origin of its perpetrators, is to fall into the trap of listening too closely to the nineteenth century travellers who elucidated it for readers on both sides of the Atlantic. Instead, the demand for labour on the plantations supplying tropical products, which were increasingly sought after in an age of global markets, worked in similar ways on slave trades and slaveries around the world.[5] However, this was also an era in which, increasingly, legal prohibition of the slave trade and slavery impacted on the ways that Americans imagined slaves and slave owners, as local, national and international law worked to fix, but ironically to make more malleable, the definition of slavery.

LEGAL PROHIBITION AND THE DEFINITION OF SLAVERY

The long history of slavery and abolition reveals the incredible diversity in the nature of slavery itself, but also in the ways that it was abolished in different contexts around the world. Abolition could be immediate, as in southern states of the United States, or gradual, as in some northern states, which, for example, began by freeing slaves of particular ages. Abolition was driven by a grass roots movement and resisted by slave-owning power brokers, as in the case of the transatlantic slave trade in Britain, or secured by the erosion of the control of slaves, who left their plantations and sought free labour employment of their own accord, as in the case of some regions of Brazil. A key factor in the abolitions of the nineteenth century onwards was the goal of legal prohibition. Sometimes this post-dated de facto freeing of slaves, but in many cases triggered it, imposing a change of practice on the ground. Legal prohibitions covered diverse jurisdictions, and were enacted on a local, regional, national or imperial basis. Seymour Drescher has surveyed many different abolition models in the Atlantic world region and has shown how political and economic change interplayed to cause legal prohibition of slavery or the slave trade. Crucially for this work, he also charts the importance in the nineteenth century of the expansion of antislavery thinking in the Atlantic world public sphere, showing that this impacted on the perceived potential for freedom understood by the enslaved.[6] This book

[5] Matthew Hopper, *Slaves of One Master: Globalisation and Slavery in Arabia in the Age of Empire* (Yale University Press, 2015), pp. 6–7, 21, 35.

[6] Seymour Drescher, *Abolition: a History of Slavery and Anti-Slavery* (Cambridge University Press, 2009), p. 363.

argues that it also changed the meaning of the term 'slavery' itself, as the legal prohibition movement of the period solidified the definition of slavery at the very time when forced and coercive labour practices were diversifying and expanding.

Legal prohibition of slavery was a significant development because it marked not only the evolution of practice and definition within particular jurisdictions, but also represented a change on a transnational level. Jenny Martinez has argued that the campaigns to abolish the slave trade were the first international humanitarian campaigns that sought to develop a body of law that would function across national boundaries. She traces the ways in which nations around the Atlantic Ocean region collaborated, with greater or lesser success, to enforce antislavery law. The ostracisation of slave traders through this law-making process meant that by the middle of the nineteenth century, slave traders were perceived by many nations as *hostis humani generis* (enemies of mankind – the moral, economic and legal equivalents of pirates).[7] However, while with hindsight we can see the development of an antislavery trajectory, the extent to which these laws affected the behaviour of individuals and nations undertaking slave trading practices is not always clear. And as Jean Allain's work has pointed out, it was only much later in the nineteenth and early twentieth centuries that international abolition law attempted a truly global, universal reach. Although in 1885, the British suggested at the Berlin conference that slavery was against the law of humanity, this declaration was not adopted as many other nations, for political reasons due to imperial competition, were loath to side with the British. However, Allain has shown that by the early twentieth century, the notion of a civilised nation dominated and nations seeking recognition of their sovereignty on a global scale had to prove they had achieved 'civilisation', including conforming to norms such as the forbidding of polygamy, suttee and slavery.[8] Therefore, for the United States, emerging from a fratricidal civil war fought over the contentious issue of slavery, the attractiveness of imperial antislavery ideology was that it allowed for favourable comparisons with other antislavery powers such as Britain, and also gave the nation a veneer of 'civilisation' on the world stage. But nations merely publicly deploying this antislavery ideology did not always result in an improvement in conditions for the enslaved.

[7] Jenny Martinez, *The Slave Trade and the Origins of International Human Rights Law* (Oxford University Press, 2012), pp. 13, 114.

[8] Jean Allain, *The Law and Slavery* (Brill, 2015), pp. 88, 124.

Although the achievement of and reinforcement of legal prohibition was, and still is, an important aspect of antislavery work, it should not be taken as the final measure of success or indeed that it signifies no further need for abolition campaigning. Joel Quirk argues that legal prohibition often only served to push abusive labour practices geographically elsewhere or give it another name.[9] This book builds on Quirk's point and suggests that because some practices continued to exist but no longer fell into the legal definition of what counted as slavery, actually this changed the very nature of what the term 'slavery' meant in public discourse, and it became much broader over time. Therefore, in popular literature, the legal definition of 'slavery' was not adhered to, but rather the term expanded to include a diverse range of practices. This evolution has important ramification for the use of the term in the twenty-first-century context, as neo-abolitionists also include many labour practices and human relationships in the scope of 'modern slavery'.

This expansion is not a rhetorical manoeuvre, but rather reveals the reality of evolving types of slavery. Kevin Grant has conceptualised these as 'new slaveries', emerging because of international legal attempts to prohibit 'slavery' and because of European imperialism. I would add that American imperialism also facilitated the evolution of slavery on a global scale. Grant argues that these new slaveries differ from 'old slavery' in only one regard, their legality. The use of *corvée* and contract labour, with some labourers dislocated from their homes, moving long distances to work, as well as coercive practices designed to encourage the development of new staple crops, were all typical in imperial regions worldwide.[10] Such labour situations did not go unchallenged by activists and in the popular press, but Grant argues that such moral panics as the Congo horror distorts our understanding of slavery in the period, because it suggests that the treatment of workers in the Congo was an isolated incident, whereas in truth it should be considered typical.[11]

However, Grant's all-encompassing definition of slavery is a controversial one. Other scholars such as William Clarence-Smith see 'slavery' as something distinct from serfdom and other forms of tied labour. Clarence-Smith works on the Indian Ocean slave trade, and he argues that in that

[9] Joel Quirk, *The Anti-Slavery Project from the Slave Trade to Human Trafficking* (University of Pennsylvania Press, 2011), p. 7.

[10] Kevin Grant, *A Civilised Savagery: Britain and the New Slaveries in Africa 1884–1926* (Routledge, 2005), pp. 2, 23.

[11] Ibid., p. 29.

context, slavery existed alongside other coercive labour types. For example, in the pearl diving industry, free labourers worked alongside enslaved Africans and indebted Arabs, who were working off their debts. This was because of the differing nature of slave work in this region. Rather than agricultural work, many slaves were employed in maritime and urban roles, and these better lent themselves to a workforce with a range of statuses.[12] The workers themselves understood their differing position in relation to their masters, but in this book I am interested less in the conditions of enslavement experienced by the labourers, but rather how definitions of and perceptions of the work they undertook evolved over the course of the late nineteenth and early twentieth centuries. I argue, as Grant does, that in this period there was a trend to expand the definitions of what counted as slavery, whether for reasons of antislavery activism or, as was often the case in the United States, more conservative goals to defend a particular region against an influx of migrants. It is to the theme of the identity of the United States, and how Americans perceived themselves as individuals, as communities and as a nation, that we now turn.

AMERICAN IDENTITY

Identifying particular labour relations as 'slavery' in the late-nineteenth-century United States, fulfilled the function of forming a bulwark against uncivilised people and practices in order to protect the nation. In the post-emancipation era, commentators in the United States were able to label others as slaves or slaveholders for ideological and economic gain, with little sense of irony given the nation's own recent slave past. As the United States politically used antislavery imperialism to define its humanitarian ideological imperative on a global scale, Americans also labelled 'others' as slaves for more pragmatic reasons. The ambivalent relationship of the country to immigration grew more fraught in this period, especially with the hardening of scientific racial discourse. Migrants from China were the most obvious victims of this trend, considered by nativist labourers to be a threat to wages and their livelihoods, but also associated with the general racial and ideological degradation of labour. Calling Chinese migrants 'slaves' was not a radical humanitarian act, demanding their protection, but a conservative one, demanding their exclusion. As Najia Aarim-Heriot has identified, stereotyping of the community of Chinese

[12] William Clarence-Smith, 'Overview', in Clarence-Smith, ed., *The Economics of the Indian Ocean Slave Trade of the Nineteenth Century* (Frank Cass, 1989), pp. 3, 7.

labourers as an invasion – a 'flood' or 'swarm' – and individuals as 'dishonest' but 'servile', was an important trend in American popular culture, especially that local to the West Coast, from the mid-nineteenth century onwards. Identifying the Chinese migrants as 'slaves' and 'enslavers' served the same rhetorical function: to 'other' them and deny them access to American citizenship. This book argues that this urge to alienate the Chinese came simultaneously from a variety of sources, the newly popular newspaper press among them.

Other roots of the depiction of Chinese as slaves and enslavers are revealed by Carter Wilson, who states that the orthodox view of modernity in the United States claims that the old planter class died and the middle class wanted to modernise labour relations. This orthodox view also asserted that, prior to the middle of the twentieth century, it was the white masses who disenfranchised the ethnic other. Wilson challenges this, saying that the white working class was not powerful enough to do that, but rather the planter class survived, reorganised African American labour, and led the nascent industrialisation which expanded the boundaries of slavery-life practices within the United States.[13] Politicians of both political parties, still struggling with the aftermath of chattel slavery within the United States itself, feared the arrival of Chinese bonded labourers would exacerbate racial tensions and might cause race wars.[14] Therefore, they were very keen that the nation be seen, at an international level, as a place that did not tolerate slavery of any type within its borders, but only if that coincided with populist aims of limiting labour competition. Coerced and bonded labour among the African American population was tacitly permitted, provided the public outcry about such practices did not become too loud.

The most significant developments in this period that changed the United States' perception of itself was the acquisition of overseas territories. As seen in Aarim-Heriot's work, racism arising from the working and political classes defined the citizenship of the United States as racially limited because powerful nations were racially homogenous. Eric Love has shown how that idea was also transmitted to discussions about the role of natives in imperial contexts, arguing that identifying the ethnic colonial other as a slaveholder reiterated the idea that they might never be properly incorporated into the American body politic. Such views,

[13] Carter Wilson, *Racism from Slavery to Advanced Capitalism* (Sage, 1996), pp. 79, 94.

[14] Najia Aarim-Heriot, *Chinese Immigrants, African Americans and Racial Anxiety in the US 1848–82* (University of Illinois Press, 2003), pp. 10, 37.

building on the doctrine of Manifest Destiny, held that any expansionism should be undertaken for the benefit of white Americans, and not to improve the lives of native peoples.[15] Michael Cullinane shows how such ideas moved from universities to the halls of political power, when during the election of 1900 anti-imperialism and liberty became key themes.[16] I argue that even conservative anti-imperialist campaigners used slavery and antislavery to reinforce their position, so that within a generation, even Americans typically hostile to abolition had been able to assimilate antislavery values at the heart of their political identity. This produced an unusual coalition of anti-imperialists that included radical voices such as Frederick Douglass, alongside white supremacists such as Ben Tillman. Anti-imperialists were a significant voice within American politics until World War I, when their unity was challenged by geopolitical demands.[17]

The imperial adventure was also conflicting for the United States because it was unsure how to assimilate a settler colonial community into its sense of self, especially in places such as Hawaii and Alaska where natives who were ethnic others also lived. Settler colonial communities often defined themselves as civilised and modern in juxtaposition with the natives and, as Walter Hixson has shown, however much the natives mimicked white society, they were unable to achieve recognition and assimilation.[18] The settler colonial community, as in European imperial contexts, made use of labour situations that were not always clearly distinct from slavery, such as, for example, in the Hawaiian sugar plantations employing Chinese and Japanese contract labourers. Another pragmatic rhetorical positioning by settler colonialists, for example in the Philippines, made use of accusations of slavery amongst natives to justify military intervention in a particular region, similar to tactics deployed and honed over decades of warfare against the Native Americans of the continental United States. As Michael Salman has shown, slavery was central to the relationship between American conquerors and Filipino natives. Slavery was legally abolished in the Philippines in 1903, but ending the practice in actuality took many more years, and Salman argues that pro-imperialists in the United States used the protracted ending of slavery and slavery-like practices as evidence

15 Eric Love, *Race over Empire: Race and Imperialism 1865–1900* (University of North Carolina Press, 2004), pp. xvi, 18.

16 Michael Patrick Cullinane, *Liberty and American Anti-imperialism* (Palgrave, 2012), p. 54.

17 Ibid., pp. 69, 179.

18 Walter Hixon, *American Settler Colonialism: a History* (Palgrave, 2013), p. 146.

of the backwards and inferior nature of the Philippine people, and their unpreparedness for self-government. This did not silence voices who feared that the Philippines were racially unprepared for the abolition of slavery, because inferior races would never accept the self-motivated moral duty of free labour.[19]

The connection between theories of human development, slavery and imperialism is explored in depth by Thomas McCarthy. He argues that, usually hostile to European imperialist theorising, the United States only experienced a union of nationalism and neo-racism at the turn of the twentieth century, as it became an imperial power. In this period, the nation came to be envisioned in racial terms, with strength linked to homogeneity, thus problematising further the position of African Americans, Native Americans and recent immigrants.[20] I argue that in this period, the definition of whiteness extended to incorporate a range of immigrant communities and linked with this is the desirability of their adopting free labour ideologies. Ideally for American conservatives, where it persisted both within and without the nation's borders, slavery and forced labour remained something associated still with the racial other. Radical voices, such as Franz Boas, Frederick Douglass and W. E. B. DuBois persisted though, drawing the attention of the public to slavery and forced labour in terms of a problem that resonated with all humanity and not solely groups in the racial hierarchy deemed to be uncivilised.[21] In order to reclaim such voices, Paul Gilroy argues, we need to move beyond national boundaries and think about the Atlantic perspective more broadly. This book extends this further and tries to develop a more global outlook. Gilroy shows that from the early nineteenth century onwards, transatlantic cultural exchange dramatically influenced both radical and conservative African American perspectives, acknowledging that for some African Americans grappling with concepts of race, nation and culture, there was no benefit in emphasising a pan-African identity, but rather working through double consciousness; they fitted themselves into an alternative racial hierarchy.[22] But both radical

[19] Michael Salman, *The Embarrassment of Slavery: Controversies over Bondage and Nationalism in the American Colonial Philippines* (University of California Press, 2001), p. 99.

[20] Thomas McCarthy, *Race, Empire and the Idea of Human Development* (Cambridge University Press, 2009), p. 8.

[21] Ibid., p. 82.

[22] Paul Gilroy, *The Black Atlantic: Modernity and Double Consciousness* (Verso, 1998), pp. 6, 24.

and conservative African American commentators felt compelled to use the story of global slavery to reflect on their own challenging, vulnerable and conflicted position within the United States and this narrative became increasingly influential for white humanitarians too.

When conceiving of slavery, by negotiating complex spaces, framed by racial theories between national identity and imperial goals, American humanitarians used European imperialist theories and the United States' own domestic experience of abolition to create a moral empire. Ian Tyrell has explored the ways in which missionaries and antislavery activists occupied the new expanded public space on an international stage, discussing regions of the world in which the United States had a direct political interest, regions where it hoped to expand its role and regions where reports about various conceptions of slavery supported Americans' sense of their own developing identity in the world. World War I represented an important hiatus, as after the shock of the devastation and extent of loss of life of the war, a sea change took place in the perceived potential of reform, especially religious reform, and of the internationalisation agenda.[23] Domestically, the late nineteenth and early twentieth centuries were a crucial period in the evolution of notions of labour, and intellectual narratives were changing on a global scale, as they were in the United States as it examined its own labour relations. There had been a long history of diverse types of unfree labour in the country, but fundamentally, those who worked for themselves were seen as more industrious than those who worked for someone else, because they might grow lazy and careless. This caricature was popular in depictions of chattel slavery. According to David Brody, the abolition message worked in the United States partly because it appealed directly to labour, suggesting that slavery was a system which degraded labour.[24] This message could hit home because it did not require a readjustment of racist beliefs on the part of the American workforce, as shown in the post-emancipation era when ordinary Americans were able to support antislavery values while tolerating slavery-like practices on their own doorstep. The importance of ordinary Americans is central to the story this book tells about conceptions of slavery, and an examination of popular cultural sources shows how ideas were created and reproduced for a diverse readership.

[23] Ian Tyrrell, *Reforming the World: the Creation of America's Moral Empire* (Princeton University Press, 2010), pp. 24, 240.

[24] David Brody, *In Labor's Cause: Main themes on the History of the American Worker* (Oxford University Press, 1993), pp. 10–12.

POPULAR CULTURE

Textual and visual artefacts of popular culture told the story of the domestic impact of antebellum chattel slavery and communicated to Americans the nature of slavery ongoing overseas. Both were underpinned by racial concepts of 'the other' and played on the American imagination of the period. The late nineteenth century saw the development of mass culture for the first time, and objects and stories depicting cultural difference, especially where it was perceived that that culture was about to be lost, whether in a domestic or global context, were tremendously popular. The idea of a *volkgeist,* or folk spirit, emerged in sociological thinking during this period, and interest in cultural output such as blues songs and Uncle Remus folktales, feared disappearing in the modernising, urbanising world, were a key part of this.[25] For white Americans, this type of popular culture tied into the romantic notions of the slave past, in which all African Americans were contented in plantation life. Kenneth Goings argues that, during the Jim Crow era, yearning for the nostalgic slave past by white households triggered the collection of black memorabilia. Owning black memorabilia for whites stood in for owning slaves, which had been unjustly taken from them. Figurines and other artifacts depicting 'Sambo', the happy slave who defended slavery no matter what his master did to him, and Uncle Mose, the loyal retainer who served quietly and happily, served to metaphorically re-enslave African Americans in the post-emancipation era. For the Lost Cause mythologizing of the American slave past, the concept that slaves had been contented and wanted to serve their masters was fundamental to the world view of southerners.[26] But some black Americans subverted such culture from white hegemonic patterns of musicality and storytelling, to reinforce the idea of distinctiveness, sourced from Africa, while for other black Americans, this type of artefact also reinforced their difference, and indeed progress, from the culture of Africans still living in Africa.

As William Van Deburg has argued, there was a pre–Civil War precedent for the development of a slavery-referring culture designed to control African Americans but providing them with avenues to autonomy. American minstrel shows thrived in the mid-nineteenth century, playing on the racial stereotypes of the era by using stock characters such as Zip

[25] Brad Evans, *Before Cultures: the Ethnographic Imagination in American Literature 1865–1920* (University of Chicago, 2005), pp. 7–9.

[26] Kenneth Goings, *Mammy and Uncle Mose: Black Collectibles and American Stereotyping* (University Press of Indiana, 1994), pp. xix, xxi, 67.

Coon and Jim Crow, and treating black women in a misogynistic way. These shows bore little resemblance to the realities of slave life, and performers of such shows were nervous of alienating a core audience by not appearing pro-slavery enough.[27] However, Van Deburg does highlight a strand of post-war African American cultural representation that challenged the conservative Jim Crow view, and these were the artefacts that celebrated pan-Africanism and depicted abolitionists as heroes.[28] As Leslie King-Hammond has shown, in rare cases, white producers of culture also showed an empathy with the lives of the enslaved and formerly enslaved in the United States. An example of this is the photography of Huestis P. Cook from the 1890s. A forerunner of the New Deal photographers of a later generation, Cook photographed the interiors of cabins of African American sharecroppers, descendants of slaves who remained in a bonded labour situation; this reflected a new type of aesthetic value and foregrounded the self-expression of this often voiceless class of people.[29] As John Michael Vlach has shown, understanding the depiction of the enslaved and formerly enslaved in this period must be done with sensitivity to the gaze of the producer and the viewer of the artefact. He challenges us to ask whether the gaze is coming from below, showing respect, or from above, taking possession due to a position of superiority.[30] Whether depicting a mode of nostalgia, acceptance or resistance, cultural artefacts from the United States of this period are unified in their concern with slavery and its legacy.

This is also true of the most important cultural output of the period, which impacted the understanding of the world of both white and black Americans, the new types of mass media. Faster global communications ensured that first newspapers and then later radio and the moving picture could transmit news faster and more efficiently and cheaply than ever before. These types of mass media had a homogenising effect on American culture, ensuring that Americans across the country had similar access to the latest reports about slavery from across the world and ironing out

[27] William Van Deburg, *Slavery and Race in American Popular Culture* (University of Wisconsin Press, 1984), p. 46.

[28] Ibid., p. 120.

[29] Leslie King-Hammond, 'Identifying Spaces of Blackness: the Aesthetic of Resistance and Identity in American Plantation Art', in Angela Mack & Stephen G. Hoffus, eds., *Landscape of Slavery: the Plantation in American Art* (University of South Carolina Press, 2008), p. 71.

[30] John Michael Vlach, *The Planter's Prospect: Privilege and Slavery in Plantation Paintings* (University of North Carolina Press, 2002), p. 1.

local differences in perception. As Andie Tucher has argued, prior to the American Civil War, local concerns were to the fore in newspaper reporting with urban and rural regions deeply suspicious of one another, and international stories were often dealt with cursorily, by copying from other newspapers.[31] However, post-war, the situation changed, and slavery in a global context provided important fodder for newspapers across the United States. This book will examine several peaks in news reporting concerning slavery, including the white slavery in Armenia in the 1870s, and even more strikingly the horrors on the rubber plantations in the Congo in the earliest years of the twentieth century. Newspaper reports and books and pamphlets based on the first-hand reports of black travellers, such as George Washington Williams and William Shepherd, that were cheap to buy, spread the campaign to expose Leopold's misdeeds. Theirs is the 'heroism' in the title of Adam Hochschild's book, before later Edmund Morel and Roger Casement took up the fight against slavery in the Congo.[32] But many pro-Leopold articles and pamphlets also emerged during the years when outrage about the slavery perpetrated in the Congo by the Belgians was at its height, because Leopold and his representatives were master manipulators of the press.[33]

The immediate political reaction to news from the Congo and the reaction of ordinary Americans was possible because of the technological development of new information systems towards the end of the century. By the 1890s, cables were much improved and journalists were able to transmit information more quickly – transmitted across the Atlantic in a couple of hours compared to news on board ship which would take seven days to cross from New York to London. According to John Britton, political tensions seemed heightened and exacerbated because of this increased speed. The news broadcast in newspapers tended to reflect popular cultural values such as an aggressive masculinity, but also Giovanna Dell 'Orto argues, constructed social meaning too. This period saw an increase in American nationalism and this was partly due to the interplay between mass media and popular opinion. Politicians and businessmen were proactive in this sphere, realising that whoever built this technology would control it, and used cable communications to further

[31] Andie Tucher, *Froth and Scum: Truth, Beauty, Goodness and the Ax Murderer in America's First Mass Medium* (University of North Carolina Press, 1994), pp. 88, 95.

[32] Adam Hochschild, *King Leopold's Ghost: a story of Greed, Terror and Heroism in Colonial Africa* (Macmillan, 1999), p. 152.

[33] Ibid., p. 237.

business interests, for example, around the Panama Canal.[34] But newspaper reports, expressed in accessible terms for the layperson, were the most powerful tool in allowing Americans to interpret the complex reports about slavery emerging from foreign correspondents. Despite a fear that the so-called 'yellow press' was eroding American values, the mass media portrayed itself as on the public's side, helping them interpret a complex world.[35] However, Karen Roggenkamp urges us to remember that in mass culture of this period, entertainment was always more important than fact, and finding a 'story', which 'sold', sometimes trumped authenticity of the narrative. This was especially true in genres such as crime fiction and its similarities to true crime accounts of murderess Lizzie Borden in the newspapers.[36] Similarly, when Armenian slavery was exposed in American newspapers of the 1870s, the descriptions of harems and enslavement of white women owed a great deal to fictional accounts describing similar adventures.

American newspapers of this period were also important in conveying messages about racial otherness of different races at home and abroad through their prolific use of cartooning. Three of the most influential were *Harper's Weekly*, *Puck* and *Judge*, all of which played on stereotypes, well known throughout society, to propagate their partisan views about slavery and imperialism.[37] Newspapers were also crucial to the creation of a distinctive African American voice, identity and community, both before the Civil War, when abolition was the focus, and after, when diverse issues such as voting, segregation, lynching and colonisation of Africa appeared frequently in the black press.[38] But, as Gerald Baldasty has shown, in both the black and white press, by the end of the nineteenth century, news had become an important commodity, valued by people at all levels of American society. Increases in literacy, urbanisation and industrialisation

[34] John Britton, *Cables, Crises and the Press: the Geopolitics of the New International Information System 1866–1903* (University of New Mexico Press, 2013), pp. 6, 18–20. Giovanna Dell'Orto, *American Journalism and International Relations: Foreign Correspondence from the Early Republic to the Digital Era* (Cambridge University Press, 2013), p. 3.

[35] Dell'Orto, *American Journalism and International Relations*, p. 64.

[36] Karen Roggenkamp, *Narrating the News: New journalism and Literary Genre in Late Nineteenth Century American Newspapers and Fiction* (Kent State University Press, 2005), pp. xii, 56.

[37] Richard Rice, 'Race and Ethnic Imagery', in David B. Sachsman, S. Kittrell Rushing & Ray Morris Jr., eds., *Seeking a Voice: Images of Race and Gender in the Nineteenth Century Press* (Purdue University Press, 2009), p. 27.

[38] Aleen J. Ratzlaff, 'Ebony Triangle: The Black Newspaper Network in Kansas 1878–1900', in Sachsman et al, *Seeking a Voice*, p. 120.

all changed the press and people's perceptions of it, as newspapers became big business. From the late nineteenth century onwards, journalism itself changed too, as journalists were encouraged to go and seek out stories for themselves, to make the news rather than passively waiting for stories to come to them.[39] This became an obvious tactic in the early-twentieth-century white slavery panic, centred initially on Chicago and then spreading to other cities. This panic was initially driven by journalism in the short-lived Chicago newspaper *The Day Book*, which had to seek sensational stories to attract both male and female readers as it was advertisement-free. But many newspapers, even the large ones surviving by their advertising revenue, such as those published by William Randolph Hearst like the *New York Journal*, published stories with an increasingly populist appeal, presenting themselves as the people's champions, rooting out and challenging political corruption. New immigrants were catered for with newspapers in their own languages, and indeed Joseph Pulitzer, himself an Hungarian Jewish immigrant, made his fortune marketing cheap newspapers to foreign-born readers before buying the Anglophone *St Louis Post-Dispatch* and the rival to Hearst, the *New York World*.[40] This book argues that stories about slavery from around the world made good copy for ambitious newspapers of this era, and that the stories they published shaped global slavery in the American imagination. However, this shaping did not occur consistently throughout the period covered by this book. Instead, this timeframe encompasses considerable evolution in representations of slavery.

CHRONOLOGY

Interrogating the evolving definition and perception of slavery must naturally take into account change over time and the chronological scope of the research becomes significant. The history of slavery and antislavery is punctuated by important dates that are thought to act as points of momentous change, 1807 being one of the most obvious. However this book will argue that although moments of legal prohibition of slavery and slavery-like practices cannot be ignored, far more important are the undercurrent of economic and cultural nuances that determine the

39 Gerald Baldasty, *The Commercialisation of News in the Nineteenth Century* (University of Wisconsin Press, 1992), pp. 4, 37.

40 Michael Emery, Edwin Emery & Nancy Roberts, *The Press and America: An Interpretive History of the Mass Media* (Allyn and Bacon, 2000), pp. 175, 217.

attitudes of ordinary people, and of their political representatives, towards slavery as an institution and as a practice. While this book chooses as its starting point the end of the American Civil War and as its end point the start of the First World War, some examples chosen for illustration come from before or after these points. This has been done deliberately so that these moments of change might be interrogated. What really did change at these crucial 'full stops' of history?

This book is about the perceptions of slavery in the United States after the emancipation of chattel slaves was passed into law following the fratricidal Civil War. It specifically addresses the tensions felt in a still-divided nation coming to terms with its 'slavery days' in the antebellum era, while simultaneously addressing continuation of forced labour practices within the United States itself, and in the world more broadly. Therefore, although the context of emancipation is fundamental to the scope of this book, it was also important to show that the intellectual and political trends in the ways that pro- and antislavery campaigners talked about enslavement domestically and globally before the Civil War were directly influential on the discourse adopted afterwards. Antebellum chattel slavery was ideologically and symbolically the reference point for much post-emancipation US debate on the topic but also the ramifications of its legacy were felt in more practical ways as the structures of enslavement, especially, although not solely, in the southern states, were resistant to dismantling and new labour forms, sometimes modelled on the control and order afforded whites by chattel slavery, were constituted. In many ways, although a tremendously important legal change took place in the post-war years, for the United States 'slavery days' were not part of the historic past during the period covered by this book.

Similarly, the choice of World War I as an end point reflects the significance of this cataclysmic conflict on the economic, political and cultural world, not only in the United States but also among the European imperial nations and those colonial subjects who fought for them. This was also a moment of cultural shock and confusion in the United States. The nation had begun to recover from the horrors of its Civil War and had confidently emerged on to the world stage, depicting itself as a modern, progressive, powerful nation to compete with its European rivals. Depressions in the 1870s and the 1890s had caused a few years of pause, but more broadly, the United States grappled with its new role as a regional and even oceanic power. The coming of the First World War created confusion about national identity both in terms of the heritage of its own immigrant population and, from 1917, its hesitant role intervening in European power politics. Despite this, there was much continuity between pre- and post-war situations regarding the interpretation of slavery and forced labour on a global scale. Rather, this is a period of the gradual evolution continuing until World War II and beyond, of the ideologies of scientific racism, of international humanitarianism and of radical resistance to labour control.

Between these two milestone moments, the end of one traumatic war and the beginning of another, this book traces some important threads of change in the way that the people of the United States conceived slavery. The manipulation of stories of chattel slavery and the emergence of new forms of forced labour to restrict the freedoms of the formerly enslaved, while they consistently resisted these controls, occupied the American imagination, simultaneously with the assimilation of a global understanding of new forms of enslavement both in territories to which the United States and her citizens laid claim and in the wider world. The ways that European imperial powers used antislavery rhetoric as part of their expansionist doctrine in this era of high empire was influential in the United States, as pro- and anti-imperialists talked about slavery to further their own narrower political ends. During this period, slavery was no longer a problem for discussion within nations (and their empires) as an international voice emerged, drawing a picture of slavery as a crime against humanity and depicting its defeat as part of the inexorable trend towards civilisation and modernity. Supporting all of these threads of discussion about slavery was the emerging discourse around scientific racism and Social Darwinism, which ranked races and peoples according to a racial hierarchy and according to racially predetermined traits and behaviours while, at the same time, recruiting a linear understanding of history in which certain races were ahead and more advanced, and others could be encouraged to catch up if the superior races performed their pedagogical duties. Let us now explore the ways that this book presents the research evidence, gathered from American newspapers (both textual and visual representations) and pamphlets and books published on both sides of the Atlantic by American and British authors, which were influential on the perceptions of an American readership of slavery and the slave trade.

THE RHETORIC OF UNITED STATES SLAVERY

Ways of writing and thinking about slavery did change dramatically as a result of the successful abolition of slavery as an outcome of the American Civil War, but a stark before and after distinction simply does not work. Rather the conceptualisation of slavery prior to the war was limited in the minds of most commentators to the chattel slavery of African Americans within the southern United States. The weight of this imaginary was very powerful and later, even when concepts of global slavery were important in the popular mind, moving away from the notion of slavery as something that had only happened in the south prior to the war was very difficult. However, this notion was highly contested during the later nineteenth and early twentieth centuries as many newly freed African Americans and their descendants struggled to resist a narrative that dismissed their experience under slavery as benevolent and nurturing, while working equally hard to resist the labour and criminal justice practices that sought to trap them (and other impoverished Americans) in forced labour situations.

When Americans did turn their attention away from their domestic situations and outwards towards slavery in the region and the wider world, the archetype of their own form of chattel slavery served as a central point of comparison, with almost all other types of slavery and forced labour being compared either directly or implicitly with the slavery of the antebellum south. The ubiquitous symbols of slavery such as chains and whips were depicted both before and after the Civil War by commentators intending to raise awareness of abusive labour practices. But because the legacy of the Jim Crow era meant that the memory of slavery became polarised and distorted, with many white Americans believing in the mythologizing about a benevolent slave past, comparisons were not being made with the true experience of chattel slavery but rather a corrupted memory of it. The reasons for comparison were also often highly political, designed to justify the furthering of the imperialist or anti-imperialist narrative, or domestically, designed to prevent the immigration to the United States of particular ethnic groups. However, also strong was the legacy of the abolitionists' way of talking about slavery, and although many abolitionists turned their attention to new causes in the later nineteenth century, their tropes and narrative structures lived on in the ways that slavery was discussed in the emancipation era. They taught later writers a great deal, for example in the use of first-person narratives to expose the true horrors of slavery, and also in how to construct an ideal victim, as in the case of the white slavery panic. This book argues that powerful notions of what it meant to name something as slavery, or someone as a slave, continued to build and evolve in the period after emancipation, but were strongly influenced by rhetorical practices from the era prior to the Civil War. However, these influences did not emerge solely from a domestic United States context, but rather from the nation's interaction with its important cultural influencer, Great Britain, and with others on the global stage.

GLOBAL AND TRANSATLANTIC INFLUENCES

Conceptions of slavery in this period did evolve in response to the further development of a European imperial world as the United States mirrored, and sometimes challenged, the ways that slavery and antislavery were depicted in the European imperial context. The British were especially influential in the construction of a modern antislavery imperialism which some in the United States desired to adopt for their own political purposes. By the end of the nineteenth century, this was not solely a British movement as an international approach to global problems which crossed national borders, such as the slave trade, was becoming increasingly tenable. Complex voices emerged on the global stage, as national political expediency was often challenged by humanitarian organisations working for the good of the enslaved. However, many of these organisations still espoused the liberal values of capitalist development and Christian civilisation, and some doubted the readiness of the enslaved to live fully free and independent lives. But an increasingly radical voice emerged in the early twentieth century which demanded a reconsideration of the racial hierarchy and the doctrine of deterministic progression.

The United States as a political and newly minted imperial nation, wanted to be part of the antislavery consensus built by the British and applied to its territorial holdings, but like the British, it realised that there was a significant gap between the idealistic rhetoric of the abolition of slavery and the pragmatic control of the labouring 'other' whether at home or abroad. Like the British, the Americans manipulated the definition of slavery for their own end and to defend their propensity to act or ignore incidents of labour abuse. While international law was beginning to formulate definitions of slavery and the slave trade, in one sense fixing it, in other ways the definition became more boundless and mutable during this period, as the term was rhetorically deployed more widely than it had been in the antebellum era, when 'slavery' in almost every case meant chattel slavery of people of African descent.

The trade in and movement of slaves became much more of a global concept. After the last transatlantic slaver voyage in 1866, attention turned to other networks facilitating the movement of bound or forced labourers, including indentured labourers. Again, the varied uses of the term 'slavery' here had political overtones. The conservative use of the term in this context often acted as a justification for the exclusion of free labourers on the grounds that they were in reality enslaved and must not be allowed to pollute the American system. However the more radical use of the term exposed labour injustices and called on governments globally to act to prevent the systemic abuses that allowed capitalists to seek vulnerable workers, coerce them to move across long distances, and then work them in horrific conditions sometimes involving restriction of movement and refusal of wages. Once again, the movement and evolution of ideas is crucial here in tracking the global trends, but so is the experience of the enslaved individuals themselves.

OTHERING OF SLAVES AND SLAVE OWNERS

American authors writing about the experiences of slaves and slave owners and traders during the late nineteenth and early twentieth century used various rhetorical techniques to signal their disapproval of the system, and in doing so often positioned themselves as different from both those who were susceptible to enslavement and those doing the enslaving. This rhetorical distancing served the function of expressing a strong disapproval of the institution of slavery, mimicking the discourse of imperial antislavery, but also refused to admit members of races vulnerable to enslavement into its own body politic for pragmatic and conservative reasons. More radical political interpretations of enslavement sought to tie it to corrupt and corrupting modern economic models of capitalism and colonialism. Both of these types of othering were undertaken using the discourse of scientific racism, showing that both slaves and slavers might be considered beyond the civilised pale. However, such ideological interpretations clashed with the realities of mobilisation of labour in an unequal world, and in order to maintain consistency, definitions of slavery became mutable to allow for such hypocritical although pragmatic prevarication.

In many ways, the othering of the slaveholder was the easiest rhetorical manoeuvre to accomplish. Building on the language of abolition and imperial antislavery thinkers, who had fashioned the British as the archetypical antislavery nation, American writers after the Civil War used racial, ethnic and religious othering to distance themselves from slavers operating in the Indian Ocean world, the Philippines and Africa. When describing harems in the Ottoman Empire, both British and American writers exoticised both the master and his sex slaves, using the tropes of fiction to titillate readers with descriptions of hidden coercion and sexual violence. In some cases othering operated on a national level, as certain nations sought to confirm or deny the sovereignty of others based on their ability to deal with the scourge of slavery and the slave trade within their borders. Ethiopians, Hawaiians and Filipinos fell victim to this type of racially informed judgement, which determined that their putative nations were uncivilised and backwards because of the continuation of forced labour and therefore unsuitable for international recognition.

Accusations of involvement in slavery were also used by European and American commentators to profess superiority over other so-called developed nations, their imperial rivals. Accusing an individual or a nation of involvement in slavery, especially if in cahoots with a racial other, was a powerful act and one that caused significant consternation. However, for much of this period, the former slave owners of the United States itself benefited from an effort to reassimilate them into the American body politic and so, rather than continuing the abolitionist antebellum process of 'othering' them and disassociating slave owning from true American values, in the Jim Crow era they were brought back into the political and cultural fold as true Americans once again. Uniting the white Americans after the fratricidal Civil War became more important than enhancing the status of the formerly enslaved.

GENDER

One of the crucial ways in which slavery was understood in this era was in the constant remaking of the vision of the ideal victim. As had been the case in the eighteenth-and early nineteenth-century abolition movements, campaigners realised that depictions of the sexual vulnerability of female victims of enslavement attracted a great deal of interest from readers, many of whom were approaching the stories of sexual abuse with a variety of motives, some humanitarian but others seeking entertainment and still others desiring ways of enforcing control of wayward women. In an era of threatening modernity, controlling women's bodies and women's behaviour was an overriding concern of the conservative patriarchy, who used the threat posed by enslavement as one way to do this. Authors portrayed white women's enslavement as especially heinous, and because of the association of whiteness with innate innocence and vulnerability, white women made the ideal victim, requiring the protection of white males, whether husbands, fathers, brothers or members of the criminal justice system. Their whiteness was especially potent when the enslaver was depicted as an ethnic other, for example, the 'lustful Turk' of eastern Europe and the Middle East forcefully taking white women into his harem, or the Jewish or southern European pimp of the domestic 'white slavery' panic in the United States itself. But representation of women's enslavement or potential enslavement was complex and involved a considerable element of victim blaming. Even white women were seen as culpable in their enslavement, being tempted because of their own moral weaknesses, to succumb to the lure of bright lights and luxury that typified fearful representations of the modern city. Such depictions of moral depravity took on even more vicious overtones when coupled with racial othering; black and Chinese women caught up in sexual slavery were frequently blamed for their own situation and thought to be unredeemable and damaged beyond repair.

In a global context, representations of female enslavement were also deployed for reactionary means, claiming that women and children participating in a particular labour form was a justification for a denial of enslavement on the part of colonial powers or their proxies, as the women's labour in this model was depicted as lighter and less severe and therefore unlike slavery. Commentators were also unsure how to react to so-called 'domestic slavery' in Africa and the Middle East in the late nineteenth century. In this form of slavery, women servants and sexual slaves were most desired, and their material and physical treatment did vary from appalling abuse, to positions of respected luxury. Despite these variations, even the best-dressed women who found themselves in this position did not have the basic freedoms of movement, of marriage, of choosing how to raise their own family and were, in essence, the property of their husbands. No wonder then that such a model represented fertile ground for feminists in the United Kingdom and the United States to comment on the position of women, and their lack of freedom, in their own countries.

This last example provides evidence that women did not allow conservative depictions of themselves in relation to slavery to exist unchallenged. Not all women engaged in this challenge: of course, some women adhered to the conservative view of slavery and women's rights shared by their male counterparts, and depicted antebellum slavery with nostalgia, as a lost golden age. But this period is an important one for the continuation in the development of women's activism regarding slavery, sexual violence and their rights in general. Few women were allowed to occupy political roles in the public sphere, but nonetheless, women from the elite classes, such as Kathleen Simon, broke through this glass ceiling. Others used a special skill to highlight the failure of the abolition of slavery, such as the photography deployed to such important effect by Alice Harris. For many women, their voices around the issue of slavery were mediated by male allies, who occasionally 'allowed' them to speak for themselves in male-authored slave narratives of the period. Nonetheless, these voices continued the radical tradition within abolitionism that started much earlier in the nineteenth century with women such as the Grimke sisters, whose vision was one of complete social change, as well as the ending of the pernicious labour form of slavery.

SUBVERTING THE NARRATIVES

In the post-emancipation era, and increasingly so in the early twentieth century, more radical voices began to address the question of global slavery, by using it to fundamentally challenge the structures of capitalism and colonialism. These voices proposed a radical reformation of human relations based on equality and the sovereignty of nations, and in many cases used a call for social activism to improve the lives of the enslaved and to eradicate slavery and other forced labour forms as part of a drive towards political revolution. Many of those authors who conceived of slavery in this way came from the newly radicalised 'New Negro' movement within the African American community, but the response of black Americans was certainly not an homogenous one in this period, nor were white Americans immune from the influence of political radicalism, especially as the new technologies of mass media increasingly allowed them to empathise with the plight of the vulnerable around the world.

WHY THIS BOOK?

This book argues that to understand the American cultural and intellectual self-image and its conception of slavery in the post-emancipation era, it is necessary to consider slavery in a global context. Although the nature of and legacy of slavery within the United States was incredibly powerful, Americans were beginning to conceive their nation as an actor on a modern global stage, and understanding mechanisms of forced labour within that world helped Americans define themselves as international actors. They built on their own memories of antebellum slavery but synthesised that with an imperialist antislavery ideology borrowed from Europe. Americans used both of these intellectual trends, along with scientific racism, to inform their othering of slaves and slave owners in the period after the Civil War, using the trope of gender to heighten concerns about slavery by crafting and developing the notion of the ideal victim. But powerful counter narratives informed by political radicalism repositioned some Americans in relation to forced labour practices and demanded a reconsideration of the entire system of capitalist, colonialist and racist hegemony.

It is important that we should understand the diverse and mutable meanings of slavery at various historical moments because slavery is ubiquitous throughout history and in all settled parts of the world. Slavery's function has varied across time and place, and by examining its story over the *longue durée* we can illustrate how to protect and defend victims, how we can use the law to prohibit the practice, and how radical activism can change the behaviour of governments around the issue. In the twenty-first century, the meaning of the word 'slavery' is as contested as it has ever been, but nonetheless, forced and coercive labour practices that many define as a form of slavery exist throughout the world, and macro and micro level antislavery activism is required now as much as it ever was. Slavery cannot be dismissed as a phenomenon of the past, nor a phenomenon of the world's poorer regions, but instead should be a concern of everyone regardless of race or nationality. The patterns that emerge in the era covered by this book – the othering of slaves and slaveholders, the flexibility of the definition of slavery in order to defend inaction in the face of injustice – still exist today and by examining their origins in the period following the end of the transatlantic slave trade, perhaps we might be better informed on how to more effectively respond to the slave system. As a work of the discipline of history, this book is underpinned by a desire to learn from the past, not assuming that values and behaviours can be simply transmitted across time, but rather showing the significance and longevity of the structural inequalities that trigger slavery that we still grapple with. The response to slavery must be an interdisciplinary one, and I hope that this book will be read by scholars of all disciplines who are interested in contributing to the fight against slavery, and that it is merely one tool in the toolkit of responses to such problems in the contemporary world.

The primary sources feature popular, populist, political and activist responses to the institution of slavery. They show the defensiveness and territoriality of nations, the economic imperative to make imperialism work, the appeal of lowest-common-denominator racial tropes, and the power of a radical rethinking of enslavement and the relations between races. Despite these sources often being written a century or more ago, their themes and concerns are still our themes and concerns when we see labour injustice in the twenty-first century. Understanding the complex responses of people in the past to enslavement can inform our own responses to the phenomenon today, making this story directly relevant. We still require a form of social activism, a new antislavery movement, to challenge the complacency that suggests slavery no longer exists, or the manipulation of the definition of slavery which denies the culpability of the world's most powerful. Let this book be a part of that social activism which seeks radical solutions to abusive labour practices the world over.

1

A Rhetorical Continuum? How Representations of Antebellum Slavery Endure in Post-War Culture

The economic, social, political and cultural legacy of chattel slavery in the United States in the era immediately following the end of the Civil War has been explored by scholars for at least a century, and the magnitude of the tremors caused by abolishing the system, and by the military conflict required to do this, cannot be underestimated. In this chapter, the evolving intersection between labour and race are explored, because the seeds of post-war discourse often had their origins in the ways that the concept of slavery was contested in the antebellum era. After the war, the United States as a nation, and white and black Americans as communities and individuals, had to come to terms with the fact that chattel slavery was no longer legal in the country and was now outlawed in the document that had become the repository for the nation's identity: the Constitution. As the Thirteenth Amendment stated, 'neither slavery nor involuntary servitude, except as the punishment of a crime, whereof the party shall have been duly convicted, shall exist within the United States or any place subject to their jurisdiction'. However, amending political and legal frameworks to outlaw chattel slavery could not change, overnight, the attitudes of American people who had been mired in the rhetorical and military struggle to such an extent that radical positions on both the pro- and antislavery sides had, in less than a generation, become firmly entrenched. As chattel slavery and the abolition movement became part of history and thus increasingly embedded in the realms of nostalgia and memory, they simultaneously remained a live issue, because their legacy impacted on emerging labour systems and race relations to such an extent that many Americans, of various ethnic backgrounds who were victims of white hegemonic power, experienced the continuation of slavery-like systems of control and organisation, variously depicted as a symbolic slavery, as akin to slavery or worse than chattel slavery. Along with nostalgic views of antebellum chattel slavery, these combined to let white Americans off the hook, allowing them to avoid adopting an anti-slavery ideology and leading to a nadir in race relations.

Antebellum chattel slavery operated as an archetype with which all other forced labour systems were compared. Its symbolic language of whips, auction blocks, bloodhounds and chains was co-opted by commentators debating the moral and economic advantages and disadvantages of new forced labour forms. Antebellum abolitionist ideas also had a long afterlife in the post-war period, morphing into new campaigns about other types of injustice, or recycled to discuss the painful legacy of chattel slavery in the United States. For some commentators, slavery was a rhetorical tool with which, through comparison, to evoke horror about the worst sorts of violence a human being could perpetrate on another, or to justify a particular type of labour because, while problematic, it was not as bad as chattel slavery. For others, despite legal and political changes, its horrors still stalked the nation. Importantly, these uses showed that chattel slavery for many, not all, became an outdated form of labour relation, an example of behaviour that now 'others', and not Americans, did. However, ambivalent views existed, as after the Civil War not all Americans rejected the use of chattel slavery in its entirety, but, increasingly, its use on American soil was seen as unacceptable in the present and consigned to the past.

Echoes of chattel slavery permeated post-war conceptions of free and forced labour in two areas: in discussions of domestic and of international labour systems. The domestic impact of the rhetoric of chattel slavery and abolition was threefold. First, mentions of slavery appeared in literature in general terms, evoked by authors discussing the potential for cultural and social reconciliation of the once-slave-holding states within the United States, to create a new post-war nation as, for the people of all races and both genders, the boundaries of the concept of freedom were tested. Second, the rhetoric of chattel slavery was deployed by campaigners and victims, and defenders and perpetrators, of the forced labour systems that formed part of the pernicious legacy of distorted relations between the races: debt bondage and convict labour. Campaigners and victims compared these labour forms to slavery, saying that they were equivalent to slavery, worse than slavery or proved that slavery itself had never been abolished. Perpetrators and defenders used the model of chattel slavery to distance their own behaviour or beliefs from those seen as heinous following the Thirteenth Amendment. Third, the rhetorical legacy of chattel slavery appeared in discussions about immigration to frame anti-immigrant discourse, especially regarding Chinese labour. In this case, the choice to label migrants as slaves or victims of slavery was made in order to deter their entry to the United States. Using the idea that the nation now wanted to define itself as a bastion of antislavery, alongside Britain and other European nations, commentators suggested that allowing bonded labourers such as the Chinese into the country would racially and economically degrade the United States. Here, antislavery was used rhetorically to defend the racial status quo, to exclude workers, most of whom were not forced labourers, and to promote nativist causes.

In debates over labour systems outside the continental United States, chattel slavery was used to redefine the position of the post-war nation in a global context. Far from refusing to acknowledge the United States' slave past, many imperialist writers were keen to fashion a nation emerging from the pain of the Civil War with its legacy of slavery and abolition adopting a new role as an international antislavery power. Activists anticipated the evolution of a new humanitarianism, built on campaigning models from prior to the Civil War. Protests and discussion about slavery in Egypt during the 1840s informed the types of activism seen in the post–Civil War era, and during the Congo crisis at the turn of the twentieth century. For writers about slavery in these parts of Africa, and elsewhere, the transatlantic slave trade and antebellum chattel slavery were models for comparison and archetypes through which discussions might be encouraged about forced labour in all other times and places. Despite a hesitant interest in Africa, the United States came of age as a world power during this era, and its contact with new forms of labour and systems of racial control in the settler colony of Hawaii, and its imperial conquest of the Philippines, was influenced by an understanding of forced labour in the light of antebellum chattel slavery. As in the domestic context, comparisons were used to either justify American complicity in coercive labour, or to 'other' particular racial groups as perpetrators of slavery and therefore uncivilised compared to the Americans who had so recently jettisoned their own ties to the system.

This chapter will trace the ways in which chattel slavery and its abolition movement became rhetorically both part of history and yet still alive in discourse within the United States. It will follow how modes, symbolism and themes concerning slavery and abolition were deliberately deployed following the war to make a symbolic new nation, to enable white Americans to reconcile as a community while excluding and alienating others, and to allow African Americans to come to terms with a different type of belonging, not to a master but to community and nation. Starting with abolition, the chapter explores how memories of the movement were manipulated by those seeking, after the war, to campaign in new ways and that while, in some ways, abolitionism was brought to a close by the Civil War, its messages and modes were reframed by new activists. There is also a continuum in the anti-abolitionist rhetoric, as ongoing accusations of abolitionists' selective compassion targeted campaigners working after the Civil War, as well as before.

After the war, the continued stridency of anti-abolition rhetoric is only one example of the power of pro-slavery ideas. Nostalgic and distorted memories of antebellum slavery had tremendous power and served an important function of healing the wounds of the Civil War, of granting the south authority in dealing with 'race problems' and of creating a new sense of unity defined by race, in effect creating a new community of whiteness. This was done by focusing on the romanticised plantation past in which the significance of place, more than people, echoed across time, but also by deploying stereotyping that elevated African American servitude to mythic levels. Pro-slavery rhetoric both before the war and since also served to challenge the binary between free and bonded labour, suggesting that free labour was often akin to enslavement. After the war, especially in the south, law enforcement and legislative systems of control responded to extreme abuses, such as murder or re-enslavement of African Americans, in similar ways to how sadistic violence against the enslaved had been treated under slavery. Morally upstanding southerners wanted to be seen to root out transgressors without overtly challenging the system that allowed such abuses to happen. Underpinning these trends are Social Darwinist views about racial hierarchy that also represented a continuum from the antebellum era. By the later nineteenth century, polygenesis was broadly discredited, but the roots of Jim Crow racism can be traced to influential antebellum literature on polygenesis such as that by anthropologist Samuel Morton and slave owner Josiah Nott, and by Louis Agassiz on enslaved individuals in South Carolina. After the Civil War, such views were also applied to new groups domestically and globally. Thus, chattel slavery informed the work of these theorists, which was then applied to other racial groups, domestically and globally, when theorising the necessity of forced labour or their tendency to trade in slaves because of racial weakness. The significance of this discourse will be explored more fully in Chapter 3; here the focus is on antebellum and postbellum continuities.

THE LEGACY OF ABOLITION

The discourse and rhetoric used on both sides of the Atlantic by the abolition movement had an important afterlife through its impact on the nascent international humanitarian movement. The practical legacy of the abolition movement is contested; much of the campaigning impulse dissipated after the American Civil War, with only a nostalgia for the heyday of the movement remaining, as activists, triggered by pamphlet or newspaper journalism, turned their attention away from slavery and towards other causes. But in other ways, within the United States, the perceived relevance of the abolition movement never entirely evaporated and throughout the post-emancipation period many reformers continued to acknowledge abolition of slavery, whether domestically or globally or both, as a live issue. Many abolitionists stopped talking about slavery-like working conditions in the United States but continued to see the movement's relevance as the United States' sphere of influence expanded in both the Pacific and Atlantic regions. An example of this is the important impact of antebellum-era abolitionist rhetoric and its anti-imperialist adaption in American discussions of the Congo, calling for reform of a colonial system that permitted torture and enslavement of black Africans. Especially pertinent is the reporting of missionary activities exposing the situation in the Congo in 1903. The *Lexington Gazette* proudly reprinted a report from London concerning a Lexington missionary, the Reverend W. M. Morrison, whose travels 'fully confirms the story of the abuses in the Congo Nation ... his personal investigation shows that the situation is growing daily worse ... as a result of the rubber monopoly's introduction of forced labour, virtually amounting to slavery'.[1] However, it is too simplistic to consider the change of use of abolitionist rhetoric during the nineteenth century from addressing domestic slavery prior to the Civil War, and then global slavery following it. Antebellum activists, influenced by the British antislavery activism of organisations such as the British and Foreign Antislavery Society, recognised that the struggle against slavery, while predominantly focused on the United States, always had to take into consideration the pernicious presence of slavery everywhere.

Moderate abolitionists' ideas were rhetorically distorted for conservative or radical purposes before emancipation and this continued in the

[1] *Lexington Gazette.* (Lexington, Va.), 06 May 1903. *Chronicling America: Historic American Newspapers*. Lib. of Congress. https://chroniclingamerica.loc.gov/lccn/sn84024716/1903–05-06/ed-1/seq-2/.

era after the war. The themes of the definitions of enslavement and freedom, the boundaries of coercion and the limits of different labour types were manipulated by commentators to show that many abolitionists had been hypocritical, too selective or lacking ambition. The conditions and experiences of enslavement of antebellum chattel slavery were compared favourably to other labour types in order to show that abolitionists had been deliberately or subconsciously in error to target it. Also, the persistent rhetoric about slavery almost always contained explicit or implicit commentary about the abolition movement, sometimes laudatory, sometimes critical. As William Green has argued in the case of abolition in the British Caribbean, the abolition movement continued to be relevant and contentious throughout the nineteenth century, because the success or failure of the movement was not judged on whether slavery had indeed been eradicated, but rather on whether the labour regime and systems of economic distribution that succeeded plantation slavery met the global trading needs.[2] The significance of the legacy of the abolition movement, the revivification of the memories of its antebellum activities, which for so long had been discredited and perceived as on the radical fringe of American political life, is that it helped frame most late nineteenth-century American discourse about slavery.

ANTISLAVERY CONTINUITIES

In the late nineteenth century, antislavery rhetoric was adopted by those campaigning for both increased and decreased American involvement in overseas territories. The broad church of abolitionism was welcoming to those of dichotomous political persuasions. As Ian Tyrrell has shown, post–Civil War reformers increasingly began to view their activism in terms of imperial rather than national agendas. He views the antislavery impulse as an unimportant part of the American reform tradition after the Civil War, as abolitionist aims were transferred to the women's movement.[3] In Chapter 5 of this book, I explore how the rhetoric of race and enslavement was an important part of anti-trafficking

[2] William Green, 'Plantation Society and Indentured Labour: the Jamaican Case 1834–1865', in P. C. Emmer, ed., *Colonialism and Migration: Indentured Labour Before and After Slavery* (Martinus Nijhoff Publishers, 1986), p. 165.

[3] Ian Tyrrell, *Reforming the World: the Creation of America's Modern Empire* (Princeton University Press, 2010), pp. 4, 19.

campaigning, as 'white slavery' became the chosen term for campaigners seeking to motivate the American public to act against forced and voluntary prostitution. Jane Addams, a prominent campaigner from Chicago against 'white slavery', explicitly drew parallels between her work and that of abolitionists, suggesting that the model of a first wave of extremists demanding immediate abolition who were then gradually joined by a second wave of moderates was repeating itself in the attempts to abolish 'white slavery'.[4] John Cumbler concurs with Tyrrell, showing that only Wendell Phillips saw a continuum between pre- and postbellum activism and argued that conditions required the persistence of an American abolition movement.[5] Evidence from the 1874 'Committee of the Anti-Slavery Reunion', proposed in Chicago, suggested that many former abolitionists saw their role as an historic rather than contemporary one. The organisation sent an announcement to abolitionists in London, explaining that they intended to hold a reunion encouraging them to 'embrace a review of the past ... a discussion of the lives of abolitionists ... recital of reminiscences ... singing the songs of liberty'.[6] Other scholars have argued that in the post–Civil war period, the people of the United States grew less concerned with Africa and its slave trade and that a conceptual break occurred at the moment of the demise of chattel slavery.[7] But while abolitionist activists and their cause may have waned in importance after the war, the influence of their methods and rhetoric, and memories of their successes and failures, continued to be felt.

One important flourishing of abolitionism in the late nineteenth century was the Congo Reform movement. It was led in the United States by campaigners such as the African American activists George Washington Williams and Booker T. Washington, the latter of whom was vice president of the Congo Reform Association and was also the American with the greatest interest in Africa during this period. According to Edward Chester, the most significant influence of the abolitionist tradition was an anti-imperialist one.[8] Much of the anti-imperialist discourse was racist

[4] Jane Addams, *A New Conscience and an Ancient Evil* (New York, 1912), p. 7.

[5] John T. Cumbler, *From Abolition to Rights for All* (University of Pennsylvania Press, 2008), p. 1.

[6] Announcement from Committee of the Anti-Slavery Reunion, Chicago 28/3/1874, MSS Brit Emp. S. 22/G 85, United States 1853–97 folder, Bodleian Library Special Collections.

[7] Edward Chester, *Clash of Titans: Africa and US Foreign Policy* (Orbis Books, 1974), p. 22; Paul Gilroy, *The Black Atlantic: Modernity and Double Consciousness* (Verso, 1998), p. 55.

[8] Michael Patrick Cullinane, *Liberty and American Anti-imperialism* (Palgrave, 2012); Chester, *Clash of Titans*, p. 176.

and exclusionary, but Williams and Edmund Morel employed the language of egalitarianism, emphasising the humanity of the African victims of Leopold's regime, calling for legislative and political change to help the weak, as well as deploying abolitionist tactics describing the dehumanising effects of such a regime on its white perpetrators, just as campaigners had had to do when confronting antebellum chattel slavery.[9] Morel, for example, recollected the heroism of the abolition movement, and the way that 'that wickedness' had been terminated by those 'few men who after incredible difficulty, heart breaking set-backs and soul-tearing toil, with pen and voice succeeded in raising the conscience of the world'; nonetheless, he wrote, 'the virus has spread'.[10]

However, it is wrong to assert, as did early historians of Anglo-American abolitionism Annie Abel and Frank Klingsberg, that while the British abolition movement was wide ranging in scope, the American focus was 'narrowly provincial'.[11] During the antebellum period, while mostly focusing on its own internal turmoil, the United States' abolition movement did attend to slavery in a global context and a sense of the transatlantic brotherhood of abolition persisted after the end of the Civil War, although some British abolitionists feared the waning of interest in the United States. In 1880, British abolitionist Joseph Cooper wrote, 'we must feel grateful to our few American friends who are exerting themselves, but those who thus act are a small minority. I think many do little and fear that more do nothing'. These concerns were shared by some African American correspondents. In 1893, Archibald Johnson wrote that 'the American colored is having a very hard time of it just now', and that he 'will like to hear that their old English friends stand by them and are true and faithful'.[12] The fear that African Americans were being abandoned by some of their white American abolitionist friends was exacerbated by the creation of myths of resistance such as the Underground Railroad that were entirely predicated on white heroism, with little attention paid or credit given to resistance of the enslaved.[13]

9 George Washington Williams, *A Report upon the Congo State and Country to the President of the Republic of the United States of America* (n.d).

10 Edmund D. Morel, *The Congo Slave State: A Protest against the New African Slavery* (Liverpool, 1903), p. 5.

11 Annie Abel and Frank Klingsberg, eds., *A Side Light on Anglo-American Relations 1839–58* (Association for the Study of Negro Life and History, 1929), p. 11.

12 Letter dated 13 Jan. 1880 from Joseph Cooper, Essex Hall, Walthamstow, to 'My Dear Friend', and Letter dated 1 Aug. 1893 from Archibald Johnson to 'Dear Sir', MSS Brit Emp. S. 22/G 85, United States 1853–97 folder, Bodleian Library Special Collections.

13 Larry Gara, *The Liberty Line: the Legend of the Underground Railroad* (University of Kentucky Press, reprint edition, 1996).

This crafting of an heroic white abolitionist narrative was one of the domestic contributory factors to the new pro-imperialist antislavery ideology, complementing the European-driven humanitarian impulse mimicked by the Americans.

Through an examination of consular correspondence and travel narratives, Ahmed E. Elbashir has shown that the United States' diplomats and newspaper readers had a lively interest in slavery and its abolition in East Africa and the Ottoman Empire prior to the Civil War.[14] Despite Elbashir's acknowledgement of the ingrained ideas of rigid racial and class hierarchy which meant that travellers were often repulsed by the sight of the slaves themselves and not by the institution of slavery, the influence of antislavery thinking on some of the authors he surveys was compelling. One such was American explorer John Lloyd Stevens, who, in the 1830s, recognised the basic humanity of the enslaved men and women he encountered at Jeddah, Saudi Arabia.[15] This type of humanitarianism persisted after the Civil War, often involving a direct remembrance of pre-war abolitionism. James Blount's historical account, published in a pamphlet in 1913 on the American occupation of the Philippines, issued a call to Americans to take up their imperial burden, and also made an explicit call to remember the abolitionist example, reminding his readers that Abraham Lincoln 'kept vigil for four years at the bedside of a sick nation through all the long agony of its efforts to throw off from its system the inherited curse of slavery. Of course human slavery was a relic of barbarism'.[16] But abolitionism was not only a powerful force in the minds of those who supported its cause. Its legacy remained alive for more conservative commentators, too.

ANTI-ABOLITION CONTINUITIES

Rhetoric deployed to challenge the methods or ideology of the abolition movement also existed in a continuum linking the periods before and after the Civil War, and writers in both eras contextualised this anti-abolition agenda using international labour concerns. George Fitzhugh was one of the most influential of the pro-slavery writers working prior to the Civil War. He was beloved by his fellow defenders of the peculiar institution

14 Ahmed E. Elbashir, *The United States, Slavery and the Slave Trade in the Nile Valley* (University Press of America, 1983).
15 Ibid., p. 32.
16 James H. Blount, *American Occupation of the Philippines 1898–1912* (Putnams, 1913, reprint Malay Books, 1968), p. 693.

and attacked vociferously by abolitionists. Much of the work focuses on Fitzhugh's arguments about the benefits of slavery to global economies and its superiority to so-called free labour, which he calls 'White Slavery', as a labour system.

But it is Fitzhugh's vilifications of abolitionist aims in a global context that are crucial, because these ideas, though often under-represented by scholars, became an important feature of the conservative stories told about the role abolition played in America's past. Fitzhugh based his critique of abolitionism on a challenge to the personal morality of those espousing its cause. He called them 'infidels', ethnically othering them because since the early modern period the term had been applied by Christians predominantly to those of other faiths in the Islamic and Jewish worlds. But the usage also reached back to the medieval etymology of the word meaning 'unfaithful' or 'not to be trusted'.[17] Fitzhugh challenged the selective compassion of abolitionists, who, he said, focused on American chattel slavery for their own nefarious political purposes, and did not pay any attention to forced labour scenarios elsewhere:

> Abolition never arose till negro slavery was instituted and now abolition is only directed against negro slavery. There is no philanthropic crusade attempting to set free the white slaves of Eastern Europe and of Asia. The world then is prepared for the defense of slavery in the abstract – it is prejudiced only against negro slavery.[18]

In a moment of foresight, Fitzhugh predicted that the abolitionists' activities would cause 'a civil and fratricidal war', but also suggested that neglect by abolitionists of the cause of global slavery would lead to the perpetuation of it as a system of labour elsewhere: 'whilst they are engaged in this labour of love, Northern and English merchants are rapidly extending and increasing slavery by opening daily markets for the purchase and sale of Coolies, apprentices and Africans'. Thus, he lamented, 'abolitionists have become the most efficient propagandists of slavery and the slave trade'.[19] Writing a generation later, revealing that many seemed to have short memories regarding slavery, Francis Newman concurred with Fitzhugh's assessment, stating that, by 1889, many people knew little of 'negro slavery' and they assumed that abolition had been a failure because it had led to the emergence of 'modified slavery' such as indentured labour.[20] Also building on Fitzhugh's themes, J. A. Moloney, a British

[17] George Fitzhugh, *Cannibals All! Or Slaves without Masters* (originally 1857, this edition Harvard University Press, 1960), p. 35.

[18] Ibid., p. 200. [19] Ibid., pp. 232–3.

[20] Francis Newman, *Anglo-Saxon Abolition of Negro Slavery* (London, 1889), pp. 2, 36.

FIGURE 1 'Slavery as it exists in England, Slavery as it exists in America', lithographic print by John Haven, printed Boston 1850. Library of Congress.

traveller in Africa, observed what he considered to be a tolerable form of slavery in which 'the slave of a powerful Arab will frequently own numerous drudges of his own'. Moloney, writing in 1893, showed the long-term influence of antebellum abolitionism because he blamed writers such as Harriet Beecher Stowe and her seminal work *Uncle Tom's Cabin* for misleading the public as to the nature of slavery. '*Uncle Tom's Cabin* should be banished from the mind', argued Moloney.[21] Henry Nevinson, usually a sympathiser with the abolitionist aim to end all forms of slavery, argued that not only was the rhetoric of some abolitionists misleading, but they were also hypocritical, because they were willing to abandon their principles for profit. Those who used to be abolitionists, he wrote, 'have all become tamer now and more ready to show consideration for human failings, provided they pay'.[22]

A generation later, the same themes are evident in the work of Marxist thinker Walter Wilson, who also used the flexible definitions of slave and free labour to criticise what he saw as the hypocrisy of the abolition movement. Wilson's overriding aim was to defend the Soviet Union against accusations of the use of forced labour by showing how prevalent it was elsewhere, and, in doing so, he conducted an important expose into the types of unfree labour still existing in the United States in the 1930s. However, as a Marxist, he felt that any form of labour exploitation amounted to slavery and, in neglecting to challenge the capitalist system, antislavery activists, prior to the American Civil War and after, had been naïve and left a job unfinished. In every capitalist country, he argued, 'free' wage labour and direct forced labour exist side by side.[23] But he went further and accused antislavery campaigners of consciously behaving hypocritically by seeming to launch humanitarian campaigns for the rights of the most vulnerable, while their true motivation was to source the 'more efficient type of labour . . . needed to man the new industries in the colonies'.[24] As explored in Chapter 2, this critique of the post-emancipation antislavery movement owed much to the new imperialist conditions emerging during this period as the United States sought to build an international reputation for itself partly modelled on that of the European nations such as Britain. But crucially, it also built on a long tradition of anti-abolition rhetoric that emerged in the 1850s and

[21] J. A. Moloney, *With Captain Stairs to Katanga* (London, 1893), p. 69.
[22] Henry W. Nevinson, *A Modern Slavery* (London & New York, 1906), p. 43.
[23] Walter Wilson, *Forced Labour in the United States* (London, 1933), p. 18.
[24] Ibid., p. 19.

persisted in the post–Civil War era, which argued for the inadequacy, duplicity and insincerity of the abolition movement. By 1927, the global humanitarian campaign to address the continued existence of slavery and slavery-like labour acknowledged that the words of the heroes of abolition had a hollow ring, given the incomplete nature of their abolition, and showing the error of the view that 'brought up on the history of Wilberforce and Lincoln, most of us had comfortably assumed that slavery was a thing of the past'.[25] Explicitly anti-abolition discourse was but one of the tools used by writers to pursue a broader pro-slavery agenda before 1860, and there is also an important broader rhetorical continuum between antebellum pro-slavery writing and the themes that emerged after emancipation in the debates about slavery and forced labour.

THE LEGACY OF PRO-SLAVERY THINKING

As already shown, crucial to the rhetorical arsenal of pro-slavery thinkers was the idea of a mutable boundary between slave and free labour. They furthered the perception that the accepted definition of slave and free labour as dichotomous was misleading and erroneous, put forward by abolitionists who wished to dismantle successful and acceptable systems of control and order that had operated for generations. Robert Steinfeld has shown that commentators, in the United States and beyond, grappled with the evolving and often troubling idea of free labour, over the *longue durée*. He traces their struggle to conceptualise slavery from its evolution in the eighteenth century as an unusual labour form, involving far smaller numbers compared to indentured servitude, to its role, through the work of nineteenth century abolitionists, as the perceived opposite of freedom.[26] As explained in Chapter 4, during the mid to late nineteenth century, indentured servitude and other systems such as peonage were increasingly identified as forced labour types akin to slavery, but also prior to the Civil War, pro-slavery advocates, such as Fitzhugh, resisted the stark distinction between free and slave labour, using two rhetorical methods. By using comparison, showing that the lived experience of the enslaved was more comfortable than that of free labourers, which will be

[25] 'Slave or Free? Native Labour: An International Problem', Official Paper of the League of Nations, no. 23, Nov. 1927.

[26] Robert Steinfeld, *The Invention of Free Labor: Employment Relation in English and American Law and Culture 1350–1870* (University of North Carolina Press, 1991), pp. 4–6.

explored in detail in the comparisons section later in this chapter, and also through trying to decontaminate the concept of slavery as a moral evil and render it as a preferable labour choice among many, all of which in some senses shared the characteristics of coercion. He argued that 'free society asserts the right of a few to the earth – slavery maintains that it belongs in different degrees to all'.[27] His conception of the cyclical nature of history and the inevitability that the flawed era of emancipation would soon have to run its course led him to suggest that 'the world will only fall back on domestic slavery when all other social forms have failed and been exhausted'.[28]

George Fitzhugh was among many pro-slavery advocates who worked with the Freedmen's Bureau after emancipation, and the influence of men such as he led Norbert Finzsch to suggest that both northern and southern military men were keen to find a quick solution to the labour problem of the south after the war and to find new ways to put the formerly enslaved to work. Thus, the Freedmen's Bureau, while maintaining the conventional rhetorical dichotomy between slave and free, blurred the lines between the two labour systems as, after the war, many of the labour contracts secured for African Americans inaugurated a system of 'compulsory free labour': debt bondage reinforced by an extra-legal system of intimidation.[29] Debates over the definition and reality of freedom after emancipation also had a gendered aspect, as the 'regime of contract', as Amy Dru Stanley called it, also extended to enforcing new ideas of marriage and proper female roles in the newly freed population.[30] Many freedmen and women resisted the imposition of these notions, but other formerly enslaved men believed that their freedom was confirmed by the new possibility of subjugating their wives, a power that, despite the existence of monogamous relationships with the permission of some masters, had largely been denied them under the system of chattel slavery.[31]

The system of extra-legal intimidation that, in the eyes of southern whites, kept the African American population under control had its

[27] Fitzhugh, *Cannibals All*, p. 19. [28] Ibid., p. 6.

[29] 'The End of Slavery, the Role of the Freedmen's Bureau and the Introduction of Peonage' in Ulrike Schmieder, Katja Füllberg-Stolberg & Michael Zeuske, eds., *The End of Slavery in Africa and the Americas. A Comparative Approach* (LIT Verlag, 2011), pp. 142–4.

[30] Amy Dru Stanley, *From Bondage to Contract: Wage Labour, Marriage and Market in the Age of Slave Emancipation* (Cambridge University Press, 1998), p. 36.

[31] Ibid., p. 47.

origins in the antebellum period. Sally Hadden has shown that throughout the chattel slavery period slave owners employed white representatives to patrol, monitor and punish their enslaved property, but when, in the later years of the antebellum period, such mechanisms of control escalated into sadistic violence, the slave-owning hegemonic power wanted to show its paternalistic side and began to prosecute the white transgressors.[32] South Carolina law enforcers demonstrated to one another their modernity and their civility by undertaking trials such as the prosecution and conviction of Thomas Motley and William Blackledge for the murder of an enslaved man in South Carolina in 1854.[33] Similarly, in the period after the war, acceptable controlling behaviour by the white population was rigidly defined by custom and shared assumptions. While few plantation owners challenged the appropriateness of black peon labour, and most considered their land to be their own fiefdom where they might enforce control, when such forced labour situations escalated into unwarranted extreme violence to the labourer, a line was drawn by the federal government. In Covington, Georgia, in 1921, in a still-insular plantation world in which white neighbours could turn a blind eye, and black peon labourers rarely left the property, John Williams became the first southern man to be convicted of first degree murder of a black man, although in fact he murdered ten, some of whom were killed by Clyde Manning, Williams's black overseer, forced to kill in order to save himself.[34]

Such horrors were obviously underpinned by the virulent racist ideology of the Jim Crow era, which saw African Americans and people of many other races dismissed as inferior to whites in the rigid racial hierarchy. This system, although bolstered by new scientific thinking in the post-emancipation era had its origins in the racial ideology upon which chattel slavery was predicated. Mid-century works such as *Types of Mankind* published by Gliddon and Nott in 1854 were crucial to the thinking of pro-slavery apologists such as John C. Calhoun, but, after the war, also influenced popular, elite and intellectual attitudes towards other races, within the new United States imperial territories, on the continent itself and when observing the behaviour of 'others' across the

[32] Sally Hadden, *Slave Patrols: Law and Violence in Virginia and the Carolinas* (Harvard University Press, 2003).

[33] For more on this case, see my chapter on 'Slave Hunting as Sport' in Andrew Dix and Peter Templeton, eds., *So the War Goes On: Violence and Its Representation in African American History from Slavery to Black Lives Matter* (Routledge, 2020).

[34] Pete Daniel, *The Shadow of Slavery: Peonage in the South 1901–1969* (Oxford University Press, 1972), pp. 115, 126.

globe. George Gliddon's thinking was developed during his time spent in Egypt, while his co-author Josiah Nott spent his career furthering such attitudes as the inherent suitability of black Africans, seen by him as a separate species, for labouring in hot climate.[35] In Chapter 3 the influence and evolution of these racial theories will be traced in more detail, showing how anti-imperialists borrowed such discourse to argue that slavery perpetuated by other races could not be allowed to pollute the United States. Here, in this chapter, the importance of ideas fermenting prior to the Civil War and their legacy in the postbellum era will be documented.

Prior to the Civil War, the significance of theories of racial hierarchy to the discourse of slave ownership was fundamental. Carter Wilson has shown that psychologically, slave owners had to dehumanise their slaves in order to be able to consider themselves as good Christians while simultaneously alienating and brutalising human beings, which was essential under the slave system to the maintenance of law and order.[36] Thus the ideas of scientific racism helped slavery function on a community and individual level. But this does not mean that such ideas were immediately abandoned following the emancipation of slaves in the United States. Rather these ideas became more entrenched than ever and served to justify a new ideology of racial separateness and non-white political inadequacy, and performed a new but similar function, that of bolstering the reputation of white Americans as representatives of the nation on a global scale; whites who were now at the top of a globally defined rather than domestically defined hierarchy.

Prior to the Civil War, concepts of race had evolved from enlightenment notions of the mutability of race into a form of scientific racial determinism. Much of this debate focused on the differences rather than the similarities of the races, as theories of polygenesis, common since the early modern period, were challenged for the first time. Academic theories, such as the Great Chain of Being, were adapted to the political expediency of the time. An example is the ongoing genocidal treatment of Native Americans throughout this period, which was often justified using racial determinism. But it was the destiny of African Americans that was most obviously affected by such intellectual debates, as discussions about the moral value of slavery were closely linked to those about human

[35] William Stanton, *The Leopard's Spots: Scientific Attitudes towards Race in America: 1815–59* (University of Chicago Press, 1960), p. 62.

[36] Carter Wilson, *Racism from Slavery to Advanced Capitalism* (Sage, 1996), p. 35.

origins. Anthropologists such as Louis Agassiz posited that humankind did not develop from a single human couple, while Alexander Winchell countered, arguing that while black races were inferior to whites, they were not descended from Adam but predated him. Prior to the Civil War, such ideologies were used to underpin the Christian justification of and support for slavery (abolitionist discourse was heathen, according to George Armstrong), but after the war they were moulded to a more useful and expedient end to emphasise separateness as, domestically, miscegenation became the great fear.[37] Even commentators who criticised American racism, such as British traveller W. Laird Clowes who opined that 'he sits on the grave of the red man, he has shut the door in the face of the yellow man ... what shall he do with the black man from Africa?', also wrote 'you cannot make a silk purse out of a sow's ear', and suggested that black Africans were inherently child-like.[38] Other sympathetic commentators who appealed for racial equality, such as Henry Ward Beecher, the son of abolitionists, acknowledged the powerful rhetoric of those dividing the races, and in some senses excused the behaviour of white southerners. In a speech in 1876 at Plymouth church, to mark the centennial of independence, Ward Beecher stated that it was difficult for men such as Wade Hampton 'to go about among his late slaves canvassing for their votes. The question before that was, are they men or monkeys'.[39] But not all writers excused the racially deterministic attitudes of southerners. Albert Bushnell Hart argued that, while there were differences between races, such as in the issue of personal morality, 'the negro is entitled to be measured not by brain calipers, not by two meter rods, but by what he can do in the world'.[40]

While domestically, racial ideology concerning African Americans largely moved away from discussions of slavery and towards an emphasis on separateness, as the United States redefined itself in relation to slavery on a global scale, racial determinism was adapted for new imperialist and anti-imperialist purposes. As Walter Hixon has argued, this was most explicitly the case in the conquest of the Philippines, where, in 1901, the killing of forty-eight American soldiers at Balangiga revived memories of

[37] David Livingstone, *Adam's Ancestors: Race, Religion and the Politics of Human Origin* (Johns Hopkins University Press, 2008), p. 145.

[38] W. Laird Clowes, *Black America: A Study of the Ex-slave and His Late Master* (London, Paris and Melbourne, 1891), pp. 160, 166.

[39] Henry Ward Beecher, *Patriotic Addresses in America and England, 1850–1885* (New York, 1888), p. 775.

[40] Albert Bushnell Hart, *The Southern South* (New York, 1910), p. 134.

Little Big Horn. Newspapers used striking headlines such as 'catastrophe at Balangiga', and depicted the defeat as a 'surprise' with the 'several hundred Bolomen' conducting 'signs of awful butchery. Our men lay stark in the streets and public square far advanced in mortification and fearfully mutilated'.[41] The model of racial stereotyping used by Americans in the Philippines was that which had been learned through warfare with the Native Americans in the continental United States. Direct comparisons were made with one Filipino military leader being compared to Geronimo. In contrast, the Hawaiian elite, such as the deposed queen Liliuoukolani, were increasingly depicted by the cartoonists of the popular press as negroid, sending out the dual message of racial inferiority and political ineptitude.[42]

Immigration to the United States was another issue taxing the racial determinists and, in the second half of the nineteenth century, they used discourse borrowed from antebellum slavery to render some of the new immigrants as 'other'. Najia Aarim-Heriot has shown that the Chinese were victims of this rhetorical link of their destiny with American negrophobia. She argues that from 1848 onwards, the labour of both blacks and Chinese was seen as 'degraded' and could never be part of the sphere of free labour.[43] Pro-slavery activists argued that the use of black labour was justified because, unlike the Chinese, by this period almost all black labour was American-born and therefore influenced by the positive values of the nation.[44] Following the war, both races were still seen as degraded labour, justifying the debt bondage systems that arose in the southern states to control the African American population, and justifying the exclusionary policies against the Chinese. Ideas of racial hierarchy, so instrumental under slavery, were merely adapted after emancipation to a different purpose. Stuart Creighton Miller showed that until the Chinese began to arrive in California in great numbers, American attitudes towards them were relatively benign. The migration coincided with the increased popularity of scientific racism and germ theory, thus making the anti-Chinese rhetoric particularly vicious. But Creighton Miller argues that it was the

[41] *Evening Star.* (Washington, DC), 12 Dec. 1901. *Chronicling America: Historic American Newspapers*. Lib. of Congress. https://chroniclingamerica.loc.gov/lccn/sn83045462/1901–12-12/ed-1/seq-17/.

[42] Walter Hixon, *American Settler Colonialism: A History* (Palgrave, 2013), pp. 156, 171–4.

[43] Najia Aarim-Heriot, *Chinese Immigrants, African Americans and Racial Anxiety in the United States 1848–82* (University of Illinois Press, 2003), pp. ix, 10.

[44] Ibid., p. 167.

link with slavery that was also timely, stating that, as after 1865 chattel slavery was 'a dead issue', more attention was paid to the 'coolie' trade.[45] I disagree with this assessment of the significance of chattel slavery post-1865, but do acknowledge, as he does, that the rhetoric about the arrival of coolies centred on their labour representing a new form of slavery. This will be explored further in Chapter 4.

The most important way that chattel slavery rhetorically influenced the post-war world was through the deployment of cultural rather than scientific tools: the use of memories and nostalgia of slavery to create and defend a sense of white community and sense of place. The plantation, the site of many of the horrors of slavery, was recreated under this use of myth as a place of joy and comfort for both races, while the formerly enslaved population were fashioned as docile and loyal. Newspapers serialised so-called 'moonlight and magnolia' stories such as that by James Franklin Fitts, *In Dixie Land Before the War*, spreading the romanticisation of the slave past to wide audiences.[46] Both of these myths (slavery as benign, slaves as happy) were instigated as a psychological coping mechanism for the southern white population who, having suffered the deprivations of the Civil War, were then unable to accept the freedmen and women as equals. The myths also served to heal the divisions within the United States as, after 1877, bringing together the white northerners and southerners in a shared national identity was judged more important than the search for justice for the formerly enslaved. As Thomas McCarthy put it, 'race lost out to reunion' and so for political reasons the memory of slavery was configured and deployed by the community.[47] In 1891, W. Laird Clowes was rather overoptimistic when he asserted that no one in the United States 'regrets that slavery has been abolished or which would restore it tomorrow even if it were able to do so by the stroke of a pen'.[48]

This nostalgic refiguring was less about the enslaved themselves and more about the places in which they worked, as after the war white southerners felt a strong desire to feel at home again in their landscape,

[45] Stuart Creighton Miller, *The Unwelcome Immigrant: the American Image of the Chinese 1785–1882* (University of California Press, 1969), p. 150.

[46] *Baxter Springs News*. (Baxter Springs, Kan.), 30 Dec. 1893. *Chronicling America: Historic American Newspapers*. Lib. of Congress. https://chroniclingamerica.loc.gov/lccn/sn83040592/1893-12-30/ed-1/seq-7/.

[47] Thomas McCarthy, *Race, Empire and the Idea of Human Development* (Cambridge University Press, 2009), p. 111.

[48] Laird Clowes, *Black America*, p. 20.

and to do this they harkened back to the supposedly lost plantation world. In reality, many plantation owners rebuilt their lives and livelihoods on the same land as their forefathers had occupied before the war, with the same labourers and their descendants working that land, but the myth of the ruined, abandoned plantation, the lost heyday, the place in the past where everyone was truly happy was a powerful one. Typical of the depictions of the abandoned plantation as a visual type was in the art of French-born George David Coulon, an example being 'Ruins of Versailles Plantation, Chalmette, Louisiana' from 1885. The title of this painting ironically referenced the grandeur of the original French Versailles, while depicting a ruined plantation house with grandeur now lost, standing alone facing the encroaching natural world.[49]

These romantic landscapes formed a central tenet of the broader, lost cause, myth. Even though the grand plantation house was only one of many landscape experiences of antebellum white and black southerners, it became, in the Jim Crow era, *the* southern experience of slavery, to such an extent that historians of slavery have only recently begun to focus on the lives of slaves who worked and lived in off-plantation spaces.[50] Literature and art constructed this myth for white consumers, but it did not emerge fully formed until after the Civil War, as the most famous mythical portrayal of southern plantation life shows. Eastman Johnson's 'Old Kentucky Home – Negro Life in the South' painted in 1859, originally depicted a scene of urban slavery but was co-opted as part of the romanticisation of the southern rural landscape. It shows racial mixing taking place, and its results in the presence of mixed-race individuals in the scene, but crucially its theatrical construction of the plantation community affected the construction of the post-war myth of a life of ease and happiness, rather than the reality of back-breaking work. Its literary equivalent was the work of Thomas Nelson Page, such as the novel *In Ole Virginia*, published in 1887, which reinforced the twin aspects of contentment of the plantation. Not only did the enslaved people there live well, but they were happy to be there and to serve their white masters.[51] Contemporary commentators recognised a distinctive southern mindset

[49] Alexis Boylan, 'From Gilded Age to *Gone with the Wind*', in Angela D. Mack & Stephen G. Hoffus, eds., *Landscape of Slavery: the Plantation in American Art* (University of South Carolina Press, 2008), p. 121.

[50] See Lawrence Aje and Catherine Armstrong, eds., *The Many Faces of Slavery* (Bloomsbury Academic, 2020) for a series of essays confronting the plantation paradigm.

[51] Kenneth W. Goings, *Mammy and Uncle Mose: Black Collectibles and American Stereotyping* (Indiana University Press, 1994), p. 10.

created, according to Albert Bushnell Hart, the son of abolitionist parents, because of the late abolition of slavery in the region. He argued that this myth of 'a prosperous happy and glorious community' had emerged because of 'the obstinate maintenance of slavery' in the region.[52] As well as art and literature, theatre made the plantation myth especially accessible to white Americans from all social orders, through performances of shows such as *Uncle Tom's Cabin*, derived from Harriet Beecher Stowe's popular antebellum novel but often as pastiches rather than true versions.[53] Throughout the late nineteenth century it was popular as a stage show, perpetuating a number of iconic myths of slavery such as the happy slaves, the tricksy runaways who triggered a dramatic pursuit with hounds, often using live dogs in the production. Such performances, along with figurines, toys and Uncle Tom wallpaper, were also popular in Britain, although there was less shyness about admitting the novel's abolitionist origins in Britain.[54] Minstrelsy, which was popular before the Civil War as well as after, also used crude stereotyping of the formerly enslaved as well as employing white actors in blackface.

John Denis Mercier and Steven Dubin both argue that stereotyping of emancipated African Americans into types created in slavery was so culturally powerful that it acted as a form of 'symbolic slavery'.[55] Dubin examined the prevalence of stereotyping in articles of material culture such as greetings cards or homeware and argues that the unconscious use of these articles around the home once again renders African Americans in the supporting role to whites and denies them a voice, just as under slavery. Therefore these objects symbolically depicting black servitude are invisible and taken for granted.[56] The nature of the black characters made them safe for whites, as the 'auntie' and 'uncle', the 'mammie' and the 'sambo' never challenged white hegemony, but more than that, they acted as collaborators and allies. When white Americans looked back at chattel slavery and saw it through the lens of these characters, they were able to convince themselves that although a key part of the historic landscape of the nation, slavery had done neither race any harm and,

[52] Bushnell Hart, *The Southern South*, pp. 81–2.

[53] William van Deberg, *Slavery and Race in American Popular Culture* (University of Wisconsin Press, 1984), p. 48.

[54] Richard Huzzey, *Freedom Burning: Anti-Slavery and Empire in Victorian Britain* (Cornell University Press, 2012), p. 21.

[55] Goings, *Mammy and Uncle Mose*, p. 20; Steven Dubin, 'Symbolic Slavery: Black Representations in Popular Culture', *Social Problem*, April 1987.

[56] Dubin, 'Symbolic Slavery', p. 127.

implicitly, it might even have been preferable to the race problem of their present day. The message was also designed for African Americans, to control and subjugate the newly emancipated and to reinvent the history of chattel slavery, denying its horror.

In this period, artefacts of African American origin such as the stories and myths told under slavery were also reconstructed with the goal of rewriting the slave past, and Joel Chandler Harris's Uncle Remus tales were part of this trend.[57] Harry Nevinson, a British investigative journalist employed at the turn of the twentieth century by *Harper's Magazine* to write an exposé on African slavery, also mentioned the Uncle Remus tales in order to rewrite the United States' troubled history with slavery. Mindful of his American audience, Nevinson blamed European colonialists and their African collaborators for the continued existence of slavery in West and Central Africa and used his narrative to call upon Americans to take up the 'white man's burden'. He wrote 'from here we can turn only to America. There the sense of freedom seems to linger. America's record is clean compared to England'.[58] He went on to give evidence of the closeness and affinity of the Congolese with the African American, arguing that the Umbundu proverbs, such as the Lion who needs no servant, were very similar to the Uncle Remus folktales. Levinson did not make explicit his argument here, but he is not suggesting that both black Africans and those within the African diaspora deserve sympathy, but rather that white Americans are making a very good job of managing the 'race problem' at home, and therefore should be encouraged to turn their attention to the issue on a global scale.[59]

Not all cultural artefacts that recalled a slave past reconstituted chattel slavery in such a positive light. A few moments of resistance can be spotted, such as in George and Huestis P. Cook's photographs of the late-nineteenth -century lives and places of the formerly enslaved in the Richmond, Virginia, area. Huestis, who took over his father's business, was especially interested in depicting African Americans in realistic settings, and therefore photographed them at work, at church, and at home, giving them agency by refusing to apply the romanticised Lost Cause filter to their lives. An example of this is the photograph 'Possum am Sweet' of 1898, depicting the home of a black couple who appear old enough to remember slavery, and therefore one of whom may have grown up in that cabin under slavery. However, while the image recalls a timelessness, a sense of the presence of the ghosts of chattel slavery within the home, it also observes that the

[57] Goings, *Mammy and Uncle Mose*, pp. xix, 9. [58] Nevinson, *A Modern Slavery*, p. 208.
[59] Ibid., p. 93.

FIGURE 2 'Couple at fireside: Possum am Sweet', photograph by Huestis Cook, 1900. © The Valentine, Richmond.

formerly enslaved have created their own domesticity and sense of family and self.[60] The power of the memory of antebellum slavery for black and white Americans is significant, and this further reveals itself in the extent to which this type of slavery became the archetypical slavery for all discussions after the Civil War, and became the point of comparison for those debating slavery and forced labour in its domestic and global forms.

CHATTEL SLAVERY AS ARCHETYPE

This chapter has explored the ways in which, in the period after the Civil War, the historical antebellum chattel slavery and the collective memory

[60] For more on Huestes Cook, see Leslie King-Hammond, 'Identifying Spaces of Blackness: the Aesthetics of Resistance and Identity in American Plantation Art', in Mack & Hoffus, eds., *Landscape of Slavery*, p. 73.

of it, impacted the conceptions of race and slavery, as the United States both examined its own cultural history and attempted to imagine itself as a new player on the global stage and, in doing so, borrowed from anti-slavery rhetoric of the European powers. Now the rhetorical power of chattel slavery will be explored in more depth, with an examination of the ways in which authors explicitly referred to this unique and, in the language of the time 'peculiar', forced labour form, linking it to other types of slavery and forced labour in the United States and in the wider world.

RHETORICAL SYMBOLISM

After emancipation, the memory and sense of awareness of antebellum slavery was invidious. The symbolism and iconography of slavery were deployed by writers for a variety of authorial purposes in the knowledge that readers of English almost anywhere in the world would be able to understand the reference. This shows how, even in the late nineteenth century, United States antebellum chattel slavery had become the archetype of slavery globally, to which authors might refer only obliquely, confident that their meaning would still be divined by their audience. The word 'slavery' had tremendous rhetorical power, and its significance was enforced by its being coupled with the symbols and icons of the recently abolished chattel form. That the language of this particular type of slavery was so powerful shows not only the dominance of the plantation form in rhetorical discourse, despite it not being the sole experience for American enslaved, some of whom served in different places and economic relationships. This reveals the powerful memories and legacies of the romanticised view of plantation life under antebellum slavery, but also the significance of the abolition movement, which was even more important than the pre-war pro-slavery ideologues in creating a lasting sense of what antebellum southern slavery was. Their rhetorical symbols – bloodhounds, chains and whips, and slave auctions – form the precise iconography of slavery that survived into the period after the Civil War and was used to such important effect when describing and defining other forms of forced labour.

Campaigners observing types of forced labour within the United States had a pre-ordained rhetorical toolkit from which to select in order to encourage their readers to rekindle in their minds the horrors of antebellum slavery. Forced labour often took place in the same landscapes, with the same victims (or their descendants), practised by the same perpetrators (or their descendants) as the chattel slavery form had decades earlier. To draw readers' attention to the pernicious nature of forced labour in the United States, it was natural and easy for authors to draw on the symbolism and iconography of the earlier model. Sometimes symbols of chattel slavery such as the whip were used explicitly to encourage the reader to draw a comparison, as in the case of Walter Wilson who wrote that convict labourers in the South after emancipation were 'whipped into signing contracts ... just as surely as Negro slaves were whipped to their tasks'.[61] Elsewhere in his book, comparisons were implicit as he described the conditions in which many convicts were kept by the brutal guards who 'knew how to handle niggers and bloodhounds', undertaking 'manhunting – the favourite sport of the southern ruling classes'.[62] These comments refer back to the continuity of the systems of slave patrolling before the Civil War and night-riding after it, but Wilson is also implying that an intimate familiarity with the long history of white hegemony under slavery in the south had prepared those white men in charge of convicts in the Jim Crow era to perform their duties successfully. It is also an interesting use of the term 'manhunting' as a considerable amount of European antislavery literature of the period seeking to justify imperialist intervention also referred to the still-extant Arab-African slave trade as 'manhunting'.[63]

The convict labour system's borrowing of the symbolism of slavery encouraged campaigners to make this rhetorical connection. John L. Spivak's novel, based on real life accounts, entitled *Georgia Nigger*, explored the role of the white overseer, showing that control of the victim's time by another was common to both: 'an hour before sundown the overseer blew his whistle', narrated the character, David.[64] He also used the shared icon of the chains of the chain gang and the chains of slavery so as to leave readers in no doubt about the pernicious nature of both systems, describing his time on the chain gang at Buzzard's Roost in stark terms. He recalled in the cage where convict labourers spent the night that the weight of the chains made it impossible to sleep and

[61] Wilson, *Forced Labour*, p. 15.

[62] Ibid., pp. 72–3. Wilson may have been referring here to the white supremacist James Vardaman, sometime governor of Mississippi, who enjoyed spending time at Parchman prison setting a prisoner free to run, and then pursuing him as prey on horseback.

[63] For example, 'The Brussels Conference and the Congo State', from the *Paris Memorial Diplomatique* 6/9/1890, bound in a collection of African pamphlets, 1884–95, Bodleian Library, Oxford.

[64] J. L. Spivak, *Georgia Nigger* (London, 1933), p. 83.

described his fellow prisoners as 'the chained things', utterly dehumanised by their experience.[65]

Rhetorically claiming an abusive situation as 'slavery' was an important tool in the campaigner's arsenal, and those trying to promote legal and political action over prostitution in the United States in the early twentieth century used the term 'white slavery' to great effect in mobilising public concern through a series of popular pamphlets and newspaper exposés. More on this will appear in Chapter 5. Some writers went beyond merely using the word 'slavery' and also used the imagery of slavery to provoke a response in their readers. Jane Addams suggested that young children were being enticed into prostitution by procurers and, at that moment, 'vice seared their tender minds with red hot irons'.[66] Surely she had the branding of the antebellum African American enslaved, a common punishment under chattel slavery, in mind when she used this metaphor.

This use of the symbolism of chattel slavery also occurred in debates about global forced labour. At the turn of the twentieth century, many of those alerting the American public to the horrors of the Belgian Congo saw themselves as neo-abolitionists and borrowed many of their rhetorical methods and chosen words from the earlier campaign. Edmund Morel was one of those; he referred to the 'cannibal troops' of Belgian King Leopold's *Force Privée* as 'the bloodhounds of the company' that kept the forced labourers working collecting rubber through fear of extreme physical violence.[67] George Washington Williams also used the symbolism of antebellum slavery to instil concern in his readers about the Congo horror. In his pamphlet 'An Open Letter to His Serene Majesty, Leopold II', Williams described the labour system that he encountered on his travels in Congo using the icons of American chattel slavery: the use of chain gangs, the prevalence of the whip as a method of punishment and inducement to work, and the offer of rewards if runaways were captured and returned to their place of work. He also described the practice of dislocation of the enslaved person, by their being transported a long distance from their place of origin, an aspect common to many types of slavery across time. Williams described this process as being 'sent down the river', referring in this case to the Congo

[65] Ibid., pp. 174–6. [66] Addams, *A New Conscience and an Ancient Evil*, p. 124.
[67] Morel, *The Congo Slave State*, p. 64.

River, but with strong echoes of the nineteenth century practice in the United States of internal slave trading where enslaved people feared being transported down the Ohio and Mississippi Rivers to the newly opened cotton fields of the deep south.[68]

The language of slave corralling and sale emerging first from the wider Atlantic world context and then later the domestic United States slave trade, was adopted by those commenting on other types of bonded labour. G. B. Densmore wrote a pamphlet designed to encourage the tightening of immigration controls against Chinese arrivals in California, and he quoted from General John Miller who depicted all Chinese as 'slaves' and the nation itself as 'the great slave pen from whence labourers for this country are being drawn'.[69] Reverend Gibson also used memories of the abuse of female slaves at auction to excoriate the Chinese for their treatment of immigrant women who supposedly became concubines or sex slaves. He wrote that 'the girls were critically examined after the manner of the African slave dealers not many years ago'.[70] As seen here, recalling the imagery of slavery was most potent when it was accompanied by a direct comparison between present labour injustice and memories of past abuses.

COMPARISON WITH ANTEBELLUM SLAVERY

The most effective way that an author called to mind the archetypical example of American antebellum chattel slavery was by making a direct comparison with it, a very common rhetorical tool in the literature of the period. This was done in three ways. First, by claiming that a system of forced labour was, in fact, slavery, the exact moral and practical copy of chattel slavery. Some commentators reinforced this assertion by arguing that slavery had never truly been ended. Second, some authors claimed that particular labour situations were like slavery: 'virtually slavery' is the form of words often used. Finally, the direct comparison of two labour systems made the argument that the subject of discussion was better or worse than antebellum chattel slavery.

[68] 'An Open Letter to the His Serene Majesty Leopold II by Col. The Honourable Geo. W. Williams of the United States of America', bound in collection of Africa Pamphlets 1885–94, Bodleian Library, Oxford.

[69] G. B. Densmore, *The Chinese in California: a Description of Chinese Life in San Francisco* (San Francisco, 1880), p. 121.

[70] Rev. O. Gibson, *The Chinese in America* (Cincinnati, 1877), p. 138.

Using the term 'slavery' in discourse for a United States audience when referring to a system of forced labour, gave it a particularly significant meaning precisely because of the memory and legacy of antebellum chattel slavery and abolition explained earlier in this chapter. Douglas Blackmon entitled his book about convict labour *Slavery by Another Name* to highlight his view of the continuation of the conditions under which slavery flourished even after emancipation. In the subtitle to his book, Blackmon does suggest that the phenomenon of convict labour was itself 'slavery' by referring to 'the re-enslavement of Black Americans.'[71] Daniel Novak concurs and states that the post-war peonage system was a 'simple and effective substitute' for slavery.[72] In some ways Blackmon's title is misleading because it was precisely by calling convict labour by the name of 'slavery' that antislavery activists sought to challenge the existence of that system. It was the choice of the specific *name* of *slavery* that was crucial. The deployment of the word with such rhetorical power was resisted by those who wished to defend the use of particular labour forms, and they appealed for strict boundaries of the definition of what constituted slavery and what did not. In 1888, Booker T. Washington was aware of this when he referred to the southern labour system as 'a kind of slavery'.[73] British neo-abolitionist Henry Fox Bourne reported the attitudes of Cecil Rhodes and his confederate Mr. Rudd, who argued that their intended use of compulsory *corvée* labour in British South Africa was not the same as slavery: 'there is constant misuse of the word "slavery" by those who want to use it as a bogey', Mr Rudd is quoted as saying by a disapproving Fox Bourne.[74] Similar disagreements took place between those defending and those exposing the forced labour practices of the Belgians and their allies in the Congo. The mutable definition of slavery became part of the weaponry of antislavery writers such as Morel, who named his most famous tract on the subject 'the Congo Slave State', suggesting that slavery was not merely a feature of the region, but fundamental to the way that it was being governed.[75] On the other side of the argument, like many pro-Belgian authors who resorted to *ad hominem* attacks on Morel's character, Demetrius Boulger took issue with Morel's

[71] Douglas Blackmon, *Slavery by Another Name: the Re-enslavement of African Americans from the Civil War to World War Two* (Anchor Books, 2008).

[72] Daniel A. Novak, *The Wheel of Servitude: Black Forced Labour after Slavery* (University Press of Kentucky, 1978), p. xv.

[73] Booker T. Washington quotation from Daniel, *The Shadow of Slavery*, p. ix.

[74] H. R. Fox Bourne, *Blacks and Whites in South Africa* (London, 1900), p. 88.

[75] Morel, *The Congo Slave State*.

chosen title for his work and at the same time used the typical anti-abolition attack, accusing him of hypocrisy. Boulger said that 'the title [of Morel's pamphlet] itself is an aggression, it also implies a falsehood ... it is not more true to say that there are no slaves in any of the British colonies and possessions in East Africa'. In an unambiguous way, Boulger entitled his own response *The Congo State Is Not a Slave State*, in case any reader should be in doubt of his position.[76]

Equally controversial was the choice of the term 'slavery' in the phrase 'white slavery' to describe forced prostitution and sex trafficking. Campaigners seeking to expose an organised international ring of procurers and traffickers saw parallels with the slave trade and were not shy of defining the phenomenon as 'slavery'. Jane Addams saw it as 'the twin of slavery, as old and outrageous as slavery itself and even more persistent'.[77] The Dillingham Commission saw the naming of prostitution as 'white slavery' as appropriate, not because it should be considered the equivalent of slavery or as slavery itself, but because like slavery, it was a trade and 'in naming the business of importing women the white slave traffic, the public has instinctively stated the fact that the business is maintained for profit. It is probably no exaggeration to say that if means can be devised of stripping the profits from it, the traffic will cease.'[78]

Newspaper journalists challenged the concept of 'white slavery' on the grounds that the evidence pointed to many of the rescued girls having entered into prostitution voluntarily and therefore this practice could not possibly be termed 'slavery'. As one reporter suggested, harking back to an important synecdoche of chattel slavery, there were no 'clanging chains' in white slavery.[79] Secondly, others criticised the term because of its tone, being sensationalist and not measured. The *Fergus County Democrat* of Lewistown, Montana, a progressive weekly paper founded in 1904 to cover state and national politics, called it 'ridiculous and melodramatic'.[80] The term was criticised as a concept dreamed up by those with political ulterior motives or those hoping to make money. The famous fundamentalist preacher Billy Sunday was named by one newspaper as guilty of using the

[76] Demetrius C. Boulger, *The Congo State Is Not a Slave State* (London, 1903), p. 2.
[77] Addams, *A New Conscience and an Ancient Evil*, p. 4.
[78] *Importing Women for Immoral Purposes, 1909 Report Presented by Mr Dillingham at 61st Congress. Senate Document no. 196*, (Washington, Government Printing Office, 1909), p. 28.
[79] *Idaho County Free Press* (Grangeville, Idaho Territory) 18/8/1913.
[80] *Fergus County Democrat*, (Lewistown, Montana) 28/10/1913.

idea of white slavery to line his own pockets. The reporter at the *Golden Valley Chronicle* wrote 'the subject of white slavery is a favourite with sensational exhorters like Billy Sunday who is set to have added $70,000 to his fat bank account this season. They seldom or never mention the slavery of white men and white children, those forms of slavery being more prosaic and commonplace and less calculated to move their listeners to indignation and tears which results in a loosening of the purse strings'.[81]

This pattern of deploying the term 'slavery' to draw attention to the system's heinousness was used effectively in other parts of the Atlantic world. It was undertaken by Joseph Beaumont in his description of the Indian and Chinese coolie trade and lived experiences in British Guiana, which was published in 1871 and entitled the *New Slavery*. Beaumont's work was illustrated with images depicting plantation culture such as overseers beating workers and fat owners enjoying a leisured life in the big house, but instead of the typical slaves of the African diaspora, he depicted plantations peopled with labourers from China or India.[82]

An even more common mode of comparison linking post-war labour to antebellum slavery claimed that the system under discussion was like slavery or 'virtually slavery'. As well as being debated within pamphlet literature and the intellectual and popular press, this was also framed in the post-war era by case law as the legal definition of what type of labour was not permitted in the United States evolved. A federal anti-peonage law had been passed as early as 1867, in response to the specific conditions in New Mexico, but its applications to the southern systems of debt bondage and sharecropping that emerged over the coming decades encompassed a number of court cases. In a 1902 case in Pensacola, Florida, concerning the turpentine industry, defence attorneys claimed that the 1867 act referred only to the type of peonage then existing in New Mexico, and that their clients' treatment of labourers was lawful. In a case the following year in Montgomery, Alabama, the judge directed the jury to leniency and emphasised that 'peonage is not slavery and a peon is not a slave' determining that peonage was only an offence when it was involuntary.[83] This decision was tested later the same year in a Georgia law court which cited twelve violations of the 1867 act. The judge

[81] *Golden Valley Chronicle* (Beach, North Dakota), 11/8/1911.

[82] Joseph Beaumont, *The New Slavery: an Account of Indian and Chinese Labourers in British Guiana* (first published 1871, The Caribbean Press,2011), p. 20.

[83] William Wirt Howe, 'The Peonage Cases', *Columbia Law Review*, April 1904, pp. 283–4.

explained that physical force and violence was used in the case at hand and explained that the victim 'is now virtually held in a condition of slavery or involuntary servitude'.[84] Thus, the legal boundaries of slavery and peonage, evolving through case law, were used by judges to control the more extreme behaviour of white masters without challenging the fundamental status quo.

Trained at Harvard, not in law but in history, Albert Bushnell Hart was especially well placed to comment on comparisons between contemporary southern labour systems and those of the antebellum era. He suggested that little had changed in cotton plantations of the south: 'conditions of the old slavery times are more nearly reproduced in the cotton field than anywhere else in the south. The old idea that the normal function of the African race is field labour is still vital'.[85] However, although he drew comparisons between the experiences of agricultural labourers in both eras, he fell short of describing the post-war system as 'slavery'. When examining the convict labour system of chain gangs, he was committed to recognising this as 'a virtual chattel slavery'.[86] Walter Wilson agreed that there was little fundamental difference between convict labour and chattel slavery, but further asserted that the capitalist system stripped even freemen of such rights, rendering them almost slaves. He illustrated this point with a quotation, taken entirely out of context, delivered in 1777 by John Adams: 'the difference as to the state [between freemen and slaves] is imaginary only.'[87]

Most frequently, writers used comparison to rank conditions in incidents of forced labour as less or more severe than chattel slavery. Their authorial purpose in undertaking these comparisons is instructive in highlighting the myriad ways in which slavery was used conceptually. Far from harking back to a mythical golden age of plantation slavery, George Holmes argued that the labour system needed to change because southern agriculture had not undertaken to modernise, and innovation and energy had seemed to pass the region by. He argued that because they had done little to change the situation, the African American labourers were partly to blame, trapped by their lack of 'instincts' and of sufficient foresight to better themselves. The black tenant farmer was worse off than under slavery, Holmes said, because 'as a slave he was better fed and better housed than he is now, he had the best medical attendance in the country and if he was disposed to neglect his master's interest, which would have been his own as well had he been free, he was

[84] Ibid., p. 286. [85] Bushnell Hart, *The Southern South*, p. 261. [86] Ibid., p. 200.
[87] Wilson, *Forced Labour in the United States*, p. 16.

restrained. Now he is almost as helpless as a child and thoughtless of the morrow'.[88] Holmes remade the classic pro-slavery argument of writers such as Fitzhugh and Ulrich B. Philips, both of whom asserted the essentially benevolent nature of the institution because it saved the black population from the negative consequences of its own supposed inherent weaknesses. Taking the opposite tack and working to defend the African American population against the systemic racism they faced, the progressive journal *Nation* nonetheless also argued that the post-war peonage system was even more pernicious than slavery in order to trigger a response from campaigners.[89]

In the late nineteenth century, as sections of American society turned their attention to labour conditions overseas, and especially the territories coming under US control for the first time, comparisons between bonded labour and slavery were made for very different authorial purposes. In her book on the Hawaiian revolution published in 1898, Mary Kraut set out both sides of the debate. She argued that when discussing the system of contract labour used on the sugar plantations of Hawaii, which were mostly run by American-born businessmen, 'opponents condemned it without reservation, declaring it to be but little improvement upon negro slavery as it prevailed in the southern states before the war'. But she went on to challenge these assertions: 'there was in reality a very great difference with all the advantage in favour of the Japanese field hand'.[90] In his ethnographic account of the Hawaiian Islands, John Musick criticised the indentured labour system, but did not blame the American sugar barons, such as the German-born Klaus Spreckels, whose plantation he visited, but rather labelled it a vestige of the former corrupt monarchical system: 'the system is far worse than absolute slavery. The owner of a slave had a personal interest in him and as a rule looked after his comfort, for on his health depended his value. But the contract labourer can have no such claim on his master'. Like George Holmes, whose argument Musick mirrored, he also excoriated the labourer for his role in the system, blaming his racial predisposition: 'a Chinaman will work at wages that would starve a Kanaka [Hawaiian native] or European to death, but a Japanese coolie can starve out even a Chinaman'.[91]

[88] George Holmes, 'The Peons of the South', Annals of the American Academy of Political and Social Science, vol. IV, 1893–4 (Philadelphia), pp. 71, 74.

[89] Daniel, *Shadow of Slavery*, p. 49.

[90] Mary Kraut, *Hawaii and a Revolution* (London, 1898), p. 87.

[91] John R. Musick, *Hawaii: Our New Possessions* (New York and London, 1898), p. 153.

Others highlighted the threat to white wages caused by labourers of other races and Samuel Gompers shared this motive for highlighting contract labour as worse than slavery: he hoped to protect the white labourer from competition, especially from the Chinese, as outlined in his famous 1898 speech about the Philippines 'Imperialism: Its Dangers and Wrongs'. Later, in 1921, during a meeting with President Harding, he protested the plan to allow coolie labour into Hawaii.[92] Gompers argued that imperialism hurt white American labour because it bound the United States to a system of contract labour in Hawaii which revolved around labourers who were 'practically slave labourers' and 'semi-barbaric'. Similarly, South Dakota senator and anti-imperialist, Richard Pettigrew, argued that Hawaiian contract labourers were 'the scum of the earth' and 'little less than slaves'.[93] Rather than being victims of a corrupt and corrupting system who deserved to be given a chance to get out of this dire situation, these contract labourers were described as slaves, or worse than slaves, because of their racial make-up, using a discourse about slavery which throughout the late nineteenth and early twentieth century underpinned conservative anti-imperialism. There will be more about this in Chapter 4.

Of concern in the parts of the world where the United States was practising new imperialism, Chinese labour also provided challenges domestically. Eric Love argued that it was the influence of working class concerns over labour rather than top down pseudo-scientific theories that motivated much of this discontent.[94] Comparisons of Chinese labourers to chattel slaves were often deployed to justify their exclusion from United States or their continuing prejudicial treatment. American diplomat Charles E. DeLong, contributing to debates in the 1870s over Chinese immigration, spoke as someone who had had experience of working in Japan, but had little respect for the Chinese. He dismissed the Chinese coolies as 'more absolute slaves than ever the negroes of the south were'.[95] Many Americans at this time perceived all Chinese to be in a state of coolie-dom in China too. Opponents to Chinese immigration were essentially suggesting that their racial predisposition to slavishness

[92] Samuel Gompers, "Imperialism, Its Dangers and Wrongs," *American Federationist*, 5.9 (November 1898), 179–83. *Schenectady Gazette*, 19 July 1921 https://news.google.com/newspapers?nid=1917&dat=19210719&id=aEshAAAAIBAJ&sjid=94EFAAAAIBAJ&pg=2884,1508426&hl=en.

[93] Eric Love, *Race over Empire: Race and Imperialism 1865–1900* (Chapel Hill, 2004), pp. 121, 163.

[94] Ibid., p. xi. [95] Creighton Miller, *The Unwelcome Immigrant*, p. 153.

underpinned Chinese labourers and their behaviour.[96] Some commentators, seeking to defend the Chinese, realised that much of the trouble over immigration was caused by a misunderstanding of the nature of Chinese labour, a labelling of coolies as the equivalent of or worse than slaves. H. C. Bennett, promulgating the notion that Chinese labourers might be good for the United States, stated that the word 'coolie' had been incorrectly used as a corollary of slavery, and in fact it simply meant 'a lower class of labourer', and not 'a slave or bondservant'.[97]

In his book published in 1874 about travelling round Cuba, British author Frederick Trench Townsend compared the Chinese coolies he encountered there to African slaves and argued that the Chinese coolies were far worse off than the enslaved Africans. No admirer of slavery in any form, he wrote 'though the fate of the poor African slave in Cuba is horrible, that of the unfortunate Asiatic who is serving under contract, is even more pitiable. The wan face, feeble frame and dejected looks of the wretched Chinaman were painful to see'.[98] Unlike most commentators, Townsend was not writing in order to persuade the public of the necessity of exclusion of the Chinese from white society, but, rather, he was a British soldier and adventurer writing in order to sell his travel account, painting Cuba as an alien last vestige of slavery. Another soldier and adventurer writing about Chinese labour in a broader context was Russell Conwell, later a Baptist minister and founder of Temple University. He was the child of abolitionist parents, and his book from 1871 explores sympathetically, for the time, the motives and experiences of the Chinese labourers. He outlined motivations for Chinese migration by comparing it to that from Europe, considering what the 'push' factors might be in both cases and also examining the detrimental effect that the coolie trade had on China itself. He traced the use of erroneous propaganda in Europe and China in encouraging migration to the United States. But it was when describing the fate of coolies taken to Cuba that he brought out the direct comparisons with African slavery. He first suggested that Chinese slavery 'is said to be less irksome than was African slavery in America' – a strange choice of adjective; does he mean for the enslaved or the enslaver? But then he went on to say that Chinese coolie labourers were treated worse: 'the buyer has

[96] John Soennichsen, *The Chinese Exclusion Act of 1882* (Greenwood, 2011) p. 92.

[97] H. C. Bennett, *Chinese Labor: a Lecture Delivered before the San Francisco Mechanics Institute* (San Francisco, 1870), p. 37.

[98] Frederick Trench Townsend, *The Wildlife in Florida with a Visit to Cuba* (London, 1875), p. 199.

exclusive and entire ownership … [coolies] see hardships that the African seldom or never saw in America'.[99] He asserted that slavery existed in China as well and that it is different to indentured servitude, saying of their status that they were 'just below that of coolies', and although it is mild, Chinese slaves are 'whipped, branded, put in stocks and pillories as often as were the American slaves in the Southern States of the American Union'. Worse than that, he claimed, women and children throughout Chinese society were seen as 'saleable things'.[100] Conwell further expanded his comparison between types of forced labour and argued that the racially driven form was morally justified: 'it would seem to me to be far more mild if the persons bargained away for such labour or for such vile uses [prostitution] were the people of an inferior or conquered race instead of being their own legitimate sons or daughters'.[101]

In his tract about the Chinese on the West Coast of the United States, Reverend O. Gibson picked up the theme of the treatment of women and girls and also criticised the tendency of the Chinese in China to buy and sell their daughters for debt, and husbands their wives. However, he explained that Chinese labourers coming to the West Coast were not slaves; even though they banded together in migrant organisations 'they are no more slaves than the members of a fire company or any other voluntary organisation'. While 'Chinese women are brought here as slaves for the vilest purpose' he wrote, the male migrants came of their own free will, and their situation was far better than enslavement because 'the Chinese people always regarded with horror the American system of African slavery'. Gibson went further to deny the validity of comparing coolies to slaves: 'this voluntary contract cannot in any way be called slavery nor can it be fairly compared to slavery'.[102] Displaying irony and implicitly drawing a comparison with the type of slavery he assumed that his audience would use as a model, Gibson wrote:

> These Chinese coolie slaves are a most remarkable class of slave. They go and come when and where they please, work or refuse to work at their pleasure; they use the proceeds of their labour as they choose, buy their own clothes, pay their own rent, go to the theatre, gamble, smoke opium, bring suits in our courts, send money home to parents and friends and act in all respects just like free men. And yet we are told that they are abject slaves.[103]

[99] Russell H. Conwell, *Why the Chinese Emigrate and the Means They Adopt for the Purpose of Reaching America* (New York and Boston, 1871), p. 181.

[100] Ibid., p. 226. [101] Ibid., p. 229. [102] Gibson, *Chinese in America*, pp. 258–9.

[103] Ibid., p. 335.

Thus rhetorically, Gibson assumed his reader has knowledge of 'true' slavery and by allowing him to compare the lived experiences of Chinese migrants with this slavery, he taught his reader that, in the late-nineteenth-century United States, despite using it twice in the first sentence, 'slave' was not an appropriate term with which to describe Chinese immigrants.

CONCLUSION

This chapter has illustrated the tremendous rhetorical power held by chattel slavery in actuality and concept in the period following emancipation. The nature of this power was framed by abolitionists in the antebellum era and their activism had a potent legacy after the Civil War as their pattern of resistance inspired later antislavery activism, whether campaigning about domestic or global slavery. The cultural symbolism of slavery envisioned in novels such as *Uncle Tom's Cabin* was continuously revisited and explored in new editions, in pastiches and in theatrical performances. The ways that antebellum abolitionists imagined slavery and their resistance to it, taught new generations how to think about forced labour, and provided a model for conservative voices to challenge the notion that slavery-like labour should be eradicated. Presenting abolitionists as naïve at best and hypocritical at worst allowed commentators to challenge the supposedly accepted narrative of chattel slavery as a closed chapter in US history. In the period after emancipation, slavery and abolition were still live issues for many, through their legacy as points of comparison and also because, for many freedmen and women and their former masters, the end of the Civil War did not bring the dramatic change in condition that was anticipated.

The memory of abolitionism and its potential to act as a model for future activism was emphasised especially to encourage American intervention to prevent enslavement overseas, as well as the alleged global sex trafficking systems identified during the white slavery panic. In these cases, commentators identified themselves as heirs to abolitionism and identified slave owners and traders as the 'other', corrupted through greed or racial inadequacy. The power of the rhetoric of antebellum abolitionists shines through here, involving the presentation of unproblematic passive victimhood, especially in abolitionist propaganda during the 1860s in the depiction of white-seeming chattel slaves which was a direct antecedent of the white slavery discourse. Antebellum abolitionists also rhetorically othered the southern slave owner and trader, distancing them from upstanding American citizens and thus making slavery opposed to American values.

In the later nineteenth and early twentieth centuries this pattern was copied by commentators discussing slavery in Africa, the Philippines and Hawaii, often invoking the figures of Abraham Lincoln and the transatlantic abolitionist community.

In the post-war era, antebellum abolitionists were most frequently criticised for their simplistic, dichotomous conception of slavery and freedom. Abolitionists were held up as a *bête noir* both by conservatives and Marxists, who felt that because African American chattel slavery dominated the discourse about free and forced labour no sensible discussion about labour options could be had. From a conservative view, abolitionists were hypocrites who, so obsessed by the fate of the African American, had neglected to expose labour abuses elsewhere. At the other end of the political spectrum, Marxists challenged the idea that slavery and free labour should be considered as diametrically opposed, and issued polemical statements that under a capitalist system all labour, including wage labour, was the moral and actual equivalent of slavery.

After emancipation, contested meanings of slavery and freedom were not merely intellectual exercises but had serious ramifications for African Americans and others. Despite attempts to bring the formerly enslaved population into the nation as full and free citizens, conceptions of racial suitability for labour and of the tainted nature of the labour force allowed pernicious systems of abuse to continue. As the southern white population negotiated boundaries of acceptable labour practice incorporating both custom and legal precedent, they stated the desirability of methods of control restricting the movement of labour, as long as such methods did not transgress norms of polite and civilised behaviour. Other campaigners identified peonage and convict labour as unacceptable by resorting to comparison with antebellum chattel slavery. But the power of the rhetoric of racial hierarchy continued in the post-war era unabated, and while under slavery it had acted as a tool of justification for paternalism, the same rhetoric was used after emancipation to justify racial separateness and the political incapacity of black Americans.

Culturally, the memory of chattel slavery was manipulated by conservative white southerners in order to control emancipated slaves and to keep them in a form of ‘symbolic slavery’. By fabricating the myth of the happy slave, living contentedly in a benevolent plantation system, white Americans deliberately perverted the history of slavery for their own psychological and practical ends. They were still in denial about their own role in a violent and brutal system, and by binding the races together in a distorted community, their refusal to acknowledge black pain also had the benefit of encouraging former slaves to tolerate the status quo.

After the Civil War, discourses underpinned by racial determinism were also deployed to comment on the labour situations in the imperial territories of the United States and on the roles of immigrants to the mainland. There are continuities between the antebellum rhetoric which described the labour of the African diaspora, and the later rhetoric targeting these new groups. The concept of slavery was used in two different ways. The first was to attack an ethnic group as inferior, being undesirable labourers (and by extension inherently racially weak and inadequate), by calling them 'slaves' when they were not. Labelling women and girls as 'white slaves' when they may have been prostitutes of their own free will, or merely young women acting independently of a male patron, fulfilled a similar rhetorical function. The second was to justify American intervention into a political theatre by manufacturing an humanitarian impulse to defend weak and inadequate 'slaves' from the threat of a more greedy, corrupt and powerful 'other'.

In the emancipation period, chattel slavery appeared as the archetypical slavery to which all others might be compared. The ways that chattel slavery was described by antebellum abolitionists also gave discussions of slavery their iconographical language of chains, whips and auction blocks. During this period the word 'slavery' itself also acquired a totemic power, as to name something as 'slavery' was compelling and controversial. Because even after abolition the very concepts of slavery and freedom were still being contested in the United States, deploying the rhetoric of slavery to talk about other labour forms was a deliberate and contentious act. Even claiming that a labour form was like slavery in a reader's mind rendered it immediately controversial. Such rhetorical tools were similarly used to entertain and to shock and titillate, as shown by travellers' accounts describing forced labour around the world, and by historical depictions such as *Uncle Tom's Cabin* at the theatre including live bloodhounds on stage.

Many commentators tried to rank slavery-like labour forms in terms of their heinousness. Stating that a system was worse than chattel slavery was done either to trigger immediate action among humanitarians who had hitherto been slow to take up that particular cause, or ironically by appealing to abolitionist sentiment to encourage a nativist agenda, thus elevating white labour above other possibly tainted ethnic groups. Among conservatives, it was designed to criticise those who had dismantled the chattel slavery system, having little care for what might replace it, whereas writers arguing that a form of labour was less severe than chattel slavery sought to deflect activists' attention by suggesting that its reputation was undeserved.

In the period prior to World War I, discourse around slavery and abolition was highly contested because the liminal nature of the national legacy of slavery for the American people was still undetermined and extremely sensitive, and because naming contemporary labour forms as slavery was mutable and questionable. Dichotomous concepts of slavery and freedom did not work for many American writers remembering 'old slavery days' and determining the most appropriate new systems of labour.

2

Global Contexts: How External Factors Drive US Perceptions of Slavery

During the post-emancipation period, important global influences affected the ways that commentators within the United States thought about and wrote about slavery. These global intellectual currents flowed into the diverse and painful streams of thought, discussed in Chapter 1, emerging as the nation came to terms with its own past as a slave-owning nation. Ideological conceptions, defined as global or local, were not divided by fixed boundaries and did not work in isolation from one another but, rather, jointly exercised a combined influence on late-nineteenth-century discourse about slavery. This chapter will explore those global influences, some of which were summarised by the British socialist and reformer Henry Nevinson in his 1906 work, *A Modern Slavery*, a summary of his investigative articles written when employed by the American magazine *Harper's Weekly*, which argued that, despite the abolition of the transatlantic slave trade, slavery by another name still existed in the Atlantic world. Nevinson summarised the reasons why, almost a century after the British abolition in 1807, slavery still deserved the world's attention, pointing out unresolved questions about race, labour and capital and the incomplete emancipation of labouring people across the globe. He suggested that while 'the real relation of the white races to the black races ... is the ultimate problem of Africa', the controversy had to be addressed on a global rather than a local scale because 'it has become a part of the worldwide issue of capital ... the question of African slavery still abides'. Unlike more Eurocentric commentators, Nevinson saw the United States as playing a crucial part in confronting these challenging problems and his tract was designed to once more awaken antislavery activity in the country.[1]

However, despite Nevinson's idealistic vision of the motives of the United States in seeking a continuation of the abolition of abusive labour practices worldwide, scholars have been quick to recognise that, as with the European imperial nations, the American political establishment had pragmatic reasons that were not always driven by altruistic motives for pushing an abolitionist agenda. Scholars have also recognised that a global focus when contending over the significance of slavery was not new in the late nineteenth century. According to Josep Fradera, in the United States prior to the Civil War, abolitionism as well as pro-slavery rhetoric was always focused on the question of expansion, conquering and settlement of new territories, and the determination of their subsequent political identity as 'slave' or 'free'. Fradera argues that chattel slavery itself, if contained within the southern states, was of concern to only a few radical abolitionists. Most campaigners began their protests only when slavery was tied to expansionism.[2] This affirms another pre- and post-war continuum because, in the post-emancipation era, conceptions of slavery were also often tied to territorial expansion. Scholars have acknowledged this connection since the early days of the twentieth century. In 1910 at the University of Chicago, Milo Milton Quaife discussed, in a PhD thesis, the denial of President Polk, as early as the 1840s, that slavery had any extra-national significance: 'what connection slavery had to do with making peace with Mexico is difficult to conceive'. But as Quaife rightly argued, Polk was wrong. National expansion was bound up with slavery from the war with Mexico onwards, and was, I argue, until the outbreak of World War I.[3]

The focus on slavery's significance within the United States was influenced by the British model of imperial antislavery, born in the late eighteenth century from abolitionist work, but epitomised in the later crusading organisations such as the British and Foreign Antislavery Society (BFASS), which, from the outset, saw its work as part of the Anglo-Saxon moral mission, and whose relationships with American abolitionists were at times precarious. Through the

[1] Henry Nevinson, *A Modern Slavery* (London and New York, 1906), p. 12.

[2] Josep Fradera, 'Reading Imperial Transitions', in Alfred McCoy and Francisco Scarono, eds., *Colonial Crucible: Empire in the Making of the Modern American State* (University of Wisconsin Press, 2009), p. 51.

[3] Milo Milton Quaife, *The Doctrine of Non-intervention with Slavery in the Territories* (Chicago, 1910), p. 11.

work of organisations such as this, and individuals like E. D. Morel, an international model of humanitarianism evolved using racial and religious othering to position whites as moral arbiters who might judge the suitability of distinct labour forms. At the end of the nineteenth century, there were three prominent campaigns against coercive and abusive labour, all centred on Africa, which influenced American thinking on slavery: the Congo Free State, British Transvaal and Portuguese West Africa. These campaigns also highlighted the hypocrisy of some European nations which, while outwardly proclaiming their opposition to the concept of slavery, in reality relied on forced labour practices resulting in experiences very similar to slavery for its victims. Some imperialists even justified slavery as being the only option for parts of the world, with the ending of slavery there seen as dangerous, unpredictable and the cause of unnecessary torment for native peoples. Contemporaries justified this gap between ideology and pragmatism using the latest Social Darwinist theories, which denied the suitability of other races for free labour and pointed to events such as the 1865 Morant Bay uprising in Jamaica as evidence of the problematic outcome of overzealous abolitionism.

This willingness by imperial powers to manipulate the concept of slavery and its admissibility for their own political and economic gain contributed to the increasingly blurred boundaries in the definitions of slavery and freedom. In many parts of the world, including the United States, formerly enslaved individuals experienced little change in day to day lived experience but their status as slaves was 'rebranded' as the diversity of types of unfree labour expanded dramatically in the period after the American Civil War. This was accompanied by the expansion of networks in the global labour market, with new types of long distance transportation intended to solve localised labour shortages. The use of indentured labour, for example, so-called coolies from India and China and the perpetuation of blackbirding in the Pacific, was a direct result of the abolition of the transatlantic slave trade, and of slavery itself. Many individuals entangled in these systems of labour movement suffered terrible personal hardship resulting from their commodification. Some were coerced using physical or mental violence and their practical labouring experience differed little from chattel slavery. However, other migrants used labour shortages to their own advantage, willingly leaving troubling situations at home and choosing to move long distances, on a temporary or permanent basis, to craft a better life for themselves and their families. By denying their identity as free people, those seeking to control, limit or end their migration emphasised the abusive and coercive nature of the labour migration system, not in order to protect these workers, but rather for protectionist and reactionary reasons to limit the numbers migrating.

At the very end of the nineteenth century, in the context of this evolving complex global conception of slavery, the United States itself become an imperial nation, and, as in the European nations, slavery in the United States framed the national vision of empire, and was used both to encourage and discourage imperialist endeavours. Of course, imperialism on both sides of the Atlantic was not an identical phenomenon and, for much of the nineteenth century, the United States was a reluctant imperialist and the country extracted principles from the Monroe Doctrine to justify isolationist policies, and looked inward to rebuild following the fratricidal horrors of the Civil War. While there was considerable intellectual cross-pollination by the political elites of both Britain and the United States, slavery did not function identically, rhetorically speaking, in both regions. However, there were similarities and it was deployed as a strategic justification for territorial expansion by pro-imperialists and used to warn against imperialism by anti-imperialist and left-wing commentators. Slavery and forced labour and their intersection with race were significant topics of debate, especially but not solely following American involvement in the Pacific, in the Philippines and in Hawaii.

This chapter, then, concerns the ways that the United States negotiated its position in the world by engaging in debates about which labour systems were appropriate in the post-emancipation environment. The dichotomous relationship juxtaposing slavery on the one hand and free labour on the other simply did not work for the United States and its forays onto the global stage. This was a period in which the transatlantic abolitionist consensus morphed into something more complex as pro- and anti-imperialists, and those concerned with the race and immigration problems at home in the United States, realised that an ideological abolitionist position was problematic, if not untenable, in an era when localised labour needs rendered necessary the continuation of the long distance movement of workers. But the period also saw the further development of a transnational response to forced labour, driven by religious, racial

FIGURE 3 'The duty of great nations', chromolithographic print by Udo Keppler, 1899. Library of Congress.

and humanitarian conceptions of the duty to protect victims of enslavement.

EUROPEAN IMPERIAL ANTISLAVERY

The necessity of the emergence of a concerted global effort to combat slavery and the slave trade was recognised early in the history of abolition. By the 1840s, this was being driven by organisations such as BFASS and inaugurated in meetings such as the 1840 World's Anti-Slavery Convention held in London. This meeting attracted five hundred delegates and stated its aims in universal terms. It is notorious for its disagreements over the role of nine female American delegates, but tensions between the British and American representatives went much deeper. In spite of their passionate antislavery beliefs, many of the United States delegates felt personally attacked by the British, who seemed to be claiming antislavery ideology as their own. The British delegates insinuated that the entire people of the nation of the United States were backwards and uncivilised, rather than focusing their attack on the immorality of slavery itself.[4]

The British sense of superiority about antislavery sentiment long outlasted the single abolitionist meeting. Richard Huzzey argued that post-1834, antislavery became a coherent ideology within British society, one that helped the British define their place as a world power, and one that excluded slave voices, and one that did not need to mount a determined abolition movement.[5] But there is no question that the 1840 meeting and its agenda were driven in part by British missionary zeal in spreading an antislavery message. This message had two fundamental and critical parts, which influenced future American writing on slavery. First that slavery and slave trading was backwards and barbaric as well as unchristian, and second that civilisation was marked by a free labour system. This latter view was new in the nineteenth-century abolition movement. Prior to this, during the Enlightenment period, there was not an inherent contradiction in the accepted view that slavery might exist within societies considered models of civilisation, such as ancient Greece and Rome. The notion that slaving was as sign of retrograde civilisation also influenced the thinking of the other European nations who had designs on the resources (agricultural, mineral and human) of Africa, the Pacific and elsewhere. Demetrius Boulger, the British apologist for the Belgian regime

[4] Maurice Bric, 'Debating Slavery and Empire', in William Mulligan and Maurice Bric, eds., *A Global History of Anti-slavery Politics in the Nineteenth Century* (Palgrave, 2013), p. 71.

[5] Richard Huzzey, *Freedom Burning: Anti Slavery and Empire in Victorian Britain* (Cornell University Press, 2012) pp. 8, 17.

in the Congo, produced a classic justification of European imperialist intervention in Africa using antislavery rhetoric to argue that to permit the continued existence of the slave trade blighted the reputation of civilised nations. His book was published in London, Calcutta and Simla suggesting that he or his publisher thought his ideas might have a wider colonial readership among the British elite in India who were grappling with their own challenges with the Indian labour force. Boulger wrote that 'to release Africa from the slave trade [was] necessary for the removal of a stain from the escutcheon of civilisation' but he had to acknowledge that differentiation between types of slavery was necessary. He wrote that 'all must not be tarred with the same brush: it is always necessary to make a clear difference between domestic slavery and the pursuit and capture of slaves by open violence and operations of war'.[6] For some who used antislavery rhetoric, an abolition of all forced labour forms was undesirable.

INTERNATIONAL HUMANITARIANISM

Throughout the late nineteenth century, the British and Foreign Antislavery Society continued to drive much of the antislavery campaigning, by creating an humanitarian and international community of action intending to shape global moral norms. Ethan Nadelmann called BFASS 'the first transnational moral entrepreneur – religious movements aside – to play a significant part in world politics'.[7] However, in looking for origins, it is important to avoid falling into the trap of creating a hagiographical account of antislavery by lauding men such as E. D. Morel more than their actions deserve. While looking for the origins of a human rights movement and of humanitarianism, it is easy to impose our contemporary values on actors in the past whose motives were complex and at times entirely distinct.[8] Authors who wrote BFASS publications in the late nineteenth century did so for a variety of reasons. In his role as assistant secretary of BFASS, J. Eastoe Teall, following the scientific and collecting impulse of the era, which facilitated a perceived dominance over the natural world through the cataloguing of specimens,

[6] Demetrius Boulger, *The Congo State or the Growth of Civilisation in Central Africa* (London, Calcutta and Simla, 1898) pp. 7, 95.

[7] Ethan Nadelmann, 'Global Prohibition Regimes: The Evolution of Norms in International Society', *International Organisation*, 44: 4 (Autumn 1990), p. 495.

[8] Abigail Green, 'Humanitarianism in Nineteenth Century Context: Religious, Gendered, National', *The Historical Journal*, 56 (Dec. 2014), p. 1157.

contributed to antislavery by publishing, in 1889, a catalogue of all the places in which slavery still existed. First listing the countries affected by slave labour, he then listed important trading routes, depots and markets. Crucially he also documented the conferences, treaties, agreements and international laws which attempted to control slavery and the slave trade so that, in one document, he catalogued both slavery and antislavery.[9] Other writers saw their function as more explicitly hortatory. Henry Fox Bourne, who spent his formative years in Jamaica and then Guyana observing the chaotic aftermath of the abolition of slavery, wrote many tracts about the horrors of the continued existence of slavery, and often directly appealed to his readers to use their influence to push the British government to reform. In a 1909 tract highlighting abuses in Portuguese West Africa, he positioned his readers in the abolitionist tradition by asking them to recall 'their forefathers' resentment of slave trading and slavery'.[10]

BFASS was not reticent about holding the British government, as well as other European nations, to account, as shown by its vigorous campaigns regarding labour abuses in the Transvaal and the Congo. On rare occasions it also challenged the United States when accusations of forced labour practices were raised. The responses from American diplomats were bureaucratic rather than enlightening. In 1883, M. Powell, of the Legation of the United States, wrote to BFASS secretary, Charles Powell, and reported that no further action would be taken 'concerning the asserted holding of slaves and employment of slave labour by United States citizens in the Comoro Islands' (off the coast of East Africa near Madagascar). Later, in 1896, the ambassador at the US Embassy in London also wrote to Powell explaining that he had forwarded the information to Washington about 'a system of slave holding [being] indirectly permitted and … progressing in Morocco'. Five months later, Allen received a further update notifying him that 'no persons in Morocco under American protection are engaged in the slave trade or hold slaves'. The US Consul in Tangier did not completely deny the possible presence of forced labour practices but ascribes them to 'Jews and Others' who 'hope to shield themselves from any unjust or wrongdoing that they may seek to engage in'. He guaranteed that

[9] J. Eastoe Teall, *Slavery and the Slave Trade 1889: Facts and Memoranda compiled from the Slave Trade Papers, the Statutes at Large and Other Sources* (London, 1889), pp. 5–53.

[10] H. R. Fox Bourne, *Slave Trade in Portuguese Africa* (London, 1909), p. 62.

his agents would be on the alert to root out such activity.[11] As well as challenging the United States where rumours of slavery arose within its jurisdiction, BFASS also recognised the growing status of the nation as a regional power and asked for help from its president to intercede to end slavery elsewhere. In 1879, the organisation wrote an official letter to Rutherford B. Hayes, whose reputation as a staunch abolitionist must have travelled across the Atlantic, asking him to intervene in Cuba 'for the emancipation of the slave population of the island' which would require 'earnest and decisive diplomatic action'. But Hayes, during the period at the end of Reconstruction, must have been too preoccupied with the domestic challenges of the so-called race problem in the United States.[12]

However, to see BFASS and late-nineteenth-century antislavery as being entirely driven by a British agenda seeking to influence other nations is erroneous. During this period, antislavery became a transnational movement for the first time, and in the new century this vision was later developed by Henry Levinson and Walter Wilson and also by abolitionist campaigners pivotal in mobilising international policy makers such as Kathleen Simon. Simon's antislavery sentiments had first been aroused during her time living with her first husband in Tennessee. Daniel Laqua has asserted that organisations such as BFASS networked across national boundaries, desiring to create new structures to influence individual national governments. This influential shared language was adopted by governments but could often be manipulated for their own ends, such as in evidence at the international call to action on the slave trade by Belgium's Leopold II at the Brussels Conference of 1889–1890. Adoption of the language of international activism could also be couched in racialised terms with childlike Africans deemed worthy of being saved from cruel Arab slavers.[13] Laqua also suggests that antislavery activists were nervous of criticising their own governments, not true of many of the BFASS authors as shown by Fox Bourne, but authors did have their own agendas in highlighting slavery in certain areas, explicitly deflecting criticism from elsewhere. A case in point is Walter Wilson, who took an internationalist

[11] MSS Brit Emp. S. 22/G85 BFASS Papers, Bodleian Library, Oxford. United States 1853–97 folder. Letter dated 22 June 1883 from M. Powell to Charles Allen; Letter dated 14 July 1896 from I. J. Bayard to Charles Allen; Letter dated Nov. 1897 from I. J. Bayard to Charles Allen.

[12] Ibid., Letter dated 6 Mar. 1879 BFASS to Rutherford B. Hayes.

[13] Daniel Laqua, 'Tensions of Internationalism: Transnational Anti-slavery in the 1880s and 1890s', *International History Review*, 3: 4 (2011), pp. 706, 711.

tone, highlighting forced labour in China and Abyssinia and numerous other locations in which American politicians and capitalists had an influence through 'Wall Street imperialism'. At the same time, throughout his tract, Wilson was very careful to reject the accusation that the Soviet Union employed forced labour, calling it 'scurrilous'.[14]

While internationalist agendas could easily be corrupted to accommodate particular political plans on the left and right, a genuine attempt at an humanitarian response had begun even before the American Civil War. According to Jenny Martinez, after 1807, slave trade courts, known as 'mixed commissions' because judges came from different countries, represent the first international human rights courts, and it was from this era that the phrase 'crimes against humanity' entered the lexicon. Another crucial step forward took place under American jurisdiction during the Civil War, with the passing of the Lieber Code, governing the conduct of the Union army, which stated that slavery 'exists according to municipal or local law only. The law of nature and nations has never acknowledged it . . . moreover a person so made free by the law of war is under the shield of the law of nations'.[15]

But how might international will be moved to thus protect slavery's victims globally? Edmund Morel came up with the radical suggestion that only by changing the entire economic relationship between Europe and Africa, and instead of focusing on Africans as labourers, recognising their potential as traders, could 'honest, upright trade methods' be brought to 'tropical Africa'.[16] But internationalist humanitarians mostly shied away from suggesting such structural reconfiguring, and instead, evoking the names of Wilberforce and Lincoln, the League of Nations turned its attention to the eradication of the slave trade and slavery wherever it still existed. Writers of a 1927 official League of Nations paper recognised that overseeing the status of native labour in colonial contexts would be crucial to dealing with forced labour.[17] While they acknowledged that local conditions were variable and could easily trigger labour abuses, the authors of the paper called for 'public opinion to be united throughout the civilised world'. They empowered the newly formed International Labour

[14] Walter Wilson, *Forced Labour in the United States* (London, 1933), pp. 119, 121, 146.

[15] Jenny Martinez, *The Slave Trade and the Origins of International Human Rights Law* (Oxford University Press, 2012), pp. 6, 13, 132.

[16] Edmund Morel, *The Congo Slave State: a Protest against the New African Slavery* (Liverpool, 1903), p. 104.

[17] *Slave or Free? Native Labour, an International Problem*: Official Paper of the League of Nations, no. 23 November 1927.

Organisation to catalogue forced labour and to gather a conference with the purpose of bringing forced labour to an end.[18] Kathleen Simon was less optimistic about the possibilities of a quick end to slavery and, in her catalogue of labour abuses published in 1929, she asserted that 'at the present rate it would take one thousand years to free all slaves', despite progress being made on an international level with twenty-five countries, 'including the United States', signing up to a convention.[19] According to Jonathon Glassman, such abolitionist discourses easily morphed into developmentalism and often led to a simplistic and distorted legacy of slavery and the slave trade. From the moment the British persuaded the Sultan to close Zanzibar's Stone Town slave market in 1873, tourists were encouraged and there they learned, and still learn today, a story framed by imperialist antislavery.[20]

As Kevin Grant has argued, it was the British who drove many of the new ideologies of humanitarianism and trusteeship through their twin promotion of the agenda of human rights presented as a veneer of the civilised nation, and of evangelical Christianity. After the First World War, they also played a key role in the creation of the international law agenda at the League of Nations. British antislavery campaigners focused on three key campaigns, highlighting the labour abuses of European imperial rivals: the Boers in the Transvaal, the Belgians in the Congo Free State and the Portuguese exporting Angolans for the West African cocoa industry on the islands of Sao Tome and Principe.[21] In all three cases, the binary dichotomy between slavery and freedom was underplayed; rather, campaigners focused on the accompanying violence and social dislocation and the long-term impingement such activities had on commerce and civilised government in the regions.[22] The antislavery literature of this period used the same rhetorical techniques as that from an earlier era challenging the transatlantic slave trade. F. W. Chesson combined a statistical survey of the number of 'kaffir children' held as slaves (said to be four thousand), with a personal first-hand testimony of the experiences of a victim of enslavement. 'Rachel's story', told by

[18] Ibid., pp. 15, 20 [19] Kathleen Simon, *Slavery* (London, 1929), p. 261.

[20] Jonathon Glassman, 'Racial Violence, Universal History and Echoes of Abolition in Twentieth Century Zanzibar', in Derek Peterson, ed., *Abolitionism and Imperialism in Britain, Africa and the Atlantic* (University of Ohio Press, 2010), pp. 175, 178.

[21] For example, Fox Bourne, *Slavery in Portuguese Africa*; F. W. Chesson, *The Dutch Boers and Slavery in the Transvaal Republic* (London, 1869); Morel, *The Congo Slave State*.

[22] Kevin Grant, *A Civilised Savagery: Britain and the New Slaveries in Africa 1884–1926* (Routledge, 2005), pp. 5–6.

a victim of extreme violence who was then seized and sold to a man who wanted a wife, presents similar themes to many accounts of modern day slavery: the victim's ignorance and confusion over their fate, and coercion and manipulation by labour merchants who lied to their victims. Rachel stated 'when we are bartered or sold one to another we are not told of it . . . we are told that after we have served our time we will get paid for our work but that we never do'.[23] This use of first-hand testimony reaches back to the antebellum abolition movement, but also forward to new abolitionism of the twenty-first century, in which publicising survivor testimony is an important means of education and fundraising. Idealism is often accompanied by pragmatism in the motivations of abolitionists.

IDEALISM VERSUS PRAGMATISM

Antislavery humanitarian activism was only part of the British influence on American thinking about slavery. Concealed behind the antislavery morality was a hardnosed pragmatism bordering on hypocrisy, as Social Darwinist thinking on the hierarchy of races infiltrated the work of those authors confronting the imperial labour problem. Even Henry Fox Bourne, the prolific antislavery campaigner, acknowledged that, in some cases, coercion was necessary. In a survey of *Forced Labour in British South Africa,* published in 1903, Fox Bourne stated that in order to provide labour for the mines of South Africa 'assistance from the government as will deter even natives willing to work from seeking employment in other pursuits and practically compel both them and the alleged idlers and wastrels to take service in the mines'. While acknowledging this necessity, Fox Bourne did not recommend such coercive practices as a desirable course of action, and instead suggested that natives would be much better put to work on food production.[24] Three years earlier, he had illustrated the prevalence of this attitude of white colonialists to forced labour in Africa: 'forced labour is freely acknowledged and applauded even by missionaries and others considering themselves philanthropists on the grounds that compulsion is necessary in teaching blacks what is called the "dignity of labour"'.[25] In the same year, he even hinted that native diamond mine workers lived on the De Beers compound in Kimberley in 'a sort of prison [whose] inmates are

[23] Chesson, *The Dutch Boers*, pp. 23–4.
[24] H. R. Fox Bourne, *Forced Labour in British South Africa* (London, 1903), p. 9.
[25] H. R. Fox Bourne, *Slavery and Its Substitutes in Africa* (London, 1900), p. 10.

for the time being in a state of complete bondage', and that in the short term this was desirable for the good of the natives because it protected them from the curse of drink.[26] As in the Atlantic World in the early modern period and beyond, alcohol, race and labour were common themes in colonial discourse.

Suzanne Miers traces the evolution of British imperial attitudes to slavery when establishing themselves in a particular region of Africa, from their first attempts at outlawing the slave trade, while responding to a public expectation that slavery itself would end while, in reality, the situation was tolerated for years, described in government literature as benign, and underpinned by the attitudes that Fox Bourne described, which stated that Africans would not work unless compelled.[27] Such beliefs were not only driven by Eurocentric racism, but could also manifest in response to local hierarchies and networks. Cassandra Mark-Thiesen has shown that in gold mining in early twentieth century Ghana, slavery and debt bondage persisted despite antislavery campaigners trumpeting free commerce because mine managers were willing to work with the local headmen, the labour brokers, who used their status in the local community to procure and control labourers.[28] This system reinforced the idea that labour in British African colonies existed on a sliding scale of coercion, rather than in a dichotomy between slave and free, and that this situation was driven by the combined needs of local labourers, headmen, the commercial company and also the colonial state.[29]

The British acknowledged that compromises had to be made to their antislavery ideology based on the experiences of travellers through the continent. Since David Livingstone reported back on his expeditions to Africa, the trend had been for travellers to espouse antislavery and to seek to expose the slave trade wherever they found it. Livingstone's escapades made newspaper headlines on both sides of the Atlantic, with the *New York Herald* of May 1874 reporting that 'the greatest difficulty that Livingstone encountered in Africa was the infamous slave trade'.

[26] H. R. Fox Bourne, *Blacks and Whites in South Africa* (London, 1900), p. 51.

[27] Suzanne Miers, 'The Anti-Slavery Game', in Keith Hamilton and Patrick Salman, eds., *Slavery, Diplomacy and Empire* (Sussex Academic Press, 2009), pp. 199–200.

[28] Cassandra Mark-Thiesen, 'Bargain of Collaboration', in Ulbe Bosma, Elise Von Nedenveen Meerkerk & Aditya Sarkar, eds., *Mediating Labour: Worldwide Labour Intermediation in the Nineteenth and Twentieth Centuries.* (International Review of Social History Special Issue, 2012), p. 22.

[29] Ibid., 'Introduction', p. 10.

The Africans Livingstone encountered were depicted as 'primitive barbarians' but the blame for this rested with Europeans who sold them alcohol.[30] Two years earlier, another newspaper exposed the amounts of money that the proprietors of the *Herald* were willing to pay for the sensational Livingstone letters. But the representations in newspaper reports did not always mirror those in the author's own words.[31] Although newspapermen depicted Africans in a less subtle way, travellers understood that they were reliant on local native hierarchical systems to provide guides and servants on their mammoth journeys, and often, as in the case of Verney Lovett Cameron, travelling in the early 1870s in East Africa to assist Livingstone, they knowingly employed enslaved guides. Cameron was opposed to the use of slave labour and discussed atrocities he saw aboard slave trading vessels in Zanzibar while musing over his fears about the spread of 'this fearful evil'. But he also did not object to the presence of slaves in his own travelling caravan and clumsily catalogued their presence (and that of some women on the expedition) alongside the animals: 'we also had twenty two donkeys and three dogs and several of the men had with them women and slaves so that numerically we were an imposing force'.[32] Slave trading took place on the periphery of the journey, as Cameron described the Wajijij traders who walked alongside them and traded 'corn, oil and goats for slaves'. On other occasions slave dealers came into camp to sell slaves, often gagged or in a neck fork, to the white men. In a metaphor of British antislavery during this period, a powerless Cameron said that he resisted the urge to set the slave children free and thrash the slave traders because he knew that this would result in a worse future for the children.[33]

Joel Quirk has suggested that the link between imperialism and antislavery is a multifarious one and that the gradual transfer of power from African to British elites and the resulting negotiations created systems of formal and informal empire which required compromise over the question of slavery.[34] The requirement for pragmatism and concession while

[30] *The New York Herald.* (New York [N.Y.]), 04 May 1874. *Chronicling America: Historic American Newspapers*. Lib. of Congress. https://chroniclingamerica.loc.gov/lccn/sn83030313/1874-05-04/ed-1/seq-6/.

[31] *The Charleston Daily News.* (Charleston, S.C.), 31 July 1872. *Chronicling America: Historic American Newspapers*. Lib. of Congress. https://chroniclingamerica.loc.gov/lccn/sn84026994/1872-07-31/ed-1/seq-1/.

[32] Verney Lovett Cameron, *Across Africa* (Harper, 1877, reprinted Rockbury Ltd., 2004), p. 63.

[33] Ibid., pp. 184, 227.

[34] Joel Quirk, *The Anti-Slavery Project from the Slave Trade to Human Trafficking* (University of Pennsylvania Press, 2011), p. 91.

maintaining antislavery beliefs exercised some British commentators at the time, as it has scholars since. Quirk argues that contemporaries came to terms with these contradictions because they distinguished between legal abolition, which provided a critical endpoint removing the status of 'slave', and effective emancipation which changed an individual's role, social relations and labouring function.[35] This argument is reinforced in Lovejoy and Hogendorn's case study of slavery in Northern Nigeria. Sir Frederick Lugard epitomises the shifting British position, which saw them keen to work for the legal status of abolition (not achieved in Northern Nigeria until 1936) and yet feeling that emancipation would bring hardship to the slaves themselves.[36] Lugard was later a significant figure in the international humanitarian movement, leading the British participation in the 1926 Slavery Convention. Joseph Alexander, cataloguing the achievements of BFASS in 1900, stated that the abolition of the legal status of slavery was contentious and asked whether this actually resulted in the ending of slavery itself? He argued that the 'emancipation of slaves' in the West Indies was clear-cut (although many scholars would not agree with him), by public proclamation on a given date, whereas, in Africa, emancipation was only gradual. This slower choice was appropriate, according to Alexander, because it was essential to achieve freedom 'without any convulsion dangerous to state or society'.[37] Thus for many exponents of antislavery in this period, the desire for order and control overrode the urge for immediate abolition.

Lovejoy and Hogendorn also trace the way that colonial officials proclaimed antislavery rhetoric without actually freeing many slaves, partly because of the fear that runaway slaves might be tempted to join the Madhist rebellion or establish lawless maroon villages, and partly because of a need to placate local allies who had a vested interest in the maintenance of the slave system.[38] Patrick Manning argues that the intellectual origins of British fears over the behaviour of emancipated slaves in Nigeria can be traced back to the conceptual fissure caused in 1865 by the Morant Bay rebellion in Jamaica, the ramifications of which caused many in Britain to be more cautious in their advocacy of antislavery ideals and to see freed slaves as a threat rather than an emblem of

[35] Ibid., p. 7.

[36] Paul Lovejoy and Jan Hogendorn, *Slow Death for Slavery: the Course of Abolition in Northern Nigeria 1897–1936* (Cambridge University Press, 1993), p. 10.

[37] Joseph G. Alexander, *Sixty Years against Slavery: A Brief Record of the Work and Aims of the BFASS 1839–1899* (London, 1900), pp. 13–14.

[38] Ibid., p. 10.

civilisation.[39] Governor John Eyre's mishandling of the protests led to full-scale rebellion, and his overreaction in using martial law upset many in Britain, but some British conservatives also persisted in their view that the Jamaican freedmen and women were not behaving with the correct propriety, humility and gratitude. Others argued that due to their racial inferiority, black Jamaicans could never have orchestrated a complex protest and military uprising and that they must have been aided by mixed race or white Jamaicans. But half a century later, the Morant Bay uprising was remembered as a threat to imperial law and order which should serve as a germane lesson to imperial administrators. Implicit in this attitude is the view expressed by Francis Newman about African slavery, which argued that abolition was a failure and that blacks were better off under slavery.[40] As shown in Chapter 4, this was accompanied by a hardening of racial views in the 1860s, led by writers on both sides of the Atlantic, such as historian Thomas Carlyle, whose 1849 work *Occasional Discourse on the Negro Question* explicitly criticised British abolitionism and influenced the behaviour of Governor Eyre. Thus, as William Green has argued, the reputation of abolitionism and its credibility in the middle part of the nineteenth century was based on the success or failure of the plantation system following the emancipation of slaves.[41]

International antislavery must be judged more harshly according to Ian Tyrrell, who labels it entirely Eurocentric and solely the product of the material interests of the imperial nations. He provides the example of the Belgian behaviour at the Brussels Conference of 1889–90.[42] This suggests that the European powers were using antislavery rhetoric in a deliberately deceitful and hypocritical way, fully aware that they had no intention of working to end slavery or the slave trade, except in cases where it coincided with their own economic interests. This view was echoed by some contemporaries, such as Henry Nevinson, who described the abuses in the cocoa plantations of the Portuguese islands off West Africa, showing how the Portuguese used centuries-old justifications for the continuation of the

[39] Patrick Manning, *Slavery and African Life: Occidental, Oriental and African Slave Trades* (Cambridge University Press, 1990), p. 165.

[40] Francis Newman, *Anglo-Saxon Abolition of Negro Slavery* (London, 1889), p. 2.

[41] William Green, 'Plantation Society and Indentured Labour: the Jamaican Case 1834–65', in P. C. Emmer, ed., *Colonialism and Migration: Indentured Labour Before and After Slavery* (Martinus Nijhoff Publishers, 1986), p. 165.

[42] Ian Tyrrell, *Reforming the World: the Creation of America's Moral Empire* (Princeton, 2010), p. 13.

use of slave labour, a system operated by them on the West coast of Africa since the early modern period. Nevinson quoted the Portuguese official: 'the slave, he said, had opportunities of coming into contact with a higher civilisation than his own . . . he might become a Christian'.[43] But Nevinson refused to accept such rhetorical game-playing and instead impressed upon his reader: 'let us at once sweep away all the talk about the natives' good. The only motive for slavery is money making and the only argument in its favour is that it pays'. The European duplicity over African slavery is certainly not new, Nevinson showed, and he did not spare his own countryman from rhetorical barbs, arguing that 'England . . . great foe of slavery all over the world was also the originator of the slave export'.[44] Writing for an American audience, Nevinson was implicitly warning those in the United States from following such a path.

BLURRED BOUNDARIES: DEFINITIONS OF SLAVERY

Despite his distaste for the new forms of slavery he found in his travels around Africa, even Henry Nevinson acknowledged that 'slavery' in Portuguese West Africa did not fit the typical conception of chattel slavery in the Atlantic world, and that domestic slavery 'or tribal slavery' as he called it, might allow for some social mobility so that a slave could become a chief and hold slaves himself.[45] Following emancipation in the United States, contesting the definition of slavery and the blurred boundaries between slave and free was an essential way for authors to negotiate their position in relation to the changing global labour market. Scholars also reject the dichotomous relationship between slavery and freedom for labour, instead preferring to see a 'sliding scale', as Ulbe Bosma puts it, in which even consensual migration might not always be truly 'free'.[46] The meaning of slavery and free labour varied depending on where in the world that labour type was being deployed. In independent and in colonial contexts, the realities of life described by the term 'free labour' were very different.[47] As the anonymous author of a 1903 pamphlet reporting on a BFASS meeting stated, quoting a Reverend Dr Henderson, 'the line between induced and forced labour will be very difficult to

[43] Nevinson, *A Modern Slavery*, p. 54. [44] Ibid., pp. 54, 137. [45] Ibid., p. 14.

[46] Bosma, von Nederveen Meekerk & Sarkar, *Mediating Labour*, p. 4.

[47] Frederick Cooper, Thomas Holt & Rebecca Scott, *Beyond Slavery: Explorations of Race, Labour and Citizenship in Post-emancipation Societies* (Chapel Hill, 2000), p. 3.

define and observe when recruiting agents are once let loose among native races'.[48]

The meaning of the term 'slavery' began to change, even before the end of chattel slavery in the United States, as the term was used metaphorically by reactionary proslavery apologists to refer to free labourers. Following the end of the Civil War, as shown in Chapter 1, the usage of the term expanded, and similar trends can be followed when tracking its deployment outside the United States. Joel Quirk argues that slavery has become an evocative concept covering a range of abuses including forced marriage, child labour and sex work, and I argue that this change began in the late nineteenth century as the British debated the boundaries between concubinage, forced marriage and enslavement in an African and Middle Eastern colonial context.[49] More significant are the ways that policy makers and campaigners spoke about slavery and used its flexible definition for their own declamatory ends. As Quirk states, when the number and types of unfree labour expanded during this period, it became less clear who the slaves that required saving actually were, and therefore it became easier for imperialists and those seeking to control labour to obfuscate by decrying the 'true' slavery while defending other coercive labour practices.[50]

One example of justification of forced or compulsory labour was the *corvée* labour deployed in British African colonies to undertake works of public infrastructure development such as the building of roads and railways. Such forced labour was justified in British eyes because it was for the public good, not only for the benefit of the imperial power but also for the native Africans.[51] This type of forced labour, to bring civilisation and commerce to hitherto underdeveloped areas, further complicates European assertions that, through their antislavery activities, they deigned to bring civilisation to the 'dark' African continent. Another common form of forced labour for the public good undertaken by European powers was the conscription of natives as soldiers. Without entering the wider debate over whether conscription is the moral or experiential equivalent of slavery, commentators such as George Washington Williams criticised the use of enslaved native soldiers in the Belgian Congo, arguing that enslaved Zanzibari soldiers 'are ignorant and cruel

[48] Anon, *Native Labour in South Africa: a Report of a Public Meeting* (London, 1903), p. 2.
[49] Quirk, *The Anti-Slavery Project*, p. 9; Cooper, Holt & Scott, *Beyond Slavery*, p. 127.
[50] Quirk, *The Anti-Slavery Project*, pp. 136, 141.
[51] Cooper, Holt & Scott, *Beyond Slavery*, p. 131.

because they do not comprehend the natives'.[52] Henry Fox Bourne condemned the use of *corvée* labour and claimed that the British should reject all forms of forced labour for their developmental and industrial projects. But elsewhere in the same pamphlet he cautioned against the overhasty abolition of domestic slavery 'before the people themselves are ready for a change ... [it] can lead to nothing but mischief'.[53] Thus, according to Fox Bourne at least, European imperial powers were right to treat differently various types of slavery and forced labour. For men like Fox Bourne, nominally abolitionists, universal and immediate abolition were no longer held aloft as attainable goals.

The main ways that authors talked about slavery, other than as labour for crops or commodities, was under three main headings, which reveal the intersection of the themes of race and gender: slave trafficking, domestic slavery and concubinage. The first of these was almost universally condemned, as seen in Chapter 3, as authors deliberately othered the Arab or Muslim slave trader. This mirrored the eighteenth-century British abolition movement which also targeted the slave trade as opposed to slavery itself, because it was easier to reconcile with beliefs over the rights over property of private individuals. The latter two types were often quietly tolerated or even explicitly justified by imperial authorities because of concerns over the suitability of Africans for free labour (more on this in Chapter 4) and because of fears over the destabilisation of the entire African society. In Africa, domestic slavery had more to do with community and kinship relations than with being unfree as a labourer and thus a slave's status was often defined by his separation from his natal community rather than through his ownership by another.[54] Domestic slavery was often different in nature from chattel slavery, although it might still involve considerable coercion and violence, and, as Quirk has argued, labelling a forced labour type as 'mild, domestic slavery' justified inaction by the imperial powers in the Middle East and in Africa.[55] Verney Lovett Cameron challenged the usual stereotype that slave traders were evil and domestic slavery was benign. While he did explicitly 'other' Tippu Tip's headmen that he met on his travels and called the slave trade 'cursed' and 'a blot on civilisation', he

[52] George Washington Williams, *An Open Letter to His Serene Majesty Leopold II*, bound in Africa Pamphlets & C. 1885–94, Bodleian Library, Oxford.

[53] Fox Bourne, *Slavery and Its Substitutes in Africa*, pp. 5, 15.

[54] Cooper, Holt & Scott, *Beyond Slavery*, p. 5.

[55] Quirk, *The Anti-Slavery Project*, p. 11.

also suggested that traders treated slaves much better than their native owners did. The worst treatment was often meted out by owners who were 'slaves themselves or freedmen who on beginning to taste the delights of freedom seemed anxious to prevent anyone lower in the scale from rising to a little state of happiness'.[56]

The end of the transatlantic slave trade coincided with an upturn in interest in Africa among the elites in owning slaves themselves as a symbol of status. No longer was big money to be made selling slaves across the ocean, so their trading interests were transferred to other commodities and instead they became slave owners. In areas where slaves undertook considerable labour, the price of land went up, further enriching the African slave owners in a nascent plantation culture.[57] This in turn triggered the development of an internal African slave trade, led by those such as Tippu Tip who were tremendously rich, often with European connections. At its height, Tip's trading empire stretched throughout the Indian Ocean world.

Domestic slavery was seen not only as the preserve of the African elite, but was also at times engaged in by Europeans, or at least white Europeans accused one another of engaging in the practice. In David Livingstone's accounts of his travels, published in 1857, he reported disapprovingly that the Boers, specifically Commander Scholz in South Africa, used the language of mildness and domesticity to describe the sort of slave ownership that they indulged in.[58] Concubinage was treated by the British colonial elite, such as Frederick Lugard in Nigeria, as an entirely separate category from slavery, even though the women involved were often forced into sex work and were not free to leave if they wished.[59] In a period of underpopulation, reproduction and building a dynasty was critical to African elites, and the role of slave concubines was central to this function. Although they were rarely allowed full autonomy, they developed strategies to improve their lot within a restricted system.[60] Thus the colonial state bolstered the patriarchal power of the male master over his female slaves, whose destiny was of little concern to administrators as, in economic terms, they were not considered a fully productive unit. Some antislavery campaigners, concerned about this pattern, highlighted the particular plight of women. The first-hand accounts,

[56] Cameron, *Across Africa*, p. 239. [57] Manning, *Slavery and African Life*, p. 107.

[58] David Livingstone, *Livingstone's Missionary Travels in South Africa* (London, 1857), p. 125.

[59] Lovejoy & Hogendorn, *Slow Death for Slavery*, pp. 111, 116.

[60] Martin Klein, 'Sexuality and Slavery in the Western Sudan', in Gwyn Campbell and Elizabeth Elbourne, eds., *Sex, Power and Slavery* (Ohio University Press, 2014), p. 71.

quoted by F. W. Chesson, of enslavement by the South African Boers, unusually all came from women and girls, including 'Adela' who was sold at age fourteen to a Boer man for thirty pounds.[61] The enslavement of eunuchs, similarly gendered as other and exoticised, was also treated by colonial administrators and by slave traders and buyers as a different category, as evidenced by J. Eastoe Teall who catalogued the markets where one could acquire eunuchs as being distinct from the general slave markets.[62]

In the first British abolition movement, and later in the white slavery panic discussed in Chapter 5, women were portrayed as the ideal victim needing defending from the aggressive trafficker or trader. But this depiction was not common in literature about Africa. Thus, in the late nineteenth century, many women undertaking forced reproductive and sexual labour were excluded from definitions of the term 'slavery'. Many other workers also found their labour 'rebranded'. In some cases, the same individuals who had been trading slaves restyled themselves as labour merchants, for example, selling contract labourers to the sugar and cocoa plantations of Angola and Sao Tome.[63] To return to the question of the effectiveness of a legal termination of slavery, it was certainly ineffective at ending the abusive labour situations in Western Africa. Henry Nevinson confirmed this, stating that the difference between contract labour in Angola and 'the old fashioned slavery of our grandfather's time is only a difference in legal terms'.[64] While acknowledging the essential difference between old and new types of slavery, Nevinson also described the rhetorical manoeuvre that allowed 'slavery by another name' to continue to exist in Africa as happened in the United States in Chapter 1. He wrote, 'call slaves by another name, legalise their position by a few printed papers and their traffic becomes a commercial enterprise deserving of every encouragement'.[65] It is this evolution of the global labour market that ensured the continuation of forced labour practices across the world, not just in the United States and Africa.

GLOBAL LABOUR MARKETS

Labour and its provision and distribution around the world was of utmost concern to political leaders and to capitalists. Economic imperatives overlapped with imperial ones, as the requirement for appropriate types of

[61] Chesson, *The Dutch Boers and Slavery*, p. 24.
[62] Eastoe Teall, *Slavery and the Slave Trade*, p. 10. [63] Grant, *A Civilised Savagery*, p. 1.
[64] Nevinson, *A Modern Slavery*, p. 37. [65] Ibid., p. 44.

labour in particular regions intersected with the ideology of conquest and civilisation. The moral benefit to the worker of undertaking regular, structured wage labour rather than subsistence farming or hunting was championed by authors who argued that Europeans and Americans were best placed to educate natives about how and why to work producing staple crops or in extraction economies such as gold and diamond mining. Similar discussions had been ongoing since at least the medieval period, when the sugar industry in the Mediterranean and Atlantic islands developed using forced labour, and then in a number of industries as the Spanish and later other European nations colonised the Americas. The transatlantic slave trade illustrated the most systematic attempt to solve a labour problem by moving large numbers of people from one location to another, using racial justification to provide moral vindication for doing so in the face of challenges from those opposed to slavery. This model persisted into the post-emancipation period, despite slavery no longer being legally and morally tolerated. As shown below, the post-emancipation systematic relocation of labour was still being triggered by the flourishing of commodity or extraction economies, and justified by both Europeans and Americans using racial logic.

Labour costs and productivity were of central concern to capitalists and imperialists and while it was acknowledged that particular landscapes and climates were best for growing certain crops, and extracting minerals was location-specific, debates were widespread as to who were the best labourers to do this work. Three clear options were offered. First, even the abolitionist H. R. Fox Bourne acknowledged that, for some commentators, the use of reluctant native labour was the most efficient option.[66] Second, for authors like Charles Forbes-Lindsay, the global labour market, coupled with the latest scientific and technological agricultural developments, offered lessons. He wrote at length about the costs of labourers in different countries and how the underproductive Filipino rice-growing field hands might be improved.

> The cost of labour in Chinese rice fields is about half as much as the cost of similar labour in the Philippines, but the adoption of economic methods would more than offset the difference. A Filipino will cultivate one hectare, yielding 1500 pounds of paddy at a cost for his labour of $20 gold and board per annum. A Louisiana field hand receives $200 a year and board but he produces 160,000 pounds of rice. He receives ten times as much as the Filipino and with the aid of scientific appliances does one hundred times as much work.[67]

[66] Fox Bourne, *Slavery and Its Substitutes in Africa*, p. 10.

[67] Charles Forbes-Lindsay, *The Philippines under Spanish and American Rules* (Philadelphia, 1906), p. 256.

While Forbes-Lindsay did not propose shipping labourers from China or the Southern states of the United States to the Philippines to improve the situation, the relative costs and skills of labourers globally were relevant to the perceived development of a native labour force. Third, the necessity of using imported labour by tapping into the global market that had developed in the wake of the legal abolition of the transatlantic slave trade was mooted. William Fremont Blackman explained, in the context of Hawaii, why the importation of labour was essential. His argument was a Social Darwinist one, that the Hawaiian race was inexorably weakened and that the immigration of races 'akin' to Hawaiians should be permitted 'in the hope of reinvigorating that decadent native stock'. Native Hawaiians were currently resistant to hard work, he lamented, a fact displayed by statistics showing that one in two Japanese, one in two Chinese but only one in twenty-five Hawaiians were plantation labourers.[68] Unlike Forbes-Lindsay above, Blackman mused over the possibilities of importing 'southern negroes' as sugar plantation labourers but in the end decided that it would be a bad idea: 'the presence of the negro in the United States constitutes a most difficult and threatening social problem', and anyway, 'they do better at home' because they would not stand up to comparison with what Blackman called 'Asiatic labour', revealingly adding 'and could not therefore be persuaded to emigrate save through deception'.[69]

The labour problem was especially acute in certain parts of the world, in those areas where the climate was deemed unsuitable for white settlement. Under the racial hierarchical models, white labourers, especially northern Europeans, were deemed superior workers on account of their moral development and rectitude, but it was ironic that such labourers were unable or unwilling to undertake work in tropical areas. Discussing labour concerns in South Africa in 1903 in an anonymous account of a BFASS meeting, an additional issue was raised of the self-segregation of workers of different racial backgrounds. The author stated that a major problem was that the 'white man will not work along with the native at the same work'.[70] Mary Kraut concurred in her assessment of Hawaiian labour, suggesting that 'Europeans or Americans have not been found in large enough numbers to work in the cane fields'.[71] Elsewhere the

[68] William Fremont Blackman, *The Making of Hawaii: A Study in Social Evolution* (New York, 1906), pp. 194–6.

[69] Ibid., p. 203. [70] Anon, *Native Labour in South Africa*, p. 1.

[71] Mary H. Kraut, *Hawaii and a Revolution* (London, 1898), p. 89.

separation of labourers into national groups was seen as a threat, especially when undertaken by politically active Japanese and Chinese labourers in the Pacific. In 1906, the US Department of Commerce and Labour called this tendency 'blood unionism'. More on labour radicalism of the period will come later in this chapter.[72] At the same time, the BFASS meeting's black delegates led by Mr Quinlan of Jamaica, protested the idea, mooted in *The Times*, that Jamaicans be shipped to South Africa as labourers in mines, calling such an idea a new 'slavery'.[73] Many American imperialists feared the political threat posed by the large scale immigration from certain nationalities, especially Japanese and Chinese, and instead preferred to fall back on the trusted option that they had relied on for centuries: African Americans. The American-born manager of an Ewa sugar plantation on Oahu, W. J. Lowrie, was quoted as recommending that Japanese and Chinese be transported out of Hawaii back to their own countries and instead 'negroes from the southern states could advantageously procured to supply their places ... the negro might cost a little more but he is capable of doing more work'.[74]

The search for labour solutions, then, was not only a response to the need for labourers to further the economic development of particular industries, but also a response to the desire to control and contain free populations. As Mandy Benton argues, master and servant laws, militia activities and vagrancy laws were all amended in the mid to late nineteenth century in response to perceived, out of control, newly freed populations.[75] Similarly, rhetorical manipulation of the idea of slavery was also used to restrain free migration. This was most obviously the case from roughly the 1870s to the 1890s with the immigration of Chinese labourers to the United States. For example, the Geary Act of 1892 extended the restrictions of the Chinese Exclusion Act of a decade earlier and stipulated that all Chinese arrivals into the United States must be photographed and registered. It was enacted specifically because the United States had a right and a duty to protect itself from the evils of what Thomas Geary called 'Asiatic Slavery'.[76] In a satirical and virulently racist account of the supposed

[72] Department of Commerce and Labour, *Third Report on Hawaii, Bulletin of the Bureau of Labour no. 6, Sept. 1906* (Washington, 1906), p. 382.

[73] Anon, *Native Labour in South Africa: A Report of a Public Meeting* (London, 1903), p. 19.

[74] John R. Musick, *Hawaii, Our New Possessions* (New York and London, 1898), p. 473.

[75] Mandy Benton, 'The Taint of Slavery', in Keith Hamilton and Patrick Salman eds., *Slavery, Diplomacy and Empire* (Sussex Academic Press, 2009), p. 147.

[76] Robert McClellan, *The Heathen Chinee: a Study of American Attitudes towards China 1890–1905* (Ohio State University Press, 1971), p. 11.

'capture of California and Oregon by the Chinese', Robert Woltor articulated the American concern about the movement of labourers around the Pacific, using the language of 'contagion', 'weeds' and 'cunning'.[77] In more measured tones, twelve years earlier, H. C. Bennett defended the Chinese in California against accusations that they were uncivilised, dirty and backwards, and more pertinently, asserted that they were not enslaved. While acknowledging that Chinese 'do sell their labour cheaper' than other races, the Chinese presence in the United States would benefit the nation, and therefore they should be allowed an opportunity to improve their status as 'the negro' had done.[78] Newspaper coverage also reflected the divided opinion of the nation on the status of the Chinese immigrant to the United States. The question of whether coolies were the equivalent to slaves exercised journalists and their readers. A regular column in the *Evening Telegraph* of Philadelphia entitled 'Spirit of the Press' purported to examine a controversy through the eyes of journalists in a number of key American newspapers. In 1870, in a piece called 'Theories and Facts about the Chinese', it examined the case for or against defining them as 'slaves'. Pitting the journalists of the *Tribune* against those of the *Star*, the report states the *Tribune*'s view first: 'Congress may doubtless prohibit the introduction of slaves into this country, but has it any right to interpose unnecessary and vexatious obstacles to the importation of free labour? This question the *Star* disposes of by asserting that the coolies are slaves'.[79] Nine years later, the issue still regularly graced the front pages of large urban newspapers with a broad, working class, labouring readership, such as the *Chicago Tribune*, which reported a meeting of Chicago Workingmen demanding the removal of 'coolie labour'.[80]

The conceptual model of the gradual evolution of slave labour into free but coercive labour forms might work for certain parts of the world, but not for the Indian Ocean or Swahili slave world. William Clarence Smith has shown that, in the nineteenth century, slavery and the slave trade expanded considerably there and that slavery co-existed with serfdom,

[77] Robert Woltor, *A Short and Truthful History of the Capture of California and Oregon by the Chinese AD 1899* (San Francisco, 1882), pp. 11, 42.

[78] H. C. Bennett, *Chinese Labour: A Lecture Delivered before the San Francisco Mechanics Institute in Reply to Hon F.M. Pixley* (San Francisco, 1870), pp. 14, 20, 23.

[79] *The Evening Telegraph*. (Philadelphia [Pa.]), 02 July 1870. *Chronicling America: Historic American Newspapers*. Lib. of Congress. https://chroniclingamerica.loc.gov/lccn/sn83025925/1870-07-02/ed-1/seq-2/.

[80] *Chicago Daily Tribune*. (Chicago, Ill.), 02 March 1879. *Chronicling America: Historic American Newspapers*. Lib. of Congress. https://chroniclingamerica.loc.gov/lccn/sn84031492/1879-03-02/ed-1/seq-7/.

corvée labour and other bonded labour forms in areas with high land to population ratios.[81] Rather than imagining this period as one of the waning of slavery and bonded labour, it is more accurate to consider the era marked by continuity rather than change. Why did this happen in a supposed era of abolitionism? The imperial ambivalence towards slavery and forced labour is visible in British attitudes in both India and Africa towards indenture and *corvée* labour, and despite the campaigns by BFASS and others to draw attention to these as a new type of slavery, in Britain's periodic permission of the transportation of coolie labourers and, in the Pacific, of blackbirders. Richard Huzzey has argued that, following the Indian Mutiny and the Morant Bay rebellion, Britons were more willing to tolerate indentured labour. But further, he claims that tolerating coercive labour practices was not seen as contradicting anti-slavery goals and, in fact, was thought to be vital in securing them.[82] This is because a certain element of stability and control was required before the practice of slave trading and slavery could be stamped out. As we shall see in Chapter 3, this rhetorical manoeuvre was essential in labelling the slaveholder and slave trader as 'other'.

However, in real terms, the system of contract labour was another coercive system, and as Hugh Tinker has stated, it might be considered 'a new system of slavery'. Labourers were once again considered commodities to be bought and sold, rather than individual human beings.[83] The abolition of slavery in the British Empire in 1834 triggered the development of new networks of forced labour migration, as Indian workers were transported around the world to cultivate sugar, coffee, tea, rubber and rice. Internal forced migration within India also resulted in further coercive labour practices on tea and coffee plantations.[84] As the British tried to accommodate this in their post-emancipation moral codes, news of the kidnapping of coolies and their forced shipping abroad, and the terrible conditions they faced while being transported and working overseas appeared in new abolitionist narratives. As with the transportation of slaves, attempts by merchants were made to ameliorate the conditions aboard ship by hiring ships' doctors and cataloguing and accounting

[81] William Clarence-Smith, ed., 'Overview', in *The Economies of the Indian Ocean Slave Trade in the Nineteenth Century* (Frank Cass, 1989), p. 3.

[82] Huzzey, *Freedom Burning*, p. 186.

[83] Arnold J. Meagher, *The Coolie Trade: Traffic in Chinese Laborers to Latin America 1847–1874* (X Libris, 2008), p. 216.

[84] Hugh Tinker, *A New System of Slavery: the Export of Indian Labour Overseas 1830–1920* (Oxford University Press, 1974), pp. 23, 29.

for every individual, but the shock, dislocation and alienation suffered by the migrants, unprepared for the enormity of their journey, was akin to that braved under Atlantic slavery. Mutinies on board coolie ships from China were common as migrants rebelled against the terrible conditions in which they travelled. Francis Bowen, a ship's captain, used to working the Atlantic slave trade routes, felt that working on the boats of the Chinese labour trade to the Chincha Islands, for the industry of guano harvesting, was too dangerous because of the ship-board mutinies, and he returned to transporting African slaves.[85] The continuities in the naming of the accommodation used by coolies in British Guiana were obvious, known by their old name of the 'Nigger Yard', and many aspects of plantation life remained very similar to pre-emancipation days.[86] As well as Guiana, many of these forced migrants ended up in Mauritius, Malaya and Natal.

Indentured or coolie migration operated in the Atlantic and Pacific with Chinese migrants moving to California, Peru, Cuba and to Hawaii, involved a challenging passage of over two months and the risks of tropical disease.[87] On the sugar plantations of Hawaii, various work systems were used: ***ukupau*** (meaning 'job done' in Hawaiian) referring to a 'task' based system, and the contract system where a large task was given to a number of labourers to spend as long as they required completing it.[88] While the use of bonded labour was determined by global labour requirements, the contract labour system was everywhere bounded by a series of local laws, regularly challenged and amended, in response to perceived abuses, and to complaints by the countries of origin of the migrants. The 1850 Hawaiian Masters and Servants Act, based on the legal system of Massachusetts and modelled for Hawaii by missionaries, and being of benefit for the American-born planters, became the origin of the contract labour system, which replaced a customary system of native serfdom.[89] The business of bringing labourers to Hawaii was a part of the forced movement of people in the nineteenth-century Pacific known as 'blackbirding', a trade in people undertaken by European and United States trading companies. The American Civil War created opportunities for lucrative new cotton and sugar markets and, as in the southern states, the blackbirding trade was underpinned by a racist ideology. In Fiji, many

[85] Meagher, *The Coolie Trade*, p. 179. [86] Ibid., p. 177.

[87] Clarence Glick, *Sojourners and Settlers: Chinese Migrants in Hawaii* (University Press of Hawaii, 1980), p. 27.

[88] Ibid., p. 33.

[89] Sally Engle Merry, *Colonizing Hawaii: the Cultural Power of Law* (Princeton University Press, 2000), p. 97.

American planters and traders were white supremacists who saw Fijians and Samoans as akin to Africans, facilitating their treatment as slaves, calling them as a group 'niggers' and, as with African American slaves in the south, giving them mocking, ironic names such as 'Jeff Davis'.[90] While racial stereotyping of groups such as the Chinese meant that their immigration to the United States always upset conservative commentators who used the language of slavery to discourage their acceptance into American society, such commentators had no qualms about the use of United States vessels to transport coolie labourers elsewhere, for example, to Cuba, where they would be auctioned off to the highest bidder just as African slaves had been.[91]

The rhetorical use of the terms 'coolie' and 'slave' to describe bonded labourers in the contract labour system was not underpinned by a formal legal definition nor an understanding of precise labour relations, but rather was used to describe economic and clandestine migrants as well as those who were really victims of coercion or violence. While migrants were often desperate, illiterate and may have been persuaded to travel by others, known as 'crimps' who derived financial benefit from the transaction, the term 'slavery' does not reflect the lived experience of many of the migrants, who were called 'coolies' for reactionary conservative ideological reasons.[92] Contract labourers had the legal status of a person, not an item of chattel and thus they were accorded civil rights under the local law, which recognised their situation as one of temporary and not permanent bondage.[93]

While in some cases contract labour practices may have been distinct from slavery, exploitation did often occur. As well as protests from campaigning organisations such as BFASS about the abusive nature of contract labour transportation, the countries of origin of the migrants also raised concerns about their treatment. From the 1880s onwards in Korea, American missionaries such as Horace Allen tried to promote the 'dollar diplomacy' agenda and encourage the migration of labourers from Korea to work in the sugar fields of Hawaii. But Allen met with opposition from the Korean government who saw the trade as like slavery, describing in

[90] Gerald Horne, *The White Pacific: US Imperialism and Black Slavery in the South Seas after the Civil War* (University of Hawaii Press, 2007), pp. 3–4, 13, 46.

[91] Najia Aarim-Heriot, *Chinese Immigrants, African Americans and Racial Anxiety in the United States 1848–1882* (University of Illinois Press, 2003), p. 78.

[92] Elliott Young, *Alien Nation: Chinese Migration in the Americas from the Coolie Era through World War Two* (University of North Carolina Press, 2014), p. 64.

[93] Meagher, *The Coolie Trade*, p. 297.

1903 the conditions of emigrants: 'it is lamentable that our brothers and sisters have become slaves like African Negroes in a strange land'. Allen suggested that the opposition to emigration by government officials was not always altruistic, stating that corrupt elite men such as Yi Yong-ik opposed the system because he personally would not benefit from it financially.[94] In the late nineteenth century, the Indian government was ambivalent about coolie emigration, on the one hand fearing it when labourers were taken from domestic industries such as tea and, on the other hand, welcoming it as a solution to domestic social problems, for example, the presence of women without masters.[95] There was resistance from local people to the actions of labour recruiters, especially to the use of coercive practices such as the use of barracoons. Crimps or labourer recruiters, often locally born, working with the connivance of corrupt local officials, who targeted the vulnerable such as refugees, or who lied to young men telling them they had a place in the army, were susceptible to being attacked by angry locals. In the 1870s, riots were common in Canton and Macau, and crimps caught in the act were lynched or beaten to death by a mob.[96]

In the few decades prior to World War I, concerns over the source and nature of labour peaked worldwide. Racial determinism imbued many of the decisions about the relative suitability of different types of labour from groups of different ethnic origins. World War I itself only further exacerbated the problem due to restricted movement of people by cutting off the labour supply. In the United States, workers were diverted from staple crop growing and harvesting to industrial activity, causing a mass migration from rural to urban areas.[97] This occurred simultaneously with fewer voluntary immigrants crossing the Atlantic. Changes in labour relations caused the United States to look outwards for solutions to its labour problems. From the 1880s onwards, domestic labour agitation increased in frequency and severity and union activity flourished.[98] It is no coincidence that the turmoil at home resulted in the burgeoning of missionary and imperial impulses at this time, with

[94] Wayne Patterson, *The Korean Frontier in America: Immigration to Hawaii 1896–1910* (University of Hawaii Press, 1988), pp. 78, 80.

[95] Tinker, *A New System of Slavery*, pp. 266, 268.

[96] Meagher, *The Coolie Trade*, p. 108.

[97] Cindy Hahamovitch, *The Fruits of Their Labour: Atlantic Coast Farmworkers and the Making of Migrant Poverty 1870–1945* (University of North Carolina Press, 1997), p. 80.

[98] Tyrrell, *Reforming the World*, p. 49.

Americans seeking to spread New England congregationalist values of moral labour around the globe.

THE UNITED STATES AND ITS IMPERIAL DESTINY

According to Frederick Jackson Turner, in the 1890s, the United States experienced the closure of its domestic frontier, completing the business of subduing and conquering the landscape and people of the continent. Simultaneously, the nation became embroiled in a series of regional infractions which resulted in its becoming an imperial nation. Thus Americans had to engage with questions over the way a colony should be governed and the ways that local native labour should be used to maximise profit and development, also facing the dilemma of how global labour movement might contribute to this economic and moral expansion. Chapters 3 and 4 of this book will analyse at greater length the ways that slavery, slaveholding and trading, and slave labour were depicted in these new environments of concern to the United States, but here the focus is on how imperial models of the European nations and their treatment of domestic and international labour questions influenced the ways that the United States behaved on the world stage.

As we have already seen, by the 1860s, Britain's ideological antislavery, tied to the nation's values, self-perception and imperial drive, was beginning to give way to a more pragmatic and problematic ambivalence towards slavery, which involved undertaking some strategic rhetorical manoeuvres to redefine labour types as not constituting slavery, or using racial hierarchy theories to justify the continued existence of slavery where it was inexpedient to remove it. The nominal emphasis on humanitarianism did not go unchallenged by Britain's European neighbours; the French rightly thought that the British were using humanitarianism to further their own political ambitions, and towards the end of the century, the Belgians could be justifiably accused of the same.[99] Eugene Schulyer, the United States ambassador to various parts of Eastern Europe, concurred and was especially concerned about the surreptitious extension of British naval power, stating that 'the real reason [behind British antislavery] was fairly well concealed under the mask of philanthropy'.[100] But despite this suspicion, since the early nineteenth

[99] Jean Allain, *The Law and Slavery* (Brill, 2015), p. 70. [100] Ibid., p. 76.

FIGURE 4 'What the United States has fought for', cartoon by John T. McCutcheon, 1914. © Wisconsin Historical Society.

century, the Americans had worked with the British to end the slave trade, agreeing in 1820 that American citizens trading in slaves could be tried as pirates and executed if convicted, and then, during the Civil War, entering into bilateral treaties to suppress the slave trade.

Antislavery campaigners addressed United States audiences by highlighting the supposed British abandonment of their opposition to slavery, accentuating the hypocrisy of the position of the European imperial nations. These authors, such as Henry Nevinson, held the United States up as an antislavery model, suggesting that it had not been tainted by such immorality. He wrote about the way that the English failed to act to prevent the Portuguese use of slave labour in the cocoa and sugar industries of the islands off West Africa. He argued that England's strategic alliance with Portugal rendered her unwilling to act. He wrote 'from her we can turn only to America. There the sense of freedom seems to linger … America's record is clean compared to England'.[101] Nevinson issued a call to arms to awaken the latent abolitionist tendencies in the United States: 'let America declare that her will is set against slavery and at her voice the abominable trade in human beings between Angola and the islands will collapse as the slave trade to Brazil collapsed at the voice of England in her days of greatness'.[102] American audiences also read the counterargument, that Europeans continued to lead the ways and ought to be trusted in their antislavery activities. Verney Lovett Cameron published his travel account in *Harper's Magazine*, and stated that Britain had led the way in being 'friends to the unfortunate slave' and should continue to do so, and he exhorted his American and British readers to 'support the King of the Belgians in his noble scheme'.[103] In 1884, under Chester Arthur's presidency, the United States as a nation did initially support Leopold II in his endeavours by being the first to recognise the Belgian claim to the Congo Free State. This is why E. D Morel addressed his tract on slavery to readers in the United States, because they had been 'deceived by the professions of philanthropy and high moral purpose' emanating from the Belgians and their defenders.[104]

By the early twentieth century, based on the European model used in Africa and the Middle East, American writers had developed their own language of imperial antislavery. But many American authors refused to participate in such national self-congratulation. In 1913, James H. Blount, writing about the short history of the American occupation of the Philippines, alerted his readers to the Filipino people's view of the Americans' 'noble acceptance of a self-imposed obligation to educate us in order that we might later deserve independence'.[105] However, Blount was cynical about the realities of the American occupation and its mission

[101] Nevinson, *The New Slavery*, p. 208. [102] Ibid., p. 209.
[103] Lovett Cameron, *Across Africa*, p. 480. [104] Morel, *The Congo Slave State*, p. 10.
[105] James H. Blount, *American Occupation of the Philippines 1898–1912* (Putnams, 1913, reprint Malay Books, 1968), p. 3.

to educate the natives and prepare them for independence. He criticised the behaviour of American soldiers and politicians, especially William Taft, accusing them of turning a blind eye to massacres and labour abuses. More fundamentally, he attacked the entire premise of American imperialism by comparing it to the British example. He deployed exactly the opposite argument to Nevinson, who had lauded American impulses over British ones, and wrote 'American imperialism is not honest like the British variety. American imperialism knows that avarice was its father and piety its mother, and it takes more after its father'.[106]

The relationship between imperialism, anti-imperialism and slavery is a complex one in the United States and reflects local conditions as well as transnational ideologies. The height of the debates over imperialism in the United States centred around the election of 1900, and at this time the anti-imperialists were especially concerned to claim the concepts of liberty and free labour as American values. But they were not humanitarians by any means. Michael Cullinane has explored the nuances in anti-imperialist thought during this period and he shows that it was politically diverse with no united vision for ending slavery.[107] Some anti-imperialists were radicals and humanitarians, while others, such as Mark Twain, claimed that the imperial moment had already passed.[108] But for many others, conservative racist and protectionist views drove anti-imperialism, based on a desire to protect domestic industries such as sugar cultivation or to prevent the arrival of cheap labourers who might undercut the American-born worker. Still others feared the political incorporation of large numbers of non-whites who might erode American values. White supremacist governor and then senator of South Carolina, Benjamin Tillman, was one such conservative anti-imperialist, whose conflicted views on slavery and expansion mirror the challenges that many Americans faced attempting to resolve the legacy of chattel slavery while confronting the reality of the United States as an imperial nation. Tillman said that it was acceptable for governments to make chattels of men at home, but not to do so overseas.[109] In the context of the war in the Philippines, further evidence of the diversity of anti-imperialist thinking at this crucial moment comes from an anti-imperialist letter from J. S. M. to the editor of the *Alexandria Gazette*, which argued precisely the opposite, that natives of foreign lands may be

[106] Ibid., p. 449.
[107] Michael Patrick Cullinane, *Liberty and American Anti-Imperialism* (Palgrave, 2012), pp. 3, 6.
[108] Ibid., p. 76. [109] Ibid., p. 60.

made into slaves through the use of 'breech loaders' but it can never 'elevate them to the dignity of citizens'.[110]

During much of the first half of the nineteenth century, the United States had adopted the position of reluctant outsider when the question of the slave trade or slavery on a global scale was raised. In 1820, the British persuaded the United States to participate in various ground-breaking international initiatives to bring an end to the Atlantic slave trade but it was not until 1862 that the United States ratified the treaty allowing for searching of slave ships and the prosecuting of captains in mixed courts. Jenny Martinez argues that American reluctance to become involved in the abolition of the slave trade, along with its embarrassing 'white man's burden element', more of which in Chapter 3, makes the abolition movement a poor model for the twenty-first century development of international human rights law, with the Nuremberg trials a far more coordinated and less problematic emblem.[111]

In the late nineteenth century, Americans who did have a vision of radically different race and labour relations acknowledged that the recalcitrance of the United States was triggered by an ideological fear of getting enmeshed in European political machinations. George Washington Williams expressed the concern of violating the Monroe Doctrine and 'of approaching the stormy circle of European politics'.[112] The 1823 Monroe Doctrine was not designed to prevent American territorial expansion, but rather to keep the 'old' and the 'new' worlds, Europe and America, as separate spheres, with no interference with each other. Indeed, in pursuing military expansionist policies in the American hemisphere, imperialists, such as Theodore Roosevelt, saw themselves as acting entirely within the strictures of the Monroe Doctrine. However, the Doctrine did limit the scope of the area of focus of the United States' overseas involvement and, accordingly, in the period prior to World War I, the country was reluctant to get involved in European, Middle Eastern and African affairs.

Anti-imperialists criticised the behaviour of Americans abroad as much as they debated the rights and wrongs of the imperial mission as a whole. The

110 *Alexandria Gazette*. (Alexandria, D.C.), 31 Jan. 1899. *Chronicling America: Historic American Newspapers*. Lib. of Congress. https://chroniclingamerica.loc.gov/lccn/sn85025007/1899-01-31/ed-1/seq-1/.

111 Martinez, *The Slave Trade and the Origins of International Human Rights Law*, p. 154.

112 George Washington Williams, *A Report upon the Congo State and Country to the President of the Republic of the United States of America*. Bound in Africa Pamphlets & C. 1894–5, Bodleian Library, Oxford, p. 3.

continued existence of slavery in the Philippines was used by the Taft regime as a justification for the United States remaining in the region, as Filipinos had not yet shown themselves suited to home rule and they could be dismissed as uncivilised slavers. It had been easy to see slavery as part of the Spanish colonial past, but once the Spanish had gone, Americans had to accommodate in their world view a very different type of slavery to their own. Military men, especially those from the south, could not understand a form of enslavement not strongly predicated on racial othering.[113] Counter insurgency and coercion were central to the ways that Americans operated in the region, as they used the latest modern systems of observation, and military and legal control, to distribute corrupt patronage and to discredit opponents.[114] The longer the Americans remained in the Philippines, the more racialised the discourse about the native inhabitants became, as they were dismissed as 'niggers' by the American soldiers, who viewed the places where the Filipinos lived as akin to 'the backcountry of Arkansas and Mississippi'.[115] Others saw the native Filipinos as analogous with the Native Americans, with guerrilla resistance in the new colonial context opening up old wounds. In 1901, the killing of forty-eight American soldiers at Balongiga revived the cultural memory of the 1876 Battle of Little Big Horn a generation earlier.[116] Many white Americans began asking themselves the same questions about the Philippines as European commentators asked about Africa: could a free labour system ever work for natives here? As Arthur Twining Hadley, president of Yale University stated, compulsory labour was better than no labour at all.[117]

Thus, Americans in their colonial arenas faced similar strife to the Europeans in theirs, despite the claims of some American imperialists to be better colonialists, able to respond more subtly to the challenges of slavery and the demand for labour. Debates centred on the racial and economic appropriateness of slavery became, as for European powers in their empires, a rhetorical tool with which to justify the chosen course of action.

113 Michael Salman, *The Embarrassment of Slavery: Controversies over Bondage and Nationalism in the American Colonial Philippines* (University of California Press, 2001), p. 85.

114 Alfred McCoy, *Policing America's Empire: the US, the Philippines and the Rise of the Surveillance State* (University of Wisconsin Press, 2009), p. 60.

115 Leon Wolff, *Little Brown Brother: How the United States Purchased and Pacified the Philippines* (Oxford University Press, 1960), p. 21.

116 Walter Hixon, *American Settler Colonialism: A History* (Palgrave, 2010), p. 174.

117 Salman, *Embarrassment of Slavery*, pp. 28, 52.

CONCLUSION

Almost as soon as it evolved during the mid-nineteenth century, the transatlantic abolition consensus, which brought the United States and Britain together to work towards an international humanitarian cessation of slavery, was over. On the British side, increasing recourse to scientific racism and evidence from Jamaica and India of social and labour unrest suggested that, in the era of high imperialism, the idealism of total abolition was unachievable. Simultaneously, for the United States, which emerged from the devastation of the Civil War imitating antislavery imperialism of Europe, a realisation struck that being part of a global commodity and labour market, and being an imperial power itself, meant that dichotomous views of slavery and freedom no longer sufficed. While in the United States the concept of slavery was used rhetorically to comprehend and justify imperial and anti-imperial views, the nation and its people struggled to assimilate the types of slavery and forced labour that they encountered elsewhere, unable to divest themselves of their entrenched view of African chattel slavery that had been their model of slavery. In some ways, after the war, the United States and its people were never fully committed participants in the global abolitionist enterprise. For example, there was no desire to boycott slave-produced goods from Cuba and Brazil, although in his personal papers in 1869, president Ulysses Grant privately acknowledged that a good reason to annex Santo Domingo was so that tropical commodities such as sugar and coffee could be grown there with no need for recourse to slave-produced goods.[118]

Where the term 'slave' became adaptable, it was used to demean and discredit free labourers, such as in the constant description of the Chinese in America as 'coolies' or even 'slaves'. These depictions built on Orientalist stereotypes of a slavish, inferior people, were used to keep free labourers out of American territories. However, some commentators, such as Frederick Trench Townsend in *Wild Life of Florida,* his 1875 travel account describing labourers of African and Chinese descent on sugar plantations in the Caribbean, were genuinely concerned to highlight labour abuses, in the same way that slavery was used rhetorically for dual purposes by the European imperial powers in Africa.[119] The coolie debate

[118] Eric Love, *Race over Empire: Race and Imperialism 1865–1900* (Chapel Hill, 2004), p. 44.

[119] Frederick Trench Townsend, *Wild Life in Florida* (London, 1875), especially chapter 14, p. 191.

became a political tool for nations and individuals to position themselves as different to others, as more humanitarian or concerned for the moral and economic development of people of one distinct race.[120]

Thus, during the mid to late nineteenth century, the meaning of abolition changed, no longer requiring the outright conversion of all working in systems of enforced labour to those ascribed to be 'free', however that was defined, but rather the transfer of slaves to systems of contract servitude and other bonded labour forms.[121] Having been in decline from the eighteenth century onwards, the significance of so-called free but bonded labour increased globally in the post-emancipation era and discussions over the destiny of these workers were to shape debates over slavery. Chattel slavery and acutely abusive labour conditions did still exist, and abolitionists worked to continue to highlight this, but complexities over the mutable boundaries between unacceptable slavery and acceptable bonded labour meant that abolitionism was no longer unambiguous in its aims.

The relationship between European and American antislavery is a complex one, with shared motivation and language yielding to hostility and the denial of a shared heritage. Campaigning organisations such as BFASS adopted a very different approach from the British government, which in turn did not see eye to eye with colonial administrators, who better understood the realities of labour requirements and stability imperatives. Antislavery campaigning contributed to the development of transnational human rights activism, and while the pragmatism and cynicism of governments and colonial administrators rendered them unable to adhere to the ideological strictures of total and immediate abolition, BFASS continued to focus on the horrors of slavery and to work for international legislative change. The organisation continued to use many of the literary methods that had worked during earlier abolition eras, and which continue to be deployed today, especially the use of first-hand testimonies of the victims of slavery.

During the second half of the nineteenth century, attitudes towards slavery among the imperial nations began to change and this affected American perceptions of enslavement in European colonies, and of the forced movement of labour and the labour practices in its own colonies. Imperialist duties to morally educate natives and to maintain law and order in colonised regions often did not marry well with the immediate

120 Young, *Alien Nation*, p. 94.
121 Hoang Gia Phon, *Bonds of Citizenship: Law and the Labors of Emancipation* (New York University Press, 2013), p. 55.

abolition of slavery and colonial administrators prioritised the former at the expense of the latter. Some did this openly, arguing that putting abolition on hold was better for the local people, whereas others engaged in rhetorical manoeuvring to defend their position, claiming that a particular form of forced labour did not equate to slavery and therefore could be allowed to continue. Fears of the European and American imperialists that the natives were unsuited to free labour and would first have to be taught how to work using coercion contributed to the pragmatism of the era which rejected ideological abolition until a controllable and stable labour system was put in place to succeed it. Some imperialists, such as Leopold II of Belgium, vocally trumpeted their antislavery credentials while continuing themselves to use a violent form of forced labour to make the colonies profitable. Once exposed, the horrors of the rubber industry in the Congo did a great deal to discredit the proclamations on slavery of all European governments.

This calculating use of the concept of slavery, denying that its lingering presence in Africa was being tolerated, resulted in the blurred boundaries of the definitions of what counted as slavery in the post-emancipation period. Many conservative and radical authors acknowledged that the period saw a proliferation in types of forced labour, and one single conception of slavery, that of the chattel slavery system used to extract staple agricultural or mining labour, no longer functioned to incorporate the entire labour environment in the modern world. One coerced labour type justified in this way was *corvée* labour, which forced workers to spend time every month on public works such as road and railway building. This use of labour was condoned in imperialist and racist terms, citing the necessity of bringing civilisation and modernity to the colonies, while at the same time refuting the suitability of white labour for the job, or realistically recognising that few white labourers would be willing to migrate to undertake heavy work in tropical heat. Most debates on the essential nature of slavery took place around three important issues: the slave trade, domestic slavery and concubinage. The slave trade was almost universally derided by European and American commentators. This was the one area in which they did heed the idealistic abolitionism of earlier in the century, although, as shown in Chapter 3, this was not because of humanitarian concerns but rather with a view to seeking economic gain, facilitated by the use of racial stereotyping of slave traders.

Concubinage, along with 'domestic slavery', was depicted by some as mild and unproblematic, vindicating the lack of imperial activity to abolish these practices. Although, in many ways, in the Victorian era, the female domestic slave and concubine represented the ideal victim, especially as shown in Chapter 5, if she happened to be white or light skinned, concubinage was juxtaposed positively against chattel slave labour systems in which large numbers of enslaved people worked on plantations or in mining, with the conditions of individual slaves being proclaimed as less severe. The threat to local law and order of bringing an end to this long-cherished procedure was brought to the fore.

As well as domestic and local concerns, the development of the global labour market in this period further contributed to the flexible and mutable definition of slavery. While the trading of slaves by racial others in Africa and the Middle East was viewed with horror by Europeans and Americans, they tolerated and, at times, actively encouraged the movement of contracted and bonded labourers around the world to meet their labour needs. Markets in labourers from the most desirable ethnicities who were thought to be the hardest working, the cheapest and the most suited to labour in the stipulated conditions, flourished with individuals bought and sold by labour brokers and capitalists, while the labourer had no self-determination to affect his or her working conditions. This differed from chattel slavery because the labour contracts were time-limited, and also because many labourers, although not all, had deliberately chosen the migratory path upon which they found themselves. Although contract labour was distinct from chattel slavery in these ways, antislavery activists used explicit comparisons linking the two, and indeed called such labour types 'slavery' when they located particularly grim working conditions. Governments of parts of the world such as Korea, China and India, which exported contract labourers, also raised concerns about the treatment of their countrymen who had travelled abroad. Conservative commentators also named contract labourers as 'slaves' or the pejorative 'coolie' when they wished to dissuade the immigration of that ethnic group, because their racial identity threatened the hegemonic power, or because their efficiency and hard work undermined local labourers who, at the end of the nineteenth century, were becoming increasingly radicalised.

As well as conceptualising slavery differently because of the changing focus of European antislavery and the maturing global labour market, the United States became an imperial nation and therefore constructed its own sense of the slave or the slaveholder as 'the other' in a range of imperial contexts. Antislavery idealists in the United States called on the nation to distinguish itself from the cynical corrupt record of the European powers, but it soon became apparent that such idealistic behaviour was not easy when acting as an imperial power rather than interested onlooker. Some anti-imperialists, who felt that direct interference in other regions was not part of the value system of the United States, used the continued existence of forced labour as a rhetorical weapon to discourage contact and the assimilation of colonies into the American body politic, while other anti-imperialists saw the hypocrisy of European powers over slavery as a reason to mistrust the entire imperialist system. Many American imperialists still believed that American values could be used to re-educate entire populations and to teach them to reject forced labour and the backwardness it represented. But fundamentally, as in the case of the European colonial powers, the desire to see colonies function as viable economic entities with stable and ordered societies overruled concerns over slavery and forced labour, and allowed the United States to proclaim itself a power opposed to slavery while tolerating coercive labour practices on its soil and in its colonial territories. It did this by rhetorically 'othering' the owners and traders of slaves, while blurring the boundaries of the definitions of slavery to permit practices that advantaged the imperial nation.

3

Othering the Slave Owner

Examining the changing perceptions of slave owners and traders in the late nineteenth and early twentieth century is a prescient way of illuminating the methods that the United States used to negotiate its role as a former slave-holding power in the era after emancipation. As shown in Chapters 1 and 2, these perceptions worked in different ways depending on whether commentators were discussing slavery in the United States or globally. Domestically, although after the Civil War abolitionist sentiments were still influential, endeavours were made to reassimilate slave owners and traders into the nation's body politic, so that they might be once again considered true Americans. This was done at the expense of African Americans, especially the formerly enslaved, whose legal and cultural position within the nation was much more contentious and vulnerable. Internationally, when turning their attention to global slavery, whether in their newly acquired colonies or in parts of the world dominated by the European imperial powers, authors from the United States did adopt some of the humanitarian and imperial antislavery conceptions of the slaver as 'other', while pragmatically adjusting antislavery rhetoric to suit the white hegemonic power. This chapter will examine the ways in which authors prevaricated between identifying slavers as the ethnic, racial and religious 'other' or choosing instead to focus on the model of the political rival as slaver.

In order to understand how this process of othering worked, it is vital to consider the slave system after the American Civil War in a global context, dominated by economic and imperial forces, interlinked in one complete trading system, reliant on the demand for luxury goods and the need for labourers to produce those goods or, in the case of the supply of lighter-skinned slaves as servants and concubines in the Indian Ocean world, to be those goods themselves. To understand the motivations and perceptions of practitioners within both systems, I emphasise the shared functions in providing people as commodities to be labourers, status symbols and breeders. As William Clarence-Smith has argued, in slavery globally, there is not always a formal nation-state–based structure driving the establishment of a slave trade or the use of slave labour, and there is also often no clear distinction between slavery and other types of coercive labour such as serfdom or *corvée* labour.[1] Although individuals such as Tippu Tip had no formal, unified political control, they were still regionally powerful and the response of Americans and Europeans to their presence was determined not only by antislavery imperialism but also by a recognition of a need to negotiate safe passage through their territory, and even, occasionally, negotiate a labour supply for the region.[2] Their otherness to European commentators was seen in terms of their ethnic origin as Arabs, their political status as regional headmen, or their religious status as Muslims. The rhetorical choice made when labelling an individual or group as slave traders or buyers was a significant and powerful act. However, in the late nineteenth century, it was not new. Abolitionists had deliberately labelled slavers as 'the other' in pre–Civil War literature, while some radical abolitionists went further and preached a complete abandonment of colour prejudice and rejection of aims of colonisation societies. They chose the tactic of religious othering, projecting the idea that slavery was a religious sin and that while it was the slave owners whose corrupt Christianity was the most heinous, all American Christians were complicit in their guilt.[3]

This chapter will first explore the question of how religion intersected with ethnic identity in a global context when American and European authors chose to 'other' slave owners and traders. Missionary involvement was crucial in determining antislavery activity as another 'crusade' against the evils of Islam or of Arabs more broadly. But missionaries also rhetorically linked the fear of the spread of slavery with other moral panics such as polygamy, headhunting and cannibalism, all of which since the early modern period and beyond had had strong racial

1 William Clarence-Smith, ed., *The Economies of the Indian Ocean Slave Trade in the Nineteenth Century* (Frank Cass, 1989), p. 4.

2 Francois Renault, 'The Structures of the Slave Trade in Central Africa in the Nineteenth Century', in Clarence-Smith, ed., *The Economies of the Indian Ocean Slave Trade*, p. 148.

3 Paul Goodman, *Of One Blood: Abolitionism and the Origins of Racial Equality* (University of California Press, 1998), pp. 1, 107.

overtones. Susceptibility to enslavement was also associated with falling prey to the evils of strong drink, something which had both racial and class connotations as the poor and the racially inferior were considered to be unable to resist the lure of intoxication and addiction.

The special vulnerability of the female enslaved in the hands of the Muslim slaver was an important trope in literature, as writers used scientific racism and the mutable definition of what counted as slavery to position themselves as separate from unfashionable practices. The hierarchy of the races was deployed to sterling effect in discussions of slave traders as backwards and uncivilised, ideas which had their origins in enlightenment thinking of philosophers such as Hume and Kant. In Africa, in American imperial holdings and domestically in struggles with Native Americans, the native was labelled as a slave trader or owner in order to justify colonial interference in a particular region. The presence of slavery could also identify an ethnic group as especially corrupt or greedy in the racial hierarchy, once again triggering the intervention of the more morally principled whites. This was visible in attacks on forced labour systems within the United States, as *padroni* and those involved in the white slave trade were labelled as dishonourable as evidenced by their deployment of these labour systems. Ironically, stereotyping of the Chinese was flexible enough to allow them to be characterised as debauched and greedy slavers at the same time as they were inherently weak and slavish forced labourers.

Labelling a slave trader as unsettling because of their race was only half the story. Equally common was the depiction of a political rival within the imperial jurisdiction as a slaver. This was part of the struggle for global resources, including minerals and agricultural products, but also human beings as labourers and consumers. Campaigns highlighted the practices of the political other, using new media such as photography as evidence of wrongdoing. Often illustrations of European and American culpability were heightened by associating their slaving practices with those of ethnic others, showing that in their forced labour activities, whites often worked alongside allies of other races thus rendering the 'sin' even more heinous in the minds of distant readers. Descriptions of slavery-like practices evolved over time and while, in some contexts, there was a distinct accommodation of white slaving activity, in other cases the hegemony was challenged by more radical authors who sought to end abuses and disseminate ideas of social justice. By the early twentieth century, several authors looked back on the chattel slavery system within the United States and rhetorically distanced the Southern planter class for their complicity in the resultant race problem that their labour choices had triggered. But when writing about global slavery, American authors, especially journalists, tended towards demonising the slaver through race and religion.

ARAB OR MUSLIM? RELIGIOUS OTHERING

Slavery in East Africa and the Middle East executed by an ethnic and religious 'other' was an easy target for commentators wishing to distance themselves from the practice, but during this period Indian Ocean slavery should not be viewed as homogenous. Enslavement had been used in the region for centuries to stock the army with new recruits and it was possible for these *devsirme* slaves to rise to senior positions. Some slaves fulfilled functions as trusted personal servants, and the use of eunuch slaves in positions of advisement and personal care to members of the elite was prevalent, as in their emasculated state, eunuchs were perceived to be unthreatening to the position of the master of the house. Among the upper classes, female sexual slavery was also common, as concubinage was thought to be a valid way for a master to increase the number of his offspring. In theory, according to Sharia law, Muslims were not permitted to enslave other Muslims, but this rule was often broken. Many non-Muslim slaves converted during their period of enslavement and manumission was common.[4] Debates often prevailed among the Ottoman elite about the role of slavery within society and, later in the nineteenth century, Ottoman political and religious leaders began to engage with abolition. Responding to British and American criticism, and the influence of discourse linking antislavery with enlightened thinking, some members of the Muslim elite did refashion themselves as modern, civilised abolitionists.[5] Unlike in Europe and the United States, there was no grass roots abolition movement, and discussions about the role of slavery within Islam usually took place in the religious realm, with some rulers, such as Ahmad Bey of Tunisia, in the 1840s, using the doctrines of Islam as justification for abolition.[6] However, Ehud Toledano has argued that there was a lack of moral condemnation of slavery in the Indian Ocean

[4] Y. Haken Erdem, *Slavery in the Ottoman Empire and Its Demise 1800–1909* (Macmillan, 1996), pp. 1–21.

[5] Seymour Drescher, *Abolition: A History of Slavery and Anti-Slavery* (Cambridge University Press, 2009), pp. 382–3.

[6] William Gervase Clarence-Smith 'Nineteenth Century Islamic Debates over Abolition of Slavery', in Keith Hamilton and Patrick Salmon, eds., *Slavery, Diplomacy and Empire* (Sussex Academic Press, 2009), p. 132.

world because it was sanctioned by Islam and that civil society in the Ottoman public sphere took no part in abolition.[7]

Such subtleties were often lost on European and American outsiders, whose remarks were immersed in the orientalist stereotypes of the time, for example, the portrayal of the 'lustful Turk'. This led some commentators to fear that slavery might never be abolished in regions of Arab and Muslim control, that slavery was an inherent part of their world.[8] The stereotypes of corrupt and sexually depraved slavery were, at different moments, applied indiscriminately to Turks, Arabs, people of mixed ethnic background or all Muslims of the Indian Ocean world. Some British political leaders, such as Sir Evelyn Baring, believed that the existence of the harem was stark evidence of a tendency towards despotism, degeneracy and cruelty, which in turn evidenced the racial inferiority of the Arab and Turkish races.[9] These beliefs about marauding Arab or Turkish slave raiders were most powerful when the victims of enslavement were lighter skinned (coming from Circassia, Georgia or Eastern Europe, for example), Christian and female. In this context, in a period when the definition of whiteness was mutable, American readers saw Armenians as proxy Westerners, as white, and prolific authors such as Frances Willard used the potent rhetoric of defending women's rights from the aggression of the sexually rapacious ethnic 'other'.[10] This chapter will examine how such rhetoric, as well as triggering horrific lynching violence in the United States, also affected the way that authors described prostitution and sex trafficking. Lighter-skinned concubines were very fashionable in parts of the Ottoman empire, with only the elite men able to afford such luxuries, while the middle classes emulated them by taking black African concubines. Although a statement of status, taking a slave wife was also a logical choice for some men. William Clarence-Smith has argued that, in parts of India, it was cheaper to buy a slave wife outright than have to pay a significant formal dowry for a free woman.[11] In this case, contrary to

7 Ehud Toledano, 'Abolition and Anti-Slavery in the Ottoman Empire', in William Mulligan and Maurice Bric, eds., *A Global History of Anti-Slavery Politics in the Nineteenth Century* (Palgrave, 2013), p. 119.

8 T. G. Otte, 'Diplomacy and Suppression of the Slave Trade in the East', in Hamilton & Salmon, eds., *Slavery, Diplomacy and Empire*, p. 102.

9 Diane Robinson-Dunn, *The Harem, Slavery and British Imperial Culture* (Manchester University Press, 2006), p. 8.

10 Ian Tyrrell, *Reforming the World: The Creation of America's Moral Empire* (Princeton, 2010), p. 106.

11 William Clarence-Smith, 'Overview', in Clarence-Smith, ed., *The Economies of the Indian Ocean Slave Trade*, p. 6.

the representations in much American literature, enslaving a woman and forcing her into marriage reflected economic pragmatism rather than an immoral desire for dominance and control. But this did not stop the flourishing of the anti-Arab trope in travel literature and newspapers.

Travel literature and newspapers both keenly reproduced accounts with lurid descriptions of the 'sour sick sultan' and his harem which contained white women as well as 'attendant slaves who were deaf-mutes whose eardrums had been pierced with a needle and whose tongues had been slit'.[12] Visual art and novels also exposed to white Christian audiences the exotic and erotic life of women in Arab and Ottoman harems, although conversation mostly focused on their personal relationships, and their 'otherness', not their coerced status.[13] These spaces were especially fascinating because they were closed, entry to outsiders was strictly forbidden. Orientalist stereotypes about the harem did not exist only in Western Europe and America. Russian literature also developed tropes about Christian maidens from the Caucasus being held against their will in Islamic harems.[14] Chapter 5 will explore the gendered aspect of perceptions of global slavery but suffice to say here that the titillation provided by tales of jealousy of wives towards concubines, and of the role of eunuchs, provided entertainment for the literate masses of Europe and America and encouraged them to see the harem as a space where enslaved women were controlled and victimised rather than being able to celebrate their autonomy.

Many writers who explored the evils of the Indian Ocean and East African slave trades referred to its perpetrators as 'Arabs' and highlighted their inherent racial difference in temperament and morality to the black Africans, who were their enslaved victims. During the 1860s, the heightened sensibility against Arab slave traders became a central tenet of Europe's antislavery imperialism, when such celebrated figures as David Livingstone, Henry Morgan Stanley, Leopold II of Belgium and Edmund Morel railed against Arab slavers.[15] Other less-well-known authors

12 *The San Francisco Call.* (San Francisco [Calif.]), 06 Jan. 1907. *Chronicling America: Historic American Newspapers.* Lib. of Congress. https://chroniclingamerica.loc.gov/lccn/sn85066387/1907-01-06/ed-1/seq-15/.

13 George Michael La Rue, 'The Fatal Sorbet: an Account of Slavery and Jealousy, Pregnancy and Murder in a Harem in Alexandria, Egypt, c. 1850', in Gwyn Campbell and Elizabeth Elbourne, eds., *Sex, Power and Slavery* (Ohio University Press, 2014), p. 204.

14 Megan Dean Farah, 'Autocratic Abolitionists', in Mulligan & Bric, eds., *A Global History*, p. 107.

15 William de Mars, 'The Congo Reform Movement', in Luc Reydams, ed., *Global Activism Reader* (Continuum, 2011), p. 58.

mirrored their depictions, presenting the Arab slave traders as 'ruga ruga' or thieves who would take anything, with slaves, ivory and honey being their favourite tradable commodities.[16] American newspapers excitedly reprinted accounts from the British press describing naval encounters off the East African coast with Arab slavers. These characters were described in highly racialised terms, for example 'with characteristic ferocity the slavers – some thirteen Arabs and seven bloodthirsty half breed cut-throats – endeavoured to spring aboard the pinnace'.[17] On his travels, Verney Lovett Cameron encountered the notorious East African slave trader Tippu Tip, and in describing him, dwelled on his appearance and racial characteristics: 'notwithstanding his being perfectly black, he was a thorough Arab, for curiously enough the admixture of negro blood had not rendered him less of an Arab in his ideas and manners'.[18] Agreeing with Lovett Cameron that there was a particularly 'Arab' form of behaviour when it came to the slave trade, J. A. Moloney asserted that black Africans slaves tended to imitate the Zanzibari Arab traders in their actions: 'through the nigger's imitative instinct he models manners and deportment of his owners'.[19] Moloney concurred with many antislavery campaigners in eliciting in his readers a sense of the horrors of the long-distance slave caravan and the mistreatment of its victims, but he also tried to educate his reader about the complexities of slavery in East Africa. He wrote, 'the slave of a powerful Arab will frequently own numerous drudges of his own'. He also teased out the entangled relationship between Arab traders and local tribal leaders in the region, stating that the slave traders' power derived from the support of the 'big negro kings', whose arrogance and complete control over their domain shocked Moloney. He described the character of Msiri, the King of the Wasanga, who treated visiting missionaries with disdain and called them 'his white slaves'.[20]

For some authors, this was a religious rather than a racial issue. In the mid to late nineteenth century, British and American argumentation about abolition was underpinned by religious moralising, associated with

[16] Verney Lovett Cameron, *Across Africa* (originally Harper, 1877; this version Rockbury Ltd., 2004), p. 110.

[17] *Omaha Daily Bee.* (Omaha [Neb.]), 15 Dec. 1887. *Chronicling America: Historic American Newspapers*. Lib. of Congress. https://chroniclingamerica.loc.gov/lccn/sn99021999/1887-12-15/ed-1/seq-6/.

[18] Ibid., p. 270.

[19] J. A. Moloney, *With Captain Stairs to Katanga* (London, 1893), p. 23.

[20] Ibid., pp. 121, 174.

FIGURE 5 'Tibo Tip's fresh captives being sent into bondage', reproduction of wood engraving by James W. Buel, 1891. Library of Congress.

Christian sentiments about preventing human suffering and facilitating the spread of Jesus's message of love to the most disadvantaged in the world. When examining slavery in the Indian Ocean world, some authors characterised abolition as a struggle between Christian and Muslim values.[21] This resulted from a misunderstanding of Islamic jurisprudence, ignoring the fact that a great deal of Islamic law on slavery was concerned with mitigating the experience of the enslaved and encouraging manumission. Catholic antislavery activists, including the influential Archbishop of Algiers and Carthage, Cardinal Charles Lavigerie, depicted the slave trade as a Muslim or Arab phenomenon and the struggle against it as a new crusade.[22] American newspapers picked up this message and published lengthy articles with strident headlines proclaiming, for example, 'Mohammedanism: the Propagator of the Slave Trade', and called for

[21] William Mulligan, 'The Anti Slave Trade Campaign in Europe 1888–1890', in Bric & Mulligan eds., *A Global History*, pp. 157–8.

[22] Daniel Laqua, 'Tensions of Internationalism: Transnational Anti-Slavery in the 1880s and 1890s', *International Historical Review*, 33: 4 (2011), p. 705.

the intervention of civilised nations to protect the 'poor, tortured slave'.[23] Missionaries of both Protestant and Catholic denominations were important carriers of the supposedly civilising message but, in some cases, such as in King Leopold's Belgian Congo, could prove awkward to the imperialists by being dogmatic about their idealistic views on preventing the use of forced labour. Elsewhere, missionaries were decisive agents in dismantling traditional economic systems and, as Adrian Graves put it, replacing 'peasants' with 'proletariat'. In the Pacific Islands, and globally, part of the missionaries' responsibility was to teach the natives the moral value of hard and consistent work.[24]

But while missionaries were not reticent about liaising with colonial authorities to put natives to work, they did consistently rail against slavery and the slave trade, seeing them not as isolated evils, but rather in tandem with other moral sins that were markers of incivility, often attached to the ethnic other, such as polygamy, headhunting, cannibalism and alcohol abuse. The first was a sin most frequently associated with Arabs and Muslims, emblematic of their corruption and greed, and the last three with pagan Africans who sinned because of their uncorrupted, child-like, even animalistic natures. Not all commentators thought that Islam was unregenerate. William Quillam, an English Muslim, tried to educate his countryman about the benefits of his religion, showing that it was a most liberating system, preventing sin, because it forbade intoxicants. Using slavery as a metaphor, he wrote 'the drink curse is a far worse slavery than that which Clarkson and Wilberforce abolished … the drunkard is a greater slave than the poor Negro'.[25] Natives were not the only group considered at risk from marauding enslavers and the pernicious influence of sin. White women were also deemed unable to resist both. Campaigners in the United States against white slavery warned women and girls that procurers used the lure of luxury goods such as clothes and also intoxication in dance halls and bars to ensnare their innocent young victims.[26] For these authors writing about the United States, the modern city itself

[23] *The New York Herald.* (New York [N.Y.]), 03 Feb. 1873. *Chronicling America: Historic American Newspapers*. Lib. of Congress. https://chroniclingamerica.loc.gov/lccn/sn83030313/1873-02-03/ed-1/seq-11/.

[24] Adrian Graves, 'Colonialism and Indentured Labour Migration in the W. Pacific 1840–1915', in P. C. Emmer, ed., *Colonialism and Migration: Indentured Labour Before and After Slavery* (Martinus Nijhoff Publishers, 1986), p. 241.

[25] Robinson-Dunn, *The Harem, Slavery and British Imperial Culture*, p. 202.

[26] Brian Donovan, *White Slave Crusades: Race, Gender and Anti-Vice Activism 1887–1917* (University of Illinois Press, 2006), p. 22.

became a marker of the threat of slavery lurking within civilisation, while for those describing colonial contexts, the presence of slavery was symptomatic of a lack of civilisation. As the United States looked around the world, this was as true of other cultures as it was in its own cities.

SCIENTIFIC RACISM, THE DEFINITION OF SLAVERY AND JUSTIFICATION FOR CONQUEST

In the late nineteenth century, the intellectual impulse to categorise and systematise the natural and human worlds was a significant cultural driver. Regarding depictions of slavery, this was done in two main ways. First, the timeline of civilisations illustrated the point of development that a particular nation or region had achieved. For example, Pacific Islanders and Africans were considered underdeveloped and untouched by civilisation, whereas the Chinese and Arabs occupied a more complicated position. The sense that history was inexorably advancing underpinned these rankings.[27] Second, human beings were systematised by the hierarchy of races, with white Anglo-Saxons at the top. Charles Darwin referred to this hierarchy in terms of 'favoured races', implying that a higher level of development was due to innate racial qualities which operated alongside economic and political realities.[28] These racial characterisations were not static – for example, the category of 'white' expanded in this period – but still, the system could be deployed by those who envisioned a hortative function for Europeans and Americans to bring civility and education to ignorant natives around the world, and in doing so, remove their vulnerability to enslavement. As Thomas McCarthy has argued, race was never truly a biological construct, with social and cultural factors playing crucial roles in the understanding of its meaning. However, in the late nineteenth century, observations of innate racial differences, regarding, for example, the suitability of one race to labour in a particular climate, were commonplace. As shown later in this chapter, this extended to discussions about the relationship between certain races and slavery, arguing that Africans were innately suited to the culture of slavery and not that of

[27] Thomas McCarthy, *Race, Empire and the Idea of Human Development* (Cambridge University Press, 2009), p. 1.

[28] James Lander, *Lincoln and Darwin: Shared Visions of Race, Science and Religion* (Southern Illinois University Press, 2010), p. 12.

free labour, and therefore they were incapable of developing an orderly civil society without coercion.[29]

In the mid-nineteenth century, the polygenist argument was contested, with some theorists suggesting that perhaps blacks and whites were not of the same species. Darwin did not subscribe to this view, but many scientists did, including Louis Agassiz, who famously asserted that when observing African Americans living in Philadelphia his belief developed that they were 'not of the same blood as us'.[30] By the late nineteenth century, Darwin's idea of natural selection superseded polygenesis, but this did nothing to alleviate the dichotomous conceptions differentiating between civilised and uncivilised races. The theories of natural selection and their relationship to racial susceptibility to slavery had more impact on the perceptions of slavery in the post-emancipation era than other intellectual frameworks. Domestically within the United States, and internationally, it led to racial anxiety for whites. Although they believed that, eventually, inferior races would be eliminated by the higher civilised races, they also feared the threat of mongrelisation and the numerical overwhelming of the higher races.[31] Many conservative Americans felt that, following the end of the slavery in the United States, the only solution to the 'negro problem', was the wholesale compulsory removal of black Americans, either to South America, the Caribbean or Africa.

However, in the post-emancipation period some writers thought more innovatively about the future of the human race. Sociologists began to challenge the idea of race as the sole marker of difference and the end of slavery and the Indian wars allowed for the questioning of simplistic dichotomies of master/slave and savage/civilised. In the late nineteenth and early twentieth centuries, a greater focus on culture emerged, on both a global and a local level. Ironically, African Americans were held up as a model of development by authors wanting to show that racial characteristics were not fixed and that education and exposure to moral fortitude could allow civilisation to develop anywhere. As Brad Evans has shown, African Americans were held up as evidence that 'they had gone beyond the originals', that is, Africans who still lived in Africa.[32] In Chapter 6, the relationship between the formerly enslaved in the United States and the enslaved in African will be explored.

[29] McCarthy, *Race, Empire*, p. 50. [30] Lander, *Lincoln and Darwin*, p. 77.

[31] Ibid., p. 281.

[32] Brad Evans, *Before Cultures: the Ethnographic Imagination in American Literature 1865–1920* (University of Chicago, 2005), pp. 4, 6, 174.

As shown in Chapter 2, in this period, the definition of slavery was not fixed and impermeable. American and European commentators pragmatically manipulated the terminology of slavery for their own gain, whether to justify inaction or intervention in the labour systems of a particular region. This functioned rhetorically alongside scientific racism as an interpretive tool for comprehending the complex systems of Indian Ocean slavery. Matthew Hopper quoting from Troutt Powell suggests that scholars have been guilty of muting the voices of the enslaved by accepting monolithic constructs of race as defined in the nineteenth century and he also accused them of over-reliance on 'the Atlantic paradigm'.[33] Turning to the historical sources, Hopper shows how authors constructed slavery in Arabia as wrongly timeless and static. American and British intervention was slow in the region because of the flourishing international markets for luxury commodities produced there using slave labour, such as pearls and dates, and the willingness to define slavery in the Arab world as more benign and less pernicious than that in the Atlantic region.[34] While some Europeans and Americans marked Arab slave owners as particularly cruel and corrupted, another trend in the literature marked them as more benevolent. To an extent, this portrayal of Arab slavery as more benign did have its roots in observed experience, as authors encountered slaves who had significantly more autonomy than those chattel slaves in the Atlantic world system. Manumission was more common, although not all slaves desired manumission, because their security and status was given to them by being part of an elite household albeit with a subservient role.[35] Liat Kozma supports this argument, that manumission behaviour read by whites as benevolence, and rhetorically used to delay intervention in Arab systems of slavery, was not always experienced as such by the enslaved individual. She argues that freedom was sometimes considered negatively because of its resulting uncertainty and loneliness. This unusual situation emerged because of the bond that Islamic law gave slaves to their master, in effect a kinship relationship. Therefore, although manumission was defined by Islamic law to be a meritorious act, it was not

33 Matthew Hopper, *Slaves of One Master: Globalisation and Slavery in Arabia in the Age of Empire* (Yale University Press, 2015), pp. x, 13.

34 Ibid., p. 11.

35 George Michael La Rue, 'Enslaved Blacks in European Households', in Terence Walz & Kenneth Cuno, eds., *Race and Slavery in the Middle East* (American University in Cairo Press, 2010), p. 116.

always considered so by the newly freed individual.[36] This subtler understanding of slavery was lost on many European and American writers who fell back on simplistic but easily identifiable stereotypes, such as the lustful or cruel Turk, or more widely, the uncivilised Filipino or Hawaiian. Authors knew that these depictions would appeal more to their readers and help sell their books or newspapers as well as implicitly justifying an interventionist imperial policy.

The origins of using theories of race and development to alienate the owners of slaves can be traced back to the Enlightenment when, for the first time, religious definitions distinguishing between in and out groups were superseded by conceptions of what it meant to be 'civilised' as a race. Using knowledge gathered from works on natural history, travel accounts and the Bible, Immanuel Kant provided what was among the earliest systematic account of race, by carefully cataloguing the characteristics of different people, sexes and races.[37] A century earlier, John Locke, who was influential in the design of the political structure of the colony of Carolina, and a shareholder in the Royal African Company, had associated slavery with inferiority, backwardness and sinfulness. But rather than examining how slave owning damaged an individual, he focused on the experiences of the enslaved, saying 'slavery is so vile and miserable an estate of man'.[38] By the time that Locke and later Kant were writing, slavery and Africa had become intrinsically linked for Europeans and Americans. By the nineteenth century, authors wrote about Africans being enslaved and being slave traders since time immemorial, furthering the idea that there was something innate in the African's nature that led them to practise the institution of slavery. Stereotypical views, that Africa and Africans had no real history because no significant progress towards civilisation had ever been made, were enhanced. Africans acknowledged the longevity of the existence of slavery on the continent and discussed its fundamental place within their societies. For example, the Hausa people of West and Central Saharan Africa have origin myths which include the figures of slave dealers.[39]

The embeddedness of slavery in certain African cultures presented an important propaganda opportunity for British imperialist antislavery writers, who viewed African complicity in slavery as a justification for

[36] Liat Kozma, 'Manumitted Female Slaves in Khedival Egypt', in Walz & Kuno, eds., *Race and Slavery in the Middle East*, pp. 198–200.

[37] McCarthy, *Race, Empire*, p. 45. [38] Ibid., p. 25.

[39] Humphrey J. Fisher, *Slavery in the History of Muslim Black Africa* (Hurst, 1988), p. 16.

their own racial hierarchical views. As Richard Huzzey argued, because for religious reasons, slavery was linked to barbarity and heathenism, then even in treaty negotiations to end slavery and the slave trade, British dealings with Africans hinged on the view that Africans were at root an uncivilised people.[40] Other European colonial powers shared this view. Although the German authorities in Tanganyika Territory never legally abolished slavery because they feared upsetting their main African allies, they used the existence of slavery to justify imperial intervention. Slavery in this part of Africa brought wealth to coastal towns because of the caravan trade, and the location of slave-raiding grounds were determined by a web of local alliances. However, enslavement by kidnap was only one method; others became slaves because of judicial process, indebtedness, famine or by being born into the state. In the late 1880s and 1890s, German antislavery was linked to justification for conquest as the region became a formal colony of the Reich. Although Bismarck was indifferent to slavery, left wing radicals in the German Reichstag suggested that 'house' or domestic slavery in the colonies was little different to wage slavery at home. But despite hesitancy, many German politicians wanted to abolish slavery in their colonies but were unsure of the mechanism by which to do this. Meanwhile, they returned to rhetoric of antislavery imperialism that was modelled so well by the British in their territories.[41]

From the 1860s onwards, the association between Africans and slavery was enhanced when international law condemned all who traded in slaves as 'criminal communities', as participation in the slave trade was rendered piracy, a capital crime.[42] The United States was initially slow to join the international effort because of President Monroe's policy to restrict activity and seize slavers on the African coast, in the Archipelagos and in the Levant, but to leave the practice alone on the continent itself.[43] However, as colonisation and conquest proceeded, African slave trading rulers would not easily give up their income and their slaves. They were no longer the ideological enemy, but allies to the colonising power and therefore slavery, while still seen as a good opportunity to distance white from

[40] Richard Huzzey, *Freedom Burning: Anti-Slavery and Empire in Victorian Britain* (Cornell University Press, 2012), pp. 52, 135.

[41] Jan-Georg Deutsch, *Emancipation without Abolition in German East Africa c. 1884–1814* (Ohio University Press, 2006), pp. 37, 53, 102, 109.

[42] Robin Law, 'Abolition and Imperialism' in Derek Peterson, ed., *Abolitionism and Imperialism in Britain, Africa and the Atlantic* (Ohio University Press, 2010), p. 164.

[43] James A. Field, Jr., *America and the Mediterranean World 1776–1882* (Princeton University Press, 1969), p. 224.

black, was no longer deployed in the same manner. An example of an African ruler who negotiated a position of power because of his attitude to slavery was Menilek of Ethiopia. In his region, slaves, gold and ivory were important trade commodities, both domestically and over long distances. In the late nineteenth century, slavery in Ethiopia was diverse as enslaved individuals were luxury status servants, concubines and eunuchs, but also employed as craftsmen. Menilek showed sensitivity to international debates on the abolition of slavery and engaged in these, promising to act. But he also owned slaves himself and was pragmatic about the radical change required to rid Ethiopia of slavery in its entirety.[44]

Reports about the behaviour of General Gordon and the Mahdi over the slave trade in Sudan caused even more consternation and confusion amongst both black and white readers. Americans were especially interested in the conflict in the Nile Valley and in the early nineteenth century it was a site for flourishing American tourism. The Mahdi's rebellion was seen in some quarters as a struggle against the colonial suppression of the slave trade, which left the Black press in the United States unsure how to reconcile this with another view of the Mahdi as black hero.[45] In 1884, the situation was further confused by General Gordon's legalisation of the slave trade, which, after his assassination, allowed American readers of the *New York Times* to see the Mahdi as a nationalist hero once again. This perception was only held briefly as, by the 1890s, the United States had become an imperial power itself, and was more sympathetic to the aims of the British in the Nile Valley, who, at the Battle of Omdurman, sought revenge on the successor to the Mahdi. General Kitchener was less interested in the slave trade, and tacitly tolerated its practice among his advisors.[46]

But despite this complexity, in the minds of Americans and Europeans the existence of slavery helped create a unified Africa: the simplification of a slave-based system and ignorance of tribal and local differences brought Africans together as one.[47] Dismantling of slavery, while a gradual process, allowed some colonialists the opportunity to take advantage of the situation and institute coercive labour practices in their wake. While

[44] Timothy Fennyhaugh, 'Slavery and the Slave trade in Southern Ethiopia', in Clarence-Smith, ed., *The Economies of the Indian Ocean Slave Trade*, pp. 114–15.

[45] Ahmed E. Elbashir, *The United States, Slavery and the Slave Trade in the Nile Valley* (University Press of America, 1983), p. 46.

[46] Ibid., pp. 52–3, 136.

[47] Patrick Manning, *Slavery and the African Life: Occidental, Oriental and African Slave Trades* (Cambridge University Press, 1990), pp. 16, 25.

'slavery' as an idea became tied to Africanness, in reality, bonded labour was simultaneously deployed by colonisers. Relocated, 'freed' slaves were susceptible to being caught up in these labour systems, as other Africans became suspicious of the rumours abounding about labour conditions. In practice, in the later nineteenth century, it became difficult to distinguish between legal and illegal labour conditions in Africa.[48] Black Africans and Arabs were not the only ethnic groups associated with slavery in Africa. In 1896, in response to an investigative enquiry from the British and Foreign Antislavery Society, a letter from the Consul General of the United States at Tangier asserted that 'no persons in Morocco under American protection are engaged in the slave trade or hold slaves'. However, the Consul followed up with the caveat that 'Jews and others might place themselves under the protection of our flag hoping to shield themselves from any unjust or wrong doing they may seek to engage in I have no doubt. I have instructed the agents to keep a sharp lookout in respect to this matter and report any cases that they may discover'.[49]

This process of using concepts of racial hierarchy and progression of civilisations to render slave traders and holders as different was a global phenomenon. Although the relationship between Anglo-Americans and Native Americans in North America cannot be equated to the relationship between coloniser and native in the high imperial period, the rhetoric to justify conquest and control through identifying a so-called backwards race with slavery was mirrored in the United States' confrontation with Native Americans. The enslavement of African Americans by the Choctaw and Chickasaw nations was disrupted first by the Indian Removal process of the 1830s, when the tribes and their slaves were forced to move west to Oklahoma territory from the eastern seaboard, and then second by the Civil War itself. Slavery as an institution among Native tribespeople survived the western migration as slave owners sought to re-establish their profitable plantations. The slavery they practised was similar to that of white slave holders, and the experiences and resistance of the enslaved was also similar. The experiences of the enslaved in the region were recorded as part of the WPA narrative oral history interviews. Immediately after the civil war, the victorious North policed

[48] Monica Schuler, 'The Recruitment of African Indentured Labourers for European Colonies in the Nineteenth Century', in Emmer, ed., *Colonialism and Migration*, p. 135.

[49] Letter from D. N. Bourke 9/11/96, appended to letter from I. J. Bayard, Embassy of the United States, London 11/1/97 to Charles Allen MSS Brit Emp s22/G85 United States 1853–97 folder, Bodleian Library, University of Oxford.

the southern states to eradicate the entrenched system of slavery, but where Native American slave holders were concerned, accusations of the continued existence of slavery-like practices justified interference in 'Indian' affairs, revealing a desire for an extension of white jurisdiction. General John Sanborn highlighted the antagonism felt towards African Americans in sections of the Choctaw and Chickasaw population, which was reiterated later in 1894 by the Dawes Commission, and he also suggested that Indian territory must be open to United States authority in order to protect the former slaves.[50]

As Linda Parker has argued, the United States applied lessons learned in conflict with native peoples in North America to its new colonial holdings in Hawaii and the Philippines.[51] Despite Hawaiians' efforts to appropriate the culture and civilisation and to mirror the modernity of Americans and Europeans, they were still seen, in the words of Walter Hixon, like Native Americans, as 'landless, premodern others'. Living in a rigidly stratified society, Hawaiian elites had, for generations, subjected commoners to systems of forced labour. Ironically, American-born sugar planters who wanted to use contract labour to farm their crops, advocated the dispossession of these so-called backwards, uncivilised Hawaiian natives.[52] William DeWitt Alexander, born in Honolulu, a child of missionary parents sent to Hawaii, was a proponent of this view, writing to dispel the application to native Hawaiians of the romantic myths of the noble savage. He speculated about earlier periods in Hawaii's history when there was a class of slaves, even lower than the commoners: 'there were also bond slaves, Kauwa, lower even that the common people who were probably made so in war. The opprobrious epithets "laepuni" and "makawela" applied to them imply that they were marked in the forehead'.[53] Although Alexander's work purported to be a history of the Hawaiian people, much of his work was taken up by cataloguing European voyages to the islands, leaving the impression that there was little history of note prior to their arrival.

Seven years later, once the American coup had deposed the native Hawaiian monarchy, a travel account by John Musick adopted a more

[50] Barbara Krauthamer, *Black Slaves, Indian Masters: Slavery, Emancipation and Citizenship in the Native American South* (University of North Carolina Press, 2013), p. 112.

[51] Walter Hixon, *American Settler Colonialism: a History* (Palgrave, 2013), p. 148.

[52] Ibid., p. 149.

[53] W. J. Alexander, *A Brief History of the Hawaiian People* (American Book Company, 1891), p. 30.

romantic tone about Hawaii's pre-contact history, but came to the same conclusion about the backwardness of the people because of their use of forced labour systems. By the time he recorded his account, the Sprecklesville plantation on Maui already had a workforce of thousands of contract labourers, imported from Japan and China. Musick called this trade in labourers 'diabolical', but then erroneously attributed it to native Hawaiians: 'it is one of the relics of monarchy, controlled and manipulated by designing men and not easy to get rid of. The system is far worse than absolute slavery'. He described in great detail the role in the pre-contact society of the oppressive 'luna' or overseer who forced the common native peoples into slavery. These 'land pirates' threatened innocent natives who merely wanted to be left in peace to cultivate their own taro patch.[54] The most detailed early history of the Hawaiian people written for American consumption was William Fremont Blackman's 1906 work, which presented the Hawaiians as a people who had made some progress to civilisation, but who were now in decline. He confirmed that, in the late eighteenth century prior to the tenure of King Kamehameha I, slaves taken in war were at the bottom of the hierarchy and the common people were bound in a system of feudal tenure and could at any time be conscripted into the army. However, by the nineteenth century, he argued, despite the reform of the land system and prevention of slavery, the racial weakness of the natives inevitably meant that 'contact with civilisation accelerates this process of decay'.[55]

Similarly, in the Philippines, the Southern Moro province was the location of what Alfred McCoy has termed 'the classical colonial script', as the supposed savage treachery of the natives, epitomised by the debt bondage and slavery found there, justified American intervention and even mass slaughter.[56] Later, when many in the United States were calling for withdrawal from the Philippines, William Howard Taft, in his 1912 presidential election campaign, justified a slower route to independence because of the Philippine Assembly's failure to deal with the issue of slavery.[57] Ironically, in the early days of American intervention in the Philippines, buoyed by successes in Cuba, the rhetoric had been mostly directed towards protecting the native peoples against the horrors of the

[54] John Musick, *Hawaii: Our New Possessions* (Funk and Wagnalls, 1898), pp. 153, 339.

[55] William Fremont Blackman, *The Making of Hawaii: a Study in Social Evolution* (New York, 1906), pp. 29, 209.

[56] Alfred McCoy, *Policing America's Empire: the US, the Philippines and the Rise of the Surveillance State* (University of Wisconsin Press, 2009), p. 207.

[57] Ibid., p. 227.

imperialist Spanish who, through the *encomienda* system, had imposed a system of slavery on the entire archipelago.[58] Increasingly the race question became fundamental in American propaganda and natives of the region were catalogued into subgroups as Negrito, Indonesian or Malayan.[59] The latter two were seen as doubly distinct by reason of their Muslim faith. Criticism of Muslim slaveholding in the Philippines was influenced by commentary on the activities of Arabs in the Indian Ocean slave trade. Like Muslim slaveholding in the Middle East, the phenomenon in the Philippines was characterised by both Presidents McKinley and Roosevelt as benign, in order to convince American readers that an easy abolition, and successful colonisation, was possible.[60] Charles Forbes Lindsay was one of those who illustrated the victims and perpetrators of slavery in the Philippines as racially different from one another, talking about how the development of the Zambales was retarded by their being an inherently 'backward race', vulnerable to the inroads of the 'Moro pirates', as he termed the slave raiders.[61] Dean Worcester, commenting on the 1904 St. Louis Anthropology Days and Olympic Games, claiming that backwardness and racial weakness were associated with slave traders and not slaves. He reported that the Filipino tribe who were present at the Expo were 'unexcelled pirates and slave traders', which was unsurprising given that the entire range of cultural practices on display at the event were selected to flaunt the racial superiority of the white man.[62]

As well as focusing on backwardness and incivility, American and European writers also rhetorically defined the use of forced labour forms as an indication of wickedness, corruption and greed. The ability of superior races to educate misguided groups was used as a justification for colonial intervention. But the pedagogical potential to elicit change was denied in other cases where slavery was discovered, and instead the

[58] Leon Wolff, *Little Brown Brother: How the US Purchased and Pacified the Philippines* (Oxford University Press, 1960), p. 16.

[59] Eric Love, *Race over Empire: Race and Imperialism 1865–1900* (University of North Carolina Press, 2004), p. 179.

[60] Michael Salman, *The Embarrassment of Slavery: Controversies over Bondage and Nationalism in the American Colonial Philippines* (University of California Press, 2001), p. 49.

[61] Charles Forbes-Lindsay, *The Philippines under Spanish and American Rules* (Philadelphia, 1906), p. 36.

[62] Gerald Gems, 'Anthropology Days, the Construction of Whiteness and American Imperialism in the Philippines', in Susan Brownell, ed., *The 1904 Anthropology Days and Olympic Games* (University of Nebraska Press, 2008), pp. 195, 200.

legal system was utilised to prosecute those charged with practising such heinous crimes. This reflects the hypocrisy of many writers who were fully aware that Europeans and Americans also used forced labour where they deemed it necessary to do so, and the selective labelling of slave owners and traders as evil lawbreakers was a calculated act of political control. This statement was commonly made when writing about Chinese emigrants and the labour agents who facilitated their movement to the United States and the Atlantic world. Racial stereotyping was simultaneously utilised to depict the Chinese as both corrupt and greedy slave traders and as weak and inherently slavish victims. But unlike the colonial narratives discussing Africa, which emphasised victimhood to justify intervention, Chinese slavishness was purported to pollute the American body politic and therefore it was argued that they must be removed and excluded from the nation because they were unassimilable. Stuart Creighton Miller traced the long history of American stereotyping of the Chinese showing how, throughout the nineteenth century, Chinese labour was associated with black slavery. In terms of the hierarchies of cultural development, the Chinese occupied an unusual position. Americans acknowledged that their civilisation was ancient, advanced and shrewd but it was deemed, by this later period, to have stagnated. In the Christian mind, the association of Chinese culture with opium added to the negative stereotyping, as nineteenth-century American diplomats described the Chinese elite as depraved, despotic and addicted to 'pernicious drugs'.[63]

In an era where many white Americans lauded racial purity, the Chinese ironically faced criticism for historically operating a closed society, in the words of G. B. Densmore 'a sealed empire where no possible admixture of foreign blood could occur'.[64] Missionaries were an important conduit, transmitting to readers in the United States information about the Chinese section of the coolie trade. To most Americans, their experience was of arrival of Chinese on their own shores as supposedly enslaved labourers, but missionaries, especially women, drew attention to the systems of labour within China that allowed slavers to ply their trade. They described how Chinese and foreign labour procurers worked alongside one another in regions such as Guangzhou.[65] Once emigration

[63] Stuart Creighton Miller, *The Unwelcome Immigrant: the American Image of the Chinese 1785–1882* (University of California Press, 1969), pp. 11, 54.

[64] G. B. Densmore, *The Chinese in California* (Pettit and Russ, 1880), p. 6.

[65] Gordon Chang, *Fateful Ties: a History of America's Preoccupation with China* (Harvard University Press, 2015), pp. 52, 75.

allowed for the establishment of Chinatowns in western cities such as San Francisco, American authors delivered often scathing commentaries on the facilitators of forced labour within the expat Chinese community. The supposedly hidden and secret nature of their communities sought to exoticise the Chinese. G. B. Densmore described how they 'depend on their own methods to keep their people in subjections' and that these methods included 'go betweens and arbitrators' as well as the 'Chinese Six Companies', depicted by hostile authors as shadowy organisations, part migrant support groups, part employment agents taking advantage of their own countrymen.[66] Not all American writers agreed with this depiction. The Reverend O. Gibson suggested that the furore was stirred up by 'Papist competitors in the labour market' and that they 'seem to be chasing a phantom': for this, Gibson was hung in effigy in San Francisco![67]

This process of accusing manipulative labour agents of taking advantage of their naïve and weaker countrymen also functioned within coercive labour situations used in many industries on the East coast. Due to the seasonal specificities of agricultural labour, and the fact that picking fruit and crops could not be mechanised, labour suppliers or '*padroni*' worked on the eastern seaboard and also in the immigrants' country of origin to provide labour for various business owners. For example, labourers leaving southern Italy were often promised a year's contract before getting on board ship. African Americans also participated in seasonal labouring, and the use of child labour was common.[68] Contract labour was outlawed in 1885, labelled as 'white slavery', but *padroni* circumvented this by employing workers directly. *Padroni* were represented as 'brutal', 'parasitic', and 'un American' and their fruit-picking employees as passive victims, with their 'submission to more powerful countrymen a racial weakness'.[69] As with Chinese immigration, both free and coerced labourers worked alongside one another and to dismiss all *padroni* as slavers was a tool of American conservatives to control labour movement.

Identifying the Chinese as being racially suited to enslavement also took on an important gendered aspect. Even the generally sympathetic Reverend Gibson accused the poorer Chinese of selling their daughters to 'panderers'.[70] There was a long history of stereotyping Chinese men for

[66] Densmore, *The Chinese in California*, p. 16.
[67] Rev. O. Gibson, *The Chinese in America* (Hitchcock and Walden, 1877), pp. 922, 336.
[68] Cindy Hahamovitch, *The Fruits of Their Labour: Atlantic Coast Farmworkers and the Making of Migrant Poverty 1870–1945* (University of North Carolina Press, 1997), p. 29.
[69] Ibid., p. 47. [70] Gibson, *The Chinese in America*, p. 35.

their barbaric treatment of women, with prostitution and concubinage highlighted as being similar to chattel slavery. Cruelty shown in China towards women who worked in laundries and who were then sexually abused was brought to the fore in the 1830s in women's magazines published in America.[71] Densmore outlined how this sexual slavery was transported to the cities of the West Coast by organised businesses. He described how the prostitutes 'confined by fear' also somehow enticed young boys of twelve years old into their den, an example of a corrupted slave further enslaving an innocent.[72] Gibson described in detail how Chinese sex slavery worked. He stated that 'of the six thousand Chinese women in America, more than nine-tenths are of that unfortunate class that have been sold into hopeless bondage worse than death', having been bought in China, and shipped to America with promises of rich husbands.[73] This statement highlights the confusion over the status of Chinese women, as they were depicted simultaneously as complete chattels, and as free migrants who have been misled about what awaited them in the United States. Gibson denied outright that male Chinese migrants were slaves, adding that 'the Chinese people always regarded with horror the American system of African slavery', but maintained the belief in widespread female Chinese enslavement.[74]

Concerns over 'yellow sex slavery' and, more widely, prostitution had direct racial overtones. Stories of Chinese women enticed into sexual slavery both exoticised and eroticised the debate over Chinese immigration and fitted easily into discourse of racial prostitution in this era.[75] In most literature of the period, victims were white, but Chinese women were also frequently depicted as vulnerable, friendless and in need of protection. However, in identifying the procurer or sex trafficker as a racial other, Americans sought to fit prostitution into their world view, which accepted the African American as a natural sexual predator. Since the end of the Civil War, the spectre of the black rapist threatening white women, especially in the south, had been used to foment anti-black violence and justify the horrific brutality of spectacle lynching.[76] Female procurers were also racially othered, with one of the most famous cases being that of Belle Moore, who, at her 1909 grand jury trial was accused of taking child prostitutes from

[71] Creighton Miller, *The Unwelcome Immigrant*, p. 76.
[72] Densmore, *The Chinese in California*, p. 77.
[73] Gibson, *The Chinese in America*, p. 134. [74] Ibid., p. 258.
[75] Donovan, *White Slave Crusades*, p. 113. [76] Ibid., p. 13.

orphanages, was identified variously as 'a mulatto', 'negro', 'negress' or 'coloured' – explicitly not white – even though in other newspaper accounts she was described as very light skinned, easily passing for white.[77]

Theodore Bingham's 1911 book about sex trafficking was an attempt to convince his readers that, contrary to the findings of the Commission to investigate white slavery, there was an organised international conspiracy to traffic white women and girls into the United States for sex slavery. He dismissed the role of female procurers such as Belle Moore and stated that 'it is now a man's trade', showing how young male procurers who had been corrupted in their teenage years worked to entice innocent women into prostitution. Bingham claimed that these 'cadets' were often of Irish, Italian or Jewish extraction.[78] According to abolitionists this was a global problem. The 1909 book *The White Slave Market* described Asian slavers buying white women in Singapore, while earlier in the novel *The Sheik's White Slave*, by Raymond Raife, an innocent and feminised white boy seeking travel and adventure was drugged and procured for personal servitude and possibly sexual purposes. The narrator, Tom, depicts his enslavement as typical of the cruelty of his captors, who also order another captive to be torn apart by lions.[79] Procurers might be an outsider of another type, as pointed out by Clifford Roe in his tract highlighting the horrors of white slavery in America. He described how prostitution functioned in different cities, with a view to the establishment of 'red light districts' to protect vulnerable girls and control vice. Many cities, such as Boston, refused to address the problem denying that prostitution existed in their environs, but Roe contradicted this, asserting that in Boston procurers were mostly Canadians.[80] But for many white slavery campaigners, procurers were only small pawns in the big business of international prostitution, and the real enemy was the modern, ruthless businessman at the head of his white slave empire. These figures were portrayed in racialised terms, described as predatory tribal chieftains: 'the big chief' – reflecting the influence of discussions of slavery in Africa on

77 Ibid., p. 89.

78 Gen. Theodore Bingham, *The Girl That Disappears: the Real Facts about the White Slave Traffic* (Boston, 1911), p. 39.

79 Margit Stange, *Personal Property: Wives, White Slaves and the Market in Women* (Johns Hopkins University Press, 1998), p. 94; Raymond Raife, *The Sheik's White Slave* (London, 1895), p. 49.

80 Clifford Roe, *The Great War on White Slavery or Fighting for the Protection of Our Girls* (New York, 1911), p. 240.

this very different type of coercive labour, and the complex interplay of the global and the local.[81] On the global stage, like other imperial powers, the United States was concerned about the relationship of its rival nations to slave labour.

THE OTHERING OF RIVALS

Competition between world powers for imperial resources was equally significant a driver of variation in the rhetorical use of the concept of slavery as was the development of a racial language of othering slave owners and traders. Accusations of an imperial rival's complicity in the slave trade or slavery itself were commonplace and such assertions worked to discredit the other imperial power, to show its hypocrisy and to label it unfit to govern by the standard of civilisation and the morality of the era. Successive European and American governments had to demonstrate that they were actively supporting the antislavery agenda, while, as shown in Chapter 2, often tacitly condoning slavery or using coercive labour systems to maintain order and control. To distance white Europeans or Americans through their involvement in slavery was a serious rhetorical decision, challenging the consensus in the notion that the civilised, superior white race had a moral fortitude which allowed them to resist the lure of the profit made from labour abuse. Usually pragmatically ventured to usurp the position of political strength of one imperial power, such rhetoric was occasionally marshalled in a more radical activist mode, through popular culture to mobilise public opinion against heinous acts in the colonial arena. In those cases, political advantage in any given region might fall to other imperial powers because of the intervention, but that was not its original aim. Rather the intention was to challenge the complacency of Europeans and Americans towards enslavement and to encourage the emergence of a counter narrative of the efficacy of colonial intervention to improve the lives of the natives.

The potential power of this use of slavery in gifting an advantage to a rival nation was fully realised in Arthur Brickman's 1868 tract about the history of Kashmir, India. His piece was a polemical rallying cry directed towards a British readership in the aftermath of the Indian Mutiny. He described the enslavement of the Kashmiri people in both literal and metaphorical terms: 'slavery in every sense of the term exists in Cashmere, no man having anything of his own, not even his soul and the care of it,

[81] Stange, *Personal Property*, p. 89.

everything, the land, the water, the food, the refuse, the weeds being the rajah's'.[82] Castigating the British for 'selling' the Kashmiris to Gholab Singh for seven and a half million rupees, Brickman acknowledged that one of the most significant dangers in the region came from other potential imperial powers: the Kashmiris, he argued, are 'ready to welcome, anyone Russian or Turk, as a deliverer from the cruel shameful bondage into which we sold them'.[83]

Therefore, when writers expressed accusations against imperial rivals of involvement in slavery and the slave trade, they knew precisely what the outcome could be: the enhancement of power of their own nation in the region. This was especially common at the turn of the twentieth century in Africa. In southern Africa, for example, the Boer War was justified in British propaganda as a war to liberate black Africans from enslavement by Afrikaners.[84] Some American newspapers echoed this by examining the issue from the Boers perspective and presented them as disgruntled slave owners, who were hostile to new laws protecting slaves and dissatisfied with having their slaves removed from them without compensation. Some Southern newspapers even went so far as to depict the First Boer War as unjust because it was waged due to the Boer refusal to liberate their slaves. The *Florida Agriculturalist* claimed that 'a good deal of sympathy has been expressed in this country' with the Boer cause because of the significant echoes for a United States readership thinking back to the situation following their own civil war only thirteen years earlier.[85] Unsurprisingly, Northern newspapers took a slightly more sympathetic view with the British, for example in 1900 the *New York Tribune* published a report from London defending the British case by explaining the true horror of the Boer's slave trading in terms familiar to American abolitionists: stating that women and children were its most significant victims.[86]

82 Arthur Brinckman, *The Wrongs of Cashmere: a Plea for the Deliverance of that Beautiful Country from the Slavery and Oppression under Which It Is Going to Ruin* (London, 1868), p. 16.

83 Ibid., p. 21.

84 Kevin Grant, *A Civilised Savagery: Britain and the New Slaveries in Africa 1884–1926* (Routledge, 2005), p. 80.

85 *Northern Ohio Journal.* (Painesville, Ohio), 31 May 1879. *Chronicling America: Historic American Newspapers*. Lib. of Congress. https://chroniclingamerica.loc.gov/lccn/sn84028194/1879-05-31/ed-1/seq-1/; *The Florida Agriculturist.* (DeLand, Fla.), 30 March 1881. *Chronicling America: Historic American Newspapers*. Lib. of Congress. https://chroniclingamerica.loc.gov/lccn/sn96027724/1881-03-30/ed-1/seq-4/

86 *New-York Tribune.* (New York [N.Y.]), 07 Jan. 1900. *Chronicling America: Historic American Newspapers*. Lib. of Congress. https://chroniclingamerica.loc.gov/lccn/sn83030214/1900-01-07/ed-1/seq-43/.

Once the fighting in South Africa was under way, most of the literature sought to demonise the Boer without reference to his treatment of Africans and some writers frequently used slavery to convey this message. As early as 1869, F. W. Chesson had alerted a British readership to the supposed love of the Boer for slavery, which, he claimed, the Boers masked by referring to slavery as 'apprenticeship'.[87] But Chesson argued that the Boers were also involved in long-distance slave trafficking because they had made a compact with the Portuguese slave traders who worked on the East coast of Africa, 'making the European soul merchants a far more revolting being than the lowest type of the negro race'.[88] The presence in South Africa of newly arrived free and contracted Chinese and Indian labourers further complicated the position and expanded the definition of slavery, just as happened in the United States with the arrival of the Chinese.

The Portuguese, who earlier in the century had been reluctant to sign the treaties abolishing the transatlantic slave trade, were by the late nineteenth and early twentieth centuries frequently accused of involvement in slaving and slavery in Africa. In 1903, Henry Fox Bourne alerted the public to the continued use of slave labour in South Africa and asserted that the Portuguese were responsible for the influx of enslaved people into the region, despite being aware of the British distaste for slavery and fearful of their public opinion.[89] Fox Bourne was one of the few who wrote, not to undertake imperial point scoring on behalf of his nation, acknowledging that the British as well as the Boers and Portuguese were at fault. However, much of his focus was on the errors of the Boers in South Africa and he accused them of continually undertaking slave raids and offering natives in their territories no legal rights whatsoever.[90]

The Portuguese use of enslavement in the cocoa industry on the West African coast also came to the attention of campaigners, and lecture tours were a popular method of spreading information about this abusive labour situation. For example, the Women's Health Protective Association heard a lecture, almost certainly in New York or Philadelphia, from General Pienaar, who was travelling the United States and Britain to share the horrors of Portuguese enslavement of West Africans. The local newspaper

[87] F. W. Chesson, *The Dutch Boers and Slavery in the Transvaal Republic* (London, 1869), p. 12.

[88] Ibid., p. 36.

[89] H. R. Fox Bourne, *Forced Labour in British South Africa* (London, 1903), pp. 40–1.

[90] H. R. Fox Bourne, *Blacks and Whites in South Africa* (London, 1900), p. 77.

reported the lecture, quoting from the General at great length and revealing that, despite his female audience, he did not hide the cruelty of the slave trade. However, he was appreciative of his audiences' concerns in one way: as well as describing brutal whippings, he also explained that the worst aspects of enslavement involved the forced separation of families. This message had impacted female audiences and created female abolitionists since the late eighteenth century. Perhaps more interesting is that a small Louisiana parish newspaper chose to print details about Pienaar's lecture, in a community which was over ninety percent black.[91]

In a move echoed in conflicts over abusive labour practices in the cocoa industry in Côte d'Ivoire today, in 1886 the Quaker-founded firm, Cadbury's, became embroiled in a slave-labour controversy when it began using cocoa from the region and then had to deny its awareness of Portuguese practices.[92] Although the Portuguese had formally abolished slavery and converted all of their slaves into contract workers, in reality nothing had changed, and slaves were still being moved around the region of central West Africa along historic slave trading routes. As Henry Nevinson cynically commented, 'call slaves by another name, legalise their position by a few printed papers and the traffic becomes a commercial enterprise deserving of every encouragement'.[93] He viewed the British and Americans as leaders in the global antislavery struggle, but also significant participants in the cocoa market, and called on them to act. Nevinson's travels in the interior of Africa exposed the activities of the Portuguese and their African allies. Journeying towards the important slave and weaponry market at Bihé, Nevinson wrote that 'if a Portuguese fort is planted in the neighbourhood so much the worse ... this I suppose is the white man's burden of which we have heard so much: it is the black man who takes it up'.[94] The slavery on the cocoa plantations was described in similar terms to the chattel slavery of the Atlantic world, with the owner of the property living in distant Lisbon, while their plantation was managed by mixed-race slave drivers and overseers. The corrupting nature of the system, and Nevinson's desire to shock his distant readership to the core, was highlighted in his description of the way that planters chose a concubine from among the prettiest slave girls. 'That is natural', wrote Nevinson, 'but it

[91] *Tensas Gazette.* (St. Joseph, La.), 08 May 1908. *Chronicling America: Historic American Newspapers.* Lib. of Congress. https://chroniclingamerica.loc.gov/lccn/sn87090131/1908-05-08/ed-1/seq-2/.

[92] Grant, *A Civilised Savagery*, p. 120.

[93] Henry Nevinson, *A Modern Slavery* (London and New York, 1906) p. 44.

[94] Ibid., p. 70.

was worse when a planter pointed me out a little boy and girl of about seven or eight and boasted that like most of the children they were already instructed in acts of bestiality'.[95] Nevinson's work reached a wide audience in the United States because his book was publicised in American newspapers. The editorial comment in a Richmond, Indiana, newspaper suggested that the slavery problem was exacerbated by a lack of exposure, which presumably Nevinson and the newspaper sought to rectify: 'this drama of enslavement of human beings goes on year by year behind the West African littora [*sic*] blistered by hot sunlight and protected by a lack of good harbours and by the disposition of the Portuguese and Belgians from any large number of visitants'.[96] Three years later, Henry Fox Bourne felt that change had not happened fast enough and in his own tract on the matter reproduced evidence from Nevinson. He also asserted that 'it seems pretty certain that they are at least as well cared for as were the slaves in former times by the better sort of masters in the United States and West Indies. But they are slaves nonetheless'.[97] This is an unusual argument from Fox Bourne, a campaigning author normally ready to castigate the treatment of slaves wherever he unearthed forced labour. However, in this section he seems to be suggesting that the focus of abolitionism should not be on ameliorating the lived experience of these workers, but rather should concentrate on the eradication of slavery as a notion.

As well as publishing books, campaigners also used the lecture tour to highlight the offences of white European slave traders and owners. In the late eighteenth and nineteenth centuries, this had been a popular method in early days of the abolition movement. At the turn of the twentieth century, one of the most successful tours was undertaken by John and Alice Harris, a husband and wife who had travelled in remote Africa and then returned to speak to audiences on both sides of the Atlantic to highlight the systems of forced labour perpetrated by Europeans. Their earlier campaigning focused on the Congo Free State, which they famously visited in 1898 as missionaries on their honeymoon and about which they shared information in a lecture tour in 1906. They proposed, a decade later, to undertake a second lecture tour of the United States to share information about other forms of slavery

[95] Ibid., p. 199.

[96] *The Richmond Palladium and Sun-Telegram.* (Richmond, Ind.), 20 Sept. 1908. *Chronicling America: Historic American Newspapers*. Lib. of Congress. https://chroniclingamerica.loc.gov/lccn/sn86058226/1908-09-20/ed-1/seq-6/.

[97] H. R. Fox Bourne, *Slave Trade in Portuguese Africa* (London, 1909), p. 54.

including those in Portuguese West Africa. Their correspondence from this time during the difficult years of World War I reveals their intention to cross the Atlantic barely two years after the sinking of the Lusitania by German U-boats. The challenges faced undertaking such a tour in wartime are evident in a letter from Gerald Christy and The Lecture Agency Ltd., asking whether it would be possible to print the promotional materials for their tour in the United States, as blockmaking and printing was difficult in England so deprived by war.[98] The Harris's activities were made even more problematic by the existence of patrons such as Josiah Wedgwood, who, writing a letter of introduction for them to contacts in the United States, stated that 'I don't regard him [John Harris] as quite sound ... I believe he is going over about some African question'.[99] Some in the United States were concerned about the propagandistic aspect of the talk and therefore John Harris proposed to avoid subjects on which the outcome of the war might have a bearing.[100] Nevertheless, the Harrises proposed to use lantern slides to illustrate their talks, one of the most popular aspects of their work that drew crowds of people wishing to view such sensational visual media. From 1888 onwards, missionaries and travellers made use of the new medium of dry plate photography to further their cause and John and Alice Harris were pioneers of this, with Alice being the photographer and John the lecturer.[101]

On both sides of the Atlantic, the disclosure of the abominations taking place in the Congo Free State under Belgium's Leopold II was the clearest example of the use of descriptions of slavery and abusive labour practices to diminish an imperial rival. Prior to the heightened public awareness of the horrors of the slave labour system used by the Belgians, discussions of slavery in the Congo placed the blame for the system squarely on the shoulders of the 'black Congo savages' to quote one lurid newspaper report of 1890, which went on to depict the ritual slaughter of enslaved Africans 'on every ceremonial occasion' proclaiming this violence worse than the existence of slavery itself.[102] However, later, at the turn of the twentieth century, Europeans were depicted more

[98] Letter from Gerald Christy 16/4/17. Item 11, MSS Brit Emp s19/D5/d, Bodleian Library, University of Oxford.

[99] Letter from Josiah Wedgwood 10/2/1917. Item 44, MSS Brit Emp s19/D5/d, Bodleian Library, University of Oxford.

[100] Letter from Harris to Sir Gilbert Parker n.d. Item 79, MSS Brit Emp s19/D5/d, Bodleian Library, University of Oxford.

[101] Grant, *A Civilised Savagery*, p. 30.

[102] *Bridgeton Pioneer*. (Bridgeton, N.J.), 14 Aug. 1890. *Chronicling America: Historic American Newspapers*. Lib. of Congress. https://chroniclingamerica.loc.gov/lccn/sn87068192/1890-08-14/ed-1/seq-4/.

frequently as culpable. The purpose of this rhetoric was twofold: to give one's own nation an advantage or, more radically, to challenge the colonial system altogether by highlighting its inherent hypocrisy. Chapter 6 explores the radical commentary on colonialism using misbehaviour over slavery and the slave trade as emblematic of its unscrupulous nature. Henry Fox Bourne suggested that, just as with the transatlantic slave trade, 'the Christian nations of Europe and their offshoots are responsible for the worst horrors of the traffic'. He documented the different types of abuses in the Congo Free State, including the levies furnished by collaborating chiefs and the soldiers who 'are abject slaves to the chiefs who are themselves under compulsion or for their own gain supply them for the state's use'.[103] He criticised the Europeans' justification of slave labour as 'teaching blacks what is called the "dignity of labour"', and also accused the *Force Publique* of being 'overseers of what are virtually slave gangs'.[104]

A decade earlier, the situation in the Congo was uncovered by the black American travel writer George Washington Williams, who was in the region to investigate the possibility of founding a settlement of African Americans, but he was so shocked by what he found there that he was motivated to record and publish details about what he had observed, writing an open letter to Leopold II about his disappointment at his hypocrisy. Williams stated that he had thought the Congo Free State to signify 'the rising of the star of hope for the dark continent', but that 'the labour system is radically unpractical'. Like Fox Bourne, he singled out the soldiers for criticism. Many of the Zanzibari soldiers are slaves, he wrote, and 'they are ignorant and cruel because they do not comprehend the natives'. But the mistreatment of the labourers also attracted his attention, as he described how 'the poor creatures are frequently beaten with a dried piece of hippopotamus skin called chicote'. He held Leopold directly responsible for the buying and selling of slaves in the Congo and, addressing the King directly, stated that these crimes have 'been done in your name and you must answer at the bar of Public Sentiment'.[105] Williams had met Leopold at the Brussels antislavery conference and Leopold assumed him to be an ally, so when Williams's highly critical

[103] H. R. Fox Bourne, *Slavery and Its Substitutes in Africa* (London, 1900), p. 8.
[104] Ibid., pp. 10–11.
[105] George Washington Williams, *An Open Letter to His Serene Majesty Leopold II*, bound in Africa Pamphlets & C. 1885-94, Bodleian Library, Oxford, pp. 1, 6, 13.

report was published it caused a furore in Belgium and embarrassed the King greatly.[106]

Three years later, Edmund Morel echoed Williams's findings and based his reports on the feedback from missionaries in the region. He explicitly addressed his tract to the public of Great Britain and the United States and quoted one unnamed missionary as stating that 'I know white men who have seen baskets of hands being carried to the Central State Station'.[107] Morel's work was so significant in changing public opinion on both sides of the Atlantic that, fearing a backlash, Leopold mobilised propagandists of his own to deny such accusations. American newspapers were not universal in their condemnation and published pieces in defence of Leopold too. The Brussels correspondent's report, which appeared in the *Minneapolis Journal*, claimed that the Belgian King's reputation was being damaged by the British because they wanted to seize the territory for themselves and that 'slavery was stopped by Leopold'. This bold statement is later qualified in the article, showing that universal abolition had not taken place, but rather 'compulsory work may of course be likened to slavery but between the hardest labour and slavery, in the heart of Africa, there is a difference so great that no twisting of phrases can bridge over it'.[108] Even more crucial and convincing in destroying Leopold's reputation were the photographic images taken by Alice Harris, showing in graphic detail the mutilation of labourers who refused to or were unable to gather their quota of rubber.

Presenting eyewitness testimony became an important mark of the veracity of stories about the Congo. The anonymous author of a pro-Belgian pamphlet from 1905, published in Edinburgh, quoted the testimony of Lieutenant Colonel James Harrison 'a country gentleman of absolute independent mind, a sportsman and traveller and a familiar figure in London social and political circles', who suggested that Roger Casement, responsible for much of publicity about the Congo, was a trader who wished to further the interests of Britain in the region. The veracity of Morel himself was dismissed in the same pamphlet because he

106 John Hope Franklin, *George Washington Williams: A Biography* (University of Chicago Press, 1985), pp. 180, 214.

107 E. D. Morel, *The Congo Slave State: a Protest against the New African Slavery* (Liverpool, 1903), p. 32.

108 *The Minneapolis Journal.* (Minneapolis, Minn.), 07 Nov. 1903. *Chronicling America: Historic American Newspapers*. Lib. of Congress. https://chroniclingamerica.loc.gov/lccn/sn83045366/1903-11-07/ed-1/seq-23/.

had never visited Africa and so could not be a reliable source of information.[109]

One of the most important ways of identifying an imperial rival as corrupt was to show them in league with black or Arab slave traders. The trope of linking the races together in proliferating slavery was very effective, as it tainted the whites by association, a rhetorical manoeuvre that functioned to so discredit white Europeans by identifying them as akin to the racial other who consorted with them. Such symbolism had its origins in the period before the Civil War, and was used by influential writers such as David Livingstone, who described the slave raiding Mambari tribe that he encountered as 'the black sheep of Africa ... what the jackal is to the lion, so are these men to those fiends in the white man's form – the European slave dealers'.[110] Livingstone did not hold back from simultaneously assigning culpability to the African and the white man. This approach was taken in many missionary reports that gained fame in the United States through being published by a number of newspapers. An example is the French missionary accounts that blamed their own government for doing little to stop the system of domestic slavery operated by free African allies.[111]

This was not just a rhetorical tool used by activists but rather reflected the reality of the colonising powers' behaviour and their involvement in slavery. Adrian Graves has shown that this system of collaboration, to ensure the continued existence of slavery, took place not just in Africa but throughout the colonial world. He described the way that white missionaries and traders imposed systems that forced the enslavement of natives in the Pacific Islands, and showed how whites worked with local native 'headmen' to ensure a steady supply of labour and to maintain control.[112] Similarly in Ceylon on coffee plantations, the white colonial authorities made use of the caste system and the strictly hierarchical native culture to help fulfil their labour needs. A white manager oversaw the plantation, working alongside his European assistants. Beneath them, the estate staff were local administrators, with labourers at the bottom. The local

[109] *A Complete Congo Controversy Illustrating the Controversial Methods of Mr Morel* (Edinburgh, 1905) pp. 4, 18.

[110] William Monk, *Dr Livingstone's Cambridge Lectures* (Cambridge, 1858), p. 97.

[111] *The Sun.* (New York [N.Y.]), 27 Dec. 1896. *Chronicling America: Historic American Newspapers*. Lib. of Congress. https://chroniclingamerica.loc.gov/lccn/sn83030272/1896-12-27/ed-1/seq-26/.

[112] Adrian Graves, 'Colonialism and Indentured Labour Migration in the Western Pacific 1840–1915', in Emmer, ed., *Colonialism and Migration*, p. 253.

administrators included *kangany* or labour recruiters, who used coercive and abusive methods to encourage the natives to work.[113] From the 1850s onwards, a similar model was adopted on Hawaiian sugar plantations. By then white Americans, or *haoles*, dominated the Hawaiian Supreme Court as judges and attorneys, some of whom were also sugar planters. This allowed a brutal slavery-like system of contract labour to continue in remote towns such as Hilo on the Big Island, where native overseers kept control on behalf of the haole owners.[114] In the later nineteenth century, this meant that white American interests were diverse and contradictory, with some wanting political control through annexation, and others fearing the end of the contract labour system should annexation take place.

Accusers did not suggest that whites were ignoring native slave raiding and slave labour practices, but rather argued that they were perpetuating the practices by their own wilful actions. In defence, some accounts justified European purchase of slaves as an act of kindness, purchase to protect and free the enslaved, for example, of the type undertaken by missionaries in the Sudan.[115] But in most case, whites accused of involvement in the slave trade participated for their own financial and strategic benefit. This was the tenor of George Washington Williams' accusations to Leopold: that the colonial government of the Congo Free State was guilty not only of 'permitting the natives to carry on a slave trade', but also 'engaging in the wholesale and retail slave trade itself'.[116] Livingstone's 'lion and jackal' metaphor explicated this argument: the whites, as the lions, were the agents undertaking the slaughter; the jackal – the African tribesmen – merely picked over the bones afterwards. Using another animal metaphor, Edmund Morel argued that the African troops used by the Belgians in the Congo were 'bloodhounds' who forced the natives to work.[117] The long association of that particular dog with slavery in the Atlantic World would not have been lost on readers in the United States or Britain because the bloodhound as a tool of a slaver was a trope made familiar by *Uncle Tom's Cabin*.

[113] Rachel Kurion, 'Labour, Race and Gender of Ceylon Plantations', in William Clarence-Smith and Steven Topik, eds., *The Global Coffee Economy in Africa, Asia and Latin America 1500–1989* (Cambridge University Press, 2003), p. 182.

[114] Sally Engle Merry, *Colonizing Hawaii: the Cultural Power of the Law* (Princeton University Press, 2000) pp. 118, 12.

[115] Abdussamad H. Ahmad, 'Ethiopian Slave Exports', in William Clarence-Smith, ed., *The Economies of the Indian Ocean Slave Trade in the Nineteenth Century* (Frank Cass, 1989), p. 97.

[116] Williams, *An Open Letter*, p. 11.

[117] Morel, *The Congo Slave State*, p. 64.

CHANGE OVER TIME: CHALLENGING THE HEGEMONY

The ebb and flow of debate over the behaviour of colonial powers was based upon struggles for influence and authority, and the depiction of slavery and the slave trade was one facet of that controversy. To a certain extent, the othering of imperial rivals over slavery brought to the fore the challenging topic of Caucasian slavers, forcing those who now defined themselves as against slavery to acknowledge that white Europeans and Americans had always been fundamental to the development and continued existence of the slave trade in the Atlantic World and that, despite efforts to refashion themselves as guardians of abolitionist values, such endeavours would only be met with partial success. The last quarter of the nineteenth century saw significant evolution in attitudes towards white involvement in slavery and the slave trade. In the earlier part of the period, idealism was still common and men such as Leopold II could convince the world that their intentions in the Congo were unequivocal and would result in the end of enslavement in the region. At least until the 1876 Brussels Conference, Leopold's reputation had not been besmirched and he was much admired by Europeans and Americans for being philanthropic, a supporter of missionaries and for his hostility to local slave traders.[118] But, by the end of the century a marked transformation had taken place and authors were more willing to disclose the practices of white slavers. Henry Nevinson's tract highlighting the Portuguese use of slave labour in the cocoa plantations off the West African coast used the memory of chattel slavery and the transatlantic system to stir his readers to indignation about the *Modern Slavery* of his work's title. He argued that little had ever changed in the behaviour of white slavers but what was new was that campaigners were now willing to expose such offences.[119] Fourteen years earlier, the Anglo-African writer Frederick Alexander Durham made similar claims in his book which proposed a new colonisation movement to Liberia to enhance that settlement, but also to solve the race problem in the United States, where lynching and prejudice were the everyday experience of African Americans. He dismissed as nonsense the racial hierarchical theories which claimed that Africans were backwards and needed to be taught good morals and behaviour, arguing that to judge immorality first one

[118] Adam Hochschild, *King Leopold's Ghost: a Story of Greed, Terror and Heroism in Colonial Africa* (Macmillan, 1999), p. 1.

[119] Nevinson, *Modern Slavery*, p. 39.

must turn to 'all those Caucasians who engaged in the infamous traffic of slavery and the slave trade and who owned slaves'.[120]

In this period, although there is continuation in accommodating slave owners and justifying their actions, much of the discourse focuses on othering them through challenging the imperial vision of the nation. Even though, in this period, imperialists mimicked the language of antislavery because of its appeal to the public globally, their true motives were exposed and they were decried as complicit in maintaining systems that allowed the slave trade and slavery to flourish. President William McKinley was an example of this, accused by rivals of being unable and unwilling to stamp out slavery in the Sulu Islands of the Philippines, to such an extent that he was deemed complicit in the slavery itself. Although McKinley had argued publicly that Moro slavery was a mild form and that it would be easy to eradicate, conditions on the ground did not allow this to be completed successfully.[121]

Domestically, in the United States, this was a period of the accommodation and assimilation of former, often unrepentant, slave owners into the body politic. During and beyond the Reconstruction era, only infrequent literature emanated from the United States to distance the southern slave owning plantocracy from other Americans. The cultural construction of Jim Crow nostalgia, and especially of the Lost Cause myth, was predicated on the idea that white unity and healing after the fissures of the Civil War were more important than spreading the antislavery message by continuing to distance the nation from its slave-owning past. Romantic notions of the ruin of the lost South, remembering fondly the way of life of antebellum days, were so powerful that some African Americans also adopted such thought processes, as revealed in the WPA narratives of the 1930s, when some, but not all, interviewees who had been slaves as children looked back on their enslavement as a golden age. The cultural output of the Jim Crow era acknowledged the existence of slavery but with a veneer of tranquillity with no sense of the violence, cruelty and despair of plantation life.[122] White Southerners such as Alice Ravenel Huger Smith, born after the Civil War, felt an obligation to honour her ancestors, motivated by loss and longing and a desire to recapture the traditional values of the older society. Her paintings, and those of other

[120] Frederick Alexander Durham, *The Lone-Star of Liberia: Being the Outcome of Reflections on Our Own People* (London, 1892), p. 76.

[121] Salman, *The Embarrassment of Slavery*, p. 39.

[122] John Michael Vlach, *The Planter's Prospect: Privilege and Slavery in Plantation Paintings* (University of North Carolina Press, 2002), p. 109.

Jim Crow era artists, depict slave owning as benevolent and paternalistic, reclaiming the reputation of slave ownership from the accusations of abolitionists and others.[123] In many of the paintings of the era, human beings, whether owner or enslaved, were not the main feature while the landscape and architecture of the Old South were far more significant in the creation of a shared white identity. African American artists used this trope, such as Edwin Harleston's 1925 depiction of Oak Hall near Charleston, South Carolina (this work is erroneously titled 'Boone Hall Plantation'). His work is often compared to the nostalgia of Alice Ravenel Huger Smith but is complicated by the knowledge that his grandfather was a white rice planter who never married, therefore his painting draws attention to miscegenation. Another act of resistance within the painting is its presentation of the plantation being overwhelmed by the foliage.[124]

Other authors, offering a counter narrative about the South, and the slavery there include Albert Bushnell Hart. He was the child of abolitionists but was rather pragmatic in his views of the race problem in the United States, and was cautious in his assertions about how the former slave owners of the south should be treated. He blamed the north for 'disturbing the pre-existing balance' when it abolished slavery, but also blamed the single-minded planters of the south and not the African Americans, for being the cause of many of their own post-war problems: 'the white man cannot build new school houses or improve his cotton seed or open a coal mine without remembering that there is a negro race and a negro problem'.[125] He argued that in the post-emancipation era, the white man must also take some moral responsibility both for the condition of Africa and for the moral condition of African Americans at home, blaming white men for taking black women as concubines and for operating an immoral system of chain gangs and convict labour. Bushnell Hart asserted that improving the morality of the African American would be impossible while they had the terrible example offered as a model by the white Americans, echoing early abolitionist rhetoric that it was the responsibility of the white Christian Americans to uphold the highest standards.[126]

As shown in Chapter 1, after emancipation, many slave owners in the United States quickly adopted forced labour practices that allowed them

[123] Ibid., p. 154.

[124] Alexis Boylan, 'From Gilded Age to Gone with the Wind', in Angela D. Mack & Stephen G. Hoffus, ed., *Landscape of Slavery: the Plantation in American Art* (University of South Carolina Press, 2008), p. 125.

[125] Albert Bushnell Hart, *The Southern South* (New York, 1910), p. 68.

[126] Ibid., pp. 95, 152.

to retain the labour that they needed and to retain the control over their workforce that they so desired. Debt bondage was commonly used, not only for the African American poor but also for new immigrants and poor white labourers. Daniel Novak argues that late in the nineteenth century, the threat to white workers motivated progressive reformers to attempt to stamp out the practice. But also, paternalism endured. Echoing the racial hierarchical argument of antislavery imperialists, Judge Thomas G. Jones, who had fought for the Confederacy during the Civil War and afterwards led anti-peonage and anti-convict labour policy-making for the federal government, argued that the 'negro race is under us, we are his custodians'. Initially, after the war, due to a focus on suffrage and then desegregation by civil rights campaigners, debt bondage was left unchallenged but, towards the end of the nineteenth century, the perpetrators of debt bondage began to be unmasked.[127] Despite the efforts of those bringing those guilty of peonage to justice, throughout this period white southerners continued to acquit their peers of the crime, thus being complicit with perpetrators of slavery-like practices.[128] The community was willing to acquiesce and accept a certain amount of law breaking for the greater good, just as in the case of the prohibition of alcohol. This was true even in a case as heinous as that of John Williams, finally brought to trial in 1921, after delays in bringing him to justice, caused by white obfuscation, led to the death of several of his workers. He was the first southern white man to be indicted for first degree murder of an African American and would be the last until 1966. He was found guilty of murdering one of his peon labourers and received a sentence of life in prison. In fact, he had killed eleven others on his plantation in Jasper County, Georgia. This case of the so-called 'murder farm' shocked American readers as they were unable to assimilate John Williams into their vision of a morally upstanding white man, and, as a result, peonage as a system was weakened.[129] However, the process of unpicking the forced labour systems, by identifying and alienating abusers, that emerged in the United States following the Civil War, was painfully slow.

It was not until the early 1930s that a concerted effort to challenge the convict labour chain gang system developed due to cultural outputs such

[127] Daniel Novak, *The Wheel of Servitude: Black Forced Labour after Slavery* (University Press of Kentucky, 1978), pp. xv, 47.

[128] Pete Daniel, *The Shadow of Slavery: Peonage in the South 1901–1969* (Oxford University Press, 1972), p. 23.

[129] Ibid., p. 126.

as films and novels. In 1932, the film 'I Am a Fugitive from a Georgia Chain Gang' was released, with a message designed to bring its audience to social justice activism. It played on the popularity of prison films, and made the African American felon the hero, humanising him as a 'forgotten man' while dehumanising the guards as animals like the bloodhounds they used.[130] The following year, John Spivak's novel *Georgia Nigger* was published, telling the true story of the treatment of convict labourers and choosing the same characterisation of a black hero while encouraging the audience to distance themselves from the perpetrators of convict labour.[131] This more radical cultural output reflects the political changes of the Great Depression and New Deal, which allowed for sympathy for the poor, downtrodden man and further othering of the culprit who had indulged in slavery-like practices.

This rejection of the southern American slave owner did not take place on a purely domestic stage. Authors writing about the global problem of slavery began to identify the United States not as a harbinger of antislavery values, but as the originator of the epitome of the chattel slave system, transatlantic slavery. Kathleen Simon, whose 1929 work defined slavery as a system in which the labourer is considered property, had first-hand experience of living in Tennessee with her first husband, and this encouraged her to view all other types of slavery through the lens of her experiences in the South.[132] She also wrote about other types of abusive labour systems, and argued that peonage, indenture and forced labour should also be abolished because they shared characteristics with chattel slavery. She argued that even though they claimed no property right over the worker, they still denied the victim their full liberty.[133] Baroness Simon's focus on American slavery was to illustrate that the United States was still paying the price for its instigation of such a system. She wrote, 'America today is paying a hundredfold penalty in political, racial and economic embarrassment for the crime of bringing into her cotton fields over five million of slaves stolen from their peaceful homes in the African continent'.[134] So, she was not solely interested in the continuation of racism within the United States in the period contemporary to her, but rather she wanted to ensure that the memory and legacy of the slave period

[130] John E. O'Connor, *I Am a Fugitive from a Georgia Chain Gang* (University of Wisconsin Press, 1981), p. 18.
[131] John Spivak, *Georgia Nigger* (London, 1933).
[132] Kathleen Simon, *Slavery* (London, 1929), p. 4. [133] Ibid., p. 174.
[134] Ibid., p. 266.

was not rewritten by narrators obsessed with the Jim Crow Lost Cause who were seeking to downplay the horrors of the slave labour system. In other words, she intended the continued and renewed 'othering' of slave owners, through the retrospective examination of chattel slavery and a more honest interpretation of its perpetration and its legacy.

CONCLUSION

Examining the different motivations of authors who depicted slavery as a means to criticise or alienate those still engaging in forced labour practices, it is clear that to truly understand the complex racial, economic and political forces at work, these must be imagined on a global scale. Authors writing about the way that the United States behaved around the world, recognised the influences that ideas about slavery emerging from the European colonial sphere had on perceptions of slavery domestically. Since at least the early modern period, slavery had been recognised as a phenomenon that crossed national borders and equally its connection to the racial and religious 'other' also long pre-dated Atlantic world slavery. It was those tropes that became most important in commentary about slavery when undertaken by non-whites. When the enslaved victim was female, even more potency was added to the argument that slavery was undertaken by those who were especially cruel and morally corrupted.

But accusing other whites of partaking in slavery and the slave trade also had an important political function, allowing one nation to position itself in a situation of moral superiority over another, and the most powerful rhetorical manoeuvre of all was to accuse European or American slavers of collaborating with an ethnic other to perpetrate the abuse. While this was ongoing in the popular press of the United States, many conservative commentators smugly downplayed, almost negating, the United States' own history of slavery at home by suggesting that the conditions on southern plantations were benign and consensual. Increasingly towards the early twentieth century, such commentary was challenged by those on the left and those with a genuinely humanitarian political perspective who used their writing to force Americans to confront their slavery past and to put it into the context of the diverse global slavery that continued to exist.

While this represented an important political trend that came to prominence in the inter-war years, prior to World War I, challenging the hegemonic consensus borne of the scientific racist belief that whites were inherently more suited to govern and to delineate systems of labour, was much more difficult. Parallel to the pattern of 'othering' the slave owner, when writing about slavery domestically and globally, American authors, both before and after the Civil War tended to resort to the use of a familiar trope, that of identifying the victim of slavery as an 'other' in order to justify the continued use of a forced labour system. It is to this pattern that the next chapter now turns.

4

Othering the Enslaved

In some ways the processes of othering the enslaved mirrored those used to distance American and British audiences from the slavers, underpinned as they were mostly by a conservative and inherently racist ideology of hierarchy, and of racial suitability and capacity. However, in the late nineteenth and twentieth centuries, the deployment of this rhetoric, when describing the enslaved in the global context, often, although not always, served a very different purpose. Authors who chose to identify the slave as the 'other' did so explicitly in order to justify the action or inaction of those in positions of power in a variety of colonial and domestic spheres. Another reason for its use was in order to retain or regain control of an increasingly chaotic labour situation. Both these rhetorical functions are connected to the period's mutable definition of slavery. This worked by denying that a coercive labour type might be counted as slavery and, thus, committing a rhetorical attack on the enslaved individual or group through dismissing their experience and victimhood. As shown in Chapter 3, the unusual case of othering of some Africans and Chinese, which involved labelling them as racially determined to be both slavers and enslaved, served to doubly alienate and exclude these groups from the American or British body politic, and render them bereft of readers' sympathy.

At first glance, this process of othering the enslaved seems at odds with an Anglo-American cultural milieu in which nations formerly involved in slavery and the slave trade sought to redefine themselves with antislavery values at the heart of their morality and their national identity. To render the victims of that pernicious system as rhetorically other seemed to defeat the purpose of the growing international humanitarian movement which was acting against all forms of forced labour. However, as we can see in the contemporary world concerning the phenomenon of modern slavery, espousing antislavery as a belief system does not require the individual to perceive slavery's victims as true equals who are to be afforded the same rights. This was especially true in the late nineteenth and early twentieth century on both sides of the Atlantic when concepts of racial hierarchy and suitability for certain types of labour held sway in many intellectual quarters.

Fundamentally, much of the discussion about slavery in this period was conservative rather than radical, aligning itself with the Social Darwinist view that suggested that racial difference rather than, for example class or education, was the foremost way of distinguishing between different groups of people. Racial othering of the enslaved was common in a number of contexts around the globe, including in the new slaveries that emerged following the end of the transatlantic slave trade. The migration of so-called coolies from India and China to sites of labour shortage across the globe, and, in a similar way, the coercive use of Pacific Islanders or 'blackbirders' to supply a labour need, as well as the recruitment of Africans in all part of the continent, were all depicted as inherently tolerant of slavery and therefore, less civilised than whites, or as requiring the application of forced labour in order to learn how to work properly and reject their hitherto lazy patterns of subsistence living.

Globally, the enslaved were rhetorically othered using a variety of intellectual manoeuvres by commentators often purporting to have the slaves' best interests at heart. One of the most common types of othering was to present the enslaved as unable to function without the paternalistic protection of Europeans or Americans. This dependency on the benevolence of whites who saw it as their duty to educate slaves in the ways of productive labour mirrored attitudes to chattel slaves held by many white Americans in the antebellum United States, where African Americans were deemed unable to survive without the protective and directive system of slavery to guide them. At other times, racial hatred of the victims of slave labour was triggered by war, and the potent mix of enmity and enslavement drove the incendiary rhetoric deployed by some in the United States against the Filipinos in the 1890s. But, in most cases, wartime propaganda and fear cannot be used as a justification, however feeble. Behind much of the rhetorical othering was the belief that whites were inherently superior and that, while it was their duty to try to civilise other races, it was also part of their mission to protect the white race and its purity. Ideas emerging out of the eugenics movement were particularly potent in the ways that they utilised a fear of racial pollution to reinforce the boundaries between forced and free labour, and between the white race and everyone else.

From the late nineteenth century onwards, it caused Americans and Britons cognitive dissonance to admit that they were tacitly or explicitly tolerating or using slavery in order to control or educate subservient populations. In order to continue to view themselves as supporters of the antislavery cause, they had to undertake a rhetorical manoeuvre to deny that certain labour forms counted as slavery. By this means, subject populations could still be coerced into work, and Europeans and Americans could maintain a view of themselves as abolitionists. As we have seen in previous chapters, defining a labour form as slavery or not was a rhetorically powerful act with consequences for the enslaved, and for the writer and their self-identity. Naming the Chinese who were free migrants as 'coolies', or explicitly as 'slaves', deliberately justified their exclusion from the American body politic and, far from inviting sympathy, alienated them further. Their only usefulness to the United States was as labourers and, because they were perceived as racially degraded labour in a similar way to the African Americans, they would never be welcomed. African Americans, by contrast, because they had been born in the United States were seen in this discourse as assimilable, and in a turn of phrase connoting possession rather than shared sense of community, were seen by white commentators as 'ours'.

In the 1890s, as the United States looked outwards to its new imperial possessions, many anti-imperialists used the rhetoric of slavery to express similar concerns. Certain Filipino tribes were depicted as slaves in order to dissuade American politicians from incorporating the Filipino people more broadly into the United States. The argument suggested that having just abolished African American chattel slavery in an horrific Civil War, requiring the process to begin all over again was undesirable. Imperialists also othered the enslaved in order to further their own ends, with American imperialists mirroring the famous precedent of King Leopold II who used the existence of slavery in the Belgian Congo as a justification for colonial intervention. The process of denying a slave's slave-hood reinforced racial ideologies and justified inaction on the part of authorities who, although nominally supporting an antislavery cause, needed to enact a pragmatic tolerance of such systems to maintain control over a chaotic, dispersed labour force. This phenomenon explains the slow abolition of slavery in parts of West Africa, as well as the flourishing of systems of convict labour and debt bondage in the United States.

Many of the attacks on the enslaved in literature of this period did not deny or justify their slave status but rather blamed the victims for the predicament in which they found themselves. Often this was linked with racial othering, for example, in depictions of Italian and other southern European immigrant labour to the United States, showing them to be inherently weak and unable to resist the power of their influential countrymen who acted as labour brokers and who entrapped them in forced labour. But in other cases, the morals of the victims were attacked. Africans caught up in coercive labour systems were blamed because of their propensity to alcoholism, which, campaigners argued, rendered them morally corrupted but also, on a practical level, desperate for the meagre wages provided by their colonial paymasters, trapping them in bonded labour. African Americans stuck in peonage or convict labour were blamed for their lack of ambition or the foresight to enable them to extricate themselves from debt bondage. Convict labourers were also easy targets for blame, despite the fact that many of them had not committed a crime at all. Women who were ensnared by domestic or international sex traffickers, a system exposed in the 'white slavery' panic of the early twentieth century, were criticised by otherwise sympathetic commentators for allowing their desire for luxury goods and for intoxication to drag them into moral turpitude.

Much of the rhetorical othering was about possession and control and reveals a paranoia on the part of the commentators about the increasing power and autonomy of the labourers they were describing. Identifying Chinese and Japanese migrants to the mainland United States and the Hawaiian Islands as coolies, the moral equivalent of slaves, removed from them the rights of citizenship and reveals how threatening their workers' solidarity and campaigning for labour rights was to the ruling classes. In Africa, too, fear of wandering, landless Africans, who squatted uninvited and undertook subsistence and not commodity farming, triggered the identification of coerced labourers as 'the other'. In the United States, the particularly vicious system of cultural control that took place in the era of Jim Crow, including the pernicious racism that was a form of symbolic slavery, emerged because of white southern fears about a vengeful, wandering free slave population, and about the denudation of their plantation labour source. However, despite the development of imperial humanitarianism, writing about the enslaved in this period was often less about describing the suffering of others, and more about trying to reinforce white hegemonic values of control and possession. The discourses of racial hierarchy and determinism offered effective ways to do this.

MECHANISMS OF OTHERING: RACE

Rhetorical othering of the enslaved served an important function for white writers. A desire to reiterate and bolster white supremacy permeated the culture of the United States in the late nineteenth century. It was a mainstream rather than an extremist, radical standpoint. This desire had its roots in the sense of inadequacy and paranoia felt by the white community, especially in the south, that was fostered in the period immediately after emancipation. According to Carter Wilson, it became such a powerful ideology that it provided the glue that allowed conflicted and factionalised political and social groups within white society to hold together in the aftermath of the Civil War.[1] However, this development was not novel in the post-war era and instead represents a long chronological pattern that operated throughout the colonial era and later, once independence had been achieved in the United States. The exclusion of those of African descent from full political equality had always allowed for the development of a stronger sense of white identity. But Brad Evans identifies a phenomenon of othering that was new in the emancipation era, resulting in a subtle change in the way that slavery and former slaves were perceived and treated. Evans suggests that from the late 1860s onwards, with emancipation and the beginning of the Indian wars, two crucial dichotomies which framed Americans' sense of self were shattered: that of master/slave and savage/civilised. As Slave Codes became Black Codes in the legal systems of control of the formerly enslaved, the freedman's labour status no longer defined him but, rather, his race did.[2] However, as Thomas McCarthy has shown, and this book also argues, race and labour status could never truly be separated. Race was never truly a biological construct devoid of social practices and relations. By the late nineteenth century, the racial other was seen as a human being at an arrested stage of human development and therefore innately suited to certain types of labour. This dovetailed well with earlier environmental determinist accounts that suggested, for example, that Native Americans were too feeble for hard labour in hot or humid climates, whereas Africans were inherently suited to it.[3]

[1] Carter Wilson, *Racism from Slavery to Advanced Capitalism* (Sage, 1996), p. 21.

[2] Brad Evans, *Before Cultures: The Ethnographic Imagination in American Literature 1865–1920* (University of Chicago Press, 2005), pp. 4, 168.

[3] Thomas McCarthy, *Race, Empire and the Idea of Human Development* (Cambridge University Press, 2009), pp. 6, 76.

The belief that Africans were suited to hard labour morphed by the end of the century into a sinister justification of forced labour in the minds of many British and American commentators. Although naïve publics in European countries sought immediate abolition of slavery in imperial contexts, imperial administrators often tended towards the theory that gradual and not immediate abolition was justified because Africans would only work if they were compelled to do so and without African workers, imperial holdings with few white settlers would not thrive.[4] They first had to be taught the economic and moral value of work and then compulsion could be gradually removed. This form of othering, derived from Social Darwinist ideas of racial development and racial hierarchy, meant that many Africans worked in slavery-like conditions under the supervision and guidance of European and American imperial control. But these Social Darwinist ideas offered the potential for improvement of the condition of the African, and of the possibility that they might be educated and civilised. Frederick Durham, a black lawyer working in London with family origins in Trinidad, trumpeting the idea that all freed slaves from America and Africa should be paid to move to Liberia, emphasised this point to his white readership: that there were some important examples of civilised, educated Africans and that with education, superstition and slavery would go away.[5]

Some thinkers dismissed the Africans' capacity for improvement altogether, thus rendering the educating mission pointless and consigning them to generations of forced labour systems. Thomas Carlyle's work, *Discourses on the Nigger Question*, from 1849, is a notorious example of this, expressing the view in political rather than labour terms: the African was simply unfit to take a part in civil society. This language of 'fitness' and 'unfitness' became an important part of the discourse around forced labour in the latter part of the nineteenth century.[6] Later, at the turn of the twentieth century, Hegel mooted the notion that Africans and Africa stood outside history altogether, in his mind thus explaining how they had not followed the European and American pattern of inevitably ending

[4] Suzanne Miers, 'Anti-Slavery Game', in Keith Hamilton and Patrick Salman eds., *Slavery, Diplomacy and Empire* (Sussex Academic Press, 2009), p. 199.

[5] Frederick Alexander Durham, *The Lone-Star of Liberia: Being the Outcome of Reflections on Our Own People* (London, 1892), p. 166.

[6] Thomas Holt, 'British Emancipation Policy 1830–1866', in Frederick Cooper, Thomas Holt & Rebecca Scott, *Beyond Slavery: Explorations of Race, Labour and Citizenship in Post-Emancipation Societies* (University of North Carolina Press, 2000) p. 54.

slavery. Indeed, Hegel asserted, 'negroes see nothing unbecoming them' in slavery.[7] Africans were not the only victims of the extreme form of racial othering. American treatment of Filipinos, at the outset driven by a civilising mission, as the colonial power got mired in a complicated and unwinnable war, descended into hardened race hatred. Those whom once America had desired to help extricate themselves from enslavement were now, regardless of their vulnerability to enslavement, dismissed as treacherous savages. During wartime, methods of surveillance and control were foregrounded, rather than missions of education and liberation. This is exactly the patterns we have since seen in United States intervention in small wars overseas and in its response to political extremism at home.[8]

While much of this othering was driven by the twin motivations of a need to control a population perceived as dangerous and the desire to maintain a modicum of economic stability, the othering of the enslaved and formerly enslaved was also framed by intellectual notions about the vulnerability of the white race. Eugenicists believed that it was their duty to intervene in public life to ensure the stability of the white race, but many were also extremely paranoid about the potential for achieving this. Their pseudo-scientific ideas were taken out of academic journals by newspaper editors and spread to the public through the medium of extended articles, often covering several broadsheet pages, such as one from 1915 entitled 'Eugenics and Ultimate Man: Heredity and Race Betterment, Continue to Stir Scientists'.[9] Similar to the seventeenth-century Puritan migrants to New England who, believing in double predestination, desperately yearned to be saved yet could never be completely sure of being a member of the chosen few, eugenicists of the early twentieth century above all feared race suicide: the idea that racially inferior groups would soon outbreed their Anglo-Saxon betters. Deploying tools of social engineering to do all they could to strengthen their race, eugenicists linked the concept of moral hygiene to that of racial purity. The unfit in all their forms – racial inferiors, the disabled, alcoholics, the list goes on – had to be prevented from breeding at all costs, and notorious forced sterilisation

[7] Laura Doyle, 'Atlantic Modernism at the Crossing', in Len Platt, ed., *Modernism and Race* (Cambridge University Press, 2011), p. 120.

[8] Alfred McCoy, *Policing America's Empire: the US, the Philippines and the Rise of the Surveillance State* (University of Wisconsin Press, 2009), p. 16.

[9] *The Washington Herald.* (Washington, DC), 26 Sept. 1915. *Chronicling America: Historic American Newspapers.* Lib. of Congress. https://chroniclingamerica.loc.gov/lccn/sn83045433/1915–09-26/ed-1/seq-34/.

programmes were instituted.[10] But eugenicists were also very active in discussions about the world of work. They believed that inferior races were genetically predisposed to accept lower wages, because their inferiority drove them to tolerate a lower standard of living.[11] This attitude underpinned much American government policy towards, and white American perception of, African Americans and newly arrived labourers such as the Chinese in California and the Chinese and Japanese in Hawaii.

Of immense concern to the eugenicist was the presence of mixed-race individuals within their society. Their existence heightened awareness of the porous boundaries of supposedly rigid racial categories. In post-emancipation America, dealing not only with the rawness of the Civil War, but also coming to terms with a past that included chattel slavery, mixed-race individuals also served as an uncomfortable reminder of the slave system itself, and of the sexual abuse at its heart, to Americans trying to redefine themselves as global humanitarians. This pattern was present in Native American as well as white American society. Circe Sturm has shown how in Cherokee society a racial bias against African ancestry had its roots in the plantation system but that mixed-race individuals were the most concerning to the Cherokee elite. Following the end of slavery, anyone with black ancestry who was mixed race was classified as black by Cherokees, and the descendants of slave women and their native masters were seen as especially threatening to the order of inheritance.[12]

Even humanitarian thinkers who rejected the idea that slavery or forced labour could ever be justified, incorporated the racial rhetoric of black dependency on white benevolence into their writing. Kathleen Simon, writing for a white British audience, found it expedient to stress the paternalistic relationship between the races, encouraging whites to metaphorically take up the white man's burden and liberate people in Africa and the Middle East from the scourge of slavery. In doing so, she depicted the British and Americans as the great emancipators and liberators. In her colourful prose, and unlike many liberal commentators of the time in refusing to distinguish between Africans residing at home and in the diaspora, she described how Liberia had needed 'warm-hearted white administrators to take the Negro Americans and the Hinterland

[10] Thomas C. Leonard, *Illiberal Reformers: Race, Eugenics and American Economics in the Progressive Era* (Princeton University Press, 2016), pp. xii, 74.
[11] Ibid., p. 136.
[12] Circe Sturm, 'Trials and Tribulations of the Cherokee Freedmen', in James F. Brooks, ed., *Confounding the Color Line* (University of Nebraska Press, 2002), p. 241.

Africans and lead them up to the higher planes of civilisation'.[13] In contrast, three quarters of a century earlier, apologist for chattel slavery George Fitzhugh positively stressed the character of American-born slaves, as were most in the United States at that time, as being used to living and working alongside whites and understanding the paternalistic relationship. He contrasted them with the slaves in Cuba, recently arrived there via the illicit African slave trade, which Fitzhugh claimed caused cruelty and neglect because it provided new recruits cheaper than the price of rearing slaves. He called the African-born Cuban slaves 'savages who do not elicit the affection of their master, who sees in them little more than brutes'.[14] Therefore many of the same themes of white paternalistic duty, that had once been at the heart of pro-slavery discourse in the antebellum United States, now appeared in the humanitarian discourse of the early twentieth century, thus rendering the victims of slavery as the 'other' by assumptions of inferiority and lack of autonomy. Lynn Hunt has argued that although the creation of selfhood from the eighteenth-century Enlightenment onwards and the emergence of human empathy it afforded was at the heart of humanitarianism, so was the belief originating in the same era that children, servants, slaves and indeed anyone who was property-less in society could not be fully morally autonomous and therefore could not act for themselves, and needed the intervention and protection of the autonomous citizen to protect and defend them.[15]

This concept of dependency and lack of autonomy of the enslaved and formerly enslaved was much debated in the post-emancipation United States. In this period, especially in the south, acceptable and unacceptable dependency were quickly delineated, with the chosen models for controlling the African American population, of wage labour and peonage, being tolerated by many white southerners. As Amy Dru Stanley has argued, black codes were used to illustrate the intolerable forms of dependency, such as vagrancy and begging, which quickly became criminalised, despite there being a fine line in many cases between labouring and begging.[16] Therefore not only were slaves and former slaves assumed to be inferior, backwards and dependent on the paternalism of whites, they also operated in a world made unstable by the whims of variable white definitions

[13] Kathleen Simon, *Slavery* (London, 1929), p. 84.

[14] George Fitzhugh, *Cannibals All! or Slaves without Masters*, ed., by C. Vann Woodward (Harvard University Press, 1960), p. 79.

[15] Lynn Hunt, *Inventing Human Rights: a History* (W.W. Norton, 2007), p. 28.

[16] Amy Dru Stanley, *From Bondage to Contract Wage Labor, Marriage and the Market in the Age of Slave Emancipation* (Cambridge University Press, 1998) pp. 103, 116.

of acceptable and unacceptable subsistence methods. This phenomenon also existed on the global stage as those who participated in many different forms of bonded labour were also, at various times, othered in order to conform to the rhetorical needs of white Americans and Europeans.

From the late nineteenth century onwards, the rhetorical needs of the white Americans and Europeans were essentially conservative in nature, designed to reinforce the hegemonic position of the individuals and nations concerned, rather than to institute any lasting, meaningful political change for the enslaved and formerly enslaved. In this period, it was possible to espouse antislavery as a moral philosophy, and to look back fondly to the British and Americans heroes of the abolition of transatlantic slavery, while being uncritical of the continued attempts to enslave Africans, people of the African diaspora, and other vulnerable groups the world over. Having started as a philanthropic and radical movement, willing to undertake indirect and direct action to push forward the abolitionist agenda, by the end of the century antislavery thinking, with a few honourable exceptions, had morphed into something far more conservative on both sides of the Atlantic. It reflected partial and pragmatic concepts of labour reform rather than universal and idealistic notions of the possibility of ending enslavement globally. As Clare Midgley has shown, writing about the British context, antislavery writers were unwilling to cause drastic upheaval, whether regarding the political role of women, or challenging the racial hierarchy. For many abolitionists, she argues, black people remained essentially dependent, passive and childlike.[17] I suggest here that this had a crucial impact on the ways that forced labour practices around the world were conceptualised in the post-emancipation era. Unable to break away from such conservative worldviews, writers instead resorted to 'othering' the victims of slavery and forced labour, or, as shown later in this chapter, blaming the victims themselves for their own hardship and lack of liberty. This phenomenon was global in focus, with labourers worldwide trapped by economic and rhetorical alienation.

Descriptions of women enslaved in the harems of the Middle East often lauded European and American men for acting as protectors and liberators, while labelling their captors, of Arab descent, as cruel and subhuman, but in performing this rhetorical act, the humanity of the female victims they were supposed to be nurturing, was diminished. Authors were fascinated with the categorisation by their skin colour of women who were trafficked

[17] Clare Midgley, *Women against Slavery: the British Campaigns 1780–1870* (Routledge, 1992), pp. 200, 205.

for sex in Egypt, because such attitudes often mirrored their own sense of racial hierarchy.[18] Uncovering the story of a white female victim was the pinnacle for a journalist or author, as in the minds of the European and American readers she presented an ideal, unimpeachable victim. For many other victims of sex trafficking of the period, their moral status was far less clear, and white authors and missionaries tended to view freed sex slaves as akin to voluntary prostitutes in need of moral re-education. Special schools were established in Cairo, Benghazi and Tripoli to mould these victims, who were often of Sudanese or Abyssinian heritage and who had already suffered terrible ordeals, into domestic servants who could be shipped to England and given a supposedly respectable profession but where, undoubtedly, they would be ostracised and mistreated because of their race. Unsurprisingly, these schools soon closed after failing to secure enough recruits to remain viable.[19]

In the Indian Ocean context, male labourers also had a challenging time. While not formerly of slave status, lascars who worked on East India Company and other commercial vessels were forced labourers, promised wages that they never received, convinced to go to sea by a *serang*, or headman, before being handed over to officers on board ship who cruelly mistreated them. From the 1860s onwards, racial attitudes hardened, leading to increasingly detrimental treatment of these men, who were considered animals and not individuals, and were savagely beaten. These violent and hostile environments saw brutal beatings inflicted by white sailors, but there is also evidence of multifarious inter-ethnic conflicts amongst the diverse population of the ships.[20] Othering these victims of forced labour situations was also a fundamental part of life. The movement of bonded labourers to cultivate cotton and sugar to supply new markets by the system known as blackbirding was allowed to continue because the racial othering of its victims justified practices that were of economic advantage to the hegemonic powers in the region. This was despite the publication of articles by authors such as Loius Becke attempting to expose the horrors of the trade to the American people. Becke's article blamed the Peruvians, the Australians and the British in turn for the

[18] Diane Robinson-Dunn, *The Harem, Slavery and British Imperial Culture* (Manchester University Press, 2006), p. 16.

[19] Ibid., pp. 44, 86.

[20] Michael Fisher, 'Working Across the Seas: Indian Maritime Labourers in India, Britain and In Between 1600–1851', in Rana P. Behal & Marcel van der Linden, eds., *Coolies, Capital and Colonialism: Studies in Indian Labour History* (Cambridge University Press, 2007), p. 37.

continuation of the trade. He proclaimed his authorial authority by stating that his knowledge of the languages of Polynesia and Melanesia had enabled him to gain employment as a labour recruiter working for blackbirders, thus reflecting an important abolitionist trope in his work: the repentant slaver, a key figure since the days of at least John Newton. The ironic juxtaposition of newspaper articles of serious and comic tone is visible here, as Becke's article appeared next to a short piece about a local church baseball game which had to be abandoned when the players were attacked by a swarm of bees.[21]

The slave traders in the Pacific sometimes fell victim to reprisal acts of violence from the captured 'blackbirds'. A newspaper report from January 1872 told the story of a crew who were set upon by 'forty kidnapped Solomon Islanders' who then 'chopped them all to pieces'. This story is particularly unusual because of its depiction of the Solomon Islanders as 'kidnapped' suggesting the reporter felt that the trade was unlawful, echoed by the subheading 'Horrors of the Slave Trade'. The article used no stereotyping or racially discriminatory language at all, but in this it was very unusual.[22]

People traders from the United States and Europe operated throughout the region and their activities were founded on the doctrines of white supremacy that supported Ku Klux Klan activity in the United States. The proposed founding of a chapter of the Klan in Fiji reveals that the systems of control and subjugation operational in the southern United States were also considered viable in Pacific contexts.[23] This was not conservative antislavery at work, but rather represents a reactionary resistance to the values of imperial abolition, with a deliberate goal of creating a new network of transportation of forced labour. Enslaved 'blackbirds' were subjugated by childlike stereotyping, with Pacific equivalents to 'Sambo', as naming practices humiliated male 'blackbirds', while women were subjected to rape in order to force them to comply.[24] Later, in 1874, when the British acquired Fiji as its own imperial territory, American

[21] *The Sun.* (New York [N.Y.]), 16 Sept. 1906. *Chronicling America: Historic American Newspapers*. Lib. of Congress. https://chroniclingamerica.loc.gov/lccn/sn83030272/1906-09-16/ed-1/seq-34/.

[22] *Nashville Union and American.* (Nashville, Tenn.), 06 Jan. 1872. *Chronicling America: Historic American Newspapers*. Lib. of Congress. https://chroniclingamerica.loc.gov/lccn/sn85033699/1872-01-06/ed-1/seq-1/.

[23] Gerald Horne, *The White Pacific: US Imperialism and Black Slavery in the South Seas after the Civil War* (University of Hawaii Press, 2007), p. 4.

[24] Ibid., p. 46.

newspapers often reported this in terms of reluctance of the British people. It quoted the British Lord of the Admiralty as calling Fijians 'unmitigated ruffians' and caricatured the antislavery imperialist British position as thinking of 'debt as a national blessing: there are slaves in Fiji and they must be emancipated of course at considerable expense'.[25]

In an attempt at trans-Pacific solidarity, David Kalakaua, the monarch of Hawaii, tried to protect the islands of Fiji and Samoa from blackbirding, but his interference brought him into conflict with the powerful British and Americans, although from the period after the overthrow of the monarchy it seems that not all Hawaiians disagreed with him, using the local newspaper to expose slavery in the Fijian sugar plantations. However, by this time, the labourers referred to were not local Fijians, who were claimed to be unwilling workers who spent time on their farms in the hills where everything grows for them, but rather the imported Indian indentured workforce. The *Honolulu Star-Bulletin* was trying to boost its own local sugar industry, at the expense of a rival region.[26]

It was these so-called coolie labourers, from China, Japan and India who faced the most consistent othering. News about Hawaii's labour situation was covered keenly by mainland newspapers and often the labourers from these countries bore the brunt of the rhetorical attacks. In an 1899 extended article entitled 'Farmers Awake, Read, Reflect!' the *Kansas Agitator* (based in an area in which sugar beet production was an important industry) published an article decrying 'Asiatic coolies who were virtually slaves' but blamed the sugar industry of Hawaii as much as the labourers themselves.[27] Much of this was undertaken, similar to the discrimination faced by African Americans in the Jim Crow south, in order to control labourers perceived as potentially troublesome by whites in positions of power. Like black Americans, the migrant labourers in Hawaii were politically in limbo because they came under the full jurisdiction of the United States but did not enjoy its full constitutional protection. Thus, as Joanna Poblete has argued when referring to Filipinos and

[25] *New-York Tribune*. (New York [N.Y.]), 05 Sept. 1874. *Chronicling America: Historic American Newspapers*. Lib. of Congress. https://chroniclingamerica.loc.gov/lccn/sn83030214/1874-09-05/ed-1/seq-6/.

[26] *Honolulu Star-Bulletin*. (Honolulu [Oahu, Hawaii), 16 Oct. 1915. *Chronicling America: Historic American Newspapers*. Lib. of Congress. https://chroniclingamerica.loc.gov/lccn/sn82014682/1915-10-16/ed-1/seq-4/.

[27] *Kansas Agitator*. (Garnett, Kan.), 08 Sept. 1899. *Chronicling America: Historic American Newspapers*. Lib. of Congress. https://chroniclingamerica.loc.gov/lccn/sn83040052/1899-09-08/ed-1/seq-1/.

Puerto Ricans in Hawaii, but can, I argue, be applied to all contract labourers on the sugar plantations there, they were neither citizens nor foreigners and unable to assert their rights as free labourers and therefore were easily vulnerable to aggression by unscrupulous masters and overseers.[28] Poblete suggests that, in some ways, labourers in Hawaii had it easier than those on the mainland because labour was in such demand in Hawaii, but Gerald Horne has argued that the Pacific structures of racial othering were so rigid that some groups of migrants that would have been considered 'white' elsewhere in the United States, such as the Portuguese, were racially othered in Hawaii.[29]

In the Caribbean and South America, coolie labourers were considered highly desirable because of a shortage of labour following the emancipation of slaves on the region's sugar plantations and in guano harvesting. In this region, as elsewhere, the Chinese developed a reputation for hard work and prudence. But there were many abusive labour practices in the region, as well as the use of racialised depictions of the workers that served to limit their ability to act as free labourers and escape their situation. In Macau, a key embarkation point for Brazil and Cuba, 'crimps' or labour agents often enlisted young men who had been in the army, and refugees from natural or economic disaster. The jobs that they promised were fictitious but, by the time the victim realised this, they had been leant clothes, food and money, which they then owed back.[30] Similarly Indian migrants travelling around the British Empire were dismissed using racialised language by John Gladstone (the Prime Minister William's father) as 'akin to monkeys'. Migrants who left Calcutta and Madras often did so under stress, feeling a sense of confusion, shock and alienation. Many of the female migrants were sexually abused in order to render them passive, while both male and female workers had their capabilities diminished by some authors who dismissed them as drunken and incapable.[31]

In response to these labour abuses, some of the anti-coolie rhetoric seen in the United States emerged from a humanitarian impulse, reflecting a genuine desire to raise awareness of violence and coercion with the contract labour system. In the years immediately after the end of the

[28] Joanna Poblete, *Islanders in the Empire: Filipino and Puerto Rican Labourers in Hawaii* (University of Illinois Press, 2014), p. 2.

[29] Poblete, *Islanders in the Empire*, p. 6; Horne, *The White Pacific*, p. 175.

[30] Arnold J. Meagher, *The Coolie Trade: Traffic in Chinese Labourers to Latin America 1847–1874* (X Libris, 2008), p. 74.

[31] Hugh Tinker, *A New System of Slavery: the Export of Indian Labour Overseas 1830–1920* (Oxford University Press, 1974). pp. 63, 117, 222.

Civil War, abolitionist rhetoric suggested that coolie labourers, travelling to Southern and Central America to fill the gap left by the freeing of the slaves, were living and working in conditions so horrific that they were tantamount to the slavery that had recently been abolished. Newspapers also published vivid accounts of the living and working conditions of Chinese labourers but, rather than eliciting the sympathy of American readers, when the coolies of Peru revolted against these conditions they were dismissed as 'a degraded class of semi-barbarians'. The desire for racial control and order amongst unruly labourers always trumped concerns over labour abuses in American rhetoric of this period.[32] An account from 1870 designed to rouse white workers to oppose Chinese coolie labour in their local area asked rhetorically 'what are those coolies, you say? They are slaves, yes bond slaves, criminals, guilty of every crime, who are sold in China . . . shipped to San Francisco where they stay until orders come for them from capitalists'. The account predicted the desolation of Stark County, Ohio, where the newspaper circulated, if Chinese coolies were used in the local factories because 'the Chinaman spends no money in America except with his own countryman'.[33] This was reiterated by an article the same year in which the author described in detail the conditions in which the Chinese were transported, to further provide evidence of their slavery. The descriptions precisely echo earlier abolitionist material so closely that they could have referred to the transatlantic slave trade: 'they were stowed away between decks in a space of sixteen inches to each individual. They were cruelly whipped, kicked and cuffed by sentries placed over them. The torment became so unendurable that many of them jumped into the sea and drowned. Shut up in the miserable pen between decks, they endured unspeakable pangs of hunger and thirst'.[34]

Any government, seeing large-scale emigration in this period, sought to label the emigrants as 'slaves' in order to alert the world to their condition and end their poor treatment. Korean migrants, many of whom went to the sugar fields of Hawaii in the early years of the twentieth century, were in this way identified as slaves by their own government. Trapped by

[32] Stuart Creighton Miller, *The Unwelcome Immigrant: the American Image of the Chinese 1785–1882* (University of California Press, 1969), pp. 150–1.

[33] *The Stark County Democrat.* (Canton, Ohio), 31 Aug. 1870. *Chronicling America: Historic American Newspapers.* Lib. of Congress. https://chroniclingamerica.loc.gov/lccn/sn84028490/1870-08-31/ed-1/seq-3/.

[34] *The New York Herald.* (New York [N.Y.]), 16 Oct. 1870. *Chronicling America: Historic American Newspapers.* Lib. of Congress. https://chroniclingamerica.loc.gov/lccn/sn83030313/1870-10-16/ed-1/seq-8/.

a complex geopolitical situation, and caught between seeking economic betterment in Hawaii and to escape the controlling Japanese regime, many Koreans experienced initial prejudice in Hawaii because they were treated as coolies, and therefore degraded labourers, but within a generation were able to establish a successful and thriving business community and integrate there.[35]

By mounting acts of resistance on board ship to their transportation to Cuba or Peru, Chinese workers risked being further dismissed as difficult and troublesome labour. In 1859, when the emigrants mutinied and set fire to the ship, all on board the *Flora Temple* perished on its journey from Macau to Havana. In Cuba, the Chinese developed a reputation for rebelliousness and plantation owners feared that they would be a bad influence on the still-enslaved Africans. In any case, the Chinese contract labourers were viewed as little different in status to the slaves alongside whom they worked. For example, plantation owners spoke of 'buying' rather than 'hiring' coolie labourers.[36] Any act of resistance served to confirm pre-existing racial stereotyping. It was the potent combination of forming a threat on the grounds of race and of class that led to the facilitation of the racialisation of a class identity that allowed coolies to be so easily ostracised and distanced from the American body politic. They were not only 'other' because they were a labouring class, but also because this status was racialised and therefore, in the minds of many, biologically determined. Positive traits and values within the American character were associated only with whiteness during this period and so non-whites such as the Chinese coolies were seen as degraded because of their race, and because of their culpability in undertaking unfree work. This combination rendered them un-American, unable to become full political participants.[37] This was not a top-down position emerging from academic and scientific writing, but rather one held by ordinary working men and women in the mines and on railroads where they worked alongside Chinese immigrants. Gordon Chang suggests that white workers in the West saw the Chinese labourers as servile, docile and essentially semi-slaves.[38] This is confirmed by Russell Conwell's 1871

[35] Wayne Patterson, *The Korean Frontier in America: Immigration to Hawaii 1896–1910* (University of Hawaii Press, 1988), p. 78.

[36] Meagher, *The Coolie Trade*, pp. 188, 201, 216.

[37] Elliott Robert Barkan, *From All Points: America's Immigrant West 1870s–1953* (Indiana University Press, 2007), p. 10.

[38] Gordon Chang, *Fateful Ties: a History of America's Preoccupation with China* (Harvard University Press, 2015), pp. 77–8.

book, *Why the Chinese Emigrate*. He dismisses the idea that the Chinese are troublesome, and instead depicts them as persistent and hardworking, but 'timid and docile'.[39] While these character traits might be a selling point for their bosses, they did not well prepare them for the role of free citizen of the United States. Conwell quoted American-born miners, who were in some confusion about the Chinese they worked with in California, calling them 'queer lookin' chicks and no mistake', but he also reported that white Americans ranked Chinese higher as workers and as men than the local Native Americans.[40]

The United States often had conflicted relations with the Chinese as a people and empire, but for commentators in the post-emancipation period it was the act of leaving one's country as a migrant that turned a Chinese person from a free labourer into a degraded coolie. According to this bigoted attitude, a Chinese man outside China could only ever be a coolie.[41] As Najia Aarim-Heriot has shown, American politicians, union leaders and journalists were quick to deploy such depictions of the Chinese for their own political or monetary gains. Progressive political economist Henry George's commonplace in his anti-coolie writing was to describe the promise of a flood of Chinese workers coming across the Pacific, with numbers reaching to five hundred million.[42] Stereotyping of the Chinese was often incoherent, irrational and contradictory. Conwell argued that the immigrating Chinese were both greedy and desperate for money, and yet he also stated that they did not care about the level of wages and so thus were suppressing wages for the ordinary working American.[43] He argued that coolies, unlike the Chinese back home, had little proper sense of religion.[44] They chose from a number of different spiritual systems but fixed on no one single one, implicitly reflecting their credulity. Then later on in his text, he described in detail the Chinese coolie and his religious practices: including his method of setting up a household altar and envisioning a spirit world similar to purgatory, while consulting mediums and astrologers.[45] Not all American politicians discouraged coolie migration, with some southern Democrats during Reconstruction lauding it in place of the black labour which had been

[39] Russell. H. Conwell, *Why the Chinese Emigrate* (Boston & New York, 1871), p. 45.
[40] Ibid., p. 127.
[41] John Soennichsen, *The Chinese Exclusion Act of 1882* (Greenwood, 2011), p. 92.
[42] Najia Aarim-Heriot, *Chinese Immigrants, African Americans and Racial Anxiety in the US, 1848–82* (University of Illinois Press, 2003), p. 113.
[43] Conwell, *Why the Chinese Emigrate*, pp. 52, 57. [44] Ibid., p. 36.
[45] Ibid., pp. 163–5.

'spoiled' by emancipation. But by the end of Reconstruction, confidence of dominance reasserted by full control of black labour once more, Chinese immigration again became distasteful, and so free Chinese immigrants were racialised and dismissed as unfree labourers, with domestic concerns in the United States being reinforced and supplemented by global 'yellow peril' arguments simultaneously in circulation.[46]

'Coolies' then were othered for a variety of reasons, the conservatism of abolition being just one. Attempts to defend the civil rights for 'coolies' without recourse to racialised discourse were very rare. Some commentators, unable to create a clear picture of their life and values, saw them as exotic creatures. Others rhetorically removed their freedom by dismissing free labourers as slave-like, for reasons of reinforcing the racial hierarchy or in order to defend the position of white labour. Still others did have humanitarian goals but could not see past the Social Darwinist rhetoric, while a final group, wishing to enforce the role of the Chinese as suitable labourers and encourage their use, depicted them as docile and pliable, preferable to any domestic labour options. So varied were the discursive reasons for othering that this was adaptable and ubiquitous: one of the universal tropes of the era.

CONFIRMATION OR DENIAL OF SLAVE-HOOD

The rhetorical choice of naming someone as a slave or denying that their experience reflected slave-hood was a powerful act but, confusingly, either pattern could be adopted as part of the process of othering the slave. Denial of slave-hood in the Jim Crow south sometimes took the form of autonomous human beings being written out of the story of the slave past. In visual depictions produced in the post-emancipation era of the plantation south, few African Americans were even present in the landscape, the focus instead being on the nostalgic memories of the southern spaces now long gone or ruined. The reality of the victims' slave-hood could not be denied, so instead their very existence was denied as they were erased from a romanticised past.[47] When describing, in a post-emancipation context, contemporary labour systems around the world, authors were more willing to manipulate the boundaries of the definitions of slavery, which also served to minimise the slave experience through the process of denial, and

[46] Aarim-Heriot, *Chinese Immigrants*, p. 122.

[47] Angela Mack, 'Introduction' in Angela Mack and Stephen Hoffus, *Landscape of Slavery: The Plantation in American Art* (University of South Caroline Press, 2008), p. 16.

which served to render free labourers unfree through defining them as slaves. This section will show how the denial of slave-hood worked to justify imperial inaction in some contexts in Africa and the Philippines, while its confirmation also justified inaction in the Philippines. It will show how free labourers were rendered rhetorically unfree as part of protectionist immigration rhetoric, while labelling the victims of violence and forced labour in the Congo as slaves mobilised an international campaign against their mistreatment.

Following the legal abolition of chattel slavery in the British Empire and in the United States, the status of various labour forms became cause for debate over whether they counted as enslavement or not. These labour forms were often as violent, coercive and restrictive of rights as chattel slavery had been, and so by denying that their victims were slaves, authors were effectively putting these workers beyond the remit of humanitarian abolitionists and 'othering' them by committing them to a life of unprotected hardship with no hope of rescue. As Joel Quirk has shown, even in cases where such labour forms were acknowledged as slavery, by the 1930s, the British were describing such 'vestiges of slavery' as 'benign', minimising the harm they did to the workforce, and juxtaposing them tellingly with 'real slavery' which was an 'ancient evil'.[48] An example of this in action is in British-occupied Nigeria, where the abolition of slavery had been partial and the colonial authorities refused to take decisive action. Throughout the twentieth century, commentators denying the continued existence of slavery did so in order to justify the inaction in the present day while lauding the supposedly successful and complete abolition in the nineteenth century.

Also justifying inaction on the part of colonial authorities and attempting to boost the reputation of the British in comparison to other colonial powers, was the rhetorical denial that indentured labour by Chinese and Indians in South Africa amounted to a new system of slavery. Elsewhere in the world, such labourers were labelled slavish in order to subjugate and limit their citizenship, but in South Africa, they were named as not slaves with the purpose of turning a blind eye to the prejudice and violence they suffered. In the early years of the twentieth century, campaigners from British trade unions became concerned about the role of Chinese labourers in the gold mines of the Transvaal. Alongside worldwide Congo activism, this was one of the most significant challenges to the abuses of labour in

[48] Joel Quirk, *The Anti-Slavery Project from the Slave Trade to Human Trafficking* (University of Pennsylvania Press, 2011), p. 148.

Africa during the period. The use of Chinese labour was seen as a betrayal of British labour, and banners appeared in protests commenting that 'slavery was abolished in 1853, revived in 1904'. Such protests were not purely humanitarian, but reflected the racist attitudes of the period, with arguments rife presenting the view that the Transvaal should be kept clear of 'Asiatics' and 'passenger Indians'.[49] The rhetorical use of slavery here mirrors exactly the conservative discourse in the United States which desired to protect native workers from the immigrant labour of the Chinese who were crossing the Pacific to the West Coast. As shown above, they came to the country of their own accord, but were labelled slaves and therefore inferior and degraded workers who must not become part of the body politic.

As the United States came to terms with its role as an imperial nation, many commentators within the country were worried about the labour situation in the new territorial holdings, and rendered free labourers in those places unfree for purposes of economic protectionism and racial othering. Defining contract labourers in Hawaii as slaves became part of the anti-imperialist's arsenal, justifying both the withdrawal of American involvement (thus to protect the nation's new antislavery patina) and preventing the eventual migration of such labourers to the United States mainland, where they might threaten the jobs of native-born Americans. Since 1888, Chinese contract labourers had been excluded legally from the mainland, and so when Hawaii was annexed by the United States barely five years later, the position of Chinese labour in the newly acquired territory was hotly debated. Eric Love has shown how the then-Secretary of State, John Foster, (in office briefly 1892–3 at precisely the period when the Hawaiian Annexation was taking place) dismissed requests from the Hawaii sugar lobby to permit Chinese labour importation to continue, and refused to condone any system which was seen to favour Chinese migrants.[50] Foster's predecessor as Secretary of State, James Blaine, had suggested that African American labour might be profitably used instead, but such a suggestion was never acted upon, nor was the idea of using white Americans to act as a bulwark against the 'yellow peril' of rampant and barbaric Chinese and Japanese labourers. But while the Secretaries of State undertook pernicious racial othering of the contract

[49] Kevin Grant, *A Civilised Savagery: Britain and the New Slaveries in Africa 1884–1926* (Routledge, 2005), pp. 69, 80, 91.

[50] Eric Love, *Race over Empire: Race and Imperialism 1865–1900* (University of North Carolina Press, 2004), p. 76.

labourers in Hawaii, they did not advocate withdrawing from the islands altogether. Others were more markedly anti-imperialist, such as Richard Pettigree, who, in 1895, defined the labourers in Hawaii as 'little better than slaves' in order to alarm the American public and to justify discontinuation of the imperial adventure.[51]

Those seeking to rhetorically 'other' the Chinese labourers in Hawaii did so not only with a concern for the islands themselves but also with the labour situation on the mainland United States in mind. With improved communications between the Hawaiian Islands and the Pacific Coast of the United States, the distance between them suddenly seemed to many as much shorter, and concerns were raised in the newspapers of California about the possibility of migration of large numbers of labourers, managing to overcome the strictures of the Chinese Exclusion Act. For example, the *San Francisco Call* wrote about the 'hordes' of slavish Chinese coolies waiting to come over from Hawaii once the islands became part of the United States.[52] Many West Coast authors reiterated this view: that the Chinese labourer, whether coming directly from China or via the Hawaiian Islands, was slave-like and therefore undesirable. However, some, like the Reverend Otis Gibson, dared to suggest an alternative view, and his 1877 tract defended the freedom of the Chinese immigrants to California and challenged those who used a definition of slavery to rhetorically other an entire race of workers. In a challenge to a clerical rival, the Jesuit Father Buchard, who called the Chinese migrants 'slaves' and 'inferior', Gibson proved that 'every man of every race in this country is his own master' and that 'the Chinamen who come here in every case come voluntarily'.[53] So in this case, the assertion of slavery revealed racial hostility, and its denial reflected a belief in the assimilability of the Chinese migrants.

But in many circumstances, especially those in Africa, the denial of slavery had sinister motives. The British and the Americans were not solely responsible for the denial of slavery. The Belgians, too, denied that the victims of their regime in the Congo were enslaved and in doing so tried to put them beyond the intervention of humanitarians. As Adam Hochschild has shown, the pro-Belgian pamphlet writers of

[51] Ibid., pp. 93, 121.

[52] Thomas J. Osborne, *Empire can Wait: American Opposition to Hawaiian Annexation 1893–1898* (Kent State University Press, 1981), p. 100.

[53] Rev. O. Gibson, *The Chinese in America* (Cincinnati: Hitchcock and Walden, 1877), pp. 245, 258.

the early twentieth century used euphemistic language to describe the native workers and to deny their enslaved status, with the term 'volunteer' being most frequently deployed to describe the members of the coerced Congo labour force.[54] One author, writing in the final years of the nineteenth century in support of the Belgian Congo, was Demetrius Boulger, and his tract on the Congo Free State and its bringing 'of civilisation in Central Africa' stretched to over three hundred pages of pro-slavery apologia. This work is especially important because it denies the enslavement of the people of Congo, but goes further and claims that the Belgians are reforming the region and acting to remove the 'stain' of the slave trade.[55] In a telling passage, Boulger argues that the supposed cannibalism of the Africans of the region justifies Belgian interference: 'of the two crimes [cannibalism and slavery] the greater must surely be to eat your brother man, than to make him a slave and treat him cruelly', thus on the one hand acknowledging enslavement to be a crime, while on the other justifying it as a way of civilising the tribes of a supposedly savage region. Boulger then goes into considerable detail about the cannibalistic practices of the region, citing evidence from European observers.[56] But even those who saw the hypocrisy of the position of the Belgians and their supporters were guilty of selective blindness when it came to African labourers. E. D. Morel, who campaigned to bring the horrors of the Belgian Congo to light in both Britain and the United States, could at the same time praise the systems of labour at work in the German colony of Togo where representatives of Booker T. Washington's Tuskegee Institute were forcing native Africans onto plantations and onto the cotton fields. The Tuskegee trainers saw forced labour both as a method of control and of education.[57] In these cases, imperial rivalry formed the backdrop to the affirmation or denial of the existence of slavery. Another form of racial othering worked by shining a light on the behaviour of the labourers themselves and blaming them, rather than political, economic or imperial structures, for the situation in which they found themselves.

[54] Adam Hochschild, *King Leopold's Ghost: a Story of Greed, Terror and Heroism in Colonial Africa* (Macmillan, 1999), p. 41.

[55] Demetrius Boulger, *The Congo State or the Growth of Civilisation in Central Africa* (London, Calcutta and Simla, 1898), p. 6.

[56] Ibid., pp. 104–6.

[57] Andrew Zimmerman, *Alabama in Africa: Booker T. Washington, the German Empire and the Globalisation of the New South* (Princeton, 2010), pp. 132, 171.

VICTIM BLAMING

The rhetorical manoeuvre of blaming the enslaved for their own abuse took two related forms. First, victims' inherent racial makeup, and their resultant weakness and inferiority, was highlighted as a causal factor, and many authors expressed this in terms of the fault, however inevitably and irresistibly, lying with the slaves themselves. Second, others focused on the behaviour and attitudes of the slaves which made them culpable in their own entrapment into coercive labour. For many this behaviour and attitude was simply a sign of their racial inferiority manifested externally so, as we have seen throughout this book, racial determinism was once again an inescapable framework, in this period, for the authors trying to understand enslavement.

In the Jim Crow south, authors such as George Holmes identified the system of peonage that had emerged after the Civil War as bad for white plantation owners and their black labourers, and also retarding the economic growth of the entire region. He suggested that hardworking immigrants from Northern Europe could easily take over and reform the south, writing that 'if German, Polish, Bohemian, Swedish agriculturalists were to invade the south they would dispossess the plantation owners by their industry'.[58] Although he felt that some of the blame should be laid at the door of white southerners whose traditions had for generations not encouraged hard work, Holmes also saw the black labourers trapped in debt peonage as responsible for this poor state of affairs. He erroneously argued that 'the blacks prefer a tenancy to selling their labour for wages', and put this down to a lack of ambition: 'most of them are so wanting in the instincts on which the rise from the kind of peonage under which they live depends that they will not do better than they are doing'.[59] Perhaps some African Americans did see debt bondage as providing them with a certain type of security, but the reason why most did not flee from their former slave masters to seek wage labour elsewhere was the psychological and physical damage inflicted under the Jim Crow system by the white hegemons. They punished wandering labourers and criminalised those who left contracts early. There was a concerted effort metaphorically and literally to keep black labour in its place and in many cases, this worked, not because of a lack of ambition or a preference for bonded labour on the

[58] George Holmes, 'The Peons of the South', *Annals of the American Academy of Political and Social Science*, IV: 1893–4 (Philadelphia), p. 73.

[59] Ibid., pp. 57, 74.

part of African Americans, but due to a justifiable fear of the carceral regime of the Jim Crow south.

While George Holmes lauded white immigrant labourers and their industry and innovation, the specific nations to which he referred were Northern European and mostly Protestant. New migrants from Southern Europe, especially the Italians, were perceived very differently and when they found themselves in contract labour situations, not free to sell their labour to another employer, commentators described them as responsible for their own situation. Their labour was needed, along with that of some African Americans who moved around for seasonal work and, without such contract labour, much of the fruit-picking industry on the East coast would have collapsed. Labour brokers or *padroni* in Italy sourced labourers for a one-year contract, advanced the worker the cost of the Atlantic passage and then bonded them until the debt was repaid. In cases of permanent migration, women and children as young as five worked in the fields and the canneries alongside the male labourers.[60] Progressive campaigners in the United States, alerted to the labour abuses by the prolific use of child labour, depicted the *padroni* as un-American, not only for their mistreatment of migrant labourers, but also, based on eugenics theory, because their practices led to the spread of disease and depravity. The eugenics crusade of the late nineteenth century led many commentators to suggest that moral and physical degradation were linked, and were especially rife in the communities of migrants from Catholic southern Europe, such as the Italian fruit pickers of the East Coast. Crucially, they blamed the labourers for allowing themselves to be conned into such a degraded position. They determined that anyone who tolerated these working and living conditions must be inherently racially weak, and susceptible to dominance by 'more powerful countrymen'.[61] In fact, as Cindy Hahamovitch has shown, such labour systems were viewed differently by the workers within them, and for many contract labourers working as fruit pickers under *padroni*, the system was not considered exploitative at all.[62] So this is another case, not only of victim blaming, but of rendering a labourer unfree by rhetorically labelling him as slave-like, when he did not define the situation as coercive.

[60] Cindy Hahamovitch, *The Fruits of Their Labour: Atlantic Coast Farmworkers and the Making of Migrant Poverty 1870–1945* (University of North Carolina Press, 1997), pp. 29, 44.

[61] Ibid., p. 47. [62] Ibid., p. 39.

A function within certain systems of slavery allowed observers to suggest that victims were truly responsible for their own downfall. Humphrey Fisher has identified that over the long chronological history of slavery in Muslim Black Africa, being sent into slavery for a limited or indefinite amount of time was frequently used as a punishment for criminality. Those slaves destined for the export market who were traded in cities such as Cairo and Kukawa (modern day Nigeria) were often criminals. In Cairo, these criminal slaves were transported either around the Mediterranean or to the Indian Ocean slave trade, while from Kukawa, many made their way to West Africa from where they crossed the Atlantic either in the legal trade before 1807, or later in the black-market slave trade. While many of these slaves were male, female criminals who had transgressed against the strict Sharia sexual codes were also caught up in the system.[63] In the early nineteenth century, this use of criminals as slaves for export mirrors the systematic use of convicts exported from the United Kingdom to perform Australian colonial labour, as sentences of execution were commuted to being sold into slavery. In both Muslim Africa and in Britain this served the triple purpose of allowing the criminal justice system to view itself as benevolent in executing fewer criminals, while providing labour where it was needed, and also removing the threat posed by criminals – who were considered immoral and inferior people – from the home country.

For moral hygienists at the end of the nineteenth century, the inherent racial weakness of the non-white was also linked to another trait which exacerbated their entrapment in forced labour situations: drunkenness. Commentators observed that biological inferiority led to susceptibility to moral degradation, of which a desire for and an intolerance of drink was merely one example. Drunkenness led to the workers being vulnerable to be taken advantage of in labour negotiations, but also addiction to alcohol caused workers to be trapped in a coercive labour situation because of their need for money to pay for their booze. The workers themselves were blamed for this, even by those polemicists who also used their rhetoric to attack alcohol and its distribution to vulnerable populations. The prolific Henry Fox Bourne, whose writing often expressed sympathy for the aggrieved native of Africa, and who was willing to criticise the actions of his fellow countrymen when he felt they were perpetuating a system of slavery, nonetheless highlighted in South Africa the desirability of restricting the freedom of the workers in the Kimberley mines. This does not

[63] Humphrey Fisher, *Slavery in the History of Muslim Black Africa* (Hurst, 1988), p. 116.

sound a likely point of view for the secretary of the British and Foreign Anti-Slavery Association to be expressing. While Fox Bourne stressed that forcing workers to remain inside their housing compound at Kimberley acted as 'a sort of prison and its inmates are for the time being in a complete state of bondage', he justified this use of coercion because it protected the natives from the 'drink curse' to which they were so susceptible. Fox Bourne suggested that the natives, like children who needed protecting so they did not hurt themselves, were only partially responsible for their own degradation but that for the British to permit such a situation to continue would allow a descent into mass criminality.[64]

Six years later, Charles Forbes-Lindsay concurred with this view when writing in his huge historical tome about enslaved labour thousands of miles away in the Philippine Islands. His tract, dedicated to President Taft, who he said had worked hard in the cause of the Filipino, justified and lauded the achievements of American colonialism in the region by highlighting the problem of slavery that had existed in the islands before the coming of the Americans. He outlined the racial differences between enslaver and enslaved, stating that the Muslim Filipinos 'of Malay blood' were responsible for much of the practice of slavery.[65] However, Forbes-Lindsay also blamed the victims of enslavement for their condition. Although he defined some Filipinos as hardworking, sober and clean family men, he showed how many of the Filipinos working on sugar plantations had fallen victim to alcoholism. Forbes-Lindsay did not suggest that this rendered them incapable of work; the opposite was true. Ironically they tended to work longer and harder: 'it is a strange economic condition in which a planter finds his most desirable labourers amongst men who drink and gamble because they will work harder than moral and sober natives in order to earn money to satisfy their vicious inclinations'.[66] Forbes-Lindsay's implication that drunk workers benefitted their masters is echoed in Henry Nevinson's commentary about watching slave-like contract labourers being shipped by the Portuguese to cocoa plantations in Sao Tome off the coast of West Africa. Nevinson's testimony bears witness to the malicious use of alcohol by labour agents that was not always the fault of the moral weakness of the victim of enslavement. He observed slaves in 'Katumbella' (modern day Catumbela, on the Angola

[64] Henry Fox Bourne, *Blacks and Whites in South Africa* (London, 1900), pp. 50–2.

[65] Charles Forbes-Lindsay, *The Philippines under Spanish and American Rules* (Philadelphia, John C. Winston and Co., 1906), p. 83.

[66] Ibid., p. 474.

coast) being 'tamed' by being beaten and given alcohol, and he described how two hundred of them 'muddled with rum and bedecked like clowns passed along that May morning to a land of doom from which there was no return'. His implication here is that alcohol was being deliberately used by the slave traders to control and pacify the workers and ensure their smooth passage to the cocoa plantations.[67] In Chapter 6, we will explore how authors, such as Nevinson, used a more radical narrative to counter assertions about native moral degradation and susceptibility to alcoholism and that they were therefore to blame for their condition of enslavement.

Another group to face victim blaming by authors writing about slavery in the early years of the twentieth century was the female victims of the 'white slave' traffickers in the United States. Although in some ways these women made the ideal victim, depicted as white, innocent country girls, unprepared for the wiles of the city dwellers, some commentators suggested that it was moral failings of these women and girls that led to their downfall. Unlike other victims of enslavement for whom their race was at the core of their moral weakness, here it was their gender that allowed authors to blame these victims for their own predicament. Margit Stange has argued that the white slave panic was essentially manufactured as a way of justifying the control and domination of single white women, whose geographical and economic freedoms had hitherto worried the male patriarchal authorities. Men were explicitly encouraged by the white slavery literature to possess and control their daughters more fully. She claims that while the procurers were always highlighted as villains in these dramatic morality tales, the women and girls themselves were also depicted as culpable because of their weakness for finery.[68] Clifford Roe's melodramatic, almost erotic account of the descent of one girl into a life of white slavery emphasises her luxury clothing: 'she was clothed in soft filmy lingerie, silk stockings and satin bedroom slippers', comfort which was juxtaposed with her mental unhappiness caused by moral turmoil.[69] Thus these tales acted as a commentary on modernity and the corrupting nature of luxury, that fits into the discourse, driven by Protestant ethics, that was so common in the United States throughout the nineteenth and early twentieth centuries. Even Theodore Bingham, whose

[67] Henry Nevinson, *A Modern Slavery* (London and New York, 1906), p. 170.
[68] Margit Stange, *Personal Property: Wives, White Slaves and the Market in Women* (Johns Hopkins University Press, 1998), pp. 83, 107.
[69] Clifford Roe, *The Great War on White Slavery* (New York, 1911), p. 27.

focus was mostly on the victimhood of the girls, acknowledged that procurers and cadets (young men posing as boyfriends) appealed to the girls' desire for 'money, elegant clothing, wine dinners'.[70] Of course, race and gender prejudice could work together to doubly 'other' certain women and to reinforce hierarchies within American society. Donaldina Cameron was one of the female authors who had no sympathy for women caught up in prostitution. She ran a mission home to turn Chinese girls convicted of prostitution into good housekeepers and blamed their 'untamed disposition' for their plight.[71] This attitude was widespread, especially amongst male authors who shared Cameron's racial views informed by Social Darwinism. Robert Woltor explicitly juxtaposed white and Chinese prostitution in his anti-Chinese propaganda pamphlet, arguing that the difference between the two types of prostitution was that the Chinese was hidden and shameful whereas the white was visible and controllable.[72] But he was writing almost a generation before the white slave panic came to a head in the early twentieth century and, for him, the racial justification of othering the Chinese at any cost superseded any attempt to comment rationally on the true nature of prostitution in the western United States.

White victims of sex trafficking could also be cruelly cast as inferior and immoral women by those purporting to help them. One chapter within Clifford Roe's volume on *The Great War on White Slavery* told the story of college-educated Paul Sinclair, a once-heroic professional baseball player who had fallen from grace and had become an opium addict and procurer. His story was framed as a narrative of redemption, the tale of a sinner who repented. His female victims, however, were tarnished for life by their entrapment, as Roe explained, a daughter who had been a white slave and then returned to her family had to enter her family home by the back door because of the shame.[73] Sinclair also, when describing the moral conduct of the women and girls that he dragged into prostitution, stated that some needed little persuasion, in his words they 'were disgustingly easy'.[74] Other authors emphasised the deceptive nature of the promises procurers made to women, showing that it was not

[70] Theodore A. Bingham, *The Girl That Disappears: the Real Facts about the White Slave Traffic* (Boston. 1911), p. 49.

[71] Brian Donovan, *White Slave Crusades: Race, Gender and Anti-Vice Activism 1887–1917* (University of Illinois Press, 2006), p. 117.

[72] Robert Woltor, *A Short and Truthful History of the Capture of California and Oregon by the Chinese* (San Francisco: A.L. Bancroft and Co, 1882), p. 24.

[73] Roe, *The Great War on White Slavery*, p. 46. [74] Ibid., p. 78.

greed but naïvety that allowed them to be ensnared: a quality that was to be lauded, as being affinitive to innocence, but one that rendered women and girls passive and in need of the protection of dominant men.[75] Bingham explained the difference in response to an attack on worldly and innocent girls, and linked it to the immigrant status of many of the victims of trafficking: 'A girl used to the ways of the United States will not submit for long, but a girl in a strange land among strange people can be cowed into doing so'.[76] This view reinforced the statement two years earlier in the report by the US Immigration Commission, which argued that procurers 'played upon the weaknesses of vanity and pride' in immigrant girls and that the easiness with which immigrant girls could be degraded was due to the lower sexual morality of those raised in Europe.[77] Few commentators were as enlightened as Jane Addams who recognised the economic and social triggers for prostitution: she stated that it was poverty that drove many women and girls to this line of work.[78] She too outlined the lure of the department store, the clothes and jewellery and beautiful possessions that are used to entrap women and girls who are 'discouraged and over-fatigued' by hard work.[79] But she also acknowledged wider societal problems, that women were often abused by men that they know, and that over-protecting girls left them with no resilience to resist the lure of procurers.[80] Clifford Roe, at times a conservative when it came to judging female victims, also did not allow male protagonists to evade his critical gaze, showing that commentators realised that it was the duty of all of society to prevent these abuses.[81] The synthesis of flexible notions of gender roles and of slavery will be explored further in Chapter 5.

FEAR OF WORKER SOLIDARITY

As well as explaining perceptions of inferiority due to gender or race and their association with moral weakness, the process of othering victims of enslavement served another important function for those in positions of power who feared the solidarity of workers. Rhetorically diminishing the

75 Donovan, *White Slave Crusades*, p. 22. 76 Bingham, *The Girl That Disappears*, p. 17.

77 *Importing Women for Immoral Purposes, 1909 Report Presented by Mr Dillingham at 61st Congress, Senate Doc. No 196* (Washington: Government Printing Office, 1909), pp. 8, 29.

78 Ibid., p. 66.

79 Jane Addams, *A New Conscience and an Ancient Evil* (Macmillan, 1912), pp. 57, 65.

80 Ibid., p. 176. 81 Roe, *The Great War on White Slavery*, p. 62.

political and economic power of particular groups of coerced workers by othering them allowed those in control to divide and rule. The perception of the violent and powerful potential of worker solidarity often vastly outstripped the reality of the actual strength that these victims of abusive situations held. According to Elliott Young, in his work on the black and Chinese workers in Peruvian plantation systems, different groups of workers were as likely to fight against one another as alongside one another.[82] However, just as during antebellum chattel slavery in the United States, when the fear of slave rebellion had driven much of the policy towards and depictions of black Americans, so in the emancipation era did fear of worker insurrection, disobedience and militancy, drive negative depictions of those groups. The process was especially potent in the Jim Crow South as there it relied on and played upon people's memories of chattel slavery and the fear that all slaves would murder their masters given the chance. Nan Woodruff has shown that in the years after the Civil War, any attempt to defend labour rights by African American workers in the south was immediately reimagined and resold as a 'negro insurrection' in the popular white mainstream press. This benefited both the capitalists (the owners of plantations, mills and industry that relied on the coerced black labourers) but also the white union leaders and members who saw themselves as in direct competition for jobs with their black neighbours.[83] Ironically, this process reinforces the point of how successful the othering process to divide and rule really was, because white and black workers could rarely conceive of themselves as a unified force. The few countervalent voices pleading for abused labour solidarity will be explored in Chapter 6.

Just as in the case of white slavery, gender and race was a potent mix when accusations of moral weakness and degeneracy were circulating. For coolie labourers working in plantations on the Hawaiian Islands, fears over their race and their willingness to stand up for their rights coalesced, causing severe alarm among the white population of the Islands, and those looking on from the mainland. Such workers who dared to resist their conditions, were accused of violent and degraded tendencies as well as laziness. This was in direct contrast to the depictions of them when they were not resisting, as racially determined to be docile, hard workers, and

[82] Elliott Young, *Alien Nation: Chinese Migration in the Americas from the Coolie Era through World War II* (University of North Carolina Press, 2014), p. 77.

[83] Nan Woodruff, *American Congo: the African American Freedom Struggle in the Delta* (Harvard University Press, 2003), p. 91.

in contrast to the depiction of the Hawaiian natives, which trope owed more to the romanticisation of the lost 'Indian' of mainland United States. Native Hawaiians were depicted patronisingly as 'ours' by whites, and thus rendered as child-like possessions who were marginalised politically. Asian migrants to the Hawaiian Islands, living under the slave-like contract labour system, were seen as a threat because of their morally undesirable habit of opium smoking but also their vocal attempts to defend their meagre rights.[84] An example of the negative perceptions of workers claiming their rights is in the work published in 1898 by John Musick, whose travel narrative and ethnographic account depicted native Hawaiians as making good progress towards civilisation, although still welcoming and childlike. But his narrative reveals disgust at the presence of Asian migrants: he recounts watching Japanese workers in Pahala coming in from the fields with their babies on their backs 'dirt begrimed, tired, wretched looking creatures, with hardly any resemblance to human beings'.[85] As well as being subhuman and inferior in every regard, according to Musick, the Japanese as a nation were politically threatening, a treacherous invader. He put this down to their position on the racial hierarchy, civilised enough to consider political overthrow of their betters, but not civilised enough to behave with proper duty, morals and decorum. He wrote, 'what nation would be more likely to seize them [the Hawaiian Islands] than a half-civilised country like Japan'.[86]

Writers like Musick, who made their living purveying historical fiction, may be expected to be selective with the truth, but because they feared its power, American government papers were equally harsh in their depiction of the Asian labour force in Hawaii. In diplomatic letters from the period leading up to the Annexation of Hawaii, two influential American politicians, the minister for Hawaii and the Secretary of State shared their fears that 'evil disposed persons might stir some of them [the forty thousand Chinese and Japanese in Hawaii] to disorder'.[87] Thirteen years later, the 'orientalising of the labouring population' was still of concern to the United States government. In its third report on Hawaii, the Department

84 Sally Engle Merry, *Colonizing Hawaii: the Cultural Power of the Law* (Princeton University Press, 2000) p. 129.

85 John R. Musick, *Hawaii: Our New Possessions* (New York & London, 1898), p. 194.

86 Ibid., p. 449.

87 Mr Stevens (John L. Stevens, Minister to Hawaii) to Mr Foster (John W. Foster, Secretary of State) 1/2/1893 in *Papers Relating to the Annexation of the Hawaiian Islands to the United States* (Washington, 1893), p. 49.

of Commerce and Labour suggested that the 'convenient and inexhaustible cheap labour markets of Asia' provide workers who live 'under penal sanction'.[88] But the real concern of the Department was the so-called blood unionism of the Japanese, who were involved in controlling labour and directing strikes. The bulletin suggested that the Japanese sense of worker solidarity, bound together as they were by blood, was far stronger than the trade unionism of American and European workers.[89] Indeed the Japanese were considered so troublesome that the author of the bulletin argued that their influence might be moderated by allowing a modification of the Chinese Exclusion act, so the more docile Chinese could balance out the militant Japanese, a proposal so far at odds with the usual American perception of Chinese immigration that it reveals the depths of fears over the Japanese, who were seen as threatening because of the mutual contempt with which they and their white masters held each other.[90]

To some extent, the fear of Asian worker resistance was a valid one, because the Japanese were willing to stand up for their rights. White plantation owners deliberately tried to segregate their workforce to prevent cross-community collaboration. Dividing their living accommodation by ethnicity served to facilitate surveillance. But whites could only hold back the tide for so long. By the end of the nineteenth century, the first labour unions in Hawaii began among the Japanese workers and then the Filipinos.[91] Japanese workers arrived with a sense of linguistic and community identity and were shocked at the brutality of their treatment by the *luna*, or overseers on the sugar plantations. The Japanese were responsible for many of the strikes at the sugar plantations, partly because they initially received the lowest wages of all migrant labour, but also were willing to resort to physical violence when their mistreatment got out of hand, with one Okinawan contract labourer using karate to challenge a sadistic *luna*.[92] But the fear of Japanese aggression and treachery was largely driven by American attitudes about their racial inferiority, and not by the reality of their performance as workers itself.

While controlling migrant labourers and limiting their militancy was an important concern during this period, sometimes white observers felt nervous about the circumstances of former slaves whose liberation had

[88] Department of Commerce and Labour, *Third Report on Hawaii*, Bulletin of the Bureau of Labor, no. 66, Sept. 1906 (Washington Government Printing Office, 1906), p. 367.
[89] Ibid., p. 382. [90] Ibid., pp. 405, 413. [91] Merry, *Colonizing Hawaii*, pp. 143, 204.
[92] Yukiko Kimura, *Issei: Japanese Immigrants in Hawaii* (University of Hawaii Press, 1988), pp. 50, 79.

been only partial. This was true both in imperial and domestic contexts. In East Africa, as former slaves sought to exert their new rights and redefine their economic roles, their former masters had difficulty in releasing the whip from their hand, so to speak. In places like early twentieth-century Kenya, where much of the land was owned and controlled by white settlers, there were few opportunities for freed slaves to make a living other than by squatting illegally on someone else's land. This situation became so notorious and ubiquitous that 'freed slave' became a synonym for 'squatter'. In this situation, former slaves found themselves redefined by the legal system as 'vagrants and masterless men'. It was here that the systems of large plantations preferred by the colonialists and the subsistence economics preferred by the peasant class butted up against one another and were found to be incompatible.[93] As Frederick Cooper has explained, the Africans here experienced a very conservative abolition of slavery, one in which their masters feared change, social and political unrest and a vengeful hopeless black population.[94]

Similarly, in the United States, African Americans also experienced a conservative backlash in the aftermath to emancipation, in which the white planter class sought to regain and maintain control and power over the labouring population on whose work their own wealth depended. As Daniel Novak has argued, the systems of debt bondage and peonage used in the south were deliberately employed to restrict the freedom of black workers: 'a simple and effective substitute for previous system of labour control: slavery'. This, along with the enforcement of a punitive regime of black codes, ensured that any worker who wanted to leave his master was effectively criminalised and might then be ensnared in the equally coercive convict labour system.[95] Pete Daniel explored further the nature of southern peonage in the years after the Civil War, showing that such abusive labour practices were most prevalent in isolated back country areas, in the cotton belt, in turpentine-harvesting regions and in railroad and road construction camps.[96] These regions, such as the backwoods of northern Florida, were often bi-racial, where few other labouring options existed and so planters and capitalists felt most keenly the threat from an

[93] Frederick Cooper, *From Slaves to Squatters: Plantation Labor and Agriculture in Zanzibar and Coastal Kenya 1890–1925* (Yale University Press, 1980), pp. 5, 111, 158.

[94] Ibid., p. 31.

[95] Daniel Novak, *The Wheel of Servitude: Black Forced Labor after Slavery* (University Press of Kentucky, 1978), pp. xv, 1, 26.

[96] Pete Daniel, *The Shadow of Slavery: Peonage in the South 1901–1969* (Oxford University Press, 1972), p. 22.

organised and mobile African American workforce. Former slaves in Oklahoma who had once belonged to Native American slave owners found themselves trapped in similar systems of bondage to other newly freed African Americans. After the Civil War, the Choctaw tribe wanted to free their slaves but simultaneously preserve the social and economic subordination of black people within their communities. One way that they enacted this was by using the Choctaw governing council to coerce freedmen and women back into forced labour just as white southerners did by labelling them 'vagrants'. In some Native American communities, the formerly enslaved could be arrested once they had been accused of vagrancy and then auctioned to the highest bidder, in a cruel imitation of chattel slavery.[97]

But black workers were not the only ones to become peons as poor white southerners could also be entrapped in this way.[98] Just as in the plantation labour system in Hawaii, those in power in the south in the late nineteenth century worked hard to ensure that the culture of segregation solidified and this meant that cross-racial worker unity was less of a threat. Groups within American society, such as recent immigrants, especially Jewish ones, who could easily be othered and whose campaigns for rights would not be supported by native-born Americans, were seen as easy pickings for the lumber industries of the south. The Jackson Lumber Company working on the border of Alabama and Florida acquired Jewish labourers directly from the slums of New York and used them as peons.[99]

Despite the selection of vulnerable and defenceless groups of workers to supplement the supply of African American labour, in the mainland south the black workers bore the brunt of the racial othering, because numerically the political and economic threat that they posed was most considerable. The narrative that without strict control, the violent and not yet fully civilised African American would take revenge for slavery, was a justification in the minds of more moderate whites for the extreme racial violence perpetrated against their neighbours. Therefore, the practical systems that sought to render newly freed slaves as once again inferior had to be accompanied by epistemological structures which also locked African Americans into the cycle of slavery-like labour systems. The cultural forms of 'symbolic slavery' as Steven Dubin has called it, such

[97] Barbara Krauthamer, *Black Slaves, Indian Masters: Slavery, Emancipation and Citizenship in the Native American South* (University of North Carolina Press, 2013), p. 108.

[98] Daniel, *The Shadow of Slavery*, p. 34. [99] Ibid., p. 86.

as material culture designed to demean the formerly enslaved and to create a sense of shared white community, using humour with an underlying violent intent, rendered black Americans invisible, taken for granted and servile, just as under slavery.[100] Kenneth Goings has further shown that material culture gave the inferiority of black people a tangible reality as their servile status was stereotyped in a post-slavery world in order to subjugate the newly freed.[101] This 'negro problem', as it was then known, became a national concern in the period following the end of the Reconstruction era, as the white community within the United States became further unified and homogenised. A significant part of the 'negro problem' was the sense that this was a body of labourers who could no longer easily be kept in their place, metaphorically and literally, and the potential of them joining together with workers of other races to campaign for their rights was a huge concern. Rhetorically othering the African American was an important way through which the risk of cross-racial worker solidarity was mitigated.

CONCLUSION

As this book shows, in this period European and American understandings of slavery and its victim cannot be separated from the antislavery impulse. However, I argue that, in many ways, antislavery rhetoric emerging from Britain and the United States was essentially conservative. Some scholars such as William Mulligan have argued that abolitionism was at its most influential in the way that people thought about slavery in the nineteenth century, so that its agenda of creating a new universal moral code, responding to the aesthetics of sensibility towards human suffering, came to dominate discourse.[102] While I agree that this agenda-setting did shape the way that slavery as an intellectual concept was viewed by many ordinary Britons and Americans, when it came to depicting the victims of slavery, the enslaved themselves, such high ideals were often lacking. Far from reflecting a genuine attempt first to understand and second to mitigate the suffering of slaves, much of the writing on slavery in this period

[100] Steven Dubin, 'Symbolic Slavery: Black Representations in Popular Culture', *Social Problems*, 34: 2 (April 1987), p. 127.

[101] Kenneth Goings, *Mammy and Uncle Mose: Black Collectibles and American Stereotyping* (Indiana University Press, 1994), p. xix.

[102] William Mulligan, 'The Anti-Slave Trade Campaign in Europe 1888–90', in William Mulligan and Maurice Bric, eds., *A Global History of Anti-Slavery Politics in the Nineteenth Century* (Palgrave, 2013), pp. 12, 157.

tells us more about the Anglo-American desire to solidify their own political and racial hegemony. Some works of more radical abolitionist writers did attempt bolder solutions to the slavery question, one of which was to rhetorically raise up the victims and make an honest appraisal of their victimhood and the structural reasons for it. These works will be explored in Chapter 6.

In most depictions of slavery, the othering of the victim tells us more about the author and his values aiming at consolidation of conservative racial and political power. Identifying the victims of slavery as the racial other, lower on the racially determined hierarchy, served to place them outside the full scope of protection of the law, or render them passive and in need of patronising, paternalistic protection from whites. Blaming such victims for their vulnerable position in society or defining particular labour systems as markedly not slavery also both served to place the forced labourer outside the protection of humanitarian elites. Rhetorically, it also allowed the British and Americans to continue to define themselves as part of an antislavery coalition while allowing coerced labour regimes to continue to exist, all without experiencing any cognitive dissonance.

Fundamentally, depictions of the slave as an 'other' around the globe were about the fears of the loss of power and jurisdiction of the dominant class and their need to assert control and a sort of metaphorical possession, once legal possession had been outlawed. Such conservative responses to the horrors of slavery reflected concerns about disorder at a local, national and imperial level. It allowed the British people to be at the same time gripped by Uncle Tom fever, when the book, theatre production, figurines, toys and wallpaper became important parts of the 'franchise', while simultaneously remaining ambivalent to the coming of the American Civil War, and the role that a desire to end slavery played in that struggle.[103] In post-war America too, the attempts to rebuild the damaged sense of community of white Americans drove their continued othering of victims of slavery both domestically and when viewing slavery around the world. Depicting the enslaved and the coerced labourer as politically radical, dangerous traitors was an important rhetorical manoeuvre designed to justify putting them outside normal systems of protection, while at the same time using labour restrictions to control and dominate them, thereby preventing disorder. This happened throughout the Anglophone world in this period, whether to Japanese labourers in the

[103] Richard Huzzey, *Freedom Burning: Anti-Slavery and Empire in Victorian Britain* (Cornell University Press, 2012), pp. 21–2.

sugar plantations of the Hawaiian Islands, to formerly enslaved and still bonded labourers in British Nigeria or to peons and convict labourers in the North American south. Moments in time when workers came together in solidarity to campaign for an improvement in working conditions, or even an overthrow of entire colonial regimes, were especially tense and saw a redoubling of efforts by white elites to use enslavement and its allied labour systems to lock down the rebellious workers. In those cases, deliberate attempts to control the discourse about the enslaved and to reinforce in the public minds their misbehaviour and their inferior status, were as important as concrete and practical actions to limit their freedom.

Policing the definition of slavery and its perimeters was crucial in cases where racial othering enabled control and possession to take place, but its effect was doubled when the theme of gendered othering was deployed. Fears of disorderly and unruly women acting beyond the control of their male protectors were a key feature of modernity on both sides of the Atlantic and thus were triggers of the white slave panic, a widespread phenomenon of the late nineteenth and early twentieth centuries. As Margit Stange has shown, many of the texts about white slavery requesting that members of the public be alert to the phenomenon were couched in terms requiring patriarchs, husbands, fathers and brothers to keep their womenfolk safe from the marauding threat of procurers and their cadets.[104] Single women, who were working and enjoying leisure pursuits, especially in the centres of cities, were presented as a key part of the white slavery problem, with victim blaming being an important part of system of control where gender was involved. Although in this context, the race of the procurers juxtaposed with the race of the victims was a crucial pillar of antislavery writing, here fear of potential victims being out of control and through their own immorality and naïvete ending up in trouble, dominated the discourse.

In the case of white slavery, naming all women involved in prostitution, whether voluntary or not, as 'slaves', facilitated mechanisms of control reflecting the overuse of the definition of slavery. In other contexts, women's enslavement was denied in order to allow their continuing control by men and prevent their being free and independent and a problem. This took place in many colonial contexts, where those in power preferred to overlook female sexual slavery, diminishing its seriousness and the victimhood of the women involved in order to preserve existing patriarchal structures of dominance. In Nigeria it was feared

104 Stange, *Personal Property*, p. 83.

that, if freed, concubines would turn to prostitution, and so the authorities responded by denying the coercive nature of concubinage and allowing it to continue.[105]

Therefore, othering the slave in this period was essentially a rhetorical function designed to protect and bolster the position of white, male power brokers whether in colonial, national or local contexts. Whether by identifying the enslaved as the racial other, by blaming them for their own situation or by worrying about their disorderly and rebellious natures, both British and American authors were able to maintain the positions of being opposed to the use of slavery, while at the same time overlooking, tolerating or even facilitating the continued existence of slavery within their jurisdictions. Fundamentally, this depended on their manipulation of the definitions of what counted as slavery and, in doing so, they rhetorically rendered many free migrants as unfree, while at the same time denying the victimhood of many others who were genuinely ensnared in slavery or slavery-like labour situations.

[105] Paul Lovejoy and Jan Hogendorn, *Slow Death for Slavery: The Course of Abolition in Northern Nigeria 1897–1936* (Cambridge University Press, 1993), p. 117.

5

Gender and the Rhetoric of Slavery

Since the late eighteenth and early nineteenth centuries, the conception of enslaved women had been a rhetorically significant one for abolitionists. Female chattel slaves in the transatlantic system were depicted as the doubly enslaved through virtue of their race and their gender, their race trapping them in a system of forced labour and their gender trapping them simultaneously in a system of forced breeding, sexual abuse and, for abolitionists, moral degradation. For such women there was no separation between the world of work and the domestic sphere; they had little sense of a private family life but, rather, in all aspects of their personhood, were owned and possessed by men. Such women became the ideal victim, passive and without agency, requiring rescue and protection. More radical abolitionists fought against this rendering of the female slave as powerless, proclaiming women's position as activists, campaigners and even resistance leaders in the struggle against slavery. Such patterns of interpretation of the intersection between slavery and gender are mirrored in the post-emancipation period, with female victims foregrounded in popular literature enabling the transmission of both conservative and radical political messages about women's place in society. Examining the position of women tells only half the story and, while as in most literature of the period, when discussing slavery, authors often treated the male experience as a normative one. In some cases, we can identify the problematising of masculinity within slavery and abolitionist discourse, alongside an analysis of the evolution of the domestic relationships of the formerly enslaved, allowing for comparisons between marriage and slavery. If they entered into marriage, even freedwomen and women born free in this period were not truly free.

This chapter will begin with an exploration of how contemporary authors treated women's experiences under slavery both as agricultural and industrial workers and as tools of sexual pleasure and reproductive labour. Women in enslavement requiring challenging physical labour were usually driven to work as hard as the men but, rhetorically, their relative physical weakness could be used by commentators to confirm or deny the definition of a particular labour form as 'slavery'. Those whose aim was to justify coercive labour proclaimed the requirements of the job so accessible that even women and children might do the work, while conversely one of the most common abolitionist tropes after emancipation was to proclaim the true horror of a particular labour practice as evidenced by its ensnaring of women – one of the very groups within society that paternalism sought to protect. But paternalistic trends also had within them the desire to limit and control, and rhetoric around enslaved women also reflected this impulse, such as through the white slavery discourse in North America (and elsewhere) which sought to confine the movement of single, financially independent women in cities by creating fear of enslavement among them and their families. Rhetorically linking prostitution, whether voluntary or not, to slavery through the use of the term 'white slavery' served to mobilise neo-abolitionists to construct these women as ideal victims. This impulse to confine and control also functioned via the discourse of social hygiene, which sought to control the breeding and reproductive freedom of the enslaved and formerly enslaved.

Women's involvement in the discourse around slavery was not merely as subjects; they also formed an important part of the abolition movement after emancipation, just as they had prior to it. From 1839, when women's participation in the Anti-Slavery Congress was contested, until 1929, when an important text on global slavery was authored by female campaigner Kathleen Simon, women's roles as both conservative and radical abolitionists were crucial. Women who found it easiest to access a platform for oral communication or publication emerged from the white middle and upper classes, but a significant proportion of former victims of enslavement also had their voices heard and were essential to the abolition movement because they were considered by readers to carry the values of authenticity and veracity. First-hand accounts, whether by observers or victims were lauded on both sides of the Atlantic. Women sometimes also presented a reactionary view within the discourse, both in an explicit pro-slavery context prior to the end of the Civil War, and later as memorialisers and commemorators of that era as a golden age. Female campaigners (as well as their male counterparts) also used the discourse of white slavery to reinforce the racial hegemony, for example, by suggesting that the emergence of white slavery in American cities was symptomatic of white women's vulnerability to attack by the racial other, often an African American.

The first case study of female enslavement to be examined for its impact on discourses about global slavery is that of the Circassian enslavement in the Ottoman empire, a phenomenon that took place over a long chronological period, but in the United States in the 1870s became a cause for concern due to extensive newspaper coverage. At a time when definitions of whiteness were still malleable, Circassian women were defined as 'white' for the purposes of rendering especially heinous this form of slavery, by the ethnic and religious other: the Turk. Although far distant in geographical terms, and from a region unfamiliar to many American readers, these female victims of enslavement were rendered as kin and as ideal victims, by the treatment in the newspapers and in literature, while at the same time, being exoticised and eroticised for the titillation of readers. This treatment shows the intersection of two rhetorical traditions: the need which this book focuses on, to render global slavery as comprehensible and its practitioners as other; and second the ongoing tradition in European discourse, from at least the late eighteenth century, of romanticising the beauty and 'fairness', in all senses of the word, of women of the Circassia region. However, discussions of the Ottoman enslavement of women in harems also took place at a broader level in this period, with the whiteness of women only enhancing their representation as the ideal victim. Debates over how much victims of sexual slavery suffered were prolific, and the conclusion often depended on the pragmatism or idealism of the author. American and British commentaries on this type of slavery often reflected a high-minded imperial antislavery outlook, but, as shown already in this book, this was hypocritical at its heart. In colonial contexts, travellers and settlers from those nations did not see the use of enslaved women for their own advantage, sexually and as labourers, as a problem.

Domestically, in the United States, the definition of prostitution as slavery was broader in scope than merely the white slavery panic. Chinese women especially, were racially othered by their depiction as a race and class of prostitutes. Their perceived servile nature rendered them passive and absent in the discourse, while they were simultaneously given agency to corrupt and pollute the American bloodstock, without hope of redemption. Not all commentators dismissed all Chinese women as prostitutes, but many refused to see, within Chinese culture, domestic relationships different to those in white American society that actually benefited women, such as the reverence with which older women were treated.

Thus, a variety of linguistic and visual tools were deployed in the late nineteenth and early twentieth centuries to control the movement and reproduction of women who were depicted as actual or potential victims of slavery. Tropes such as the motif of the harem, could be manoeuvred to function as either conservative and radical discursive tools, with the harem rendered by temperance campaigners as a site of protection and security, and by suffragists as a metaphor for entrapment, luxury and stagnation. As shown in Chapters 3 and 4, the othering of both slave and slaveowner, which predominantly had racial characteristics, was enhanced and made more rhetorically powerful when tied to Americans' paranoia about gender roles. The troubled performance of masculinity, including fears over emasculation in both white and black American culture, resonated through these discussions as much as did tensions over the behaviour of women. These concerns took on a global context in this period, as global slavery became part of the American mainstream for the first time after emancipation, and as powerful white orientalist discourse influenced perceptions of enslavement and defined new black orientalist fantasies, permeated by melodrama and exoticisation. But nowhere was the enhancing role of gender adding grist to the mill of the othering discourse so easily visible as in the white slavery discourse, where victims of white slavery, often rendered as naïve, innocent and ideal, once corrupted and fallen were considered beyond redemption, whereas, in some narratives, their male procurers, as long as they could be given an identity considered white and civilised, were depicted as penitents, and therefore had available to them the moral and legal fruits of redemption. However, despite the prevalent notion of victim blaming and spoiling, the power of white slavery rhetoric, and other discourse about enslaved women, partly evolved from its ability to create in its readers a sympathetic ideal victim.

CONSTRUCTION OF THE IDEAL VICTIM

The pernicious combination of abuse because of race and gender resulted in enslaved women under the chattel slave system being victims of a type of double jeopardy, doubly persecuted. From the late eighteenth century onwards, abolitionists recognised this, but also appreciated that female victims were also more potent symbols of the heinous nature of the slave trade and slavery. In the United States, it was not only white masters who abused their slaves in this way. Mixed-race black and Native American women were often raped and beaten by their masters whether they were white or Native.[1] This led to female slavery being foregrounded by those opposed to this type of labour and, even in discussions around modern slavery, female victims receive more attention. It is important to remember that men too were specially victimised in ways that deliberately challenged their sense of gender identity, as their roles as fathers and protectors were not only denied them but subverted, for example, when male slaves were punished by having to watch their female slave partners be beaten or even sexually abused by their slave masters.

In the period after emancipation, as antislavery writing continued to mirror many of the patterns from the era prior to the Civil War, the focus remained on women in slavery and how their peculiar experiences symbolised broader truths about certain labour systems. Many commentators recognised that females were vulnerable to the most abuse, partly because of their inherent physical weakness, partly because of their increased susceptibility to sexual abuse and partly because dominance of women was an easy way for masters to achieve the submission of entire kinship groups of enslaved individuals. This was also true in the systems of indentured labour that emerged in the period after the abolition of the transatlantic slave trade. Hugh Tinker argued that for Indian migrant workers travelling globally on coerced indentured contracts, labour agents saw the migration of women, especially those willing to marry the male labourers, as essential for maintaining a sense of moral order. This resulted in many 'depot marriages' as they were known, where male and female labourers paired off at the port of disembarkation for mutual protection.[2] However, campaigners trying to improve the conditions of indentured migrants argued that women were especially mistreated, for example, as in the mission to reform the endless indentures worked in Natal by Indian migrants, women often had the least power and were the last to be helped.[3] This assessment is reinforced by the evidence provided by female workers from the Tamil areas of South India who were persuaded to migrate to Sri Lanka, then Ceylon, to work on the coffee plantations. They were encouraged by a *kangany*, a recruitment agent of

[1] Tiya Miles, 'Uncle Tom was an Indian: Tracing the Red in Black Slavery', in James F. Brooks, ed., *Confounding the Color Line* (University of Nebraska Press, 2002), p. 150.

[2] Hugh Tinker, *A New System of Slavery: the Export of Indian Labour Overseas 1830–1920* (Oxford University Press, 1974), pp. 90, 140.

[3] Ibid., p. 293.

a higher caste, who specifically recruited women because the wages they could command were much lower, and they would be more likely to remain working for many years without causing trouble. Despite their status as more desirable labourers, the women who did make the journey to Ceylon faced sexual abuse from men, whether fellow workers or the overseers.[4]

Although he made no explicit mention of sexual abuse, and did spend most of his four-hundred-page tract writing about the male experience as normative, Walter Wilson briefly mentioned the plight of female convict labourers in the system that emerged in the United States after the Civil War. For him, it was the requirement that women undertake the same sorts of physical labour as men (road and railroad construction, for example) that provoked comment. He equated the entire system with slavery but proclaimed that female prisoners were treated especially badly. He stated that because of the excessive demands of the overseers of convict labour, female prisoners were essentially 'work animals'.[5]

The prizing of slave women as less troublesome workers was nothing new. Humphrey Fisher identified that, since medieval times, female slaves who were deaf and dumb were prized in Africa as domestics, not only because of their inability to talk back, but also their inability to share the slaveowners' intimate family secrets. But casual sexual abuse was also an important part of the story. Elite Muslim men, such as the West African ruler Mansa Musa, going on pilgrimage to Mecca, took large retinues of servants of all types with them, including slave women for personal sexual entertainment.[6] For Mansa Musa, sexual abuse of female slaves was part of his status display to other males, as well as for his own titillation. Across the *longue durée*, this behaviour was underpinned by extreme misogynistic attitudes doubled by racism. Imperial observers of slavery in Africa, while criticising the immorality of the slave trade, simultaneously described women that they encountered in the most prejudiced terms, thus implicitly justifying their abuse by rendering them 'other'. J. A. Moloney talked about the Wagogo tribe in these terms, implicitly contrasting Africans with European and American women whose beauty is adorned and inauthentic: 'young women and girls are distinctly

[4] Rachel Kurian, 'Labour, Race and Gender of Ceylon's Plantations', in William Clarence-Smith and Steven Topik, eds., *The Global Coffee Economy in Africa, Asia and Latin America 1500–1989* (Cambridge University Press, 2003), p. 181.

[5] Walter Wilson, *Forced Labour in the United States* (London, 1933), p. 62.

[6] Humphrey J. Fisher, *Slavery in the History of Muslim Black Africa* (Hurst, 1988), pp. 181, 202.

handsome as niggers go and cultivate the graces of beauty unadorned'. However, a few sentences later he commented that 'as with most African tribes this [the attractiveness] ceases with the twentieth year and a female of thirty has degenerated into a repulsive crone'.[7] As Elizabeth Elbourne has argued, race and sex operated together in the colonial era because the perceived perverse sexuality of the racial other justified slavery.[8] For many slave abusers in the post-emancipation era however, rape was a tool of control. An example of this is in the late nineteenth century Pacific system of blackbirding when 'blackbirders', slave traders by another name, forced labourers to leave the Pacific Islands to work in Central and Southern America. They gained control over the male labourers by subjugating females through rape. Blackbirder William 'Bully' Hayes, a notorious and violent pirate from Ohio, enhanced his economic gains by his exploitation of women and girls, as well as poor treatment of fellow sailors.[9]

Those seeking to justify labour types as different from slavery, or explicitly not slavery, also made rhetorical use of women to illustrate their arguments. Demetrius Boulger was one such writer who defended Leopold II's Belgian Congo from the plethora of pamphlets suggesting that far from ending slavery in the Congo Free State, Leopold's regime was itself enslaving the population. Boulger praised Leopold's 'prescience, energy and courage', and proclaimed that he intended to stop the slave raiding from Zanzibar which often targeted women and children. Then, those whom he had freed from the threat of slavery would be given moral and honest work harvesting rubber or '*caoutchouc*' as he called it. And lest the readers be concerned about this activity, Boulger stated that this harvesting could be undertaken so easily that women and children might do it, the supposed lightness of the work justifying claims that it could not involve slave labour.[10]

Further complicating the rhetorical presentation of enslaved women in this period is the acknowledgement by contemporaries and by scholars since, that even women who had a nominally free status cannot be considered free in the modern sense of being fully independent and

[7] J. A. Moloney, *With Captain Stairs to Katanga* (London, 1893), p. 52.

[8] Elizabeth Elbourne, 'Introduction', in Gwyn Campbell and Elizabeth Elbourne, eds., *Sex, Power and Slavery* (Ohio University Press, 2014), p. 4.

[9] Gerald Horne, *The White Pacific: US Imperialism and Black Slavery in the South Seas after the Civil War* (University of Hawaii Press, 2007), p. 48.

[10] Demetrius Boulger, *The Congo State or the Growth of Civilisation in Central Africa* (London, Calcutta and Simla, 1898), pp. 1, 90, 283.

autonomous agents. In order to defend his case for the continued existence of chattel slavery, George Fitzhugh used the argument that many groups within society lacked true freedom. He asked, 'how shall we class wives, children, wards, apprentices, prisoners, soldiers and sailors? They are not free … are they therefore slaves?'[11] For many women who had been formerly enslaved, despite their nominal change of status from slave to freedwoman, their experience in fact reflected a continuum of unfreedom throughout their lives.[12] Although discussing Sally Hemings, an enslaved individual, David Brion Davis raised a valid point that might be applied to all women in the nineteenth century: that sexually, they had a debateable ability to consent.[13] This had important ramifications for the British and American perceptions of women who had been freed from slavery, such as those liberated from harems in Africa and the Middle East. Despite the British proclaiming themselves protectors of women and their virtue, according to imperial antislavery authors, women freed from slavery ought not to be allowed complete freedom because the women's morality and reproduction needed to be monitored and controlled.[14] Later, this chapter will further explore the eugenicist imperative to control the breeding of women of different classes and races.

According to Amy Dru Stanley, it was desirable in the minds of American abolitionists, that, in the United States context, after emancipation, the ownership of a formerly enslaved woman passed seamlessly from her slave master to her husband. To this end, the Freedmen's Bureau attempted to educate slaves on their future gender roles and on the nature of marriage, causing some freedmen to treat their new wives poorly because they were inculcated with the belief that their own freedom and status as men depended on their subjugation of their wives.[15] Albert Bushnell Hart's view is even more pessimistic, suggesting that the legacy of the system of slavery in the South, and of the racist Jim Crow culture that emerged following emancipation (both of which 'disturbed the balance of race relations'), served to corrupt the domestic life and familial

[11] George Fitzhugh, *Cannibals All! or Slaves without Masters*, ed. C. Vann Woodward (Harvard University Press, 1960), p. 80.

[12] Elbourne, 'Intro', p. 17.

[13] David Brion Davis, 'Slavery, Sex and Dehumanization', in Campbell & Elbourne, ed., *Sex, Power and Slavery*, p. 44.

[14] Diane Robinson-Dunn, *The Harem, Slavery and British Imperial Culture* (Manchester University Press, 2006), p. 45.

[15] Amy Dru Stanley, *From Bondage to Contract: Wage Labour, Marriage and the Market in the Age of Slave Emancipation* (Cambridge University Press, 1998), pp. 18, 36, 47.

relationships of both whites and blacks in the southern states. Regarding labour, he seemed to have little problem with 'negroes' of both genders working in the fields, but he disliked the way that poor white women were consigned to such manual labour as well.[16] However, he did elaborate on some of the family problems caused amongst African Americans for whom work for both parents outside the home was essential for their financial survival. Because of this, Bushnell Hart suggested, African Americans were able to maintain little sense of family life.[17] Sexual morality was also a concern for Bushnell Hart and he professed reluctance to acknowledge what he saw as the 'terrible truth' of black Americans' lower sexual morality but he did attempt to contextualise it, deriding the habit, even after slavery's end, of white southern men of cohabiting with black concubines. Bushnell Hart's issue was with the resultant miscegenation rather than immorality, as evidenced by his suggestion that an increase in numbers of white prostitutes might solve the problem.[18]

Control and limitation of black male and female sexuality was a significant concern in the late nineteenth and early twentieth centuries, as was the monitoring of their reproduction and breeding. This became significant in the discourse around slavery because of abolitionists' fears that emancipated slaves would breed in a disorderly manner and this would lead to the pollution of blood stocks. However, disorderly women were also feared in another context, and their lack of control was a threat to the strength of the white race and led directly to the white slavery discourse. As Magaly Rodriguez Garcia has shown, although in the 1870s there was a genuine humanitarian urge that founded the first anti-trafficking movements, much of the discourse was about moral purity. As traffickers were identified as the racial other, and many of the victims of trafficking as white, labelling prostitution as white slavery was a useful rhetorical device to mobilise both conservative and radical abolitionists behind the cause. In a period when women's work of any kind was often viewed with suspicion, anti-trafficking campaigners used the white slavery panic to call for women to be employed in morally safe and secure work.[19] Joel Quirk concurs and sees the white slavery panic as a direct antecedent to modern human trafficking campaigning

[16] Albert Bushnell Hart, *The Southern South* (New York, 1910), p. 45. [17] Ibid., p. 116.

[18] Ibid., p. 152.

[19] Magaly Rodriguez Garcia, 'The League of Nations and the Moral Recruitment of Women', in Ulbe Bosma, Elise van Nederveen Meerkerk & Adilya Sarkar, eds., *Mediating Labour: World Wide Labour Intermediation in the Nineteenth and Twentieth Centuries* (International Review of Social History, 2012), pp. 100, 126.

with all its ambiguities of motivation. Quirk suggests that the use of slavery, as a rhetorical device around which to discuss prostitution, shifted the focus onto young girls who had been coerced rather than the autonomous, consenting adult women who worked willingly in prostitution. The literature reflected a conservative moral position, underpinned by middle-class manners, but also allowed for voyeurism and titillation.[20] Therefore, the gendered literature about sexual slavery was popular and captivating to audiences because of its multivalent nature.

Thomas Leonard argued that, in the United States, this impulse for control and order was part of the conservative Progressive reform tradition, which used the theories of euthenics to conceptualise a woman's position in the world, thus explaining why such campaigners were so threatened by the notion of uncoerced prostitution, revealing the necessity of viewing it with a white slavery lens. Reformers argued that women's breeding hygiene must be protected for the future of the race, and this was linked to their wage-earning capabilities because women in the workplace were less able to protect their heredity. Socialist thinkers such as Florence Kelley, who worked alongside white slavery campaigner Jane Addams in Hull House in Chicago, argued that the welfare of the race rather than a woman's economic independence ought to come first. In 1909, in *Everybody's Magazine*, another female campaigner, Rheta Child Dorr, a suffragist and muckraking journalist, argued that the working woman was 'the white Chinaman of the industrial world. She wears a coiled up queue and wherever she goes she cheapens the worth of human labour'.[21] Women's value to a race feeling threatened by encroaching ethnic others was as breeders, and according to many at the turn of the twentieth century, this reproductive labour was not merely a private matter of concern to a woman and her husband, but rather something to be monitored in the new modern scientific era.[22] Thus arguments about whether sex work counted as 'slavery' only if the woman was coerced or if she were too young to properly consent, did not acknowledge that many readers imagined white slavery as a way to keep in order errant women moving too far outside the protection of a patriarchal society.

[20] Joel Quirk, *The Anti-Slavery Project from the Slave Trade to Human Trafficking* (University of Pennsylvania Press, 2011), pp. 218–20.

[21] Thomas C. Leonard, *Illiberal Reformers: Race, Eugenics and American Economics in the Progressive Era* (Princeton University Press, 2016), pp. 178, 176.

[22] Elbourne, 'Introduction' in Campbell & Elbourne eds., *Sex, Power and Slavery*, p. 21.

The racially determined failure of women to fulfil their duty as breeders linked to slavery discourse in another way, as a lack of available native labour in imperial sites, such as Hawaii, encouraged some commentators to appreciate the role played by imported labour. In his work surveying the different labour options in sugar and coffee plantations in Hawaii, William Fremont Blackman lauded the Chinese as a hard workers, although commented that when they were allowed to be free labourers as opposed to bonded ones, they were more productive. However, Fremont Blackman did not see the Chinese as a long-term labour solution. He dismissed the possibility of importing African Americans from the mainland because they were of more use where they were away from the competition from 'Asiatic Labour' and anyway, they were 'constituting a most difficult and threatening social problem in the southern United States', which ought not to be imported into Hawaii. But he did suggest that great success had been had with Italians as a migrant labour force, and that inevitably, in the future, it would be necessary to use white labour, provided it could be 'seasoned' so that work in the tropics was a possibility.[23] Fremont Blackman suggested that this question had been initially raised because of the declining numbers of native Hawaiians, a problem that he put down to 'sexual irregularities' such as promiscuity, including an early age of sexual activity which induced exhausted fertility in women. He also determined that the natives' frequent mixed-race relationships rarely bore children, an implicit argument against miscegenation.[24] This narrative of the lack of fecundity among less-developed races contradicts that used by some Social Darwinists who argued that without a change in behaviour it was the white race that would commit race suicide by not having enough children. But Fremont Blackman's tract does reiterate the widely held view that women were central to the health of the race, and if they were unable to bear enough healthy children then decline was imminent, and therefore labour would have to be sought by other means. Similar narratives around the question of lack of sustainability of the population and the inevitable decline that would result circulated about the Native American population living on the mainland.

[23] William Fremont Blackman, *The Making of Hawaii: a study in Social Evolution* (New York, 1906), pp. 203, 205.

[24] Ibid., pp. 213, 216.

WOMEN AS CAMPAIGNERS

The role of women, in systems defined as slavery for the purposes of control, and women's behaviour as a trigger for the enslavement of others, were the most significant ways in which women appeared in slavery and abolition narratives of this period, but their role as campaigners and activists was also frequently acknowledged. Authors often demonstrated that women's gender and life experience gave them a unique and special insight into the horrors of slavery and therefore significant power to campaign to oppose it. This in turn led to the emphasis on the first-hand accounts of women's experience of slavery in order to appeal directly to female readers. This development can be seen in the literature around the abolition of chattel slavery in the United States, with stories of women like Margaret Garner, the slave whose resistance led her to run away taking her children with her, and when it became clear that they would be recaptured, she killed her children rather than see them re-enslaved. The discourse around Garner's victimhood and resistance became a powerful part of the feminine abolitionist discourse of the nineteenth century.[25] As well as eyewitness accounts, one other woman's voice represented a significant part of pre-emancipation abolitionist discourses. The author of *Uncle Tom's Cabin*, Harriet Beecher Stowe, was the first international abolition celebrity whose fame exceeded even some of her male counterparts, such as William Lloyd Garrison, who respected the vital role that women played in the movement.[26]

The role of women as contributors to the campaign against slavery and for abolition had not always been respected in this way as, in 1840, at the outset of the World's Antislavery Convention, the position of the female delegates from the United States was contested. The British and Foreign Antislavery Society refused to acknowledge their right to contribute to political discussions taking place at that forum.[27] By the end of the nineteenth century, on both sides of the Atlantic, women's position in the political sphere around the question of slavery was no less contested, just as earlier in the century, their activism connected with suffragism, temperance and a broader campaign for women's rights. Middle-class women

[25] Paul Gilroy, *The Black Atlantic: Modernity and Double Consciousness* (Verso, 1993), p. 67.

[26] Simon Morgan, 'Political as Personal', in William Mulligan and Maurice Bric, eds., *A Global History of Anti-Slavery Politics in the Nineteenth Century* (Palgrave, 2013), p. 90.

[27] Maurice Bric, 'Debating Slavery and Empire', in ibid., p. 62.

took the lead in fundraising and boycotting activities, and although women from the working classes were involved in these campaigns, they were not treated as equals. Towards the end of the nineteenth century, for many women, abolitionism became a secondary cause compared to the feminist movement for equal rights and the vote.[28] However, through their work to expose the horrors of slavery, individual women were still lauded as voices of the oppressed, such as the photographer Alice Harris, who travelled with her husband John as a missionary and, together with him, published many works and gave many lectures showing the Congo Free State to be operating its rubber industry based on the coerced slave labour of thousands of natives. During the First World War, Alice Harris figured prominently in the advertising materials for their lecture tours in the United States, because of it being newsworthy that a woman should have undertaken such travels. The advertisements did not foreground her views on slavery, although that was the main reason for the Harris's undergoing their lecture tour, but rather highlighted the exotic adventures that she would recount: 'a woman's journey of 5,000 miles in West Central Africa', in which she 'makes her hearers familiar with the production of rubber, palm oil, cocoa and gum capal. She describes in a most interesting manner native customs such as fetish worship and cicatrizing'. The advert quietly acknowledged Alice's purpose, but proclaimed it uninteresting compared to her travel stories: 'Mrs Harris, whilst bent on social and labour studies had some more thrilling experiences'.[29]

Just as some male authors in the United States, writing about slavery, had a conservative agenda, women also engaged with the legacy of a slavery past in a nostalgic way. As men did, they felt that the post-Civil War South was a shadow of its former self and they celebrated and memorialised the former landscapes of slavery such as the plantations, and in doing so romanticised the slave past leaving open the opportunity of a return to it. John Michael Vlach has shown that many of the artists producing 'moonlight and magnolia' artistic representations of the southern landscape were women, who saw themselves as custodians of the memory of this southern heyday. Not all these women were even American-born, for example Fanny Palmer who produced light-hearted vignettes of slaves' lives was from

[28] Clare Midgley, *Women against Slavery: the British Campaigns 1780–1870* (Routledge, 1992), pp. 84, 196.

[29] 'Advert for lectures by Mrs Harris', item 87; MSS Brit Emp s19/D5/5, Bodleian Library, Oxford.

Leicester in England.[30] On the other hand, Alice Ravenel Huger Smith was a descendent of two of the most important planter families in South Carolina, the Ravenels and the Hugers, both of which could trace their lineage back to Huguenot migrants who arrived before the Revolutionary War. Alice Smith's art reflected her desire to honour her ancestors, something which she perceived as an obligation. Her depiction of slaves portrayed them as types, not individuals, whose lives were mostly defined by their work in the rice fields.[31] Although Smith's concerns were regionally specific, her work helped create an intellectual environment in which Americans viewed slavery abroad in the context of antebellum chattel slavery.

SLAVERY, GENDER AND RACE IN A GLOBAL CONTEXT

When Americans viewed enslavement overseas after the emancipation of the chattel slaves at home, they did so through the lens of their own race problems. This meant that, for many Americans, the ideal victim of slavery was one that could be categorised as 'white'. The definition of whiteness did not remain static, but for one group of enslaved women it served as an important mobiliser of sympathy for them while simultaneously rendering them sexually available and their stories titillating, without triggering incongruent and psychologically damaging fantasies about miscegenation in conservative Americans. Thus, in the United States during the 1870s, the female white slavery system in Circassia, in which light-skinned women were enslaved to become harem 'wives' to Turkish men, became a media sensation. The portrayal of this type of slavery foregrounded the sexual nature of the women's work, and alongside the similar orientalist paintings so popular in the era, eroticised the women's victimhood, rather than focusing on the long-term economic and political causes of their situation.

In his study of Victorian-era Ottoman slavery, Hakan Erdem has shown that contemporary understandings of Circassian slavery were simplistic and misleading. The mechanisms of enslavement were, in reality, complex. While some women were kidnapped into slavery by force, many were part of a formal tribute payment to the Ottomans, while still

[30] John Michael Vlach, *The Planter's Prospect: Privilege and Slavery in Plantation Paintings* (University of North Carolina Press, 2002), p. 122.

[31] Ibid., p. 154.

others were sold as children by their parents in a deliberate attempt to seek a better life in cases where the parents could not afford to keep the children at home. Self-enslavement was also frequently practised. Deliberate slave breeding was also undertaken in the Circassia region, although it was very rare elsewhere in the Ottoman Empire, and this led to the slave trade's eventual decline.[32] Circassian men were also enslaved, and often achieved positions, such as Bey and Pasha, of power in the empire, but it was the Circassian female slaves upon whom international focus fell. By the late nineteenth century, forced enslavement was in decline in the region and by the time of the Young Turks' rule, Circassian slavery was almost entirely voluntary.[33]

The foregrounding of the white slavery of Circassian women suggests the deployment of the argument that this form of enslavement was more heinous because it involved the subjugation of whites by those of other races, and so inverted the natural hierarchy. Some commentators felt that it was completely wrong for white people to be enslaved at all. For example, the Scottish bishop, Reverend Michael Russell, when touring Egypt, described Ethiopian women for sale in Cairo in erotic terms, but was repulsed by the sight of Caucasian female slaves at the same market.[34] A newspaper article, first published in 1894 in New York and then syndicated by many other regional papers, explored the enslavement of both white and black women in Cairo. The trade was portrayed as secretive, and against the law, but occurring with the full knowledge of the European elites who saw Cairo as their sunshine playground. When describing the black enslaved women, the author of the article used eroticised terms, referring to them as 'black beauties' or 'ebony-skinned'. The article bravely approached the subject of gender politics more broadly, asking 'how is it possible for a people [i.e. the Egyptians] which considers women naturally a slave to believe that it is wrong to traffic in slave girls?' It concluded by pessimistically announcing that 'it will be a century before complete reform can be accomplished'.[35] On the other hand, other commentators such as Mark Twain made a joke out of

32 Y. Hakan Erdem, *Slavery in the Ottoman Empire and Its Demise 1800–1909* (Macmillan, 1996), pp. 46–9, 53.

33 Ibid., pp. 106, 151.

34 Ahmed Elbashir, *The United States, Slavery and the Slave Trade in the Nile Valley* (University Press of America, 1983), p. 29.

35 *The Morning News*. (Savannah, Ga.), 22 Sept. 1894. *Chronicling America: Historic American Newspapers*. Lib. of Congress. https://chroniclingamerica.loc.gov/lccn/sn86063034/1894-09-22/ed-1/seq-5/.

the phenomenon in a letter from Constantinople in 1867 to his wife, Jane Clemens. He commented how his roommate had bought so many souvenirs that 'that fellow will buy a Circassian slave next'.[36] A decade later, a *New York Times* article, an early example of muckraking journalism, talked about the lack of protection afforded to the beautiful white women of Georgia and Circassia who were enslaved in the Ottoman empire.[37] This was then taken up by the American media. Some newspaper accounts even turned the story of Circassian slavery into a melodrama, such as the account of 'The Sad Story of the Harem', which appeared in *The Wellington Enterprise* of 1880. It told the story of the author's female friend, a governess to a child fathered by Mahmoud Pacha, whose mother was a Circassian slave woman. Her enslavement is described in the most benign, tragic and romantic terms: 'he bought a very interesting and youthful Circassian slave; after a year of domestic happiness, finding her of a loving and teachable character, he determined to marry her'. After giving birth to his child, the slave's health began to decline, leading to her wasting away. Simultaneously the Pacha's father insisted he take a second wife, and only at that point was the 'Circassian's degradation complete'. She died alone but visited at times by her still-loving but estranged husband.[38] Such stories had the effect of distancing the American reader from the true horrors of global sexual slavery, and blurring the line between fiction and reality.

Apart from the panic about white people being enslaved in the Ottoman Empire, the response by British and American commentators to the female sexual coercion in harems was ambivalent. Despite the gendered nature of women as ideal victims, and the stereotyping of the so-called 'lustful Turk' as the ideal sinful perpetrator, for various cultural and political reasons sexual slavery in the Ottoman empire was often depicted as benign. On the one hand, Joel Quirk argues, antislavery propaganda was a useful tool in the imperialist's arsenal in foregrounding a common European political heritage that excluded 'others' such as the Turk from international law. On the other hand, systems of domestic and sexual work undertaken by female slaves were portrayed as benign, and the

[36] Mark Twain, 'To Mrs Jane Clemens and family, Constantinople, 1 Sept. 1867', Mark Twain's Letters, vol 2, ed. Albert Bigelow Paine: http://www.gutenberg.org/files/3194/3194-h/3194-h.htm.

[37] Elbashir, *The United States, Slavery and the Slave Trade*, p. 48.

[38] *The Wellington Enterprise*. (Wellington, Ohio), 13 May 1880. *Chronicling America: Historic American Newspapers*. Lib. of Congress. https://chroniclingamerica.loc.gov/lccn/sn84028271/1880–05-13/ed-1/seq-1/.

security and safety of the enslaved in their family or kinship groups was emphasised.[39] Despite being a vociferous antislavery campaigner, Henry Nevinson explained to his readers that in West and Central Africa domestic slavery was very different to the long-distance slave trade, and implied that it was less serious because of the ability of former slaves, both male and female, to achieve very high status within the system.[40] Conceptually, in Ottoman regions and in East Africa, William Clarence-Smith distinguishes female slaves, along with eunuchs, as 'luxury slaves' who were fundamental to the economics of the slave trade as a whole. He states that it is impossible to divorce race from gender in understanding the status these people had, and that the elite who could afford the most expensive slaves bought white slave concubines, whereas the middling sort could emulate such luxury, but by purchasing cheaper black African concubines.[41] Beverley Mack concurs, explaining that Hausa women from present day northern Nigeria, who were trafficked as sex slaves to the North African slave markets in Tripoli and Benghazi, achieved large sums for their sellers.[42]

Is the assumption that the lives of these women were akin to slavery correct? Some scholars argue that while there is evidence of their inferior bonded status, that they ought not be considered slaves in the same way that agricultural or industrial workers might be enslaved. Paul Lovejoy and Jan Hogendorn suggest that in the case of late nineteenth-century northern Nigeria, when the British were trying to deal with the disorder caused by large numbers of runaway slaves, that concubines were recognised as legally enslaved, but treated as a separate category entirely. The colonial state reinforced the notion of the hegemony of their masters over the female slaves, but not because they were slaves, but rather because they were women.[43] Elsewhere, the legal and cultural position of concubines was a liminal one, part slave, part woman, but totally bonded. Abdul Sheriff-Suria argues that because of a shortage of 'free' women and prostitutes in nineteenth-century Zanzibar, concubinage was

[39] Quirk, *The Anti-Slavery Project*, pp. 58, 95, 98.

[40] Henry Nevinson, *A Modern Slavery* (London and New York, 1906), p. 14.

[41] William Clarence-Smith, 'Overview' in William Clarence-Smith ed., *The Economies of the Indian Ocean Slave Trade in the Nineteenth Century* (Frank Cass, 1989), p. 6.

[42] Beverley Mack, 'Women and Slavery in Nineteenth Century Hausaland', in Elizabeth Savage, ed., *The Human Commodity: Perspectives on the Trans-Saharan Slave Trade* (Frank Cass, 1992), p. 101.

[43] Paul Lovejoy and Jan Hogendorn, *Slow Death for Slavery: the Course of Abolition in Northern Nigeria 1897–1936* (Cambridge University Press, 1993), p. 116.

common, and that residents of Zanzibar from India and Europe, as well as locals, all purchased slave wives for sexual services.[44] In a society that tolerated polygamy, such slave wives were, in practice, controlled by female mistresses, the so-called free wives of the master, but slave wives did have an official status within the household and their marriage was officially recognised. The children of free and slave wives also slotted into a similar hierarchy in the household.[45] In some cases, elite women owned slaves of their own, and while usually unable to buy them on the open market, were often given them as part of their dowry. Then wife and slaves would in their entirety be incorporated into the household and responsibility of her new husband.[46]

In this system, women were valued and offered security and protection and, for them, freedom was not necessarily something to be desired but, rather, epitomised isolation and vulnerability. For example, in Egypt, manumitted female slaves were sometimes left without community and support networks and they sought security in concubinage and sexual slavery.[47] Underpinning the harem system were assumptions about status and dynasty building. Despite what British and American commentators wished to assert, constructing a harem was less about sexual pleasure and more about a desire to father sons and build a family and a dynasty. In this system of slavery, the female slaves, although coerced, were incorporated into the family group.[48] Some commentators used this fact to claim that this form of slavery was benign, but in the antebellum period exactly the same arguments were made by pro-slavery apologists, saying that the paternalism of the master seeing his slaves as part of his family ameliorated the system.

As well as functioning as a way of recruiting more wives with a view to dynasty building, concubinage was also a way for poorer men to acquire more subordinates in their households. In the nineteenth century, as costs of dowries rose in Egypt, concubinage became more popular because it was cheaper for a man to purchase and keep a slave wife than a free one.

[44] Abdul Sheriff-Suria, 'Concubine or Secondary Slave Wife? Zanzibar in the Nineteenth Century', in Campbell & Elbourne eds., *Sex, Power and Slavery*, pp. 101–2.

[45] Ibid., p. 118.

[46] Mack, 'Women and Slavery in Nineteenth Century Hausaland', p. 94.

[47] Liat Kozma, 'Manumitted Female Slaves in Khedival Egypt', in Terence Walz and Kenneth Cuno, eds., *Race and Slavery in the Middle East* (American University in Cairo Press, 2010), p. 208.

[48] Martin Klein, 'Sexuality and Slavery in the Western Sudan', in Campbell & Elbourne eds., *Sex, Power and Slavery*, p. 66.

Also, as it was the master's duty to arrange marriages for all his household, buying slave wives for his offspring seemed an economically prudent choice. Even the male slaves within his household were provided with wives in polygamous contexts.[49]

However, in some parts of the East African and Indian Ocean slave system, women were used purely as sex slaves with little gain to them in status and security. Writing about Morocco, Mohammed Ennaji argues that such practices persisted both in urban elite society and in rural areas, where there was a strong distinction between the free wife who was 'used' for breeding and the concubine used for sexual pleasure.[50] Despite this distinction, Ennaji suggests that materially, sex slaves might be rewarded with luxury items because their appearance enhanced the master's status and his derivation of pleasure. So, the concubine might be better dressed than the wife.[51] Women caught up in this system might be the racial or ethnic other or may be Moroccan. Seemingly little racial prejudice existed determining a different treatment for slave women of different races. However, a lack of security permeated a slave wife's life in Morocco, especially in rural regions where a man who got into financial difficulty could sell his wife to someone else.[52]

Many of these complexities passed contemporary British and American commentators by, and through a process of othering the slave owner, they rendered women in harems, whether concubines or slave wives as unfree victims, especially if they were lighter skinned. This was part of the imperialist antislavery rhetoric emerging first from the British context, and then, in the period after emancipation, imitated by American authors. As Westerners struggled to understand the challenging and diverse Indian Ocean slave system, they fell into easy comparisons with the Transatlantic slave trade and undertook easy stereotyping through the orientalist fantasy of the so-called 'Lustful Turk'.[53] However, if this was designed to render for the British and American readership a more manageable and abolishable slavery, this tactic mostly failed because influential commentators on the ground, such as the third Lord Vivian, British

[49] Kenneth Cuno, 'African Slaves in Rural Egypt', in Walz and Cuno eds., *Race and Slavery in the Middle East*, pp. 93, 88.

[50] Mohammed Ennaji, *Serving the Master: Slavery and Society in Nineteenth Century Morocco*, translated Seth Graebner (Macmillan, 1998), p. 33.

[51] Ibid., p. 16. [52] Ibid., p. 83.

[53] T. G. Otte, 'Diplomacy and Suppression of the Slave Trade in the East', in Keith Hamilton & Patrick Salmon, eds., *Slavery, Diplomacy and Empire* (Sussex Academic Press, 2009), pp. 101–2.

plenipotentiary at the Brussels conference of 1889–90, adapted their rhetoric instead to acknowledge the impossibility of abolition of domestic slavery and therefore its benignity.[54]

The hypocrisy of the imperial powers must also be acknowledged when considering the treatment of female enslaved around the globe. While simultaneously attacking the practices of ethnic others such as the Ottoman elites for maintaining harems and sexual slaves, British and Americans were themselves participating in female enslavement. Imperial control has been maintained across time and place through aggression aimed at women, with the dual purpose of taking sexual and reproductive advantage, but also through instilling fear and obedience in men who fear that women from their kinship groups may be abused in this way. Female slaves in the late nineteenth century were used thus, simultaneously with the rhetoric about the antislavery imperial mission coming to a head.

Some colonial systems of control were so oppressive that all of those living within them were in some senses denied their freedom and therefore, as Joost Coté argues, concubinage, common in the late nineteenth century Javan context, in all its complex forms, must be seen in this light. Most discussions of forced labour by the Dutch considered the status of the unfree male worker, but as Coté shows, concubinage underpinned the whole colonial system. Garrison concubinage was rife and resulted in offspring whose status was unclear and threatening to the racial control.[55] In Central Africa, sexual abuse and forced marriage of women by white Europeans was rife, as slave women were bought by white officers to be turned into wives for their men, in much the same way as an Ottoman master might provide wives for his dependents.[56] This might be justifiable by asserting that buying slave women gave them some sort of freedom and prevented them falling into a much worse fate. Under the racism and misogyny of the time, an African woman's highest achievement in life might be marrying a white man. But there is no doubt that coercion and force took place and that women were not autonomous and able to control their own sexual and reproductive labour, but rather were beholden to another, different master.

[54] Ibid., p. 110.

[55] Joost Coté, 'Slaves, Coolies and Garrison Whores in Colonial Discourse of Unfreedom in the Dutch East Indies', in Campbell and Elbourne eds., *Sex, Power and Slavery*, pp. 561, 569.

[56] William J. Samorin, *The Black Man's Burden: African Colonial Labor on the Congo and Ubangi Rivers 1880–1900* (Westview Press, 1989), p. 216.

Not all slave women in Central Africa were bought for sexual or reproductive work. Others were used as army auxiliaries forced into servile and menial work, which might also include sexual slavery. Women's role was to support the soldiers in any way possible, for example in the gathering and preparation of food and the laundering of clothes. But they might also be used for heavier labouring tasks because they were cheaper labour than African men, requiring less provision, or fewer wages, if any were paid. Often women undertook work in the construction and maintenance industries.[57] The burgeoning rubber industry in the Congo Free State was run on coercion and abuse towards both the native men and women. Unlike much plantation work, such as cotton, rice or sugar, rubber workers could not be kept together in a single field under surveillance, but rather had to range over a wide area to gather the rubber sap. This meant that the Belgian soldiers and their African allies found it difficult to monitor the male rubber workers and ensure that they were working as hard as possible. Threat of extreme violence worked in many cases, but in others, workers were simply able to flee. Therefore, the kidnap of women from the tribal villages served an important purpose to encourage the native men to produce the required amount of rubber. To refuse to do so, or to miss targets meant the death of a wife, mother or sister.[58] When it was exposed by authors such as George Washington Williams and E. D. Morel, such psychological trauma suffered by both men and women in this system naturally caused worldwide outrage. Morel highlighted that many of the abuses were perpetrated by African troops working for the Belgians, 'cannibal troops' as he called them, but ironically pointed out that they too had been forcibly conscripted.[59]

As well as including first-hand testimony from European and American missionaries, Morel used the tried and tested abolitionist method of reproducing eyewitness accounts from the women themselves, to emotionally persuade his readers of the true horrors that were being perpetrated in the Congo Free State. He published the testimony of an unnamed African girl who had managed to escape to the English region and there shared her story in which women and girls were kidnapped as a ransom as part of the rubber industry. She described how 'we were fastened together

[57] Ibid., pp. 214, 217.

[58] Adam Hochschild, *King Leopold's Ghost: A Story of Greed, Terror and Heroism in Colonial Africa* (Macmillan, 1999), p. 160.

[59] Edmund Morel, *The Congo Slave State: a Protest against the New African Slavery* (Liverpool, 1903), p. 18.

by a rope round our necks', for British and American readers the symbolism of which would have recalled the capture of slaves for the transatlantic slave system.[60] Although still mediated through the male authorial voice, works presenting the stories of enslaved women were rare examples of the stories of the habitually silenced being shared in this period. These stories were deployed for the same reasons that female slaves in the eighteenth and early nineteenth centuries became such important parts of the movement for the abolition of the slave trade and slavery, because to white audiences they were often less problematic as victims than males of other races and also because female readers were particularly sensitive to these accounts.

An example of a late-nineteenth-century author to use this technique to great effect was F. W. Chesson. Chesson was a prominent British anti-slavery activist, but one who had, during the 1850s, been influenced in his methods by his meeting in England with Harriet Jacobs, the abolitionist campaigner and former victim of the antebellum chattel slave system. He keenly perceived the importance of transatlantic and even global networks of abolitionism and felt that women's voices played an important part in building those connections. In 1860, Chesson's main focus was alerting a wide readership to the victims of Boer enslavement in the Transvaal and he told the stories of three native women to illustrate this. The first was Rachel, whose story explored the physical violence she received at the hands of one master, before being sold on to a man who wanted to use her as a slave wife. 'When we are bartered or sold one to another we are not told of it', she explained, illustrating the powerlessness of her position, before proceeding to describe the false promises that kept her enslaved. 'We are told that when we have served our time we will get paid for our work but we never do'.[61] Chesson, like many abolitionists before him, illustrated the horrors of the system by presenting the stories of younger victims and their poignant separation from their families, such as Adela who was sold aged 14 for thirty pounds, and Sophia who keenly recalled being taken from her mother's home.[62] By naming these women and girls, Chesson has given them an identity, and an agency, allowing them to share their own particular stories rather than being an anonymous mass of female slaves. Although globally they form a significant part of the story of

[60] Ibid., p. 53.

[61] F. W. Chesson, *The Dutch Boers and Slavery in the Transvaal Republic* (London, 1869), p. 23.

[62] Ibid., pp. 24–5.

women's resistance to enslavement, not all antislavery campaigners used first-hand accounts, and interestingly, Kathleen Simon did not do so, preferring to rely on a catalogue recording instances of slavery and of abolition activity.

SLAVERY, GENDER AND RACE IN THE UNITED STATES

Another context, at the turn of the twentieth century, in which women were occasionally allowed to voice their own stories was in the white slavery panic, but, as in the case of Chesson's narrative, these accounts were problematic and multi-faceted. While giving victims of sex trafficking agency of sorts, the narratives also provided opportunities for the titillation of male readers and encouragement of greater control. These challenging depictions of sex trafficking are illuminated by addressing the problem of definitions. Naming something as 'white slavery' meant that a powerful rhetorical act was undertaken by the author, reflecting either conservative or radical antislavery motives. The term 'white slavery' itself was used widely in the period to refer both to coerced victims of sex trafficking, and also to prostitutes who had entered the trade voluntarily and who certainly did not see themselves as enslaved. As with twenty-first century sex work, the mutable boundary of coercion and agency is crucial in interpreting the experiences of victim and perpetrator. However, in many ways, the use of the term 'white slavery' circumvented such complexities and rendered all those caught up in sex work as victims who needed to be rescued.

Taking the two words of the term separately helps us better understand the motives of those who deployed it. Calling sex work 'white slavery' denoted that the victims of this type of enslavement were of a particular race and, like Circassian slaves in the Ottoman Empire, were especially important because of their whiteness. They benefited from its association with innocence and virtue as well as notions of racial superiority. The term was used in this way in many hundreds of articles in *The Day Book*, the Chicago publication most associated with exposing and exacerbating the white slavery panic. A typical article suggested that 'Thousands of White Slaves Sought for Traffic in 1917', arguing that 'New York alone will want 1200 slaves'.[63] The term implicitly suggests that non-white women

[63] *The Day Book*. (Chicago, Ill.), 24 Aug. 1916. *Chronicling America: Historic American Newspapers*. Lib. of Congress. https://chroniclingamerica.loc.gov/lccn/sn83045487/1916-08-24/ed-1/seq-14/.

were not victims of this type of enslavement. It cannot be denied that some non-white women were prostitutes and, therefore, the term 'white slavery' manifests an argument that their sex work is acceptable because of their already morally degraded state, in a sense arguing that it matters less when non-white women fall victim to sexual slavery. Jane Addams was a rare author who challenged this view by drawing a direct link between prostitution of black women and the antebellum system of chattel slavery. She writes, 'the negroes themselves believe that the basic cause for the high percentage of coloured prostitutes is the recent enslavement of their race with its attendant unstable marriage and parental status, and point to thousands of slave sales that but two generations ago disrupted the negroes' attempts at family life'.[64] But few commentators desired to explore non-white victims, for fear of disrupting the rhetorically powerful trope which relied on the whiteness of its victims.

If the procurer or perpetrator was not white, the perceived vulnerability of white victims, as in Circassia, was more serious in white slavery the world over. In the United States, Jack Johnson the black sports star was convicted of white slavery under the Mann Act of 1910 because of conservative hostility towards his consensual relationships with white women. This was not solely a phenomenon of the United States, Britain and Europe. A book published in 1909 entitled the *White Slave Market* depicted predatory Asians buying white girls in Singapore. Despite protestations from some of the most vocal campaigners, such as Clifford Roe and Jane Addams, that white girls were not the only victims of sex trafficking and therefore the term 'white slavery' was a misnomer, its use persisted.[65] This is partly because, as Brian Donovan has argued, at the turn of the twentieth century the construction of the native-born white woman or girl as the ideal victim of slavery helped reconstruct the racial category of 'white', welcoming new ethnic groups in, such as Russians, Poles, Italians and Hungarians, while at the same time defining the boundaries of whiteness more rigidly through Social Darwinist anti-miscegenation ideas about blood purity.[66] At a time when the conservative white population of the United States was

[64] Jane Addams, *A New Conscience and an Ancient Evil* (Macmillan, New York, 1912), p. 119.

[65] Margit Stange, *Personal Property: Wives, White Slaves and the Market in Women* (Johns Hopkins University Press, 1998), p. 94.

[66] Brian Donovan, *White Slave Crusades: Race, Gender and Anti-Vice Activism 1887–1917* (University of Illinois Press, 2006), p. 5.

FIGURE 6 '*Uncle Tom's Cabin* – As it will be played if Johnson wins', front cover illustration in *Puck*, by Louis Glackens, 1910. Library of Congress.

feeling threatened by social change, urbanisation and changing racial hierarchies, such community-reinforcing moral panics served an important cultural purpose.

The second word in the term 'white slavery' also deliberately spoke both to the radical and conservative white communities. To more radical campaigners the term awakened the need for a new abolition, bringing to mind the pre–Civil War activism and calling for an almost nostalgic return to those glory days. But for conservative white Americans using the term 'slavery' in this context allowed for the term to be reclaimed and redefined. No longer was 'slavery' something that spoke only about black victimhood or about the perpetrating of abuses by white Americans. Rather this was something that was reconstructed into a horror that now attacked the white community at its most vulnerable heart (its women and girls). Often that attack was undertaken by a racial other, thus reinforcing the ideas of racial hierarchy and superiority. The author for whom the term 'white slavery' had most resonance was Jane Addams. Addams was a social worker, feminist and peace activist who worked in the slums of Chicago with women and girls of all races and ethnic backgrounds. She helped found the Hull House Centre, which undertook both community work and research. But in trying to inspire her readers to match her activism, she looked back to the golden age before the Civil War, not the golden age of slavery but the golden age of abolitionism. Writing in 1912, at the height of the flourishing of the Lost Cause myth of the South, she wrote of the heroic generations that had gone before, but they were not the plantation owners – the flower of southern chivalry – but rather those that 'uprooted the enormous upas of slavery'.[67] She referred to prostitution as 'the twin of slavery as old and outrageous as slavery itself and even more persistent'.[68] She advocated an imitation of abolitionist tools, the use of first-hand narratives to educate the general public; and she also wanted to see a new underground railroad which might 'cherish and educate individual slaves'.[69]

For Addams and other campaigners, the question of coercion was a crucial one in their activism on white slavery. The presence of coercion could make the difference between slavery and prostitution, while for others all sex work came under the white slavery umbrella. For Addams, in some ways, the societal problem was not the coercion of women and girls into prostitution but rather their moral enslavement in the modern urban environment through having new choices. Addams wrote, 'we all know that the American girl has grown up in the belief that the world is hers from which to choose ... her interest and ambition almost invariably become thoroughly worldly ... she obtains an exaggerated idea of the

[67] Addams, *A New Conscience and an Ancient Evil*, p. 3. [68] Ibid., p. 4. [69] Ibid., p. 5.

luxury of the illicit life all around her'.[70] However, Addams denied that this meant that the women themselves were to blame for their predicament, an assumption often made, she said, by the courts. Instead she blamed extreme poverty, mental distress or abuse and coercion (often by men already known to the victim) for the enslaved woman's plight.[71]

Theodore Bingham, the former Commissioner of Police of Greater New York and vigorous white slavery campaigner was also concerned with the question of coercion, but from a more paternalistic viewpoint, arguing that it was the duty of everyone to protect, secure and defend vulnerable young girls from organised criminal networks so they did not become victim to white slavery. He argued that, unlike the stereotypical victim who was a naïve country girl, 95 per cent of victims were foreigners newly arrived with little spoken English, who were easily persuaded to submit to procurers.[72] Bingham also stated that coercion was used to keep the girls continuously trapped in sexual slavery; he wrote, about a case in Chicago, that 'women were kept veritable prisoners'.[73] Clifford Roe agreed that coercion and force were used regularly by female procurers as well as male. He called the traps used by 'lady panders' more horrific than those found 'in worst annals of Turkish misrule'.[74] But for Roe, the cage that kept white slaves trapped was the sense of moral disgrace and the rejection by society that followed. Because of society's expectations and the ostracisation of any woman who transgressed sexual norms, Roe argued that prostitutes considered themselves slaves, whether they were forced into their situation or not, because they could never be allowed to reinvent themselves in a new life.[75]

Commentators differed in their suggestions for solutions, but most of these hinged on a change in the behaviour of women and girls, or in the oversight of their protectors, fathers and brothers, rather than an exposure of the predators who had enslaved them. White slavery was seen as especially threatening at that moment in American history where both conservative and radical authors were grappling with the meaning of modernity and its affect on American society and culture, specifically on economic and personal relations between the genders and family

[70] Ibid., p. 67. [71] Ibid., p. 109.

[72] Theodore Bingham, *The Girl That Disappears: the Real Facts about the White Slave Traffic* (Boston, 1911), p. 16.

[73] Ibid., p. 33.

[74] Clifford Roe, *The Great War on White Slavery or Fighting for the Protection of Our Girls* (New York, 1911), p. 106.

[75] Ibid., p. 32.

structures. The city became especially important as the main locus of this threat and, for authors engaged in alerting the public about the white slavery panic, the city became emblematic of everything that was degenerate within American society. During this period, the desire for control, reform and order, partly framed by the rise in influence of eugenics theory but also triggered by the fast pace of change in a rapidly industrialising world, led commentators to depict cities as environments that threatened women through their lure of luxury and intoxication. At this time, cities also had closer links with recent immigrant groups as sites of 'ghettoes' for the poorer populations from Italy and Ireland and of Jews from Eastern Europe, all of whom fitted the bill as the stereotypical foreign procurer. The cities' sinfulness was juxtaposed with the rural hinterland from where the ideal victim of white slavery often came, and where such luxury and intoxication were, according to white slavery mythmaking, in short supply.

Sinfulness associated with sex and drinking was not the only perceived threat from the urban monster. In the town and the city single women could easily find employment and therefore have income to spare and this was seen as even more worrying and, through this threat to the patriarchy, women voluntarily working in diverse roles were caught up in white slavery discourse as a problem, as potential victims.[76] The Dillingham report on white slavery listed urban sites haunted by procurers, claiming that a woman could be safe in very few places. Significantly, 'employment agencies' were the first places listed, followed by 'immigrant homes, moving picture shows, dance halls, sometimes waiting rooms in large department stores, railroad stations, manicuring and hairdressing establishments'.[77] As Jane Addams wrote, a girl or woman may be safe at home or in the factory, but in very few places between.[78] However, some contemporary commentators challenged the ubiquitous urban versus rural divide, and stated that American-born country girls could be lured into what he called 'difficulty' (i.e., a sexually compromised position) in urban environments, but that these individuals were not the ones who were destined for white slavery. He wrote that 'a girl used to the ways of the United States will not submit for long'.[79] This statement resonated

[76] Donovan, *White Slave Crusades*, p. 22.

[77] *Importing Women for Immoral Purposes 1909. Report from US immigration Commission 1907–1910* (Washington, Government Printing Office, 1909), p. 16.

[78] Addams, *A New Conscience and an Ancient Evil*, p. 29.

[79] Bingham, *The Girl That Disappears*, p. 17.

not only with the urban versus rural divide, but also suggested that immigrant girls (especially the ethnic other) were the most vulnerable to white slavery.

Complicating the picture were enslaved Chinese women and girls. By some commentators they were considered entirely outside the white slavery panic, yet for others their presence and the problems they were supposed to cause had to be tackled simultaneously. Scholars, too, have tended to see the plight of Chinese female migrants to the United States alongside that of their male counterparts, rather than in the same context as female sex slaves. However, there is a consensus that many Chinese women, while not all, were forced to migrate and were indeed used as sex slaves. As Arnold Meagher has written, this was true of Chinese migrations throughout the Atlantic region, and not just to the United States. He has shown that the Chinese government often tried to prevent the migration of women and girls by associating emigration with dishonour, and this may be the origin of the notion that all Chinese women who did migrate were immoral. In many cases women were deliberately imported for prostitution or as second wives and, according to Meagher, for these roles they were bought and sold like slaves.[80]

Regarding the United States case, Najia Aarim-Heriot, who often exposed the negative portrayal of the Chinese as slaves, actually concurred when it came to women, stating that Chinese women were imported as captives for an organised trade, and not as free workers earning wages.[81] Contemporary accounts support this assertion, with the Reverend Otis Gibson's 1877 account of the *Chinese in America* arguing that 'of the six thousand Chinese women in America, more than nine-tenths are of that unfortunate class that have been sold into hopeless bondage worse than death', that is, into sexual slavery. He also explained the mechanism by which this enslavement occurred. These vulnerable women were bought in China and shipped to America, lured by the promises of rich husbands, convinced of the morally secure position into which they were entering by plausible female Chinese 'procuresses'.[82] Gibson suggested that not all girls entered into formal prostitution, and that some found themselves as concubines, a fate which the pragmatic Gibson, surprisingly given his

80 Arnold Meagher, *The Coolie Trade: Traffic in Chinese Laborers to Latin America 1847–1874* (X Libris, 2008), pp. 64, 84.

81 Najia Aarim-Heriot, *Chinese Immigrants, African Americans and Racial Anxiety in the United States 1848–82* (University of Illinois Press, 2003), p. 159.

82 Rev. O Gibson, *The Chinese in America* (Cincinnati, 1877), pp. 134–5.

religious role, acknowledged as an improvement on 'general and promiscuous intercourse'. However, in the worst cases, the girls and women entered into coercive and abusive situations of forced prostitution, which he likened to the African chattel slavery of the past: 'We have heard dark hints of a room called the Queen's Room where the girls were critically examined after the fashion of African slave dealers many years ago'.[83]

Otis Gibson, unlike many of his contemporaries, wrote about Chinese women as victims of structures of enslavement, rather than portraying them as conniving in their own downfall. He even suggested that prior to arriving in the United States they were innocent and that their corruption happened because of the reluctance of the city officials to crack down on prostitution.[84] But for many in this period, fears over the gender and sexuality of the ethnic other combined to make a potent mix and resulted in the inability of many Americans to empathise with victims from other races. Just as from the chattel slavery period onwards African American women were stereotyped as jezebels, Chinese women were also depicted as doubly other because of their race and sexuality. They were deemed to be deliberately polluting, spreading disease via their sexual promiscuity and while this was thought less of a problem when their clientele was drawn from their own race, it was taken much more seriously when they began to attract white men to their brothels.[85] However, Otis Gibson again jumped in to scotch these rumours. He acknowledged that many people believe that Chinese courtesans corrupt white men and boys, but he stated that, on the contrary, they first have had 'a few lessons in sinful pleasure in these Christian saloons, these ante-rooms of hell'.[86]

Gibson's clear thinking in this regard was not echoed by many of his contemporaries. Many authors got mired in the rhetoric of the evils of prostitution, which they disagreed with from a moral or religious standpoint and thereby associated with chattel slavery. But they still wanted to assert the culpability of the victims in their own downfall and the corruption of others. In 1880, G. B. Densmore, writing about the Chinese community in San Francisco, argued that prostitutes there were 'virtually slaves' and 'their confinement was more by fear than anything else'. He gave an account of a twelve-year-old Chinese girl brought to the United

[83] Ibid., p. 138. [84] Ibid., p. 157.

[85] Erika Lee, *At America's Gates: Chinese Immigration during the Exclusion Era* (University of North Carolina Press, 2003), p. 26.

[86] Gibson, *The Chinese in America*, p. 357.

States for the sole purpose of sexual slavery. But only a few pages later he confidently asserted that some of the Chinese prostitutes that he had met enticed young boys of twelve into their dens.[87] This approach was echoed in many newspaper reports, which acknowledged Chinese prostitutes as slaves, but argued that 'they train children to follow their vile calling … and the prostitutes are spreading dreadful diseases even among mere boys'.[88]

Some authors used the existence of Chinese forced prostitution as a convenient justification to rhetorically attack the entire Chinese immigrant community. A classic racist trope of othering an entire community through criticising the inability of the men to fulfil their proper paternalistic role and to protect their women was deployed here. Reference to innate racial characteristics that influence the relationships between men and women was common. But even in cases such as Russell Conwell's criticism of the Chinese and their supposed disregard for female virtue shown by their defective gender relations and the way that they 'treat their women as slaves' were tempered by his acknowledgement of other reasons for prostitution among the Chinese community. He suggested that 'the sale of girls for doubtful purposes and the killing of female infants' was evidence of the inherent corruption and greed within Chinese culture but said that evidence of these practices was seen 'only where abject poverty is concerned'.[89] The Chinese culture of arranged marriage was portrayed by Conwell as being like slavery because it turned women into 'saleable things'. The willingness of families to sell their children to become concubines or to enter into forced marriage was criticised as epitomising the breakdown of familial bonds, and also as akin to slavery because the girls were kept in harem-like conditions on being sold: 'in their closest confinement'.[90] While Conwell did admit that economic want was often a reason for the sale of a daughter into sexual slavery or forced marriage, he still detested the practice. Unlike for many commentators who depicted this intra-familial system as a mild form of slavery, such practices were worse than if the victims of enslavement had been of another conquered

[87] G. B. Densmore, *The Chinese in California: A Description of Chinese Life in San Francisco* (San Francisco, 1880), pp. 77–85.

[88] *Memphis Daily Appeal*. (Memphis, Tenn.), 29 July 1885. *Chronicling America: Historic American Newspapers*. Lib. of Congress. https://chroniclingamerica.loc.gov/lccn/sn83045160/1885-07-29/ed-1/seq-2/.

[89] Russell Conwell, *Why the Chinese Emigrate and the Means They Adopt for the Purpose of Reaching America* (Boston, 1871), pp. 54, 71.

[90] Ibid., pp. 227, 229.

tribe or race. He wrote, 'it would seem to me to be far more mild if the persons bargained away for such labour or for such vile uses were the people of an inferior or conquered race instead of being their own legitimate sons and daughters'.[91]

The concern about white slavery, prostitution, and more broadly, female entrapment, thus came from a wide range of political perspectives. The campaigns and commentators cannot easily be categorised as emerging from the right or the left, or their ideas from racially tolerant or intolerant perspectives. Like the progressive movement, of which this activism was a key part, it had global ramifications because of the simultaneity of white slavery panics in Britain, Europe and the Americas, but also was so successful as a concept because of its wide political umbrella allowing those from a range of positions to assert their civic activism without compromising their political and psychological beliefs. White slavery as a motif was used by organisations as diverse as the Ku Klux Klan, the Women's Christian Temperance Union and on the political left by the Immigrant Protective League.[92] More radical commentators, such as Theodore Bingham, used the white slavery panic to highlight corruption and misguided government policy. He showed how the Tammany Hall machine in New York had been accused of ignoring the question and how the commission set up to investigate organised white slavery gangs had overlooked obvious evidence, had connived with corrupt officials and had only succeeded in driving the sex trafficking rings underground.[93] Another author with a more radical agenda, Jane Addams was unafraid to highlight the corruption at every level of political decision-making and law enforcement around this issue. She claimed that the police regularly turned a blind eye to forced prostitution when local politicians owned the saloons where assignations took place, telling the story of a morally upstanding young police officer who was transferred because he happened to arrest a theatre owner who was 'under political protection'. She wrote 'the young officer had naively undertaken to serve the public without waiting for his instructions from his political bosses'.[94]

Others investigating white slavery had more conservative agendas, hoping to use the public fear of its spread to trigger a more restricted immigration policy. Typical of this was the report produced as part of the Dillingham Commission's work on immigration. Bingham saw the

[91] Ibid., p. 229. [92] Donovan, *White Slave Crusades*, p. 2.
[93] Bingham, *The Girl That Disappears*, pp. 19–20.
[94] Addams, *A New Conscience*, p. 45.

Commission as a failure to expose the true extent of the white slavery problem. Nonetheless, it did acknowledge that 'the recruiting of alien women and girls ... is carried on both here and abroad'.[95] It explored the difference in experience of women and girls from different ethnic groups, showing that the French were more likely to be prostitutes in their own country, before emigration, whereas 'the Hebrew' was less so, often converted to it in the United States by procurers.[96] But the report concluded that the problem of white slavery was fundamentally an immigration problem because most of the women ending up in prostitution did so willingly because of their need for economic security: 'they have already entered this life at home and come to this country, as they would go elsewhere influenced primarily by business considerations'.[97] Therefore, the report implicitly argued, to control so-called white slavery, immigration must be more strictly controlled in turn. Such political solutions emerge explicitly from the white slavery literature, but cultural solutions, the implicit rhetorical tools of control, are also found hidden within the texts.

LINGUISTIC TOOLS OF CONTROL

In the post-emancipation era, shared by accounts of gendered slavery across the globe, were a number of rhetorical techniques that allowed the authors to assert the desirability of the maintenance of notions of typical and traditional masculinity and femininity. While some authors chose a factual and documentary mode of storytelling to convince their readers, even these were infiltrated by tropes of writing more usually associated with literary fictional accounts. In both the textual and visual representations of female slavery in the Islamic slavery context, the use of romanticisation and melodrama came to the fore but, somewhat more surprisingly, in the genre of white slavery narratives these techniques were equally prevalent. When applied to enslaved individuals in unfamiliar contexts, the technique had the effect of distancing the reader through exoticisation and othering of both victim and perpetrator. A different mechanism was at work in the white slavery narratives, as such accounts became simultaneously a call to action for campaigners, while providing almost pornographic satisfaction.

[95] *Importing Women for Immoral Purposes 1909*, report from US Immigration Commission (Washington, Government Printing Office, 1909), p. 8.

[96] Ibid., p. 14. [97] Ibid., p. 14.

In both cases, these literary techniques portrayed the restriction of the freedom of women as a necessary precaution to prevent them from entering into full blown slavery, especially sexual slavery, a fate seen by contemporaries as 'worse than death', because of loss of reputation and of sexual purity. In many cases it was the reputation of white women, in the broadest new definition of whiteness, that was the concern of authors, because in the cases of women who were the ethnic other, their innocence and purity was deemed already lost because of their own inherent racial traits towards lasciviousness, or those of the men of their race with whom they lived. This was not always the case: some Americans desired the imposition, on other parts of the world, of control through patriarchal systems that imitated those in use on mainland United States. Sally Engle Merry has shown that the gradual colonisation of Hawaii using American and European notions of civility meant that the relationship between native men and women changed. Increasingly, as American norms were adopted by the elites, women's bodies became important sites of regulation and correction.[98] While the use of the law that Merry discusses is a crucial method of implementation of this change, more subtle cultural modes were engaged, such as the creation of a narrative around the defective womanhood of Hawaiian natives. This was put down to an excess of freedom, rather than to their vulnerability to enslavement. The context of these beliefs about gender was that all women of whatever race, were in essence unfree, and were an item for trade, opportunity, investment, profit, or a tool for dynastic furtherance.[99] Most of the women's value to men was derived from their sexuality, and therefore that sexuality must be limited. The commentators surveyed here mostly chose to do this by using rhetoric with the goal of instilling fear into women themselves, but also of urging men to adopt this patriarchal role within their own families on society's behalf. As Thomas Leonard has shown, such arguments were further strengthened by the euthenics movement. This was built on the concept of the weakness of women and their vulnerability to corruption. It suggested a limited acknowledgement of the free will of a healthy, adult woman but were that women to exercise her right

[98] Sally Engle Merry, *Colonizing Hawaii: the Cultural Power of Law* (Princeton University Press, 2000), p. 16.

[99] Stange, *Personal Property*, p. 4.

to damage her own body and morals, she must not be allowed to damage that of her offspring.[100]

Some commentators, who wrote in the early years of the twentieth century about the white slavery panic, rejected the notion of women's sole culpability, and instead focused on the procurers, traffickers and pimps who facilitated the sexual slavery. As shown in Chapter 3, conservative authors commonly 'othered' the men and women involved in entrapment of white slavery victims, suggesting that they were usually from a different race, or from a recent immigrant class, and therefore uncivilised compared to native-born Americans. Unusually, one narrative told a different story about the life of a procurer, and it shows that the indelible moral stain that sexual slavery gave to women and girls was not reflected in the judgement passed on male procurers. Clifford Roe's account of the repentant procurer stands out as a pseudo-religious tale of confession and forgiveness, and affords the protagonist the positive future that his victims of enslavement were denied. Chapter 4 of Roe's extensive compendium about the fight against white slavery outlines the story of Paul Sinclair. There are important class implications as the first thing that readers find out about Sinclair is that he was college-educated. His colourful past also included time as a professional baseball player and an opium addict – an occupation that would have clearly signalled to the reader the beginning of his downfall. He described the way that he procured girls (through placing newspaper advertisements looking for chorus girls). In doing so he passed judgement reflecting his low opinion of the women and girls who worked for him: some needed little persuasion to enter prostitution and thus were dismissed as 'disgustingly easy'.[101] But what is most significant was Roe's judgement on Sinclair: that his almost Damascene confession and repentance make him deserving of forgiveness and redemption. Roe wrote that 'the foregoing confession marks the conversion of another slave trader. These fellows are not altogether bad and often make our best fighters against the panders when converted'.[102]

The hypocrisy of such forgiveness is brought into sharp relief in another chapter of Roe's work, written by the Reverend D. G. Shearer, who tells the story of Mildred, partly in his and partly in her own words. He described Mildred's return to the bosom of her family after escaping a life of sexual slavery, but still having to enter her home by the back door to avoid shame.[103] Shearer's account is typical of the white slavery

[100] Leonard, *Illiberal Reformers*, p. 94.

[101] Roe, *The Great War on White Slavery*, pp. 78–9. [102] Ibid., p. 92. [103] Ibid., p. 46.

panic literature, designed to alert fathers and brothers to the danger that 'our girls', of Roe's title, might be in. However, his description of Mildred's life as a prostitute used a style that mimics erotic fiction, depicting her lazily and luxuriously enjoying a quiet moment in her boudoir: 'clothed in soft filmy lingerie, silk stockings and satin bedroom slippers'.[104] Mildred's relationship with her madam and the men in charge of containing her within the brothel was outlined in the most melodramatic terms, as was her final rescue by a band of Christian missionaries waiting for her outside in the street.[105] Such sections of Roe's work were no doubt designed to provide entertaining ways of making didactic material more accessible to a wider range of readers. But, as in works of fiction, they have the effect of giving Mildred's victimhood a patina of unreality and implicitly suggesting adventure and excitement, rather than coercion and abuse in the real world.

Another arena in which the romanticisation and eroticisation converged in these stories to make them unreal, was in the discussions about slavery in East Africa and the Middle East. Orientalism was a construct used subconsciously by both black and white travellers to frame their descriptions of the slavery they encountered there. The fascination in African American culture with the history and slavery of Egypt, imbued with both sympathy and fantasy, identification and disidentification, was influenced by black orientalism. Also, a part of this important relationship was the notion that blackness, masculinity and its performance could be practised and developed in safe spaces abroad.[106] Simultaneously, orientalism was affecting the presentation of Africa and the Middle East and its slavery by white commentators, who themselves were exploring masculinity and white identity in their travels.

Orientalism was significant in the rhetorical explorations of the harem by British and American authors. Actual access to such secretive spaces was forbidden, but this did not prevent writers and artists of the mid-to-late nineteenth century having a fascination with the inner workings of such highly gendered spaces. The harem itself soon became a metaphor to be used in both conservative and radical writing about gender. In Victorian England, the 'women question' frequently involved recourse to the harem as an epitome of the control and enslavement of women and, with its overtones of exotic otherness, became something with which

[104] Ibid., p. 27. [105] Ibid., p. 32.

[106] Scott Trafton, *Egypt: Land, Race and Nineteenth Century American Egyptomania* (Duke University Press, 2004), pp. 23, 26.

British men were reluctant to identify. John Stuart Mill explicitly compared white women and their political destiny to those women in a harem, and later suffragists used the harem, and the slaves within, to make their case for increasing rights for women in Britain.[107] This literature was especially potent because of its implicit criticism of the uncivilised and cruel Eastern barbarism which permitted such a system, and the comparison drawn with the British society where men would never allow women to be enslaved in this way.[108] American feminists, such as Frances Willard, also made frequent reference to the harem trope, especially when it was shown that white women were sometimes enslaved there. When she wrote about the Circassian girls being 'unwilling slaves of their brutal captors', her main focus was drawing a comparison with the vulnerability of disempowered white American women to assault by African American men, such rhetoric drew her into dispute with Ida B. Wells.[109] William Laird Clowes, in his tract promoting the financed migration of African Americans back to Africa, among other arguments, used the suggestion that 'the situation of white women in many parts of the South is a very perilous one' as a justification for the removal of an entire race. To his credit, though, unlike Willard who supported the use of extra-legal violence to control the African American population, Clowes argued that the 'racial crimes and outrages' (i.e., lynching) 'sullies the south [and] is a disgrace to the fair name of Anglo Saxon civilisation'.[110] White victimhood proved once again to be a powerful sales tool for writers during this period.

CONCLUSION

Both before and after the emancipation era in the United States, women occupied an important position in antislavery narratives, with the transgression of acceptable and civilised gender norms being a powerful motivating tool for the recruitment of both male and female abolitionists. Women were constructed as the 'ideal victim' of cruel slavers because of their vulnerable physical position, their susceptibility to moral disgrace and their position as mothers to future generations. Most significantly

107 Robinson-Dunn, *The Harem*, pp. 115–16. 108 Ibid., p. 119.

109 Ian Tyrrell, Reforming the World: the Creation of America's Moral Empire (Princeton University Press, 2010), p. 106.

110 W. Laird Clowes, *Black America: a Study of the Ex-slave and His Late Master* (London, Paris and Melbourne, 1891), pp. 135, 130.

though, this narrative removed any agency from these women, arguing that their victimhood required the intervention of outside forces precisely because they lacked autonomy to protect themselves or to carve out for themselves any position of power and influence within slavery's sphere. As this chapter has shown, this narrative wilfully or ignorantly misunderstood the nature of much of the slavery that women endured in the late nineteenth century.

By naming concubinage or prostitution as slavery, commentators motivated others to act to prevent the system, but also rendered the females involved in these systems as passive and vulnerable. This allowed commentators to argue for the control and restriction of the movement and freedoms of women in order to protect them from such systems, an argument that appealed to male readers in an era of unsettling modernity in which men's roles and identities were challenged and negotiated. The status of women, whether nominally free or not, revealed that in late nineteenth and early twentieth-century society, the boundaries between bondage and freedom could be blurred. No woman could ever claim to be truly free of the control of another in this period, and so this complicates our attempts to understand the idea of slavery and its rhetorical uses. The desirability of male control of women was heightened by the growing significance in both American and British cultures of eugenics discourse. This put forward the reasoning that women needed to be morally pure because they were the guardians of the blood lines of future generations, and their role as breeders must be considered before their individual personal rights and autonomy. In this narrative, women were the bulwark against the encroachment of other races and ethnic groups in the breeding war to racially dominate. The consequence of defeat in this war, so fearful white commentators suggested, was annihilation of the race.

It would be wrong to deny that females, caught up in slavery and slavery-like systems of labour, experienced terrible conditions, but for some their gender enabled them to achieve positions of strength. Even for female contract indentured migrants, who often suffered sexual abuse, their situation could be mitigated because of their 'value' as wives and mothers, and perceived civilising influence on male migrants. As agricultural and industrial labourers, masters thought female workers were less trouble, and so were an attractive proposition. However, for many enslaved, their work was also sexual and reproductive and it was in this context that the identity markers of race and gender worked together so powerfully to 'other' particular types of women. Many female enslaved were abused precisely because they were both women and of a different race or ethnicity, making them doubly inferior.

However, as early as the late eighteenth century, public activism against slavery was an area in which women were able to have a voice in the political space, and the period following emancipation was no different, as their antislavery activism became one facet of women's political protest in this period, intersecting especially with other campaigns for suffrage and temperance. Women's campaigning about slavery was in some ways distinct from that by men, but in other ways reinforced their patriarchal desires for control. In order to symbolically draw attention to the unfree nature of women the world over, some women activists highlighted the horrors perpetrated on the female enslaved, whereas others used similar cases to argue for increased control and a furthering of progressive agendas such as temperance in order to limit the influence of the new, modern, urban world on master-less women vulnerable to enslavement. Women's commentary on slavery was likely to be as traditional and even as nostalgic as that of men.

After the American Civil War, the most potent rhetoric about women's slavery was that which exposed enslavement of white women. White slavery as an idea combined commentary on race and gender that activists used to mobilise campaigns based on the incongruity of allowing white people to live as slaves. This idea was so powerful that it migrated across times and places, describing the concubinage of Circassian women in the Ottoman empire, and the supposedly forced prostitution of American women and girls in the United States. The term itself is crucial, because it shows how malleable notions of both slavery and whiteness had become in this period, thus lending itself to adaption in such different contexts. In both cases, the depiction of an ideal victim, a vulnerable, naïve white girl, was as much a construct as was the portrayal of the enslaver as a male racial other. The female character in these tales was a tool with which to comment on the uncivilised, backwards and cruel nature of the enslaver. A rare exception to this appeared in the white slavery literature emerging from the United States; where female procurers and white male panders were presented, the latter, if willing to repent, were deemed by campaigners as examples of redemption.

Campaigners were sometimes forced to acknowledge that the ideal victim was only a fiction, and that many women in prostitution in the United States worked of their own free will, or they were partly culpable in their own enslavement because of their greed, lust or other sinfulness. More complicated still were attempts to incorporate discussions of

Chinese prostitution into the white slavery narrative, with commentators divided on whether the Chinese racial traits made them inherently likely to abuse their women, or whether the women themselves were corrupting and manipulative, coercing innocent white boys into their immoral ways. Such differing representations were often determined by the political allegiance of the author, whether he or she was intending a conservative or more radical response to the problem of enslavement and prostitution. Most conservatives hoped for a return to traditional domestic values, or a decrease in immigration, and more radical commentators appealed for protection for the vulnerable, and equality and rights for the victims of enslavement. Much of the portrayal of female slavery during this period relied on exaggerated textual and visual tropes that served to romanticise, eroticise and exoticise the situation, showing an inherent resistance in society to the recording of women's victimhood in a documentary manner. These tropes also allowed campaigners to further demonise the predatory male who sought to violate the white woman, whether he was a 'lustful Turk' in distant lands or, in the domestic United States context, a rampaging African American man. But more radical voices did challenge these notions and crafted the antislavery narrative for their own purposes; not to reinforce the patriarchy or the racial hierarchy but rather to argue for a more profound reconsideration of human relations.

6

Resistance and the Slavery Counter-Narrative

The previous five chapters have built a picture of continuous manipulation of the depiction of slavery, its perpetrators and its victims, for the goal of reinforcing either a conservative or progressive racial, imperial and gendered narrative. In the United States, this narrative evolved in response to and imitation of patterns of discourse about slavery, antislavery and imperialism in Britain, but were then adapted to specific American requirements. These needs were to reconcile a nation riven in two by civil war, and unsure of its place on the global stage following its painful legal abolition of slavery. However powerful this narrative became during the period on which this book focuses, all voices to the contrary were not silenced and, indeed, the clamour for a rival narrative about slavery and antislavery grew in the period following the turn of the twentieth century. This chapter will explore first how this rival narrative of resistance became so dominant and then will catalogue the forms it took, showing how, once again, the definition of, and legacy of, slavery in the United States and globally was manipulated for diverse political ends.

During this period in the United States and Europe, political discourse was marked by the rise of a more radical form of humanitarianism which genuinely aimed at racial and gender equality and full exposure of abuse. This is not to claim that every act or profession of humanitarian action was accompanied by such drastic reconsiderations of human relations; far from it. As Patrick Manning has argued, humanitarianism in this period was often limited in scope. He shows that 'charity is a response to misfortune rather than injustice' and that charity sought to improve the lives of a few individuals rather than institute systems to prevent anyone falling victim to slavery in the future.[1] As this book has shown, humanitarian rhetoric about slavery was used to mask more pragmatic or downright regressive goals. But in some rare cases, a broader vision was beginning to develop. This humanitarianism is epitomised by the writing of Kathleen Simon, the aristocratic British abolitionist who became an activist following her experience of living in Tennessee with her first husband and observing the legacy of slavery with her own eyes. Simon's book on *Slavery* published in 1929 begins with a call to arms. She encouraged her readers not to be passive observers or to treat her work as merely pedagogical in nature but, rather, she wanted them to become activists like herself. She encouraged her readers to ask, 'what can I do?' to help the enslaved.[2] Simon was a campaigner for the political underdog for much of her career, refusing to acknowledge the necessity of a colour bar in the British Empire, as well as supporting the Irish nationalists and, when many of her class were silent, speaking out vociferously against the Nazis.

However, political radicalism and support for the working man did not always go hand in hand with a radical narrative about slavery and other forms of forced labour. In the United States, powerful unions often used definitions of slavery in a regressive way to discourage immigration and, by labelling them unfree labourers, encourage prejudicial treatment of foreign-born workers. As David Brody has argued, around the time of the Civil War many in the labour movement hoped that the battle against slavery was the first of many successive labour reforms. But, by the 1880s, trade union political activity under Marxist socialist influence had moved away from a focus on reform.[3] Eric Love concurs with this assessment, suggesting that no radical voice in the discourse around slavery and other coercive labour types was present because of the racism coming from the white labouring classes and the public leaders, union and otherwise, who exploited their fears.[4] This is well illustrated by the positioning of an article in Chicago's *Day Book* of 1914 deriding white wage slavery, and referencing Abraham Lincoln's abolition of chattel slavery: 'Nothing is

[1] Patrick Manning, *Slavery and African Life: Occidental, Oriental and African Slave Trades* (Cambridge University Press, 1990), p. 174.

[2] Kathleen Simon, *Slavery* (London, 1929), p. xii.

[3] David Brody, *In Labor's Cause: Main Themes on the History of the American Worker* (Oxford University Press, 1993), pp. 53–4.

[4] Eric Love, *Race over Empire: Race and Imperialism 1865–1900* (University of North Carolina Press, 2004), p. xvi.

clearer than the truth of what Lincoln said – this nation cannot live half slave and half free. It has purged itself of chattel slavery and it will purge itself of wage slavery'. It is followed immediately on the same page by a racist stereotypical cartoon of 'Funny little Sambo', depicting a black child with grossly over-sized lips and feet in foolish posture, precisely the type of material that divided white worker from black and contributed to the perpetuation of the inequalities of capitalism.[5] Lincoln's name was also used in an article about the fate of a group of indigent white labourers in the New York district of Park Slope, who were being sold, with the consent of the local Board of Trade, to the highest bidder in return for food and shelter. The article presented it as ironic that black slavery had been abolished, while white slavery still continued.[6]

During the early twentieth century, the term 'white slavery' did at times gain currency referring to unfair wage labour, a metaphorical use of the word slavery, to depict an inherent inequality within capitalism. For example, in *The Day Book*, an article argued that those who work for a wage not sufficient to live on are 'white slaves'. But unlike Frederick Douglass, who had also used the term, this author was a proponent of the conservative vision of white slavery, arguing that 'before their emancipation the black slaves of the south got enough to eat and a place to sleep. The white slaves of today, theoretically have their liberty, but they don't get enough wholesome food and are not properly housed or clothed'.[7] Other more left-leaning publications, such as the *Workman's Advocate*, acknowledged more radical ways of challenging 'wage slavery', stating for example that 'the socialists are much maligned because they call for an abolition of slavery: wage slavery'. The article grandly called for readers to take up arms for the 'final emancipation'.[8]

Despite this challenging climate, it is possible to identify countervalent voices appealing for new thinking about slavery and the systems that

[5] *The Day Book*. (Chicago, Ill.), 30 Jan. 1914. *Chronicling America: Historic American Newspapers*. Lib. of Congress. https://chroniclingamerica.loc.gov/lccn/sn83045487/1914–01-30/ed-2/seq-31/.

[6] *The Tacoma Times*. (Tacoma, Wash.), 11 Feb. 1909. *Chronicling America: Historic American Newspapers*. Lib. of Congress. https://chroniclingamerica.loc.gov/lccn/sn88085187/1909–02-11/ed-1/seq-1/.

[7] *The Day Book*. (Chicago, Ill.), 06 March 1913. *Chronicling America: Historic American Newspapers*. Lib. of Congress. https://chroniclingamerica.loc.gov/lccn/sn83045487/1913–03-06/ed-1/seq-25/.

[8] *Workmen's Advocate*. (New Haven, Conn.), 13 Oct. 1888. *Chronicling America: Historic American Newspapers*. Lib. of Congress. https://chroniclingamerica.loc.gov/lccn/sn90065027/1888–10-13/ed-1/seq-1/.

allow it to perpetuate. This chapter will explore first those who pitted themselves against the prevalent antislavery imperialist narrative on both sides of the Atlantic, including those who saw the struggle against slavery as part of a broader challenge to capitalism itself. The most obvious point of attack against this narrative was through identifying its hypocrisy, and this became a powerful tool to mobilise the public, especially in the early years of the twentieth century after the exposure of the horrific treatment of the native peoples in the Congo Free State. Second, the focus changes to examine writers who challenged the patriarchal view that suggested women's autonomy left them vulnerable to enslavement and therefore, ironically, their freedoms should be curtailed. Many such campaigners, such as feminist activist Jane Addams, coupled their challenge against the conservative understanding of white slavery with broader activism on women's rights, including appeals for equality and for the women's vote. Others called for a complete rethink of the relations between the sexes, including innovative sex education to teach boys how to control themselves rather than teaching girls how to protect their modesty. Still others concluded that the rhetorical construct of white slavery was not synonymous with prostitution and that prostitution ought to be legally permitted with mandated protection from violence for the sex workers.

Many of the most radical commentators during this period pitted themselves against the racial orthodoxy, challenging the views that whites were naturally superior and that Christianity was the only valid religion. Others suggested that the race problem of the United States was not, in the parlance of the time, a 'negro problem' but rather a white problem. They saw a continuity between the radical activism of the pre-Civil War period and that which was still required in the later nineteenth century. Resistance to the narrative of the once-noble, decaying southern landscape was also manifest as artists and private individuals tried to assert the existence of spaces of blackness in the South, reclaiming that locale for a diverse population.

However, it was black writers themselves whose work was the most radical and dangerous and, indeed, the most feared by the white hegemons. They suggested ambitious new programmes of international equality, of which Pan-Africanism became the most visible. Many, such as Frederick Douglass, challenged the working-class white voice which rejected immigration and demonised immigrants, instead expressing welcome and solidarity. African Americans made it their business to expose abuses domestically and globally, with their activism in the struggle against debt bondage in the Deep South helping change attitudes nationwide. They were also important contributors to the rhetoric which punctuated the smugness of white abolitionists, whose hypocrisy when it came to slavery knew no bounds. But most crucially, the activism of the enslaved was the most radical of all. The very act of speaking up about slavery, of sharing their own first-hand experience, of adding their disempowered voice to the clamour for justice and in doing so empowering themselves, represents the most profound rhetorical moment of this period. Through this, they proclaimed themselves activists and not victims. Like antebellum slaves, the post-emancipation era enslaved proclaimed the injustice of their condition by running away and deploying violent acts, as well as through authorship. The more educated also made use of letter writing, and other forms of political mobilisation, including collective direct action, were accessible to all regardless of literacy.

Therefore, to see much of the humanitarian activity of this period as radical is problematic. However, this does not mean that genuine deep-seated humanitarianism is not in evidence and it is to the voice of the enslaved and the formerly enslaved that we must turn to find it. While this narrative is not always tied to political radicalism and, indeed, white radicals often used notions of slavery for troubling ends, in the era after World War I the rejection of progressive positivism did facilitate a rethink in human relations and allowed challenges to accepted ways of thinking that had seemed omnipresent before the war. But slavery as a labour type seemingly has the power to emerge relatively unscathed from all manner of political and intellectual revolutions, as has been the case since at least the eighteenth century, and despite the counter narrative exposed in this chapter, at the end of the period of study, and to the present day, slavery as a labour form, and its troubling legacy, is still with us.

CHALLENGING ANTISLAVERY IMPERIALISM

Socialist and communist authors developed a radical commentary about slavery that relied on its definition as a metaphorical one, which has had a lasting influence on thinkers on the political left even today. The notion that the capitalist system generated inherently abusive labour relations led some authors to identify those abuses as a symptom of the corruption of capitalism itself, while others went further and argued that under such a system, all labour was essentially unfree and therefore enslaved. This problematises an analysis of slavery discourse of the period because it not only shifts the goalposts, but removes them altogether. While it is important to acknowledge that boundaries between slavery and freedom are blurred and mutable, to deny an essential difference between enslavement and the other forms of labour that allow the worker more autonomy makes challenging labour abuses where they occur nearly impossible.

Even the most radical contemporary commentators realised that identifying only the truly abusive labour systems as slavery was important rhetorical work that would contribute to their cause. This writing became especially prevalent under the cultural shift accompanying the New Deal, an era important in understanding the intellectual trajectory that discourse about slavery took in the previous decades. South African black communist leader Albert Nzula is one such writer, whose work in 1933 on this topic was originally published in Russian. He used the concept of slavery both symbolically and realistically in his work. He began with the metaphorical statement linking slavery to a sense of political disempowerment. He wrote that 'whether educated or uneducated, rich or poor, we are all subject to these badges of slavery ... we are slaves as long as we think we can only beg and pray to this cruel government'.[9] But the main rhetorical goal of his book was to link the systems of forced labour in use in Africa to European and American imperialism. He identified the Belgian Congo and British South Africa as particularly heinous examples, but also outlined some private commercial enterprises such as the Lever Bros palm oil concession in 1911 on the Congo as a form of bonded labour because it controlled the trading stations where its own workers had to buy their supplies.[10] Nzula recognised the importance of the more moderate abolitionist Kathleen Simon's work in identifying vestiges of slavery still extant in Africa, but criticised her for denying the full horrors of the system that allowed its continuance.[11]

The same year, an American communist, Walter Wilson, published his tract about labour abuses in his own region. The book was compiled with support of the Labour Research Association, a statistical research group formed by members of the American Workers' Party. Interestingly both Wilson and Nzula (in translation) named their books 'Forced Labour' rather than 'slavery'. This may reflect their shared left-wing goal of the encompassing of all labour relations under capitalism as unfree or may also reflect an uncertainty present by the 1930s of the validity of naming a plethora of labour types as 'slavery'. Another likely reason is the contemporary interest in forced labour camps in the Soviet Union, which had

[9] A. T. Nzula, I. I. Potekhin & A. Z. Zusmanovich, *Forced Labour in Colonial Africa* (original publication, 1933; Zed Press, 1979), p. 8.

[10] Ibid., p. 66. [11] Ibid., p. 86.

been recently exposed in the British and American press. Wilson, like Nzula, names slavery as connected both to capitalism and imperialism. In the late nineteenth century, American challenges to imperialism had been more conservative, raising moral or racial objections to, for example, the annexation of Hawaii, although some more politically idealistic thinkers opposed imperialism on the grounds that it represented a challenge to the Republican tradition.[12]

But American anti-imperialism had morphed into something new and more radical by the time Wilson was writing. For him, imperialism and capitalism were intrinsically linked corrupt systems that fed off one another and benefitted the industrialists while rendering all workers unfree. He wrote, 'under capitalism labour is bound in any case to be exploited'. Unlike Nzula, he explicitly addressed the juxtaposition of the capitalist United States with the communist Soviet Union and used his book to assert that there is 'tyranny' in the United States and not in the Soviet Union, arguing that an alertness to forced labour in the USSR had led to its exposure elsewhere.[13] The main message is that supposedly free labour is not truly free. However, Wilson did proceed to identify particular forms of unfree labour, within the United States and globally, that he regarded as particularly heinous. In the United States he discussed peonage and prison labour as epitomising corruption, while globally, like Nzula, he attacked both nation-led imperialism and commercially driven enterprises. Mindful of his American audience, he picked three culprits who would have been well known to those reading his work in the United States. He accused Herbert Hoover, an executive of a mining company in China, of allowing the use of coolie labour, while identifying the Guggenheim family's ownership of tin mines in Bolivia that allowed the semi-slave conditions of the natives there. In Venezuela, the Mellon family had oil interests in which peon labour was used to construct the roads. Wilson held 'Wall Street imperialism' responsible for some of the worst of the labour abuses.[14]

Part of Wilson's argument mirrored that of a number of other less radical commentators who had written earlier in the century, who stated that it was the hypocrisy of antislavery imperialism that most troubled them. He attacked those progressives who sought social

[12] Thomas J. Osborne, *Empire Can Wait: American Opposition to Hawaiian Annexation 1893–1898* (Kent State University Press, 1981), p. xv.

[13] Walter Wilson, *Forced Labour in the United States* (London, 1933), p. 9.

[14] Ibid., p. 122.

reform on a global scale and saw the white race as responsible for it, but who refused to do anything about peonage and convict labour in the United States arguing that such 'humanitarians' are hypocritical because they just want to see a 'more concealed form of forced labour'.[15] Wilson is suggesting here that for many influential Americans, the reputation of the nation on a global scale, of its being able to depict itself as an antislavery nation, was more important than the good of the American people who were victim to such labour abuses.

The trope of the hypocritical abolitionist dated back to the mid-nineteenth century, when proslavery apologists deployed it to deflect criticism away from the institution of slavery itself (see Chapter 1). However, the trope was also used in the United Kingdom at that early stage in a more radical context by the Chartist movement of the 1840s, which sought universal male suffrage, among other reforms. The Chartists were largely taken from the working classes and they attacked the hypocrisy of middle-class abolitionists whose attention was diverted away from British men and women and towards the African diaspora. While Chartists concurred that chattel slavery was an abusive labour form, they denied that it was unique as a condition of labour exploitation and urged for attention to be given closer to home.[16] Their radical rhetoric, in turn, then influenced conservative American proslavery apologists such as George Fitzhugh, who referenced claims to abolitionist hypocrisy through the ignorance of the white working class in his book *Cannibals All.*[17]

Little had changed by the turn of the twentieth century. The boundaries between slavery and freedom were still being contested and manipulated by those who wished to justify inaction, or even the deployment of unfree labour. Henry Nevinson was the author who did most to expose this type of antislavery hypocrisy, which involved simply recategorising something as not slavery in order to render it outside the realm of abolition interest. Nevinson's book was published simultaneously on both sides of the Atlantic in London and New York. He was British, but his journeys in Africa which resulted in his publication were funded by *Harper's Weekly*

[15] Ibid., p. 19.

[16] Richard Huzzey, *Freedom Burning: Anti-Slavery and Empire in Victorian Britain* (Cornell University Press, 2012), p. 90.

[17] George Fitzhugh, *Cannibals All: or Slaves without Masters*, ed., by C. Vann Woodward (Harvard University Press, 1960), p. 12.

Magazine which serialised his account. Nevinson was scathing about the imperial authorities and their activities in Africa, targeting the Portuguese but also the British. Writing of the British he said that they 'call slaves by another name, legalise their position by a few printed papers and the traffic becomes a commercial enterprise deserving of every encouragement'.[18]

It was around the issue of the hypocrisy and abuses in the Belgian Congo that the most vociferous campaigning gathered. This provided an example of a battle between defenders and accusers that was waged in print, with increasing polarisation of views as time went on. One of the most radical responses to the horrors in the Belgian Congo was that taken by the missionary couple John and Alice Harris. Like many others, they saw it as their job to spread as much information as possible about the situation in the Congo, but their extensive lecture tours, taking them to both sides of the Atlantic accompanied by the many photographs taken by Alice Harris, allowed them to reach larger audiences. Alice Harris's presence was important because of the rarity of female travellers, and so many audience members attended talks just to gawp at her, and in presenting herself and allowing this to happen, she communicated her and her husband's message to those harder to reach. Other missionaries, such as W. D. Armstrong also used innovative and horrific 'atrocity photos' to bring a greater awareness to the public on both sides of the Atlantic.[19] But not all missionary voices about the Congo were appealing for fundamental change. Some were content to turn a blind eye to slavery in order to further their Christian message, and others, some unwittingly, were part of the implicit effort to discredit native eyewitness testimony, and instead prioritise white voices.

While many authors addressed an audience of the general public in order to raise awareness about the Congo, George Washington Williams, the African American politician and writer who travelled in Africa in the 1880s, took a different approach and wrote instead directly to the Belgian King Leopold II himself. For Washington Williams, the hypocrisy of the Belgians was based on their false claims, made at the Berlin Conference of 1883, that they would end slavery in the Congo. In his open letter to Leopold, Washington Williams did not hold back, telling him that 'you have no legal claim to the territory' because Henry Morton Stanley, on

[18] Henry Nevinson, *A Modern Slavery* (London and New York, 1906), p. 44.

[19] Kevin Grant, *A Civilised Savagery: Britain and the New Slaveries in Africa 1884–1926* (Routledge, 2005), pp. 30, 57.

FIGURE 7 'Nsala of Wala with remains of daughter', photograph by Alice Harris, 1904. © Anti-Slavery International.

Leopold's behalf, had tricked native chiefs into signing treaties. He accused Leopold of violating the Berlin Conference Act by 'permitting the natives to carry on the slave trade and by engaging in the wholesale and retail slave trade itself'. Finally Washington Williams said that judgement must be passed: 'all the crimes perpetrated in the Congo have been done in your name and you must answer at the bar of Public Sentiment for the misgovernment of a people'.[20] His direct and impassioned writing about this matter influenced many of the later white authors such as E. D. Morel who followed.

Challenging antislavery imperialism had a long history dating back almost to the legal abolition of slavery in the British Empire itself. The goals of some authors were narrow in focus: pedagogical activism around one particular issue, while for others, a broader exposé of slavery on a grand scale was attempted. For the most ambitious, an

[20] George Washington Williams, 'An Open Letter to His Serene Majesty Leopold II', in *Africa Pamphlets 1885–94*, Bodleian Library, Oxford.

entire reconsideration of human relations was called for, with slavery being deployed with revolutionary fervour. Alongside antislavery, another entrenched intellectual construct of the late nineteenth and early twentieth centuries was the patriarchal notion of gender relations. Authors had to be just as profound when using slavery in their challenges to that notion.

CHALLENGING PATRIARCHY

It is important to state at the outset, that challenging patriarchal notions of the gender hierarchy and distinct gender roles was, in this period, a task as difficult as challenging racial assumptions. Intellectual, legal and cultural structures interlocked to provide a systemic block to women and their allies who were appealing for a different way of thinking. It is no surprise then, that when discussing slavery in most global contexts in this period, American and British authors made few attempts to challenge or dismantle the patriarchy. For them, the gendered order was a given, something to be deployed in justification of their own beliefs on slavery and abolition rather than an opportunity for radical activism. This is not to say that, from the late eighteenth century onwards, women themselves had not taken a key role in the abolition movement, and indeed their activism, including petitioning and sugar boycotts, was crucial in achieving, in 1807, the legal end of the slave trade by the British Parliament. This trajectory was continued throughout the nineteenth century by female campaigners who felt that abolitionism gave them a political voice which they could use to further other causes of equality such as suffrage. And bringing women's voices to the fore as authors, such as Kathleen Simon, as photographers and lecturers, such as Alice Harris, or as eyewitnesses to slavery in the work of F. W. Chesson, was itself a radical act because of the norms that suppressed women's political expression and rendered them supposedly unreliable witnesses, even when communicating their own observations. Even into the early twentieth century, the expectation that women ought to remain in the domestic sphere persisted, and it is these norms that Alice Harris played on so effectively to attract people to the lectures given by her and her husband. A female adventurer was far more of a 'draw' to the crowds than a male one, and the Harrises then communicated their antislavery message successfully to larger audiences. Without explicitly describing the patriarchal system that entrapped women, people like the Harrises confronted the prejudice and inequality along gender lines that existed in their society.

The exception to the general silence within the discourse on the issue of gendered norms is around the theme of the white slavery panic of the early twentieth century. Interestingly, both male and female authors depicted themselves as custodians of women's rights and desirous of an improvement in the lot of female victims of enslavement, which would be brought about by a reconsideration of gendered norms. But within the same text, authors of both genders were also susceptible to falling back on assumptions and assertions that sought to keep women in their place and to render them dependent on men, or to present female victims of enslavement as a titillating subject for the male gaze. One of the most radical thinkers in the field of white slavery was Jane Addams. In her 1912 book *A New Conscience and an Ancient Evil*, Addams based her entire argument on equating white slavery with the chattel slavery of African Americans in the antebellum era. Her calls to activism required a new abolition movement, based on the successes of the earlier one, a glorious antecedent. Her book was based on the testimony of department store girls, factory girls, immigrant girls, hotel and restaurant workers and so her methodology was a feminist one, desiring to bring the silenced and ignored voices to the fore.[21] She wanted all activists to be primed ready for surveillance and to fight, writing that she sought 'scouts and outposts' in the fight against the evil of white slavery.[22]

One of the most important appeals within Addams's book called for 'a little more humanity in its [society's] dealing with this class of women', referring to those individuals who were trafficked or otherwise forced by circumstances or by individuals to become prostitutes. This plea for a reconsideration of the dismissal of prostitutes as immoral, fallen women, was even more strident placed as it was following an indictment of the corruption in the system of law and order that allowed pimps and traffickers to be protected. She recounted the story of a young police officer who, when trying to arrest someone for white slavery who was under protection of law enforcement and the local political elite, was transferred for his 'mistake'.[23] Addams also stands out for her enlightened stance on the question of race. Despite the 'white slavery' moniker, she acknowledged that African American women were victims of enforced prostitution too, and indeed were especially vulnerable: 'who because of her traditions is often treated with so little respect by white men that she is

[21] Jane Addams, *A New Conscience and an Ancient Evil* (New York, 1912), p. ix.
[22] Ibid., p. 5. [23] Ibid., pp. 45, 47.

constantly subjected to insult'.[24] This is a rather flimsy turn of phrase about 'her traditions' with which to express the systematic racism of the era, but nonetheless, Addams stands out from her fellow authors of the white slavery panic in that she was willing to acknowledge African American victimhood at all.

Like the nineteenth-century abolitionists before her, Addams perceived women's suffrage as being crucial in bringing about broader social reform. She was a passionate believer in equal suffrage and wrote that corruption would be eliminated were this to happen: 'women with political power would not brook that men should live openly on the wages of captured victims'.[25] However, it is incorrect to say that Addams was completely free of the prejudices that infiltrated her time and class. Like other progressive thinkers, she felt that victims of forced prostitution were, to an extent, culpable in their own downfall because of their willingness to be enticed by the promise of luxury goods and by a procurer touting alcohol, to which they were predisposed and unable to resist. This view was somewhat contradictory to her other statements asserting the similarity of prostitution to chattel slavery.

The biological and moral vulnerability of women and people of other races to excessive consumption of alcohol was commonly accepted during this period and part of the rhetoric of less radical progressives as well as of activists such as Addams. Another author who aligned the temperance movement with a radical struggle against slavery was the English Muslim convert William Quilliam, who wrote that Islam and reform were perfectly compatible. He discouraged Muslims in Africa and the Middle East from fighting alongside the European powers and earned himself the name of traitor in the process. Quilliam's profound dislike of alcohol and of enslavement led him to assert that Islam is a most liberating system because it forbids intoxicants: 'the drink curse is a worse slavery than that which Clarkson and Wilberforce abolished ... the drunkard is a greater slave than the poor Negro'.[26]

Writing the previous year, Clifford Roe also conceived of the struggle against white slavery as a 'war' as elucidated in his chosen title. He saw his activism as international in scope, influenced by the exposure of child prostitution in London by W. T. Stead, but was also globally aware, exploring the impact of international trafficking rings. His publication is

[24] Ibid., p. 169. [25] Ibid., p. 197.
[26] Diane Robinson-Dunn, *The Harem, Slavery and British Imperial Culture* (Manchester University Press, 2006), p. 165.

a handbook with contributions from several other authors, such as the Rev J. G. Shearer, and this explains its varied nature. One of the contributions was from William Alexander Coote, who was co-founder and secretary of Stead's organisation, the National Vigilance Association. For someone who eschewed formal education, Coote's interest in education as reported in Roe's book is notable. He explained that one way of minimising the impact of white slavery and its concurrent outbreaks of sexual transmitted diseases was to improve sex education. He recommended to his audience that they 'strip the subject of all false delicacy, all twadding and nonsense'.[27] Although Coote insisted that girls and boys should be taught separately in the accepted and traditional pedagogical style, his subsequent suggestions were more forward thinking. He stated that the biology of reproduction in animals should be ignored, and instead much more practical lessons should be taught, which might be of use to help the developing young men and women learn how to be with one another in the world, akin to the relationship education of the twenty-first century.[28] However, this training was not as radical as it may at first have seemed and Coote went on to confirm that much of this work was needed to reinforce the contemporary vogue for heroic, healthy masculinity, and that boys must be taught about their bodies and about sexual desire, but only to a limited extent. They might learn of the 'primordial urge' but in an aim to prevent masturbation, still thought of as sinful, they must be taught 'that the fires of passion must be banked' and that moral and self-control were values to be lauded.[29] Coote did not expound how such limited pedagogical initiatives might reduce the vulnerability of girls and women to white slavery.

The same year as Roe's book was published, another volume emerged purporting to outline 'the real facts about the white slave traffic'. Theodore Bingham wrote from a law enforcement perspective and, like Coote, criticised American public reticence to discuss matters of sex as 'inherited Puritanism' and said that this was damaging attempts to end white slavery.[30] Bingham's solution presented a radical reconsideration of white slavery. His work was more subtle in its definition of white slavery than many others, clearly distinguishing between human trafficking and

[27] Clifford Roe, *The Great War on White Slavery or Fighting for the Protection of Our Girls* (New York, 1911), p. 412.

[28] Ibid., p. 414. [29] Ibid., p. 416.

[30] Theodore Bingham, *The Girl That Disappears: the Real Facts about the White Slave Traffic* (Boston, 1911), p. 11.

forced sexual slavery on the one hand, and voluntary prostitution on the other. Bingham realised that, while many Americans found voluntary prostitution undesirable and saw it as a moral stain, it needed to be dealt with in a different way than the violent and organised criminality of white slavery. He presented the enlightened examples of the Ohio cities of Toledo and Cleveland, where a specific neighbourhood was 'segregated', in his terms, that is, set aside for prostitution: an early red-light district. Bingham argued that the existence of these spaces had eliminated white slavery (forced prostitution) from the towns.[31] Wasting police and court time on 'exacting tribute from these unfortunate women' – rounding them up and fining them in the courts – was not appropriate, he argued, and instead only made a great deal of money for professional bail bondsmen.[32]

Bingham was asking for nothing less than an entire societal reconsideration of the payment for sex. He wanted to decriminalise the transaction for voluntary sex workers and instead treat them in ways that would ensure their physical protection. By thus separating out the trade into voluntary and coerced, Bingham felt that it would be easier to shine a light on the coerced white slavery system. And just in case the reader had failed to realise that they were being embroiled in a scheme requiring a substantial change of mindset, Bingham spelled this out at the end: 'And don't you see my reader, this all comes back to you. These things [white slavery] would not be possible if it were not for the hypocrisy that surrounds the social evil with secrecy'.[33] For all his visionary thinking, though, Bingham's proposals were flawed in other ways, with the racial ideology of his time infiltrating his book, resulting in the othering of procurers, identifying them as mostly Irish, Italian or Jewish.[34] Resisting the hegemonic systems of the time that were underpinned by the racial hierarchy was an even greater task than challenging the patriarchy.

CHALLENGING RACIAL ORTHODOXY

Much of the work undertaken by American authors, challenging the racial orthodoxy in relation to slavery and slavery-like systems of labour, reflected an overriding concern with the legacy of slavery within the United States itself, and a desire to confront inequalities within the nation directly caused by the inability of the federal government to impose a solution on the rebellious states that might benefit all Americans,

[31] Ibid., pp. 70–1. [32] Ibid., p. 77. [33] Ibid., p. 87. [34] Ibid., p. 39.

whatever the colour of their skin. The methods that these authors adopted were varied, but the main ones emerging as a common thread across this period were a realignment of the memories and values of the pre-war abolition movement to fit the new post-emancipation vestiges of slavery, reassignment of culpability, and an assertion of the cultural rights of people of the African diaspora as Americans. However, it did also become apparent that some of these abolitionist tactics could be applied to global slavery and, so, for some more radical authors, audiences and issues became internationalised in this period.

As we saw in Chapter 1, the pre-war abolition movement had a long legacy in the United States just as did the rhetoric deployed by the proslavery side. While some of the personnel withdrew from the movement or their interests morphed into activism in other areas, focusing on labour reform or suffrage, the radical legacy of abolitionism was somehow kept alive in the Jim Crow era, showing that, despite the overwhelming power of scientific racism and racist ideology in the period, some within the United States still saw their personal and national identity as inclusive of a story of abolition and not of slave holding. While much popular culture reflected Jim Crow nostalgia for a benign, paternalistic slave past, other authors presented a counter narrative built on the influence of literature such as *Uncle Tom's Cabin* and pushed a nostalgia for abolition and slave resistance. Prior to the Civil War, radical abolitionism had never attracted a large following, and for many, ending slavery became decoupled from the idea of racial equality. But a small band of radicals always pushed for full citizenship and acknowledgement of African American personhood, alongside a complete abandonment of colour prejudice, arguing not only for a practical change in status of the enslaved people of colour, but a rethinking on the part of whites about their own colour identity and their relationship to other Americans.[35] From the 1830s onwards, this led to a reconsideration of the validity of ideas of racial determinism and a new emphasis on environmentalism and re-education. This emphasis resulted in a parting of the ways between the conservatives who preached the impossibility of equality in the United States and the desirability of the African diaspora returning to their natal homeland, and the radicals who pushed for a change in the attitudes of the white population in order to solve the problem. Those abolitionists who fought for genuine equality labelled the others 'the aristocrats', a class-riven nickname indicating their elitist and

[35] Paul Goodman, *Of One Blood: Abolitionism and the Origins of Racial Equality* (University of California Press, 1998), p. 1.

anti-reformist tendencies. They also deliberately tried to model integrationist practices in their meetings, including allowing diverse races, and both genders to speak together, the latter seen as especially radical and rejected by the more moderates.[36]

Some abolitionist works by members of the movement, recalling their experiences prior to the war, such as William Still's *The Underground Railroad,* were published during the post-emancipation era, valorising the actions of a few heroic fugitive slaves and their white supporters. Still, an African American who participated in freeing others using the Underground Railroad, had kept diaries during the antebellum era, and his book published in 1872 was a best seller that went through several editions.[37] During this period, though, in many cases it was still white voices which shouted the loudest in recalling the legacy of the abolition movement and African Americans continued to struggle to get their voices heard in the American mainstream. However, for many white abolitionists in the period after the Civil War, it was important to broaden the struggle and to speak about slavery, and the successful fight to defeat it, in inspirational terms. Although it became clear that the South was not going to become an equal society which offered civil rights to its freed people, some abolitionists felt that challenging this was a task to which they were unequal and instead turned their attention to loftier goals. An example of this is Julia Ward Howe, who famously said that 'all humanity must be seen as neighbours', foreshadowing the international and global agendas of antislavery campaigners.[38] However, Howe's primary goal was women's suffrage, and in this she was similar to many abolitionists who turned away from the cause of slavery in the years after the American Civil War. For others, the interest became minority groups who were being persecuted the world over: an important new international focus, but one that also marked a refusal by some to confront the aftermath of slavery head on. In the late nineteenth century, support for Irish, Greek and Polish nationalists, for the Cretan rebellion against the Turks, was common amongst American former abolitionists.[39] They still saw their role as political campaigning, but for them, at least until the news of the Congo

[36] Ibid., pp. 141, 249.

[37] William Van Deberg, *Slavery and Race in American Popular Culture* (University of Wisconsin Press, 1984), p. 76.

[38] John T, Cumbler, *From Abolition to Rights for All* (University of Pennsylvania Press, 2008), p. 143.

[39] Ibid., p. 143.

Horror broke in the later years of the century, slavery was no longer the main trigger for radical action.

Concerns over the impact slavery had had on the United States, especially on the states that had formed part of the Confederacy, dominated political and cultural discourse. Much of this debate did little to challenge the racial orthodoxy of the time, instead it further entrenched ideas of racial difference, and the alienation between black and white Americans. Its purpose was rather to create a sense of shared white identity that allowed for healing of some wounds following the fratricidal civil war, while in the process ignoring wounds of other Americans, and created still more. Authors propounding this vision of the new United States, determined that the so-called 'negro problem' was an inevitable outcome of a war that triggered the regretful ending of slavery, and that a maintenance of the values that had allowed chattel slavery to perpetuate for so long would insulate white Americans from the negative aspects of its legacy. Those responsible for any deleterious outcomes were the 'uppity' former slaves who no longer knew their place and, at times of political tension, their northern allies who were blamed for facilitating a power grab by African Americans unprepared for office, in revenge for slavery.

Outside observers, and more radical thinkers, challenged this conception of the 'negro problem', and instead suggested alternative culpability and alternative solutions. Albert Bushnell Hart, who saw his authorship as in the mould of the pre-war radical abolitionists as his parents had been, argued that 'the negro does not make all the trouble'. He called for a complete reconceptualisation of the race issue facing the United States, saying that actually this should be conceived as a 'Caucasian question', and that it was white Americans who could never leave behind race difference: 'the white man cannot build new school houses or improve his cotton seed or open a coal mine without remembering that there is a negro race and a negro problem'.[40] Bushnell Hart was also radical in his proposition of a practical solution, stating that 'negro uplift' also required action on behalf of white Americans. He instructed them that community and not competition was fundamental to moving beyond slavery and into true freedom for all: 'you are not made poor because your neighbour gets on in the world'.[41]

Because he was a more moderate progressive, Bushnell Hart's plea for solidarity was not expressed in radical political terms, but other authors went further and foregrounded a shared sense of alienation between the

[40] Albert Bushnell Hart, *The Southern South* (New York, 1910), p. 68. [41] Ibid., p. 371.

poorer classes of Americans in order to find a solution to the troubled legacy of enslavement in the nation. One such author was Walter Wilson who put the 'assemblage of horrors' of convict labour, peonage and chain gangs firmly in the context of American class privileges 'for the money bag'. He contrasted the differing treatment of wealthy criminals such as Al Capone who, two years before Wilson's book was published, had been sentenced to prison for tax evasion, and the convict labourers who suffered horrendous punishments and indeterminate sentences.[42] Radical voices in the early twentieth century attempted to use union power to challenge segregation and foster a sense of cross-racial solidarity. This was undertaken by both the Knights of Labor and the International Workers of the World, with the latter explicitly founded in 1905 to address this race issue.[43] However, until at least the middle of the twentieth century, challenging the dominant hegemonic ideology that the white masses of the working class perpetuated Jim Crow culture proved difficult for countervalent thinkers.[44] Certainly during the period immediately following emancipation through to the 1920s, the majority of white Americans were unable to genuinely accept African Americans as 'their neighbour' in Bushnell Hart's terms. But this did not stop political radicals from trying, and they achieved some success, especially in the later period following the Wall Street Crash.

Simultaneously, awareness was growing of the slavery-like conditions in which convict labourers were housed and worked, to the extent that by the period after the Crash, the public mood was altered by popular cultural representations of these conditions, undertaken through an effort to humanise the victims of this abusive labour form. This reveals another radical attempt to reconsider slavery-like labour systems and their impact on their victims, because through the humanisation of the mostly African American male labourers, the racist ideology underpinning the system might be challenged. Although Walter Wilson's geographical framework was global one, one of his main areas of activism was in forcing recognition of the vestiges of slavery still extant within the United States. Wilson, in line with his desire to encourage class solidarity, acknowledged that all prisoners, not only African American ones, were mistreated under the convict labour system and throughout his book he was less concerned with labelling convict labour a continuation of chattel slavery than he was

42 Walter Wilson, *Forced Labour*, pp. 7, 27.

43 Carter Wilson, *Racism from Slavery to Advanced Capitalism* (Sage, 1996), p. 137.

44 Ibid., pp. 79–80.

with using it to epitomise the essentially corrupt nature of the capitalist system. Having said that, he did make a direct connection between the two labour systems, saying that the convict lease system has become 'a partial substitute for chattel slavery'. But he also stated that the worst cruelties were almost always reserved for the black prisoners, especially those of the South where segregation excluded African Americans from jury service.[45] He highlighted examples of torture being routinely used to extract confessions, including prisoners in Helena, Arkansas, who were being threatened with the electric chair.[46] The use of this type of torture by the post-emancipation carceral regime has clear antecedents in the ways that physical coercion was used prior to the end of chattel slavery.

Newspaper mirrored the furore against convict leasing, publishing extended articles linking its abuses to slavery and explicitly calling for its abolition. While some did not express the explicit connection between a need for labour and the corrupt criminal justice system, they did outline the abuses, such as the use of the sweat box and refusal to treat sick prisoners, as well as expressing the racial dimension, namely, that abuses had continued because 'the negro is more easily imposed upon'.[47] By the turn of the twentieth century, even Southern newspapers were referring to their own state's convict leasing system as 'odious'. This particular author still maintained that putting prisoners to work was advantageous and fair, but that it was immoral to lease them to private companies for financial reward.[48] This shows how far thinking had come on the topic in a generation.

Earlier, a Louisiana newspaper had published a report praising the convict leasing system as efficient and effective, stating that the taxpayers favoured it regardless of the opinions of the convicts themselves.[49] But by the later period, these voices were rare. However, few went as far as Walter Wilson who took this a step further and instead of criticising only the treatment of the victims of this type of forced labour, criticised the entire system itself and requested its dismantling. Wilson argued that

[45] Walter Wilson, *Forced Labour*, pp. 29–30. [46] Ibid., p. 31.

[47] *The Colville Examiner*. (Colville, Wash.), 25 Jan. 1913. *Chronicling America: Historic American Newspapers*. Lib. of Congress. https://chroniclingamerica.loc.gov/lccn/sn88085318/1913-01-25/ed-1/seq-7/.

[48] *The Grenada Sentinel*. (Grenada, Miss.), 05 Oct. 1901. *Chronicling America: Historic American Newspapers*. Lib. of Congress. https://chroniclingamerica.loc.gov/lccn/sn85034375/1901-10-05/ed-1/seq-2/.

[49] *The Bossier Banner*. (Bellevue, Bossier Parish, La.), 13 June 1874. *Chronicling America: Historic American Newspapers*. Lib. of Congress. https://chroniclingamerica.loc.gov/lccn/sn85034235/1874-06-13/ed-1/seq-4/.

the fundamental problem with convict labour was that it offered a challenge to free labour. He raised the cases of companies such as the Tennessee Coal, Iron and Railroad Company, which was founded on convict labour and dealt on the Stock Market in convict labour futures just as were wheat and corn futures.[50] The naming by Wilson of this particular company is unsurprising because in the early 1890s it had become notorious throughout the United States because of the industrial unrest caused by unscrupulous use of convict labour to strike break in the Coal Creek coal fields of Tennessee. Others shared Wilson's strong dislike of convict and chain gang labour but saw the victims of 'slavery' therein in terms influenced by eugenic thinking. In a 1910 letter to the *Los Angeles Times*, a U. P. Marsway argued:

> a community, state or nation that builds an elaborate system of workhouses and penitentiaries and votes to have convict and chain gang slave labour to do their public road making must by all laws of compensation have them filled to overflowing and it is this never-ending flowing of criminal sewage from source to sea that makes for our national disgrace in heading the crime column.[51]

The era in which Walter Wilson wrote was marked by increased political radicalism in the United States, partially due to the economic difficulties in which many white Americans found themselves, suddenly aware of the deprivation and iniquities in American society that had been common knowledge to African Americans and new immigrants for generations. However, cultural rather than overtly political tools of rhetorical persuasion became an important part of the arsenal of forced labour activists around this time. Documentary novels, in which fact and fiction became difficult to distinguish, humanised the victims of convict labour and especially of the chain gang systems of prison labour. An important example is the novel *Georgia Nigger*, written in 1932 by John Spivak, accompanied by his own documentary photographs of real-life instances of the punishments and living conditions of convict labourers. As well as being serialised in Communist party newspapers, the novel was published in parts in more mainstream newspapers, thus reaching a diverse political audience. Spivak chose Georgia for his story because he claimed 'it does not stand alone ... it was chosen because it is fairly

[50] Walter Wilson, *Forced Labour*, p. 41.

[51] *Los Angeles Herald*. (Los Angeles [Calif.]), 25 March 1910. *Chronicling America: Historic American Newspapers*. Lib. of Congress. https://chroniclingamerica.loc.gov/lccn/sn85042462/1910-03-25/ed-1/seq-4/.

representative'.[52] Georgia was also discussed in a newspaper article from fifty years previously with its chain gang system then described as 'a drove of slaves'.[53] The novel is the story of one victim of this system of new slavery, David (the name perhaps chosen to resonate with the Old Testament story of the underdog remaining undefeated by superior odds), and it was written as a direct address to the audience in the first or second person, to bring the reader closer to the experience of David. This technique is deployed especially vividly to describe the living conditions of the labourers, for example the sleeping arrangements in which men were chained together: 'some turn restlessly and when you turn the sweat from your half naked body leaves a damp clot on the torn mattress'.[54]

The conditions which 'David' narrates are, of course, amongst the worst that might be imagined, with the implication being that African Americans were valued in this system even less than they had been under slavery. They had been worth a lot of money then, now 'Limpy [a convict labourer murdered by his master] had cost Deering only five dollars'.[55] Much of the personal violence and institutional inequality was meted out by the 'crackers' in the novel, an uncivilised class of whites who might nonetheless have considerable political and economic power. But the focus of the novel is the personal crushing of a man's spirit, his attempts to resist the system, with odds stacked against him, by running away and asserting his autonomy, but one that finally got the better of him. At the end of the novel, David is caught, having run away from the Buzzard's Roost chain gang, and his punishment is a day and a night in the 'sweat-box': 'a living mummy in an upright coffin'.[56] At the end of his ordeal, Spivak writes, 'the boy fell out unconscious': no longer referring to him as David, he had become 'the boy' pacified by his punishment. The closing scene has David realise that his fellow escapees have also been recaptured, and 'he turned his face to the bars'.[57]

Spivak concluded his book with evidence of the factual convict leasing system on which he had based his narrative. He presented twenty-six different images and textual documents, ranging from accounts of escapes, to photographs of punishment devices, men being punished and

[52] John Spivak, *Georgia Nigger* (London, 1933), unnumbered postscript.
[53] *The Wheeling Daily Intelligencer*. (Wheeling, W. Va.), 08 Oct. 1879. *Chronicling America: Historic American Newspapers*. Lib. of Congress. https://chroniclingamerica.loc.gov/lccn/sn84026844/1879-10-08/ed-1/seq-1/.
[54] Spivak, *Georgia Nigger*, p. 9. [55] Ibid., p. 100. [56] Ibid., p. 238. [57] Ibid., p. 240.

punishment logs, photos of the bloodhounds used to track escaped convicts, letters from convicts, accounts of murdered prisoners, and an account of the death of a man from tuberculosis, who died in a labour camp when he ought to have been transferred to hospital. These items act as an accessible bibliography to the novel itself, offering proof that incidents in the novel that could have been wrongly labelled by readers as fabricated excesses in the pulp fiction genre, have their origin in truth.

The same year, an even more popular account was written by prisoner Robert Eliot Burns, purporting to tell a first-hand account of life on a prison chain gang, and this work achieved an even wider audience because it was adapted for the new popular medium of the motion picture. This time, the lead character was a white American and this may go some way to accounting for its more popular reception. In 1932, the Warner Bros film *I Am a Fugitive from a Georgia Chain Gang* was released, with the Jewish actor, Paul Muni, cast in the lead role, and although it was a film of social consciousness, it built on the popularity of prison films at that time, and also spoke to the cultural zeitgeist driven by authors such as John Dos Passos and John Steinbeck, who wrote novels in which unpredictable forces threatened an individual.[58] The film put chain gangs into their long historical context, of the failure of the United States to deal with post-Civil War lawlessness, the disappointment of soldiers returning from war finding poverty, and also called the chain gang contract system 'a legal alternative to slavery'.[59] Press releases emphasised the authenticity of the film, and the uncivilised and retrograde brutality of the torture. The film achieved some of its radical aims by puncturing the assumptions that underpinned the acceptance of chain gang labour at the time. It also gained a crusading reputation because Georgia prison officials who felt their reputation had been smeared sued the film-makers. The studio settled out of court to avoid an expensive court case, but the film's political work had been done.[60] The notoriety of the book and film allowed its author to remain a free man in New Jersey, because the state's governor refused to upset public opinion by extraditing him back to Georgia.

Another important strand of radical thought challenging racial ideology, attempted to tackle head on the scientific justification for the determination of the hierarchy of the races. While sometimes lacking explicit reference to enslavement, this thinking contributed to a reassessment of

[58] John E. O'Connor, *I Am a Fugitive from a Georgia Chain Gang* (Screenplay) (University of Wisconsin Press, 1981), p. 9.
[59] Ibid., p. 14. [60] Ibid., p. 43.

the intellectual conditions that permitted the racial othering that was essential to the perpetuation of slavery-like practices in the United States. It also enabled a challenge to be mounted to the notion that slavery had been a benign institution and one that was preferable to the post-emancipation state of affairs in the South. One important thinker who did reference slavery in his efforts to challenge scientific racism was Franz Boas. He was a German-born immigrant of Jewish ancestry whose enlightened thinking on matters of race and religion marked him out as different to other anthropologists of his generation. Boas led the intellectual challenge to the Jim Crow doctrine that suggested that chattel slavery had essentially been a massive apprenticeship scheme to African Americans, who were unable to lift themselves up alone without the support of patriarchal whites. Boas actively objected to the 'slavery as school' analogy and instead emphasised its degrading nature. His most radical statement was to argue for fundamental racial equality of the black and white races, a position unacceptable to many white academics of the period. He supported this by using evidence of the existence of advanced civilisations within Africa.[61] The foreword to Boas's book about the condition of African Americans written by Mary Ovington stated 'although their hereditary aptitudes may lie in slightly different directions, it is very improbable that the majority of individuals composing the white race should possess greater ability than the Negro race'.[62] He also issued a call to action for researchers to help further the spread of this message. He saw the role of scientists as exposing the inequality of opportunity, rather than the inherent racial difference experienced by Americans of the African diaspora. He wrote 'every demonstration of the inequality of opportunity will therefore help to dissipate prejudices that prevent the best possible development of a large number of our citizens'.[63]

As well as a desire to demonstrate the essential humanity and equality of African Americans, radical thinkers in the United States, at this time, also turned their attention to demonstrating the right of black Americans to full citizenship and to call the nation, especially the South, their home; to consider it as much their land as that belonging to the proponents of Jim Crow segregation. Not everyone shared this optimism, and some indeed

[61] John David Smith, 'A Different View of Slavery: Black Historians Attack the Proslavery Argument 1890–1920', *Journal of Negro History*, 65: 4 (Autumn, 1980), p. 300.

[62] Franz Boas, 'Foreword', in Mary White Ovington, *Half a Man: The Status of the Negro in New York* (New York, 1911), p. viii.

[63] Ibid., p. viii.

FIGURE 8 'Slavery is dead?' print from wood engraving by Thomas Nast, illustration in *Harper's Weekly*, 1867. Library of Congress.

saw the only possibility of liberation of African Americans if they moved away from the inherent prejudice of the United States. One such was Frederick Durham, a black lawyer educated in London, who asserted that the present violence suffered by African Americans coupled with the memories of enslavement should be enough to urge them to leave the country 'with her lynchings and other oppressions and persecutions, which is their land of bondage'.[64] Durham's comments on political equality were valid until 2009 and the election of Barack Obama: 'it is foolish for any Africo American [sic] to hope that some day he will be elected to the presidentship of the United States'.[65] Durham's motivation in writing was to advertise the potential of the colony of Liberia as a place for black solidarity and freedom. However, for others, to assert African American citizenship and rights within the United States was the more strident and daring rhetorical act. During this troubled post-emancipation period claiming the Southern States as a black homeland as well as a white one was a radical political statement.

Although many of the cultural outputs, produced by white Americans, were designed to reinforce racial segregation and to disenfranchise African Americans, rendering them aliens in their own land, there were rare exceptions and challenges to the hegemonic norms. American plantation art of the late nineteenth and early twentieth centuries was dominated by the nostalgic yearning for the benign slave past, as seen in the artwork of Alice Ravenel Huger Smith. However, the African American sense of space, the 'spaces of blackness' as Leslie King-Hammond calls them, and the aesthetics of resistance which worked towards claiming their own unique Southern identity were not totally silenced. The work of white photographer Huestis P. Cook, son of well-known Civil War photographer George Smith Cook, is important in that regard. On the death of his father in 1902, Huestis took over his father's Richmond, Virginia studio, but before then he had already taken one of his most influential pictures. His photograph from 1898 captioned 'Possum am Sweet', an interior shot of a former slave cabin in Virginia, decorated with newspaper and magazine sheets, and housing a sharecropping husband and wife, speaks to a cultural world that is both uniquely Southern and uniquely black.[66]

[64] Frederick Durham, *The Lone-Star of Liberia: Being the Outcome of Reflections on Our Own People* (London, 1892), p. xvi.

[65] Ibid., p. 288.

[66] Leslie King-Hammond, 'Identifying Spaces of Blackness: the Aesthetics of Resistance and Identity in American Plantation Art', in Angela D. Mack & Stephen G. Hoffus, eds.,

Cook made much of his living depicting African American life in his home state in a documentary and non-judgemental way, allowing the assertion of identity and shared sense of landscape to come through at a time when such assertions were rejected by the majority of the Southern white community.

Another counter-narrative to the hegemonic power of former Confederates and their descendants emerged in the Jim Crow era, bringing together two groups targeted by scientific racism: African Americans and Native Americans. During this period, claiming Native American ancestry became a symbol of power and prestige for the formerly enslaved for two reasons. It enabled them to challenge the scientific notions of racial fixity, and simultaneously also became an important marker of resistance. A cultural production in which this blending was seen, from the late nineteenth century onwards, was the costumes on show at New Orleans' Mardi Gras celebrations.[67]

But for some people of Native ancestry, such as the Lumbees of North Carolina, associating themselves with slavery and blackness was uncomfortable, showing that to some extent they had internalised the views of racial hierarchy that positioned people of African descent at the bottom. Similarly the contested position of people of mixed Native and African descent within tribal groupings such as the Cherokee who, from 1992 under the leadership of Wilma Mankiller, effectively disbarred the Cherokee freedmen from full tribal membership, illustrates an alliance with the hegemonic racial norms. For some African American thinkers, such as Booker T. Washington, distancing themselves from Native Americans and rhetorically rendering them inferior was an important response to the alienating structures of racial discourse and a challenge to the system of segregation.[68] It is therefore vital to remember that African Americans did not speak with one voice during this period, and they disagreed over which rhetorical message to prioritise. But the activism of non-whites on the issue of slavery, whether African Americans, Africans living in Africa or other native or ethnic peoples,

Landscape of Slavery: the Plantation in American Art (University of South Carolina Press, 2008), p. 71.

[67] Laura Lovett, Race and Resistance under Legalised Segregation', in James Brooks, ed., *Confounding the Color Line* (University of Nebraska Press, 2002), p. 198.

[68] Ibid., p. 203.

was the most radical response of all because of its fundamental challenge to the accepted order.

RESISTANCE BY PEOPLE OF COLOUR

Resistance to the prevalent narratives outlined in this chapter so far, became even more potent, powerful and dangerous when undertaken by non-white actors. In speaking out politically, on a theoretical level, by sharing their own story or undertaking direct action to change the conditions within which victims of slavery lived, these individuals were both taking greater risks than their white counterparts and undertaking an implicitly revolutionary act. They were not expected to have a political voice; their activism was not recognised by white hegemonic powers and yet still they spoke and acted to change the labour system on either a local, national, international or global level. While radical antislavery voices often had shared goals and methods, they did not comprise an homogenous movement speaking with the same voice. Rather, it was riven with complexity and division. In fact one newspaper made a plea in 1911 for greater race solidarity (or sense of community identity) 'to make our influence more keenly felt'.[69]

Within this movement it is important to consider two important yet distinct strands of resistance and radical speech and action. First is that activism undertaken by those still enslaved. This chapter mounts a challenge to the still sometimes rehearsed argument of the passivity of the enslaved and instead foregrounds the actions and words that they used to challenge their own situation and in doing so amend the definition of slavery by provoking a reconsideration of what were considered just and unjust labour systems. This political mobilisation took many forms but for Americans in the late nineteenth and twentieth centuries the ones that affected their world view most strikingly were letter writing, violence, withholding of labour, collective political action and running away. African American authors who were either freedmen and women or descendants of slaves increasingly challenged perpetuation of slavery and abusive labour practices on a global scale as well as the incomplete emancipation they saw first-hand at home. In fact, these individuals were among the most vocal, the most radical and most effective voices in

[69] *Franklin's Paper the Statesman.* (Denver, Colo.), 19 Aug. 1911. *Chronicling America: Historic American Newspapers*. Lib. of Congress. https://chroniclingamerica.loc.gov/lccn/sn91052311/1911-08-19/ed-1/seq-3/.

highlighting slavery as a continuing concern for the American people as a whole. They confronted collective systemic ways of silencing them and continued to speak out on matters that concerned African Americans, such as the peonage and convict labour systems. But they also challenged the perpetuation of the accepted norms within American discourse on aspects such as immigration, with denials of the slavish nature of Chinese immigrants, and encouraged a reframing of cultural practices to facilitate the welcoming of new migrants.

Second, African American thinkers also led the way in a transnational consideration of racial identity and its relationship to slavery. Pan-Africanism and its links to an increasingly international sense of activism are important in understanding black authors' responses to slavery and slavery-like practices in Africa, and they led the way in demanding international action in the Congo, and the reconsideration of imperial relations that had allowed the horrors to happen. Their radicalism also spoke directly to, and held up a mirror to, the smugness of white Americans and British people who felt that their job of abolition had been finished, and who trusted their political leaders who told them that the imperialist missions were essentially driven by a desire to eradicate slavery and other coercive labour practices from newly occupied territories. This political militancy, with its global reach and ambitious anticolonial message, became increasingly more strident in the early years of the twentieth century, especially following World War I, and became even more dangerous as judicial and extra-judicial racial violence was deployed to silence those asking questions about the broken promises of the emancipation movement from over half a century earlier. For a white person to write about racial equality and the hypocrisy of antislavery imperialism in this period was unusual and daring and would set them outside the excepted realms of their peers. For an African American to do so was far braver and more serious.

White activists within the abolition movement on both sides of the Atlantic had always struggled to conceptualise the proper place of the enslaved within the movement. Indeed, in terms of historiography, it has only been in the most recent decades that activism and resistance by African Americans has been recognised on an equal footing with that of their white allies and patrons. It is no wonder, then, that in the nineteenth century, slave eyewitnesses were often considered problematic by many within the movement. Mary Prince, for example, was always considered as an outsider by the female abolitionists with whom she worked in London. Her word needed verifying because as a black woman she was an unreliable witness.[70] Similarly, later in the Congo, the testimony of white missionaries was at times prioritised over black observers, reflecting the racial discourse of the day that suggested inferior abilities, weaker moral compass and a general lack of trustworthiness of the ethnic other. But it was not simply that the accounts of black people were treated as less dependable. Ironically, for activists attempting to end systems of slavery, women like Prince found that their status as enslaved or formerly enslaved placed them in a disadvantaged position within the movement. White abolitionists tended to treat them as victims of slavery, passive and in need of white aid, rather than allowing them to share the platform as activists.[71] But just as in the antebellum era, slaves in the post-emancipation period resisted this tendency within the abolition movement and continued to assert their political autonomy and to fight for their own freedom and that of their fellow enslaved.

Two of the most common tactics shared by slaves on both sides of the chronological divide of the American Civil War were the use of violence and running away. Slavery, wherever it existed in the world, was a system which was maintained partly through the fear of overwhelming physical violence on the part of the masters and overseers. Without this, the system would have broken down completely as there would have been few obvious reasons for the enslaved to remain in place and to undertake their work. Therefore, to undertake resistance that might result in the punishment of the individual or members of their family or kinship group was an intensely daring and radical act, a calculated moment of resistance that reveals the fundamental desire of the enslaved to challenge the system within which they lived. But violent resistance must not be seen solely in the context of confronting the slavery system. In this period, especially from the 1890s onwards, the instances of violent resistance to many types of labour abuses, even amongst the so-called free labouring population in places like the United States, were increasingly common, often undertaken with an increasing awareness of political radicalism and knowledge of the power of collective action in protesting local conditions but at the same time contributing more broadly to a larger sense of defiance and objection to the capitalist system.[72]

[70] Clare Midgeley, *Women against Slavery: The British Campaigns 1780–1870* (Routledge, 1992), p. 88.

[71] Ibid., p. 91.

[72] Elliott Robert Barkan, *From All Points: America's Immigrant West 1870s–1952* (Indiana University Press, 2007), p. 89.

For the abolition movement prior to the American Civil War, the trope of the runaway slave was a tremendously important one. Rather than foregrounding the subaltern resistance that such an act demonstrated, abolitionists mostly used slaves running away to give a lie to the often-claimed proslavery argument that slaves were happy and did not wish to see slavery ended. Slaves running away has always been a complex form of resistance. For some, it was a means to protect themselves from beatings, rape or other mistreatment. They ran away literally to save their lives. For others the act was a deliberate removal of labour from the master, a punishment for a perceived slight or mistreatment, an often-temporary assertion of power and illustration to the master that he could not have everything his own way. Slaves ran away singlely or in groups, and from the 1830s onwards many aimed not only for their own freedom and safety but also to contribute to the burgeoning abolition movement, through communicating their story in writing or in person. For the enslaved in the later period, running away was similarly a complex act, but one that nonetheless represented a fundamental challenge to the slave system, whether that was the actor's intention or not. For example, in British Nigeria, runaway slaves banded together and regularly caused public order problems much to the annoyance of Governor Frederick Lugard and the British High Commission. The runaways established their own slave villages in the area around Nassarawa, where increasing numbers then sought sanctuary. Unfortunately their activities led to a general fear of slave revolt, and increased restriction on movement through the use of vagrancy laws, mirroring the patterns of resistance and repression seen in the antebellum and Jim Crow United States.[73]

In defiance of the stereotype of them as 'slavish' and cowardly, one of the groups who most frequently deployed violence in the struggle against the conditions in which they were transported, lived and worked, were Chinese, Indians and Pacific Islanders, bonded labourers who were transported to the Americas to fulfil indentured contracts. Their labour, seen by many globally in the mid-nineteenth century as a valid replacement for African slave labour, was perceived through inherently racist lenses and many antislavery activists looked the other way and ignored mistreatment of the so-called 'coolie' labour force.[74] But despite the relative silence

[73] Paul Lovejoy & Jan Hogendorn, *Slow Death for Slavery: The Cause of Abolition in Northern Nigeria 1897–1936* (Cambridge University Press, 1993), p. 50.

[74] Arnold J. Meagher, *The Coolie Trade: Traffic in Chinese Labourers to Latin America 1847–1874* (X Libris, 2008), p. 21.

about their plight, the indentured labourers themselves actively resisted the conditions they endured and, in doing so, attracted the attention of campaigning organisations who finally came to their defence. One of the most significant points of tension was at the port, when the 'coolies' were embarking for their long sea journeys. Shocked by being kept in barracoons (prison-like pens) awaiting the arrival of ships, many 'coolies' used violence to challenge their enslavement, the targets of their violence being the 'crimps' or labour dealers who had misled them and sold them into indentured servitude. The situation at the ports of Hong Kong, Canton and Macau deteriorated so markedly that opium traders became nervous that their own trade would be affected. The labourers' resistance attracted the attention of the British and Foreign Anti-Slavery Society who began to monitor contract emigration out of Hong Kong and, horrified at what they saw, campaigned for its ending, which was finally enacted in 1874.[75]

For many coolies, the opportunities to protest their situation arose later once they had arrived at their new place of habitation. Perhaps they preferred to wait to judge their labour conditions for themselves. On finding that they were held in a form of bonded labour, they then began to mobilise. For some of the labourers, just as for some African Americans prior to the end of chattel slavery, using the skill of literacy to resist their situation seemed the most apposite way of proceeding. For white activists putting pen to paper was an important part of their political resistance but for groups of unfree labourers doing so rendered a fundamental challenge to the system. The act of writing itself, regardless of the content of the text, demanded a reconsideration of the racial and class system that placed them at the bottom. For Indian labourers in the Caribbean, letter writing became an important part of identity creation as well as political resistance. Many of them were contracted for at least five years, forbidden to move outside their plantation and breaking their contract was made a criminal offence. Cultural practices allowed them to maintain a sort of autonomy which effectively enabled them to transcend their coolie status. From the 1880s onwards, letter writing to journals and newspapers became a key part of their protest, and through doing this they were able to refute their supposedly lower-class status through a rejection of illiteracy, as well as undertaking protests about low wages, late payment, dangerous work environments and poor living conditions.[76]

[75] Ibid., pp. 101, 108, 122.

[76] Prabhu P. Mohapatra, 'Following Custom? Representation of Community Among Indian Immigrant Labour in the West Indies 1880–1920', in Rana P. Behal &

The Chinese community in the United States used similar tactics. Their letter-writing campaigns also asserted their status as free and autonomous labourers, belying the dismissive definition of 'coolies'. Their activism resisted the discrimination that they found in the United States, using literacy to reinforce their claims to class and status, and to reinforce their petitions for citizenship. Chinese residents in the United States also used letter writing as a form of activism to challenge the exclusionary policies that separated families and prevented further migration. But it was also used as a form of intra-community activism, with more experienced immigrants sharing with others news of how to cope with the immigration interview, or who to hire as a sympathetic attorney.[77] Other migrants manipulated the increasingly bureaucratic system by playing the American immigration controllers at their own game. They constructed elaborate, fraudulent family histories, along with accompanying documentary evidence, in order to facilitate the migration of other Chinese people, actually unrelated to them but known as 'paper sons' due to their fictitious identities that allowed them entry into the United States.[78] For these Chinese migrants, asserting their freedom and rejecting the stereotype of slavery that had been attached to them was a key purpose behind their political activism. For other groups, who were suffering labour conditions much more closely aligned with slavery, other methods of community action achieved a modicum of success.

Political mobilisation of enslaved groups took three distinct forms: first, collective action to campaign for labour rights; second, to campaign for other civil rights; and third, to bring about complete transformation of the political system through revolution or cultural change. These types of activism were especially common in, although not exclusive to, times and places where the system of slavery was already beginning to break down, either by large numbers of slaves being manumitted and not replaced, or by slaves freeing themselves by leaving their place of work. For example, in the later nineteenth century under the Ottoman rule, slaves who had been freed or had simply left their masters, organised themselves into lodges for mutual defence and protection. This was a matrilineal system as each lodge had a freed female slave as its president, combining the roles

Marcel Van Der Linden, eds., *Coolies, Capital and Colonialism: Studies in Indian Labour History* (Cambridge University Press, 2007), p. 188.

77 Erika Lee, *At America's Gates: Chinese Immigration During the Exclusion Era* (University of North Carolina Press, 2003), pp. 132, 135.

78 Elliott Young, *Alien Nation: Chinese Migration in the Americas from the Coolie Era through World War II* (University of North Carolina Press, 2014), p. 146.

of union leader and priestess. These lodges had considerable financial power and were able to buy the liberty of other slaves.[79] Rebecca Scott has shown that in 1880 a similar breakdown in law and order accompanied the legal end of slavery in Cuba and that as the newly freed workers became unionised, their activism immediately sought redress for the inequalities of the system. They began petitioning for compensation, using the legal system in their new capacity as citizens. Protests tended to operate in a cross-racial way, despite planters' best efforts to trigger inter-racial hostility.[80]

Another group of recently freed slaves who took advantage of the legal system to further their cause, in a radical departure from its intended use, were women who challenged the perpetuation of the post-emancipation view that ownership of their person simply transferred from their master to their newly freed husband. Some freedwomen took the radical decision not to marry for feminist reasons, that is, to maintain their independence from the control of men. Conversely others used the law, and the policies of the Freedmen's Bureau, to enforce the marriage contract which their errant husbands sought to break. This activism reveals the adaptability and pragmatism of freed slave women who were even prepared to challenge traditional notions of family and a woman's role in order to protect themselves in their new freed state.[81]

But for others, activism took place within a system that on the surface seemed tightly controlled and designed to minimise protest and collective activity. For Japanese indentured workers in Hawaii, their contracts trapped them in appalling working and living conditions. They dreamed of earning large sums of money, and some wished to return to Japan after doing so, but this dream was not the reality for most. Plantation conditions horrified many and they banded together to protest against their treatment, soon realising that withholding their labour through striking was the quickest way to get a response from their overseers and master. The Japanese workers were often paid lower wages than other groups, and so this resulted in frequent protests. One American newspaper documented the supposed change in Japanese labourers from firstly passive and slavish to those willing to stand up for their rights. It wrote, 'they were not

79 Y. Hakan Erdem, *Slavery in the Ottoman Empire and Its Demise 1800–1909* (Macmillan, 1996), p. 74.

80 Rebecca Scott, *Degrees of Freedom: Louisiana and Cuba after Slavery* (Harvard University Press, 2005), pp. 220, 231.

81 Amy Dru Stanley, *From Bondage to Contract: Wage Labour, Marriage and the Market in the Age of Slave Emancipation* (Cambridge University Press, 1998), p. 50.

recognised among the responsible people of the islands any more than the Asiatic buffalo imported to work in the rice fields'. But following their defeat of China, Japanese workers were saying, 'we work but we are no longer mere coolies, slavishly lacking human rights. We can fight; we are of the nation that just whipped China'.[82]

Although they sometimes achieved an improvement in conditions, there was also the risk of a fierce crackdown by the authorities. In 1909, when 1,500 workers went on strike at the Aiea sugar plantation, founded in 1899 near Pearl Harbor, many of them ended up in nearby Honolulu jail and there were treated with great racism by the guards and tortured with loud noises to prevent them from sleeping.[83] Prior to the significant 1909 strike, the Japanese indentured workers had already got a reputation for 'blood unionism' which led them to be involved in directing strikes. According to the report from the Department of Commerce and Labor, the Japanese ties were stronger than the 'trade unionism' of the American and European workers.[84] Ironically, newspaper reports confirmed that the Japanese striking labourers in 1909 seeking redress for their grievances, carried both the Japanese and the American flags. Earlier Japanese protests were triggered by the overthrow of the monarchy and the rumour spreading among Japanese labourers that they were now free American citizens who were entitled to nothing less than a dollar a day.[85]The same Department of Commerce and Labor report went on to confront what it saw as the degradation of the Asiatic labourer, and, in an attempt to downplay the political awareness and power of the Japanese workers, the report concluded by saying that the strikes were not driven by any sense of class consciousness but rather in response to personal provocation. Only occasionally were they driven to strike for more wages, for better food or accommodation, suggesting that the workers' motives

[82] *Evening Star.* (Washington, D.C.), 14 July 1897. *Chronicling America: Historic American Newspapers*. Lib. of Congress. https://chroniclingamerica.loc.gov/lccn/sn83045462/1897–07-14/ed-1/seq-9/.

[83] Yukiko Kimura, *Issei: Japanese Immigrants in Hawaii* (University of Hawaii Press, 1988), pp. 89, 91. Some estimates (for example, local newspaper the *Honolulu Record*) have the striking plantation worker numbers much higher, at 7000.

[84] Department of Commerce and Labor, *Third Report on Hawaii, Bulletin of the Bureau of Labor, no. 66, Sept. 1906* (Washington Government Printing Office, 1906), p. 382.

[85] *Los Angeles Herald.* (Los Angeles [Calif.]), 22 May 1909. *Chronicling America: Historic American Newspapers*. Lib. of Congress. https://chroniclingamerica.loc.gov/lccn/sn85042462/1909–05-22/ed-1/seq-1/; *The Oregon Mist.* (St. Helens, Columbia County, Or.), 06 July 1900. *Chronicling America: Historic American Newspapers*. Lib. of Congress. https://chroniclingamerica.loc.gov/lccn/2004260421/1900–07-06/ed-1/seq-1/.

were for their own selfish good, rather than the good of all, somewhat contradictory in light of the earlier comment about 'blood unionism'.[86]

For other groups of people trapped in bonded labour situations or the traumatic aftermath of slavery, their radical activism did take the form of seeking a complete revision in the values of society either through protest or through armed revolution. For the British imperialists in Nigeria who had delayed a total emancipation of the slave population due to fears of a loss of labour and a breakdown of law and order, the Madhist rebellion of 1881 was a nightmarish scenario. They worried constantly that the enslaved from Nigeria might run away to join the rebellion which then in turn might threaten their colony and result in the complete overthrow of British Imperial rule.[87] American audiences interpreted the uprising differently as it was portrayed in the American press as being a protest against the suppression of the slave trade. The black press was unsure how to reconcile two contradictory views of the Mahdi, as a black freedom fighter or as a slave trader.[88] A generation later, across the other side of the Atlantic, those in authority in the United States also feared a new militancy amongst African American soldiers returning from fighting in World War I. This group required social change at home, a reconsideration of their status as Americans and an end to the inequalities perpetuated by the Jim Crow legal and cultural systems. This was a period in which the United States was in some ways more confident in its role on the global stage, but at the same time confronting new tensions at home, with the practitioners of the New Negro movement demanding a consideration of an international pan-African political agenda. White Southern planters felt that their authority and autonomy was being significantly challenged.[89]

The late nineteenth and early twentieth centuries saw important developments in the black American intellectual movement. It took an increasingly radical turn and in the form of an increasing pan-Africanism, along with a sense of shared injustice that can be characterised as anti-imperial antislavery. The urgency of crafting a sense of educated, civilised black nationalism came to the fore and was discussed in 1893 and 1895 at both the Chicago and Atlanta Congresses. At both of these meetings, anti-European and anti-imperial feeling were

[86] Ibid., p. 493. [87] Lovejoy & Hogendorn, *Slow Death for Slavery*, p. 39.

[88] Ahmed E. Elbashir, *The United States, Slavery and the Slave Trade in the Nile Valley* (University Press of America, 1983), p. 46.

[89] Nan Woodruff, *American Congo: the African American Freedom Struggle in the Delta* (Harvard University Press, 2003), pp. 38–9.

expressed very strongly, as Europeans were blamed both for the trans-atlantic slave trade and the perpetuation of slavery and inequality in Africa.[90] A few years later, in 1900, the Pan African Congress in London called for nothing less than a complete end to racial discrimination.[91] Cultural identity was as important in this struggle as political power, and W. E. B. Du Bois recognised this. Du Bois had fought against the tendency of intellectuals, such as Franz Boas, to divorce questions of race from culture and instead, for him, culture and civilisation were aligned. He felt it crucial to assert the existence of an African narrative of progress and historical change to contradict the stereotype that black people had no history.[92] His African history pageant in 1913, held in New York City, celebrated the Nile cultures, the riches and sophistication of Mansa Musa of Medieval Mali and, most interestingly, the struggle against slavery depicted as a moment of African heroism.[93] Du Bois was also greatly impressed with George Washington Williams's writing of black history, challenging the neglect of the black story in narratives of the United States. Du Bois called him 'the greatest historian of the race'.[94] Protests against a misuse in the cinema of the history of American slavery also became part of the African American radical story, as the National Association of the Advancement of Colored People led the campaigns against the depiction of slavery, its legacy, and of freedmen and women, first in *The Birth of a Nation* (1915) and then later *Gone with the Wind* (1939).[95]

African cultural awareness had contributed a radical message to black nationalist thinking earlier in the nineteenth century, as Martin Delany wrote works of black self-fashioning, building on the notion of a black Egyptomania, in which he argued that the 'sons of Ham' became the kings and gods of antiquity. But many later Afrocentrist thinkers felt that Ethiopia was a more relevant point of comparison.[96] Delaney and other early black nationalists, such as Paul Cuffee, argued for emigration back to

[90] P. Olisanwuche Esedebe, *Pan Africanism: the Idea and Movement 1776–1963* (Washington, 1982), p. 46.

[91] Ibid., p. 55.

[92] Brad Evans, *Before Cultures: the Ethnographic Imagination in American Literature 1865–1920* (University of Chicago Press, 2005), pp. 155, 157, 167.

[93] Van Deberg, *Slavery and Race*, p. 120.

[94] John Hope Franklin, *George Washington Williams: A Biography* (University of Chicago, 1985), p. 133.

[95] Van Deberg, *Slavery and Race*, pp. 123, 126.

[96] Scott Trafton, *Egypt Land: Race and Nineteenth Century American Egyptomania* (Duke University Press, 2004), pp. 75, 239.

FIGURE 9 'Evolution of the African race', print, artist & publisher unknown. Nashville, c. 1910. Library of Congress.

Africa and used the language of liberation metaphorically, intending that African Americans return to Africa to civilise Africans from the so-called barbarism of religious ignorance.[97] Later black travellers, such as George

[97] Floyd Miller, *The Search for a Black Nationality: Black Emigration and Colonisation 1787–1863* (University of Illinois Press, 1975), p. 15.

Washington Williams, challenged that view and called for 'kindness, firmness and justice' for native Africans, but he did not contradict the accepted view of the time that the overall purpose of governance was to provide a passive labouring population.[98] However, Washington Williams's activism on the matter of the Congo Free States is very significant and radical. Adam Hochschild recognises him as one of the most important voices in the campaign to end the labour abuses there and as the author who first drew the world's attention to the Congo.[99] While Marcus Garvey continued to push the colonisation message with his Back to Africa movement, by the early twentieth century thinking had moved on and at the 1919 Pan African Congress, debate was led by W. E. B. Du Bois, who pushed a radical socialist anti-imperial agenda.[100]

By the early twentieth century it was black internationalism that represented the most radical strand of African American thinking, spearheaded by men such as Du Bois. The period immediately after World War I was especially contentious, as we have already seen, for the returning African American soldiers, but it was also an important period for battles for intellectual control of the American mindset as, for many white Americans, this period marked a 'return to normalcy' while other radical voices sought new beginnings marked by pacifism and internationalism.[101] Before their intellectual split, under the guidance of Du Bois, Booker T. Washington began thinking internationally. He, like Delaney before him, saw African Americans as an elite labour force whose expertise could be influential throughout the colonial world. But this had reactionary implications for the spread of coercive labour practices because students from his Tuskegee Institute worked in Togo to assist the German authorities in their efforts to make cotton production pay.[102] Meanwhile Du Bois rejected Washington's approach and instead worked alongside other radical activists to link the questions of forced labour and colonial coercion. At the 1911 Universal Races Congress in London, Du Bois and Gandhi were

[98] *A Report Upon the Congo State to the President of the Republic of the United States of America by Colonel the Honourable Geo. W. Williams*, bound in Africa Pamphlets & C. 1884–95, Bodleian Library, Oxford.

[99] Adam Hochschild, *King Leopold's Ghost* (Macmillan, 1999), p. 4.

[100] Lawrence Peskin & Edmund Wehrle, *America and the World* (Johns Hopkins University Press, 2012), pp. 187–8.

[101] Ibid., p. 148.

[102] Andrew Zimmerman, *Alabama in Africa: Booker T. Washington, the German Empire and the Globalisation of the New South* (Princeton University Press, 2010), p. 63.

brought together, united by their anti-imperial vision and desire for genuine equality of all races.[103] Du Bois's thinking was shaped by such meetings but also by his doctoral studies, although his universalistic pluralism did not come from his supervisor, William James at Harvard, but was determined by the German historical tradition.[104]

For many, practical collaboration outweighed any desire for conceptual change. In 1893, Archibald Johnson wrote to the British Foreign Anti-Slavery Society and urged them to keep in mind the plight of their African American friends labouring under the horrors of lynching and other prejudices. For him transatlantic solidarity was not only a practical consideration, because he published news from the Society in his black newspaper, but also an intellectual sustaining one.[105] Such internationalism began to impact on political structures in the period after World War I. The League of Nations published a report in 1927 on native labour entitled 'Slave or Free?' and in it asserted that slavery was still a very important matter that needed to be eradicated but that 'it is difficult for one territory to act in disregard of its neighbours'. So, the solution was to unite public opinion against it 'throughout the civilised world' and to that end, the International Labour Organisation sought to have the eradication of slavery and forced labour as its primary goal.[106]

One important voice of radical resistance was Frederick Douglass whose activism encompassed almost every aspect of the African American challenge to their own continued enslavement and that of others around the globe. He represented the most significant continuum between pre- and post-Civil War antislavery activism and was a rare writer and speaker able to comment with authority on domestic United States matters as well as tapping into the new internationalism. Like other black thinkers, he was influenced by pan-Africanism and especially Egyptomania but rejected the Back to Africa movement and other black-only community initiatives such as the Exoduster migration. His conception of enslavement in the post-emancipation period was shaped by his earlier activism which sought to define an abolitionism that operated within the constitution. He distinguished between voluntary bondsmen

103 Paul Gilroy, *The Black Atlantic: Modernity and Double Consciousness* (Verso, 1998), p. 144.

104 Evans, *Before Cultures*, p. 167.

105 Letter dated 1 Aug. 1893 'Archibald Johnson to Dear Sir' MSS Brit Emp. S. 22/G85. United States 1853–97 folder. Bodleian Library, Oxford.

106 *Slave or Free? Native Labour: an International Problem*, Official paper of the League of Nations, no. 23 Nov. 1927, p. 15.

such as indentured servants, and chattel slaves who were denied all agency and whom he called 'hereditary bondsmen'.[107] Before the war, he insisted that abolitionists should focus on the chattel principal as it resulted in the most abuses, although he also used the term 'white slavery' to refer to wage labourers in the South, despite it being also deployed by proslavery advocates.[108] After emancipation, Douglass worked hard to alert his audiences to the limits of freedom and the essentially bonded nature of many African Americans in the years after the Civil War. He wrote that freedom was a 'hard bargain ... I endured all the evils of being a slave and yet suffered all the care and anxiety of a responsible freeman'.[109]

Despite Frederick Douglass's continuing desire to limit the definition of slavery in order to better fight it, his ideas were inspiring for many groups struggling against oppression. In the Philippines of the early twentieth century, where members of the social elite were grappling with ways of challenging American control, Douglass's ideas, as well as the less radical political ideas of Spanish liberal thinkers, influenced the perspectives of nationalists such as Jose Rizal.[110] In trying to rethink his own nation's identity, Douglass had given an important speech trying to reframe the American debate about labour and to welcome the Chinese immigrants who were so instrumental in the same year in building the Transcontinental railroad. In 'A Composite Nation' delivered in Boston in 1869, Douglass said, 'I want a home here not only for the negro, the mulatto and the Latin races, but I want the Asiatic to find a home here in the US'.[111] While some Americans did profess to welcome immigration during this period, few did so in such explicitly racial terms, preferring instead to emphasise economic justifications. Where immigration and race were linked, it was usually in a negative context. Douglass's radical reframing of the immigration debate, stating that such groups should be welcomed despite racial difference, offered a new interpretation of the racial hierarchy.

As we have already seen, in this period, not all acts of resistance challenging systems of forced labour were undertaken using direct action outside the law. As newly freed people, African Americans used the law to assert

[107] Hoang Gia Phon, *Bonds of Citizenship: Law and the Labors of Emancipation* (New York University Press, 2013), pp. 14, 163.

[108] Ibid., p. 169. [109] Ibid., p. 208.

[110] Paul Kramer, *Blood of Government: Race, Empire, the United States and the Philippines* (University of North Carolina Press, 2006), p. 56.

[111] Najia Aarim-Heriot, *Chinese Immigrants, African Americans and Racial Anxiety in the United States 1848–82* (University of Illinois Press, 2003), p. x.

the rights being denied to them. This tactic was frequently and successfully deployed to challenge the peonage system that emerged to replace chattel slavery in the agricultural areas of the South. Booker T. Washington, who saw peonage as 'a kind of slavery', was instrumental in bringing the case of Alonzo Bailey to national attention. Bailey was an agricultural worker in Alabama who signed a contract and secured an advance on his wages, before quitting his employment. By Alabama law, he could then be forced back to work, thus becoming a peon. Washington helped pay for his case which finally, at appeal, saw the decision that contract labour law in Alabama was ruled unlawful.[112] African Americans worked with white allies in the fight to expose the horrors of peonage. One of the most important figures was the first female Assistant United States Attorney, Mary Grace Quackenbos, who investigated peonage in the United States and beyond.[113] Case law was gradually developed in the years around the turn of the twentieth century across the Southern States and it determined the definition of peonage and showed that the 1867 Act, which declared it unlawful, should apply in those cases.[114]

In sum, radical campaigners had a wide variety of focuses and agendas, from the local to the global, from the narrow to the revolutionary. But all shared the desire of activists such as Ida B. Wells who saw their goal as puncturing the smugness of white reformers. Those reformers who saw their humanitarianism as part of the imperial mission or the patriarchal maintenance of order were consistently exposed as hypocrites by radical authors. The authors and speakers discussed in this chapter wished to foreground the link between humanitarianism and political reform for indigenous or minority groups and to challenge the notion that internationalism and antislavery politics had to be Eurocentric in focus and the product of material interests.[115]

CONCLUSION

In this period, we see the emergence of a radical humanitarianism, which was willing to interrogate the hegemonic structures of America and Europe and to fight for genuine rights and equality for the

[112] Pete Daniel, *The Shadow of Slavery: Peonage in the South 1901–1969* (Oxford University Press, 1972), pp. 70, 76.

[113] Ibid., p. 101.

[114] William Wirt Howe, 'The Peonage Cases', *Columbia Law Review*, April 1904, p. 286.

[115] Ian Tyrrell, *Reforming the World: the Creation of America's Moral Empire* (Princeton University Press, 2010), pp. 8, 13.

oppressed around the world. Publicity surrounding slavery in the Congo rubber industry, and then the subsequent change to the intellectual milieu following war, meant that the post–World War I era saw an increase in radical humanitarian activities, led by men such as E. D. Morel who had been a pacifist during the war.[116] Increasingly, those with new humanitarian agendas worked within international organisations, and authors gained a great deal of publicity through their wide-ranging works challenging the horrors of slavery. Kathleen Simon broadened the definition of slavery during this post-war period, as the recognition spread that slavery was no longer the monolithic chattel slavery (and in fact never had been) and rather, as Joel Quirk says, was a conceptual ambiguity. The League of Nations' temporary Slavery Commission vowed to 'investigate slavery in all its forms'.[117] Intellectual and political trajectories altered considerably in the aftermath of World War I as modernism, especially inspired by French socialist ideas, replaced the progressive positivism of the Gilded Age. Combined with a willingness to celebrate black culture and history, this intellectual mindset led to a reconsideration of racial and imperial structures that had once seemed unassailable.

In the early twentieth century, the death of Leo Tolstoy, who argued that the world is divided into slaves and masters, triggered articles in mainstream American newspapers describing the new phenomenon of 'modern slavery', which is 'far more cruel and extensive than slavery of any previous age'.[118] But espousing politically radical ideas such as socialism did not automatically equate to campaigns for racial equality or challenging systems of forced labour on a global scale. American unions, in particular, withdrew from visionary politics into a more isolationist position, and the labour unrest following World War I meant that many African Americans were reluctant to join the unions in which they were welcomed.[119] Persistent division along racial lines in the United States and worldwide, allowed slavery and other forms of bonded labour to continue unchallenged despite the presence of political radicalism. This should

[116] Hochschild, *King Leopold's Ghost*, p. 288.

[117] Joel Quirk, *The Anti-Slavery Project from the Slave Trade to Human Trafficking* (University of Pennsylvania Press, 2011), pp. 143–4.

[118] *The Nebraska Independent. [volume]* (Lincoln, Nebraska), 21 March 1901. *Chronicling America: Historic American Newspapers*. Lib. of Congress. https://chroniclingamerica.loc.gov/lccn/2017270205/1901-03-21/ed-1/seq-2/.

[119] Brody, *In Labor's Cause*, p. 120.

not be a surprise in the context of the long history of slavery and abolition. As Seymour Drescher has shown, the abolition movement was initially born in a revolutionary moment in the late eighteenth century, and yet slavery as a system of labour emerged unscathed from that period of political upheaval and, indeed, endures in diverse forms to this day.[120]

[120] Seymour Drescher, *Abolition: A History of Slavery and Anti-Slavery* (Cambridge University Press, 2009), p. 246.

Conclusion

Within the United States, the years from 1865 to 1920 represent a period during which the various understandings of the notion of slavery evolved and simultaneously became more entrenched and important within the political culture of the nation. The influence of both abolitionist (of moderate and radical hues) and proslavery discourses, that had their origins in the pre-Civil War era was marked, but there was also a new conception of the changing definition of slavery in a global context. In both domestic and global situations, it was difficult for commentators to overcome the era's pervasive racial and gender ideologies, meaning that during this period even antislavery discourse had a strongly conservative, reactionary tone and message. However, radical antislavery rhetoric increasingly became a part of the intellectual world of the early twentieth century, challenging traditional hierarchies and, in some cases, the entire capitalist system itself.

One of the most significant rhetorical continuums, running before, during and after the Civil War, was the emergence of an abolitionist discourse that attempted to fashion the United States as an antislavery power. Supposedly unproblematic depiction of victimhood of enslaved individuals, as passive victims unable to help themselves without the aid of humanitarian whites, became a significant part of the discussions around slavery. In a domestic context, commentators' blindness to the fate of African Americans, accompanied by denial by many that slavery still haunted the United States in the guises of debt bondage and convict labour, also shows the essential conservatism of the discourse around slavery in this era. This trend was magnified further by the emergence of the Jim Crow Lost Cause myth, which expressed the idea that 'our old slavery days' had been a golden age, the loss of which was to be mourned. This had the effect of diminishing the horrors of slavery, rendering it benign and consensual. Such depictions of slavery called for the maintenance of a *status quo* in which white supremacy reigned in the South, while other representations, of free labourers as slaves, in the case of Chinese labourers called for change to immigration laws, and in the case of the white slavery panic called for increased control of wayward women. Such examples show that in the post-emancipation period, the meaning of the word 'slavery' itself was contentious. No longer was African American chattel slavery the type of slavery to which all Americans referred when they used the term, an important change in the later nineteenth century.

When looking outside their own borders, Americans began to reject dichotomous notions of slavery and freedom, and instead attempted, in imitation of British policy from earlier in the century, to fashion themselves as an antislavery power on the world stage. The term 'slave' became adaptable and allowed the Americans to adopt a humanitarian stance while simultaneously reinforcing racial notions of the civility and superiority of the white race *vis-à-vis* other races who were still predisposed to enslave others. But Americans, like European imperialists, realised that often pragmatic decisions rather than idealistic ones were apposite, and their ability to genuinely make a difference to the lives of enslaved individuals across the globe was limited. The need for labour forces who would work productively, while remaining under the control of the superior white race, often rendered meaningless the Americans' newly adopted antislavery rhetoric. In order to reconcile the position of their antislavery claims with the realities of life on the ground in their colonial holdings, Americans and Europeans manipulated the definition of slavery, pushing many abusive and coercive slavery-like labour forms outside its scope. As the United States came to terms with its new imperial identity, it realised that creating productive labourers and viable, stable colonies took priority over idealistic goals to eradicate unfree labour.

One important rhetorical tool which commentators deployed in the post-emancipation era to distance themselves from the practices of enslavement was that of othering the slave trader or slave owner. For Americans conscious of their own late abolition of chattel slavery, this rhetorical manoeuvre was essential in order that they be considered authentic by other antislavery imperialist powers such as Britain. Slavery, as an idea, was a weapon used to attack those perceived as racial or religious enemies, and this weapon was even more powerful when the purported victim of enslavement could be depicted as the 'ideal victim', a role for which white women were well suited. This reinforced the notion of the people of the United States as protectors, and as part of the group of superior white nations whose role was to eliminate such retrograde practices as slavery and the slave trade.

Politically, while such nations promoting antislavery imperialism often worked in consort in a loose alliance, in this period of high imperialism at the end of the nineteenth century they were also rivals competing for the economic and strategic gains that colonies could offer. Thus, accusing European nations of undertaking nefarious practices, such as slavery and slave trading, performed an important purpose for the United States. For more radical commentators, it allowed them to expose the essential hypocrisy of much antislavery discourse of the period and, for other moderate writers, it allowed the creation of an hierarchy of humanitarianism in which the commentators' nation and people were more morally upstanding, more forward looking and more civilised, than their fellows of other nations.

Depictions of the victims of enslavement were often conservative in their purpose, designed to reinforce the perceived superiority of an imperial nation, or to shore up the racial and gendered hierarchical notions of order and control. Such depictions were almost always about the maintenance of power in the hands of hegemonic groups, rather than a genuine attempt to rethink concepts of free and unfree labour, or to help improve the lives of the victims of slavery in the United States or globally. Some radical writers fell outside this category but, for most, the definition of slavery became a tool with which to assert the antislavery imperialist status quo. An important way to undertake this was to depict the victim of slavery as passive, unable to help themselves, requiring intervention of others to protect them. Another common method of othering was blaming the victims' moral or political weakness for the unfree labour situation in which they found themselves.

Commentators also acknowledged that a newly freed labour force outside the control of imperial or domestic authorities was problematic, both for the labourers themselves, whose moral weakness rendered them unable to do productive work without encouragement by their betters, but also, more broadly, for those in positions of power who felt politically and racially vulnerable because of shifts in patterns of free and unfree labour. Confirming or denying that labour forms counted as slavery enabled better control in these troubling situations. Denying the presence of slavery rendered a labour form outside the abolitionist remit, and left the colonial or local power able to deploy it at will. Conferring the definition of slavery on free labourers rendered them submissive and dependent, either due to their race or their gender or both, on the humanitarianism of those in a position to help them out of the trap of enslavement. Thus, in the post-emancipation period, rhetorically, the perimeters of the definition of slavery became highly contested places where hegemons desired to assert their power.

This policing of the perimeters of the definition of slavery was especially keenly undertaken when female victims of slavery were present, especially if they were also identifiable as white. Both before and after the Civil War, for women in the abolition movement, slavery offered a rare opportunity to assert their political voices on the public stage. For other more conservative women, the depiction of enslavement allowed them to look back to a nostalgic past. But as most authors and creators of cultural artefacts about slavery were men, female slavery was depicted in a way that reinforced the notion of the inferiority of women, and their dependence on the protection of men. For those who espoused the doctrines of eugenics, white women's sexuality was especially closely scrutinised, because of their role as breeders, to produce more racially and morally pure children who would act as a bulwark against the encroachment of breeding of the so-called inferior races. Labelling concubinage and prostitution as 'slavery' allowed men to intervene and call for harsher penalties for enslavers but also to campaign for restrictions on the movement of all women outside the home and outside the protection of fathers, brothers and husbands. For especially potent rhetoric, this was coupled with an enslaver who was depicted as the racial other; for example, an African American or a recent immigrant. Non-white female victims of enslavement were not treated in this way, as being desirous of protection, as white men already considered them tainted because of their race. Chinese prostitutes, for example, were simultaneously depicted as temptresses and slaves and, while some commentators were sympathetic to their plight, there was no systematic call, mirroring the white slavery panic, pleading for an end to their abusive situations.

Despite the overwhelmingly conservative nature of much of the discourse around slavery, especially in the early twentieth century, some more radical voices did emerge. Beginning with the furore about slavery in the rubber industry of the Congo Free State, a genuinely humanitarian antislavery discourse emerged in the discussions about the global nature of slavery. This sought to define slavery as any type of unfree labour, and aimed to eradicate it from all parts of the world where it existed, including in the United States. These authors accepted that slavery's definition had evolved considerably from that of the earlier nineteenth century, in which chattel slavery as a model dominated and, instead, they focused on the abusive and coercive nature of unfree labour, as not only its 'ownership' aspect. Some of this radical commentary was driven by left-wing political radicalism, to the extent that an ideological connection with capitalism was drawn, at times accompanied by a denial of the existence of slavery-like labour systems in communist or socialist contexts. But for other radical thinkers of the period, the collectivisation of labour took place in a segregated context, and this resulted in their refusal to tackle slavery and its legacy, and generated a conservative definition of slavery designed to prevent the acceptance of free migrant labour by labelling it as 'slave labour'. Although radical anti-slavery discourse, which offered a fundamental challenge to the system, did become increasingly prevalent, its influence did little to shake the foundations of either the capitalist system within which unfree labour operated, or to bring to an end coercive and abusive labour forms, many of which are extant, and their legacies being felt, throughout the world today.

During the period which followed, the patterns observed in this book continued to evolve. Domestically, in the United States, conservative efforts to ensure that, conceptually, experiences with chattel slavery are consigned to the history books continue. While the memories of slavery have been preserved by various initiatives, such as the Works Progress Administration oral history interviews, this has had the effect of historicising the legacy of slavery and, to some extent, preventing engagement with its ongoing legacy. These problematic interviews, while in many ways rich and insightful, also further entrenched Jim Crow attitudes towards 'our old slavery days', although a few exceptional African American interviewees were able to assert their own counter-narrative about slavery's pernicious influence on their lives. For many individuals who contributed to, and later made use of these recordings, slavery and its experiences became something in the distant past, a time which came to a definite full stop and which now, having been preserved through the recordings of the oral histories, might be put to one side without being properly acknowledged and the racial divide reconciled.

Not all efforts to tell the history of chattel slavery had the same rhetorical effect. African Americans increasingly defined the agenda for discussions about the legacy of slavery in the United States. Their work often had the impact of collapsing the length of time between two remote periods. An example is Zora Neal Hurston's interviews undertaken in 1928 with Cudjo Lewis, recorded in the manuscript *Barracoon*, but only recently published. Hurston was trained as an anthropologist by Franz Boas and was immersed in the Harlem Renaissance tradition of the 1920s and 1930s. Her rendering of Lewis's words in his dialect provided a more sympathetic hearing than many of the WPA narrative collectors afforded their participants, and alerts us to the illegal transatlantic slave trade that continued long after official abolition. Like many other African American authors, Hurston's work punctuated the failures to fully and immediately abolish the slave trade, and gave a human face to the sufferings endured by the enslaved and the partially freed.

From the mid-1930s onwards, concerns over a hardening of racial ideology and the use of slave labour gained a new focus as the political situation in Nazi Germany attracted international condemnation. International responses to Hitler's white supremacy and his use of labour camps varied, with some conservatives refusing to condemn the regime but then, first the conduct of the war, and then news of the Holocaust itself, redefined the world's conceptions of horror, injustice, violence and genocide. Slave labour utilised by twentieth-century dictatorships as a war measure, or during peacetime, changed the nature of discourse about slavery and its legacy. Simultaneously, as colonial structures began to fall apart, without antislavery imperialism having completed its work, slavery and other unfree systems of labour continued unchecked around the world.

In the fifty years or so immediately following the American Civil War, two important transitions occurred that have informed our interpretations in the twenty-first century of modern slavery. First, the solidification of a problematic transatlantic conservative antislavery rhetoric, that then, in more recent times, fed into the sphere of international development. Although, gradually, racial determinism was rejected, this conservative antislavery rhetoric solidified the hierarchies of nations, and placed antislavery at the heart of immigration and international development policy. Adherence to the free market and its accompanying labour systems, which are devoid of collectivisation, was required of nations, especially those in the Global South, which require support from the wealthier nations or transnational institutions such as the World Bank. Modern slavery and its attendant threat to security from traffickers are put forward as justifications for tighter immigration controls and, just as in the Chinese case in the late-nineteenth-century United States, voluntary migrants are sometimes labelled as enslaved, while truly enslaved individuals go unnoticed. The distinction is still blurred between voluntary sex work and forced prostitution, and voluntary sex work is named as slavery for rhetorical purposes now, as it was at the height of the white slavery panic. Once again, in the contemporary world, what can be defined as slavery is controversial and contentious, showing that such a definition is always historically contingent and never universal.

The most important argument made in this book, therefore, is as true today as it was in the late nineteenth and early twentieth centuries. To call a labour form 'slavery' or 'not slavery' is a rhetorically powerful act. In the post-emancipation era, deliberate manipulation of the definition of slavery for the purposes of personal or national self-fashioning was common, as writers in the United States and beyond struggled to conceptualise a world in which chattel slavery was unlawful. As many at home refused to acknowledge the true horrors of chattel slavery, while denying full freedom to many of the formerly enslaved, the United States tried to fit the model of British antislavery imperialism to its own forays into empire building and, in doing so, used challenging slavery as a justification for imperial interventions hitherto considered un-American. But, while the context of the illegality of slavery was new, many patterns of discourse around slavery pre-dated the American Civil War, revealing a rhetorical continuum with understandings of modern slavery in the contemporary world. And in refusing to listen to many African American and native African voices of protest when they talked about slavery and its legacy, the mainstream United States mishandled the traumatic aftermath of the racial horror that is chattel slavery, resulting in the riven and divided society it has become today. It is time to acknowledge the rhetorical power, in the past and today, of talking about this 'peculiar' labour form, and, within the United States and globally, to use it as a prism through which we might address the fundamental inequalities in race and gender.

Bibliography

PRIMARY SOURCES

MANUSCRIPT

Letter from London Embassy of the US to Charles Allen, Secretary of BFASS, 14/7/1896, MSS Brit Emp s. 22/G85

Letter from M/ Powell, legation of the US to Charles Allen, 22/6/1883, MSS Brit Emp s. 22/G85

Letter from Joseph Cooper to My Dear Sir, 13/1/1880, MSS Brit Emp s. 22/G85

Letter from Archibald Johnson to Dear Sir, 1/8/1893, MSS Brit Emp s. 22/G85

Letter from Charles Allen to I. J. Bayard, Embassy of the US in London, 11/1/1897, MSS Brit Emp s. 22/G85

Letter from BFASS to Rutherford B. Hayes, 6/3/1879, MSS Brit Emp s. 22/G85

Handwritten announcement from the Committee of the4 Anti-Slavery Reunion, dated 28/3/1874, Chicago MSS Brit Emp s. 22/G85

John Harris letter to NAACP, 25/4/1917, MSS Brit Emp s19/D5/5

John Harris letter to Foreign Office, 23/4/1917, MSS Brit Emp s19/D5/5

Letter from Josiah Wedgwood to 'Dear Molly', 10/2/1917, MSS Brit Emp s19/D5/5

Advertisement for lectures given by 'Mrs Harris', MSS Brit Emp s19/D5/5

PRINTED

Addams, Jane, *A New Conscience and an Ancient Evil*, New York: Macmillan, 1912.

The African Trade Section of Liverpool Chamber of Commerce: the Trade in Spirits with West Africa, Liverpool, 1895.

Alexander, Joseph, *Sixty Years against Slavery: a Brief Record of the Work and Aims of the BFAS 1839–1899*, London: British and Foreign Antislavery Society, 1900.

Alexander, W. D., *A Brief History of the Hawaiian People*, New York: American Book Company, 1891.

Bell, Hesketh, *The History, Trade, Resources and Present Condition of the Gold Coast Settlement*, Liverpool, 1903.

Bennett, H. C., *Chinese Labour: a Lecture Delivered before the San Francisco Mechanics Institute in reply to Hon. F.M. Pixley*, San Francisco, 1870.

Bennett Bean, Robert, *The Racial Anatomy of Philippine Islanders*, Philadelphia & London, 1910.

Bingham, Theodore, *The Girl That Disappears: the Real Facts about the White Slave Traffic*, Boston, 1911.

Blount, James H., *American Occupation of the Philippines, 1898–1912*, New York, 1913.

Boulger, Demetrius, *The Congo State or the Growth of Civilisation in Central Africa*, London, Calcutta & Simla, 1898.

Boulger, Demetrius, *The Congo State Is Not a Slave State*, London, 1903.

Brinckman, Arthur, *The Wrongs of Cashmere: a Plea for the Deliverance of that Beautiful Country from the Slavery and Oppression under Which It Is Going to Ruin*, London: Thomas Bosworth, 1868.

The Brussels Conference and the Congo State from the Paris Memorial Diplomatique, 6/9/1890.

Bushnell Hart, Albert, *The Southern South*, New York, 1910.

Campbell-Copeland, Thomas, *American Colonial Handbook: a Ready Reference Book of Facts and Figures Historical, Geographical and Commercial about Cuba, Puerto Rico, and the Philippines, Hawaii and Guam*, New York & London, 1899.

Carpenter, Edward James, *America in Hawaii*, London & Boston, 1899.

Chesson, F. W., *The Dutch Boers and Slavery in the Transvaal Republic*, London, 1869.

Coman, Katherine, 'The History of Contract Labor in the Hawaiian Islands', *Publications of the American Economic Association*, 4: 3 (1903), 1–61.

A Complete Congo Controversy Illustrating the Controversial Methods of Mr Morel, Edinburgh: Oliver and Boyd, 1905.

Conwell, Russell H., *Why the Chinese Emigrate and the Means They Adopt for the Purpose of Reaching America*, Boston & New York: Lee & Shepherd, 1871.

Coolie Labour and the Indian Recruiting Ground: Report of the Committee on Emigration from India for the Crown Colonies and Protectorates, 1910.

Densmore, G. B., *The Chinese in California: Description of Chinese Life in San Francisco*, San Francisco: Pettit and Russ, 1880.

Department of Commerce and Labor, *Third Report on Hawaii*, Bulletin of the Bureau of Labor, no. 66, Washington, 1906.

Durham, Frederick Alexander, *The Lone-Star of Liberia: Being the Outcome of Reflections on Our Own People*, London, 1892.

Eastoe Teall, J., *Slavery and the Slave Trade in 1889: Facts and Memoranda Compiled from the Slave Trade Papers, the Statutes at Large and Other Sources*, London, 1889.

Federation pour la Defense des Interets Belges a L'Etranger, *Mr Morel's Errors*, Brussels, 1904.

Fitzhugh, George, *Cannibals All! or Slaves without Masters*, ed., C. Vann Woodward Cambridge, MA: Harvard University Press, 1960.

Forbes-Lindsay, Charles, The *Philippines under Spanish and American Rules*, Philadelphia: John C. Winston and Co., 1906.

Fox Bourne, Henry, *Regulation of the Liquor Traffic in Africa*, London, 1895.

Fox Bourne, Henry, *Blacks and Whites in South Africa*, London, 1900.

Fox Bourne, Henry, *The Claims of the Uncivilised Races*, London, 1900.

Fox Bourne, Henry, *Slavery and Its Substitutes in Africa*, London, 1900.

Fox Bourne, Henry, *Forced Labour in British South Africa*, London, 1903.

Fox Bourne, Henry, *Slave Trade in Portuguese Africa*, London, 1909.

Fox Bourne, Henry, *The Romance of Trade*, London, n.d.

Fremont Blackman, William, *The Making of Hawaii: a Study in Social Evolution*, New York, 1906.

Gibson, Rev. O., *The Chinese in America*, Cincinnati: Hitchcock and Walden, 1877.

Harris, John H., *Native Races and Peace Terms*, London, 1916.

Hildreth, R., *The White Slave: a True Picture of Slave Life in America*, London, 1852.

Hoffnung, A., *The Recent Revolution in Hawaii*, Woking, 1893.

Holmes, George, 'The Peons of the South', *Annals of the American Academy of Political and Social Science*, IV, (1893–4), 65–74.

Hopkins, Gerald Manley, *Hawaii: the Past, Present and Future of its Island Kingdom*, London, 1866.

Importing Women for Immoral Purposes: 1909 Report from US Immigration Commission, Washington, 1909.

Kraut, Mary H., *Hawaii and a Revolution*, London, 1898.

Laird Clowes, William, *Black America: a Study of the Ex-slave and His Late Master*, London, Paris & Melbourne, 1891.

Lardner, H. R., *The Agricultural and Commercial Problems in Sierra Leone*, Sierra Leone, 1893.

Liberia Bulletin, no. 14, Feb. 1899.

Livingstone, David, *Livingstone's Missionary Travels in South Africa*, London, 1857.

Lovett Cameron, Verney, *Across Africa*, London & New York, 1877.

Moloney, J. A., *With Captain Stairs to Katanga*, London, 1893.

Monk, William, ed., *Doctor Livingstone's Cambridge Lectures*, Cambridge, 1858.

Morel, Edmund D., *The Congo Slave State: a Protest against the New African Slavery*, Liverpool, 1903.

Musick, John R., *Hawaii: Our New Possessions*, New York & London: Funk and Wagnalls, 1898.
Native Labour in South Africa: a Report of a Public Meeting, London, 1903.
Nevinson, Henry W., *A Modern Slavery*, London & New York, 1906.
Newman, Francis, *Anglo-Saxon Abolition of Negro Slavery*, London, 1889.
Nzula, A.T., I.I. Potekhin & A.Z. Zusmanovich, *Forced Labour in Colonial Africa*, London, 1933, this edition 1979.
Oliver, S. P., *The French Soudan Up to Date January 1894*, Woolwich, 1894.
Papers Relating to the Annexation of the Hawaiian Islands to the United States, Washington, 1893.
Raife, Raymond, *The Sheik's White Slave*, London, 1895.
Renner Maxwell, J., *The Negro Question*, London, 1892.
Roe, Clifford, *The Great War on White Slavery or Fighting for the Protection of Our Girls*, New York, 1911.
Simon, Kathleen, *Slavery*, London, 1929.
Slave or Free? Native Labour: an International Problem, Official Paper of the League of Nations, no 23, 1927.
Spivak, John L., *Georgia Nigger*, London, 1933.
Tomlinson, Thomas, *The Congo Treaty*, London, 1884.
Townsend, Frederick Trench, *Wild Life in Florida: with a Visit to Cuba*, London: Hurst and Blackett, 1875.
Ward Beecher, Henry, *Patriotic Addresses in America and England*, New York, 1888.
Washington Williams, George, *A Report upon the Congo State and Country to the President of the Republic of the United States of America*, n.d.
Washington Williams, George, *An Open Letter to His Serene Majesty Leopold II*, n.d.
White Ovington, Mary, *Half a Man: the Status of the Negro in New York*, New York, 1911.
Wilson, Walter, *Forced Labour in the United States*, London, 1933.
Wirt Howe, William, 'The Peonage Cases', *Columbia Law Review*, April 1904.
Woltor, Robert, *A Short and Truthful History of the Capture of California and Oregon by the Chinese AD 1899, by Robert Woltor, a Survivor*, San Francisco: A.L. Bancroft and Co, 1882.

SECONDARY SOURCES

Aarim-Heriot, Najia, *Chinese Immigrants, African Americans and Racial Anxiety in the US, 1848–82*, Champaign: University of Illinois Press, 2003.
Abel, Annie, & Frank Klingberg, eds., *A Side-Light on Anglo-American Relations 1839–58*, Chicago: Association for the Study of Negro Life and History, 1929.
Aje, Lawrence & Catherine Armstrong, eds., *The Many Faces of Slavery*, London: Bloomsbury Academic, 2020.
Allain, Jean, *The Law and Slavery*, Leiden: Brill, 2015.

Alter, Stephen, *Darwinism and the Linguistic Image: Language, Race and Natural Theology in the Nineteenth Century*, Baltimore, MD: Johns Hopkins University Press, 1999.

Barkan, Elliott Robert, *From All Points: America's Immigrant West 1870s-1952*, Bloomington: Indiana University Press, 2007.

Beaumont, Joseph, *The New Slavery: an Account of Indian and Chinese Labourers in British Guiana* (first published 1871), Guyana: The Caribbean Press, 2011.

Behal, Rana, &Marcel van der Linden eds., *Coolies, Capital and Colonialism: Studies in Indian Labour History*, Cambridge: Cambridge University Press, 2007.

Blackett, R. J. M., *Building an Anti-Slavery Wall*, Baton Rouge: Louisiana State University Press, 1983.

Blackmon, Douglas, *Slavery by Another Name: the Re-enslavement of African Americans from the Civil War to World War Two*, New York: Anchor Books, 2008.

Bőger, Astrid, *Envisioning the Nation: the Early American World's Fairs and the Formation of Culture*, Chicago: Campus Verlag, 2010.

Bosma, Ulbe, Elise van Nederveen Meerkerk & Aditya Sarkar eds., *Mediating Labour: Worldwide Labour Intermediation in the Nineteenth and Twentieth Centuries*, Special Issue. Cambridge University Press, 2012.

Britton, John, *Cables, Crises and the Press: the Geopolitics of the New International Information System 1866–1903*, Albuquerque: University of New Mexico Press, 2013.

Brody, David, *In Labor's Cause: Main Themes on the History of the American Worker*, Oxford: Oxford University Press, 1993.

Brooks, James, ed., *Confounding the Color Line: the Indian-Black Experience in North America*, Lincoln: University of Nebraska Press, 2002.

Brownell, Susan, ed., *The 1904 Anthropology Days and Olympic Games*, Lincoln: University of Nebraska Press, 2008.

Campbell, Gwyn, & Elizabeth Elbourne, eds., *Sex, Power and Slavery*, Athens: Ohio University Press, 2014.

Chang, Gordon, *Fateful Ties: a History of America's Preoccupation with China*, Cambridge, MA: Harvard University Press, 2015.

Chester, Edward, *Clash of Titans: Africa and US Foreign Policy*, Maryknoll, NY: Orbis Books, 1974.

Clarence-Smith, William, ed., *The Economics of the Indian Ocean Slave Trade in the Nineteenth Century*, London: Frank Cass, 1989.

Clarence-Smith, William & Steven Topik, eds., *The Global Coffee Economy in Africa, Asia and Latin America 1500–1989*, Cambridge: Cambridge University Press, 2003.

Cooksey, Susan, Robin Poyner & Hein Vantee, eds., *Kongo across the Water*, Gainesville: University Press of Florida, 2013.

Cooper, Frederick, *From Slaves to Squatters: Plantation Labor and Agriculture in Zanzibar and Coastal Kenya 1890–1925*, New Haven: Yale University Press, 1980.

Cooper, Frederick, Thomas Holt & Rebecca Scott, *Beyond Slavery: Explorations of Race, Labour and Citizenship in Post-Emancipation Societies*, Chapel Hill: University of North Carolina, 2000.

Creighton Miller, Stuart, *The Unwelcome Immigrant: the American Image of the Chinese 1785–1882*, Berkeley: University of California Press, 1969.

Cullinane, Michael Patrick, *Liberty and American Anti-imperialism*, London: Palgrave, 2012.

Cumbler, John T., *From Abolition to Rights for All*, Philadelphia: University of Pennsylvania Press, 2008.

Daniel, Pete, *The Shadow of Slavery: Peonage in the South 1901–1969*, Oxford: Oxford University Press, 1972.

Dell'Orto, Giovanna, *American Journalism and International Relations: Foreign Correspondence from the Early Republic to the Digital Era*, Cambridge: Cambridge University Press, 2013.

Deutsch, Jon-Georg, *Emancipation without Abolition in German East Africa, c. 1884–1914*, Athens, Ohio University Press, 2006.

Dix, Andrew & Peter Templeton, eds., *So the War Goes On: Violence and Its Representation in African American History from Slavery to Black Lives Matter*, Abingdon: Routledge, 2020.

Donovan, Brian, *White Slave Crusades: Race, Gender and Anti-Vice Activism 1887–1917*, Champaign: University of Illinois Press, 2006.

Drescher, Seymour, *Abolition: a History of Slavery and Anti-Slavery*, Cambridge: Cambridge University Press, 2009.

Dru Stanley, Amy, *From Bondage to Contract: Wage Labor, Marriage and the Market in the Age of Slave Emancipation*, Cambridge: Cambridge University Press, 1998.

Dubin, Steven, 'Symbolic Slavery: Black Representations in Popular Culture', *Social Problems*, 34: 2 (1987), 122–140.

Elbashir, Ahmed E. *The United States, Slavery and the Slave Trade in the Nile Valley*, Lanham, MD: University Press of America, 1983.

Emery, Michael, Edwin Emery & Nancy Roberts, *The Press and America: An Interpretive History of the Mass Media*, Boston: Allyn and Bacon, 2000.

Emmer, P. C., ed., *Colonialism and Migration: Indentured Labour Before and After Slavery*, Leiden: Martinus Nijhoff Publishers, 1986.

Engle Merry, Sally, *Colonizing Hawaii and the Cultural Power of the Law*, Princeton: Princeton University Press, 2000.

Ennaji, Mohammed, *Serving the Master: Slavery and Society in Nineteenth-Century Morocco*, translated by Seth Graebner, London: Macmillan, 1998.

Esedebe, Peter Olisanwuche, *Pan-Africanism: the Idea and Movement 1776–1963*, Washington: Howard University Press, 1982.

Evans, Brad, *Before Cultures: the Ethnographic Imagination in American Literature 1865–1920*, Chicago: University of Chicago Press, 2005.

Field, James A. Jr., *America in the Mediterranean World 1776–1882*, Princeton: Princeton University Press, 1969.

Fisher, Humphrey J., *Slavery in the History of Muslim Black Africa*, London: Hurst, 1988.

Gara, Larry, *The Liberty Line: the Legend of the Underground Railroad*, Lexington: University of Kentucky Press; reprint edition, 1996.

Gilroy, Paul, *The Black Atlantic: Modernity and Double Consciousness*, London: Verso, 1998.

Glick, Clarence, *Sojourners and Settlers: Chinese Migrants in Hawaii*, Honolulu: University Press of Hawaii, 1980.

Goings, Kenneth, *Mammy and Uncle Mose: Black Collectibles and American Stereotyping*, Bloomington, IN: Indiana University Press, 1994.

Gompers, Samuel, 'Imperialism, Its Dangers and Wrongs', *American Federationist*, 5: 9 (November 1898), 179–83.

Goodman, Paul, *Of One Blood: Abolitionism and the Origins of Racial Equality*, Berkeley: University of California Press, 1998.

Grant, Kevin, *A Civilised Savagery: Britain and the New Slaveries in Africa 1884–1926*, Abingdon: Routledge, 2005.

Green, Abigail, 'Humanitarianism in Nineteenth Century Context: Religious, Gendered, National', *The Historical Journal*, 57 (Dec. 2014), 1157–1175.

Hadden, Sally, *Slave Patrols: Law and Violence in Virginia and the Carolinas*, Cambridge, MA: Harvard University Press, 2003.

Hahamovitch, Cindy, *The Fruits of Their Labour: Atlantic Coast Farmworkers and the Making of Migrant Poverty 1870–1945*, Chapel Hill: University of North Carolina Press, 1997.

Hakan Erdem, Y., *Slavery in the Ottoman Empire and Its Demise 1800–1909*, London: Macmillan, 1996.

Hamilton, Keith, & Patrick Salmon, eds., *Slavery, Diplomacy and Empire*, Eastbourne: Sussex Academic Press, 2009.

Hixon, Walter, *American Settler Colonialism: a History*, London: Palgrave, 2013.

Hochschild, Adam, *King Leopold's Ghost: a Story of Greed, Terror and Heroism in Colonial Africa*, London: Macmillan, 1999.

Hope Franklin, John, *George Washington Williams: a Biography*, Urbana, IL: University of Chicago Press, 1985.

Hopper, Matthew, *Slaves of One Master: Globalisation and Slavery in Arabia in the Age of Empire*, New Haven: Yale University Press, 2015.

Horne, Gerald, *The White Pacific: US Imperialism and Black Slavery in the South Seas after the Civil War*, Honolulu: University of Hawaii Press, 2007.

Hunt, Lynn, *Inventing Human Rights: A History*, London: W.W. Norton, 2007.

Huzzey, Richard, *Freedom Burning: Anti-Slavery and Empire in Victorian Britain*, Ithaca, NY: Cornell University Press, 2012.

Kimura, Yukiko, *Issei: Japanese Immigrants in Hawaii*, Honolulu: University of Hawaii Press, 1988.

Kramer, Paul, *Blood of Government, Race and Empire: the United States and the Philippines*, Chapel Hill: University of North Carolina Press, 2006.

Krauthamer, Barbara, *Black Slaves, Indian Masters: Slavery, Emancipation and Citizenship in the Native American South*, Chapel Hill: University of North Carolina Press, 2013.

Künnemann, Vanessa, & Ruth Mayer, eds., *Trans Pacific Interactions: the United States and China 1880–1950*, London: Palgrave, 2009.

Lander, James, *Lincoln & Darwin: Shared Visions of Race, Science and Religion*, Carbondale: South Illinois University Press, 2010.

Laqua, Daniel, 'Tensions of Internationalism: Transnational Anti-Slavery in the 1880s and 1890s', *International Historical Review*, 33: 4 (2011), 705–26.
Lee, Erika, *At America's Gates: Chinese Immigration during the Exclusion Era*, Chapel Hill: University of North Carolina Press, 2003.
Lee, Joann, & Faung Jean, *Asian American Experiences in the United States*, Jefferson, NC: McFarland, 1991.
Leonard, Thomas C., *Illiberal Reformers: Race, Eugenics and American Economics in the Progressive Era*, Princeton: Princeton University Press, 2016.
Livingstone, David, *Adam's Ancestors: Race, Religion and the Politics of Human Origin*, Baltimore, MD: Johns Hopkins University Press, 2008.
Love, Eric, *Race over Empire: Race and Imperialism 1865–1900*, Chapel Hill: University of North Carolina Press, 2004.
Lovejoy, Paul, & Jan Hogendorn, *Slow Death for Slavery: the Course of Abolition in Northern Nigeria 1897–1936*, Cambridge: Cambridge University Press, 1993.
Mack, Angela, & Stephen G. Hoffius, eds., *Landscape of Slavery: the Plantation in American Art*, Columbia: University of South Carolina Press, 2008.
Manning, Patrick, *Slavery and African Life: Occidental, Oriental and African Slave Trades*, Cambridge: Cambridge University Press, 1990.
Martinez, Jenny, *The Slave Trade and the Origins of International Human Rights Law*, Oxford: Oxford University Press, 2012.
McCarthy, Thomas, *Race, Empire and the Idea of Human Development*, Cambridge: Cambridge University Press, 2009.
McClellan, Robert, *The Heathen Chinee: a Study of American Attitudes towards China 1890–1905*, Athens: Ohio University Press, 1971.
McCoy, Alfred, & Francisco Scarone, eds., *Colonial Crucible: Empire in the Making of the Modern American State*, Madison: University of Wisconsin Press, 2009.
McCoy, Alfred, *Policing America's Empire: the US, the Philippines and the Rise of the Surveillance State*, Madison: University of Wisconsin Press, 2009.
Meagher, Arnold J., *The Coolie Trade: Traffic in Chinese Laborers to Latin America 1847–1874*, London: X Libris, 2008.
Merry, Sally Engle, *Colonizing Hawaii: the Cultural Power of Law*, Princeton, NJ: Princeton University Press, 2000.
Midgley, Clare, *Women against Slavery: the British Campaigns 1780–1870*, Abingdon: Routledge, 1992.
Miller, Floyd, *The Search for a Black Nationality: Black Emigration and Colonization 1787–1863*, Urbana: University of Illinois Press, 1973.
Milton Quaife, Milo, 'The Doctrine of Non-intervention with Slavery in the Territories', PhD for University of Chicago, 1910.
Mulligan, William, &Maurice Bric, eds., *A Global History of Anti-Slavery Politics in the Nineteenth Century*, London: Palgrave, 2013.
Nadelmann, Ethan, 'Global Prohibition Regimes: the Evolution of Norms in International Society', *International Organisation*, 44: 4 (1990), 479–526.
Novak, Daniel, *The Wheel of Servitude: Black Forced Labor after Slavery*, Lexington: University of Kentucky Press, 1978.

O'Connor, John E., *I Am a Fugitive from a Georgia Chain Gang: the Screenplay*, Madison: University of Wisconsin Press, 1981.

Okihiro, Gary, *Island World: a History of Hawaii and the United States*, Berkeley: University of California Press, 2008.

Osborne, Thomas J., *Empire Can Wait: American Opposition to Hawaiian Annexation 1893–1898*, Kent, OH: Kent State University Press, 1981.

Patterson, Wayne, *The Korean Frontier in America: Immigration to Hawaii 1896–1910*, Honolulu: University of Hawaii Press, 1988.

Peskin, Lawrence, & Edmund Wehrle, *America and the World*, Baltimore, MD: Johns Hopkins University Press, 2012.

Peterson, Derek, ed., *Abolitionism and Imperialism in Britain, Africa and the Atlantic*, Athens: Ohio University Press, 2010.

Phon, Hong Gia, *Bonds of Citizenship, Land and the Labors of Emancipation*, New York: New York University Press, 2013.

Platt, Len, ed., *Modernism and Race*, Cambridge: Cambridge University Press, 2011.

Poblete, Joanna, *Islanders in the Empire: Filipino and Puerto Rican Laborers in Hawaii*, Champaign: University of Illinois Press, 2014.

Quirk, Joel, *The Anti-Slavery Project from the Slave Trade to Human Trafficking*, Philadelphia: University of Pennsylvania Press, 2011.

Reydams, Luc, ed., *Global Activism Reader*, London: Continuum, 2011.

Robinson-Dunn, Diane, *The Harem, Slavery and British Imperial Culture*, Manchester: Manchester University Press, 2006.

Roggenkamp, Karen, *Narrating the News: New Journalism and Literary Genre in Late Nineteenth Century American Newspapers and Fiction*, Kent, OH: Kent State University Press, 2005.

Sachsman, David B., S. Kittrell Rushing & Ray Morris Jr., eds., *Seeking a Voice: Images of Race and Gender in the Nineteenth Century Press*, West Lafayette, IN: Purdue University Press, 2009.

Salman, Michael, *The Embarrassment of Slavery: Controversies over Bondage and Nationalism in the American Colonial Philippines*, Berkeley: University of California Press, 2001.

Samorin, William J., *The Black Man's Burden: African Colonial Labor on the Congo and Ubangi Rivers 1880–1900*, Boulder, CO: Westview Press, 1989.

Savage, Elizabeth, ed., *The Human Commodity: Perspectives on the Trans-Saharan Slave Trade*, London: Frank Cass, 1992.

Schmieder, Ulrike, Katja Füllberg-Stolberg & Michael Zeuske, eds., *The End of Slavery in Africa and the Americas. A Comparative Approach*, Berlin: LIT Verlag, 2011.

Scott, Rebecca, *Degrees of Freedom: Louisiana and Cuba after Slavery*, Cambridge, MA: Harvard University Press, 2005.

Smith, John David, 'A Different View of Slavery: Black Historians Attack the Proslavery Argument 1890-1920', *Journal of Negro History*, 65: 4 (1980), 298–311.

Soennichsen, John, *The Chinese Exclusion Act of 1882*, Santa Barbara, CA: Greenwood, 2011.

Stange, Margit, *Personal Property: Wives, White Slaves and the Market in Women*, Baltimore, MD: Johns Hopkins University Press, 1998.

Stannard, David, *Before the Horror: the Population of Hawaii on the Eve of Western Contact*, Honolulu: University of Hawaii Press, 1989.

Stanton, William, *The Leopard's Spots: Scientific Attitudes towards Race in America 1815–59*, Chicago: University of Chicago Press, 1960.

Steinfeld, Robert, *The Invention of Free Labor: Employment Relation in English and American Law and Culture 1350–1870*, Chapel Hill: University of North Carolina Press, 1991.

Suranyi, Anna, *The Atlantic Connection 1450–1900*, Abingdon: Routledge, 2015.

Tinker, Hugh, *A New System of Slavery: the Export of Indian Labour Overseas 1830–1920*, Oxford: Oxford University Press, 1974.

Trafton, Scott, *Egypt Land: Race and Nineteenth Century American Egyptomania*, Durham, NC: Duke University Press, 2004.

Tucher, Andie, *Froth and Scum: Truth, Beauty, Goodness and the Ax Murderer in America's First Mass Medium*, Chapel Hill: University of North Carolina Press, 1994.

Tyrrell, Ian, *Reforming the World: the Creation of America's Moral Empire*, Princeton: Princeton University Press, 2010.

Van Deburg, William, *Slavery and Race in American Popular Culture*, Madison: University of Wisconsin Press, 1984.

Vlach, John Michael, *The Planter's Prospect: Privilege and Slavery in Plantation Paintings*, Chapel Hill: University of North Carolina Press, 2002.

Walz, Terence, & Kenneth Cuno, eds., *Race and Slavery in the Middle East*, Cairo: American University in Cairo Press, 2010.

Wilson, Carter, *Racism from Slavery to Advanced Capitalism*, Thousand Oaks, CA: Sage, 1996.

Wolff, Leon, *Little Brown Brother: How the US Purchased and Pacified the Philippines at the Century's Turn*, Oxford: Oxford University Press, 1960.

Woodruff, Nan, *American Congo: the African American Freedom Struggle in the Delta*, Cambridge, MA: Harvard University Press, 2003.

Young, Elliott, *Alien Nation: Chinese Migration in the Americas from the Coolie Era through World War II*, Chapel Hill: University of North Carolina Press, 2014.

Zimmerman, Andrew, *Alabama in Africa: Booker T. Washington, the German Empire and the Globalisation of the New South*, Princeton: Princeton University Press, 2010.

Index

abolition, 5, 12, 51, 68, 72, 81, 85, 92, 103, 134, 149, 152, 165, 186, 225, 236, 240, 255, 272
  and international law, 6
  challenges to, 36
  success of, 19, 25
abolitionism
  rhetoric of, 23, 30
abolitionists, 1, 33, 98, 185
  eyewitness testimony, 205, 206
  and hypocrisy, 56, 64, 229, 232
  narrative, 2
  and religion, 44, 110, 113
  rhetoric, 20, 21, 32, 36, 39, 63, 77, 107, 142, 158, 161, 186, 193, 196, 269
  success of, 37, 40, 69, 82, 204, 253
  transatlantic, 64, 68, 70, 75, 102, 140, 206
  transatlantic networks, 2
Addams, Jane, 34, 53, 56, 175, 194, 208, 210, 212, 216, 228, 236
African Americans, 9, 11, 12, 13, 14, 16, 20, 25, 31, 34, 35, 41, 42, 43, 44, 45, 48, 49, 53, 58, 59, 64, 90, 94, 107, 117, 122, 127, 128, 136, 140, 141, 142, 143, 144, 148, 149, 150, 154, 155, 159, 164, 166, 169, 170, 176, 179, 180, 181, 187, 193, 195, 214, 220, 221, 224, 228, 233, 236, 237, 240, 241, 242, 243, 244, 245, 246, 248, 250, 251, 252, 253, 256, 260, 261, 262, 263, 264, 265, 267, 269, 270, 272, 273, 274, 275
Africans
  and alcohol, 80, 150
  as collaborators, 49, 120, 133, 138, 205
  as slave owners, 3, 86, 113, 119, 121, 190
  as slaves, 3, 8, 32, 43, 58, 61, 75, 79, 82, 84, 102, 111, 116, 150, 151, 162, 168, 201, 204
Angola, 87, 98, 172
Anti-Slavery convention, 2

Balongiga, 101
barracoons, 95, 256
Beecher Stowe, Harriet, 39, 48, 196
Black Codes, 151
blackbirding, 69, 93, 157, 159, 191
Boas, Franz, 11, 248, 261, 274
Boulger, Demetrius, 55, 56, 72, 73, 168, 191
British and Foreign Antislavery Society, 68, 72, 73, 74, 75, 81, 83, 89, 90, 92, 94, 103
Brussels Conference, 75, 82, 136, 137, 140, 204, 278
Bushnell Hart, Albert, 44, 48, 58, 142, 192, 242

Cairo, slave trade in, 171, 199
Caribbean region
  slavery in, 3, 33, 102, 117, 160, 256
Carlyle, Thomas, 82, 152
Civil War, American, 6, 18, 19, 30, 31, 36, 63, 76, 93, 97, 141, 154, 242, 254, 269
concubines, 54, 86, 108, 111, 112, 121, 142, 184, 193, 201, 203, 213, 215
Confederacy, 143, 242

Congo, 7, 15, 30, 32, 34, 53, 55, 69, 73, 74, 77, 84, 98, 104, 112, 115, 134, 135, 136, 137, 139, 140, 149, 165, 167, 176, 191, 197, 205, 228, 230, 233, 241, 253, 254, 263, 267, 272
Congo Horror, 7, 53
convict labour. *See* labour, convict
Cook, Huestis P., 14, 49, 250
coolies, 37, 92, 94, 164
crimps, 95, *See* labour agents
Cuba, 61, 75, 93, 102, 124, 155, 160, 162, 258

debt bondage, 29, 41, 45, 57, 79, 124, 143, 149, 150, 169, 179, 228, *See* Peonage
Dillingham Commission, 56, 216
Douglass, Frederick, 10, 11, 227, 228, 264, 265
Du Bois, W.E.B., 261, 263
Durham, Frederick, 140, 152

Egypt, 30, 43, 157, 199, 202, 220
Egyptomania, 261, 264
emancipation, 18, 41, 65, 67, 81, 151, 164, 179, 227, 252, 253, 260
Ethiopia, 23, 121, 261
eugenics, 148, 170, 212, 222, 272
eunuchs, 87, 110, 112, 121, 201

Fitzhugh, George, 36, 37, 40, 41, 59, 155, 192, 232
Forbes-Lindsay, Charles, 88, 89, 172
Fox Bourne, Henry, 55, 74, 75, 78, 79, 85, 88, 132, 134, 136, 171, 172
free and unfree labour, 2, 5, 11, 31, 37, 39, 40, 41, 45, 64, 69, 70, 72, 83, 85, 91, 99, 101, 104, 117, 149, 231, 245
freedmen and women, 41, 46, 63, 82, 180, 252, 261
freedmen, Cherokee, 251
Freedmen's Bureau, 41, 192, 258

harem, 4, 16, 22, 112, 156, 187, 192, 200, 203, 204
Harleston, Edwin, 142
Harris, Alice, 197, 233, 235
Harris, John, 197, 233
Hawaii, 10, 30, 60, 70, 89, 90, 93, 94, 123, 139, 159, 166, 167, 177, 180, 183, 195, 218
  annexation of, 45, 59, 123, 231
  Japanese labourers in, 154, 177, 178, 258
human trafficking, 193, 238
humanitarianism, 1, 6, 8, 12, 21, 23, 32, 36, 39, 40, 65, 71, 73, 76, 78, 81, 99, 102, 103, 104, 107, 145, 147, 154, 155, 160, 164, 165, 166, 167, 182, 193, 225, 226, 229, 232, 267, 269, 270, 272

immigration, 8, 20, 30, 45, 89, 90, 105, 165, 216, 217, 224, 226, 228, 265, 274
  Chinese, 54, 60, 90, 94, 127, 128, 164, 178, 257, 270
imperialism, 11, 16, 26, 230, 231, 271
  American, 7, 76, 99
  and anti-imperialism, 10, 60, 99
  antislavery, 8, 21, 80, 108, 112, 231, 234, 274
  British, 225, 275
indentured labourers, 22, 37, 40, 59, 62, 69, 92, 159, 165, 189, 222, 255, 256, 258, 259, 265
internationalism, 263, 264, 266

Jim Crow
  era, 23, 42, 47, 52, 142, 150, 159, 164, 169, 176, 240, 248, 251
  racism, 169, 192, 243, 248, 260, *See* racism and segregation
  romanticisation, 141, 145, 240, 269, 273

kangany. *See* labour agents
Ku Klux Klan, 158, 216

labour
  degraded, 12, 45, 149, 162, 163, 166, 176
  shortages, 69
labour agents, 127, 160, 172, 189, *See* crimps, *kangany*, *padroni*
labour, convict, 29, 52, 55, 58, 64, 142, 143, 144, 149, 150, 179, 190, 232, 243, 245, 253, 269
League of Nations, 76, 77, 264, 267
Leopold II of Belgium, 53
Lincoln, Abraham, 36, 40, 64, 76, 226, 227
Livingstone, David, 79, 80, 86, 112, 138, 139
Lost Cause, 13, 49, 141, 210
Lovett Cameron, Verney, 80, 85, 98, 113
Lustful Turk, 24, 111, 200, 224

Manifest Destiny, 10
manumission, 110, 114, 118
marriage as slavery, 84, 185, 192, 203, 204, 215, 258
Marxism, 39, 226
mining, 231
 coal, 242, 245
 gold, 79, 88
miscegenation, 44, 142, 193, 195, 198, 208
missionaries, 12, 78, 93, 94, 108, 113, 115, 126, 134, 135, 137, 138, 139, 140, 157, 205, 220, 233
modernity, 9, 19, 23, 42, 104, 123, 173, 183, 211, 222
Monroe Doctrine, 70, 100
Morel, Edmund D., 15, 35, 53, 76, 112, 137, 139
Morocco, 74, 122, 203

National Association of the Advancement of Colored People, 261
nationalism, 11, 15
 Black, 260
Native Americans, 11, 43, 45, 101, 109, 122, 123, 151, 163, 251, *See* slavery, and the Cherokee, slavery and the Lumbee
nativism, 8, 30, 65
Negro Problem (so-called), 117, 142, 181, 228, 242
neo-abolitionists, 7, 53, 186
Nevinson, Henry, 39, 49, 67, 68, 82, 83, 87, 98, 99, 133, 134, 140, 172, 173, 201, 232, 233
Nigeria, 81

Ottoman Empire, 4, 22, 36, 199, 200, 207

padroni, 127, 170
pan-African, 14, 228, 260, 264
pan-Africanism, 11
paper sons, 257
peonage, 55, 57, 58, 59, 64, 143, 144, 150, 155, 169, 179, 231, 232, 243, 253, 266, *See* Bondage, Debt
Philippines, 10, 11, 22, 30, 36, 44, 60, 64, 70, 88, 89, 98, 99, 101, 123, 124, 141, 165, 265
photography, 14, 25, 109, 135
plantations
 artistic portrayals of, 47, 142, 197, 250
 cocoa, 82, 87, 133, 173
 coffee, 138, 189
 cotton, 58
 rubber, 15
 sugar, 10, 59, 89, 90, 93, 102, 159, 160, 172, 178, 183, 259
polygenesis, 31, 43, 117
progressivism, 18, 56, 59, 143, 163, 216, 223, 225, 229, 237, 242, 267
prostitution, 34, 53, 56, 62, 111, 128, 129, 174, 175, 183, 184, 186, 187, 193, 194, 208, 210, 213, 214, 215, 216, 217, 219, 222, 223, 224, 228, 236, 237, 239, 272, 274

Quackenbos, Mary Grace, 266

racial hierarchy, 11, 19, 21, 31, 42, 43, 45, 64, 96, 109, 122, 148, 150, 152, 156, 157, 164, 177, 210, 224, 239, 251, 265
racial stereotypes, 13, 16, 102, 111, 112, 119, 214, 255, 261
racism
 scientific, 19, 22, 26, 43, 45, 102, 109, 118, 240, 248, 251
 and segregation, 180, 244, 250, *See* Jim Crow
Ravenel Huger Smith, Alice, 141, 142, 198, 250
Rebellion
 Mahdist, 121, 260
 Morant Bay, 69, 81, 82, 92

Sao Tome, 77, 87, 172
serfdom, 7, 91, 93, 108
Simon, Kathleen, 25, 75, 77, 144, 154, 186, 207, 226, 230, 235, 267
slave trade
 Arab, 112, 113, 138
 transatlantic, 2, 5, 26, 30, 67, 69, 77, 86, 88, 89, 132, 136, 148, 161, 189, 261, 274
slave traders, 6, 80, 85, 87, 104, 108, 109, 113, 119, 122, 125, 126, 132, 134, 140, 158, 173, 191
slavery
 antebellum, 24, 25, 31, 45, 50, 51, 53, 57
 and the Constitution, 28

chattel, 1, 3, 12, 18, 19, 20, 28, 29, 30, 31, 34, 35, 41, 42, 46, 48, 49, 52, 53, 54, 55, 56, 58, 63, 64, 65, 68, 83, 85, 99, 102, 104, 105, 109, 128, 133, 140, 144, 149, 154, 165, 176, 180, 192, 196, 198, 208, 214, 226, 232, 236, 242, 244, 248, 256, 266, 270, 273, 275
Cherokee, 154, *See* Native Americans
Circassian, 187, 198, 199, 200, 207, 221, 223
definition, 2, 5, 6, 7, 21, 26, 27, 55, 83, 105, 116, 118, 132, 147, 167, 183, 252, 265, 267, 269, 270, 271, 272, 273, 275
domestic, 2, 24, 32, 41, 73, 83, 85, 104, 120, 138, 201, 204
and family, 24, 50, 174, 185, 190, 193, 201, 202, 208, 211, 219, 254, 257, 258
in newspapers, 4, 14, 15, 16, 17, 19, 60, 91, 112, 113, 114, 119, 131, 134, 137, 138, 159, 167, 187, 244, 245, 256, 267
legal prohibition of, 5, 6, 17
Lumbee. *See* Native Americans
radical responses to, 10, 11, 21, 22, 25, 28, 76, 99, 108, 109, 130, 144, 173, 182, 185, 216, 225, 226, 227, 228, 229, 231, 232, 233, 235, 236, 237, 238, 240, 242, 243, 245, 247, 248, 252, 254, 258, 260, 261, 263, 264, 266, 269, 271, 272
running away from, 48, 53, 255
sexual, 24, 110, 128, 183, 187, 194, 200, 202, 205, 208, 211, 213, 215, 218, 219, 239
and suffragists' campaigning, 188, 221
symbolic, 29, 48, 64, 150, 180
symbolism of, 52, 63
symbols of, 20
as uncivilised practice, 8, 11, 23, 30, 72, 91, 101, 109, 117, 119, 120, 123, 219, 221, 223, 246, 247
and victimhood, 63, 126, 147, 174, 182, 183, 184, 196, 198, 210, 220, 221, 222, 224, 237, 269
Social Darwinism, 19, 174
solidarity, 150, 159, 175, 176, 178, 181, 183, 228, 242, 243, 250, 252, 264
South Africa, 87, 131, 230
Southern states, 5, 18, 45, 59, 68, 90, 93, 123, 193, 250, 266
Spivak, John L., 52

Tanganyika, 120
Tippu Tip, 85, 86, 108, 113
Togo, 168, 263

Uncle Tom's Cabin, 3, 39, 48, 63, 65, 139, 196, 240
unions, 95, 163, 165, 176, 178, 226, 243, 267
and blood unionism, 90, 178, 259

victim blaming, 24, 170, 173, 183, 188

wages, 8, 22, 59, 60, 150, 154, 157, 163, 169, 178, 190, 205, 213, 237, 256, 258, 259, 266
Washington Williams, George, 15, 34, 53, 84, 100, 136, 139, 205, 233, 261, 263
Washington, Booker T., 34, 55, 168, 251, 263, 266
white identity, 142, 151, 220, 242
white slavery, 15, 34, 37, 53, 56, 63, 127, 176, 183, 186, 193, 194, 198, 207, 208, 210, 211, 212, 216, 217, 219, 223, 227, 236, 238, 239
depiction in literature, 173
procurers, 53, 56, 115, 126, 128, 129, 173, 174, 175, 183, 188, 211, 212, 217, 219, 223, 239
white slavery panic, 4, 17, 20, 24, 63, 87, 150, 187, 193, 207, 212, 213, 216, 219, 220, 236, 237, 270, 272, 275
whiteness, 11, 23, 24, 31, 111, 162, 187, 198, 207, 208, 218, 223
Wilson, Walter, 39, 52, 58, 75, 190, 230, 243, 244, 245
World War One, 10, 12, 18, 19, 66, 68, 77, 94, 95, 100, 135, 145, 197, 229, 253, 260, 263, 264, 267
WPA narratives, 122, 274

Zanzibar, 77, 80, 191, 201

CPSIA information can be obtained
at www.ICGtesting.com
Printed in the USA
LVHW092011300820
664593LV00008B/239

SUGARCANE PHYSIOLOGY

A Comprehensive Study of the
Saccharum Source-to-Sink System

ALEX GETCHELL ALEXANDER
B.S., M.S., Ph.D.

AGRICULTURAL EXPERIMENT STATION,
UNIVERSITY OF PUERTO RICO

ELSEVIER SCIENTIFIC PUBLISHING COMPANY
AMSTERDAM – LONDON – NEW YORK 1973

ELSEVIER SCIENTIFIC PUBLISHING COMPANY
335 Jan van Galenstraat
P.O. Box 211, Amsterdam, The Netherlands

AMERICAN ELSEVIER PUBLISHING COMPANY, INC.
52 Vanderbilt Avenue
New York, New York 10017

Library of Congress Card Number 78-190675

ISBN 0-444-41016-3

Printed in The Netherlands

FOREWORD

In antiquity, the Greek philosopher Protagoras proposed that "man is the measure of all things". Within the realm of modern plant physiology the same tribute is applicable to the *Saccharum* species and mixtures of species known as sugarcane. From the context of a purely crop science to highly fundamental plant systems analyses, sugarcane research has extended the outer frontiers of plant physiological understanding.

Having joined in 1962 a small group of investigators working to bolster Puerto Rico's declining sugar industry, the author was at once impressed by the sheer magnitude of the sugarcane source-to-sink system. Given good cultural conditions sugarcane will produce annually up to 90 tons of storage tissue per acre in a commercial operation – an accomplishment matched by few, if any, plant species. Within the leaves sheltering these stalks there was recently discovered a "new" photosynthetic mechanism helping to provide abundant sugar for storage in addition to growth and metabolic needs. Transport of this sugar from leaf to storage tissues is itself no small achievement. In Cuba alone some 8000000 tons of sucrose were translocated in 1970, through a conducting phloem system peculiarly complicated in tropical grasses, and by mechanisms mainly known to the plant itself.

While composing the story of the *Saccharum* source-to-sink system several groups of readers having divergent needs and interests were kept constantly in mind. Foremost is the college-trained plantation manager, and perhaps the average cane grower of the future, who no longer has the time or means to keep abreast with developments in crop physiology. To him, subjects such as photosynthesis, sugar metabolism, or sugar transport might invoke only memories of classroom lectures and examinations, but they are also factors of intimate concern to the science of sugar planting. The student of plant physiology – graduate or advanced undergraduate – is a second reader having an interest in the sugarcane story. Since the mid-1960's sugarcane has entered the world's greenhouses, laboratories, and classrooms as a teaching model and object of fundamental plant research. It is not unlikely that sugarcane will help instruct the young physiologists and agronomists who must soon give an answer to the worldwide call for more carbohydrate and protein. A third reader is any plant scientist embarking for the first time on professional research with sugarcane. At the very least, La caña is a physiological "personality" whose idiosyncracies must be learned and understood if very much satisfaction is to be gotten in return for one's efforts. Understanding the plant as whole probably constitutes a lifetime effort; indeed, many excellent scientists have devoted their entire career to sugarcane. A comprehensive reference work on sugarcane physiology is therefore needed to provide a rapid and correct perspective.

The present book is, in fact, what the author would like to have had when first encountering sugarcane a decade ago.

An attempt was made to present a historical perspective consistent with *Saccharum* species evolution and the development of sugarcane research along with general plant physiology during the past four decades. It was thought also that students of sugarcane in a number of cane-growing nations have only limited access to plant physiological literature. The present literature review was completed in May, 1971.

A.G. ALEXANDER
Everett, Washington

Dedicated
to
my parents
Alex and Ruth Alexander

ACKNOWLEDGEMENTS

As is typical for works of this sort it is not possible to properly credit all individuals and institutions who have lent valuable assistance. However, the author must acknowledge complete indebtedness to Mrs. C. L. Rosario who somehow deciphered and typed beautifully the entire manuscript. To the Station's library assistants, and to the staff of the Science Library, Washington State University, the author is similarly indebted. To Mrs. C.A. Alexander, Director of the National Agricultural Library, Beltsville, Md., and to Library of Congress staff members, Washington, D.C., special thanks are due for their help in locating numerous antiquated and rare works relating to plant physiology.

A number of prominent sugarcane scientists kindly consented to review individual chapters and to discuss directly with the author various aspects of the book. In Australia, Drs. K.T. Glasziou, C.R. Slack, M.D. Hatch, and T.A. Bull, all of whom have greatly advanced sugarcane as a basic research specimen, read portions of the manuscript and gave valuable consultation. Similarly, in Hawaii, Dr. L.G. Nickell made available much technical information and reviewed parts of the chapter dealing with tissue culture. Through their kindness and by exceptionally good fortune, the author was able to confer personally with Drs. H.P. Kortschak, G.O. Burr, D.J. Heinz, and Constance E. Hartt, at the Experiment Station, H.S.P.A., with Dr. H.F. Clements, University of Hawaii, and with Dr. R.E. Coleman at the Plant Industry Station, Beltsville, Md. Personnel of the Tate and Lyle Research Centre, London, were extremely generous in consultation and cooperated significantly in compiling manuscript information. I particularly want to thank Dr. A.J. Vlitos and Dr. R.H. Tilbury who provided much technical information and reviewed portions of the manuscript dealing with postharvest physiology. Dr. J.P. Nitsch, Phytotron Director at Gif-sur-Yvette, Paris, and Dr. L.P. Hebert, Superintendent of the Sugarcane Field Station, Canal Point, Florida, gave graciously of their time and institutions' literature.

Above all, the author is immeasurably indebted to Mr. Arturo Roque, former Director of the Agricultural Experiment Station at Río Piedras, under whose directorship the Station was a haven for all genuinely concerned with fundamental plant research.

A.G. ALEXANDER

CONTENTS

Foreword V
Acknowledgements IX

INTRODUCTION

Chapter 1 – **Origin of the *Saccharum* source-to-sink system**

1. Introduction 3
2. Phytogeologic history of the cultivated canes 5
   A. The original noble canes 5
   B. Geologic transition of Malaysia 7
   C. Flora migrations in the Cretaceous and Pleistocene 9
   D. Prehistoric movement of primitive cane 10
   E. Origin of the noble canes as cultivated garden or chewing forms 11
   F. Migrations and development of noble canes 11
   G. Probable ancestry of cultivated canes 12
3. Allied genera and speciation of the genus *Saccharum* 14
   A. The world's major grasses 14
   B. Allied genera; the *Saccharum* complex 15
   C. *Saccharum* speciation 18
4. The wild sugarcanes 20
   A. General 20
   B. Geographical distribution of wild canes 21
   C. Polynesian canes 23
   D. Contribution of wild canes to the development of *S. officinarum* 24
5. Development of modern cane varieties 25
   A. Origin of the commercial cane hybrids 25
   B. Advent of the controlled cross 27
   C. Intergeneric crosses 28
   D. Interspecific crosses 35
   E. The introgression theory (*S. officinarum* X *Miscanthus*) 37
6. Cytogenetics of cultivated canes 39
   A. General 39
   B. Cytogenetic origin of *S. officinarum* 40
   C. Basic chromosome numbers 40
   D. New approaches to sugarcane improvement 42
   E. Induced sugarcane mutations 43
7. Chromosome transmission and inheritance 45
   A. Maternal (*S. officinarum*) transmission of somatic chromosome numbers 45
   B. Gene transmission and character inheritance 49
8. Regional improvement of cultivated canes 51
   A. Breeding for qualitative character improvement 51
   B. The Northern Caribbean sugarcanes 52
   C. Louisiana canes 54
   D. Hawaiian cane breeding 56
   E. Performance history of improved canes 58

9. *Saccharum* evolution of a superior source-to-sink system . . . 60
A. Physiological efficiency . . . 61
B. "Source" and "sink" concepts . . . 62
C. Sugarcane growth and the C_4 pathway . . . 63
D. Isozyme (isoenzyme) analysis as a potential research tool . . . 65

PART I – SOURCE REACTIONS AND THE ORIGIN OF SUCROSE

Chapter 2 – **Photosynthesis in chlorophyll-bearing plants**
1. Introduction . . . 69
2. Energy capture from solar radiation . . . 71
A. Photosystem I (Photoact I) . . . 72
B. Photosystem II (Photoact II) . . . 74
C. Cyclic photophosphorylation . . . 75
D. Noncyclic photophosphorylation . . . 76
E. Ferredoxin and the photoreduction of $NADP^+$ . . . 77
F. Cyclic and noncyclic photophosphorylation as distinct reactions . . . 79
G. The chemiosmotic hypothesis . . . 83
3. CO_2 assimilation . . . 83
A. Theories of photosynthetic carbon reduction . . . 84
B. The reductive pentose phosphate cycle . . . 85
C. The carboxylation phase . . . 86
D. The reductive phase . . . 87
E. The regenerative phase . . . 88
F. Steady-state *vs.* nonsteady-state experiments . . . 91
G. Low activity of carbon reduction enzymes . . . 91

Chapter 3 – **Photosynthesis: CO_2 assimilation in sugarcane**
1. Introduction . . . 93
2. The C_4 pathway of CO_2 assimilation . . . 94
A. Initial work by Kortschak and co-workers . . . 94
B. Essential steps of the C_4 pathway . . . 98
C. Extension of the C_4 pathway to other plants . . . 102
3. Enzymology of the C_4 pathway . . . 102
A. Synthesis of CO_2 acceptor . . . 102
B. Ribulose diphosphate carboxylase . . . 104
C. Malic enzyme . . . 105
D. Initial search for transcarboxylase activity . . . 106
E. Reactions incidental to the C_4 pathway . . . 108
F. Evidence for light regulation of C_4 pathway enzymes . . . 109
4. Characteristic features of C_4 pathway plants . . . 112
5. Photosynthesis and photorespiration . . . 113
6. Evidence of Calvin-cycle CO_2 fixation in sugarcane stalks . . . 115
7. Carbon flow to 3-phosphoglyceric acid: Cooperation of mesophyll and parenchyma-sheath chloroplasts . . . 115
A. Operation of two chloroplast types . . . 117
B. Differential enzyme retention by disrupted leaf tissue . . . 120
8. CO_2 assimilation by isolated sugarcane chloroplasts . . . 121
A. Isolation of viable chloroplasts and enzyme localization . . . 121
B. Chloroplast permeability . . . 122
9. Energy conversion in sugarcane . . . 122
A. Inefficient use of solar energy . . . 122
B. Sugarcane chloroplasts . . . 124

C. Photosynthesis inhibitors in cane chloroplast preparations 125
D. Absence of Photosystem II in C_4 species parenchyma-sheath chloroplasts . . . 125
E. Chlorophyll and enzyme gradients relating to basipetal transport 127

Chapter 4 – **Rate of photosynthesis**
1. Introduction 129
2. Photosynthesis as a function of light intensity 130
A. Saturating light intensity and the compensation point 130
B. Light response of individual leaves 135
C. Light intensity *vs.* respiration during photosynthesis 142
D. Photosynthesis in relation to chlorophyll content 143
3. Photosynthesis response to CO_2 supply 144
A. CO_2 and HCO_3^- as photosynthetic carbon sources 144
B. Effects of CO_2 concentration on rate of photosynthesis 146
C. CO_2 fertilization; light × CO_2 supply 151
D. CO_2 as a limiting photosynthesis factor among species 152
E. CO_2 transport in relation to foliar water regime 155
F. The CO_2 compensation point 156
G. CO_2 transport as a function of discrete resistances 157
4. Photosynthesis decline in nutrient-deficient plants 158
A. General aspects of CO_2 assimilation as affected by nutrition 159
B. Effects of K, Mg, and Ca deficiency 160
C. Effects of N and P deficiency 164
5. Assimilation rate in relation to water supply 167
A. General 167
B. Soil moisture effects 169
6. Photorespiration 172
A. Photorespiration and O_2 supply 172
B. Photorespiration and glycolate metabolism 173
7. Product repression 174
A. General 174
B. Sucrose repression of sugarcane photosynthesis 175
C. Oxygen inhibition of photosynthesis 178
8. Photosynthesis control in sugarcane 179
A. Leaf geometry *vs.* light intensity and CO_2 supply 180
B. Temperature effects 182
C. Photosynthesis potential *vs.* leaf rank 183
D. Plant age and seasonal effects 183
E. Effects of sugar concentrations in source and sinks 185
F. Effects of photosynthesis conditions on initial yield of C_4-dicarboxylic acids . . 187
G. Varietal effects 189
H. Additional factors affecting photosynthesis in sugarcane 192

Chapter 5 – **Polysaccharide biosynthesis**
1. Introduction 195
2. Sugarcane starches in perspective 196
A. Distribution among *Saccharum* species 196
B. Physiological role 198
C. Foliar starch production in relation to sucrose synthesis and transport 198
D. Evidence of foliar starch in *S. officinarum* 202
E. Insoluble cane photosynthate; α-glucan 204
3. Mechanisms of starch biosynthesis 206
A. Starch phosphorylase 206

B. Starch synthetase (UDPG–, ADPG–starch transglucosylase) 208
4. Polysaccharide synthesis by sugarcane leaf preparations 210
A. The phosphorylase reaction 210
B. Phosphorylase properties 211
C. Phosphorylase distribution; spatial and functional considerations 213
D. Evidence of starch synthetase (UDPG–starch transglucosylase) 214
E. The Q enzyme; polysaccharide elaboration 217
F. Foliar polysaccharide formation in context 220
5. Polysaccharide synthesis under conditions of variable water, N, P, and K supply . . . 221

Chapter 6 – **Sucrose biosynthesis**
1. Introduction 225
2. Historical aspects of sucrose biosynthesis 226
A. Early concepts of sucrose as a primary and a secondary photosynthate 227
B. Sucrose synthesis by chemical means; isosucrose 228
C. Biological synthesis of sucrose 230
D. Recognition of the sugar phosphates 231
E. Failure of invertase to account for sucrose synthesis 233
3. Sucrose phosphorylase 234
A. Discovery of sucrose phosphorylase 235
B. Properties and mode of action of sucrose phosphorylase 236
4. UDPG-transglycosylase mechanisms in sucrose synthesis 238
A. Discovery of UDPG 238
B. Implication of UDPG in sucrose synthesis 238
C. Enzymatic synthesis of sucrose and sucrose phosphate 241
D. UDPG in sucrose phosphate synthesis 245
E. Enzymatic synthesis of UDPG 245
F. Nucleoside specificity in sucrose synthesis 246
5. Sucrose synthetase and sucrose phosphate synthetase 249
A. Early evidence of sucrose synthetase in plant tissues 250
B. Sucrose synthetase and sucrose-*P* synthetase in pea, bean, and broad bean preparations 251
C. Purification of sucrose-*P* synthetase from wheat germ and spinach 251
D. Sucrose synthetase and sucrose-*P* synthetase of potato tubers 253
E. Localization studies of sucrose-forming enzymes 254
6. The sucrose–starch interconversion 256
A. Historical 256
B. Relationship of sucrose synthetase to starch formation 257
C. Potato tuber sucrose synthetase: Temperature, varietal, and maturation effects . . 258
7. Sucrose synthesis in sugarcane leaves 261
A. Historical 261
B. Discovery of sucrose synthetase in sugarcane 263
8. Sucrose synthesis in sugarcane storage tissue 264
A. Enzymes of the sugar accumulation cycle 264
B. Sucrose synthetase inhibition by phenol oxidation products 267
C. The synthesis and role of sucrose phosphate 269

PART II – SUGAR TRANSLOCATION AND STORAGE

Chapter 7 – **Paths of sucrose transport**
1. Introduction 273
2. Developing the normal flow of ^{14}C 274
A. ^{14}C methodology for tracing sucrose 274

B. Veinal loading and initial movement of ^{14}C in the leaf . . . 276
C. Movement from sheath to stalk . . . 279
D. Movement within the stalk . . . 280
E. Sucrose as the principal photosynthate moved . . . 284
F. Velocity and rate of sucrose transport . . . 285
G. Translocation to adjacent stalks in the stool . . . 288
3. Translocation in detached leaves . . . 289
A. Basipetal transport . . . 289
B. Polarity of ^{14}C transport . . . 291
C. Reversal of transport polarity in the dark . . . 292
D. Translocation with specific leaf areas darkened . . . 293

Chapter 8 – **The rate of sucrose transport**
1. Introduction . . . 295
2. Theory of assimilate movement in higher plants . . . 295
A. General . . . 295
B. Development of the mass flow concept . . . 297
3. Effects of water stress on sucrose transport . . . 302
A. Context of plant water stress . . . 302
B. Biochemical aspects of water stress . . . 304
C. Water stress and sucrose transport in sugarcane . . . 305
D. Effects of restricted sucrose transport upon storage . . . 307
4. Effects of light on sucrose transport . . . 309
5. Temperature effects on sucrose transport . . . 314
6. Effects of nutrient deficiencies on sucrose transport . . . 318
7. Effects of leaf competition . . . 321
8. Effects of wind and mechanical injury . . . 322
9. Effects of the stool complex . . . 323
10. Mechanism of translocation in sugarcane . . . 324

Chapter 9 – **Sugar accumulation in storage tissue**
1. Introduction . . . 327
2. Theory of solute uptake . . . 328
A. Passive *vs.* active entry of non-electrolytes . . . 328
B. Sugar–boron carrier complexes . . . 330
3. Sugar accumulation against a concentration gradient . . . 332
A. Initial studies with tissue slices [Bieleski (178–180)] . . . 332
B. Sugar uptake by mature and immature tissues . . . 333
C. Relative movement and fate of different sugars in immature storage tissue . . . 335
D. Tissue maturity and sugar uptake . . . 336
E. Effects of inhibitors on sugar accumulation . . . 336
F. Kinetics of sugar accumulation . . . 337
4. Elaborating the sugar accumulation concept [Glasziou (579, 581, 582)] . . . 341
A. Evidence of active accumulation of a sucrose derivative . . . 341
B. Efflux of sugars from the inner space . . . 341
C. Criteria of the sugar accumulation and transformation hypothesis . . . 343
D. Studies of glucose and fructose in the inner space . . . 344
5. The sugar accumulation cycle [Hatch, Sacher, Glasziou (689, 690, 1268)] . . . 348
A. Enzymology of the sugar accumulation cycle . . . 348
B. Role of invertase in sugar accumulation . . . 351
C. Sucrose phosphate as an intermediate in sugar accumulation . . . 354
6. Summary of the sucrose storage process . . . 356

Chapter 10 – **Regulation of sugar storage**
1. Introduction 359
2. Theory of enzyme regulation by sugars and hormones 360
A. Glucose regulation (the "glucose effect"; catabolite repression) 360
B. Hormonal enzyme regulation 362
C. The allosteric transition hypothesis 364
3. Inversion control 365
A. Discovery of auxin–carbohydrate mediated invertase control [Sacher *et al.* (1267, 1269)] 366
B. Relationships of regulatory mechanisms to age and parentage of tissue 368
C. Interrelationships of auxin and N source in invertase synthesis 369
D. Regulation of spatially distinct invertases 371
4. Glucose and glucose-derivative regulation of invertase 372
A. Studies by Glasziou and co-workers (586, 585, 589) 372
B. Loci of the auxin–carbohydrate control system 374
C. Development of a configuration model for invertase regulators 376
D. Mechanism of glucose and sugar-derivative action 378
E. Glucose and fructose specificity 380
5. Mechanism of hormonal action 381
A. Stability *vs.* synthesis of mRNA [Glasziou *et al.* (588, 591); Gayler and Glasziou (567, 566)] 381
B. mRNA as a rate-limiting factor in auxin and GA enzyme regulation 381
C. Stability studies subsequent to chemical blockage of RNA synthesis 382
6. Sucrose inversion and growth 386
A. Invertase and growth responses to controlled environment. 386
B. Relationship between invertase and GA-induced growth 390

PART III – *SACCHARUM* SINK PHYSIOLOGY

Chapter 11 – **Maturation and natural ripening**
1. Introduction 397
2. Theory of sugarcane ripening 398
3. Maturity 400
4. Mechanism of sugar storage in mature stalk tissue 402
A. General 402
B. Relationships of invertase level to sucrose accumulation in mature storage tissue . 405
5. Storage potential of *Saccharum* species 407
6. Moisture 410
A. Water and sugarcane ripening [Hartt (648, 654–656)] 411
B. Similar responses to deficient and excessive water supply 414
7. Nitrogen and potassium in sugarcane ripening 416
A. Nitrogen 416
B. Potassium 420
8. Ripening control through crop logging 422
A. The primary index 423
B. The nitrogen index 424
C. The moisture index 425
D. The K and K–H_2O indexes 426
E. Crop log ripening 430
F. Crop logging *vs.* analyses of 8–10 tissues and soils 432
G. Growth and yield equations 433
9. Maturation effects of photoperiod, daily temperature, and seasonal temperature . . 434

Chapter 12 – **Chemical ripening and sucrose control**
1. Introduction 441
2. Early concepts of artificial ripening 442
   A. Cultural ripening 442
   B. Ripening with molasses 442
3. The "promising" ripener; 1950–1970 443
   A. Ripening with 2,4-D 443
   B. Maleic hydrazide 448
   C. Sucrol (Esso 59-G) 451
   D. TBA (Trysben), Pesco 1815, and Kuron 452
   E. Boron 453
   F. Monopotassium phosphate 454
   G. Other early chemical trials 455
   H. Recent evaluations of D.A.-5, C.P. 41845, and Cycocel 455
4. Ripening with gibberellic acid 457
   A. Historical 457
   B. GA effects on sugarcane 458
   C. GA effects upon sugar production and utilization 459
   D. Delayed GA growth effects: The post-growth stimulatory phase 464
5. Chemical control of sucrose 467
   A. Increased synthesis with phosphatase inhibitors 468
   B. The enzyme index 470
   C. Invertase and amylase control 472
6. Chemical control of the apical meristem 475
   A. Theoretical considerations 475
   B. 6-Azauracil 476
   C. 6-Azauracil × GA 479
   D. 6-Azauracil × nitrogen 480
7. Chemical screening 483
   A. Limitations of the chemical ripener trial 483
   B. The screening program 485

Chapter 13 – **Chemical desiccation**
1. Introduction 489
2. The search for sugarcane desiccants 491
3. Diquat and Paraquat: Properties and mode of action 495
   A. Chemical configuration and phytotoxicity 495
   B. Mode of action 497
   C. Relationship of phytotoxicity to light 498
   D. Theory of dipyridyl action 498
4. Yield effects of Diquat and Paraquat 500
   A. Growth and yield responses in Natal 500
   B. Desiccation experiments showing quality losses 502
5. Fundamental dipyridyl effects in sugarcane 504
   A. Visual effects of Paraquat and Diquat 505
   B. Curtailed sucrose production 507
   C. Dipyridyl blockage of regenerative CO_2 assimilation reactions 509
   D. Dipyridyl induction of abnormal enzyme behavior 513
   E. ATPase suppression and photosynthetic phosphorylation 516
   F. Chemical control of adverse dipyridyl activity 518
6. Sugarcane topping 519

Chapter 14 – **Flowering**
1. Introduction . . . 523
2. The flowering stages . . . 525
   A. Measurement of distinct flowering stages . . . 527
   B. Abnormal development of the flowering stages . . . 529
3. Flowering as a function of photoperiod . . . 530
   A. Day length as one of several controlling factors . . . 531
   B. Flowering in relation to latitude and length of day . . . 533
4. Additional factors influencing floral initiation and rate of tassel development . . . 535
   A. Temperature . . . 535
   B. Night length (nyctiperiod) and latitude . . . 541
   C. Physiological maturity *vs.* age . . . 542
5. Flowering control: The breeder's viewpoint . . . 543
   A. Flowering induction by controlled photoperiod . . . 545
   B. Controlled flowering in *S. spontaneum* . . . 547
6. Flowering control: The grower's viewpoint . . . 549
   A. Effects of flowering on cane quality . . . 550
   B. Flowering control by moisture stress . . . 551
   C. Flowering control with chemicals . . . 554
   D. Defoliation and spindle removal . . . 557
   E. Relative effectiveness of defoliation and chemical treatments . . . 560
   F. Flower control with nitrogen . . . 561
7. Mechanism of sugarcane flowering . . . 562
   A. The inductive stimulus . . . 563
   B. Gibberellin effects . . . 564
   C. Importance of red and far-red light . . . 565
   D. Enzyme behavior during flowering . . . 566
   E. Stability of the flowering stimulus . . . 569
   F. Summary of the cane flowering mechanism . . . 570

Chapter 15 – **Postharvest physiology**
1. Introduction . . . 573
2. Nature and magnitude of postharvest deterioration . . . 574
   A. Historical . . . 574
   B. After-ripening . . . 576
   C. The role of environment . . . 577
   D. Burned cut *vs.* burned standing cane . . . 579
   E. Deterioration of frozen cane . . . 580
   F. Magnitude of postharvest sugar losses . . . 580
3. Invertases and postharvest inversion . . . 582
   A. Invertases present in harvested cane . . . 582
   B. Distribution of invertases within the sugarcane stalk . . . 583
   C. Relationships of invertase type and distribution to burning and storage factors . . . 586
   D. Inversion as a function of variety, temperature, moisture, and condition of cane . 591
   E. Inversion as a function of enzyme and substrate level . . . 595
   F. Inversion control in stored cane . . . 595
4. Inversion control in milled juice . . . 596
   A. Inversion control with sodium metasilicate . . . 597
   B. Silicate mode of action . . . 600
   C. Possible "sucrase"-type reactions in milled juice . . . 601
5. Biodeterioration in mechanically-harvested cane . . . 602
   A. Cause of "sour cane"; *Leuconostoc mesenteroides* . . . 603
   B. Dextrans; their nature and effects on sucrose solutions . . . 605
   C. Control of biodeterioration . . . 608

Chapter 16 – **Cell and tissue physiology**
1. Introduction . . . 611
2. Fundamentals of tissue culture with virus-induced tumors . . . 613
   A. Tissue culture development with isolated *Rumex* tumors . . . 613
   B. Analysis of variable factors in tumor tissue culture . . . 614
3. Morphogenesis in monocot tissue cultures . . . 617
   A. General background . . . 617
   B. Morphogenesis in maize . . . 618
   C. Morphological changes in cultured monocot cells . . . 621
   D. Cytological and chromosomal aberrations . . . 621
   E. Hypothetical means of ploidy change . . . 622
   F. "Loss" of totipotency . . . 623
4. Nutritional and metabolic aspects of sugarcane cell cultures . . . 624
   A. General . . . 624
   B. Development of a suitable medium . . . 625
   C. Carbohydrate sources; starch . . . 628
   D. Importance of arginine in the growth medium . . . 630
5. Totipotency control and polyploidy in sugarcane cells . . . 630
   A. General . . . 630
   B. Totipotency control . . . 632
   C. Polyploidy by tissue culture . . . 633
6. Organ differentiation from callus tissue . . . 638
   A. General . . . 638
   B. New plant induction from callus tissue cultures . . . 640
7. Arginine biochemistry in sugarcane cell cultures . . . 643
   A. Cell growth response to arginine . . . 644
   B. Comparative uptake and assimilation of arginine by cane, duckweed, and carrot cells . . . 645
   C. Arginine incorporation into cell proteins . . . 646
   D. Arginine catabolism products . . . 647
8. Chemical effects on sugarcane cell cultures . . . 651
9. Amylase secretion by tissue cultures . . . 654

BIBLIOGRAPHY . . . 657

Author index . . . 723
Subject index . . . 731

INTRODUCTION

Chapter 1

Origin of the *Saccharum* Source-to-Sink System

1. INTRODUCTION

Books dealing with the agriculture of sugarcane – its growth and management, its genetics, breeding, and disease control – find a convenient point of departure in its unusual history as a crop plant. As crops go, it is a most captivating history, one in which countless millennia of geologic habitat change, natural evolution among wild grasses, long centuries of association with primitive man, and intensive hybridization in the present century have all combined to produce a magnificient agricultural specimen. Many excellent monographs and books have treated sugarcane's origin in this context (838, 1256, 1362, 224, 225, 113). In another sense the plant has also evolved as a unique source-to-sink system. It is unique in that no other organism on earth has so perfected the art of synthesizing, translocating, and storing sugar in massive quantities. In this context much less has been written; indeed, it was only during the 1960's that sugarcane at last found its way into the world's laboratories where its physiological pedigree could be examined for its own merits, quite aside from a strictly crop orientation. In the present chapter the origin of sugarcane is reviewed as a basis for the source-to-sink chapters which follow, and as a convenience for students of plant physiology having limited access to sugarcane literature.

For those unfamiliar with sugarcane it can be stated quite simply that the original "noble" canes resulted from a fortuitous combination of natural events, the craving of man's proverbial "sweet tooth", and unlimited time. Artschwager and Brandes (113) hypothesize that a common wild ancestor, presumably a form of *Saccharum spontaneum*, originated in southern Asia and spread southeastward across an ancient land mass which during the early Cretaceous epoch extended from southern Asia to Australia. The origin of the early Cretaceous *Saccharum* from a subtribe of Andropogoneae in Asia is still a matter of conjecture, but Celarier (309) suggests that the ancestral genus evolved from *Erianthus* with germplasm contributions from *Miscanthus*. Inundations during the late Cretaceous isolated a part of these forms on the great Australia shelf, the latter being alternately insular and continental as the sea level varied during the subsequent ice ages. Early forms of *Saccharum* probably evolved independently under insular conditions and intermingled when land bridges were reestablished. The wild species *S. robustum* evolved in the region of New Guinea and possibly hybridized with other wild grasses. From *S. robustum* primitive man gradually "selected" the sweetest, softest, and thickest canes which he cultivated in his village gardens for chewing purposes. Eventually such forms became dependent upon man for their propagation as the species *S. officinarum*, the original "noble" canes.

The original *officinarum* forms were inbued with many desirable characters including sweetness, lack of fiber, thick stalks and vigor, and as such they were cultivated in commercial plantings almost to the present time. However, the discovery of sugarcane fertility during the 1880's[1] signaled a new era in sugarcane culture which featured extraordinary new progeny from controlled *inter*specific and *intra*specific crosses. A key phenomenon of the interspecific cross, such as the crossing of *S. officinarum* with the wild *S. spontaneum* or *S. robustum*, was the "nobilization" process in which the female parent (*S. officinarum*) contributed its somatic rather than its gametic chromosome number to the progeny. Therefore, while male parents contributed "wild" characters such as vigor and disease resistance in the normally-reduced chromosome complements, *S. officinarum* chromosomes carrying high quality characters were transmitted intact (unreduced), thereby building polyploid offspring with enormous yield and quality potential. The interspecific cross is rare in other crops but it has been commonplace in sugarcane for about 60 years. The intergeneric cross, almost unheard of in most crops, has been demonstrated between *Saccharum* and a half dozen "allied" genera.

Some authors have held that sweet and succulent hybrids produced in nature during the long evolution of *S. officinarum* could not have withstood the selection pressure for survival unless aided by man. However, other evidence suggests that plants having a marked ability to produce carbohydrate, to store it, and to quickly remobilize it for shoot production held a positive advantage for survival over their evolutionary competitors. A probable "ace" favoring primitive sugarcanes was the C_4 mechanism which permitted a more efficient assimilation of CO_2 in the source (or leaf) tissues. This mechanism is also known in related genera such as *Sorghum*, *Zea*, and *Amaranthus* (*cf.* Chapter 3, pp. 102, 112, 113), but there is no evidence at all appertaining to the circumstances of its transmission to sugarcane. It may have entered an ancient *Saccharum* genome from *Erianthus* in Asia during the early Cretaceous. In addition, a distinctive "sugar accumulation cycle" is operative in the sugarcane sink (or stem) tissue which provides for massive sucrose storage and its rapid remobilization. Key regulatory features of the process include acid and neutral invertases. Differential distribution of acid invertase among primitive and modern sugarcanes, and between young and mature storage tissues, is suggestive that high-sucrose accumulating species would be favored for survival in the evolutionary process (*cf.* this chapter, p. 63).

---

[1]The first artificial plant hybrid was produced by Fairchild in 1708 (1362, p. 2). A few workers may have always known that sugarcane could produce seed, but the world at large continued to propagate the plant by stem cuttings until Soltwedel (426) "discovered" cane fertility in 1888.

2. PHYTOGEOLOGIC HISTORY OF THE CULTIVATED CANES

Deerr (426), reviewing in 1911 the 19th century literature on cane varieties, concluded that most cultivated canes originated in the "South Pacific", while a lesser number originated in India. He questions earlier beliefs that *Cheribon* canes are indigenous to Java, or the *Bourbon* cane to the Malabar coast. Evidence that sugarcane might be indigenous to the western hemisphere was dismissed as "quite unsatisfactory". Apparently, early writers did not always make clear whether a variety's "origin" meant its indigenous habitat or the port from which its delivering ship had sailed. Deerr clearly regarded the Indian canes as a distinct group even though the members' speciation was obviously unknown to him: ". . . If, as seems reasonable, this speculation connecting these canes with the South Pacific is correct, then all the standard varieties of cultivated cane originated in the South Pacific, that is to say east of Wallace's line, and they form, at the very least, a type of cane very far removed from those found to the West."

A. *The original noble canes*

As pointed out by Grassl (609), *S. officinarum* canes were selected for use in gardens and are adapted for survival as garden or horticultural plants. Brandes (229) notes that the "garden sugarcanes" of Melanesia and their descendents are variously termed "thick-stemmed tropical", "original", and "noble" sugarcanes, all of which broadly cover "the horticultural species *S. officinarum* L.". The garden sugarcanes, along with their migrating and transported descendents, are ". . .by all odds the most important base from which our present cultivated hybrid varieties derive".

In 1932 Bremer (236) extended the "original" classification to the cultivated canes of northern India, a move which Brandes (229) describes as "logical but confusing". It is now clear that the North Indian canes did originate as selections from natural hybrids, but they are both genetically and morphologically distinct from the New Guinea canes previously termed "original". During the subsequent decades the "original" designation failed to satisfy the needs of a rapidly-growing body of sugarcane scientists. As indicated by Brandes, ". . .Carried to its logical conclusion the extension of meaning as used by Bremer would result in a long series of related but more or less discrete original sugarcane groups that came into existence prehistorically by promiscuous hybridization or selfing along the track of the migrating original sugarcanes from the Melanesian archipelago."

A more suitable description relative to the *S. officinarum* forms which came to dominate most sugarcane regions was found in the term "noble", adapted from the English language by Dutch growers in Java. Here, too, some confusion is found although the meaning of the expression "noble cane" is nowhere in doubt today. At first the concept of "nobilization" simply referred to the processes of ennobling the wild *S. spontaneum* forms, or other wild canes, through their hybridization with *S. officinarum.* Apparently there was no intention for the term to become synonymous with all future cultivated forms having *S. officinarum* parentage, but "noble" could hardly have been a better choice for this purpose, and ". . .there is little likelihood that the word will be misappropriated for other groups of cane" (229). At the present the nobilization process is almost synonymous with the increase of chromosome numbers in progeny from species crosses and backcrosses. However, it is interesting to note that scientists who have traveled to the New Hebrides, the Solomon Islands, New Guinea, and adjacent areas to personally gather *S. officinarum* varieties have preferred the collective name "native garden sugarcanes" or simply "native sugarcanes" (229).

Brandes lists among the desirable qualities of noble canes, that is, the thick-stemmed "horticultural" species *S. officinarum*, features of high weight per plant and high tonnage per acre, "self-cleaning" (ability to drop their aged leaves), disease resistance, and "a surprising degree of adaptability to harsh alien climates". The species likewise excels in high processing qualities such as minimal fiber, high juice purity, low invert sugars and low starch.

Price (1188) states that the designation "*S. officinarum*" properly belongs to "chewing" canes having their origin in New Guinea. He describes *S. officinarum* varieties as having wide leaves, large and frequently multicolored stalks, and soft, juicy pith. Although the designation "noble canes" was coined by the Dutch as a suitable descriptive term for *S. officinarum* clones, Grassl (609, 607), however, points out that not all noble sugarcanes are true *S. officinarum* forms. This view is substantiated by evidence of introgression between *Saccharum* and *Miscanthus* following the origin of *S. officinarum.* The resultant clones having high sterility levels, although "noble" canes, are not regarded as valid forms of *S. officinarum* (609).

Highly specialized requirements of the modern sugar industry necessitated that *S. officinarum* should be hybridized with other species, most notably the mosaic-resistant *S. spontaneum* L. Nature is believed to have accomplished hybridization on her own accord (1147) in the instances of *S. sinense* and *S. barberi.* In general, hybrid seedlings are more resistant to diseases and are more adaptable to climatic variables than the noble parent, while at the same time desirable noble traits are retained undiminished owing to somatic transmission of the *S. officinarum* chromosomes.

In describing sugarcane more recent authors have used "noble" and *Saccharum officinarum* almost synonymously. In the former Netherlands East Indies the term "original" was used to distinguish domesticated canes, that is, canes gradually selected and grown by indigenous peoples for their chewing qualities, from the new seedling varieties produced intentionally by controlled crosses (229). Posthumus (1177) has emphasized that "original" did not necessarily mean "ancient", and that the slower processes of natural selection have not ceased in Indonesia.

Brandes describes at some length the natural barriers which fix and maintain discrete species orientation within a genus. The genus *Saccharum* does not comply especially well to formal speciation owing to lack of clear-cut separations of the type found, for example, between species of the related genus *Sorghum.* A convenient example of a natural isolation mechanism operating among *Saccharum* species is the variation of reproductive season. At any given locality, one *Saccharum* species may flower early (*S. spontaneum*) and another late (*S. officinarum*) with the result that nature has interposed a barrier between the two[2]. The effectiveness of this barrier is affirmed by the considerable ingenuity and effort expended by cane breeders in closing the flowering gap on even the most minute scale (*cf.* Chapter 14, pp. 543–545).

Conditions preventing clear distinction among *Saccharum* species are much more complex in the cultivated *officinarum*, *sinense*, and *barberi* species than in the "wild" *spontaneum* and *robustum* species (229). Brandes lists several such conditons or deviations: (a) High polyploidy permitting interspecific or even intergeneric crossing in nature; (b) long-term vegetative propagation with attendant mutations in unstable clones; (c) incompatibility of male and female gametes; (d) self-fertilization; (e) male sterility; and (f) absence of floral organs or inability to produce flowers owing to alien environment. Ultimately such conditions must result in "...the development of a miscellaneous assortment of moderately definable groups each composed of individuals with some characteristics in common and the development of more numerous odd or integrating forms interspersed in and between them" (229).

Daniels *et al.* (407) have shown that *S. spontaneum* forms include both long-day and intermediate-day clones, and that initiation of flower primordia can be obtained with constant, increasing, or decreasing day lengths. Moreover, significant interactions of day and night temperature with day length occur which explain the failure of canes to flower in the spring when day length *per se* is favorable. It was shown that artificial environments leading to flower production could be created for some 20 clones of *S. spontaneum.* By this means the flowering gap between *S. officinarum* and *S. spontaneum* may be closed for limited amounts of plant material.

Quite obviously the noble sugarcanes, the modern hybrids having noble parentage, and related wild and cultivated species constitute a thoroughly complex group whose final classification may be decades in the making. It is appropriate at this time to scan the evolutionary history of sugarcane and to trace as best we can the processes by which these plants came into being.

B. *Geologic transition of Malaysia*

Geologic and hydrographic data summarized by Molengraaff (1029) reveal the

---

[2]Warner and Grassl (1535, p. 794) observed *S. officinarum* blooming synchronously with *S. spontaneum* on the lowlands of New Guinea. The area was 4–5 degrees south latitude and considerable overlapping of flowering was attributed to the broad flowering season.

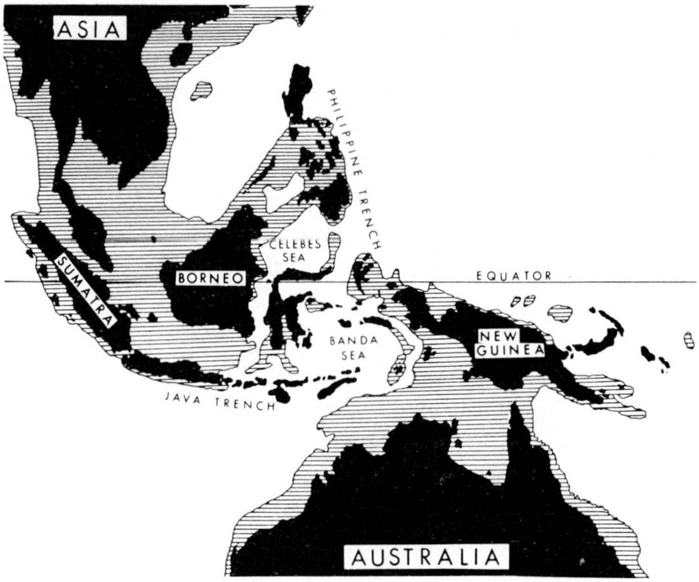

Fig. 1-1. The Malaysian region showing the Asiatic and Australian shelves (shaded) and the intervening deep-sea areas. [Based on a world map produced by the National Geographic Society, Cartographic Division, December, 1970. Also after Merrill (1012) and Molengraaff (1029).]

presence of two continental shelves in the Asiatic–Australian region (Fig. 1-1). An intermediate "Australasian mediterranean sea" intervenes between the present Borneo–Java area and New Guinea–Australia. The two shelves or banks are attached to the continents of Asia and Australia. The Asiatic bank (Sunda shelf), being the largest in the world, underlies the Sunda Islands, Sumatra, Java, Borneo, and numerous Pacific Islands extending eastward to Bali. The Australian bank (Sahul shelf) underlies New Guinea. Both shelves have been geologically stable since the late Pleistocene. They are uniformly flat and submerged only to very shallow depths. At the present time a sea level drop of only 20 meters would unite New Guinea with Australia, and a drop of 45 meters would join the greater Sunda Islands with Asia (1012). Sea level fluctuations during the Pleistocene[3] effected periodic land connections between New Guinea and Australia, and between southeast Asia and the Sunda Islands, Sumatra, Java, and Borneo. The alternate isolation and intermingling of evolving flora must have figured in the development of *Saccharum* germplasm as it did in the flora of the Philippine Islands (1012). The area intermediate between the two great shelves consists of inclosed deep-sea basins which are unstable and remain "orogenetically active" and insular as in earlier geologic epochs (Fig. 1-1).

In his phytographic review of Malaysia, Merrill (1012) concluded that the Malaysian

[3]The great Ice Age, including four glacial and three interglacial phases (719).

region as a whole, including the Philippine area, constituted a part of the great Asiatic–Australian continent during the Cretaceous epoch. Archipelago conditions developed during the late Cretaceous or the Eocene, that is, much of the former land mass became permanently inundated. Since that time Australia and Asia have remained separated. Land connections reformed temporarily over the two stable continental shelves during the Pleistocene, but insular conditions have persisted in the intervening and unstable deep-sea area. A breaking up of land connections between Southeast Asia, Formosa, and the Philippines occurred during the early Tertiary era and insular conditions have persisted to the present. An arbitrary biogeographic boundary known as "Wallace's Line" extends along the approximate western edge of the unstable insular area. "Weber's Line" follows the approximate eastern boundary of the same area (1012).

C. *Flora migrations in the Cretaceous and Pleistocene*

Merrill (1012) describes the Cretaceous as "...a period of remarkable climatic uniformity, in which strictly tropical types of vegetation existed far to the north and south". Seward (1316) presents a more transitory view of the Cretaceous in which the earliest stages saw the dawn of the modern plant world[4]. Climatic conditions favored the rapid and extensive movement of flora in both the eastern and western hemispheres. In the course of plant evolution many essential features of modern plants had appeared during the early Cretaceous. Angiosperms were predominant, and genera living today were becoming increasingly abundant (314). Malaysian plant forms at the time of the late-Cretaceous inundations were probably quite modern in appearance. The widespread incidence of common families and genera in Asia, Africa, and Malaysia can be traced to flora movements prior to the late-Cretaceous breakup of the ancient Asiatic–Australian continent. Only minimal biological intermingling between the Asian and Australian land masses and between eastern and western Malaysia are believed to have occurred since that period (1012).

Merrill (1012) emphasized the effects of Malaysian geologic changes on flora and fauna which are still evidenced by modern plant and animal forms in the Philippine Islands: "With this geologic history in mind it becomes very evident why we find the Asiatic types of plants and animals rapidly dwindling in numbers in the islands east of the Macassar Strait with a corresponding but even more rapid decrease of Australian types as we go westward from New Guinea, and their almost entire absence from the Sunda Islands." The intermediate position of Celebes between Australia and Southeast Asia, according to Merill, led A.R. Wallace to describe it as an "anomalous island",

[4]Botanists visiting a northern European forest at this time would have found many ferns, conifers, and other ancient gymnosperms intermingled with modern flowering types, but they would have been struck most of all by an abundance of warm-climate plants prospering far to the north of their present latitudes (1316, p. 384).

with reference "both to what it has and by what it lacks". Wallace was impressed by differences in the plant and animal forms found in eastern and western Malaysia, and observed that the Macassar Strait and the Lombok Passage formed a natural boundary between the two regions. The demarcation line bearing his name was established by Huxley, but both the line and Wallace appear to have been thoroughly criticized (1012).

D. *Prehistoric movement of primitive cane*

Artschwager and Brandes (113) hypothesize at least two periods of sugarcane movement. The earliest period dates back to the early Cretaceous and in this the phytogeographic conclusions drawn by Merrill (1012) and by Molengraaff (1029) figure prominently. The enormous Asiatic–Australian continent of the Cretaceous period afforded a continual land bridge by which primitive Asiatic canes moved unaided by man to the region presently known as Melanesia. Artschwager and Brandes hypothesize the existence of a common wild ancestor throughout the entire region.

The advent of insular conditions in the region of the former great Asiatic–Australian continent posed enormous restrictions against the movement of flora – the latter by the late Cretaceous including primitive ancestral forms of sugarcane. Plant species adapted for growth in or around shallow tracts of brackish water have some advantage in that their seeds or fruits may survive long periods adrift in ocean currents. Seed produced by early *Saccharum* forms could not have withstood prolonged saline emersion. As they do today, wild *Saccharums* probably preferred fresh-water habitats along flood plains and river beds. In this respect they may be likened to fresh-water species of fish, such as the cyprinoids (1012), which are effectively confined to "land" by intervening salt water. The primitive cane stalk, although frequently hollow, had little inclination to drift, and the "fuzz" did not lend itself to dissemination by wind or birds over broad expanses of water.

It is reasonable to conclude that distinct wild forms of sugarcane must have evolved at isolated spots in Asia, New Guinea, and insular Melanesia (113). Considering the vastness of evolutionary time and the presence of other wild grasses, considerable modification of the original stock must have taken place by natural selection and hybridization. Many authorities agree that even intergeneric hybridization could have occurred, as well as interspecific hybridization with *Saccharum* species now extinct. At some later period primitive man himself took part in selection and dissemination processes. The advanced forms of garden or "chewing" canes cultivated or at least maintained by indigenous peoples certainly reflect prolonged selection, however unintentional and unrefined the methods. The most prized garden canes accompanied man on his early travels to Fiji, Tahiti, and the Hawaiian islands, and westward to Southeast Asia, India, and Africa (113).

Oddly enough, there is no plausible evidence that sugarcane made its way to the western hemisphere with any of the hypothesized movements of man. Asiatics crossing the Bering Strait must have been totally unfamiliar with the plant. Polynesian movements eastward to South America, or Egyptian excursions westward to the Caribbean or northeastern South America, were probably accidents rather than planned migrations, and in any case the *Saccharum* species these peoples might have known did not make the trip. Early Norsemen who possibly saw the plant during their raiding voyages to the Mediterranean area appear to have had less than minimal interest in horticultural affairs. Creole or a similar clone of Asiatic origin was brought to the western hemisphere by Columbus on his second voyage in 1493.

E. *Origin of the noble canes as cultivated garden or chewing forms*

As suggested above the early peoples inhabiting New Guinea and insular Malaysia took sufficient interest in the wild canes amongst them to select and maintain the most desirable forms in village gardens. Probably there was no formal criteria for a plant's acceptance other than that it tasted good, or grew easily from cuttings, or perhaps that it survived the rigors of overland or inter-island travel. The result of these selective processes, which continue to the present, was the native garden canes, *i.e.*, the original noble canes, now classified within the species *S. officinarum*. They tended to be sweet rather than starchy, thick-stemmed rather than thin, and soft rather than fibrous. Moreover, they became totally dependent upon native gardeners for their propagation by cuttings, no longer being able to maintain themselves in the wild. Add to this the vigor of *S. robustum* plus the disease resistance of *S. spontaneum* and one has the essence of a modern cane with commercial potential.

Considering the unlimited span of time involved, no conscious effort at selection was needed for superior types to have emerged. Also considering the warlike nature of man, it can safely be assumed that superior types were continually discovered, lost, and discovered again in the form of war booty. The social–political affairs of primitive peoples must certainly have contributed to the movement and interexchange of the developing garden canes. Very likely the most desirable canes faired better than their cultivators in times of conflict, and served as a valuable medium of exchange in times of peace.

F. *Migrations and development of noble canes*

Artschwager and Brandes (113) depict the first major migrations of the noble canes as passing southeastward from New Guinea to the New Hebrides and New Caledonia. These movements, totally dependent upon man, began some 17 000 years ago, practically within the "memory" of modern men when considered in the vastness of evolutionary time. Secondary migrations moved westward and northwestward into India via the Malay peninsula and Burma. Each of these areas appears to have become important centers of diversification. With reference to the equator the noble canes originated at about 5° south latitude, moved first to about 21° south latitude, and later advanced from about 5° south to approximately 21° north latitude (Fig. 1-2).

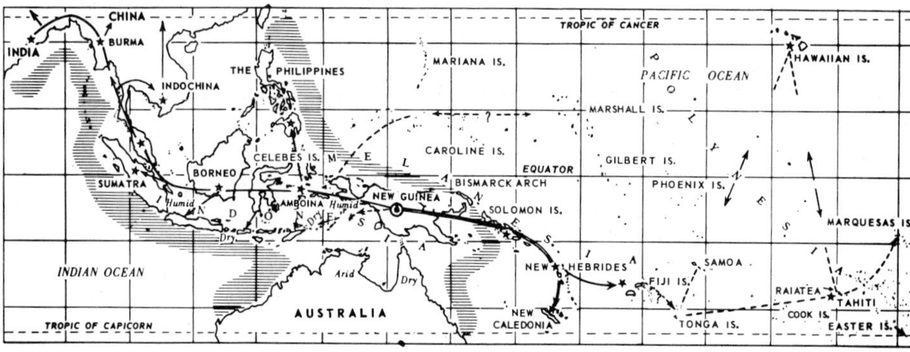

Fig. 1-2. Origin, migration, and centers of diversification of the noble sugarcanes. (⊙) Probable site of origin of *Saccharum officinarum*, through natural hybridization of *S. robustum*, about 8000 B.C. to 15 000 B.C. (══) Initial migratory track of *S. officinarum*, beginning about 8000 B.C. (——) Secondary paths of migration, beginning about 6000 B.C. (- - - -) Subsequent paths of movement, about 500 A.D. to 1100 A.D. (★) Centers of diversity which developed along the migratory tracks. Shaded portion of map indicates outline of the former great Asiatic–Australian Continent. [After Artschwager and Brandes (113).] Reproduced by permission of the *U.S. Government Printing Office*, Washington, D.C.

G. *Probable ancestry of cultivated canes*

Some authors claim separate origins of sugarcane in India and New Guinea. A more logical explanation is found in the Cretaceous isolation of a common wild ancestor into distinct Asiatic and Malaysian evolution centers. Differential selection pressures combined with interspecific hybridization may then have produced the distinctive sugarcanes presently found in northern India.

In 1936, Brandes and Sartoris (225) described *S. spontaneum* and *S. robustum* as the most probable wild ancestors of modern cultivated sugarcanes. The possibility that other wild or extinct species may have played a part in sugarcane development was not, however, excluded: "Assuming immediate descent from existing wild forms would be premature, for there is no doubt that most if not all present varieties of sugarcane are the result of extensive hybridization, the history of which has not been traced and therefore cannot be used as a basis upon which to determine questions of derivation with accuracy."

In 1948 Parthasarathy (1148) distinguished two broad groups of cultivated sugarcane: (a) North Indian canes having *S. barberi* and *S. sinense* parentage, and characterized by thin, hardy stalks; and (b) noble canes of *S. officinarum* parentage characterized by thick stalks. North Indian canes, including all those recorded in Indian antiquity, were regarded by Barber (143) and Jeswiet (807) as being indigenous while noble types were thought to be introduced at a much later date. However, cytogenetic and morphological evidence points to a later origin of North Indian canes than noble canes (807). The origin of Indian canes was earlier attributed by Parthasarathy (1147) to hybridization between *S. officinarum* and *S. spontaneum* forms in eastern India.

In 1957, Mukherjee (1055) placed the cultivated sugarcanes in three species: (a) Noble canes belonging to *Saccharum officinarum* L., not known in the wild state; (b) the North Indian canes, belonging to the group *S. barberi* Jesw., having thinner stalks and generally poorer quality than the noble canes; and (c) the *S. sinensis* (Roxb.) group constituting the Chinese canes and the *Pansahi* Indian canes, ". . .which are somewhat similar in appearance to the North Indian canes. . .". On a worldwide basis Mukherjee described the cultivated canes as products of extensive hybridization among *S. officinarum, S. spontaneum, S. barberi*, and *S. sinensis.*

Parthasarathy (1147) believed that the cultivated canes of northern India were derived by extensive natural hybridization of *S. officinarum* with *S. spontaneum*, the latter growing wild over much of India from the slopes of the Himalayas to the tropical south. Both morphological and cytogenetic evidence supported this conclusion. Moreover, a common ancestry was hypothesized for *S. officinarum* and the genus *Sclerostachya* via an unknown species having the basic chromosome number $x = 5$. This further supports the view that *S. officinarum*'s presence in India dates from great antiquity, and that it contributed to a later evolution of the North Indian group.

Grassl's (609) treatment of *S. spontaneum* stresses its development from an initially small botanical group to a huge one containing innumerable forms of varying rank and importance. Although Linnaeus originally described an Indian *S. spontaneum* as the type form, other *spontaneum* forms collected in distant areas differed so much in appearance that they were given their own species names. More recently a reverse tendency has been operative. Grassl lists 16 species ". . .that have been reduced to *S. spontaneum* or are likely to be after further study. . . .".

Aside from *S. spontaneum*, the only other wild species of sugarcane is *S. robustum* (228). It is found in New Guinea, New Britain, and the New Hebrides, probably growing also in the Solomon Islands and perhaps as far west as Borneo (95). Brandes (228) distinguishes *S. robustum* from *S. spontaneum* on the basis of its large vegetative structure, *i.e.*, very thick stalks exceeding in height all other species of sugarcane. In addition, the *sanguineum* form of *S. robustum* features a distinctive blood-red color in the stalk interior.

S. sinense, comprising a homogeneous and morphologically indistinct group of canes, and *S. barberi*, having greater chromosomal and morphological heterogeneity, are believed to have originated in India through natural hybridization of indigenous *S. spontaneum* with imported *S. officinarum* (228). For years *S. barberi* was confined to India while *S. sinense* was common in China, Burma, and India. Both *S. barberi* and *S. sinense* forms achieved commercial importance in South Africa, Brazil and the

United States, as well as in India and China, but these have largely been replaced by new hybrid clones. According to Brandes (228), *S. sinense* is still grown in China and the Ryukyu Islands. *S. barberi* clones have been used as breeding stock in India and the United States (225, 1301). These are almost indistinguishable morphologically from *S. sinense* and *S. spontaneum* (228), but they nonetheless constitute a distinct group of cultivated canes (1332).

From the above discussion it is evident that the systematic grouping of species within the genus *Saccharum* has been a difficult task and remains inconclusive. This is due in part to prolonged vegetative propagation of highly polyploid forms and to early classification based on inadequate representative types. Grassl (609), for example, does not regard *S. edule* as an authentic *Saccharum* species, while *S. barberi*, thought by some workers to belong in *S. sinense*, is a "potentially valid" species in its own right. Morphological features used by Jeswiet (806) to construct a species key have shown wide overlapping among all *Saccharum* members (113). Bor (212) reclassified many *Erianthus* species in *Saccharum*. Other authors believe that *Saccharums* in general evolved from a common gene pool (1357, 1147).

3. ALLIED GENERA AND SPECIATION OF THE GENUS *SACCHARUM*

A. *The world's major grasses*

The genus *Saccharum* belongs to the family Gramineae, in the tribe Andropogoneae, subtribe Saccharininae. In 1950 Hartley (645) surveyed the major grass tribes and listed the six largest as percentages of the total grass flora:

Tribe	Percent
Paniceae	24.7
Festuceae	16.5
Andropogoneae	11.9
Agrosteae	8.2
Eragrosteae	8.1
Aveneae	6.3

Hartley maintained that each major tribe is distributed in accordance with "a few readily recognizable factors", of which climatic variables, especially winter temperature, have special importance. However, with respect to Andropogoneae and in marked contrast to Agrosteae and Festuceae, species distribution could not be explained on the basis of winter temperature. Nearly 20 percent of test localities showed species numbers which significantly deviated from calculated values ". . .in relation to the

50 °F isotherm". Andropogoneae members showed a definite preference for warm climates with the exception of the American tropics where few species are found. Hartley regarded this as evidence of incomplete development of Andropogoneae in the western hemisphere.

Celarier (309) also depicts most of the Andropogoneae tribe, including the genus *Saccharum*, as being of relatively recent origin. He further recognizes in the group's rapid expansion and development processes a unique subject for evolution experiments, one which few investigators had acted upon prior to the work of Mangelsdorf and Reeves (972, 1224). Brandes (228), on the other hand, regards the extensive polyploidy of *Saccharum* and the absence of surviving diploid progenitors as evidence of considerable antiquity in its developmental history.

Hartley has further shown that rainfall was not a major factor in determining Andropogoneae distribution (645). Other authors have noted an apparent preference of this tribe for drier climates (309, 173). Since Andropogoneae species were found in abundance in tropical savannahs as well as in tropical forests, Hartley surmised that dominant vegetation had little to do with their distribution. In summarizing his evidence, Hartley (645) concluded that the Andropogoneae are a natural tribe of relatively recent origin in Southeast Asia, not yet fully developed in the western hemisphere, and whose species are sensitive to cold while not being governed by low temperatures in their geographic migrations.

In general, however, the Andropogoneae grasses are already highly specialized, and at least the most advanced members are particularly well adapted to dry subtropical regions and tropical savannahs (309, 173). Originating relatively recently in the tropical forests of Southeast Asia, the Andropogoneae have spread widely, and some species reside even in temperate North America and Eurasia. Flowering characters are generally far advanced among all Andropogoneae members, but primitive features also persist as do several divergent lines of specialization. Celarier (309) divides the Andropogoneae into two principal subtribes[5], the supposedly primitive Dimeriinae, geographically restricted to the "Indo-Malaya area, China, and North Australia", and the Saccharinae. The latter subtribe is in turn divided into two groups, the Saccharininae and the Eulaliininae.

B. *Allied genera; the Saccharum complex*

It is among the Saccharininae that many genera of direct concern to the sugarcane scientist are found, including *Saccharum, Erianthus, Narenga, Imperata, Sclerostachya, Miscanthus, Eccoilopus, Eriochrysis,* and *Spodiopogon* (309). Species of

---

[5]The subtribe and generic divisions of Andropogoneae have been treated by numerous authors [reviewed by Celarier (309)]. Final classification based upon thorough cytotaxonomic studies will probably not be forthcoming for many years.

Sclerostachya, Narenga, and *Erianthus* have been used as staminate parents in crosses with *S. spontaneum* (816, 1147). Mukherjee (1055, 1054), after examining herbarium specimens in New York and Calcutta, regarded as firm the "*Saccharum* complex" comprised of *Saccharum, Erianthus, Sclerostachya*, and *Narenga*, the latter genus having but two species which were formerly placed in *Saccharum*. At an earlier period *Sclerostachya fusca* was included also in *Saccharum* (1148). Kandasami (816) and other authors include *Sorghum* among the genera related to sugarcane.

The separation of *Saccharum, Erianthus, Sclerostachya*, and *Narenga* as distinct genera (459) was not at all clear to early botanists. According to Mukherjee (1055), the genus *Saccharum* as established by Linnaeus in 1753 was comprised of the species *S. officinarum* and *S. spicatum*, the latter subsequently becoming *Imperata arundinacea*. By 1803 Michaux (1020) established the genus *Erianthus*, also with two species, *E. saccharoides* and *E. brevibarbis*. In 1820 Roxburgh listed eleven species under *Saccharum* which presently are classified within four genera (*Saccharum, Imperata, Sclerostachya*, and *Erianthus*). By 1855 a total of 62 species were included under *Saccharum*, all of which by 1957 had been redistributed under *Saccharum, Erianthus, Sclerostachya, Narenga, Eriochrysis, Pollinia, Miscanthus*, and *Eulalia*. By 1896 Hooker (746), with some hesitation, separated *Erianthus* from *Saccharum* on the basis of the awned glume characteristic of *Erianthus*. Some 40 years later Bor (210) created the genus *Narenga* on the basis of former *S. narenga* characters, thereby completing the generic quartet *Saccharum, Sclerostachya, Erianthus*, and *Narenga*. The validity of this grouping is supported by Dutt and Rao (459) and by Mukherjee (1054, 1053).

Among the morphological characters distinguishing generic members of the *Saccharum* complex are relatively clear vegetative features and somewhat less clear flowering features (1055). *Saccharum* types are distinct in their annual growth in which the stem achieves heights up to 15 feet, the latter being hollow with varying amounts of sucrose and displaying prominent nodes and internodes. The root zone has two to three rows of "root eyes". Axillary buds have prominent wings and prophylls, and the leaf lamina is virtually glabrous above a deltoid ligule. An auricle is usually present at the blade–sheath juncture. *Erianthus*, on the other hand, generally has biennial stems of which all produce flowers. Its stem formation is "poor", *i.e.*, with solid pith, little sucrose, and nodes and internodes of little prominence. Only a single row of eyes are found in the root zone and these do not usually give rise to roots. A characteristic feature is the passage of the leaf blade into the sheath without a visible auricle. The ligule is usually truncate. Buds are without wings. The inner surface of the leaf lamina above the blade joint is "densely villous" (1055). Mukherjee describes *Sclerostachya* as being similar in appearance to *Erianthus*, but distinguishing features include an eyeless root zone, poorly developed buds, and a deltoid ligule similar to that of *Saccharum*. *Narenga* is conspicuous largely because of its prominent bearded nodes and a hairy leaf sheath.

Given suitable conditions, most of the "allied genera" will cross with one another and produce viable seed. Venkatraman (1487), for example, accomplished intergeneric hybridization between *S. officinarum* and *Sorghum durra* as early as 1930. In 1937 he reported successful crosses between *S. officinarum* and bamboo (*Bambusa arundinacea*), the latter parent belonging to a different subfamily of the Gramineae. Among some 29 hybrids obtained, Venkatraman found bamboo characters in the manner of underground branching, bud and shoot formation, stem and root anatomy, and chromosome number. Moreover, the hybrids "...further show abnormalities even more numerous than those met within the intergeneric crosses with *Sorghum*".

Mukherjee (1055, 1054) examined herbarium specimens of the four genera *Saccharum, Erianthus, Sclerostachya*, and *Narenga*, and claimed the following numbers of valid species for each: *Saccharum* = 5, *Sclerostachya* = 3, *Erianthus* = 28, and *Narenga* = 2. The most widely distributed genera is *Erianthus*, being discontinuously scattered in Asia, America, the Mediterranean region and the Polynesian Islands (Table 1-1). In

TABLE 1-1

GEOGRAPHIC DISTRIBUTION OF SPECIES IN THE GENERA *ERIANTHUS*, *SACCHARUM*, *SCLEROSTACHYA*, AND *NARENGA*

[After Mukherjee (1055).] Reproduced by permission of the *Botanical Gazette*, University of Chicago Press.

Locality	*Erianthus*		*Saccharum*		*Sclerostachya*		*Narenga*		Total species
	Total	Endemic	Total	Endemic	Total	Endemic	Total	Endemic	
Americas	11	11	0	0	0	0	0	0	11
Africa	1	1	1	0	0	0	0	0	2
Madagascar	2	2	1	0	0	0	0	0	3
Mediterranean	2	0	1	0	0	0	0	0	3
India	10	1	4	1	2	1	2	0	18
Burma, Siam, Malay and Indochina	4	0	3	0	2	1	2	0	11
Malayan archipelago	3	1	3	1	0	0	0	0	6
China and Formosa	7	1	3	0	0	0	2	0	12
Polynesia	2	1	2	0	0	0	0	0	4
Ceylon	1	0	1	0	0	0	0	0	2
Afghanistan and Baluchistan	3	0	2	0	0	0	0	0	5
Russia	1	0	1	0	0	0	0	0	2

the instance of *Erianthus* the question of a single or multiple origin remains unresolved. Mukherjee (1055) noted that "*Saccharum* is mainly Malaysian, .. *Sclerostachya* is Indomalayan, and *Narenga* is mainly Indochinese". Because India possessed the largest total number of species from the four genera, and on the basis of endemic species evidence, Mukherjee proposed that India is the center of maximum variation among the *Saccharum* complex, particularly the zone Bengal–Assam–Sikkim.

C. *Saccharum speciation*

To say that *Saccharum* nomenclature has undergone change would be a gross understatement. The literature reveals much confusion which can be traced in part to prolonged vegetative propagation with parallel mutations and to the taxonomists' reliance upon herbarium specimens rather than living plant materials (459). Nor are living collections complete. A final classification is, quite frankly, impossible at this time, but some of the work should be noted.

In 1876 Roxburgh placed ten species within the genus *Saccharum*, while Hooker (747) divided *Saccharum* into two groups: (I) *Eusaccharum*, with *S. officinarum, S. spontaneum, S. arundinaceum*, and *S. narenga* and (II) *Sclerostachya*, including *S. fuscum* and *S. ridleyi.* In 1925 Jeswiet (806) placed the four North Indian groups (Mungo, Saretha, Sunabile and Nargori) together in the species *S. barberi*. The fifth or Pansahi group was thought sufficiently distinct to warrant classification as *S. sinense.* Jeswiet also removed several *Saccharum* species to *Erianthus*, finding numerous distinguishing characters between the two genera where Hooker had found only "...the presence of an awn to the 4th glume which is all but illusory...". Various other authors reduced the *Erianthus* species to *Saccharum* (459). Bor (211), on the other hand, created the new genus *Narenga* from the former *Saccharum narenga.* Dutt and Rao concluded that *Saccharum officinarum* L., as it had stood in the Flora of British India, should be divided into three separate genera: (a) *Saccharum*, with five species, (b) *Sclerostachya*, with two Indian and one Egyptian species, and (c) *Narenga*, having but one species.

In 1968 Grassl (609) placed four species in the genus *Saccharum: S. officinarum*, the type cane of the genus; *S. robustum*, the wild ancestor of *S. officinarum; S. spontaneum*, another wild species but farther removed and more primitive than *S. robustum;* and *S. barberi*, a cultivated group whose origin remains unclear. The cane available to Linnaeus when he established *S. officinarum* in 1753 appears to have been *Creole*, a clone brought to the western hemisphere by Columbus in 1493. Grassl believes that Linnaeus intended the genus type to include North Indian canes and in this connection *Creole* was an unfortunate choice, being recognized as a species hybrid by sugarcane workers prior to 1940. The clone *Cristalina*, belonging to the horticultural or garden cane group (the noble canes), is regarded as a more suitable type cane (609).

The classification of *S. barberi* involves a number of unresolved problems. Parthasarathy (1147) thought it to be a hybrid group of *S. officinarum* and *S. spontaneum* parentage, a view with which Stevenson (1362) concurred. Grassl (609) did not believe that hybridization with *S. officinarum* was unessential for the origin of *S. barberi*; rather, he hypothesized that an initial hybridization and selection within *S. spontaneum* established part of the "circumscription" of *S. barberi.* The *S. barberi* (Jesw.) form was thought to belong in *S. sinense* prior to 1925, and its reclassification was regarded as an improvement by Grassl in its distinction from the Pansahi canes.

Grassl's position implies two separate and distinct origins for sugarcane, one in northern India and the other in New Guinea. In this context the species *S. barberi* is "potentially valid" until the origin of North Indian sugarcanes is clarified.

Grassl (609) concurs with *S. robustum* being the wild ancestor of *S. officinarum*. The favored type specimen is the clone *28 N.G. 251*, ". . .a basic individual unmodified by hybridization with recently introduced species such as *S. spontaneum* or *Miscanthus floridulus*"[6]. The actual appearance of *S. officinarum* is attributed to hybridization between distinct geographical groups, which also explains the difficult recognition and delineation of such groups. Other hybridizations of *S. robustum* with *M. floridulus*, and probably *S. spontaneum*, appears to have complicated enormously the separation of species from the "very extensive hybrid swarms" (609). Grassl further claims that, because *S. officinarum* arose by hybridization and selection within the species *S. robustum*, both groups can be combined taxonomically within a single species. However, such a grouping would be highly complex since now there would be both cultivated and wild forms of *S. officinarum*. It would be necessary to adopt trinomial nomenclature involving subspecies designations (*S. officinarum* subspecies *officinarum*, *S. officinarum* subspecies *robustum*).

The view that *S. officinarum* is a hybrid and therefore not a valid species, constituted as it is from various parts of *S. robustum*, was not accepted by Grassl (609): ". . .All species were hybrids at one time. The important point here is that the hybridization resulted in a new group which is easily distinguished from the wild group because of much lower fiber content, increased juiciness and sugar throughout the stalk, and other characteristics which are the result of a slightly larger size of all parts. These differences became established genetically, and consequently we can conclude that a new species has originated with the help of primitive man."

The edible-inflorescence form, *Saccharum edule*, has also posed classification problems. The plant is cultivated by natives in New Guinea for its edible flowers which do not ordinarily emerge[7]. Warner and Grassl (1535) suggest that *S. edule* is a relatively simple mutant of *S. robustum*. Grassl (609) maintains that *S. edule* is not an authentic *Saccharum* species, but rather it is a group of canes produced by hybridization between *S. robustum* and *Miscanthus floridulus*. With the view that it is incorrectly placed under *Saccharum*, Grassl proposed instead the horticultural group name *Troboeg* for use by sugarcane breeders.

Kandasami (816) examined the gametic contributions of both male and female parents in a series of intraspecific and interspecific *Saccharum* crosses, and in *Saccharum* crosses with other genera. He concluded that a given clone's gametic behavior

---

[6]Grassl makes no mention of a contributing *Erianthus* form, nor of the claims by Brandes and his colleagues (227) which implicate an *Erianthus* role in development of large cultivated canes.

[7]Lennox and Pemberton reportedly collected fuzz from a *S. edule* tassel and succeeded in producing a few viable seedlings (1535).

might be used as a species identification criterion along with its morphological and anatomical features. In intraspecific crosses involving five forms of *S. spontaneum* only haploid gametes functioned on the part of both parents. Selfing of *S. spontaneum* (Coimbatore) gave evidence of functional diploid gametes and in addition yielded a small number of triploid ($3n$) forms. An abundance of diploid plants were obtained having $n + n$ gametic constitution.

In crosses of *S. barberi* and *S. robustum* with *S. spontaneum*, Kandasami again obtained only haploid gametes. In *S. officinarum* crosses with *S. spontaneum* functional diploid gametes were contributed by the female (*S. officinarum*) parent. When *S. spontaneum* forms were crossed with hybrid varieties containing some *S. spontaneum* chromosomes, again only haploid gametes were evidenced to be functional. However, in intergeneric crosses of *S. spontaneum* x *Sclerostachya, Narenga*, and *Erianthus*, both $2n + n$ and $n + n$ gametes were functional. Since the operation of both $n + n$ and $2n + n$ gametes was observed in varietal crosses within a species, and even in selfs, Kandasami concluded that gametic type is not a valid parameter in identifying the parental genetic relationships.

4. THE WILD SUGARCANES

A. *General*

During the 1920's and 1930's the cumulative knowledge of "wild" sugarcanes was enormously advanced, largely as a result of expeditions to their primitive habitats for the purpose of collecting plant materials. The success of these expeditions, accomplished at no small effort and personal discomfort, perhaps resulted as much from humanitarian and diplomatic efforts as from the botanical skills of workers seeking out the wild *Saccharum* species. In 1936 Brandes and Sartoris (225) wrote: ". . .When the work was started few, if any, botanists regarded 'wild sugarcane' as anything more than a single species, *S. spontaneum*, which would come 'true to seed'. On the contrary, the conception has now grown that wild sugarcane comprises a large complex group of plants with an infinite assortment of characteristics." In gathering these materials the human factor in relations with so-called "primitive peoples" was heavily stressed: ". . .It remains only to mention the importance of making friends in the remote, seldom visited places and establishing correspondence with them. . . Demands on official-looking letterheads signed by unknown functionaries do not carry the weight of an unpretentious request from one whose claim is based on intimate, friendly contacts in the lonely places where short-wave radios are the chief companions. . . One can unblushingly ask a man to take a trip almost as formidable as the Lewis and Clark expeditions across North America and he sees nothing extraordinary in it. The chances are that sooner or later along will come a small packet of seeds or a 5-gallon oil tin full of cuttings packed in charcoal from some far place where the spirit of international service is not beclouded."

In some instances the power of entrenched officialdom, so often the curse of scientists who wish to accomplish something in a hurry, lent valuable aid to the *Saccharum* explorer: "...The Governor of New Caledonia sent word by telegraph and runner to the gendarmes of thirty native villages, ordering them to meet one of the writers at specified times and places and conduct him to the village gardens. By reason of this service 138 garden and two wild varieties were collected in a trip of 5 weeks by motor car, horse and launch covering 2000 kilometers.... Assembling a world collection of plants leads one into contact with officials from the headmen of villages to the headmen of civilized states and to establish friendly relations with them is essential always" (225).

B. *Geographical distribution of wild canes*

The ancient habitat of *S. spontaneum* and *S. robustum* included southern Asia and island groups situated adjacent to southeastern Asia in the Pacific and Indian Oceans (225). Brandes and Sartoris describe a somewhat larger distribution for *S. spontaneum* than *S. robustum*, the former apparently extending from Afghanistan in the west to the Malay peninsula, Taiwan, and the South Pacific islands in the east. Whether evolution of wild species occurred throughout this region or within restricted areas remains a matter of conjecture. Artschwager and Brandes (113) regard the subsequent nobilization processes as having occurred within discrete centers such as the New Hebrides and New Caledonia, the Malay peninsula, Burma, and India. Barber (143) and Jeswiet (807) trace the origin of *S. officinarum* to the mountainous islands of the Malayan archipelago, Polynesia, and New Guinea, but not to India. Although situated in close proximity to confirmed *Saccharum* habitats, Australia does not appear to have supported any of the wild *Saccharum* species (225).

No true *Saccharum* species or even a very close relative has ever been found in the "wild" state in the western hemisphere (225, 227). Despite early reports to the contrary (878), it appears that sugarcane first journied to the New World as a companion of Columbus (225). Brandes and Sartoris noted a tendency for the annual plant *sorgo* (sweet sorghum) to be called "sugarcane" in some parts of the United States. Further confusion arises from the term "canebrake", frequently used in the southern states, "...in a way that suggests that canebrakes are made up of sugarcane or that cultivated fields of sugarcane are canebrakes, neither of which is correct". The true canebrake is a wild growth of canes or reeds typically of *Arundinaria* or *Panicum* parentage (225).

Brandes *et al.* (227) placed the center of diversity for wild canes in "Melanesia", a region extending from New Guinea to the Fiji Islands and having clearly defined ethnography, flora, and fauna. "The diversity of the wild sugarcane types reaches its climax in this region, and without much doubt the widespread cultivated forms had their origin here." The dominant and most "conspicuous" type is *S. robustum*, the varieties of *S. robustum* Jeswiet being outstanding. The latter are "robust types with stalks about the diameter of the medium thick canes of commerce". The term *robustum* is apparently derived from the vigorous growth habit characterized by exceedingly tough stalks which achieve a height of 25–30 feet. Stalks are usually pithy, but in some clones they are solid. Leaves are of medium width and quite long. ". . .The most distinctive vegetative character is the shape of the stalk. The nodes are swollen, having a larger diameter than the internodes. The growth ring is a definite swollen band which is colored red or reddish-brown" (227).

The *S. robustum* habitat is along river banks where it survives periodic inundation. "One of the unusual characteristics in the natural habitat is that it forms long stolons up to 60 feet which grow out over the mud flats of the rivers. During flood stage these stolons float on the surface of the water" (227). Roots and sometimes shoots develop from stolons in the natural habitat but seldom in plantings removed to other regions. *S. robustum* also forms thick canebrakes along the rivers but stalks become few and scattered in dry or elevated areas.

Brandes *et al.* (227) described some 24 wild clones collected in New Guinea which were thought to be *S. robustum*. From the text of this and other early reports it is clear that the authors who at great effort had gathered these canes "on the spot" were seldom totally certain of their speciation. Included among the probable *S. robustum* clones were "a few with edible or abortive inflorescences". These are probably synonymous with *Saccharum edule*, a separate species cultivated exclusively for its abortive but edible flowers (1535)[8]. Another instance of an uncertain form was the wild cane, *Fiji 2*, collected in the Fiji Islands in 1935. Brandes observed flower characteristics similar both to *S. officinarum* and *Erianthus*. These and certain vegetative features led him to propose that it was ". . .a hybrid or an intermediate form between *Erianthus maximus* and forms of *S. officinarum* and/or *S. robustum*". More recent reports show a reluctance of *S. robustum* to cross with other *Saccharum* species or allied genera (1362); presumably, natural hybridization of *S. robustum* with other forms was rare.

Brandes and his associates also attached considerable importance to wild *Erianthus* species found in Melanesia. A number of variants belonging to the species *E. arundinaceus* were described, and in particular the "variety" *28 N.G. 7* (Imp. 852) was thought to have ". . .several advantages for crosses with sugarcane over other species which have been tried". In 1786 Forster (535) described wild canes in the Society Islands which he thought were *S. spontaneum*, but in fact were *Erianthus* (227). *Erianthus maximus*, found in Tahiti and Raiatea, closely resembles sugarcane and was thought by various early workers to be *Saccharum*.

Brandes and his co-workers (227) described the wild sugarcanes of Asia as "varia-

---

[8] According to Brandes, ". . .the abortive inflorescence looks somewhat like a banana with the skin removed".

tions of *S. spontaneum*" and surmised that they had given rise to the cultivated canes of northern India. Although numerous and varied, the Asiatic *S. spontaneum* canes all feature generally slender and straight stalks which range from 18 inches to more than 20 feet in height. Among the varied forms of special interest to early workers were the cold-tolerant varieties, as for example the members of subspecies *S. spontaneum indicum* Hack., growing wild up to 40° north latitude, up to 5000 feet elevation, and surviving winter temperatures as low as −20 °F (227). From this group Brandes collected *Amu Dary* Nos. 59 and 60 which proved to be winter hardy in field plantings at Arlington, Virginia (39° north latitude). The cold-tolerant varieties are small with slender stalks, their leaves are very narrow, and they are distinguished by "the pointed nature of the first and second glumes; the tip of the second glume being awn-like" Other *S. spontaneum* types described by Brandes include (a) the *Dacca* and *Local* forms, indigenous to India, being small and slender and no more than 6–8 feet tall; (b) *S. spontaneum* Burma and Aegyptiacum, being indigenous to Burma and Africa, respectively; and (c) *S. spontaneum* Tabongo found in Celebes, the Philippines, Taiwan, New Guinea, and southeastern China (Canton). Brandes placed the large *spontaneum* types in Asia (which includes Java and Sumatra), while forms like Tabongo were classified as insular.

Wild canes collected in Taiwan are predominantly *S. spontaneum* forms (326, 946). The plants grow extensively at low altitudes in most parts of the island with heavy concentrations being found around ponds, water reservoirs, and along the banks and exposed beds of practically all rivers. An interesting exception is the island of Penhu, where no trace of *S. spontaneum* is found, but where *Erianthus* forms grow extensively. Breeders in Taiwan have used *S. spontaneum* germplasm to advantage in improving the vigor and disease resistance of new progeny (946).

C. *Polynesian canes*

Many of the original garden forms of *S. officinarum* and related wild canes have declined as civilization spreads through their natural habitats. In 1965 Daniels (406) summarized the cultivated and wild forms collected in the Fiji Islands for the purpose of preserving these canes for germplasm in future breeding programs. Of *S. officinarum* proper there were 27 clones, used mainly for chewing, of which four clones showed signs of introgression with a wild ancestor. The latter may have been *Miscanthus floridulus* in accordance with the introgression theory of Grassl (608), or *Erianthus maximus*, as proposed earlier by Grassl (606). Such atypical clones of *S. officinarum* led Artschwager and Brandes (113) to describe Fiji as a "satellite center of diversity".

The Fiji collection was gathered between 1951 and 1962 and included 23 "wild" canes which Daniels grouped in the species *Erianthus maximus*. It was proposed that the *E. maximus* clones (or "vithos") originated as products of *Saccharum* x *Miscanthus* introgression, although in 1947 Lennox (928) classified them as forms of *S. robus-*

tum. Daniels gives the following description of the wild forms: "*E. maximus* is a tall grass with stalks up to 5 meters in length in its native habitat. The stalks have the same range of bright colors as *S. officinarum*, are 1–3 cm in thickness and superficially resemble the stalks of *Saccharum robustum*. The stalks are free thrashing and internally they are solid early but tend to pithiness with age. The plants show great vigor, but the stalks contain so little sucrose that they are entirely unsuitable for sugar production. . . *E. maximus* is such a handsome plant and so much like sugarcane that sugar technologists have collected clones for inclusion in breeding programmes or for cytogenetical investigation. . ." However, *E. maximus* forms in Fiji show a high level of infertility. For this reason extra importance is attached there to the atypical *S. officinarum* (*S. officinarum* x *Miscanthus*) as a potential source of wild germplasm (406). During the period 1951–1962 many attempts were made to hybridize *S. officinarum* with *E. maximus*, but the wild parent proved to be almost sterile and only a few progeny were obtained, most of these showing little vigor and a recumbent habit.

Among other large grasses on Fiji, Daniels mentions eight clones of *Miscanthus floridulus* which he classifies as "reeds". The stalks are generally thinner and shorter than *E. maximus* and are enclosed by persistent leaf sheaths. The stalk is pithy, turns red upon illumination after stripping, and appears to have found its greatest use in Fiji as a home-building material. Moreover, as a long-day plant it flowers too early in Fiji to be crossed with *S. officinarum*. On the other hand, Grassl's (608) introgression theory depicts a major contribution by *M. floridulus* in New Guinea, and Fiji workers have not discounted future hybridization with *S. officinarum* providing that flower synchronization can be achieved by photoperiod control.

Additional forms in the Fiji collection included six clones of *Saccharum edule* which all have edible inflorescences, and one clone of *Imperata conferta* or plume grass. Daniels notes that Fijians prize the abortive *S. edule* flowers which they cook for food. Apparently grown for this purpose alone, fields of *S. edule* sometimes cover several hundred acres. Artificial crosses of *Imperata* with *Saccharum* are known and *I. conferta* is regarded as indigenous to Fiji. However, no natural hybridization between *Imperata* and *Saccharum* has been discovered there (406).

D. *Contribution of wild canes to the development of S. officinarum*

Brandes and his colleagues attached great importance to the role of *S. robustum* in the development of large cultivated canes of the *S. officinarum* group: "Certain characteristics of *S. officinarum* such as its tremendous size, the shedding of its leaves, and the complete absence of, or greatly reduced, fertile lemna, not to mention other characteristics of lesser significance, can now, with confidence, be considered as having come from the wild canes known as *S. robustum.*" In addition to its growth and morphological features, Brandes saw the broad natural range of *S. robustum* as a factor implicating its contribution to the large cultivated canes. "...Extending as it does from Papua to New Hebrides and possibly New Caledonia and Fiji Islands, it is overlapped in the west by the range of *S. spontaneum* and *E. arundinaceus*, and in the east by modified forms of *E. maximus*. This same general region is likewise noted for the large number of cultivated forms grown in native gardens and is the place from which the cultivated varieties of *S. officinarum* were distributed to other parts of the world." On the other hand, such features of *S. officinarum* as the "venation of the spikelet parts", which in no way could be accountable to *S. robustum*, were thought to originate in species of *Erianthus* (227).

Brandes regarded *E. maximus* as the *Erianthus* form most likely to have played a role in the development of large cultivated canes. He listed a number of morphological similarities between *E. maximus* and *S. officinarum* while attaching minimal importance to their chief morphological differences, *i.e.*, "...the presence of an awn on the fertile lemna". In general, however, he took a broad view of the role played by *Erianthus* in the development of noble canes: "When we suggest that species of *Erianthus* have played a part in the origin of the large cultivated canes, we do not imply that the cultivated canes are immediate hybrids, but that such hybrids may occur and that the existence of such hybrids, even if very rare, because of the perennial nature of the plants might exert such an influence on the parent population as to keep them in a highly plastic condition."

5. DEVELOPMENT OF MODERN CANE VARIETIES

A. *Origin of the commercial cane hybrids*

In 1911 Deerr (426) summarized the principal cultivated canes whose history could still be traced at the close of the 19th century. Common names and vivid morphological descriptions were given along with commentaries supplied by growers who had known the canes since childhood. No cytological data was available at that time, and, by present standards, the literature available to Deerr seems sparse. In 1911 Deerr could write: "The development of the scientific study of the cane only dates back a generation....", yet he personally felt that "...a voluminous and polyglot literature has now accumulated."

Deerr found the nomenclature of cane varieties in an advanced state of confusion. So effectively isolated were the cane-growing regions of the 18th and 19th centuries that a given variety might thrive for generations in one area, unknown to the rest of the world, except by word of mouth of the occasional traveler, who in any case was untrained in systematized botany and commanded but a small audience in the low-pressure industry of the day. When canes did travel to a new region they often received a new name, or retained an old name already several times removed from the original one. "In these ways (Deerr wrote), names for the principal varieties have multiplied until a variety may have as many as twenty titles, and to add to the confusion some of these titles may be applied to other quite distinct varieties."

Nonetheless Deerr succeeded in organizing into plausible groups the most important varieties cultivated in the major cane-growing areas of the 19th century. One exception was the canes of India whose classification he regarded as "a hopeless task". He made use of descriptive lists from botanical gardens and experiment stations in Jamaica, Louisiana, Demerara, and Java, compiled by such authors as Fawcett, Stubbs, Harrison and Jenman, and Soltwedel. In addition, he maintained a fluent correspondence with administrators, businessmen and growers, and with surviving botanists who in 1911 could claim to have witnessed the birth of modern botany. In some instances Deerr's best leads as to the origin of a variety were letters from persons recalling events in the sugar industry dating back to the 1860's or the 1850's.

Deerr classified the cane varieties into 26 major groups on the basis of morphological features, use, and centers of cultivation. Among the most important groupings were the *Otaheite, Cheribon, Indian, Javanese, New Guinea, Pacific Island, Hawaiian,* and *Brazilian.* Members from each of these groups contributed to the parentage of modern hybrids, and a few may still be cultivated in isolated instances. Of perhaps lesser importance were the *Tanna Canes*, grown extensively in Mauritius at the beginning of this century; the *Uba Cane* of Natal; the *Salangore Cane* remarkable for an excessive quantity of "cane itch and for its large amounts of wax"; the *Bamboo Canes* (at the time having no known genetic proximity to the genus *Bambusa*); the *Elephant Cane*, of perennial growth habit reaching a height of 30 feet in 5 or 6 years and possessing "...absolutely no importance as a sugar producer" (426); the *Creole Cane*, long associated with New World colonies but originating in eastern Asia; and the *Red Canes*, having some historical importance in India and Australia.

Considerable importance was assigned to another varietal type depicted simply as a "sport", *i.e.*, "a plant which in some way is notably different from its parent, and whence it originates *'per saltum'* ". Deerr regarded some of the finest varieties of his day as having originated by bud variation. For reasons unclear to the early growers, and fundamentally not much clearer today, a given stool can send up a shoot totally distinct from its peers in morphology, vigor, quality, and flowering habit. "...In no other way is it possible to account for the terms White, Black, and Striped Cheribon; Transparent, White and Purple Transparent; Striped Bamboo, Rose Bamboo, and Purple Bamboo; and it must have been with full knowledge of their origin that these names were given" (426).

In the light of our present dependence upon interspecific and intraspecific crosses for new cane varieties, it is surprising that sugarcane was considered infertile prior to 1888. This view was generally accepted (426) in spite of observations to the contrary by Dutrone [1790], Porter [1843], and Parris [1859]. Deerr atributes the "rediscovery" of cane fertility to Soltwedel in Java [1888] and to Harrison and Bovell in

Barbados [1889]. During the following 20 years numerous crosses were performed by the pioneers of cane breeding in Java, the British West Indies, Mauritius, Martinique, and Hawaii. Private growers conducted much of the early cane breeding. Even today, as this author has observed, private cane breeding is still performed in Puerto Rico.

Early hybrids of commercial importance were grouped by Deerr in the category "Seedling Canes", subdividing them into the Demerara, Barbados, Mauritius, and Java groups. Many of the early crosses were adventitious, *i.e.*, the male parent was unknown. In Java the practicality of using male sterile canes as maternal parents was quickly recognized and adopted. Interesting enough, from strictly empirical observations, a problem still burdening cane breeders today was also quickly recognized and the only practical solution adopted: "Briefly it appears . . .that the cane is enormously subject to variation and there is but little tendency towards the inheritance of the properties of either parent; in all cases where successful seedlings have been obtained it has been by growing a very large number of seedlings and eliminating almost all" (426). Harrison was cited as having grown more than a million seedlings to obtain a small number giving superior performance. Deerr justified the production of massive F_1 populations not only because in this way valuable seedlings had somehow emerged, but because ". . .it is only the outstanding canes of merit grown under experiment station conditions that have any chance of success on the estate level".

B. *Advent of the controlled cross*

According to Jeswiet (807), one of first attempts to improve sugarcane by controlled crosses was performed in Java during the 1880's as a consequence of "sereh-disease" attacks upon the *Black Cheribon* cane, the principal variety then cultivated in Java. During the resultant crisis Soltwedel introduced nursery isolation methods which saved *Black Cheribon*, but only at considerable expense, and the process was unpopular with sugar growers. Searches conducted throughout the Malayan Archipelago revealed new varieties which, although none were completely immune to sereh-disease, brought to the forefront new genetic material having variable tonnage and quality potential. Among these were *Fiji*, *Striped Batjan*, *Striped Preanger*, and others from the Malayan Archipelago, and *Chunnee* from India, varieties in themselves no match for *Black Cheribon*, but having enormous importance as parent material in future crosses. Breeding methods in Java thereafter developed along two lines: (a) Varietal crosses performed exclusively within the species *S. officinarum*; and (b) the crossing of different species from the genus *Saccharum* with *S. officinarum* (807).

Price (1188) notes that in Java, "where wild relatives of sugarcane could hardly go unnoticed", intergeneric as well as interspecific crosses were attempted. By the mid-1880's, according to Price, Soltwedel had attempted to cross *S. officinarum* with *Erianthus arundinaceus* [1885] and with *S. spontaneum* [1887]. The initial efforts failed but the interest therein generated led ultimately to "unparalleled success". The wild clone *Kassoer*, a natural F_1 hybrid of *S. officinarum* x *S. spontaneum*, was used successfully by Moquette and Wakker to produce hybrids with *S. officinarum* [1893]. In 1897 Kobus initiated crosses of *S. officinarum* with *Chunnee* (*S. sinense*), producing F_2 and first backcross generations. Price further relates that by 1911 Wilbrink produced plants from *Kassoer* x *S. officinarum* crosses, which Jeswiet subsequently examined and therein discovered the hybrid nature of *Kassoer* [1916]. Jeswiet also recognized that Wilbrink's seedlings were first backcross progeny. Following the backcross technique already used by Kobus with *Chunnee* for eliminating undesirable characters, Jeswiet continued backcrossing Wilbrink's seedlings with *S. officinarum* (noble canes) and thereby further "diluted" the *S. spontaneum* influence in a process which Java breeders began to term "nobilization" (1188).

In 1921 one of Jeswiet's crosses produced a clone, *P.O.J. 2878*, enormously superior to the noble varieties then available and which Rosenfeld in all seriousness termed the "Wonder Cane" (1256). Its success in Java and throughout the sugarcane world in general is unparalleled. In a survey by Arceneaux (95) covering major commercial varieties grown during the period 1940–1964, *P.O.J. 2878* appeared in the recorded parentage of 23 commercial canes, including such widely-scattered varieties as *B. 41227, C.B. 36-24, Co. 449, C.P. 34-120, F. 134, H. 38-2915, M. 336*, and *P.R. 980.*

Price (1188) underscores the complexity of a modern variety bred since the advent of *P.O.J. 2878* with the pedigree example of *H. 49-5*, as illustrated in Fig. 1-3. *H. 49-5* is a modern Hawaiian variety which Arceneaux (95) ranked as having intermediate "usefulness" during the period 1940–1964. It can be seen that, of the four species contributing to its genetic make-up (*S. officinarum, S. sinense, S. spontaneum*, and *S. robustum*), *S. officinarum* readily predominates. The Pansahi group shown under *S. sinense* might be regarded by some authors as a fifth species contribution, *i.e.*, as *S. barberi. S. spontaneum* enters the pedigree three times – twice via *P.O.J. 2878* and once through an Indian *S. spontaneum. S. sinense* enters twice via the Saretha group and once by the Pansahi group. *S. robustum* is represented once by a New Guinea form of the wild species.

C. *Intergeneric crosses*

Some authors maintain that the lack of clear species delineation in *Saccharum* is due in part to the ease with which crossing over occurs between *Saccharum* species. To a lesser degree intergeneric crosses may also have occurred in nature. Artschwager and Brandes (113) note the likelihood that natural intergeneric exchanges took place during the long history of sugarcane development and migration. A few workers have turned to allied genera in efforts to improve the genetic make-up or stability of modern breeding lines. Their partial successes underscore the fact that exchanges between *Saccharum* and related genera can transpire, albeit with some difficulty.

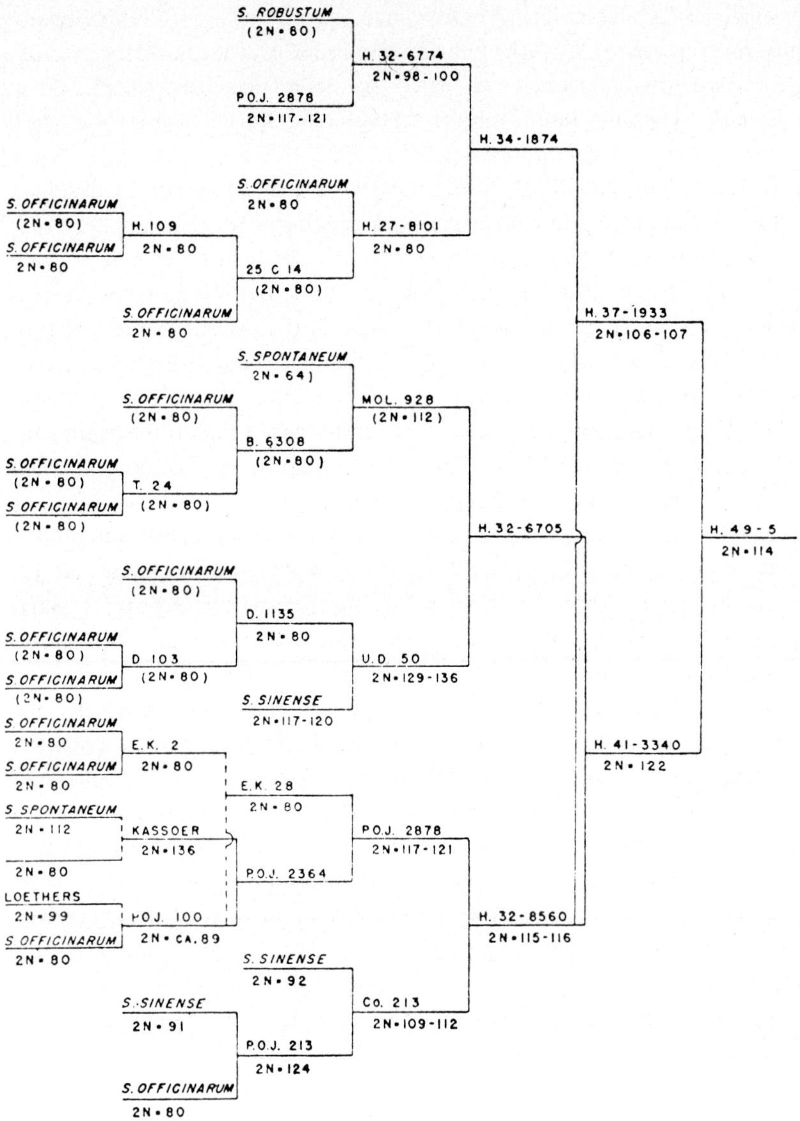

Fig. 1-3. Pedigree of the Hawaiian variety *H. 49-5.* Male parents are shown above, female parents below. Broken lines signify areas of uncertainty. [After Price (1188).] Reproduced by permission of *Economic Botany.*

Among the allied genera, crosses with *Sorghum* appear to have been more successful than any other. By 1930 workers at Coimbatore had produced F_1 hybrids by crossing *P.O.J. 2725* with a *Sorghum* variety known locally as "Periamanjal" (1424). Literally thousands of seedlings were obtained, among which *Sorghum* morphological features were clearly evident. Two years later Venkatraman and Thomas (1484) described in detail the surviving sugarcane–*Sorghum* hybrids, and in 1934 Viswa Nath *et al.* (1505) reported that a long-sought character of early maturation had been established in sugarcane x *Sorghum* progeny. In 1938 Moriya (1035) published the first cytological descriptions of *Saccharum–Sorghum* hybrids.

In 1936 Janaki-Ammal and Singh (798) reported a new *Saccharum* x *Sorghum* hybrid for which a "simpler" sugarcane parent was substituted for the complex *P.O.J. 2725.* An Indian form of *Saccharum spontaneum* L. ($2n = 56$) was crossed with *Sorghum durra* ($2n = 20$) to produce the hybrid. In addition to having a less complex chromosome make-up, the sugarcane parent showed an early flowering habit typical of *S. spontaneum* forms. The resultant hybrid contained the awned 4th glume characteristic of *Sorghum* and callus hairs characteristic of *Saccharum.* Root-tip preparations showed the hybrid chromosome number $2n = 38$, an amount equal to the sum of the *S. spontaneum* and *Sorghum* haploid numbers. All seedlings from this cross resembled the *Saccharum* parent more closely than *Sorghum.*

Three morphologically-distinct types of F_1 hybrids were described by Moriya (1036) in 1940 following initial *P.O.J. 2725* x *Sorghum vulgare* crosses in Taiwan: (a) Hybrids having the external appearance of sugarcane; (b) short and bushy (dwarf) types, comprising 60 to 70 percent of the F_1 generation; and (c) hybrids intermediate between the sugarcane and dwarf types, all being abnormal insofar as sugarcane characters were concerned. Proportionately more dwarf types were obtained than sugarcane or intermediate (62.9 percent *vs.* 13.5 and 23.5 percent, respectively) although the extent of dwarfing varied with the variety of the *Sorghum* parent.

Cytological examination of the F_1 plants revealed $2n = 118$ chromosomes in the normal or sugarcane-like hybrids (1036). Moriva attributes this number to maternal doubling, *i.e.*, $2n$ for sugarcane, n for *Sorghum.* Both the dwarf and intermediate types of F_1 plants showed $2n = 64$ chromosomes, presumably a combination of n sugarcane plus n *Sorghum* complements. Ten meiotic univalents found in the normal hybrids were ascribed to the *Sorghum* parent. Meiotic univalents, bivalents, and occasional multivalents were found in the dwarf and intermediate hybrids in numbers exceeding ten. Moriya interpreted the higher number as tacit evidence of autopolyploidy in *P.O.J. 2725.* By this reasoning, some of the sugarcane chromosomes in the haploid set might conjugate autosyndetically to form bivalents or multivalents, while the *Sorghum* chromosomes remained univalents.

Subsequent studies by Venkatraman (1487) in which *P.O.J. 2725* and *P.O.J. 213* were crossed with bamboo (*Bambusa arundinaceae*) indicate that *Saccharum* can extend its genetic exchanges considerably beyond the allied genera which constitute the *Saccharum* complex. Twenty-nine hybrids were obtained using the sugarcane varieties as female parents. The improbability of such events occurring in nature is suggested by the fact that very few cane flowers were still available at the crossing period (December), and suitable bamboo flowers had to be shipped to Coimbatore by rail in special containers.

During the 1965 and 1966 breeding seasons at Coimbatore, Thuljaram Rao and his colleagues performed *Saccharum* x *Bambusa* hybridization experiments in which the resultant hybrid embryos were nonviable (1430, 1431). Initial work indicated that viable embryos could be obtained by dissecting them out and culturing them in nutrient media. Subsequently it was shown that hybrids from the cross *S. officinarum* (var. *Chittam*) or *S. spontaneum* Coimbatore x *Bambusa arundinaceae* Willd. produced hybrid embryos viable both *in vitro* and *in vivo*. However, the authors concluded that natural *Saccharum* x *Bambusa* hybridization was highly improbable. Failure of the seedlings to grow was attributed to "disharmony between embryo and endosperm growth". Although fertilization was observed frequently, development of either the embryo or the endosperm led to degeneration of the other tissue. Optimum embryo growth was obtained in an artificial medium, *i.e.*, via ovary culture, in which excellent development was attained so long as the endosperm was absent.

Raghavan (1210) attributes to high polyploidy the ease of sugarcane's interspecific crosses and the relative ease with which sugarcane enters into intergeneric crosses. In his view, high polyploidy has made autosyndesis almost mandatory. Hence, chromosomes from either parent can pair among themselves, and sterility will not necessarily occur regardless of the proximity of parent relationship. On the other hand, a serious restraint is imposed on the cane breeder owing to the fact that in sugarcane crosses there is seldom a synapsis between the two parental complements of chromosomes (1210). In genetic terms the outcome is far from favorable: "Variations giving the parental combinations and their Mendelian segregation are almost impossible (Raghavan states). No prediction can be made as to what will result from any particular cross. The high polyploidy, heterozygosity and autosyndesis all combine to make the chances of the reappearance of a particular synthesized variety almost impossible" (1210).

In Taiwan, Li and his colleagues (939) obtained three F_1 hybrids by crossing male-sterile *P.O.J. 2725* with *Miscanthus japonicus* Anders. This occurred during the systematic crossing of wild sugarcane relatives with commercial cane varieties at the Taiwan Sugar Experiment Station, a procedure designed to maintain breeding stock with genetic diversity and hybrid vigor. During earlier investigations Li *et al.* (937) obtained two F_1 types from the cross *P.O.J. 2725* ($2n$ = 107) x *M. japonicus* ($2n$ = 38): (a) An "OOM" type having 126 somatic chromosomes, of which 107 were contributed by the female parent and 19 by the male parent (*M. japonicus*). This type was depicted earlier by Moriya (1036) as "nobilized". (b) An "OM" type was obtained with 72–74 somatic chromosomes received from the reduced gametes of both parents. Moriya described this type as "intermediate".

In subsequent crosses of *P.O.J. 2725* with *M. japonicus* some 40 seedlings were obtained, one of which resembled the *Miscanthus* male parent in morphological features and was free of certain leaf diseases common in Taiwan sugarcanes but not in *Miscanthus.* In outward appearance this selection seemed to be an intermediate between the OM hybrid and *Miscanthus*; however, it was found to have 96 rather 72–74 somatic chromosomes. It was hypothesized that the reduced gamete of *P.O.J. 2725* (n = 58) combined with the unreduced gamete of *M. japonicus* ($2n$ = 38). This view was later substantiated by cytological examination.

In summarizing their data, Li *et al.* (939) concluded that partial homology exists between certain chromosomes of *Miscanthus* and *S. spontaneum*, and between *Miscanthus* and *S. officinarum* chromosomes. Moreover, similar homology appeared to exist among the *Miscanthus* chromosomes themselves. These conclusions were based upon the relatively small number of univalents in the OOM hybrid type as compaired with the expected number which would appear had the *S. officinarum* chromosomes of *P.O.J. 2725* not been "homologous" with those of *M. japonicus.* Partial homology was indicated by the inconsistency of chromosome pairing.

Saccharum crosses with *Erianthus, Imperata* and *Zea* were reported by Janaki-Ammal (800) in 1941. The following year she reportedly crossed *S. officinarum* with *Narenga porphyrocoma* to yield the intergeneric hybrid *"Saccharum–Narenga"* (801).

The *Saccharum–Erianthus* cross, performed with *S. spontaneum* "Glagah" ($2n$ = 112) and *Erianthus ravennae* ($2n$ = 20), yielded fertile F_1 hybrids with 66 chromosomes. They resembled the sugarcane parent morphologically in general proportion to the parental chromosome contribution (56 for *Saccharum*, 10 for *Erianthus*). F_2 seedlings included diploids, triploids, and a tetraploid (chromosome numbers = 68–76, 104–108, and 136, respectively). Diploid seedlings predominated and showed clear segregation of *Erianthus* characters, *i.e.*, presence of awn, compound inflorescence, and typical callus hairs and glumes. Sucrose content was much lower in the F_1 hybrids than in the sugarcane parent, but only slightly lower in the F_2 hybrids. In F_1 hybrids evidence was found of autosyndesis pairing in the gametic complement of *S. spontaneum*. Whereas many *Erianthus* chromosomes were lost or distributed at random in meiosis, others joined with *Saccharum* chromosomes to form trivalents and quadrivalents.

The grass *Imperata cylindrica* is described by Janaki-Ammal as ". . .a troublesome weed of cultivated land. . . whose ecotoype forms range. . . from dwarfs of a few inches in height to swamp forms over 9 feet tall with inflorescences up to 20 inches in length". The author used a local Malayan form ($2n$ = 20) as the pollen parent in crosses with *P.O.J. 2725.* Thirty-five seedlings were obtained having generally high sucrose content, a few exceeding 19 percent sucrose. Cytological evidence indicated four types of seedlings: (a) Vegetative ($2n$ = 106); (b) selfed or diploid parthenogenetic seedlings ($2n$ = 108–112); (c) triploid "selfs" ($2n$ = 156); and (d) true *Saccharum–Imperata* hybrids ($2n$ = 120–134). Sugarcane characteristics predominated in the vegetative and true hybrids as did a high proportion of *Saccharum* chromosomes in all hybrids. F_2 seedlings of true *Saccharum–Imperata* showed segregation of *Imperata* characters.

In performing the *Saccharum–Zea* crosses, Janaki-Ammal used *Saccharum officinarum* "Vellai" ($2n$ = 80) as the female parent and a sweet corn variety, *Golden*

Beauty (2*n* = 20 + 2B), as the male parent. Actual pollination was performed in an enclosure rather than in the field, and emerging *Saccharum* stigmas were dusted daily with pollen for 10 days. Two seedlings were produced and only one survived. An obstacle to *Saccharum* x *Zea* crosses appears to lie in the differing sugar concentration required at the outset by germinating pollen (800), being much lower in the *Zea* stigma than was actually encountered in the *Saccharum* stigma. The surviving seedling had 52 chromosomes. Virtually all anatomical and morphological measurements showed the hybrid to be smaller than either parent. However, of some 15 qualitative characters examined, ten resembled *Saccharum* and three resembled *Zea*. There was one intermediate and one new character (*i.e.*, a depressed shape of the bulliform or motor cells). The hybrid's stem was extremely woody. During the next four years the *Saccharum–Zea* hybrid grew slowly but produced no inflorescence, being propagated exclusively from tillers. Janaki-Ammal noted similarities of this hybrid with the Java *Troboeg* (the cane *S. edule*).

In summarizing the crosses between *Saccharum* and genera residing outside of the *Saccharum* complex, Janaki-Ammal concluded that *Saccharum* lends itself to plant improvement by crossing far more readily than was generally recognized. In explaining this potential the extensive polyploidy of *Saccharum* was assigned a key role: "...in *Saccharum* high polyploidy has removed all obstacles to hybridization with other groups of Gramineae except those that depend upon the simply ascertainable conditions of pollen germination". This investigator recognized in the high polyploidy a versatility of reproduction "...capable of producing from apparent hybridization with diploid species of other genera true diploid crosses, true triploid crosses, and diploids and triploids which are not crosses at all". The fertility of subsequent hybrids was thought to depend on the "internal pairability of the chromosomes derived from the pollen parent, in other words on their capacity for autosyndesis". However, it should be noted that in controlled hybridization the allied genera have contributed little or no germplasm to the pedigrees of modern varieties of commercial importance.

In 1942 Janaki-Ammal (801) published morphological and cytological descriptions of the *Saccharum–Narenga* hybrids produced by Barber (141) in 1913 at Coimbatore. As a commercial cane the hybrid had no future owing to its low sucrose content, and its complete sterility excluded further use as a parent. Its propagation for possible economic use ceased after some 100 F_1 seedlings had been duly examined. Janaki-Ammal's work was performed a few years later with surviving seedlings from the original progeny.

The *Saccharum–Narenga* hybrid, having 55 chromosomes, originated from the cross *Saccharum officinarum* Vellai (2*n* = 80) x *Narenga porphyrocoma* Hance (2*n* = 30). F_1 seedlings showed qualitative characters from each parent, but in overall appearance they favored the *Saccharum* or female parent. Quantitative characters were generally intermediate between the two genera. *Narenga porphyrocoma* Hance had recently been reclassified from *Saccharum narenga* owing largely to the incongruity of certain morpholical features with those of established *Saccharum* species (210). This parent features a generally weak structure, a much reduced inflorescence, highly coriaceous glumes, few or no branches, no non-flowering stalks, and a fourth glume absent in *S. officinarum*.

Saccharum–Narenga hybrids approached the maternal sugarcane parent in vigor and flowering behavior while showing considerable variation among themselves (801). Sucrose content of millable stalks varied from 6 to 11 percent. A single character, the minute celia normally found on *Narenga* lodicules, but not in *Saccharum*, was exaggerated in all F_1 hybrids. Cytological examinations revealed that *Narenga*'s 30 chromosomes formed 15 bivalents and behaved normally during meiosis. Although *Saccharum officinarum* Vellai is male sterile, in this instance the sterility was due to defective pollen-grain division; the 80 maternal chromosomes formed 40 bivalents and performed normally at meiosis. Evidence of autosyndesis was found in *Saccharum–Narenga* hybrid preparations (801). Chromosomes associated as bivalents, trivalents, and quadrivalents, and a few remained as univalents. The male and female sterility which precluded further development of the new intergeneric form was attributed to autosyndesis of both parental sets of chromosomes. Janaki-Ammal observed after tetrad formation "...a general deterioration in the pollen grains, generally beginning before the first division in the pollen grain". Interesting enough, a change in the pollen grain cytoplasm was manifested by the appearance of starch grains during the deterioration period, a feature not observed in degenerating *Saccharum* pollen grains (801).

In 1951 Raghavan (1210) reviewed the cytogenetic work performed up to that time at Coimbatore, including intergeneric crosses of *S. officinarum* with *Narenga, Erianthus* and *Sclerostachya*, and hypothesized a common generic ancestor having a basic chromosome number of five. The total failure of inbreeding as a means to improve Indian canes prompted further study of interspecific and intergeneric crossing to obtain superior clones. A measure of success was found in the hybrids *Co. 205, Co. 419, Co. 421*, and others produced by utilizing *S. spontaneum* as the male parent in crosses with *S. officinarum*.

Prompted by Parthasarathy's view (1147) that functioning reduced gametes are an implication of close genetic relationship, Raghavan (1210) crossed *S. officinarum* (Vellai) with *Sclerostachya* and obtained reduced female gametes functional on the *Saccharum* side. This was taken as tentative evidence of a close relationship between *S. officinarum* and the genus *Sclerostachya.* In second and third backcrosses in which $2n$ = 40 chromosomes (10 from *S. officinarum* and 30 from *Sclerostachya*) it was found that five of the ten *Saccharum* chromosomes had paired with five *Sclerostachya* bivalents giving five trivalents. The remaining chromosomes from each parent retained their respective univalent and bivalent configurations. From this evidence Raghavan concluded that the basic *S. officinarum* complement of ten chromosomes actually contains a complement of five chromosomes homologous to *Sclerostachya*. Subsequent crossing of the backcrossed progeny ($2n$ = 50) with a different genus, *Narenga* ($2n$ =

30), produced trivalents and a "total number of bodies being 18–20". These results favored homology of the ten *Saccharum* chromosomes with *Narenga* chromosomes.

Jagathesan and Sreenivasan (785) reported incompatibility systems operating in *Narenga* (four clones) and *Sclerostachya* (seven clones). Both genera were shown to be completely self-incompatible and partially cross compatible. The authors claim that one form of *Narenga* possesses heterogenetic pollen grains in which an extra fragment chromosome ensures partial intraspecific compatibility. Incompatibility in both genera is traced to an inhibition of pollen tube growth. According to Lundquist (967), self-incompatibility occurs in grasses with unusual frequency and is controlled by a two-loci system.

D. *Interspecific crosses*

The clone *Vellai*, a hybrid of *S. spontaneum* which Janaki-Ammal (800) identifies with the Hawaiian cane *Lahaina*, was crossed with *Narenga narenga* (presently *S. narenga*) by Barber (141) in 1913. *Vellai* was later used as the female parent in crosses with two species of *Sorghum* and with *Erianthus arundinaceus* at Coimbatore (1488). The history of *Vellai* dates back at least to 1766 when Bougainville introduced it from Otaheite to Mauritius (426). Bligh brought it to Jamaica from Otaheite in 1791 (464). This variety is also known as *Otaheite, Bourbon*, and *Caña Blanca* (800). Characterized by a thick, soft stalk with high sucrose content, it is still maintained in many parts of the world, including a few private gardens in Puerto Rico, for chewing purposes.

Raghavan (1210) describes a number of interspecific crosses performed at Coimbatore involving forms of *S. officinarum, S. spontaneum, S. robustum* and *S. barberi.* The work was designed (a) to clarify the unverified thesis that North Indian canes originated by "promiscuous hybridization" between *S. officinarum* and indigenous forms of the wild *S. spontaneum*, and (b) to establish the basic *Saccharum* genome. Efforts to establish the basic number are instructive even though they were not completely successful. They included crossing the *S. spontaneum* variety *Coimbatore* ($2n$ = 64) with *S. barberi* ($2n$ = 92) and successively backcrossing the hybrid with *S. spontaneum* to reduce *S. officinarum* chromosomes to their basic number. Conversely, *S. barberi* ($2n$ = 92) was crossed with *S. officinarum* with the view that subsequent hybrid backcrosses with *S. officinarum* would reduce *S. spontaneum* chromosomes to their basic number.

The interspecific cross studies at Coimbatore clearly underscored the complex genetic relationships among *Saccharum* species. In the cross *S. barberi* x *S. spontaneum*, yielding the hybrid *P. 3146*, evidence was found of gamete reduction, while non-reduction appeared to occur on the female side in an undetermined number of *Saccharum* species (1073). Various authors find this to be most common in *S. officinarum*. Raghavan concluded from available evidence that non-reduction of pollen gametes will also occur when *S. officinarum* is used as the male parent. In another *S. barberi* x *S. spontaneum* cross, six functional reduced gametes were obtained, thereby implying a close genetic relationship between the two species. However, a cross between *S. officinarum* and *S. barberi*, yielding the hybrid *S.G. 377-1*, produced evidence of further genetic complication involving the doubling of *S. officinarum* chromosomes contributed by both parents. As noted elsewhere (*cf.* this chapter, pp. 45, 46), the transmission of somatic chromosome numbers from the maternal (*S. officinarum*) parent is well substantiated; however, in the *S. officinarum* x *S. barberi* cross Raghavan was forced to conclude from his data that in *S. barberi* there are more *S. spontaneum* chromosomes than *S. officinarum* chromosomes, and hence a close genetic proximity must exist between *S. barberi* and *S. spontaneum.* Recalling that in *S. officinarum* x *S. spontaneum* crosses the female parent (*S. officinarum*) normally contributes the unreduced gametes, Raghavan proposed that a limit must exist for the number of *S. spontaneum* chromosomes acceptable to *S. officinarum*, beyond which ". . .*S. officinarum* is disturbed and so begins to function as a diploid on its gametic side". He subsequently states: ". . .If in *barberi* there are more *S. spontaneum* chromosomes than *S. officinarum* would relish, presumably it at once functions as a diploid. But if the number of *S. spontaneum* chromosomes is considerably reduced *S. officinarum* is not presumably disturbed by their presence and would function with its haploid egg gametes". Raghavan also noted the similar behavior of the *S. officinarum* diploid gamete in crosses with *S. spontaneum* and *S. barberi*, and cited this as further evidence of a close relationship between the two *Saccharum* species.

In the interspecific cross *S. barberi* (*Saretha*, $2n = 93$) x *S. robustum* ($2n = 72$), producing the F_1 hybrid *P. 3134*, workers at Coimbatore found the hybrid chromosome number $2n = 82$ $(46 + 36)$ which corresponds to the sum of parental haploid numbers (1210). Since in *S. officinarum* crosses with *S. barberi* there is an F_1 number exceeding the sum of parental haploids, but less than the sum of the *S. officinarum* diploid plus *S. barberi* haploid numbers (225), Raghavan was able to postulate on the genetic proximity of *S. officinarum, S. barberi*, and *S. robustum* (1210). In essence, if *S. robustum* and *S. officinarum* are very closely related, "the behavior of *S. robustum* with *S. barberi* should not be the same as that of *S. officinarum* with *S. barberi*". In the *S. officinarum* x *S. barberi* cross there is evidence of a functional non-reduced female gamete (possibly due to a predominance of *S. spontaneum* chromosomes over *S. officinarum* chromosomes in *S. barberi*), but examination of the hybrid *P. 3134* showed that only haploid gametes were functional. Two possible explanations were forwarded: (a) *S. robustum* may contain certain chromosomes homologous to *S. spontaneum.* If, as the author suspected (1210), *S. barberi* contains more chromosomes from *S. spontaneum* than from *S. officinarum*, a homology between *S. robustum* and *S. barberi* would render unacceptable the origin of *S. officinarum* from *S. robustum.* Raghavan therefore reasoned that a *S. robustum–S. barberi* homology could not have explained the functioning of haploid gametes in the

S. barberi x *S. robustum* cross. (b) A second explanation proposed that discrete haploid and diploid gametes are formed primarily in *S. officinarum*, to a lesser extent in *S. spontaneum*, and not at all in *S. robustum* and *S. barberi.* Under such conditions this criteria is of value in determining genetic relationships only where *S. officinarum* has contributed to a particular cross. The degree and proportions of diploid gametes formed in all *Saccharum* species remained unclear at the time of Raghavan's writing [1951], but their occurrence today in most modern commercial varieties is logically traced to the *S. officinarum* parentage.

Basic chromosomes of *S. officinarum*, which were thought to be components of *Sclerostachya* (1210), also showed homology with *Narenga* chromosomes. This view is supported by Janaki-Ammal's (799) observation of functional reduced female gametes on the *Saccharum* side of the cross *S. officinarum Vellai* x *Narenga.*

Raghavan (1210) presented as further evidence of a close relationship between *S. officinarum, Sclerostachya*, and *Narenga* the findings by Dutt and Narasimhan (458) relative to starch distribution among the respective canes. The absence of appreciable starch in any of these three groups, while appearing frequently in *S. spontaneum* and *S. barberi*, appears to be a genetic feature rather than a chance phenomenon. Moreover, the appearance of functional reduced gametes in *S. officinarum* when crossed with *Sorghum, Erianthus, Zea*, and *Bambusa*, a feature already noted in crosses with *Sclerostachya*, might be taken as evidence of a genetic relationship to all of these genera. However, the lack of homology between *S. officinarum* chromosomes – when reduced to their basic number – and chromosomes of other genera might preclude a common ancestral origin (1210).

Although starch content is clearly a varietal character with marked differences among discrete clones, Hogarth (740), in Queensland, was unable to correlate starch content with other major characters such as sugar content, sugar per acre, and cane per acre. A high degree of genetic determination was obtained for starch on a level comparable to that for C.C.S. values. Theoretically, the low degree of association should have permitted selection for low starch without complications with regard to yield and sucrose characters. However, because of a reduced selection differential for high yield and high sugar characters, Hogarth suggested that milling techniques rather than selection of low-starch varieties offer a better means to lower starch content.

E. *The introgression theory (S. officinarum x Miscanthus)*

Loh and Tseng (949), in establishing general guidelines for cane breeding in Taiwan, maintained that *S. spontaneum* and *Miscanthus* species are more readily nobilized by *S. officinarum* than are *S. narenga* and forms of *Erianthus. Miscanthus japonicus* was found especially suitable for hybridization with *S. officinarum.* According to Loh and Tseng (949), earlier work in Taiwan produced two types of hybrids from the cross *P.O.J. 2725* with *Miscanthus japonicus* (937). One type resembled *Miscanthus*, having low sucrose content and a slender stalk. The other type, with more sucrose and a larger stalk, resembled *S. officinarum* and possessed both reduced gametes (from *Miscanthus*) and unreduced gametes (from *S. officinarum*). The *Miscanthus*-like hybrids had only reduced gametes from both parents.

In 1946 Grassl (606) concluded that *Erianthus maximus* was the second most important wild ancestor of the noble canes (*S. officinarum* L.). Subsequent studies with newer collections suggested that *E. maximus* was actually a hybrid originating from the cross *S. officinarum* x *Miscanthus floridulus*, in which the *Saccharum* parent contributed most of the chromosomes (607). In 1965 Grassl (608) proposed that *Erianthus maximus* was a natural hybrid originating with the cross *S. officinarum* L. x *Miscanthus floridulus*, and that forms of *E. maximus* should be reclassified as hybrids. Evidence suggestive of an introgression between *M. floridulus* and *S. officinarum* in the Pacific area, and between *M. floridulus* and forms of *S. robustum* in New Guinea, was also presented.

According to Loh (948), the first artificial hybridization of *Saccharum* with *Miscanthus* was performed in 1933. Li and his co-workers (939) crossed *P.O.J. 2725* with *M. japonicus* in 1951. However, *Miscanthus* x *Saccharum* crosses only infrequently produced hybrids and these were usually sterile. The specific cross *S. officinarum* x *M. floridulus* was not reported prior to the paper by Grassl (608). Moreover, *Miscanthus* and *Saccharum* differ widely in morphological characters and environmental requirements (608), features which Grassl considers prohibitive against grouping into a common species. Evidence offered by Grassl for reclassifying certain *Erianthus maximus* forms as *Miscanthus–Saccharum* hybrids include: (a) Male sterility of Florida-grown clones; (b) extensive variation in external morphology; (c) intermediate quality of juice; (d) lateness of flowering; (e) chromosome counts indicating neither a stable species nor a complex polyploid group; (f) presence of introgression signs in the putative parents.

Interesting enough, the *S. edule* canes (having edible inflorescence) were viewed by Grassl (608) as BC_1 forms from the *Saccharum–Miscanthus* hybridization. Historically, *S. edule* canes were taken as hybrids or varieties of both *S. officinarum* and *S. spontaneum*. Typical *Miscanthus* leaf morphology and other features in *S. edule* plants tend to support the possibility of *Miscanthus* parentage.

In summarizing his introgression studies Grassl claimed that introgression of *M. floridulus* features into *S. officinarum* have modified many of the native garden canes which technically retain their "noble cane" classification. He cites the discovery of similar but more complex hybrids among the native garden canes in New Guinea highlands. Some of these forms were "escapes" from cultivation or from living fences, and in New Guinea hybridization had occurred predominantly with *S. robustum* rather than *S. officinarum*. However, the evolution of complex highland types, that is, above about 100 feet elevation where *S. robustum* seldom grows, probably involved recurrent backcrossing into *M. floridulus* under a decided influence of primitive man who showed great interest in these canes. Natural selection also played a role in the isolated-valley habitats characteristic of New Guinea uplands, which in turn depended on man as their primary means of material exchange (608). At low and intermediate elevation, Grassl speculates that the presence of *S. robustum* and relative absence of *M. floridulus* assured greater backcross frequency with *S. robustum.* The origin of cane forms with edible inflorescences is traced to the extensive crossing of *S. robustum* with *M. floridulus* at these levels. From a taxonomic point of view the complex introgression canes would be treated as "subgroups of *S. robustum*. . . . or nothormorphs of the hybrid group under the formula name" (608).

6. CYTOGENETICS OF CULTIVATED CANES

A. *General*

Modern sugarcane varieties are derived through controlled crosses involving as many as four *Saccharum* species in the genetic source material (1188). Modern varieties likewise bear high aneuploid chromosome numbers owing to chromosomal increases accompanying certain crosses and backcrosses. However, as observed by Price (1188), the chromosome behavior is similar to that of allopolyploids in spite of their great complexity, with the result that such varieties may respond to inbreeding much like diploids. With reference to specific gene behavior little evidence has been found of genetic exchange between *S. officinarum* and *S. spontaneum* chromosomes in the meiotic stages of modern sugarcane. Although linkages between desirable and undesirable genes of *S. spontaneum* which ordinarily do not break during crossing over can be broken by irradiation, such treatments have not appreciably increased the production of superior new hybrids (1188).

Price (1188) depicts *S. officinarum* as being cytogenetically less complex than other *Saccharum* species. Typical *S. officinarum* clones have the chromosome number $2n$ = 80, and 40 bivalents regularly form during meiosis. A small number of original or "atypical" noble canes possess variable chromosome numbers and distinctive morphological features stemming from interspecific and possibly intergeneric hybridization.

Roach (1245) suggests that the highly desirable heterosis in sugarcane breeding results from a complementary action of genes transmitted from different parental forms. Accordingly, the complementary gene action might best result from crossing diverse genotypes. This is a keystone of the much-written need for expanding the rather limited genetic base of modern hybrid varieties.

Owing to a predominance of bivalents in modern cane varieties which cytologically resemble allopolyploids, Price (1188) maintains that an inbreeding approach to homozygosity should be predictable. He notes that selfing diploids will reduce heterozygosity by about one-half each generation. Therefore the modern canes whose chromosomes form bivalents should yield to an inbreeding approach to homozygosity much the same as would diploids.

B. *Cytogenetic origin of S. officinarum*

Parthasarathy (1148), in 1948, summarized research in India aimed at clarifying the still obscure genetic origin of *S. officinarum*. Considered to be an octoploid ($2n = 80$) with a basic number of x = ten chromosomes, successive backcrosses with the wild *Sclerostachya fusca* produced a homology between parental chromosomes which began to manifest itself in diploid and haploid progeny. In the haploid condition five chromosomes of *S. officinarum* consistently paired with five chromosomes of the *Sclerostachya* parent. Parthasarathy therefore proposed a basic number of ten chromosomes composed of two discrete sets of x = five chromosomes each. Identification of the lower compliments plus proof of a common *Saccharum–Sclerostachya* ancestor having x = five chromosomes would require a series of interspecific and intergeneric crosses utilizing reduced *S. officinarum* complements (1148).

Celarier (309), in 1956, published a comprehensive cytological review of the subtribe Saccharinae in which chromosome numbers and meiotic behavior of certain genera were presented for the first time. Twelve genera and 28 species were listed for the subtribe, and all genera in which more than one species was studied contained extensive polyploidy. The basic chromosome number occurring with greatest frequency was either five or ten. Celarier found all chromosomes to be small, but some were so much smaller than others that a "phylogenetic" trend seemed to manifest itself from the large to smaller chromosomes. Morphological differences within the subtribe were described and ordered along phylogenetic lines. On this basis Celarier hypothesized an evolutionary pathway for Saccharinae which is shown diagramatically in Fig. 1-4. In this scheme the reader will note the intermediate position given *Erianthus* between *Eriochrysis* and *Saccharum–Narenga*. Distinguishing morphological characters are lacking in *Erianthus* while *Saccharum* and *Narenga* are shown to differ slightly in panicle structure.

C. *Basic chromosome numbers*

Price (1190) concluded from chromosome counts in a large number of *Saccharum, Miscanthus, Miscanthidium, Narenga* and *Sclerostachya* forms that the noble canes constitute the one large group of similar clones. This was the only group in which the chromosome number $2n = 80$ was consistent. *Narenga* and *Sclerostachya* forms were consistent with $2n = 30$ chromosomes. *Miscanthus floridulus* had $2n = 38$, *Miscanthidium erectum* had $2n = 30$, and *Miscanthidium violaceum* had $2n = 28$ chromosomes.

Nishiyama (1118) described four methods by which the basic number in a

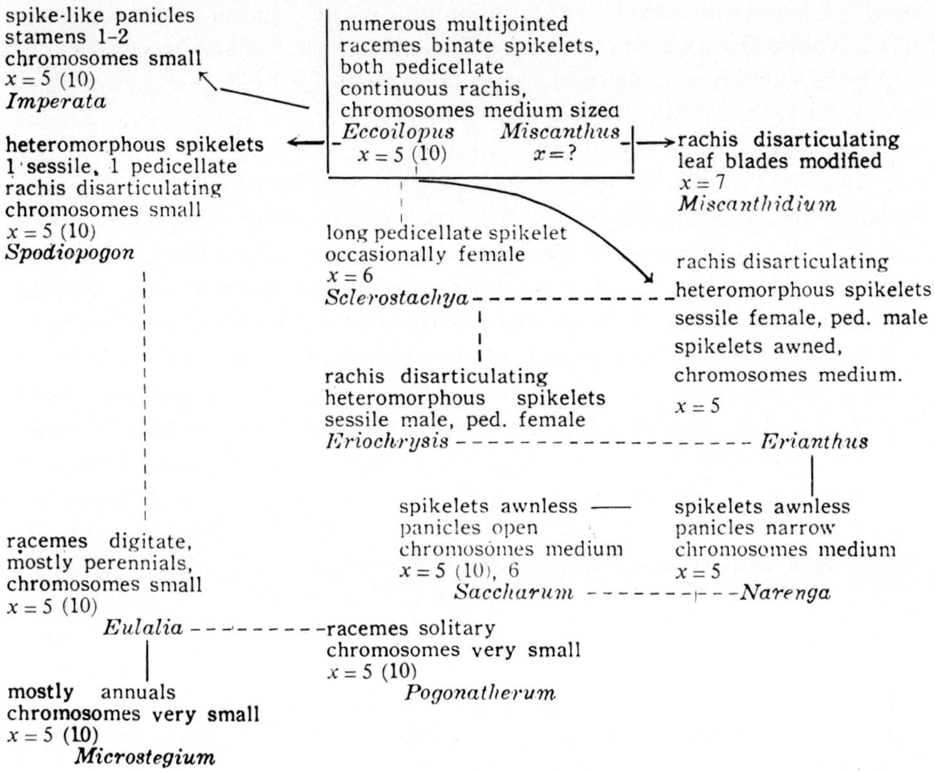

Fig. 1-4. Hypothetical pathway for the evolution of Saccharinae. [After Celarier (309).] Reproduced by permission of *Cytologia*.

polyploid series can be ascertained: (a) An arithmetical determination of the largest common division in the polyploid series; (b) the genome method of analysis whereby the basic chromosome number is indicated in the meiotic chromosome homologies of F_1 hybrids; (c) analysis of "secondary polyploidy" as shown by the secondary association of chromosomes; and (d) application of karyotype analysis. Nishiyama notes that each of the first three methods have been applied in efforts to determine the basic *Saccharum* number, but no consistent figure has emerged. Hence, Bremer (234) proposed basic numbers of five and ten, Dutt and Rao (454) reported eight, Darlington and Janaki-Ammal (408) reported ten and twelve, Parthasarathy (1148) claimed two sets of five chromosomes each, and Raghavan (1210) suggested two sets of five chromosomes each for *S. officinarum* and three sets of five chromosomes each for *S. narenga.* Loh (950) assigns three basic chromosome numbers to *S. spontaneum*, six, eight and ten.

Nishiyama (1118) attempted to establish the basic *Saccharum* chromosome number by genome analyses based upon meiotic chromosome homologies in F_1 hybrids. A series of interspecific crosses were performed and the resultant F_1 chromosome numbers were examined on a theoretical basis, taking into account the possibility of autosyndesis occurring in different species [as Janaki-Ammal (801) had demonstrated in the intergeneric hybrid *S. officinarum* x *Narenga porphyrocoma*]. The crosses and subsequent conclusions drawn from the chromosome pairing are as follows: (a) *S. officinarum* (n = 40) x *S. spontaneum Coimbatore* (n = 32); two basic numbers were evidenced, ten in *S. officinarum* and eight in *S. spontaneum.* (b) *S. officinarum* (n = 40) x *S. spontaneum Glagah Java* (n = 56); some chromosomes failed to pair (probably *S. spontaneum*), but in theory three basic numbers were possible, eight, ten and twelve. (c) *P.O.J. 2725* ($2n$ = 107) x *S. spontaneum Ponape* (n = 40); a basic number of ten was indicated for both parents. (d) *S. robustum* (n = 40) x *S. spontaneum Coimbatore*; autosyndesis was evidenced in chromosomes from both parents, and for each parent a basic number of ten was probable. (e) *S. spontaneum Karenki* (n = 48) x *S. spontaneum Glagah Java*; basic numbers of eight and ten were evidenced. Nishiyama concluded from the genome analysis that there are two basic numbers in *Saccharum*, eight and ten, and that polyploidy in *Saccharum* consists of multiples and combinations of these two basic numbers.

D. *New approaches to sugarcane improvement*

Price (1189) traces the spectacular gains made in developing new clones to two major events in the history of varietal improvement: (a) The discovery (or rediscovery) of fertility in sugarcane, followed by a shift of emphasis from exploration and importation to controlled crossing and selection; and (b) the breeding of *P.O.J. 2878*, characterized by disease resistance and vigor transmitted from a wild parent (*S. spontaneum*), which motivated cane breeders throughout the world to follow the example of interspecific hybridization. Major advances followed each of these events and Price was of the opinion that "another giant stride is needed". He proposed two unconventional approaches to accomplish this. The first approach was based on the thesis that modern sugarcane clones are cytogenetic balances between *S. officinarum* chromosomes and *S. spontaneum* chromosomes in which extra transmissions from the former have masked undesirable characters in the latter. New balances might therefore be attained by creating new levels of polyploidy. The second approach envisions induced translocation of genetic material, in the process of which it should be possible to retain desirable chromosome segments and eliminate undesirable segments. This would further enable new genes from diverse species to become incorporated into new sugarcane genotypes. In this context Price thought it probable that new canes could be bred on an 80-chromosome level.

It is difficult to argue with Price's views, at least on theoretical terms. Major improvements are needed in sugarcane in almost every region where it is grown. In a few areas, as for example Puerto Rico, the immediate survival of the sugar industry depends on varietal as well as cultural improvements. Moreover, as various authors have pointed out (1189, 1362, 225), in the process of interspecific hybridization in sugarcane only a few clones from wild species have actually contributed to the modern cane genome. For example, *S. spontaneum* Java, which enters the pedigree of many commercial varieties via the natural hybrid *Kassoer*, has contributed only one gamete to modern canes (1189). A Philippine form of *S. spontaneum* ($2n = 80$) contributes only one gamete. Similarly, the Coimbatore form of *S. spontaneum* has transmitted germplasm through only one gamete, although via several F_1 hybrids. Price continues in this vein: "...Only a few gametes from *S. sinense* have introduced *S. spontaneum* chromosomes into modern sugarcane... One *S. robustum* gamete has been utilized in Hawaiian breeding and another in Australian breeding. No germplasm at all has reached modern varieties from genera outside *Saccharum*. (There is no credence in pedigrees of commercial sugarcanes that include *Sorghum, Zea, Euchlaena, Coix*, or any of the true bamboos[9].) Surely, the great genetic diversity of wild plants that hybridize with sugarcane has been sparsely used."

An interesting paradox of this condition, that is, the non-use of abundant interspecific germplasm, lies in the fact that interspecific hybridization has been performed in sugarcane for more than five decades, whereas in most crops the concept is still novel. Five *Saccharum* species (counting *S. sinense*) have contributed to the ancestry of modern varieties. In this connection the enormous successes already obtained have perhaps obscured the need to continue sugarcane breeding in any other way[10]

E. *Induced sugarcane mutations*

In 1959 Price and Warner (1186) evaluated the prospects for sugarcane improvement by induced mutations, *i.e.*, by radiation treatment of genetic material, a technique first discovered by Muller (1057) and by Stadler (1355). The possibility that agricultural crops might be improved by this means had prompted serious research by the close of the 1950's (775, 571). In essence, at the expense of various side effects, the radiation method may increase the frequency of genetic mutations which otherwise occur but rarely in nature. However, by 1959 informed workers had already cautioned that rapid and spectacular results could not reasonably be expected from radiation technology (1361). During the subsequent decade this approach to variety improvement has had no great impact on sugarcane breeding programs.

Methods examined for increasing mutation frequency include ionizing radiations (X-rays, γ-rays, pile neutrons) and chemical treatment of specific bud tissues. X-rays reportedly produced changes in stalk color among striped canes at Mysore (1489). Various authors have examined the possibility of mutant induction in sugarcane with

---

[9]The qualification in parentheses is given by Price. The considerable work in intergeneric crosses and the ease with which *Saccharum* species participate in such crosses certainly implies that new germplasm is available outside *Saccharum*.

[10]Sugarcane improvement by cell and tissue culture methods has advanced appreciably during the drafting of this manuscript. This topic is treated in detail in Chapter 16.

γ-rays (1465, 1138, 1497). Thuljaram Rao *et al.* (1429) obtained a red rot-resistant mutant of *Co. 449* by low level γ-irradiation of bud tissue. Other authors claim that various chemical agents compare favorably with radiation (754, 850). One advantage of chemicals is their relative ease of administration to a wider range of plant materials.

Price and Warner conceived two approaches whereby sugarcane might be improved via induced mutations: (a) The first, aimed at improvement of existing sugarcane varieties through mutagenic treatment of cuttings, was viewed as an extension of bud selection methods whereby mutant types would be selected from vegetatively-reproduced varieties. However, the authors foresaw prohibitive difficulties in recognizing and isolating mutants having appreciably superior agronomic characters. (b) By the second approach radiation technology would be incorporated into conventional breeding programs. It was thought that, by the processes of segregation, recombination, and selection through successive generations, unsuitable mutations could be rejected and favorable ones accumulated. The main advantage of radiation, at least in theoretical terms, was pictured as induced changes of a nature which ordinarily do not occur, or occur too infrequently to be of importance. The breaking of linkages between adjacent genes, permitting the formation of new recombination types, would in theory constitute a major improvement upon conventional meiotic processes. In particular, the transfer of favorable genes from otherwise unfavorable chromosomes and the subsequent deletion of undesired chromosome segments seems to offer an important means of cane improvement. In effect it should overcome part of the *Saccharum* handicap of low meiotic synapsis.

As opposed to *chromosome mutations, i.e.*, changes affecting segments of chromosomes rather than specific gene changes, of which the translocation type mentioned above offers a theoretical means of sugarcane improvement, Price and Warner also discussed *gene mutations.* However, little hope was seen for the induction of gene mutations *per se* to hold any particular advantage for the cane breeder[11]. This is to say that desirable mutant alleles are probably already present in breeding lines with little expectation of finding expression in conventional progeny.

Hrishi *et al.* maintain that vegetatively-propagated crops such as sugarcane are as suitable for mutation breeding as seed-propagated crops (754) Disadvantages arise from the recessive nature of gene mutations (1186) and tissue changes amounting to "tissue mutation" rather than true genetic mutation. At times authentic mutated

[11] During the discussion period for this paper, G.C. Stevenson remarked that precautionary heat treatments against ratoon stunting disease had possibly produced a mutagenic effect as shown by increased flowering by varieties previously reluctant to flower (*Badila* in particular). Remarks by G.W. Burton, based on radiation studies of non-*Saccharum* grasses, emphasized favorable results which "chromosome engineering" might produce in sugarcane. He emphasized that *S. spontaneum* chromosomes should be irradiated in the univalent condition to avoid masking effects by the second member of the chromosome pair. Moreover, since mutant characters tend to be recessive, progeny should also be examined through the second (R_2) generation in order to recognize new mutant forms.

segments are too small to be seen. Some authors feel that mutation induction is of value only when performed in a conventional breeding program, and that it is desirable only when directed at specific meiotic stages of reproduction (1186). Natural mutants such as the bud "sports" described by Deerr (426), which must have originated as the result of strictly empirical influence upon vegetative tissue, occur much too infrequently to be meaningful in a modern breeding program.

At Coimbatore Hrishi *et al.* (754) evaluated chemical treatments as a means to induce sugarcane mutants. The alkylating agents MMS (methyl methane sulfonate) and MES (methyl ethane sulfonate), and phenols (pyrogallol and pyrocatechol) were examined as bud treatments. Chemicals were administered to the buds on variety *Co. 419* at various levels in aqueous solution or phosphate buffer. Bud scales were removed and the single-budded setts were presoaked in distilled water for 24 hours. Results showed a number of growth and morphological aberrations in the young plants, primarily bud inactivation, tissue damage or "tissue mutations", reduced height and leaf area, reduced number of millable canes and tillers, and ring color mutations. The studies were of a preliminary nature and no evidence was found of a superior mutant being induced by these methods.

7. CHROMOSOME TRANSMISSION AND INHERITANCE

A. *Maternal (S. officinarum) transmission of somatic chromosome numbers*

Virtually all modern sugarcane varieties are produced by the controlled crossing and backcrossing of parents having different chromosome numbers (1188). Some of these crosses, particularly *S. officinarum* x *S. spontaneum*, result in a peculiar increase in chromosome numbers first described by Bremer (235) in 1922. As a result modern varieties tend to have high aneuploid chromosome numbers, with somatic numbers usually in the order $2n$ = 100–125 (1188). Precise chromosome counts are rendered more difficult by the small size and "stickiness" of *Saccharum* chromosomes. In spite of general difficulty in distinguishing univalents from small bivalents, and larger bivalents from multivalents, the chromosome configurations of certain varieties such as *H. 49-5* have been interpreted "with complete confidence" (1188).

Chromosome counts from first anaphase and diakinesis-metaphase stages of *H. 49-5* and three other Hawaiian varieties were presented by Price as indicative of meiotic chromosome associations for the four varieties. Price found that "bivalents prevailed, univalents were relatively infrequent, and multivalents were rare". Nishiyama (1118) observed occasional trivalents and quadrivalents in metaphase I preparations from *S. officinarum* or *S. robustum* x *S. spontaneum* crosses. Multivalents were usually formed by weak linkages between two bivalents or between one bivalent and one univalent.

Li *et al.* (939) observed tetravalents and a single pentavalent in meiotic pollen mother cell preparations of *P.O.J. 2725* x *Miscanthus japonicus* progeny. A ring structure was observed in all multivalents. The authors suggested that the tetravalent ring was comprised of two *S. officinarum* chromosomes and two *S. spontaneum* chromosomes. The pentavalent was thought to involve the union of two *Miscanthus* chromosomes, two of *S. officinarum* origin, and one of *S. spontaneum* origin. An important feature of this work is the implication of at least partial homology among *Saccharum* chromosomes at the generic as well as specific level.

The pedigree for *H. 49-5* given by Price (Fig. 1-3) illustrates an odd feature of *Saccharum* having the effect of additive chromosome behavior. The varieties *Kassoer* and *P.O.J. 2364* are seen to have received the somatic rather than gametic chromosome number for *S. officinarum.* These varieties therefore contain the sum of the maternal somatic number plus the paternal gametic number ($2n + n$ chromosomes). In general, *S. officinarum* will consistently transmit its somatic number when acting as the female parent in *S. officinarum* x *S. spontaneum* crosses (1118, 1187). This is not a consistent feature of *intra*specific crosses (1118), nor does male transmission of the somatic number generally occur (1188). Price also notes the infrequency of $n + n$ hybrids and aneuploids. This behavior is substantiated by a number of prior studies (1185, 1187, 816, 1118).

Price attributes to maternal transmission of $2n$ chromosomes the rapid success of backcrossing in nobilizing *S. spontaneum* forms (1188). An early change in chromosome ratios between *S. officinarum* and wild canes will occur during the first two generations, a feature of no small importance to breeders seeking to introduce new *S. spontaneum* forms into their genetic source material. However, the rapid change of chromosome ratios does not occur during nobilization of other *Saccharum* species (1188). Prior work by Price (1187) indicates that *S. officinarum* x *S. robustum* yields $n + n$ hybrids. *S. officinarum* x *S. officinarum* also produced $n + n$ hybrids, being in this instance the anticipated progeny.

Narayanawsami (1073) has described several abnormalities in the embryo-sac mother cells of *S. officinarum*, in particular a postmeiotic fusion of the two innermost megaspores. Bremer (237) failed to confirm these observations and claimed that embryo sacs with $2n$ egg cells were sometimes produced by postmeiotic endomitosis. At times $4n$ cells were produced. Price (1187) stated that "Bremer's postmeiotic endomitosis. . . can hardly be denied", but proposed further verification.

Parthasarathy (1149) attempted to explain the formation of gametes having $2n$ = 86 chromosomes on the basis of two meiotic processes, the effect of which is an *en bloc* elimination of chromosomes thereby establishing "reversible polyploidy": (a) An elimination of 16 bivalents by the formation of two spindles in metaphase I; and (b) the cell bearing 43 chromosomes undergoing endomitosis in accordance with the theory of Bremer (237). Parthasarathy obtained his evidence by selfing the male-sterile *Co. 421* and performing a series of crosses with *Co. 421* as the female parent. In each case he obtained two types of seedlings, one having thick stalks and $2n = 118$ chromosomes, and the other having thin stalks with $2n = 86$ chromosomes. Photographic evidence of two spindles and two metaphase plates in a single cell was produced. The proposed *en bloc* elimination of chromosomes underscores the contention that both desirable and undesirable characters are being retained and discarded together in *Saccharum* (1188).

Use of *S. robustum* in breeding modern canes has been generally limited (95). A notable exception is the Hawaiian variety *H. 37-1933* which contains *S. robustum* genetic material. This variety attained unusual prominence in Hawaii and elsewhere. In a practical vein Price (1188) cautioned against undue impatience among breeders seeking new hybrids by breeding with *S. robustum*, implying that such hybrids may in fact be forthcoming in time. Arceneaux (95) likewise favors an increased usage of *S. robustum* germplasm in long-term breeding programs.

Recent chromosome transmission studies by Roach (1245) in Queensland showed that *S. officinarum* ($2n = 80$) crosses with different *S. spontaneum* clones ($2n = 64$ and 96) were consistent with the transmission pattern in which hybrid chromosome numbers equalled the sum of maternal somatic and paternal gametic numbers. However, *S. officinarum* ($2n = 80$) crosses with four different *S. spontaneum* clones in which all had $2n = 80$ chromosomes yielded hybrids with varying proportions of $2n + n$ and $n + n$ chromosome numbers. The proportions appeared to depend on: (a) The *S. officinarum* parent used as the female; (b) the *S. spontaneum* parent used as the male; and (c) non-gametic factors of unknown origin. The latter condition was surmised from two crosses of *Badila* x *U.S. 56-13-7*, and is one of the few instances where an author has pointed to non-genotype influence on the proportion of $n + n$ hybrids produced. Roach mentions the time of crossing, location of crossing, and greenhouse environmental conditions where the fuzz was seeded as possible contributing factors.

Meiotic chromosome association studies of F_1 hybrids revealed considerable inconsistency among hybrids of the same *S. officinarum* x *S. spontaneum* cross (1245). Meiosis appeared to be more irregular in hybrids from crosses showing $n + n$ chromosome transmission than from crosses which do not. Partial or attempted allosyndesis was offered by Roach as a possible explanation. The appearance of a few miniature clones with $2n = 48–50$ chromosomes was observed in several crosses indicating possible intergeneric hybridization (resulting from contaminated pollen), or possible aneuploid derivatives from *S. officinarum*. One instance of a $n + n$ intergeneric hybrid was reported, *i.e.*, from *S. officinarum* x *Erianthus arundinaceus*.

Roach, quite significantly, emphasized that much additional data must be gathered on patterns of intrageneric and intergeneric chromosome transmission, and that this information should be incorporated in a new taxonomic classification reflecting genetic as well as morphological distinctions. Although cane breeders have come to recognize the narrowness of the genetic base of modern sugarcane hybrids, there is, in his view, much need of a taxonomic classification which will serve as a breeder's guide in selecting the correct germplasm from the vast quantities now available. By this means a "...logical rather than random testing of germplasm" should help to increase the genetic diversity needed in sugarcane breeding.

Among progeny from the cross *S. officinarum Korpi* ($2n$ = 80) x *Erianthus procerus* ($2n$ = 40), Roach found three atypical seedlings having $2n$ = 70 chromosomes (Fig. 1-5). This is an excellent example of cytological technique coming to the investigator's

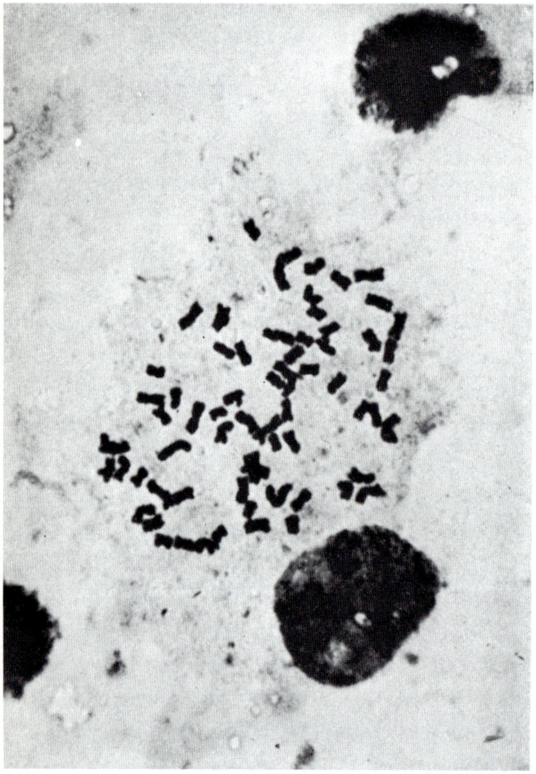

Fig. 1-5. Somatic metaphase in a seedling from the cross *Korpi* x *Erianthus procerus*, $2n$ = 70 (x 1000). [After Roach (1245).] Reproduced by permission of *I.S.S.C.T.*

aid in establishing parentage, a tool not available to the early workers who attempted to sort out *Saccharum* species by empirical means. Roach believed it highly unlikely that *E. procerus* had in fact been the pollen parent for the 70-chromosome seedlings, while on the other hand he was quite certain that some form of *Erianthus* had served as the male parent. The most plausible explanation involved contaminant pollen entering the cross from a parent with a chromosome number in the order of $2n$ = 60. *Erianthus* clones having this number were being nobilized at the same time and in the same area but at a different site.

B. *Gene transmission and character inheritance*

Efforts to relate qualitative character segregation with specific genes in *Saccharum* have met with little success. *Saccharum* species apparently do not lend themselves to simple genetics and the transfer of individual genes from one breeding line to another has not been accomplished by cane breeders (1188). Exceptions to this view include the work of Skinner (1332) in Queensland who showed that hair presence is determined by a small number of important genes. With reference to Jeswiet's hair group numbers 56 and 60, Skinner hypothesized that group 56 was determined by one or two major genes in different crosses, and that group 60 was determined by one, two, or three major genes in different crosses. Skinner's evidence also indicated that the genes determining the two groups were completely independent in inheritance and that the genes gave simple diploid segregations.

Studies by Li and Shang (938) with *S. robustum* and two varieties backcrossed to male sterile *P.O.J. 2725* offered evidence in support of the following hypotheses: (a) Cane hardiness is quantitatively inherited. (b) Sugar content is controlled by approximately four polymeric genes. (c) Stalk color is controlled by an inhibitor, "Aa", and two complementary genes, "Bb and PLpl". (d) Color of growth rings (brown *vs.* non-brown) may be accountable to the complementary genes "C and D" having a 33.3-percent crossover. (d) Node morphology (prominent *vs.* flat) is controlled by two duplicate genes "P^1 and P^2"

Price (1188) points out that such hypotheses can be substantiated only by adequate test crossing. Moreover, in his view, ". . .every attribute of sugarcane behaves as if it were controlled by many genes". Within the context of traditional breeding methods for sugarcane Price also supports the use of massive progeny populations: "Sugarcane breeders must continue to rely upon selection in large populations for every accomplishment." It is possible that new developments in cell and tissue culture technology (*cf.* Chapter 16, pp. 631–635) will render this viewpoint obsolete.

Price has suggested that the breeding and selection processes which produced modern sugarcane varieties effectively retained whole noble chromosomes bearing favorable characters and eliminated whole *S. spontaneum* chromosomes bearing unfavorable characters. This view is based on $n + n$ and $2n + n$ evidence from F_1 hybrids which suggests virtually no pairing between *S. officinarum* and *S. spontaneum* chromosomes. More recent varieties having a predominance of bivalents but few multivalents conform to this thesis. Price therefore concludes: "With minimal interspecific chromosome pairing, genetic exchange between chromosomes of the two species must be negligible." He further assumes that linkage of desirable and undesirable genes in *S. spontaneum* chromosomes is not ordinarily broken in backcrosses with *S. officinarum.* An important assumption here is that whole retained chromosomes would bear undesirable traits as well as favorable ones, and whole deleted chromosomes would eliminate desirable traits along with the unfavorable ones. Price recommends irradiation as a possible means to transfer specific desirable *S. spontaneum* genes to

S. officinarum chromosomes: ". . . .Used for specific purposes, irradiation may gratify the plant breeder." Price was at least consistent with other authors who foresaw useful applications of irradiation.

Roach (1244) examined the transmission of quantitative characters in *S. officinarum* x *S. spontaneum* crosses and found that contribution of the somatic chromosome complement by the maternal parent produced a more rapid increase of sugar and decrease of fiber than did transmission of the gametic complement by the male parent. Eight F_1 populations from two *S. officinarum* clones crossed with four *S. spontaneum* clones (pollen parents) were evaluated for four yield–sugar classes, that is, "high" and "low" characters for both yield and sugar in their respective combinations. No evidence was found that hybrid sugar yields were related to the yield potential of either parent. However, male–female interactions were highly significant in determining sucrose yield per acre. In most hybrids, heterosis was evident for early growth, stalk length, yield per acre, percent flowering, and pollen production.

In the instance of progeny from the cross *Badila* x *51 N.G. 2*, in which *S. spontaneum* was expected to predominate, the $n + n$ hybrids were consistent with the anticipated quantitative characters. In the cross *Korpi* x *51 N.G. 2* the $2n + n$ hybrids showed closer resemblance to the *S. spontaneum* parent. In general, the investigations showed that features of stooling and quality exceeded mid-parent values; stalk thickness, flowering time, total sugars and sucrose approximated mid-parent values; and fiber content and erectness were below mid-parent values.

In 1950 Loh and Tseng (949) proposed five parental categories based on the manner of gene transmission for sucrose content (SS) and vegetative vigor (VV): Sucrose carriers, vigor carriers, sucrose acceptors, vigor acceptors, and inert carriers. An underlying assumption was that sucrose genes and vigor genes do not ordinarily accompany one another in the same parent. By this reasoning virtually all commercial varieties are either sucrose carriers or inert carriers, whereas the other types seldom attain commercial prominence. Moreover, desirable crosses were depicted as crosses between a sucrose carrier and a sucrose acceptor, or between a vigor carrier and vigor acceptor. Crosses between two carriers or between two acceptors were thought to be undesirable. Sex of the parent was also emphasized, some varieties making excellent female parents only, others performing well only as male parents. Although Loh and Tseng had been trying to set broad guidelines to ease the enormous burden of selecting from millions of seedlings, Stevenson (1362) regarded their interpretations as overly simplified, and in particular he questioned their use of Mendelian symbols which implied sucrose and vigor inheritance as single factors rather than as complexes of factors.

Babu (128), at Coimbatore, attempted to establish *S. spontaneum* genotypes for the two qualitative characters "habit" and "occurrence of sprawlers" on the basis of their segregation in first generation progeny of selfs and crosses. Three Indian clones of *S. spontaneum* were employed. The characters "rhizomic" (dominant) and "bushy" (recessive), plus sprawler absence (dominant) and sprawler presence (recessive), were found to segregate in a 3:1 ratio in both selfs and crosses. All parents were extremely heterozygous for the two characters. One of the cross progeny showed the homozygous condition for rhizomic and sprawler absence.

8. REGIONAL IMPROVEMENT OF CULTIVATED CANES

A. *Breeding for qualitative character improvement*

As stated by Lalouette (884) "...the production of sugarcane seedlings is a relatively easy matter, the problem is to produce the right sort of seedlings". Virtually all modern sugarcane varieties or clones (varieties grown as horticultural entities are clones) have derived from the breeders' intentional use of interspecific hybridization. Price (1188) distinguishes between "original" sugarcanes, whose improvement occurred during prehistoric times through *intra*specific breeding, and later through *inter*specific breeding, and modern clones derived through intentional use of *inter*-specific hybrids. He has also described the *S. officinarum* x *S. spontaneum* hybridization as a major feature in the evolution of modern varieties. "...In the original cross and in the first backcross, the female *S. officinarum* transmits its somatic rather than its reduced chromosome number to the progeny. Thus, while the chromosome complement of *S. spontaneum* is first halved and then approximately quartered, the somatic number of *S. officinarum* chromosomes is transmitted intact and then increased." Nobilization of *S. spontaneum* is accomplished relatively rapidly by recurrent backcrossing to *S. officinarum* or noble canes. This process involves a parallel increase of the *S. officinarum* chromosomes (1188).

Nobilization programs in Mauritius have utilized forms of *S. spontaneum, S. robustum*, and imported clones of *S. sinense* (884). Seedlings are selected on the basis of vigor. A highly standardized breeding program tailored to local conditions and complete with data processing facilities was recently established.

In Taiwan, sugarcane breeding was initiated in 1913 but gained little initial success owing to inadequate breeding lines and poor flowering performance (950). Early efforts to produce wind-resistant or "hard" seedlings were negative. Reorientation of the program in 1946 resulted in improved wind-resistant and self-cleaning types. Diseases (mosaic, red rot, yellow spot) have largely been brought under control. During the 1960's new high-yielding hybrids were produced by vigorous selection of progeny from a few "elite" parents (950). Recently, interest has increased in the use of wild germplasm to expand the genetic base of breeding lines.

Between 1958 and 1965 workers in Taiwan studied the transmission of agronomic characters in crosses of *N.Co. 310* and *N.C. 19* with a local form of *S. spontaneum*. Features such as tillering, stalk size, flowering, sucrose content, fiber content, and pithiness were readily transmitted from the wild parent to the F_1 progeny. Inferior characteristics were further improved by backcrossing. However, wide variations appeared in the transmitted characters among the different backcross generations. Loh[12] recommends the use of *S. robustum* forms noted for their hardness of rind and vigor for breeding "long-cycle" varieties, *i.e.*, for growing seasons of 18 to 24 months duration. He also notes that *Chunnee* hybrids are exceptionally winter hardy in Taiwan, and *S. spontaneum* hybrids are adaptable to adverse environments. Loh (950) was one of the few authors to specifically recommend the increase of photosynthetic tissue area as a sugarcane breeding objective.

"Foreign" varieties introduced to India have tended to show low vigor in that country (1281). As a result efforts are being made to maintain as breeding stock varieties from Barbados and Queensland for high yield characters, and from Clewiston and Queensland for quality characters. Canal Point and Clewiston varieties have shown promise in resistance breeding for subtropical India. For tropical India parental stocks from Barbados and Queensland have shown good tonnage, vigor, and quality characters.

In addition to yield and quality features, the capacity to resist disease is an inherited character highly prized by cane breeders. Brandes *et al.* (227), in 1947, after summarizing new and old forms of wild cane collected for breeding purposes, observed that ". . . .it is difficult to judge at the present stage just how the characters of the wild parent operate to bring about amelioration of disease hazards. In the case of root diseases it seems to be in some cases simply ability to 'grow away' from the parasite, in unfavorable situations by vigor and regenerative power of the parts attacked. In the case of virus diseases such as mosaic, in which outstanding tolerance of hybrids has been achieved, the plants appear to have an innate physiological defence against the injurious effects of infection". In Louisiana, the search for mosaic resistance has not ceased since the early years of this century when the disease all but ruined the sugar industry. A more recent spread of sugarcane mosaic to all but the northern areas of Louisiana has prompted new efforts to produce hybrids having both resistance and higher quality (231). Both interspecific hybrids and wild clones of *S. spontaneum* were evaluated for resistant germplasm. While none of the parent forms are completely immune to the predominant "H" strain, resistant clones have appeared with increasing frequency.

B. *The northern Caribbean sugarcanes*

Although it is generally acknowledged that *Saccharum* species are not indigenous to the western hemisphere, in modern times a major cane-growing industry has emerged

---

[12]Loh, C.S., 1969. Sugarcane breeding. Retrospect and prospect, *Proc. Int. Soc. Sugar Cane Technol.* 13: 1069–1086.

in the north Caribbean area which accounts for approximately 25 percent of the world's cane sugar production (96). The principal areas, including Cuba, Mexico, the Dominican Republic, Jamaica, Puerto Rico and Haiti, have depended largely upon outside sources for its cultivated canes. Among the latter, *P.O.J. 2878* and certain Barbados varieties have been grown extensively. *P.R. 980*, bred in Puerto Rico, achieved local importance.

Prior to the early 1950's local breeding efforts were handicapped by environmental conditions generally unfavorable for flowering. These have been partially overcome by the use of mountain nurseries for growing parent stocks. According to Arceneaux (96), a wide range of flowering parental forms were maintained near Preston, Cuba, from 1953 until the Castro revolution. Nurseries were established at elevations ranging from 150 to 730 meters above sea level. Although this program was interrupted in its early stages, a number of promising selections identified by the initials U.C.W. were removed to the U.S.D.A. collection for testing in Florida, Jamaica, Puerto Rico and the Dominican Republic. One of the objectives at Preston had been to incorporate wild germplasm from *Saccharum spontaneum* (*Mandalay*) into north Carribean breeding stock. The first success was achieved when *S. spontaneum* pollen transported from Florida to Colombia effected a cross with *Caña Blanca.* Seedlings from this cross and a subsequent *Cristalina* x *S. spontaneum* cross were removed to Canal Point.

More recent work at Central Romana, Dominican Republic, also employed nurseries at various altitudes in a breeding program which Arceneaux terms as "very satisfactory". Additional parent varieties brought in from Canal Point and Barbados contributed significantly. The C.P. forms, bred for subtropical conditions, produced seedlings essentially free of flowering problems when crossed with canes bred for tropical conditions. Arceneaux reports that a residue of 519 seedlings (about 1 percent of the total of original Central Romana progenies) produced two main subgroups when evaluated against local standard varieties under field conditions: (a) 64 seedlings producing significantly greater sugar per acre, and (b) 168 seedlings producing significantly lower sugar per acre. Composite pedigrees were examined with reference both to ancestral forms of original species and to ancestral forms desired from interspecific and intraspecific crosses. Seeking "clues that might permit a more discriminating use of the parent material", Arceneaux found that specific ancestral forms appeared within the two contrasting groups with marked inconsistency, at times deviating widely from a 1:1 ratio. Original varieties more prevalent in the superior group included *Cristalina* (94:37), *Chunnee* (134:90), *Okinawa Tekcha* (14:5), and the hybrid canes *D. 74, U.S. 1694*, and *M. 2.*

In Puerto Rico, efforts to develop a cane suitable for all parts of the island culminated in the variety *P.R. 980.* This variety originated in 1947 from the cross *Co. 281* x *P.O.J. 2878.* In 1966 González-Ríos wrote: "This variety seems to be, until now, the best cane that has been produced in Puerto Rico" (598). The *P.R. 980* pedigree illustrated in Fig. 1-6 shows an entry of wild germplasm from both parents: *S. sponta-*

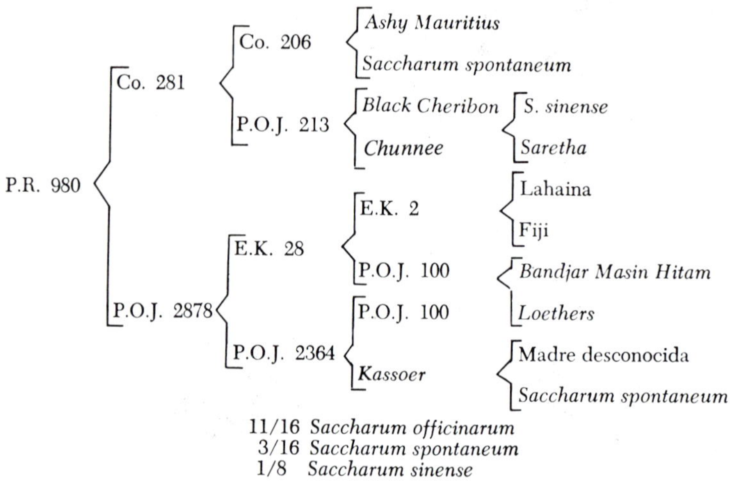

Fig. 1-6. Pedigree of the sugarcane variety *P.R. 980*, indicating the sources of its wild genes which constitute 5/16 of its total germplasm. [After González-Ríos (598).] Reproduced by permission of P. González-Ríos.

neum from *P.O.J. 2878* via *Kassoer*, and from *Co. 281* via an unknown ancestor; and *S. sinense* from *Co. 281* via *Black Cheribon*. The *P.R. 980* germplasm is derived 2/16 from *S. sinense*, 3/16 from *S. spontaneum*, and 11/16 from *S. officinarum* (598).

C. *Louisiana canes*

In the instance of the Louisiana sugarcanes relatively complete acreage records have been kept during a cultural history of more than two centuries (990). First planted in 1751 by Jesuit missionaries from Santo Domingo, as few as ten varieties occupied more than 35 percent of the acreage up to about 1940. As shown by Matherne (990) in Fig. 1-7A, the clone *Creole* was grown for nearly a century with *Otaheite* being its lone important competitor. These gave way to the *Louisiana Purple* and *Louisiana Striped* varieties during the mid-nineteenth century. In 1894 twenty new varieties were introduced from the Royal Agricultural Society of Demerara, of which *D. 74* rapidly became the predominant variety following its release to growers in 1898.

Varietal data illustrated in Fig. 1-7B reflect the pressures of a rapidly-developing industry and an important weakness of nobilized canes, *i.e.*, an inability to cope with certain diseases. About 1920 the early noble canes began producing exceptionally low yields, and by 1925 Brandes and Klaphaak (223) confirmed the widespread incidence of sugarcane mosaic disease. According to Matherne (990), sugar yields in Louisiana dropped from 324 000 tons in 1921 to 47 000 tons in 1926, through the combined inroads of red rot, root rot, and mosaic. The need for resistant varieties led to the establishment of a breeding station at Canal Point, Florida. The *P.O.J.* varieties *213*

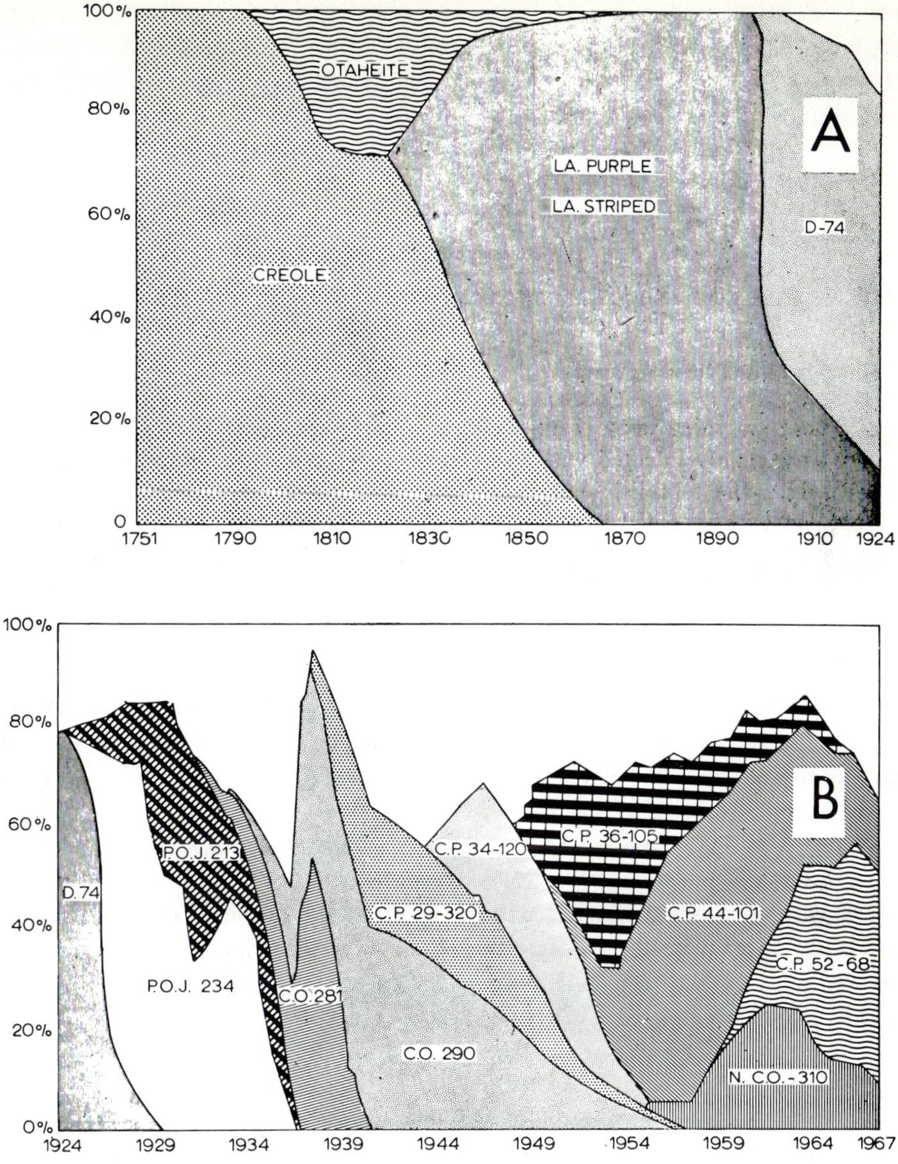

Fig. 1-7. Changes in the predominance of major sugarcane varieties in Louisiana, as percentage of the total state acreage. (A) The period 1751 to 1924, showing the long reign of *Creole* and the infrequency of new varietal introductions. (B) The period 1924 to 1967 characterized by increased numbers of varieties with relatively short cultivation spans. [After Matherne (990).] Reproduced by permission of *I.S.S.C.T.*

and *234*, lacking the thick joints and low fiber prized by Louisiana growers in their earlier noble canes, but showing some tolerance to mosaic, were widely established but only briefly cultivated. *P.O.J. 213* soon succumbed to red rot and *P.O.J. 234* was replaced by *C.P.* varieties having superior mosaic resistance and cultural features. The *C.P.* varieties were introduced after 1930 and cumulatively occupied an important share of the Louisiana acreage.

D. *Hawaiian cane breeding*

In 1965 Heinz (713) reviewed sugarcane breeding in Hawaii and emphasized that the development of a broad genetic base was instrumental in the rapid evolution of new and better Hawaiian varieties. The use of wild germplasm has been emphasized by Hawaiian workers for many years, reflecting perhaps the imposition in 1905 of an embargo against importations of new sugarcane varieties. From 1905 to 1925 local sugarcane breeders labored under the handicap of limited foreign breeding material. By 1925, however, Hawaiian-produced seedlings occupied more than a third of the total cane acreage. Heinz attributes this success to the single clone *H. 109* which was produced in 1905 and gave superior performance in the leeward areas.

Following the establishment of suitable quarantine procedures in 1925 there was an influx of new germplasm into Hawaii and from that date the cane breeders achieved a continual series of new and higher yielding varieties. The following 25 years saw an increasing proficiency in cane breeding which by 1949 had placed Hawaiian-bred clones in more than 99 percent of the commercial acreage. By 1963 Heinz reports more than 89 percent of new plantings were made with varieties germinated in 1947 or later. These varieties were developed to meet the needs of a 24-months crop with relatively less emphasis given to disease and insect problems. Yield capability amounting to 0.4 to 0.8 ton of sugar per acre per month and prolonged soundness of the stalks were features given special emphasis. Adaptability to the island's diverse soil and climate conditions was largely achieved. The trend in Hawaii has thus developed toward the rapid breeding and release of new varieties adapted specifically for Hawaiian agronomic and ecological conditions.

The requirements of the accelerated breeding program in Hawaii were such that only a large and diverse source of germplasm would assure an acceptable frequency of new hybrids (713, 1534). A large "germplasm pool" was thus established and maintained. Much of the wild genetic material was gathered by Warner and Grassl (1535) during the 1957 Melanesian expedition. Over 600 clones were represented in the pool, including *Saccharum* species (*officinarum, spontaneum, robustum*, and *sinense*), hybrids of these species, foreign varieties, and clones of allied genera (Table 1-2).

Hawaiian usage of wild germplasm began in 1931 with the introduction of a New Guinea form of *S. robustum*. Fuzz was collected at Port Moresby and germinated under quarantine at Mapulehu, Molokai. The best clones from the fuzz plantings were maintained and crossed with *S. officinarum* varieties, with interspecific and noble hybrids of Hawaiian origin, and with introduced foreign canes. *S. robustum* constitutes

TABLE 1-2

SUGARCANE CLONES INTRODUCED INTO HAWAII, AS OF DECEMBER, 1963

[After Heinz (713).] Reproduced by permission of D.J. Heinz.

Genera and species	Clones	
	Number imported	Number producing seedlings
Erianthus arundinaceus	7	4
Erianthus bengalense	2	0
Erianthus maximus	2	2
Miscanthus hybrids	3	3
Narenga porphyrocoma and hybrids	4	1 or more
Sclerostachya hybrids	2	2
Sclerostachya fusca	5	0
Sclerostachya sp.	2	0
Saccharum officinarum	110	59
Saccharum sinense	24	13
Saccharum spontaneum	42	26
Saccharum robustum	17 clones plus 2035 seedlings	Over 100

by far the largest source of wild genetic material with over 2000 clones being introduced as cuttings or germinated fuzz. Additional *S. robustum* material, collected during the 1937, 1951, and 1957 expeditions to New Guinea, had progeny in various stages of development in 1965 when Heinz presented his paper (713). A number of *S. spontaneum* clones were also introduced as collected material and foreign hybrids, and also in the genotype of *P.O.J.* clones. Although the *S. spontaneum* chromosomes carried by *P.O.J.* types dates from 1925, and *P.O.J. 2878* dates from 1927, much *spontaneum* material did not arrive in Hawaii until after 1945. Progeny from the later germplasm was not expected to emerge until after 1965 (713). Clones of allied genera introduced into Hawaii include *Erianthus arundinaceus, E. maximus*, and hybrid forms of *Miscanthus, Narenga*, and *Sorghum*.

Although in general the world's commercial canes have only a narrow genetic base (1189, 95), Hawaiian sugarcane breeders have attempted to widen the base within the limits of conventional breeding technology (713). With possibly one exception, *H. 54-775*, all commercial or semi-commercial varieties could claim a known *spontaneum* ancestor by 1965 (Fig. 1-8). Subsequent to 1965 Hawaiian cane breeding has emphasized *spontaneum* sources of germplasm in implementing the "melting pot" concept. Heinz (717) identifies 15 *spontaneum* clones plus numerous local *robustum* strains employed in the current [1971] breeding program. Since approximately 40 new clones are introduced each year the latest published data (Table 1-2) are already outdated.

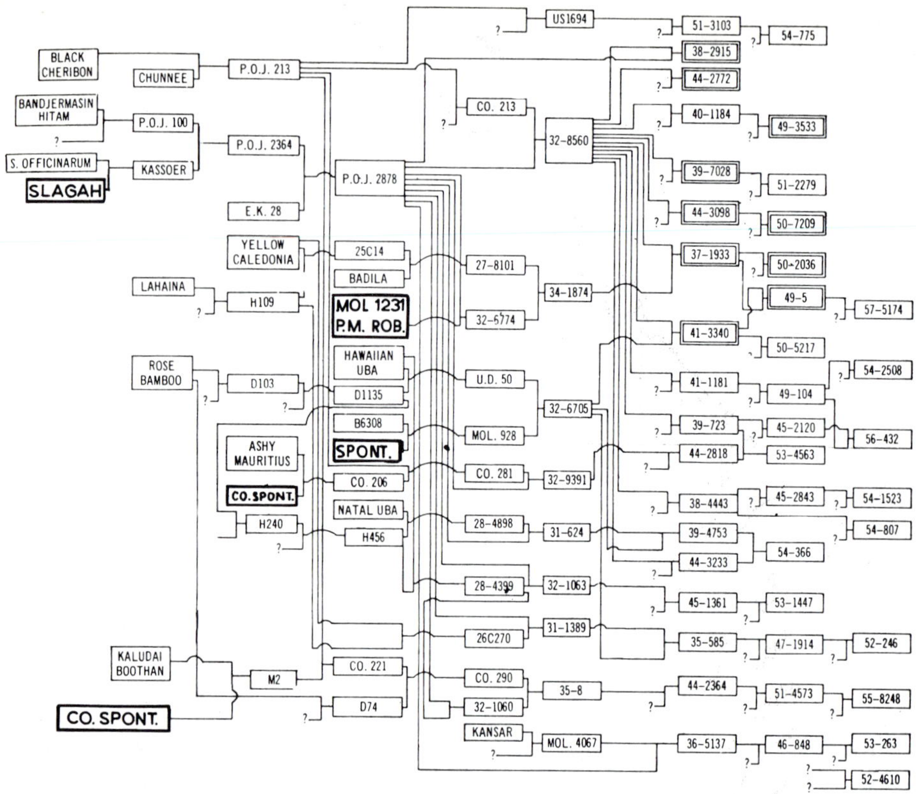

Fig. 1-8. Pedigrees of Hawaiian varieties grown commercially or having commercial potential as of 1963. The ten varieties occupying the greatest acreage are enclosed by double lines. Shaded boxes signify wild *Saccharum* species. [After Heinz (713).] Reproduced by permission of D.J. Heinz.

As pointed out by Heinz (713), the important yield increases in Hawaii, which have been more or less continual since the release of *H. 109*, can be traced not only to the incorporation of wild germplasm but also to the methods of incorporation which are specifically tailored to meet Hawaiian cultural and ecological requirements. The "melting pot" technique provides for rapid incorporation of wild germplasm into the Hawaiian gene pool. Regional breeding and testing stations coupled with plantation testing increase the likelihood that the improved hybrids will show specific adaptation to the Islands' soil and climate variables (973). A pedigree cannot in itself measure the contribution of a given ancestral form, but the Hawaiian experience seems to show that a great deal can be wrung from limited ancestral material if wisely handled.

E. *Performance history of improved canes*

In 1965 Arceneaux (95) presented a "merit" survey of some 114 sugarcane varieties utilized commercially during the quarter century 1940–1964. Based upon utilization records gathered from 16 major sugarcane-growing regions[13], Arceneaux's criteria was in effect a "...compromise between cultural history on the one hand and contemporary usefulness on the other...". Usefulness *per se* becomes highly relative with the passage of decades and recent varieties are at a disadvantage in not having had time to prove themselves fully. Interesting enough, sugarcane varieties showed a tendency to remain in the general region where they were bred. Hence "H." varieties (Hawaiian) remained largely in Hawaii, "C.P." (Canal Point) varieties stayed predominately in Louisiana, and "B." varieties (Barbados) were mostly situated in the British West Indies. An exception to this was the *P.O.J.* group, especially *P.O.J. 2878*, which ranged widely throughout the regions covered by Arceneaux's study[14].

Arceneaux's work dealt largely with canes obtained by controlled crosses; however, seven original clones (six of *S. officinarum* and one of *S. sinense*) were retained in commercial use throughout the 25-year period. Only one, *Badila*, attained a first-rank status, the others "... maintained relatively minor positions, and as a group these varieties are quite obviously on the way out". On the other hand the predominant role played by a few *S. officinarum* clones in the parentage of newer varieties was strikingly evident (Table 1-3). *Black Cheribon*, for example, was confirmed in the pedigree of 66 of the varieties examined; 25 more had "strong presumptive evidence" of *Black Cheribon* parentage. *S. spontaneum* (India) contributed to the ancestry of 62 of the commercial varieties of *S. spontaneum* (Java) likewise appeared in the ancestry of 62, in this instance via the presumed wild ancestor of the single clone *Kassoer* (95). *S. sinense* contributed through the Indian variety *Chunnee*. *S. robustum* entered the ancestry of only two commercial varieties and *Sorghum vulgare* was reported in the ancestry of three of the varieties studied.

Arceneaux (95) commented pointedly on the prominence of *S. officinarum* and the paucity of *S. spontaneum* material entering into the genetic make-up of modern varieties: "If we consider the vast botanical resources, among natural forms of *S. spontaneum*, it is obvious that we have barely scratched the surface in view of the small number of original clones represented in our commercial canes." With reference to the clone *Kassoer*, an F_1 hybrid from the cross *S. officinarum* x *S. spontaneum* (Java), Arceneaux notes that "...it should be possible to develop artificially some better starting point of the nobilization process". Referring to earlier work by Arceneaux *et al.* (93), they proposed "...a more exhaustive exploitation of forms of *S. sinense* and

---

[13]Served by the principal cane breeding stations of the world.

[14]A similar trend is found in the varietal selection for most of the fundamental research with sugarcane. Hence, a major percentage of our basic knowledge of this plant has come from *H. 37-1933* (Hawaii), and from *Pindar* (Queensland), with *N.Co. 310* and *P.R. 980* appearing less frequently in the literature. In Puerto Rico, basic research utilized whatever variety was conveniently at hand.

TABLE 1-3

IMPORTANT COMMERCIAL CANES DESCENDED FROM SPECIFIED ORIGINAL FORMS OF RECOGNIZED SPECIES

[After Arceneaux (95).] Reproduced by permission of *I.S.S.C.T.*

Clone or original form	Number of descendents	Clone or original form	Number of descendents
Saccharum officinarum		*Sorghum vulgare*	
Black Cheribon	66	Dura	3
Bandjarmasin Hitman	65	Lahaina	5
Loethers	64	Meligeli	5
Cristalina	46	Striped Preanger	4
Ashy Mauritius	21	Badila	4
Kaludai Boothan	21	Yellow Caledonia	2
Green Sport	12	Korpi	2
Vellai	11	Fiji	1
Striped Mauritius	8	Goru	1
		Batjan	1
Saccharum spontaneum		Oramboo	1
India	62	From one or the	
Java	62	other region	78
		From both regions	46
Saccharum sinense		Uba	3
Chunnee	60	Tekcha	1
Saretha	7		
Saccharum robustum			
Molokai 1231	2		

forms of *S. spontaneum* from the upper latitudes in the development of cold resistant canes would seem to offer very interesting possibilities indeed". Arceneaux *et al.* further emphasized the value of traditional germplasm in limited research programs requiring new commercial varieties in the shortest possible time. But again, ". . .where substantial resources and appropriate investigational facilities are available development of new basic material from original sources, especially *S. spontaneum* and possibly *S. robustum* as well should not be overlooked as a tool for long range varietal improvement".

9. *SACCHARUM* EVOLUTION OF A SUPERIOR SOURCE-TO-SINK SYSTEM

Most of the literature appertaining to the origin, cytogenetics, and breeding of *Saccharum* species makes little or no mention of sugarcane in its physiological–biochemical context, that is, as a very unique source-to-sink system, perhaps the finest devised by nature with or without the aid of man. This observation does not minimize in any way the accomplishments of taxonomists, cytologists, and breeders, or of the cane growers themselves who have improved the plant since prehistoric times. Their progress with sugarcane as a crop plant has undeniably been great. On the other hand, most of the scientific investigation of *Saccharum* species has centered around the questions "what?" and "how much?"; very seldom has serious attention been given to "how?" and almost never to "why?". The latter question, the most difficult question, still lurks ominously in the background when one reads of "characters", "genes", "genomes" and "germplasm". When reading the literature on cane cytogenetics and breeding one begins to feel that, if only the correct genes are brought together at the right place and time, all else in the matter of sugar growing will somehow take care of itself. Of course this is not true. Perhaps this is best shown by the work of knowledgeable cane breeders who have expressed less than total satisfaction with conventional methods of cane improvement (1362, 1189, 713).

A. *Physiological efficiency*

During the 1960's a few authors began to relate "physiological efficiency" to yield and quality factors structured into new cane hybrids by conventional breeding methods. In the culture of a given crop the factors of leaf area, photosynthetic assimilation rate, and duration of the growth period obviously must interact to produce the dry matter or "yield" value otherwise attributed simply to gene control. In recent years features such as CO_2 supply, leaf area, and leaf angle incident to solar radiation have begun to be considered by breeders of maize and sorghum (8, 1349). Stevenson (1362, p. 7) described yield as being "dependent upon the integration of a series of physiological processes. . .", and suggested that each of these processes would have to be understood as a prerequisite to fundamental genome analysis. Juice quality was also seen to have ". . . physiological limits to the upper range of variability".

Watson (1539), working with kale and sugar beet, examined the relationships of net photosynthesis rate to the leaf area per unit area of land, *i.e.*, the *leaf-area index.* By thus relating the size of photosynthetic system with dry matter production a greater discrepancy was obtained than net assimilation values (based on activity rates) would have shown. The key factor was leaf-area variation which ranged from inadequate in young plants to excessive in well-developed stands. Watson concluded that "heavy" crops may require leaf thinning in order to achieve maximum yield.

The leaf-area index has probably never been excessive in modern cane fields. Loh (950) estimates that as many as 90 000 millable stalks per hectare must be raised to approach maximum tonnage. Heavy tillering is a desired feature in most seedling selection programs. Loh specifically recommends a greater production of photosynthetic area to insure tiller survival. Hartt (665) has cautioned against cane selection based on the "self-cleaning" feature. Conceivably, too much of the essential green canopy may drop away before its photosynthetic usefulness has been fulfilled.

Stevenson's dissertation on quality inheritance, published in 1965, makes a strong case for the operation of environmental and physiological factors in addition to – and interacting with – purely genetic characters (1362, pp. 134–138). He writes: "Juice quality is essentially a relative character, whose expression is controlled by a strong and very evident variety–environment interaction. Even where favorable genes are present in a suitable array, good juice quality will not develop in the absence of the appropriate ripening conditions." And subsequently: "In order to reach a full understanding of how varieties may differ in juice quality, and of the factors which contribute to such differences, it would be necessary to integrate a chain of physiological processes, some of which are as yet only partly understood. Only then could any sort of fundamental genotype analysis be attempted." Stevenson makes special reference to variable leaf area, net CO_2 assimilation rate, growth vigor, and number of tillers (the latter an expression of growth, leaf area, and photosynthate requirement) as attributes through which heritable characters govern cane quality.

Stevenson gives the example of Brix inheritance (polygeneric) to illustrate quality expression in seedlings where the upper limits are determined by physiological means. It is pointless, he explains, to look for seedlings having Brix values in the order of 25–27 percent among progeny whose parents did not exceed 21–22 percent Brix. An upper limit must exist beyond which high Brix values represent excessive desiccation rather than an inherited character: ". . . The physiological explanation is that as soon as a limiting (water) concentration within the plant is reached, further reduction of CO_2 stops, and it is only under conditions where secondary loss of water takes place from the sugar solution as it exists in the plant that higher concentrations are attained."

In principle Stevenson is quite correct, but his physiological explanation is not very impressive. There is little evidence that sucrose concentrations in sugarcane stalks govern the rate of carbon assimilation in sugarcane leaves. There is, however, a reasonable argument-favoring product repression in the leaves when sucrose accumulates more rapidly than it can be translocated (666). Moreover, as Hartt and her colleagues reported shortly after Stevenson's book was published, the moisture status of sugarcane differentially affects both CO_2 assimilation rate and the rate of sucrose movement from leaf to storage tissue (675, 676). It is conceivable that low moisture may cause a slackening of CO_2 assimilation while at the same time permitting greater sucrose accumulations in the stalk by virtue of more efficient "unloading" from conducting phloem to storage parenchyma (675).

B. *"Source" and "sink" concepts*

In his "prospect" for sugarcane breeding, Loh (950) noted in addition to photosynthesis the work performed in Queensland by Glasziou and his colleagues relative to sugar storage processes and the "sink" concept of sugar storage. He appears to have been one of the few breeders to see a relationship of all this to breeding objectives. The fact that *S. officinarum* forms tend to accumulate sucrose where *S. spontaneum* produces fiber was traced to a predominance of neutral invertase in *S. officinarum* and of acid invertase in *S. spontaneum*. Taken to its logical conclusion such reasoning would place the mechanism for gene control of sucrose[15] squarely on the invertase synthesis and regulation systems operative in storage tissues. This is perhaps an oversimplification of the case since both acid and neutral invertases are required for sugar storage (*cf.* Chapter 9, pp. 349–351), and acid invertase is intimately involved in rapid growth processes (567, 590). However, the examination of inheritance in physiological–biochemical terms as well as in genetic terms is certainly a step in the right direction.

The effectiveness of sucrose accumulation and its role in the evolution of *Saccharum* species was vividly underscored by Bull and Glasziou (258) in 1963. In this study various species of the genera *Erianthus, Miscanthus*, and *Saccharum* were examined for their contents of sugars, moisture, and fiber. The results were interpreted from the viewpoint of selection pressure and the survival of a type cane under favorable ecological conditions and almost unlimited evolutionary time. In essence, survival, and therefore retention in the evolutionary scheme, was related to the capacity for mobilizing sugars essential for shoot production. Selection pressure was thought to favor the carbohydrate most readily remobilized from storage, that is, sucrose, a view inconsistent with that of Stevenson (1362) who believed human intervention best explained the survival of high sucrose types. This work is appropriately examined in a later chapter (*cf.* Chapter 10, 368, 369, 393), but in any case it is heartening to find a plausible physiological explanation for sugarcane's evolution, taking nothing away from the purely random events of nature and the selection processes of primitive man so often postulated by other authors.

C. *Sugarcane growth and the C_4 pathway*

Although sugarcane's efficient carbon fixation mechanism must reasonably contribute to the plant's high level of sugar synthesis and storage, a similar relationship of photosynthesis to growth has not withstood critical examination. Recent work by Bull (260) in Queensland tends to minimize the C_4 pathway of photosynthesis as a factor in cane growth superiority over other species. Quite logically, some authors have

---

[15] Stevenson (1362, p. 34) suggests that the genes responsible for high sucrose inheritance in *S. officinarum* are relatively few in number and are situated at more than one locus. He reasons that these are mutant genes which originated as mutant alleles from "wild" genes favoring photosynthate conversion to fiber rather than photosynthate storage. The mutant genes appear to have originated separately in *S. officinarum* and *S. robustum*, whereas the *S. spontaneum* genome still leans toward fiber production. Stevenson regarded the mutant "sweet" plants as being at a disadvantage in the evolutionary sense, their survival being dependent upon man.

associated the rapid growth rates of certain tropical grasses with their typically high light saturation levels and an inherent capacity to assimilate carbon at rates several times higher than temperate species (854, 271, 700). Bull (260), however, cites the work of Slatyer (1347) with C_4 and C_3 pathway species of *Atriplex* showing that the C_3 or Calvin-cycle species was able to overcome an early growth lead by the C_4 species by virtue of its larger leaf area. In his own studies Bull found that high photosynthesis rates in recently-expanded cane leaves were characteristic only of young plants growing in summer. Mature leaves in summer and young leaves in winter gave less efficient assimilation values comparable to those of C_3 plants. Bull attributed this to increased stomatal resistance characteristic of the lower light regimes while discounting the view that more efficient water usage may give sugarcane an advantage at times when water stress would limit stomatal opening (880, 446). Moreover, growth data showed maximum rates of dry matter production occurring in sugarcane at the season when photosynthesis rates coincided with those of C_3 plants. Bull found no conclusive evidence of growth superiority that could be linked to the C_4 pathway. These findings were essentially consistent with those of Slatyer (1347) and Warren Wilson (1536).

Nonetheless, superior growth by sugarcane over most other plant species is an undisputed fact. Bull suggested that this may be due to the extended growing season enjoyed by cane rather than to any inherent superiority linked to the C_4 pathway. He

TABLE 1-4

COMPARISON OF PHOTOSYNTHESIS RATES, DRY MATTER PRODUCTION, AND LEAF AREA AMONG VARIETIES OF DIFFERENT *SACCHARUM* SPECIES

[After Bull (260).] Reproduced by permission of T.A. Bull.

Species	Variety	Photosynthesis* ($mg/dm^2/h$)	Dry matter** (g/pot)	Blade area** (dm^2/pot)
S. officinarum	*Chittan*	46	415	150
	H.Q.-409	53	350	116
S. robustum	*U.S. 57-86-3*	53	291	128
S. spontaneum	*SES 327*	57	497	173
	SES 356	50	208	86
Commercial	*B. 49-119*	48	423	144
	Pindar	52	431	136
	Trojan	47	322	116
	L.S.D. at 1%	10	82	28

*Single leaves from 6-week-old plants.
**At 5 months.

further proposed that temperature tolerance may confer a selective advantage on certain C_4 species. Sugarcane will survive and continue rapid photosynthesis at high temperatures lethal to many Calvin-cycle plants (260); conversely, the C_3 species tend to withstand cool temperatures more effectively than sugarcane.

Comparisons drawn between *Saccharum* species revealed higher dry matter production by *S. officinarum* and commercial varieties than by certain *S. robustum* (*U.S. 57-86-3*) and *S. spontaneum* (*SES 356*) varieties, although photosynthetic activity was essentially constant in individual leaves (Table 1-4). Photosynthetic differences between varieties were similar to those found within a single variety. Leaf area showed a high correlation with dry matter yield during the first five months. Bull therefore proposed that rate of leaf area production is of greater importance than differences in photosynthesis rate.

In his concluding remarks Bull reiterated the concept of selection pressure: ". . .Present evidence indicates that the C_4 pathway confers no advantage to plant growth which cannot be circumvented by C_3 species should the required selection pressure arise." The origin of the enormous growth capacity among *Saccharum* species thus remains an open question. In accordance with Bull's reasoning, C_3 species tolerant of high temperatures might also take advantage of the long tropical or subtropical growing seasons, but this has not been accomplished to the degree shown by C_4 plants.

D. *Isozyme (isoenzyme) analysis as a potential research tool*

The recent introduction of isozyme analysis to sugarcane research (1420, 593) offers promise for a greater understanding of genotype development and the evolutionary processes of *Saccharum* species. In essence, isozymes may represent variant forms of an enzyme type performing a specific catalytic role in biochemical reactions. The presence or absence of specific isozymes, however minor in a quantitative sense, may possibly account for major qualitative differences in *Saccharum* performance through regulatory roles in the plants' growth and development processes. Initial studies with peroxidase and esterase isozymes have been performed in Hawaii (1420), and with phosphorylase isozymes in Queensland (593)[16]

Thom and Maretzki (1420) evaluated isozyme pattern responses in 15 clones under conditions of variable nitrogen and light supply. Although this work was of an exploratory nature, isozyme patterns showed some sensitivity to each of the variable parameters. Total soluble protein values were characteristic for different tissues but not for

[16]P.G. Roughan, J.C. Waldron and K.T. Glasziou [*Proc. Int. Soc. Sugar Cane Technol.* 14: in press (1972)] successfully employed β-amylase patterns in identifying interspecific and intergeneric cane hybrids in Queensland. Isozyme patterns were also used in investigating starch inheritance within interspecific crosses (*S. officinarum* x *S. spontaneum*).

different clones or variable age of plants. Peroxidase isozyme patterns varied quantitatively among the 15 clones, but not as an age factor, and only moderate differences could be attributed to reduced solar radiation (partial shading). Increased nitrogen supply brought about a change in one clone (*H. 61-5433*), amounting to a new intensely-staining band not present in normal light and nitrogen environments. Esterase isozyme patterns were also characteristic for specific clones and did not differ as an age factor.

PART I

SOURCE REACTIONS AND THE ORIGIN OF SUCROSE

Chapter 2

Photosynthesis in Chlorophyll-Bearing Plants

1. INTRODUCTION

Generally speaking, photosynthesis is the process by which chlorophyll-bearing plants convert light energy to chemical potential energy stored in organic matter. Carbohydrates are far and away the most spectacular products studied thus far, although fats, fatty acids, amino acids, proteins, vitamins, and other compounds are increasingly recognized as important photosynthetic products. In simple chemical terms photosynthesis is frequently depicted according to the equation

$$CO_2 + H_2O \xrightarrow{h\nu} (CH_2O) + O_2 \tag{1}$$

in which the elements carbon, hydrogen and oxygen, in the form of carbon dioxide (CO_2)[1] and water, are converted to carbohydrate and molecular oxygen. The production of oxygen as a "by-product" has itself been a matter of utmost importance in the evolution of life to its present status on earth.

Eqn. 1 was partially established in 1796 when Ingen-Housz (772) concluded that plants produce oxygen and organic matter through the decomposition of atmospheric carbonic acid. The participation of water was quantitatively established by de Saussure (430) in 1804, and in 1845 Mayer (994) recognized that light was the source of photosynthetic energy. With this knowledge the correct summary reaction of photosynthesis could be written. What remained to be clarified was the nature of photosynthetic mechanisms and products, a topic which has attracted scientists for more than a century and which does so unabatedly to this day.

It is difficult to scan current issues of biological research journals and not find material relative to the energy-conversion or CO_2-assimilation mechanisms of photosynthesis. These reactions are so meaningful to all higher plant forms that several chapters are devoted to developing their context as an integral part of sugarcane life processes. When some future generation writes the final book on sugarcane every chapter may well be touched in some way by photosynthesis.

By 1960 the essential outlines of photosynthesis as we know it today had been

---

[1] Abbreviations: CO_2, carbon dioxide; $h\nu$, light; 3-PGA, 3-phosphoglyceric acid. NAD, NAD^+, NADH, nicotinamide adenine dinucleotide and its oxidized and reduced forms (formerly written DPN, DPN^+, DPNH); NADP, $NADP^+$, NADPH, nicotinamide adenine dinucleotide phosphate and its oxidized and reduced forms (formerly written TPN, TPN^+, TPNH) [abbreviations on recommendations of the IUPAC–IUB Commission on Biochemical Nomenclature]. ADP, adenosine 5′-diphosphate; ATP, adenosine 5′-triphosphate; DCMU, 3-(3,4-dichlorophenyl)-1,1-dimethylurea; P_i, orthophosphate; Fd, ferredoxin; TPP, thiamine pyrophosphate..

drawn by several teams and numerous individuals working with extracts or chloroplast preparations of primitive and higher plant species. Most of the chloroplast enzymology had yet to be confirmed as did the existence of alternate carbon fixation reactions. Nonetheless some important concepts were solidly established:

(1) From the early work of Blackman (193), Blackman and Smith (195), and Warburg (1526) it was shown that photosynthesis comprises two classes of reactions conveniently termed as "light" and "dark". In 1932, some 25 years after Blackman's work, Emerson and Arnold (489) demonstrated that the light and dark reactions could be separated in time. Nearly 30 more years passed before it was known with certainty that these reactions were also spatially separated from one another. Emerson and Arnold also recognized the need for a dark period many times longer than the light exposure in order to obtain efficient light utilization. They theorized that a light-excited photochemical system was regenerated in darkness to its former receptive state.

(2) CO_2 assimilation into carbohydrates proceeds in a multi-phasic sequence of dark reactions which, taken together, constitute a *reductive pentose phosphate cycle* (1209, 150, 1208). Between 1943 and 1958 Calvin, Horecker, Ochoa, Racker and their co-workers established a carboxylative phase dependent upon ATP (1201, 1555, 791, 1208). It was shown that the incorporation of CO_2 into the reactions of photosynthetic cells depends upon an ATP-mediated phosphorylation of ribulose monophosphate to ribulose diphosphate, which in turn is cleaved to yield two molecules of 3-phosphoglyceric acid (3-PGA). As discussed in the following chapter, this phase is somewhat modified in sugarcane where C_4-dicarboxylic acids predominate as the earliest stable products. Through a series of kinetic studies, Calvin, Bassham, and Benson (149, 287, 167) evidenced a reductive phase of CO_2 assimilation in which 3-PGA is reduced to triose phosphate with the aid of reduced pyridine nucleotide (NADPH) and ATP. Since the reductive phase is mediated by reactions of the glycolytic pathway, but proceeds in the opposite direction, the need was quickly recognized for isolating chloroplast reactions from those of the intact cell. A third phase distinct from carboxylation and reduction was tentatively established upon discovery in photosynthetic tissues of components of the pentose pathway. This afforded a mechanism for regenerating the CO_2 acceptor through the formation of pentose monophosphate from part of the hexose phosphate pool. Regeneration can be viewed as a back reaction involving part of the hexose phosphates otherwise passing into end-product biosynthesis.

(3) Although the reductive pentose phosphate cycle involves only dark reactions, CO_2 assimilation does not reside exclusively in chlorophyll-bearing cells. Discovery of ribulose diphosphate carboxylase in *Escherichia coli* (1504, 547), and of the complete cycle in the nonphotosynthetic sulfur bacterium *Thiobacillus denitrificans* (1453, 118) established that CO_2 assimilation is removed from the realm of specifically light-dependent photosynthetic reactions.

(4) In green plants the light reactions proper of photosynthesis convert the radiant energy of sunlight to chemical energy. The first stable, chemically-defined products are ATP and NADPH rather than intermediates of CO_2 assimilation (101). Both ATP and NADPH are subsequently employed in the reductive pentose phosphate cycle. Two light reactions, cyclic and noncyclic photophosphorylation, are widely regarded as the means available to plants for energy conversion, although there has not been full agreement as to which is predominately used. Eqns. 2 and 3 summarize the overall light reactions:

$$n\cdot\mathrm{ADP} + n\cdot\mathrm{H_3PO_4} \xrightarrow{h\nu} n\cdot\mathrm{ATP} \tag{2}$$

$$2\ \mathrm{NADP^+} + 2\ \mathrm{H_2O} + 2\ \mathrm{ADP} + 2\ \mathrm{H_3PO_4} \xrightarrow{h\nu} 2\ \mathrm{NADPH} + 2\ \mathrm{ATP} \tag{3}$$

The photolysis of water (Eqn. 3) with concurrent evolution of oxygen has frequently been termed the *Hill reaction* after the experiments of Hill (731, 732) showed that illuminated chloroplasts evolved oxygen when a suitable electron acceptor was present. Hill used a reducible ferric salt as the electron acceptor. The electron donor was identified as water in 1941 by Ruben *et al.* (1262) working with labeled oxygen.

(5) The site of both light and dark reactions in green plants is the chloroplast. Even without substantial experimental evidence early workers associated the chloroplast with sugar synthesis (1272, 1170). This view was discarded in the light of newer evidence (1247, 1205, 964, 1091, 733) but eventually was reaccepted with the advent of labeled-carbon techniques and improved methodology for preparing viable chloroplasts (97, 98, 63, 99, 574, 1442).

(6) Within the chloroplast the enzymes needed for CO_2 assimilation are situated in the water-soluble portion and can carry CO_2 activity to the level of sugar in darkness. However, evidence from reconstituted chloroplast systems in which ATP and NADPH supply was lowered to catalytic levels has shown that ATP and NADPH must be continuously regenerated by light reactions in order for the dark assimilation of CO_2 to continue (955).

2. ENERGY CAPTURE FROM SOLAR RADIATION

All life on earth owes its continued existence to complex photochemical processes conveniently termed "energy conversion". By these processes the radiant energy of sunlight is converted to chemical energy in the form of stable high-energy compounds, primarily NADPH and ATP, which are generated through a series of electron-transfer steps coupled to photosynthetic phosphorylation. Chlorophyll *a* is the essential absorptive pigment. Only about half of the solar spectrum is absorbed (wavelengths shorter than 700 nm) and in nature only a fraction of this half is used. According to

Kok (846), only about 1 percent of the incoming solar energy is employed by the plant kingdom in support of life; nonetheless this energy conversion far exceeds the total industrial output by man.

Shortly after the discovery of photosynthetic phosphorylation in chloroplasts, evidence of a light-induced phosphorylation was reported by Frenkel (538) working with cell-free preparations of the photosynthetic bacteria *Rhodospirillum rubrum*. Photosynthetic phosphorylation was soon established in cell-free preparations of virtually all kinds of chlorophyll-bearing organisms, including photosynthetic bacteria (1574, 570, 1503, 66), and algae (1241, 1167, 1409), and in isolated chloroplasts of such higher plants as spinach (1168, 1596), lettuce (1091), bean (857), and tobacco mutants (741). It is now widely accepted that the chemical energy required for photosynthesis is produced by reactions in the chloroplast independently of respiration. Thus, the earlier concept that chloroplasts and mitochondria might collaborate in the photosynthetic production of ATP was rendered academic, at least for the time being. In such a scheme NAD^+ would be reduced photochemically in chloroplasts while reoxidation with oxygen would occur via oxidative phosphorylation in mitochondria (1503). An analogous scheme which would permit common expenditure of energy from diverse sources is still an attractive way to account for the diurnal, nocturnal, and seasonal energy requirements for sugarcane growth and maturation.

It is sometimes difficult for workers with intact higher plants to grasp the significance of research with isolated chloroplasts, especially when they are prepared from one-celled plants. In fact, recent isolation of functional chloroplasts, together with new techniques by radioactive phosphorus, is an essential tool in the critical examination of photosynthetic energy conversion. Hence, chloroplast research is of very real importance to life at all levels. Certain intermediates of cellular respiratory reactions cannot with certainty be separated from intermediates of photosynthetic energy conversion, or from intermediates of 3-PGA reduction in the reductive pentose phosphate cycle. However, since chloroplasts cannot respire, owing to lack of the terminal cytochrome oxidase (734, 797, 966), such confusion is avoided with chloroplast preparation. Permeability barriers in the form of cellular membranes are also avoided with isolated chloroplasts. The investigator is enabled to supply intermediates in substrate quantities, in contrast to the fleeting catalytic quantities of intact cells, and hence the production of high-energy products can be examined on a large scale. Furthermore, to the extent that purely photosynthetic reactions collaborate with other energy-yielding systems to pay common energy debts, some control mechanism must exist which might seriously compromise chloroplast-reaction studies in intact cells.

A. *Photosystem I (Photoact I)*

In the initial step of photosynthesis one chlorophyll *a* molecule apparently enters a state of excitation through the absorption of one quantum of red light. The excited molecule then converts its absorbed energy into chemical energy by transferring an unstable electron to a suitable acceptor (846). In Fig. 2-1 the acceptor is designated

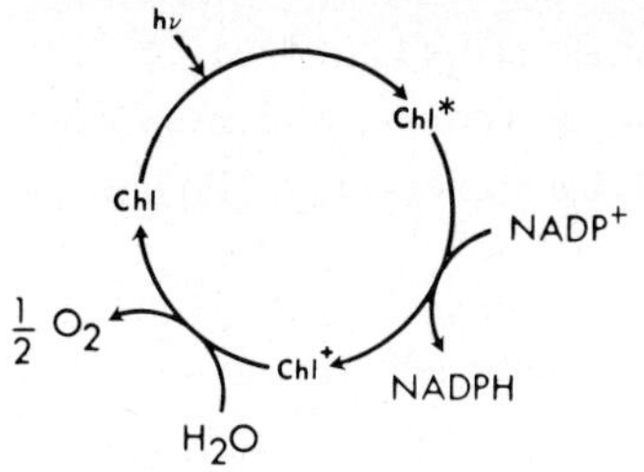

Fig. 2-1. Schematic representation of a photochemical reduction process in chlorophyll. Upon absorption of a quantum of light, a chlorophyll molecule becomes excited and donates an electron to the acceptor molecule $NADP^+$. The oxidized chlorophyll is subsequently reduced by water acting as a weak reductant in an oxygen-evolving reaction. The electron has thereby moved against a thermogradient by utilizing the absorbed light energy. The net result is that $NADP^+$ is photochemically reduced to NADPH in a process by which solar energy is converted to chemical energy. [From Bonner and Varner (205), after Kok (845).] Reproduced by permission of the *Academic Press, Inc.*, New York.

$NADP^+$, with water acting as a weak reductant which returns the oxidized chlorophyll to its original state. In effect, light energy has been used to move an electron against a thermogradient, O_2 is evolved from water, and NADPH is formed at the expense of solar radiation. Only a small fraction of the excited chlorophyll *a* molecules (one in about 400 or 500) is able to convert the energy of its excited state to chemical energy. This fraction serves as a trapping center to receive the energy from the remaining chlorophyll *a*, or possibly from other excited pigment molecules (chlorophyll *b* and chlorophyll *c*). Should the trapping center already be converted, the incoming quanta of energy can be degraded or it can escape as fluorescence.

As elucidated by Kok (846) and others, Photosystem I is heavily dependent upon two agents, P700 and X, whose identities remain obscure. P700, acting essentially like a cytochrome with a redox potential of +0.43 V, was discovered by Kok (845) more than a decade ago. Highly sensitive spectroscopic techniques detected an unusual chlorophyl *a* molecule believed terminal for Photosystem I during the excitation-induced bleaching and dark recovery of a red absorption band at about 700 nm. The bleaching itself is regarded as a direct photochemical event rather than a physiological reaction. It is insensitive to low temperature and produces a high quantum yield (approx. 1). P700 functions as a one-electron redox agent losing a single electron along with its red absorption band when reversibly oxidized by ferricyanide. During *in vivo* photosynthesis the electron is removed from P700 by a photon[2] rather than a chemi-

[2] A photon, or light quantum, is a distinct unit of light energy, $E = h\nu$, in which h is Planck's constant and ν is the light frequency inversely proportional to its wavelength.

cal oxidizing agent. The electron acceptor is not yet identified and hence is written as "X". It is known that the photoreduced form of X is a powerful reducing agent with a potential of 0.6 V or lower. The end result of Photosystem I is that an electron has been caused to move against a thermogradient over a voltage range of at least 1 V. The motivating entity is the absorbed quantum, representing an energy of 40 kcal/mole of 1.8 eV, more than half of which is ultimately retained as chemical energy. The remaining energy is lost in stabilization of the photoproducts.

B. *Photosystem II (Photoact II)*

In the brief discussion of Photosystem I oxygen evolution and possible involvement of chlorophylls *b* and *c* were touched upon as if they were incidental to the primary photoact. Actually, abundant evidence now supports the existence of a second photosystem, or Photoact II, which is sensitized by accessory chlorophylls (*b* and *c*) as well as by chlorophyll *a*, and which accounts for the evolution of oxygen. Viewed in this manner (846), Photoact I primarily receives those photons absorbed by chlorophyll *a*, it reduces a low-potential reactant (X), and it oxidizes a reactant of intermediate potential (P). In Photoact II chlorophyll *a* and accessory pigments collaborate to sensitize the reduction of a second electron carrier (Y) while oxidizing water to oxygen. By a dark reaction the photoreduced Y is reoxidized by photooxidized P; in exergonic dark reactions the weak photooxidant P is reduced by the weak photoreductant Y. According to the hypothesis of Kok (846), this step creates a link between the two photoacts, establishes the site of ATP formation, and completes an essential chain of transport by which light-driven electrons pass from water to X (Fig.2-2).

Although nearly all forms of life on earth owe a tremendous debt to the photosynthetic evolution of oxygen, its mechanisms are only partially understood. So long as several major components of Photosystem II remain unidentified it is impossible to explore with certainty the intrinsic mechanisms of electron transport. Some of the known electron carriers, including plastoquinones, cytochromes, ferredoxin, plastocyanine, $NADP^+$ reductase, and others are presented in Fig.2-2 in a sequence based on their normal potential. No specific trapping pigment comparable to P700 of Photosystem I is known in Photosystem II. A specific requirement of Photosystem II for manganese (830, 831, 320) and its extreme sensitivity to the poison DCMU (320, 1562) have been established. Hydroxylamine, *o*-phenanthroline, urethans, salicylaldoxime and aminotriazines inhibit at higher concentrations than DCMU. The system is insensitive to cyanide except at very high concentrations, a fact casting doubt on the early belief that hydrogen peroxide, destroyed by Fe-containing catalase, serves as a principal intermediary. Aging and moderate heating destroy Photosystem II as does strong visible light and weak ultraviolet light. This sensitivity to a host of chemically unrelated factors is itself indicative of Photosystem II complexity.

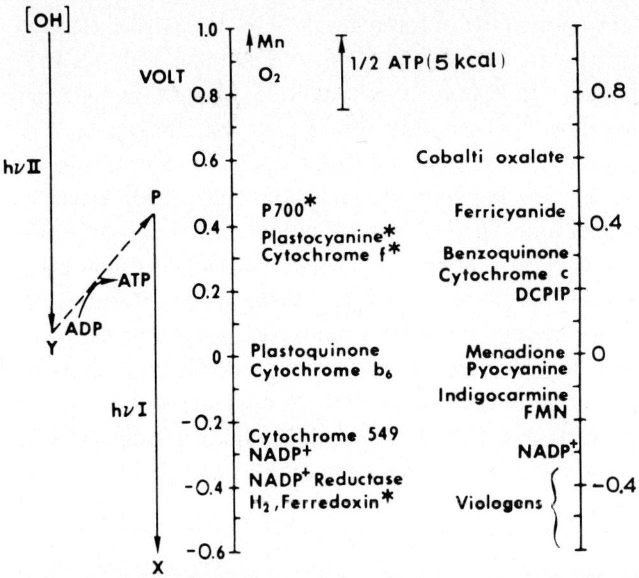

Fig. 2-2. Hypothetical diagram of Photoacts I and II (left), with chloroplast electron carriers arranged in accordance with their normal potential (center), and chloroplast electron donors and acceptors arranged according to their normal potential (right). The broken line (left) signifies exergonic dark reactions in which a weak photooxidant P is reduced by the weak photoreductant Y. DCPIP = 2,6-dichlorophenolindophenol; FMN = flavin mononucleotide. [From Bonner and Varner (205), after Kok (846).] Reproduced by permission of the *Academic Press, Inc.*, New York.

C. *Cyclic photophosphorylation*

The energy-conversion step proper envisages, as we have seen, the transfer of a high-energy electron to an acceptor molecule having a strongly electronegative oxidation–reduction potential. This high-energy electron originates when a quantum of light (a photon) excites a chlorophyll *a* molecule which in turn sends an electron into an outer orbit with a higher energy level. In essence a flow of photons is converted to a flow of electrons and the way is open for creating a powerfully electronegative reductant in the chloroplast through the mediation of a limitless supply of solar energy.

As first hypothesized by Arnon and his colleagues (102, 104, 107), this mechanism requires no additional input of energy once the strongly electronegative reductant is formed. Subsequent electron transfers from the electronegative reductant to acceptors having more positive redox potentials yield energy within the chloroplast. A number of electron-transfer steps are eventually coupled with a phosphorylation reaction. In theory, the electron transfer series operates in a cycle, and more than enough free energy is liberated for one phosphorylation. The now electron-deficient chlorophyll molecule receives back the emitted electron at the end of the transfer cycle and the process of quantum absorption is repeated. This process was termed *cyclic photo-*

phosphorylation in view of the cyclic route of travel imagined for the emitted electron (102, 104).

The concept of photosynthetic phosphorylation constituted a significant advance beyond earlier concepts of cellular phosphorylations. Known mechanisms of ATP formation by fermentation (substrate level phosphorylation) and oxidative phosphorylation in mitochondria occur at the expense of free energy liberated when electrons pass from a high-energy electron donor to an acceptor. The new mechanism consumes radiant energy rather than a chemical substrate. It operates within the chloroplast, independently of mitochondria or of enzyme systems external to the chloroplast. It neither consumes nor produces oxygen, and ATP is produced without the aid of an oxidation–reduction sequence requiring an external electron donor and acceptor. Although at the time of its inception cyclic photophosphorylation left unclear the number of electron transfer steps and the nature of the coupled phosphorylation reaction, it provided the first insight into fundamental mechanisms of photosynthetic phosphorylation.

D. *Noncyclic photophosphorylation*

Prior to 1957 there was no direct evidence of a coupling between the electron transport system driven by light and the phosphorylation reactions yielding ATP. In that year Arnon and his co-workers (101) reported another type of photophosphorylation in which a light-driven transfer of electrons from water to $NADP^+$ was coupled stoichiometrically to ATP formation with a concurrent production of oxygen. The coupling of ATP synthesis to electron transport had the overall effect of increasing the rate of electron flow (101, 103, 120, 415) and of oxygen evolution. It was also found that a nonphysiological electron acceptor such as ferricyanide could receive electrons from water in place of $NADP^+$. From this evidence it was concluded that coupling of the phosphorylative reaction was essential for the most effective movement of electrons (107), and the well-known Hill reaction (731, 732, 733), which yielded oxygen but not ATP, could be regarded as an electron transport mechanism uncoupled from photophosphorylation (101).

In formulating a new concept of electron transport, Arnon (102, 104) did not visualize the originally-emitted electrons returning to the electron-deficient chlorophyll molecules; rather, the emitted electrons were thought to be replaced by electrons from water, and oxygen was thereby evolved. The one-directional electron flow prompted Arnon to name the process *noncyclic photophosphorylation*. Originally it was believed that an electron passed directly from the excited chlorophyll molecule to $NADP^+$ or ferricyanide. More recent evidence has shown that ferredoxin is an intermediate electron acceptor (1399), and that reduced ferredoxin itself reduces $NADP^+$ by a light-independent mechanism. Thus a common denominator of both cyclic and noncyclic photophosphorylation emerged in the form of ferredoxin, a physiological reactant whose role in energy conversion is significant to all life processes relating to photosynthesis.

E. *Ferredoxin and the photoreduction of NADP*$^+$

By 1960 there was general agreement that chloroplasts contained a protein or enzyme-like "factor" which catalyzed the photochemical reduction of $NADP^+$. Still lacking precise knowledge of the properties and function of this factor, and indeed unaware that it was synonymous among many plant species, investigators assigned it different functions under the names *methemoglobin-reducing factor* (412), *TPN*$^+$-*reducing factor* (100), *photosynthetic pyridine nucleotide reductase* (PPNR), *i.e.*, synonymous with chloroplast ferredoxin (1296), the *heme-reducing factor* (413), and the *red enzyme* (572, 1530). All of these are now identified either directly as ferredoxin or as compounds functionally analogous to ferredoxin.

Ferredoxin is the name given by Mortenson and his colleagues (1038) to a protein containing iron but which is neither a heme nor a flavin protein. It was isolated from a nonphotosynthetic, obligately-anaerobic bacterium whose natural habitat is in the soil free of all exposure to light. There was at first no inkling that this protein was identical to the chloroplast factor or that it operated in electron transport in organisms other than the nonphotosynthetic bacteria *Clostridium pasteurianum* (1038) and *Micrococcus lactilyticus* (1468). However, in 1961 Losada *et al.* (956) published evidence of a bacterial protein (then called "pyridine nucleotide reductase") isolated from a chloroplast-free bacterium which replaced the endogenous protein of chloroplasts in catalyzing the photoreduction of $NADP^+$ and the evolution of oxygen. In 1962 Tagawa and Arnon (1399) reported that a protein (ferredoxin) obtained from a nonphotosynthetic organism performed a similar role in the $NADP^+$-reducing action of isolated chloroplasts.

Ferredoxin was soon recognized as a key factor in the two photophosphorylation reactions which taken together account for the products of photosynthetic energy conversion. It appears to be the most reductive compound active in the chloroplast photosynthetic apparatus (105). Arnon *et al.* (108) reported in 1967 that no electron carriers more negative than ferredoxin had yet been isolated from living cells[3]. Other substances effective *in vitro* in energy conversion, including ferricyanide, menadione, flavin mononucleotide (FMN) and phenazine methosulfate (PMS) were viewed as substitutes for ferredoxin.

The effectiveness of ferredoxin in photophosphorylation is reflected by the conditions under which energy conversion is being measured. In Eqns. 4 to 7 [after Arnon *et al.* (108)] the essence of cyclic and noncyclic photophosphorylation catalyzed by ferredoxin is presented. The cyclic reaction, Eqn. 4, was measured aerobically with catalytic amounts of ferredoxin plus an inhibitor of oxygen evolution.

---

[3]In 1971 D.I. Arnon (*Proc. Natl. Acad. Sci. U.S.* 68: 2887) reported as "speculative" claims of reductants stronger than ferredoxin existing in chloroplasts.

$$n\cdot\text{ADP} + n\cdot\text{P}_i \xrightarrow[\text{Fd}]{h\nu} n\cdot\text{ATP} \tag{4}$$

Noncyclic photophosphorylation, giving the stoichiometry of ferredoxin reduction, ATP formation, and oxygen evolution is represented in Eqn. 5.

$$4\,\text{Fd}_{ox} + 2\,\text{ADP} + 2\,\text{P}_i + 2\,\text{H}_2\text{O} \xrightarrow{h\nu} 4\,\text{Fd}_{red} + 2\,\text{ATP} + \text{O}_2 + 4\,\text{H}^+ \tag{5}$$

In this reaction, under aerobic conditions and in the absence of $NADP^+$, oxidized ferredoxin, Fd_{ox}, is photoreduced to Fd_{red}. Arnon *et al.* (108) successfully coupled the photoreduction of ferredoxin to its reoxidation by molecular oxygen (Eqn. 6), therein accomplishing measured noncyclic photophosphorylation with catalytic

$$4\,\text{Fd}_{red} + \text{O}_2 + 4\,\text{H}^+ \longrightarrow 4\,\text{Fd}_{ox} + 2\,\text{H}_2\text{O} \tag{6}$$

$$\text{Summation (5 + 6): ADP} + \text{P}_i \xrightarrow[\text{Fd, O}_2]{h\nu} \text{ATP} \tag{7}$$

amounts of ferredoxin (Eqn. 7). The oxygen-linked noncyclic reaction (Eqn. 7) is similar to cyclic photophosphorylation (Eqn. 4) in that only ATP is produced, but unlike cyclic photophosphorylation it requires a continuous production and consumption of oxygen.

Noncyclic photophosphorylation (Eqn. 9) was also accomplished in the presence of $NADP^+$, under argon, by coupling Eqn. 5 (photoreduction of ferredoxin) with its reoxidation by $NADP^+$. This reaction (Eqn. 8) is mediated by a flavoprotein enzyme (fp) termed "ferredoxin–$NADP^+$ reductase" (1323).

$$4\,\text{Fd}_{red} + 2\,\text{NADP}^+ + 4\,\text{H}^+ \xrightarrow{\text{fp}} 4\,\text{Fd}_{ox} + 2\,\text{NADPH} \tag{8}$$

$$\text{Summation (5 + 8): } 2\,\text{NADP}^+ + 2\,\text{ADP} + 2\,\text{P}_i + 2\,\text{H}_2\text{O} \xrightarrow[\text{Fd, fp}]{h\nu} 2\,\text{NADPH} + 2\,\text{ATP} + \text{O}_2 \tag{9}$$

Since reduced ferredoxin has a greater affinity for ferredoxin–$NADP^+$ reductase than for oxygen (1402), continued availability of $NADP^+$ ensures that $NADP^+$ will be reduced (Eqn. 8) rather than oxygen, thereby supplying the NADPH essential for CO_2 assimilation.

With ferredoxin rather than $NADP^+$ acting as the electron acceptor in photochemical reactions of chloroplasts, the pathway of electron flow (solid line) is summarized as follows [after Arnon (107)]:

Electron donor system ⟶ ferredoxin ⟶ ferredoxin–$NADP^+$ reductase ⇄ free $NADP^+$
⇢ free NAD^+

Assuming the participation of ferredoxin, Arnon (107) demonstrated that the reducing potential created in chloroplasts during photophosphorylation is more than 100 mV greater than the redox potential of $NADP^+$. In noncyclic photophosphorylation the photoreduction of 2 moles of ferredoxin corresponds to one new pyrophosphate bond of ATP. Thus, with water as the electron donor [E'_0 = + 0.82 (pH 7)], the photoreduction of ferredoxin [E'_0 = − 0.43 V (pH 7)] and the concurrent photophosphorylation (potential equal to approximately 0.2 V) comprise a conversion of solar energy to chemical energy having a potential span close to 1.45 V (107).

F. *Cyclic and noncyclic photophosphorylation as distinct reactions*

Prior to the discovery of cyclic and noncyclic photophosphorylation, evidence suggestive of multiple light reactions collaborating in the photochemistry of photosynthesis was already accumulating. Working with whole cells, Warburg *et al.* (1527) observed that catalytic amounts of blue light increased the quantum efficiency of photosynthesis in *Chlorella* illuminated by red light. Subsequent "enhancement" effects of supplemental wavelengths were observed by Emerson *et al.* (493), Emerson and Chalmers (494), Blinks (196), Myers and French (1069, 1068), Duysens *et al.* (460, 462, 461), and others. After the basic facts of energy conversion were established and the importance of ferredoxin recognized, questions still remained concerning the extent to which cyclic and noncyclic photophosphorylation was accomplished by discrete mechanisms.

Evidence that ferredoxin-mediated cyclic and noncyclic photophosphorylation operate as distinct mechanisms was also obtained with chemical inhibitors. Cyclic photophosphorylation is inhibited by antimycin A and 2,4-dinitrophenol (1400, 1401), and by desaspidin (106), while the noncyclic system remains unaffected. The results are similar for both oxygen- and $NADP^+$-linked noncyclic photophosphorylation. Conversely, powerful inhibitors of noncyclic photophosphorylation (DCMU, *o*-phenanthroline) stimulate cyclic photophosphorylation. Since the inhibitors antimycin A, 2,4-dinitrophenol, and desaspidin also inhibit oxidative phosphorylation by mitochondria, the results were suggestive that chloroplasts carry an inhibitor-sensitive site between cytochromes b_6 and f which corresponds to the inhibition site in mitochondria.

Physical evidence of the different natures of cyclic and noncyclic photophosphorylation is found in the differential response to monochromatic light in the red and far-red region (1401). Arnon *et al.* (108) observed that the rate of ferredoxin-catalyzed noncyclic photophosphorylation by spinach chloroplasts, as evidenced by the μmoles of ATP formed, declined as the wavelength of monochromatic light was increased from 664 to 679 nm (Fig. 2-3). The reaction nearly ceased above 708 nm. By contrast, cyclic photophosphorylation increased as the wavelength was extended from 664 to 708 nm. The two distinct responses were termed "red drop" and "red rise" for the

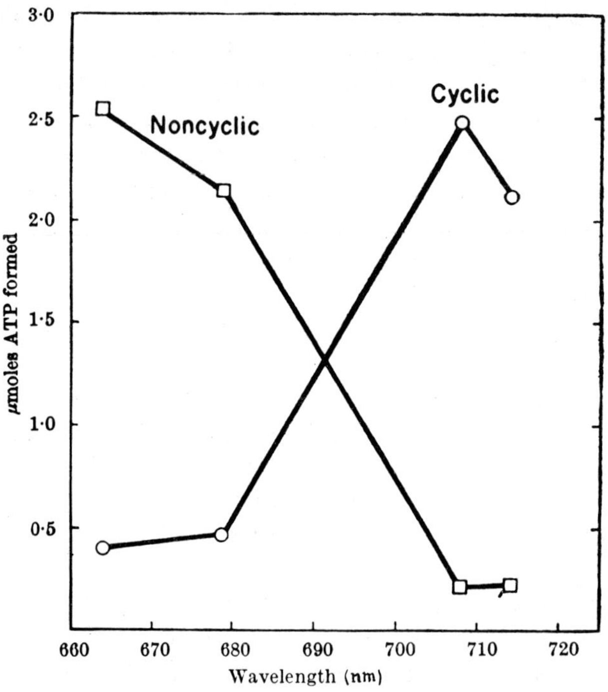

Fig. 2-3. Effects of red and far-red monochromatic light on two photosynthetic phosphorylation systems catalyzed by ferredoxin. Noncyclic photophosphorylation appears as a "short-wavelength" system decreasing sharply as wavelengths approach 700 nm. Cyclic photophosphorylation is shown as a "long-wavelength" system most effective at wavelengths above 700 nm. [After Arnon *et al.* (108).] Reproduced by permission of *Nature*.

noncyclic and cyclic reactions, respectively. Since the number of light quanta supplied at each wavelength was equal, and because light absorption by chloroplasts drops rapidly at wavelengths exceeding 679 nm, the real difference between the cyclic and noncyclic responses is far greater than shown by Fig. 2-3 when viewed in terms of solar energy absorbed.

As discussed earlier in this chapter only one light reaction, constituting chlorophyll *a* excitation by captured photons followed by electron transfer, was considered in accounting for the products of cyclic and noncyclic photophosphorylation (102, 104). In the cyclic mechanism the electron-deficient chlorophyll molecule was replenished with an electron from within the photosynthetic apparatus; in the noncyclic reaction electrons were replenished by water through the mediation of an unknown cytochrome. However, during subsequent years no evidence of strongly-oxidizing cytochrome was found in the chloroplast. In 1961 Losada *et al.* (956) published evidence that noncyclic photophosphorylation is itself comprised of two light reactions; one being a photooxidation of water yielding oxygen and a reduced electron carrier, the other a photoreduction of $NADP^+$ which is coupled with ATP formation. This conclusion was based on the observation that, under carefully contrived conditions, oxygen evolution from illuminated chloroplasts was coupled with a reduction of an indophenol dye, but no ATP was produced. Other workers could not establish conclusively whether photoreduction of $NADP^+$ by water and by indophenol proceeded via a single mechanism, although differential inhibition by low levels of desaspidin did suggest that the two photophosphorylation reactions were different (1553, 139, 615).

Arnon *et al.* (106) eventually proposed a new hypothesis suggesting that electron transfer from reduced indophenol dye to $NADP^+$ employs part of the cyclic photophosphorylation pathway. The new hypothesis regarded cyclic and noncyclic photophosphorylation in chloroplasts as parallel but independent mechanisms for ATP formation which do not share a common phosphorylating site. In 1971 Arnon[4] presented the conception of three light reactions based on more recent evidence from isolated chloroplasts. Accordingly, two short-wavelength reactions (IIa and IIb) in Photosystem II are linked in series, with the single photoreaction of Photosystem I constituting the third component (Fig. 2-4). "According to this concept, in System II (Fig. 2-4, left) Photoreaction IIb oxidizes water and reduces Component 550 (a newly discovered non-cytochrome component of chloroplasts), while Photoreaction IIa oxidizes plastocyanin (PC) and reduces ferredoxin. These two light reactions are joined by a 'dark' electron transfer chain which includes (but is not limited to) cytochrome b_{559} and is coupled to the noncyclic phosphorylation site."

It has been suggested (107, 108) that physiological photophosphorylation, *i.e.*, the reaction of intact plants, proceeds via the ferredoxin-catalyzed cyclic mechanism. Cyclic photophosphorylation could be instrumental in supplying the large amounts of energy needed for protein synthesis and other endergonic processes distinct from carbohydrate production (107, 104, 101). It has also been suggested (104) that "long-wavelength" and "short-wavelength" designations might be suitable for cyclic and noncyclic photophosphorylation, respectively.

To summarize, the photochemical "common denominator" of cyclic and noncyclic photophosphorylation is the photoreduction of ferredoxin by electrons from excited chlorophyll molecules. What finally distinguishes the noncyclic system is its ultimate dependence on water as an electron source for ferredoxin reduction, with oxygen evolving as a by-product. In cyclic photophosphorylation there is no dependence on an exogenous electron supply; rather, electrons are recycled among the constituents of the photosynthetic apparatus.

The issue of energy conversion has by no means been laid to rest. Some workers

---

[4]Arnon, D.I., 1971. The light reactions of photosynthesis, *Proc. Natl. Acad. Sci. U.S.* 68(11): 2883–2892.

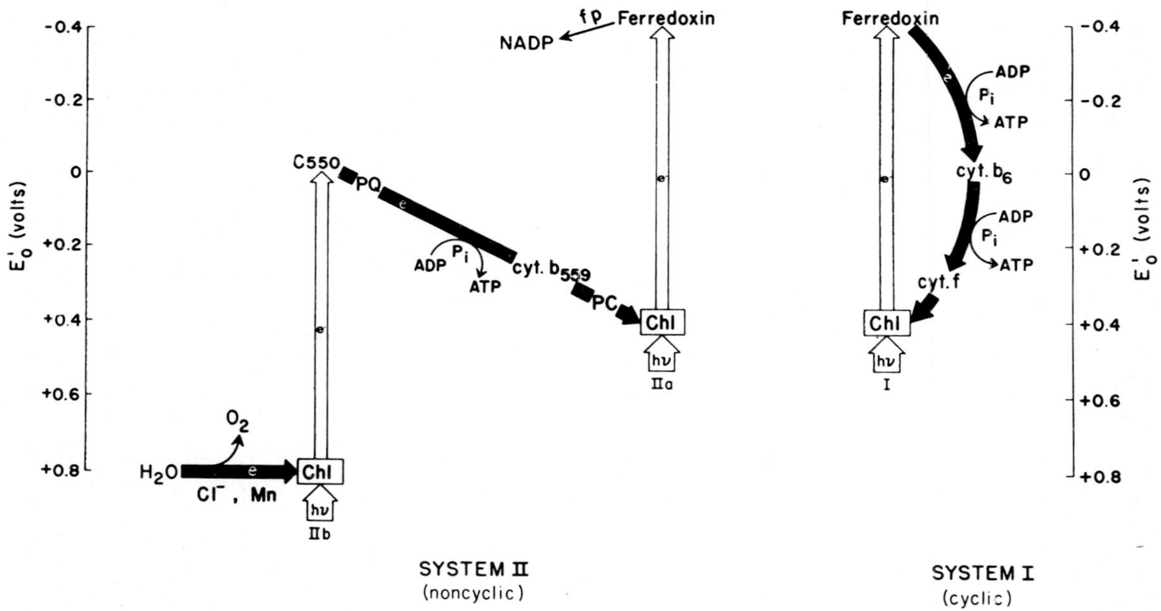

Fig. 2-4. Schematic representation of three light reactions in plant photosynthesis as depicted by Arnon[4]. Notations C550, PQ, and PC signify Component 550, plastoquinone, and plastocyanine, respectively. In the new conception cytochromes b_6 and *f* are included in cyclic photophosphorylation. The presence of cytochrome ***f*** and P700 in System I anticipates that neither is required for the photoreduction of ferredoxin–$NADP^+$ by water via System II, as previously thought. (Reproduced by permission of D.I. Arnon.)

feel that cyclic photophosphorylation provides 1 mole of ATP and noncyclic photosynthetic phosphorylation 2 moles of ATP in achieving the 3-mole total envisaged by the Calvin cycle (153). Others disagree with this interpretation (532, 275). Tanner *et al.* (1409) recently reported evidence that the cyclic mechanism does not contribute ATP stoichiometrically to photosynthetic CO_2 fixation in *Chlorella*.

G. *The chemiosmotic hypothesis*

A different interpretation of hydrogen ion transport in ATP synthesis has been proposed by Mitchell (1026), in which a chemiosmotic mechanism for the coupling of a proton gradient across a lipophilic, carrier-containing membrane impermeable to hydrogen ion diffusion is visualized. In essence, plastoquinone is believed to acquire a hydrogen ion from outside the membrane and an electron from manganese (supplied by water in Photoact II). The carrier is reduced by accepting the electron; the hydrogen ion is not accepted and is deposited inside the membrane, thereby creating a pH gradient which is lower on the inside. This gradient constitutes a potential force for hydroxyl and hydrogen ion removal in the "dehydration" process by which ATP is formed. The pH gradient itself is regarded as a form of potential energy (790), although stoichiometry exists in the number of hydrogen ions translocated and ADP molecules phosphorylated.

Considerable evidence has been cited in support of the chemiosmotic hypothesis, including measurable pH gradients (790), uncoupling by membrane destroyers (781, 1090), and acid-induced synthesis of ATP (788, 789, 1467, 1466). Schwartz and Ebert (1310) measured proton movement across chloroplast membranes (influx in light, efflux in darkness) and found that, above a minimal potential value, the proton gradient across the membrance generates ATP in the ratio of one ATP molecule synthesized for two protons consumed ($H^+/ATP = 2$). An attractive aspect of the hypothesis is that it takes into account the total geometry of photophosphorylation in subcellular structures. In the words of Jagendorf (790), ". . .the chloroplasts are drawn closer to the rest of biology".

3. CO_2 ASSIMILATION

From the preceding section we have seen that a classic problem of plant photosynthesis is the derivation of ATP and NADPH needed for subsequent CO_2 assimilation into organic compounds. Most photosynthetic plants use CO_2 as the source of carbon, and water as a reductant supplying hydrogen atoms (comprised of electrons and protons) for biosynthesis reactions. The principal by-product, oxygen, is itself of immeasurable importance to life on this planet.

A. *Theories of photosynthetic carbon reduction*

According to Bassham and Calvin (149), Liebig (942) proposed in 1843 the first theory implying a stepwise conversion of atmospheric CO_2 to sugars. The theory was based on the fact that plant acids are intermediate between CO_2 and carbohydrate in oxidation level and from the example of ripening fruits which are at first acid and later sweet. Many years later Liebig's theory of intermediate acids was shown to have a factual basis.

In 1870 Baeyer (130) advanced the *formaldehyde theory* purporting a CO_2 reduction to formaldehyde following initial decomposition to carbon monoxide and oxygen. Thereafter the formaldehyde was condensed to carbohydrate. This theory did account for the stepwise conversion of CO_2 to sugar in a relatively simple manner but efforts to demonstrate a photosynthetic role of formaldehyde were generally unsuccessful. The theory was laid to rest when $^{14}CO_2$ experiments with plant extracts showed insignificant amounts of radioactivity in an aldehyde-trapping derivative by comparison with other compounds intermediary in CO_2 assimilation.

The first critical evidence of stepwise photosynthetic CO_2 assimilation came in 1905 from the kinetic studies of Blackman *et al.* (194). Blackman *et al.* recognized that photochemical events occurred in light independently of temperature, and that one or more reactions occurred in darkness which were sensitive to temperature. A number of dark reactions are recognized today in energy conversion as well as the CO_2 reductive phase of photosynthesis.

Although the reductive pentose phosphate cycle is now widely accepted as a major system of CO_2 assimilation, an entirely different concept was forwarded, and is still supported, by Warburg and his colleagues (1529, 1531). Rather than 3-PGA being the first stable product, in turn reduced by NADPH, they believe that the reductive step in CO_2 assimilation involves a light-induced removal of oxygen from an "activated" form of CO_2. The activated CO_2, depicted as $(H_2CO_3)^*$, is bound to chlorophyll and is reduced to carbohydrate (H_2CO) in a photochemical reaction using a single quantum of light (Eqn. 10).

$$(H_2CO_3)^* + 1\,N_\circ \cdot h\nu = (H_2CO) + O_2 \qquad (10)$$

The evolved oxygen originates from activated carbon dioxide rather than water. Two dark reactions are visualized, one producing activated carbon dioxide from ordinary CO_2 in a hydrated form, the second an energy-producing reaction in which two-thirds of the carbohydrate formed in light is oxidized by molecular oxygen. Energy liberated from this reaction is used in the activation of more CO_2. Ultimately, 1 mole of CO_2 is assimilated at the expense of only 3 light quanta, a concept which clashes with other views placing the minimal quantum requirement of photosynthesis at 8 (1204).

Warburg's many contributions to biochemistry unquestionably extend to photosynthesis. Nonetheless, his views of CO_2 assimilation have not gained wide acceptance owing to lack of critical evidence. Tracer experiments have shown that the oxygen evolved in photosynthesis comes largely (1262), if not solely (248), from water. Neither the activated carbon dioxide $(H_2CO_3)^*$ nor the initial carbohydrate (H_2CO) has been isolated and critically examined. By contrast there is increasingly abundant evidence confirming the intermediates of the reductive pentose phosphate cycle. Most of the latter, along with their essential enzymes, have been isolated, characterized, and studied kinetically in whole cells and chloroplast preparations from numerous plant species.

B. *The reductive pentose phosphate cycle*

The concept of CO_2 assimilation which gained the widest acceptance was developed by Bassham and his colleagues (148, 152) during the 1950's. More than a decade earlier, Ruben *et al.* (1262), reasoning without precise evidence, concluded that the CO_2 acceptor was phosphorylated by ATP prior to receiving CO_2, and that a later phosphorylation took place at the site of the new carboxyl group. Ruben *et al.* recognized that the new carboxyl could be reduced to a carbonyl group by a reductant such as reduced pyridine nucleotide, but he did not visualize a regeneration of CO_2 acceptor. In fact, the first inkling of a cyclic pathway for CO_2 assimilation came when 3-PGA and other constituents of glycolysis were identified as early products of photosynthesis. In 1957 Bassham and Calvin (149) proposed a cyclic pathway of CO_2 fixation frequently termed the *reductive pentose phosphate cycle* (Fig.2-5). The cycle

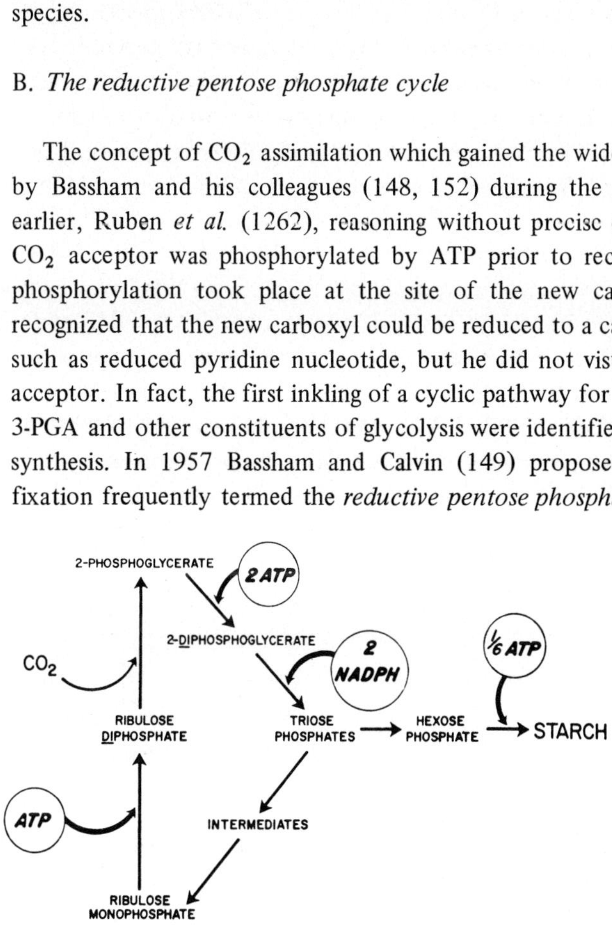

Fig. 2-5. Abbreviated scheme of the reductive pentose phosphate cycle showing the three principal phases (carboxylative, reductive, regenerative) and the expenditure of ATP and NADPH. 1 mole of ATP is utilized in the carboxylative phase and 2 in the reductive phase. 2 moles of NADPH are expended in the reductive phase. One complete turn of the cycle results in the assimilation of 1 mole of CO_2 at the cost of 3 1/6 moles of ATP and 2 moles of NADPH. [After Arnon (107).] Reproduced by permission of *Physiological Reviews*, Bethesda, Md.

consisted of carboxylative, reductive, and regenerative sequences which, taken together with available enzyme and kinetic data, presented a convincing story of CO_2 assimilation.

Fig. 2-5 illustrates the three phases of CO_2 assimilation in Arnon's (107) depiction of ATP and NADPH expenditure. In the carboxylative phase CO_2 is not accepted until ribulose monophosphate is phosphorylated by ATP to yield ribulose diphosphate. The latter is carboxylated enzymatically with CO_2 and is cleaved to yield two molecules of 3-PGA. In the reductive phase ATP is expended in phosphorylating 3-PGA to a *di*phosphoglycerate which in turn is reduced by NADPH to yield triose phosphates. The third phase was established following discovery of the pentose cycle intermediates sedoheptulose monophosphate and ribulose diphosphate among early labeled products. By diverting part of the triose phosphate toward synthesis of pentose phosphates rather than hexose phosphates, a mechanism was provided for regenerating the CO_2 acceptor which thereby completed a cycle for carbon reduction.

C. *The carboxylation phase*

Bassham and Calvin observed that only 5 seconds exposure to $^{14}CO_2$ sufficied to show 3-PGA as the first prominently-labeled product of photosynthesis in one-celled plants. Lesser products included sugar phosphates, malic acid, and traces of amino acids. Since degradation experiments with 3-PGA repeatedly showed most of the ^{14}C lying in the carboxyl position, while the *alpha* and *beta* carbon atoms were only slightly labeled,

```
  *  CH2O–P
     |
 **  CHOH
     |
***  COOH

     3-PGA
```

it was at first suggested that an unknown 2-carbon acceptor was carboxylated to give 3-PGA. However, as more data accumulated it was found that among the sugar phosphates ribulose diphosphate alone seemed to accept CO_2.

During this period the reactions by which atmospheric CO_2 enters the metabolism of photosynthetic plants were measured for the first time. Two new enzymes, phosphoribulokinase and ribulose diphosphate carboxylase (287, 1555, 791, 1209) jointly account for this entry via carboxylation of a phosphorylated pentose, ribulose 1,5-diphosphate. Phosphoribulokinase catalyzes the ATP phosphorylation of ribulose 5-phosphate (Eqn. 11).

$$\text{Ribulose phosphate} + \text{ATP} \xrightarrow[\text{Phosphoribulo-kinase}]{Mg^{2+}} \text{ribulose 1,5-diphosphate} \qquad (11)$$

Upon accepting CO_2 in a reaction catalyzed by ribulose diphosphate carboxylase, the pentose diphosphate splits to yield 2 moles of 3-PGA (Eqn. 12).

$$\text{Ribulose 1,5-diphosphate} + CO_2 \longrightarrow \text{3-PGA (2)} \qquad (12)$$

McMahon and Bogorad (1004) recently studied the synthesis of ribulose diphosphate carboxylase in etiolated leaves of *Zea mays* under conditions of variable illumination and in the presence of photosynthetic and metabolic inhibitors. They concluded that, although brief illumination leads to an increase of ribulose diphosphate carboxylase, the level of this enzyme is controlled by processes independent of photosynthesis.

The phosphorylation and carboxylation reactions summarized by Eqns. 11 and 12 were soon found in nonphotosynthetic cells (1202), and the entire CO_2 assimilation cycle was found in the nonphotosynthetic sulfur bacterium *Thiobacillus dinitrificans* (1453, 118). Reductive pentose phosphate cycle reactions were eventually discovered even in cells lacking chlorophyll, underscoring the fact that this pathway is not unique to photosynthesis (107).

D. *The reductive phase*

Phosphates of triose and hexose were also identified among the early products of CO_2 assimilation (149). When the hexoses were degraded they were found to have a label distribution similar to that of 3-PGA, *i.e.*, carbon atoms 1, 2, 5 and 6 were only slightly labeled while carbon atoms 3 and 4 were heavily labeled.

$$\overset{*}{C}H_2OH - \overset{*}{C}O - \overset{*}{\overset{*}{\overset{*}{C}}}HOH - \overset{*}{\overset{*}{\overset{*}{C}}}HOH - \overset{*}{C}HOH - \overset{*}{C}H_2O - P$$

Fructose 6-phosphate

From this evidence it was postulated that 3-PGA was reduced to triose phosphate and that 2 moles of triose phosphate condensed to form a single mole of hexose diphosphate, and ultimately hexose monophosphate, via reactions constituting a reversal of the Emden–Meyerhoff pathway (glycolysis). Although in some instances the labeled carbon distribution in 3-PGA need not correspond to that of the two halves of hexose phosphate, it is generally accepted that the reductive phase of photosynthetic carbon assimilation is identical to the corresponding series of glycolytic reactions[3].

Oddly enough the only reductive step in the entire reductive pentose phosphate cycle occurs when 1,3-diphosphoglyceric acid is reduced by NADPH to triose phosphate (glyceraldehyde 3-phosphate). All other photosynthetic reactions are in some way dependent upon this one. It ensures that atmospheric carbon can in fact be reduced to carbohydrate.

E. *The regenerative phase*

The discovery of ^{14}C in di- and monophosphates of sedoheptulose was major evidence of molecular rearrangement during CO_2 assimilation. Degradation data showed that the 7-carbon sugar, heavily labeled in carbon atoms 3, 4 and 5, could not have been formed from the early hexose or pentose products available; that is, neither a $C_1 + C_6$ nor a $C_2 + C_5$ addition would produce sedoheptulose with the correct labeling. However, condensation of a triose phosphate with either of two 4-carbon pieces from the hexose (carbon atoms 1 to 4 or 3 to 6) would yield a sedoheptulose having the label sequence found experimentally. It was later recognized that sedoheptulose 7-phosphate was an intermediate in a reaction sequence from hexose phosphates to triose phosphates to pentose phosphates. In essence, these reactions made possible the replenishment of pentose phosphate needed to accept CO_2 in the carboxylation phase.

Prior work by Racker *et al.* (1207) and by Horecker *et al.* (751) had established that carbon atoms 1 and 2 of a ketose phosphate, such as fructose 6-phosphate, could be removed as a 2-carbon fragment via action of the enzyme transketolase. A thiamine pyrophosphate glycoaldehyde is formed with the 2-carbon section and a 4-carbon aldose phosphate is produced simultaneously (Eqn. 13).

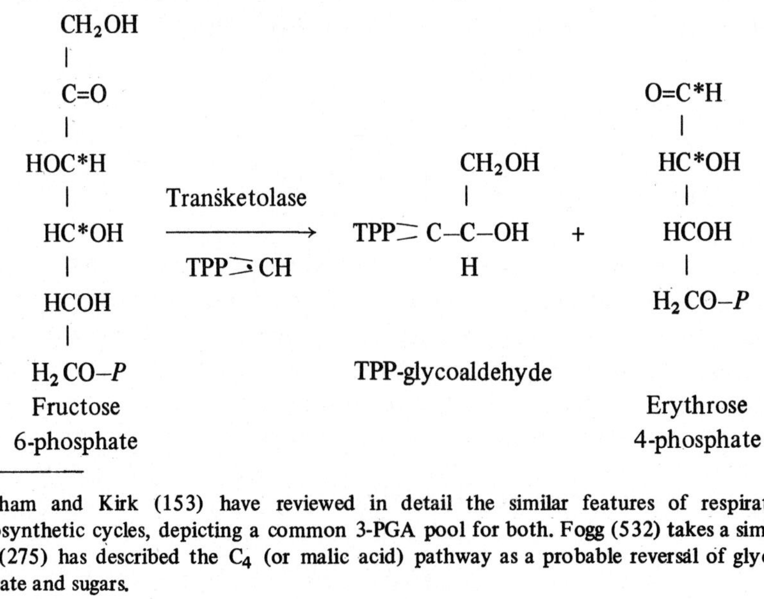

(13)

---

[3] Bassham and Kirk (153) have reviewed in detail the similar features of respiratory and photosynthetic cycles, depicting a common 3-PGA pool for both. Fogg (532) takes a similar view. Burr (275) has described the C_4 (or malic acid) pathway as a probable reversal of glycolysis to pyruvate and sugars.

In Eqn. 13 the aldose phosphate product is erythrose 4-phosphate, a 4-carbon sugar which is condensed with dihydroxyacetone phosphate to yield sedoheptulose 1,7-diphosphate in a reaction catalyzed by aldolase (Eqn. 14):

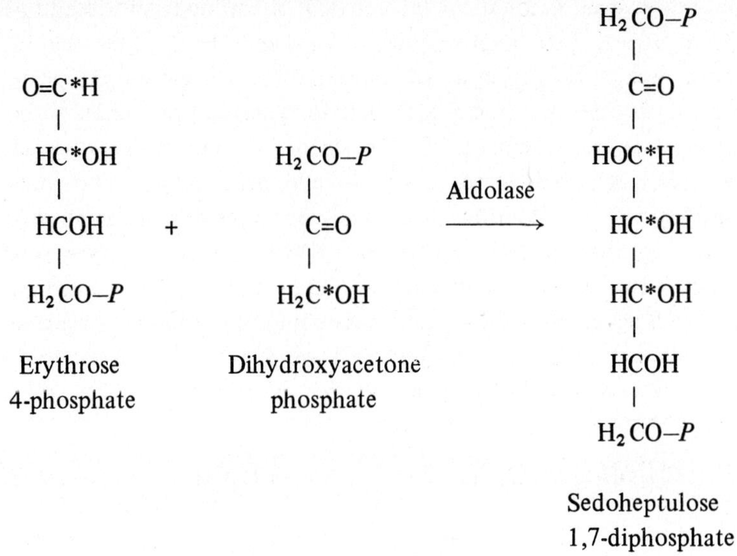

(14)

Sedoheptulose 7-phosphate is then formed by action of a hydrolytic enzyme, phosphatase, removing the phosphate group from carbon atom 1.

A 5-carbon sugar, ribose 5-phosphate, is produced from thiamine pyrophosphate plus sedoheptulose 7-phosphate in a reaction catalyzed by transketolase (152). In Eqn. 15 the ribose 5-phosphate in turn is converted to ribulose 5-phosphate by mediation of the enzyme phosphoribose isomerase (124).

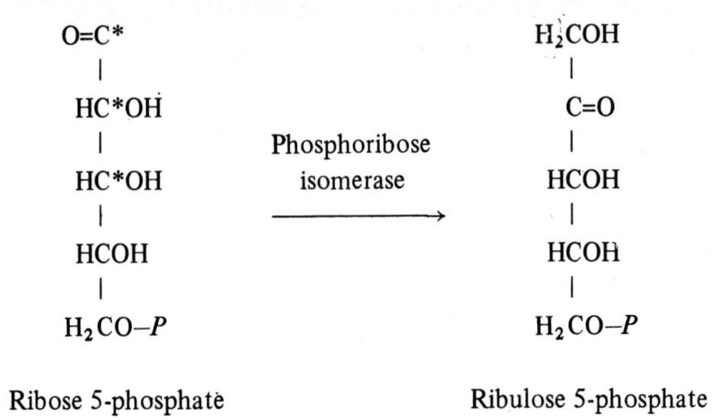

(15)

It can be seen that the keto group shifts from the C-1 position of ribose 5-phosphate to the C-2 position of ribulose 5-phosphate.

The reactions catalyzed by transketolase, aldolase, phosphatase and phosphoribose isomerase provide a sequence by which the CO_2 acceptor ribulose 1,5-diphosphate can be formed. However, the transketolase reaction is so highly reversible that the sequence does not in itself account for the net flow of carbon from triose to pentose characteristic of steady-state photosynthesis. Bassham (152) states that a TPP-glycoaldehyde molecule could react about as readily with the aldose phosphate from which it was just cleaved as it could with dihydroxyacetone phosphate or another suitable reactant. A common pool of TPP-glycoaldehyde can react almost equally well with fructose 6-phosphate, sedoheptulose 7-phosphate, and xylulose 5-phosphate. This explains a *feedback* of ^{14}C from the C-1 and C-2 positions of pentose phosphate to the C-1 and C-2 positions of hexose phosphate which at times achieves significant magnitude (149, 818). According to Bassham (152), the net flow of carbon from triose to pentose is accomplished by a net production of xylulose 5-phosphate from TPP-glycoaldehyde and glyceraldehyde (Eqn. 16), which is then converted to ribulose 5-phosphate by action of the enzyme ribulose phosphate–xylulose phosphate isomerase (Eqn. 17).

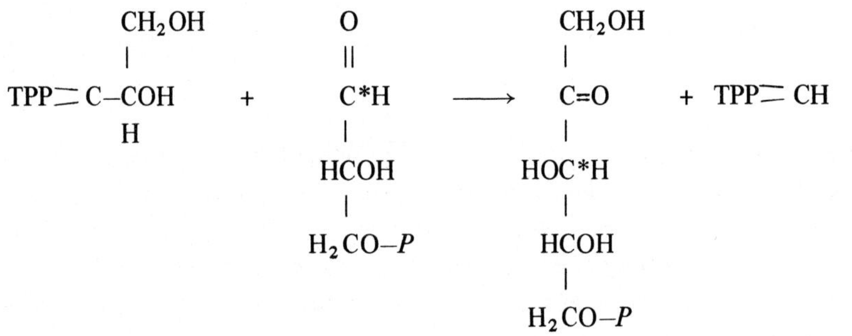

(16)

TPP-glycoaldehyde Glyceraldehyde phosphate Xylulose 5-phosphate

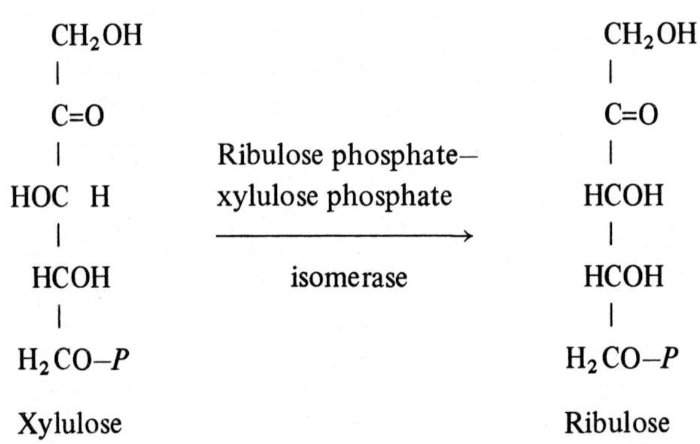

(17)

Xylulose 5-phosphate Ribulose 5-phosphate

The ribulose phosphate–xylulose phosphate isomerase reaction was described by Srere *et al.* (1353). Evidence of this reaction has also been found in sugarcane leaves (45). This is the final step in a series of reactions whereby five molecules of glyceraldehyde 3-phosphate are converted to three molecules of ribulose 5-phosphate.

F. *Steady-state vs. nonsteady-state experiments*

During the early investigations in which Bassham and Calvin (149) identified the intermediate reactants of the "carbon-reduction cycle", many experiments of a *nonsteady-state* type were performed in which it was not possible to maintain *steady-state* conditions of photosynthesis. It was later recognized that steady-state conditions are critical in determining the *normal* flow of carbon from one compound to another. Ordinarily, cultures of the single-celled green algae *Chlorella* or *Scenedesmus*, suspended in a weak phosphate buffer, were illuminated with bright incandescent lamps and aerated with 1 to 4 percent natural CO_2 for about an hour. After a high level of photosynthetic activity was reached, the algae were flushed with air, treated with $H^{14}CO_3$ solution, shaken briefly in light, and then run into boiling ethanol to quickly terminate all reactions. Radioactive products were subsequently analyzed by paper chromatography. These experiments precluded a constant CO_2 pressure during the change from natural to tracer CO_2 (from $^{12}CO_2$ to $^{14}CO_2$) but were suitable for identifying numerous simple compounds including those labeled within a few seconds.

In other experiments Bassham and Calvin created true steady-state conditions, that is, a linear relationship was established between the amount of $^{14}CO_2$ incorporated into organic compounds and time of exposure. This was accomplished by injecting a $^{14}CO_2$ solution into an illuminated transparent tubing which contained a stream of algae pumped toward boiling methanol at a constant rate of flow. Exposure time thus became a function of the distance between injection point and methanol.

G. *Low activity of carbon reduction enzymes*

The first biochemists seeking clues to photosynthetic mechanisms with isolated chloroplasts did so with the knowledge that respiratory and fermentation systems had already been reconstructed outside the intact cell. However, as recently as 1953 the task of separating the complete photosynthetic process from intact cells appeared to be insurmountable (1206). A year later, with improved techniques, Arnon *et al.* (63, 98, 97) succeeded in reducing CO_2 to the level of carbohydrates with isolated spinach chloroplasts. But the *in vitro* reaction rates were still very low by comparison with those of whole cells. The literature for several more years reflected a genuine note of disappointment among investigators who regarded chloroplasts as the site of photosynthesis but could demonstrate *in vitro* only a shadow of the *in vivo* assimilation potential. As recently as 1969 Latzko and Gibbs (899) reported that CO_2-assimilating enzymes in cell-free extracts of *Chlorella, Euglena, Tolypothrix* and spinach leaves were insufficiently active to support *in vivo* rates of CO_2 fixation.

Much of the problem stemmed from the fact that CO_2-assimilating enzymes were removed in an aqueous phase as the chloroplasts were being prepared. Treatment of whole chloroplasts with water or a dilute salt solution yielded broken chloroplasts consisting of insoluble *grana* and a yellow extract containing water-soluble, CO_2-fixing enzymes (955, 1448). The grana fraction contained chlorophyll and was capable of evolving oxygen, but it lacked the necessary enzymes for CO_2 assimilation. Restoration of CO_2-fixing ability was achieved when the grana and aqueous extract were recombined. Trebst *et al.* (1447), working with the grana-free aqueous extract in darkness, achieved CO_2 assimilation with ATP and NADPH formed previously by both photochemical and nonphotochemical means. Thus it was established that CO_2 assimilation was mediated in the chloroplast by water-soluble enzymes, themselves independent of light but employing the ATP and NADPH products of a prior light reaction.

There is generally good agreement among students of photosynthesis as to the nature and function of CO_2-assimilating enzymes. Although detailed examination is beyond the scope of this chapter, the essential enzymes originally postulated by Bassham and Calvin (149) include the following: *Ribulose diphosphate carboxylase* (*carboxydismutase*) (1201, 992, 1554, 1555, 791, 1553), *phosphoglyceryl kinase* (122, 11), *triose phosphate dehydrogenase* (1382, 1383, 626), *triose phosphate isomerase* (1414), *aldolase* (1382, 1413, 753), *phosphatase* (11, 597), *transketolase* (1207, 751), *transaldolase* (750), *phosphoribose isomerase* (749, 769, 124), *ribulose phosphate–xylulose phosphate isomerase* (1353, 1384), and *phosphoribulokinase* (769).

Chapter 3

Photosynthesis: CO_2 Assimilation in Sugarcane

1. INTRODUCTION

At an international conference on the photosynthetic unit held in May, 1970, Black (192) summarized a newly-developing concept whereby higher plants may be grouped into two major categories in accordance with their manner of assimilating carbon dioxide. The division was further based upon anatomical, physiological, and biochemical information gathered during more than four decades. However, one of the foremost distinguishing factors, *i.e.*, the path of carbon flow from atmospheric CO_2 to sugars in sugarcane and related species, could not have been offered as recently as 1965. It was only during the past several years that a new "cycle" of carbon fixation, quite distinct from that of Calvin and Bassham, has been pieced together. Its various steps have been secured and its requisite enzymology has been described in a growing number of species. In a large measure the discovery of this new pathway, the "C_4 pathway", began as a sugarcane phenomenon.

If the photosynthetic apparatus of unicellular organisms were duplicated in its entirety by sugarcane there would still remain some imposing questions relative to photosynthesis in *Saccharum* species. Seasonal and intervarietal fluctuations, factors of age, light quality and light intensity, relationships to product levels and to moisture regimes, and control mechanisms balancing photosynthetic and respiratory functions are all subjects requiring further elaboration. Sugarcane's massive productivity of sucrose, which can approach 20 percent by weight of the ripened stalk, is itself suggestive of a photosynthetic potential exceeding that of most plant species. Net CO_2 assimilation rates exceed by 1.5 to 2 times the rates usually found in other plants (274, 722, 854, 698, 808).

Several striking features of the C_4 plants prompted the tentative grouping by Black (192) and his colleagues. As already noted for sugarcane, the C_4 species as a group will assimilate CO_2, under intense illumination, at rates several times faster than species utilizing the reductive pentose phosphate cycle. Photorespiration, or lack of it in C_4 species[1], is thought by some workers to account for this difference in carbon-reduction rates. Studies by Black and his associates suggest that a smaller photosynthetic unit exists in the C_4 pathway species. This concept is supported by: (a) A hyperbolic

[1]There is increasing evidence of a photorespiratory system operating in C_4 pathway species (446 and C.R. Slack, Personal communication, January, 1971). In some studies the lowering of oxygen level below 2 percent has not brought about CO_2 assimilation increases in Calvin-cycle plants approaching the normal rates in C_4 species. Moreover, lowering oxygen tension does not increase the light intensity for saturation of CO_2 fixation.

CO_2 assimilation response to increasing light intensity; (b) the parallel hyperbolic response shown only by cyclic photophosphorylation (catalyzed by Photosystem I) in isolated chloroplasts; (c) C_4 plants contain a higher concentration of P700, and bear a higher ratio of chlorophyll *a* to *b*; and (d) a higher ratio of ferredoxin to chlorophyll exists in the C_4 plants. Black (192) estimates from P700 data that the photosynthetic unit could be at least one-third smaller in sugarcane and other plants using the newly-discovered pathway. This view is consistent with the recent findings of Woo and his co-workers (1585) showing the absence of Photosystem II in parenchyma-sheath chloroplasts of C_4 species.

These and other features are discussed at length in the following chapter which deals specifically with photosynthesis rates in the two systems. In the present chapter we shall relate the story of how the C_4 pathway came to be known. It is not yet possible to tell how the C_4 "machinery" itself came into being, or to trace anything like a common biochemical ancestry for the two principal paths of carbon flow. But the discovery of carbon movement through the C_4-dicarboxylic acids, the development of related steps, and the extension of the cycle from sugarcane to other tropical grasses and, indeed, to other species having little in common with sugarcane, can quite appropriately be told at this time.

2. THE C_4 PATHWAY OF CO_2 ASSIMILATION

When Kortschak and his co-workers (852, 853) tried to demonstrate that the Calvin cycle was operative in sugarcane leaves their efforts did not meet with success. In the words of Kortschak (854), "...We decided to repeat some of this work (Calvin's) on sugarcane, anticipating that a few months time would be enough to show the presence of the same pathway. As you know, this attempt was a failure. Much time was spent trying to find conditions under which PGA would predominate at short times. The fact that fixation of CO_2 into malic acid was well known as a dark reaction made us feel that perhaps for some reason we were not actually examining a normal photosynthetic process." What Kortschak had encountered were reactions quite normal to sugarcane but which assumed only minor importance, if any importance at all, in Calvin-cycle plants. Subsequent studies by Hatch and Slack (693, 1342) in Australia confirmed Kortschak's findings and established beyond question that sugarcane and certain other species assimilate CO_2 via reactions yielding C_4-dicarboxylic acids as predominate early products rather than 3-PGA.

A. *Initial work by Kortschak and co-workers*

When Kortschak and his colleagues began their photosynthetic $^{14}CO_2$ studies with sugarcane leaf sections in Hawaii (852), there was no reason to think that their technology, once perfected, would yield a CO_2-fixation pathway appreciably different than that of Calvin and Bassham. What was apparent were peculiarities of the plant itself and leaf samples generally unfamiliar to other workers. When extracting leaf sections, for example, they found that 5 minutes boiling in 95 percent ethanol had little effect on the rugged cane leaf whereas the same treatment for algae or a leaf from soybean or spinach left the sample colorless and completely extracted. The leaves themselves were selected from a complex interspecific hybrid, *H. 37-1933*, comprised of germplasm from *officinarum, spontaneum* and *robustum* species. Care was taken to assure leaf samples of uniform rank and age, and the leaf sections themselves were cut under water from the leaf center (midway between leaf tip and dewlap).

Methods devised for exposing the leaf sections to $^{14}CO_2$ included: (a) A porous filter method for brief exposures of 2-inch segments requiring precise timing; (b) a steady-state method for longer exposures, in which 3-inch segments supported in an 18-liter, aquarium were exposed to $^{14}CO_2$ after 10 minutes equilibration in a high CO_2 atmosphere (0.10 percent); and (c) a third procedure or "dip" method involved rapid entry of a cane leaf into a closed glass container of $^{14}CO_2$ followed by periodic recovery of the leaf sample.

Preliminary experiments exposing blade sections to $^{14}CO_2$ for intervals up to 15 seconds invariably showed more radioactivity passing into malic and aspartic acids than into 3-phosphoglyceric acid (3-PGA). There was never more than 34 percent of the total activity incorporated into 3-PGA[2]. Subsequent experiments gave similar results. Fig. 3-1 illustrates the early predominance of malate and aspartate over 3-PGA, with

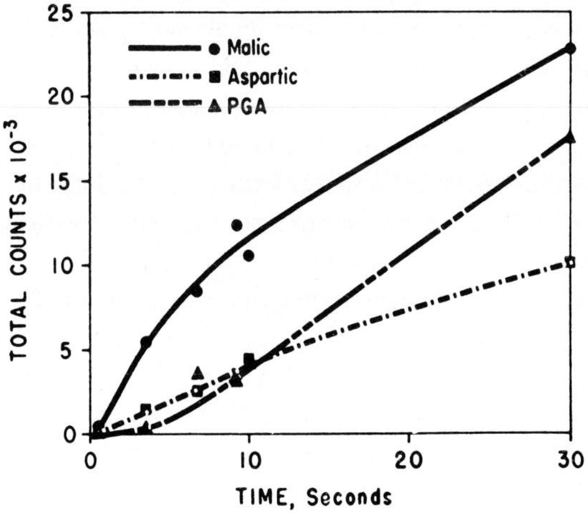

Fig. 3-1. Early products of photosynthesis in sugarcane leaves, illustrating the initial predominance of malic and aspartic acids over 3-phosphoglyceric acid (PGA). [After Kortschak *et al.* (852).] Reproduced by permission of *Plant Physiology.*

---

[2]Results of preliminary tests published in 1957 led Kortschak *et al.* (851) to depict phosphomalic acid as an early product of photosynthesis in sugarcane. The compound believed to be phosphomalic acid has since been correctly identified as 3-PGA (852).

the latter beginning to surpass aspartate only after about 10 seconds had elapsed. Kortschak *et al.* (852) concluded that, in contrast to other plants, sugarcane formed malic and aspartic acids as the first stable products of CO_2 assimilation. Thus, the ribulose diphosphate carboxylase reaction so laboriously established in other species could not have played the key role of CO_2 reception in sugarcane. What then of the subsequent reductive phase and regenerative reactions essential to replenish the CO_2 acceptor? What was the acceptor? Indeed, the operation of the reductive pentose phosphate cycle could no longer be taken for granted as a valid explanation of carbon reduction in sugarcane.

Kortschak's conclusions were not hastily drawn. He and his co-workers (Constance E. Hartt and G.O. Burr) felt that malic acid might be an important product of CO_2 fixation in dark reactions independent of photosynthesis. Steps were therefore taken to compare light and dark malate synthesis by leaf segments in identical $^{14}CO_2$ atmospheres. The photosynthetic production of malic acid was substantiated by results showing the dark fixation of $^{14}CO_2$ to be only 0.5 percent of the light fixation, and that the dark assimilation into malic acid was only 1 percent of that in light. Measures were also taken to prove that malic acid was not an artifact produced when the blade section was immersed in boiling alcohol. Analyses showed no qualitative difference between ^{14}C-containing malate in tissues killed by boiling alcohol or by quick freezing in a dry ice–acetone medium.

Kortschak *et al.* (852) were also aware that failure to detect greater amounts of 3-PGA might be interpreted as the work of a specific phosphatase acting to hydrolyze the compound as soon as it was formed. This view was taken by Bonnet (208) following a personnal communication with Calvin in which the latter had written:

"The failure of a number of workers to catch the intermediate phosphate seems to me to be due to the presence of a highly active phosphatase enzyme system which resists the destruction by either temperature or solvents (or both) long enough to hydrolyze the very small pools of intermediate organic phosphates leading to the free sugars and sugar acids."[3]

Known specific phosphatases in sugarcane include uridine diphosphatase (688), sucrose phosphatase (704), and alkaline pyrophosphatase (698), each reported by workers in Australia. A ribose 5-phosphatase (862) and several ATPases (17, 48) were found in cane leaf extracts in Puerto Rico. In 1964 Alexander (48) described a nonspecific acid phosphatase preparation from sugarcane leaves which not only hydrolyzed all organic phosphates tested, including 3-PGA and 2-PGA, but declined in activity as leaf sucrose was increased by withholding nitrogen. However, Kortschak *et al.* (852) concluded from their $^{14}CO_2$ studies that phosphatase did not play a role in producing low 3-PGA values. If it had, the radioactivity would have appeared in free

---

[3]Letter to Dr. J.A. Bonnet, former Soil Scientist and Head of the Soils Department, Agricultural Experiment Station, U.P.R., dated August 14, 1961.

glyceric acid and this compound in no instance contained more than 15 percent of the radioactivity found in 3-PGA.

Calvin's group (148, 286) had also found malic acid as an early photosynthetic product, but it appeared in such small quantities relative to 3-PGA that no great importance was attached to it. However, Bassham *et al.* (148) had further observed the formation of malate by the unicellular algae *Scenedesmus* to be selectively inhibited by malonic acid with little effect on 3-PGA formation and total photosynthesis. When Kortschak pretreated his cane leaf sections in malonic acid prior to $^{14}CO_2$ exposure, he found that malic acid, 3-PGA, and total photosynthesis all showed an equal degree of nonselective inhibition. This supported the view that sugarcane photosynthesis proceeded by reactions qualitatively different from those of the Calvin cycle.

Kortschak *et al.* (852) interpreted their findings on the assumption that no change was effected in proceeding reactions when $^{14}CO_2$ was introduced, even though the time course of 0.6 to 9.8 seconds was nonsteady-state owing to drastic CO_2 increases characteristic of the porous filter method employed. The interval from 10 to 810 seconds was close to steady-state with added $^{14}CO_2$ raising the total CO_2 concentration only by 0.03 percent. Their assumption seemed to be borne out when tests using 4.8 and 0.13 percent CO_2 gave comparable results at 9.3 and 10 seconds, respectively, and when increased CO_2 concentration did not give the increased assimilation into 3-PGA described by Bassham *et al.* (150).

That the radioactivity found in malic acid eventually passed to sucrose was shown in dark-metabolism experiments followed by exposure to light (Table 3-1). It is evident that malic acid was the main source of ^{14}C found in sucrose. Reexposure of dark fixation experiments to light was accompanied by an intervening induction

TABLE 3-1

PHOTOSYNTHESIS PRODUCTS IN SUGARCANE LEAVES SHOWING EVIDENCE OF ^{14}C MOVEMENT FROM MALATE TO SUCROSE FOLLOWING INITIAL INCORPORATION INTO THE C_4 ACID

[After Kortschak *et al.* (852).] Reproduced by permission of *Plant Physiology*.

Product	Total counts × 10^{-3} after indicated light exposure (minutes)*			
	0	1	3	5
Malate	21	15	8	8
Glucose-1-*P*	0	4	9	1
Sucrose	0	6	15	16
All others	8	9	4	8
Total	29	34	36	32

*Leaf sections of equal area were exposed to $^{14}CO_2$ in darkness for 10 minutes, then illuminated in air at 2000 foot candles.

period' before photosynthesis again proceeded normally. This time lag featured a temporary and unexplained accumulation of glucose 1-phosphate (Table 3-1), which might be due in part to the relative inability of leaf phosphatase to hydrolyze this compound (11). It should be noted that the pools of C_4 acids labeled in darkness are not necessarily synonymous with the pools directly involved in photosynthetic CO_2 fixation.

An important conclusion from the initial work in Hawaii (852) is that malic and aspartic acids are converted to sucrose via 3-PGA and the hexose phosphates. During the initial 20 seconds exposure to $^{14}CO_2$ the combined radioactivity lost from malic and aspartic acids at a given point approximated the gain by 3-PGA, and the rate of loss by 3-PGA about equaled the radioactivity gained by hexose phosphate. Since virtually all of the absorbed $^{14}CO_2$ passed through malate and aspartate before passing through 3-PGA, Kortschak and his colleagues discounted the possibility that the Calvin cycle contributed a second source of 3-PGA via carboxylation and splitting of ribulose diphosphate. In the new scheme 3-PGA assumed not the role of a stable first product but one of an intermediary whose mechanism of origin and its essential enzymology remained obscure.

From this point the task of clarifying sugarcane CO_2 assimilation fell to M.D. Hatch, C.R. Slack, and their co-workers in Australia. In the words of Kortschak (854), "...Having spent years on the problem, seeing no further light ahead using the same old methods, and having no one experienced in enzyme chemistry in our group at the time, I urged Dr. Hatch to continue this study".

B. *Essential steps of the C_4 pathway*

Hatch and Slack (693) confirmed Kortschak's finding of malic and aspartic acids as early stable products of photosynthesis by sugarcane leaf segments (variety *Pindar*). In addition they found an unstable third compound and identified it as oxaloacetic acid. Degradation studies enabled them to measure radioactivity in the different carbon atoms of the 4-carbon dicarboxylic acids. They confirmed that the C-4 atom of malic and aspartic acid is labeled prior to the C-1 carboxyl group of 3-PGA. In later studies Johnson and Slack (809) established that, under steady-state conditions, virtually all the label incorporated from $^{14}CO_2$ into the C-1 atom of 3-PGA enters via the C-4 atom of the dicarboxylic acids.

Hatch and Slack were perhaps the first to strive for steady-state conditions comparable to those of the intact physiological system. Rather than dismantle the CO_2 fixation process to study its component parts, as for example others had done in working out photosynthetic electron transport or the respiratory pathways, they proceeded with the assumption that only physiologically important carboxylations were operative under steady-state physiological conditions. Light intensity at the leaf surface was raised to 8200 foot candles as compared to about 2000 foot candles used by Kortschak (852) and Calvin's group (148, 150). The minimum preillumination period was increased to 45 minutes and CO_2 concentration at zero time was 0.055 percent. In addition to testing leaf sections, Hatch and Slack also worked with intact blades still attached to the stalk. Under these conditions the total fixation of $^{14}CO_2$ by leaf segments remained linear for about 150 seconds, and nearly identical results were obtained with attached leaves over the time-course from 4 to 90 seconds.

Different killing and extraction methods were also adopted. This precaution ultimately led to discovery of oxaloacetic acid as a photosynthetic product since the unstable oxaloacetate was completely destroyed by boiling ethanol and chromatography procedures suitable for malic and aspartic acids. Radioactive oxaloacetate was identified as its 2,4-dinitrophenylhydrazone after killing leaves at $-80\ ^{\circ}C$ in the presence of this reagent. A lesser proportion of the radioactive derivative was recovered when leaves were killed in boiling ethanol containing 2,4-dinitrophenylhydrazine. Hatch and Slack therefore attached major importance to methodology in dealing with sugarcane photosynthesis. At this time [1966] they felt that the C_4 pathway might be operative in other plant species, and that this pathway could give 3-PGA as the first detectable labeled product when only standard killing procedures are used.

Taking into account the possibility of secondary or independent side reactions, Hatch and Slack surmised that malate or oxaloacetate was the primary carboxylation product and that aspartate was likely formed from this by a side reaction. The ^{14}C would then pass from a pool of C_4-dicarboxylic acids to 3-PGA, then to hexose phosphates and finally to sucrose and glucan. Malate and aspartate were also formed in the dark but at a greatly reduced rate with no radioactivity at all passing into 3-PGA. At this point the evidence was consistent with the view that a compound analogous to the pentose monophosphate of Calvin's cycle is phosphorylated by photosynthetically-produced ATP and serves as a carboxyl recipient prior to the production of 3-PGA.

The essentiality of a light reaction gained support from experiments in which $^{14}CO_2$ exposure in the light was followed by exposure to unlabeled CO_2 in either light or darkness. In the unlabeled CO_2 atmosphere the total radioactivity in leaf segments remained constant regardless of illumination treatment. However, in light the radioactivity continued to move from malic and aspartic acids to 3-PGA, hexose phosphate, and end products, whereas in darkness there was no label movement into end products and radioactivity increased in the dicarboxylic acid pool. This increase occurred at the expense of 3-PGA.

In establishing the most probable pathway of photysynthetic carbon movement in sugarcane, Hatch and Slack needed to decide whether carbon passed from the dicarboxylic acids to 3-PGA via a decarboxylation release and refixing of CO_2, for which non-photosynthetic pathways were already known, or by a transcarboxylation reaction. They favored the latter choice on the basis of labeling data and because photosynthesis can achieve its net gain of carbon for the plant only if there is no release and loss of CO_2. Quite significantly, they found that labeling of the C-2 and C-3 carbon atoms of 3-PGA is much more rapid than for the non-carboxyl atoms of malate. After 45 seconds only 4 percent of the malic acid activity had moved to C-2 and C-3, while these contained 39 percent of the activity in 3-PGA. Therefore, the involvement of known decarboxylation pathways became doubtful since the decarboxylation of malate or oxaloacetate to pyruvic acid, which in turn is converted to 3-PGA, would have led to the appearance of their C-1 to C-3 atoms in the analogous C-1 to C-3 positions of 3-PGA. To the contrary, the data indicated that C-4 atoms of dicarboxylic acids are the source of the C-1 atom of 3-PGA. Hatch and Slack proposed that a transcarboxylation reaction transfers the C-4 carboxyl group of a 4-carbon dicarboxylic acid to a 2- or 5-carbon acceptor which in turn provides the C-2 and C-3 atoms of 3-PGA.

Since at this point there was still no clear picture of carboxyl movement between the C_4 acids and 3-PGA, this interpretation might have gained strength if the work was repeated with isolated chloroplasts. As it was, no complete distinction could be drawn between photosynthetic, glycolytic, or respiratory involvement of the supplied ^{14}C. Studies with chloroplast preparations would also have given an answer to proposals such as that of Galmiche (555) who felt that in maize the ^{14}C incorporation into malate results from exchange reactions in the cytoplasm, constituting only a delay of CO_2 penetration to the chloroplasts, and that CO_2 assimilation into 3-PGA "...is the effective part of photosynthetic reactions occurring in chloroplasts". On the other hand, the efforts by Hatch and Slack to study CO_2 assimilation under simulated physiological conditions would have been pointless had they disassembled the photosynthetic apparatus from intact leaf tissue. Their early decision to work with intact tissues was substantiated amazingly well by labeling and enzyme studies during the subsequent 3 years.

With the transcarboxylation step tentatively established that the C_4 pathway could be written with four summary reactions (Eqns. 1 to 4):

$$\text{Pyruvic acid} + \text{ATP} + \text{P}_i \rightleftharpoons \text{phosphopyruvic acid} + \text{AMP} + \text{PP}_i \quad (1)$$
$$\text{Phosphopyruvic acid} + \text{CO}_2 \rightleftharpoons \text{oxaloacetic acid} \quad (2)$$
$$\text{Malic acid} \rightleftharpoons \text{oxaloacetic acid} \rightleftharpoons \text{aspartic acid} \quad (3)$$
$$\text{Oxaloacetic acid} \rightleftharpoons \text{3-PGA} + \text{pyruvic acid} \quad (4)$$

These reactions are shown schematically in Fig. 3-2. As depicted by Hatch and Slack (693), two cycles are linked to one another by a transcarboxylation reaction. One cycle serves to fix CO_2 and acts as a source of carboxyl groups to react with a carboxyl acceptor in the other cycle. The second cycle regenerates carboxyl acceptor for the transcarboxylation reaction. It was thought that some of the 3-PGA might be converted into a 3-carbon acceptor of CO_2, a function which could replace carbon lost from the first cycle by side reactions. Oxaloacetic acid was designated as the most

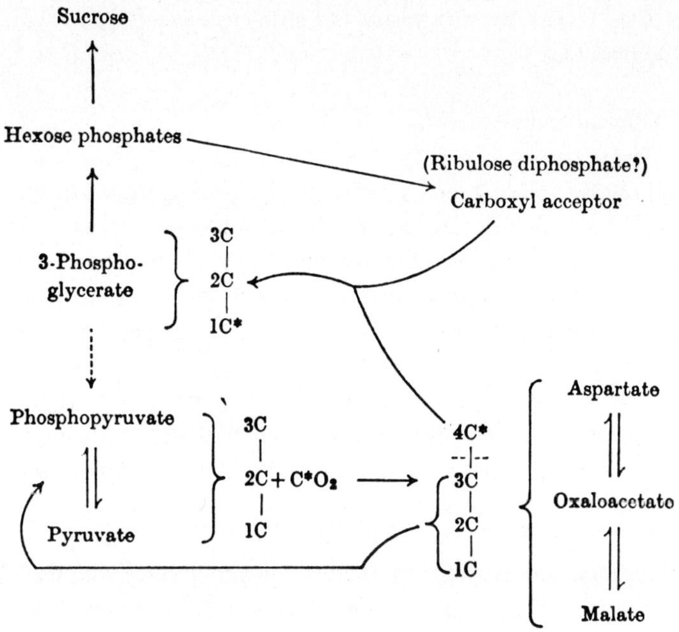

Fig. 3-2. The pathway of photosynthetic carbon dioxide fixation in sugarcane leaves as proposed by workers in Queensland in 1966. The broken line indicates a minor pathway. [After Hatch and Slack (693).] Reproduced by permission of the *Biochemical Journal.*

likely carboxyl donor on the basis of its known activity in transcarboxylation reactions (760, 1586). The carboxyl acceptor was visualized as a 2-carbon compound such as glycoaldehyde phosphate, or as the 5-carbon ribulose diphosphate which accepts CO_2 in the Calvin cycle.

Burr (275), in 1970, stressed three requirements having to be met in order for the C_4 pathway (or malic acid pathway) to account for CO_2 assimilation in sugarcane at rates typically recorded: (a) Absence of respiratory CO_2 in light; (b) insensitivity of all essential enzymes to oxygen inhibition; and (c) absence of a photo-oxidation site. Burr further suggests that under suitable conditions of environment, *i.e.*, oxygen inhibition of ribulose diphosphate carboxylase, the C_4 pathway may provide the dominant carboxylation system in Calvin-cycle plants having both the C_4 and Calvin-cycle mechanisms. As an alternative pathway of carbon flow Burr proposed the reaction

$$\text{Malic acid + acetyl-CoA} \longrightarrow \text{pyruvate + glyceraldehyde}$$

in which carbon would pass from malate to acetyl-CoA without liberation of free CO_2. Reduced ferredoxin is required. In the presence of ferredoxin acetyl-CoA is known to accept CO_2. With reference to respiratory CO_2, it was concluded that an active C_4

pathway would prevent CO_2 release by this means in Calvin-cycle plants photosynthesizing in air (about 300 ppm CO_2).

C. *Extension of the C_4 pathway to other plants*

After Hatch and Slack (693) published their kinetic and ^{14}C-labeling studies of the sugarcane C_4 pathway in 1966, the new scheme of CO_2 fixation was extended to numerous other species and its essential reactions were substantiated by enzyme studies. In 1967 Slack and Hatch (1342) reported carboxylase activity characteristic of the C_4 pathway in the tropical grasses maize (*Zea mays*) and sorghum (*Sorghum vulgare*). A survey by Hatch *et al.* (695) also revealed the pathway in tropical grasses and a monocot species of *Cyperus*, but not in other monocots or in several dicotyledonous plants examined. Shortly thereafter the photosynthetic labeling of C_4-dicarboxylic acids was reconfirmed by Kandler and Senser (817) in *Saccharum* and *Sorghum*, while in *Oryza sativum* the Calvin cycle was found to be operative.

In 1968 Johnson and Hatch (808) published evidence of the C_4 pathway in species of the dicotyledons *Amaranthus* and *Gomphrena* (family Amaranthaceae), and *Atriplex* (family Chenopodiaceae), and in other species of the monocotyledons *Cyperus* and *Kyllinga* (family Cyperaceae). Each of these plants displayed a characteristic early labeling of the C_4-dicarboxylic acids. In addition, evidence of the Calvin cycle was found in certain genera of the Cyperaceae (*Gahnia, Lepidosperma*, and *Cyperus*). Since the latter yielded no radioactivity in oxaloacetate, malate, or aspartate, while 3-PGA and the sugar phosphates were readily labeled, the possibility that 3-PGA might be found solely as a result of inadequate handling of C_4 pathway products was dispelled. Rather, there was increasing evidence that differences in such features as leaf anatomy, light response curves, CO_2 compensation points, response to lowered oxygen tension, and phôtosynthesis rates tend to distinguish C_4 pathway plants from those using the Calvin cycle.

3. ENZYMOLOGY OF THE C_4 PATHWAY

A. *Synthesis of CO_2 acceptor*

In 1967 Hatch and Slack (694) described an enzyme from leaves of sugarcane and other tropical grasses that catalyzes the critical conversion of pyruvic acid to phosphopyruvic acid, the essential acceptor of CO_2 in the C_4 pathway (Eqn. 2). Initially it appeared to be identical with an enzyme described by Cooper and Kornberg (387) in *Escherichia coli* which catalyzes the reaction:

$$\text{Pyruvate} + \text{ATP} \longrightarrow \text{phosphopyruvate} + \text{AMP} + P_i$$

Upon further purification Hatch and Slack found that orthophosphate was also a reactant (696), a fact previously obscured by the presence of pyrophosphatase. A new reaction was written according to Eqn. 1, but the name *phosphopyruvate synthase* was retained in accordance with the terminology of Cooper and Kornberg (387). In 1969 Andrews and Hatch (77) reported isotope-exchange studies indicating that this reaction proceeds via several steps:

$$\text{Enzyme} + \text{ATP} + P_i \rightleftharpoons \text{enzyme}-P + \text{AMP} + PP_i$$
$$\text{Enzyme}-P + \text{pyruvate} \rightleftharpoons \text{enzyme} + \text{phosphoenolpyruvate}$$

Terminology was changed so that *phosphopyruvate synthase* now became *pyruvate, P_i dikinase.* This enzyme was not detected in preparations from Calvin-cycle plants. Kortschak (854) expressed doubt that it is entirely absent from the latter, since its absence (or that of any other C_4 pathway enzyme) would mean that Calvin-cycle plants could perform none of their CO_2 assimilation via the C_4 pathway.

Pyruvate, P_i dikinase has some unusual properties, including less stability when frozen or at 0 °C than at 22 °C, and rapid loss of activity within 3 hours under the best possible conditions (696). With the exception of ATP all the reaction products in each direction are inhibitory (67). The enzyme requires Mg^{2+} which cannot be replaced by Mn^{2+} or Ca^{2+}. Because the ΔF for hydrolysis of phosphopyruvate to pyruvate (–13.6 kcal/mole) greatly exceeds the ΔF for hydrolysis of ATP to AMP plus pyrophosphate (–7.6 kcal/mole) at pH 7.0, the reaction equilibrium would lie strongly toward free pyruvic acid. The synthesis of phosphopyruvate must therefore require continuous removal of products in accordance with Eqn. 2. Arsenate was found to maintain phosphopyruvate synthesis in the absence of enzymes needed to remove the product, apparently by shifting the equilibrium away from free pyruvate[4]. This observation was interpreted by Hatch and Slack in support of orthophosphate as a reactant (696). Studies with [^{32}P]orthophosphate indicated that one of the pyrophosphate groups originates from orthophosphate. In some respects the enzyme behaves as a phosphatase.

In 1968 Slack (1343) reported a pronounced light sensitivity of pyruvate, P_i dikinase in *Amaranthus.* Activity declined about 50 percent within 15 minutes of dark exposure but recovered quickly in light. In 1969 Hatch, Slack and Bull (698) reported that in maize and *Amaranthus* the enzyme's content was 5 to 10 times higher in plants grown for 7 weeks with high light intensity (130 000 lux for 12 hours daily) than in plants grown under low light intensity (8600 lux for 12 hours daily). From this it appears that pyruvate, P_i dikinase requires light for both activation and synthesis.

---

[4]C.R. Slack (personal communication) states that the As–P_i complex formed in place of PP_i is labile and therefore acts to displace the equilibrium toward phosphopyruvate.

B. *Ribulose diphosphate carboxylase*

Within the Calvin cycle the most critical enzyme is probably ribulose diphosphate carboxylase (RuDP-carboxylase). In the C_4 pathway the carboxylative reaction (Eqn. 2) is catalyzed by the enzyme phosphoenolpyruvate carboxylase [PEP-carboxylase (1342, 808)]. A traditional weak point in the theory of CO_2 assimilation via the reductive pentose phosphate cycle is the low magnitude of the carboxylase reaction by comparison with the rate of photosynthesis (289, 1366, 151). By contrast, workers in Australia (1342, 808) reported the PEP-carboxylase reaction in certain tropical grasses may approach a velocity 6 times greater than photosynthesis, and up to 60 times greater than the rate of RuDP-carboxylase activity. In leaf extracts of *Amaranthus* and *Atriplex* the RuDP-carboxylase activity was far lower than that of Calvin-cycle plants and constituted only about one-tenth of the maximum Calvin-cycle photosynthesis rate (Table 3-2). It can also be seen from Table 3-2 that wheat, oat, and silverbeet

TABLE 3-2

COMPARISON OF ENZYME ACTIVITIES AND PHOTOSYNTHESIS RATES IN *AMARANTHUS* AND *ATRIPLEX* SPECIES WITH TROPICAL GRASSES AND CALVIN-CYCLE PLANTS

[After Johnson and Hatch (808).] Reproduced by permission of *Phytochemistry*, Pergamon Press, Ltd., Oxford.

Tissue source	Maximum photosynthesis*	Enzyme activity (μmoles/mg chlorophyll/min)		
		Ribulose diphosphate carboxylase	Phosphopyruvate carboxylase	Phosphopyruvate synthetase
Amaranthus palmeri	4.8	0.6	21	3.7
Atriplex semibaccata	4.0	0.2	18	1.4
Tropical grasses**	2.9–3.5	0.3–0.6	15–18	1.2–3.5
Calvin-cycle plants***	1.6–1.7	4.2–4.7	0.3–0.35	0

*At light saturation and 0.03 percent (v/v) carbon dioxide.
**Sugarcane, maize, and sorghum.
***Wheat, oat, and silverbeet.

species representing the Calvin cycle contained low levels of PEP-carboxylase and no phosphopyruvate synthetase (pyruvate, P_i dikinase). This attests to the little opportunity afforded these plants to fix CO_2 via the C_4 pathway.

In 1964 Alexander (11) described the enzyme "pyruvic carboxylase" in aqueous extracts of lyophilized sugarcane leaf tissue. Apparently this enzyme is identical to the PEP-carboxylase found by Hatch and his colleagues. We were primarily concerned with sugar degradation at the time and the assay was designed to detect acetaldehyde formed by enzyme action against pyruvic acid. The reaction was not specific for pyruvate as evidenced by aldehyde formation when either α-ketoglutaric or oxaloacetic acid was substituted for pyruvate. No trace of pyruvate could be found when the enzyme acted upon oxaloacetate. Interest in the carboxylase waned after no consistent relationship could be drawn between its activity and changing sucrose levels induced by empirical treatments, *i.e.*, by supplying the plants with variable nitrate and potassium (11), or by spraying them with maleic hydrazide, 2,4-dichlorophenoxyacetic acid, or indole-3-acetic acid (19).

The interconversion of oxaloacetic, malic, and aspartic acids, as depicted by Eqn. 3, is well known throughout the plant kingdom. The two requisite enzymes, malate dehydrogenase and aspartate aminotransferase seem to be present in all plant species. However, in the C_4 pathway there appears to be an extremely rapid equilibrium between the CO_2 acceptor and an unidentified symmetric compound. Hatch and Slack (693) found that within 3 seconds after exposure of cane leaf segments to $^{14}CO_2$, about 10 percent of the total ^{14}C had appeared in the malate C-1 atom (the secondary carboxyl atom in terms of carbon flow). This initial movement was considerably more rapid than the labeling of the C-2 plus C-3 atoms of 3-PGA. The latter required up to 20 seconds to accumulate 10 percent of the total ^{14}C. Kortschak (854) suggested that fumaric acid is probably the symmetric compound. The essential enzyme, fumarase, was found in sugarcane leaves in 1964 (11).

C. *Malic enzyme*

Other enzymes with probable roles in the C_4 pathway include adenylate kinase and alkaline pyrophosphatase (698). Both appear to be present in adequate quantities. Adenylate kinase and alkaline pyrophosphatase activities were found to be at least 35- and 5-fold higher, respectively, in C_4 pathway plants (including sugarcane) than in Calvin-cycle plants.

A catalyst of questionable stature is malic enzyme (1342). Since it catalyzes the direct conversion of pyruvate to malate, it could be functional in the C_4 pathway if present in adequate amounts. Although quantitatively higher in tropical grasses than other plants, there still is only enough to account for about 15 percent of the total CO_2 uptake. Thus the importance of malic enzyme remains questionable, although it is also possible that preparation methods have not been entirely suitable for this system. Mere traces of the enzyme were found in leaf preparations some years ago in Puerto Rico (11).

Workers at the Tate and Lyle Research Centre (89) regard the malic enzyme "...as the final component of the enzyme pathway, 'shuttling' CO_2 from the atmosphere to the site of CO_2 fixation by ribulose diphosphate carboxylase". Differential grinding experiments showed the malic enzyme being released at the same stage of tissue disruption as RuDP-carboxylase, and somewhat later than PEP-carboxylase. This is consistent with the view that RuDP-carboxylase resists ready extraction from plant tissues.

Although malic enzyme appears to be more abundant in C_4 pathway plants than Calvin-cycle species, Johnson and Hatch (810) assigned only a minimal role to the enzyme in CO_2 fixation. Rather, it was proposed that malate is formed from oxaloacetate by an NADP-specific malate dehydrogenase. The latter system was isolated from maize leaf extracts along with malic enzyme but separated from NAD-malate dehydrogenase. The two dehydrogenases differed insofar as a thiol was essential for the NADP-malate dehydrogenase reaction. The K_m for malate formation via malic enzyme was pH-dependent and optimal pH varied with malate concentration. Malic enzyme activity was enhanced further by Mg^{2+} than by Mn^{2+}. NADP-malate dehydrogenase was light sensitive, being inactivated in darkness and readily reactivated in light, or by thiol additives *in vitro.* This enzyme was readily synthesized along with chlorophyll in etiolated leaves upon reillumination. The *in vivo* light regulation of NADP-malate dehydrogenase was thought to be governed in a manner similar to that of pyruvate, P_i dikinase. With suitable concentrations of $NADP^+$ and malate (699) the NADP-malate dehydrogenase reaction toward malate proceeds up to 30 times faster than in the reverse direction. This enzyme offers a reasonable accounting of oxaloacetate conversion to malate, with malic enzyme possibly acting to remove some of the malate carboxyl groups for refixation by RuDP-carboxylase (810).

D. *Initial search for transcarboxylase activity*

The C_4 pathway reactions by which carbon is passed from a 4-carbon dicarboxylic acid to 3-PGA (Eqn. 4) were perhaps the most difficult to establish enzymatically. We have seen that Hatch and Slack (693) had to select between a decarboxylation sequence, in which carbon is lost, and a transcarboxylation sequence whose intermediates and enzymology were obscure. Hatch and Slack chose transcarboxylation on the basis of labeling data and the photosynthetic need for a net increase of assimilated CO_2. Transcarboxylation to a 2-carbon acceptor such as glycoaldehyde phosphate, or to the 5-carbon ribulose diphosphate, was suggested. Kortschak (854) found indirect evidence of a 2-carbon acceptor when he infiltrated sugarcane leaves with a labeled 2-carbon compound, glyoxylic acid. After 1 hour he found label distributions in sugars, malate, and aspartate which matched closely the label distributions obtained with infiltrated [^{14}C]pyruvate.

More recent ^{14}C studies by Johnson and Hatch (809) showed no detectable radioactivity in glycolaldehyde, hydroxypyruvate, or their phosphorylated derivatives. Hydroxypyruvate or phosphohydroxypyruvate were regarded as suitable precursors of 3-PGA if the acceptor of the C-4 carboxyl group was a 2-carbon compound. Since failure to detect radioactive hydroxypyruvate or phosphohydroxypyruvate could have been due to their small pool size, Johnson and Hatch proceeded to seek evidence for their presence by comparing the movement of radioactivity into serine (which could be formed directly from phosphohydroxypyruvate or hydroxypyruvate rather than from 3-PGA) and into 3-PGA. Using pulse-chase exposure techniques (exposure first to $^{14}CO_2$ followed by air, or $^{12}CO_2$)[5], radioactivity decline was observed in 3-PGA. This was accompanied by increased radioactivity in serine, and it was tentatively concluded that serine was formed via 3-PGA.

In 1969 Hatch and Slack (699) reported the presence of a NADP-specific malate dehydrogenase and glycerate kinase in leaves of both C_4 pathway plants (including sugarcane) and Calvin-cycle plants. Evidence was presented for their location in chloroplasts. It was suggested that NADP-malate dehydrogenase, about 5 times more active in C_4 pathway plants than Calvin-cycle plants, contributes to malic acid synthesis where the C_4 pathway is operative. Interest was taken in glycerate kinase because of its possible involvement in carboxyl transfer from the C_4 acids to 3-PGA. It was found to be less active in the C_4 pathway species than those of the Calvin cycle, and no proof of a role in carboxyl transfer was presented. It is also possible that this enzyme participates in a photosynthetic bypass cycle described by Tolbert (1443), in which glycolate derived from sugar phosphates appears to be converted to 3-PGA.

Galmiche (555) has questioned the carboxyl movement from malate to 3-PGA in maize on the basis that the C-2 and C-3 atoms of 3-PGA incorporate radioactivity much more rapidly than the C-2 and C-3 atoms of malate. Hatch *et al.* (695) observed this phenomenon in sugarcane. As mentioned earlier relative to Fig. 3-2, the two-cycle scheme proposed by Hatch and Slack (693) envisages some of the 3-PGA being converted to the CO_2 acceptor phosphopyruvic acid. This movement could be necessary to replace carbon lost by side reactions such as amino acid synthesis. Considering the needs of an intact physiological system, the apparent imbalance becomes logical and can be accountable to accelerated labeling of 3-PGA precursors such as ribulose diphosphate.

The most probable acceptor of the C-4 carboxyl group from the dicarboxylic acids appears to be ribulose diphosphate. Labeling data for 3-PGA and hexose phosphates were found to be consistent with an involvement of ribulose diphosphate in the pathway of carbon flow (693, 809). Slack and Hatch (1342) confirmed that C_4 pathway plants contain phosphoribulokinase, the enzyme needed to convert ribulose 5-phosphate to ribulose 1,5-diphosphate. In their assay of phosphoribulokinase, Slack and Hatch (1342) included excess amounts of phosphoribose isomerase, an enzyme which converts ribose 5-phosphate to ribulose 5-phosphate, and which they prepared from the Calvin-cycle plant silverbeet. Kumar and Alexander (861) found this enzyme in sugarcane leaves. In addition, a ribose 5-phosphatase capable of hydrolyzing the pentose monophosphate to free ribose has been isolated from sugarcane leaves (862).

Evidence of a major flow of pentose phosphate cycle intermediates was found by Alexander and Montalvo-Zapata (45) working with sugarcane leaves in which photo-

[5]Another type of pulse-chase experiment was also employed in efforts to identify the acceptor of the C-4 carboxyl group. Leaves exposed to $^{14}CO_2$ were transferred to a CO_2-free atmosphere rather than normal air. This procedure was designed to deplete the pool of 4-carbon dicarboxylic acids and thereby cause the carboxyl acceptor to accumulate.

synthesis had been terminated by the bipyridylium herbicide Paraquat. When chromatographed, aqueous extracts of treated leaves showed detectable accumulations of a sugar tentatively identified as ribose (*cf.* Chapter 13, pp. 509–512). Its identity was later substantiated by gas–liquid chromatography[6]. Diquat, a related bipyridylium compound, also causes this sugar to accumulate (47). Alexander and Montalvo-Zapata theorized that the herbicides or their photoreduced free radicals irreversibly inactivated phosphoribose isomerase, allowing ribose 5-phosphate to accumulate, which in turn was hydrolyzed by ribose 5-phosphatase. This view was substantiated by the finding of phosphoribose isomerase (861) and ribose 5-phosphatase (862), and the demonstrated essentiality of light for Paraquat action (51).

An attractive aspect of ribulose diphosphate serving as the carboxyl acceptor is that all subsequent reductive and regenerative reactions of CO_2 assimilation, along with their requisite enzymology, might then conform to the Calvin cycle. It should be stressed, however, that in the C_4 pathway ribulose diphosphate would not act as the main recipient of atmospheric CO_2 as it does in Calvin-cycle plants, but rather it would act in a carboxyl-transferring sequence subsequent to the reception of CO_2 by phosphopyruvate.

Much of the difficulty in establishing the carboxyl movement to 3-PGA was ultimately laid to the enzyme RuDP-carboxylase. Present in both C_4 pathway and Calvin-cycle plants, but seldom found in very high concentrations, it may have a peculiar configuration relative to the chloroplast structure which defies adequate extraction by methods used to date. Evidence of the enzyme's localization in only one of two chloroplast types has mounted in recent years.

E. *Reactions incidental to the C_4 pathway*

The radiotracer pulse-chase experiments reported by Johnson and Hatch (809) in 1969 underscore a direct and rapid movement of carbon along the C_4-dicarboxylic acid pathway. Most of the relevant ^{14}C work published since 1965 implies the same. Once the initial misgivings of Kortschak and his co-workers were dispelled by their mounting evidence, no subsequent report cast serious doubt on the primary thesis of carbon flow, that is, from oxaloacetate or malic acid to 3-PGA to hexose phosphates to sucrose or glucan. Johnson and Hatch confirmed that, in essence, the lone route of fixed CO_2 to 3-PGA is via the dicarboxylic acids. Labeling patterns for dihydroxyacetone phosphate, fructose 1,6-diphosphate, and pentose mono- and diphosphates strongly suggest that their functions as CO_2-assimilation intermediates in C_4 plants closely parallels their intermediary roles in Calvin-cycle plants.

However, aside from the main flow of carbon, Johnson and Hatch (809) also found evidence of amino acids forming as secondary or "side" products. Alanine, glutamate,

---

[6]Unpublished.

glycine and serine were identified as recipients of ^{14}C. Apparently the amino acid arginine, currently gaining significance in sugarcane biochemistry through the work of Maretzki and his co-workers in Hawaii (977, 975, 976), has not been detected in photosynthesis studies with ^{14}C.

As mentioned previously, serine was found to increase at the expense of 3-PGA during pulse-chase experiments designed to identify the carboxyl transfer intermediates. The observation that 50 percent of the serine label at 60 seconds was detected in the C-1 atom was interpreted as inconsistent with its formation via glycolate reactions. The fact that glycine incorporated much more radioactivity during a CO_2-free air treatment than with normal air was not explained, but it does suggest a fluent amino acid-forming potential sensitive to the plant's external atmosphere. In 1964 Alexander (11) reported transaminase activity in cane leaf extracts that converted L-aspartic acid to oxaloacetic acid in the presence of excess α-ketoglutarate. The responsible enzyme was probably the aspartate aminotransferase measured by Slack and Hatch (1342), whose photosynthesis role appears to involve an interconversion of dicarboxylic acids. When one considers the broad range of nitrogen metabolism activity and photosynthetic activity which occurs in sugarcane during a 12-month crop cycle, plus the rather close correlation of decreasing photosynthesis to decreasing foliar nitrogen with age (674), it seems probable that some important physiological data will eventually appear relative to photosynthetic amino acid production.

F. *Evidence for light regulation of C_4 pathway enzymes*

In 1968 Hatch *et al.* (698) reported effects of variable light treatments on four enzymes considered specifically operative in the C_4 pathway: Pyruvate, P_i dikinase, PEP-carboxylase, adenylate kinase, and alkaline pyrophosphatase. Glyceraldehyde 3-phosphate dehydrogenase was also measured. Maize and *Amaranthus* plants were grown at high or low light intensities (approximately 130 000 lux and 8600 lux, respectively) for 7 weeks. Plants from each treatment were transferred to the other treatment and enzyme content was measured before and after transfer.

An interesting result of this work was the failure of RuDP-carboxylase to change appreciably in response to the light variables (Table 3-3). Assuming that light is but one of several factors able to perform essential regulation, one would not anticipate light effects on an enzyme operative in numerous plant species ranging from the equator to far northern and southern latitudes. On the other hand, Hatch *et al.* could find no evidence that RuDP-carboxylase made a greater contribution toward CO_2 assimilation in plants adapted to low light. Pyruvate, P_i dikinase was rapidly inactivated when plants of both species were transferred from high to low light intensities. The enzyme regained most or all of its activity upon reillumination.

Light effects upon photosynthetic enzyme level or activity were reflected in the net CO_2 assimilation rates of attached leaves (698). In these experiments differential

TABLE 3-3

EFFECT OF LIGHT INTENSITY AND CHANGES OF LIGHT INTENSITY ON THE ACTIVITY OF PHOTOSYNTHETIC ENZYMES

Maize and *Amaranthus* plants were grown with a 12-hour light period at either "high" light intensity (sunlight, approximately 130 000 lux) or "low" light intensity (8600 lux) for 7 weeks. "High" and "low" controls were retained in their original light regime throughout the 6-day period. Fully-expanded leaves were sampled at approximately 11:00 a.m.
[After Hatch *et al.* (698).] Reproduced by permission of *Phytochemistry*, Pergamon Press, Ltd., Oxford.

Light regime	Enzyme activity (μmoles/min/mg chlorophyll) at 0, 3 and 6 days																	
	Pyruvate, P_i dikinase			Phosphopyruvate carboxylase			Ribulose diphosphate carboxylase			Glycer-aldehyde-3-*P* dehydrogenase			Adenylate kinase			Pyrophosphatase		
	0	3	6	0	3	6	0	3	6	0	3	6	0	3	6	0	3	6
	Amaranthus																	
High	3.6	3.1	3.5	17.0	15.0	14.5	1.3	1.1	1.3	23	19	18	70	67	54	52	49	51
Low	0.4	0.42	0.4	1.4	1.4	1.4	1.1	1.4	1.4	10	10	8	26	30	24	21	27	25
High to low	3.6	1.64	0.6	17.0	8.8	4.8	1.3	1.4	1.4	23	14	16	70	49	21	52	46	36
Low to high	0.4	1.5	2.0	1.4	11.5	14.6	1.1	1.6	1.3	10	16	12	26	49	50	21	38	40
	Maize																	
High	2.8	2.9	3.0	20	19	18	0.8	1.1	0.7	25	23	21	53	54	64	46	46	52
Low	0.52	0.57	0.46	4.7	4.0	3.8	1.1	1.3	0.9	13	11	12	30	30	27	28	33	29
High to low	2.8	1.08	0.88	20	8.4	5.9	0.8	1.0	0.9	25	12	13	53	34	35	46	34	41
Low to high	0.52	–	3.2	4.7	–	14.9	1.1	–	1.0	13	–	16	30	–	49	28	–	57

species responses were also evident (Fig. 3-3). Maize plants transferred from a high-light regime to a low-light regime lost more than half of their prior photosynthesis rate while much less pronounced effects were obtained with *Amaranthus.* Moreover, in the low-light regime the optimal light intensity for CO_2 fixation was about half of that required for control plants retained at the higher light intensity.

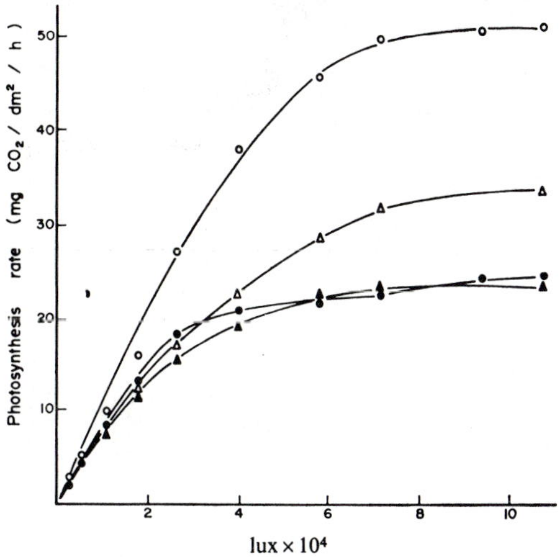

Fig. 3-3. Effect of lowered light intensity on the maximum photosynthesis rates and light-saturation properties of maize and *Amaranthus.* (○ and ●) maize, at high light and transferred to low light; (△ and ▲) *Amaranthus*, at high light and transferred to low light. [After Hatch *et al.* (698).] Reproduced by permission of *Phytochemistry*, Pergamon Press, Ltd., Oxford.

In contrast to RuDP-carboxylase, the enzymes glyceraldehyde 3-phosphate dehydrogenase, pyrophosphatase, and adenylate kinase approximately doubled their content at high light intensity (Table 3-3). For pyruvate, P_i dikinase and PEP-carboxylase the high light treatment produced still greater increases in the order of 5- to 12-fold. All enzymes except RuDP-carboxylase shifted to levels characteristic of the new light regime within 6 days of plant transfer. The most pronounced changes occurred with pyruvate, P_i dikinase and PEP-carboxylase, enzymes operative specifically in the CO_2-fixation phase of the C_4 pathway, regardless of whether plants were moved from low to high or high to low light intensities. Hatch *et al.* (698) interpreted these findings as indicative of enzyme adjustment to support the maximum rate permissible by the available solar energy. None of the light-intensity variables caused appreciable changes in the pathway of carbon flow as evidenced by ^{14}C measurements. Liberally interpreted this goes a long way in explaining the capacity of sugarcane and other tropical grasses to conduct photosynthesis at rates several times greater than many other plant species.

From the same series of experiments Hatch *et al.* (969) interpreted the photosynthetic behavior of leaves adapted to low light in terms of a changed balance between the energy-conversion and CO_2-assimilation phases. Since their results indicated that the potential rate of the light-dependent phase remains essentially constant, they concluded that changes in maximum CO_2-fixing capability and light-saturation characteristics are explained wholly by lowered potential of the CO_2-fixation phase. In support of this thesis the authors cited the work of Hesketh and Moss (721) whose light-saturation curves for Calvin-cycle plants closely resembled their own data for plants adapted to low light.

The light control mechanism discussed above is considered operative over prolonged periods of at least several days. Another light control apparatus appears to operate in C_4 pathway plants over shorter periods in the range of a few minutes to several hours. Slack (1343) has shown that pyruvate, P_i dikinase in *Amaranthus* is extremely sensitive to light, being inactivated in darkness and recovering activity within about 15 minutes after reillumination. According to Hatch *et al.* (698) unpublished evidence by their group shows that pyruvate, P_i dikinase and PEP-carboxylase are both inhibited by photosynthesis products, a finding possibly related to Hartt's observation (666) that leaf sucrose accumulations inhibit photosynthesis in sugarcane. Invertase, although not ordinarily considered a photosynthetic enzyme, experiences up to 7-fold activity variations on a diurnal basis (1340, 54). Alexander and Montalvo-Zapata (51) observed cane invertase inactivation by prolonged darkness (73 hours), followed by comparatively rapid recovery beginning within 6 hours after reillumination.

In 1969 Slack (1345) reported enzyme-localization studies of RuDP-carboxylase, phosphoribulokinase, pyruvate, P_i dikinase and adenylate kinase in the C_4 pathway plant *Amaranthus palmeri*. Mesophyll and parenchyma-sheath chloroplasts were isolated by non-aqueous density fractionation. Results indicated that RuDP-carboxylase and phosphoribulokinase are localized primarily in parenchyma-sheath chloroplasts. The C_4 pathway enzymes pyruvate, P_i dikinase and adenylate kinase appeared to be concentrated in the mesophyll chloroplasts.

4. CHARACTERISTIC FEATURES OF C_4 PATHWAY PLANTS

We have seen that workers distinguishing the C_4 pathway of CO_2 assimilation from that of the Calvin cycle have relied heavily on characteristic enzymology and ^{14}C-labeling patterns. It is now apparent that the C_4 pathway plants have certain other distinctive features, including higher maximum photosynthesis rates coupled with a different light response curve (808, 721, 723), a lower CO_2 compensation point (448), a different response to low oxgen tensions (446), and a unique leaf anatomy (808, 1179) relative to plants in which the Calvin cycle is secure.

Downton and Treguna (448), using the low CO_2 compensation point as an indicator of C_4 pathway plants, found that these have an unusually well developed parenchyma bundle sheath with a characteristic high chloroplast concentration by comparison with species having a high CO_2 compensation point. With some practice the two groups can be distinguished by examining the leaf against a light background. Leaves from high compensation point plants have a uniform green color, except around the vascular bundles which appear translucent, whereas C_4 pathway plants show a dark green network. The close contiguity of chloroplasts and conducting tissue is believed to increase the efficiency of photosynthate transport (448), thereby reducing the likelihood of product repression. Although plant morphological features in themselves can hardly account for the more rapid photosynthesis rates of C_4 pathway plants, it does seem probable that these go hand in hand with the strictly biochemical aspects needed to make the C_4 pathway operate.

5. PHOTOSYNTHESIS AND PHOTORESPIRATION

A distinctive feature of C_4 pathway plants is their seeming failure to perform photorespiration, that is, they do not increase respiration in light as evidenced by increased CO_2 liberation and oxygen consumption (782). When Calvin-cycle plants are placed in an oxygen-free atmosphere, photorespiration cannot take place, and the photosynthesis rates (measured by CO_2 uptake) appear to increase by as much as 50 percent. Hence, photorespiration has been aptly described by Rabinowitch (1203) as "...a nightmare oppressing all who are concerned with the exact measurement of photosynthesis". The fact that similar conditions have not appeared to increase the already high CO_2 uptake by sugarcane and other C_4 pathway plants has been the object of much speculation. This point will probably remain obscure until the mechanism of photorespiration has been thoroughly examined.

Some workers believe that respiration rates are essentially constant in both light and darkness, and this may be the case in some plant species (599). However, in their recent review of photorespiration, Jackson and Volk (782) conclude: "... it is quite clear that substantial changes in respiratory processes occur upon illumination, and that under certain conditions the light respiratory rate may be a significant fraction of the photosynthetic rate". One hypothesis holds that dark respiration is inhibited by light and in most plants a second respiratory mechanism becomes operative (737, 1131, 486). The second mechanism appears to give respiration rates greater than those of the dark process (422, 424). This increase has important bearing on the controversy over quantum yield of photosynthetic energy conversion (599), and on the measurement of CO_2 transport resistances within CO_2-assimilating cells (881, 882).

Another way of distinguishing photorespiration variances among plants is by their differing CO_2 compensation points. The latter term has reference to the plants' ability to lower CO_2 concentration in a closed chamber. Plants of the C_4 pathway can lower CO_2 concentration to about 5.0 ppm (854), whereas Calvin-cycle plants reach the CO_2 compensation point at about 50 ppm. Lake (881) developed mathematically the gas exchange of leaves in which the individual resistances between ambient CO_2 and the chloroplasts are treated in algebraic terms. He found that, under conditions of light-saturated photosynthesis, most of the dicotyledonous plants examined produced respiratory CO_2 at rates two or more times greater than in the dark. The calculated CO_2 compensation point value for *S. officinarum* was about one-tenth of that for species of *Dactylis, Nicotiana, Pelargonium*, and *Lypersicon* (881).

Several proposals have been forwarded to account for the apparent lack of photorespiration in sugarcane and other C_4 pathway plants. El Sharkawy and Hesketh (486) tended a morphological view holding that in tropical grasses most of the respiratory CO_2 could be trapped by chloroplasts before it escapes to the atmosphere. Treguna (1451) attributed the lack of photorespiration in maize to insufficient flavin mononucleotide (FMN) after he had increased the CO_2 compensation point by foliar treatments with FMN. Downton and Treguna (448) suggest that the substrate of CO_2 production, rather than being decarboxylated, is utilized in photosynthesis by C_4 species.

Another interpretation was given by Kortschak (854) which takes into account the more efficient photosynthetic reactions of C_4 plants. He feels that photosynthetically-produced pyruvate may be partially diverted into the respiratory pathway of Calvin-cycle plants, whereas in plants using the C_4 pathway there is more efficient movement of carbon toward carbohydrate. This interpretation is supported by the fact that the carboxylation of phosphopyruvate (Eqn. 2) is considerably more efficient than the carboxylation of ribulose diphosphate. On the other hand, an opposing argument holds that the more efficient PEP-carboxylase reaction might simply remove the internal respiratory CO_2 before it can reach the external atmosphere.

An accepted view at present favors an active photorespiration mechanism in C_4 plants, but one operating at relatively low rates (782). Particularly in sugarcane and maize, these rates are sufficiently low to permit the refixation of liberated CO_2 by PEP-carboxylase. Jackson and Volk (782) note the difficulty in measuring photorespiration in C_4 or "low compensation" species which deplete ambient CO_2 almost to zero and perform highly efficient photosynthesis. Nonetheless, photorespiratory enzymes (synonymous with those of the glycolate pathway), along with their sites of glycolate oxidation (peroxisomes) appear to exist in C_4 species. Low enzyme levels and sparcity of peroxisomes, as evidenced by electron micrographs, may help explain the low rates of photorespiration in C_4 pathway plants.

Whittingham (1569) has suggested differing enzyme potentials which may account for photorespiratory differences noted between tobacco and maize or sugarcane. Noting the work of Goldsworthy (596) in which similar affinities for CO_2 were demonstrated, that is, each of the three species lowered CO_2 close to zero in an oxygen-free atmosphere, he described experiments in which tobacco and maize were exposed to an atmosphere containing 1 percent $^{12}CO_2$ and 99 percent O_2. Under these conditions, stimulatory for a potential photorespiration apparatus, tobacco produced CO_2 at rates several times greater than those of maize, even though both species experienced reduced photosynthesis. Whittingham also observed that feeding either ^{14}C or labeled glycolate to tobacco leaves in CO_2-free air led to major CO_2 increases, whereas maize produced very little. He suggested that these discrepancies between the C_4 species and tobacco relate to different activity potentials of the two carboxylating enzymes (PEP-carboxylase and RuDP-carboxylase) rather than to the total absence of a system from either group of plants.

6. EVIDENCE OF CALVIN-CYCLE CO_2 FIXATION IN SUGARCANE STALKS

Recent studies by Kortschak and Nickell (856) have shown active CO_2 fixation of the Calvin type in chlorophyll-bearing stalk parenchyma tissue. The experiments were performed with cultured tissue isolates grown on an artificial medium. Such isolates are initially white but assume a green appearance upon development of chloroplasts during the tissue-culture phase. Two important implications of this work are immediately apparent: (a) A photosynthetically active tissue is available for close examination under *in vitro* conditions. In a large measure this fulfills conditions thus far unattained or only partially attained with isolated chloroplasts (88, 727). (b) Existence of a full complement of Calvin-cycle CO_2 fixation enzymes, as shown by Slack *et al.* (1344) in maize parenchyma-sheath chloroplasts, is verified in sugarcane parenchyma tissue.

Further to this, the possibility of a variant CO_2 assimilation system distinct from that normally present in stalk chloroplasts is open for speculation. As discussed in Chapter 16 (*cf.* pp. 621–623; 633–638), an enormous variability exists in the cytological and "ploidy" characteristics of cultured sugarcane cells. This may also extent to the biochemical level. Tacit support for this thesis may be found in a slight deviation noted by Kortschak and Nickell (856) from the normal Calvin-cycle flow of carbon. They found that ^{14}C appeared early in glucose, but not in fructose, as distinct from both the C_4 and Calvin-cycle pathways which quickly place carbon in fructose.

7. CARBON FLOW TO 3-PHOSPHOGLYCERIC ACID: COOPERATION OF MESOPHYLL AND PARENCHYMA-SHEATH CHLOROPLASTS

By 1968 the essential outlines of the C_4-dicarboxylic acid pathway were established. However, a significant question still remained incident to the enzymes required for moving ^{14}C from dicarboxylic acids to 3-PGA at the high rates observed in $^{14}CO_2$ experiments. As noted earlier, Hatch and Slack (693) postulated that ^{14}C may pass into 3-PGA by two distinct routes; however, they favored a transcarboxylase reaction largely because the alternative step, *i.e.*, via a RuDP-carboxylase reaction, could not be accomplished at suitable rates by the small quantities of RuDP-carboxylase found in

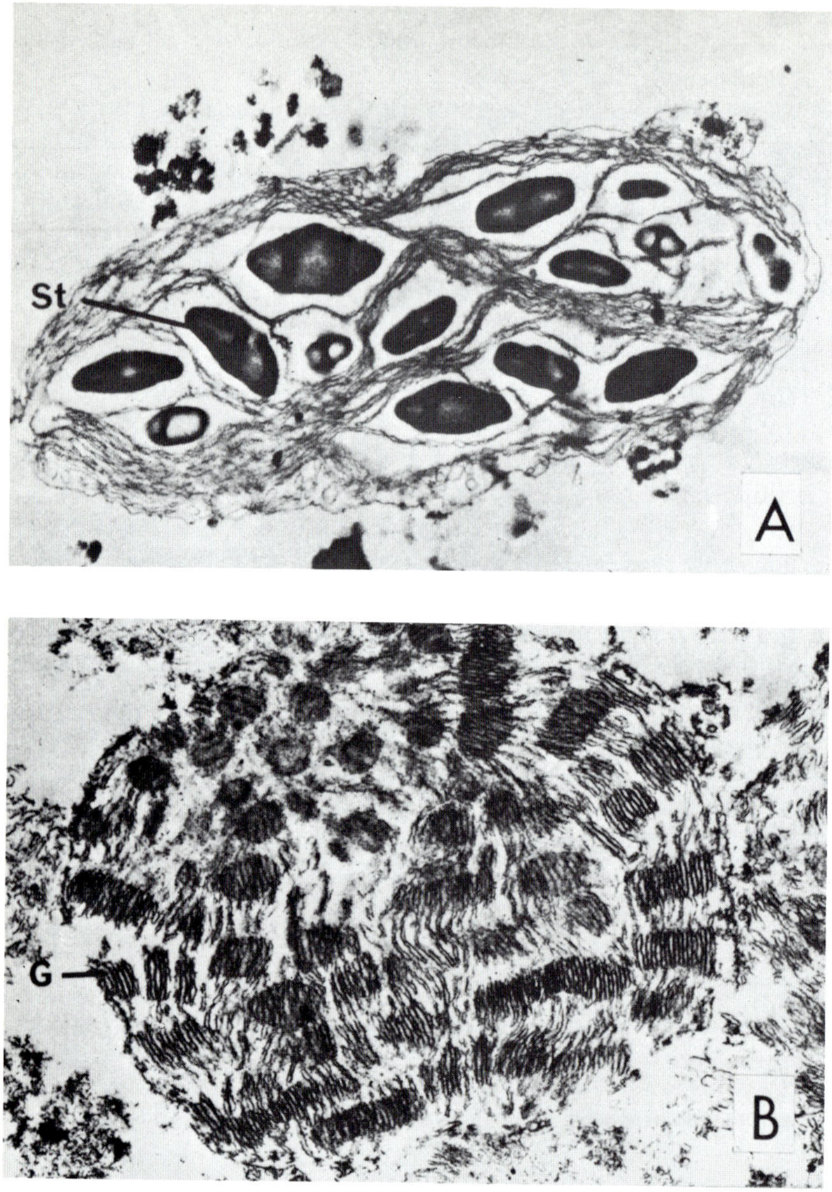

Fig. 3-4. Electron micrographs of two chloroplast types obtained from maize leaves by density fractionation in non-aqueous media. (A) Grana-free, starch-containing chloroplasts of the parenchyma sheath type having a density greater than 1.36. (B) Grana-containing, starch-free chloroplasts of the mesophyll type having a density less than 1.30. St = starch grains; G = grana. [After Slack *et al.* (1344).] Reproduced by permission of the *Biochemical Journal.*

leaf preparations. This was a difficult choice because the transcarboxylase step with its supporting enzymes was unknown. During the years immediately following the transcarboxylation concept was all but abandoned.

The question was resolved in part by examining two concepts: (a) An apparent need for improved extraction methods for RuDP-carboxylase, whose measured work potential has seldom been adequate even in Calvin-cycle plants when conventional enzyme-isolation methods are employed. (b) Two morphologically-distinct types of chloroplasts are functional in two cell types of C_4 pathway plants.

A. *Operation of two chloroplast types*

In 1969 Slack *et al.* (1344) reported extensive findings on mesophyll and parenchyma-sheath chloroplasts from maize which suggest that the two chloroplast types have cooperative roles in maintaining carbon flow through the C_4-dicarboxylic acid pathway. Employing density-fractionation techniques in non-aqueous media, the mesophyll and parenchyma-sheath chloroplasts were sufficiently separated so that their distinguishing structures and grana constituents could be examined (Fig. 3-4). Moreover, the evaluation of enzyme complements characteristic of each chloroplast type was rendered possible. Although some contamination of one chloroplast group by the other was unavoidable, the authors concluded that mesophyll chloroplasts contain a complete complement of photosynthetic enzymes, *i.e.*, pyruvate, P_i dikinase, NADP-specific malate dehydrogenase, glycerate kinase, and nitrite reductase. Most of the adenylate kinase and pyrophosphatase were also localized in the mesophyll chloroplasts. On the other hand, the enzymes RuDP-carboxylase, ribose phosphate isomerase, phosphoribulokinase, fructose diphosphate aldolase, alkaline fructose diphosphatase, and NADP-specific "malic" enzyme appeared to be localized entirely in the parenchyma-sheath chloroplasts. Distributed more or less equally between the two chloroplasts groups were phosphoglycerate kinase and NADP-specific glyceraldehyde phosphate dehydrogenase.

Subsequent experiments in which $^{14}CO_2$ was supplied to illuminated leaves for 25 seconds showed that labeled malate, aspartate, and 3-PGA appeared predominately in the enzymatically-complete chloroplasts, *i.e.*, the mesophyll type. Conversely, the parenchyma-sheath chloroplasts contained most of the labeled fructose phosphates and ribulose phosphates. Also noted was a fractionation pattern for dihydroxyacetone phosphate which was intermediate between those of the C_4-dicarboxylic acids and sugar phosphates. On the basis of this evidence it seemed likely that the two chloroplast groups performed complementary roles in the normally-functioning mechanism of CO_2 assimilation. Accordingly, appropriate routes for the transfer of carbon from the C_4 acids to sugars were proposed (Fig. 3-5).

With reference to the scheme shown in Fig. 3-5, Slack (1346) postulates that about half of the 3-PGA formed in the parenchyma-sheath chloroplasts is transferred to

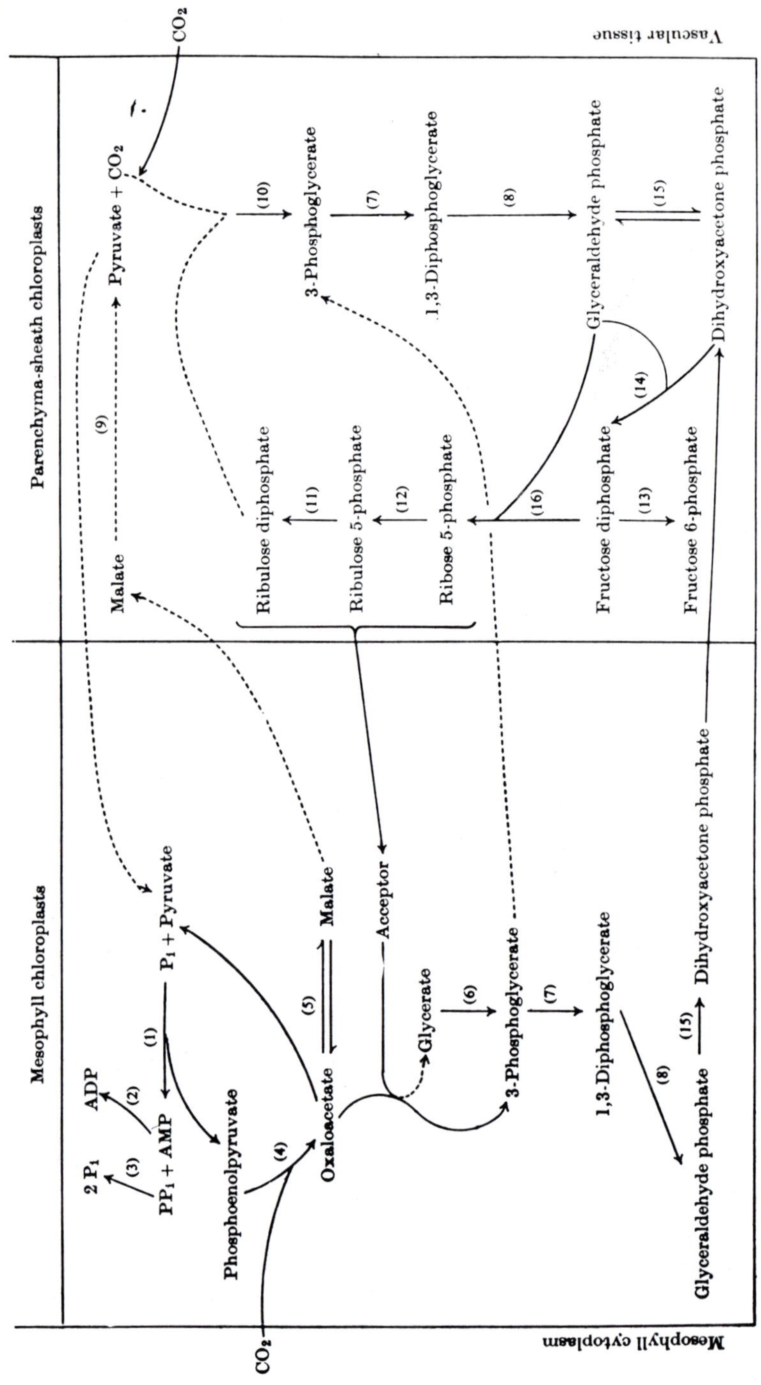
Mesophyll chloroplasts
Parenchyma-sheath chloroplasts
Vascular tissue
Mesophyll cytoplasm
CO2
2 P1
ADP
PP1 + AMP
P1 + Pyruvate
Phosphoenolpyruvate
Oxaloacetate
Malate
Acceptor
Glycerate
3-Phosphoglycerate
1,3-Diphosphoglycerate
Glyceraldehyde phosphate
Dihydroxyacetone phosphate
Malate
Pyruvate + CO2
Ribulose diphosphate
Ribulose 5-phosphate
Ribose 5-phosphate
Fructose diphosphate
Fructose 6-phosphate
(1)
(2)
(3)
(4)
(5)
(6)
(7)
(8)
(9)
(10)
(11)
(12)
(13)
(14)
(15)
(16)

mesophyll chloroplasts and therein elaborated to triose phosphate. The remaining half of the 3-PGA is reduced in the parenchyma-sheath chloroplasts. This hypothesis is based on the presence of 3-PGA kinase and glyceraldehyde phosphate dehydrogenase in both chloroplast types. Slack further suggests that the flow of malate from mesophyll to parenchyma-sheath cells provides for the transfer of one mole equivalent of CO_2 and one of NADPH. Moreover, the possibility that parenchyma-sheath chloroplasts are incapable of photoreducing $NADP^+$ appears to have been considered by Slack as well as by other workers. In this context the reduction of half of the 3-PGA in the mesophyll chloroplasts becomes a necessity.

An important aspect of the biochemical data was their implication that RuDP-carboxylase must be localized in the parenchyma-sheath chloroplasts. Both the CO_2 receptor sugars and sugars expected to appear subsequent to 3-PGA were found predominantly in this group rather than in mesophyll chloroplasts. This concept was strengthened by the work of Bjorkman and Gauhl (188) who found considerably more RuDP-carboxylase in tropical grasses than was earlier believed. Slack and his colleagues confirmed this finding in their own laboratory. Relative to the elusive carboxylase, Slack wrote: "The enzyme is entirely localized in chloroplasts of the parenchyma sheath and these cells are extremely difficult to break, hence a normal type of leaf homogenization results in only a partial breakage of these cells" (1346).

Shortly after Slack and his co-workers (1344) published on the cooperative functions of mesophyll and parenchyma-sheath chloroplasts, similar conclusions were drawn by Berry *et al.* (172) working with *Zea mays* and *Gomphrena globosa.* These authors used a different technical approach than that of Slack *et al.* and they placed somewhat more emphasis on RuDP-carboxylase in the carboxyl-transfer step. Their model depicts CO_2 generation via oxidative decarboxylation of malic acid by malic enzyme, the CO_2 then being "refixed" by RuDP-carboxylase to form 3-PGA. Berry *et al.* propose that CO_2 fixation (by β-carboxylation) is performed in mesophyll cells, and that carboxyl-transfer plus subsequent steps leading to starch occur in bundle-sheath cells (equivalent to sheath-parenchyma cells of sugarcane).

Both groups of authors propose that physical structures may aid the rapid exchange of photosynthetic intermediates between the mesophyll and parenchyma-sheath chloroplasts. Berry *et al.* (172) suggest that plasmodesmata facilitate transport of C_4

Fig. 3-5. Schematic representation of the C_4-dicarboxylic acid pathway illustrating the possible operation of two chloroplast types in a cooperative movement of carbon. Broken lines signify possible alternate routes of carbon flow. Numbers identify the enzyme that catalyzes each specific reaction: (1) Pyruvate, P_i dikinase; (2) adenylate kinase; (3) pyrophosphatase; (4) phosphopyruvate carboxylase; (5) NADP-specific malate dehydrogenase; (6) glycerate kinase; (7) phosphoglycerate kinase; (8) NADP-specific glyceraldehyde phosphate dehydrogenase; (9) NADP-specific malic enzyme; (10) ribulose diphosphate carboxylase; (11) phosphoribulokinase; (12) ribose phosphate isomerase; (13) alkaline fructose diphosphatase; (14) fructose diphosphate aldolase; (15) triose phosphate isomerase; (16) reactions similar to those functional in the Calvin cycle. [After Slack *et al.* (1344).] Reproduced by permission of the *Biochemical Journal.*

acids from the mesophyll site of fixation. Slack and his co-workers (1344), noting the work of Rosado-Alberio *et al.* (1254) and others who described a conductive peripheral reticulum in maize mesophyll chloroplasts, proposed that the reticulum represents the "terminals of tubules connecting the two types of chloroplast". This reticulum is apparently a phenomenon of C_4 species chloroplasts.

B. *Differential enzyme retention by disrupted leaf tissue*

The task of improving methodology for photosynthetic enzyme preparation has been approached by Tate and Lyle scientists in England (89). Studies both with enzymes and isolated chloroplasts were seriously restricted by release of phenolic compounds from disrupted leaf tissue. Efforts to counter phenolic interference included: (a) Studies of phenol synthesis; (b) use of chemicals to block the endogenous phenol activity; and (c) reversal of photosynthesis inhibition.

While investigating alternate methods for measuring CO_2 assimilation, the release of foliar enzymes by differential grinding was closely examined (89). A progressive release of PEP-carboxylase[7] was correlated with the disruption of specific tissues. Moreover, whereas most of the chlorophyll was recovered in the mesophyll (or grana-containing) chloroplasts, a predominance of carboxylase activity was released along with total protein (Fig. 3-6). This could be interpreted as evidence against the localization in parenchyma-sheath chloroplasts of C_4 pathway carboxylation reactions. Among the enzymes obtained differentially in progressive stages of grinding was the

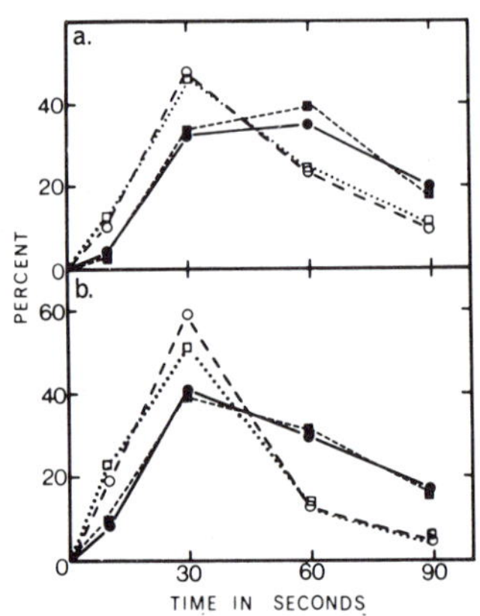

Fig. 3-6. Release of photosynthetic constituents of sugarcane leaves during progressive stages of grinding. (a) Chlorophyll (○, ●) and photosynthetic carbon reduction cycle activity (□, ■). (b) Protein (□, ■) and phosphoenolpyruvate carboxylase (○, ●). Open symbols, experiments performed with thioglycolate; closed symbols, without thioglycolate. [After Anon. (89).] Reproduced by permission of *Tate and Lyle, Ltd.*, London.

---

[7]Indicated in Fig. 3-5 as phosphopyruvate carboxylase.

malic enzyme which appeared after most other CO_2 "shuttle" enzymes had been released. This lends support to the view that low levels of the malic enzyme in conventional preparations may be due to strong retention by leaf cells.

8. CO_2 ASSIMILATION BY ISOLATED SUGARCANE CHLOROPLASTS

A. *Isolation of viable chloroplasts and enzyme localization*

Tate and Lyle scientists recently accomplished CO_2 assimilation with chloroplast preparations from sugarcane leaves (88, 135, 89). The CO_2 fixation was dependent upon light and phosphoenolpyruvate (PEP). The chloroplasts themselves were isolated in the presence of thioglycolate and polyethylene glycol. Malic acid was the main product. Aspartate and glutamate were also obtained in trace amounts. The results with isolated chloroplasts were consistent with the physiological pathway developed by Slack *et al.* (1344). Presumably, phosphoenolpyruvate is carboxylated at the usual chloroplast site through the mediation of PEP-carboxylase. Thereafter, a conversion of oxaloacetate to malate is visualized via direct photoreduction of reduced ferredoxin (135). It is also suggested that malate might then be decarboxylated by malic enzyme to produce pyruvate and CO_2. The Tate and Lyle group depict the latter CO_2 being liberated at the site of the RuDP-carboxylase reaction, but they do not specify a chloroplast type for the location of this step.

Enzyme localization studies with C_4 pathway and Calvin-cycle plants showed a consistency in the loci of individual enzymes at the subcellular level (88). Pyrophosphatase and PEP-carboxylase were obtained from chloroplasts, and NAD-dependent malate dehydrogenase was found in mitochondria. Peroxidase and polyphenol oxidase were believed to be situated in the cytoplasm. Tropical grasses (sugarcane, maize, and sorghum) contained generally higher levels of PEP-carboxylase, NAD-dependent malate dehydrogenase, and malic enzyme than did *Spinaceae* and *Chenopodium album.* The temperate species contained high levels of RuDP-carboxylase. The contents of other enzymes measured were about equal among C_4 and Calvin-cycle species.

Difficulties in isolating active chloroplasts from sugarcane leaves have not been overcome (89). Because of phenolic inhibition and possibly other inherent problems, an alternate method utilizing pea or spinach chloroplasts was adopted in studies of sucrose metabolism control. The suspended chloroplasts contained enzymes needed to assimilate CO_2 and to synthesize sugar, but sucrose was not formed owing to accumulation of early CO_2 fixation intermediates in the external medium. The inhibitory effect was overcome by layering the chloroplasts on filter paper supports. With the volume of external medium thus reduced to a minimum, it was possible to perform CO_2 fixation, accumulate hexose monophosphates, and synthesize sucrose under conditions permitting close examination of factors rate limiting for each process (89).

B. *Chloroplast permeability*

The findings of Slack and his co-workers (1344) relative to the cooperative functions of mesophyll and parenchyma-sheath chloroplasts strongly implied a rapid exchange of photosynthetic intermediates between the two chloroplast types. Physical structures possibly assisting this operation have been described, including plasmodesmata (172) and a conductive peripheral reticulum (1254). Recent studies of chloroplast membranes at the Tate and Lyle Research Centre led to the development of a method for measuring membrane permeability (89). Based upon the ability of ions to move between platinum electrodes, across the chloroplast membranes, it has been possible to distinguish between movement effects of outer and internal membranes. Some evidence suggests that ion flow is confined to specific sites on the membrane, a thesis consistent with the "tubule" suggestion of Slack *et al.* (1344). Structural complexity and ion specificity of chloroplast membranes are also suggested by the ion-flow data (89).

9. ENERGY CONVERSION IN SUGARCANE

Throughout this chapter the term "photosynthesis" is used sparingly; indeed, the various reactions of CO_2 assimilation might be viewed by some as secondary events by comparison with the energy-conversion phase. Unfortunately, the mechanisms by which solar energy is converted to chemical energy in sugarcane have not been examined to any appreciable degree. At the moment there is no reason to believe that this is accomplished differently than in *Chlorella*, spinach, and other Calvin-cycle plants long the objects of energy-conversion studies.

However, in an empirical sense, the cultural management of a modern sugarcane crop has increasingly become a management of energy-conversion processes. In simplest terms, the moisture–nitrogen–growth relationships regulated with an eye toward maximum tonnage and quality involves the most judicious and efficient use of solar energy as it becomes available to the grower in the form of carbohydrate. The early ecological studies by Clements (*cf.* Chapter 11, pp. 422–424) which led ultimately to the primary index, and indirectly to our present crop-logging concepts based on a series of indexes, were focused upon solar energy usage in the forms of heat and light. Consciously or otherwise, the effective utilization of energy-conversion processes remains a foremost characteristic of sugarcane culture from seedling selection to the milling of mature stalks.

A. *Inefficient use of solar energy*

Regardless of the enormous capacity of *Saccharum* species to produce organic matter[8], which in essence is energy "fixed" in fiber and carbohydrate, sugarcane is similar to other plants in that it is not an efficient system for converting kinetic energy to fixed or chemical energy forms, *i.e.*, to carbohydrate or ATP. According to Van Dillewijn (1475, pp. 318–320), early studies published by Komatsu *et al.* (847) in 1933 showed that nearly 99 percent of the solar radiation received by a cane plant in the course of a year is reflected by the leaves or utilized in transpiration. In one study, only about 1 percent of the incident sunlight was used in photosynthesis (Fig. 3-7A). Of this 1 percent only a relatively small portion was used in dry matter production (Fig. 3-7B), the remainder being expended in various growth and life-maintenance processes.

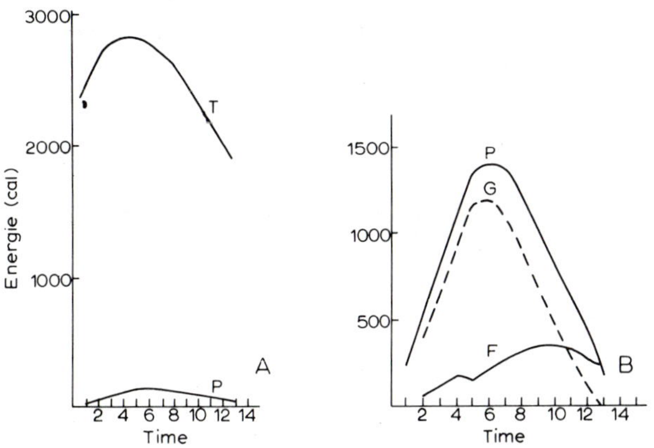

Fig. 3-7. (A) Photosynthetic utilization of solar energy in Taiwan by the sugarcane variety *P.O.J. 2878.* T = total energy received per stalk; P = energy utilized in photosynthesis. Energy in calories is shown on the ordinate, time in number of 3-week periods is shown on the abscissa. (B) Rate of energy accumulation and utilization by a sugarcane stalk. P = rate of energy accumulation in photosynthesis; F = rate of energy utilization in dry matter production; G = rate of energy utilization in growth. [From Van Dillewijn (1475), after Komatsu *et al.* (847).] Reproduced by permission of the *Ronald Press Company*, New York.

It is evident from the energy accumulation and utilization data shown in Fig. 3-7 that increasing amounts of energy were accumulated from photosynthesis during the first 6 months, but most of this energy was utilized in growth processes. During the second 6 months less energy was obtained from photosynthesis, still less energy was used in growth, and more energy was expended in forming dry matter. The same study showed that between 10 and 11 months the descending growth expenditure curve intercepted the dry-matter expenditure curve and from that point onward the amount of energy utilized in dry matter accumulation exceeded that utilized in growth.

[8]Seventy to eighty tons of topped stalks per acre for a 12-month crop is not an uncommon yield under suitable culturai conditions.

Although the data shown in Fig. 3-7 represent only a single variety (*P.O.J. 2878*), two points are well made: (a) that sugarcane "harvests" but a small fraction of the solar energy available, and (b) sugarcane proceeds to make widely-divergent expenditure of this energy during its natural growth and ripening phases.

Solar radiation relationships to photosynthesis were reported recently by Chu (325), also working in Taiwan. Maximum photosynthetic efficiency (4.9 percent) in field-grown cane was found only under low light intensity, with efficiency decreasing as a function of increased light intensity. The leaf-area index was positively correlated with CO_2 assimilation efficiency. Young plants showed greater photosynthetic activity than aged plants, a finding consistent with recent work in Australia (260). In general, a linear relationship was obtained between solar radiation and photosynthesis rate up to 0.4 ly/min. Average compensation points varied between morning and evening by a factor of 0.05 ly/min, with higher values obtained in the morning.

B. *Sugarcane chloroplasts*

Although by 1929 Emerson (487, 488) had established that photosynthesis rate is a "smooth function of the chlorophyll content" (in *Chlorella*), there appears to have been no intensive examination of sugarcane chlorophyll prior to 1967 when chloroplast studies were initiated at the Tate and Lyle Research Centre (81, 88). Martin (984), in 1938, vividly illustrated chloroplast concentrations in the parenchyma cells surrounding vascular bundles in a sugarcane leaf blade. Van Dillewijn (1475, p. 44) mentions the "chlorophyll-bearing bundle sheath" without attaching significance to the chloroplasts therein localized.

In 1968 workers at the Tate and Lyle Research Centre (81) described two types of chloroplasts present in sugarcane leaves: (a) The mesophyll type comprising "thylakoid aggregations" formed into grana stacks, and (b) a non-grana type which is localized in the bundle sheath and contains abundant starch granules. The presence of starch granules in one type but not in the other was used to advantage in chloroplast resolution by means of density-gradient centrifugation. The heavier, starch-bearing chloroplasts are obtained as "pellets" along with cellular debris. By use of 73 percent sucrose the debris can be separated from chloroplasts. This method was used by Slack and his co-workers with the analogous maize chloroplasts, although with somewhat limited success owing to the loss of starch grains during homogenization and to the adsorption of cellular components on the mesophyll-type chloroplasts (1344). These preparations could not perform photophosphorylation. However, some evidence was found that electron transport via ferricyanide is coupled with phosphorylation. In some experiments ferricyanide reduction was enhanced by added ADP and inorganic phosphate. Significant advances were also made in the area of chloroplast membrane structure and permeability (88).

C. *Photosynthesis inhibitors in cane chloroplast preparations*

An initial lack of positive photophosphorylation reactions prompted the Tate and Lyle workers to suggest that cane leaves may contain inhibitors which are released during grinding. This postulate was verified in subsequent studies (88) which revealed inhibitory compounds active against both oxygen-producing and CO_2 fixation systems. Baldry and co-workers (136) have shown that *o*-phenols inhibit both carboxylation and oxygen-evolution reactions at levels in the order of 10^{-5} M. Compounds obtained by high-voltage electrophoresis and showing ultraviolet fluorescence were fractionated and tested for inhibitory action. Characterization experiments showed that the most active inhibitors were chlorogenic and caffeic acids. It was proposed that phenolic compounds liberated from disrupted leaf tissues are converted to quinones through the mediation of phenol oxidase, and that the quinones selectively inhibit photosynthetic enzymes via –SH group reactions. Inhibition was partially reversed by including polyethylene glycol and thioglycolate in the reaction medium, but inhibitor activity has continued to interfere in photosynthesis studies with isolated cane chloroplasts (89).

Baldry *et al.* (137) tested a series of chemical additives for their regulatory effects on phenol oxidase preparations from sugarcane leaves. Inhibitory action was obtained with thioglycolate, β-mercaptoethanol, polyethylene glycol and bovine serum albumin. Parallel measurements of CO_2 assimilation showed a negative response to sulfhydryl compounds at low levels, but in the presence of Mn^{2+} there was an increase in oxygen consumption sufficient to mask photosynthetic oxygen evolution. CO_2 assimilation was increased by sulfhydryl compounds in crude enzyme preparations from cane leaves. No effect was obtained with similarly prepared spinach (Calvin cycle) enzymes. Although phenol oxidase was restricted by high pH, copper chelates, low oxygen tension, and powerful reducing agents, such treatments proved to be impractical with isolated chloroplasts.

D. *Absence of Photosystem II in C_4 species parenchyma-sheath chloroplasts*

Woo *et al.* (1585) were unable to detect an active Hill reaction in parenchyma-sheath chloroplasts of C_4 species of *Zea, Sorghum*, and *Atriplex*. The authors examined photochemical properties, fluorescence spectra, and cytochrome contents of mesophyll and parenchyma-sheath types, both of which showed Photosystem I activity. An elaborate chloroplast isolation method was described which appears to give more precise separation of the two groups than density-fractionation methods based on differential starch contents. In essence, mesophyll chloroplasts were readily released by conventional grinding which left the bulk of parenchyma-sheath cells unbroken, the latter being disrupted for chloroplast extraction by subsequent blending.

Hill reaction activity was closely correlated with the presence of grana. In *Zea* and *Sorghum* species the parenchyma-sheath chloroplasts were devoid of grana and little or no oxygen evolution was recorded. The grana-containing mesophyll chloroplasts of each species gave abundant Hill reaction activity. In *Atriplex*, parenchyma-sheath chloroplasts produced oxygen at rates comparable to the mesophyll chloroplasts. Moreover, chloroplasts inactive in *Zea* and *Sorghum* were enabled to photoreduce $NADP^+$ if supplied with the electron donor ascorbate–2,6-dichlorophenolindophenol. Woo *et al.* therefore concluded that Photosystem II was either absent or inactive in parenchyma-sheath chloroplasts of *Sorghum* and *Zea.*

This conclusion was supported by light-induced absorbance changes with cytochrome *f* in *Sorghum* parenchyma-sheath chloroplasts (Fig. 3-8). Taking reduced cyto-

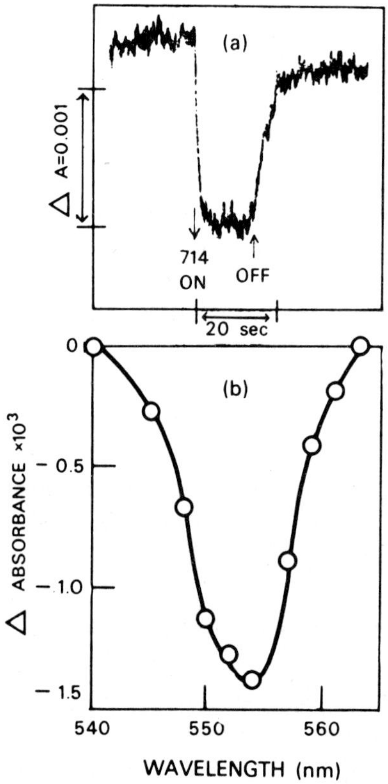

Fig. 3-8. Absorbance changes in bundle-sheath chloroplasts of *Sorghum bicolor.* (a) Induced by 714 nm light of intensity, 6.2×10^3 ergs/cm^2/sec, at 554 nm and 20 °C. (b) Spectrum of absorbance change induced by 714 nm light at 20 °C. [After Woo *et al.* (1585).] Reproduced by permission of *Proceedings of the National Academy of Sciences*, Washington, D.C.

chrome *f* to be localized in Photosystem I, the authors oxidized the cytochrome by illumination with 714 nm light (Fig. 3-8a), thereby obtaining a concurrent rapid decrease in absorbance which returned to a steady-state when the light was turned off. Woo *et al.* worked on the assumption that only light absorbed by Photosystem I could have oxidized the cytochrome. By varying the wavelength of the measuring beam (Fig. 3-8b), a spectrum was obtained for the absorbance change which corresponds with the absorption spectrum of cytochrome *f*. Similar results were obtained with *Sorghum* mesophyll chloroplasts and with both chloroplast types of *Atriplex*.

Woo *et al.* (1585) point out that the absence of grana and an active Photosystem II in parenchyma-sheath chloroplasts of certain C_4 species (including sugarcane) and the localization of Calvin-cycle enzymes in the parenchyma-sheath chloroplasts (1344, 188, 1346) pose questions as to the source of reducing power for 3-PGA reduction. Several workers are cited holding that the reducing power may arise by oxidative decarboxylation of malate donated by mesophyll chloroplasts. This interpretation is essentially in keeping with the cooperative chloroplast roles proposed by Slack and co-workers (1344, 1346) and with the enzymology developed by these authors.

E. *Chlorophyll and enzyme gradients relating to basipetal transport*

Kumar *et al.* (863) observed quantitative correlations between chlorophyll content and the levels of sucrose, amylase, ATPase, and acid phosphatase in detached sugarcane blades (variety *P.R. 980*). A theory was advanced in which the driving force for basipetal sucrose transport originates largely in the upper portions of the blade and is reflected in the higher ATPase levels in this region. Conversely, the foliar amylase levels which increased toward the leaf base were thought to favor sugar movement by hydrolyzing diurnal accumulations of polysaccharide.

Evidence was also found of variable chlorophyll distribution as a function of leaf rank, time of day, and position within the blade. In addition to finding higher chlorophyll content toward the blade apex, leaf $^+2$ was shown to contain more chlorophyll than younger or older leaves, and somewhat less chlorophyll was found at 8:00 a.m. than at 6:00 a.m. or at 1:00 p.m. Since ATPase activity is presumably an indicator of the photophosphorylation potential in cane chloroplasts, the formation of ATP along a gradient inversely related to the leaf sucrose gradient lends tacit support to a concept of photosynthetic ATP participation in sucrose movement.

Chapter 4

Rate of Photosynthesis

1. INTRODUCTION

Optimum conditions for photosynthesis are difficult to define among plant species. They are equally difficult to define among individual plants within a species having different cultural histories and exposed to distinct ecological variables. With reference to sugarcane, Kortschak (854) wrote in 1968: "... It should be emphasized, though, that there is no such thing as 'the' photosynthetic rate for a species, or even for a variety. Having made several thousand determinations by now, we could go out in a field and with considerable confidence select leaves whose rates, measured under the same conditions, would differ by a factor of 2. I am sure that this is also true of other plants."

Within a given plant photosynthesis rate will vary with time of day and with the leaf selected. It will vary with the leaf's age, its position relative to shade, its geometry relative to solar radiation, its chlorophyll content, moisture content, nutritional status, and numerous other factors. When all of these are given due consideration and all possible steps have been taken to insure their consistency, the rate of CO_2 assimilation may still vary enormously with the intensity of light received and with the available concentration of CO_2.

Rabinowitch (1204) stressed the need for closely similar conditions of CO_2 concentration, temperature, and previous plant history if valid photosynthetic comparisons are to be drawn between distinct plant species. Another important consideration is the respiration rate of each plant or group of plants being compared. Product level may also affect photosynthesis via its influence upon respiration: "...Plants allowed to photosynthesize efficiently for some time often accumulate assimilates and then respire many times stronger than similar plants 'starved' for an extended period of time."

A rise in temperature generally causes a greater increase in respiration than photosynthesis, whereas inhibitors such as cyanide may have but little effect on photosynthesis (in weak light) while strongly suppressing respiration (1204). Moreover, inadequate supplies of CO_2 may seriously decrease photosynthesis without affecting respiration. The density of cells in the suspension under scrutiny is also important. According to Beer's law (1204, p. 983), light absorption in an optically-dense system increases at a rate slower than proportionally with the concentration. It will be seen that these and other factors all contribute to a phenomenon of *light saturation* which underlies the species photosynthetic response to illumination.

Although no attempt is made in this chapter to survey the vast literature appertaining to photosynthesis rates, data are frequently drawn from maize and other crop plants to help fill out the picture of rate-governing factors. We shall see that there are both direct and indirect factors bearing heavily on photosynthesis potential, and that, historically, numerous measurements of this potential have had to be performed by indirect means. In recent years the advent of infrared CO_2 analytical techniques used in conjuction with transparent assimilation chambers mounted around both intact and detached leaves have yielded precise and reproducible information relating to CO_2 assimilation rates. The use of radioactive CO_2, so instrumental in defining the mechanisms of photosynthesis, has also found its place in studies of photosynthesis rates.

We are fortunate in that sugarcane photosynthesis has been studied by physiologists in temperate countries having little direct interest in sugarcane as a crop. Although the C_4-dicarboxylic acid pathway was unknown when most of the work reviewed here was performed, considerable use has been made of sugarcane along with maize and other plants in crop photosynthesis studies. In such work a new note of interest now arises by virtue of the distinct pathway of carbon movement operating in the tropical grasses and certain other species.

For convenience the terms "photosynthesis" and "CO_2 assimilation" are used loosely and interchangeably throughout this chapter even though practically nothing is known about the light reactions proper in sugarcane chloroplasts. At this time any discussion of photosynthetic phosphorylation rates, the mechanism governing these rates, and the relationships of ATP and NADPH synthesis to CO_2 assimilation would amount to little more than speculation.

2. PHOTOSYNTHESIS AS A FUNCTION OF LIGHT INTENSITY

A. *Saturating light intensity and the compensation point*

According to Rabinowitch (1204), the Russian botanist Volkov was the first to recognize a relationship between photosynthetic activity and the amount of solar radiation received by the photosynthesizing plant. In 1886 he observed that submerged water plants evolved more oxygen when illumination intensity was increased. The phenomenon of *light saturation* was discovered 17 years later by Reinke (1229) who detected a progressive decline of photosynthesis rate curves as illumination intensity approached that of full sunlight. The fact that light saturation may be followed by *light inhibition* was shown by Ewart's (515) experiments in the closing years of the nineteenth century. Blackman and his associates (194, 195) soon demonstrated that photosynthesis requires no minimum level of light in terms of a precise point of intensity. They also noted that the "true" rate of photosynthesis is one which is based on a correction for current respiration. By this reasoning the phenomenon of light saturation may be viewed as a broad plateau of light intensities rather than a precise optimum point.

In later years light curves were also evaluated as possible rate-limiting systems in accordance with Blackman's theory of limiting factors. According to Rabinowitch (1204, p. 964) an exception to this was Lubimenko's claim of a light threshold for photosynthesis based on observations of certain land plants showing light curves with a sigmoid shape. This response is characteristic of the purple bacteria (1204, p. 964).

Whether light inhibition of photosynthesis at high intensities is due to overheating, as claimed by Blackman, or to photo-oxidative reactions, as suggested by Rabinowitch, is a mute point in the present limited discussion. It is important to note that most precise measurements have shown a linear response to increasing light intensity which *gradually* curves from an ascending to a horizontal plane. Thus, light saturation is approached over a range of intensities and is not ordinarily achieved in an abrupt manner as depicted by Blackman. Rabinowitch claimed that the heterogeneity of light absorption alone, even in relatively homogeneous chloroplast preparations, would prevent accurate measurement of Blackman's angular saturation curves even if the latter were a valid representation of the photosynthesis relationship to light intensity.

Rabinowitch also states that no exact description of the linear phase of a photosynthesis response curve to light intensity is possible: "... No exact definition of the linear range can be given, since all light curves probably are hyperbolae (or curves of a higher order) and can only approach straight lines asymptotically. A formal definition of the upper limit of the linear range could thus be given only in terms of a definite deviation from linearity." The work of Wassink (1538) with nine horticultural plants is cited in which deviation of 16 percent from proportionality was found. Emerson and Lewis (491) obtained linearity with *Chlorella* up to 1300 lux in white light. Other workers (843, 844, 1473) claim that the linear phase may be subdivided into two segments in which the initial response plotted in the lower segment may be up to twice as steep as that of the upper segment.

The light intensity at which photosynthesis is balanced by respiration has been termed the compensation point (1204, p. 981). Under these conditions the net gas exchange is zero. Rabinowitch notes that the compensation point may also be described as the CO_2 concentration at which gas exchange becomes zero at a given light intensity. Assuming that the maximum quantum yield of photosynthesis is nearly equal among all species, and that CO_2 is available in nonlimiting supply, Rabinowitch maintained that variations in the compensation point will depend primarily on rate of respiration and absorbance of the preparation. Since respiration is proportional to cell concentration, while light absorption subscribes to Beer's law, *i.e.*, absorption decreases less than proportionally with increased cell concentration, the compensation point of a dispersed suspension will be found at a lower light intensity than the compensation point of a more dense suspension. On the other hand, density decreases resulting from lower chlorophyll concentrations within the cells without parallel decreases in cell number will cause the compensation point to be shifted toward higher intensities. In effect, the loss of photosynthetic yield will not be compensated by even greater losses in total respiration (1204, p. 983). Respiration in chlorophyll-deficient cells is reportedly equal to or greater than respiration in normal green cells (1120, 492).

The relationship of the compensation point to temperature and CO_2 supply is illustrated in Fig. 4-1. Higher temperature may produce an upward movement of the

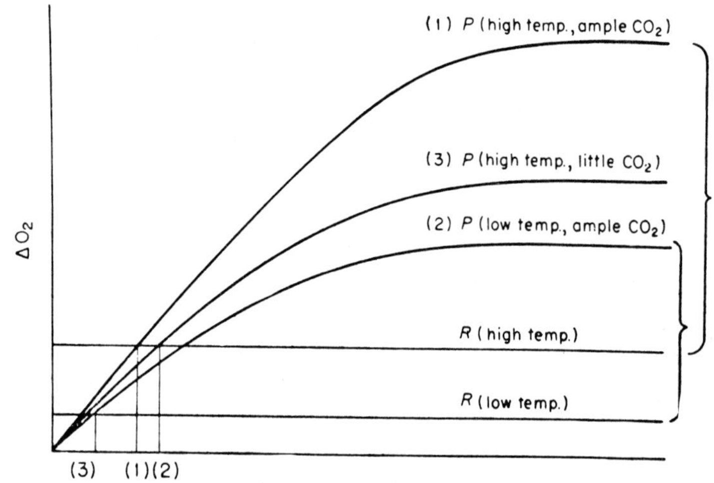

Fig. 4-1. Shift of compensation point with changing carbon dioxide concentration. (1) ⟶ (2) decreasing CO_2; (3) ⟶ (1) increasing temperature. [After Rabinowitch (1204).] Reproduced by permission of *Interscience Publishers, Inc.*, New York.

compensation point at low light intensities. In effect, the ratio between respiration and photosynthesis is altered in favor of respiration by the temperature rise. On the other hand, Rabinowitch (1204) states that lowered CO_2 supply will decrease photosynthesis without affecting respiration. It is possible that under conditions of insufficient CO_2 supply the photosynthetic response curves will bend in weak light so that the compensation point is markedly elevated or never reached at all (Fig. 4-1). Under conditions of CO_2 "deficiency" the compensating light intensity may be independent of temperature (1021). Presumably, the temperature coefficient of the CO_2-supplying process is then essentially equal to that of respiration.

The phenomenon of photosynthetic light saturation was observed by Reinke (1229) to occur at light intensities common at noontime, or approximately at 60 000 lux in temperate regions. Absolute values for saturating light intensity will depend upon numerous external and internal variables. For example, the red algae whose habitat is deep under the sea will achieve saturation with light intensities in the order of 1000 lux (1204, p. 989). Species adaptability to sun or shade markedly affects their photosynthetic response to the intensity or duration of illumination. Rabinowitch (1204) cites the work of Böhning (200) who found that leaves of shade-adapted *Pyrus malus* declined in continuous illumination of 32 000 lux during a period of 20 days. In trees adapted to sunlight there was no photosynthesis decline over a similar period even at 50 000 lux. Studies by Kramer and Decker (858) showed that three species of hardwood (heliophilic) trees were relatively adapted to high light intensities by comparison with white pine, an "umbrophile" adapted to low light intensities. Light adaptibility is also known in algae both as an individual and phylogenetic feature.

Rabinowitch (1204, p. 986) stressed the role of specimen absorbance in producing distinct saturating light intensities: ". . .Saturation begins when the most exposed chlorophyll molecules receive a certain light flux, and becomes complete when the most deeply shaded molecules obtain this saturating intensity. The intensity of incident light at which this complete saturation occurs obviously must depend on whether we use a thick or thin leaf, a dense or dilute cell suspension." Relative to this, Irvine (780) has shown a relationship between leaf thickness and photosynthesis rate in sugarcane. It is possible that different saturating light intensities will characterize the mesophyll chloroplasts and the parenchyma-sheath chloroplasts found in sugarcane leaves (*cf.* Chapter 3, pp. 117–120).

In addition to the "density effect" and the phenomenon of light adaptability discussed above, the factor of age will also affect saturating light intensity. Among many plant species, including sugarcane, the chlorophyll content *per se* will tend to

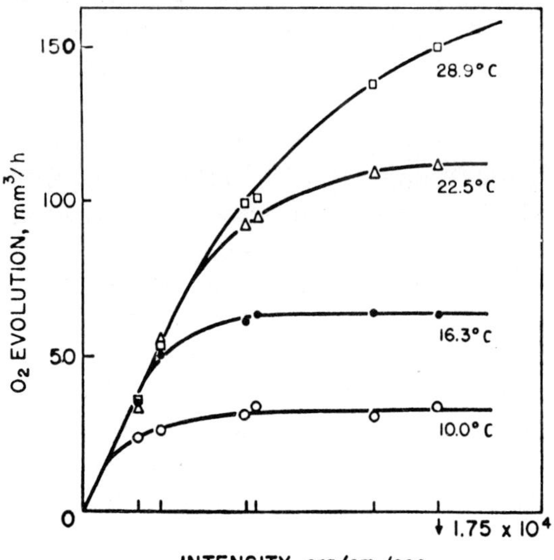

Fig. 4-2. Light curves of *Chlorella* at different temperatures. [From Rabinowitch (1204), after Wassink *et al.* (1537).] Reproduced by permission of *Interscience Publishers, Inc.*, New York, and *Enzymologia.*

decline among the older leaves, and their physical position along the plant stem relative to incoming solar radiation becomes progressively noncompetitive as more of the younger leaves emerge above. Kortschak and Forbes (855) have shown that age of the sugarcane plant has even greater influence than leaf age on photosynthesis rate.

As is true of the compensation point, external factors affecting the saturating light intensity are markedly influenced by temperature and CO_2 supply. The effects of temperature on light curves of *Chlorella*, as obtained by Wassink and his colleagues (1537), are shown in Fig. 4-2. Oddly enough, seasonal temperatures (in Hawaii) tend to favor photosynthesis when the means are low rather than high (855). Sugarcane response to CO_2 has further been shown by Hartt and Burr (674) to vary as a varietal feature.

Probably all of the factors depicted by Rabinowitch and others as having significant bearing on the photosynthesis response to light by plants in general must also relate to sugarcane photosynthesis. The fact that sugarcane's overall rate of photosynthesis is several times greater than most other plants (911, 854), plus its employment of the C_4 pathway of CO_2 assimilation, may or may not alter this statement in the light of future evidence. Very little precise information has been made available with sugarcane chloroplast preparations. However, reliable data has been obtained in recent years with intact or detached blades in CO_2 assimilation chambers (*cf.* this chapter, pp. 175–177).

The sugarcane habitat varies from tropic conditions in which low-temperature restrictions are virtually unknown, to subtropic and temperate conditions (such as those of Florida and Louisiana) where low temperature determines the length of growing season, growth rate, and probably bears heavily on sugar transport and storage mechanisms. Even within the tropics a mountainous sugar-growing region will show temperature effects on sugar production when data from the uplands are compared with those from the valleys or coastal lowlands (963).

Whereas sugar yield is admittedly an indirect measure of CO_2 assimilation, it is a generally reliable one nevertheless. Singh and Lal (1327) demonstrated as early as 1935 that photosynthesis is essentially constant in sugarcane between 30 and 40 °C, although measurable decline was detected above 34 °C. The temperature effects on sugarcane photosynthesis as an integral part of sugar transport, storage, and utilization should certainly yield to further exploration.

With respect to chlorophyll content of the sugarcane leaf, unpublished work by Kumar and his associates in Puerto Rico have shown that chlorophyll varies as a function of leaf age and is also distributed in a positive or increasing gradient between the base and apex of a given blade. A greater chlorophyll content in the outer reaches of the leaf may explain in part the basipetal transport of sucrose toward the base and thereafter to storage tissues.

M. Tió-Lladó, R. Montalvo-Zapata, A.G. Alexander and A. Kumar (unpublished) have shown that chlorophyll decline and sugar-forming capability were parallel features of general cane growth restriction caused by industrial air contamination in the Arecibo area of Puerto Rico. As shown by Table 4-1, the unknown atmosphere contaminant had severely lowered the chlorophyll content of leaves $^{+}1$ to $^{+}3$ of 13-month-old sugarcane. The youngest leaves, *i.e.*, those ranked $^{+}1$, were less severely affected owing to their shorter period of exposure to the injurious factor. The corresponding loss of sugar-forming capability is clearly evidenced by sucrose levels found in the blade lamina (Table 4-1). The corresponding sucrose percent cane values were lowered to about 26 percent of the control levels. Other studies by Kumar have shown that cane chlorophyll content is sensitive to variable levels of nitrate supplied in sand culture (unpublished).

TABLE 4-1

EFFECTS OF INDUSTRIAL AIR CONTAMINATION ON THE FOLIAR CHLOROPHYLL AND SUCROSE CONTENTS OF SUGARCANE IN THE ARECIBO REGION OF PUERTO RICO*

[After Tió-Lladó *et al.* (unpublished).] Reproduced by permission of the authors.

Leaf	Chlorophyll (mg/g × 10^4)		Sucrose (mg/g fresh wt.)	
	Control	Damaged	Control	Damaged
$^{+}1$	125	21	10.1	2.7
$^{+}2$	144	68	9.1	1.5
$^{+}3$	163	96	8.7	1.8

*Variety *P.R. 1016*, age 13 months.

In terms of saturating light intensity the variations anticipated by Rabinowitch on the basis of species and sample differences may generally hold true for a normal sugarcane crop once it has formed a typical green canopy. The uppermost leaves usually receive good light exposure. In many sugarcane regions subject to the "trade winds" local competitive leaf shading is probably minimized by an almost continuous leaf motion. However, beneath the canopy surface light penetration becomes progressively sporadic until a point is reached where mature but potentially productive leaves receive little or no direct light exposure. Anyone who has made his way through a field of mature cane will verify that it is a rather dark and dingy place even at noontime on a clear day. In this sense the interior of the green canopy is not unlike the ocean depths insofar as poor light penetration is concerned, but in this instance there is no reason to suppose that an adaptation to weak light occurs.

B. *Light response of individual leaves*

Soon after Rabinowitch reviewed the relationship of light to photosynthesis rates in chlorophyll-bearing organisms, interest mounted rapidly in the light response curves of higher land plants. Böhning and Burnside (201), in 1956, reported on light relationships to apparent photosynthesis in leaves of "sun" and "shade" plants. Several species were shown to achieve light saturation near 2500 foot candles. Other authors began to make use of individual leaves in developing light-absorption models for agricultural crops (1276, 548, 433). In the Netherlands De Wit (433) examined the CO_2-assimilating capability of crop surfaces under long-day and short-day conditions, *i.e.*, in June and December, respectively. He found that the photosynthesis potential was nearly 6 times greater in June than in December. The higher potential was not achieved in practice owing to limitations of sugar transport, lower CO_2 supply, and a general inability for a closed crop surface to perform photosynthesis at rates comparable to the sum of its individual leaf potentials. Similar trends were recorded by Saeki (1276) in Japan who studied the interrelationships between total photosynthesis and the leaf area and light distribution in a plant community. In 1959 Gaastra (548) included stomatal diffusion resistance among the parameters of temperature and CO_2 supply in evaluating the relationships of light to photosynthesis rates in crop plants.

Böhning and Burnside (201), in 1956, were perhaps the first workers who seriously attempted to standardize environmental conditions under which compensation points, saturating light intensities, and maximum photosynthesis rates could be examined at normal atmospheric CO_2 levels. Prior to this, the work summarized by Thomas (1423) in 1955 gave the most accurate picture available of photosynthesis light curves in agricultural land plants. Recognizing the biological differences of individual plants and variations inherent in experimental procedure, Böhning and Burnside compared a number of typical "sun" and "shade" plants under near-constant experimental conditions. Data relative to compensation points, light saturation, and maximum photosynthesis rates was obtained using a transparant (plexiglass) leaf chamber, a compressed air supply to assure a uniform CO_2 concentration, a Drierite column to remove moisture, an air-flow measuring device, and an infrared gas analyzer. Individual leaves could be studied in the chamber while still attached to the plant. Artificial light treatments were of sufficiently short duration to prevent solarization of shade plants. It was found that, under similar conditions of light, temperature, moisture, and CO_2 supply, light saturation and compensation points for the sun species were 2000–2500 foot candles and 100–150 foot candles, respectively. The shade species attained light saturation at a maximum of 1000 foot candles and the compensation point was in the order of 50 foot candles. In certain shade species light saturation occurred at light intensities as low as 400 to 500 foot candles.

Böhning and Burnside questioned the interpretation of Decker (420) who held that shade plants must be more efficient utilizers of light on the grounds that many important tasks are accomplished in nature by apparently inefficient means. The saturation light intensities obtained by Böhning and Burnside were quite low; however, these authors, like Thomas (1423), were primarily interested in ecological effects upon plant processes, particularly the ". . .fallacy of attempting to draw broad ecological inferences from . . . comparisons of single factors". In this they were very successful.

In sugarcane, Kortschak *et al.* (851) had performed photosynthesis experiments with individual leaves by 1957, and during the 1960's advanced photosynthesis studies were performed with detached blades standing in water or sugar solutions (852, 666). In 1963 Hartt (666) reported photosynthesis and sugar-transport experiments with detached sugarcane leaves in which the lamina to the left and to the right of the midvein were given differential treatments. By 1966 this work had been extended to include parameters of CO_2 concentration, age of leaf, and variety, in addition to extreme light intensities, for detached sugarcane leaves (853).

Preceding by several years the sugarcane photosynthesis and sugar transport studies in Hawaii, and the C_4 pathway studies in Australia, the work of Hesketh and his colleagues (720, 721) with maize, sugarcane, and numerous other species advanced enormously our understanding of photosynthesis–light relationship in single-leaf models. In contrast to the low light saturation values obtained by Böhning and Burnside (201), and by Verduin and Loomis (1490), Hesketh and Musgrave (720) reported that a single maize leaf will increase its net photosynthesis with increasing illumination to a minimum of 10 000 foot candles. Verduin and Loomis (1490), as early as 1944, had used small cellophane envelopes to isolate portions of field corn leaves in order to measure CO_2 absorption during photosynthesis. By determining the CO_2 content of an air stream before and after passage through the chamber it was possible to estimate the quantity of CO_2 assimilated. Although the data were highly variable, particularly at high light intensities, the authors concluded that individual leaves must achieve light saturation at about 2500 foot candles.

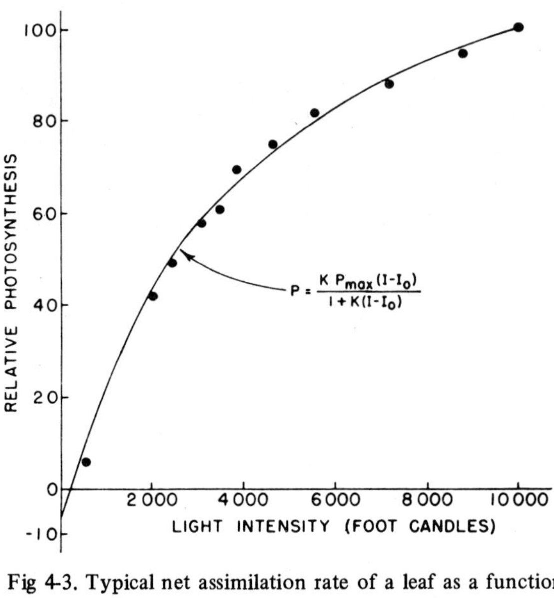

Fig 4-3. Typical net assimilation rate of a leaf as a function of light intensity. [After Hesketh and Musgrave (720).] Reproduced by permission of *Crop Science.*

In the experiments by Hesketh and Musgrave (720) net CO_2 assimilation was measured by three different means: (a) Continually from midday to sunset, under clear sky, with light intensity declining from 10 000 to zero foot candles; (b) under clear sky but with modifying layers of cheesecloth; and (c) with variable cloudiness. A light meter was used in conjunction with a newly-developed technique of leaf or ear isolation in a sealed chamber. By a rapid method of photosynthesis measurement it was possible to examine in isolation the photosynthesizing tissue under essentially natural field conditions. It was repeatedly shown that a maize leaf continued to respond to light intensity increments up to the maximum illumination of 10 000 foot candles (Fig. 4-3).

From his treatment of photosynthetic data with equations based on physical–chemical kinetic theory, Rabinowitch (1204) had concluded that the derivations could in most cases be reduced to a rectangular hyperbola. When Hesketh and Musgrave fitted the data in Fig. 4-3 to the same theoretical equations, they obtained a close fit for the values as predicted by Rabinowitch. Only small corrections were needed for the changes in respiration which accompanied changes in light intensity. Moreover, the hyperbola that most nearly fit the data had not achieved a maximum at 10 000 foot candles. The rate of photosynthesis change in the range of 9000 to 10 000 foot candles was found to be quite small, amounting to only 1 to 6 percent by calculation. Hesketh and Musgrave maintained that extrapolation of the photosynthetic response beyond 10 000 foot candles would produce deviations owing to the inability of the leaf to disperse the increased solar energy by transpiration. On the other hand, the authors attributed their success in achieving photosynthetic response to high light intensity [which was well beyond the intensity limits met by other workers (1589, 1063, 548)] to their elimination of leaf-to-leaf variation, *i.e.*, to the isolation of the single intact leaf. In addition, the relatively rapid method employed for photosynthesis measurements tended to eliminate errors due to slow air exchange, inadequate cooling, inadequate light supply, and insensitive CO_2 analyses. It was also found that a wind speed of 1/3 mph was sufficient to provide adequate CO_2 within the chamber.

In 1963 Hesketh and Moss (721) published exhaustive studies on the variations in photosynthesis response to light within a species (maize) and among species, including comparisons of maize and sugarcane. Other species included deciduous and evergreen trees, annual crop plants, and perennial crop plants. Individual leaves or small numbers of attached leaves were enclosed in water-cooled transparent chambers through which air was drawn and CO_2 analyzed at intake and exhaust. Radiation flux density was measured perpendicular to the leaf with an Eppley pyrheliometer and expressed in values of ly/min (langley = 1 cal/cm^2). The conditions under artificial light were such that from each ly/min the bathed and illuminated leaf received 7/10 as many quanta, between 400 and 700 nm, as did those illuminated by the sun. In addition, air-flow rates were adjusted so that the maximum difference in CO_2 concentration between input and exhaust was 40 ppm. The change in CO_2 concentration (Δ CO_2) was measured with an infrared gas analyzer. Hesketh and Moss calculated net photosynthesis (P) from the equation

$$P = (\Delta\ CO_2 \cdot F \cdot K)/A$$

where P = net photosynthesis as mg of CO_2 assimilated per standard unit of leaf area per hour ($mg/dm^2/h$); $\Delta\ CO_2$ = change in CO_2 concentration between intake and exhaust as ppm by volume $\times 10^{-6}$; F = air flow through the chamber (l/h); K = [(44 000 mg CO_2)/22.4] x (273/294), an approximate empirical conversion factor from liters of CO_2 to mg of CO_2 for the rotameters used to measure air-flow rates; and A = leaf area (dm^2).

With each leaf or CO_2 concentration, P was examined at 5 or more radiation flux densities. Under field conditions the CO_2 concentrations were varied by adding CO_2 to a transparent chamber placed over several corn plants or similarly by plant exhaustion of CO_2 within the enclosed area. Chlorophyll concentration and leaf morphology, and hence the light-intercepting capability of the leaf, was incorporated into the $P_{max}\ K$, whose value was taken as constant for a uniform population within a single species.

Zea mays experiments with outwardly identical leaf populations showed that some variation had entered owing to errors in measurement and biological differences regardless of the care taken to minimize variations in light, CO_2, temperature, soil moisture and sampling procedure. Differences between outwardly comparable leaf populations were manifested in divergent shapes of the light curves for leaves having a high P value as compared with leaves having a lower P value. However, these differences were not significant and the light curves generally substantiated the proposition that $P_{max}\ K$ varies but little. Moreover, the authors concluded that a valid description of light response curves is obtained with the equation

$$P = P_{max}\ K\ (I - I_0)/[I + K\ (I - I_0)] \quad (1)$$

where I_0 is the observed light intensity at $P = 0$, *i.e.*, the *light compensation* point; $I - I_0$ is the excess of radiation flux density (I) above the light compensation point (I_0); and $P_{max}\ K$ is the slope as $I \longrightarrow I_0$.

Citing the work of Saeki (1276) and De Wit (433) concerning the prediction of potential crop yields based on light response data incorporated into mathematical models, Hesketh and Moss further concluded that leaf variability is an important factor in bright sunlight but it is much less important in weak light.

Variation studies among species revealed greater P differences than those obtained within a species (Table 4-2). Owing to shade effects, tree leaves produced lower photosynthesis rates in groups than when examined separately. The authors did not alter their conclusions on this basis and it was shown that Eqn. 1 (above) was as valid for

TABLE 4-2

VARIATION IN NET PHOTOSYNTHESIS (*P*) AMONG DIFFERENT SPECIES IN NATURAL AND ARTIFICIAL LIGHT*

[After Hesketh and Moss (721).] Reproduced by permission of *Crop Science.*

Species	Common name	In sunlight		
		P(1.0)	*P*(0.5)	Replicates
Castania mollisima	Chinese dogwood	6.5	6.0	1
Cornus florida	Dogwood	7.5	6.5	1
Helianthus annus	Sunflower	42.0	30.0	2
Liriodendron tulipifera	Tulip tree	15.0	13.5	2
Nicotiana tabacum	Tobacco	21.0	19.0	2
Saccharum officinarum	Sugarcane	49.0	35.0	1
Tsuga canadensis	Hemlock	4.4	3.6	5
Zea mays	Maize	46.0	32.0	8
		In incandescent light		
		P(1.4)	*P*(0.7)	Replicates
Dactylis glomerata	Orchardgrass	17	12	2
Lycopersicum esculentum	Tomato	19	19	1
Nicotiana tabacum	Tobacco	17	16	2
Phaseolus vulgaris	Bean	12	12	1
Philodendron sp.	Philodendron	0	0	1
Saccharum officinarum	Sugarcane	42	28	3
Trifolium pratense	Red clover	20	19.5	2
Zea mays	Maize	48	36	6

*300 ppm CO_2, 25–31 °C.

light-saturated tobacco as it was for light-unsaturated maize, whose net photosynthesis continued to rise at high light intensity.

Sugarcane was found to behave similarly to maize in that it did not become light-saturated. Sunflower responded in like manner, while nine other species did experience light saturation. As shown in Table 4-2, net photosynthesis (*P*) increased in light-unsaturated plants to values greater than 40 mg/dm^2/h at 1 ly/min, whereas light-saturated species ranged only from 4 to 21. It is noteworthy that the mean *P* value of 47 obtained for maize is more than double the value reported by Verduin and Loomis (1490) in 1944 ($P = 20$) and given wide acceptance for a number of years.

Separation of the two light response groups was visualized as an arbitrary graduation rather than a clear distinction owing to the fact that the light response curves tended to converge in weak light. This was suggestive of a consistency for initial slopes and $P_{max}K$ values. Furthermore, it was thought that Eqn. 1 could be fit to all of the light response curves, regardless of species, by varying P_{max} while holding $P_{max}K$

constant. These findings generally substantiated the kinetic treatment of limiting factors by Rabinowitch (1204) from which Eqn. 1 was derived. Use of this equation also implies that high net photosynthesis rates such as those obtained with sugarcane, maize, and sunflower will not be achieved if light saturation occurs.

By treatment of individual leaves with artificial light of increasing intensity, Hesketh and Moss were able to distinguish graphically between the light-saturating and non-light-saturating groups of species (Fig. 4-4). Sugarcane, representing the non-

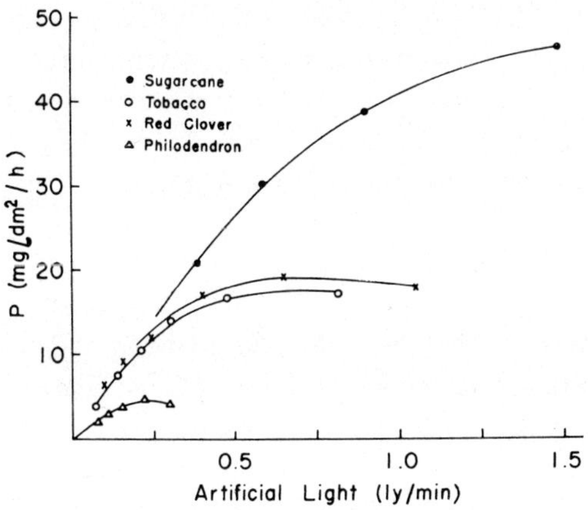

Fig. 4-4. Net photosynthesis (P) in four plant species as a function of the radiation flux density of artificial (incandescent) light. [After Hesketh and Moss (721).] Reproduced by permission of *Crop Science.*

saturating group (sugarcane, sunflower, maize) continued to increase net photosynthesis up to full sunlight, while representatives of the remaining nine species experienced light saturation and ceased to increase net photosynthesis at rates less than half of that achieved by sugarcane. The response of philodendron leaves was particularly striking in that they were saturated at less than 0.25 ly/min and achieved a P value approximately 1/10 of that obtained by sugarcane. A somewhat similar graph was presented by Moss (1041) showing a P value close to 60 for sugarcane at an incandescent light concentration of 2.0 ly/min. Oak and maple were much lower, in the order of the philodendron values shown in Fig. 4-4, while orchardgrass gave an intermediate response.

From their results with different species Hesketh and Moss concluded that diverse photosynthesis response curves will fit the rectangular hyperbola predicted by Rabinowitch (1204), and that light saturation is a species phenomenon occurring in some but not all plant species. In the absence of light saturation net photosynthesis values as high as 40 mg/dm^2/h can be attained. It was further proposed that species differences in light saturation and maximum rates of photosynthesis might relate to physical difference in CO_2 diffusion resistance, or to CO_2 concentration at the site of its assimilation in the leaf.

In a subsequent paper Moss (1041) described measurements of CO_2 diffusion as a function of the plant's environment. It was found that light increased CO_2 uptake by lowering CO_2 levels at the chloroplast and by lowering stomatal resistance to gas flow. The effect of decreased stomatal resistance was in turn governed by the rate of increased water loss by opened stomata. Higher levels of atmospheric CO_2 resulted in greater CO_2 absorption. This was attributed to an increased gradient between the leaf and atmosphere. Precise estimation of the CO_2 increase was rendered difficult by an apparent rise in CO_2 concentration at the chloroplast and by greater stomatal resistance. The latter could nonetheless be estimated by measuring the changed water loss. Higher temperature promoted both transpiration and CO_2 absorption. Turbulence produced in a still atmosphere had the effect of an added CO_2 supply.

C. *Light intensity vs. respiration during photosynthesis*

As noted elsewhere (*cf.* Chapter 3, pp. 113, 114) the concurrent evolution of CO_2 by respiratory processes during photosynthesis may impose serious restrictions against analyses based upon CO_2 absorption. Blinks (196), working with algae, and Decker (421, 423), working with higher plants, observed that subsequent to a period of photosynthesis the initial rate of respiration in the dark may be greater than that of the extended dark respiration. Decker also noted that the degree of the initial CO_2 "surge" in darkness paralleled the intensity of preillumination. Tregunna *et al.* (1450) observed similar effects in detached tobacco leaves. These authors felt that the post-illumination increase in CO_2 evolution was a vestige of prior respiratory stimulation in the light. However, this view has not been sustained by other workers whose results are suggestive of respiratory suppression during photosynthesis (248, 605, 981).

Subsequent studies of photostimulated respiration by Tregunna *et al.* (1450) greatly clarified the relationships between photosynthesis and respiration in light. Much of the work was performed with leaves of maize, soybean, and peperomia having both abundant and deficient levels of chlorophyll. Experiments designed to compare the effects of prior illumination on the subsequent rate of CO_2 evolution in darkness showed that the initial rate of dark CO_2 production was related to prior illumination as a function of the leaf capacity to perform photosynthesis. Species differences were evidenced by light-increased CO_2 evolution in green soybean and peperomia leaves and light inhibition of CO_2 evolution in maize leaves. The possible role that the C_4 pathway of CO_2 assimilation might have played in producing the different maize response can only be speculated upon since the existence of this pathway in maize, sugarcane, and other plants was not yet recognized (in 1964). It is of interest to note here the suggestion of Galmiche (555) in 1968 who proposed that in maize the movement of ^{14}C into malic acid results from cytoplasmic exchange reactions which in essence constitute a delay of CO_2 penetration to the chloroplasts.

Studies by Tregunna *et al.* (1450) with detached tobacco leaves in which a Geiger tube was used to measure $^{14}CO_2$ concentration changes gave evidence that ". . .some recent product of photosynthesis was the substrate for the initial postillumination production of carbon dioxide. All above results indicated that there was a close relationship between the photosynthetic apparatus of the leaves and the production of carbon dioxide both during and immediately following a period of illumination". These findings are consistent with Verduin's (1491) conclusion that in nature plant photosynthetic and respiratory rates are adapted to the "factor intensities" prevalent in their respective habitats.

Recent findings by Hew and Krotkov (726) with green and yellow (non-green) plants are suggestive of different processes of CO_2 evolution by leaves having the distinct chlorophyll regimes. Citing previous reports that CO_2 production is increased by O_2 in the atmosphere surrounding illuminated plants, but not darkened ones, green and non-green leaves of sunflower, poinsettia, peperomia, and geranium were placed in different O_2 atmospheres (21 percent or 100 percent O_2) and the rates of CO_2 evolution were examined in light and darkness. It was found that CO_2 production was related both to chlorophyll content and O_2 supply in addition to the illumination factor. The equal rates of CO_2 evolution by non-green leaves in light and darkness and their insensitivity to O_2 supply was taken as evidence of a single CO_2-evolving process operating both in light and darkness. However, because green leaves produced more CO_2 in light than in darkness and were affected by O_2 supply, the greater CO_2 evolution was thought to originate from a different process than that operating in darkness. The authors made note of the fact that only in normal green leaves was CO_2 production stimulated by O_2 and light. This was taken as additional evidence of a close relationship between the plants' photosynthetic and respiratory mechanisms. It was further suggested that the CO_2 may derive from early photosynthesis products rather than from elaborated sugars. In this connection the work of Zelitch (1611) was cited in which he suggested that glycolic acid may at times perform such a substrate role. Glycolate as a source of photosynthetically-reproduced CO_2 is treated at length elsewhere (*cf.* this chapter, pp. 173, 174).

D. *Photosynthesis in relation to chlorophyll content*

Little information is available concerning sugarcane photosynthesis as related to chlorophyll content. However, evidence from other species points toward chlorophyll content as a rate-determining factor when others factors are nonlimiting. The fact that chlorophyll is an "internal factor" seriously complicated early efforts to measure its effects on CO_2 assimilation (193, 487). Willstätter and Stoll (1576) appear to have been the first to measure leaf pigment content with sufficient precision so that the photosynthesis–chlorophyll relationship could be approached on an acceptable experimental basis (487). They were able to demonstrate a stability of chlorophyll content even during prolonged photosynthesis under high light intensity. This disproved earlier beliefs depicting chlorophyll as a continually decomposed and resynthesized entity as photosynthesis progressed. It was further shown that the ratio of chlorophyll *a* tq chlorophyll *b* also remained unchanged. On the other hand, Willstätter and Stoll worked with leaves of widely-differing origin, age, and condition, and hence were not able to prove conclusively a relationship between chlorophyll content and photosynthesis potential.

Chlorophyll studies were greatly advanced by Emerson (487, 488) who avoided much of the earlier difficulty by working with cultures of *Chlorella vulgaris*, and by maintaining other factors nearly constant. The culture's medium, its temperature, light exposure, and CO_2 supply were all carefully regulated. Under these conditions Emerson showed that the maximum rate of photosynthesis is a "smooth function" of the chlorophyll content per unit volume of cells (487). Under varying light and temperature conditions maximum photosynthesis was obtained at about the same level of each variable over a broad range of chlorophyll concentrations (488).

The question arises as to whether a positive chlorophyll relationship to photosynthesis rate exists for higher land plants in nature where numerous factors change and interact more or less continually. Presumably it does. Hartt and Burr (674) reported a lower rate of photosynthesis in sugarcane leaves containing visibly less chlorophyll than green leaves. However, when all leaves were deep green in color there was no appreciable difference in photosynthesis. Kumar and his associates (863) found chlorophyll gradients in sugarcane leaves which varied between the apex and base of individual leaves and among leaves of differing rank. Hesketh (722), however, reported that chlorophyll content per unit of leaf area did not vary appreciably among nine plant species given variable light and CO_2 treatments. Singh and Lal (1327), working with wheat, linseed, and sugarcane, reported higher chlorophyll levels in mature or relatively old leaves than in younger leaves but observed no proportionate increase in photosynthesis among the aged leaves.

3. PHOTOSYNTHESIS RESPONSE TO CO_2 SUPPLY

A. *CO_2 and HCO_3^- as photosynthetic carbon sources*

As pointed out by Verduin (1491) and by Rabinowitch (1204), some controversy has persisted relative to the activity of HCO_3^- in the photosynthesis of aquatic and land plants. In his discussion of "area-based" photosynthesis rates Verduin treats atmospheric CO_2 and bicarbonate CO_2 as having equal availability. According to Verduin, Ruttner (1265) claimed that this was true of certain submerged algae and phanerogams. Rabinowitch reopened the question of carbonate ion roles in photosynthesis. He proceeded ". . .on the old assumption that the rate of photosynthesis is primarily a function of the concentration of the molecular species CO_2 in the immediate surroundings of the cells, and that the main effect of the presence of HCO_3^- ions is to prevent this concentration from depletion during photosynthesis". Verduin suggested that, if this was the correct role of HCO_3^-, the availability of CO_2 in an aqueous habitat would be less favorable owing to an increased relative length of the CO_2 diffusion path when the CO_2 content of the water is equal to that of air.

Steemann Nielsen (1358) treated CO_2 assimilation by aquatic plants in considerable detail. In particular he took issue with Rabinowitch (1204) who assumed that free CO_2 was the lone carbon source for aquatic plants. He proposed instead that "...water plants possess a special mechanism for utilizing HCO_3^- ions in the surrounding water for photosynthesis". To support his claim Steemann Nielsen cited results from experiments utilizing *Potamogeton lucens* leaves. These were placed between two cylinders in such a manner that the lower surface was immersed in bicarbonate-containing lake water, and the upper surface in distilled water. It was shown that the lower surface absorbed HCO_3^- ions (plus cations) and discharged OH^- ions (plus cations) from the upper surface. Steemann Nielsen cited other investigators whose work suggests an importance of HCO_3^- ions in the photosynthesis of many – but not all – water plants. Osterlind (1130), for example, suggests that the plankton *Scenedesmus quadricauda* utilizes HCO_3^- ions more readily than free CO_2.

Steemann Nielsen also stressed the importance of CO_2 diffusion in both land and aquatic plants as a means of illustrating the role of HCO_3^- ions in photosynthesis. He maintained that in leaves of land plants CO_2 diffuses through the stomata and intercellular spaces to the cells containing the assimilation sites. Such diffusion of CO_2 proceeds rapidly in the gaseous phase whereas its only movement as a fluid solute may occur as it passes through the cell walls to arrive at the chloroplasts. The solute phase was regarded as being much slower than the gaseous phase, but the very short distance (about 1 μm according to Steemann Nielsen) prevents this slowness from becoming critical. However, in leaves of aquatic plants the CO_2 would transcend different membrane barriers covering a distance frequently in the order of 40 μm. Over this path the CO_2 must pass entirely in solution. Steeman Nielsen continues: "...It is therefore a matter of course that such plants must require high CO_2 tensions in the water if CO_2 is the only carbon source... At a tension of 0.03 percent, which is found in water being in equilibrium with the atmosphere at about 15 °C, photosynthesis in the plants just mentioned (*M. spicatum* and *P. lucens*) is nearly without any importance if free CO_2 is the only carbon source."

Other authors have considered a bicarbonate role in photosynthesis and recent evidence suggests that it is probably involved when maximum photosynthesis rates are obtained. As early as 1936 Burr (265) noted an insufficient rate of CO_2 hydration in leaves to account for measured rates of photosynthesis. He proposed that either CO_2 is assimilated independently of a union with water, or the enzyme carbonic anhydrase performs an essential role in photosynthesis. Carbonic anhydrase was recently shown to be a chloroplast constituent of Calvin-cycle plants (513). The operation of this enzyme in CO_2 assimilation was substantiated by reports (770, 513) of photosynthesis restriction in Calvin-cycle species by the carbonic anhydrase inhibitor Diamox (5-acetamido-1,3,4-thiadiazole-2-sulfonamide). Working with isolated spinach chloroplasts, Everson (514) found evidence of carbonic anhydrase requirement for full photosynthetic activity. In essence, the enzyme was thought to catalyze bicarbonate formation from water (at pH 6.0) by the reaction:

$$CO_2 + H_2O \rightleftharpoons H^+ + HCO_3^-$$

the latter occurring both at the chloroplast surface and within the chloroplast interior. Carbonic anhydrase was seen to promote photosynthesis under conditions such that CO_2 from bicarbonate is the immediate substrate for ribulose diphosphate carboxylase, or if CO_2 diffusing into the chloroplast is converted back to HCO_3^-. If HCO_3^- rather than CO_2 was the immediate carboxylase substrate, carbonic anhydrase would be needed only under conditions of low chloroplast permeability to HCO_3^-.

Using as comparative examples the published photosynthesis curves for the unicellular land algae *Hormidium flacidum* and the higher aquatic plant *Myriophyllum spicatum*, Steemann Nielsen demonstrated that 22 times as much CO_2 is needed to attain saturation in the aquatic higher plant than in the terrestrial unicellular algae. The author also speculated upon the order of CO_2 concentration needed to avoid a diffusion gradient from the external CO_2 source to the internal site of CO_2 assimilation. Interesting enough, he states specifically that this can be answered only after greater knowledge of carboxylation is available. As discussed in previous chapters the CO_2 fixation and assimilation reactions are among the most critical and troublesome mechanistic steps in both Calvin-cycle and C_4 pathway plants.

Of the factors affecting CO_2 availability, Verduin (1491) makes special note of the following: (a) CO_2 concentration, (b) CO_2 "diffusivity", and (c) the length of the CO_2 diffusion path. It may be recalled that Galmiche (555) regarded differential diffusion rates of CO_2 in sugarcane leaves as an explanation for its appearance in malate, in preference to the accepted explanation that a pathway of carbon flow different from that of the Calvin cycle was operative. Citing data obtained from Lake Erie in the United States, Verduin notes that the higher CO_2 content of water, by comparison with air, is countered by the lower diffusibility of the CO_2 in water. Thus, by appearances, western Lake Erie contains about 160 times more CO_2 than air, while the CO_2 diffusibility in air is 10^4 times greater than in water. Verduin proposes that aquatic plants may counter the obvious disadvantage by shortening the diffusion path.

B. *Effects of CO_2 concentration on rate of photosynthesis*

Although variations in natural CO_2 supply do not produce dramatic changes in photosynthesis rates in the order of those produced by variable illumination, there is ample evidence that CO_2 content of the ambient air can affect net photosynthesis and CO_2 assimilation efficiency. Moreover, the effects produced by variable CO_2 levels are intimately related to light intensity, and to a lesser degree to temperature and the plant's moisture regime. These conclusions originated largely in recent times with the advent of improved technology for measuring gas exchange in higher plants.

Early workers were generally aware that CO_2 supply could significantly affect photosynthesis rates, although Verduin and Loomis (1490) in 1944 obtained very little photosynthesis response by maize leaves to increased CO_2 supply. Kursanov (865), in 1934, reported experiments with the attached green fruits of apple, cucumber and pea in which the photosynthesis rates were estimated by measuring CO_2 uptake. However, no allowance was made for respiratory CO_2 evolution, and, when carbohydrate movement to the fruits was restricted, the apparent photosynthesis (CO_2 uptake) increased significantly. These authors were aware of an atmospheric CO_2 source for photosynthetic activity in leaves and they attributed the relatively low "photosynthesis" of apple and cucumber fruits to a lower number of stomata. Other workers recognized that optimal CO_2 concentrations existed (250, 1576) beyond which increased CO_2 supply produced a suppression of photosynthetic activity (202). Blackman (193) was the first to emphasize that accurate estimation of CO_2 effects, or the effects of any other factor measured individually, necessitates careful control of all other factors contributing to photosynthesis rates. Blackman's concept of *limiting factors* subsequently received both support and criticism (1325).

Boysen Jensen (219), in 1933, published findings with leaf chambers which were based on the assumption that the rate of photosynthesis was directly proportional to the *average* CO_2 concentration within the chamber. On this basis he corrected the photosynthesis rate obtained for the decline of CO_2 level in the chamber. Bonde (202) questioned this method and examined photosynthesis rate relationships to CO_2 level at "normal" CO_2 concentrations, *i.e.*, close to 0.03 percent, by plotting his data against the actual average CO_2 concentration in the leaf chamber. The experiments were performed with excised *Sinapsis alba* leaves with illumination and temperature held constant. The results indicated that CO_2 is assimilated by *Sinapsis* leaves as a logarithmic function of the CO_2 concentration of the surrounding atmosphere. The upper limits were about 3 times greater than normal CO_2 concentrations in air. Bonde therefore concluded that "...The rate of photosynthesis at normal carbon dioxide concentration with optimal illumination is at least partially limited by insufficient carbon dioxide supply."

A discussion of CO_2 level in photosynthesis is virtually inseparable from the question of light intensity (*cf.* this chapter, pp. 130–132). Blackman (193) depicted the photosynthetic response to light intensity and CO_2 concentration in terms of a chart of limiting factors. In a large measure the response pattern he visualized is essentially correct, with the exception that a gradual rounding of the curve is attained rather than a sharp angle as saturation is approached. An exception to this is found in the assimilation curves obtained by Emerson and Green (490) with *Chlorella* which conform precisely with the Blackman pattern.

Absolute saturation by CO_2 is not readily attained with most plants. Thomas and Hill (1422) obtained photosynthesis curves in full sunlight in which CO_2 concentration up to 3700 ppm failed to produce saturation. Hoover *et al.* (748), in 1933, were among the first to produce a "typical" assimilation curve. Wheat plants were supplied with circulating air in a closed system and CO_2 content was measured continually by infrared light absorption. When photosynthesis was plotted as the ordinate against CO_2 level as the abscissa, with illumination constant and CO_2 increasing, photosynthesis rate initially described a steep, straight line. Thereafter the rate increase was progressively flattened until a horizontal line was obtained. The effect of increased light intensity was to lengthen the steep and straight portion of the curve without changing its slope. The horizontal portion was retained but at increasingly higher levels. This response has been verified by other investigators working with many plant species. Nonetheless, the exact relationship of light to CO_2 activity has posed a tremendous challenge to students of photosynthesis (1204, 1041, 721, 1039).

Thomas (1423) has correctly asserted that the ability of a leaf to assimilate CO_2 depends upon its previous history. In sugarcane this is especially true if its history precludes adequate climate, water, and nutrients for producing a large and healthy canopy, a full complement of chlorophyll, and the essential apparatus for moving and storing photosynthate. However, the statement by Thomas that ". . .healthy plants growing under field conditions probably have greater capacity for assimilation than greenhouse plants, chlorotic plants, or excised leaves" is open to question. Greenhouse-grown plants properly raised hardly belong in the same category with "chlorotic plants" or detached leaves. More to the point is the fact that consistently adequate water supply is seldom assured, and healthy field-grown plants will impose the handicap of self-shading. This is most certainly true of sugarcane where each leaf has but a brief tenure in the uppermost position where its reception of sunlight is essentially unrestricted. Maize, as indicated elsewhere in this chapter, is another plant whose laboratory process in assimilating CO_2 exceeds all reasonable expectations of the field-grown specimen.

Verduin and Loomis (1490) concluded from their experiments with maize that ". . .the light saturation value for fully-expanded maize leaves was in the neighborhood of 2500 foot candles, or 25 percent of full sunlight". Since this light intensity was obtained at ground level under the expanded maize canopy, it was assumed that ordinary midday illumination was fully adequate for the maize plant. Moreover, although air movement and soil moisture affected to some degree the CO_2 content of the ambient air, photosynthesis was not found to be affected when CO_2 declined below its average air value. Under more exacting experimental conditions, Hesketh and Musgrave (720) found that maize did not become light saturated even at 10 000 foot candles. Under such high light intensity the light-unsaturated plant might conceivably be sensitive to CO_2 level. This was vividly demonstrated by Moss *et al.* (1039) working with maize under field conditions.

Moss (1041) presented a different view of maize photosynthesis which held that CO_2 supply must take into account the simultaneous rate of CO_2 absorption and water loss by leaves, which in turn are affected by light intensity. Light was shown to increase CO_2 absorption by decreasing the CO_2 level at the chloroplast and by decreasing stomatal resistance to gas flow. A major effect of light was the initiation of stomatal opening. By measuring moisture loss as the stomata opened it was possible to estimate the magnitude of the effect of decreased stomatal resistance. Similar responses were obtained with sugarcane and sorghum (1041).

Moss (1041) also found that higher CO_2 concentrations in the atmosphere lead to increased CO_2 absorption. This results from an increased CO_2 gradient between the leaf and air. However, complications relative to internal CO_2 diffusion rate were encountered which prevented CO_2 absorption at theoretical levels. These apparently were related to increased CO_2 concentration at the chloroplast and to greater stomatal resistance. To clarify the effects of CO_2 and other factors on photosynthesis rate (P), Moss referred repeatedly to the hypothetical equation

$$P = \frac{D\,([CO_2]_A - [CO_2]_{chl})}{L + S + M} \tag{2}$$

where L and S represent the effective diffusion path lengths through the air and through the stomata, respectively. L/D is a measure of the resistance of air to water vapor flow, and S/D is a measure of the stomata resistance. $[CO_2]_{chl}$ is equated with $[CO_2]_A$ under conditions of a closed system in which the leaf removes all possible CO_2. The CO_2 concentration at the chloroplast is then theoretically equal to that of the atmosphere, since there is no net influx of CO_2 into the leaf. Moss believed that Eqn. 2 goes a long way toward explaining why plants ever become light saturated, or why different species do not respond equally to light.

Assuming that once the stomata are open the primary effect of light is to change $[CO_2]_{chl}$, Moss proposed that either $[CO_2]_{chl}$ is zero, *i.e.*, it could not decrease, or it is another minimum value "... determined either by the capacity of the chemical system of the species or by affinity of the enzymes for CO_2". With reference to species light response, it was proposed that $[CO_2]_{chl}$ could have an equal minimum value for all species while differences in P between the species might originate via differences in L, S, or M. Variations in the latter might in turn be caused by differences in leaf thickness, number and size of stomata, or respiration rates.

That differing physical barriers may in fact exist in leaves was shown by the work of Hesketh (722) in 1963. It was found that tobacco leaves enclosed by an atmosphere of 800 ppm CO_2 produced a light response curve nearly identical with corn contained in an atmosphere having only 300 ppm CO_2. However, with philodendron leaves increasing CO_2 did not increase net photosynthesis. Commenting on this, Moss (1041) noted that those plants which do not respond to increasing CO_2 under light-saturating conditions must bear non-physical explanations incident to the photosynthetic processes *per se* which will not yield to environment manipulation.

In contrast to the work of Verduin and Loomis (1490), which suggested that in maize the midday illumination was adequate for maximum photosynthesis by all leaves from top to ground level, Moss *et al.* (1039) obtained distinct responses among different leaf surfaces at different times of thc day. These further varied with CO_2 supply and transpiration. Transpiration experiments were performed in which the CO_2 concentration of one chamber was higher than in another chamber for several hours. It was found that plants exposed to higher CO_2 levels maintained a lower rate of transpiration. This was suggestive of a restriction against stomatal opening by high CO_2. Moss *et al.* verified this by painting the leaf surface with a "collodion solution" and allowing the solvent to evaporate; thereafter the film was peeled off and stomata imprints in the film were measured with the aid of a microscope. Results shown in Table 4-3 indicate that the stomatal apertures were altered markedly by small changes in CO_2 concentration. Quite significantly, this effect was especially true among leaves situated at the top of the plants where they experienced a fuller light exposure. The changes were notably smaller within and beneath the foliar canopy but the relationship of stomata opening to CO_2 held true to a lesser degree. The diurnal changes evidenced in Table 4-3 are also of interest. Among top leaves a progressive restriction

TABLE 4-3

EFFECTS OF CO_2 SUPPLY ON ASSIMILATION, TRANSPIRATION, AND STOMATAL APERTURES OF CORN

[After Moss *et al.* (1039).] Reproduced by permission of *Crop Science.*

Time	CO_2 (ppm)	Assimilation (g/chamber)	Transpiration (g/chamber)	Stomatal aperture for leaf		
				Top	Center	Bottom
7 a.m.	55	6	0	6.3	3.8	2.0
8 a.m.	120	7	0	5.2	4.9	3.6
9 a.m.	260	103	5000	3.4	3.1	3.6
12 noon	535	113	4200	2.5	1.8	1.0
1 p.m.	575	118	2700	2.0	2.6	2.8
3 p.m.	310	76	3500	4.7	2.9	1.7

of stomatal apertures was recorded from 7:00 a.m. to 1:00 p.m.; among bottom leaves the trend was less distinct and in fact there was no aperture restriction until some time between 9:00 a.m. and 12:00 noon, well after the upper stomata had been partially closed.

Botanists and ecologists have for years recognized that many plant species simply cannot survive or reproduce in the shade of a forest canopy. That portions of a given plant may experience similar difficulties in performing essential life processes is strongly implied by the work of Moss *et al.* (1039) with maize. Interesting enough, these authors found the light intensity to be so low on certain cloudy days (between July 15 and October 1) that the entire maize canopy performed below the compensation point. Moss and his co-workers wrote: "...Certainly leaves down in the plant cover must contribute little to the net assimilation of the plant on cloudy days and may play a minor role in dry matter production even on clear days." This trend of thought must apply equally well to the sugarcane plant. Sugar losses during the "rainy season" are frequently blamed upon excessive moisture and its attendant rise in inversion, increased soluble nitrogen in the soil, and increased growth. It is probable that the photosynthetic processes themselves would not support normal sugar accumulation even if the wet season brought only clouds without the rainfall.

C. CO_2 *fertilization; light* x CO_2 *supply*

The concept of "CO_2 fertilization" as a means to increase crop yields has been much debated but remains largely at the academic level. Moss *et al.* (1039) performed CO_2 experiments with maize which vividly demonstrated the capability of increased

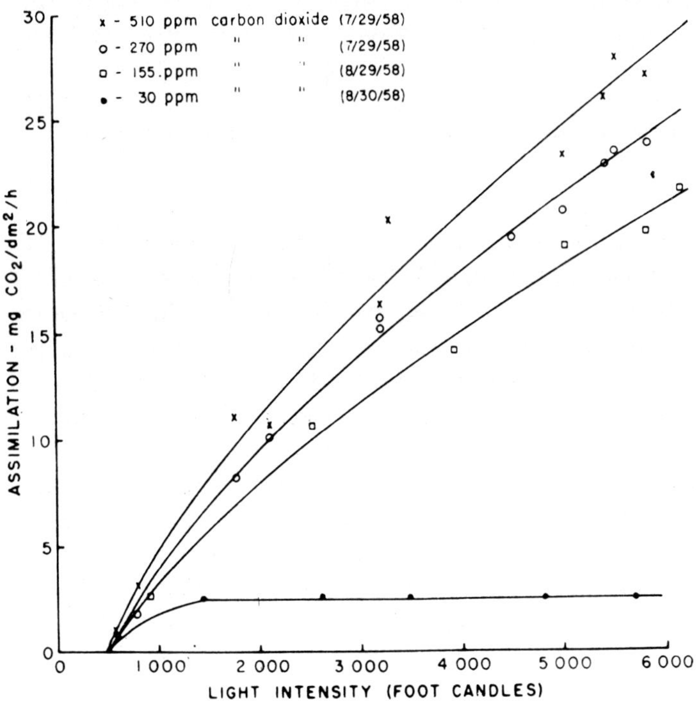

Fig. 4-5. Apparent photosynthesis in corn plants as a function of light intensity at four CO_2 concentrations. [After Moss *et al.* (1039).] Reproduced by permission of *Crop Science*.

CO_2 supply to increase CO_2 assimilation rates. It was also shown that the effectiveness of added CO_2 in this plant is greatly dependent upon light intensity. In Fig. 4-5 the photosynthesis response to variable CO_2 levels is plotted as a function of light supply. Maize plants were maintained in portable assimilation chambers for 1 hour with the indicated CO_2 levels held constant. The light intensities shown are averages for the same period. It is quite evident that at 30 ppm of CO_2 there was very little apparent photosynthesis and increasing light intensities above 1500 foot candles produced no additional CO_2 assimilation. At higher CO_2 levels there again was little apparent photosynthesis at low light intensities, but with increasing light supply there were enormous increases in CO_2 assimilation. The rate of photosynthesis in these experiments was close to 50 percent greater at 510 ppm CO_2 than at 155 ppm CO_2. Light saturation occurred only at the lowest CO_2 level.

Moss *et al.* underscored the fact that the photosynthesis curves tended to spread with increasing light intensity, suggesting that a greater CO_2 "fertilization" was achieved at higher light intensities (1039). It should be noted that these experiments were performed under field conditions in which light values greater than 6000 foot candles were difficult to obtain for extended periods. The authors concluded that ". . . any economical fertilization with CO_2 would have to be applied during midday hours on clear days". In general, light conditions suitable for crop "treatment" with CO_2 would be more prevalent among tropical species such as sugarcane than among temperate species.

D. *CO_2 as a limiting photosynthesis factor among species*

Differing photosynthetic capacity has long been recognized among plant species. We have touched upon the theoretical causes as reviewed by Rabinowitch (1204), Blackman's concept of limiting factors (193), and the mathematical treatment of photosynthetic variables by Moss (1041) and by Hesketh and Moss (721). The kinetic examination by Rabinowitch set forth the prediction that maximum photosynthesis will be determined by chlorophyll content, or by the relationship between absorbed quanta and photosynthesis. In accordance with this theory inherent differences in these factors would express themselves under conditions of extremely weak illumination. We have seen also that a number of investigators sought proof for the Rabinowitch equations by examining at low light intensities various species having broad differences in maximum photosynthesis potential. Moreover, since the equations also predict that maximum photosynthesis may be determined by "dark reaction" factors, such as the quantity of CO_2 or CO_2 receptor, or by the rate of CO_2 diffusion to the assimilation site, other workers have studied the response of these factors to CO_2 under conditions of low CO_2 supply.

In 1963 Hesketh (722) published findings with nine species (including sugarcane) which seemed to indicate that factors associated with the light reaction, *i.e.*, chlorophyll content and proportionality between absorbed quanta and photosynthesis, were not critical in determining species response differences. Rather, the critical differences appeared to lie in the conductivity of CO_2 within mesophyll tissue and in the kinetics of dark reactions.

Hesketh felt that the critical characteristic in determining maximum photosynthesis (P_{max}) was $Q_{max}K$, the slope of the response curve as (I) approaches zero. The value of $Q_{max}K$ did not vary appreciably among the species, nor was there any striking relationship between chlorophyll content and photosynthetic efficiency (Table 4-4). It was also found that radiation absorption and thickness of the leaf lamina had little apparent bearing on the photosynthetic differences, *i.e.*, the most efficient species were those having the least apparent ability to intercept light. For these reasons Hesketh concluded that such factors relating to the light reaction were probably not critical determinants of photosynthetic rate. Alternately, factors relating to CO_2, as depicted by the equation

$$Q' = Q'_{max}K'X(1 + K'X) - 1 \tag{3}$$

where Q' = net photosynthesis plus respiration in the absence of CO_2; Q'_{max} is Q' as X, the concentration of CO_2, approaches infinity, and $Q'_{max}K'$ is the slope of the response curve as $X \longrightarrow 0$, were of major importance in determining photosynthetic rate. Contrary to the initial slope of the light response curve in which differences were very small, the initial slope of the CO_2 response curve was essentially borne out at the higher CO_2 level, 300 ppm, at which concentration species differences were most pronounced. The $Q'_{max}K'$ of the CO_2 reaction thus included the $Q_{max}K$ of the light reaction, the equilibrium constants of intermediate dark reactions, and the constant relating to CO_2 diffusion from the air to the assimilation site. Hesketh concluded that the dark reaction kinetics and resistances to CO_2 diffusion into the leaf must explain much of photosynthetic differences among species. This view is based upon the assumption that stomata are open in intense light.

No clear relationship was found between photosynthesis rate and stomata arrangement. Species such as sugarcane, maize, and orchardgrass have stomata aligned in rows whereas other species have stomata situated more or less at random over the leaf surface. Hesketh noted the small stomatal area ($b \times n$) found in sugarcane and maize leaves as compared with other species examined (Table 4-5). He interpreted this to mean that sugarcane and maize, having CO_2 assimilation rates in the order of 50 to 60 mg $CO_2/dm^2/h$, should have greater photosynthesis to transpiration ratios than species assimilating roughly half this amount of CO_2. The work of Zelitch and Waggoner (1609) was cited in which transpiration was shown to be controlled by stomatal area.

Significantly, Hesketh attached little importance to the concept of product repression in photosynthesis. Noting similarities in photosynthesis rate over periods of 3 to 5 hours for maize, sunflower, tobacco, and castor bean in 300 ppm CO_2, he concluded

TABLE 4-4

PHOTOSYNTHETIC FEATURES OF LEAVES AMONG DIFFERENT PLANT SPECIES

[After Hesketh (722).] Reproduced by permission of *Crop Science.*

Species	Q at 300 ppm CO_2	Q' at 800 ppm CO_2	Chlorophyll (mg/dm^2)	Radiation absorptivity	Thickness lamina (mm)	Fresh wt. (g/cm^2)	Mean L.C.P.* ($ly/min \times 10^2$)
Castor bean	18–26	59–78	2.4–2.9	1.01	0.28–0.33	1.4–1.7	4.5
Maize	31–64	60–90	2.1–3.0	1.00	0.20–0.30	1.5–1.9	3.4
Maple	5–7	–	–	1.00	0.15–0.20	–	1.3
Oak	7–12	–	–	1.02	0.23–0.30	–	1.9
Orchardgrass	22–26	–	–	–	0.20–0.30	–	1.6
Red clover	23–34	–	–	–	0.20–0.30	–	1.8
Sugarcane	42	–	–	–	0.25–0.30	–	–
Sunflower	37–43	89–108	2.8–2.9	1.02	0.36–0.43	2.2–2.4	4.0
Tobacco	18–27	65–69	3.0–3.2	1.03	0.38–0.46	2.4–2.5	4.7

*Light compensation point at 300 ppm CO_2.

TABLE 4-5

ESTIMATED Q_{max} K VALUES FOR NINE PLANT SPECIES BASED ON RADIATION DENSITIES AND STOMATA DATA OF UPPER AND LOWER LEAF SURFACES*

[After Hesketh (722).] Reproduced by permission of *Crop Science.*

Species	Q_{max} K (mean values)	Stomata (n thousands)		Larger axis (b microns)		$b \times n$, both surfaces
		Upper	Lower	Upper	Lower	
Castor bean	88	27	17	15	15	660
Maize	109	7.0	4.9	34	43	450
Maple	229	0	25	0	7	175
Oak	115	0	37	0	8.8	325
Orchardgrass	129	14	20	18	18	610
Red clover	115	17	21	10	7.5	325
Sugarcane	–	6	10	19	19	304
Sunflower	113	23	25	16	16	770
Tobacco	94	11	22	14	14	460

*0.12 Q_{max} K was taken as the approximate percent efficiency for conversion to sucrose of artificial light absorbed by leaves at wavelengths between 400 and 700 nm.

that these rates must exceed those possible in nature, and that therefore a midday depression due to accumulated sucrose is unlikely: "...Apparently, if ample water is available or the leaf is not suddenly stressed, constant photosynthetic rates are possible over very long periods of time." In the instance of sugarcane, Hartt has built a strong case for diurnal sucrose repression of photosynthesis (*cf.* this chapter, pp. 175–177) which appears to be worsened by inadequate water supply (675). Workers in Australia (594, 1518) found no evidence of direct end-product repression of photosynthesis in sugarcane. Hesketh was probably correct in assigning field-grown plants only a moderate capability for fulfilling their theoretical photosynthesis potential.

E. *CO_2 transport in relation to foliar water regime*

Aside from its role in photosynthetic energy conversion, water has attracted increased interest among students of CO_2 assimilation. Many workers have directed their attention to stomatal resistance and mesophyll resistance to CO_2 diffusion (1204, 1358, 1041, 721, 722). Moss (1041) observed that decreased stomata resistance was so closely paralleled by increased water loss that the latter could be used as a reliable gage of the decreasing resistance effects. Steemann Nielsen (1358) stressed the difficulty of CO_2 movement as a solute toward the chloroplasts of aquatic plants in his efforts to prove that free CO_2 was not the lone carbon source of photosynthesis in such plants. Other workers dealing with water–CO_2 relationships in land plants have treated both CO_2 and water as gases, the latter being in a vapor phase. Hesketh (722) carefully specifies that the leaf must have "ample water" in order to maintain high photosynthesis rates over an extended period of time. The possibility that water vapor affects CO_2 movement to the assimilation site assumed added significance after Hesketh demonstrated the potentially critical nature of CO_2 dark reaction kinetics and CO_2 movement through mesophyll in governing photosynthesis rate. Other investigators stressed the need of abundant water in connection with photosynthate transport (674, 675).

In 1967 Zelitch (1612) reviewed the importance of CO_2 and water vapor diffusion as gases through open stomata. Particular attention was given to the diffusion effects upon transpiration and photosynthesis. Zelitch concluded that with stomata being small and essentially constant in number (he gives the figure 10 000 per cm^2), the increased size of stomatal openings in response to light is "...an adaptation which permits greater rates of photosynthesis by decreasing the diffusive resistance to CO_2 uptake". However, under field conditions of high light intensity, "...most of the water escaping from the soil readily diffuses through these leaf pores".

Zelitch treated the experimental approaches toward regulating photosynthesis and transpiration in terms of a series of resistances. In essence, he maintained that transpiration control via stomatal resistance is an accomplished fact in nature. By providing a resistance to water movement from internal moist conditions to the dry exterior, and by closing when the leaf wilts, stomata are depicted as functional "hydrostats" (1517). Support for the hydrostat role is found in the work of Waggoner and Simmonds (1516) who described a potato mutant which wilts excessively and produces poor growth because of an inherited inability to close its stomata.

Efforts to accomplish transpiration control with plastic films or "anti-transpirants" have been described (554), the object being to restrict water movement without restricting CO_2 diffusion. Chemical inhibitors which prevent stomatal opening in the light have also been reported (987, 1608). The inhibitory action of α-hydroxysulfonates on glycolate oxidase has contributed to the evidence favoring a glycolic acid metabolism role in stomatal opening (1612). Sodium azide is an effective inhibitor of stomatal opening in light and at high levels also interferes with their closing in darkness (1612, 1519). Zelitch (1612) states that ideal transpiration control would involve the inhibition of guard cell metabolism by agents which do not harm other leaf cells. In practice this amounts to direct treatment of the guard cells with non-translocating inhibitors. Phenylmercuric acetate has shown promise in this respect by closing tobacco-leaf stomata without being transported to other cells (1610, 1609).

F. *The CO_2 compensation point*

Zelitch (1612) proposed that plants having low CO_2 compensation points and high photosynthetic efficiency are behaving in accordance with the expected effect of high photorespiration. As discussed earlier in relation to light intensity (*cf.* present chapter, pp. 130–132), the CO_2 compensation point in a given plant is attained when the CO_2 concentration in the surrounding enclosed atmosphere has declined to a steady-state concentration. Plants such as maize, sugarcane, and sorghum are particularly efficient in photosynthesis and have compensation points in the order of 5 ppm CO_2 (1040). Most other species have CO_2 compensation points in excess of 50 ppm (1612). Under conditions of high light intensity, sugarcane, maize and sorghum (all C_4 pathway plants), have photosynthesis rates 2 to 3 times greater than plants such as tobacco, wheat, and orchardgrass (721).

Zelitch continued: "... The value of the CO_2 compensation point correlates well with previously-stated knowledge about photorespiration in various species. In those species exhibiting considerable photorespiration it seemed reasonable to assume that photorespiration could cause diminished CO_2 uptake from the atmosphere through loss of fixed carbon which decreases the CO_2 concentration gradient on the pathway from the air to the chloroplasts." Maize, sugarcane, and sorghum do not evolve appreciable CO_2 in the light in a CO_2-free atmosphere (1612).

The CO_2 compensation point is also affected by temperature and foliar water content. Zelitch (1612) cites data for five species showing compensation points at least 2 times higher at 35 °C than at 25 °C. Moss (1041) has shown CO_2 assimilation to be doubled in maize between 20 and 30 °C, but only when water is not limiting. In this instance the increased water loss as the stomata opened (in response to light) was taken as a measure of the effect on gas flow of the newly-decreased stomatal resistance. The relationship is apparently species-orientated since tobacco leaves were found to assimilate less CO_2 at 30–35 °C than at 25 °C. Zelitch proposed that the lower photosynthesis rates in the less efficient species stemmed from a combination of high temperature and increased photorespiration.

G. *CO_2 transport as a function of discrete resistances*

From the foregoing discussion we have seen that various workers were concerned with the capacity of CO_2 to pass from the external atmosphere to fixation sites in the leaf (1041, 1358, 555, 722). Still greater importance is attached to this concept today; indeed, some authors feel that in much of the early sugarcane photosynthesis work too little attention was given to stomatal aperture function and adequate air turbulence at the leaf surface. This might have led to decreased transpiration and photosynthesis with parallel increases in leaf temperature and stomatal resistance. Other workers [1, 2] (822, 881, 594) depict CO_2 transport in terms of a series of physical and biochemical resistances operating along the course of CO_2 movement. Meidner [1], for example, distinguishes between a gaseous CO_2 diffusion from the leaf boundary layer through leaf pores and intercellular spaces, and the mesophyll movement of dissolved CO_2 in

---

[1] Meidner, H., 1969. Rate limiting resistances and photosynthesis, *Nature* 222: 876–877.

which a liquid phase diffusion is modified by water status, streaming, and enzymic action. In addition, purely biochemical resistances are seen in the availability of carboxylation enzymes at the assimilation site. A present conception[2] of CO_2 resistances (r) likely to be operative in the sugarcane leaf is shown schematically as follows:

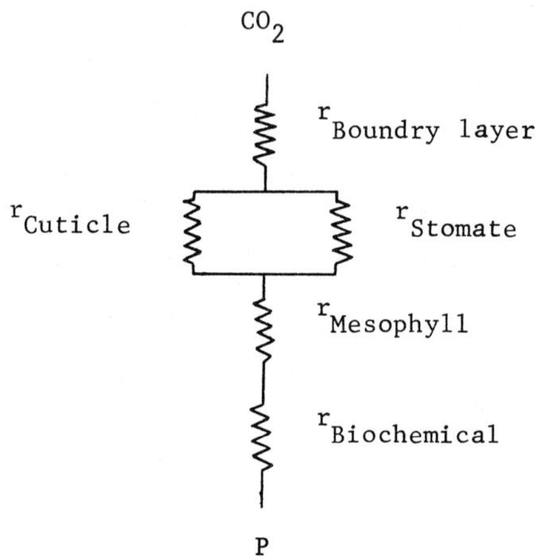

Bull[2] (594) stresses the importance of the total CO_2 transport pathway and its different resistances in photosynthesis rate measurements for sugarcane. It follows that considerable care must be taken both in estimating individual resistances and in controlling them for physiological studies of CO_2 assimilation rates.

4. PHOTOSYNTHESIS DECLINE IN NUTRIENT-DEFICIENT PLANTS

Although nutrient deficiencies may reduce crop yields in many ways, those deficiencies that restrict photosynthesis must rank among the most serious since loss of photosynthetic activity will ultimately reflect upon every yield parameter. On the other hand, yields may be lowered by inadequate nutrient levels without appreciably affecting photosynthesis. An important point here is the fact that plants need not be deprived to the point of visible deficiency in order for photosynthetic restriction to occur. Plants experiencing "hidden hunger" might appear to be green and healthy while the processes of carbohydrate synthesis, translocation, and storage operate at suboptimal rates.

A second point is that the effects of nutrient deficiency upon photosynthesis are not specifically confined to CO_2 assimilation. Any functional aspect of the normal source-to-sink system that is placed under stress by inadequate nutrient supply will

[2] Bull, T.A., 1971. Personal communication, March, 1971.

frequently find expression, if not its cause, in some phase of energy conversion or CO_2 assimilation. To the extent that the driving forces of sucrose transport are derived from photosynthetic phosphorylation, it can be said that any factor affecting chlorophyll content and its concomitant light reactions hangs ominously over the entire scene of source-to-sink activity. For sugarcane this activity encompasses the entire plant throughout its entire life history. The implications of a sugarcane photosynthetic apparatus operating under nutritional stress are enormous; its full effects have not yet been measured either by the sugar producer or by the professional physiologist.

A. *General aspects of CO_2 assimilation as affected by nutrition*

The literature relating to empirical effects of nutrient deficiencies on photosynthesis is voluminous and no more than general outlines can be given here. However, it is safe to state that little information is available concerning mechanisms of nutrient action in the CO_2 assimilation process. Information suggesting that Fe, Mn, and Mg perform roles incident to the energy conversion process is somewhat more extensive but this also is by no means complete.

Many nutritional effects appear to be indirect ones relating to the size and vigor of the plant and its chlorophyll-bearing tissues. Deficiencies of N, S, Mg, Fe and Mn which lead to foliar chlorosis pose a more direct restriction by lowering chlorophyll content (1423). Subnormal CO_2 assimilation rates have been recorded in barley (613) and sugarcane (76) deficient in N, P, and K. In the instance of maize, K deficiences of insufficient severity to produce visual symptoms can materially lower the CO_2 assimilation rate (1152). It is interesting to note that Eckstein (469), while examining chlorophyll content and CO_2 assimilation in wheat, observed a high-K suppression of chlorophyll content, but he also noted that there was no apparent relationship between chlorophyll content and net assimilation as evidenced by organic matter synthesis. In this connection Eckstein cited the findings of Emerson (487), and of Gassner and Goeze (560), showing photosynthesis rates to be very low even in the presence of high chlorophyll content. Willstätter and Stoll (1576) reportedly found evidence that a direct proportionality need not exist between chlorophyll content and CO_2 assimilation.

Loustalot *et al.* (958), studying the effects of variable N and K levels in tung seedlings on apparent photosynthesis, detected no significant interaction between N and K. Of the two elements, low N supply restricted photosynthesis more severely than low K. Schwabe (1309), after comparing N, P, and K data from bracken with similar data from flax and barley, concluded that the three species respond similarly to N, P, and K deficiencies[3]. Thomas and Hill (1422) observed that S deficiency lowered

[3] In these studies and many others performed under field conditions dry weight values were taken as an acceptable expression of CO_2 assimilation.

photosynthetic activity in sugar beets, alfalfa, and tomatoes without significantly affecting respiration. Enriching the air with CO_2 failed to counter the S-deficiency effect in sugar beets.

Childers and Cowart (321), studying the nutrition and photosynthesis rates of 2-year-old apple trees, observed a close relationship between N nutrition and photosynthesis. He attributed this to N effects upon chlorophyll content. Similar results were obtained by Heinicke (711) under field conditions; the greener the apple leaf, the greater the photosynthesis rate. Although this work was published in 1935, the authors were aware of "...a close correlation between the ability of a leaf to assimilate carbon dioxide and its ability to give off water in transpiration". In later years, much importance was to be attached to the relations between transpiration and CO_2 assimilation by investigators having much greater control over their experimental conditions than was possible for Heinicke and his colleagues (321, 711, 712).

B. *Effects of K, Mg, and Ca deficiency*

In 1966 Peaslee and Moss (1152) published results of maize photosynthesis studies showing close relationships of foliar K or Mg concentrations to CO_2 assimilation rate. Plants were grown in a greenhouse by sand–soil culture techniques designed to give low nutrient-supplying capacity[4]. Data from the experiments showed that quantitative relationships existed between the foliar K and Mg concentrations and photosynthesis rates in the same leaves. The primary effect of Mg deficiency appeared to be a deterioration of chlorophyll. Low photosynthesis in K-deficient leaves was associated with stomatal closure.

Fig. 4-6 illustrates the CO_2 assimilation rate relationship with extractable foliar K. Extremely rapid losses of photosynthetic activity occurred as K levels decreased from 1.0 to 0.2 mg K/g of fresh tissue. Above 2.0 mg of K the nutrient effect was negligible. It is important to note that all leaves appeared to be normal and no K-deficiency symptoms were visible in the leaves examined. Moreover, there were appreciable variations in chlorophyll content.

In offering an explanation for the low-K effect on CO_2 assimilation Peaslee and Moss made note of two facts: (a) Provision of K-deficient leaves with supplemental K led to a significant recovery of photosynthesis within 24 hours, and (b) transpiration increased in the recovering leaf. It was thought that low K had affected the stomata. Subsequent experiments in which K-deficient leaves were immersed in K solutions revealed a 10-fold increase of leaf permeability within 6 hours. This affirmed the authors' contention that low K had seriously affected leaf permeability and photo-

[4]Individual containers held 2 kg of quartz sand at the bottom, and 500 g of soil were layered over this followed by a cover of 700 g of sand. Potassium levels varied from 0 to 525 mg of K per container. The containers of the Mg series received from 0 to 50 mg of Mg. Nutrient sources were KH_2PO_4 and KNO_3 for K, and $MgSO_4$ for Mg. Treatments were given at 5-day intervals.

synthesis in a reversible manner. It was also shown that the K relationship to photosynthesis could not be altered by Na, a complementary monovalent cation, or by divalent Ca ions (Fig. 4-6). Further to this, Moss (1043) published in 1967 photo-

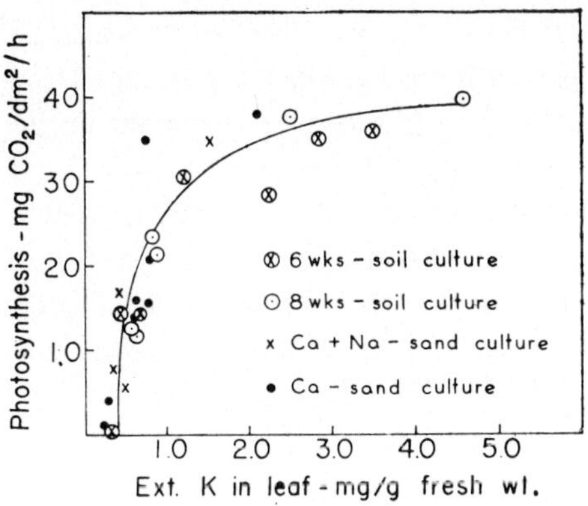

Fig. 4-6. Relationship between extractable potassium and photosynthesis rates in maize grown in soil or supplied with variable calcium or calcium plus sodium in sand culture. [After Peaslee and Moss (1152).] Reproduced by permission of the *Soil Science Society of America.*

graphs of open and closed stomata in well-fertilized and K-deficient leaves, respectively. Singh (1328), working with sugarcane, found that K fertilization increased CO_2 assimilation efficiency during approximately the first half of the cane life cycle and decreased assimilation during the second half.

In 1960 (76) photosynthesis studies were reported in Hawaii which suggested that K-deficient sugarcane plants were unable to maintain normal photosynthesis rates. Photosynthesis in leaf samples showing no visible deficiency symptoms and containing 0.91 percent K (control = 1.70 to 1.73 percent K) was restricted by about 10 percent. Severe K deficiency producing typical symptoms and accumulating less than 0.40 percent K decreased photosynthesis from 84 to 98 percent. Potassium had no appreciable effect on chlorophyll content. The same report also contained information relative to nutrient deficiencies and moisture stress as they affect sucrose transport, but no connection was drawn at this time between low K and restricted photosynthesis on the one hand and a low K, moisture-stress relationship on the other.

In more recent experiments with detached blades of sugarcane plants given low K supplies, Hartt (677) found that low K decreased photosynthesis but a much more pronounced effect was exerted upon basipetal sucrose transport. Translocation restrictions were recorded at K levels not sufficiently low to produce either deficiency symptoms or restricted photosynthesis. In leaves only "slightly" deficient in K the translocation effect occurred in light but not in darkness. More severe K deficiency reduced sucrose transport both in light and darkness. In addition, low K restricted sucrose translocation to a greater degree than it decreased moisture content:

". . .There was a much better correlation between the decrease in potassium and translocation than between the decrease in moisture and translocation."

Hartt's findings are consistent with those of Peaslee and Moss in that K deficiency altered photosynthesis rate without causing permanent injury to the photosynthetic apparatus. In essence, both the maize findings by Peaslee and Moss and the sugarcane findings by Hartt point to a K effect upon leaf permeability, which in turn affects leaf moisture status. In sugarcane the ensuing restriction upon sucrose movement implies that product repression of photosynthesis might have occurred. On the other hand, lowered leaf permeability must also influence CO_2 diffusion potential, thereby creating potential restrictions upon the CO_2 assimilation rate.

Peaslee and Moss (1152) found that low Mg significantly lowered CO_2 assimilation rate and chlorophyll content of maize leaves (Fig. 4-7). In contrast to the reversible

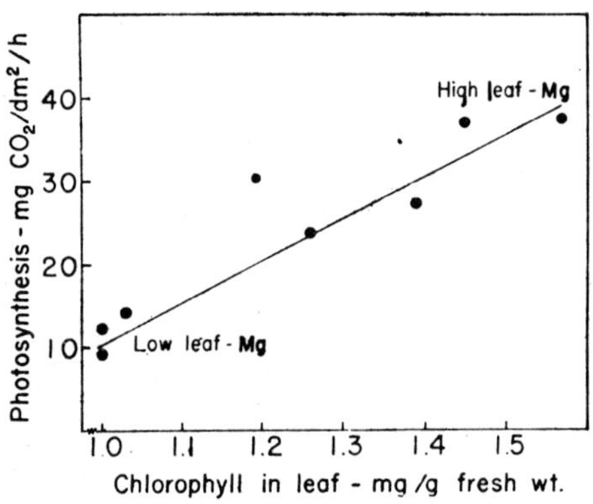

Fig. 4-7. Chlorophyll content and rates of photosynthesis in maize leaves containing variable amounts of magnesium. [After Peaslee and Moss (1152).] Reproduced by permission of the *Soil Science Society of America*.

effects of low K on maize photosynthesis, the Mg-deficient leaves did not recover their photosynthetic capability, and in fact the excised leaves deteriorated within 24 hours. Also unlike plants given low K, the Mg-deficient series clearly showed Mg-deficiency symptoms and a high level of leaf permeability. The latter did contain lower amounts of chlorophyll. Lal and De (883) similarly correlated high chlorophyll content and high CO_2 assimilation rates in young sugarcane leaves having correspondingly high Mg content.

Peaslee and Moss concluded: ". . .the major photosynthetic function of Mg is in the chlorophyll molecule, and any enzyme functions are either not involved with initial energy transfers during photosynthesis or they are affected by Mg deficiency subsequent to chlorophyll deterioration". These authors also visualized quantitative relationships between K and Mg in maize leaves and the rates of photosynthesis serving as field guides for critical K and Mg levels. Moss (1043) noted that under field conditions the highest foliar K concentration at which corn yield ceases to increase is about 1.3 percent on a dry weight basis, whereas the critical K concentration for photosynthesis lies between 1.1 and 1.5 percent.

In 1965 Hartt and Burr (674) reported positive correlations between low photosynthesis and low K or Ca content of sugarcane leaves. Working with the varieties *H. 37-1933* and *H. 50-7209*, it was found that K deficiency suppressed photosynthesis when the foliar K percentage fell to about 0.40 percent. The variety *H. 37-1933* was apparently more sensitive to low K than was *H. 50-7209*. The latter variety tended to retain higher K levels, but photosynthesis restriction was nonetheless evident in the older blades (Table 4-6).

TABLE 4-6

RELATIONSHIPS OF LEAF POTASSIUM CONTENT TO THE PHOTOSYNTHESIS RATE IN SUGARCANE*

[After Hartt and Burr (674).] Reproduced by permission of *I.S.S.C.T.*

Age (months)	Blade rank	Photosynthesis (ml $CO_2/dm^2/h$)		K (% dry wt.)	
		Control	K	Control	–K
3.8	4	16.6	16.6	–	–
4.3	4	19.6	20.4	2.11	1.68
4.7	4	20.3	21.6	2.45	1.15
5.1	4	24.0	21.3	2.50	0.89
5.5	4	25.0	22.1	2.35	0.73
5.8	4	22.6	18.2	2.25	0.52
6.3	4	26.3	23.2	2.10	0.60
6.6	4	20.5	20.2	1.91	0.56
6.8	4	23.2	16.8	1.73	0.59
7.1	4	15.2	17.9	2.15	0.59
7.3	4	20.8	17.1	1.78	0.59
7.3	8	21.0	1.9	2.14	0.14
7.4	5	18.5	7.2	1.81	0.30
7.4	6	20.7	11.9	1.84	0.30
7.4	7	17.2	2.1	1.61	0.14

*Variety *H.50-7209*. Plants were grown in complete and potassium-free nutrient solutions.

Effects of Ca deficiency on sugarcane photosynthesis, as evidenced by declining foliar Ca values, are shown in Fig. 4-8. In this experiment comparisons were drawn between leaves $^+4$ and $^+8$ of the variety *H. 50-7209*. As anticipated, the Ca effect was apparent in the younger blades before it was noted in leaf $^+8$. Deficiency symptoms visible in leaf $^+8$ included browning of the blade edges and some specking. In both leaf ranks the photosynthetic depression was associated with foliar Ca levels in the order of 0.043 to 0.034 percent (674).

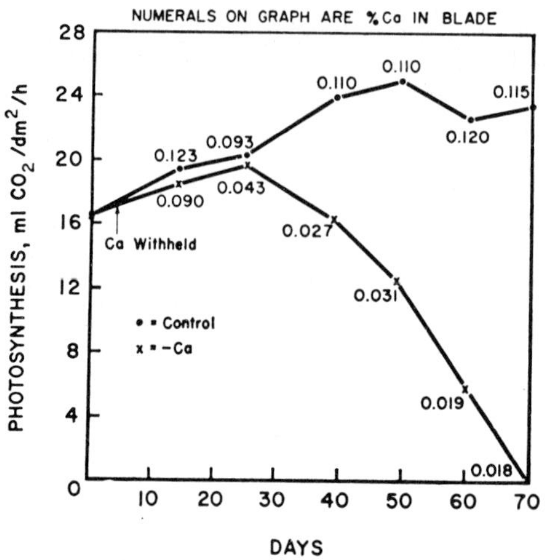

Fig. 4-8. Relationship of variable calcium content of sugarcane leaves to the rate of photosynthesis. [After Hartt and Burr (674).] Reproduced by permission of *I.S.S.C.T.*

C. *Effects of N and P deficiency*

Loss of chlorophyll to the point of visible yellowing is a traditional symptom of inadequate N supply in numerous plant species. In most instances a parallel loss of net CO_2 assimilation or assimilation efficiency is a safe assumption. With respect to sugarcane, studies by Singh (1329, 1328) published in 1941 were the first to correlate reduced photosynthesis rates with N deficiency. An earlier report by Singh and Lal (1325) had pointed up certain shortcomings in Blackman's law of limiting factors as applied to sugarcane photosynthesis, but this work centered upon light, CO_2, and temperature factors rather than nutritional aspects. Singh (1328) found that N fertilization of sugarcane increased CO_2 assimilation efficiency with concurrent increases of growth and dry matter at all stages of the life cycle. Hartt and Burr (674) noted similar N effects in the earlier stages.

In another paper, Singh (1329) described the decline of growth parameters, carbohydrates, chlorophyll content, and CO_2 assimilation efficiency in N-deficient sugarcane. Lal and De (883), in 1953, correlated subnormal photosynthesis in N-deficient sugarcane with a marked decline in pigment content. This effect was most severe in the leaves of intermediate rank and least severe in leaves $^{+}1$ and $^{+}6$. Both chlorophyll *a* and *b* were lowered by N deficiency. The generally constant respiration in these leaves was attributed to a preference for hexoses rather than nitrogenous compounds as respiratory substrates. It was also observed that chlorophyll *a* and *b* and CO_2 assimilation gradually declined in sugarcane plants after the third month. This appears to be an authentic age effect. It should be noted that the normal cultural plan for sugarcane calls for N to become limiting for optimum growth several months before harvest, an event which might lower chlorophyll content and net CO_2 assimilation, particularly in the older leaves, regardless of the overall age factor.

Singh (1329) found that P deficiency increased the percentage of starch and total carbohydrates in sugarcane dry matter. Extractable juice and sucrose were decreased by low P. Excessive P supplies reversed these effects. Differences in CO_2 assimilation rates were recorded before distinct growth effects were obtained with variable P, as well as with variable N and K. Low P was shown to reduce the number of leaves and stem circumference and to lower CO_2 assimilation efficiency throughout the sugarcane life cycle.

Photosynthetic ^{14}C studies in Hawaii (76) with N-, P-, and K-deficient sugarcane grown in water culture showed that low levels of each element reduced CO_2 assimilation rates (Table 4-7). Low P was more restrictive against photosynthesis than N and K

TABLE 4-7

PHOTOSYNTHESIS DECLINE IN SUGARCANE PLANTS DEFICIENT IN NITROGEN, PHOSPHORUS, AND POTASSIUM

[Anon. (76).] Reproduced by permission of the *Hawaiian Sugar Planters' Association*, Honolulu.

Treatment	Photosynthesis	
	TC*/cm²	Percent decrease
Control	556	–
–N	257	41
–P	208	63
–K	449	19

*TC refers to total counts per minute.

deficiencies in the 2-month-old plants. In subsequent trials plants were grown in water culture with a single element withheld. Leaf samples showing marked reduction of the respective nutrient level were transferred to a photosynthesis chamber and evaluated for CO_2 assimilation under conditions of controlled temperature, light intensity, and CO_2 concentration. Results are presented in Fig. 4-9. It can be seen from the tabulated data that low P markedly reduced the chlorophyll content, depressed N content, and severely curtailed photosynthesis. In this study low N reduced chlorophyll content to about 1/3 of the control level while photosynthesis rate declined to less than half of the control rate. After steady-state photosynthesis had proceeded for 175 seconds, the blades were extracted with boiling alcohol and the sugars were examined by paper chromatography. Nutrient deficiencies were found to have lowered the amounts of early photosynthesis products to an essentially equal degree. An exception was noted in the case of P-deficient leaves whose extracts contained extremely low amounts of phosphoglyceric acid, glucose 1-phosphate, and fructose 1,6-diphosphate. The loss of organic phosphates was not accompanied by loss of sucrose.

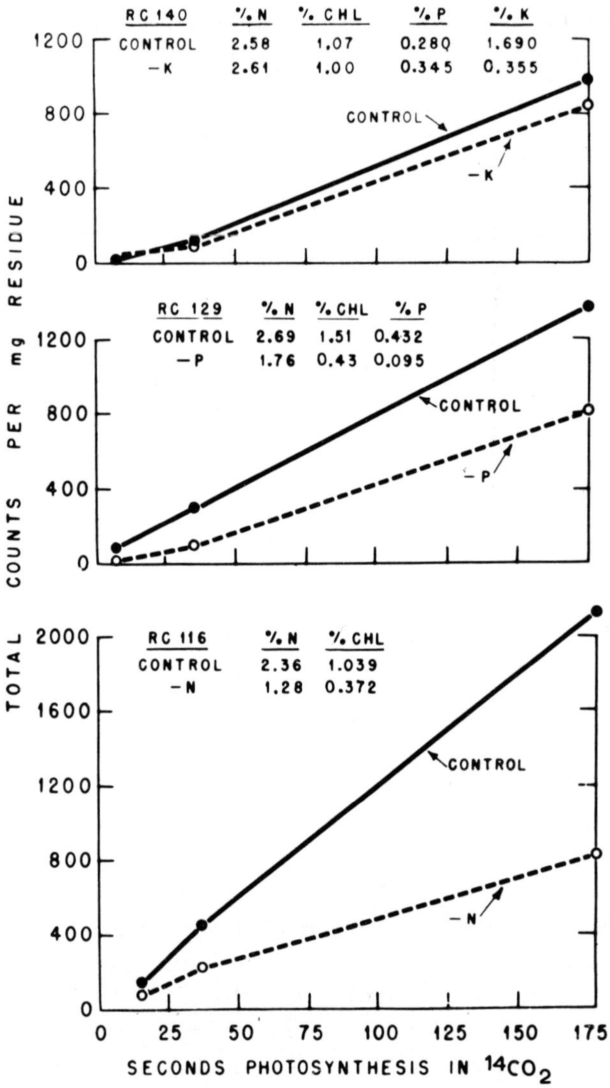

Fig. 4-9. Effects of deficiencies of nitrogen, phosphorus, and potassium on steady-state photosynthesis in sugarcane after exposure of leaves to $^{14}CO_2$. [Anon. (76).] Reproduced by permission of the *Hawaiian Sugar Planters' Association*, Honolulu.

Hartt and Burr (674) reported pronounced relationships between CO_2 assimilation rate, N supply, and the percentage of N in sugarcane leaves (Fig. 4-10). The data presented in Fig. 4-10 are the means of 12 varieties. Between 9 and 15 months a major decline was recorded for total N and CO_2 assimilation rate (A). At 6 months of age there was a direct relationship between photosynthesis rate and percentage of total N in the leaf (B). A positive correlation was retained between N supply and photosynthesis.

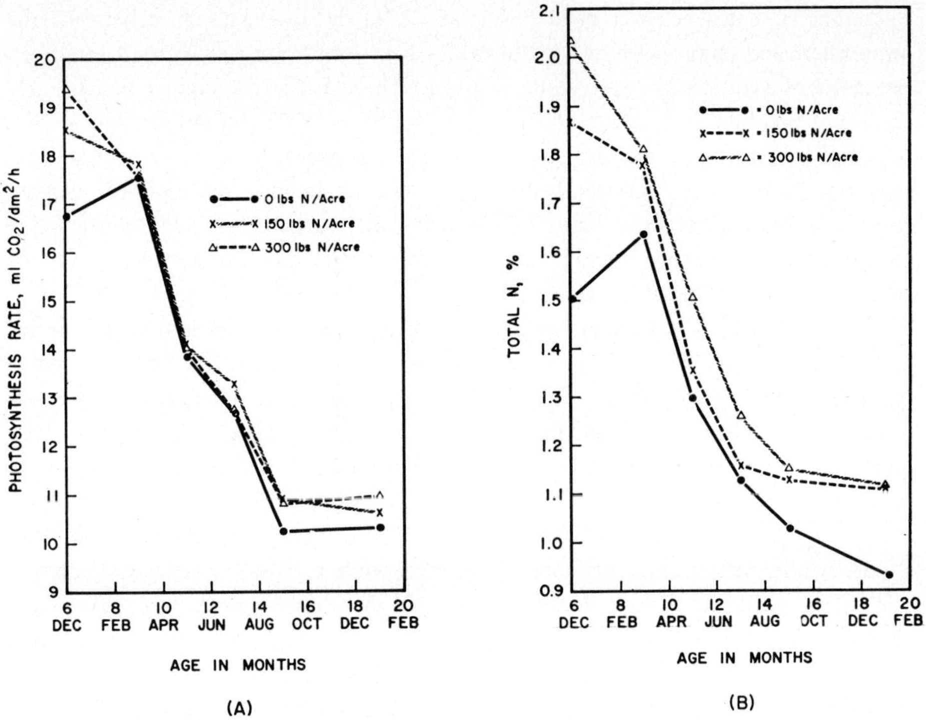

Fig. 4-10. Relationship of nitrogen content of sugarcane leaf blades to photosynthesis rate. (A) Rate of photosynthesis at saturating light intensities. (B) Percentage of total nitrogen in the same blades. [After Hartt and Burr (674).] Reproduced by permission of *I.S.S.C.T.*

With respect to P deficiency, Hartt and Burr (674) found that at 2 months of age plants deprived of P experienced a greater loss of photosynthesis than those deficient in N or K. However, no consistent effect of P deficiency on photosynthesis was found in older plants. In the latter instance the P effects appeared to be confined to primary stalks while photosynthesis remained unaffected by low P supply in secondary stalks.

5. ASSIMILATION RATE IN RELATION TO WATER SUPPLY

A. *General*

Photosynthesis rate as a function of water deficit has been studied by numerous workers. It has been estimated that less than 1 percent of the water absorbed by a plant is utilized chemically in photosynthesis (1014). However, the plants' internal water deficits involving much larger percentages of water also affect photosynthesis by less direct means. These effects are usually associated with stomatal closure, reduced hydration of chlorenchyma protoplasm, and CO_2 diffusion resistance between the atmosphere and chloroplasts. Added to this is the loss of water needed to maintain the processes of vein loading and solute transport through the conducting tissue. Early studies in this field were reviewed by Miller (1022) in 1938, and more recent work is reviewed by Ashton (116). The present discussion is primarily confined to sugarcane. Empirical relationships between water supply and net assimilation have been studied for many years throughout most of the sugarcane world. Since 1955 considerable fundamental information has also been gathered relative to sugarcane photosynthesis under conditions of variable water supply.

Water, or lack of it, unquestionably affects the rate of CO_2 assimilation in sugarcane. Hartt (648, 654, 656) has shown that photosynthetic activity does proceed in leaves at or below the wilting point, but at rates significantly lower than in leaves adequately supplied with water. In 1939 Hartt (656) commented on the results of her work on water and cane ripening: "...The plants supplied with water were definitely better producers of cane sugar than the plants deprived of water, for the blades of the former made ten times as much sucrose as the blades of the latter, the green-leaf cane of the former gained a large amount of sucrose while that of the latter lost sucrose, and the juice extracted from the dry-leaf cane of the former had a better quality ratio than that from the latter." And subsequently: "...The third study of water and cane ripening confirms the conclusions of the first two studies: a plentiful supply of water is essential for the formation of sucrose in the blades, for its transport to the stem, and for the expression of sugar in the juice."

By the time that Hartt published the first of her three papers in the series on water and cane ripening (648), other workers had proposed that low water supply enhanced sucrose formation in plants. Iljin (771) concluded from a survey of plant species in moist and dry habitats that more sugar is produced in leaves under dry conditions. According to Hartt, little or no consideration had been given at that time [1929] to factors of light intensity or sugar transport. Other workers claimed that wilting hastens the loss of starch from leaves (648). Schroeder and Herrmann (1307) reported that in wilting nasturtium leaves there is an increase in sucrose content at the expense of starch. As discussed elsewhere (*cf.* Chapter 5, pp. 197–202) the question of polysaccharide conversion to sucrose in sugarcane leaves is still a valid problem relating both to sucrose translocation and photosynthetic product repression. Hartt considered this question in her recent studies of sucrose transport in sugarcane (675, 676).

However, in her earlier paper (648) the tentative view was taken that abundant water favors photosynthesis whereas water deficits favor sucrose synthesis. At this time [1934] the primary photosynthate was not yet known. Hartt assumed that it was glucose whereas in fact it was sucrose. It was further suggested that sucrose is formed via condensation reactions catalyzed by invertase. Although the latter view has changed with time, it is nonetheless significant that the correct context of water roles in photosynthesis, carbohydrate interconversion, and sugar transport in sugarcane was being formed more than 35 years ago. The elaboration of this same context remains a major task of sugarcane physiologists today.

B. *Soil moisture effects*

Working with the sugarcane variety *H. 37-1933*, Ashton (116) studied the photosynthetic effects of high and low soil water contents given in a series of five alternating cycles. In these experiments CO_2 assimilation (apparent photosynthesis) was estimated with an infrared spectrophotometer which measured the CO_2 taken from an enclosed chamber during a 13-minute photosynthesis period. Measurements were recorded at half-hour intervals. Control plants were maintained with a high soil moisture status by daily watering. Each cycle consisted of a 7-day period of high soil moisture maintained by daily irrigation, followed by a 6- to 8-day period of drying to the permanent wilting point. The soil used was a Manoa loam, of volcanic origin, contained in 16-inch pots filled to a depth of 10 inches. Plants were about 1 year old when the photosynthesis experiments were performed.

Results showed that photosynthesis rate slackened as the soil moisture declined from maximum water-holding capacity to the permanent wilting percentage (Fig. 4-11). However, the rate of decline was not uniform and the original level of photosynthesis was retained until soil moisture stress had developed materially between field capacity and the permanent wilting percentage. At this point, which is not known precisely, there was a decrease in photosynthesis rate which approached zero at permanent wilting. Several days passed after irrigation before the plants regained their original level of CO_2 assimilation (Fig. 4-11). In general, this verified the earlier findings of Hartt (648, 654, 656) which were based on sugarcane carbohydrate production under conditions of variable soil moisture supply.

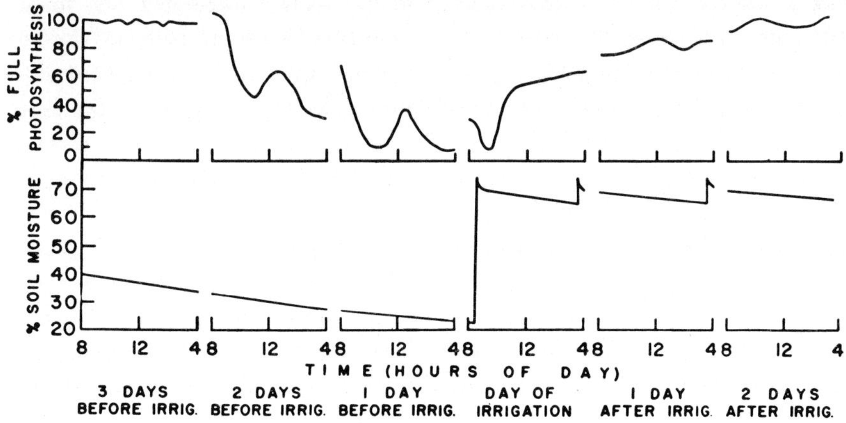

Fig. 4-11. Daily courses of photosynthesis in sugarcane under conditions of increasing soil moisture tension [After Ashton (116).] Reproduced by permission of *Plant Physiology*.

Loustalot[5] had obtained somewhat similar results working with pecan trees. His work had shown that pecan leaves performed subnormal photosynthesis and respiration when soil moisture was either too low or too high. Loustalot further noted a relationship between the degree of photosynthesis decline and severity of moisture stress. Moreover, there was a delay in recovery which differed between morning and afternoon photosynthesis rates.

Ashton (116) observed that, as the alternating cycles of soil moisture progressed from the first to the fifth cycle, there was a cumulative increase in the daily rate of photosynthesis (Fig. 4-12). The increase of photosynthesis rate in response to irriga-

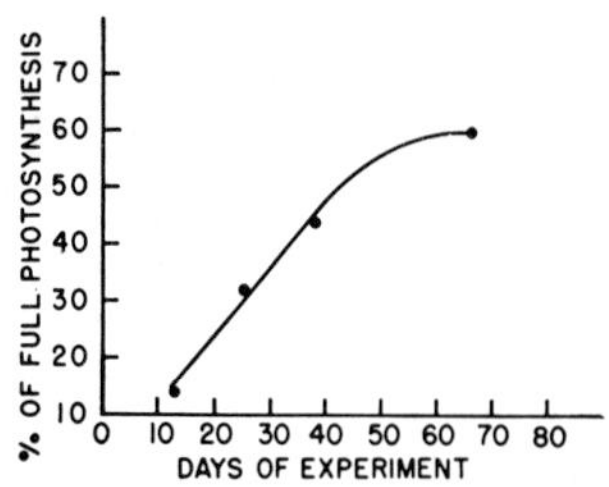

Fig. 4-12. Cumulative increase in the daily rate of photosynthesis in sugarcane given cycles of alternating low and high soil moisture supply. Values shown were recorded on the day of irrigation. [After Ashton (116).] Reproduced by permission of *Plant Physiology*.

tion came primarily on the day of irrigation and during the first and second days thereafter. Some 80 to 90 percent of normal activity was recovered within 2 days. It was also found that as the number of cycles increased there was a progressive lessening of the time interval between irrigation and the initial photosynthesis response to irrigation. Curiously, an overnight recovery of photosynthesis rate occurred in plants experiencing moisture stress the previous afternoon. Ashton attributed this to an improved water balance in the plant. Presumably the nocturnal stomata closure permitted plants to deploy their dwindling water intake toward reactivation of photosynthesis mechanisms. The latter was sufficiently viable to accomplish some CO_2 assimilation when the stomata opened briefly in the morning. Under such conditions the brief renewal of photosynthesis might also be explained in terms of improved CO_2 diffusion from the air to the chloroplast.

Ashton's study also showed that sugarcane plants responded to reduced illumination under conditions of severe moisture stress. Even a brief period of reduced light intensity, produced by clouds or by the midday shading of lower leaves by upper leaves, led to increased photosynthesis rates when soil moisture was close to the permanent wilting percentage. This was similarly attributed to improved water balance within the plant.

---

[5] Loustalot, A.J., 1945. Influence of soil moisture conditions on apparent photosynthesis and transpiration of pecan trees, *J. Agric. Res.* 71: 519–532.

The diurnal course of photosynthesis in sugarcane given adequate water and in sugarcane deprived of water is shown in Fig. 4-13. In this instance the soil moisture percentage remained slightly above the permanent wilting point all day, being 27 percent at 3:30 p.m. It is evident that both the normal (control) and water-deficient plants increased photosynthesis until about 9:00 a.m., and both decreased photosynthesis after about 4:00 p.m., in connection with normal morning and evening changes in illumination intensity. During the intermediate 7 hours the water-deficient plants experienced a general loss of photosynthetic activity which correlated closely with foliar wilting during this period. Wilting was most severe in the topmost leaves but extended downward to leaf $^{+}5$. The partial recovery of photosynthetic activity in water-deficient plants between 11:30 a.m. and 1:00 p.m. (Fig. 4-13) was associated with a midday loss of wilting. Ashton indicates that no wilting was evident in any of the leaves at 12:00 noon.

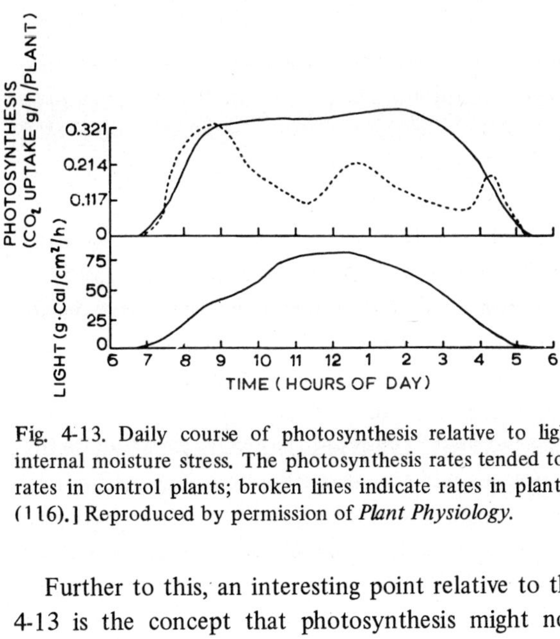

Fig. 4-13. Daily course of photosynthesis relative to light intensity in sugarcane experiencing internal moisture stress. The photosynthesis rates tended to recover at midday. Solid lines indicate rates in control plants; broken lines indicate rates in plants under moisture stress. [After Ashton (116).] Reproduced by permission of *Plant Physiology.*

Further to this, an interesting point relative to the CO_2 assimilation curves in Fig. 4-13 is the concept that photosynthesis might normally be expected to decrease around midday by virtue of foliar sucrose accumulations to the level of repression. Midday slackening of photosynthesis rate has been recorded by a number of workers (1598, 1003, 600). Hartt (666) published evidence that sucrose can restrict photosynthesis if not translocated readily from the leaves. Hartt also cites evidence that a sugarcane leaf can continue photosynthesis at a maximum rate (*i.e.*, at light saturation) for only about 2 hours, after which there is a rapid loss of CO_2-assimilating activity. Under these conditions (with 20-cm sections of blade) there is little opportunity for sucrose transport. Workers in Australia (1518) have questioned the importance of a sucrose role in photosynthesis repression. However, examination of the diurnal photosynthesis response curve for control plants in Fig. 4-13 reveals that very little increase in photosynthesis was obtained after 9:00 a.m., whereas light intensity almost doubled after 9:00 a.m. This may be taken as tacit evidence of product repression against photosynthesis in the plants given daily irrigation.

6. PHOTORESPIRATION

A. *Photorespiration and O_2 supply*

A discussion of photosynthesis rates in most plants other than sugarcane would have to include photorespiration as one of the key qualifying features. The increased production of CO_2 in illuminated plants may complicate enormously conventional measurements of CO_2 assimilation based on CO_2 uptake from an enclosed atmosphere. In Chapter 3 it was noted that sugarcane and other C_4 pathway plants do not show extensive photorespiration, and some of the theories advanced to explain this phenomenon were briefly discussed (*cf.* Chapter 3, pp. 113–115). These explanations are based on morphological factors (486), insufficient flavin mononucleotide (FMN) (1451), differing enzyme potentials (782), diversion of the substrate source of CO_2 into photosynthesis reactions (448), and a more efficient movement of carbon in C_4 pathway plants than in Calvin-cycle plants. The latter hypothesis was advanced by Kortschak (854) and is consistent with our present understanding that the C_4 pathway carboxylation reaction may be more efficient. Aside from the knowledge that photorespiration is not a major complicating feature of photosynthesis in sugarcane, maize and other C_4 pathway plants, this fact has been helpful in studying photorespiration and mechanisms of O_2 action upon CO_2 assimilation.

By 1966 Tregunna and his colleagues (1449, 1450) had observed changes in photosynthesis rate, the CO_2 compensation point, and CO_2 evolution from photorespiratory plants resulting from changes of O_2 concentration in the atmosphere. Dark respiration was shown to require only about 1 percent O_2 in the atmosphere whereas the burst of CO_2 evolution in darkness was stimulated by increased O_2 up to 100 percent. These findings were interpreted to mean that reactions responsible for photorespiration and the excessive CO_2 output in subsequent darkness were distinct from reactions of normal dark respiration. On the other hand, Zelitch (1607) had by this time introduced the concept that photorespiration is largely a result of an active glycolate pathway in leaves.

Forrester *et al.* (534) demonstrated an O_2 stimulatory effect on photorespiration and an apparent inhibitory action upon photosynthesis. They then demonstrated that the inhibitory effect can be examined directly in a plant which does not perform photorespiration (*i.e.*, one which does not produce internal CO_2 in the light). Maize was selected for this purpose because of its lack of a measurable CO_2 compensation point and its lack of a measurable CO_2 "burst" such as that produced by photorespiring plants during the initial exposure to darkness following light treatment (1042). Their experiments were designed to reveal whether CO_2 is not produced by maize leaves in light, or whether CO_2 is produced in light but is reutilized before it can escape into the atmosphere. Test plants other than maize included the monocots barley, wheat, oats, and timothy (*Phleum pratense* L.).

Their data showed a failure of maize leaves to produce CO_2 at any of the variable O_2 levels provided, *i.e.*, at 1, 21, or 100 percent O_2. The CO_2 compensation point remained at zero and no postillumination burst of CO_2 was obtained during the first 60 seconds of darkness. Photosynthesis rate was inhibited by O_2 and the effect was only partially reversible. Subsequent steady-state respiration in darkness was not influenced by O_2. This response was obtained in each of the 12 maize varieties tested. The authors concluded that no measurable photorespiration had taken place concurrently with photosynthesis. Each of the other monocots did perform photorespiration in the light and the process was stimulated by increasing O_2.

Forrester *et al.* (534) were not certain at that time [1966] whether any plants other than maize were free of photorespiration, but they were aware from personal communications with Hartt and with Zelitch that this might also be true of sugarcane. These investigators therefore speculated that the well-known high productivity of maize and sugarcane might stem from a characteristic absence of photorespiration. To demonstrate this point comparisons were given for maize and soybean which showed that, in 24 hours under prescribed experimental conditions, maize leaves would assimilate about twice as much carbon as soybean leaves. This was shown in atmospheres containing 1 and 21 percent O_2. At 100 percent O_2 maize assimilated about 5 times more CO_2 than soybean.

B. *Photorespiration and glycolate metabolism*

Goldsworthy (595), in 1966, and Moss (1045), in 1968, published evidence from tobacco leaves linking photorespiration with glycolate metabolism. Earlier work by Moss had revealed strong glycolic acid oxidase activity in tobacco leaves (1044). Subsequently, Moss observed that photorespiration was retarded by inhibiting glycolate oxidase with α-hydroxy-2-pyridinemethanesulfonic acid. Photosynthesis was suppressed by the inhibitor and the CO_2 compensation level was increased indefinitely among treated leaves. Subsequent accumulation of glycolate was dependent upon light intensity as well as inhibitor concentration. On the basis of glycolate accumulations it was calculated that photorespiration employing glycolate as substrate could exceed the dark respiration by at least 2-fold. However, it was thought that respiration based on glycolate metabolism was not of sufficient magnitude to account for the typically large differences in photosynthesis between maize and tobacco. Moss, unlike Forrester *et al.* (534), did not consider photorespiration to be a complete answer for the photosynthesis differences between species. On the other hand, differences in CO_2 compensation points might be explained on this basis: ". . .Although it seems unlikely that differences in net photosynthesis between efficient species such as maize and inefficient species such as wheat or tobacco could be due to differences in photorespiration alone, it is possible that the difference in CO_2 compensation concentration between these species is due to differences in respiration."

Evidence indirectly relating glycolate oxidase to photorespiration in maize was reported by Tregunna (1451) in 1966. In the absence of added FMN, a cofactor for glycolate oxidase, maize did not oxidize glycolate. When FMN was provided (by placing the cut end of a maize leaf in a FMN solution) there was a marked increase in the CO_2 compensation point which presumably reflected an operative glycolate pathway and active photorespiration. Moss (1045) concluded from this and other evidence that glycolate metabolism may well account for much of the internal CO_2 released in leaves. He qualified this view with the stipulation that the parallel increase of CO_2 compensation point with increasing respiration requires a constant diffusion resistance between the respiratory site and the CO_2 assimilation site.

7. PRODUCT REPRESSION

A. *General*

Photosynthetic CO_2 assimilation is accomplished through a series of enzymatically-catalyzed reactions operating in sequence toward the ultimate production of sucrose or polysaccharides. In the final analysis, these reactions are the means by which a multitude of empirical factors are able to exert an apparent regulatory action on photosynthesis. Any one of the reactions is conceivably rate limiting for the overall assimilation process. These steps, individually or in sequence, are for the most part reversible; in fact, the stepwise performance of CO_2 assimilation when taken in the reverse direction becomes almost indistinguishable from the glycolytic breakdown of sucrose or polysaccharides. Moreover, like most enzyme reactions, the rate of each step may become limited by its own product should the latter accumulate in excessive amounts. Since end products such as sucrose, glucans, and starch must by definition accumulate at least temporarily, plant scientists have quite rightly questioned whether the end products themselves perform a key role in governing the rate of photosynthesis.

Loomis (952), in 1949, proposed that the accumulation of photosynthetic end products, and specifically the utilization of end products, ". . .is the final limiting factor concerned in plant development under field conditions". His own findings relative to increased sugars and declining dry matter accumulation in bagged maize ears (*i.e.*, having restricted translocation) were cited as tentative evidence for this. Loomis also conceived "back reactions" occurring when photosynthate accumulates. However, Verduin and Loomis (1490) noted that bagging the silking ear shoots of maize to prevent pollination produced large increases of leaf sugar without decreasing CO_2

absorption. They therefore concluded that end-product repression of photosynthesis was not operative in maize.

Moss (1043), in 1967, suggested that carbohydrate accumulation induced by nutrient deficiencies may be restrictive against photosynthesis. Referring specifically to the example of maize, Moss wrote: "...Potassium deficiency in corn at flowering time, for instance, results in barren or poorly fertilized ears. The ear is a storage site for carbohydrates, and if no ear, or if only a small ear is formed, sugars build up in the leaves and photosynthesis is suppressed. Thus, a temporary potassium deficiency at tasseling can impair flowering and development of a storage site for photosynthate from leaves." Alexander, working with sugarcane grown in sand culture, frequently observed that inadequate nitrogen leads to foliar sucrose accumulations and restricted net growth (11, 37, 41, 31). Sucrose accumulation has also been observed in sugarcane leaves grown with inadequate phosphorus, potassium, and calcium (31). No photosynthesis measurements were performed during these studies.

Franck (537) proposed that photosynthetic enzymes may be inhibited by intermediate respiratory products and by photosynthetic by-products. The "short induction period" or initial depression of photosynthesis at the beginning of an illumination period was attributed to a "deactivation of the oxygen-liberating enzyme during dark periods and its reactivation during illumination". Franck maintained that certain substances which he termed "photoperoxides", and which he theorized are removed by the oxygen-liberating enzyme, will now accumulate and "...oxidize easily oxidizable substances and convert them into narcotic-acting substances". According to this theory the endogenous "narcotics" acted to "...cover the chlorophyll complexes and check thereby their photochemical activity". Franck depicted the "narcotics" as plant acids whose inhibitory properties are quickly eliminated by further oxidative reactions following the recovery of the oxygen-liberating enzyme. In this context various workers have speculated upon the production of toxic peroxides during the energy-conversion phase of photosynthesis but little evidence of their existence has been found. One explanation for the severe toxicity of the bipyridylium herbicides is based upon peroxide formation (*cf.* Chapter 13, pp. 497).

B. *Sucrose repression of sugarcane photosynthesis*[6]

Possibly the most convincing evidence of end-product repression in photosynthesis was that published by Hartt (666) in 1963. Using blades from several varieties it was shown that a sugarcane leaf can continue photosynthesis at a maximum rate at light saturation for about 2 hours. Thereafter the rate drops rapidly, even though tests with

---

[6] T.F. Neales and L.D. Incoll [The control of leaf photosynthesis rate by level of assimilate concentration in the leaf: A review of the hypothesis, *Bot. Rev.* 34: 107–125 (1968)] reviewed a large body of evidence suggestive of photosynthetic product repression but concluded that the hypothesis is by no means proven. In particular, the operation of discrete feedback systems from sink to source may offer equally valid explanations of photosynthesis rate variation.

Nujol–dodecane indicated that the stomata had remained open. In these studies measurements were performed with 20-cm sections of blade and no sucrose translocation was possible. Hartt also found that simulated wind injuries in which the leaf lamina, midrib, or entire blade is broken by folding led to restricted CO_2 assimilation and slackening of sucrose transport. The extent of photosynthesis inhibition roughly paralleled the extent to which sucrose translocation was restricted by the leaf injury. Inhibition was not related to loss of moisture. Taken together, these results pointed toward an inhibitory action by the accumulated leaf sucrose.

In subsequent experiments (666) sugarcane blades were detached from the plant, recut under water, and divided longitudinally so that the leaf and right lamina could be illuminated separately while standing in water or sucrose solutions. Conditions of the photosynthesis experiments were such that during a 10-minute interval the left lamina of duplicate blades assimilated a little more than 17.0 ml of CO_2 per dm^2 per hour while standing in water (Table 4-8). Extension of the assimilation period to 3 hours produced a rate suppression amounting to about 34 percent. This implies that sucrose

TABLE 4-8

EFFECT OF LEAF SUCROSE CONCENTRATION ON THE RATE OF PHOTOSYNTHESIS IN SUGARCANE

[After Hartt (666).] Reproduced by permission of *Naturwissenschaften*, Springer-Verlag, Berlin.

Tissue*	Photosynthesis time (at 6500 foot candles)	Sucrose (% dry wt.)	Photosynthesis rate (ml $CO_2/dm^2/h$)
(1) Leaf A	10 minutes in water	3.59	17.25
Leaf B	10 minutes in water	3.84	17.35
(2) Leaf A	3 hours in water	6.60	11.40
Leaf B	3 hours in 5% sucrose	12.65	1.77

*(1) Left lamina; (2) right lamina.

accumulated during the extended experiment and prevented further photosynthetic activity of the magnitude attained during a brief experiment. Moreover, the lamina standing in a 5-percent sucrose solution experienced a photosynthesis inhibition amounting to about 90 percent (Table 4-8). Hartt concluded that the accumulation of sucrose in leaves during the day may inhibit CO_2 assimilation, and that the coordination of photosynthesis with the translocation of sucrose is essential to attain maximum yield.

Kortschak (854) proposed an explanation for curtailed photosynthesis based on the inhibition of sucrose phosphate phosphatase by sucrose, as shown by Hawker (704). This conclusion was substantiated by Hartt and Burr (674) who observed photosynthesis decline (or solarization) produced by successive doses of CO_2 and accompanied by end-product accumulation in treated leaves. It was suggested that in some instances increased sugar transport might automatically increase photosynthesis rate. In this context the rate relationships of CO_2 assimilation to sugar transport might be improved materially by selecting varieties on the basis of translocation capability, and by examining the effect of cultural practices upon sugar movement within the cane plant (674).

Studies by Waldron *et al.* (1518) have supported Hartt's findings to a limited extent but end-product repression was not established as an operative control mechanism for sugarcane photosynthesis. Prolonged illumination of detached blades led to increased sucrose and hexose contents with parallel decreases in photosynthesis rates. However, after a 12-hour dark treatment photosynthesis increased without appreciable changes having occurred in sugar levels. In addition, leaf discs immersed in 0.4 M sucrose, glucose, or mannitol solutions in Warburg flasks did not show a photosynthetic repression as evidenced by O_2 evolution. It was concluded that, under conditions of prolonged illumination, end-product repression could not explain the photosynthesis patterns obtained with sugarcane.

Recent experiments by Glasziou and Bull (594) strengthened the case against end-product repression of sugarcane photosynthesis. To avoid water stresses characteristic of detached blades the work was performed with attached leaves on stalks having various other portions shaded or removed. The latter treatments produced significant increases in photosynthesis directly correlated with an improved moisture status in the remaining assimilating leaves. However, certain evidence pointed toward control systems operating by means other than stomatal aperture: (a) Mature plants forced into a restricted growth regime by prolonged cool treatment (17 °C days, 10 °C nights) did not immediately increase photosynthesis upon return to a normal temperature regime even though transpiration rate was doubled. With passage of time the photosynthesis rate doubled while transpiration remained constant. (b) Variable humidity experiments with single attached blades (above 80 percent and below 40 percent) showed transpirational decline close to theoretical values, while assimilation rates remained appreciably below theoretical values calculated from prevailing conditions of CO_2 supply, season, and age of plants. A possible explanation for this is the operation of photosynthesis controls which are independent of stomatal resistance.

Additional experiments were performed to ascertain possible product repression as a function of xylem sugar content (133). For this purpose blades from induced side shoots were employed which have photosynthesis rates similar to those of leaves on the main stalk. After recording an initial photosynthesis rate, the shoot was detached while submerged and water was forced upward from the base by means of a peristaltic pump following reestablishment of a steady assimilation rate. The upper leaf tissues were trimmed to allow rapid flushing of the severed xylem vessels without affecting photosynthesis rate. Replacement of the water with 0.2 M glucose or sucrose solutions produced rapid inhibition of photosynthesis and a marked increase of leaf resistance from 4 to 25 sec/cm. Xylem samples taken with microcapillary tubes from photosynthetically-repressed leaves showed no detectable sugar. The authors concluded: "...These results leave us with no evidence that sugar in the leaf xylem is responsible for reduced rates of photosynthesis."

C. *Oxygen inhibition of photosynthesis*

The concept of product repression is usually applied to photosynthesis in terms of diurnal carbohydrate accumulations. However, oxygen (O_2) is also an important product and one having potential inhibitory action against photosynthetic processes.

It is generally accepted that the O_2 in the earth's atmosphere originated through photosynthetic activity. Warburg (1525), in 1920, reported the discovery that high O_2 concentrations inhibit O_2 evolution by photosynthetic processes in *Chlorella.* This was confirmed by later workers who obtained significant inhibition by O_2 levels in the order of 21 to 100 percent. The effect was most pronounced at saturating light intensities (187). The earliest report of O_2 inhibition of photosynthesis in a higher plant was published by McAlister and Myers (996) working with wheat leaves. In this instance CO_2 assimilation was significantly lower in a normal atmosphere than in one containing only 0.5 percent O_2. The inhibition was obtained at both high and moderate light intensities in 0.03 percent CO_2.

Theories advanced to explain the "Warburg effect", as it came to be called, were reviewed by Turner and Brittain (1464) in 1962. These include a hypothetical inhibition of enzymes operating in the carbon reduction cycle (1463), enzyme inhibition in the O_2-evolving apparatus, and back reactions in which O_2 uptake produces the effect of reversing photosynthetic processes. The latter would include such reactions as photo-oxidation, photorespiration, and the Mehler reaction (1404). None of the theories have received general acceptance (187).

Working with both algae and higher land plants, Bjorkman (187) found O_2 inhibition to be most prevalent among the higher land plants. He therefore concluded that the photosynthesis apparatus of algae differs from that of higher plants in its sensitivity to O_2. The studies with higher plants included O_2 concentrations ranging from 0 to 21 percent in a CO_2 atmosphere of 0.03 percent. Photosynthesis was significantly inhibited by O_2 levels less than 2 percent. Inhibition in the order of 30 percent was obtained with the highest O_2 level. The inhibitory action was rapid but readily reversible. In addition, the degree of inhibition was independent of light intensity.

In Bjorkman's experiments diverse species of higher plants showing broad differences in photosynthetic response to light intensity, CO_2 level, and light saturation were notably consistent in their response to O_2. This suggests that O_2 affects photosynthesis by reactions other than those sensitive to light intensity and CO_2 concentration. The photosynthesis quantum yield was inhibited to the same degree as the light-saturated rate at all O_2 levels tested. In constrast to the results obtained with higher plants, experiments with green algae (*Chlorella* and *Ulva*) under identical conditions showed no appreciable O_2 inhibition of photosynthesis.

Photosynthetic inhibition by O_2 was also examined in relation to specific wavelengths and fluorescence intensity (187). In higher plants an increase in fluorescence intensity accompanied the rising O_2 concentrations, but this response was not recorded in *Chlorella*. The inhibitory action of O_2 was considerably higher at wavelengths which preferentially excite Photosystem I. Moreover, a greater CO_2 assimilation rate induced with a weak far-red beam in a background of red light was stronger under conditions of low O_2 concentrations than in air.

Bjorkman presented evidence favoring a plastocyanin role in reversible light absorbance changes. Such variations were sensitive to changing O_2 concentration only when Photosystem II was excited, and the reducing effect on plastocyanin declined as O_2 level was increased. Taken together, Bjorkman's data pointed to an O_2 inhibitory site located in the electron carrier chain operating between Photosystems I and II. It was proposed that O_2 may act as an electron acceptor at this site, producing a back reaction of reducing power with molecular oxygen. Unaccounted for in this hypothesis is the consistency of quantum yield inhibition and the light-saturated rate of CO_2 assimilation.

In 1966, apparently unaware of Bjorkman's work, Forrester *et al.* (533) published their findings on O_2 inhibition of photosynthesis in detached soybean leaves. Concurrent but differential effects were produced by O_2 on dark respiration and photorespiration. The detached blades were examined with an infrared CO_2 analyzer and a Clark oxygen electrode in both open and closed systems. The rate of apparent photosynthesis was retarded by O_2 while the rate of dark respiration was unaffected after a few minutes in darkness. Part of the photosynthetic inhibition was shown to result from increased photorespiration. In addition, the O_2 stimulatory effect on photorespiration was accompanied by an increase in the CO_2 compensation point. The fact that O_2 had no effect on dark respiration [also observed by other workers (1464, 1204)] while stimulating photorespiration was taken as evidence that these were two distinct processes. The authors subsequently treated this concept in greater detail (534).

Forrester *et al.* (533) also presented evidence that dark respiration, subject to CO_2 concentration, was suppressed in the light. Their observations were consistent with those of Tregunna *et al.* (1450) who found that CO_2 production at minimal O_2 was zero, that is, the CO_2 compensation point extrapolated to zero in the absence of O_2. This was confirmed by Forrester *et al.* who further observed that both the CO_2 evolution "burst" and the CO_2 compensation point increased as O_2 was raised from 1 to 100 percent, the line extrapolating to zero at zero O_2.

8. PHOTOSYNTHESIS CONTROL IN SUGARCANE

While it is true that photosynthesis is influenced by a multitude of internal and empirical factors, the photosynthetic processes must ultimately be examined in the context of a plant's growth and development needs. Photosynthesis is neither an isolated phenomenon nor an end in itself; it is part of an enormously complex physiological system, and therefore its rate must be governed in accordance with the needs and limitations of this system. With the possible exception of end-product repression, our discussion of sugarcane photosynthesis up to this point has been removed from the context of its control, that is, from the manner of its integration among all the other processes of sugarcane growth, development, and maturation. Most certainly such factors as light intensity, CO_2 concentration, nutrition, moisture, temperature, and product accumulation all appear to affect photosynthesis rate, but it is equally certain that the means by which all of these factors are harmonized within the intact physiological system remain obscure.

The first attempts to construct a photosynthesis control model for sugarcane based either upon metabolic imbalances or upon a negative sink-to-source feedback mechanism were reported by Waldron and his co-workers (1518) in 1967. Photosynthesis rates were measured in detached leaves, in small groups of plants, and in larger groups of plants grown in greenhouses and controlled-temperature chambers. These experiments were designed to examine photosynthetic efficiency and regulation factors operating in both intact and detached leaf tissues. Their findings did not lend support to the concept that photosynthesis is controlled by sucrose.

A. *Leaf geometry vs. light intensity and CO_2 supply*

Singh and Lal (1325, 855), in 1935, published exhaustive studies of sugarcane photosynthesis as affected by light intensity and CO_2 supply. A positive correlation was obtained between light intensity and CO_2 assimilation rate regardless of the CO_2 concentration. As light intensity increased the optimum CO_2 level also increased. Temperature was also shown to be an important factor and optimum photosynthetic activity was recorded at 34 °C with 0.05 percent CO_2. At CO_2 levels simulating those of the sugarcane field (about 0.061 percent CO_2), photosynthesis was considerably lower than at 0.33 percent.

Taking note of the fact that normal leaf geometry in sugarcane produces variable shading, Waldron *et al.* (1518) studied the effects of variable light intensity on CO_2 assimilation by small groups (four plants) having varying degrees of shade. It was found that where mutual leaf shading occurred the rate of photosynthesis was a linear function of light intensity up to full sunlight. There was no light saturation. This was consistent with the results obtained by Moss (1041) with sugarcane and maize. However, when leaves were so arranged in the assimilation chamber that no shading occurred, light saturation was obtained at an intensity of 0.6 cal/cm^2/min (Fig. 4-14). In this instance leaves were arranged on a frame so that each blade received maximum sunlight. Under these conditions the photosynthesis rate (mg CO_2/dm^2/h) at light saturation exceeded the rate obtained at much higher light intensity (about 0.9 cal/cm^2/min).

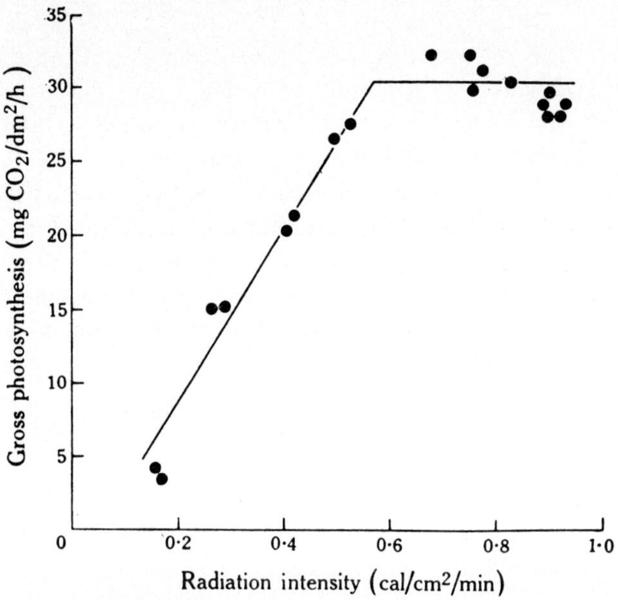

Fig. 4-14. Relationship between net photosynthesis and radiation intensity in sugarcane leaves where mutual shading was prevented by arranging the blades on a frame. [After Waldron *et al.* (1518).] Reproduced by permission of the *Australian Journal of Biological Sciences.*

It was further shown that detached leaves in an enclosed chamber gave photosynthesis rates which were proportional to both CO_2 concentration and light intensity. In an open system, the photosynthesis rate of intact plants was about doubled when CO_2 supply was increased from 125 to 237 ppm. Whereas both the light and CO_2 responses were consistent with findings of other workers, the light saturation of sugarcane leaves has been less frequently observed. Hartt and Burr (674) obtained evidence that light saturation may occur as a varietal feature. The implication here is that greater rates of CO_2 assimilation (and hence greater sugar yields) might be attained with much smaller quantities of light and CO_2 if leaves were more favorably positioned relative to the incident solar radiation. Ultimately, more favorable "leaf spread" might be a means toward greater yields by crop plants in general. It is certainly a valid objective for sugarcane breeders (86, p. 68).

Moss (1041), studying the effects of air movement on photosynthesis rates of detached sugarcane leaves, found that stirring of calm air produces a stimulatory effect comparable to adding CO_2 to quiet air. This is an interesting point in view of the fact that in many regions air turbulence is nearly a constant factor. A reasonable assumption is that CO_2 supply, leaf geometry, and competitive shading are all affected in the cane field by air turbulence.

B. *Temperature effects*

Controlled-temperature experiments were performed by Waldron *et al.* (1518) in order to clarify the relationship between photosynthesis efficiency and air temperature (Fig. 4-15). Mature sugarcane plants were equilibrated for 24 hours at 18, 26, and 34 °C in one study, and between 5 and 18 °C in another study. Net photosynthesis was determined on the basis of 1 cal/cm^2/min under conditions of competitive leaf shading, *i.e.*, under conditions giving photosynthesis rate as a linear function of light intensity up to full sunlight. One hour was allowed between individual measurements for leaf and air temperature equilibration. Results indicated that between 8 and 34 °C sugarcane photosynthesis has a Q_{10} value of 1.1 (Fig. 4-15).

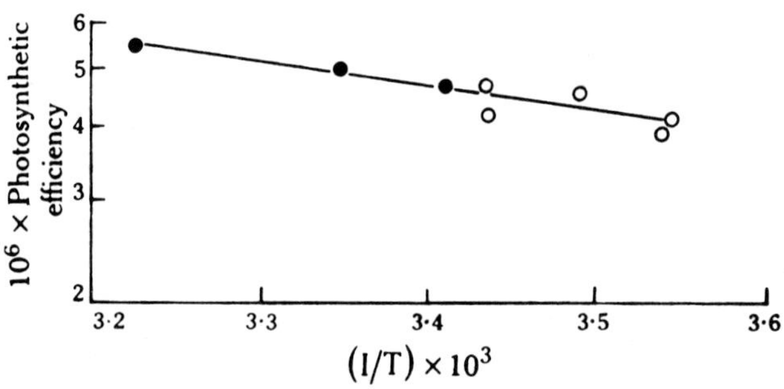

Fig. 4-15. Relationship between photosynthesis efficiency in sugarcane and air temperature over the range 5 to 34 °C. Measurements were performed under conditions such that leaves had attained their full area and competed with one another for light. (●) Plants examined over the temperature range 34 to 18 °C; (○) plants studied over the range 18 to 5 °C. Photosynthetic efficiency is expressed as the number of grams of carbohydrate fixed per calorie of visible solar radiation. [After Waldron *et al.* (1518).] Reproduced by permission of the *Australian Journal of Biological Sciences.*

Singh and Lal (1325) reported that, in mature sugarcane leaves, rising temperature produces both an accelerating and depressing effect upon photosynthesis. Their data revealed a point at higher temperatures where the acceleration due to increased temperature is balanced by a depressing action. It was surmised that the point at which the two responses balance one another, and hence the point at which maximum photosynthesis is attained, is close to 34 °C. Above 34 °C a gradual decline in photosynthesis was anticipated and on this basis 30 °C was proposed as the most suitable temperature for studying photosynthesis in sugarcane. Kortschak *et al.* (852) performed sugarcane CO_2 fixation experiments between 27 and 30 °C. Moss (1041) found that young maize plants increased net photosynthesis as air temperature was increased up to 30 °C at any given CO_2 level. This was attributed in part to increased stomatal opening. However, at 40 °C photosynthesis had begun to decline even though stomatal opening was greatest at 40 °C.

C. *Photosynthesis potential vs. leaf rank*

Sugarcane photosynthesis as a function of leaf and plant age has been touched upon briefly (*cf.* Chapter 1, p. 64). Workers in India (1329, 1328) reported a stimulatory effect of N fertilization on CO_2 assimilation efficiency at all stages of the life cycle. Potassium fertilization reportedly increased CO_2 assimilation during the early stages and later decreased assimilation, although chlorophyll content was higher during the later stages (1328). In these studies N deficiency lowered CO_2 assimilation efficiency and leaf chlorophyll content (1329). Yamasaki and Arikado (1593, 1595) reported greater photosynthesis rates in young leaves than in older leaves, with maximum assimilation occurring in September. They hypothesized a relationship operating between high CO_2 assimilation and flower initiation during this period. Waldron *et al.* (1518) evaluated both the light-intercepting capability of leaves ranked in sequence along the stalk and the CO_2 assimilation potential of each leaf when spread on a frame to receive maximum sunlight. Data presented in Table 4-9 indicate that leaves 0 to $^{+}2$

TABLE 4-9

RADIATION INTENSITY RECEIVED BY THE LEAVES OF A SUGARCANE PLANT

[After Waldron *et al.* (1518).] Reproduced by permission of the *Australian Journal of Biological Science.*

Leaf No.	Mean radiation intensity for whole blade ($cal/cm^2/min$)	Leaf No.	Mean radiation intensity for whole blade ($cal/cm^2/min$)
0	0.61 ± 0.10	5	0.39 ± 0.20
1	0.62 ± 0.10	6	0.32 ± 0.16
2	0.57 ± 0.08	7	0.17 ± 0.06
3	0.46 ± 0.18	8	0.14 ± 0.02
4	0.49 ± 0.24	9	0.13 ± 0.10

intercepted more solar radiation than those attached below, but leaves $^{+}3$ and $^{+}4$ also received relatively large amounts of light. The six uppermost leaves were shown to intercept about 70 percent of the incident solar radiation. It was further shown that the net photosynthesis potential for leaves 0 to $^{+}6$, and for leaves $^{+}7$ to $^{+}9$, amounted to approximately 31 and 20 mg $CO_2/dm^2/h$, respectively. These results underscore the commanding position of the younger leaves (0 to $^{+}6$) which, in addition to intercepting most of the sunlight, have a greater capability to utilize this sunlight than do the older leaves situated in the shade below.

D. *Plant age and seasonal effects*

In 1969 Kortschak and Forbes (855) described the effects of shade and age on photosynthesis in detached sugarcane blades. In these studies the effects of age and season were separated statistically, and the leaf age *per se* was constant at about 1 month. Quite significantly, it was found that the age of the plant had a greater effect on photosynthesis than other variables such as season, shade, and time of day. As shown in Fig. 4-16, photosynthesis rate declined from a peak at 5 months to a low at 15 months which amounted to a loss of some 20 percent[7]. A small recovery was observed at around 20 months which was generally consistent among varieties and was not taken as an artifact of the experimental conditions. It should be emphasized that the photosynthesis decline shown in Fig. 4-16 was a characteristic of the plants' age as a whole rather than leaf age.

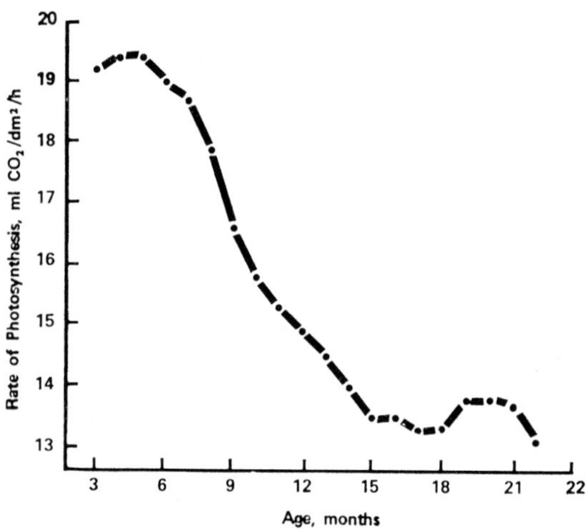

Fig. 4-16. Photosynthesis in sugarcane as a function of plant age. Indicated values are corrected for seasonal effects. [After Kortschak and Forbes (855).] Reproduced by permission of *Progress in Photosynthesis Research*, Tübingen.

Seasonal studies of sugarcane photosynthesis rates in Hawaii (855) revealed a moderate depression during the summer months (Fig. 4-17). Because average summer temperatures in Hawaii exceed winter temperatures by about 5 °C, it was thought that the higher temperature should have produced greater photosynthesis (1325). Kortschak and Forbes attributed the decline to lesser amounts of sunlight owing to increased shade. The lag of photosynthesis rate behind the change in solar radiation (Fig. 4-17) was consistent with the effects produced by artificial shading. The authors suggested that growth of sugarcane at high light intensities reduces photosynthetic

---

[7]Kortschak and Forbes express CO_2 assimilation rate in terms of ml $CO_2/dm^2/h$. The rate values must be multiplied by 1.80 to be made comparable with photosynthesis rates expressed as mg $CO_2/dm^2/h$.

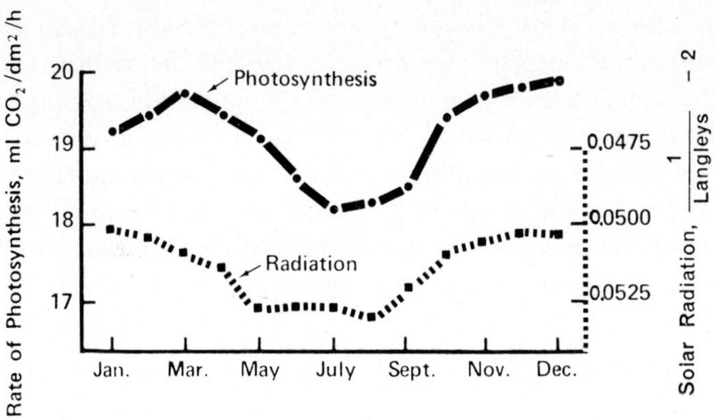

Fig. 4-17. Relationship of photosynthesis in sugarcane to solar radiation and time of year. [After Kortschak and Forbes (855).] Reproduced by permission of *Progress in Photosynthesis Research*, Tübingen.

efficiency, and several months are required before the effect is noticeable under Hawaiian conditions.

In Queensland, Bull (260) performed photosynthesis measurements in conjunction with growth-rate measurements over a normal growing period from October to the following September. Potential photosynthesis rates declined from an early-season high (90 $mg/dm^2/h$) to much lower values between April and September (30–40 $mg/dm^2/h$). Significantly, neither dry matter nor leaf area production showed appreciable increases until photosynthesis rates were at their minimum (in single leaves). Data compiled over several years showed than mean monthly values for photosynthesis rates and leaf resistance correlated closely with seasonal changes in radiation flux density, rainfall, and temperature.

With respect to diurnal changes in photosynthesis rate, Kortschak and Forbes (855) found the lowest CO_2 assimilation occurring about 3 hours after sunrise. This was followed by a maximum rate between 4 and 5 hours after sunrise, and finally by a second minimal period some 8 to 11 hours after sunrise. Under prevailing Hawaiian conditions this pattern was observed to shift on a seasonal basis so that in summer the second minimum rate corresponds to the traditional midday decline.

E. *Effects of sugar concentrations in source and sinks*

The potential of sucrose to limit photosynthesis rates was discussed in the previous section dealing with end-product repression. In particular, the findings of Hartt (666) seemed to indicate that foliar sucrose accumulations could restrict photosynthesis regardless of the cause for sugar having accumulated. Hartt's premise was that sugar translocation is a potentially limiting factor and some minimal flow of sugar out of the leaves must be maintained if CO_2 assimilation is to continue at a maximum rate.

Waldron *et al.* (1518) elaborated on this concept by measuring sugar changes in immature internodes while restricting photosynthesis by cold-temperature "shock" treatments. This is a valid approach since sucrose movement from the leaves is but a part of the overall source-to-sink system which must function properly if excessive foliar sugar accumulations are to be avoided. Plants subjected to low temperatures (17 °C day, 10 °C night) gradually declined in photosynthetic efficiency and transpiration. These changes were accompanied by increased sucrose content in the expanding internodes (Fig. 4-18). Return of the plants to normal temperature regimes (24 °C day, 19

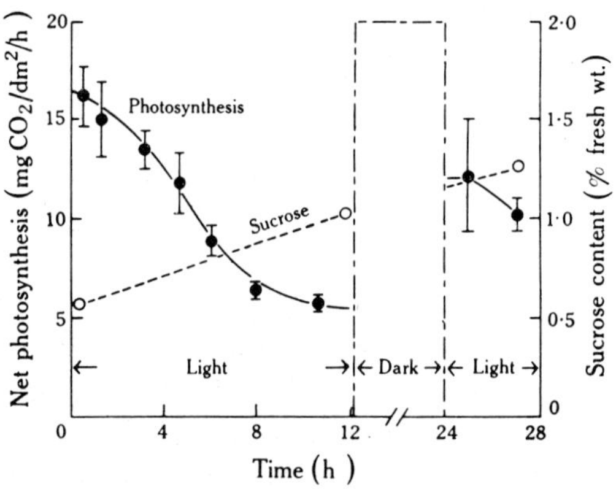

Fig. 4-18. Photosynthesis rate and sucrose content of detached sugarcane leaves subjected to prolonged light treatment followed by a period of darkness. An artificial light source provided 0.35 cal/cm^2/min. [After Waldron *et al.* (1518).] Reproduced by permission of the *Australian Journal of Biological Sciences.*

°C night) led to increased transpiration and increased photosynthetic efficiency. The data were somewhat limited in scope but the authors nonetheless drew several important conclusions: (a) Since transpiration rose more rapidly than photosynthesis upon reexposure to normal temperatures, stomatal resistance was not regarded as a critical factor in the readjustment of photosynthesis rates; (b) since there was no appreciable exchange of new leaves for old during the time-course of the study, the recovery of photosynthetic activity was due to reversible changes in the old leaves. The second conclusion may be easier to substantiate than the first. Potassium deficiency, for example, is known to produce reversible changes in photosynthetic behavior patterns that have taken weeks to establish (677). With reference to stomatal resistance, Hartt (853) was unable to attribute photosynthesis decline, after 2 hours of light saturation, to stomatal closure. Other workers (594, 721, 1041) have produced evidence relating CO_2·availability to stomatal opening.

Waldron and his co-workers observed that prolonged illumination of detached blades led to increased sugar content with parallel slackening of photosynthesis rates.

This was consistent with the findings of Hartt (666). However, photosynthesis rates recovered after 12 hours of darkness even though high sugar levels were still retained in the blades. The authors also noted that, under continuous high light intensity, conditions designed to prohibit or delay water stress would sometimes extend the period of constant photosynthesis up to 24 hours. Subsequent decline of photosynthesis was initially accompanied by increased stomatal resistance. Moreover, treatment of the blades with ammonia vapor (832) frequently restored photosynthesis by inducing the stomata to open. These results suggested that product accumulation was not the restrictive factor, but that moisture stress with its concomitant restriction upon stomatal opening operated as a reversible control mechanism governing photosynthetic activity.

As the illumination period was further extended (beyond 22 hours), it was no longer possible to obtain complete reversal of the photosynthesis decline by ammonia treatment. In other words, an irreversible factor was introduced into the inhibition process. The authors surmised that either product repression or damage to the photosynthesis apparatus might account for the irreversible effect. In their concluding remarks Waldron *et al.* distinguished between the control mechanism operating under low-temperature conditions and the mechanism operating under conditions of excessive sugar accumulation. They then proposed that the reversibility of the low-temperature effect should have a biochemical basis: "...The present evidence is inadequate to distinguish between a model based on negative feedback from sinks to source for the regulation of photosynthesis in sugarcane, and an alternative model based on effects of temperature shock on the induction of metabolic imbalances which differentially alter rates of photosynthesis, stalk elongation, and sugar storage. However, the results clearly show that the reversible loss in photosynthetic efficiency due to low-temperature shock to intact plants is not mediated by changes in stomatal resistance, and is presumably a biochemical phenomenon."[8]

F. *Effects of photosynthesis conditions on initial yield of C_4-dicarboxylic acids*

Virtually all of the photosynthesis experiments discussed in this chapter were based upon the rate of CO_2 uptake or the amounts of carbohydrate or dry matter produced. In these instances the mechanism of photosynthesis was a lesser issue subordinate to the various conditions which contribute to the regulation of photosynthesis rates. However, in one study Kortschak and Hartt (853) measured malic acid and aspartic acid production during the brief time course of 7 to 15 seconds as a function of photosynthetic conditions. At that time the C_4-dicarboxylic acids were newly-

---

[8]H. Beevers [*Physiological Aspects of Crop Yield*, Chapter 8, Metabolic sinks, pp. 169–180, Am. Soc. Agron., Madison, Wisc. (1969)] in his discussion of source–sink interactions, suggests a photosynthetic rate regulation by sink "demands" under conditions favoring rapid interactions, as in *Triticum* species.

discovered as early products of CO_2 assimilation in sugarcane. It was necessary to establish whether they were consistently the early products and not mere artifacts of the conditions prevailing at the time of their discovery. In addition, by concurrently measuring phosphoglycerate and glycerate, a clue was offered as to whether the Calvin cycle was operative as a second assimilation pathway, and, if so, under what conditions might the ratios of initial products vary.

Kortschak and Hartt found the movement of ^{14}C into malic and aspartic acids to exceed the movement into phosphoglyceric acid and glyceric acid under all conditions tested (Table 4-10). The conclusion correctly drawn at the time was that the early

TABLE 4-10

EFFECTS OF LIGHT INTENSITY, CO_2 CONCENTRATION, AGE OF LEAF, AND VARIETY ON INITIAL PRODUCTS OF PHOTOSYNTHESIS IN SUGARCANE

[After Kortschak and Hartt (853).] Reproduced by permission of *Naturwissenschaften*, Springer-Verlag, Berlin.

Conditions		Percent of total counts in acids		
		Malic	Aspartic	Phosphoglyceric + Glyceric
Standard*		50	25	17
Extremes of variables:				
Light intensity (lux)	5 000	40	36	14
	80 000	43	22	28
CO_2 concentration (%)	0.01	46	5	27
	4.80	39	18	21
Leaf age (weeks)	1	43	24	20
	10	39	25	23
Variety	*H.50-7209*	44	18	25
	Unknown seedling	39	18	21
Attached leaf in field		41	18	11

*Standard conditions: Variety, *H.37-1933*; light intensity, 20 000 lux; CO_2 concentration, 1.0%; leaf age, 3 to 5 weeks; time-course of experiments, 7 to 15 seconds.

fixation of CO_2 into malic and aspartic acids is a general characteristic of sugarcane photosynthesis. In this system phosphoglyceric acid appears as an intermediate product prior to hexose phosphate formation but after the C_4-dicarboxylic acids have appeared. A slow movement of ^{14}C into aspartic acid under conditions of low CO_2 supply was taken as a characteristic of the plants selected rather than a CO_2 effect. The doubling of activity in phosphoglyceric acid and glyceric acid as light intensity was raised from 5000 lux to 80 000 lux (Table 4-10) was not mentioned by the authors. Although this might be viewed as tacit evidence of Calvin-cycle reactions being operative under weak light, no conclusive evidence has yet been found that the

Calvin cycle performs jointly with the C_4-dicarboxylic acid pathway in sugarcane leaves. Carbon assimilation of the Calvin type has been established in chloroplast preparations from the sugarcane stem (856).

In general, the movement of ^{14}C into malate and aspartate was remarkably consistent among the different treatments when one considers the striking influence that light, CO_2 concentration, and age of leaf have on net photosynthesis. It appears that the early carboxylation reactions may proceed in relative independence of the photosynthesis conditions critical for overall CO_2 assimilation rate. If so, this is itself an important consideration since the carboxylation reactions have been taken by some workers as valid rate-limiting steps in the CO_2 assimilation process.

G. *Varietal effects*

Because the breeding of new varieties has been one of the most effective means of increasing sugar yield, the extent to which CO_2 assimilation rate or efficiency will vary as a varietal feature is an extremely important question. Little pertinent work has been done in this area. For the most part sugarcane breeders have been content with such indirect assimilation measurements as the stalk tonnage or sucrose yield of new selections. However, Hartt and Burr (674), working with detached sugarcane leaves, demonstrated that CO_2 assimilation may vary materially among different varieties. For example, data presented in Fig. 4-19 clearly show a differential response to light

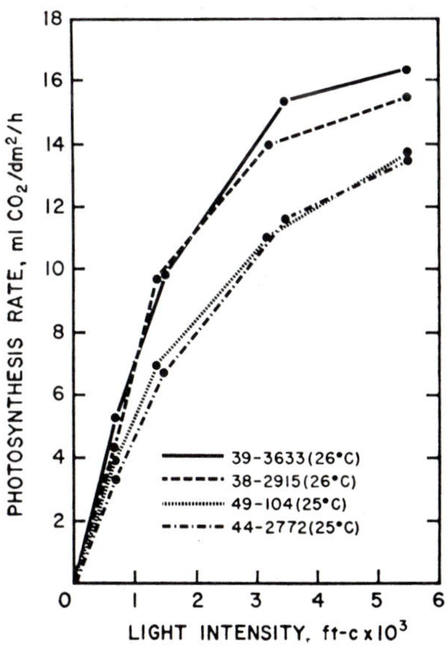

Fig. 4-19. Variable photosynthetic responses of different sugarcane varieties to increasing light intensity. [After Hartt and Burr (674).] Reproduced by permission of *I.S.S.C.T.*

intensity by four sugarcane varieties. In related experiments one variety, *H. 49-104*, was found to be light saturated below 6000 foot candles while the majority of varieties tested were light saturated between 6000 and 8000 foot candles. The variety *H. 52-123* was saturated at 10 000 foot candles and *H. 41-1045* remained unsaturated at 14 000 foot candles. Hartt and Burr suggested that photosynthesis experiments comparing varietal or other factors should be performed close to the saturating light intensity.

Hartt and Burr also observed varietal differences in response to CO_2 concentrations greater than that of the normal atmosphere. Photosynthesis rate in the variety *H. 37-1933* was increased by CO_2 concentrations in the order of 0.06 to 0.07 percent, whereas the variety *H. 38-2915* did not respond to CO_2 concentrations greater than 0.03 percent.

In 1967 Irvine (780) reported extensive sugarcane photosynthesis studies conducted under field conditions in Lousiana. These were designed to measure varietal differences in CO_2 assimilation rate and to evaluate the leaf characteristics potentially responsible for such differences. Of the ten varieties studied, four were natural *S. officinarum* hybrids "...characterized by thick stalks, wide leaves, and low content of sucrose and fiber. The remaining six varieties were interspecific hybrids of different genetic complexity, characterized by thinner stalks, more narrow leaves, and higher sucrose and fiber content than the 'noble' varieties". In these experiments air was enriched with $^{14}CO_2$ and passed over intact leaves enclosed in a transparent chamber. The CO_2 content was 0.031 to 0.033 percent, and leaf blades were oriented for maximum light reception. Leaves were exposed to the air—$^{14}CO_2$ mixture for 30

TABLE 4-11

RATE OF PHOTOSYNTHESIS AND LEAF CHARACTERS OF TEN SUGARCANE VARIETIES

[After Irvine (780).] Reproduced by permission of *Crop Science.*

Variety	Photosynthesis rate (mg/dm²/h)	Porosity (l/sec)	Stomatal number (mm²)	Stomatal length (μm)	Thickness (mm)	Density thickness (mg/cm²)	Leaf area per stalk (cm²)
F. 36-819	86.40 a*	0.056	212	22.5	0.277	0.0229	5220 a*
C.P. 44-155	66.40 b	0.020	272	21.0	0.236	0.0197	3475 cd
C.P. 36-13	66.20 b	0.020	230	22.5	0.234	0.0208	3980 bcd
C.P. 58-48	62.42 b	0.031	254	19.5	0.254	0.0215	3913 bcd
C.P. 52-68	59.35 bc	0.031	204	26.0	0.244	0.0214	3079 d
C.P. 59-43	51.22 cd	0.031	192	23.0	0.244	0.0205	3717 bcd
La. Purple	42.22 de	0.030	224	21.5	0.213	0.0188	3858 bcd
Otaheite	39.17 e	0.006	334	22.5	0.229	0.0208	4764 ab
Badila	34.87 e	0.017	316	20.0	0.218	0.0208	4449 abc
Crystalina	34.44 e	0.012	269	21.5	0.223	0.0205	5588 a

*Mean values sharing the same letter are not significantly different at the 5-percent level.

seconds. Blade samples were analyzed for radioactivity, porosity, area, stomata number and length, and leaf density thickness.

Irvine's results showed that photosynthesis rate per unit of leaf area varied significantly among the ten sugarcane varieties. The *S. officinarum* hybrids (*Badila*, *Crystalina*, *Louisiana Purple*, and *Otaheite*) showed markedly lower photosynthesis rates than the interspecific hybrids (Table 4-11). Of the latter, the parent variety *F. 36-819* was clearly superior to all others tested. A significant correlation was found between photosynthesis rate and leaf thickness, and between photosynthesis rate and leaf porosity. Irvine, noting that both leaf thickness and porosity are more easily determined than photosynthesis rate, suggested that the two leaf parameters might be useful in selecting sugarcane varieties having high photosynthesis potential. There was no apparent correlation between photosynthesis rate and stomata number, stomata length, or leaf density thickness.

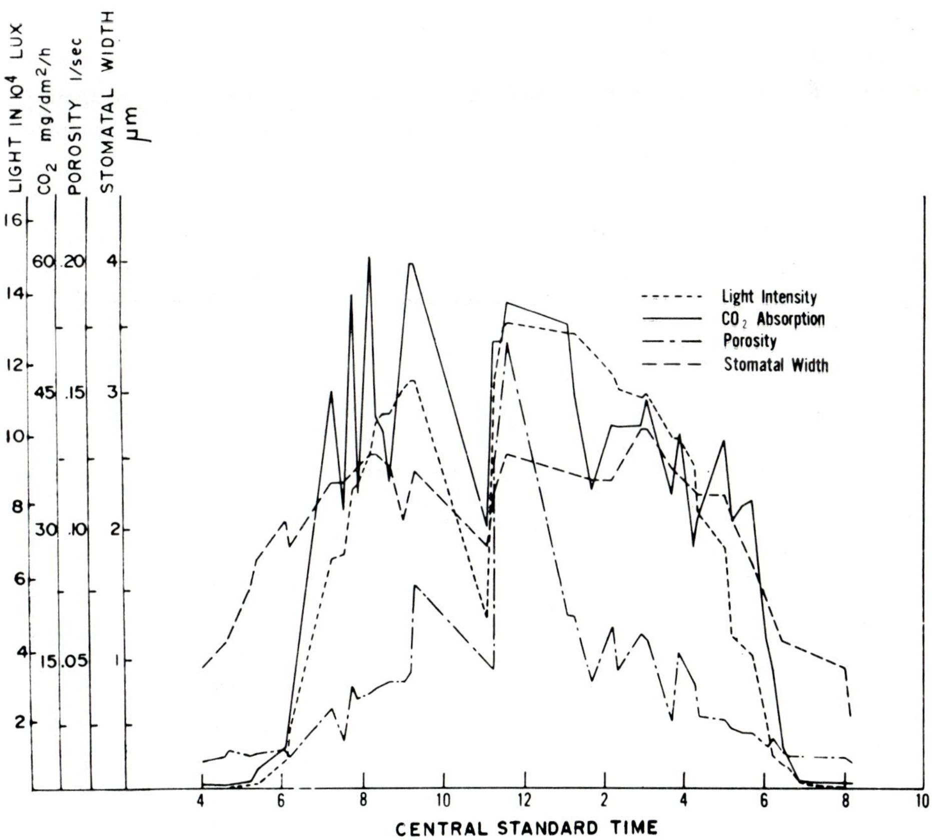

Fig. 4-20. Diurnal changes in light intensity, carbon dioxide absorption, porosity and stomatal width of sugarcane leaves (variety *C.P. 58-48*). [After Irvine (780).] Reproduced by permission of *Crop Science*.

Diurnal variations in photosynthesis rate were also examined by Irvine using the interspecific hybrid *C.P. 58-48*. Data presented in Fig. 4-20, gathered on June 21, showed maximum photosynthesis during the late morning hours, but so long as no cloud cover occurred there was no evidence of "bimodal" distribution of photosynthesis rates. It is unfortunate that the analyses were not repeated on at least one of the other nine varieties. Experiments with artificial shade confirmed that even small losses of sunlight can lower assimilation rates.

H. *Additional factors affecting photosynthesis in sugarcane*

One of the most thorough reports available on factors affecting photosynthesis in sugarcane was presented by Hartt and Burr (674) in 1965 during the 12th Congress, I.S.S.C.T. Reference has already been made to a number of their findings. A possible limitation of this work stems from the fact that only a small number of varieties could be tested and these only under Hawaiian conditions.

In addition to the rate-affecting factors previously noted, Hartt and Burr demonstrated differential effects of various blade portions and evaluated the light intensity factors of saturation and compensation point. The importance of moisture percentage and of solarization, *i.e.*, prolonged exposure to light, was also examined. It was reported that within a given blade the photosynthesis rate varied as a gradient with the center or widest part of the leaf being the most active. Younger leaves were found to have lower photosynthesis rates than mature leaves. The compensation point for blade $^{+}5$ of the variety *H. 50-7209* was between 120 and 125 foot candles. Blade $^{+}4$ of variety *H. 37-1933* gave a compensation point lying between 47 and 150 foot candles. Among some 12 varieties it was found that the saturating light intensity was generally between 6000 and 8000 foot candles, although the variety *H. 41-1045* was not saturated even at 14 000 foot candles.

With respect to leaf moisture, it was shown that the percentage of moisture in the blade may parallel a decrease in CO_2 assimilation rate in the same blade (Table 4-12). In these experiments variable osmotic concentrations were obtained by supplying NaCl to the plants in nutrient solutions. The highest osmotic concentration, 6.4 atmospheres, depressed photosynthesis rate in both primary stalks and suckers.

Hartt and Burr described a solarization effect upon photosynthesis rate which could not be correlated with saturating light intensity or stomatal closure (674). When repeated doses of CO_2 were supplied to the same portion of blade there was at first an increase of activity followed by a decline, the decline being described as solarization. In one set of experiments it was shown that the stomata remained open after 35 doses of CO_2 had been supplied, *i.e.*, sufficient to produce more than 50 percent inhibition of photosynthesis. Further studies suggested that solarization was caused by accumulating end products which subsequently inhibited further photosynthesis. The authors stressed the importance of continued translocation in maintaining the maximum photosynthesis rate in a given leaf.

TABLE 4-12

EFFECT OF LEAF MOISTURE CONTENT ON PHOTOSYNTHESIS RATE IN SUGARCANE*

Plants were grown in nutrient solutions in which osmotic levels of 0.4 and 6.4 atm were created with NaCl. [After Hartt and Burr (674).] Reproduced by permission of *I. S. S. C. T.*

Blade No.	Moisture (%) with		Photosynthesis rate (ml $CO_2/dm^2/h$)	
	0.4 atm	6.4 atm	0.4 atm	6.4 atm
2	71.0	68.2	9.28	5.66
3	70.1	62.1	8.00	6.29
4	68.5	56.4	12.09	5.88
5	68.7	57.6	15.32	6.50

*Variety *H. 37-1933.*

Burr (274) stresses greater leaf area with better leaf arrangement as a means of improving photosynthetic efficiency, and hence growth and sugar yield. Under Taiwan conditions the variety *F. 146* was shown to have near vertical leaves which favor light reception, *i.e.*, 4.1 m^2 of leaf blades were optimally illuminated per 1.0 m^2 of ground area (leaf-area index = 4.1). By contrast, horizontal leaves maintained a much inferior rate of net photosynthesis which could not have supported optimal growth.

Chapter 5

Polysaccharide Biosynthesis

1. INTRODUCTION

Although sucrose must invariably emerge as the principal actor in any story of sugarcane physiology, it is necessary to digress at some point and review our understanding of the polysaccharides produced by sugarcane during its normal growth and maturation phases. This should not imply that starches and other insoluble polysaccharides are not important to the sugarcane plant or to its ultimate success in producing sucrose. Starches have been known for years in certain varieties and their annoyance to factory operators is well documented. Indeed, until quite recently physiologists were not certain whether sucrose or starch was the main product of sugarcane photosynthesis.

In 1907 Browne and Blouin (252) gave the following description of cane photosynthesis in young leaves and shoots: "...The process of assimilation now begins; the carbonic acid of the air and the water taken up through the roots undergo a transformation in the chlorophyll-bearing tissues of the leaf, *with the result that starch and also probably sugar are formed...*"[1] According to Hartt (652), Komatsu depicted in 1933 starch or a similar polysaccharide as the primary product of photosynthesis while his colleague, Ozawa, assumed that a simple sugar was the primary product (847). Hartt (652), in 1936, pondered long over the question whether starch, sucrose, or hexose was the primary assimilate. Her own data suggested that it was hexose.

Investigators have dealt with three general types of polysaccharides formed in sugarcane: (a) "Starches" distributed throughout the plant, including the green leaves, but especially predominate in mature storage tissue; (b) "dextrans" which are produced in mature stalks both before and after harvest; and (c) "glucans" appearing daily as insoluble photosynthates or residues in leaf tissues. These groupings are admittedly arbitrary. Interrelationships between simple sugars and polysaccharides, especially appertaining to synthesis, structure, and function, have not been clearly defined. The polysaccharides do appear to have a common basis in their insolubility and their composition of glucose residues joined through $1 \longrightarrow 6$ or $1 \longrightarrow 4$ glucosidic linkages. It is reasonable to assume that common precursor pools are expended, perhaps competitively, in the biosynthesis of sucrose and polyglucosides.

Polysaccharides produced during the postharvest deterioration period appear to have no physiological role in the normal living cane. Such compounds are frequently associated with the bacterium *Leuconostoc mesenteroides* which infects the harvested

---

[1] Italics by the author.

stalk, multiplies rapidly in the cane and milled juice, and produces low molecular weight glucosides or dextrans. These are appropriately discussed in Chapter 15 in relation to postharvest physiology and will not be treated further in this section.

2. SUGARCANE STARCHES IN PERSPECTIVE

A. *Distribution among Saccharum species*

The occurrence of "traditional" starches in sugarcane, *i.e.*, high molecular weight, elaborately-branched glucosides producing a typical deep blue color with iodine, was historically associated with *Saccharum* species other than *officinarum.* According to Van Dillewijn (1475), starch was observed in *Erianthus* by Kramers in Java during the 1890's. Dutt and Narasimhan (458) reported that virtually all of some 85 *S. barberi* varieties contained large quantities of starch in both lower and upper portions of the stalk. Starch was also abundant in *S. sinense*, but less so than in *S. barberi*, while *S. spontaneum* contained still smaller quantities of the polysaccharide (Fig. 5-1). Other studies by Dutt and Narasimhan revealed little or no starch in 78 varieties of *S. officinarum.*

The preferential distribution of starch among "primitive" *Saccharum* species appears to complement a cane evolution theory proposed by Bull and Glasziou (258) which stresses the preferential selection of high-sucrose containing canes. By this reasoning *S. officinarum* would not constitute a single species, but rather a group of naturally-selected strains having had extraordinary success in accumulating sucrose. Starch accumulations in more primitive or "wild" types, including *Erianthus* [the allied genus from which Celarier (309) states that *Saccharum* might have evolved], is consistent with the expected low availability of soluble sugar reserves.

The variety *Natal Uba* (*S. sinense*) appears to have been a prime offender with respect to starch production (522, 624, 1587). Haddon (625) found starch distributed along the entire length of 8-month-old stalks but attributed the starch to low-pH soil conditions. Alfaro (59) drew similar conclusions relating high starch content to acid soils in Cuba. Weller (1557) observed that starch accumulated in all parenchyma cells of *Natal Uba*, in contrast to other varieties (including *Hawaiian Uba* and *Puerto Rico Uba*), in which starch was localized in parenchyma cells surrounding the vascular bundles. Weller believed that a different type of starch was present in *Natal Uba* but provided no definitive evidence to support this claim. Von Stieglitz (1510), in Queensland, confirmed the unusual accumulations of starch in *Natal Uba* but found no evidence of a starch–soil pH relationship.

More recent findings have shown that starch is present in *S. officinarum*, but in relatively small quantities which do not seriously interfere with milling operations. Nicholson and Horsley (1093) describe analytical methods for starch when mixed with

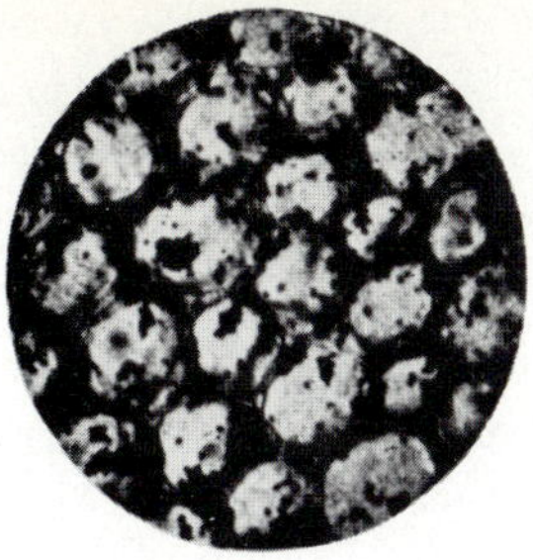

KATHA
(*S. barberi*)

UBA
(*S. sinense*)

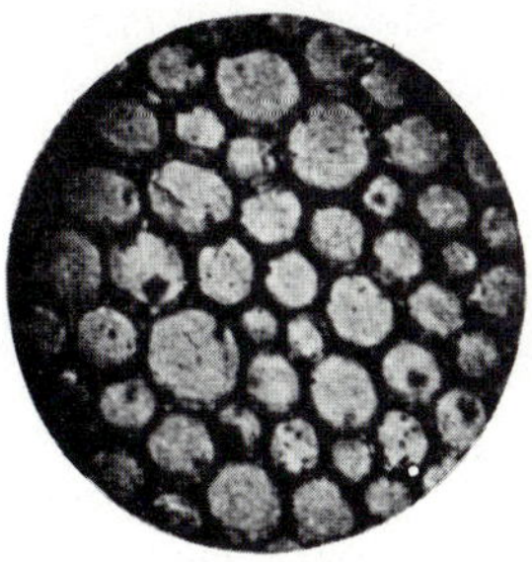

COIMBATORE
(*S. spontaneum*)

VELLAI
(*S. officinarum*)

Fig. 5-1. Accumulations of starch in the stems of *Saccharum* species. [After Dutt and Narasimhan (458).] Reproduced by permission of *Current Science*, Bangalore.

dextran and sucrose. In unheated crude juice the cane starch was described as a visible granular material which could be isolated from dextran by centrifugation or filtration. Balch (134) removed starch from aqueous extracts by alcohol precipitation following removal from raw juice on diatomaceous filter aid. Sutherland (1391), on the other hand, obtained two polysaccharides from mill syrups by fractional alcohol precipitation and subsequent moving-boundary electrophoresis. One polysaccharide appeared to be a dextran and the other a hemicellulose. Since crude polysaccharide preparations failed to give a blue color with iodine, doubt was expressed as to whether starch *per se* was present at all.

Another polysaccharide, *pullulan*, apparently distinct from both dextran and starch, was recently isolated from harvested *S. officinarum* (80). This compound was hydrolyzed by the enzyme *pullulanase*, produced by a strain of *Aerobacter aerogenes*, whose action pattern is specific for $1 \longrightarrow 6$ glucosidic linkages. Efforts to isolate cane starch and to analyze its amylose–amylopectin ratios as a varietal feature met with only limited success (80). In a later report the *pullulan* was described as an α-polyglucan (84) and progress in the hydrolysis of cane starch by bacterial α-amylases was described. Sutherland (1390) obtained a crude water-soluble polysaccharide having a high ash content and varying amounts of galactose, glucose, arabinose, xylose, and traces of rhamnose. The polysaccharide appeared to be a major factor in determining the viscosity of mill syrup. In addition to the strictly glucosidic polysaccharides the appearance of cane fructosides is at least theoretically possible, perhaps originating by fructose condensation upon an initial sucrose molecule as depicted by Hehre (709).

B. *Physiological role*

The physiological role of starch and other polysaccharides in the cane stalk is quite uncertain. Most of the current literature portrays cane polysaccharides from a factory viewpoint and the impression given is that they serve no purpose other than to harass the factory operators. Since sucrose is the only carbohydrate conducted in appreciable amounts to the storage areas (665, 697) it must be assumed that starch biosynthesis follows an outer space sucrose inversion and subsequent conversion of fructose to glucose. Polysaccharide synthesis presumably occurs in the inner space in place of the sucrose reassembly as depicted by Glasziou and his colleagues in Australia (*cf.* Chapter 9, 343–345). The deposition of large polysaccharide molecules rather than sucrose would not appear to be especially advantageous to the plant even though the necessary enzymology, including the catalyst starch phosphorylase or starch synthetase, would be no more elaborate than the enzymic mechanisms needed for sucrose synthesis. However, the efflux of glucose would then depend upon inner space amylases, both α- and β- if the polysaccharide is highly branched, plus maltase, rather than a single invertase system. It is therefore in the remobilization of hexose for growth or respiratory processes that starch might prove to be the more cumbersome storage carbohydrate.

A different view is presented by the work of Dutt and Narasimhan (458) who suggest that cane starch accumulations might be stimulatory for germination. Noting the experiments of Carlson (306) with roses, in which shoot growth was exceptionally profuse from cuttings whose nodes contained heavy starch accumulations, Dutt and Narasimhan compared the starch content and root development in two varieties having distinct germination rates. Cuttings from the variety *Katha* (*S. spontaneum*), producing early and extensive sett-roots, contained higher starch concentrations than the *Burma* form of *S. spontaneum* in which root development was notably slow. The authors made no mention of endogenous amylase levels.

C. *Foliar starch production in relation to sucrose synthesis and transport*

S. officinarum varieties contain foliar starch as a somewhat fleeting and secondary photosynthate. The term "starch" is used loosely here since no clear distinction has yet been drawn in cane between the *glucan* photosynthates and the elaborated starches evidenced as granules in cane chloroplasts. The latter are presumably comprised of straight-chain amylose and highly-branched amylopectin constituents. Polysaccharides representing photosynthetic end products accumulate daily in the leaves and are removed as sucrose during the same day and subsequent night.

Although the role of starch in leaves is no more evident than it is in storage tissues, several features of the foliar cane polysaccharides have gradually emerged. Foremost is the fact that, in sugarcane, starch is not the primary end product of photosynthesis that it appears to be in many plant species. Historically, Sachs (1270, 1271) concluded more than a century ago that starch was the first major product of photosynthesis in green plants. The possibility that sucrose was the primary assimilate was first suggested by Brown and Morris (249) in 1893. De Vries (432), in 1878, associated starch formation with the chloroplast and also recognized that translocation would not be feasible unless some manner of polysaccharide disintegration first occurred. He proposed that starch was hydrolyzed or "digested" and that the glucose residues moved to the plant roots where they were reassembled into sucrose. In 1907 Browne and Blouin (252) incorrectly assumed that both sucrose and starch are enzymatically hydrolyzed in sugarcane leaves and that the reducing-sugar products are then translocated to areas of utilization (and presumably also to areas of storage). These authors correctly recognized the independent synthesis of foliar starch and sucrose, and that sucrose could

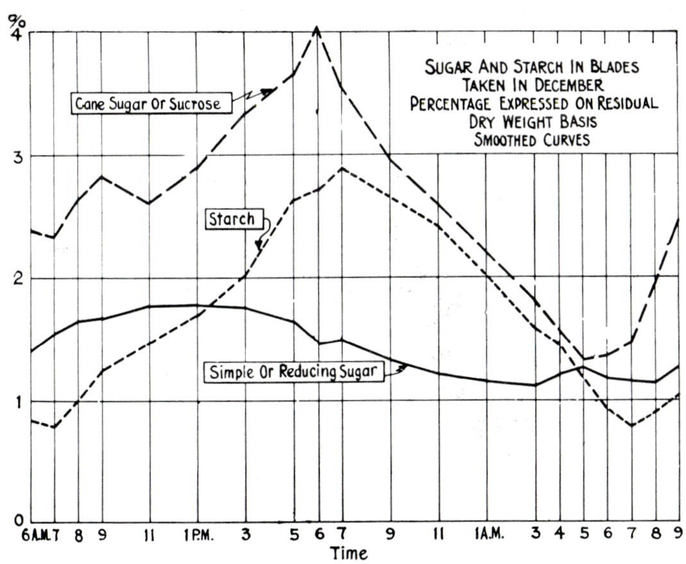

Fig. 5-2. Variations in sucrose, starch, and hexose contents of sugarcane under Hawaiian conditions during a 27-hour period in December. [After Hartt (652).] Reproduced by permission of the *Hawaiian Sugar Planters' Association*, Honolulu.

be formed thereafter from starch. However, they had no way of knowing that sucrose was the only important form of transiting carbohydrate in sugarcane. This was not established until the mid-1960's when, armed with labeled carbon dioxide, workers in Hawaii (667) and Australia (692) independently demonstrated that ^{14}C-labeled photosynthate is translocated primarily in the form of sucrose.

Additional important features of foliar polysaccharides are the interconversion of starch and sucrose, and the nocturnal translocation of starch (or glucans) in disaccharide form. For many years plant physiologists have been intrigued with the problems inherent in the sucrose–starch interconversion (1084, 110, 5). Hartt, in Hawaii, appears to have been the only sugarcane physiologist who recognized both the necessity of removing starch from cane leaves and the significance of these reactions to the larger problem of moving sucrose from source to sink. Even so, our knowledge of these features remains extremely limited. Hartt (652), in 1936, published results of seasonal carbohydrate studies in which sucrose, starch and hexose constituents appeared to fluctuate both on a seasonal and diurnal basis. From Fig. 5-2, illustrating foliar sugar changes during a 27-hour period in December, it is evident that starch literally increased all day and decreased all night. Hartt recognized the similarity of sucrose and starch curves and the likeness of both curves to that of a temporary storage product. It was tentatively concluded that simple sugars are the primary photosynthetic products and that their "condensation" to sucrose and starch might help to alleviate product repression of photosynthesis.

Citing Ahrens (4) whose findings implied a conversion of starch to sucrose in wilting leaves, plus similar work by Schroeder and Herrmann (1307), Hartt surmised "...that the conversion of starch to cane sugar (sucrose) occurs in plants thus seems well established". Hartt questioned not the fact of starch–sucrose interconversion but the biochemical mechanisms involved. These are still being questioned more than 30 years later.

Early concepts purporting a direct interconversion between starch and sucrose (1059, 1583) have not received support in recent times. Experiments by Arreguin-Lozano and Bonner (110) with the potato tuber were suggestive of a phosphorylase-coupled interconversion of starch and sucrose which is powerfully influenced by temperature. Hasselbring (653) described a temperature-sensitive conversion of starch to sucrose in stored *Narcissus* bulbs involving an initial conversion of starch to hexose. However, plant phosphorylases of the type discovered by Hanes (634) in 1940 would be hindered by limit dextrans in direct enzymatic conversion of polysaccharide to sucrose. Moreover, some fraction of the glucose residues would have to be converted to fructose. Physiological experiments with immature sugarcane (15) have shown only an indirect relationship between sucrose formation and phosphorylase activity involving time differentials of at least 7 days.

The stepwise conversion of starch to "cane sugar" visualized by Hartt in 1936 envisaged first a conversion of starch to glucose, then conversion of some glucose to fructose, followed by union of the two hexoses to form sucrose. While in essence this is consistent with present knowledge of polysaccharide synthesis and degradation, the enzymology required to accomplish these transformations was established in cane only during the past decade. Enzymes essential for starch conversion to sucrose include α- and β-amylase, maltase, hexokinase (glucokinase), and sucrose synthetase (UDPG–fructose transglucosylase). Sucrose phosphorylase and sucrose phosphate phosphatase might also be involved. Presumably this sequence would be reversible, in which case either starch phosphorylase or starch synthetase would catalyze the reconstitution of starch in cooperation with a branching factor (Q enzyme).

Modern conceptions of the starch–sucrose interconversion were reviewed by Akazawa (6) in 1965. Essentially a cellular conservation mechanism, its necessity rests upon the fact that most plants produce starch in their leaves but translocate carbohydrate in the form of sucrose. Two possible mechanisms are depicted by Akazawa (Eqns. 1 and 2). The first mechanism encompasses the earlier thinking of Hartt plus the enzymes enumerated above. A key feature of Eqn. 1 is the operation of invertase. Since this enzyme is virtually non-existent in sugarcane leaves, the mechanism as shown is not applicable to the conversion of foliar cane sucrose to starch. However, a

$$[\text{sucrose}] \xrightarrow{\text{invertase}} [\text{glucose} + \text{fructose}] \xrightarrow[\text{(ATP)}]{\text{hexokinase}} \begin{bmatrix} \text{glucose 6-phosphate} \\ + \\ \text{fructose 6-phosphate} \end{bmatrix} \rightarrow \quad (1)$$

$$[\text{glucose 1-phosphate}] \xrightarrow[\text{(ATP or UTP)}]{\text{pyrophosphorylase}} \begin{bmatrix} \text{ADPG} \\ \text{or} \\ \text{UDPG} \end{bmatrix} \xrightarrow{\text{starch synthetase}} [\text{starch}]$$

$$[\text{sucrose}] \xrightarrow[\text{(ADP or UDP)}]{\text{sucrose synthetase}} \begin{bmatrix} \text{ADPG} \\ \text{or} \\ \text{UDPG} \end{bmatrix} \xrightarrow{\text{starch synthetase}} [\text{starch}] \quad (2)$$

reverse reaction entailing known amylases rather than invertase, and sucrose synthetase (also known) rather than starch synthetase, is very possibly operative in sugarcane leaves.

Akazawa's statement that "...invertase is widely present in plants, but there is no proof of its function in sucrose breakdown..." was certainly ill-timed. By 1965 workers in Australia (586, 585, 689) had established discrete spatial and functional invertase reactions essential both for sucrose accumulation and efflux in cane storage tissue. Eqn. 1 is probably quite valid in sugarcane storage tissue up to the formation of hexose phosphate. The ultimate product is stored (vacuolar) sucrose rather than starch. Eqn. 2 might be operative in leaves as a simple reversal of the starch synthetase reaction coupled directly with sucrose synthetase. However, Akazawa raises the point that coupling the two reactions yields a thermodynamic balance favoring starch synthesis. This might not be strictly true under conditions of increased polysaccharide accumulation such as normally occurs in cane foliage by late afternoon (652). Furthermore, there is no evidence to show that starch synthesis is favored over sucrose synthesis in *S. officinarum* at any time of day.

A remarkably consistent parallel between foliar amylase activity and changing sucrose levels led Alexander to suggest that starch formation and breakdown is of paramount importance to the sucrose-forming capacity of sugarcane (11, 15, 24, 34)[2]. This conclusion was drawn in spite of repeated failure to detect more than traces of starch in the stalks of Puerto Rico varieties under scrutiny. It was assumed that amylase was sufficiently abundant to hydrolyze virtually all starch at the instant of synthesis. In this context the starch-forming apparatus might seriously affect sucrose production via competition for UDPG and glucose 1-phosphate without actually accumulating starch in leaf of storage tissues. Moreover, amylase level *per se* could provide a biochemical explanation for the differential starch patterns noted by Dutt and Narasimhan (458) among *Saccharum* species. Hartt (653) reported that amylase was less active in the high starch variety *Natal Uba* than in six other varieties grown under similar conditions. Quite clearly the enzyme syndrome for polysaccharide synthesis and degradation as an evolutionary factor among *Saccharum* species is ripe for exploration.

D. *Evidence of foliar starch in S. officinarum*

Visible evidence of starch in sugarcane leaves was published by Laetsch *et al.* (879) in 1965. Leaf tissue preparations from the field-grown varieties *B. 57150* and *B. 5744* were examined by light and electron microscopy in the first definitive studies of the cane chloroplast ultrastructure. Of the two types of chloroplasts encountered, *i.e.*, grana-containing chloroplasts from leaf parenchyma and grana-free (lamellar) chloroplasts from bundle-sheath cells, the latter or grana-free type contained an abundance of starch grains (Fig. 5-3). Similar bodies of starch were observed frequently in the cytoplasm of bundle-sheath cells. In these studies insoluble polysaccharides and starch were localized with the periodic acid–Schiff's (PAS) reaction. Starch was also localized with iodine.

The work by Laetsch and his colleagues in Trinidad (879) gave the first visible proof that starch was an important photosynthetic product of *S. officinarum*[3]. Although the author's enzymic studies had clearly shown a potential for polysaccharide synthesis in commercial varieties, the work in Trinidad showed that the enzymes were more than

---

[2]In the author's experience foliar amylase in sugarcane is very nearly as sensitive to leaf sucrose level as invertase is to the sucrose content of immature storage tissue. Indeed, the enzymes themselves are quite similar with respect to certain physical and chemical properties (18, 33).

[3]Browne and Blouin (252) had found starch in sugarcane leaves prior to 1907: "...The presence of starch in cane leaves can be very easily demonstrated by dissolving the chlorophyll in boiling alcohol and then applying tincture of iodine, when the starch grains will be colored blue."

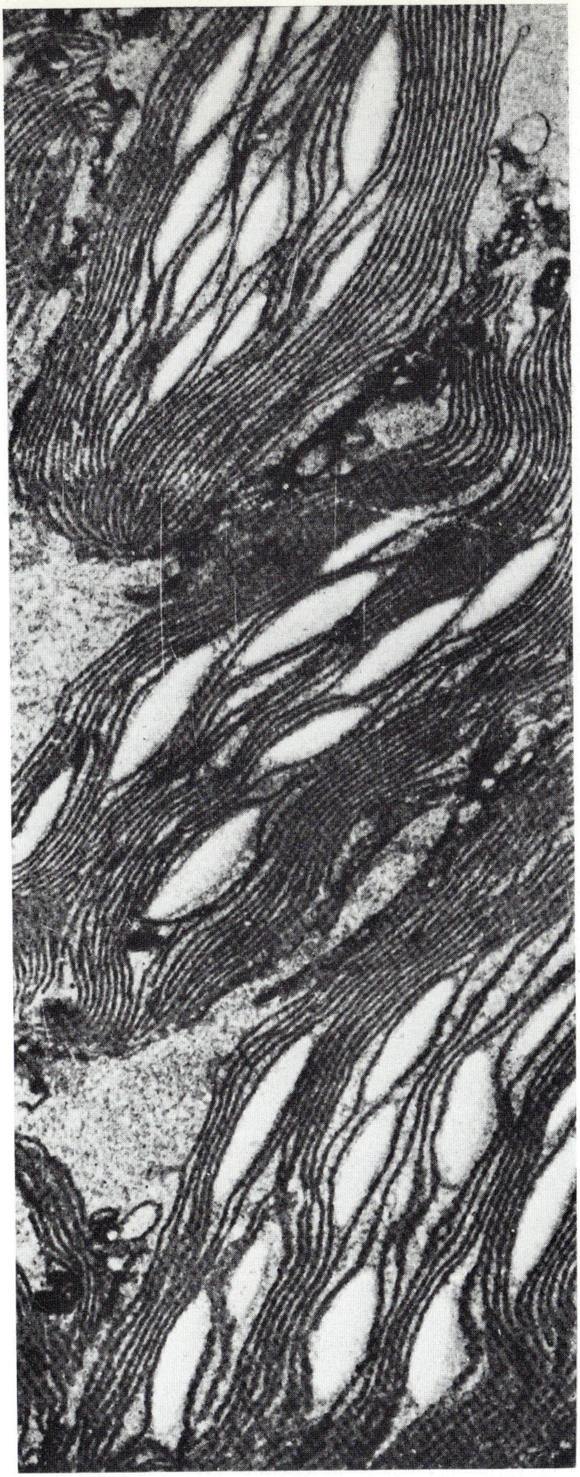

Fig. 5-3. Electron micrograph showing starch grains in the non-grana (lamellar) type of chloroplast in sugarcane leaves. Magnification: 12 000 x 3. [Front cover, *Annual Report of the Tate and Lyle Central Agricultural Research Station*, Carapichaima, Trinidad, 1965. Courtesy of the Tate and Lyle Research Centre, Ravensbourne, Keston, Kent, England.]

vestigial relics from primitive *Saccharum* species. On purely physiological grounds the chloroplast starch findings may have been a milestone in elucidating the mechanism of source-to-sink sugar transport. A predominance of cane chloroplasts in the single layer of parenchyma cells surrounding the bundle sheath (Fig. 5-4) is suggestive that the bio-

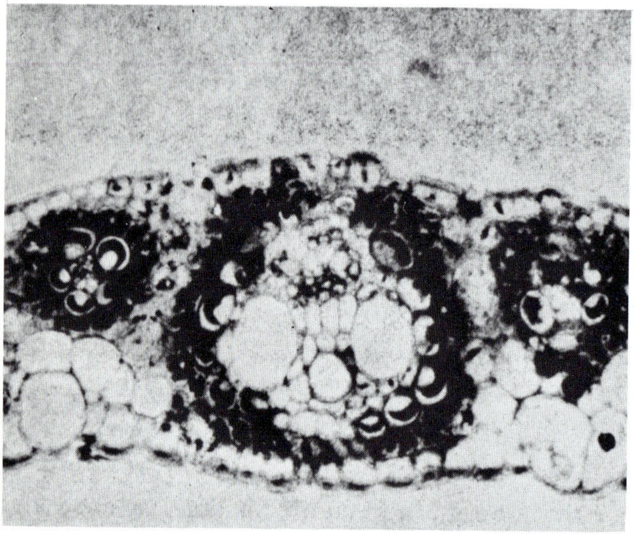

Fig. 5-4. Cross section of a sugarcane leaf illustrating the distribution of chloroplasts in parenchyma cells surrounding the bundle sheath. [*Annual Report of the Tate and Lyle Central Agricultural Research Station*, Carapichaima, Trinidad, 1965. Courtesy of the Tate and Lyle Research Centre, Ravensbourne, Keston, Kent, England.]

chemical solutions to sucrose synthesis, starch synthesis, and starch–sucrose interconversion are spatially situated so as to accommodate active vein loading and active sugar transport. This view is consistent with Hartt's concepts of nocturnal polysaccharide conversion to sucrose (432, 675) and subsequent transport in the disaccharide form (675). The energy source for vein loading and basipetal transport, never adequately explained in spite of the enormous advances achieved in Hawaii and Australia, might conceivably originate in these chloroplasts, *i.e.*, via photosynthetic energy conversion. In addition to the purely physiological–biochemical aspects, the relationships of chloroplast starch to varietal growth and yield potentials beckon to be explored. This is especially true since chlorophyll analyses can be performed on seedlings within a few days after germination.

E. *Insoluble cane photosynthate; α-glucan*

It has long been recognized that glucose polymers are a frequent product of photosynthesis by intact cells and isolated chloroplasts (574). Allen *et al.* (63) reported in

1955 that under conditions favorable for complete photosynthesis the only insoluble product formed by isolated chloroplasts was a glucose polymer. Everson *et al.* (511) recently took note of the fact that sucrose is not usually formed to an appreciable extent in isolated chloroplasts (803, 1520), although the latter contain the correct enzyme complement for sucrose synthesis (184, 640). In the instance of spinach chloroplasts (511) sucrose formation occurs as a seasonal phenomenon. Hodgkinson and Veale (739) reported that ethanol-insoluble photosynthate increased in illuminated lucerne leaves and declined in darkened leaves. There was no build-up of insoluble photosynthate in continuously-darkened plants. The authors concluded that starch had accumulated during the illumination period and was broken down to maltose and glucose in the dark. In 1966 Hatch and Slack (693) proposed a two-cycle scheme of the C_4-dicarboxylic acid pathway, subsequently verified (1342, 696, 697, 698), in which the second cycle yields the photosynthetic end products sucrose and α-glucan while regenerating an acceptor for the C-4 carboxyl group of dicarboxylic acids. Presumably the α-glucan is analogous to the insoluble leaf photosynthate described by Hartt *et al.* (667), and the insoluble storage tissue residues formed from translocated sucrose (665, 675).

Kortschak *et al.* (851) reported that some 13.5 minutes after exposing sugarcane leaves to $^{14}CO_2$, the radioactivity found in photosynthesis products insoluble in 95 percent boiling ethanol constituted approximately 10 percent of the amount found in sucrose. Hartt *et al.* (667) observed that 5 hours after treating cane leaf tissue with $^{14}CO_2$ the total counts (TC) found in alcohol-insoluble residue increased from 7000 to 12 000. During the same interval sucrose TC values dropped from 118 000 to 25 000. Insoluble compounds were also formed in immature internodes and roots from translocated [^{14}C]sucrose. After 6 weeks, 20 percent of the ^{14}C found in mature internodes (joints 11 to 15) was incorporated into insoluble compounds. Hartt (675) later proposed that foliar polysaccharide is converted to sucrose during the night as part of a metabolic regulation of solution flow.

Hatch and Slack (693), in Australia, noted that the products of $^{14}CO_2$ fixation in detached cane leaf segments were initially C_4-dicarboxylic acids, followed by 3-phosphoglycerate, hexose monophosphates, and sucrose. During a time course of 40 to 50 seconds of steady-state photosynthesis there appeared detectable quantities of a ^{14}C-labeled residue described as glucan. By 150 seconds this product contained about 7.5 percent of the total incorporated ^{14}C. It was insoluble in 80 percent boiling ethanol and remained insoluble during subsequent extractions with boiling water. Upon treatment of the residue with 72 percent (v/v) H_2SO_4, virtually all of the radioactivity was recovered in a single compound which co-chromatographed with glucose in the solvents propan-1-ol–aqueous NH_3–water (6:3:1, by vol.), and in ethyl acetate–pyridine–water (8:2:1, by vol.). Hydrolysis of the glucan with 6 N HCl yielded no radioactivity in amino acids.

It should be noted that the workers in Hawaii and Australia were not primarily interested in the insoluble photosynthesis products. Indeed, the discovery of a new carbon-assimilation pathway was fresh upon the scene, with all that this implies in carbon movement prior to any polysaccharide synthesis. Yet several important conclusions can be drawn from this and other work incidental to the foliar polysaccharide. First, it is sucrose rather than "starch" which appears as the initial major storage carbohydrate in sugarcane photosynthesis. Second, under natural conditions, glucan will increase to levels having physiological importance while remaining considerably below those of sucrose. Third, each day's output of insoluble polysaccharide is converted to sucrose and translocated away from the photosynthesizing tissues. Remaining residues such as the starch grains photographed in chloroplasts by Laetsch *et al.* (879) are presumably resistant to rapid enzymatic hydrolysis. Whether or not these are sufficiently abundant to interfere with continued photosynthesis remains to be determined.

3. MECHANISMS OF STARCH SYNTHESIS

Two general types of polysaccharide-forming mechanisms are widely distributed in plants: (a) A phosphorylase-mediated and phosphate-sensitive system producing glucoside by "condensation" of Cori ester glucose[4] upon an appropriate primer molecule; (b) a starch synthetase-mediated system in which glucose from UDPG or ADPG is transferred to an appropriate acceptor molecule. The latter mechanism is the predominating one in recent literature. Since indirect evidence of both mechanisms has been obtained from sugarcane, it is appropriate to review briefly the background of each.

A. *Starch phosphorylase*

As we have already seen, the fact of polysaccharide synthesis and its essential "condensations" involving simple sugars was recognized long before the actual mechanisms were discovered. Early attempts to demonstrate starch synthesis by the reverse amylase reaction were invariably negative. However, in 1937 Cori *et al.* (388) demonstrated that glucose-1-*P* was a product of glycogen breakdown by muscle extracts, and in so doing enormously advanced the understanding of polysaccharide synthesis and breakdown. This was the first acceptable alternative to the prior belief that glycogen degradation was mediated by amylases. A key feature distinguishing polysaccharide breakdown by amylase and by phosphorylase is that the amylase

[4]Abbreviations: glucose-1-*P*, glucose 1-phosphate (also "Cori ester"); ADPG, adenosine diphosphate glucose; UDPG, uridine diphosphate glucose; ATP, adenosine 5′-triphosphate; AMP, adenosine 5′-monophosphate; UTP, uridine 5′-triphosphate; UDP, uridine 5′-diphosphate; FAD, flavin adenine dinucleotide.

equilibrium heavily favors hydrolysis, whereas the "phosphorolysis" equilibrium is highly flexible and under suitable conditions can favor either direction [Fruton and Simmonds (540, p. 441)]. A phosphorylase isolated from muscle and liver tissues is known to catalyze the synthesis of glucose-1-*P* from glycogen in the presence of inorganic phosphorus. Under *in vitro* conditions the concentration of inorganic phosphate and glucose-1-*P*, along with the medium's pH, will govern the phosphorylase equilibrium[5]. Comparable energy levels of the glucosidic and phosphate–ester linkages (6, 278) encourage the reaction's reversibility. Polysaccharide is therefore synthesized or broken down in accordance with Eqn. 3:

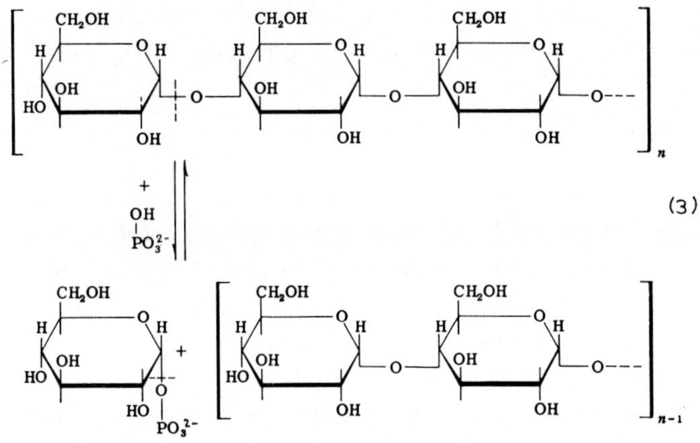

(3)

In 1940 Hanes (634, 635) isolated a phosphorylase from the pea seed and potato tuber which catalyzes starch synthesis and degradation in plants. In the presence of inorganic phosphate the enzyme catalyzes a starch breakdown which liberates glucose-1-*P* from the nonreducing end of the starch molecule. Since only the α-(1 $\longrightarrow$ 4) linkages are attacked, a restriction (limit dextrin) is imposed upon the enzyme's activity similar to that encountered by β-amylase in the presence of polysaccharide side branches (940). The reverse reaction produces an unbranched polysaccharide from glucose-1-*P* which yields a deep blue color with iodine. Evidence of this or an analogous phosphorylase has been found in sugarcane leaf preparations (32, 15).

Several differences have been noted in the properties of plant and animal phosphorylases. Cori and Green (389) isolated two distinct forms of phosphorylase (*a* and *b*)

[5] In describing the reaction's equilibrium some authors have correctly assumed that the polysaccharide concentration changes but little by comparison with that of glucose-1-*P* and inorganic phosphate, and therefore can be regarded as a relative constant [Fruton and Simmonds (540, p. 441), Akazawa (6, p. 278)]. However, in terms of cane leaf polysaccharide which varies significantly during the course of the day, the diurnal polysaccharide level should assert an important influence upon the phosphorylase equilibrium.

from muscle, the *b* enzyme being inactive until converted to *a* by mediation of phosphatase and kinase reactions in the presence of ATP or AMP. To the latter enzyme there is also attached the prosthetic group pyridoxal 5′-phosphate (390). The potato phosphorylase appears to be a single entity bound with pyridoxal 5′-phosphate, but it lacks a phosphatase–kinase reaction or an activation requirement for AMP (916). Moreover, the plant phosphorylase has different primer requirements than animal phosphorylase. Maltodextrans containing four to six residues very effectively prime the amylose synthesis reaction (1564); even maltotriose is effective to a lesser degree. However, there is increasing evidence that animal phosphorylase is active only in glycogen breakdown and not in the polysaccharide's synthesis (1030, 894, 1305). Similar conclusions based on inorganic phosphate content have been drawn relative to starch synthesis by phosphorylase in tree bark (516) and the pea seed (1259).

B. *Starch synthetase (UDPG–, ADPG–starch transglucosylase)*

A different means of glycogen synthesis was discovered by Leloir and his associates (921–923) during the late 1950's which appears to have answered certain doubts about the phosphorylase mechanism. The reaction is independent of inorganic phosphate level. Glucose is contributed via UDPG[6] and the critical enzyme is UDPG–glycogen transglucosylase. Extension of this work to starch biosynthesis soon showed that a similar reaction occurred in many plant species (427, 924, 5). Leloir *et al.* (924) established that the enzyme starch synthetase (UDPG–starch transglucosylase) catalyzed the formation of α-(1 $\longrightarrow$4) glucosidic linkages via the following reaction (G = glucosyl):

$$\text{UDPG} + \text{acceptor (G)}_n \longrightarrow \text{UDP} + \text{starch (G)}_{n+1} \tag{4}$$

This enzyme is technically an amylose synthetase whose ultimate production of starch is presumably linked with a polysaccharide branching factor, or Q enzyme, of the type described by Gilbert *et al.* (576, 577) in the potato and by Alexander (22) in sugarcane.

Certain plants appear to synthesize starch more effectively by utilizing ADPG (Fig. 5-5) rather than UDPG. The reaction is unknown in glycogen formation. Recondo and Leloir (1222) reported in 1961 that bean preparations synthesized starch more effectively when ADPG was supplied in place of UDPG. A chemically-synthesized source of the compound was employed initially but it was later found as an endogenous constituent of maize (1223) and rice (1064, 1065). Enzymatic synthesis of ADPG by the

---

[6]UDPG has recently been evaluated as a constituent of cellulose synthesis in higher plants (686, 1126). Ordin and Hall (1126) published evidence that UDPG is utilized to form several β-linked polysaccharides in plants, one of which is cellulose.

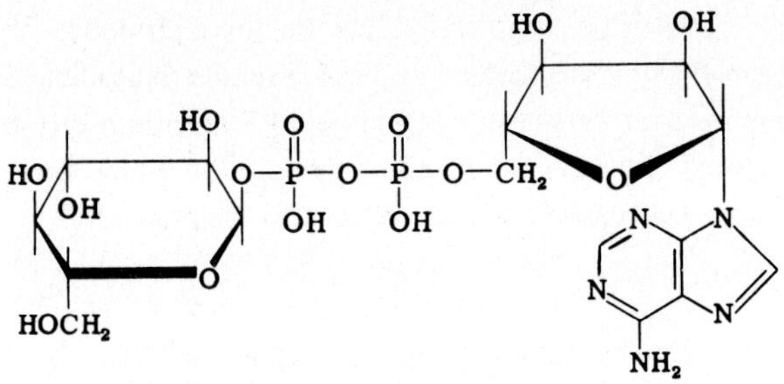

Adenosine diphosphate glucose

Fig. 5-5. Structural representation of adenosine diphosphate glucose. [From Bonner and Varner (205, p. 280), after Akazawa (6).] Reproduced by permission of the *Academic Press, Inc.*, New York.

enzyme ADPG pyrophosphorylase has been demonstrated in wheat flour (501) and rice (1067). According to Akazawa (6), even more effective glucose transfer has been shown with deoxy-ADPG in the starch-forming mechanism of maize (543). The latter compound has not been isolated from plant tissues.

In discussing the possible mechanisms of starch synthesis by sugarcane, none of which are known with appreciably certainty, one has to consider sugarcane's peculiar problem of having to translocate its daily output of insoluble polysaccharide. We have seen that Hartt (652), using conventional carbohydrate analyses, demonstrated a major movement of starch during the night (Fig. 5-2). Years later, working with radioactive carbon, Hartt and her co-workers confirmed the nocturnal sugar movement from leaf to stalk tissues (667, 675) and in addition showed that sucrose is the only sugar translocated in appreciable amounts (106). Thus the sugarcane problem is one of starch conversion to sucrose rather than of sucrose conversion to starch.

In physiological terms the "problem" would be less crucial if sucrose were the only photosynthate accumulating in cane leaves. Sucrose is readily soluble and easily moved. It might be converted to starch quite leisurely in the stalk without affecting photosynthesis. However, insoluble polysaccharide accumulations in the very limited storage space of sugarcane leaves would conceivably pose a serious restriction upon continued photosynthesis. With all that this implies in adverse restrictions upon the enormous cane growth, respiratory, and sugar-accumulating activity, it follows that some provision must be made to remove starch with reasonable consistency. One obvious approach would be utilization of highly-active amylases to destroy as much polysaccharide as possible at its inception and to complete the task at night. β-Amylases (18, 11) are certainly present in abundance and at least one α-amylase (22) is found in cane leaves. The rapid breakdown of initial amylose is also consistent with the view that elaborated starch granules formed during prolonged storage of starch will be more resistant to hydrolysis (1522). All enzymic systems needed for reassembly of simple sugars into sucrose are available in the cane leaf. Thus, on these grounds, the question of the specific mechanism for polysaccharide synthesis is rendered academic; whether formed by starch phosphorylase or starch synthetase, the reverse reaction which has concerned so many students of glycogen and starch metabolism would be of only secondary importance so long as a powerful amylase complex is maintained.

4. POLYSACCHARIDE SYNTHESIS BY SUGARCANE LEAF PREPARATIONS

A. *The phosphorylase reaction*

The discovery in 1963 (11) of highly active amylase in sugarcane leaves, without parallel evidence of accumulating starch, prompted attempts to measure cane polysaccharide synthesis *in vitro* (32, 15). Semi-purified aqueous leaf extracts were shown to produce a blue-staining polysaccharide in the presence of glucose-1-*P* and small amounts of primer. The original experiments were performed with the "sweet" variety *M. 336* grown by sand culture in the greenhouse. The responsible enzyme was tentatively described as starch phosphorylase (15). During the ensuing two years optimum conditions for both the *in vitro* and *in vivo* reaction were evaluated and attempts were made to modify the foliar starch–sucrose equilibrium with various irrigation and nutritional treatments (15, 24). A significant error was the exclusive use of local *S. officinarum* varieties which at no time showed more than traces of starch in stem tissue by the iodine test. Other *Saccharum* species should at least have been examined. Nonetheless, certain aspects of the work are worth recounting.

Aqueous enzyme extracts were initially prepared from freeze–dried, finely-ground tissues harvested from various parts of the plant. In later studies leaves $^{+}1$ to $^{+}4$ were generally accepted as the most convenient source. The phosphorylase enzyme was precipitated from clarified extracts with solid ammonium sulfate at pH 5.6, 22 °C. On the basis of solubility there appeared to be two phosphorylases, one precipitated between 0 and 30 percent saturation and the other obtained predominately between 70 and 90 percent saturation (Fig. 5-6). Polysaccharide synthesis was determined colorimetrically by measuring the increased blue value of clarified reaction digests following treatment with standardized iodine–potassium iodide solution. This method was particularly effective with sugarcane preparations and has been used to assay potato phosphorylase (110) as an alternative to measuring increased inorganic phosphate (391, 610, 635). The standard reaction mixture was comprised of succinate buffer (pH 6.25), glucose-1-*P*, undialyzed enzyme preparation, and a small amount of soluble potato starch serving as primer. Traces of molybdate were added to inhibit contaminant phosphatase (264) and iodide was added to suppress amylase (15). Enzyme action was computed both in terms of specific activity and as milligrams of starch formed per gram of cane tissue. It should be reemphasized that the term "starch" is used here for convenience rather than accuracy. The polysaccharide formed during the brief reaction period was presumably a straight-chain glucoside comparable to amylose.

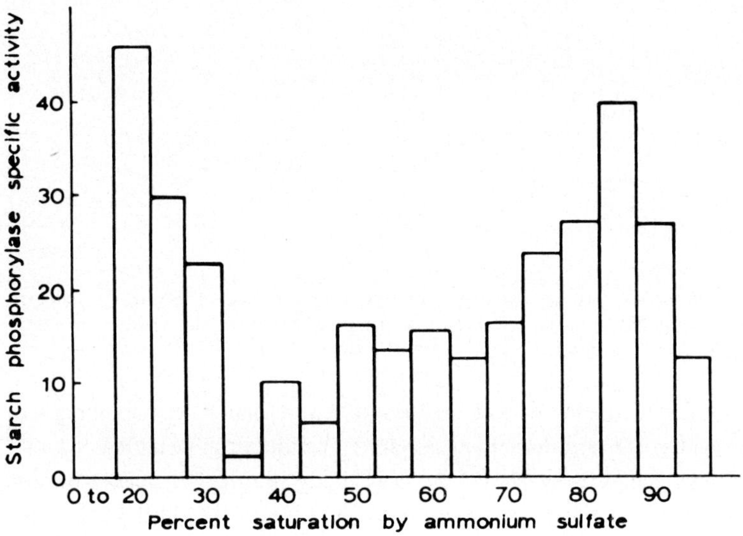

Fig. 5-6. Starch phosphorylase activity in protein increments precipitated from sugarcane leaf extracts with solid ammonium sulfate. [After Alexander (32).]

B. *Phosphorylase properties*

The two phosphorylase fractions already mentioned above, *i.e.*, obtained by salt fraction between 0–30 and 70–90 percent saturation, were usually combined in a single preparation largely free of amylase and phosphatase. These two enzymes abound in cane leaves but both are precipitated primarily between 35 and 55 percent saturation. Small amounts of the two systems present in the phosphorylase preparation were effectively inhibited by molybdate and iodide. However, Q enzyme was present and apparently achieved some branching by the close of the reaction period.

The effects of product elaboration, or branching, by Q enzyme are illustrated in Fig. 5-7. After 20 minutes had elapsed the formation of new polysaccharide was markedly restricted. The possibility of an amylase becoming active in spite of the added iodide inhibitor was considered since a number of amylases are known to be present in cane, but this was not borne out by the small reducing sugar increases in the phosphorylase reaction medium. A similar phosphorylase decline after initially rapid activity was observed by Arreguin-Lozano and Bonner (110), who attributed the effect to Q enzyme. The catalyst apparently does not become active until a substantial substrate level is present (in this case the substrate being the newly-formed phos-

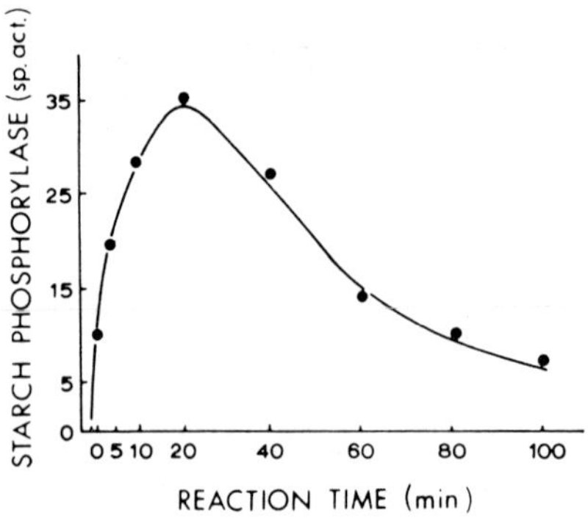

Fig. 5-7. Activity pattern of sugarcane starch phosphorylase as a function of time. Initial high activity declines following the appearance of polysaccharide product in the reaction medium. [After Alexander (32).]

phorylase product). The formation of α-(1 ⟶6)-linked side chains thereupon reduces the number of free glucoside terminals upon which new residues can be added.

The rate of polysaccharide synthesis by cane phosphorylase increased almost linearly as glucose-1-*P* was raised to 10 μmoles/ml (Fig. 5-8). Little additional activity

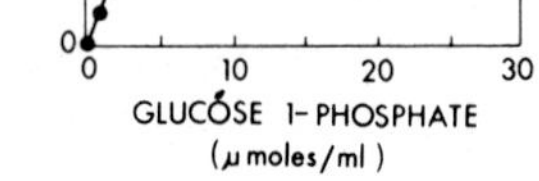

Fig. 5-8. Rate of polysaccharide synthesis by sugarcane starch phosphorylase as a function of glucose 1-phosphate level in the reaction medium. [After Alexander (32).]

was obtained with 30 μmoles of glucose-1-*P*. Optimum temperature for the reaction was 32 °C. Optimum pH was 6.25. The enzyme was relatively unstable even when refrigerated, losing 44 percent of its activity within 24 hours at 2 °C, and 65 percent at room temperature. The enzyme was therefore prepared fresh daily. Dialysis of the phosphorylase preparation against distilled water produced severe inactivation amounting to a loss of about 65 percent within 1 hour. Hanes (635) also reported major inhibition of the potato enzyme by dialysis. However, potato phosphorylase was quite stable up to 20 days in storage at 20 °C.

Cane phosphorylase activity was moderately stimulated by calcium and bromide ions, and by β-glycerophosphate. Green and Cori (611) found that reducing agents and especially glutathione or cysteine increased solubility of muscle phosphorylase. According to Fruton and Simmonds (540, p. 441), β-glycerophosphate is a non-competitive inhibitor of muscle phosphorylase *a*, although Green and Cori used the compound to neutralize solutions and to create buffers for dialysis procedures during the preparation of crystalline phosphorylase. The most effective activator of cane phosphorylase found at the author's laboratory was the substituted urea herbicide Diuron [3-(3,4-dichlorophenyl)-1,1-dimethylurea]. Mere traces of the herbicide added to reaction mixtures produced nearly 3-fold activity increases (29). It is noteworthy that Diuron also restricts the sucrose-forming mechanisms of cane leaves (29), which raises again the question of the closeness of cane sucrose- and starch-forming pathways. In a hypothetical direct exchange between the two mechanisms, *i.e.*, use of a common glucose-1-*P* pool, hindrance of either system could produce an increased rate of output by the other under conditions of limited glucose-1-*P* supply.

C. *Phosphorylase distribution; spatial and functional considerations*

The presence of starch in sugarcane is easily demonstrated by splitting the stalks longitudinally and treating the cut surface with iodine solution. Since starch is almost totally insoluble, and hence immobile, its discovery in any given tissue indicates the presence of a starch-forming mechanism. However, this means little in terms of absolute starch-forming potential inasmuch as varying starch levels might simply reflect variable amylase content.

Employing field-grown plants of the variety *Uba Marot* (predominantly *S. officinarum*), various tissue samples were analyzed to determine the richest phosphorylase source (Table 5-1). Maximum specific activity was recorded among internodes

TABLE 5-1

STARCH PHOSPHORYLASE ACTIVITY AMONG DIFFERENT TISSUES OF 12-MONTH-OLD SUGARCANE

[After Alexander (32).]

Enzyme action	Enzyme source								
	Meristem	Leaves			Internodes		Nodes		Sheaths
		−1+0	2+3	6+7	1–3	8–10	1–3	8–10	6+7
Specific activity	13.9	16.7	14.6	2.5	22.4	21.2	6.9	11.7	8.9
Potential synthesis (mg starch/g tissue/20 min)	55.6	12.5	11.0	1.4	5.6	5.9	3.5	2.3	1.8

subtending leaves $^{+}1$ to $^{+}3$ and $^{+}8$ to $^{+}10$. Owing to the low protein content of these tissues their net potential for polysaccharide was very low. Meristematic tissue revealed moderate specific activity but high starch-forming potential by virtue of its high content of catalytic protein. By virtue of enzyme content, tissue abundance, and ease of harvest, leaves $^{+}1$ to $^{+}3$ were selected as a convenient source of cane phosphorylase.

For the sake of biochemical perspective a distinction must be drawn between the synthesis of transitionary polysaccharides and synthesis of the storage polysaccharides more rightfully termed starch. In storage tissues such as the potato tuber, or the seeds of bean, pea, rice or barley, there is ample time and space for storing large amounts of elaborated polysaccharide. Amylase activity is generally low until growth is resumed or germination processes initiated. Thus the accumulation of starch in appropriate storage organs is a logical and widely-recognized fact of plant physiology. However, the starch-forming system in sugarcane leaves is not complemented by adequate storage space, nor is there time for extensive starch elaboration owing to the presence of abundant foliar amylases. On the other hand, it is erroneous to conclude from the lack of accumulated starch that foliar polysaccharide synthesis is of no importance to sugarcane. A transitory polysaccharide, whether existing for a few days, hours, or a fraction of a second, is nonetheless produced at the expense of precursors highly essential for sucrose synthesis. Even after rapid hydrolysis the diurnal conversion of glucose residues to new glucose-1-*P* or UDPG requires additional expenditure of ATP, and nocturnal conversion of polysaccharide to sucrose could hardly proceed less cheaply. There is in fact no apparent reason why it should not be more efficient to form only sucrose from the start. In any case, the starch-forming mechanism poses a peculiar challenge to this plant whose botanical and agricultural success is utterly dependent upon sucrose synthesis.

D. *Evidence of starch synthetase (UDPG–starch transglucosylase)*

The point has been made that since the early 1960's investigators have attached decreasing importance to starch synthesis from glucose-1-*P* via phosphorylase systems. Rather, a reaction involving UDPG or ADPG, plus a phosphate-insensitive enzyme, has been increasingly recognized. The critical catalyst in this mechanism is starch synthetase (UDPG–starch transglucosylase). In the presence of UDPG and an appropriate acceptor it catalyzes the synthesis of α-(1 $\longrightarrow$ 4) glucosidic linkages as depicted in Eqn. 4. This more recent view of starch formation has been favored by Akazawa *et al.* (5), Nelson and Rines (1085), Pottinger and Oliver (1178), Whelan (1565), and others.

Some evidence of a sugarcane starch synthetase was obtained by Alexander (32) with dialyzed leaf enzyme preparations from the predominantly *S. officinarum* varieties *M. 336* and *Uba Marot* (Table 5-2). A series of additives consisting of UDPG, UTP, UDP, ATP, and FAD were tested in several combinations with glucose-1-*P* plus an enzyme preparation identical to that used in the prior phosphorylase assays. Undialyzed protein catalyzed a moderately strong phosphorylase reaction, *i.e.*, in the

TABLE 5-2

STARCH FORMATION BY DIALYZED AND UNDIALYZED CANE ENZYME PREPARATIONS IN THE PRESENCE OF DIFFERENT ADDITIVES

[After Alexander (32).]

Experiment No.	Treatment No.	Composition of reaction medium*	Starch formation (activity units/mg protein)
1. Undialyzed enzyme	1	Enzyme, primer, plus glucose-1-*P*	19.7
	2	plus UDPG (1 μmole/ml)	4.8
	3	plus UDPG (10 μmoles/ml)	0
	4	plus glucose-1-*P*, plus UTP (1 μmole/ml)	3.7
	5	plus UTP (10 μmoles/ml)	4.7
	6	plus UDP (1 μmole/ml), plus ATP (0.5 μmole/ml)	6.9
	7	plus UDP (10 μmoles/ml), plus ATP (5 μmoles/ml)	0
	8	plus FAD (0.1 μmole/ml)	0
2. Dialyzed enzyme**	9	Enzyme, primer, plus glucose-1-*P*	6.9
	10	plus UDPG (1 μmole/ml)	26.7
	11	plus UDPG (10 μmoles/ml)	2.7
	12	plus glucose-1-*P*, plus UTP (1 μmole/ml)	10.7
	13	plus UTP (10 μmoles/ml)	3.6
	14	plus UDP (1 μmole/ml), plus ATP (0.5 μmole/ml)	19.8
	15	plus UDP (10 μmoles/ml), plus ATP (5 μmoles/ml)	6.9
	16	plus FAD (0.1 μmole/ml)	18.6

*All reaction mixtures included 10 μmoles/ml glucose-1-*P*, 0.5 ml of enzyme solution containing 0.5 to 0.7 mg of protein, and 0.1 ml of 2 percent soluble starch solution as primer. Final volume was 3.0 ml. All assays were run in duplicate or triplicate for 25 minutes at 30 °C.

**Enzyme preparations for Expt. 2 were dialyzed for 5 hours against two changes of distilled water.

presence of glucose-1-*P*, activator, and water (Table 5-2, treatment No. 1). So long as undialyzed preparations were used the additive compounds served only to inhibit this activity, with repression being complete in the presence of 10.0 μmoles/ml UDPG, or as little as 0.1 μmole/ml FAD. UDP and ATP also inhibited at levels of 10.0 and 5.0 μmoles/ml, respectively. On the other hand, strong starch-forming activity was obtained with UDPG when dialyzed enzyme preparations were used (Table 5-2, treatment No. 10). The 5-hour dialysis treatment eliminated more than 60 percent of the phosphorylase reaction, a response anticipated on the basis of earlier results. The positive response to 1.0 μmole/ml UDPG indicates an active mechanism in cane leaves for the transfer of glucose from UDPG to polysaccharide. The transfer is believed to be catalyzed by an enzyme analogous to the starch synthetase already described in the present chapter (Eqn. 4).

Of further significance was an increased polysaccharide-forming activity when UTP, or UDP plus ATP, were added to the standard reaction mixture (Table 5-2, treatments Nos. 12 and 14). This suggests that the dialyzed cane preparation catalyzes UDPG synthesis in accordance with Eqn. 5:

$$\text{UTP} + \text{glucose-1-}P \longrightarrow \text{UDPG} + \text{UDP} \qquad (5)$$

Moreover, the formation of starch from a mixture of glucose-1-*P*, UDP, ATP and activator implies that the following reactions occur in sequence (Eqns. 6–8):

$$\text{UDP} + \text{ATP} \longrightarrow \text{UTP} + \text{ADP} \qquad (6)$$
$$\text{UTP} + \text{glucose-1-}P \longrightarrow \text{UDPG} + \text{UDP} \qquad (7)$$
$$\text{UDPG} + \text{activator} \longrightarrow \text{polysaccharide} + \text{UDP} \qquad (8)$$

Eqns. 6 and 7 are well established in higher plants (303, 264, 1461, 450, 1133) including sugarcane (689, 12), while Eqn. 8 is essentially identical to that established by Leloir and his colleagues (921–924), Akazawa *et al.* (5), and others (427) as the starch synthetase reaction (Eqn. 4). The only qualification suggested for Eqn. 8 is that, in sugarcane leaves, neither product accumulation nor a reverse reaction is anticipated owing to continual amylase action against the polysaccharide product.

Table 5-2 emphasizes the importance of dialysis in distinguishing between the starch phosphorylase and starch synthetase mechanisms. The two systems would not appear to operate jointly *in vitro* inasmuch as the dialysis step which activated the synthetase reaction was inhibitory for phosphorylase. Perhaps an endogenous inhibitor was released during extraction which prevents the transglucosylase reaction. Conversely, an activator or cofactor of phosphorylase is probably lost during dialysis. It is also possible that traces of sulfate ion in the undialyzed preparation are inhibitory for starch synthetase.

In addition to all this one must consider the *in vivo* phosphorylase and synthetase systems as they operate in larger and more complex reaction sequences. Their behavior as individual entities *in vitro* may be quite different from that in the intact physiological system. Dugger and Humphreys (450) stressed this point when they found that several enzymes related to sucrose formation behaved differently when assayed individually than when coupled to an intact sucrose-forming mechanism.

It was interesting to note that FAD inhibited the undialyzed phosphorylase while being strongly stimulatory for the dialyzed preparation (Table 5-2). It has been suggested that FAD might affect glucose levels in sugarcane as an essential cofactor of glucose oxidase (13). Also relevant is an observation from earlier studies (12) in which sucrose-forming reactions suppressed by dialysis *in vitro* were more effectively reactivated by FAD than by other additives such as UTP, UDPG, boron, and cysteine–NAD.

E. *The Q enzyme; polysaccharide elaboration*

To this point our discussion of sugarcane foliar polysaccharides has been based on the principle of "easy come, easy go", and the assumption that enzymatic breakdown begins almost at the instant of polysaccharide inception. That this is not always true was shown by Laetsch and his co-workers when they discovered starch grains in sugar-

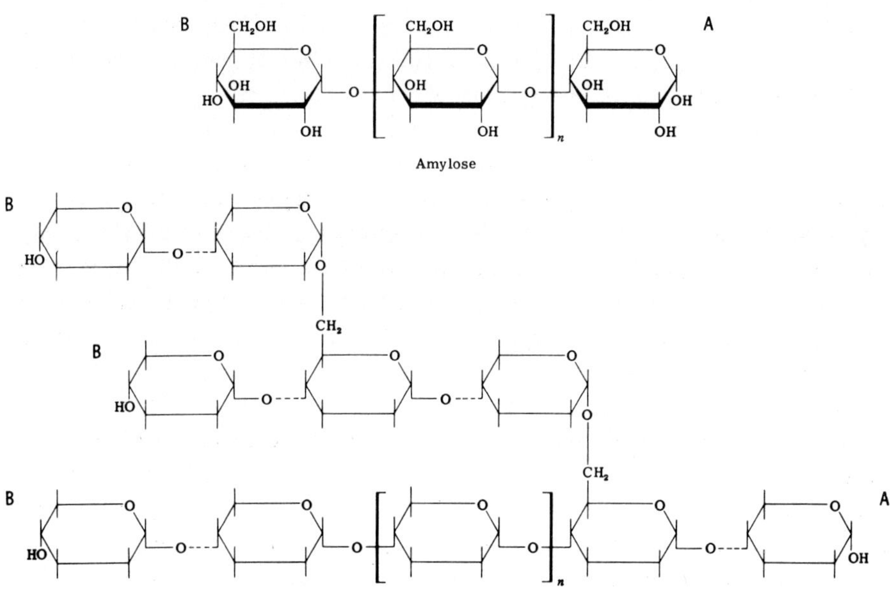

Fig. 5-9. Structural representations of the amylose and amylopectin components of starch. [From Bonner and Varner (205, p. 263), after Akazawa (6).] Reproduced by permission of the *Academic Press, Inc.*, New York.

cane chloroplasts (Fig. 5-3). Moreover, the synthesis of polysaccharide and subsequent accumulations of starch in stalk tissues has long been recognized in most *Saccharum* species. Therefore, a mechanism must exist in cane tissues for transforming an initial straight-chain molecule into the highly elaborated configuration traditionally designated as "starch".

It is generally accepted that starch is composed of two major polysaccharides: (a) Straight-chain *amylose*, and (b) highly-branched *amylopectin*. Essential structural features of the two components are depicted in Fig. 5-9. Early students of starch-forming mechanisms were perplexed by the prolific branching of the polysaccharide chains. The phosphorylase discovered in muscle by Cori and co-workers (388, 391), and in higher plants by Hanes (634, 635), catalyzes the synthesis of a straight-chain polymer linked only through α-(1 $\longrightarrow$ 4) glucosidic bonds. Leloir *et al.* (924) established that similar linkages are produced by the starch synthetase reaction. Thus, the phosphorylase and synthetase enzymes could not in themselves account for the multitude of α-(1 $\longrightarrow$6) glucosidic linkages characteristic of amylopectin.

More recently a branching enzyme has been obtained from potato extracts which acts in conjunction with phosphorylase to produce a branched polysaccharide of the amylopectin type (577, 1153). This catalyst has been named the *Q enzyme*. It appears to function as a transglucosidase by transferring relatively short portions of a long, (1 $\longrightarrow$4)-linked amylose chain to the C-6 position of glucose units within the chain. In effect, the (1 $\longrightarrow$ 4)-linked amylose chain is shortened and extensive branching is brought about through (1 $\longrightarrow$ 6) linkages. The Q enzyme is generally regarded as hydrolytic in action, that is, the scission of α-(1 $\longrightarrow$ 4) bonds is attended by the addition of elements of water. This view is contested by Peat (1153).

Initial experiments with cane leaf phosphorylase showed that the product forms a blue-violet color with iodine even though straight-chain amylose produces a deep blue color. According to Meyer (1015), the blue-violet color is typical of branched polysaccharides, which suggests that the cane phosphorylase product is already branched to some degree by the close of the standard 20-minute reaction period. Studies were therefore initiated which led to the discovery of a Q enzyme–α-amylase complex in sugarcane leaves.

Q enzyme was isolated from aqueous extracts of lyophilized leaf tissue (22) in accordance with the method used by Barker *et al.* (144) to characterize the potato enzyme. This procedure involves precipitation of protein from the plant extract by lead acetate at pH 7.2, followed by elution of the precipitate with bicarbonate in the presence of CO_2, and subsequent fractionation of the bicarbonate extract with neutral ammonium sulfate. Barker *et al.* obtained several protein fractions in this manner (Q_1, Q_2, and Q_3), which contained Q enzyme (Q_1) and starch phosphorylase (Q_2) in the presence of only trace amounts of amylase and maltase. Q enzyme was assayed by measuring the progressive loss of blue color as soluble potato starch was incubated for 50 minutes in the presence of dialyzed enzyme preparation. Since blue-value decline can also be brought about by amylase, it was necessary to measure simultaneously the reducing-sugar content of the reaction mixture.

Fractionation of the Q enzyme-containing bicarbonate solution into 5-percent increments showed that the bulk of branching activity was obtained in the 0 to 35 percent fraction. β-Amylase and phosphatase were largely bypassed by discarding all other protein. Some phosphorylase was present in addition to an acid, α-amylase (optimum pH = 4.0). The α-amylase caused considerable difficulty when Q enzyme was measured in acid media; however, it posed no problem at pH values above 6.5, and the Q enzyme was usually assayed close to its pH optimum at 7.5.

Maximum Q enzyme activity was attained at 30 °C but the reaction was readily detected as low as 7 °C. Optimum substrate concentration (soluble potato starch) lay between 2.0 and 2.5 mg/ml of digest. α-Amylase was inactive at 7 °C and was partially inhibited by soluble starch levels above 0.5 mg/ml. Prolonged dialysis had little effect on Q enzyme but the treatment retarded α-amylase after 6 to 10 hours. Distribution experiments showed that Q enzyme was heavily localized in mature leaves (+6 and +7), and that very little enzyme was present in leaves +1 and +2 or the apical meristem (Fig. 5-10). Virtually no Q enzyme was found in sheaths +1 and +2, +8 to +10 internodes, or in +8 to +10 nodal tissue.

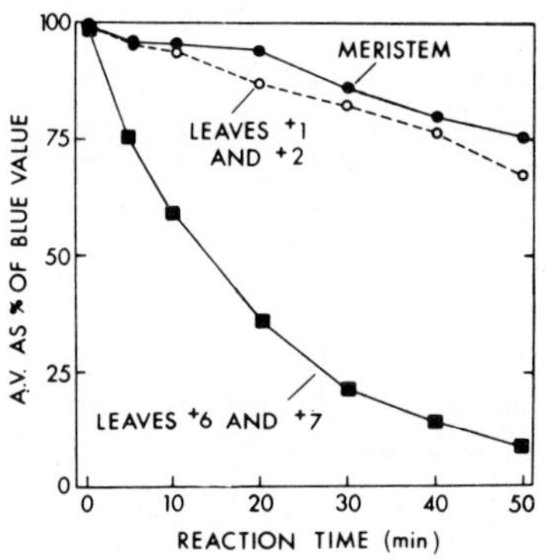

Fig. 5-10. Activity of the Q enzyme (or branching factor) among different sugarcane tissues. The enzyme is situated predominantly in aged leaves. A.V. = absorption value. [After Alexander (22).]

Q enzyme was competitively inhibited by lead ions. The contaminant α-amylase was inhibited by fluoride or copper ions at low levels having no effect on Q enzyme. The localization of an enzyme in aging leaves is unusual for sugarcane. This may relate in some way to the exceptionally low sucrose-synthesizing activity found in these same tissues (12). The predominance of Q enzyme in aged leaves is consistent with the thesis that starch accumulation is unessential for the rapid growth and sugar-forming mechanisms typical of younger cane tissues. Presumably the Q enzyme exists only in a repressed state in the spindle tissues. This enzyme is conceivably a relic of earlier cane forms in which neither abundant growth nor massive sucrose accumulation was a characteristic feature.

F. *Foliar polysaccharide formation in context*

Regardless of the number of polysaccharide-forming systems active in sugarcane, those operating in the leaves will logically bear certain close relationships to one another and to other carbohydrate-forming and metabolizing reactions. The common precursors glucose-1-*P* and UDPG, with all that these entail in supporting enzyme systems, will help to assure behavior conformity with the prevailing trends in sucrose formation so long as they exist in rate-limiting supply. This is particularly true since the foliar polysaccharide must soon be translocated and it can only be translocated as sucrose. Tentative support for a close sucrose–polysaccharide relationship has been cited from Puerto Rico (15, 24) and Hawaii (652, 665, 653).

In 1965 Alexander (32) summarized schematically the sucrose–polysaccharide relationships as they appear to exist in sugarcane leaves (Fig. 5-11). Evidence for each of

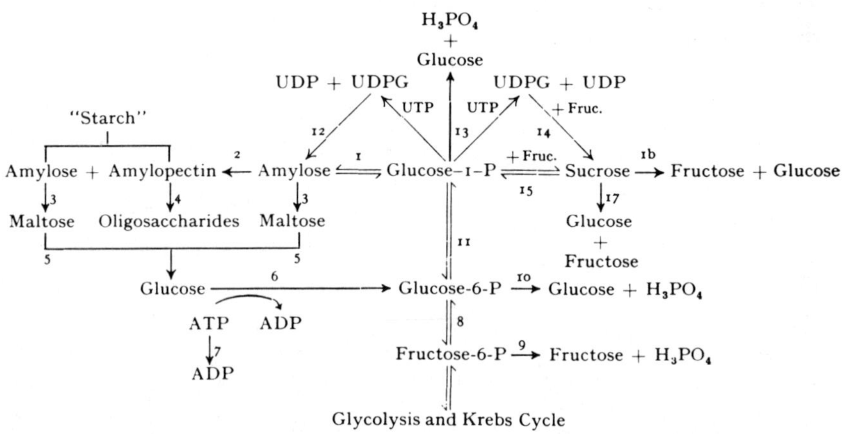

1. Starch phosphorylase
2. Q enzyme
3. Beta-amylase
4. Alpha-amylase
5. Maltase
6. Hexokinase
7. ATPase
8. Phosphohexose isomerase
9. Fructose-6-P phosphatase
10. Glucose-6-P phosphatase
11. Phosphoglucomutase
12. Starch synthetase
13. Glucose-1-P phosphatase
14. UDPG-Fructose transglycosylase
15. Sucrose phosphorylase
16. Beta-fructosidase
17. Alpha-glucosidase

Fig. 5-11. Schematic representation of enzymic reactions leading to the synthesis and metabolism of storage carbohydrate in sugarcane. [After Alexander (32).]

the indicated enzymes has been obtained with the exception of phosphoglucomutase. Indirect evidence for UDPG synthesis from UTP and glucose-1-*P* has been cited above (Eqns. 6 and 7). The critical position of glucose-1-*P* is clearly evident. A number of reactions other than starch formation are capable of affecting the level of this compound, not the least of which is the hydrolysis catalyzed by glucose-1-*P* phosphatase. Also evident is the expected employment of amylase, maltase, and hexokinase in returning the glucose residues to active metabolic pathways. These reactions need not await the accumulation of elaborated starch, *i.e.*, amylose plus highly-branched amylopectin. It is presumed that, at least in starch-free *S. officinarum* varieties, polysaccharide degradation proceeds day and night, beginning as soon as amylose or a comparable substrate appears in the morning and ending at night only when the previous-day's polysaccharide output has been hydrolyzed.

5. POLYSACCHARIDE SYNTHESIS UNDER CONDITIONS OF VARIABLE WATER, N, P, AND K SUPPLY

The presence of one and perhaps several polysaccharide-forming mechanisms in the green tops of *S. officinarum* varieties aroused considerable interest in Puerto Rico relative to their possible competition with sucrose-synthesizing reactions. Since both glucose-1-*P* and UDPG are involved in producing each storage carbohydrate, it was thought that competition of a serious nature might exist whenever the endogenous precursor levels were lowered to rate-limiting proportions by inadequate synthesis or excessive phosphatase activity. This hypothesis was tested at the greenhouse level with immature plants subjected to variable water, N, P and K treatments given in sand culture (15, 24). It was expected that such treatments would eventually alter the rate of sucrose biosynthesis and, to the extent that common precursor pools were being employed, changing sucrose production would be reflected in changing levels of phosphorylase. No measurable starch content was expected and none was obtained. Certain positive results were obtained with respect to sucrose and phosphorylase.

Nutritional treatments involved lowering N supply from 10.0 to 1.5 meq/l, and K from 5.0 to 0 meq/l during the initial study (15). Water stress was created by lowering the daily water supply from 3 liters to 1 liter over a period of 49 days. Four-month-old plants of the variety *M. 336* were employed, with samples of leaves $^{+}1$ to $^{+}4$ being frozen for sugar and enzyme analyses at intervals of 7 or 14 days.

Small but generally consistent sucrose increases were obtained with each treatment. A sucrose-forming mechanism tentatively described as "sucrose phosphorylase" (12) was unaffected, while amylase and acid phosphatases were generally suppressed by each of the three treatments. More to the point was the fact that both the high and low extremes for sucrose were followed, after 7 or 14 days, by phosphorylase level changes which were inversely related to sucrose production. Phosphorylase apparently fluctuated as a result, rather than as the cause, of sucrose changes. This was taken as at least indirect evidence of a common factor such as glucose-1-*P* or UDPG operating in rate-limiting supply for both starch and sucrose-forming reactions. If this were true, the sucrose mechanisms were clearly in a preferential or "higher priority" position than the starch mechanisms under the prevailing conditions. Periods of high amylase activity were accompanied, or followed closely, by increased phosphorylase activity. This is the type of response expected under conditions of product repression; however, since no starch was detected either in leaf or sheath tissue, the interpretation given was that amylase acted as part of an overall design to keep the greatest possible amount of glucose available for active metabolism. We have never been able to establish a more plausible role for sugarcane amylases.

A subsequent study (24) evaluated phosphorylase–sucrose relationships in two varieties (*M. 336* and *Uba Marot*) supplied with high and low levels of N and P in sand culture. Treatments were given in 2 x 2 x 2 factorial combinations. These were begun at 4 weeks of age and a single harvest was taken at 12 weeks. Nitrate was provided at 12.0 and 1.5 meq/l, and P at 6.0 and 0 meq/l. The N variables were designed to ensure distinct rates of sucrose synthesis. In addition, it was considered that the expected differential quantities of organic acids produced as a result of nitrate metabolism (328, 1194, 1495, 1514) might affect the ratio of mineral P to organic P. The relatively extreme differences in P supply were specifically intended to alter this ratio. Hanes (635) concluded from his experiments with potato phosphorylase that the reaction proceeds in either direction until the ratio of mineral P to organic P achieves a value not altered by variable starch, mineral phosphate, or organic phosphate concentrations.

The fact that starch is sometimes formed when inorganic P levels are theoretically too high to permit synthesis via a phosphorylase reaction led several workers (516, 1259) to question phosphorylase as polysaccharide-forming enzyme even before starch synthetase was discovered. The equilibrium between starch and the several ionic phosphate species was depicted by Hanes (635) as follows:

$$\begin{array}{lcl} \text{Starch} + (HPO_4)^{2-} & \rightleftharpoons & (C_6H_{11}O_5\cdot O\cdot PO_3)^{2-} \\ \quad\quad\quad\;\; \updownarrows & & \quad \updownarrows \; H^+ \\ \quad\quad (H_2PO_4)^- & & (C_6H_{11}O_5\cdot O\cdot PO_3H)^- \end{array}$$

It is at once evident that (a) the equilibrium should respond to absolute levels of P at the reaction site, and (b) the ionic phosphate species will be subject to variations in the medium's pH (636).

During the variety x N x P study it was found that N produced the greatest influence over sucrose and phosphorylase levels while P supply had the least effect (Table 5-3). There were no pronounced treatment effects on leaf sucrose. With reference to meristem sucrose the varietal factor was clearly predominant. As a main effect *Uba Marot* contained less than 1/3 of the sucrose level found in *M. 336*. Equally striking was the fact that high P very severely suppressed sucrose in *Uba Marot* while in *M. 336* high P (plus high N) produced a large sucrose increase. This illustrates the fallacy of drawing conclusions with data from a single variety.

TABLE 5-3

EFFECTS OF VARIABLE NITRATE AND PHOSPHORUS SUPPLY ON THE SUCROSE, PHOSPHORYLASE, AND AMYLASE CONSTITUENTS OF TWO SUGARCANE VARIETIES GROWN IN SAND CULTURE

[After Alexander (24).]

Treatment*			Sucrose content (mg/g)		Enzyme specific activity	
Var.	X nitrate	X phosphate	Leaf	Meristem	Phosphorylase	Amylase
Uba Marot	1.5	0	45.1	26.5	10.2	46.3
	1.5	6.0	42.2	10.1	9.6	40.3
	12.5	0	48.8	14.2	12.8	45.0
	12.5	6.0	47.4	7.9	12.8	52.8
Uba Marot mean			45.9	14.7	11.4	46.2
M. 336	1.5	0	42.8	38.6	8.2	42.0
	1.5	6.0	44.9	37.1	7.8	38.9
	12.5	0	54.6	49.2	16.4	68.5
	12.5	6.0	55.5	63.8	19.3	87.7
M. 336 mean			49.5	47.2	12.9	59.3

*N and P levels are given as meq/l. Variable N and P treatments were initiated at 4 weeks of age and concluded at 12 weeks. There were four replicates of each treatment.

Although *Uba Marot* is constituted mainly of *S. officinarum* germplasm, it enjoyed some notoriety among Puerto Rico growers as a starch producer when it was grown on a commercial scale many years ago. Until recently *M. 336* was the "sweetest" variety grown on a commercial scale in Puerto Rico and it has never presented a starch problem. Phosphorylase data shown in Table 5-3 indicate that the enzyme was somewhat more active in each variety under conditions of adequate N supply, and that in *Uba Marot* high N approximately doubled the phosphorylase level. A similar variety x N effect is shown for amylase. In this instance high P further enhanced the high N effect. Even though no formal conclusions can be drawn from such limited data there is a strong implication that the varietal sucrose and starch differences can be explained largely on an enzyme basis. The enzymes themselves are responsive to the same varietal and nutritional factors already recognized as having important empirical effects upon cane carbohydrates.

Chapter 6

Sucrose Biosynthesis

1. INTRODUCTION

Sucrose is formed as a result of photosynthetic carbon assimilation in virtually all higher plants. Its importance as the most abundant sugar in plants and as the world's principal commercial sugar is exceeded only by its physiological status as a reserve constituent in cell respiration. Energy liberated via respiratory processes is utilized for numerous metabolic activities. Of these the synthesis of amino acids, proteins, fats, and other organic compounds ranks among the most important. Yet the manner by which sucrose itself is synthesized has long eluded plant scientists. In recent times the discovery that sucrose is the principal form of transient carbohydrate, plus the fact that it is not the form most readily accumulated in cellular storage compartments, has shown that a sucrose molecule might be synthesized, inverted, and resynthesized several times before fulfilling its physiological destiny.

It can be argued that the sucrose-synthesis research spanning nearly half of our century was largely a failure since the limited and laborious mechanistic advances bore little relationship to the *in vivo* reactions occurring in nature. Of course this is not true. On purely technical grounds the synthesizing of sucrose is such a complicated matter that enormous strides in the field of plant physiology were required before the natural mechanisms could be seen in anything like a correct perspective. Although the exploration of sucrose biosynthesis by scores of plant scientists and chemists is a long story at best and at times a disappointing one, it is one worth telling by any measure. The present chapter attempts to recount this story and to describe those mechanisms in sugarcane which are the measure of nature's success in her efforts to produce and accumulate sucrose.

It will be seen that for many years physiologists were uncertain as to whether a simple sugar, the disaccharide sucrose, or starch was the primary product of photosynthesis. Some workers maintained that fructose and glucose appeared only after sucrose was formed. Eventually a theory prevailed which held that D-glucose and D-fructose were produced first and then combined through enzymic mediation to form sucrose. Efforts to condense the two moieties by chemical means were largely unsuccessful, and several claims that invertase catalyzed such a reaction could not be substantiated.

With passage of time most workers concluded that hexose phosphates and a series of phosphorylation and sugar-interconversion reactions were involved in an elaborate sequence of reactions incident to sucrose formation and breakdown. During the 1940's, after starch and glycogen biosynthesis via phosphorylase was widely recognized, the reverse phosphorolysis of sucrose was demonstrated with a bacterium preparation containing the enzyme *sucrose phosphorylase.* It was indeed a natural catalytic system capable of producing authentic sucrose, but it could not be found in tissues of higher plants. Mechanisms accountable for sucrose in its natural abundance were not discovered until the mid-1950's. Thereafter, the enzymes *sucrose 6-phosphate synthetase* and *sucrose synthetase* were finally isolated from numerous plant species and were shown to be distinct entities having a common capacity to synthesize authentic sucrose linkages.

The reader will find that much of the correct sucrose-formation context was established prior to 1940 even though actual mechanisms escaped the biochemists and physiologists of the day. Thus, differing synthetic capability among plant varieties, species, or families, and among differing latitudes and changing seasons, even among different hours of the day, were gradually recognized and accepted. No longer was a single plant expected to tell the complete story of sucrose biosynthesis. Extremely complex sugar interconversions were demonstrated and interpreted in physiological rather than strictly chemical terms. The importance of distinct plant tissues, their relationships to water, light, and nutrient supplies, and the need for infinite care in sampling, preparing, and analyzing the tissues were lessons being learned and incorporated into plant carbohydrate research. These lessons, no less than the mechanisms themselves, are still being learned in sucrose research today.

2. HISTORICAL ASPECTS OF SUCROSE BIOSYNTHESIS

In Chapter 5 the discovery of reversible phosphorolysis as a means for glycogen and starch formation was reviewed (*cf.* pp. 206–208). The work of Cori and co-workers (389, 391), Kiessling (837), and Hanes (634, 635) revealed that phosphorylase systems were present in both animal and plant tissues which catalyzed the synthesis of α-(1 ⟶4) glucosidic linkages, ultimately yielding the reserve polysaccharides glycogen or amylose.

The question of sucrose biosynthesis posed an equally difficult problem. Although early workers recognized the possibility of reverse phosphorolysis reactions taking part in sucrose formation, this view evolved only gradually and several other concepts were tested and eventually discarded before a valid mechanism was finally isolated from the bacterium *Pseudomonas saccharophila.* It is noteworthy that two of the present senior sugarcane physiologists, Drs. C.E. Hartt and H.F. Clements, took part in early studies of sucrose formation in cane and other plant species. The very exacting requirements for meaningful carbohydrate analyses, particularly without the aid of radioactive carbon, and without detailed knowledge of photosynthetic pathways, was difficult but fitting preparation for the decades of productive sugarcane research that followed.

A. *Early concepts of sucrose as a primary and a secondary photosynthate*

Long before the mechanisms of sucrose formation were recognized, conflicting opinions were published relative to the importance of sucrose as a photosynthate and its role in higher plants. Some workers held that sucrose is the primary sugar of photosynthesis (250, 1144, 417). Clements (332) traced this assumption to the belief that fructose and glucose were the only hexoses found in plant leaves. It was also believed that interchange between the two sugars was accomplished by enol conversion of glucose to fructose and mannose. Clements discounted this view along with the argument that sucrose must be the primary photosynthate because of its greater abundance in leaves. His own observations with the potato, soybean, and sunflower indicated that sucrose was not the first sugar of photosynthesis and that its function in the leaf is one of temporary storage. Miller (1022), working with sorghum and corn, also concluded that a predominance of sucrose over reducing sugars is not a valid argument in favor of sucrose as the primary photosynthate.

Another argument favoring sucrose as the primary sugar was formulated on the basis of its greater variability in leaves as compared with simple sugars. According to Clements (332), Stanescu (1356) classified plants according to the extent of soluble-sugar and polysaccharide variations (*i.e.*, as *saccharophiles* and *amylophiles*). Clements used his own data to discount plant groupings on a sugar basis "...since under varying conditions of environment the plant will respond differently. Thus at times the curves for starches and hemicelluloses vary more than those of the simple forms. These facts indicate that sucrose does not always vary more than simple sugars." Earlier work by Clements (331) had shown that carbohydrate constituents will vary quantitatively on the basis of day length. Tottingham *et al.* (1446), working with sugar beet, also noted sugar variations induced by variable climate.

Efforts to assign sucrose a specific position incident to photosynthesis were frequently based on differing assumptions as to the mechanism of its synthesis. Moreover, there was a tendency to accept the findings from one or several species as conclusive for the entire plant kingdom. Thus the view that fructose and glucose originated only after sucrose had been formed implies a direct production of disaccharide via CO_2 assimilation mechanisms. Clements (333), after eliminating the pentoses, mannose, and sucrose as sugars not always present during active photosynthesis by some 42 plant species, concluded that glucose and fructose are jointly the first sugars produced. By this view sucrose would have had to arise by condensation of the two hexose moieties. In the sugar beet, Ruhland (1264) maintained that reducing sugars were transported to the sugar beet root and there resynthesized into sucrose.

As early as 1916 Davis and Sawyer (418) recognized that important changes in leaf sucrose may occur on a seasonal and diurnal basis. Having measured sucrose, reducing sugars, and starch ("dextrin") in the leaf blades and "stalks" of the potato, they concluded that sucrose is the primary leaf sugar during the period of tuber initiation.

Diurnally, sucrose predominated in leaves between sunrise and 2:00 p.m. Hexoses and starch increased between 2:00 and 6:00 p.m. (in July), and starch virtually disappeared before 2:00 a.m. An enzymic conversion of starch to dextrose was proposed via the mediation of taka-diastase, or a similar enzyme, plus nonlimiting amounts of maltase.

Clements' (333, 332) proposal that simple sugars rather than sucrose constitute the primary photosynthesis product was supported by the work of Strakosch (1372) who observed only simple sugars appearing in leaf mesophyll cells of *Beta vulgaris*. However, an entirely different concept of sucrose origin and function was advanced by Priestley (1191) in 1924. Priestley maintained that sucrose is not functionally related to photosynthesis at all. He believed that it forms as a by-product of aging cell protoplasm, and that sucrose is released as the cells become vacuolated. Priestley's theory was advanced from a chemical viewpoint which conveniently overlooked the massive sucrose accumulations of such plants as sugar beet and sugarcane. Considering that much of his data was taken from plant roots and stems having little storage sucrose, plus the fact that no one had yet demonstrated sucrose synthesis in the test tube, his arguments were not nearly so misleading as they would seem today.

B. *Sucrose synthesis by chemical means; isosucrose*

It is sometimes written that early efforts to produce sucrose by chemical means met with little success. This is quite true. The union of glucose and fructose proved to be an enormous task. However, such formidable efforts were made toward this end that our understanding of sucrose chemistry was greatly advanced. Some of the work is worth recounting if only to reaffirm the resourcefulness of nature wherein the event has been commonplace for some countless millions of years.

During the final quarter of the nineteenth century various workers in France reported on the chemical condensation of glucose residues in the presence of acid (1192, p. 99). Non-crystalline, sirup-like products were obtained which were slightly reducing and non-fermentable. Acid hydrolysis led to the regeneration of glucose. According to McDonald (1192, p. 99), Fischer (525) synthesized the maltose derivative isomaltose by reacting glucose with four times its weight of HCl (sp. gr.=1.19) at room temperature for 15 hours. The product was not crystalline but characterization was achieved by its phenylosazone (m.p.=138 °C). It is now known that Fischer's method also yields gentiobiose and possibly other condensation products. Crystalline isomaltose was prepared by controlled acid hydrolysis of dextran and amylopectin by Wolfrom *et al.* (1584) in 1949.

Prior to 1901 all efforts to synthesize sucrose by condensation of dextrorotatory glucose with levorotatory fructose were negative. In that year sugar methylation studies were initiated by Purdie and Irvine (1195, 1196) which led to increased understanding of the glucose and fructose forms present in sucrose. Although the glucose residue was a "normal" type, the fructose residue was "abnormal" in that it differed in certain respects from the levorotatory form. Upon acid hydrolysis of octamethylsucrose, Purdie and Irvine (1196) unexpectedly obtained a methylated fructose that was dextrorotatory; hence no inversion in the usual sense occurred. In 1970 Purdie and Paul (1197) claimed that two isomeric tetramethylfructoses do in fact exist, one being dextrorotatory and the other levorotatory. Additional evidence of a dextrorotatory or "γ-form" of fructose was published in 1916 by Irvine and Robertson (776) who concluded that sucrose was a derivative of this form. Their view was substantiated by Haworth and Law (706) working in the same laboratory.

Irvine *et al.* (777), in 1929, reported the successful condensation of glucose and fructose to form an isosucrose. These investigators had arrived at the conclusion that "...the synthesis of sucrose thus resolves itself into the union, through the loss of water, of equimolecular proportions of normal glucose and γ-fructose, or, alternatively, of reducing derivatives of these sugars followed by elimination of the substituting groups". They believed a total of four isomeric glucofructoses might be formed via condensations of this nature. The main difficulty lay not with glucose, for which derivatives of the normal type could be obtained, but with the highly unstable γ-fructose derivatives. Irvine *et al.* decided to use a sirup which contained a mixture of partially-acetylated fructoses, including γ-forms, which is obtained during the acetylation of fructose by the Hudson and Brauns (758) method. Pictet and Vogel (1173) employed this sirup with success as a reagent in synthesizing a compound depicted as "saccharose D". After much effort, Irvine and his co-workers obtained a separate tetraacetylfructose related to γ-fructose. Then they attempted to synthesize sucrose with this compound via a reaction with tetraacetylbromo(or chloro)glucose in the presence of a base. The synthetic reaction was also attempted with tetraacetylchloro-γ-fructose. All of these efforts were negative, that is, no condensation of glucose and fructose residues took place.

For reasons unclear to the authors this failure lay with the halogen derivative of glucose which was unable to condense with tetraacetyl-γ-fructose. However, another condensation method in which tetraacetylchloro-γ-fructose was used as the halogen carrier to react with tetraacetylglucose was successful. The product of this reaction was depicted as a crystalline octaacetylisosucrose. Other disaccharides were believed to have arisen but only the latter was obtained in crystalline form. Subsequent de-acetylation led to the isolation of an isosucrose in needle-shaped crystals.

Irvine *et al.* (777) regarded their new synthetic disaccharide as a β-glucosido-β-(γ)-fructose. They reasoned at the time that sucrose was either α-glucosido-α-(γ)-fructose, or β-glucosido-α-(γ)-fructose. The configuration of authentic sucrose, α-D-glucopyranosyl-(1→ 2)-β-D-fructofuranoside (540, p. 415; 205, p. 240), was not confirmed by periodic acid oxidation until 1943 (529). The difference between the new compound and Pictet's *saccharose D* appears to be a matter of purity, but possibly it differs with respect to glycosidic linkage as well.

Irvine and his co-workers realized that the glucose–fructose disaccharide they had synthesized was not identical to the natural sucrose or "cane sugar" of their day. No sucrose octaacetate was detected as would have been the case had authentic sucrose been formed. Isosucrose gave a slight reducing reaction with Fehling's solution upon prolonged boiling, indicating a greater instability than sucrose. This was verified by a more rapid rate of acid hydrolysis for isosucrose. Finally, the acetylated derivative was characterized by a different melting point and specific rotation than that of sucrose octaacetate. In a paper published in 1929, Irvine and Oldham (778) described the conversion of sucrose octaacetate into equimolar tetraacetylglucose and tetraacetyl-γ-fructose, but efforts to reconstitute sucrose from this mixture, *i.e.*, to form sucrose octaacetate, yielded only the octaacetate of isosucrose.

In the same year that Irvine *et al.* (777) published their work with isosucrose, Pictet and Vogel (1177) claimed to have synthesized sucrose by condensing tetra-*O*-acetyl-D-fructofuranose with tetra-*O*-acetyl-D-glucopyranose in the presence of a dehydrating agent. However, Zemplén and Gerecs (1613), using the Pictet and Vogel method, were unsuccessful in their efforts to synthesize authentic sucrose.

Twenty-five more years were to pass before sucrose was finally synthesized by chemical means. Lemieux and Huber (925, 926), in 1953, synthesized authentic sucrose by reacting 3,4,6-tri-*O*-acetyl-1,2-anhydro-α-D-glucopyranose with 1,3,4,6-tetra-*O*-acetyl-D-fructofuranose. The synthesis was performed in a sealed tube maintained at 100 °C for 104 hours. Chromatographic analysis of the products showed a 5.5-percent yield of sucrose octaacetate. By treatment of the same anhydride with 1,2,3,6-tetra-*O*-acetyl-β-D-glucose at 120°C for 13 hours, Lemieux (927) achieved the synthesis of octaacetyl-β-D-maltose.

C. *Biological synthesis of sucrose*

The enormous quantities of sucrose produced in nature left little doubt among early workers that a formidable mechanism of sucrose synthesis existed in plant tissues. Empirically, the mechanism was readily demonstrated by placing intact leaf petioles or blades in hexose solutions, whereupon the tissue's sucrose content rapidly increased (930, 1000, 1502, 657). Unfortunately, attempts to produce sucrose from monosaccharides with tissue extracts met with no more success than did parallel efforts by chemical means. Bonner (204) suggested in 1950 that the grinding or general disruption of plant tissues inactivates the sucrose-synthesizing mechanism. Today we know that several enzymes related to sucrose synthesis categorically resist isolation in viable form by conventional means.

For a time there was confusion as to whether sucrose was produced from glucose, from starch, from glucose plus fructose, or whether hexoses in general appeared as polysaccharide degradation products. Some early workers had felt that starch itself was converted directly to sucrose (1059, 1583). Virtanen and Nordlund (1502) claimed that in wilting leaves starch is converted into sucrose. Nelson and Auchincloss (1084), working with potato tubers, found sucrose to be formed from glucose or fructose rather than from starch. Nurmia (1124) reported a rapid interconversion of fructose and glucose in leaves of red clover (*Trifolium pratense*) and horse bean (*Vicia faba*). These reactions were paralleled by sucrose synthesis.

With reference to sugarcane, Hartt (657) found that detached leaf blades and sheaths readily synthesized sucrose when the cut ends were immersed in a 5-percent glucose solution. The synthesis occurred as a result of glucose uptake rather than by rearrangement of endogenous sugars induced as an osmotic effect. Hartt went on to compare sucrose synthesis rates among different tissues according to "synthetic efficiency", that is, by the percentage of absorbed glucose converted to sucrose. Hartt was aware that interconversion of glucose and fructose must take place, but she felt that glucose might be the most effective substrate since only one additional sugar would then be needed, *i.e.*, fructose monophosphate, whereas both glucose and fructose monophosphate must be formed when only fructose is the initial substrate (660).

Working with wheat and clover, Virtanen and Nordlund (1502) observed sucrose synthesis proceeding at equal rates from both glucose and fructose. Clements (333), on the other hand, concluded from studies of 42 plant species that fructose does not form from glucose. Clements felt that glucose and fructose originate simultaneously as the first sugars of photosynthesis. His interpretation was based on the fact that mannose was absent from leaves of each species, plus the assumption that mannose would arise from glucose along with fructose. Clements published this work in 1932 and was therefore unaware of the hexose phosphate roles in sugar transformations subsequently established by Cori and Cori (391) and by Hanes (634, 635).

D. *Recognition of the sugar phosphates*

By the mid-1930's many investigators had accepted the thesis that highly complex interconversion of simple and elaborated carbohydrates must proceed routinely in plant tissues. Yet the mechanistic details remained elusive. Thus, Virtanen and Nordlund (1502) wrote in 1934: "There is every reason to assume that all the individual carbohydrates in plant material are capable of conversion into each other, though the experimental evidence at hand is insufficient to warrant definite conclusions in individual cases."

Numerous investigators now recognized the presence of hexose phosphates in plant tissues (859, 1125, 868, 261, 678, 439, 869). Evidence of phosphorylation *per se* in higher plants was first reported by Bodnár (198), in 1925, who observed that inorganic phosphorus added to ground peas in the presence of toluene passed into a different form. A phosphate involvement in glucose fermentation by yeast extracts had been discovered some 17 years earlier by Harden and Young (641). Burkard and Neuberg (261), in 1934, described phosphate esters of both glucose and fructose in leaves of sugar beet. They believed that hexose monophosphates were produced in beet leaves and that sucrose arose from these products. Hassid (678) obtained glucose and fructose phosphates from pea leaves and arrived at a similar conclusion with respect to sucrose synthesis. He regarded the unstable furanose form of fructose in the sucrose molecule as evidence of phosphorylation occurring prior to sucrose synthesis. McCready and Hassid (1000) found that barley plants produced sucrose when supplied with mannose and galactose as well as with fructose and glucose. Maltose and lactose also served to promote sucrose synthesis, indicating that hydrolytic reactions occurred in addition to hexose interconversion prior to sucrose formation. It was also suggested that oxygen, but not light and chlorophyll, was essential for sucrose synthesis. In spite of these important advances the phosphorylation mechanism remained obscure.

The first inkling of a possible phosphate role in sucrose formation appears to have been recorded by Oparin and Kursanov (1125) in 1931. They described two forms of fructose originating from sucrose hydrolysis; first an "am-fructose", and later a β-fructose, with the equilibrium favoring β-fructose. The slowness of "enzymic resynthesis" was attributed to a stereoisometric change of the first-formed fructose to β-fructose. Oparin and Kursanov claimed to have restricted this reaction by incorporating H_3PO_4 into the sucrose molecule. Under these conditions a "polysaccharide" identical to sucrose was produced from simple sugars by invertase in the presence of phosphatase. It does not appear from the available abstract that a phosphorolysis reaction was considered during these investigations. Lebedev and Dikanova (909) were unable to corroborate this work even though invertase was allowed to remain in contact with substrate for two years. In 1940 Kryukova (860) observed that plant phosphorylation inhibitors (sodium fluoride and monoiodoacetic acid) restricted sucrose formation in plant tissues, and on this basis it was concluded that phosphorylation is an essential step in sucrose synthesis.

With specific reference to sugarcane, Hartt (657–660) developed a strong argument in support of hexose phosphorylation as an essential part of hexose interconversion and sucrose synthesis. The following evidence was presented (660): (a) Plants grown without phosphorus (P) experienced lower rates of hexose interconversion and sucrose synthesis than did plants supplied with adequate P. Kursanov and Kryukova (868) had also shown that leaves of P-deficient plants lose their ability to form sucrose from hexose. (b) Addition of P plus glucose to detached blades increased the rate of sucrose formation. Curiously, such additions gave a greater response for normal leaves than for those from P-deficient plants. (c) The inclusion of alkaline phosphatase along with glucose decreased sugar interconversion and synthesis. The implication here is that all organic phosphate pools subject to non-specific hydrolysis might be depleted by the supplemental phosphatase. (d) Inhibition of hexokinase with fluoride lowered the rates of sugar interconversion and sucrose synthesis. Indirect evidence was also offered relating to the diurnal fluctuation of interconversion and synthesis rates. The rhythm of fluctuation was shown to be identical to P-movement rhythms described by Biddulph (174) in the bean plant.

E. *Failure of invertase to account for sucrose synthesis*

While in essence the catalytic nature of sucrose formation became widely accepted, the identification of a specific sucrose-forming enzyme continued to elude plant scientists for many years. Some investigators believed that invertase catalyzed sucrose synthesis by reversal of the long-known hydrolytic reaction; indeed, countless enzymes in nature do catalyze easily-reversible reactions. Certain hydrolytic enzymes such as the lipases and emulsin are known to have synthetic capability. Moreover, Oparin and Kursanov (1125), Kursanov and Kryukova (868), and Kursanov (866) maintained that invertase was active in sucrose synthesis as well as hydrolysis. Support for this view was taken from the fact that invertase is widely distributed among plants containing abundant sucrose. Kursanov (867) reported in 1936 that introduction of small amounts of yeast invertase into leaves of *Cyclamen*, *Crinum*, and *Primula* produced an accelerated invertase activity favoring sucrose synthesis and hydrolysis to an equal degree. Hydrolysis alone was increased by incorporating additional enzyme.

During the same year Rubin (1263) claimed that slow growth is associated with a predominately synthetic action of invertase in certain varieties of onion. Working with sugarcane invertase, Hartt (647, 649) obtained indirect evidence of the enzyme's involvement in sucrose formation. The fact that invertase was highly active in immature storage tissue, but declined as the joints matured, was taken as evidence of invertase participation in sucrose formation.

Other findings by Hartt were suggestive of a potassium regulatory role in sugar transformations catalyzed by sugarcane invertase (651, 646, 647). It was observed in 1929 (646) that K-deficient plants contained "weaker" invertase than plants given adequate K supplies. This was verified in 1933 (647). Even though the direct role of cane invertase in sucrose synthesis has not been substantiated, several invertase roles have been established in the sucrose accumulation process (689, 582, 584). It is interesting to note that as early as 1933 Hartt (647) ascertained some sort of relationship between invertase and sucrose storage: ". . .It is evident that wherever sucrose is actively formed and stored, the activity of invertase is great, whereas where the process of storage is practically completed, invertase decreases in activity." It seems that Hartt very nearly discovered the "sugar accumulation cycle" more than 30 years before it was developed in detail by Glasziou and his co-workers in Australia (*cf.* Chapter 9, pp. 348–357).

A somewhat different concept of invertase synthetic potential has been evaluated by Myrbäck (1070), who treats yeast invertase as a transferase rather than a strictly hydrolytic enzyme. The yeast transferase reaction depicts the passage of β-fructofuranosyl residues from substrates to receptors or co-substrates. Dedonder (425) proposed that water is itself a special receptor. Distinct ratios of transferase products to hydrolysis products have been described by Aronoff and Bacon (109) as a function of substrate concentration.

The transferase concept of "sucrase" has also been supported by Feingold and his colleagues (518) who synthesized the sucrose isomer "galsucrose" (α-D-galactopyranosyl β-D-fructofuranoside) with an enzyme described as "levansucrase". This enzyme catalyzed the transfer of β-fructofuranosyl from raffinose to the oxygen of the anomeric carbon of galactose, and thus created a sucrose-like disaccharide in which galactose rather than glucose was linked to fructose. Hydrolysis of the product by yeast invertase yielded galactose and fructose. Hydrolysis by "levansucrase" yielded galactose, fructose, "oligofructosyl galactosides" and levan.

Nonetheless, no sustained evidence of an invertase role in the synthesis of sucrose *per se* can be found in the literature. We have seen that Lebedev and Dikanova (909) failed to synthesize sucrose from simple sugars with invertase over the unusual time course of two years. Leonard (929) was unable to substantiate an invertase synthetic reaction in sugar beet and corn leaves. Nurmia (1124) concluded that in *Trifolium* and *Vicia* species sucrose was not formed by invertase but rather by a specific sucrose-synthesis system.

It is widely accepted today that the invertase equilibrium leans heavily toward hydrolysis and that no appreciable sucrose arises from this reaction. Invertase, like amylase and maltase, catalyzes the cleavage of glycosidic linkages by introducing elements of water:

$$>CH{-}O{-}HC< \xrightarrow{+H_2O} >CHOH + HOHC<$$

Hassid and Putman (682) depict hydrolysis as approaching completion when invertase acts upon a dilute sucrose solution. A theoretically finite level of sucrose must remain in solution at equilibrium, the precise amount being determined by the reaction's free energy change and product concentration (682). The ΔF value for sucrose hydrolysis, about −6500 calories per mole, strongly favors an equilibrium to the right. Moreover, the fact that one of the reactants is water, whose concentration is enormous in an aqueous medium, greatly enhances a strictly hydrolytic reaction. Under these conditions invertase has but little expectation of performing sucrose synthesis. Hassid and Putman (682) envision no *direct* importance of hydrolytic enzymes in synthesizing any of the complex carbohydrates.

3. SUCROSE PHOSPHORYLASE

By 1940 the biosynthesis of glycogen and starch by reversible phosphorolysis was widely recognized. The possibility that sucrose might be synthesized by a similar type of reaction was not lost on plant scientists of the day. Yet regardless of the discovery of fructose and glucose phosphates and their ready interconversion in plant tissues, no one had found a viable enzyme which was capable of uniting the hexose phosphates to produce a glucose–fructose disaccharide and its attending inorganic phosphate.

In 1944 Hartt (660) presented an elaborate scheme summarizing the current knowledge of sugar and phosphate interconversions, and pointedly deploted the absence of a sucrose-yielding reaction. It is true that the Russian workers Kursanov (869) and Kryukova (860), in 1940, had presented strong evidence of sucrose synthesis being dependent upon phosphorylation. Hassid (678) had arrived at a similar conclusion in 1938. However, it was in a bacterium, *Pseudomonas saccharophila*, that an appropriate sucrose phosphorylase was finally discovered. Unlike its starch-forming counterpart, no direct evidence of sucrose phosphorylase was ever found in higher plant tissues. Eventually even starch phosphorylase came to be questioned insofar as an appreciable synthetic reaction is concerned. Be that as it may, sucrose phosphorylase was the first authentic sucrose-forming catalyst found in nature and its discovery constitutes a milestone in the history of sucrose biochemistry.

A. *Discovery of sucrose phosphorylase*

In 1943 Doudoroff *et al.* (439) published the first widely-accepted evidence of "enzymic phosphorolysis"[1]. Working with a dry preparation of the bacterium *Pseudomonas saccharophila* Doudoroff (443), a phosphorolysis reaction was discovered in which sucrose was converted to glucose 1-phosphate (glucose-1-*P*) and fructose. Quite significantly, it was also shown that with glucose-1-*P* and fructose acting as substrates sucrose was synthesized by reverse phosphorolysis in a competing system of hydrolytic and phosphorolytic reactions:

$$\begin{array}{l}\text{Sucrose} + H_3PO_4 \rightleftharpoons \text{glucose-1-}P + \text{fructose}\\ \quad + \\ \quad H_2O \\ \quad \downarrow \\ \text{glucose} + \text{fructose}\end{array} \qquad (1)$$

Sucrose was identified by simultaneous increase of reducing value and change in optical rotation following inversion with yeast invertase. Doudoroff *et al.* (439) did not identify a specific phosphorolytic enzyme in this report. During the same year [1943] Doudoroff (440) described an enzyme, sucrose phosphorylase, obtained from dried *P. saccharophila* cells and partially purified by fractional ammonium sulfate precipitation.

---

[1]Doudoroff and his colleagues appear to have been "beaten" by about a year with respect to the discovery of the sucrose phosphorolysis reaction. Kagan *et al.* (814) had published evidence of a similar reaction by cell suspensions of the bacterium *Leuconostoc mesenteroides* which operated at the expense of inorganic P and sucrose. However, the Russian workers do not appear to have demonstrated a reverse reaction whereby sucrose would be formed from glucose 1-phosphate and fructose.

B. *Properties and mode of action of sucrose phosphorylase*

Sucrose phosphorylase appears to be an inductive enzyme in that it is readily synthesized when the organism's culture medium contains sucrose or another sugar, such as raffinose, containing a sucrose linkage. It is not induced in the presence of starch, maltose, or glucose. The enzyme has been found in *P. saccharophila*, *Leuconostoc mesenteroides*, and *Pseudomonas putrefaciens* (442). Some indirect evidence of the sucrose phosphorylase reaction has been reported in sugarcane (1337, 1137). Bonner (204, p. 41) suggests that it may eventually be found in higher plants if appropriate conditions for its isolation can be discovered.

The equilibrium constant may be expressed by the following mass law equation:

$$K = \frac{[\text{Sucrose}]\,[\text{HPO}_4^{=}]}{[\text{Glucose-1-}P]\,[\text{Fructose}]}$$

The value of K at 30 °C, subject to the medium's pH, has been given as 0.053 at pH 6.6 (682) and 0.09 at pH 5.8 (204, p. 39). The *P. saccharophila* enzyme is specific for the glucose portion of its substrate and will not combine with monophosphates of galactose, mannose, or xylose. It will not react with α-L-glucose 1-phosphate (1007). However, fructose may be replaced as the glucose acceptor by L-sorbose, D-xylulose, L-arabulose, and L-arabinose, so that four non-sucrose disaccharides will arise from the sucrose phosphorylase reaction (540, p. 448). The enzyme has no appreciable action on starch, maltose, lactose, or raffinose. There is a strict retention of configuration in each of the synthetic reactions in which α-glucosidic bonds participate in the interconversion of α-D-glucose 1-phosphate and disaccharides. Fruton and Simmonds (540, p. 447) depict the phosphorylase reaction with sucrose in the following structural sequence (Fig. 6-1):

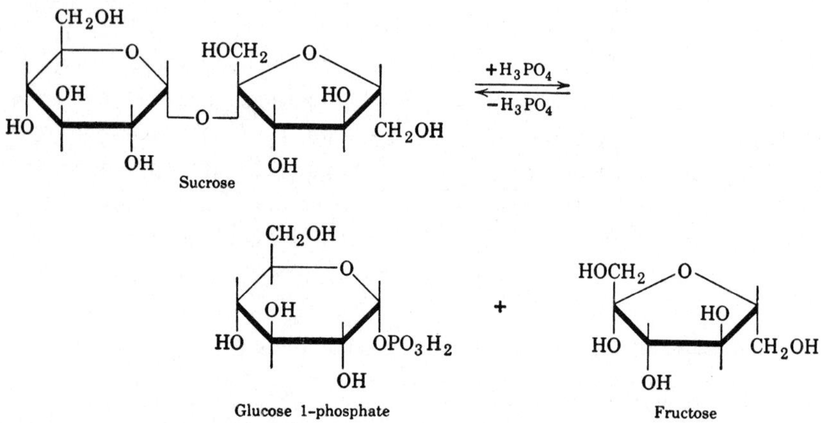

Fig. 6-1. Structural representations of sugar changes incident to the action of sucrose phosphorylase. [After Fruton and Simmonds (540, p. 447).] Reproduced by permission of *John Wiley and Sons, Inc.*, New York.

Sucrose phosphorylase had scarcely been discovered before investigators questioned whether its mode of action is similar to that of the polysaccharide-forming enzymes. In particular, cleavage of the phosphate bond in glucose-1-*P* and the essentiality of phosphate became focal points of attention. Studies by Doudoroff *et al.* (441) with ^{32}P showed that the enzyme catalyzed a glucose transfer and could therefore be classified as a transglucosidase. In the absence of ketose sugars a rapid exchange of ^{32}P occurred between inorganic phosphate and glucose-1-*P* in the presence of *P. saccharophila* enzyme. It was also shown that with phosphate-free enzyme preparations there was an interconversion of sucrose and the sucrose analog "glucosidosorboside". In this reaction there was a transfer of the glucose moiety from the fructose end of sucrose to sorbose to yield a new dissacharide:

$$\text{Glucosyl 1-fructoside} + \text{sorbose} \rightleftharpoons \text{glucosyl 1-sorboside} + \text{fructose} \qquad (2)$$

It follows that the enzyme catalyzes a reaction of the aldehydic group of D-glucose with an appropriate acceptor, and that an essential "activation" of the aldehydic group is accomplished by converting glucose to either glucose-1-*P* or a glucoside. Hence, phosphate is not indispensable and the term "phosphorylase" is opened to question since in the phosphorolysis of sucrose the employment of phosphate as a glucose acceptor is rendered a matter of convenience rather than necessity. Thus the reaction mảy be termed "transglycosidation" or "transglycosylation", and the enzyme a "transglycosidase".

There is evidence that the sucrose and starch phosphorylases do not operate by strictly identical mechanisms even though both enzymes appear to attack glucose-1-*P* at the same linkage. ^{32}P studies by Cohn and Cori (363) have shown that, in the absence of a polysaccharide primer, starch phosphorylase does not catalyze an exchange between organic and inorganic phosphate. For both the potato and muscle phosphorylases the presence of phosphate or glucose-1-*P* is essential for enzyme activity. On the other hand, evidence obtained by Cohn (364) is suggestive that sucrose phosphorylase and its starch-forming counterpart both cleave the same glucose-1-*P* linkage (Fig. 6-2). Experiments with ^{18}O-labeled inorganic phosphate

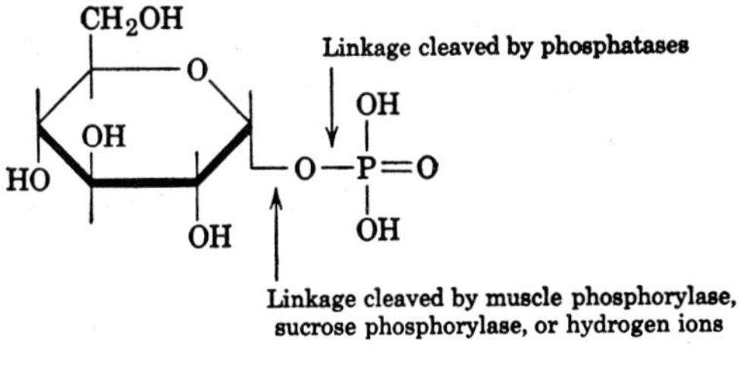

Fig. 6-2. Mode of action of various enzymes on glucose 1-phosphate. [After Fruton and Simmonds (540, p. 450).] Reproduced by permission of *John Wiley and Sons, Inc.*, New York.

showed that each enzyme acts upon the linkage between carbon 1 of glucose and the phosphate-group oxygen. This is the same cleavage which occurs during acid hydrolysis. It was also shown that when phosphatase catalyzes the glucose-1-*P* hydrolysis a cleavage occurs between the oxygen and phosphorus atoms (Fig. 6-2).

4. UDPG-TRANSGLYCOSYLASE MECHANISMS IN SUCROSE SYNTHESIS

A. *Discovery of UDPG*

In 1949 Leloir and his co-workers (300) reported the presence of an unidentified "thermostable factor" essential for the conversion of galactose-1-*P* to glucose-1-*P* by the enzyme *galactowaldenase.* In two subsequent reports the factor was identified as uridine diphosphate glucose (UDPG) and its role as an enzyme cofactor was established (302, 301). UDPG was isolated from baker's yeast and partially purified by fractional precipitation plus ion-exchange chromatography. The cofactor's nomenclature arose from early evidence that it contained uridine, two phosphate groups, and glucose. Acid hydrolysis of UDPG yielded uridine 5′-phosphate (UMP) plus lesser amounts of uridine 5′-diphosphate (UDP) and ribose phosphate. Coenzymatic activity was destroyed by bromine, which acted upon the uracil component, and by alkali, which presumably altered the molecular configuration.

Paper chromatographic studies of purified UDPG showed that the cofactor was accompanied by two contaminating substances (1133). One of these was identified as uridylic acid. The second substance appeared to be structurally identical to UDPG, with the exception that an unidentified component substituted for glucose. In addition to uridine 5′-phosphate, alkaline degradation of UDPG yielded a cyclic glucose phosphate ester, which in turn yielded glucose-1-*P* (25 percent) and glucose-2-*P* (75 percent) when broken down with acid or alkali.

The mechanism of coenzymatic action by UDPG was not at first clear. Cardini *et al.* (302) did underscore the point that glucose phosphate was an integral part of the cofactor: "The fact that glucose phosphate can be recognized as part of the coenzyme suggests that this portion may exchange with the substrate during the reaction cycle." These authors were also aware that UDPG might be widely distributed in nature. A similarity was noted between UDPG and a compound described by Park and Johnson (1142) in *Staphylococcus aureus.* Moreover, the presence of UDPG in animal tissues and in yeast which does not utilize galactose led Caputto *et al.* (301) to suggest that it may serve in some capacity other than the coenzyme of galactowaldenase.

B. *Implication of UDPG in sucrose synthesis*

In 1952 and 1953 Buchanan and his colleagues (255–257) recognized UDPG as an active metabolite of photosynthesizing green leaves. Almost immediately it was proposed that UDPG might take part in sucrose synthesis in a mechanism alternative to the sucrose phosphorylase system. By this time the absence of the latter in plants was becoming increasingly conspicuous.

Buchanan *et al.* (257) described the gradual discovery of UDPG among phosphorylated products of algae or green leaves exposed to $^{14}CO_2$: "It has been noted. . . that on radiograms of the products of photosynthesis a dark area appeared in a position occupied by no known sugar phosphate. Extracts of the area gave glucose on very mild acid hydrolysis or on treatment with a phosphatase preparation. This has hitherto been referred to as an 'unknown glucose phosphate'. It was found that this substance was more labile to acid than glucose-1-*P*, itself a readily hydrolyzable phosphate, and furthermore that other labile glucose derivatives were formed as intermediates during the acid hydrolysis." Noting that the accumulation of labeled glucose precedes the accumulation of ^{14}C in sucrose, Buchanan *et al.* (257) suggested a "precursor relationship to sucrose synthesis". Intensive decomposition studies of the radioactive material accumulated over a time course of 60 seconds revealed at least eight labeled areas upon rechromatography. Within three of these the radioactivity was localized in glucose, mannose, and galactose; two of the others yielded glucose and galactose upon hydrolysis with phosphatase. From this evidence the authors surmised that compounds analogous to the "uridine diphosphate glucose type" were produced.

Working with preparations of *Scenedesmus* and sugar beet, Buchanan *et al.* (257) proceeded to identify UDPG as an active metabolite containing hexoses rapidly labeled during photosynthesis in $^{14}CO_2$. Evidence of a uridine diphosphate galactose was also obtained. In addition, mannose- and adenosine-containing compounds having chromatographic properties similar to nucleotides were found.

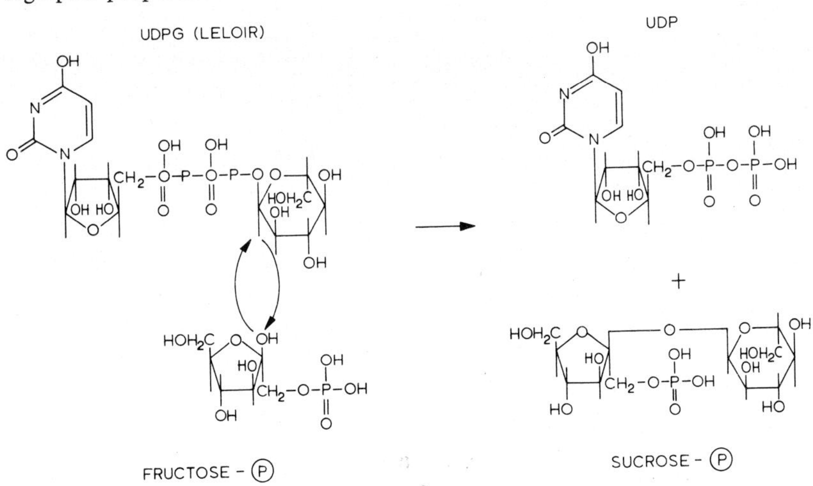

Fig. 6-3. Schematic representation of sucrose synthesis from phosphorylated intermediates. [After Buchanan *et al.* (255).] Reproduced by permission of *The Johns Hopkins Press*, Baltimore, Md.

At about the time that the above studies were being conducted, Buchanan *et al.* (255) speculated upon the roles of UDPG and UDP-galactose in plants while contributing to a major symposium on phosphorus metabolism. It was proposed that UDP-galactose participates in the synthesis of galactose from glucose. The authors suggested that UDPG and UDP-galactose are involved in polysaccharide synthesis, "functioning in a manner similar to that of glucose-1-*P* in the numerous phosphorylase reactions". The suggested role of UDPG in sucrose synthesis is presented in Fig. 6-3. A significant point here is that UDPG was no longer viewed strictly as a coenzyme but as a contributor of glucose residues in reactions leading to the formation of sucrose and other complex carbohydrates. Support for this view was taken from data showing that the labeling of UDPG and UDP-galactose was more rapid than the labeling of sucrose, and from the growing consensus that sucrose synthesis involves phosphorylated glucose and fructose (255).

By 1951 Leloir (917) had stressed the importance of substrates as integral parts of coenzyme structure. He described glucose 1,6-diphosphate as a coenzyme for the conversion of glucose-1-*P* to glucose-6-*P*. Moreover, the involvement of uridylic acid in the galactowaldenase reaction suggests a coenzymic role. The possibility of UDPG taking part in natural Walden inversions is clearly implied by the latter reaction. In addition, Leloir placed special emphasis upon recurrence of the nucleoside pyrophosphate configuration within the structure of coenzymes.

Burma and Mortimer (264) reported in 1956 radiotracer studies with sugar beet leaf preparations which greatly substantiated the thesis that UDPG is synthesized in plants and that it is a major reactant in sucrose biosynthesis. When radioactive glucose-1-*P* was supplied to excised leaves, sucrose was formed with the label equally distributed between the glucose and fructose moieties. It was further observed that when uridine 5′-triphosphate (UTP) is "fed" along with glucose-1-*P* the sucrose yield declines in favor of increased UDPG formation. Working with leaf homogenates, it was found that a mixture of radioactive glucose-1-*P* and UTP was converted to labeled UDPG, and that a combination of ATP and UDP could serve in place of a direct UTP supply.

In addition to UDPG being formed from glucose-1-*P* plus UTP and ATP, it was observed that sucrose labeled in the glucose moiety was formed from labeled glucose-1-*P* plus UTP and fructose-6-*P* (264). The essentiality of UDPG in the reaction sequence was confirmed when omission of UTP terminated the production of sucrose. Conversely, UDPG substituted freely for glucose-1-*P* plus UTP in sucrose synthesis. It was also shown that sucrose phosphate (sucrose-*P*) was the initial sucrose form produced. Attempts to replace fructose-6-*P* with fructose or fructose 1,6-diphosphate terminated the production of sucrose. Traces of sucrose-*P* were found but it was believed that the bulk of sucrose-*P* was rapidly dephosphorylated to give free sucrose.

Quite significantly, Burma and Mortimer (264) also accounted for the resynthesis of UTP from UDP and ATP. By this means a continual regeneration of the glucose donor for sucrose synthesis, *i.e.*, UDPG was assured. The authors visualized an ATP role in UTP regeneration in addition to the ATP energy expenditure toward hexose phosphate synthesis. They speculated that the required ATP might arise through photosynthetic phosphorylation, reactions which had not yet been demonstrated in sugar beet, but which had recently been discovered in *Chlorella, Rhodospirillum rubrum*, and spinach chloroplasts.

Ganguli (556), working with homogenates from *Impatiens holstii*, a plant producing large quantities of sucrose which exudates and forms crystals at the leaf and leaf petiole edges, isolated a pyrophosphorylase which catalyzed the synthesis of UDPG and inorganic pyrophosphate from UTP and glucose-1-*P*. The reaction was reversible and was stimulated by Mg^{2+}. Addition of [^{14}C]glucose-1-*P* to the reaction led to the synthesis of [^{14}C]UDPG. An additional enzyme was found, "nucleotide diphosphate kinase", which catalyzed the reversible formation of UTP plus ADP from UDP plus ATP.

C. *Enzymatic synthesis of sucrose and sucrose phosphate*

All of the work recounted thus far implicating UDPG involvement in the synthesis of complex sugars was conducted without precise knowledge of any of the enzymes involved. Until 1953 bacterial sucrose phosphorylase remained the sole enzyme that was known with certainty to catalyze a synthesis of authentic sucrose. Thus the enzymic reactions of sucrose formation retained their obscurity even while great advances were made with respect to the essential intermediates of these events. When at last enzymes were found which could catalyze the enormous sucrose productivity of green plants, one of the troublesome problems of modern plant physiology seemed about to be laid to rest.

In 1953, following earlier work in which they had obtained trehalose phosphate from UDPG and glucose-6-*P* (918), Leloir and Cardini (920) reported the discovery of a wheat-germ enzyme which catalyzed sucrose formation from UDPG and fructose:

$$\text{UDPG} + \text{fructose} \rightleftharpoons \text{sucrose} + \text{UDP} \tag{3}$$

Unlike the reverse phosphorolysis which characterizes the sucrose phosphorylase reaction, the new enzyme promoted a transfer of glucose from UDPG to fructose, yielding equal amounts of sucrose and UDP. Sucrose was verified chromatographically and by identification of its acid hydrolysis products. Significantly, glucose-1-*P* could not replace UDPG as the glucose donor, nor could fructose be replaced by sorbose, aldoses, arabinose, or by the hexose 1- or 6-phosphates. Moreover, a reverse reaction was demonstrated which began with UDP plus sucrose and ended with authentic UDPG. For confirmation of UDPG the product was used to perform coenzymic activity with galactowaldenase.

In a subsequent paper [1954] Leloir and his co-workers (303) described in detail the enzyme's preparation and conditions of maximal activity. At this time the name *UDPG–fructose transglycosylase* was first proposed. The reaction equilibrium was shown to favor sucrose synthesis with the value of K being about 5.0 at 37 °C and pH 7.4. This contrasts with sucrose phosphorylase ($K = 0.053$ at pH 6.6 and 30 °C) whose displacement in favor of monosaccharides disposes the enzyme toward a sucrose utilization role rather than one of sucrose synthesis. However, Leloir *et al.* (303) noted that UDPG–fructose transglycosylase gave K values ranging from 2.0 to 8.0 under similar conditions in different experiments. This probably reflected a rather close relationship between K and the pool size of a number of reactants not appearing in the equation.

UDPG–fructose transglycosylase was detected in numerous plant tissues and particularly among those having low invertase content. Seeds were generally the best source. Qualitative tests were positive with seed extracts of pine, pea and fenugreek, and with corn germ, potato sprouts and barley shoots. It is interesting that quantitative tests revealed sugarcane roots to be an abundant source. Quantitative estimates were also made with shoots of pea, beet, and sorghum. Oddly enough, the tissues of greatest interest to this narrative, *i.e.*, sugarcane leaves, gave negative or non-reproducible results which the authors attributed to interfering enzymes. The latter could hardly have included invertase. Although not specifically mentioned, varietal factors or inconsistencies in diurnal sampling periods could explain the difficulty with sugarcane.

It was noted above that fructose-6-*P* could not replace fructose in the UDPG–fructose transglycosylase reaction. Nonetheless, Leloir and Cardini reported in a later paper that certain preparations did form sucrose with either fructose or fructose-6-*P* (920). The fact that these preparations contained phosphatase led the authors to presume that the transglycosylase reaction proper was preceded by enzymatic hydrolysis of the fructose phosphate:

$$\text{Fructose-6-}P + H_2O \longrightarrow \text{fructose} + \text{inorganic phosphate} \quad (4)$$

$$\text{UDPG} + \text{fructose} \rightleftharpoons \text{sucrose} + \text{UDP} \quad (5)$$

However, continued investigation showed that a sucrose phosphate could be produced from fructose-6-*P* plus UDPG. A phosphatase reaction occurred after the synthetic reaction with the result that free sucrose was produced from sucrose phosphate:

$$\text{UDPG} + \text{fructose-6-}P \rightleftharpoons \text{sucrose phosphate} + \text{UDP} \quad (6)$$

$$\text{Sucrose phosphate} \longrightarrow \text{sucrose} + \text{inorganic phosphate} \quad (7)$$

Each of the four reactions was catalyzed by crude wheat germ preparations.

The presence of a second enzyme capable of synthesizing the sucrose linkage was at least implied by the fact that Reaction 4 proceeded at less than half the rate of Reaction 5. When Leloir and Cardini compared sucrose synthesis rates with fructose and fructose-6-*P* they obtained activity ratios varying from 5.8 to 0.33. This was taken as proof that two distinct enzymes were involved. In order to obtain enzyme preparations free of phosphatase and UDPG–fructose transglycosylase, wheat germ extracts were repeatedly precipitated by treatment with ammonium sulfate and by dialysis; however, some phosphatase was retained even in the purest preparations so that a mixture of products, sucrose and sucrose phosphate (sucrose-*P*), was obtained. Substitution of fructose-1-*P* for fructose-6-*P* led to severe reductions in the amount of free sucrose obtained in the product mixture. The Michaelis constant for sucrose-*P* synthesis was 2.2×10^{-3}. The optimum pH was 6.4.

Regardless of the fact that they were dealing with a mixture of products, Leloir and Cardini obtained sufficient sucrose-*P* to determine its structure with reasonable certainty (Fig. 6-4). Phosphatase treatment yielded a compound identical to sucrose with

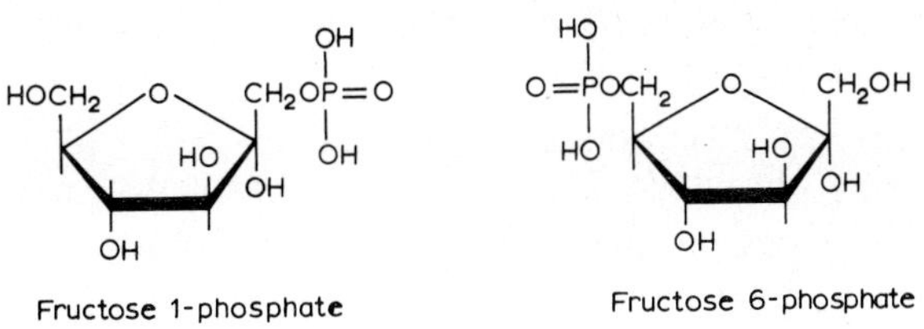

Fig. 6-4. Structural formulas for fructose 1-phosphate and fructose 6-phosphate. Fructose 6-phosphate enters readily into plant reactions leading to sucrose phosphate. [Based on structures by Fruton and Simmonds (540, p. 458).] Reproduced by permission of *John Wiley and Sons, Inc.*, New York.

respect to reducing power and ultraviolet light absorption, increased reducing power with acid hydrolysis, and migration behavior during paper chromatographic analyses. Mild acid hydrolysis of the sucrose phosphate produced free glucose plus a fructose ester having properties identical to fructose-6-*P* when treated with acid, or when treated with isomerase and glucose dehydrogenase plus NADP.

Leloir and Cardini observed that the sucrose-*P* was more stable to acid than was free sucrose, a fact explained by the presence of a phosphate group at the C-6 position. It was concluded that the synthetic reaction product was sucrose with a phosphate group at the C-6 position of the fructose moiety. This product was not regarded as being identical to the sucrose-*P* described by Buchanan (256) which yielded fructose-1-*P* upon hydrolysis.

In 1955 Bean and Hassid (160) confirmed the synthesis of sucrose from UDPG and D-fructose using a partially-purified enzyme preparation from green peas. In addition, sucrose-*P* was produced enzymatically from UDPG and fructose-6-*P*. It was also shown that three other disaccharides were formed when D-xylulose, D-rhamnulose, and L-sorbose were substituted for D-fructose:

$$\text{UDPG} + \text{D-xylulose} \rightleftharpoons \text{D-glucosyl D-xyluloside} + \text{UDP} \quad (8)$$

$$\text{UDPG} + \text{D-rhamnulose} \rightleftharpoons \text{D-glucosyl D-rhamnuloside} + \text{UDP} \quad (9)$$

$$\text{UDPG} + \text{L-sorbose} \rightleftharpoons \text{D-glucosyl L-sorboside} + \text{UDP} \quad (10)$$

The disaccharide D-glucose L-sorboside, formed by Reaction 10, was believed to be identical to that produced from glucose-1-*P* plus D-xylulose by a *P. saccharophila* preparation as described by Hassid *et al.* (680). Bean and Hassid (160) concluded that the three new disaccharides were synthesized through the mediation of UDPG–fructose transglycosylase.

Sucrose and sucrose-*P* were identified by paper chromatography and appropriate treatment with invertase or phosphatase. Bean and Hassid were apparently the first to recognize a stimulatory effect of Mg^{2+} on sucrose synthesis. It was proposed that, under conditions of the assay, a significant quantity of fructose-6-*P* may be formed. This in turn would lead to higher sucrose-*P* levels and ultimately to greater sucrose in the presence of UDPG.

Evidence of sucrose-*P* synthesis in *Canna indica* leaves was obtained by Putman and Hassid (1199) using a darkened infiltration technique with labeled sugars. When ^{14}C-labeled glucose, fructose, and sucrose were infiltrated into leaf discs during 6-hour respiration periods in darkness, each of the radioactive hexoses produced a rapid increase of labeled sucrose and labeled hexose monophosphates. Infiltration of [^{14}C]fructose led to a decrease of [^{14}C]fructose activity and a concurrent increase of [^{14}C]sucrose. A similar response was obtained with [^{14}C]glucose. When the labeled sucrose product was hydrolyzed, the glucose and fructose moieties in each instance contained comparable amounts of ^{14}C. Putman and Hassid concluded: "The sucrose does not seem to be formed by a mechanism involving either free fructose or free glucose. The synthesis of the disaccharide probably involves a dephosphorolytic condensation of phosphorylated derivatives of glucose and fructose." Similar conclusions denying free fructose a role as the immediate glucose acceptor were drawn by Vittorio *et al.* (1506) and by Porter and May (1176) working with tobacco leaves.

An observation having far-reaching implications relative to sucrose synthesis as a part of sugar storage processes was recorded during the studies with *Canna indica* (1199). Putman and Hassid noted that when ^{14}C-labeled sucrose was infiltrated into the intact leaf cells, there was an immediate hydrolysis which yielded free fructose and glucose. This was believed to occur before the sugars entered the cells. Thereafter the hexose products were rapidly reconstituted as sucrose following entry into the intact cells.

Additional evidence of a sucrose-forming system which utilizes fructose phosphate rather than free fructose was reported by Edelman *et al.* (471) in 1955. Studies of ^{14}C-labeled fructose and glucose incorporation into the sucrose and cellulose constituents of wheat seedlings showed that sucrose always contained a nearly equal amount of ^{14}C in each moiety. The authors had expected that the disaccharide would be labeled predominately in the glucose portion by virtue of the low-labeling tendency for free fructose in the plant. The similar label distribution was therefore taken to mean that free fructose was not involved in sucrose synthesis.

D. *UDPG in sucrose phosphate synthesis*

The view that UDPG should also play a role in sucrose-*P* synthesis was forwarded by Buchanan (256) in 1953. It had been shown by Calvin and Benson (285) in 1949 that sucrose was the first free sugar to be formed by *Chlorella* assimilating $^{14}CO_2$. In view of the phosphorylated precursors available, this was taken as evidence of early sucrose-*P* synthesis followed by rapid conversion to free sucrose. However, Buchanan (256) suspected that a different sucrose phosphate existed in nature having a phosphorylated fructose moiety. This belief was based on studies of microbial sucrose utilization, but Buchanan also cited the findings by Putman and Hassid suggestive of a phosphorylated sucrose derivative formed during sucrose synthesis. Buchanan, employing an invertase-free phosphatase preparation, hydrolyzed a number of phosphorylated $^{14}CO_2$ fixation products and examined them for the presence of free sucrose. In the instance of sugar beet he found significant amounts of sucrose, indicating that a sucrose phosphate had indeed been formed incident to the synthesis of hexose monophosphate. The authenticity of sucrose was established by co-chromatography and enzymatic hydrolysis.

When Buchanan hydrolyzed the sucrose-*P* with phosphatase he obtained free sucrose. Acid hydrolysis gave glucose plus a fructose phosphate which did not co-chromatograph with fructose-6-*P*. He therefore proposed a sucrose-*P* structure in which the fructose moiety was phosphorylated at the C-1 position. On this basis Buchanan described two mechanisms which he believed would account for sucrose-*P* synthesis in green plants: (a) A reaction of glucose-1-*P* with fructose-1-*P* yielding sucrose-*P*, the latter being converted in turn to sucrose via dephosphorylation; and (b) a reaction of UDPG with fructose-1-*P*. UDPG for the second mechanism would be formed from glucose-1-*P*.

E. *Enzymatic synthesis of UDPG*

Data reported by Turner in 1954 (1460) and in 1957 (1461) had shown that crude pea extracts readily formed sucrose from glucose-1-*P* plus fructose, but the mechanism appeared to be much more complicated than the system involving sucrose phosphorylase. Turner visualized a sucrose synthesis accomplished through the mediation of UDPG, and a synthesis of UDPG from UTP plus glucose-1-*P*. Considerable supporting evidence was found in the apparent operation of glycolytic and phosphorylation reactions, a requirement for NAD and Mg^{2+}, and stimulatory action by added adenosine phosphates. Confirmation that pea extracts contain a viable glycolytic mechanism capable of producing UTP was published by Hatch and Turner (687) in 1958.

In 1958 Turner and Turner (1458) described an enzyme isolated from pea extracts which catalyzed the synthesis of UDPG from UTP plus glucose-1-*P*. The enzyme was named *UDPG pyrophosphorylase.* A purified preparation was obtained free of interfering enzymes by fractional precipitation at 4 °C with ammonium sulfate, followed by dialysis of the protein at 4 °C against phosphate buffer. The reaction equilibrium favored the synthesis of UTP (pyrophosphorolysis of UDPG):

$$\text{UDPG} + \text{inorganic pyrophosphate} \rightleftharpoons \text{UTP} + \text{glucose-1-}P \qquad (11)$$

The apparent equilibrium constant was affected by the Mg^{2+} concentration and pH of the reaction medium. The value of K was approximately 7.2. Optimum pH was about 7.5 and Mg^{2+} was required for activity. The enzyme was sensitive to high temperature (60 °C) but remained stable for 3 months at −15 °C. Active preparations were obtained from all plant tissues examined, including wheat and maize shoots, pea and sugarcane roots, wheat leaves, silver-beet leaves and potato tubers. A phosphatase active against UTP was also present in most of the preparations. Recent studies (428, 501) have shown that both ADPG and UDPG pyrophosphorylases are active in corn endosperm.

In 1960 Dugger and Humphreys (450) reported that boron increased sucrose synthesis by pea and sugarcane seedling homogenates. Sucrose synthesis from UDPG, fructose, and UTP was more than doubled. The stimulatory action of boron was apparently related to its effect on UDPG pyrophosphorylase. It was further shown that UDPG–fructose transglycosylase and UDP kinase were sensitive to added boron. The element inhibited sucrose synthesis from UTP, glucose-1-*P* and fructose in coupled reactions requiring ATP. By means not entirely clear, boron served to maintain a consistent level of UDPG. When assayed individually, ATP inhibited both UDPG–fructose transglycosylase and UDPG pyrophosphorylase. Boron increased UDPG pyrophosphorylase activity but inhibited UDPG–fructose transglycosylase. Although these results seemed to indicate an important role of boron in carbohydrate metabolism, this role does not appear to have been examined further.

F. *Nucleoside specificity in sucrose synthesis*

Following the discovery of starch synthetase (427, 924), an enzyme catalyzing the transfer of glucose from UDPG to an appropriate primer, Recondo and Leloir (1222) examined the enzyme's behavior when combined with a series of synthetic nucleoside diphosphate sugars. One of these, adenosine diphosphate glucose (ADPG), was found to be about 10 times more effective than UDPG as a glucose donor (Fig. 6-5). The glucose was transferred from ADPG to polysaccharide in a pattern similar to the glucose movement from UDPG, that is, it was distributed between the amylose and amylopectin components. However, the addition of ADPG to ^{14}C-labeled UDPG caused a decrease of ^{14}C incorporation into starch, while the inverse treatment of labeled ADPG with UDPG produced no change.

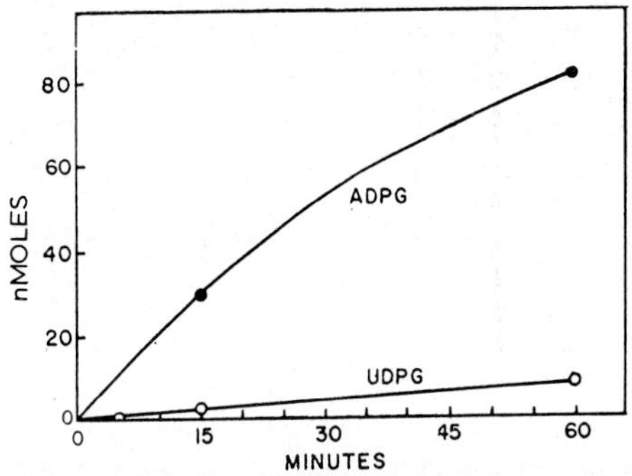

Fig. 6-5. Relative effectiveness of adenosine diphosphate glucose (ADPG) and uridine diphosphate glucose (UDPG) as glucose donors in the starch synthetase reaction. [After Recondo and Leloir (1222).] Reproduced by permission of the *Academic Press, Inc.*, New York.

No nucleoside diphosphate formation was detected when starch synthetase was incubated with inosine diphosphate glucose (IDPG), cytidine diphosphate glucose (CDPG), guanosine diphosphate glucose (GDPG), ADP-maltose, ADP-galactose, or UDP-galactose. Moreover, negative results were obtained with β-anomers of ADPG and UDPG, and an isomer of ADPG having the glucose linkage at the C-6 position. Little or no activity was obtained when ADPG was tested with sucrose synthetase, sucrose-*P* synthetase, and galactowaldenase. Although Recondo and Leloir (1222) concluded that ADPG and UDPG react with the same enzyme, they raised the question as to whether ADPG performs an *in vivo* role in starch synthesis. The presence of ADPG pyrophosphorylase in plant materials was forwarded in support of an ADPG role as an active metabolite.

In a subsequent report by Conchie *et al.* (386) it was shown that arbutin, a compound formed from UDPG in the presence of wheat germ and locust enzyme preparations, was present as a natural constituent of seeds and locust. Trivelloni *et al.* (1452) examined the response of similar enzyme preparations to ADPG. With locust enzyme ADPG failed to increase glucoside formation; with wheat germ enzyme the glucoside arbutin and the corresponding gentiobioside were formed. These products were identical to compounds produced from UDPG. Glucoside and gentiobioside synthesis was notably faster when ADPG was substituted for UDPG, but the differences in rate of glucose transfer were somewhat less than in starch synthesis.

Similar experiments examining the effects of nucleoside diphosphate sugars on sucrose synthetase were reported by Cardini and Recondo (305) in 1962. A sucrose-forming enzyme obtained from wheat germ was assayed in the presence of CDPG, GDPG, UDP-galactose, UDP-xylose, and ADP-xylose. Galactose derivatives and UDP-xylose markedly slowed activity as compared with UDPG. The other compounds gave negative results. Sucrose was the only product synthesized with radioactive nucleotides labeled in glucose, and there was no liberation of [^{14}C]glucose. In competetion experiments employing nucleotide pairs with one labeled member, it was found that UDPG inhibited [^{14}C]glucose incorporation into sucrose from all nucleotides tested, but in the reverse experiments with ^{14}C-labeled UDPG there was no inhibition by any of the nucleotides. It was further shown that UMP, UDP, and UTP inhibited equally well as UDPG. On the other hand, AMP, thymidine 5′-monophosphate (TMP), and deoxy-UMP gave no interference with glucose incorporation into sucrose from UDPG, ADPG, thymidine diphosphate glucose (TDPG), and deoxy-UDPG.

The wheat germ preparation used by Cardini and Recondo (305) contained sucrose-*P* synthetase operating at somewhat lower rates than sucrose synthetase. Very little activity was obtained with any nucleotide other than UDPG. This is consistent with the findings of Slabnik *et al.* (1339) showing that sucrose-*P* synthetase from potato tuber specifically requires UDPG as the glucosyl donor, while sucrose synthetase is non-specific and reacts equally well with ADPG. Cardini and Recondo (305) concluded from this that UDPG is the natural substrate for sucrose synthetase. Other nucleoside diphosphate sugars were shown to replace UDPG, but their donation of glucose was inhibited by UMP, UDP, UTP, or UDPG, compounds all presumably situated close to the reaction site. The authors suggested that experiments of this type provide a basis for explaining such processes as the sucrose–starch interconversion in plants. It is noteworthy that De Fekete *et al.* (428) and Murata *et al.* (1066) soon demonstrated that ADPG formation from sucrose and ADP provides a pathway for glucose transfer from sucrose to starch.

In 1965 Milner and Avigad (1023) reported on the nucleoside diphosphate specificity of a highly purified sucrose synthetase obtained from sugar beet root. This preparation was free of invertase and phosphatase. The reactions were designed to test the nucleoside diphosphate effectiveness as glucosyl acceptors. It was found that thymidine 5′-diphosphate (TDP) was highly effective whereas ADP was considerably less efficient than had been reported with the corn endosperm enzyme. Nonetheless, reaction systems to which UDP, TDP and ADP had been added formed new products which co-chromatographed with UDPG, TDPG, and ADPG, respectively. Sucrose was produced by a reaction mixture containing fructose, TDPG and purified sucrose synthetase.

Avigad (119) published in 1964 findings from kinetic experiments with invertase-free sucrose synthetase from Jerusalem artichoke tubers. It was shown that UDP and TDP, along with UDPG and TDPG, act as competing substrates for an active enzyme site. With UDPG the maximum velocity at pH 7.2 was 3.7 times greater than with TDPG. For sucrose cleavage the $V\ max.$ value (maximum velocity at infinite concentration) with UDP was 1.7 times greater than with TDP. Apparent K_m values obtained with uridine and thymidine nucleotides were of the same order of magnitude.

Milner and Avigad (1023) proposed that TDPG synthesis by sucrose synthetase might serve as a pathway for the provision of glucose to various biosynthetic reactions in plant tissues. In support of this thesis the work of Neufeld and Hassid (1089), and of Ginsburg (578), relative to TDPG as an active intermediate in the synthesis of TDP-rhamnose and TDP-galactose, was cited. The authors also noted their own findings of TDP-sugar derivatives occurring naturally in sugar beet roots.

5. SUCROSE SYNTHETASE AND SUCROSE PHOSPHATE SYNTHETASE

Following the "pioneer" studies by Leloir and his co-workers (302, 301, 1133), by Buchanan *et al.* (225–257), by Burma and Mortimer (264), and others during the mid-1950's, widespread interest developed in the reactions supporting sucrose and polysaccharide synthesis by transglycosylation. The output of new pertinent information from diverse plant species continues unabated at this writing. By 1960 Yamaha, Leloir and Cardini (304, 1591, 1592) had established the role of UDPG in β-glucoside synthesis from diphenols and had isolated a specific enzyme, UDPG–diphenol transglucosylase, from wheat germ (1591). Yamaha and Cardini (1592) had further shown that gentiobiosides can be formed from phenol glucosides and an appropriate enzyme was isolated from wheat germ extracts. As already noted (pp. 246, 247), Recondo and Leloir (1222) reported that bean preparations performed starch synthesis more effectively when UDPG was replaced with ADPG. The synthesis of ADPG by the enzyme ADPG pyrophosphorylase has been reported in wheat, rice, and other plants.

With respect to sucrose, the distinction between free sucrose synthesis and the formation of sucrose-*P* remained vague for a number of years. It is true that two distinct reactions were known in wheat germ but definitive work was complicated by the presence of acid phosphatase or invertase. This raised the specter of product hydrolysis in sucrose-forming digests, or of the added fructose-6-*P* being hydrolyzed to free fructose at the reaction site an instant before sucrose was assembled. The need for purified enzyme preparations in fundamental plant research has seldom been greater. Axelrod (123) questions the overall need of two enzymes having the same apparent goal, and whether one or both are functional *in vivo.* He further points out the additional energetic impetus arising from the phosphatase reaction converting sucrose-*P* to free sucrose. The coupling of hexose phosphates from photosynthesis prior to their hydrolysis to free monosaccharides is depicted in terms of free energy conservation.

A possible explanation for multiple synthesis mechanisms may lie in the complexity of sucrose transport and accumulation systems in the intact higher plant. Glasziou and his associates in Queensland have shown that sucrose is broken down and resynthesized during the process of moving from conducting tissue to cellular storage compartments in sugarcane stems (*cf.* Chapter 9, pp. 348–357). An "activated" form of sucrose believed to cross certain barrier membranes, and at first depicted as "sucrose–X", appears in fact to be sucrose-*P*. Sucrose-*P* might perform a similar role during the process of active vein loading in the leaves. Each of the sucrose-forming mechanisms might therefore perform a legitimate function depending on the site of sucrose synthesis in an intact source-to-sink system.

Axelrod gives the following systematic names for the two sucrose-forming enzymes: (a) UDP-glucose:D-fructose 6-phosphate 2-glucosyltransferase (sucrose phosphate synthetase), and (b) UDP-glucose:D-fructose 2-glucosyltransferase (sucrose synthetase). In the literature the two catalysts are frequently termed UDPG–fructose-6-*P* transglycosylase and UDPG–fructose transglycosylase, respectively. For convenience the names sucrose-*P* synthetase and sucrose synthetase are retained during the remainder of this discussion.

A. *Early evidence of sucrose synthetase in plant tissues*

Turner (1462) reported in 1953 strong sucrose-forming activity by crude pea extracts incubated in a mixture of glucose-1-*P* and fructose. Inorganic orthophosphate was liberated by the reaction. Sucrose synthesis was completely inhibited by iodoacetate and fluoride. Although such evidence might be taken to favor a sucrose phosphorylase reaction, Turner concluded that a far more complex mechanism of sucrose synthesis was operative.

The level of endogenous sucrose contained in the crude extract increased considerably when both glucose-1-*P* and fructose were added, but when glucose-1-*P* alone was added the sucrose level declined. Only a small sucrose increase was recorded when fructose was added alone. Furthermore, the increased glucose-1-*P* supplies which lowered sucrose simultaneously raised the level of liberated inorganic phosphate. Turner concluded that no direct relationship existed between the quantity of sucrose formed and inorganic phosphate liberated. He suggested that a sucrose-forming mechanism different than the reaction between glucose-1-*P* and fructose was operating in the pea extracts. In support of this view he cited the work of Hassid and Putman (684) with intact leaves, and of Calvin and Benson (285) with algae.

In 1954 Turner presented evidence of UDPG participation in sucrose synthesis by pea extracts (1460). Fructose rather than fructose phosphate appeared to be the essential ketose. Moreover, evidence suggestive of an active glycolytic system operating during sucrose formation was found. In a later report (1461) Turner strengthened his prior contention that a sucrose synthetase rather than a sucrose-*P* synthetase catalyzed the final step in sucrose formation by pea extracts. Free fructose could not be replaced by fructose-1-*P*, fructose-6-*P*, or by fructose 1,6-diphosphate. Turner noted the work of

Leloir and Cardini relative to a fructose-6-*P* utilizing system but did not discount the possibility that free fructose might be formed in such a system at the site of sucrose synthesis. Additional support for active glycolytic and phosphorylative mechanisms was taken from the fact that sucrose synthesis was dependent upon a diphosphopyridine nucleotide and was stimulated by addition of adenosine phosphates. A requirement for Mg^{2+} by the pea sucrose-forming mechanism was also demonstrated.

B. *Sucrose synthetase and sucrose-P synthetase in pea, bean, and broad bean preparations*

Hassid and Bean (683) reported in 1955 the presence of sucrose-forming enzymes in partially-purified extracts of pea seeds. Both fructose and fructose-6-*P* served as substrates when combined with UDPG and pea extract. UDPG was depicted as a coenzyme for the sucrose synthetase reaction, *i.e.*, sucrose produced from UDPG plus free fructose. UDPG was also described as the coenzyme for sucrose-*P* synthesis from UDPG plus fructose-6-*P*. Mg^{2+} stimulated the sucrose synthetase reaction and was essential for sucrose-*P* synthetase activity. Both enzymes were present in a single preparation obtained by ammonium sulfate fractionation of clarified aqueous extracts. Sucrose-forming activity was precipitated between 20 and 50 percent saturation. The pea preparation also catalyzed the synthesis of D-glucosyl D-xyluloside from UDPG plus D-xylulose, and of D-glucosyl D-rhamnuloside from UDPG plus D-rhamnulose.

In 1959 Nakamura (1071) described a sucrose synthetase obtained from soybean and broad bean. It was reported that the same enzyme reacted with both free fructose and fructose-6-*P*, although, as already noted, other workers were supporting the view that a second enzyme, sucrose-*P* synthetase, catalyzes the fructose-6-*P* reaction with UDPG. Optimum pH for sucrose synthetase was between 7.4 and 7.8 in Tris buffer. Mg^{2+} stimulated sucrose synthesis about 10-fold. The K_m values for UDPG and fructose were 0.73×10^{-3} M and 1.15×10^{-3} M, respectively. It was further noted that the reaction rate for sucrose-*P* synthesis, from UDPG plus fructose-6-*P*, was much lower than for sucrose formation. A regeneration of UDPG from UDP plus glucose-1-*P* was demonstrated in the presence of ATP. Taken together, these findings were consistent with a growing body of opinion holding that distinct sucrose synthetase and sucrose-*P* synthetase enzymes were operative in plant tissues, and that the regeneration of glycosyl donor involved phosphorylation reactions incident to conventional glycolytic processes.

C. *Purification of sucrose-P synthetase from wheat germ and spinach*

During the initial studies by Leloir and Cardini (920) of sucrose 6-phosphate synthesis by wheat germ extracts, the responsible enzyme, sucrose-*P* synthetase, was purified approximately 5- to 10-fold. Sucrose synthetase and phosphatases hydrolyzing both sucrose-*P* and fructose-6-*P* were retained in the preparations. In 1960 Mendicino (1011) extracted sucrose-*P* synthetase from wheat germ and achieved a 220-fold purification. The new preparation was essentially free of sucrose synthetase, acid phosphatases, and invertase. It was thus conclusively established that different enzymes perform the synthesis of free sucrose and sucrose-*P*. Mendicino also obtained a partially-purified sucrose-*P* synthetase from spinach leaves.

The wheat germ synthetase was obtained by prolonged (2 hours) extraction in phosphate buffer (1011). The clarified extract was subjected to repeated fractional precipitation with ammonium sulfate and was dialyzed against distilled water. Precipitate obtained by freezing and thawing the enzyme-containing solution was discarded. The preparation was further fractionated with a protamine sulfate solution at pH 7.4. Extensive washing of the fractions was possible since the enzyme–protamine complex was not water soluble. The precipitate carrying sucrose-*P* synthetase was then redissolved in Tris buffer, pH 7.0, and dialyzed against 0.001 M Tris buffer for 1 hour.

Sucrose-*P* synthetase retained viability for 2 months at $-10\ ^\circ$C. Reaction digests with the purified enzyme failed to produce orthophosphate from fructose-6-*P*, glucose-6-*P*, UDPG, UDP, or sucrose-6-*P*. Neither sucrose nor sucrose-6-*P* was hydrolyzed by the enzyme, nor was sucrose or sucrose-*P* produced when free fructose or fructose-1-*P* was substituted for fructose-6-*P*. The apparent Michaelis–Menten constant for UDPG was 7.4×10^{-3} M. Although the initial reaction rate increased with increasing supply of fructose-6-*P*, high concentrations of the reactant eventually inhibited sucrose-*P* synthesis. High UDP levels were also inhibitory. The apparent K_m for fructose-6-*P* was 3.0×10^{-3} M. The apparent equilibrium constant for the reaction was 53 at pH 5.5 and 3250 at pH 7.5.

The isolation of sucrose-*P* synthetase from spinach was of particular interest because earlier workers had failed to detect it in leaf tissues following its initial discovery in seeds[2]. In 1953 Buchanan (256) had suggested that sucrose-1-*P* might be formed from UDPG and fructose-1-*P* after he had discovered a sucrose phosphate in sugar beet leaves. However, Mendicino was unable to obtain a sucrose phosphate ester from UDPG and fructose-1-*P* with the spinach enzyme preparation, the latter producing both sucrose and sucrose-6-*P* with fructose-6-*P*.

Mendicino (1011) also appears to have been the first to describe a specific sucrose-6-*P* phosphatase in plant tissues. The enzyme, obtained from wheat germ, dephosphorylated sucrose-6-*P* and fructose-6-*P*. Its reaction rate was about 2.5 times greater against sucrose-6-*P*. A specific sucrose-6-*P* phosphatase has been isolated by Hawker and Hatch (703) from sugarcane.

Earlier investigators of the wheat germ mechanisms could not state with certainty

---

[2]At about the time that Mendicino's paper appeared [1960], Rorem *et al.* (1253) reported the isolation of both sucrose synthetase and sucrose-*P* synthetase from sugar beet leaf tissue. Efforts to obtain invertase-free preparations of the enzymes failed. These investigators were apparently not aware of Mendicino's work with spinach leaves.

whether one enzyme or the other produced sucrose, or whether both operated jointly toward this end. The purification of sucrose-*P* synthetase and the discovery of a complementary phosphatase would have established the predominance of the sucrose phosphate mechanism if no other sucrose-forming enzyme had been found. However, sucrose synthetase was also obtained from wheat germ extracts. Mendicino observed that only sucrose-*P* synthetase was precipitated by treatment with protamine, and sucrose synthetase remained in the supernatant fluid. The latter enzyme was purified by ammonium sulfate precipitation and by prolonged dialysis against Tris buffer. Although this enzyme was still accompanied by wheat germ phosphatases, its sucrose-forming activity remained consistently at about half of that obtained with sucrose-*P* synthetase.

D. *Sucrose synthetase and sucrose-P synthetase of potato tubers*

In 1968 Slabnik *et al.* (1339) isolated both of the sucrose-forming enzymes from potato tubers and purified them sufficiently to examine their properties. Purification procedure included repeated fractional precipitation with ammonium sulfate followed by dialysis against Tris–HCl buffer containing EDTA and mercaptoethanol. Most of the sucrose-*P* forming activity was obtained in the 0 to 30 percent fraction and sucrose synthetase was obtained in the 30 to 40 percent fraction. The enzymes were further purified by elution through a DEAE-cellulose column with Tris–HCl buffer.

The sucrose-forming enzymes from potato showed important property differences which were interpreted as possible indicators of distinct physiological roles. Both enzymes, but especially sucrose synthetase, were active over a broad pH range. Sucrose synthetase was resistant to high temperature but was inhibited by a number of phenolic glycosides. These did not inhibit sucrose-*P* synthetase. Mg^{2+} increased

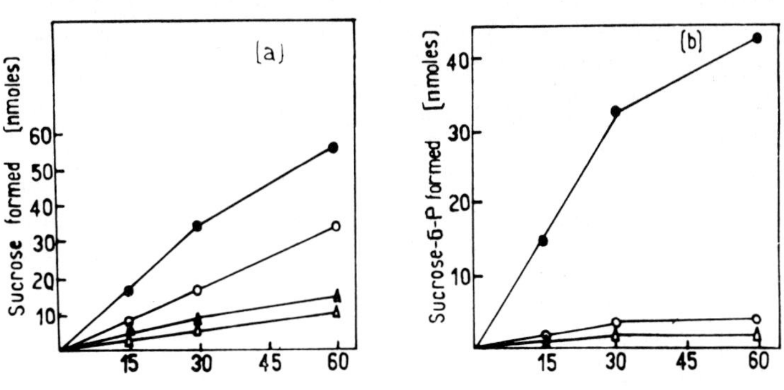

Fig. 6-6. Time course for the synthesis of sucrose and sucrose 6-phosphate from different sugar nucleotides of equal concentration. (●) UDPG; (○) ADPG; (▲) TDPG; (△) GDPG. [After Slabnik *et al.* (1339).] Reproduced by permission of *Plant Physiology*.

sucrose synthetase activity. The inhibition of this enzyme by mercuribenzoate was taken as evidence of a sulfhydryl structure; however, the potato enzyme was less sensitive to this reagent than a sucrose synthetase isolated by Slack (1341) from sugarcane stem tissue.

Slabnick *et al.* (1339) attached strong significance to the fact that the two potato synthetases showed different specificities for their glucosyl donor (Fig. 6-6). Whereas sucrose-*P* synthetase reacted only with UDPG, sucrose synthetase used other sugar nucleotides as donors, particularly ADPG. Moreover, ADP inhibited competitively the sucrose synthetase reaction while having no effect on sucrose-*P* synthetase. From these observations it was proposed that "...the role of sucrose synthetase could be a bridge between sucrose and starch formation, whereas the role of sucrose-6-*P* synthetase would be the synthesis of this disaccharide". Noting that sucrose-*P* is excluded from the sucrose–starch interconversion (428, 1023; *cf.* Chapter 5, p. 201), Slabnick *et al.* further proposed that the common inhibition of sucrose synthetase and starch synthetase, utilizing UDPG or ADPG, supports a relationship between sucrose and starch biosynthesis. Thus the main role of sucrose-*P* synthetase was depicted as sucrose formation while its counterpart's role was assigned to the area of sucrose–starch interconversion.

Recent studies by Pressey (1183, 1184) with potato sucrose synthetase and sucrose-*P* synthetase concurred with the thesis of specialized functions for each of the two sucrose biosynthesis systems. Sucrose synthetase was found to be more active in sucrose cleavage than in sucrose synthesis, whereas sucrose-*P* synthetase was active solely in sucrose synthesis. Each system, but especially sucrose-*P* synthetase, increased in cold storage and was sensitive to storage temperature. Warm temperatures suppressed the enzyme levels in stored tubers. Although varietal differences were noted, between *Kennebec* and *Norchy*'s tubers, sucrose-*P* synthetase tended to be much more abundant than sucrose synthetase in all stored potatoes.

E. *Localization studies of sucrose-forming enzymes*

In 1965 Bird *et al.* (184) published the results of intracellular localization studies relating to the sites of sucrose-forming activity. Chloroplasts were prepared in a non-aqueous medium from expanding *Nicotiana tabacum* leaves. Both sucrose synthetase and sucrose-*P* synthetase were active in the chloroplasts. Additional relevant enzymes included UDPG pyrophosphorylase, phosphoglucomutase, glucose-6-*P* isomerase, and sucrose-6-*P* phosphatase. It was found that sucrose-*P* synthetase was more active than sucrose synthetase. In view of the tissue source, this is tacit support for the contention that sucrose-*P* synthetase is primarily concerned with sucrose formation while sucrose synthetase is more closely related to starch synthesis (1339, 428). Evidence was also obtained indicating that sucrose synthetase and sucrose-*P* synthetase were present in the cell cytoplasm as well as chloroplasts. UDPG pyrophosphorylase was confined to the chloroplasts.

A totally different type of localization study was recently reported by Nomura *et al.* (1121) working with germinating rice seeds. Following up a prior study of induced α-amylase in germinating rice seeds, the authors found that reserve endosperm starch is converted to glucose via induced amylase and maltase, and that glucose is transported to the scutellum where it is converted to sucrose. Maltase achieved its highest activity within 4 days after sowing the rice seed and began to decline at about the 10th day. The developmental pattern for maltase closely paralleled that of α-amylase. Glucose was therefore the major soluble sugar constituent of the endosperm during the later germination stages even though sucrose had constituted the major sugar in the pre-germination period.

It was felt that sucrose must be the transient form to embryonic tissues, but little evidence of sucrose synthetase was found in the endosperm. A subsequent search revealed highly active sucrose-forming systems in the scutellum[3]. The apparent

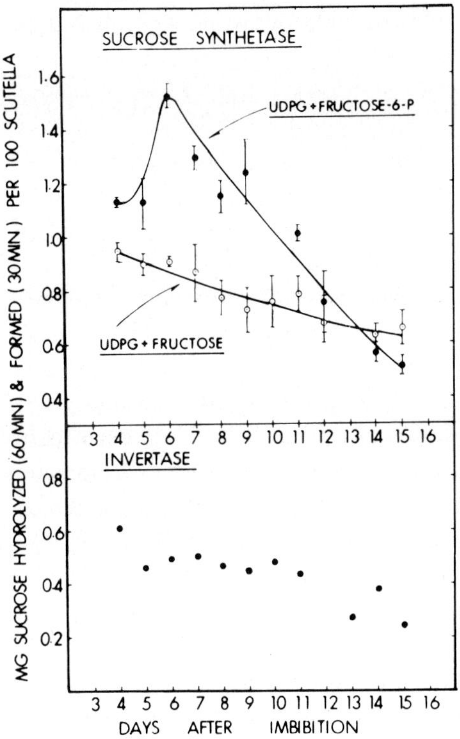

Fig. 6-7. Sucrose synthetase and invertase activity in extracts of germinating rice seed scutella. [After Nomura *et al.* (1121).] Reproduced by permission of *Plant Physiology.*

---

[3]Cardini and Recondo (305) reported that the scutellum and endosperm of sweet corn contained comparable sucrose synthetase activity.

sucrose-forming activity shown by scutellum extracts closely paralleled the rate of sucrose movement from scutellum to embryo tissues. Moreover, by using both fructose-6-*P* and free fructose in the reaction digests, it was shown that sucrose-*P* formation predominated early in the germination period, whereas sucrose synthetase, the catalyst hypothetically related to starch formation, declined gradually throughout the germination period (Fig. 6-7). Significantly, simultaneous invertase measurements of scutellum invertase indicated no particular increase in sucrose-hydrolyzing potential during the germination period (Fig. 6-7). These results were consistent with the findings of Edelman *et al.* (472) with sucrose-forming enzymes in the scutellum of germinating wheat and barley seeds. Nomura and his colleagues concluded that glucose is derived from the endosperm by amylotic breakdown and is "mobilized" in the scutellum where it is resynthesized to sucrose. Sucrose would then be translocated to the embryonic tissues for utilization in metabolic processes. There were a number of inconclusive points in this work but it does underscore the concept of multiple sucrose-forming reactions responding to physiological needs in spatially-distinct source-to-sink regions.

6. THE SUCROSE–STARCH INTERCONVERSION

A. *Historical*

The problem of diurnal starch accumulation in sugarcane leaves and its subsequent (nocturnal) conversion to sucrose, and hence to a transportable form, has been brought out and discussed in terms of temporary polysaccharide synthesis and storage (*cf.* Chapter 5, pp. 198–202). The effects of foliar polysaccharides on the rate of photosynthesis have also been discussed. However, regardless of whether polysaccharides originate in leaf or storage tissues, or whether they are fully-elaborated starches or polysaccharides of lesser complexity, the plant mechanisms for accomplishing their conversion to soluble sugars will need to be understood before sucrose physiology itself can be fully understood. In recent years a growing body of evidence has begun to implicate in sucrose–starch interconversion the enzymes responsible for catalyzing sucrose synthesis.

In 1949 Hehre (708) reported a bacterial enzyme, "amylosucrase", which catalyzed the synthesis of amylopectin- or glycogen-like polysaccharides from sucrose. Obtained from the bacterium *Neisseria perflava*, the enzyme attracted interest as an apparent link between sucrose and starch in the plant kingdom, and because it did not require mediation by glucose-1-*P*. In 1951 Hehre (709) published a review article in which enzymes catalyzing dextrin and levan synthesis from sucrose ("dextransucrase" and "levansucrase") were described, along with amylosucrase and amylomaltase systems which produce polysaccharides from sucrose, maltose, and "cycloamylose". The mechanism of levansucrase action was subsequently described in detail by Hestrin *et al.* (724) in 1956. A levansucrase preparation from *Aerobacter levanicum* was shown to produce a branched polysaccharide group linked to the anomeric carbon of an aldose. Proof of the branched structure was obtained by methylation and infrared analyses.

Ewart *et al.* (516), summarizing the enzymic mechanisms of starch–sucrose interconversion as they were understood in 1953, depicted dextransucrase and levansucrase as catalyzing irreversible reactions in the sucrose conversion to dextran and levan, respectively. Amylosucrase was shown mediating an irreversible production of amylose from sucrose. Both sucrose and amylose were believed to be synthesized from a common glucose-1-*P* pool by the appropriate phosphorylase system.

Physiologists have been intrigued for years with the fact that polysaccharides are reversibly converted to simpler sugars in certain storage organs such as the potato tuber and numerous seeds. As early as 1882 Müller-Thurgau (1059) observed that potato tubers stored at low temperatures, between 0 and 6 °C, lost starch and accumulated sugars. This phenomenon has been studied by various workers to the present time. Arreguin-Lozano and Bonner (110), choosing an enzyme aproach to examine the mechanism, compared the activities of starch phosphorylase, sucrose phosphorylase, phosphatase, and β-amylase in potato tubers stored in the cold and at room temperature. It was found that tubers stored above 10 °C retained their starch, but those stored between 10 and 0 °C experienced a rapid loss of starch with a parallel rise of sucrose. Significantly, the sucrose–starch changes appeared to be mediated by changes in glucose-6-*P* which increased tremendously between 9 and 16 °C. At low temperatures (9 °C and 0 °C) fructose-6-*P* increased markedly. No changes in the starch phosphorylase level were produced by variable temperature, but at high temperature an inhibitor of the enzyme was produced. Both sucrose phosphorylase and phosphohexose isomerase were sensitive to the temperature changes. Although this work remained inconclusive, Arreguin-Lozano and Bonner suggested that the low-temperature breakdown of starch was induced by a loss of the phosphorylase inhibitor, and by an increased activity of related enzymes which utilize glucose-6-*P*. With the discovery of the UDPG-utilizing synthetases considerably more insight was soon to be gained relative to sucrose–starch interconversion.

B. *Relationship of sucrose synthetase to starch formation*

The possibility that sucrose metabolism is related to starch synthesis has long been implied by physiological experiments, but it was not until the discovery of UDPG as a common substrate for both sucrose- and starch-forming reactions that an enzymatic explanation began to emerge (303, 920, 427, 924). De Fekete and Cardini (428), in 1964, drew attention to the fact that, in spite of similar substrate requirements, certain differences between the sucrose and starch synthetase mechanisms offered clues to the means by which starch and sucrose are interconverted. These differences included a preference of starch synthetase for ADPG rather than for UDPG (1222), and the inhibition by ADPG and other adenine nucleotides of glucose transfer from UDPG to starch (1222, 542). Moreover, ADP has been shown to inhibit competitively sucrose synthetase while having no effect on sucrose-*P* synthetase (1339), while UDPG appears to be the natural substrate for sucrose synthesis by both enzymes (305).

These and other consideration led De Fekete and Cardini (428) to propose that ADPG may act as a substrate for starch synthesis while UDPG is a substrate for sucrose synthesis. A series of experiments were performed with sweet corn endosperm preparations in an effort to demonstrate an interrelationship of the active nucleotides. These experiments were based on the hypothesis that the process would initiate via an inversion of the sucrose synthetase reaction and proceed to a measurable sucrose-to-starch transformation. It was shown that endosperm preparations containing the total protein plus starch granules catalyzed ^{14}C transfer from sucrose to the starch granule. ADP or UDP was required, with ADP being more effective than UDP. A similar transfer did not occur from labeled glucose-1-*P* to starch unless Mg^{2+} and ATP were present. In addition, the K_m values for UDPG–fructose transglycosylase with ADP, UDP, ADPG, and UDPG were estimated and their reciprocal inhibitions measured. On the basis of these results De Fekete and Cardini proposed two reaction sequences to account for glucose transfer to the starch granule:

$$\text{Sucrose} \rightleftharpoons \text{ADPG (or UDPG)} \longrightarrow \text{starch} \tag{12}$$

$$\text{Sucrose} \rightleftharpoons \text{UDPG} \rightleftharpoons \text{glucose-1-}P \rightleftharpoons \text{ADPG} \longrightarrow \text{starch} \tag{13}$$

Enzymes essential for each of the reactions were found in the corn endosperm preparations.

C. *Potato tuber sucrose synthetase: Temperature, varietal, and maturation effects*

In 1960 Schwimmer and Rorem (1311) established the presence of sucrose synthetase and sucrose-*P* synthetase in the potato tuber and explored the possibility that sucrose accumulation at low temperature was related to a synthetase-induction mechanism. Peeled tubers were stored for 21 days at 25 °C or 2 °C. Partially-purified enzyme was obtained by fractional precipitation of clarified crude extracts followed by dialysis against cold distilled water. Precipitate obtained during dialysis was removed with the centrifuge and suspended in water. The potato preparation formed sucrose or sucrose-*P* when either fructose or fructose-6-*P* was added to a buffered reaction mixture containing enzyme and UDPG. The possibility of phosphatase action against sucrose-*P* was not discounted. Invertase was present in the preparation.

No appreciable differences were found in sucrose-forming activity by the two enzymes preparations. Protein from tubers stored at 2 °C, in which sucrose accumulates, and from tubers stored at 25 °C, in which sucrose does not accumulate, produced essentially comparable amounts of sucrose. The apparent optimum pH was identical for both preparations and each contained similar amounts of invertase. However, experiments with a second variety (*White Rose*) having low storage quality showed that the latter formed sucrose at rates 3 to 4 times greater than the tuber with high storage quality (*Washington Russet*). The authors concluded that low-temperature induction of sucrose synthetase was not a factor in low-temperature sucrose accumulation. It was suggested that varieties which tend to accumulate greater amounts of sucrose contain more sucrose-forming enzyme as a varietal feature.

The findings of Schwimmer and Rorem were substantiated by Lavintman and Cardini (906) working with aging potato tuber slices. These authors found no evidence of variable sucrose synthetase or sucrose-*P* synthetase activities in tubers stored at low temperature. Observed increases in sucrose synthetase in aged tubers were attributed to an activation of pre-existing enzyme. This conclusion was based on the failure of protein synthesis inhibitors (actinomycin D and chloramphenicol) to lower sucrose synthetase levels, even though they prevented a *de novo* synthesis of proteins induced by treatment with 2,4-dinitrophenol.

In 1968 Slabnik *et al.* (1339) reported that potato sucrose synthetase supports only a low rate of sucrose cleavage. This observation cast some doubt on the involvement of sucrose synthetase in a sucrose–starch interconversion of the type proposed for Jerusalem artichoke (119), sweet corn (428), and rice grains (1066). This was a particularly important observation owing to the prominence of the potato tuber as a source of starch and the longstanding recognition that sucrose–starch interconversions do occur in potato by one means or another (1311, 110).

However, Pressey (1183) published in 1969 findings with a highly-purified potato sucrose synthetase which showed that, at physiological pH, sucrose cleavage could be expected to occur more rapidly than sucrose synthesis. An unusual feature of the enzyme was a large discrepancy in pH optima for the sucrose synthesis and cleavage reactions. The two reactions further differed in their response to mercaptoethanol and Mn^{2+}. Sucrose cleavage was increased by mercaptoethanol but was inhibited by Mn^{2+}, while synthesis was increased markedly by a combination of the two additives. Individually, Mn^{2+} or mercaptoethanol gave a small stimulation of the sucrose-forming reaction. Pressey regarded these findings as consistent with the view that sucrose synthesis and cleavage involve more complex events than simple reversal of the sucrose synthetase equilibrium (1339). Nonetheless, Pressey was unable to resolve distinct sucrose synthesis and cleavage reactions. He concluded that a single enzyme was responsible for both activities and cited as supporting evidence the consistency of reaction ratios over a wide range of sucrose synthetase activity. In addition, both reactions were shown to have identical stabilities with respect to pH and temperature.

Pressey (1183) explained the high sucrose accumulations in immature or early-harvest potatoes in terms of a temporary storage form awaiting conversion to starch. It was suggested that, as a primary transport form, sucrose movement to the tuber might exceed the rate of conversion to starch, as depicted by Burton (279). He also suggested a temporary storage of sucrose regardless of translocation, as Shannon (1319) had proposed for the developing corn kernel. To initiate the ultimate conversion of sucrose to starch, Pressey considered both invertase and sucrose synthetase to be suitable catalysts, but he discounted invertase by virtue of his findings of an endogenous invertase inhibitor in developing tubers (1180, 1181). Pressey substantiated the endogenous invertase inhibitor concept in recent studies demonstrating a similar substance in red beet, sugar beet, and sweet potato roots (1182). He favored sucrose synthetase in this important role owing to high synthetase activity in developing tubers, and to the fact that at physiological pH the reaction equilibrium favors sucrose cleavage rather than synthesis. Pressey's conclusion that sucrose synthetase is a major factor in potato tuber development, which in simplest terms amounts to starch accumulation, places the cleavage role in a perspective consistent with that taken by De Fekete and Cardini (428) with sweet corn, and by Murata *et al.* (1066) with rice.

A somewhat different interpretation of the temperature effect on sucrose synthesis in potato tubers was forwarded by Tishel and Mazelis (1441) in 1966. Data were presented which suggested marked changes among enzymes indirectly involved in sucrose formation, while leaving open the question of direct temperature effects on sucrose synthetase and sucrose-*P* synthetase.

Clarified homogenates from freshly-harvested tubers (var. *White Rose*) were assayed for glucose-6-*P* dehydrogenase, aldolase, invertase and phosphohexose isomerase, either before or after dialysis (1441). Tissue samples were taken from whole tubers and halved tubers stored at 2 °C or at room temperature. A technique was perfected whereby halves of the same tuber, which ordinarily behave as whole tubers, were compared under two storage regimes. It was found that within 4 days sucrose accumulated in potato halves stored at low temperature. This was followed by reducing sugar increases. The authors were unable to explain the sugar changes in terms of lowered respiration rates at low temperatures. It was suggested that the 2 °C treatment induced a series of events in the order of decreased aldolase, increased sucrose, increased invertase, increased reducing sugars, and finally decreased phosphohexose isomerase. In this scheme invertase would account for the appearance of reducing sugars after sucrose; presumably the initial sucrose rise reflected increased synthetase activity paralleled by a low capability to invert the sucrose. Tishel and Mazelis suggested that an aldolase decline induced by low temperature might trigger the sucrose-forming mechanism. This view is at least consistent with that of Slabnik *et al.* (1339) who maintained that sucrose cleavage, even by the same enzyme that forms sucrose, involves more than a simple shift in the reaction equilibrium.

Invertase and phosphohexose isomerase changes in response to low temperature were clearly demonstrated by the work of Tishel and Mazelis (1441). This alone casts doubt on the premise of sucrose–starch interconversions being only a matter of varietal and maturity factors. Relevant to this was the observation of sucrose and invertase increases closely paralleling one another. In whole tubers this relationship was established by the 7th day; in halved tubers low temperature hastened the sucrose accumulation by several days, an event accompanied by equally earlier invertase changes. The inference here is that sucrose induced the synthesis of invertase.

7. SUCROSE SYNTHESIS IN SUGARCANE LEAVES

A. *Historical*

As noted earlier in this chapter, the first enzyme known definitely to catalyze sucrose synthesis was discovered by Doudoroff *et al.* (439) in the bacterium *Pseudomonas saccharophila.* Given the name sucrose phosphorylase, the enzyme catalyzed a reaction in which the glucose from glucose-1-*P* was transferred to D-fructose:

$$\text{Glucose-1-}P + \text{D-fructose} \rightleftharpoons \text{sucrose} + \text{inorganic phosphate} \tag{14}$$

In 1953 Buchanan *et al.* (255) concluded from the results of $^{14}CO_2$ photosynthesis experiments that UDPG is an immediate precursor of sucrose in green plants. Shortly thereafter, Leloir and his co-workers (303, 920), Bean and Hassid (160), and others (264, 1011) demonstrated the presence of two enzymes in extracts from wheat germ, peas, sugar beet and other plants which catalyze sucrose formation by reactions utilizing UDPG as the glucosyl donor. For simplicity these enzymes have been depicted herein as "sucrose synthetase" and "sucrose-*P* synthetase", after reactions employing free fructose or fructose-6-*P*, respectively, as the glucosyl acceptors.

Numerous attempts have been made to discover sucrose phosphorylase in tissues of green plants. These have generally met with failure. Pandya and Ramakrishnan (1214, 1137), and Skukla and Prabhu (1337) claim to have found a sucrose phosphorylase in sugarcane which catalyzes a sucrose-forming reaction identical to that of the *P. saccharophila* enzyme. According to Skukla and Prabhu, the principle difference between the sugarcane phosphorylase and the bacterial phosphorylase is that the equilibrium constant for the former is 5.6, whereas the latter has a value of 0.058. The high value of K for the sugarcane enzyme is itself suggestive of a more complicated reaction. The purest forms of sucrose phosphorylase known tend to favor a breakdown rather than synthesis of sucrose. Skukla and Prabhu also noted a trisaccharide among the reaction products which co-chromatographed with raffinose.

Turner (1459), in 1953, also reported the synthesis of sucrose from glucose-1-*P* plus fructose, using pea preparations to which yeast extracts had been added. However, he was at once aware of complications and concluded that glycolytic and phosphorylative reactions indirectly related to sucrose formation were taking place. Turner (1461) later reported that sucrose was synthesized from UDPG plus fructose in accordance with the reaction described by Cardini *et al.* (303). He attributed the sucrose obtained in earlier experiments to the presence of UDPG in the supplemental yeast extracts.

Alexander (12), in 1964, reported sucrose-forming activity with sugarcane leaf homogenates and undialyzed crude extracts, but less than 3 percent of this activity was obtained with partially-purified protein solutions. Sucrose was readily formed from glucose-1-*P* and fructose (Table 6-1) and it was at first presumed that a sucrose

TABLE 6-1

SUCROSE SYNTHESIS BY SUGARCANE LEAF EXTRACTS WITH GLUCOSE 1-PHOSPHATE, FRUCTOSE, AND VARIOUS ADDITIVES

Quantities added (μmoles/ml): Glucose-1-*P* and fructose, 10 each; for Mg, ATP, cysteine–NAD, NAD, UTP, UMP, and UDPG, 2.5 each. The standard reaction proceeded for 4 hours at 30 °C in Tris buffer, pH 7.5. [After Alexander (12).]

Treatment	Sucrose formed (μmoles/ml)
Leaf extract	0
Leaf extract + glucose-1-*P* + fructose	0.78
+ fructose + Mg	0.93
+ ATP	0.93
+ Mg, ATP	1.04
+ cysteine–NAD	0.86
+ UDPG	1.04
+ UMP	0.86
+ UTP	1.14
+ ATP, cysteine–NAD	1.07
+ ATP, UMP	1.53
+ ATP, UTP	1.12
+ ATP, UDPG, cysteine–NAD	1.29
+ ATP, UTP, cysteine–NAD	0.78

phosphorylase reaction was responsible. However, stimulation of the reaction with UTP, or UMP added with ATP, was taken as evidence of a UDPG-forming mechanism and hence of a contribution by UDPG–fructose transglycosylase toward the net sucrose yield. The presence of an essential cofactor was implied by the rapid loss of activity upon dialysis against phosphate buffer or distilled water. Part of the activity was returned by adding UTP, UDPG, and cysteine–NAD to the dialyzed preparation. Boron was also effective in returning part of the activity lost via dialysis. The latter observation is consistent with the work of Dugger and Humphreys (450) showing a boron role in governing the activity of enzymes indirectly related to sucrose formation. Flavin adenine dinucleotide (FAD) was still more effective in reactivating the dialyzed preparations and from this it was suggested that a flavoprotein having a specific requirement for NAD might be involved in reactions related to sucrose synthesis.

These findings were interpreted to mean that both phosphorylase and UDPG–fructose transglycosylase reactions were operative in sucrose formation and that the net sucrose yield was governed in part by glycolytic reactions affecting the levels of endogenous sucrose precursors. In subsequent years, however, the possibility of a sucrose phosphorylase being active in sugarcane leaves has been all but abandoned.

Alexander also recorded a pH optimum of 8.0, although sucrose was readily formed between pH 7.0 and 9.0. Distribution experiments revealed the greatest activity in apical meristem tissues. Homogenates from older leaves ($^+6$ and $^+7$) and sheaths were only slightly active. Preparations from $^+8$ to $^+10$ node and internode tissues were about comparable in activity to young leaves ($^+1$ and $^+2$).

B. *Discovery of sucrose synthetase in sugarcane*

In 1963 Frydman and Hassid (541) reported the discovery of UDPG–fructose transglycosylase (sucrose synthetase) in sugarcane leaf extracts. It was at first believed that this was the only sucrose-forming enzyme operative since the replacement of fructose with fructose-6-*P* terminated all sucrose-forming activity. However, the use of isolated chloroplasts as enzyme source revealed that both fructose and fructose-6-*P* served as glucosyl acceptors from UDPG. Frydman and Hassid were unable to detect sucrose-*P* in the reaction mixtures to which fructose-6-*P* had been added, so they were uncertain as to whether sucrose-*P* had been hydrolyzed after being synthesized, or whether fructose-6-*P* had been hydrolyzed prior to the synthesis of sucrose. Other workers had been confronted with a similar problem with sucrose formed by phosphatase-containing preparations (689).

Haq and Hassid (640) reported in 1965 that both sucrose synthetase and sucrose-*P* synthetase are present in sugarcane leaf chloroplasts. Extracted from homogenized leaves with 0.35 M NaCl solution containing 0.02 M Tris (pH 8.3) and 0.01 M sodium ascorbate, the chloroplasts were suspended in cold distilled water. This preparation catalyzed the synthesis of sucrose from UDPG plus fructose, and from UDPG plus fructose-6-*P*, but no sucrose-*P* was detected in the reaction mixture. However, it was found that if the NaCl chloroplast preparation was extracted with acetone rather than suspended in cold distilled water, the resulting enzyme preparation, free of chlorophyll and fatty materials, produced both sucrose and sucrose-*P* from UDPG plus fructose-6-*P*. Moreover, only sucrose was formed when the acetone-extracted chloroplasts were incubated with UDPG plus fructose. It should be noted that the amount of sucrose-*P* produced was quite small, representing only about 1 percent of the substrate's total radioactivity.

Haq and Hassid had no way of knowing whether the sucrose-*P* obtained represented the maximum productivity of the sugarcane enzyme. It appeared likely at the time that some of the disaccharide was being lost during product isolation. They demonstrated that a phosphatase was present which hydrolyzed sucrose-*P* to a greater extent than fructose-6-*P*. Substrate specificity of the phosphatase could not be determined owing to an insufficiency of sucrose-*P*. The authors did not discount the possibility of a phosphatase specific for sucrose-*P* being present in sugarcane similar to that already discovered by Mendicino (1011) in wheat. In 1966 Hawker and Hatch (703) succeeded in isolating such a phosphatase from sugarcane.

8. SUCROSE SYNTHESIS IN SUGARCANE STORAGE TISSUE

A. *Enzymes of the sugar accumulation cycle*

Hatch *et al.* (689) reported in 1963 that enzymes having direct and indirect bearing on sucrose synthesis had been found in storage tissue preparations from *S. officinarum* and *S. spontaneum* varieties. Prior studies of sugar accumulation mechanisms had shown a need for enzymes catalyzing the synthesis and breakdown of sucrose, the synthesis and breakdown of hexose phosphates, and the interconversion of glucose and fructose. Many of the essential enzymes were identified. Among these were sucrose synthetase, UDPG pyrophosphorylase, acid and neutral invertases, hexokinase, glucose-6-*P* isomerase, and phosphoglucomutase. Some evidence of sucrose-*P* synthetase was also found. Repeated efforts to detect sucrose phosphorylase in leaf and storage tissues were unsuccessful. In most instances the enzymes were precipitated from expressed juice of rind-free internodes, at pH 7.0 and 0 °C, with saturated ammonium sulfate solution. Invertase was also obtained from homogenated cellular debris.

Sucrose synthetase was isolated from the cane storage tissue. In the presence of enzyme preparation and D-fructose, added UDPG was almost quantitatively converted to sucrose when given sufficient incubation time (Table 6-2). A phosphatase was present which readily hydrolyzed UDP to UMP. UTP was slowly hydrolyzed. Under these conditions the reverse synthetase reaction, *i.e.*, UDPG synthesis from [^{14}C]sucrose plus UDP, could not be demonstrated. Optimum pH of the sucrose synthetase reaction was 8.2, as compared with 7.4 for the wheat germ enzyme, and 8.0 for the sucrose-forming reaction in sugarcane leaf homogenates (12). The K_m for fructose was 3×10^{-3} M. The K_m for UDPG was too low to calculate with precision.

When fructose-6-*P* was substituted for fructose in the reaction digest a small quantity of sucrose corresponding to 1 percent of the substrate radioactivity was produced during a 1-hour period. About 3 percent of the labeled fructose-6-*P* was converted to a compound having the properties of sucrose-*P*. The compound cochromotographed with authentic sucrose after treatment with alkaline phosphatase and was hydrolyzed by invertase.

TABLE 6-2

SUCROSE SYNTHESIS FROM UDPG AND FRUCTOSE BY ENZYME PREPARATION FROM SUGARCANE STALK TISSUE

[After Hatch *et al.* (689).] Reproduced by permission of *Plant Physiology*.

Expt. No.	Reaction conditions	Incubation (minutes)	Sucrose formed (μmoles/reaction)
1	Standard reaction	30	0.30
	Standard reaction	60	0.55
	Standard reaction	150	0.72
	Standard reaction minus UDPG	60	0
	but 0.2 μmole UDPG	15	0.14
	but 1.4 μmoles UDPG	30	0.29
	plus 0.025 M pyrophosphate	60	0.03
2	Standard reaction	60	0.23
	Standard reaction plus glucose-1-*P*, UTP, Mg^{2+}	60	0.17
	minus UDPG plus glucose-1-*P*, UTP, Mg^{2+}	60	0.18
	minus UDPG plus glucose-1-*P*, Mg^{2+}	120	0
	minus UDPG plus UTP, Mg^{2+}	120	0.051*

*Calculated on the basis that sucrose was equally labeled in the glucose and fructose moieties.

TABLE 6-3

UDPG-FRUCTOSE TRANSGLYCOSYLASE ACTIVITY IN STALK TISSUE FROM DIFFERENT SUGARCANE TYPES

[After Hatch *et al.* (689).] Reproduced by permission of *Plant Physiology*.

Cane variety*	Maturity	Sucrose formed	
		nmoles/mg protein/h	nmoles/g fresh wt./h
CO 281	Mature	51	53
Badila	Mature	8	24
Chunnee	Mature	27	81
Fiji 28	Mature	28	57
Fiji 10	Mature	20	20
Mandalay	Mature	0	0
NCO 310	Immature	2	26
CO 281	Immature	8	18

**Mandalay* is *Saccharum spontaneum* and *Chunnee* is *S. sinsense.* The remaining varieties are either *S. officinarum* or hybrids.

Hatch *et al.* (689) detected sucrose synthetase activity in preparations from both mature and immature storage tissue of distinct *S. officinarum* varieties and hybrids (Table 6-3). Activity was relatively low on a protein basis in immature storage tissue extracts but was absent only in the *spontaneum* variety *Mandalay.* It was reported that interference in the synthetase reactions by invertase was avoided by performing the assays in Tris–HCl buffer. An inhibitory action by phenol oxidation products in immature storage tissue preparations, as shown later by Slack (1341), was not clearly evident at this time.

Sugarcane storage tissue was found to contain a UDPG pyrophosphorylase similar to the enzyme described in other plants by Neufeld *et al.* (1088), Turner and Turner (1458), and by Dugger and Humphreys (450). This enzyme catalyzed sufficient UDPG synthesis from UTP plus glucose-1-*P* to maintain sucrose synthetase activity in the absence of added UDPG. Mg^{2+} was required for the pyrophosphorylase reaction. Very little sucrose was formed in the absence of Mg^{2+}. An inhibition of sucrose synthetase by pyrophosphate (Table 6-2) was believed to stem from UDPG pyrophosphorylase action on UDPG. When sucrose was synthesized from a mixture of UTP, Mg^{2+}, and [^{14}C]fructose, without added UDPG, the fructose and glucose moieties were equally labeled. Inclusion of glucose-1-*P* in this mixture led to predominant labeling in the fructose moiety. It appeared that in the absence of glucose-1-*P* there was phosphorylation of fructose followed by the conversion of fructose phosphate to glucose-1-*P* via isomerase and phosphoglucomutase reactions.

Substantial evidence was presented by Hatch *et al.* (689) in support of rapid hexose phosphate synthesis and transformation in sugarcane storage tissue. Preparations from mature and immature storage tissues catalyzed the conversion of [^{14}C]fructose to [^{14}C]glucose, and the production of both glucose and fructose from [^{14}C]fructose-6-*P*. When ATP and Mg^{2+} were included in reaction mixtures of [^{14}C]glucose plus [^{14}C]fructose, the label from both sugars appeared in the respective hexose phosphates. Taken together these results clearly indicated the presence of hexokinase, glucose-6-*P* isomerase, and phosphoglucomutase in the sugarcane preparations.

Hawker and Hatch (701), while studying the mechanism of sugar storage in mature joints as compared with immature storage tissue, found that sucrose synthetase is localized essentially in the vascular tissue. They examined parenchyma tissue, conducting tissue which had been carefully sectioned out, and parenchyma-free vascular bundles. Whole tissue and longitudinal tissue sections were also studied. Each type of sample material was washed and extracted in accordance with the rind-free storage tissue method. Virtually all of the sucrose synthetase was found in vascular material, primarily in parenchyma-free conducting tissue. By contrast, all of the neutral invertase and most of the acid invertase was found in parenchyma tissue. It is obvious that crude extracts and less exacting enzyme preparations would have extracted the invertases along with sucrose synthetase, thereby posing important restrictions against interpreting the enzyme data.

In elongating internodes whose parenchyma is extremely delicate and thin-walled it is not possible to remove vascular tissue by dissection. However, Slack (1341) successfully demonstrated that elongating internodes, like mature storage tissue, contain sucrose synthetase predominately in vascular strands. This was shown by differential cell rupture techniques in which parenchyma cells burst more readily under pressure with pestle and mortar than vascular cells. In practice it was found that the "light squash" technique released 65 percent of the tissue's acid invertase and only 7 percent of the sucrose synthetase. When the method was applied to immature tissue the results were less conclusive owing to the fact that cells of both vascular and parenchyma tissues were still fragile.

The precise location and function of sucrose synthetase in sugarcane vascular strands remains unknown. However, noting the absence of UDP phosphatase from the vascular strands, Slack proposed that the enzyme could provide a source of UDPG if situated in the presence of UDP and sucrose. In this context the work of Kursanov was mentioned in which sugar beet vascular strands were found to contain more UDP and UDPG than other tissues. Slack also envisioned a possible connection between sucrose synthetase and UDPG pyrophosphorylase in maintaining the high sucrose levels characteristic of sieve tubes. This point could be of major importance in explaining the mechanisms of sucrose flow along the pathways of sugar transport.

B. *Sucrose synthetase inhibition by phenol oxidation products*

In 1966 Slack (1341) reported that conventional isolation methods had led to serious loss of sucrose synthetase during extraction from sugarcane immature storage tissue. This possibly accounted for the smaller amounts of sucrose synthetase activity obtained by Hatch *et al.* (689) from elongating internodes as compared with mature internodes. Slack examined the inhibition mechanism and developed isolation procedures which minimized enzyme repression.

Slack also observed a rapid browning of macerated immature storage tissue which occurred as a result of a highly-active phenol oxidase system acting upon endogenous phenolic substrates. Alexander (27) reported this reaction in preparations from immature storage tissue and described the responsible enzyme as "polyphenol oxidase" or "tyrosinase". The enzyme is found in leaves to a lesser degree. Slack observed that much more sucrose synthetase activity was obtained when the synthetase was prepared under conditions restrictive to phenol oxidase. This was accomplished by adding cysteine or sodium diethyldithiocarbamate (DIECA) to the extracting medium (0.2 M potassium phosphate buffer saturated with nitrogen).

Slack proposed that sucrose synthetase was inhibited either by intermediate quinones arising from phenol oxidation, or by formation of an inactive enzyme complex with the dark-colored phenol oxidation products. Subsequent experiments were performed in which unpurified enzyme extracts were incubated with phenols, oxidized phenols, or *p*-benzoquinone (Table 6-4). The results were suggestive of enzyme inhibition by intermediate quinones rather than by the final (polymerized) products. This interpretation was supported by the fact that the strong synthetase inhibition produced by catechol and endogenous phenolic extracts was lessened if the phenolic

TABLE 6-4

INHIBITION OF SUCROSE SYNTHETASE FROM SUGARCANE STORAGE TISSUE BY PREINCUBATION OF EXTRACTS WITH PHENOLS AND *p*-BENZOQUINONE

[After Slack (1341).] Reproduced by permission of *Phytochemistry*, Pergamon Press, Oxford.

Preincubation solutions	Inhibition (%)
Phenol extract from 25 mg fresh tissue	98
Phenol extract from 25 mg fresh tissue with 5 mM DIECA	10
Phenol extract from 0.1 mg fresh tissue	72
Oxidized phenol extract from 50 mg fresh tissue	70
Oxidized phenol extract from 50 mg fresh tissue with 5 mM DIECA	3
Catechol, 100 mM	100
Catechol, 1 mM	94
Cathechol, 1 mM containing 0.005 M DIECA	10
p-Benzoquinone, 1 mM	96
p-Benzoquinone, 0.1 mM	72

TABLE 6-5

EFFECT OF THIOL INHIBITORS ON SUCROSE SYNTHETASE FROM SUGARCANE STORAGE TISSUE

[After Slack (1341).] Reproduced by permission of *Phytochemistry*, Pergamon Press, Oxford.

Expt. No.	Reagent added		Inhibition (%)
1	*p*-Chloromercuribenzoate	100 μM	93
		25 μM	63
	$HgCl_2$	50 μM	94
		10 μM	21
	$CuSO_4$	200 μM	65
		20 μM	5
2	*p*-Chloromercuribenzoate	10 μM	100
		1 μM	89
		1 μM + 1 mM cysteine	10
		1 μM + 0.1 mM 2-mercaptoethanol	12
		1 μM + 0.1 mM 2,3-dimercaptopropanol	0
		0.1 μM	0

compounds were oxidized prior to mixing with enzyme. Moreover, there was little phenolic inhibition in the presence of DIECA, and inhibitory action could be obtained with *p*-benzoquinone, a compound which produced no browning reaction.

Exploring the proposition that quinones inhibited sucrose synthetase, Slack added 2-mercaptoethanol to a sucrose synthetase preparation inhibited with *p*-benzoquinone. A partial reversal of the inhibition by 2-mercaptoethanol strongly supported Slack's contention that the inhibitor operated via oxidation of sulfhydryl groups on the enzyme. The possibility of new configurations developing between enzyme sulfhydryl groups and the quinone was also forwarded.

Further inhibition studies showed that sucrose synthetase was suppressed by thio inhibitors via thio-reversible mechanisms (Table 6-5). Of the two experiments summarized in Table 6-5, the first involved a spectrophotometric assay of sucrose synthetase with large excesses of yeast hexokinase, phosphohexose isomerase, and glucose-6-*P* dehydrogenase. Although yeast hexokinase is known to be inhibited by *p*-chloromercuribenzoate (131), Slack showed that this could not explain the sucrose synthetase inhibition since *p*-chloromercuribenzoate did not affect the rate of $NADP^+$ reduction upon addition of fructose to the reaction mixture.

C. *The synthesis and role of sucrose phosphate*

In 1964 Hatch (691) reported the isolation of enzymes catalyzing the synthesis and breakdown of sucrose-*P* in sugarcane leaf and stem tissues. Sucrose-*P* synthetase (UDPG–fructose-6-*P* transglycosylase) was extracted from frozen, homogenized tissues with potassium phosphate buffer at pH 8.0. The clarified extract was treated with solid ammonium sulfate to obtain sucrose-*P* synthetase between 40 and 50 percent saturation. Alkaline phosphatase was also present in this preparation. Other phosphatases were present which hydrolyzed sucrose-*P* even though at this time a specific sucrose-*P* phosphatase had not yet been described in sugarcane. Experiments were also performed with storage tissue slices.

The synthesis of sucrose-*P* was attended by some difficulty which was attributed in part to interfering enzymes. With both leaf and storage tissue preparations the rate of sucrose-*P* formation declined rapidly with time. Nonsaturating substrate levels were used so it might have been possible for enzymes depleting the fructose-6-*P* level (phosphatases and phosphohexose isomerase) to lower the rate of sucrose-*P* formation. The hydrolysis of sucrose-*P* to free sucrose and subsequent inversion of sucrose were also taken as contributing factors. These also probably account for the failure by Frydman and Hassid (541) to detect sucrose-*P* formation by sugarcane leaf extracts.

Studies with ^{14}C-labeled sugars and sugar phosphates incorporated into storage tissue slices led Hatch to conclude that the synthesis of sucrose-*P* plays a significant role in sugar accumulation by cane storage tissue. Essential features of the accumulation processes are summarized in Fig. 6-8. In accordance with this scheme, Hatch

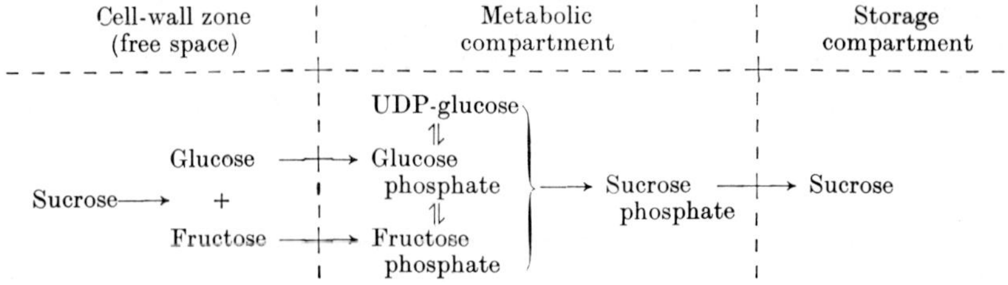

Fig. 6-8. The sugar accumulation process in sugarcane storage tissue illustrating the role of sucrose phosphate. [After Hatch (691).] Reproduced by permission of the *Biochemical Journal.*

proposed that sucrose-*P* should accumulate at least as readily as sucrose barring restriction of movement into the metabolic compartment. However, less inward movement was detected for sucrose-*P* than for sucrose. A restriction related to the presence of a phosphate group on the fructose moiety was strongly implied by the fact that free fructose was incorporated into the cells far more readily than was fructose-6-*P*.

Hatch also pointed out that sucrose might be stored via sucrose-*P* without the mediation of invertase, and that some plant tissues (tobacco leaf, sugar beet root, artichoke tuber) do store sucrose in the absence of abundant invertase. The possibility of direct sucrose phosphorylation seemed doubtful owing to the absence of a requisite sucrose kinase. Another pathway would involve the cleavage of sucrose by synthetase, followed by phosphorylation of the fructose moiety prior to synthesis of sucrose-*P*. This was taken by Hatch as the more probable mechanism by virtue of the presence of essential enzymes and a sucrose synthetase equilibrium constant favorable to sucrose cleavage. Nonetheless, the extent of sucrose accumulation by this means remained in doubt. Three factors weighing against an extensive accumulation of sucrose via sucrose-*P* include: (a) An active involvement of free-space invertase; (b) localization of sucrose synthetase in vascular tissue; and (c) a UDP phosphatase is known which, if appropriately situated in the cell, would prevent sucrose cleavage by sucrose synthetase.

PART II

SUGAR TRANSLOCATION AND STORAGE

Chapter 7

Paths of Sucrose Transport

1. INTRODUCTION

Thanks to the studies by Hartt, Burr, Kortschak and their co-workers with radioactive photosynthate, the pathways of sucrose movement are understood perhaps better than any other aspect of sugarcane physiology. This does not imply that the partial processes of sugar movement are equally well understood, or that their separation in writing from the events of photosynthesis and sucrose biosynthesis is anything but a matter of convenience for the student of sugarcane physiology. Indeed, within the cane source-to-sink system the events comprising sucrose transport are only beginning to be understood in their full context relevant to sugar synthesis and storage.

As a tropical grass intensively selected for its manufacture and accumulation of sucrose, the modern commercial cane is confronted with transport problems unknown to many temperate and dicotyledonous species. The high photosynthetic potential of tropic grasses in general and the need to maintain a flow of photosynthate from leaf to storage tissue are indisputed facts. Competition among individual leaves for conducting elements, integrity of the blade union with sheath, and of the sheath union with stalk, veinal branching at each node, and a great length of conducting tissue are all features characteristic of the *Saccharum* species. Many plants do not transport sucrose so far as sugarcane does from one end of a leaf to the other. Moreover, although a mature cane plant will commonly extend its green top 12 to 14 feet above the ground, there is evidence that even the lowest internode continues to receive some fresh sucrose via conducting tissues that must now traverse some 30 or more joints having discrete node and internode structures.

The amount of photosynthate moved by sugarcane is likewise difficult to match. In Puerto Rico during 1970, the island's least productive year in decades, about 400 000 tons of sucrose were translocated from leaves to storage tissues. In Hawaii over a million tons of sucrose are conducted through sugarcane each year (667), and in Cuba the annual flow has approached eight million tons. It is not surprising that, granted adequate pathways of sugar transport, the development of sufficient driving forces to move this sucrose, and the control of its movement in the best interests of the overall source-to-sink system, constitutes one of the most intriguing aspects of sugarcane physiology yet to be resolved.

Having established that sucrose is the principal compound translocated in sugarcane, Hartt *et al.* (667) traced its movement downward through the leaf and leaf sheath to the stalk, then to the center of the stalk and downward. The bulk of sucrose seemed to move toward the plant base and roots, while lesser amounts entered a system moving upward toward the spindle and apical meristem. Some sucrose reached the latter tissues before any arrived at the roots. Part of the daily sucrose product appeared to find temporary storage in the leaf sheath, but this was soon translocated to the ripening internodes of the stalk. The present chapter recounts our understanding of the routes taken by sucrose as it moves from leaf to storage tissue. In Chapter 8, factors governing the rates of sucrose translocation in sugarcane are treated in detail.

2. DEVELOPING THE NORMAL FLOW OF ^{14}C

Even before the advent of radioactive carbon as a research tool, much information had been gathered about sugar movement by conventional chemical analyses of different tissues. However, an important restriction of chemical analyses is the limited number of sugars that can be assayed directly and the relatively small number of plant samples that can be processed at one time. Hence, the investigator working with properly-replicated experiments is usually confined to a limited amount of data taken at a few points in time, and can hardly achieve a true measure of carbohydrate flow. When ^{14}C became available in 1946, it was possible to improvise time-course experiments that would identify the specific photosynthates, their rate and direction of movement, leaf of origin, and conditions under which movement was achieved with least restriction upon photosynthetic processes. Some significance can be attached to the fact that radiotracer techniques were very quickly adopted by physiologists who had known sugarcane for many years.

Much of the early work by Hartt, Burr, and others dealt with the normal flow of photosynthate, that is, sucrose translocation in intact plants given adequate water and nutritional supplies under normal climatic conditions. It is important to recognize that the rate of sucrose movement throughout the sugarcane stool is highly sensitive to changes in illumination, water supply, and nutritional status of the plant. This sensitivity has important implications relating to the agronomic control of sucrose yield and is treated in some detail in the following chapter.

A. ^{14}*C methodology for tracing sucrose*

As is true for photosynthesis research, the sugarcane plant offers certain advantages and disadvantages for radiotracer studies of sugar transport. Hartt *et al.* (667) clearly preferred the long symmetrical blade with parallel conducting elements, undissected by lobes or cross venation. The plant is so large that uniform leaf tissues can be taken for several kinds of analyses. By ranking numerically the leaves and internodes, one can easily select comparable tissue samples from any plant in a given population. Certain disadvantages are inherent in the plant's unwieldly size and its typical monocotyledonous structure. The xylem and phloem tissues are repeatedly segmented along the stalk. In addition, they are very difficult to separate from one another to study their respective transport roles, *i.e.*, water and mineral movement in the xylem, movement of photosynthate and other elaborated compounds in the phloem.

Hartt *et al.* (667) usually employed the interspecific variety *H. 37-1933*, grown outside in 4-gallon containers of continuously-aerated nutrient solution, or grown in the field with standard fertilization. $^{14}CO_2$ was generated from barium [^{14}C]-carbonate and stored over mercury prior to use. The radioactive CO_2 was administered by syringe injection of measured amounts into a glass cylinder (661), or a wood and plastic chamber containing some portion of an attached leaf blade. The blades passed into the chamber through a split rubber stopper, or over a hinged chamber edge coated with rubber, the latter giving an air-tight, gasket-like seal. Apparently there was little or no physical damage to the leaf that would later affect sugar transport. Chamber volumes ranged from 65 to 900 ml. In most experiments Hartt and her co-workers used a wood and plastic chamber, of 900 ml volume, in which 20 cm of leaf was exposed to the $^{14}CO_2$ atmosphere. The exposure period was usually 5 minutes. The time allowed for sugar transport, including exposure to $^{14}CO_2$, ranged from 10 minutes to 6 weeks.

At harvest, short-duration experiments were terminated simply by cutting off the leaf blade; for longer experiments entire stalks were harvested. Tissue samples were dried at 80 °C, ground with a Wiley mill, and counts were taken of weighed powder samples or powder extracts. Up to 2000 counts[1] were taken over a period no longer than 10 minutes; recounts were performed after turning the planchets. Background counts were also recorded periodically. These were averaged and subtracted from average gross counts. Net counts of less than 5 per minute were treated as zero. Ethanol extracts were clarified and assayed for total reducing sugars by conventional means (266, 267), as was fructose (1252) after paper chromatography. Paper chromatograms were run twice in one dimension on Whatman No. 41 H paper, using the solvent isoamyl alcohol, isopropanol, and water (4:4:1, v/v). The first run served to isolate the sugars as a group from which total sugar counts could be taken. After the second run, chromatograms were recounted and the percentages of total counts in individual sugars (sucrose, glucose, and fructose) were calculated.

At about the time that Hartt and her colleagues presented their initial translocation findings for publication, Hatch and Glasziou (692) were investigating ^{14}C movement in sugarcane in Australia. Their methodology differed from that of Hartt *et al.* (667) in several respects. Plants of the hybrid variety *Pindar* were grown for 12 weeks in a normal greenhouse and then transferred to a constant-temperature greenhouse 5 days

[1] Abbreviations used by Hartt and co-workers: RSA, relative specific activity, *i.e.*, net counts per minute at infinite thickness; RTC, relative total counts, equal to RSA x total dry weight (mg); TC, total counts; CPM, counts per minute; SA, specific activity, equal to CPM/mg of tissue.

before treatment. Translocation studies were conducted in full sunlight at 29 °C. $^{14}CO_2$ was usually applied as the barium carbonate (released at zero time by syringe injection of acetic acid) in a plastic bag enclosing a complete 20-cm section of blade situated about 60 cm above the dewlap. Also applied were solutions of radioactive sucrose, glucose, and fructose, either to severed or non-severed midribs. Exposure time was 15 minutes. Samples consisting of 5-cm sections of the midrib were taken consecutively beginning 1 cm below the treated area. The tissue samples were extracted in boiling 95 percent ethanol, and aliquots of the ethanol extracts were taken for radioactivity measurements in a gas-flow counter. Individual sugars were separated by paper chromatography, located with *p*-anisidine phosphate, and analyzed for radioactivity. The identity of sucrose was confirmed by isolating the radioactive spot corresponding to sucrose, hydrolyzing it with yeast invertase, and chromatographing the products with authentic glucose and fructose. This procedure also gave the ratio of ^{14}C carried by the hexose moieties.

B. *Veinal loading and initial movement of ^{14}C in the leaf*

Sucrose was found to be the only compound carrying major quantities of ^{14}C through the sugarcane plant (667, 692). Unless otherwise specified, all subsequent references to translocating ^{14}C assume that sucrose is the carrier.

Hartt *et al.* (667) recognized at once that photosynthate begins to move in the leaf as soon as it is formed rather than accumulating until nightfall. Within 5 minutes of the initial leaf exposure to $^{14}CO_2$ radioactivity was detected 55 cm below the exposure area. It was also noted that within the exposure site the radioactivity of a given spot increased after several minutes had elapsed. This activity increase was thought to represent the entrance of [^{14}C]sucrose into conducting tissue, an assumption based on the fact that leaf veins protrude slightly above the mesophyll cells (663, 664). The mechanism of vein loading in sugarcane remains almost totally obscure.

Among other plant species, vein loading has been the object of numerous histochemical investigations. It is here that perhaps the entire question of translocation force will one day be resolved. Essentially, there has never been a clear picture as to whether loading and subsequent transport is a passive process, accountable to simple diffusion, or whether it is an active process dependent upon energy from metabolic reactions[2]. Adherents of active transport fall into two groups; those favoring an active driving force along the entire path of translocation, and those partial to an active driving process centered in the phloem of the source regions, including the vein endings of the leaf blade (156, 499, 622, 643, 873, 1058, 1524, 1618). Some studies have suggested that, in the phloem external to source regions, metabolic processes serve mainly to retain structural organization while within the source areas they act to move the translocate (568, 1394).

[2]Reviewed by O. Biddulph [Chapter 7 in *Physiological Aspects of Crop Yield*, pp. 143–164, Am. Soc. Agron., Madison, Wisc. (1969)].

Chilling experiments designed to inhibit metabolism have tended to favor active vein loading in the source area (156, 622, 1058, 1524, 1616). Swanson and Geiger (1394), for example, found that subjection of a 2-cm length of sugar beet leaf petiole to physiologically-inhibitive temperatures caused little or no impairment of sucrose translocation. Kursanov (874, 873) reported that treatment of sugar beet leaves with ATP increased the movement of organic substances into conducting tissue and increased their subsequent movement toward the roots. Kursanov *et al.* (870) studied the incorporation of radioactive photosynthate into leaf veins of rhubarb and concluded that the process could not be attributed to free diffusion; rather, it appeared to be a metabolically-controlled process. Vickery and Mercer (1496) distinguished between a rapid osmotic and a slower non-osmotic uptake of sucrose by *Phaseolus* leaves. The non-osmotic process was inhibited by cyanide, azide, and 2,4-dinitrophenol, but not by phlorizin.

Having entered the cane leaf veins, [^{14}C]sucrose passed through the parallel veins of the treated lamina moving in the direction of the dewlap (667). When ^{14}C was incorporated into only one side or lamina of the blade, the radioactive carbon remained within that side during its subsequent travels to midrib, sheath, and stalk. Hartt *et al.* (667) detected only small amounts of labeled sucrose passing over into the opposite side of the midrib. Much of the ^{14}C massed in the lower midrib where sizeable quantities of sucrose could still be detected 2 hours after initial exposure of blades to $^{14}CO_2$ (Fig. 7-1). The appearance of labeled sucrose in the midrib is explained anatomically

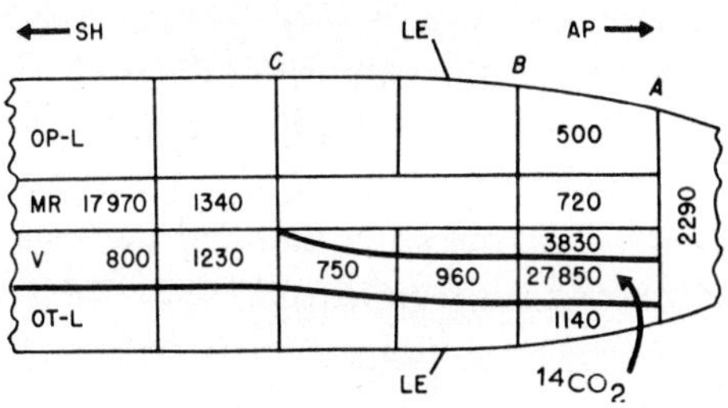

Fig. 7-1. Paths of labeled photosynthate movement in the sugarcane leaf. Radioactive carbon is shown schematically following veins in the lamina enroute to midrib and sheath. OP-L = opposite lamina; MR = midrib; V = veins below fed part; OT-L = outer lamina; LE = leaf edge; AP = apex; SH = sheath. Line A: cut across upper edge of fed part. Line B: cut across lower edge of fed part. Line C: cut across juncture between veins below fed part and midrib. [After Hartt *et al.* (667).] Reproduced by permission of *Plant Physiology*.

by the gradual union of veins with midrib along the flow course from leaf tip to dewlap. Consequently, sucrose formed near the leaf tip has a greater likelihood of entering the midrib than sucrose formed near the base. Some sucrose can find its way to the midrib by lateral conduction through leaf bundles extending diagonally between parallel leaf veins (111). After 20 minutes exposure, some radioactivity was detected 55 cm below the fed area, indicating that the early *velocity* of movement was 2.5 cm, or about 1 inch, per minute (667).

Age of the leaf greatly affected the sucrose movement. A relatively old mature blade, *i.e.*, from leaf $^{+}12$, moved a lesser amount and at a slower rate than younger mature blades in the order of $^{+}5$ to $^{+}8$. This was attributed to the older leaves having to compete with streams of sucrose descending from the younger leaves above (667). It is also probable that in the field the older leaves are in poorer physical condition, bear a higher incidence of insect and fungal damage, and receive insufficient illumination for the photosynthetic processes to operate at full potential.

The observations made by Hartt and her co-workers on early sucrose movement in leaves was generally verified by Hatch and Glasziou (692), with the exception that the latter workers detected a more rapid rate of movement. Hatch and Glasziou recognized the possibility that ^{14}C might be carried by compounds other than sucrose. They were also concerned with the integrity of the sucrose molecule in transit, since their earlier work with the sugar accumulation cycle had shown that sucrose is hydrolyzed and later reassembled as part of the storage process. They found that when all of the label was applied in sucrose it remained in sucrose. When applied as a solution of fructose or glucose (7×10^{-3} M), a predominant portion remained in the applied form, but lesser amounts appeared in sucrose. However, when smaller quantities of labeled glucose were given (0.7×10^{-3} M), nearly all of the radioactivity appeared in sucrose.

Hatch and Glasziou (692) also performed experiments designed to show whether [^{14}C]hexoses were converted to sucrose prior to vein loading, or afterward while moving through the veins[3]. Leaves were first treated with ^{14}C-labeled fructose. Then the ratio of ^{14}C in fructose plus glucose to the ^{14}C in sucrose was compared at uniform distances after 20 minutes and again after 180 minutes (Fig. 7-2). Although during the initial 20 minutes there was an increase in the ratio of [^{14}C]hexose to [^{14}C]sucrose (Fig. 7-2a), after 180 minutes the ratio declined at all distances from the treatment area. This value approached zero at 20 cm and beyond (Fig. 7-2b). Hatch and Slack concluded that glucose and fructose *per se* can enter the veins, and sub-

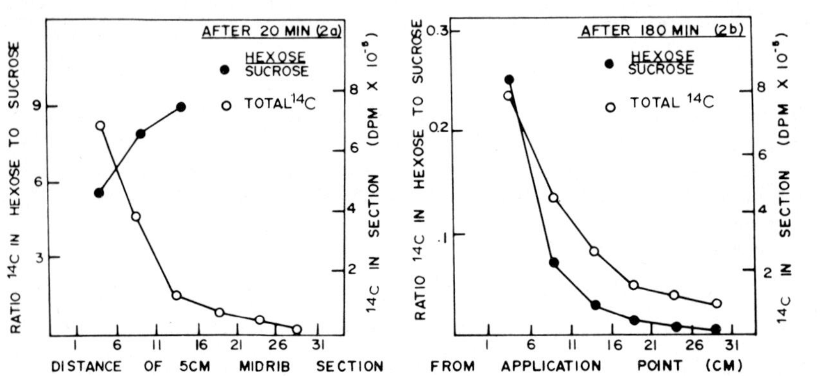

Fig. 7-2. Movement of radioactivity in the midrib of sugarcane leaves following treatment of the leaves with ^{14}C-labeled fructose. DPM = disintegrations/minute. [After Hatch and Glasziou (692).] Reproduced by permission of *Plant Physiology.*

[3]O. Biddulph [*Physiological Aspects of Crop Yield*, p. 145, Am. Soc. Agron., Madison, Wisc. (1969)] views sugar movement to sieve tubes in phosphorylated form with sucrose synthesis occurring just prior to, or during, entry.

sequent conversion to sucrose occurs in transit. Furthermore, labeled fructose or glucose given individually did not yield a label in the other hexose. This was taken as evidence that the hexoses are not degraded to a common translocating molecule in equilibrium with fructose and glucose.

C. *Movement from sheath to stalk*

Hartt *et al.* (667) observed that when one lamina was exposed to $^{14}CO_2$ over an area extending from the outer edge inward, but not inclosing the midrib, radioactivity remained on the exposed side during its downward journey to leaf sheath and stalk (Fig. 7-3). Some radioactivity was detected in the lower midrib; however, a greater

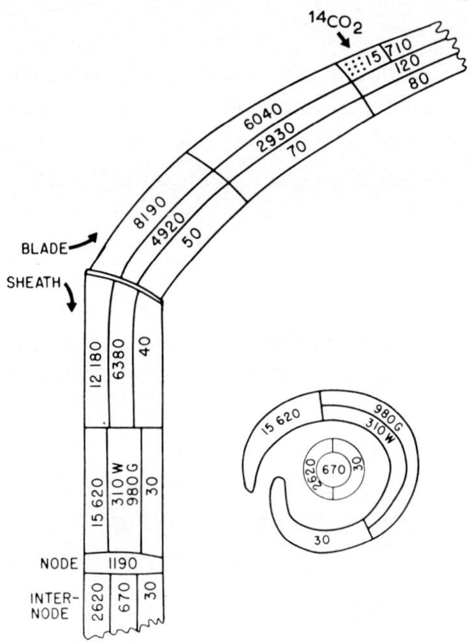

Fig. 7-3. Path of photosynthate movement in the sugarcane leaf blade and sheath enroute to the stalk. ^{14}C-labeled sucrose formed on one side of the blade remains primarily along that side in its downward movement. W = white, inner part of lower leaf sheath. G = green, outer part of lower leaf sheath. [After Hartt *et al.* (667).] Reproduced by permission of *Plant Physiology*.

amount passed directly into the sheath without having entered the midrib. At this time the labeled sucrose began to spread away from the center of the lower sheath. The sugarcane leaf sheath assumes a greater mass toward its base (111), presumably to strengthen the leaf-to-stalk union. In addition to the thickening, there is also an enfolding of lower sheath tissues over one another, so that some portions of the sheath are effectively excluded from light and therefore contain no chlorophyll. Hartt *et al.* described these as the *green* and *white* sheath areas. Quite significantly, the flow of labeled sucrose shifted away from the white sheath areas in favor of the green, an observation which Hartt and her colleagues interpreted on the basis of spreading veins, but which also suggests a relationship between the photosynthetic processes in chlorophyll and efficiency of sucrose transport.

A confinement of labeled sucrose to one side of the leaf, sheath, and stalk resulted from unilateral $^{14}CO_2$ treatment of the lamina. In nature the entire blade is exposed to $^{12}CO_2$ and the wrapping of sheath tissues around the stalk assures a relatively balanced distribution of sucrose to the entire stalk circumference.

D. *Movement within the stalk*

Labeled sucrose was found to pass from the lower leaf sheath into the subtending node, and then into the adjoining internode (667). The initial movement was inward toward the center of the stalk (Table 7-1). After about 5 hours the sucrose distribution between the stalk rind and stalk center was nearly equal as evidenced by uniform RSA data. The early RSA concentration in the center was attributed to the natural distribu-

TABLE 7-1

MOVEMENT OF RADIOACTIVITY (RSA) IN SUGARCANE INTERNODES DURING VARIOUS INTERVALS OF TIME

[After Hartt *et al.* (667).] Reproduced by permission of *Plant Physiology.*

Internode and portion	Midrib side*	Opposite side**
	From blade 12, 90 minutes	
Internode 13		
Rind (1 mm)	0	10
Next 2 mm	10	180
Remaining center	30	480
	From blade 7, 194 minutes	
Internode 7		
Rind	250	110
Center	360	210
Internode 8		
Rind	10	10
Center	150	90
	From blade 8, 5 hours	
Internode 8		
Rind (1 mm)	1600	3000
Next 2 mm	1300	2100
Remaining center	1600	2900

*Directly below midrib of treated blade.
**Overlapping attachment of sheath edges.

tion of large leaf traces. These pass downward from the leaf, move horizontally inward to the stalk center, and resume their descent through a series of internodes (111).

Having found its way to the stalk center, sucrose turned and moved down the stalk. All of the sucrose continued to descend for a distance of at least several internodes. Eventually, some of it began moving upward (Fig. 7-4) from the general area in which

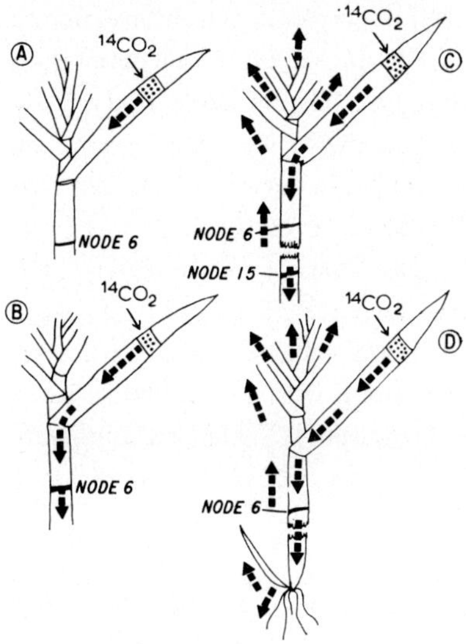

Fig. 7-4. Relative descending and ascending movement of ^{14}C-labeled photosynthate in sugarcane. Over a time-course of 10 minutes to 2 hours, ^{14}C fed to blade $^{+}6$ moved downward about 60 minutes before upward flow was detected. By 2 hours, some ^{14}C had passed downward a total of 174 cm, while radioactivity was also found in the upper stalk, leaves, spindle, base of stalk, roots and suckers. (A) 10 minutes after treatment; (B) 60 minutes; (C) 90 minutes; (D) 120 minutes. [After Hartt *et al.* (667).] Reproduced by permission of *Plant Physiology*.

the leaf traces lose their identity (667). Part of the ascending sucrose entered the spindle leaves, immature storage tissue, and meristematic area before any of the descending sucrose arrived at the roots. Labeled sucrose also appeared to move out of the roots into the nutrient solution (667). The journey of ^{14}C from treated lamina to the roots required 2 or more hours, depending upon the length of stalk.

During the first 90 minutes of exposure to $^{14}CO_2$, radioactive sucrose tended to accumulate at the nodes along the stalk rather than in the internodes (667). This was attributed to a lesser [^{14}C]sucrose concentration in storage tissue than in conducting tissue, and relatively greater concentrations of conducting tissue in the nodal regions. Hartt *et al.* (667) found that, within 90 minutes, more than 70 percent of the ^{14}C-labeled sucrose might leave the exposure or "fed" area, although this same region might still show the highest RSA values in the plant.

Lateral movement of sucrose in the stalk was examined by Hawker (702) in

Australia. Most plants are believed to conduct lateral solute movement via the plasmodesmata (1547) rather than through the aqueous phase of cell walls. Working with stalk tissue slices bathed in sugar solutions, Hawker demonstrated the presence of high sucrose concentrations in the cell walls. These concentrations were believed to help maintain high sucrose levels in the vacuoles of parenchyma cells, and were interpreted as evidence of sugar movement via the cell walls rather than via plasmodesmata.

The upward movement of sucrose is not very well understood. Ascending sucrose was not mentioned at all by Hatch and Glasziou (692). This movement should have begun by the close of their longer experiments (3 hours), especially in their 12-week-old plants in which the downward conduction through stalk tissue must still be minimal. Presumably, the upward transport is accomplished through the same xylem tissues that carry the ascending water and nutrients. As metabolically active sink areas, the immature storage and meristematic tissues contain high levels of invertase (16, 689) which probably hydrolyze sucrose as an initial step in converting it to amino acids and other compounds essential for growth. Hartt *et al.* found labeled glucose, fructose, lipids and traces of malic or other metabolic acids, along with a predominance of [^{14}C]sucrose, in the spindle area after 5 hours of ^{14}C transport (Table 7-2). Immature

TABLE 7-2

TRANSLOCATION OF RADIOACTIVITY TO DIFFERENT AREAS OF THE CANE PLANT AS EVIDENCED BY PERCENTAGE OF COUNTS IN ETHANOL EXTRACTS 5 HOURS AFTER TREATMENT OF BLADE 8 WITH $^{14}CO_2$

[After Hartt *et al.* (667).] Reproduced by permission of *Plant Physiology.*

Tissue	Radioactivity in component					
	Phosphates, amino acids, etc.	Sucrose	Glucose	Fructose	Malic acid	Lipids
		Descending transport				
Blade 8, fed area	6	64	8	12	6	4
Blade 8, below	4	84	4	5	3	1
Sheath 8	3	72	11	11	4	3
Internode 8	4	93	2	1	0	0
Internode 13	0	100	0	0	0	0
Internode 15	0	100	0	0	0	0
Internode 19	0	100	0	0	0	0
		Ascending transport				
Internode 7	4	81	7	5	2	1
Spindle	10	66	8	6	1	8

storage tissue is also one of the areas where Hatch and co-workers (689, 691, 690, 1268) developed the *sugar accumulation cycle*, a process requiring both acid and neutral invertase. It is very probable that the upward flow of sucrose is related to the growth status of the plant. An actively-growing plant should require a greater sugar flow toward the spindle area than a mature plant in the advanced stages of ripening. This topic is treated in detail in Chapter 9.

After 5 hours translocation (667) it was no longer possible to distinguish between transient sucrose and that already gone into storage, *i.e.*, between sucrose in conducting phloem and that residing in the storage vacuoles of parenchyma cells. From the data summarized in Table 7-3, it can be seen that radioactive sucrose had moved

TABLE 7-3

PERCENTAGE OF RADIOACTIVITY IN SUCROSE AMONG DIFFERENT SUGARCANE TISSUES 5 HOURS AFTER TREATMENT OF BLADE 8 WITH $^{14}CO_2$

[After Hartt *et al.* (667).] Reproduced by permission of *Plant Physiology*.

Cane tissue	Sucrose		[^{14}C]Sucrose	
	mg	counts/mg	mg	% of total*
Blade, fed area	45	77 000	6.3	2.8
Blade, below fed area	147	8 700	0.7	1.0
Sheath 8	134	7 700	0.6	0.8
Internode 8	4 420	240	0.02	0.9
Internode 13	11 714	25	0.002	0.2
Internode 19	7 886	92	0.007	0.6

*The original SA of sucrose was 1220 000. This was decreased to 77 000 by translocation of [^{14}C]sucrose and formation of [^{12}C]sucrose, amounting to a decrease to 6.3 percent.

away from the leaf as far as internode No. 19, but that this sugar accounted for only 0.007 percent of the total sucrose contained in the internode. By contrast, the portion of leaf exposed to $^{14}CO_2$ contained more than 6 percent of its total sucrose in radioactive form. This broad discrepancy of relative concentrations is less accountable to transport factors than it is to a dilution effect caused by the unlabeled sucrose already accumulated along the path of translocation. Hence, the absolute quantity of [^{14}C]sucrose in internode No. 19 was more than 20 percent of the quantity found in the ^{14}C-treated leaf area. After 24 hours, 8 to 10 internode tissue accounted for 25 percent of the total ^{14}C. After 6 weeks, internodes 11 to 15 contained 18 percent of the total counts, 80 percent being soluble in alcohol and presumably representing sucrose in "permanent" storage.

Hatch and Glasziou (692) tried to determine whether the sugar accumulation cycle, found earlier to be operative in storage-tissue discs, likewise accounted for sucrose storage in intact sugarcane. Although no very satisfactory method was found to distinguish between conducting sucrose and storage sucrose, they did observe randomization of ^{14}C in the fructose and glucose moieties of parenchyma sucrose. This contrasted with virtually no randomization of ^{14}C in conducting sucrose. They also found a higher proportion of label in free hexoses and non-sugar parenchyma compounds. This suggests that the transient sucrose was hydrolyzed upon entry into parenchyma cells.

E. *Sucrose as the principal photosynthate moved*

As mentioned briefly above, Hartt *et al.* (667) found that sucrose was the lone compound translocated in sizable amounts (Table 7-2), an observation confirmed by independent studies in Australia (692). This is also true of many other species, including willow, soybean, sunflower, Jerusalem artichoke, grape, tobacco, wheat, barley, bracken, pine, dwarf mistletoe, and potato [reviewed by Hartt *et al.* (667)]. In the grapevine sucrose is the principal sugar translocated (1392) although fructose and glucose constitute the bulk of sugar in the grape berry at all times (840). Kursanov (871) reported that in many plant species there is a predominance of hexose phosphates along with sucrose in a mixture of sucrose, glucose, fructose, hexose phosphates, organic acids and amino acids. Stachyose and verbascose have also been identified among translocating compounds in pumpkin (1193). Raffinose is known to be translocated in soybean and raspberry (263). Webb and Burley (1548) reported that in the apple there is more activity in sorbitol than in sucrose, both in the ^{14}C-treated leaf and in tissues some 60 cm away. Nelson *et al.* (1082) working with soybean, examined the possibility of nutritional status having an influence on the form of photosynthate moved. Both sucrose and serine were found to be radioactive in soybean plants given adequate nutrient supply, but in N-deficient plants nearly all of the ^{14}C appeared in sucrose. Nitrogen deficiency causes sucrose to accumulate in leaves of sugarcane grown by sand culture (11, 31).

Hatch and Glasziou (692) did not discount the possibility that a sucrose derivative is the carrier of ^{14}C through sugarcane. The latter contention assumes a rapid equilibrium between sucrose and the derivative in the conducting tissue, such that the derivative would be found only in small amounts. One possible derivative is the trisaccharide raffinose. It is present in leaf and immature storage tissue of sugarcane (35) and carries an intact sucrose moiety. Each of its three linkages are readily hydrolyzed by cane invertase preparations (43). Invertase might conceivably mediate the interconversion with sucrose, via free hexoses, in the storage tissues where the bulk of cane invertase resides.

Hartt and her co-workers (667) observed that, as ^{14}C moved farther away from the point of absorption, a greater percentage of the alcohol-soluble radioactivity was found in sucrose. Thus, after 5 hours, 100 percent of the counts were in sucrose for internode extracts, 72 percent for sheath extracts, and only 64 percent for extracts of the treated leaf area (Table 7-2). These authors stated that small amounts of radioactive fructose and glucose may be attributed to sucrose conversion. Quite possibly the labeled hexoses represent the hydrolyzed remains of labeled hexose phosphate pools from photosynthetic CO_2 assimilation. Similarly, small amounts of labeled aspartic acid and malic acid detected below the $^{14}CO_2$-treated leaf areas might be pool remnants of C_4 pathway intermediates.

F. *Velocity and rate of sucrose transport*

Hartt *et al.* (667) distinguished between *velocity* of sucrose movement, defined by Swanson (1393) as the linear distance moved per unit of time, and *rate* of movement, which is the *amount* of sugar moved per unit of time (665). In Hawaii the parameter of time was measured from the instant of $^{14}CO_2$ exposure to the blade to the time of cutting the leaf from the stalk or the stalk from the stool. Distance was measured from the lower edge of the exposure chamber to the leading edge of radioactivity. Measured velocities for sucrose in sugarcane have ranged from 42 to 150 cm/hour (661, 664). From the mean of 12 measurements made with normal plants, it was estimated that the average downward velocity of sucrose translocation in sugarcane is 84 cm/hour. Upward velocity was approximately 37 cm/hour (667). Hatch and Glasziou (692) reported a somewhat higher velocity of [^{14}C]sucrose transport, 4.5 cm/minute, and a velocity of 4 to 6 cm/minute for labeled hexoses.

It appears that there is nothing very constant about the velocity of ^{14}C movement among different plant species, or within sugarcane itself. According to Hartt *et al.* (667), reported velocities range from 0.24 cm/hour for *Salix* (294) to 5040 cm/hour for soybean (1080, 1081), with intermediate velocities ranging in the order of 20 to 144 cm/hour. So many physiological factors affect the speed and rate of sucrose translocation that a separate chapter is devoted to this aspect alone. However, it appears that ^{14}C movement in sugarcane cannot approach the velocity reported for soybean.

An interesting feature of ^{14}C velocity in sugarcane is its sensitivity to $^{14}CO_2$ exposure time (667), rather than to dosage size as was suggested by Canny (291, 292). Hartt and her co-workers obtained no velocity distinctions with dosages ranging from 40 to 400 microcuries during an exposure interval of 5 minutes. However, lengthening exposure time from 5 to 10 minutes reduced the ^{14}C velocity from 98 to 72 cm/hour, and a 37-minute exposure lowered velocity to 42 cm/hour.

Rate of sucrose transport is not so readily determined as velocity (665). One of the methods adopted in Hawaii involved taking successive small samples from the blade area exposed to $^{14}CO_2$. This was accomplished by punching out small segments, working from the top down in an effort to avoid disrupting translocation, and then measuring the loss of counts from the exposure area. This method has shown that more than half of the ^{14}C exits from the exposure area within about 2 hours. A better overall picture of translocation was obtained by subdividing an entire plant, as illustrated schematically in Fig. 7-5. From this it can be seen that in 90 minutes more than 70 percent of the [^{14}C]sucrose moved away from the fed area. Considerable

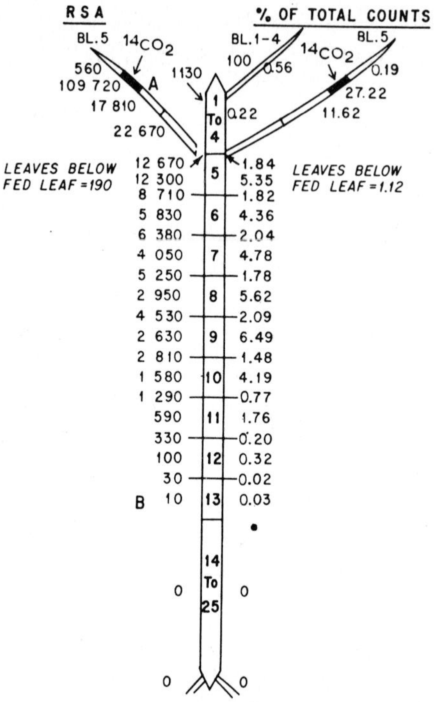

Fig. 7-5. Relative velocity and rate of [^{14}C]sucrose movement in sugarcane. Shown at the left are RSA values 90 minutes after treatment of blade $^{+}$5. Percentages of total counts are shown at the right. [After Hartt *et al.* (667).] Reproduced by permission of *Plant Physiology*.

variation was encountered with this method owing to climatic and edaphic factors, varying number of suckers and lalas, and age differences among treated blades. Old blades, *i.e.*, $^{+}$12 or older, moved less ^{14}C and at a slower speed than leaves of intermediate rank. This observation was consistent with ^{14}C transport data from rye (995) and tobacco (811).

The most precise estimate of translocation rate is achieved by calculating the absolute amount of ^{14}C moved per hour (667). This estimate must take into account the specific activity of moving sucrose, of sucrose in the exposure area, and specific activity of total sucrose in tissues below the exposure area, as well as the expanse of treated and conducting leaf area. In one experiment it was calculated that, from an area of 82 cm^2, a minimum of 10.7 mg of [^{14}C]sucrose moved down the blade, through the leaf sheath, and into the respective node and internode in 1 hour (667). For an average blade having an area of 570 cm^2, sucrose could traverse this pathway at the rate of 74 mg/hour (665).

The translocation profile developed by Hartt *et al.* (667) indicates that sucrose movement is linear at 1 hour, but thereafter deviates increasingly to the right up to 5 hours (Fig. 7-6A). The deviation after 1 hour was attributed to sucrose ascending toward the spindle area. It is interesting to note that even very old internodes (Nos. 27 and 28) received newly-formed sucrose, underscoring the fact that no part of the sugarcane plant ever quite retires from biochemical activity. A "depression" at internode No. 11 and a subsequent "peak" at internode No. 19 was mentioned by the authors; however, Fig. 7-6A at 5 hours appears to show little difference in sucrose

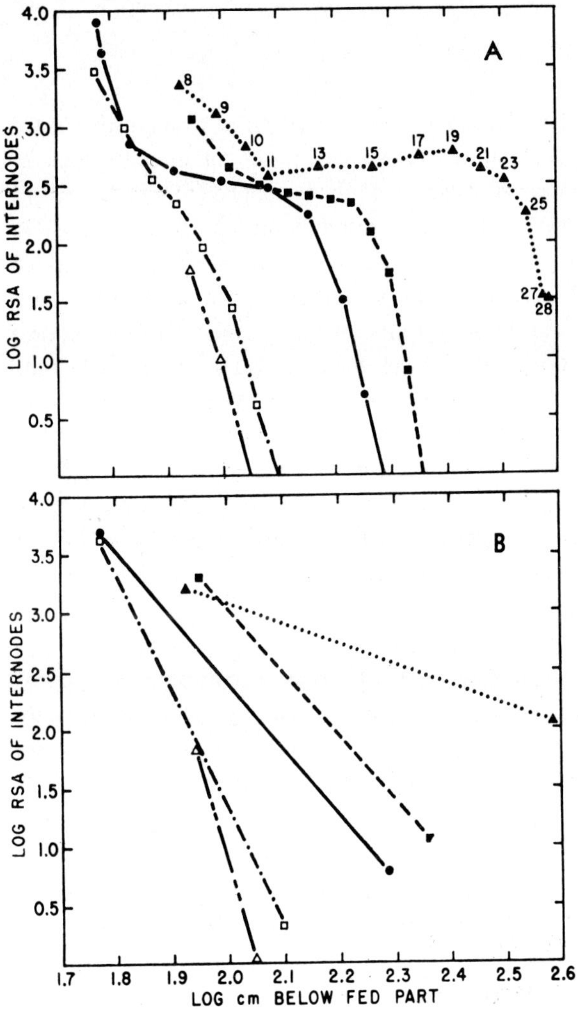

Fig. 7-6. Profile of [^{14}C]sucrose movement in sugarcane internodes from 1 to 5 hours after treatment of the leaves with $^{14}CO_2$. △——△, 1 hour; □–.–□, 1.5 hours; ●–●, 3 hours; ■—■, 4 hours; ▲· · · · ·▲, 5 hours. (A) Development of profile, in which indicated numbers refer to specific internodes. (B) Decrease in the overall slope with time. [After Hartt *et al.* (667).] Reproduced by permission of *Plant Physiology*.

values from internodes Nos. 4 to 19, and it can be assumed that these intermediary sections were supplying all of the sucrose moving upward to be metabolized for growth or other purposes. It would be highly instructive to develop similar radioactivity profiles for ripened sugarcane and similar plants reverting to growth following heavy rainfall. Fig. 7-6B presents regression lines calculated from Fig. 7-6A. This shows that the entire slope decreased with time (although there was no decrease between 3 and 4 hours) and a very rapid decrease occurred between 4 and 5 hours.

G. *Translocation to adjacent stalks in the stool*

An interesting finding by Hartt and her co-workers was the rather prompt appearance of ^{14}C throughout an entire cane stool following exposure of a single stalk to $^{14}CO_2$. Radioactivity was also received in lalas (shoots developed from buds near the top of the stalk) and in suckers (shoots developed from buds at the base of the stalk or from harvested stubble). In one experiment (270), it was found that ^{14}C incorporated into blade No. 3 of a single stalk had moved as far as blade No. 2 in 15 other stalks growing from the same stool. In another experiment some 17 percent of total counts reached the suckers in 14 days where they accumulated primarily in millable stalk tissue. More than half of the ^{14}C was found in sucrose. Radioactivity appeared in suckers between 4.5 and 5.5 hours after treatment of the primary stalk with $^{14}CO_2$.

Hartt *et al.* (667) concluded that ^{14}C moving in the suckers was not carried by xylem, the logical tissue for upward conduction from the stool base, but rather by phloem. This interpretation was based on the extremely low percentage of counts found in xylem constituents removed by compressed air. Their findings were in contrast to those of Jones *et al.* (811) who reported that ^{14}C assimilated by a single tobacco leaf was later moved up the stem in the xylem.

Within the sugarcane stool the younger stalks and suckers contributed a greater percentage of newly-formed sucrose toward sugar-utilizing processes (667). Older stalks tended to accumulate more sucrose in storage. The latter required much more time to send [^{14}C]sucrose to the roots than did the young stalks (Table 7-4). This

TABLE 7-4

TRANSLOCATION OF ^{14}C-LABELED PHOTOSYNTHATE FROM BLADE 5 TO DIFFERENT STALKS OF THE SUGARCANE STOOL COMPLEX DURING A 5-HOUR INTERVAL

Blade 5 of each stalk received 200 μCi of $^{14}CO_2$ in 5 minutes under bright sunlight. [After Hartt *et al.* (667).] Reproduced by permission of *Plant Physiology*.

Stalks	Distance to roots (cm)	Velocity (cm/min)	Time needed to reach roots (hours)
Old	451	0.9	8.35
Young	235	1.1	3.55

appears to be due to the greater length of old stalks rather than to differences in transport velocity. The authors suggested that the increased time involved in moving new photosynthate to the roots might have a bearing on aging. It seems doubtful that there is a preference for new sucrose over that stored in the oldest internodes in meeting the needs of root growth.

3. TRANSLOCATION IN DETACHED LEAVES

Between 1960 and 1964, Hartt and Kortschak (669) performed numerous translocation experiments with detached leaves. The reader will probably wonder whether a leaf cut from its plant will still function as it did while part of the intact organism. Schumacher and Hülsbruch (1308) cautioned against too liberal interpretation of translocation data from isolated plant parts. Other workers, including Leonard (931) and Thaine *et al.* (1415), have successfully used severed leaves for translocation research. Geiger and Batey (569) studied sucrose transport in sugar beets severely pruned to single source and sink leaves attached to the storage root, a system which could easily be more misleading than use of detached leaves. From their own observations Hartt and Kortschak concluded that the severed cane leaf does behave normally in many important respects.

By use of detached blades a great deal of information was gathered relative to sugar movement in light and darkness, polarity of translocation, applicability of the mass flow and diffusion theories of translocation, sugar absorption and accumulation by the leaf, origin of the driving force, and effects of various chemical additives on sugar transport. It would seem that this technique has special merit in studies of the driving force (670) and possible collaboration of photosynthetic and respiratory processes in vein loading. An important limitation of detached blades is the loss of the "pulling" forces normally exerted by the remainder of the plant.

The methodology used by Hartt and Kortschak (669) for unattached leaves was for the most part identical to that described earlier (667). Detached blades recut twice under water were thereafter retained standing in water in a photosynthesis chamber. Light intensity was decreased from 8000 to 2000 foot candles. Leaves were taken from the hybrid variety *H. 50-720* as well as from the interspecific variety *H. 37-1933.* All treated leaves were removed from the plant before being exposed to $^{14}CO_2$.

A. *Basipetal transport*

The translocation of sucrose by detached blades is illustrated in Fig. 7-7. As translocation progressed from 30 minutes to 5 hours, RSA values decreased in fed areas and a radioactivity gradient developed with higher label concentrations accumulating in the basal leaf area. As in studies with attached leaves (667), a small amount of radioactivity appearing in the leaf tip or apex was attributed to intercellular leakage rather than to upward transport through conducting tissue. Translocation velocity was considerably slower in detached blaaes, about 0.4 cm/minute as compared with 2.5 cm/minute with normal blades (667). Since $^{14}CO_2$ exposure time was usually 5 minutes, as in earlier experiments, the loss of velocity must have been due to reduced light intensity, or to detachment of the blade from driving forces external to the leaf. In a subsequent paper, Hartt *et al.* (670) gave additional evidence of a driving force residing within the leaf.

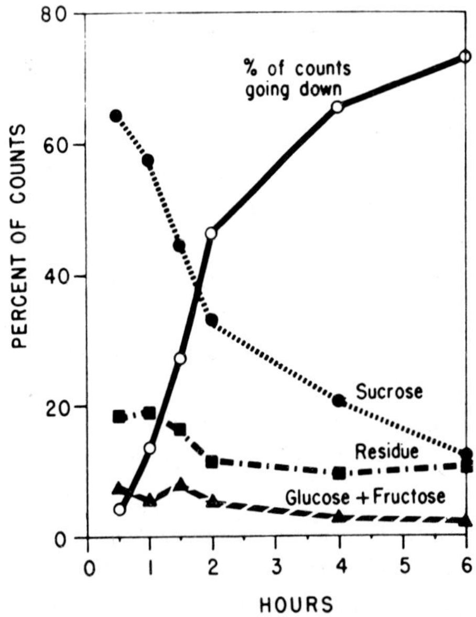

Fig. 7-7. Translocation of ^{14}C in detached blades of sugarcane at 2000 foot candles over a time course of 30 minutes to 6 hours. Blades severed at the base were treated with $^{14}CO_2$ about 50 cm above the cut. Total translocation is expressed as percent of counts moving down the blade. Sucrose, residue, and glucose plus fructose are expressed as percent of ^{14}C remaining in the treated area. [After Hartt and Kortschak (669).] Reproduced by permission of *Plant Physiology.*

One atypical aspect of sucrose movement in the detached blade was its retention within the leaf tissue; it did not pass from the lower or severed end into the surrounding water. After 6 hours the accumulating sucrose in the basal area appeared to restrict further movement from above. This seemed to confirm that continued translocation requires a sink (an area using or storing the translocate) in addition to a productive source.

It was noted (669) that darkening either the basal area or apex with aluminum foil created an artificial sink in the detached blade into which new [^{14}C]sucrose continued to flow (Fig. 7-8). Earlier work with attached blades had shown that removal of the leaf tip, the area above the treated tissues, restricted further downward movement of sucrose (670); however, this restriction did not occur in detached blades when the apex was removed. This plus the failure of sugar to move out of the severed blades underscored the artificial nature of the leaf pathway when disconnected from the plant. Nonetheless, these experiments substantiated the earlier findings (667, 692) in several important respects: (a) Photosynthate follows leaf veins to the midrib; (b) the predominating movement is basipetal; and (c) the predominant compound moving is sucrose.

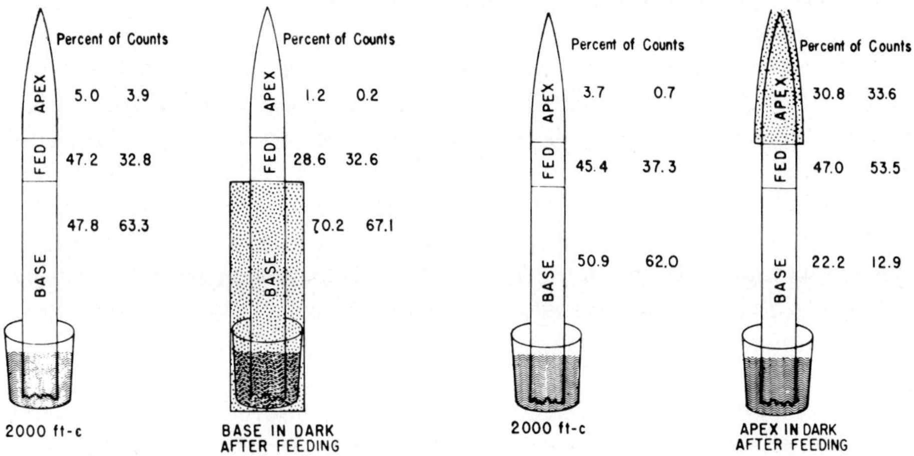

Fig. 7-8. Translocation of ^{14}C in detached sugarcane blades in which the base or the apex is darkened. Darkening the base decreased acropetal movement and increased basipetal movement. Darkened base or apex tissue acted as a sink. [After Hartt and Kortschak (669).] Reproduced by permission of *Plant Physiology.*

B. *Polarity of ^{14}C transport*

In a most interesting series of experiments Hartt and Kortschak (669) demonstrated a clear polarity of sucrose movement in the phloem, in contrast to nonpolar movement of phosphorus in the xylem. The normal downward movement of sucrose through leaf blade to leaf sheath and stalk seems logical if for no other reason than the storage area is situated below the blade. However, in detached blades inverted so that the severed base was at the top, ^{14}C moved acropetally (toward the top) in the direction of the morphological base. In these experiments a portion of the tip was cut off and this end stood in water while the morphological base was exposed to the air. In this way it was shown that a polarity exists for sucrose transport which is independent of leaf orientation and independent of a connection with the stalk.

Since photosynthate is known to move in the phloem (1393), Hartt and Kortschak (669) tried to determine whether polarity also existed for elements moving through the xylem. When detached blades were stood upright or inverted in water containing radioactive phosphorus (^{32}P), the labeled phosphorus was absorbed and moved upward regardless of leaf orientation. The xylem movement thus did not exhibit polarity. Since upward movement of water and minerals through the xylem is considered to be dependent upon "transpirational pull", Hartt and Kortschak (669) felt that polarity could serve as a basis for distinction between solutes moving in the transpirational stream and those moving in the phloem.

C. *Reversal of transport polarity in the dark*

Hartt and Kortschak found that complete darkening of blades detached shortly after 8:00 a.m. led to acropetal or upward sucrose movement toward the apex. At first this was believed due to intercellular leakage similar to that observed in illuminated experiments, or to leakage into the xylem. However, with the cut base or cut apex standing in water, darkening the blade after $^{14}CO_2$ exposure invariably resulted in movement toward the morphological apex. This movement was unaffected by changing orientation of the blade. The acropetal translocation in darkness was therefore a polar phenomenon, resembling basipetal polarity in light by its independence of gravity, orientation, or transpirational pull.

It was also noted that darkening of blades cut around 8:00 a.m. resulted in a general decrease of total ^{14}C translocation, but that blades cut in the afternoon performed normal ^{14}C translocation in the dark (669). The ability to move sucrose in darkness gradually increased with time of day. This increase was also dependent upon attachment to the plant, since blades cut early in the morning and held in light until afternoon did not increase their capacity to move sucrose in darkness. Hartt and Kortschak interpreted these findings on the basis of diurnal changes in sugar gradients. For blades cut early in the morning there is little difference in sucrose percentages between base and apex. Blades cut in the afternoon have up to twice as much sucrose in the apex, thus creating a positive gradient. This gradient would not develop in blades cut in the morning and exposed to light because sucrose then accumulates near the severed base (669).

Unfortunately, no experiments were reported with darkened blades still attached to the plant. It would seem that the acropetal movement in darkness is more likely an artifact of blade detachment at a particular time of day than an example of normal night transport in a physiological system. Nonetheless, Hartt and Kortschak contributed important evidence toward an active transport system dependent upon light and operating in competition with a second mechanism linked to a metabolic energy source and functional in darkness.

One might speculate that basipetal transport is an ATP-utilizing system. If ATP were either produced more abundantly in the apex, or utilized (or hydrolyzed) less readily in the apex by competing mechanisms, then the energy basis of basipetal transport would be established. In this respect the diurnal distribution of ATPase along the length of the blade could be instructive. Failure of sucrose to move down the darkened blade suggests a restriction of photosynthetic phosphorylation; acropetal movement in the dark suggests that the competing mechanism is still functional, and increasingly so toward the apex. The latter mechanism could constitute simple hydrolysis of ATP, or a complete respiratory system. That the latter might in fact be operative at higher rates was suggested by increased amino acids and organic phosphates found in darkened tissues exposed to ^{14}C (669).

D. *Translocation with specific leaf areas darkened*

As mentioned earlier in this chapter, physiologists have long pondered whether the driving force of translocation resides near the vein endings of source areas or whether there is active driving force all along the path of transport. Some theories hold that seive plates themselves may act as metabolic pumps (520, 1350). Hartt and Kortschak (669) found some evidence of lengthwise driving force in detached leaves, although they did not interpret their data from this viewpoint. Darkening only the treated area, which was situated a little higher than midway up the blade, restricted downward translocation but did not affect movement toward the apex. In this respect the length of blade from tip to darkened area could still be considered normal. Basipetal translocation stopped when both the ^{14}C-treated area and the apex were darkened, but some movement continued toward the apex. Darkening the treated area with apex removed stopped virtually all translocation.

It appears that Hartt and Kortschak achieved with dark treatments what Swanson and Geiger (1394) had failed to achieve with localized petiole chilling in the sugar beet, that is, their restriction of physiological activity in a small area along the transport pathway resulted in decreased movement between source and sink areas. Ordinarily, the low-temperature treatments should restrict a much broader range of reactions than does darkness. In these instances they were less effective in slowing transport than the light treatments which do not affect so many important metabolic reactions. This may be interpreted as evidence of a photochemically-linked driving force operative along the entire length of the sugarcane leaf.

Chapter 8

The Rate of Sucrose Transport

1. INTRODUCTION

In the preceding chapter the paths of sucrose transport were outlined on the basis of ^{14}C experiments performed in Hawaii and Australia. For the most part these studies were conducted under normal conditions of climate, water supply, and nutrition. Having established the routes that sucrose takes in its journey from leaves to storage tissues, or to areas of intense utilization, the fact remains that it may not follow these pathways in anything like a constant or predictable flow. There are many factors responsible for this. Some are inherent in sugarcane's environment, others in the plant's physical structure, and still others relate to its many biochemical requirements during growth and maturation. In the present chapter we will review some of the outstanding factors contributing to the rate of sucrose transport.

Translocation has held the interest of numerous investigators working with equally numerous plant species. Many important questions remain unanswered, particularly in the realm of transport mechanisms. Relatively few workers have approached translocation in sugarcane. Fortunately, those who have were generally succesful in isolating the important contributing factors and studying them as controlled variables. From these results we have gained a rough outline of the potential for sucrose flow. We have a better understanding of the causes for frequent failure to meet this potential under field conditions. Moreover, from these studies and from work performed with other species, a picture of sucrose transport mechanisms for sugarcane is beginning to emerge.

2. THEORY OF ASSIMILATE MOVEMENT IN HIGHER PLANTS

A. *General*

A maze of contradictory reports has accompanied the study of transport mechanisms almost from the time that physiologists first wondered whether plants circulate their sap as animals circulate blood. In the words of Crafts[1], "Probably in no part of the field of plant physiology have so many theories been proved wrong, so many experiments obviously been misinterpreted, and so little solid evidence presented." Much of the difficulty is laid in the differing physical structures and biochemical

---

[1] Crafts, A.S., 1961. *Translocation in Plants*, Holt, Rinehart and Winston, New York.

requirements among plant species. Functional phloem elements lie inclosed within living tissues where they serve as an intricate part of a complex circulatory system. They have not survived the histological dissection, staining, and physical pressures of the mounted specimen in a natural state. Among earlier workers, Small (1348) alone appears to have succeeded in preparing intact sieve tubes for microscopic examination. Because of these difficulties the general features of assimilate transport were established only gradually from bits and pieces of experimental evidence.

In 1962 Canny (293) summarized many years of translocation research with a listing of 12 conclusions given qualified acceptance by many plant scientists[2]. He stated that sucrose is the primary carbohydrate moved, along with related polymers, amino acids, viruses, and other substances, and that transport occurs through the phloem along a downward gradient of sucrose. Actual movement occurs in groups of sieve tubes where different substances move simultaneously in opposite directions. Owing to a semipermeable membrane, the sucrose solution within sieve tubes is maintained under high turgor pressure. This would account for exudations by cut tissues and for the general loss of integrity of sieve strands when dissected. Translocation is sustained by respiratory energy. As sucrose is moved through the phloem, a constant proportion is depicted as being metabolized to CO_2 in reactions possibly related to the production of transport energy (290, 294). When radioactive tracer compounds are introduced into the phloem their subsequent distribution is such that the logarithm of radioactivity is described as a nearly linear function of distance. The radioactivity thereby develops a characteristic *profile*, having an upper plateau and a slope whose straight line is independent of the carrier's chemical identity (291). There is very little transport into mature leaves; into fruits there is a dry-weight movement of approximately 4 g/cm^2 of phloem/hour (293). Velocity of transport is in the order 1 to 5 cm/hour (in *Salix* and *Vicia*)[3].

A major confirmation of two-directional movement in sieve tubes was achieved by Thaine (1416) working with petiole phloem from *Primula obconica*. Thaine hypothesized that tubular strands extend from cell to cell across the sieve tube endings, thereby giving the structural basis for transcellular protoplasmic streaming. Proof of the concept required that particles should be seen moving from cell to cell along the strands within living sieve tubes. Thaine (1417) had demonstrated by phase-contrast microscopy the presence of extremely small and thread-like structures passing through the tubular strands, presumably in a longitudinal manner surrounded by a fluid matrix facilitating intracellular streaming.

The final proof was nonetheless difficult to produce. Even slight damage will ordinarily disrupt the spatial and pressure continuity of particle flow, and vaguely-discernible particles in movement become almost invisible in a still photograph. How-

[2]There is no theory acceptable to all authorities. Recently, O. Biddulph [*Physiological Aspects of Crop Yield*, Chapter 7, pp. 143–164, Am. Soc. Agron., Madison, Wisc. (1969)] compiled into one chapter the factors which a reasonable theory must take into consideration.

[3]In sugarcane, Hartt *et al.* (667) placed the velocity of downward sucrose movement at about 2.5 cm/minute; Hatch and Glasziou (692) reported somewhat faster movement.

ever, Thaine did observe the hypothesized tubular strands. Also observed was transcellular particle movement within the strands and, in addition, he succeeded in recording the movement on 200 feet of 16-mm ciné film. The movement was continuous in parallel strands situated in sieve tubes crossing sieve plates. There was also movement in the opposite direction within the same sieve tube, at times within adjacent strands. The particles themselves resembled plant mitochondria in size and were linearly arranged about 3 μm apart. Velocity of movement was in the order 3 to 5 cm/hour. These observations were confirmed by Canny (293).

B. *Development of the mass flow concept*

Assimilate transport in the phloem has been explained from many viewpoints. Diffusion, protoplasmic streaming, variable turgidity, surface equilibrium of the protoplasm, and mass flow along a hydrostatic pressure gradient have all had their advocates. The concept of mass flow is one of the most widely-held explanations for phloem translocation (1620, 500). This theory was considerably strengthened by Barrier and Loomis (147) who observed an apparent "loading" of ^{32}P into leaf veins. Employing radioautograph techniques, vivid photographs were published showing the accumulation of ^{32}P in veins of excised beet leaf blades, over a 24-hour period, while no translocation from the blades occurred. Barrier and Loomis assumed that respiratory energy was expended in veinal accumulation of the ^{32}P-labeled molecules. Nakata and Leopold (1072), and Leonard and King (932), substantiated the concept that mass flow involves metabolic loading of solutes and unloading at a suitable sink area. Both vein loading and translocation in *Phaseolus* were considered relative to a polarizing force in the outer parts of the veins (932). In addition, Leonard and King (932) found that rate of ^{32}P transport from blades to petioles was affected by the nature of the leaf treatment. Hence, spraying with tap water, in contrast to distilled water, reduced movement to petioles. Addition of Tween 20 to distilled water greatly increased the translocation of ^{32}P.

On the basis of "cytophysiological" studies of *Cucurbita pepo* phloem, Duloy *et al.* (451) claimed that mass flow rather than active transport offers the best explanation of solute transport. Sieve tubes having the appearance of "conduits", with little evidence of respiratory activity, were bordered by metabolically-active companion cells and highly-vacuolated parenchyma cells. This suggested a "division of function" accommodating the mass flow concept.

Bieleski (181), working with excised phloem and vascular tissues in celery and apple, developed methods suitable for measuring radioactive phosphate and sulfate accumulations in distinct cell types. In excised celery vascular tissue, and to a similar extent in apple, the most actively accumulating cells were those of the young secondary phloem situated at the sides of vascular bundles. Intact plants used the same tissues for major translocation activity. Sieve tubes were especially active in accumulating radioactive compounds – about 20 times more active than cortical parenchyma cells. Bieleski concluded that in the mechanism of phloem transport a primary role is performed by accumulation processes.

Nelson and his co-workers (1082, 1083) have shown that, at least in soybean and tobacco, the movement of assimilated carbon may be selective, *i.e.*, it may be translocated in several possible forms depending on the physiological condition of the plant. In soybean given adequate nutrient levels, ^{14}C supplied to leaves was recovered from stems in sucrose and serine (1082), Virtually all ^{14}C was recovered in sucrose among N-deficient plants. With adequate nutrients but with modified greenhouse environments malic acid was at times the only recoverable form of ^{14}C. Ten-fold variations in $^{14}CO_2$ supply had little qualitative effect on the carrier product in soybean. The proportion of serine transported along with sucrose varied as a function of plant age. In tobacco leaves (1083), Nelson found that ^{14}C was carried mainly in sucrose, although rate of sugar movement declined with increasing leaf age. In pine seedlings (*Pinus resinosa* and *Pinus strobus*) the rate of ^{14}C movement was markedly affected by the degree of root development and to a lesser extent by the seedlings' prior illumination history.

Regardless of transport mechanism the movement of sucrose and other organic material seems first and foremost to require a relationship of source to sink, *i.e.*, between areas of synthesis on the one hand and areas of utilization or storage on the other. Secondly, the sharing of phloem tissue by many compounds other than sucrose is a normal occurrence in many plants (876, 870). Sucrose appears to move along a concentration gradient while other phloem constituents can be carried along and "unloaded" in highly-concentrated deposits in sink areas. Since all living cells require sugar whether they bear chlorophyll or not, the phloem assumes a carbon-distributing role for cells which cannot synthesize their own carbohydrate. Crafts[i] proposed one mechanism based on a functional symplast and mesoplasm continuity in which sieve tubes act as a specialized elongated cell system. Within this system a carbohydrate gradient is transformed to a fluid hydrostatic gradient with high mobility potential between source and sink.

Advocates of the pressure flow concept do not appear to have found a satisfactory explanation for the exceptional permeability of the sieve plates. Taking as factual a semipermeable ectoplast in the sieve tube, Crafts visualized a linear flow velocity through protoplasmic strands at the sieve plate that would have to achieve hundreds of centimeters per hour. Formulas for calculating resistance to such flows are not applicable to sytoplasm nor have they been satisfactory in calculating cytoplasmic space from known flow velocities and pressures (392). A possible answer to rapid phloem exudation is found in Mendelssohn's (1009) data on *superfluidity* of molecules in a highly-ordered state. By this reasoning, if protoplasmic water exists in an ordered rather than randomized state (1397), water movement might be attained at rates unaccountable to normal concepts of physics.

In 1958 Spanner (1350) offered a different concept of transport based on electroosmosis. In essence, a pumping mechanism operative at each sieve plate would overcome local resistance while contributing force to the moving stream. Spanner maintained that the essential components are present in sieve plates, that is, a charged porous membrane and a membrane potential difference. The potential difference would be maintained by a cyclic movement of potassium ions into the sieve tube about the sieve plate, returning to a point below the plate via companion cells or phloem parenchyma. The potassium ion circulations would electrically polarize the sieve plate and rapid electroosmosis through the plate would occur. Spanner's theory has gained only limited support, however, and Crafts[1] notes his own earlier work demonstrating an absence of transport polarity in sieve tubes[4]. This observation was confirmed by Weatherley *et al.* (1543).

In his conclusions, Crafts[1] places considerable emphasis on rapid exudation from cut phloem (which can be observed even in wilted leaves), and states that whatever mechanism accounts for this phenomenon must automatically explain normal phloem transport. He concluded that the force of phloem transport arises from osmotic turgor development in the source areas, while absorption of the sieve tube sap in sink areas relieves the pressure and activates flow.

Evidence favoring turgor pressure as the driving force of translocation was presented by Zimmermann (1619) from experiments with normal and defoliated ash trees. He found that the total molar gradient of sucrose, raffinose, stachyose, and D-mannitol is basipetally positive during the summer, but upon defoliation the gradient disappears. Zimmermann's findings suggest that an α-D-galactosidase is positioned in the sieve tube cytoplasm which removes D-galactose residues from passing oligosaccharides, *i.e.*, producing sucrose from raffinose and raffinose from stachyose. This enzyme, by the way, has not been found in sugarcane leaf or leaf sheath tissue, although Hartt has suggested that sucrose conversion may occur in transit. Hatch and Glasziou (692) were unable to find evidence of sugar interconversion with a common transiting carbohydrate in sugarcane.

Evidence that energy expenditure is required by transport mechanisms was obtained from the respiratory inhibitor studies of Ziegler (1617) and Willenbrink (1573). In 1958 Ziegler reported comparatively strong respiratory activity in xylem and phloem tissue of *Heracleum* petioles. Cyanide treatment severely retarded O_2 consumption in both tissues. Ziegler interpreted his results as evidence for a mass flow mechanism. Willenbrink also observed higher respiration rates in conducting tissue of *Pelargonium* petioles, as compared with low rates in cortex parenchyma. HCN reversibly blocked assimilate transport but no effect was obtained with N_2, H_2 or CO. The inhibitors 2,4-dinitrophenol, arsenite, azide, and iodoacetic acid blocked transport completely and irreversibly. Willenbrink concluded that translocation in the phloem is dependent upon respiration.

---

[4]Crafts, A.S., 1936. Further studies on exudation in cucurbits, *Plant Physiol.* 11: 63–79.

By elaborating on Thaine's studies of transcellular streaming, and by incorporating the salient facts that a succesful transport system must accommodate, Canny (293) proposed a translocation theory given tentative acceptance among plant scientists. The transcellular strands and bi-directional movement observed by Thaine are taken to be of general occurrence; his velocities of particle movement are regarded as minimal for the physiological system. In their natural state the transcellular strands would occupy close to half the sieve tube lumen, surrounded by a sucrose solution containing lesser amount of other solutes (Fig. 8-1). A boundary is depicted between strands and sucrose solutions having greater permeability than that normally found between protoplasm and vacuole. Under these conditions, the transcellular strands will partially equilibrate with the sucrose solution of each sieve element through which they extend. Local differences in concentration will tend to disappear, the strands acting as a stirring mechanism for the entire sieve tube. The main feature of the transport system, movement of solutes, will occur *only* if there is a concentration gradient, and only *down* the concentration gradient[5]. For each solute this gradient will be determined by the rate and direction of its utilization. By this means movement can occur simultaneously in both directions so long as the biochemistry of the plant creates suitable sinks (utilization areas). Bi-directional movement can occur within a single sieve tube if the respective sinks are at opposite ends, and if concentration gradients extend in opposite directions. Canny's theory of translocation also accommodates some level of solute exchange with tissues surrounding the sieve tubes.

Canny distinguishes four gradients of sucrose concentration: One in the phloem tissue, one in the sieve tube reservoirs, and two in the transcellular strands. Of the latter two, one moves down and the other moves up the general gradient. Each of the gradients would be extremely difficult to measure since they are complicated by solute and water contents of phloem cells, and are generally inaccessible in their functioning state to conventional sampling methods. An exception to this might be found in the plant aphid, whose stylet has access to the nearly pure sieve-tube reservoir solution, but for reasons of possible stylet permeability even the aphid is held suspect (293).

In simplest terms, the transport operation might begin with the removal of sugar at the sink from a gradient-free, sink-to-source pathway (a phloem status which could exist for sugarcane during the early morning hours). At this time the sucrose concentration in all sieve-element reservoirs are presumably equal and the strands are streaming in both derections. Removal of sugar at the sink would produce a concentration drop in the reservoir sucrose solution of the terminal sieve element. There would follow a transfer of sugar *from* the next element and water movement *to* the next element. Canny (293) visualized a "wave of adjustment of the concentrations . . . along the sieve tube at something less than the rate of streaming, and a new

[5] In sugarcane a classical problem relevant to sucrose translocation stems from the fact that sucrose must move against a concentration gradient as part of the storage process (178, 180).

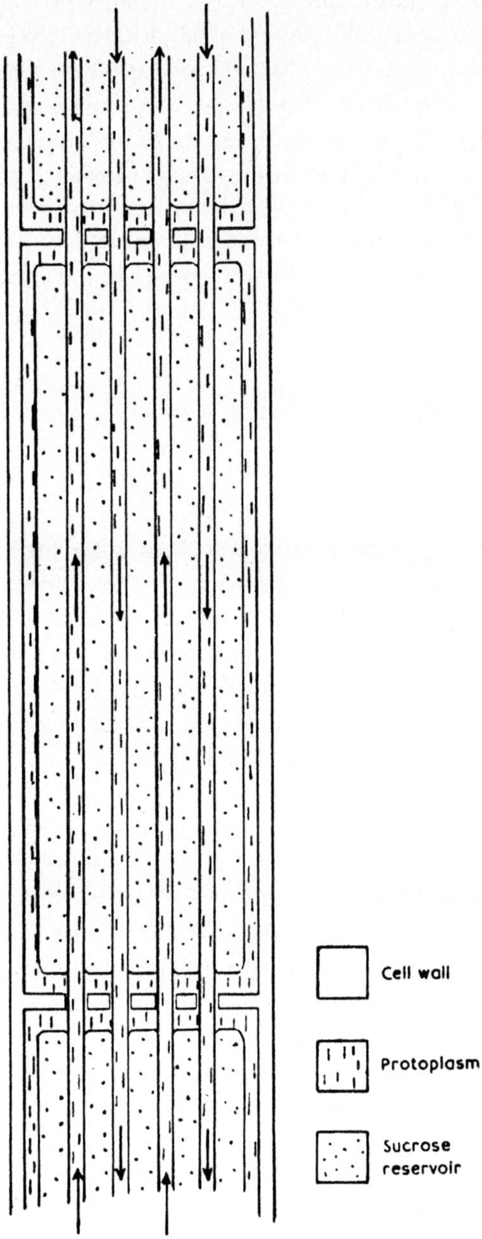

Fig. 8-1. Hypothetical representation of the structure and internal movement of a sieve tube. Strands are shown in the uncollapsed state transversing the sieve plates in accordance with the presumed continuity of driving force which propels the streaming solution. [After Canny (293).] Reproduced by permission of *Annals of Botany*, Oxford University Press, London.

steady state will be reached in which there is a gradient of concentration from source to sink". The slope of the gradient will increase with the rate of sugar utilization. In essence, the gradient will result from imperfect mixing within the extended sieve tube regardless of the mixing effect of the streaming strands (293). Assuming that movement within the sieve tube is more rapid than the loss of solute, Canny surmised that the reservoirs of elements close to the sinks will never lose a large percentage of their surcrose, an event which would result in a correspondingly large decline in movement to the next element. Local reservoir depletion is rendered unlikely in view of the large surface area of the sieve tube, relative to its diameter, from which sucrose can exit at low rates (293).

3. EFFECTS OF WATER STRESS ON SUCROSE TRANSPORT

A. *Context of plant water stress*

Plant physiologists have treated few topics more thoroughly than water stress, particularly water deficit and its effects upon various aspects of growth. Direct effects of water deficiency are difficult to distinguish from secondary ones; indeed, all life processes will eventually reflect the water stress if it is prolonged indefinitely. Wardlaw (1532) notes that photosynthesis, translocation of sugars, and growth have each been designated as the first process to be affected by water stress. He has shown that water deficit in wheat can reduce photosynthesis by half without affecting growth, or without affecting movement of photosynthate once it has entered the conducting tissues. On the other hand, water deficit in *Lolium temulentum* (1533) caused measurable reduction in leaf and root growth before photosynthesis was affected. In sugarcane there appears to be an extremely complex interrelationship between photosynthetic rate, leaf sucrose content, and moisture supply which varies diurnally even while plants are making normal growth. Response patterns to increasing water deficit probably vary with each species.

An apparent weakness of much water-stress research is the lack of clearly-defined parameters which describe the conditions of water within plant tissues. Wilson (1578–1580) distinguishes three essential components of leaf water potential: (a) Osmotic potential, due to solutes; (b) matrix potential, relating to water adsorption on the tissue matrix; and (c) turgor pressure potential. In this context hydrostatic pressures originating in capillary forces are assigned to matrix potential. Wilson cautions that conventional methods for measuring osmotic potential give all or part of matrix potential as well (1578). Mathematical methods have been developed (1580) for measuring the three components of leaf water potential based on three characteristic features of the tissue at full turgor. These include the sum of osmotic and matrix potentials, the proportion of total water content in bound form, and the coefficient of tissue enlargement. On this basis it follows that the usual practice of withholding water will not guarantee a consistent pattern of physiological changes even within a single species.

A longstanding question among students of water stress has been the pathway of transpirational water flow from the xylem to the evaporative leaf surface. This movement has far-reaching significance for photosynthesis, transport of assimilates, and drought resistance. Many workers have held that water moves by osmotic flow from one protoplast to the next. This view was discounted by Strugger (1378) more than 20 years ago on the basis of fluorescent dye movements pointing to a mass flow of water along the cell walls. Although some workers supported Strugger's thesis (549), his views were not generally accepted.

In 1961 Strugger and Peveling (1379) reported findings with the electron microscope which seemed to show accumulations of colloidal gold and silver particles in the cortical cell walls of transpiring *Helxine* shoots. This was taken as strong evidence of a mass flow of water within the wall, although only one tissue of a single species was used, and the densely-packed material was not unequivocally identified as the gold and silver particles taken up during immersion in sols. In 1964 Gaff *et al.* (550) substantiated the mass flow concept with electron microscopic data showing an "extrafascicular" movement of colloidal gold particles in *Helxine* tissues immersed in gold sols. It was observed that particle conduction was confined to discrete areas of the wall, presumably capillary spaces, of about 300 Å diameter. However, the results were inconclusive for such other species as *Beta vulgaris, Australina muelleri*, and *Eucalyptus globulus*.

In the context of the cell wall as interpreted by Scholander *et al.* (1306), the transfer system discovered by Gaff and his co-workers would serve as an extension of the xylem in which channels of flow intercommunicate freely through the cell wall. Gaff and Carr (549) found that in leaves of *Eucalyptus globulus* the cell-wall water could constitute up to 40 percent of the total leaf content at full turgor. This large amount of water was thought to have implications as a buffer against water loss from the protoplast, and was taken as evidence of the cell wall rather than the protoplast acting as the main pathway of extrafascicular water flow.

Teoh *et al.* (1412) also underscored the significance of water retention by cell walls in studies of root materials from several monocots and dicots. They concluded that the greater tenacity of drought-resistant species for holding cell-wall water helps to account for survival of xerophytes under arid or semi-arid conditions, regardless of whether specialized morphological adaptations are available to the plant. Thus a xerophyte is better equipped than a mesophyte to resist wilting within an equal deficit regime. In this respect the *apparent free space* (A.F.S.) or "outer space" of plant tissues, ranging from about 12 to 35 percent in roots (1412), holds special importance in that its localization within the cell wall (280, 936, 402, 1279, 1280) probably facilitates the mass flow of water along the wall (1412). Noting the relative order of water exchangeability developed by Petinov (1165), Teoh *et al.* (1412) suggested that the water of the cell wall and vascular system is relatively free, and thus might move from the wall structure to other cellular components where vital processes are subject to dehydration under drought conditions.

B. *Biochemical aspects of water stress*

An important biochemical effect of water deficit is the abnormal production of nitrogen compounds. Proteolysis and interrupted synthesis of proteins characteristically accompany water stress in a number of species (821, 1169, 1615, 146). RNA synthesis and degradation are affected by water shortage in the tomato (561). In citrus (318), marked increases and decreases in nitrogen metabolism were observed to follow one another when water supply was limiting. Levels of free amino acids can change quite drastically, particularly the level of proline (821, 318, 146).

Barnett and Naylor (146) reported proline accumulations up to 100-fold in shoots of Bermuda grass subjected to water stress. Asparagine and valine also increased while glutamic acid and alanine decreased. Low water supply also promotes amide accumulation (821, 318, 1049), possibly by incorporation of free ammonia from deaminated amino acids, which in turn arise from water-induced proteolysis (1049). Proline turnover in water-deficient Bermuda grass was so slow relative to other amino acids that Barnett and Naylor (146) suggested a storage role for proline under these conditions. They also found that amino acid synthesis continues under water stress while protein synthesis is inhibited and protein levels decline. However, no significant varietal differences were found in relation to amino acid and protein metabolism even though two varieties were selected with known variances in water-stress resistance.

Maretzki *et al.* (978) found that ^{14}C-labeled amino acids in sugarcane cell cultures tended to decrease as osmotic pressure of the suspension medium was increased. Those amino acids whose quantitative changes were not accompanied by comparable specific activity changes were regarded as possible sites of metabolic shifts related to water stress.

Respiration is almost always retarded by losses of relatively large amounts of water from plant tissues. Effects of lesser water restriction tend to be variable and some degree of respiratory stimulation has been recorded[6] (244). Zholkevitch and Koretskaya (1615) observed that water restriction led to a decline of phosphorylated compounds in pumpkin, and from this Kursanov (872) concluded that phosphorylation and oxidation may be uncoupled during drought. Flowers (530) reported evidence of mitochondrial malfunction in potato discs caused by water stress. Working with mitochondria isolated from soybean hypocotyls, Flowers and Hanson (531)

[6]Crafts, A.A., 1968. In *Water Deficits and Plant Growth*, Vol. 2, Academic Press, New York, pp. 85–133.

found that water stress induced by sucrose or KCl retarded respiration. This effect could not be attributed to lower water potential *per se* since hydrostatic pressure did not reverse a net decline of phosphorylation which paralleled lower oxidation. However, sucrose and KCl did inhibit the mitochondrial enzyme malate dehydrogenase, and from this it was suggested that the primary oxidation effects are exerted not by lowered water potential but by solute action against enzyme activity.

C. *Water stress and sucrose transport in sugarcane*

In 1967 Hartt (675) reported that restricted moisture supply has a deleterious effect upon the velocity and rate of sucrose translocation. Sugarcane thereby joined a number of species (1246, 1543, 1570, 1614) in which moisture stress appears to have adverse effects upon transport, in contrast with other plants seemingly more responsive in moving carbohydrate when water is limiting (466, 485, 1001, 1312). Hartt also found that, through relatively greater changes in growth processes and inversion, there can be a greater net accumulation of stored sucrose even though the velocity and quantity of movement is lessened. From this it is evident that unless considerable care is taken the data from water-stress experiments can be interpreted either way.

Withholding moisture is an accepted approach toward increased ripening in the field (342, 1219, 763, 648, 654, 656). It is generally assumed that this practice restricts further growth and allows sucrose to accumulate in the stalks. Its counterpart, heavy rainfall on the ripening cane, causes renewed growth accompanied by severe sucrose losses. Apparently, little thought was given to translocational effects of water stress in sugarcane prior to the work of Hartt (675). That low water might restrict sucrose transport was suggested by the sand-culture studies of Alexander (15), in which gradual decrease of water supply led to sucrose accumulation in the leaves. However, no distinction was drawn at the time between increased sugar synthesis and slackened sugar transport.

Employing the interspecific variety *H. 37-1933*, Hartt (675) studied ^{14}C transport in sugarcane experiencing water stress. Low moisture stress was produced by three methods: (a) Adding NaCl to nutrient solutions[7]; (b) by severing the stalk; and (c) by withholding water in the field. ^{14}C translocation was measured for 1.5 hours, 5 hours, 24 hours, or 6 weeks. Complete plants were harvested, subdivided, and sampled. Tissue samples were oven dried and ground to a powder prior to extraction with ethanol for sugar analyses. Counts were taken directly with powder and with ethanol extracts of

---

[7]Use of NaCl to increase osmotic concentration may have certain disadvantages owing to reduced K uptake. Greenway (612) found that NaCl markedly lowered the K content of root, leaf, and sheath tissues of *Hordeum vulgare* grown in water cultures. Pitman (1175) reported that the Na/K uptake ratio of *Hordeum vulgare* seedlings was related to transpiration rate. Tanimoto and Nickell (1407) developed a rapid test for sugarcane drought resistance by adding NaCl in increments to potted plants. No mention was made of NaCl effects upon the plants' K nutrition.

the milled tissues. Paper chromatograms were also prepared and counts were taken directly on the paper.

Hartt (675) found that the early rate of ^{14}C movement was greatly restricted when the nutrient solution tension (atmospheres) was increased by NaCl 48 hours prior to $^{14}CO_2$ treatment. Fig. 8-2 shows that within 90 minutes the control plants (in 0.4 atmosphere) moved proportionately greater amounts of ^{14}C-labeled photosynthate

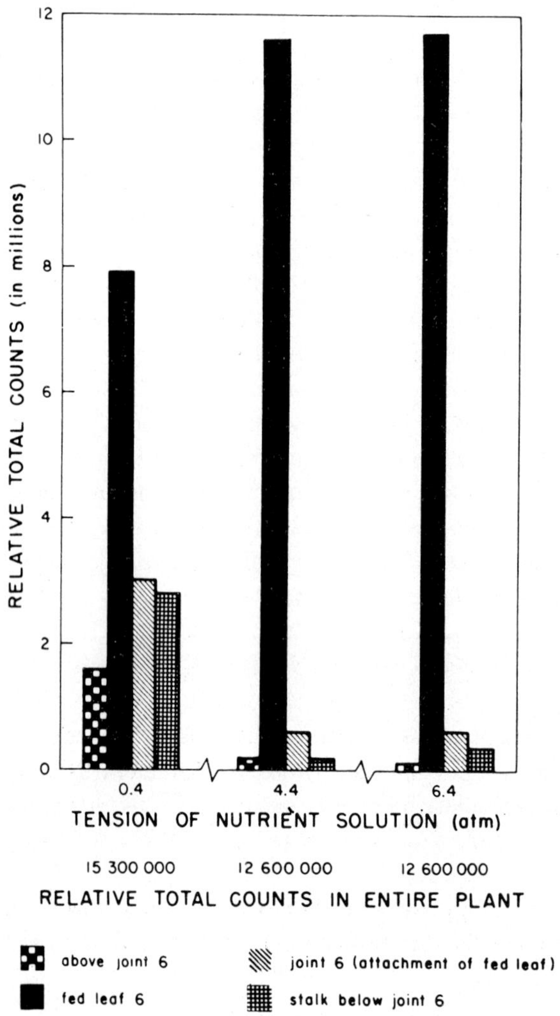

Fig. 8-2. Effects of moisture supply on [^{14}C]sucrose transport in sugarcane over a time course of 90 minutes. Moisture tensions were developed by immersing roots in NaCl solutions 48 hours prior to $^{14}CO_2$ treatment. Radioactive CO_2 was administered to blade $^+6$ for 5 minutes in sunlight. [After Hartt (676).] Reproduced by permission of *Plant Physiology*.

out of the treated leaf (No. 6) into the stalk tissues residing both above and below the point of leaf attachment. By this time nearly 50 percent of the ^{14}C had left the treated blade of control plants, as compared with less than 10 percent leaving the blade in plants given NaCl-treated nutrient solutions. As time progressed the higher moisture tensions continued to restrict ^{14}C transport. At 24 hours the plants under water stress had accumulated somewhat more sucrose than control plants in the internode corresponding to the treated leaf, but movement toward roots and spindle areas was definitely restricted. The intermediate tension (2.4 atmospheres) restricted downward transport at least as severely as the high tension (4.4 atmospheres). For upward transport the restriction was increasingly severe as tension was raised from 0.4 atmosphere (normal osmotic concentration) to 2.4 atmospheres to 4.4 atmospheres. Velocity of ^{14}C movement was not appreciably affected by the reduced availability of water. At 90 minutes the velocity was 1.3, 1.0, and 1.1 cm/minute, respectively, for the low; intermediate, and high tensions. This suggests that some fraction of the total quantity of sugar moved is translocated independently of water stresses affecting the bulk of translocate.

Moisture percentages calculated between 41 and 46 hours after exposure to $^{14}CO_2$ clearly reflected the plants' inability to absorb water under NaCl-induced tensions. In 46 hours the total water consumption by control plants was 825 ml; under 6.4 atmospheres tension the water concumption value was only 125 ml. The younger, elongating internodes were most severely affected by water stress, as evidenced both by low moisture consumption and retarded rates of elongation. Visible wilting characterized by rolling of the young leaves was evident for plants subjected to 6.4 atmospheres.

D. *Effects of restricted sucrose transport upon storage*

Hartt (675) studied the ^{14}C profile development for stalks in which water supply was restricted by severing the plant, or by NaCl-induced stress (4.4 and 6.4 atmospheres). Within 90 minutes a lag in profile development was recorded for the 4.4 and 6.4 atmospheres of tension. Fig. 8-3 illustrates the profile lag for cut stalks as compared to controls after 5 hours. During this period the cut plants lost their normal moisture gradient in addition to experiencing a general moisture decline.

In Fig. 8-4, Hartt (675) has summarized four experiments in which the quantity of ^{14}C movement under conditions of restricted water supply is calculated as the percentage of ^{14}C movement in control plants. Moisture supply was varied by NaCl-induced tension, severing the stalk, and by withholding irrigation to field-grown plants. Moistures stress created a generally adverse storage trend regardless of method. Within 90 minutes, an inability of ^{14}C to move from treated leaves was evident for plants subjected to an osmotic pressure of 4.4 atmospheres (Fig. 8-4A). At this time none of the plants had moved the label farther than the first internode below that of the treated

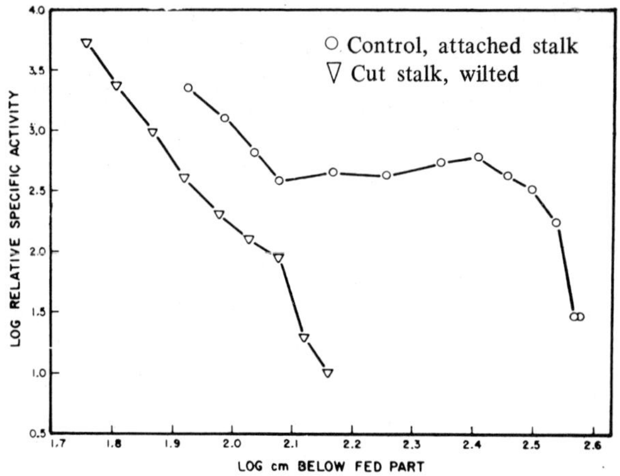

Fig. 8-3. Effects of moisture supply on the profile development of [^{14}C]sucrose transport over a time course of 5 hours. Radioactive CO_2 was administered to a segment of blade $^+$8 for 10 minutes in bright sunlight. The cut stalks were severed under water and the cut ends remained immersed during the entire translocation period. [After Hartt (675).] Reproduced by permission of *Plant Physiology*.

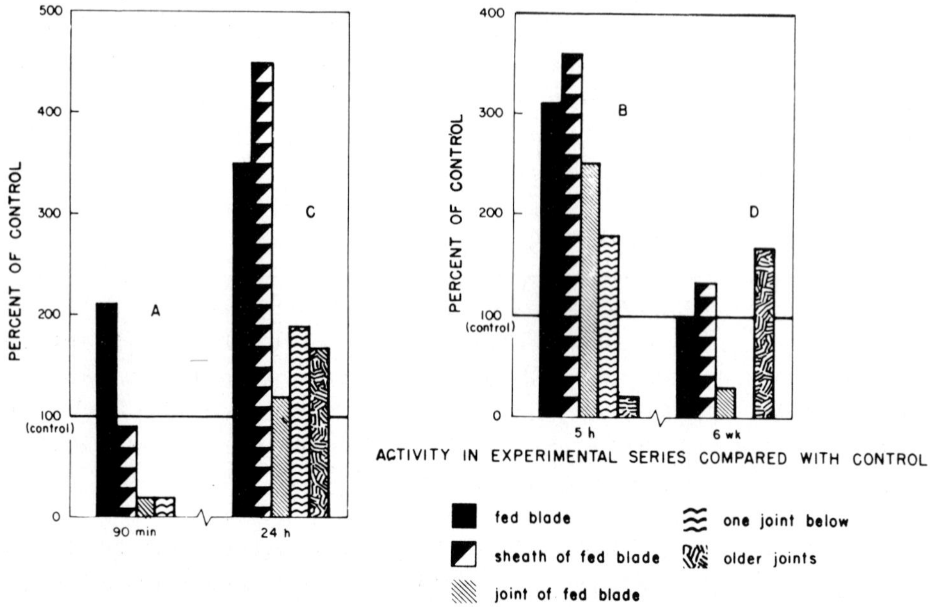

Fig. 8-4. Time effects on the relationships of moisture supply to sucrose transport and storage. (A) 90 minutes: NaCl treatment of plants in culture solution produced a 10-fold increase of moisture tension over 48 hours and [^{14}C]sucrose transport was measured during the final 90 minutes. (B) 5 hours: A normal turgid stalk is compared with a stalk severed under water to produce wilting. (C) 24 hours: Plants were immersed in NaCl solution for 43 hours; [^{14}C]sucrose transport was measured during the final 24 hours. (D) 6 weeks: In field plots, irrigated control plants were compared with non-irrigated plants. [After Hartt (675).] Reproduced by permission of *Plant Physiology*.

leaf. After 5 hours the plants that had been cut and wilted showed difficulty in transporting ^{14}C out of the treated leaf and leaf sheath, as well as from the corresponding internode plus the internode immediately below. Conversely, older internodes were accumulating less ^{14}C than controls, although small amounts of the radioactive sucrose were now moving down the stalk (Fig. 8-4B). Quite significantly, the plants subjected to 4.4 atmospheres for 24 hours contained more ^{14}C than controls in the older internodes as well as in the treated leaf and its corresponding internode (Fig. 8-4C). After 6 weeks the plants with restricted irrigation contained as much ^{14}C in the treated blade as did the controls, and in addition they had stored significantly more labeled sucrose in the older internodes than did the control plants (Fig. 8-4D).

The fact that retarded transport ultimately increased the quantity of sucrose in storage was verified by subsequent experiments of 1 month duration. Hartt (675) interpreted this effect as true ripening; water content was decreased, sucrose increased, and the ratio of sucrose to reducing sugars increased. A curious feature here is that low water supply also restricts sugar synthesis as well as movement (675, 674); hence, the increase of storage sucrose must signify that production losses are less severe than the losses due to slower transport. Hartt concluded that the growth restriction allowed more sucrose to become available for storage, and that slower transport gave the additional sucrose more time to accumulate in storage tissues. A weak point of this view is that optimum sucrose production requires a maximum tonnage of stalk tissue as well as an affluent storage mechanism. Growth restriction would thus be valid only toward the final weeks of the production cycle. Another questionable point is whether sucrose does in fact need more time to accomplish efficient storage. If so, the normal storage process as depicted in the sugar accumulation cycle (*cf.* Chapter 9, pp. 348–353) may not be operating efficiently. This would imply a weak link in the essential enzymology of incident storage reactions under normal conditions, or possibly improved enzymology under conditions of water stress. New studies designed to measure low-water effects on enzymes functional in the storage process should help to clarify this question.

4. EFFECTS OF LIGHT ON SUCROSE TRANSPORT

In the preceding chapter the work of Hartt *et al.* (667) was discussed briefly in relation to the polarity of cane sucrose movement in light and darkness. Light was shown to be an essential factor in maintaining basipetal movement. Some of the data presented was suggestive of an ATP involvement as the energy source for sugar transport. In addition, the origin of driving force has been shown to reside in the leaf itself. However, in spite of implications to the contrary, Hartt (665) discounted photosynthesis as an energy source for translocation. Her conclusion was based on the fact that very little sunlight is required to move sucrose. She found that 100 foot candles (well below sugarcane's light compensation point) was equally effective as full sunlight in satisfying the light requirement for translocation in detached blades. Hartt therefore assumed that light played only an activating role in sucrose transport. Conversely, the essentiality of this small amount of light was taken to mean that respiration does not play a part in translocation (665).

Aside from chlorophyll, two other types of light-absorbing pigments were considered as possible activating systems for sugar transport: Phytochrome and the yellow pigments. The latter, which absorb blue light, were eliminated when transport was found not to be restricted to blue light. Hartt (665) therefore proposed that phytochrome or some other low-energy system is responsible for activating translocation. The fact that translocation does not take place in far-red light offers some support to this thesis. However, one could also interpret this as tacit evidence for the essentiality of noncyclic photosynthetic phosphorylation. Arnon *et al.* (108) found that in spinach chloroplasts the production of ATP nearly ceased as the wavelength of monochromatic light was increased from 664 to 708 nm.

In subsequent experiments Hartt (672) evaluated ^{14}C-labeled photosynthate transport as a function of light quality. Using detached blades from the varieties *H. 37-1933* and *H. 50-7209*, differing light exposures were provided with red, green, blue, and cool-white fluorescent lamps. Far-red illumination was obtained from incandescent lamps and sunlight. Basipetal translocation was stimulated more by red or blue illumination than by green or cool-white illumination. Far-red light was equivalent to total darkness in that both failed to support translocation. Hartt observed more effective basipetal translocation occurring in red light free of blue light than in cool-white fluorescent light. From this she postulated a stimulatory effect of red light on sucrose translocation. Although Hartt was unable to determine whether chlorophyll or other pigments were involved in stimulating transport, she did demonstrate that light quality affects sucrose movement by means other than physicochemical changes in protoplasmic properties.

Recognizing that light had markedly affected sucrose transport in earlier studies, Hartt (673) initiated additional experiments with detached blades designed to show whether light produced effects upon translocation other than those relating to CO_2 assimilation. From these and subsequent experiments (672) have come our best picture of light roles in sugarcane assimilate movement. Hartt took into consideration such factors as the time of day when blades were detached, time-course of ^{14}C translocation, light intensity, effects of intermittent illumination, and the light compensation point for transport initiation as compared to the light compensation point for CO_2 assimilation. The translocation features found to be most affected by light were polarity and the percentage of ^{14}C moved.

Blades detached in the morning were found to translocate ^{14}C more effectively than those removed in the afternoon; however, in darkness the afternoon blades were superior for translocation. This substantiated earlier findings by Hartt and Kortschak

(669) suggesting that the capacity to move sucrose in darkness increased when sampled leaves remained attached to the stalk for increased periods during the day. Light significantly increased basipetal translocation in leaves, with morning blades being superior to afternoon blades.

The importance of the leaf apex and polarity of movement was underscored when it was found that darkening the apex plus the $^{14}CO_2$-exposed area led to a loss of sufficient "push" to move all of the photosynthate out of the leaf. A reversal of polarity occurred between 2.5 and 3 hours when the sugar which had not moved out of the leaf, plus some that had, began moving toward the apex. The ensuing acropetal transport was most pronounced in morning blades, and total transport (basipetal plus acropetal) was always greater in light than in darkness. As little as 5 minutes of light exposure (2000 foot candles) interspersed with 25-minute periods of darkness sufficed to maintain the acropetal flow. The "factor" controlling polarity was saturated at only 50 foot candles. Polarity of movement was therefore controlled by much less light than was needed to drive basipetal transport.

Photosynthetic measurements with an infrared analyzer revealed CO_2 assimilation being saturated between 5000 and 7000 foot candles. Basipetal transport was saturated at a maximum of 250 foot candles, and its compensation point was established at about half this value. This seemed to establish a light effect upon translocation which occurs independently of the CO_2 assimilation reactions producing sucrose. Hartt (673) concluded that light did not simply produce a "washing out" of [^{14}C]sucrose by the continuing production of sucrose in natural CO_2, as had been suggested earlier by Hartt *et al.* (670).

It was again proposed that translocation is photochemically controlled, but critical evidence for such a mechanism has not yet been presented. Hartt did suggest than an electrokinetic mechanism might be operative in the manner of that described by Fenson (519). After reexamining electroosmosis and streaming potentials in xylem and phloem, Fenson had concluded that bioelectrical forces are of adequate magnitude to cause transport, and that they operate in a direction to assist assimilate movement. The necessary potentials would be produced through metabolic activity and membrane diffusion.

A possible role of ATP was also suggested by Hartt (673). Working with the sugar beet, Kursanov (876) had demonstrated increased sucrose movement in leaves enriched with ATP. The energy-rich third phosphate group appeared to be involved in activating this movement since neither ADP nor AMP gave appreciable transport stimulation. Hartt and Kortschak (669) reported earlier that an inhibitor of photosynthetic phosphorylation, 3-(*p*-chlorophenyl)-1,1-dimethylurea (CMU) (787), decreased basipetal translocation in detached sugarcane blades. Treatment of the cut end with ATP had little effect on ^{14}C movement but the authors expressed doubt as to whether ATP was absorbed.

In a subsequent report on light effects Hartt (673) finally suggested that photosynthetic phosphorylation might be the source of energy for translocation. This process occurs independently of CO_2 assimilation, but it would not appear to be very productive at the low light intensities which control polarity. A possible explanation might be found in Canny's (293) hypothesis which holds that the sugar gradient needed for transport is initiated when sugar is removed from the sieve elements adjacent to the sink. In sugarcane a low light intensity might suffice to intitiate the gradient by slight increases of sucrose utilization, with the energy for mass flow being derived at higher light intensities. This is especially attractive for the intact plant since early-morning light greatly stimulates inversion potential within actively-elongating immature storage tissues (1340, 54).

Fig. 8-5 illustrates diurnal changes in sucrose content of leaf and immature storage

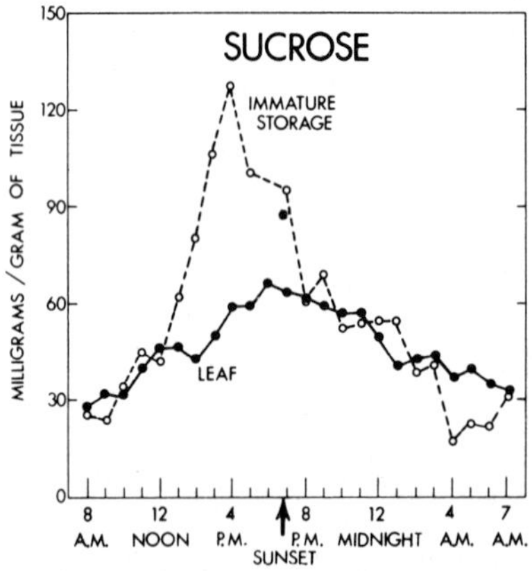

Fig. 8-5. Diurnal and nocturnal changes in sucrose content of sugarcane leaf tissue and immature storage tissue. [After Alexander *et al.* (54).]

tissue as reported by Alexander *et al.* (54). Tissue samples were harvested at 1-hour intervals from 12-week-old plants of the variety *P.R. 980.* Clearly evident is a several-fold increase and decline of sucrose in immature storage tissue and a lesser increase and decline in leaves. The sucrose changes were a function of photosynthesis and translocation rather than of invertase activity (54). Changing sucrose content in the immature storage area appears not to have been a direct function of photosynthesis for several reasons: (a) Sucrose loss from immature storage tissue began several hours before photosynthate accumulation reached a maximum in leaves. (b) Sucrose movement into immature storage tissue began in the early morning at least 2 hours before sunrise. This apparent response to mere traces of light lends support to Hartt's (675) thesis that translocation can be activated by extremely low light intensities. (c) Sucrose continued to move out of the leaves throughout the night. The nocturnal transport is additional evidence of respiratory involvement in sugarcane translocation processes.

Evidence of light effects on sucrose storage and utilization processes is presented in

Figs. 8-6 and 8-7. Slack (1340), and later Alexander *et al.* (54), found that invertase activity varies up to 7-fold in immature storage tissue during daylight hours. From the 24-hour study summarized in Fig. 8-6 it can be seen that a major invertase peak occurred around 9:00 a.m., and that day activity was still relatively high between 11:00 a.m. and 1:00 p.m. Plants maintained concurrently in darkness did not produce an activity peak at 9:00 a.m.

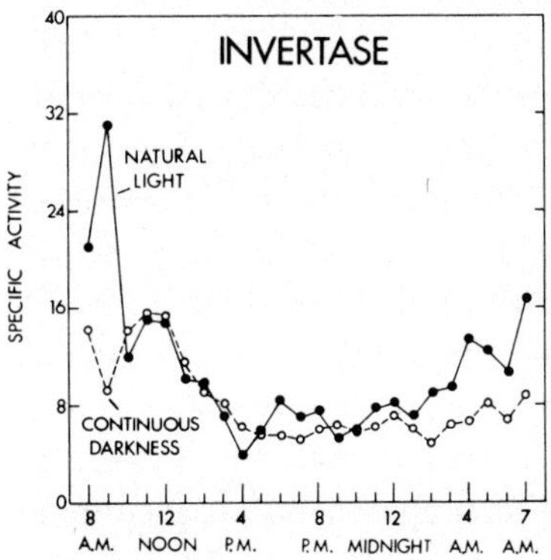

Fig. 8-6. Diurnal fluctuations in the acid invertase activity of immature storage tissue. [After Alexander *et al.* (54).]

In Fig. 8-7 the products of invertase action, glucose and fructose, are shown to fluctate markedly in illuminated plants but not in darkened ones. This apparently reflects an increased demand for hexose by light-stimulated growth processes (54). The respective hexose pools would then experience a continuous flux between input, from invertase action, and utilization via hexokinase-mediated phosphorylation and sub-

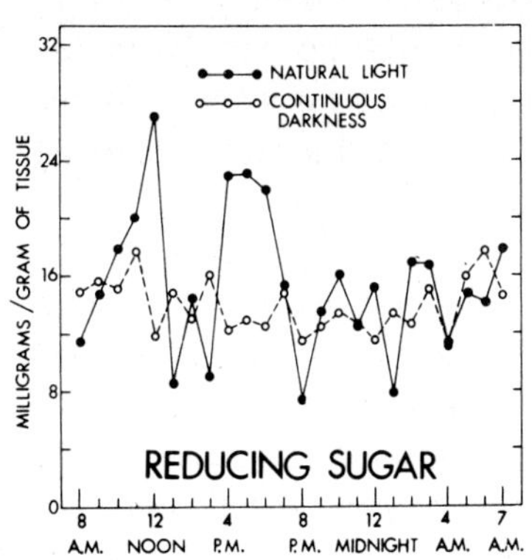

Fig. 8-7. Diurnal and nocturnal hexose levels in immature storage tissue of sugarcane given variable illumination. Reducing sugars were fairly constant over the 24-hour interval in darkened plants but not in plants exposed to a normal day–night illumination sequence. [After Alexander *et al.* (54).]

sequent respiratory metabolism. A hexokinase (glucokinase) has been found in sugarcane leaves (11). The relatively constant hexose levels in the absence of light might also be due in part to lack of a light-generated ATP pool of sufficient size to accommodate the full hexokinase potential.

5. TEMPERATURE EFFECTS ON SUCROSE TRANSPORT

Many plant scientists hold that growth and assimilation processes may relate more closely to the plant's effectiveness in utilizing or storing photosynthate than to its maximum photosynthetic potential (767, 768, 1428, 276). Humphries (767) described a series of controlled-temperature experiments with detached but rooted leaves of *Vicia* in which an active physiological sink was provided by the developing roots. By varying the temperature of nutrient solutions around the roots, Humphries altered both the rate of carbohydrate utilization and the rate of photosynthesis. By use of a relatively simple source–sink apparatus a remarkable regulatory potential of temperature was thereby underscored. In addition to direct effects upon carbohydrate utilization, low root temperature is possibly regulatory for mineral uptake and movement (766, 784, 1117). Lowered mineral uptake might in turn affect photosynthesis, directly (1454), or indirectly by lowering the rate of photosynthate export from leaves (1455). According to Burt (277), in the potato tuber the initiation of the sink itself is favored by low temperature and low mineral supply, whereas high temperature and high nutrient levels favor carbohydrate utilization by the sink.

In 1965 Hartt (671) reported a series of controlled-temperature studies of ^{14}C-labeled photosynthate movement in sugarcane grown in nutrient solution. Root and air temperatures were regulated independently by means of specially-constructed climate houses, with plant containers being immersed in troughs of water having thermostatically-controlled temperature. Translocation experiments were performed under full sunlight, and efforts were made to control the range of daily temperatures rather than to hold a single temperature constant. These studies were remarkably productive, particularly in the area of transport mechanisms where Hartt was able to distinguish between physiochemical and chemical aspects of assimilate movement.

Air temperature directly affected the percentage of ^{14}C moving out of leaf blades, and the percentage of ^{14}C moving down the stalk. According to Swanson (1393), optimum temperature for translocation from bean leaves lies between 20 and 30 °C. Hartt's data indicated that the optimum temperature for sugarcane may be close to 33 °C for both upward and downward transport. Velocity of ^{14}C translocation was also affected by temperature, being 1.40, 1.56, and 2.00 cm/minute at 20, 24, and 33 °C respectively. As insurance against the possibility of temperature effects upon transport being secondary to temperature relationships with growth and water content, Hartt also measured ^{14}C movement in detached blades. Definite ^{14}C movement was detected at 22 °C, but movement completely stopped when the temperature was lowered to 5 °C. This was taken to mean that the sugarcane translocation process has a temperature coefficient (Q_{10}) greater than 1.0. According to Hartt (671), a Q_{10} value less than 1.0 has been reported for translocation in tomato (1558).

Fig. 8-8, illustrating the effects of variable air temperatures on the translocation profile in the sugarcane stalk, also suggests that temperature affects assimilate movement independently of its relationship to growth (671). Overall slope of the profile did not vary, but at any given distance along the stalk the relative specific activity (net counts per minute at infinite thickness) consistently showed a positive correlation with temperature.

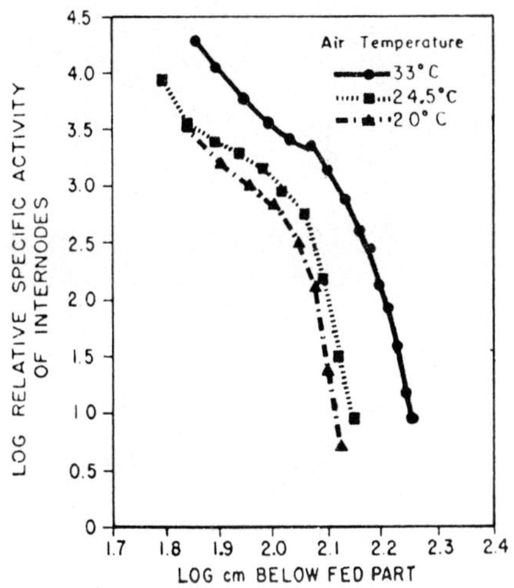

Fig. 8-8. Effect of air temperature of the translocation profile of [^{14}C]sucrose in sugarcane. The profile slope remained unaffected by air temperature, but relative specific activities at given distances along the stalk were positively related to air temperature. [After Hartt (671).] Reproduced by permission of *Plant Physiology.*

The Q_{10} values recorded by Hartt (671) are particularly significant in view of the fact that temperature coefficients of physiological reactions are usually greater than 2.0 (804). Hartt obtained Q_{10} values of 1.1 to 1.5, and 1.05 to 1.7, for ^{14}C movement out of the blade and ^{14}C movement down the stem, respectively. Waldron *et al.* (1518) reported a similar value (Q_{10} = 1.1). In contrast, much larger values (Q_{10} = 3.9 to 16.2) were obtained by Hartt for movement up the stem. This suggests that a physical or a physicochemical process is operative for downward translocation, but that a chemical process, involving enzyme-catalyzed reactions, accounts for upward transport. This is strong support for Canny's (293) translocation hypothesis which requires that assimilate-utilizing reactions initiate a concentration gradient by removal of sugar at the physiological sink. In this instance the sink would be developing leaves and elongating storage tissue of the spindle area. Hartt (671) further substantiated her thesis by pointing out the lowering of [^{14}C]sucrose transport to meristematic areas when growth is restricted by P deficiency (271). The low Q_{10} values for downward transport might possibly be taken as evidence of light-driven translocation from the leaf since the photochemical reactions relative to ATP formation are essentially independent of temperature (107). A similar interpretation was given by Jenson and Taylor (804) for their low Q_{10} values (1.3 to 1.7) for water translocation through stems of sunflower and tomato.

Hartt (665) also found that low-temperature treatment of roots decreased translocation from the leaf (Fig. 8-9). In less than 10 hours a very powerful restriction was

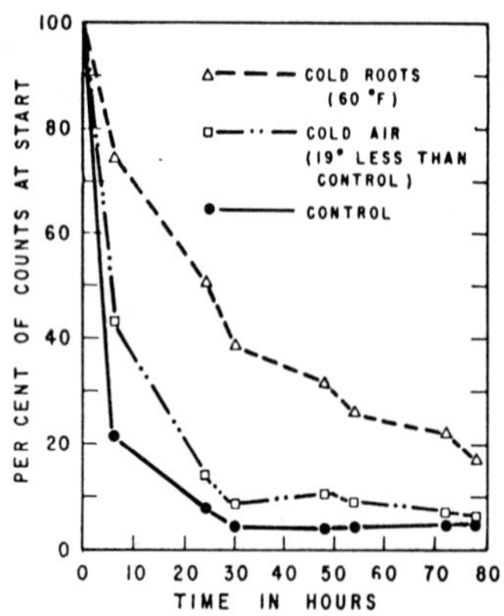

Fig. 8-9. Sucrose transport repression as a function of cool temperature and of root-chilling treatments. [After Hartt (671).] Reproduced by permission of *Plant Physiology*.

exerted by root chilling in contrast to only moderate restriction when air temperature was lowered. This response was apparently related to the plant water status at the time that ^{14}C-labeled photosynthate movement was being studied. Transport was restricted by low root temperature only at high light intensities, *i.e.*, at a time when the plants were experiencing considerable moisture stress. Root chilling had no effect on transport during cloudy days with intermittent sun. In general, low temperature appears to produce an adverse effect on water uptake and movement in plants (804).

The low-temperature effects elaborated by Hartt (671) have practical implications relative to sucrose yield. By retarding transport, sucrose is allowed to accumulate in the leaves where it might act as a deterrent to photosynthesis[8] (666). The circulatory system also fails to operate normally when roots are cooled, as indicated by foliar accumulations of ^{32}P taken up from the nutrient solution, and by a parallel slowing of

[8]Waldron *et al.* (1518) contested this view, reporting that photosynthate repression was not the controlling factor for photosynthesis in detached leaves given prolonged light treatments.

the return of organic phosphates through the phloem (671). On the other hand, low night temperatures (presumably restrictive against a much lower rate of sucrose transport) are known to increase sucrose yield in Puerto Rico. After exhaustive statistical analyses of climate and weather data, Lugo-López and Capó (963) concluded that cool night temperatures with relatively broad ranges between maximum and minimum values increased sucrose yields more than any other factor. This is apparently due to increased ripening as a consequence of growth reduction. Samuels (1291) has described cool temperature as a major factor in the ripening of sugarcane.

Alexander and Samuels (34) found that neither a high-tonnage variety (*P.R. 980*) nor a "sweet" variety (*P.R. 1059*) was able to accumulate normal amounts of sucrose in storage tissue with temperature held constant between 80 and 85 °F. However, when temperature was held between 50 and 55 °F, *P.R. 1059* accumulated far more sucrose than did *P.R. 980.* Within the lower temperature regime there appeared to be a general deficiency of enzymes in the high-tonnage variety *P.R. 980*, but not in *P.R. 1059* (Table 8-1). In essence, the leaf enzyme content of *P.R. 980* plants kept continuously warm did not equal the content of *P.R. 1059* plants kept continuously chilled. It was concluded that varietal factors can bear heavily on sugar and enzyme response to temperature.

TABLE 8-1

ENZYME CHANGES IN SUGARCANE SUBJECTED TO CONTINUOUS WARM AND COOL TEMPERATURES

All plants were grown in sand culture in an ordinary greenhouse for 12 weeks. They were then transferred to walk-in, controlled-temperature chambers where treatments were given for 10 weeks. All plants received abundant water and a complete nutrient solution throughout their entire growth period. [After Alexander and Samuels (34).]

Tissue	Var.	Temp. (°F)	Enzyme (specific activity)					
			Phosphatase	ATPase	Amylase	Peroxidase	Phenol oxidase	Invertase
Leaf	*P.R. 980*	55–60	4.3	7.0	26	21	9	–
		80–85	6.5	8.4	55	27	14	–
	P.R. 1059	55–60	11.0	16.0	78	52	20	–
		80–85	9.0	11.6	165	34	20	–
Immature storage	*P.R. 980*	55–60	13	16	52	15	16	6.1
		80–85	22	23	71	23	16	8.2
	P.R. 1059	55–60	15	20	66	22	15	0.9
		80–85	18	20	70	22	15	6.9

6. EFFECTS OF NUTRIENT DEFICIENCIES ON SUCROSE TRANSPORT

Major restrictions on sucrose translocation have been associated with inadequate nutrient supply. Hartt (665) reported a decline in both the rate and velocity of ^{14}C movement by plants deficient in N, P, and K (Table 8-2). ^{14}C data presented in Table 8-2 show that in deficient plants sucrose was retained in the treated blade over a

TABLE 8-2

EFFECTS OF NITROGEN, PHOSPHORUS, AND POTASSIUM DEFICIENCIES ON [^{14}C]-SUCROSE TRANSPORT IN SUGARCANE

[After Hartt (665).] Reproduced by permission of the *Hawaiian Sugar Technologists' Association*, Honolulu.

Tissue	Percent of total radioactivity			
	Control	–N	–P	–K
Leaves and joints $^{+}1$–$^{+}5$	1.8	0.1	0.2	0.1
Leaf $^{+}6$, above treatment	0.03	0.2	0.2	0.2
Leaf $^{+}6$, treated area	41	69	75	77
Leaf $^{+}6$, below treatment	14	27	19	18
Sheath $^{+}6$	14	4	4	5
Internode $^{+}6$	10	0.2	0.3	0.6
$^{+}7$	7	0	0.2	0.4
$^{+}8$	5	0	0	0
$^{+}9$	3			
$^{+}10$	2			
$^{+}11$	1			
$^{+}12$	1			
$^{+}13$	0.4			
$^{+}14$	0.15			
$^{+}15$	0.11			
$^{+}16$–$^{+}21$	0			
TC*/plant ($\times 10^6$)	100	79	66	108

*TC = total counts.

period of 90 minutes while in control plants some ^{14}C had moved along a transloca-tion course about nine internodes in length. The relative consistency of response among the different nutrient deficiencies implies that their effect was incidental to the loss of plant vigor rather than to direct influences upon transport mechanisms.

An important nutritional effect reported by numerous workers is the loss of storage sucrose owing to lack of K. The essentiality of K for high juice quality was well established prior to 1934 (651, 650). Low sucrose yields associated with K deficiency (1287, 1286, 1289, 1285, 161), or imbalance of the K/N ratio (761), are quite possibly related to inadequate sucrose transport between leaf and stalk tissues. In essence, this constitutes a physiological manifestation of the delayed maturation effect described by Acevedo-Ramos (2). Samuels and Landrau (1286) reported K fertilization increased juice quality along with tonnage in more than 200 field experiments. This strongly implies that the effect of low K is more complex than simple growth restriction, and that some critical transport process is not functioning normally between source and sink areas.

Nelson *et al.* (1081) emphasized the relationship of N status to ^{14}C-labeled photosynthate movement in studies of normal and N-deficient soybean grown in nutrient solutions. In plants given an adequate nutrient solution the ^{14}C was recovered from the stem in sucrose and serine. In N-deficient plants nearly 100 percent of the stem ^{14}C was recovered as sucrose. Analyses of differently-aged plants showed that serine was translocated with sucrose but not in the same proportions found in the leaves. Since metabolic conversion of sucrose to serine in transit was too slow to account for the quantities extracted, it was concluded that assimilate transport is selective, depending upon the growth conditions available to the plant. In this instance N status was shown to affect the qualitative make-up of assimilate flow as well as the rate and velocity of movement.

A possible clue to the mechanism of nutritional stress as it relates to cane sucrose transport was suggested by Alexander (31). Gradual development of N, P, K, and Ca deficiencies in sand culture was shown to be accompanied by increased sucrose accumulations in leaves (Table 8-3). Although daily nutrient treatments approached

TABLE 8-3

EFFECTS OF GRADUALLY DECREASING NUTRIENT SUPPLIES ON THE FOLIAR SUCROSE CONTENT OF SUGARCANE GROWN IN SAND CULTURE

All plants received adequate nutrient levels until 14 weeks of age. Control plants continued to receive the complete nutrient complement while N, P, K, and Ca were lowered individually in separate populations at 2-week intervals. [After Alexander (31).]

Treatment	Age of plants (weeks) 14	16	18	20	22	24	26	28	30	Mean
	mg sucrose/g dry wt.									
Control	69	53	89	96	89	82	76	80	90	80
–N	65	75	97	148	116	112	135	123	110	109
–P	67	68	101	132	96	84	78	120	110	95
–K	59	65	94	114	111	115	104	108	117	99
–Ca	65	70	113	125	94	87	90	119	141	100

deficiency levels toward the close of the study, sucrose increases were recorded much earlier when nutrient supplies were still adequate. This suggested that a rather delicate change had been triggered in the transport mechanism by shifts in nutritional balance rather than by outright nutritional deficit. Foliar enzyme analyses showed positive correlations between increased sucrose and decreasing enzyme activity, particularly with reference to β-amylase (Fig. 8-10). It is evident from Fig. 8-10 that the initial lowering of each nutrient was followed closely by the initial decline of amylase, and by the close of the study low amylase activity was a feature of each of the four nutritional-stress regimes.

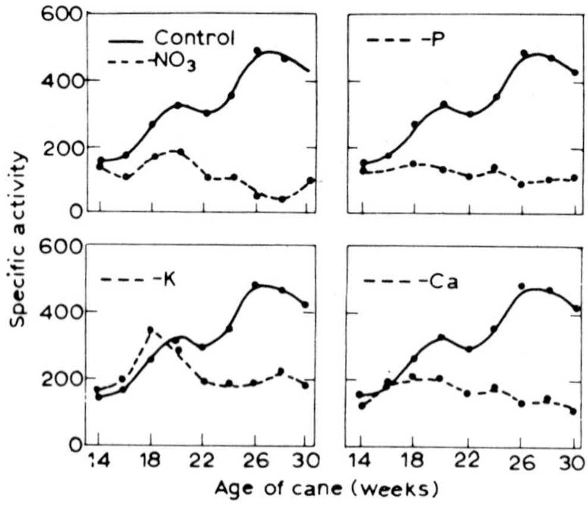

Fig. 8-10. Amylase decline in sugarcane leaves as a function of nutritional stress. The enzyme was sensitive to lowered supply of each of the four major nutrients. NO_3=nitrate. [After Alexander (31).]

Lessened amylase activity potential may possibly affect the conversion of insoluble photosynthate residues to a soluble, and hence movable, form. Insoluble photosynthesis products have been reported in sugarcane by Hartt *et al.* (667) and by Hatch and Slack (693). Similar insoluble residues are also formed in the stalk from translocated sucrose (665). These residues are probably polysaccharides constituting chains of glucose residues having variable length and branching properties. Hartt (675) suggests that they are converted to sucrose and thereby contribute to nocturnal translocation processes. This concept is supported by the work of Geiger and Batey (569) with sugar beet. Observed diurnal changes in foliar amylase (A.G. Alexander, unpublished) also support its role in leaf sucrose accumulation and transport. On the other hand, early concepts of direct sucrose–starch interconversion (1059, 1583) have not received wide support. The amylase-mediated conversion of glucans to sucrose could hardly be a direct one since the logical amylase product would be maltose. Other essential enzymes would include maltase, glucokinase, phosphoglucomutase (or phosphohexose isomerase), and sucrose synthetase. The enzymes UDPG–fructose-6-*P* transglycosylase and sucrose-*P* phosphatase might also be involved. A phosphorylase-linked mechanism such as that found to be temperature controlled in potato tubers (960) might also be operative, in which case amylase would affect the equilibrium constant by hydrolysis of the polysaccharide product. The rather consistent correlation of low amylase activity with foliar sucrose accumulations (34, 31, 11) does suggest a rate-limiting role of amylase at some point in the reaction sequence.

7. EFFECTS OF LEAF COMPETITION

In a series of ^{14}C experiments with variably-defoliated plants, Hartt *et al.* (670) discovered a major competition among cane leaves in their movement of sucrose toward storage areas. This competition resides primarily in the uppermost leaves, *i.e.*, in leaves elevated above the blade exposed to $^{14}CO_2$ in Fig. 8-11. Thus, removal of the

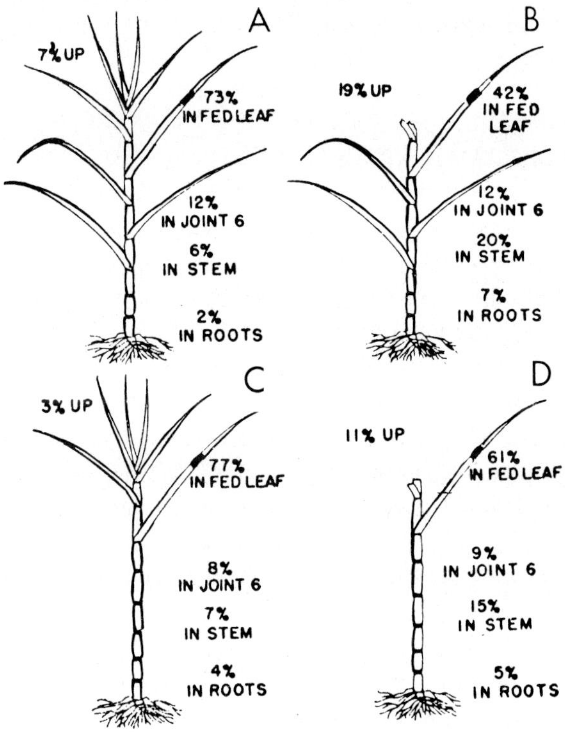

Fig. 8-11. Effect of defoliation on [^{14}C]sucrose transport from blade $^{+}6$. (A) No defoliation. (B) Blade $^{+}5$ and higher blades were removed. (C) All blades removed below blade $^{+}6$. (D) All leaves removed except leaf $^{+}6$. [After Hartt *et al.* (670).] Reproduced by permission of *Plant Physiology*.

upper leaves caused a greater portion of the ^{14}C to move out of the treated blade and down through leaf sheath and stalk tissues. Upward movement of ^{14}C in the stalk was also increased by removal of higher leaves. Similar transport stimulation was observed when all leaves except the treated one were removed. Wardlaw (1532) noted that in *Lolium temulentum* the removal of all but the treated leaf increases the demand for assimilates from that leaf. Hartt *et al.* (670) found that removal of the lower leaves had little effect on sucrose translocation, a fact which eliminates the possibility of older leaves acting as a sucrose sink for the leaves above. On this basis Hartt *et al.* concluded that a mature leaf experiences increasing competition from the younger leaves above with passage of time.

Since removal of all but the $^{14}CO_2$-treated blade did not retard the capacity of this blade to translocate sucrose, Hartt *et al.* (670) concluded that transpirational pull of the surrounding leaves does not affect translocation. The critical area of competition appeared to be the site of leaf sheath attachment to the stalk. Sucrose passing down the blade and sheath of an older leaf seemed to have difficulty in exiting from the leaf owing to the mass of sucrose already flowing downward from above. On the other hand, the same series of experiments suggested that the major force of translocation resides within the blade itself (670).

8. EFFECTS OF WIND AND MECHANICAL INJURY

The aging sugarcane leaf experiences increased difficulty in maintaining an unbroken line of conducting tissue between the apex and its union with the stalk. Under various kinds of physiological stress the more mature leaves will discolor, desiccate, and loosen their attachment to the stalk, even as the younger leaves above continue to resist the adverse environment. Under the most ideal conditions a mature leaf eventually has to drop away, a highly desirable feature from the standpoint of harvesting a clean stalk. On the other hand, Hartt (665) suggests that the tendency of breeders to select for readily-defoliating plants might cost the industry some otherwise excellent sugar-producing clones. It is doubtful whether the leaf's potential duration as a photosynthetic asset is ordinarily achieved.

As a rule, the fully-emerged leaf is exposed to more or less continual buffeting by the wind. Hartt (666) tried to ascertain the effect of wind damage on sucrose transport by inflicting various injuries to the blade immediately after exposing it to $^{14}CO_2$. These injuries included bending the midrib, bending the lamina, bending the midrib plus lamina sharply at right angles, and fraying the lamina at different positions along the blade. Restriction of the midrib alone retarded translocation. Restricting the lamina alone caused more severe retardation, while bending sharply both the midrib and lamina virtually halted all sucrose transport.

Hartt (666) also noted that restrictions imposed upon midrib and lamina inhibited photosynthesis as well as translocation. Presumably, the accumulating sucrose itself suppressed photosynthesis much as it normally would on a diurnal basis (666). Oddly enough, sucrose accumulations in physically-injured leaves occurred in the sheath rather than behind the point of leaf folding. In these instances the point of sheath union with the stalk acted as a "bottleneck". This suggests that slackened transport is due primarily to a loss of driving force rather than to the morphological injury *per se.* Hartt attached major importance to these findings and proposed that sucrose transport might be the limiting factor in sugarcane photosynthesis.

9. EFFECTS OF THE STOOL COMPLEX

A sugarcane stool will ordinarily number from eight to fifteen stalks in a group complex. Technically this constitutes a single plant. It is interesting to note that workers treating one of the stalks with $^{14}CO_2$ usually detected radioactivity in other stalks of the same stool within a few hours. Eventually the entire stool would contain some trace of radioactivity. Interstalk translocation has also been reported in rye (995) and in rice (1322).

Yang (1597), after treating with $^{14}CO_2$ one of five shoots from a single cane stalk, detected radioactivity throughout the entire plant within 100 hours. Since the photosynthate formed in one shoot was translocated to all other parts of the same stalk, Yang concluded that photosynthate is gradually exchangeable among all areas of the same plant.

Yang also observed that older leaves, $^{+}4$ to $^{+}6$, bore an essentially even distribution of ^{14}C from base to apex, whereas a descending gradient of radioactivity occurred from the base to apex of leaf $^{+}3$. Leaf $^{+}2$ contained more ^{14}C in the center than at either end, and leaf $^{+}1$ contained more radioactivity at the apex than in the central and basal areas. Yang interpreted these varying patterns in younger leaves in terms of a decreasing need for imported photosynthate as leaf tissue becomes more mature. He surmised that growth processes are initially more intense near the leaf tip and move progressively toward the base. Relevant to this, the chlorophyll gradients observed by Kumar *et al.* (863) in Puerto Rico suggest that photosynthetic capability may decrease between the apex and base of newly-emerging cane leaves.

Shen (1322), working with complete stools of rice, found discrete centers of active growth or storage which received ^{14}C-labeled photosynthate in varying amounts according to the stage of plant development. Aside from age, the quantity of light available also affected ^{14}C movement toward different areas of the stool. In full sunlight labeled photosynthate moved readily into adjacent tillers. Under partial shade the main ^{14}C flow was toward active centers in the primary stalk. After tillering was complete no ^{14}C was exchanged with tillers regardless of light supply. In rice it appears that the available exchange pathways are not used randomly, but only when one area cannot meet its own photosynthate requirements while another area has more sucrose than it needs. Shen (1322) also noted, as did Yang (1597), that young expanding leaves held priority for retaining their own photosynthate. When leaf development ceased after heading the uppermost leaf became a major photosynthate contributor toward grain yield while sugar from other leaves compensated for respiratory losses.

Hartt *et al.* (670) found that cane *lalas* (shoots arising from the upper stalk buds) and suckers (shoots arising from basal stalk buds) affected the translocation of ^{14}C-labeled photosynthate. Descending transport was increased by the presence of young lalas, by young suckers, and by both lalas and suckers. In prior studies Hartt *et al.* (667) found that a single blade from one stalk of a 16-cane stool transported ^{14}C to every other stalk in the stool within 20 hours. Between 5.5 and 6 hours were required for detectable radioactivity to reach millable suckers. ^{14}C tended to accumulate in nodes rather than internodes of the adjacent stalks. Hartt *et al.* (667) observed that interstalk movement occurred in the phloem rather than in the xylem as reported by Jones *et al.* (811) in tobacco. The young, vigorous cane suckers appeared to provide more new photosynthate to the stool as a whole than did older stalks. This included sugar for root-growth processes. Older stalks contributed relatively more new sucrose to storage and less to growth than did suckers.

10. MECHANISM OF TRANSLOCATION IN SUGARCANE

Hartt's development of sucrose transport between source and sink is consistent with the mass flow concept being operative in sugarcane. Moreover, in the sucrose movement from leaf lamina to midrib, to leaf sheath, to internodal phloem, and its subsequent descent toward the roots with partial ascension toward the spindle area, there is no evidence that Thaine's (1416, 1417) picture of transcellular streaming, as elaborated by Canny (293), is less applicable for sugarcane than it is for a multitude of other plants. There are, however, two important aspects of the sugarcane transport processes that are not explained by Canny's hypothesis; namely, a reliance upon light for a portion of transport driving force, and the unloading of sucrose from the phloem into storage tissue against a large concentration gradient.

Thus, at each end of the source-to-sink pathway we find a sugarcane elaboration of assimilate transport, each requiring specifically sugarcane research to complete the translocation picture. Fortunately, the problem of sugar movement against a concentration gradient was recognized and thoroughly examined by workers in Australia. The process of sugar accumulation was systematically approached and many aspects were clarified. This work is treated fully in the following chapter.

With regard to light reactions contributing toward driving force, it is reasonable to think that solar energy trapped by the photosynthetic light reactions proper is contributed toward development of the necessary pressure gradient, in the same sense that respiratory energy would be used for a similar purpose. We have seen that Hartt and her colleagues, after encountering evidence for the light involvement over a period of years, finally concluded that photosynthetic phosphorylation might provide the requisite ATP. There is presently no better explanation of the light effect upon sucrose transport.

The precise action of photosynthetic ATP remains open to conjecture. In developing turgor pressure the use of ATP would involve the entire circulatory system, including water uptake and ascension through xylem tissue. A complication of normal water movement from xylem to phloem elements was suggested by the root-chilling studies of Burr *et al.* (270), showing ^{32}P accumulating in leaves rather than passing normally into the phloem system along with ^{14}C-labeled photosynthate. A possible clue to foliar ATP activity in relation to water supply was suggested by Alexander *et al.* (55) who found that night flooding severely restricted ATPase in sugarcane leaves. Kursanov (876) proposed multiple effects of ATP on assimilate movement, including transport processes *per se* and increased rates of phloem loading, based upon phosphorylation of photosynthetic products (875). It is conceivable that sucrose enters the cane leaf veins in a phosphorylated form, but no evidence of this has been reported. Moreover, a contribution of photosynthetic ATP toward phosphorylative reactions immediately preceding sucrose biosynthesis is a definite possibility having indirect bearing on the rate of sucrose transport.

In sugarcane the metabolic sink envisioned by Canny's hypothesis would be the apical meristem, the adjoining immature storage tissue, and the rapidly-growing immature leaves not yet capable of meeting their own requirements for photosynthate. Hartt has shown that sucrose passing into this sink constitutes an ascending fraction of the main sucrose flow which had already descended toward mature storage tissue. Thaine's discovery of bi-directional streaming within a single sieve tube, and Canny's explanation on the basis of multiple gradients in opposite directions, provides the theoretical basis of bi-directional movement in sugarcane. Sucrose conceivably could reverse its downward direction and move upward without leaving the sieve element. The requirements for this include: (a) Adjacent transcellular strands within each tube; (b) a semipermeable membrane separating adjacent strands; and (c) presence of an opposite concentration gradient in some of the strands created by sucrose utilization in the spindle area. The initiation of upward transport might therefore depend more upon the rate of sucrose utilization above than upon photosynthetic production of ATP and sugar.

Under otherwise normal conditions some degree of sucrose movement would initiate and continue under light intensities too low for photosynthesis. The requirements for this are growth activity, the unstored remnants of yesterday's sucrose lying in the phloem between source and sink, and respiratory production of energy. To the phloem sucrose reservoirs might be added the insoluble leaf residues, or glucans, which Hartt suggests are converted to sucrose during the night.

A major challenge for students of cane sucrose transport is the experimental confirmation of transcellular strands within sugarcane sieve tubes, and proof of bi-directional streaming within these strands. Added to this is the mechanism of sucrose exchange between transport streams flowing in opposite directions. Moreover, the enzymology of assimilate movement between source and sink has scarcely been touched. Particular attention should be given to the conversion of glucans and raffinose to sucrose, and to possible sucrose conversion reactions occurring in transit. We are fortunate in having a nearly complete enzyme picture with respect to the transfer of sucrose from phloem to storage tissue.

In the final analysis the transport mechanism of sugarcane remains a matter of speculation, just as it does in the plant kingdom as a whole. Biddulph[2], in 1969, quite succinctly stated the main problem of plant translocation mechanics. In his view there has never been sufficient evidence to refute the pressure flow concept based on a phloem turgor pressure gradient between source and sink (proposed by Münch, in 1930), nor adequate explanation for overcoming flow resistances featured in such a system: "The heart of the matter is, of course, the mechanism that propels the materials . . . across the sieve plates, for if it were not for this resistance to movement the Münch hypothesis would appear adequate." And subsequently: ". . . Yet there exists the hard facts of the high theoretical resistance that should be offered by the sieve plates, if they are structurally as pictured by anatomists. For the sieve tubes to function in the Münch manner the resistance offered to flow through each sieve plate must somehow be substantially reduced or some other compensating factors must be disclosed."

Chapter 9

Sugar Accumulation in Storage Tissue

1. INTRODUCTION

In Chapters 7 and 8 the paths and rates of sucrose translocation were discussed as part of the intricate source-to-sink mechanism operating in sugarcane. We have seen that newly-formed sucrose moves in large quantities through the leaf blade and sheath toward the mature storage tissues which constitute the bulk of the ripening plant. Some of this sugar then moves upward toward utilization areas in the region of the apical meristem. The present chapter deals with the storage processes within these areas which accomplish the transfer of sucrose from conducting phloem to the vacuoles of storage cells.

Following Burr's development of a well-defined circulatory system throughout the stool complex (270–272), Bieleski (178) approached the problem of sucrose storage against a concentration gradient. By this time [1960] interest had intensified in absorption mechanisms (diffusion, mass flow, active transport), and new terms had appeared in the literature (*outer space, inner space, apparent free space*) which reflected changing concepts of solute accumulation (983, 151). Bieleski's studies with tissue slices bathed in aqueous sugar solutions indicated that sucrose, fructose, and glucose are accumulated from the medium by a process dependent upon aerobic respiration. Subsequent studies (584, 581, 582, 579, 691, 1268, 689, 690) by Glasziou and his colleagues in Australia led to a stepwise development of the *sugar accumulation cycle*. This work included detailed treatment of the essential enzymes (582, 689, 690) kinetic features (1268, 180), and reaction sequences (584, 691, 1268) of the cycle. More recent experiments have dealt with sucrose storage in mature stalk tissue (701 702).

Important gaps remain to be filled before the picture of sucrose storage is complete particularly in the area of accumulation mechanisms (701, 592). Field responses implying water and temperature effects upon sucrose storage need to be investigated in the context of storage processes. New interpretations are needed for such longstanding questions as the low sucrose response to high N and to low K. Growth-regulating compounds giving much new information about sugar movement and storage in the grape (1274, 689, 1324, 1544–1546) and other plants (621, 725, 859) have yet to be evaluated in relation to sugarcane storage processes. Nonetheless, remarkable advances have been made during the 1960's and early 1970's toward understanding sucrose accumulation in sugarcane. The reader will find that the basic foundations for new developments in sugar storage have been thoroughly laid.

2. THEORY OF SOLUTE UPTAKE

A. *Passive vs. active entry of non-electrolytes*

In 1940 Lundegardh[1] advanced the hypothesis that electrolyte ions are prevented from penetrating a body of protoplasm owing to a highly-resistant, lipoid-type membrane situated at the interface between the protoplasm and its surrounding medium. The hypothetical membrane was believed to contain fixed negative valences which restricted the movement of ions of an electrolyte to depths no greater than a few molecular layers. Lundegardh pictured an active accumulation process having as its first step a passive adsorption of metallic cations on the membrane in exchange for hydrogen ions. Later workers held that ions can also diffuse into the protoplasm without great difficulty (1151).

In general terms, sugars can be regarded as large, highly-polar, non-electrolytes having little proficiency in permeating the plasma membrane. Students of plant cell osmotic properties have frequently used sucrose as a standard non-permeating solute. In order to account for solute entry across an impermeable membrane two hypotheses have been widely considered [reviewed by Höber (736)]: (a) Passive diffusion by the penetrating molecule, made possible by special physicochemical properties of the plasma membrane, and (b) active transfer of molecules into the cell by virtue of physiological reactions occurring at the cell surface. Sugars might logically conform to the passive hypothesis, moving through a lipoid-sieve membrane.

However, studies with diverse tissue types have demonstrated active sugar uptake. Experiments on sugar absorption by isolated small intestine tissues of the guinea pig (539, 805, 839) showed that glucose, fructose and galactose are actively absorbed by a respiration-mediated process, and that a prior conversion of fructose to glucose occurs. Riklis and Quastel (1236) reported glucose absorption from similar tissues which proceeds via an active, inhibitor-sensitive process, and also by a passive, inhibitor-insensitive process. Rate of glucose uptake relative to initial glucose concentration conformed to an equation of the Michaelis–Menten type. Other animal tissues, *i.e.*, erythrocytes and kidney tubules (616, 1275) absorb glucose at rates unaccountable to diffusion and can do so against a concentration gradient.

Plants have also given evidence of active sugar uptake by different tissues. It has long been known that leaves or leaf parts given an external sugar supply will accomplish sugar absorption [experiments reviewed by Yarwood (1599)], although the mechanism of uptake has never been clear. Early experiments by Boehm (199) and by Meyer (1013) showed that leaves supplied with sugars accumulated starch. Boehm maintained that sucrose was first hydrolyzed in the external solution, and that the fructose and glucose moieties were subsequently absorbed. On the other hand, Meyer noted that sucrose was more effective than either of the hexoses in promoting starch

---

[1] Lundegardh, H., 1940. Investigations as to the absorption and accumulation of inorganic ions, *Ann. Agric. Col. Sweden* 8: 233.

formation and concluded that sucrose was taken up directly. Weatherley's (1540) findings with *Atropa belladonna* leaves suggested direct sucrose absorption.

Dormer and Street (438), and later Street and Lowe (1377), reported that excised tomato roots utilized sucrose more readily than glucose or fructose. Moreover, sucrose uptake nearly ceased under conditions of phosphorus deficiency, although phosphorus absorption resumed when an external source of the nutrient was provided (1377). Dormer and Street advanced a theory in which sucrose uptake involves the operation of a specific sucrose phosphorylase at the absorbing cell surface.

The possibility of active sugar uptake was not at first recognized by early workers although Parkin (1143), in 1899, observed that air seemed essential for starch accumulation by leaves floating on sucrose solutions. In 1937 Phillis and Mason (1171) reported that oxygen and light promoted sugar uptake and starch formation by cotton leaf discs. Also working with cotton leaf discs, Weatherley (1541), in 1954, observed weight increases by fully-turgid tissues floating on a 5-percent sucrose solution. The weight increase included dry weight as well as water. Prolonged experiments with *A. belladonna* revealed up to 4-fold gains in dry weight, an accomplishment explained only by assuming that a considerable accumulation of sugar had occurred after water uptake had ceased. Weatherley concluded that sugar uptake by floating leaf discs is probably an active process rather than passive absorption. Subsequent studies with leaf discs (1542) revealed passive water absorption following active sugar uptake. Active uptake by plant tissues of certain inorganic ions (965) and amino acids (991, 1549, 186) was also established during the mid-1950's.

Bieleski (178) was the first to describe active sugar uptake by sugarcane tissues, a process whose net sugar movement involves a passive diffusion phase as well. Bieleski regarded the active sugar uptake as having features in common with other active accumulation processes [reviewed by Brown and Danielli (251) and by Robertson[2]], and active phloem transport (499). As shown by the stalk sections illustrated in Fig. 9-1, the mechanisms for unloading sucrose from conducting phloem in sugarcane must accomplish a transverse displacement from clusters of phloem elements interspersed among huge parenchyma storage cells. Moreover, the sucrose concentration in the conducting solution is much lower than that of the adjoining storage cells. In a well-ripened stalk the latter may be literally packed with sucrose.

Working with storage tissue slices bathed in aqueous sugar solutions, Bieleski succeeded in restricting sugar uptake by creating anaerobic conditions. Chemical metabolic inhibitors likewise restricted sugar uptake (179). An important exception was the inhibitor phloridzin which had little effect on the sugarcane process even though it severely retards absorption by animal tissues. Bieleski (179) concluded that sugars are maintained in the cane storage cell by virtue of a continuously active storage mechanism rather than by an impermeable barrier to diffusion. Later studies (179,

[2]Robertson, R.N., 1956. The mechanism of absorption. In *Encyclopedia of Plant Physiology* (Ruhland, W., ed.), Vol. 2, pp. 449–467, Springer-Verlag, Berlin.

180, 581) empirically established a selectively-permeable barrier membrane between the storage vacuole and outer space. The membrane was permeable to existing hexoses but impermeable to sucrose in either direction. It was also shown (178) that relatively little sucrose is taken up directly, even during the initial passive diffusion phase.

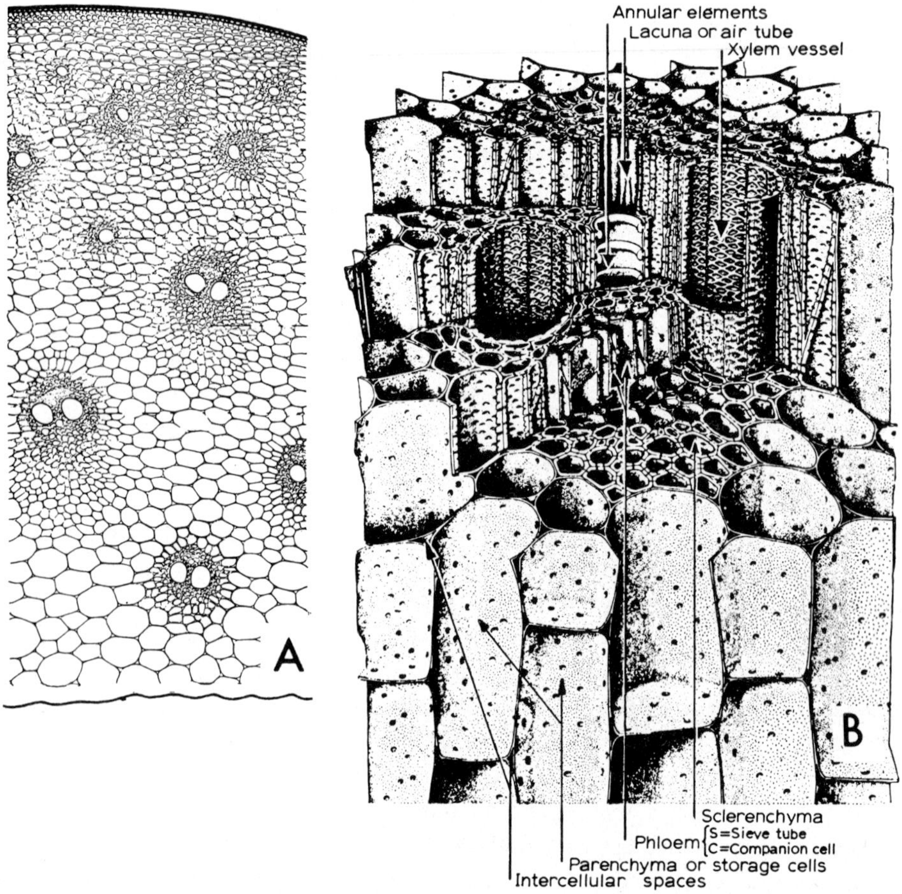

Fig. 9-1. (A) General cross-section of the sugarcane stalk showing the rind, storage, and conducting tissues. (B) Three-dimensional view of stalk conducting tissues, consisting of xylem vessels and phloem elements, and the adjoining parenchyma storage cells. [From Payne (1151), after Martin (983).] Reproduced by permission of *I.S.S.C.T.*

B. *Sugar–boron carrier complexes*

Between 1953 and 1957 considerable research was performed by Gauch, Dugger, and their co-workers relating boron to sugar uptake and translocation. Gauch and Dugger (562) reported that small quantities of boron markedly speeded the absorption and movement of applied sucrose, particularly toward physiological sinks where sugars were rapidly utilized in growth and respiratory processes. They proposed that boron reacts with sugar to form a sugar–borate complex which is readily ionizable. The complex would then pass more freely through cellular membranes than would non-borated sugar.

The ionizable complex visualized by Gauch and Dugger is based upon a borate ion reaction described by Zittle (1621). The reaction occurs readily in OH-rich compounds having two OH groups in the *cis* position. Although this requirement is not fulfilled by sucrose, Gauch and Dugger felt that a reaction with sucrose does take place involving the *trans*-1,2-diol groups to form the structure

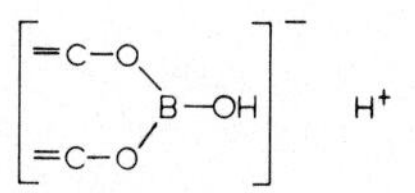

whose precise form will vary with changing conditions, particularly with variable pH. They did not discount the possibility that a sugar–borate complex might remain intact until the sugar is utilized and the borate ion set free, but they favored a membrane role of boron in which the borate ion is freed at the inner surface. The latter hypothesis is consistent with Epstein's (497) concept of active ion-carrier movement across root membranes.

The proposed carrier role of boron received added support from Mitchell *et al.* (1025) who found that boron enhanced the movement of indole-3-acetic acid (IAA), α-naphthalene acetic acid (NAA), and 2,4,5-trichlorophenoxyacetic acid (2,4,5-T) when each compound was supplied to bean leaves in sucrose solutions. In variable-illumination experiments, 2,4-dichlorophenoxyacetic acid (2,4-D) movement (ammonium salt) was increased up to 50 percent in darkened plants when boron was added to the sugar–herbicide solution. With illumination, boron alone added to 2,4-D solution more than doubled stem curvature, and boron plus sucrose added to 2,4-D solution more than tripled stem curvature, as compared to 2,4-D treatment without additives. The positive effect of boron without added sucrose suggests a boron reaction with endogenous sugars. Significantly, sucrose added without boron to the 2,4-D solution reduced stem curvature to about 25 percent of that obtained with 2,4-D alone.

Sisler *et al.* (1330) continued studies of the boron–sugar relationship by supplying sugar solutions to cut petioles of tomato plants grown in boron-deficient and normal culture solutions. So long as low-boron plants had not yet developed deficiency symptoms, the inclusion of boron (50 ppm) facilitated the movement of supplied sucrose. Control plants given 0.5 ppm in their nutrient solution did not yield a consistent response to the boron additive. Plants showing boron deficiency symptoms took up less than normal amounts of sugar when boron was included in the sugar solution, and boron failed to increase the rate of sugar transport. In other experiments sugar movement was examined after 4 hours of leaf exposure to $^{14}CO_2$. A greater percentage of ^{14}C-labeled photosynthate was translocated by boron-sufficient plants than by those deficient in boron. The same relationship was obtained with only 20 minutes exposure to $^{14}CO_2$.

In a subsequent paper Dugger *et al.* (449) proposed a relationship of boron to the enzyme starch phosphorylase. By decreasing the formation of starch from glucose 1-phosphate, a larger pool of the sugar phosphate is presumably made available for other reactions, including sucrose synthesis. The increased production of a soluble sugar from a less soluble sugar phosphate might then result in greater sugar translocation from source to sink.

3. SUGAR ACCUMULATION AGAINST A CONCENTRATION GRADIENT

A. *Initial studies with tissue slices* [Bieleski (178–180)]

During prior experiments relating to the respiration of harvested stalks, Bieleski (182) observed that discs of storage tissue placed in distilled water lost little of their sugar contents to the water. He surmised that the tonoplast[3], or vacuolar membrane, might be so impermeable that endogenous sugars could not pass outward, but this raised the question of how sugar originally accumulated behind the membrane. Another possibility was the presence of an accumulation mechanism actively opposing outward sugar flow. With these considerations in mind, Bieleski (178) initiated studies of the accumulation processes which, taken together with the work of other scientists in Australia, led to our present understanding of sugar uptake by cane storage tissues.

Bieleski worked with rind-free storage tissue taken from basal internodes at least 6 months old, and also with immature storage tissue taken from the spindle area. Initial studies were performed with commercially-grown samples of the variety *Pindar*. The tough, outer sclerenchyma was split away from the internal parenchyma tissue. The latter was quartered longitudinally or sliced transversely into quadrant-shaped pieces. Core samples were also taken of the parenchyma with a cork borer and sliced into discs with a razor blade. Tissue samples were washed for 15 to 20 hours in five to seven changes of distilled water and blotted dry prior to being weighed out into experimental samples.

---

[3]Definitions appertaining to the sugar accumulation process: *Tonoplast*, a vacuolar membrane [Henderson and Henderson (719)], also the probable site of energy-dependent sucrose movement into cane storage tissue (581, 579); *bathing solution*, a dilute aqueous solution of sugars within which storage tissue slices or discs were emersed; *outer space* (including "metabolic compartment"), cytoplasmic portion of the storage tissue into which sugars of the bathing solution pass rapidly in a reversible diffusion; *inner space*, vacuoles of the storage tissue into which sugar from the external solution, or outer space, pass slowly by non-reversible active accumulation against a concentration gradient.

The ratio of tissue to bathing solution was varied between 1:2 and 1:3 (w/v). The sugar concentration (glucose or sucrose) of the external solution varied from less than 1/2 to about 1/20 of the tissue sugar concentration. Bieleski determined the endogenous sucrose content by measuring the refractive index of expressed sap, a method having considerable precision by virtue of the fact that sucrose was the only major soluble constituent (178). Each flask with its contents was routinely weighed and reweighed so that corrections could be made for evaporation losses.

Experiments were performed at room temperature under conditions of constant aeration. The tissues' own buffering action, about pH 5.4, was employed rather than buffer solutions in order to avoid respiratory increases. No agents were added to prevent microbe growth, but this also was avoided by frequent changes of distilled water. No significant infection was observed with immature storage tissue for 24 hours, or with mature storage tissue up to 100 hours. The older tissues appeared to have a natural inhibitory action against microbe development. With varying modifications Bieleski's technique was employed throughout subsequent studies of the sugar accumulation cycle.

It can be argued that Bieleski completely divorced his tissue samples from anything like the intact storage system. Gone were the natural relationships of source to sink, of storage-process integration with the physiological circulatory system, and the myriad of rate-compromising factors relative to photosynthetic and respiratory activity external to the storage area. Nonetheless, Bieleski accomplished the isolation of storage-process essentials, quite in the sense that other workers had isolated photosynthetic processes in cell-free chloroplast preparations. In this respect the sugar-accumulating ability of tissue slices closely reflected the storage capacity of parent material remaining in the field. In kinetic terms, the problems incident to sugar accumulation by bathing tissue slices appear to be a fair representation of the problems confronting an intact storage system.

B. *Sugar uptake by mature and immature tissues*

Bieleski (178) found that mature tissue slices having an endogenous sugar content close to 10 percent rapidly accumulated sucrose, glucose, and mannitol from the surrounding medium. An equilibrium was reached within 1 hour and no further uptake occurred during the subsequent 24 hours. The quantity of sugar absorbed was directly proportional to its concentration in the external solution. Anaerobic conditions failed to decrease the rate of uptake or the quantity accumulated at equilibrium. Upon return of the tissue to distilled water, each compound was rapidly and totally lost from the tissue. From these results Bieleski concluded that the sugar uptake was a passive diffusion into the tissue's apparent free space (A.F.S.).

Similar experiments with immature storage tissue revealed sugar uptake occurring in two stages (Fig. 9-2). The first, ceasing within an hour, seemed identical to that of the mature tissues and was therefore taken as passive movement into the A.F.S. The second stage occurred more slowly but at a constant rate during a time interval of 20 to 60 hours. Using dilute external solutions (0.25 percent), a concentration increase of 2- to 20-fold was obtained above that of the endogenous sugar. This was interpreted as

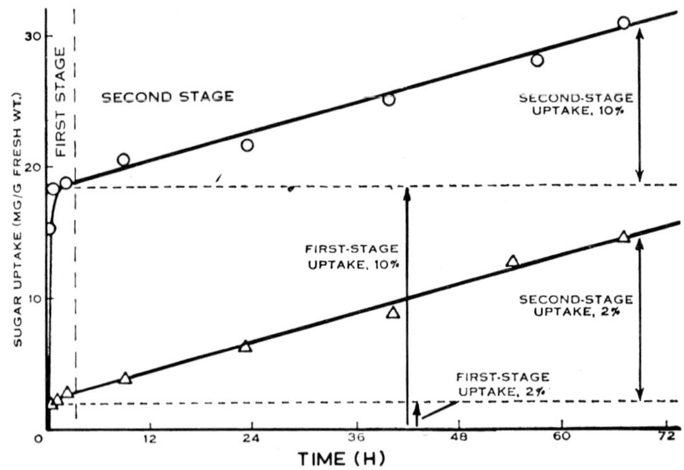

Fig. 9-2. Two-stage sugar uptake by immature storage tissue slices from sucrose solutions of varying concentration: (△) 2 percent sucrose; (○) 10 percent sucrose. The first-stage (passive) uptake is proportional to the sugar concentration of the external solution, and the second-stage (accumulation) uptake is largely independent of concentration. [After Bieleski (178).] Reproduced by permission of the *Australian Journal of Biological Sciences.*

evidence of an active uptake into the "osmotic volume" (storage vacuoles) of the tissue by a metabolic process. Mannitol, metabolically inert to many tissues (178), achieved the first stage of uptake but failed to make the second-stage movement. Bieleski also observed that when the immature storage tissues were returned to distilled water, an amount of sugar equal to the first-stage uptake returned to the water, leaving within the tissues an amount equal to the second-stage accumulation. The sucrose lost from the A.F.S. was gradually taken up again at the original rate until the final equilibrium was established.

Conducting further experiments with immature storage tissue slices, Bieleski found that anaerobic conditions markedly restricted the second-stage (active) uptake, but did not affect the first-stage (passive) uptake. When active accumulation ceased, those sugars already accumulated "leaked" back into the external solution. Bieleski further observed that when the accumulation of either glucose or sucrose alone was stopped by anaerobic environment, the sugar leaking back to the medium was accompanied by some quantity of the second sugar. By aerating the anaerobiosis-treated tissue in distilled water (to remove possible products of anaerobic respiration), and transferring the aerated tissue to a fresh, aerated sugar solution, the original sugar accumulation was reestablished. These experiments demonstrated that the anaerobic inhibition of sugar uptake and the subsequent sugar leakage were totally reversible.

C. *Relative movement and fate of different sugars in immature storage tissue*

Working with immature storage tissues, Bieleski (178) performed comparative uptake studies with 0.25 percent solutions of glucose, fructose, sucrose, glucose 1-phosphate (glucose-1-*P*), and mannitol which revealed a greater accumulation proficiency for fructose or glucose than for sucrose. Bieleski distinguished between sugar accumulating on a weight basis and a molar basis. It was shown that glucose accumulation occurred at a rate close to 25 percent greater than sucrose on a weight basis, and more than double the sucrose rate on a molar basis (Fig. 9-3). Combinations of the two

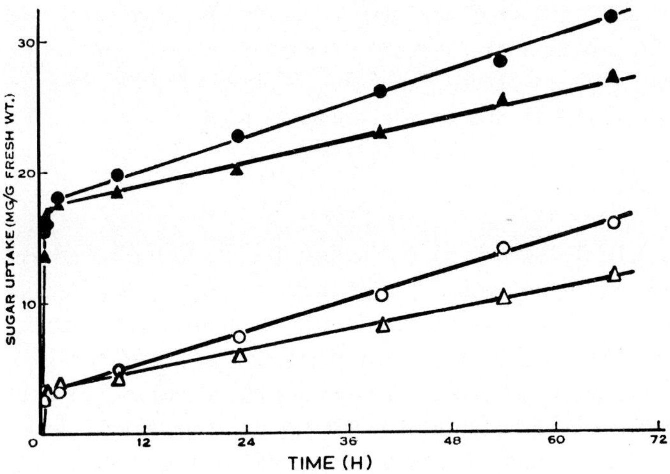

Fig. 9-3. Comparative uptake rates for sucrose and glucose by immature storage tissue slices: (△) 2.0 percent sucrose; (○) 2.0 percent glucose; (▲) 10.0 percent sucrose; (●) 10.0 percent glucose. [After Bieleski (178).] Reproduced by permission of the *Australian Journal of Biological Sciences.*

sugars in the external solution led to the same net uptake on a molar basis that was recorded for glucose alone. Individually, glucose accumulation was suppressed when sucrose was also present[4]. Bieleski surmised that glucose *per se* might not be accumulated. Moreover, glucose-1-*P* was not taken up or hydrolyzed under normal conditions. This finding is of special interest in accounting for the storage of hydrolyzed "glucans", or other glucose polysaccharides, and true starches residing in the sugar cane stalk[5]. Little evidence was found of mannitol accumulation by the sugarcane tissues.

---

[4] Subsequent kinetic studies (180) contradicted the sucrose effect on glucose uptake.

[5] Bieleski did not elaborate upon glucose-1-*P* behavior, but large quantities of starch are formed in certain varieties (1587, 522, 134). It would appear that a mechanism of glucose-1-*P* accumulation in storage vacuoles, where starch biosynthesis could occur, might be a varietal feature not present in *Pindar*.

In accounting for the fate of sugars absorbed from the external solution, Bieleski was aware that in some tissues most or all of the sugar taken up could theoretically be used in starch formation or in respiratory reactions. Tissue slices tested by the iodine method did not give a positive reaction for starch. Microscopic examination likewise failed to show any trace of the polysaccharide. However, sugar accumulation, amounting to 1 percent of the fresh tissue weight, was accompanied by a 30- to 40-percent increase in respiration. Sucrose, glucose, and mannitol each effected greater respiration. Glucose produced the largest rate increase and mannitol the least. Sugar lost via respiration accounted for 12 percent of the net uptake by storage tissue. Efforts to recover the absorbed (A.F.S.) sugar by repeated washing in distilled water failed to account for some 8 percent of the sugar taken up. The discrepancy was observed in spite of the fact that all but 0.3 percent of the tissue sugar was removed by prolonged washing. Bieleski concluded that the missing 8 percent had been used in maintaining the respiration needed for active sugar accumulation.

D. *Tissue maturity and sugar uptake*

A most interesting facet of Bieleski's work was the variable effect of tissue maturity on sugar movement from external solutions. With advancing age the first-stage uptake was increased, whereas the rate of second-stage movement (active accumulation) declined with increasing age. Time of year also affected the storage process. Mature stalk tissue sampled in March (midway through the growing season in Queensland) accumulated sugar at close to 1/3 of the rate for immature storage tissue. Mature tissues taken between June and August could not perform sugar accumulation. By this time the endogenous sugar content was greater than 16 percent. It appears that the loss of sugar-accumulating ability was not due to the increased concentration gradient between external solution and tissue, since Bieleski raised the external sugar concentration as high as 25 percent without inducing uptake. The close parallel between the performance of laboratory tissue slices and intact field tissue prompted Bieleski to suggest that laboratory techniques might be used in screening new varieties for storage potential.

E. *Effects of inhibitors on sugar accumulation*

Shortly after his work on sugar accumulation appeared in print, Bieleski published another paper dealing with inhibitor effects on storage processes (179). The inhibitors tested were known to be active against three critical areas of plant or animal biochemistry: Aerobic respiration (anaerobic conditions, cyanide), phosphate transfer (2,4-dinitrophenol, arsenate), and –SH group enzymology (*p*-chloromercuribenzoate, cupric ion, mercuric ion).

The inhibitor studies underscored a need for active metabolic reactions in maintaining normal accumulation rates. They further suggested several possible explanations for the loss of accumulation potential with age. In general, each of the three inhibitor groups prevented accumulation and induced sugar leakage at concentrations inhibitory to most other processes in plant tissues. The sensitivity of sugarcane tissue was less than that reported for animal tissues. Bieleski's (179) data with immature storage tissue revealed no direct inhibitor action against membrane permeability; rather, metabolic processes were believed to be so restricted that insufficient energy was available for sugar accumulation. The attending lack of storage-process energy might then permit a leakage of sugars from the vacuole to the outer space. It was concluded that the rate of active accumulation is the determining factor as to whether sugar will be accumulated, maintained at equilibrium, or lost by leakage. However, data obtained with mature tissues was much less consistent. Bieleski suggested that, as the cell ages, it becomes more impermeable and less dependent upon accumulation mechanisms for retaining the inner space sugar.

While inhibitors of animal transport mechanisms were also effective against sugarcane accumulation (although at higher concentrations), an important exception was the inhibitor phloridzin. No effect was obtained with 10^{-6} to 10^{-5} M concentrations even though comparable amounts severely restrict sugar accumulation by animal tissues. Increasing the phloridzin level to 2×10^{-3} M still did not give complete inhibition. Bieleski suggested that the tissue itself may serve to inactivate the inhibitor. Certain evidence indicated that the inhibitor had difficulty reaching the locus of active accumulation. Citing reports (1540, 1377, 1418) that other plant species had failed to show inhibition comparable to that of animal tissues, even at high concentrations, Bieleski concluded that the sugar-accumulation process might differ in plants with respect to phloridzin sensitivity.

F. *Kinetics of sugar accumulation*

In 1962 Bieleski published the results of kinetic studies on sugar accumulation (180), two years after his first report had appeared concerning active accumulation against a concentration gradient. The kinetic data established three important features of the previously-obscure accumulation process: (a) A hyperbolic relationship was found between the external sugar concentration and rate of uptake, suggesting that the rate-limiting step is best described as an enzyme–substrate reaction rather than as diffusional movement into the tissue; (b) from initial uptake through the rate-limiting step, the individual sugars (glucose, fructose, sucrose) behave as distinct entities with little interconversion taking place; (c) subsequent to the rate-limiting step there is a major interconversion of sugars which yields sucrose as the predominant product, or only product, regardless of the sugar form originally supplied.

Using radioisotope techniques, a hyperbola form was obtained for sucrose, glucose, and fructose when the accumulation rate of each sugar was plotted against its concentration. The double reciprocal plot of this data [after Lineweaver and Burk (945)] gave a straight-line intercept of the y axis for each sugar (Fig. 9-4). The y-axis intercept and

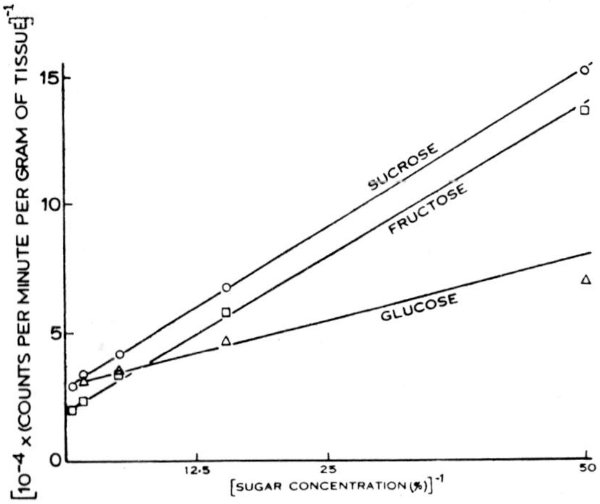

Fig. 9-4. Double reciprocal plot of sugar accumulation data showing rate variation as a function of sugar concentration. A sugar uptake rate of 1.5 mg/g of tissue = 1000 counts per minute per g of tissue. [After Bieleski (180).] Reproduced by permission of the *Australian Journal of Biological Sciences.*

slope of each line allowed the values for K_m (sugar concentration at half-maximum velocity) and V (maximum velocity at infinite concentration) to be calculated for each sugar's accumulation rate. The K_m for sucrose, glucose, and fructose was established at 0.85, 0.31, and 1.23 mg/ml, respectively; V was 5.91, 5.81, and 8.71 mg/g/day, respectively. The hyperbolic relationship discounted diffusion as the rate-limiting process since in that case the uptake rate would have been in direct proportion to external concentration. In order to account for the continuity of accumulation, Bieleski bypassed a simple sugar–receptor complex in favor of a sugar–receptor complex acting as a transitory intermediate:

$$\text{Sugar} + \text{receptor} \rightleftharpoons \text{sugar–receptor} \rightarrow \text{sugar product} + \text{receptor} \tag{1}$$

The reader will note the similarity of Bieleski's accumulation sequence (Eqn. 1) to the relationship of an enzyme to its substrate (Eqn. 2):

$$\text{Substrate} + \text{enzyme} \rightleftharpoons \text{substrate–enzyme complex} \rightarrow \text{product} + \text{enzyme} \tag{2}$$

Bieleski assigned a catalytic role to the sugar receptor, thereby establishing a reaction whose rate is expressed as a straight-line relationship,

$$\frac{1}{v} = \frac{K_m}{V} \cdot \frac{1}{s} + \frac{1}{V} \tag{3}$$

in which v = reaction rate, V = maximum rate at infinite concentration, s = substrate concentration, and K_m = dissociation constant of the enzyme–substrate complex. Bieleski's data did in fact describe such a straight-line relationship for sugar accumulation, in which v = accumulation rate, s = sugar concentration, and V = accumulation rate at infinite sugar concentration.

The interaction of individual sugars during their uptake was interpreted as further evidence of an enzyme-like reaction governing the rate of accumulation. Detailed analysis of the glucose-inhibited accumulation of sucrose showed that the glucose effect described a competition of two sugars for the same receptor. Bieleski noted that the kinetic data for the sugar accumulation process in sugarcane closely paralleled that of analogous processes in yeast [Rothstein (1257)] and bacteria [Monod (1034); Rickenberg *et al.* (1232)]. K_m values were very comparable. These investigators had depicted the receptor as one or several inducible enzymes (*permeases*) with specific roles for different kinds of accumulating compounds. Bieleski accepted the possibility that a permease was active in sugarcane storage reactions.

A most important aspect of Bieleski's kinetic studies was the interpretation he developed for the predominance of sucrose as the accumulated sugar. His proposed mechanism takes into account contemporary findings with plant and animal tissues as well as his own sugarcane data, but it does not correspond fully with Glasziou's (579, 581) mechanism (*cf.* this chapter, pp. 343–347), even though Glasziou appears to have attained similar kinetic data by independent studies. Relevant to this is the question as to why glucose rather than sucrose is the preferential sugar for uptake. Bieleski suggested that glucose could be used preferentially in the synthesis of a labile sucrose–carrier complex which, upon passage of the permeability barrier, is broken down to yield sucrose. The essential steps and sugar interrelationships of the accumulation process were given as follows:

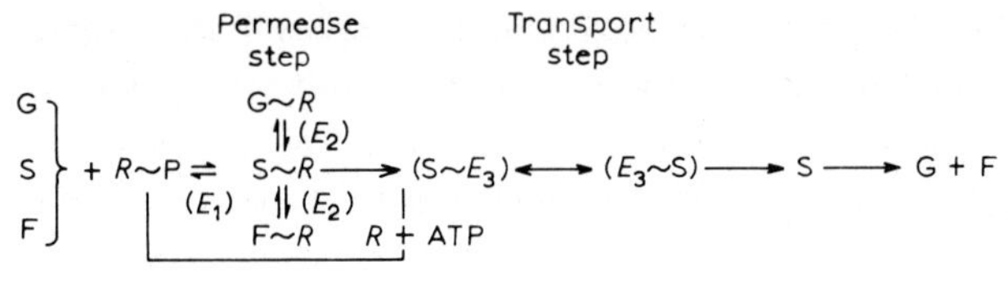

It can be seen that at least two kinds of enzyme reactions are envisioned in three stages. The first step is the linkage of sugar to an activated acceptor (R~P). It is enzymatic (E_1) and has properties of a permease reaction which is rate limiting for accumulation. The second enzymatic step (E_2) involves the interconversion of activated sugars. In the third stage, an enzyme situated at the barrier membrane receives the activated sucrose on its surface. The sucrosyl group is then shifted to a new site on the enzyme surface, positioned at the inner side of the membrane. The transport step proper would thus constitute a transfer of the sucrosyl group. Ultimately, sucrose is released to the inner space where it may be stored or hydrolyzed to yield fructose and glucose.

According to Bieleski, the permease step receives support from Cohen and Monod (362) working with bacteria, and the accumulation scheme is similar to one proposed by Porter and May (1176) in accounting for sugar metabolism features in tobacco leaves. It differs from the stepwise accumulation process proposed by Glasziou (579) in several respects. In particular, the formation of activated sucrose (sucrose–X) visualized by Glasziou is not necessarily an enzymatic reaction, nor is its formation considered to be rate limiting. To the contrary, Glasziou (581) suggested that the rate-limiting features of sugar uptake are the enzymatic reactions dealing with sugar phosphorylation and interconversion[6]. In addition, Glasziou assumed that the inner space fructose exists in a single pool whereas Bieleski (180) held that at least two independent fructose pools are situated in the vacuole.

In Bieleski's scheme the rate-limiting step is the union of sugar with an activated acceptor ($R{\sim}P$), prior to which there is no appreciable interconversion of sugars. Glasziou (581) maintained that glucose is converted to fructose prior to the formation of sucrose–X. Putting this another way, glucose becomes a better source of sucrose–X than is sucrose, which explains the preferential uptake of glucose over sucrose. Furthermore, Glasziou (581) felt that sucrose–X is formed by two parallel pathways, one of which predominates at low sucrose concentrations in the outer space. In general terms, Bieleski's mechanism is supported by the fact that sucrose is the major sugar translocated by plants, and therefore its accumulation process should relate closely to sucrose-forming reactions. This view was taken in preference to the possibility that all sugars are converted to a common compound during their accumulation (180).

Bieleski's work was the first of its kind with sugarcane and yet he encountered a storage problem that still remains unclear, *i.e.*, the mechanism for sugar accumulation in mature stalk tissue. The immature storage tissue which best performed the active, second-stage accumulation against a concentration gradient is more accurately described as a metabolic sink, an area of sugar utilization rather than a storage area in the practical sense. Although the ^{14}C studies by Hartt have clearly shown that new photosynthate does accumulate in the most mature tissue as well as in younger internodes (*cf.* Chapter 7, pp. 282–284), it also appears that certain enzymes known to be operative in immature storage tissue processes tend to be lost as a function of tissue aging. Glasziou (579) suggested that the lowered ability of aged tissue to synthesize sucrose from glucose might relate to insufficient conversion of glucose to fructose. Possibly some enzyme constituent of aged storage tissues, which did not survive in Bieleski's tissue-slice preparations, remains to be discovered in sugarcane stalks. Such a catalyst might logically relate to an energy-generating mechanism distinct from the respiratory processes measured by Bieleski.

---

[6]H. Beevers [*Physiological Aspects of Crop Yield*, Chapter 8, pp. 169–180, Am. Soc. Agron., Madison, Wisc. (1969)] depicts sugar absorption by castor bean cotyledon as a process similar to Glasziou's sugar accumulation cycle, with the exception that sucrose remains intact through all stages in castor bean.

4. ELABORATING THE SUGAR ACCUMULATION CONCEPT [Glasziou (579, 581, 582)]

Glasziou's work in Hawaii (579) and Australia (581) verified the salient features of Bieleski's (178) results. The added use of ^{14}C-labeled sugars enabled Glasziou to draw firm conclusions as to the sites of active accumulation and hexose interconversion. He developed the concept of an activated sucrose derivative moving across the tonoplast membrane. Certain relationships of tissue maturity to the origin and efflux of hexoses were recognized. Glasziou (582) also discovered an inversion mechanism active within the inner space. From these studies some tentative relationships of a cyclic storage system to the processes of respiration and photosynthesis began to emerge.

A. *Evidence of active accumulation of a sucrose derivative*

Working with tissue discs from freshly-cut, year-old stalks of the variety *H. 37-1933*, Glasziou (579) supplied the tissues with ^{14}C-labeled glucose and sucrose in the bathing medium. Other experiments involved leaf exposure to $^{14}CO_2$ with subsequent analyses of accumulated sugar. At the end of each experiment the actively-accumulated sugars were separated from passively-accumulated sugars by prolonged washing in running water. The labeling patterns of storage sugar were found to be the same regardless of ^{14}C source. Most of the accumulated ^{14}C appeared in sucrose. Young tissues accumulated sucrose at a rate 6 times greater than mature tissues; glucose accumulation was about 15 times greater in young tissues (Table 9-1).

TABLE 9-1

ACCUMULATION RATES OF ^{14}C-LABELED GLUCOSE AND SUCROSE INTO THE INNER SPACE OF INTERNODAL TISSUE DISCS

[After Glasziou (579).] Reproduced by permission of *Plant Physiology.*

Internode	Sugar uptake (μM/g dry wt./day)		Tissue sugar content (% dry wt.)	
	Sucrose	Glucose	Sucrose	Reducing sugars
5	3.65	30.8	11.5	15.7
7	2.76	26.8	34.6	7.8
10	0.61	4.9	55.2	1.6
15	0.61	2.1	54.5	0.36

B. *Efflux of sugars from the inner space*

In order to study the outward movement of accumulated sugars, Glasziou first created a pool of labeled inner space sugar by exposing leaf No. 7 to $^{14}CO_2$ for 24 hours prior to harvesting the storage tissue samples. Some of the samples were analyzed directly for sugar while others were placed in water for analyses of exiting sugar. For immature storage tissue the effluent sugars were proportionately less sucrose and more fructose; for mature tissues a still greater proportion of fructose was emanated. Glasziou noted that the distribution of ^{14}C in the exiting sugar may be different from ^{14}C distribution in the inner space sugar.

Calculations were made in accordance with Fick's Law which assumed a permeability preference by the tonoplast for different sugars. Results indicated that the minimum outward movement occurs from tissues having just completed rapid elongation. The fall of efflux rate was paralleled by increased content of both hexoses and sucrose, suggesting that membrane permeability declines with advancing age. In general, the rate of outward diffusion was not closely correlated with sugar content of the tissue. With increasing tissue maturity this diffusion at first decreased, and then later increased, the increase being accompanied by a lowering of accumulation rate. The barrier membrane was more permeable to reducing sugar than to sucrose and more permeable to fructose than glucose.

Glasziou (579) pointed out that the net rate of change for sugar concentration of the inner space should be the sum of accumulation rates minus the sum of efflux rates. Glasziou tested this assumption by first accumulating ^{14}C-labeled photosynthate in the inner space, then incubating the tissues for 4 hours in unlabeled sucrose solutions after the outer space sugars were removed by washing. By radioactivity analyses of the external medium, Glasziou was able to show that sucrose concentrations up to 2.0 percent in the bathing medium had no effect on efflux rate. The maximum sucrose concentration, 2.0 percent, was 10 times the saturation level for sugar accumulation as established by Bieleski (178)[7].

By defoliating plants and initiating tissue harvests some 24 hours after exposure to $^{14}CO_2$, Glasziou was able to demonstrate a rapid mobilization of sucrose for new growth. This constituted an efflux of sucrose from the inner space at the same rate which occurred when tissue samples were immersed in water. A rapid increase of ^{14}C-labeled hexose and loss of ^{14}C-labeled sucrose within 6 hours of defoliation suggests that sucrose acts as the source of glucose and fructose. It was also shown by rate analysis of [^{14}C]sucrose appearance in wash water that the outer space sucrose probably exists in more than one pool.

Evidence for active movement of a sucrose derivative through the tonoplast membrane was obtained from hexose-absorption experiments in which one sugar or the other, or both, contained radioactive carbon (579). Labels from glucose or fructose

---

[7]From this it might be surmised that cane storage tissue can withstand considerable utilization of outer space sugar without experiencing appreciable change in the rate of sugar transformation in the storage vacuole. Putting this another way, a tremendous utilization rate of outer space sugar must proceed, as for example during growth renewal caused by heavy rainfall, in order for the well-known seasonal losses of accumulated sucrose to occur.

given alone in the bathing medium were later found equally distributed among the two moieties of sucrose. When only one of the supplied hexoses contained ^{14}C, the accumulating sucrose was asymmetrically labeled, with counts predominating in the moiety that contained ^{14}C in the bathing medium. Glasziou recognized that the storage form of supplied ^{14}C was inevitably sucrose, although the storage tissue also contained unlabeled mixtures of endogenous sucrose, glucose, and fructose. He surmised that sucrose storage must occur in a compartment spatially distinct from sites of hexose interconversion and sucrose synthesis. This compartment was taken to be the vacuole, and the cytoplasm was regarded as the area of hexose interconversion.

Also relevant was the fact that, although glucose was taken up at a rate close to 10 times greater than the rate for equimolar sucrose, it was nonetheless converted to sucrose prior to deposition in the vacuole. Sucrose was taken up and accumulated as sucrose, but since this occurred against a severe concentration gradient, the form of sucrose in movement must have differed in some respect from the form residing in the vacuole. From these considerations Glasziou (579) concluded that sugar accumulation is more than just an active process, it must also involve an "activation" of sucrose prior to its storage in the inner space. This activated form was at first regarded as an unknown sucrose derivative and as such was depicted as "sucrose–X" in several papers (584, 579). Later experiments indicated that the sucrose derivative is sucrose phosphate (691).

C. *Criteria of the sugar accumulation and transformation hypothesis*

In summing up his sugar storage experiments in Hawaii, Glasziou (579) drew several conclusions which accommodated his and Bieleski's data in a working hypothesis of the sugar storage process: (a) Accumulation is an energy-dependent process with a rate-limiting step whose kinetics concur with the Michaelis–Menten criteria for enzymes; (b) regardless of the ^{14}C source supplied to incubated tissues, nearly all of the label appears in sucrose within the inner space. Since this is true even when glucose is the lone sugar supplied, the fructose moiety must be derived from glucose–fructose interconversion reactions prior to sucrose synthesis; (c) although both glucose and sucrose in the bathing medium are stored as sucrose, the accumulation rate for glucose is close to 10 times greater than for sucrose; (d) the net rate of sugar movement is the algebraic summation of distinct efflux and accumulation reactions; (e) the rate of sugar loss from the inner space may be independent of inner space sucrose concentration.

The essential features of sugar movement between outer space and inner space were depicted with the following reaction sequence:

$$\begin{matrix}\text{Outer space}\\ \text{sugar}\end{matrix} \xrightarrow[\text{accumulation}]{\text{Active}} \begin{matrix}\text{inner space}\\ \text{sugar}\end{matrix} \xleftrightarrow{\text{Diffusion}} \begin{matrix}\text{outer space}\\ \text{sugar}\end{matrix} \tag{4}$$

Glasziou felt that the sugar storage data excluded several relevant theories of assimilate movement across barrier membranes. In particular, the role of a rate-limiting carrier mechanism seemed not to apply. The chief discrepancy here lies in the fact that glucose competitively inhibits sucrose uptake (178), whereas a carrier transporting both sugars should give a constant uptake ratio of sucrose to glucose. Sucrose inversion in the outer space might account for the glucose inhibition but would not explain the differing relative rates of sugar accumulation, *i.e.* glucose accumulating at 10 times the rate of sucrose. In addition, the operation of a diffusion-type carrier would be affected by varying sugar concentrations in the external solution, but this did not comply with experimental data. It should be noted, however, that the sugarcane storage process may well be an exceptional case, and Glasziou's interpretations were not offered to refute some general absorption and translocation theories developed by other workers [Gauch and Dugger (562); Dugger *et al.* (449); Esau *et al.* (499, 498); Biddulph *et al.* (175–177); Kursanov (876)].

Glasziou further concluded that sucrose synthesis does not occur in the inner space. The main evidence for this was the fact that labeled glucose given alone yielded nearly all of its ^{14}C in accumulated sucrose, the latter having a labeled fructose moiety which was procured via glucose transformation rather than from the pool of endogenous inner-space fructose. It follows that sugar transformations must occur in the outer space. The outer space in turn is in diffusion equilibrium with sugars of the bathing medium.

An alternative mechanism was proposed having as its main feature a hypothetical activation of sugars prior to their union with a carrier. A four-stage sequence was presented to account for sugar transformations, activation, and combination with carrier in the outer space:

I.	Sugar + R–X	$\longrightarrow$	sugar–X + R
II.	Sugar–X + carrier	$\longrightarrow$	sugar–carrier + X
III.	Sugar–carrier	$\longrightarrow$	sugar (accumulated) + carrier
IV.	Sugar (outer space)	$\longleftrightarrow$	sugar (inner space)

Glasziou (579) states that the net free energy change for Reactions I to III would permit accumulation against a major concentration gradient. Reaction IV describes sugar efflux as a reversible diffusion process. At this stage of development [1960] the nature of the carrier and activated sugar remained obscure, as did the site of the rate-limiting reaction for sugar accumulation.

D. *Studies of glucose and fructose in the inner space*

Employing the sugarcane variety *Pindar*, Glasziou (581) continued at Brisbane, Australia, the sugar accumulation studies begun in Hawaii. The particularly high levels of hexose in immature storage tissues were taken as possible evidence of an accumulation-control mechanism based upon the rate of sucrose inversion in the inner space. Another possibility considered at the time was that reducing sugars might be stored when the incoming flow of photosynthate exceeded the ability of the storage mechanism to accumulate the sugar as sucrose. Glasziou (581) soon demonstrated that sucrose is practically the only form of sugar accumulated in the vacuole, and that hexoses arise therein as products of a powerful inversion mechanism.

The hypothesized storing of hexoses when outer space sugar becomes excessive was discounted when Glasziou found that the sugar concentration in the external medium had little effect on sugar movement into the inner space. However, prolonged ^{14}C-distribution experiments with accumulated [^{14}C]sucrose revealed an increased percentage of the label passing from sucrose to hexose in the inner space. Equal distribution of the label between fructose and glucose suggested that each sugar arose within the inner space as a product of sucrose inversion. Virtual steady-state conditions existed between the levels of sucrose, glucose, and fructose for a period of at least 24 hours. The inner space loss of ^{14}C from the pool of accumulated [^{14}C]sucrose was described by the equation

$$\frac{-dS^*}{dt} = \frac{(R_1 + R_2)S^*}{S} \tag{5}$$

where S^* is the radioactivity in sucrose, S is the inner space sucrose concentration, R_1 is the rate of sucrose transfer to the hexose pool, and R_2 is the rate of sucrose transfer to the outer space. Additional proof of the steady-state condition was shown by the plot of log S^* against time, which gave the expected straight line with negative slope (581). The half-time for label movement from the sucrose pool, given by

$$t_{1/2} = 0.693 \frac{S}{R_1 + R_2} \tag{6}$$

was shown to be about 6 hours (Fig. 9-5), and the turnover time (1.44 $t_{1/2}$) about 8.6 hours (581). Glasziou also pointed out that if the tonoplast is impermeable to sucrose movement toward the outer space, the value for R_2 becomes 0, and absolute values can be calculated for R_1 (the inversion rate), for S, for K' (velocity constant), for K'', for turnover time of observed sucrose loss to the hexose pool, and maximum turnover time (the interval required for total sucrose loss to the hexose pool). The steady-state sequence would encompass the following steps as the lone pathway for loss of accumulated sucrose:

$$\text{Precursor} \longrightarrow \begin{matrix}\text{sucrose}\\ \text{pool}\end{matrix} \xrightarrow[K'']{} \begin{matrix}\text{glucose + fructose}\\ \text{pool}\end{matrix} \xrightarrow[K'']{} \text{product} \tag{7}$$

However, neither the impermeability nor consistency (with age) of the tonoplast

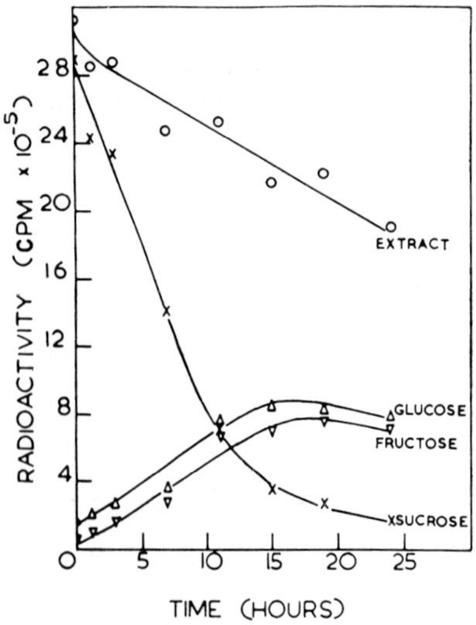

Fig. 9-5. Movement of ^{14}C in inner space sugars. The loss of ^{14}C from sucrose is accompanied by increased labeling of glucose and fructose. Over a time course of 19 hours, the total activity shifted from 93 percent in sucrose to less than 9 percent in sucrose, and from less than 7 percent in hexoses to 52 percent in hexoses. CPM = counts per minute. [After Glasziou (581).]. Reproduced by permission of *Plant Physiology.*

membrane has been proven by critical experimentation. Its behavior could conceivably be affected by outer space sugar in equilibrium with the phloem imports of a physiologically-intact plant, by maturation of the physiological system, and by a host of environmental changes.

In the latter context both the importance and limitations of Glasziou's concept of inner space inversion are underscored. In essence, Glasziou has described the behavior pattern of once-stored sucrose which is called upon to participate in growth processes. Requisite to this participation, one must consider the movement of vacuole sugar to the phloem, the reloading of phloem, and translocation of sugar to the active sink. In a practical sense the postharvest inversion which plagues most plantation managers will also proceed by this or some similar sequence.

Glasziou (581) presented additional evidence relating to pathways of sugar accumulation. Essentially, his earlier thesis of an activated "sucrose–X" was retained, but by selecting younger storage tissues for their higher reducing-sugar contents, he discovered several divergences from the Michaelis–Menten criteria which had pointed to an enzyme-like character of sugar uptake. This was especially true when high concentrations of sucrose or glucose were given in the bathing solution. The resulting Michaelis–Menten relationship was divergent for high sucrose but not for high glucose. This was true even when glucose was supplied at double the maximum sucrose concentration.

Glasziou observed that even though 6 times more [^{14}C]glucose reached the inner space than [^{14}C]fructose, hydrolysis of the inner space sucrose showed only a moderate excess of labeled glucose over labeled fructose. Calculations based upon a sucrose origin of the [^{14}C]fructose suggested that more than 10 percent of the labeled glucose had reached the inner space by an alternate pathway. Accumulation by the second pathway reached significant proportions only under conditions of high glucose supply. Moreover, accumulation experiments with tissues of variable maturity revealed a consistency in the site of rate-limiting sucrose uptake over a wide range of maturity. For glucose, as indicated by relative K_m values, the site of the rate-limiting reaction was shifted within the reaction sequence as a function of maturity. A second sucrose uptake pathway was therefore postulated which would explain the increased rate of sucrose uptake when the sugar level approaches saturation for the low-concentration reaction. Of the parallel pathways for sucrose–X formation, one would predominate at low sucrose concentrations in the outer space. The K_m for the rate-limiting step was estimated to be in the order of 2.5×10^{-3} M.

Fig. 9-6 summarizes schematically the sugar interconversion and accumulation reac-

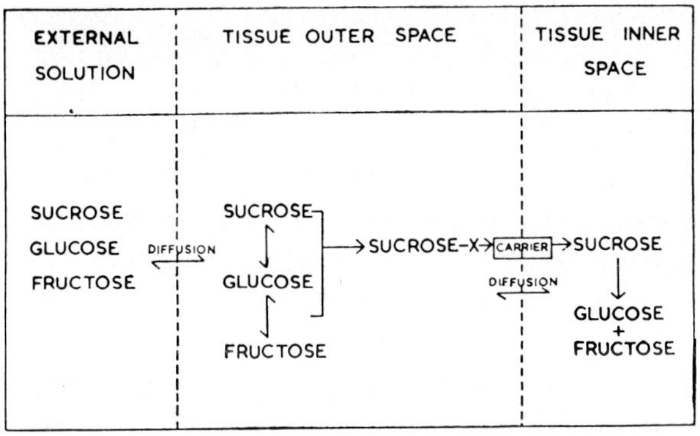

Fig. 9-6. Schematic summary of the sugar interconversion and accumulation processes in sugarcane storage tissue. Sugar efflux is shown as a diffusion process. [After Glasziou (581).] Reproduced by permission of *Plant Physiology*.

tions pictured by Glasziou (581). It was assumed that breakage of the sucrose–X bond provided sufficient free energy to drive the sequence toward sucrose accumulation in the vacuole (inner space). It is seen that both sucrose and glucose are potential sources of sucrose–X, but experimental data points to glucose as the preferential source. Efflux of inner space hexose is depicted as a diffusion process as is the efflux of all three sugars from the cytoplasm (outer space).

5. THE SUGAR ACCUMULATION CYCLE [Hatch, Sacher, Glasziou (689, 690, 1268)]

Up to this point our discussion of sugar storage processes has dealt with the work of Bieleski and of Glasziou performed over a 3-year period. These investigators were the first to define and evaluate the essential reactions for storing sugarcane's vast sucrose output. In addition, valid theories relative to the accumulation mechanism were forwarded to account for the experimental evidence then available. Subsequent papers were issued by Hatch, Sacher, and Glasziou which further developed the storage reactions as a distinctly cyclic process. Salient features of this work include: (a) Elaboration of specific enzymes involved in sucrose storage; (b) establishment of sucrose inversion in the outer space as the rate-limiting step; and (c) clarification of the activated sucrose derivative (sucrose–X) and its principal reactions.

A. *Enzymology of the sugar accumulation cycle*

Employing rind-free storage tissues of the varieties *CO 281* and *NCO 310*, Hatch *et al.* (689) evaluated three categories of enzymes: (1) Those relating to sucrose synthesis and breakdown; (2) enzymes active in the synthesis and breakdown of hexose phosphates; and (3) enzymes catalyzing the interconversion of glucose and fructose. The enzyme sucrose phosphorylase, known to catalyze sucrose synthesis in *Pseudomonas saccharophila* (681), could not be demonstrated in leaf or storage-tissue preparations. Some indirect evidence of the enzyme has been reported in sugarcane leaves (1137, 1338, 12), but it appears not to have general occurrence in higher plants (575, 681). Another sucrose-synthesizing enzyme, UDPG–fructose transglycosylase (sucrose synthetase) was found in storage tissue. As discussed in Chapter 6, this enzyme is widely distributed among higher plants.

The sucrose-forming reaction catalyzed by UDPG–fructose transglycosylase did not appear to be reversible, as evidenced by failure to detect labeled UDPG from [^{14}C]sucrose plus UDP. In the forward reaction the incorporation of [^{14}C]fructose into sucrose was heavily dependent upon the supply of UDPG, the latter achieving saturation of the enzyme at 1×10^{-3} M, whereas the fructose K_m was 3×10^{-3} M. Optimum pH for the reaction was 8.2. Analyses of preparations from eight varieties showed considerable activity variation, with none at all being detected in the lone *S. spontaneum* variety tested. A *S. sinense* variety showed moderate activity.

Evidence of sucrose phosphate synthesis was obtained when fructose was replaced with labeled fructose-6-$\dot{P}$. This is a reaction of considerable importance as shown by the work of Hatch (691) relating to a sucrose phosphate role in sugar accumulation. The compound believed to be sucrose phosphate remained immobile on paper chromatograms irrigated with a solvent giving fluent elution of sucrose and hexose [ethyl acetate–pyridine–water (8:2:1, v/v)]. Upon treatment with alkaline phosphatase the compound became mobile and could then be hydrolyzed by invertase. It thus appeared that the synthesis of sucrose phosphate was catalyzed by UDPG–fructose-6-*P* transglycosylase, although Hatch *et al.* (689) did not include kinetic data for the reaction with fructose-6-*P*.

In 1966 Slack (1341) presented evidence of an inhibitory action against UDPG–fructose transglycosylase by phenol oxidation products in elongating internode tissue. This tissue is the site of intense polyphenol oxidase activity (27) and browning occurs almost immediately upon excision of young internode samples. Slack found the inhibition to be reversed by thiol compounds. He concluded that sucrose synthetase is a sulfhydryl enzyme, and that inhibition occurs via a reaction between quinones (intermediary oxidation products) and sulfhydryl groups on the enzyme. These studies also revealed a localization of the enzyme in vascular strands.

Evidence that UDPG pyrophosphorylase is active in cane sucrose synthesis was also obtained (689). This enzyme is found in sugar beet leaves (264), mung bean (1088), and the pea seed (1458). A combination of glucose-1-*P*, UTP, and Mg^{2+} effectively replaced UDPG in the reaction. The enzyme showed activity comparable to that of UDPG–fructose transglycosylase when allowance was made for partial inhibition by one or several additives. Some sucrose formation was observed in the absence of glucose-1-*P*. Other experiments indicated the presence of a kinase which utilized UTP as well as ATP.

The effectiveness of these enzymes as a group was illustrated by experiments with ^{14}C-labeled fructose and glucose incubated with enzyme preparations from mature and immature storage tissues. The label from each hexose soon appeared in the corresponding hexose phosphate. ATP and Mg^{2+} were required. Labeled glucose was formed from labeled fructose, and both glucose and fructose were formed from [^{14}C]fructose-6-*P*. Thus, a complete set of catalysts needed for the synthesis, interconversion, and breakdown of hexose phosphates was shown to be operating in the sugarcane storage tissues. These are technically hexose phosphate-metabolizing enzymes, but they illustrate the reliance of sucrose-synthesizing reactions upon the adequate performance of a team of supporting catalysts.

Of particular importance to the sugar accumulation cycle was the discovery of an *acid* invertase (pH optimum = pH 5.0 to 5.5) and a *neutral* invertase (pH 7.0) in storage tissue preparations. The acid invertase was first noted by Glasziou (582) in extracts from immature storage tissue. This enzyme is analogous to the system reported by Alexander (16), and appears to constitute a group of distinct proteins when viewed from the standpoint of substrate preference (16), action pattern (43), and electrophoretic mobility (33). When compared with yeast invertase, Alexander (43) found that the cane invertase preparation showed considerably greater action potential against hydrolyzable bonds other than the β-fructosidic linkage of sucrose. Glasziou found that the neutral invertase was situated in mature storage tissue only. The acid and neutral invertases have moderately divergent K_m values for sucrose

(2.5×10^{-2} M and 1.3×10^{-2} M, respectively). Each invertase is active over a broad pH range which overlaps the pH curve of the other enzyme. Neutral invertase was severely inhibited by Tris (0.05 M), but only 25 percent inhibition was recorded against the acid invertase. Kestose (0.05 M) inhibited neutral invertase but had no effect on the acid enzyme.

Some evidence suggests that the sugarcane acid invertase is a transferase for which elements of water serve as but one of several types of hexose receptors (35). Edelman (470) has shown that fungal invertase catalyzes the transfer of ^{14}C-labeled hexoses to sucrose in the presence of unlabeled sucrose. Hatch *et al.* (689) were unable to demonstrate this property with cane invertase preparations. A fraction of the total invertase was detected in association with washed cell fragments, apparently as a bound form of the low-pH enzyme. This fraction represented about 5 percent of the total invertase. It possessed a lower optimum pH (4.4) and a higher K_m value (8×10^{-3} M for sucrose) than the main body of acid invertase. This enzyme might perform a specific role within the cell wall. A bound enzyme would account for the slightly higher invertase yields obtained by Alexander (16) when lyophilized tissue powder was subjected to sonic disintegration prior to extraction.

A pronounced seasonal effect on the acid invertase was also reported (689). The time of highest invertase activity paralleled the time of most rapid growth. The enzyme was hardly detectable during the cooler and drier conditions characteristic for Queensland between May and October (Fig. 9-7). In a subsequent paper Hatch and

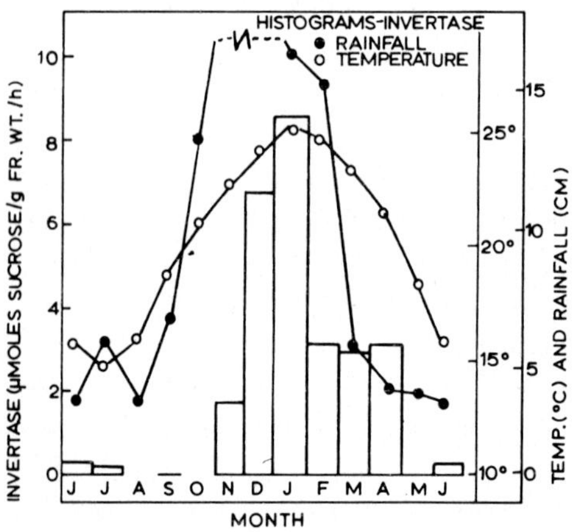

Fig. 9-7. Seasonal effect on acid invertase activity of immature storage tissue. The period of highest activity corresponds to the season of rapid growth. Only traces of the enzyme were found during the Queensland dry and cool season between May and October. [After Hatch *et al.* (689).] Reproduced by permission of *Plant Physiology.*

Glasziou (690) reported a strong correlation between invertase content and elongation rate of immature internodes, suggesting that, under certain conditions, invertase may be a growth-limiting factor.

B. *Role of invertase in sugar accumulation*

Glasziou's (581) development of the accumulation scheme depicted in Fig. 9-6, including the concept of parallel pathways for synthesis of sucrose–X, was soon followed by the studies of Sacher *et al.* (1268) which elaborated both the pathways of sugar accumulation and the importance of invertase as a regulatory system. The essence of this work includes the following points: (a) Based upon enzyme studies and sugar transformations, the concept of direct sucrose activation to sucrose–X was modified in favor of differential hexose phosphorylation and a subsequent reconstitution of hexose to yield sucrose phosphate; (b) conclusive evidence for spatial separation of three distinct compartments is given in terms of *outer space* (including cell walls), *metabolic compartment*, and *inner space*; (c) acid invertase was localized in the outer space where it can control the flow of sucrose from conducting phloem to immature storage tissue; and (d) neutral invertase was assigned a similar regulatory effect over sugar movement in mature storage tissue.

The possibility of direct sucrose conversion to sucrose–X was not accepted for several reasons. In some experiments where immature storage tissue contained little acid invertase in the outer space, the rate of sucrose uptake was clearly limited. In tissues having abundant invertase there was an accumulation of reducing sugars where formerly sucrose was present alone. The concept of a single rate-limiting carrier for sugar uptake was therefore discarded.

Strong evidence for spatially distinct metabolic and storage compartments was shown by the asymmetric label distribution in sucrose accumulated from mixtures of [^{14}C]sucrose and unlabeled fructose. The observation that labeled glucose or labeled fructose supplied alone yielded sucrose with equally-labeled moieties was taken to mean that a ^{14}C movement occurred from free-space hexose to sucrose without equilibrium with endogenous reducing sugar. A similar movement had been found by Putman and Hassid (1199) in *Canna indica* leaves. Any explanation of the labeled sugar behavior must assume that diffusion occurs into the free space (including the cell wall), and that metabolically-mediated reactions occur in an outer space distinct from an inner space.

Sacher *et al.* (1268) found the acid invertase of immature storage tissue to be heavily concentrated in the outer space where it performs a major role in sucrose accumulation. Qualitative localization of the enzyme in the outer space was accomplished by measuring labeled hexose in an external medium supplied only with labeled sucrose. The latter experiences partial inversion upon entrance into the outer space, and some of the labeled products would appear in the external medium by reverse diffusion. Quantitative estimates of invertase activity could not be determined from external hexose levels owing to the fact that some hexose passes into the vacuole as resynthesized sucrose. Experimental data showed that glucose was utilized about 3 times more rapidly than fructose, as evidenced by the predominance of labeled fructose over labeled glucose in the bathing medium. By assuming that the level of inversion in the bathing solution itself was negligible, the net uptake of sucrose from the medium was taken as a reliable estimate of invertase activity in the outer space. An alternate method for estimating outer space invertase relied on the summation of labeled hexose in the medium plus accumulated radioactivity in the tissue. The two invertase methods were found to be in close agreement. The presence of an acid invertase in the outer space also agreed with the findings of Putman and Hassid (1199) with *Canna indica* leaf tissue.

Sacher *et al.* (1268) observed that the accumulation curve for sucrose closely paralleled the activity curve for outer space invertase (Fig. 9-8). The correlation is even

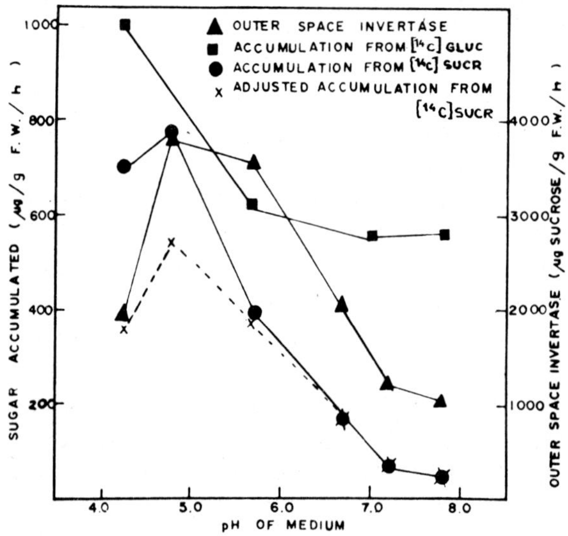

Fig. 9-8. Outer space invertase activity and sugar accumulation as a function of pH. The sucrose accumulation curve closely resembles the curve for outer space invertase at different pH values. [After Sacher *et al.* (1268).] Reproduced by permission of *Plant Physiology.*

more apparent when correction is made for the low-pH enhancement of glucose uptake, an event which Sacher *et al.* (1268) regarded as irrelevant to the normal accumulation process. Noting the findings by Hatch *et al.* (689) showing Tris buffer to be increasingly inhibitive against invertase at higher pH, Sacher and his co-workers demonstrated that Tris inhibition of outer space invertase was accompanied by slower sucrose uptake, but not by slower glucose uptake. From these results it was concluded that sucrose inversion in the outer space is an integral part of the sugar accumulation process, and under certain conditions inversion can be a rate-limiting factor.

Another catalyst having possible significance in sugarcane storage processes is the enzyme *trehalase.* It was recently isolated from sugarcane roots, stalks, and leaves by Glasziou and Gayler (592). A similar enzyme is bound in mammalian kidney and intestinal membranes (616, 1275) where it is believed to mediate glucose transfer. In sugarcane, trehalase predominates in immature storage tissue but declines to negligible levels as the tissue matures. It acts upon the substrate trehalose, producing glucose, with a pH optimum near 6.2 and a K_m value of 1.0×10^{-4} M. Trehalase appears to be situated near vacuolar invertase but differs from invertase in that it is not subject to product repression by glucose nor is it inhibited by cycloheximide. Glasziou and Gayler noted that the rate of trehalase activity is much too low to account for more than a small fraction of the observed levels of glucose taken up. However, it was suggested that trehalase might perform a role in hexose movement out of the vacuole, probably as an unbound cytoplasmic enzyme (592).

Sacher *et al.* (1268) summarized schematically their understanding of the sugar accumulation process (Fig. 9-9). By comparison with Glasziou's (581) earlier scheme (Fig. 9-6) the reader will note several important new features: (a) A clear distinction is made for the first time between conducting phloem and storage parenchyma; (b) the parenchyma itself is assigned three compartments, within which a clear distinction is drawn between the *outer space* and *metabolic compartments*[8]; (c) the roles of outer

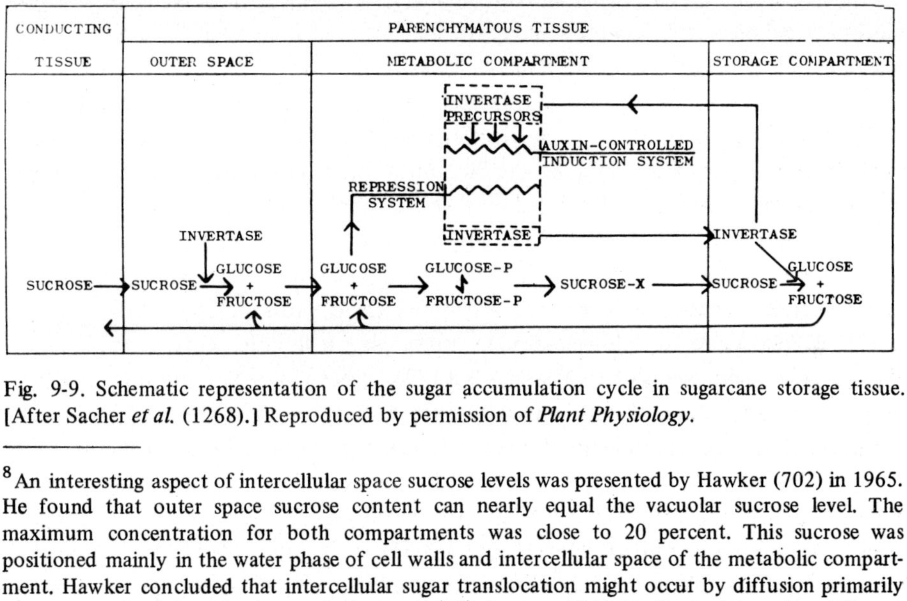

Fig. 9-9. Schematic representation of the sugar accumulation cycle in sugarcane storage tissue. [After Sacher *et al.* (1268).] Reproduced by permission of *Plant Physiology.*

[8] An interesting aspect of intercellular space sucrose levels was presented by Hawker (702) in 1965. He found that outer space sucrose content can nearly equal the vacuolar sucrose level. The maximum concentration for both compartments was close to 20 percent. This sucrose was positioned mainly in the water phase of cell walls and intercellular space of the metabolic compartment. Hawker concluded that intercellular sugar translocation might occur by diffusion primarily along the cell walls. Glasziou and Gayler (1159) later verified Hawker's data using different methods and confirmed that the diffusive movement applied only to mature tissue. Sucrose may thus be seen to move by independent processes of active accumulation and diffusion, the relative importance of the two processes being determined by current levels of cell wall acid invertase and neutral invertase, *i.e.*, the enzymes presumably governing the rate of active accumulation. Should this occur during periods of high sucrose demand in other parts of the plant, the sucrose needs may be met by diffusive drainage of sucrose from the vacuoles and intercellular space of mature stalk tissue. At other times the diffusion process may operate between intercellular space and vacuole, in conjunction with active sugar accumulation, as an effective means of maintaining the sucrose level of storage vacuoles.

space invertase and of vacuolar invertase are clearly indicated; (d) a cyclic nature of the storage process is depicted for the first time; and (e) an auxin-controlled induction system and a repression system is included within the metabolic compartment. The latter feature is an extremely important concept with far-reaching significance for sugarcane growth and maturation control. It will be given detailed treatment in the following chapter.

C. *Sucrose phosphate as an intermediate in sugar accumulation*

The discovery by Hatch *et al.* (689) of a UDPG–fructose-6-*P* transglycosylase reaction yielding a chromatographically-immobile compound having properties similar to sucrose phosphate has been mentioned briefly (*cf.* this chapter, pp. 348, 349.) The necessity of an "activated" sucrose derivative for the accumulation process had been recognized for several years (579). That sucrose phosphate could serve this purpose, with free energy for active accumulation provided by breakage of the phosphate bond (581), became a distinct possibility.

Working with enzyme preparations from leaf and storage tissue, Hatch (691) found additional evidence that sucrose phosphate performs an intermediary role in sucrose accumulation: (a) Enzymes capable of synthesizing and hydrolyzing sucrose phosphate were found in storage tissue; (b) labeled sucrose phosphate was formed when [^{14}C]glucose was supplied to tissue slices; (c) vacuolar sucrose derived from fructosyl-labeled sucrose phosphate retained the label in its fructose moiety, whereas vacuolar sucrose derived from fructosyl-labeled sucrose was labeled in both moieties.

The assay of UDPG–fructose-6-*P* transglycosylase (sucrose phosphate synthetase) was rendered more difficult by several interferring enzymes of common occurrence. Rapid decline of reaction rates was attributed to loss of fructose-6-*P* through the action of phosphatases, phosphohexose isomerase, invertase, and sucrose-*P* phosphatase. This lends support to Glasziou's (579) suggestion that enzymes relating to sugar phosphorylation and interconversion may be rate-limiting factors in sugar accumulation. Hatch implied that similar systems may explain the failure of other workers (541) to detect sucrose phosphate synthesis by sugarcane leaf extracts. In later studies with leaf preparations, Hawker (705) greatly improved the assay method for UDPG–fructose-6-*P* transglycosylase by incorporating EDTA into the reaction mixtures. Sucrose-*P* phosphatase was inhibited by the additive and sucrose phosphate synthesis was increased up to 100 percent. A specific sucrose-*P* phosphatase had not yet been described when Hatch performed his experiments, but confirming evidence of this enzyme in sugarcane was soon presented by Hawker and Hatch (703).

Hatch (691) found that sucrose phosphate appeared to be restricted in its movement into the metabolic compartment as evidenced by a lesser accumulation of sucrose from sucrose phosphate than from sucrose. That the phosphorylated fructose moiety might be responsible for impeded movement was suggested by a similar restriction of fructose-6-*P* uptake by storage tissue as compared to fructose uptake (691).

When Hatch concluded his experiments relating to sucrose phosphate he was aware that invertase was rapidly being established as an important factor in sugar accumulation by sugarcane storage tissue. In his commentary he cites other workers whose evidence points to an invertase requirement for metabolic utilization of sucrose (1199, 685, 718, 1248, 544). However, several plant tissues were noted [artichoke tuber (473), tobacco leaf (1176), sugar beet root (129)] which contain little or no invertase but nonetheless accumulate sucrose. Some evidence has been published suggestive of sucrose movement into leaf-tissue cells without prior hydrolysis (1176)[6].

Hatch proposed two mechanisms by which sucrose could actively accumulate via sucrose phosphate without the mediation of invertase: (a) Direct phosphorylation without interconversion of the glucose and fructose moieties; and (b) a splitting of sucrose by UDPG–fructose transglycosylase followed by phosphorylation of fructose and synthesis of sucrose phosphate. An enzyme essential for the first system, sucrose kinase, has not been found in plant tissues. Favoring the second system is the presence of all requisite enzymes in sugarcane storage tissue. Studies by Cardini *et al.* (303) on UDPG–fructose transglycosylase revealed an equilibrium constant permissive of a sucrose-splitting reaction (691). Hatch states that this mechanism could be operative in sucrose accumulation without interconversion of its hexose moieties, providing that UDPG is employed in forming sucrose phosphate without prior equilibration with the hexose phosphate pool. Neither of the two mechanisms would appear to contribute heavily to sucrose storage in sugarcane. In any case an active role of invertase has definitely been established for sucrose storage in sugarcane.

Hatch presented an abbreviated scheme showing the intermediary position of sucrose phosphate in sugar accumulation (Fig. 9-10). The main feature was the replacement of sucrose–X with sucrose phosphate. Virtually all sucrose arriving from the phloem is inverted. The only sugar accumulating in the storage compartment (vacuole) is sucrose. In addition, hexose phosphates are shown in equilibrium with one another and with UDPG.

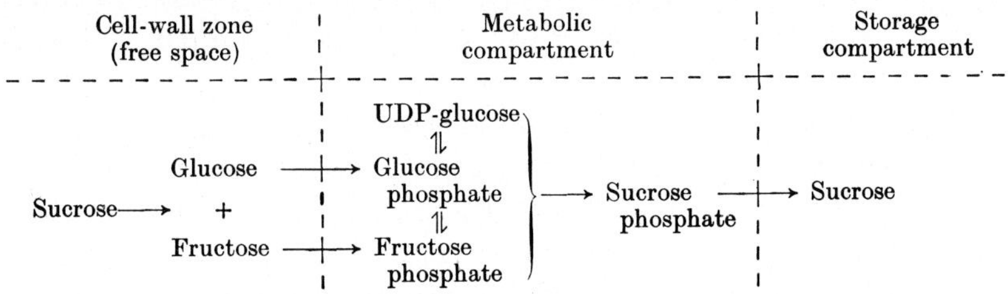

Fig. 9-10. The sugar accumulation process as depicted by Hatch showing the intermediate position of sucrose phosphate. [After Hatch (691).] Reproduced by permission of the *Biochemical Journal*, London.

6. SUMMARY OF THE SUCROSE STORAGE PROCESS

Essential outlines of the sucrose storage process in sugarcane have been established. As a freshly-formed photosynthate, sucrose embarks upon extended travels through conducting phloem and ultimately experiences major transformations in storage cells before it comes to "rest" in the vacuole. The storage process includes inversion of sucrose to its component hexose moieties, interconversion and phosphorylation of fructose and glucose, synthesis of sucrose phosphate, and active accumulation across the vacuolar membrane. A striking feature of the storage process is that sucrose is effectively moved against a massive concentration gradient. In order to leave the storage vacuole sucrose must again experience inversion to fructose and glucose.

Upon arrival at the storage parenchyma cell, sucrose is inverted through the mediation of an acid invertase (optimum pH = 5.0 to 5.5) situated in the cell-wall area of the outer space. The products, fructose and glucose, readily diffuse inward to the metabolic area of the outer space, and with equal ease can diffuse back out to the external medium. This movement is strictly passive. Sucrose *per se* can likewise move between the external medium and outer space, but only at about 1/10 of the rate shown by glucose. The sugars (fructose, glucose, sucrose) are now residing within the storage tissue, but they are not "stored" in the usual sense because there is no barrier against their diffusion back to the external medium.

Within the outer space (metabolic compartment), fructose and glucose experience rapid interconversion and phosphorylation. Several groups of enzymes are present which assure adequate amounts of UDPG, fructose, and fructose-6-*P* for sucrose synthesis. This is true even when only one of the sugars has been supplied in the external medium. Among the essential enzymes there appears to be an abundance of hexokinase (phosphorylation of glucose and fructose), phosphohexose isomerase (interconversion of glucose-6-*P* and fructose-6-*P*), UDPG–fructose transglycosylase and UDPG–fructose-6-*P* transglycosylase (sucrose and sucrose phosphate synthesis), numerous non-specific phosphatases and a specific sucrose-*P* phosphatase. There is no known kinase for the direct synthesis of sucrose phosphate from sucrose plus ATP. The requisite ATP for hexokinase reactions is provided by respiratory reactions. Taken together these enzymes catalyze the reconstitution of sucrose *per se*, or of sucrose phosphate, the latter being hydrolyzed by sucrose-*P* phosphatase.

Sucrose phosphate (sucrose–X) is enabled to pass from the outer space to the inner space, a step which free sucrose cannot accomplish owing to the greater sucrose concentration of the inner space. This is an active accumulation step. It appears to rely upon free energy released by breakage of the phosphate bond of sucrose phosphate. Having arrived inside the storage vacuole the sucrose molecule is effectively stored.

The mechanism of active sucrose accumulation is the same in both mature and immature storage tissues; however, the fate of accumulated sucrose differs in the two tissues owing to distinctive invertase complements and growth requirements. In immature storage tissue where rapid cell expansion is a predominant feature, accumulated sucrose is rapidly hydrolyzed by vacuolar acid invertase and the hexose products move freely to the cytoplasm for use in growth processes. The hexoses may also be reaccumulated as part of the overall cyclic mechanism. In mature stalk tissue where growth processes have practically ceased there is a striking decline of vacuolar acid invertase and a neutral invertase becomes predominant. This enzyme is apparently situated in the cytoplasm. The neutral invertase operates in conjunction with the cell wall acid invertase to govern the active accumulation of sucrose into the vacuole. In very mature tissues, having sucrose levels approaching 15 to 20 percent, there is a further placement of sucrose in the intercellular spaces. The latter sucrose, depending upon the plants' physiological status as determined by its environment, assumes an important role in sugar movement. This may occur by passive diffusion between the intercellular space and vacuole, and by translocation to areas of intensive sugar metabolism.

With reference to the cyclic movement of sugars in immature storage tissue, two functions appear to be served: (a) A buffer system is created which prevents large fluctuations in cytoplasmic sugar supplies, and (b) large fluctuations in the vacuole osmotic potential, which serves as a driving force for cell expansion, are prevented. The buffer system is regulated in part by a complex feedback control system for vacuolar acid invertase. The operation of this control mechanism is treated in detail in the following chapter.

Chapter 10

Regulation of Sugar Storage

1. INTRODUCTION

A sucrose molecule deposited within the sugarcane stalk is a product of many reactions and a veteran of many travels. This is no less true among the intercellular compartments than throughout the different tissues and extensive conducting system of the intact plant. Although its residence within the vacuole is potentially a permanent one, in another sense sucrose is never fully retired from active service to the plant. Sugarcane expends considerable effort in storing sucrose, but at the same time provision is made to retract it from storage when the need arises. A rapid sucrose turnover is especially common in immature internodes whose hexose requirements are high and whose subtending leaves are not yet ready to produce sucrose in appreciable quantities.

However, with due regard to sugarcane's extensive use of sucrose, a salient feature of this plant is its ability to accumulate and maintain large quantities of sucrose in the same tissues whose growth required an earlier sucrose expenditure. Quite possibly we may never discover or understand all of the events which account for sucrose storage in such massive amounts. On the other hand, investigators who have outlined the storage processes in sugarcane have also produced much new information relative to storage control. The purpose of this chapter is to review regulatory mechanisms operative in the sugar storage processes outlined in the previous chapter.

In essence there are two categories of information relevant to the control of sugar storage. (a) Inversion control, appertaining specifically to rate-limiting reactions of the sugar accumulation cycle, and (b) environmental control, acting indirectly through photosynthesis, respiration, and growth processes. The first category is the main topic of this chapter. Other tentative control systems could be mentioned, *i.e.*, those relating to genetic make-up, hormone balance, maturity, and metabolites, but for the present it is assumed that each of these is operative within categories (a) and (b). Relatively little is known about environmental effects upon the sugar accumulation reactions *per se*, although much empirical information has been published relating net sucrose storage to water, temperature, and nutritional factors. These are taken up in a subsequent chapter dealing with sugarcane ripening.

When discussing invertase control in its correct context relative to sugar storage, one might expect that outer space invertase would provide the main topic. This enzyme does control the overall rate of sucrose entry into the cell (1268), while vacuolar invertase operates in the redirection of sucrose from storage. It appears that only the vacuolar invertase is subject to rapid control by highly-sensitive regulatory mechanisms (585, 1267, 1340, 1268). Moreover, the storage space invertase is found in considerably greater quantities than the outer space enzyme (1268, 590). Therefore, while outer space invertase is largely concerned with the incoming sucrose from conducting tissue, vacuolor invertase regulates the return of sucrose from a storage condition to a status of reinvolvement in metabolic activity. By this reasoning the concept of vacuolar invertase acting as a key regulatory factor of metabolic processes emerges. This view is supported by the work of Hatch and Glasziou (690), and by Glasziou and Bull (590), showing a close correlation between invertase behavior and growth rate of elongating internodes.

2. THEORY OF ENZYME REGULATION BY SUGARS AND HORMONES

A. *Glucose regulation (the "glucose effect"; catabolite repression)*

Scientists developing the sugar accumulation cycle were aware of a regulatory action of glucose upon vacuolar invertase. The glucose effect was operative in addition to, and in conjunction with, a hormone-sensitive mechanism of invertase control. However, the concept of enzyme regulation by carbohydrates did not originate with sugarcane invertase; reports suggestive of such systems were extant from the early years of this century [literature reviewed by Epps and Gale (496)]. Initial observations were related to apparent changes in microbial N metabolism when carbohydrate was included in the test medium (822, 823). Kendall (824), in 1922, suggested a protein-preserving action of carbohydrate, whereas Bergman and Rettger (171) found that carbohydrate effects can occur specifically upon a protease enzyme. For a time the mechanism of carbohydrate action was interpreted in terms of greater acidity resulting from sugar fermentation (171, 1212).

During the 1930's several investigators reported discrete effects of glucose upon an indole-forming enzyme ("tryptophanase") in cultures of *Escherichia coli* (638, 639, 523). Glucose was seen as inhibiting an adaptive portion of the enzyme (523). Evans *et al.* (503) later claimed that tryptophanase is purely adaptive, and that its regulation by glucose depends upon the presence of tyrosine or phenylalanine. The glucose effect was incomplete in the absence of these amino acids.

A regulatory relationship of glucose to deaminase[1] (1359) and aspartase (551) was also described with *E. coli* preparations during the late 1930's. In each instance the glucose action was shown to occur as growth was in progress rather than after growth had ceased. The possibility of an anaerobiosis effect was discounted when it was shown that passage of ample oxygen through the medium had no bearing on the

[1] Gale, E.F. and Stephenson, M., 1938. Factors influencing bacterial deamination. II. Factors influencing the activity of *dl*-serine deaminase in *Bacterium coli*, *Biochem. J.* 32: 392–404.

glucose–enzyme relationship. Some evidence (552) still purported to show that low pH accounted for the glucose action. However, in subsequent experiments, Epps and Gale (496, 553) demonstrated that the formation of a number of *E. coli* enzymes is suppressed by glucose independently of potential fermentative acidity. Five years later, in 1947, Monod (1032) reported a similar glucose effect on enzymes for the metabolism of other sugars.

Taken together, the work of Epps and Gale (496, 553) and Monod (1032) gave the first definition of "glucose effect" *per se*, that is, the inhibition by glucose of synthesis mechanisms for inducible enzymes. The first clear picture of the glucose mode of action emerged in 1961 when Magasanik (968) proposed his *catabolite repression* hypothesis. This hypothesis was the first to recognize that glucose is not necessarily the lone repressor, and it extended the range of regulatory potential far beyond the N-metabolic and amino acid reactions which had attracted numerous early workers. Principal features of the concept include the following: (a) Glucose regulation is effective upon noninducible enzymes as well as inducible ones. In addition, many inducible ones (nitrate reductase, amino acid decarboxylases, tetrathionate reductase) are not affected by glucose. (b) Any compound serving as an efficient source of intermediary metabolites, and of energy, is a potential regulator of glucose-sensitive enzymes. (c) A common property of glucose-sensitive enzymes is their capacity to convert substrates into products *which are more readily obtainable by glucose metabolism* (1077). This relationship is especially true for enzymes which metabolize sugars or sugar alcohols. (d) Glucose-insentitive enzymes cannot form their products independently via glucose metabolism. (e) Glucose, being more rapidly metabolized than most other carbon compounds, normally forms intermediary metabolites at rates exceeding the cellular capacity to utilize them. Cells supplied with glucose in a mixture of carbon sources can thus economize by preferentially forming enzymes orientated to glucose metabolism. (f) Glucose contributes to cell economy by inhibiting formation of enzymes at a time when this formation would not contribute to cell growth[2].

From this reasoning the concept of *catabolite repression* was first formulated (1077, 1078), in which catabolites produced rapidly from glucose would accumulate and repress further synthesis of enzymes augmenting the already large pools of catabolites. Accordingly, the repressor products of catabolic enzymes would restrict enzyme synthesis in their own pathway of origin, and also the formation of enzymes by any catabolic pathway having the potential to produce them.

Magasanik (968) visualized a number of conditions for which the rate of catabolic reactions would be particularly important to biological experiments. Any conditions leading to reduced rates of protein and nucleic acid synthesis without comparable

---

[2] In this view glucose acts in the sense of a repressive end product of a reaction series against the individual reactions of that series; glucose inhibition of an enzyme does not mean that the enzyme is nonessential.

slackening of catabolism would lead to metabolite accumulations and subsequent suppression of catabolic enzymes. Under these conditions, Magasanik maintained, compounds normally having insufficient concentration to act as supressors would assume repressor activity. The work of Mandelstram (971) was cited in which N-deficient cells producing little protein were able to produce β-galactosidase only in the *absence* of an energy source. A similar relationship of the enzyme to P deficiency was described (968). Citing β-galactosidase as an example, Magasanik cautioned against the use of catabolic enzyme synthesis rates as indicators of genetic or biosynthetic potential.

A relationship of *repressor* to *inducer* has been depicted by Jacob and Monod (783) in the instance of β-galactosidase synthesis. By this theory, the enzyme's formation is induced when an inducer compound prevents a repressor from blocking synthesis. The repressor is thought to be a specific RNA produced under the mediation of a repressor gene. The repressor compound would block the formation of β-galactosidase, a trans-acetylase, and a permease by "interacting" with the specific chromosomal area where these activities are performed. Szilard (1398) proposed that the enzyme repressors *per se* are inactive until combined with the "metabolite moiety" or ultimate product of that particular reaction sequence.

In the present chapter we shall see that glucose is not the only repressor of cane invertase synthesis, and that each active repressor bears certain common pyranose or furanose ring configurations. In general, the catabolic repression theory helps to explain much of the experimental evidence pointing to invertase regulation in sugar-cane.

B. *Hormonal enzyme regulation*

It is widely assumed that hormones[3] regulate biochemical processes by action upon specific enzymes, although until quite recently there was little evidence giving direct support to this view. Plant growth hormones, or *auxins*, have been implicated in the regulation of inducible enzymes. Recent evidence points to hormonal regulation of the specific messenger RNA (mRNA) required for synthesis of a given enzyme. Workers in Australia have shown that, apart from the glucose role in cane invertase regulation, there is a hormone-sensitive mechanism governing the synthesis of invertase mRNA. Because of the strong correlation of invertase activity with growth rate, this work has

---

[3]Abbreviation and definitions: Hormone, "a substance normally produced in cells and necessary for the proper functioning of other distant cells to which they are conveyed and of the body as a whole" [Henderson and Henderson (719)]; auxin, plant growth hormone [Henderson and Henderson (719)], "any organic compound which, in low concentrations, promotes growth along the longitudinal axis of shoots" [Fruton and Simmonds (540, p. 972)]; IAA, indole-3-acetic acid; NAA, α-naphthalene acetic acid; GA, gibberellic acid; RNA, ribonucleic acid; mRNA, messenger RNA.

helped to clarify one of the mechanisms by which growth hormones may exert control over growth and maturation of sugarcane.

Although the recent work by Gayler and Glasziou (567) appears to show a direct linkage of hormonal invertase regulation with overall growth control, the growth responses of auxins were studied for many years with little light being shed on their mechanism of action (540, p. 972; 1561, 933, 1419). The study of plant tropisms (curvatures of stems or roots in response to light or gravity) culminated in the *negative geotropism* hypothesis which holds that shoot curvature upward from the earth is accountable to higher concentrations of growth-promoting auxin on the lower side of the shoot. It was recognized that growth increases were due to cell elongation rather than increased cell numbers. In addition to cell elongation, auxins sometimes act to stimulate cell division or to retard growth. Flowering has for a number of years been attributed to flower-forming hormones, or *florigens*, although the auxin-like compound gibberellic acid (GA) is also known to induce flower formation. The most widely distributed natural auxin is indole-3-acetic acid (IAA). A synthetic aromatic auxin, α-naphthalene acetic acid (NAA), produces effects similar to IAA. The compound indolyl-3-acetonitrile has generally weaker growth activity but is readily oxidized to IAA. Certain other compounds, such as the gibberellins, produce auxin-like growth stimulation. GA and a number of gibberellins produced by the fungus *Gibberella fujikuroi* are believed to be closely related to natural plant hormones (540, p. 975).

The biochemical mode of action of auxins and "related" growth-regulatory substances has never been clearly defined. A longstanding hypothesis offered in explanation of auxin activity holds that a physiochemical mechanism alters cell membranes and interfaces (848, 849, 1482). Glasziou *et al.* (580) lent support to this hypothesis with studies of bean endocarp which was maintained in the presence and absence of auxin. However, it was difficult for these workers to explain overall auxin control of metabolic processes by a system localized at the cellular membranes.

Changes in such features as cell wall elasticity, pectin methylation, and protoplasmic streaming tell little about the essential metabolic events. Auxin-increased respiration rates are suggestive of roles in this area by virtue of the generally parallel relationship of growth and respiratory activity. Participation of an oxidative source of energy during increased growth is implied by the nature of various respiratory inhibitors (1122). Auxin-increased respiration has also been correlated with increased water uptake, and with increased amino acid uptake by cells (1228). Nooden and Thimann (1122) presented evidence that protein synthesis is among the requirements for cell elongation. It has further been shown that GA-stimulated elongation of lentil epicotyl cells is accompanied by increased synthesis of DNA (1119).

Auxins have been found to increase RNA synthesis in tissues of higher plants (834, 986, 1403, 1550). Leaf senescence, regarded as an expression of RNA- and protein-synthesis decline (528), is temporarily arrested by gibberellin (242, 527) and auxins

(1128). Considerable evidence now supports a hormonal control of leaf senescence based upon a DNA-dependent synthesis of RNA (528, 1129, 527). GA has been shown to increase RNA synthesis as well as cell elongation and DNA synthesis in lentil epicotyls (1119). Roychoudhury and Sen (1261) reported that auxin stimulates the release as well as the synthesis of RNA. Brachet (220) has described at length the roles of RNA in protein synthesis, growth, and morphogenesis.

Williamson and Schweet (1575), working with puromycin-inhibited protein synthesis of rabbit reticulocytes, discovered a dynamic equilibrium between ribosome attachment and detachment reactions, with the ribosomes moving along a strand of mRNA during growth of polypeptide chains. Other studies suggested that protein synthesis occurs on polyribosomes made up of two or more ribosomes [reviewed by Marks *et al.* (980)], and that an important role of "S-RNA" is maintenance of polyribosome structure (980).

Numerous reports have appeared relative to auxin-induced changes in enzyme behavior. A pertinent example is given by Alexander (19) who treated immature sugarcane with an aqueous 0.175 percent solution of IAA and measured the activity of numerous foliar enzymes over a period of 27 days. Of the 20 enzymes assayed, 15 were significantly increased within 9 days (11 during the first day), 4 enzymes remained unaffected, and one catalyst (condensing enzyme) was suppressed.

A fundamental question incident to auxin–enzyme relationship is whether the observed changes in activity are due to *de novo* synthesis or to activation of enzymes already formed. When *de novo* synthesis results from the action of the enzyme's specific substrate, the enzyme is said to be induced (1478). Varner (1478, p. 18) does not consider rapid enzyme changes as proof of synthesis, and as recently as 1965 he regarded only the formation of radish nitrate reductase (164), in response to added nitrate, as unquestionably *de novo* synthesis. Neilands and Stumpf (1079, p. 379) point out that the inducers and substrates need not be identical, and in the absence of inducer some enzyme formation may occur at extremely low rates. Yeast invertase (a β-fructosidase) appears to be substrate induced since preautolysis of yeasts with sucrose will increase invertase content up to 3-fold (1087, 502). Sugarcane invertase may also appear to be inducible by virtue of its rapid diurnal fluctuations (1340, 54). However, the picture here is vastly complicated both by spatially- or chemically-distinct substrates (leaf and transient sucrose, outer space sucrose, activated sucrose or "sucrose–X", and inner space sucrose), and invertase [outer space (acid), inner space (acid), and inner space (neutral)].

C. *The allosteric transition hypothesis*

The control mechanism of an enzyme's synthesis appears to reside at the formation of specific mRNA for that enzyme. In 1963 Monod *et al.* (1033) published evidence that regulatory agents for biologically-active proteins induce a conformational alteration (allosteric transition) in the protein when it "binds" with the agent. By this means the metabolite is believed to act as a physiological signal rather than by direct participation in the reaction itself. According to Monod and his co-workers, the control system is so organized that structural information coded in the deoxyribonucleotides of the gene is transcribed into a ribonucleotide sequence, *i.e.*, the messenger. The messenger then attaches to a ribosome where transcription into a polypeptide sequence occurs. Amino acids are positioned in the sequence by appropriate base pairing between messenger and S-RNA. Varner (1478, p. 18) suggests that control occurs as a portion of the nuclear DNA is transcribed to form an enzyme-specific mRNA.

The allosteric transition hypothesis thus accounts for metabolite activation or inhibition, at a genetic-level synthesis of mRNA, through mediation of a conformational protein alteration. Literature has subsequently appeared lending support to this concept. Chrispeels and Varner (324) noted that a GA-enhanced synthesis of barley aleurone α-amylase was inhibited by abscisin and by GA removal at mid-course during synthesis. Mid-course addition of 6-methylpurine or 8-azaguanine gave delayed inhibition, but actinomycin D had little effect. Cycloheximide gave immediate inhibition. These results were interpreted as evidence of a GA effect upon the synthesis of mRNA for α-amylase. Abscisin was believed to prevent mRNA synthesis or its incorporation into a functional enzyme-synthesizing unit.

Also pertinent is the work of Venis (1483) showing that IAA induces a system which in turn produces benzoylaspartate in pea stems. The IAA effect was shown to depend on RNA synthesis. IAA activity was also severely restricted by actinomycin D, and by puromycin (believed to interfere with amino acid transfer). Venis concluded that IAA acted by causing a new mRNA to be synthesized, and therefore a new enzyme protein was produced. On the other hand, studies by Gayler and Glasziou (567), relating to invertase and peroxidase synthesis in sugarcane internodal tissue, revealed that both NAA and GA increased the invertase-synthesizing capacity without affecting peroxidase. Their results were taken as evidence of hormonal stabilization of invertase mRNA rather than an effect upon mRNA synthesis.

3. INVERSION CONTROL

In Chapter 9 we saw that the acid and neutral invertases present in sugarcane storage tissue play specific roles in at least two spatially-distinct sites relative to the sugar accumulation cycle. Sucrose, as freshly-formed photosynthate, is translocated through the phloem of the leaf, leaf sheath, and stalk, ultimately arriving at the parenchyma cells of storage tissue. It is not accumulated as such but is first inverted through the mediation of an outer space acid invertase situated in the cell wall. This reaction is rate limiting for sugar uptake. Once it is stored in the vacuole, sucrose cannot diffuse back into the metabolic compartment, nor presumably to the conducting phloem, without first being inverted through the mediation of a vacuolar invertase.

Between 1962 and 1969 a great deal of work was published concerning invertase control by endogenous mechanisms in sugarcane storage tissue (1267, 1269, 586, 585, 589, 567, 588). A large share of these studies was performed by the same investigators who had developed the sugar storage process and were aware of the important role played by invertase. Two types of regulation were definitely established: (a) A feedback repression by invertase products, including potential repression by other sugars or sugar metabolites; and (b) hormonal control involving stabilization of mRNA for invertase.

A. *Discovery of auxin–carbohydrate mediated invertase control* [Sacher *et al.* (1267, 1269)]

In 1962, shortly after Glasziou described invertase activity within the storage vacuole (582), Sacher and Glasziou (1267) published a brief report describing increased invertase activity in storage tissue discs incubated in a dilute solution of NAA. Incubation in glucose solutions led to activity suppression. The glucose effect persisted when NAA was included in the glucose solution.

Immature internodal tissue from the variety *N.Co. 310* was used as invertase source. Tissue discs were washed, randomized and assorted into lots of specified number and weight. They were incubated in 20-ml volumes of water or additive solution with continuous shaking for a period of 18 hours. Solutions were changed twice during this period. Tissue discs were washed, ground with a mortar, and the juice separated from cell debris by passage through fine muslin. Juice was dialyzed to remove sugars prior to enzyme analysis. Invertase contained in both the juice and cell residue was assayed using 1.0 percent [^{14}C]sucrose at pH 5.5 and 30 °C under toluene. Samples of the reaction mixture were taken at variable intervals, chromatographed on No. 1 Whatman filter paper, and analyzed for radioactive sugars.

Results of a typical experiment are presented in Table 10-1. It can be seen that 18 hours incubation in water alone had no appreciable effect, although changes of significant magnitude reportedly occurred at times in both directions. This was attributed to the variable action of endogenous auxin (1267). Preliminary experiments had shown a NAA-stimulatory effect with optimum NAA concentration in the order of 1.42×10^{-5} M. This level more than doubled invertase activity in the experiment summarized in Table 10-1, and at other times it increased the enzyme up to 3-fold. Glucose lowered the enzyme level and NAA was unable to reverse the glucose suppression. Similar results were obtained with sucrose and fructose. Galactose and mannitol gave lesser suppression.

NAA had no effect on invertase activity of the dialyzed tissue homogenates. This was suggestive of NAA action on an enzyme-synthesis mechanism operative within the

TABLE 10-1

INCREASE OF SUGARCANE INVERTASE ACTIVITY BY AUXIN AND REPRESSION OF THE ENZYME BY GLUCOSE

[After Sacher and Glasziou (1267).] Reproduced by permission of *Biochemical and Biophysical Research Communications*, Academic Press, Inc., New York.

Treatment of tissue discs	Invertase activity (μg sucrose hydrolyzed/g fresh wt./h)
Control (freshly cut)	3807
18 hours in water	3743
18 hours in NAA (1.42×10^{-5} M)	8315
18 hours in glucose (1%)	1843
18 hours in glucose + NAA	1872

tissue discs rather than an activation of invertase already formed. The action of glucose was taken as evidence of a possible *in vivo* suppression by a hexose or a hexose derivative. From these results Sacher and Glasziou (1267) concluded that auxin-regulated invertase synthesis is instrumental in cellular mechanisms directing the fate of sucrose in growth or storage. The auxin role would be complemented by a "feed-back" repression system relying upon invertase products.

The concept that NAA and glucose suppression was active against an enzyme-synthesis mechanism rather than the isolated enzyme is supported by Alexander's (16) work with partially-purified preparations of the same or analogous acid invertase. It was shown that 36 hours dialysis against distilled water removed all but about 5 percent of the original activity. However, activity was readily restored upon addition of various sugars, including glucose and fructose, to the dialyzed enzyme preparations. This could hardly have come about if hexoses were inhibitors of previously-formed invertase. It was concluded that the active cane invertase is a carbohydrate–protein complex (16), possibly similar to the enzyme–carbohydrate complex proposed by other workers (1386, 1200, 3) for yeast invertase.

Additional evidence of an auxin- and sugar-mediated control system was presented by Sacher *et al.* (1269) in 1963. The variety *Pindar* was included in these studies along with *N.Co. 310*. Tissue discs were prepared as described in the earlier work and the invertase activity unit was defined as the amount of enzyme hydrolyzing 1.0 μg of sucrose per hour in a 0.15 M sucrose solution at pH 5.5. The effects of IAA, GA, and N source on invertase level were studied in addition to NAA and glucose effects.

Earlier observations on NAA regulation of invertase synthesis and glucose suppression were verified. IAA showed regulatory effects similar to NAA, although the optimum IAA level fluctuated among different tissue samples as an apparent function of daily and seasonal environmental changes. Seasonal changes in invertase content had been noted earlier by Hatch *et al.* (689), but extensive day to day fluctuations appear to have been observed for the first time. Later studies by Slack (1340) showed that invertase activity may vary as much as 7-fold on a morning-to-afternoon basis. Sacher *et al.* (1269) concluded that the variable responses to NAA and IAA might relate to endogenous growth substances whose levels are sensitive to the external environment.

B. *Relationships of regulatory mechanisms to age and parentage of tissue*

The tendency for acid invertase levels to vary was underscored in experiments with tissues having variable anatomical development. Sacher *et al.* noted that an immature internode is not a homogenous unit; rather, an intercalary meristem is localized at the base, above this there is an area of cell elongation, and still higher above lies an area of cell maturation. The invertase levels found in the three tissue types are presented in Table 10-2 along with modifying effects of IAA. A striking variation is evidenced by

TABLE 10-2

RELATIONSHIP BETWEEN THE AGE OF SUGARCANE TISSUE, ITS INVERTASE CONTENT, AND RESPONSE OF THE TISSUE TO INDOLEACETIC ACID

[After Sacher *et al.* (1269).] Reproduced by permission of *Physiologia Plantarum.*

Tissue	Treatment	Invertase content (units/ml juice)
Internode base, with intercalary meristem	Fresh tissue	1850
	10 hours in water	1750
	10 hours in IAA	1130
Internode center	Fresh tissue	815
	10 hours in water	1510
	10 hours in IAA	1020
Internode top	Fresh tissue	254
	10 hours in water	375
	10 hours in IAA	338

high activity at the bottom and low activity at the top of the immature internode. Added IAA clearly suppressed the enzyme at the base but had little apparent effect at the top where natural repression had already occurred. This seemed to verify within a single elongating internode the earlier observation (690) that acid invertase tends to disappear from storage tissues as they mature. Sacher and his co-workers also observed that no acid invertase was found in mature internodal tissue of variety *N.Co. 310,* either before or after incubation in NAA, suggesting that the maturation decline is not readily reversed by auxin.

Sacher *et al.* attached major importance to the fact that auxin–sugar regulation of invertase was operative in the variety *Mandalay*, a member of the *spontaneum* species which is known to retain acid invertase in mature storage tissue (690). Results shown in Table 10-3 confirm an NAA effect on invertase synthesis and a glucose suppression

TABLE 10-3

EFFECT OF AUXIN AND GLUCOSE ON THE ACID INVERTASE CONTENT OF JUICE FROM THE "WILD" SUGARCANE VARIETY *MANDALAY* (BELONGING TO THE SPECIES *S. SPONTANEUM*)

[After Sacher *et al.* (1269).] Reproduced by permission of *Physiologia Plantarum.*

Treatment	Invertase content (units/ml juice)
Fresh tissue	3860
18 hours in NAA (1.4×10^{-5} M)	5200
18 hours in NAA plus glucose (0.055 M)	422

of the enzyme. Hence, the possibility that "wild" species of *Saccharum* do not contain an auxin–carbohydrate regulatory system was not substantiated. In relation to this, Bull and Glasziou (258) had found evidence that the evolution of *S. officinarum* was by natural selection processes which favored plants having a large capacity for sucrose storage. By this reasoning, *S. officinarum* appears not as a separate species but as a group of extensively-selected strains particularly well adapted for storing sucrose. *S. spontaneum* types store relatively little sucrose and retain acid invertase in mature storage tissue. Bearing in mind the extensive polyploidy of *Saccharum* species, Sacher *et al.* interpreted the presence of an auxin–sugar control mechanism in both wild and cultivated types as evidence that the gene dosage for invertase regulation acts as a determining factor for sucrose-storing capability.

C. *Interrelationships of auxin and N source in invertase synthesis*

Other experiments by Sacher and his colleagues were designed to clarify possible relationships of N source to auxin-induced invertase synthesis. GA and IAA were used separately or combined, while glycine, nitrate, and urea served as N-source variables. Tissue samples were pretreated in a 1-percent glucose solution with the expectation that invertase content and possibly auxin content could be reduced to a low value. This stage included variable N supplements. In a second stage glucose was removed and tissues were incubated with IAA, GA, or mixtures of the two growth-stimulatory substances. Results presented in Table 10-4 show that glycine, but not nitrate and urea, produced exceptionally large invertase increases as a main effect in tissues previously depleted by glucose plus glycine. Considerable evidence of auxin interactions is also shown. A positive IAA effect was confined to the tissues pretreated with

TABLE 10-4

EFFECTS OF INDOLEACETIC ACID, GIBBERELLIC ACID, AND NITROGEN SOURCE ON THE SYNTHESIS OF INVERTASE IN DEPLETED SUGARCANE TISSUES

Tissues from the variety *Pindar* were pretreated in glucose solution for 16 hours at 30 °C to deplete invertase and endogenous auxin contents. [After Sacher *et al.* (1269).] Reproduced by permission of *Physiologia Plantarum.*

Part A		Part B	
Pretreatment	Invertase (units/ml juice)	Treatment	Invertase (units/ml juice)
Glucose (0.06 M)	1020	Water	2820
		IAA	2510
		GA	1770
		IAA + GA	2440
Glucose plus glycine (0.05 M)	685	Water	7820
		IAA	7380
		GA	6180
		IAA + GA	6070
Glucose + complete nutrient supplement containing nitrate (0.003 M) and urea (0.0035 M)	640	Water	1990
		IAA	3020
		GA	2470
		IAA + GA	2840

nitrate plus urea. The IAA response was not altered appreciably by GA. A GA stimulation of invertase synthesis was also confined to the nitrate- and urea-pretreated tissues, and in this instance the effect was enhanced by combination with IAA. However, GA produced a negative effect in tissues pretreated with glycine plus glucose or with glucose alone.

The dependence of both IAA and NAA on a nitrate-N source in promoting invertase synthesis has several complex implications extending beyond the scope of this review. However, two immediate conclusions do seem justified from this data: (a) The manifold increase of invertase by glycine pretreatment points to an intimate relationship of auxin with protein synthesis from pools of free amino acids; (b) the lesser increase by virtue of nitrate- and urea-N sources implies that at least several divergent N-metabolism pathways are operative leading to free amino acids. These pathways probably contribute N to processes other than amino acid synthesis, a debilitating effect on invertase formation which was partially countered by IAA and NAA stimulation of the invertase-forming mechanism.

Sacher *et al.* (1269) offered the view that neither nitrate N nor urea N enter readily into the normal metabolic pathways of cane storage tissue. The stimulatory action of IAA was seen to be most effective when amino N is limiting for protein synthesis. It was also pointed out that the glycine stimulation of invertase synthesis does not occur when glucose is included in the medium. This was interpreted to mean that a pool of invertase precursors is formed from glycine, but that glucose prevents either the synthesis of enzyme from its precursors or the release of newly-formed enzyme molecules.

The concept of invertase precursors existing in rate-limiting supply was given added support by Alexander (36) who treated immature sugarcane with varying combinations of GA and the pyrimidine analog 6-azauracil. Apparently, 6-azauracil acts in accordance with other base analogs which prevent the normal synthesis of RNA (1231, 1211, 598, 969, 970, 841, 836). When applied to cane as an aqueous foliar spray it is specifically lethal to meristematic tissue at concentrations ranging from 0.01 to 0.05 percent (41). Moderate growth stimulation has been recorded in the range of 0.001 to 0.005 percent (Alexander, unpublished). In the GA-series control plants, *i.e.*, those sprayed only with distilled water, all trace of invertase was removed by 0.05 percent 6-azauracil. However, plants receiving 0.10 percent GA in combination with 6-azauracil retained about 1/3 of their invertase activity, suggesting that GA had effectively overcome part of the inhibitor's suppression against an invertase-forming mechanism. This was true in spite of the fact that GA itself suppressed invertase activity as a main effect. Another experiment with the same foliar inhibitor levels included variable nitrate supply in the nutrient solution. Plants receiving insufficient nitrate (0.5 meq/l) lost more than 50 percent of their invertase activity when treated with 0.01 percent 6-azauracil, and all activity was lost in response to 0.05 percent. Plants given a high nitrate supply (50.0 meq/l) retained more than 50 percent of their invertase activity when treated with 0.05 percent 6-azauracil. Unlike GA, nitrate increased invertase activity as a main effect. High nitrate presumably increased the size of essential amino N pools, not by varying the N source, but rather by virtue of a 100-fold increase in total N supply.

In both experiments the loss of invertase was paralleled by slackened growth and increased sucrose content of immature storage tissue. This conforms fully with the slower growth and increased sugar storage noted by Sacher *et al.* under conditions of invertase restriction.

D. *Regulation of spatially distinct invertases*

Experiments described up to this point were concerned with the total extractable invertase obtained from incubated tissue discs. Prior work by Hatch and Glasziou (690) had shown that acid invertase was situated both in the outer space (including the cell wall) and in the storage vacuole. With this in mind, Sacher *et al.* (1269) used ^{14}C-labeled sucrose in efforts to determine the area of auxin and glucose regulation. Tissue samples were incubated for 4 hours in [^{14}C]sucrose to determine outer space invertase, after which inner space invertase activity was calculated from the concentration and radioactivity of inner space sugars. Clear evidence was found of a glucose regulation of invertase within the inner space. Results were less conclusive with respect to the site of the auxin–invertase relationship. In another report, Glasziou and Waldron (586) cite the lack of evidence for rapid changes in outer space invertase. They concluded that the auxin–carbohydrate control mechanism is mainly involved in regulating sucrose inversion in the storage vacuole rather than in the outer space where sucrose is received from conducting tissues.

4. GLUCOSE AND GLUCOSE-DERIVATIVE REGULATION OF INVERTASE

A. *Studies by Glasziou and co-workers* (586, 585, 589)

The experiments by Sacher and Glasziou (1267), and by Sacher *et al.*. (1269), demonstrated conclusively that IAA and the synthetic auxin NAA had regulatory potential over invertase synthesis. The action of glucose was less certain. Subsequent work by Glasziou *et al.* (586, 585, 589) showed that glucose performed a regulatory role over invertase synthesis quite distinct from that of auxin. The main features of this work include the following: (a) Possible regulatory mechanisms acting by means other than invertase synthesis were experimentally eliminated; (b) the glucose effect was shown to be a reversible inhibition of invertase synthesis; (c) conversion of a sugar to its methyl glycoside was found to destroy the inhibitory property, while reduction to a polyhydric alcohol produced an inductive potential; and (d) auxin and sugar differences in chemical configuration and effective concentration indicated an involvement of more than one mechanism of invertase regulation.

Using immature internodes from field-grown cane of the variety *Pindar*, Glasziou and Waldron (585) performed a series of experiments designed to clarify the role of sugars in invertase regulation. Considerable difficulty was experienced relative to inconsistent behavior of the control tissues in water. These sometimes showed constant invertase levels for 18 hours; at other times there was rapid increase or decrease in enzyme level. Field-grown samples were used so that their inherent variability would prevent overemphasis of a control system characterizing only a specific experimental condition. It should be noted, however, that the kind of variability present in commercial stands of cane would detract from this objective unless exceptional care was taken in the harvest and preparation of tissue samples.

Glasziou and Waldron found that glucose caused a major invertase suppression at concentrations less than 0.01 M, and the maximum effect was obtained at about 0.03 M. Time-course data for loss of invertase described a first-order reaction in experiments having no time lag for initial glucose effect. Other experiments revealed no glucose effect for a period of several hours. The likelihood that glucose activity might relate to osmotic concentration was also considered. However, potassium and calcium salts failed to give comparable restriction although some effect against invertase was evident. A number of compounds given at higher concentrations than glucose failed to restrict invertase as effectively as glucose (Table 10-5). Osmotic suppression was therefore rendered improbable.

TABLE 10-5

EFFECTS OF SUGARS, SUGAR DERIVATIVES, AND POLYHYDRIC ALCOHOLS ON LEVELS OF ACID INVERTASE IN IMMATURE STORAGE TISSUE OF SUGARCANE

[After Glasziou and Waldron (585).] Reproduced by permission of the *Australian Journal of Biological Sciences.*

Compound	Molarity	Invertase content	
		As % of water control	Relative to glucose
2-Deoxy-D-glucose	0.006	10	0.14
	0.06	10	0.20
D-Mannose	0.055	25	0.55
2-Amino-D-glucose	0.028	40	0.97
	0.055	29	0.89
D-Galactose	0.055	67	0.94
L-Ascorbic acid	0.06	36	1.10
D-Arabinose	0.06	52	–
	0.12	47	–
D-Galacturonic acid	0.06	39	1.20
Melibiose	0.03	72	1.40
Maltose	0.06	53	1.70
Raffinose	0.02	108	–
	0.04	84	3.8
	0.20	21	2.0
Lactose	0.03	108	–
	0.04	95	4.3
	0.20	59	5.4
α-MethylL D-mannoside	0.06	106	3.1
	0.12	83	3.2
L-Arabinose	0.04	152	6.9
	0.077	109	–
	0.20	84	7.7
i-Inositol	0.06	96	2.8
	0.12	99	3.9
Mannitol	0.055	145	2.9
Glycerol	0.06	137	2.8
α-Methyl D-glucoside	0.005	109	1.6
	0.05	151	4.4
D-Arabitol	0.06	160	4.4
	0.12	179	7.6
Ribitol	0.06	150	4.4
	0.12	208	8.1
D-Sorbitol	0.06	186	5.1
	0.12	214	9.1
Galactitol	0.06	183	5.0
	0.12	254	11.0

A number of other sugars and related compounds were found to affect invertase (Table 10-5). These included 2-amino-D-glucose (glucosamine), 2-deoxyglucose, and mannose as inhibitors. The polyhydric alcohols ribitol, galactitol, and D-sorbitol were stimulatory. Additional study of the glucosamine effect showed that this derivative gave results almost identical to glucose at pH values of 4.5, 5.5, and 6.7, and over a broad concentration range. In living tissues, ^{14}C-labeled glucosamine was converted to two radioactive compounds plus free glucose, but no changes occurred in nonmetabolizing tissues killed in ethanol. One of the labeled compounds was identified as 2-amino-D-glucose phosphate (585); the other remained unidentified although it did form a phosphorylated derivative. Glasziou and Waldron (586) concluded that free glucose and free glucosamine act directly to lower invertase content. Because in nature glucose would serve as the normal feedback repressor of invertase, glucosamine was taken to be a structural analog. Phosphorylated sugars were excluded as possible regulatory substances on the basis of their kinetic properties.

Glasziou and Waldron (585) also evaluated the relationships of invertase level to total protein content, changing acidity, and K_m. They found that, while incubation in water led to major invertase increases, and incubation in glucose solution caused enzyme losses, neither treatment affected total protein content. In another study (588), use of the protein inhibitors chloramphenicol, puromycin, actinomycin D and fluoride caused rapid loss of invertase. Invertase was considerably less stable at pH 4.2 than at 5.2, but since the pH of tissue juice remained constant at 5.0 during 8 hours of tissue incubation, no pH effect was believed to occur. There was no change in the stability of extracted invertase in the presence of glucose or mannitol (0.10 M). Neither high – nor low – molecular weight substances induced invertase activation or repression (588). From these results it was concluded that the observed changes in invertase behavior were related to changes in the balance between invertase synthesis and destruction.

B. *Loci of the auxin–carbohydrate control system*

In 1966, as noted above, Glasziou *et al.* (588) reported on the behavior of vacuolar invertase when subjected to several inhibitors of protein and RNA synthesis. The experiments were performed with tissue slices from the base of elongating internodes (variety *Pindar*). Inhibitors included chloramphenicol, fluoride, puromycin, and actinomycin D. A number of important conclusions were drawn: (a) Changes in observed invertase activity resulted from changes in the balance between invertase synthesis and destruction. (b) The glucose effect was localized upon the rate of invertase synthesis rather than invertase destruction. (c) Glucose was shown *not* to affect mRNA synthesis; rather, evidence pointed to a glucose-accelerated destruction of the mRNA needed for enzyme synthesis. (d) The main auxin effect is produced either upon the rate of mRNA synthesis, or upon the combination of mRNA with ribosomes.

Numerous experiments showed the maximum rate of invertase loss to be about the same when glucose, chloramphenicol, and actinomycin D were supplied under optimum conditions. The consistency of results obtained when either glucose or a protein inhibitor was present indicated that glucose acted upon the rate of invertase synthesis rather than upon its destruction. It was noted that at times the sum total of added and endogenous sugar did not suffice to repress invertase, apparently owing to permeability changes which prevented glucose entry into the metabolic compartment. However, under other conditions, when mRNA was not limited and invertase formation continued in spite of actinomycin D treatment, glucose proved to be repressive. From this it was taken that glucose did not affect mRNA synthesis.

Under similar conditions of non-limiting mRNA, no effect on invertase synthesis was obtained with NAA. It was thus implied that NAA does not accelerate mRNA breakdown nor does it alter the substrate or enzyme pools which limit the rate of peptide bond formation. Glasziou *et al.* (588) noted that NAA levels giving early invertase increases can also be repressive later in the experiment. No NAA increase in tissue permeability could be shown, on the basis of effluxing sugar, and no conclusions could be drawn as to whether invertase was altered by auxin in the bathing medium or by auxin accumulated or metabolized in a tissue compartment.

From these observation Glasziou and his co-workers were encouraged to speculate that auxin must affect the rate of mRNA synthesis. This concept was substantiated with fluoride-inhibition studies inspired by the work of Colombo *et al.* (382) and Marks *et al.* (980) concerning the fluoride inhibition of reticulocyte protein synthesis. These workers had used fluoride to prevent protein formation by causing the polysomes to disrupt. In these instances there was no reticulocyte ribonuclease present to destroy mRNA. The polysomes were reformed and protein synthesis resumed upon removal of fluoride. A similar situation existed with cane storage tissue to the extent that fluoride inhibited invertase synthesis, but ribonuclease was present in abundance (588). Glasziou *et al.* apparently succeeded in depleting endogenous sugar levels by incubating tissues for 12 hours in dilute fluoride and glycine solutions, and they further disrupted polysomes through cane ribonuclease activity with a concurrent loss of mRNA. The system thus created was such that, with glycine providing essential carbon and amino N, the removal of fluoride gave an invertase-forming mechanism which was rate-limiting for mRNA, and hence susceptible to NAA stimulation, if in fact this was the mode of NAA action upon invertase level. Their results showed that NAA did give major invertase increases within 3 hours after removal of fluoride. On this basis Glasziou *et al.* (588) concluded that mRNA production, or its union with ribosomes, constitues the area of auxin effect on invertase synthesis in cane storage tissue.

Interpreting their results in a broader sense, Glasziou and his co-workers did not feel that the observed auxin effect on the rate of mRNA synthesis was fundamental to the general auxin responses of other plant tissues. Regulation of mRNA synthesis would not necessarily be the prime mode of auxin activity, but where mRNA level is altered certain short-term effects are visualized upon enzymes having a high turnover rate. This view is shared by other authors (833, 835, 1122).

C. *Development of a configuration model for invertase regulators*

Taking into account the proposed pool of invertase precursors (1269), and the specificity of glucose action against invertase synthesis, Glasziou and Waldron (585) began to develop a conformational scheme which would explain the regulatory action of glucose. With respect to the glucose concentration at the regulatory site, special importance was attached to the following factors: (a) Glucose concentration in the storage compartment; (b) permeability of cell membranes; (c) glucose utilization rate in the metabolic compartment; and (d) rate of sucrose and fructose conversion to glucose during efflux from the tissue. The bathing medium was regarded as having infinite volume owing to frequent changes during the experiments. It was further understood that within the control system (tissue in water only) the potential for invertase synthesis was already suppressed to an unknown degree by endogenous glucose.

Compounds in competition with glucose at the regulatory site were placed in several categories on the basis of configuration or "fit": (a) Compounds which fit the site and retain a configuration essential for inhibiting invertase synthesis; (b) substances which fit the site but no longer retain a good configuration for inhibition; and (c) compounds having the essential inhibitory configuration but fit poorly into the control site. Although data available to Glasziou and Waldron (585) in 1964 were inadequate for definitive descriptions of the inhibitory configuration, it was believed that certain sugars, polyhydric alcohols and α-methyl D-glucosides might act through metabolic conversion to glucose. In this instance the configuration around carbon atoms 1 and 2, plus the C-1 oxygen and the glucopyranose ring oxygen, were taken to be of major importance.

With respect to the behavior of compounds listed in Table 10-5, Glasziou and Waldron considered the ascorbic acid configuration (carbonyl oxygen at C-1) to be acceptable for inhibition, while substitution of $-OCH_3$ for $-OH$ (as in α-methyl glycosides) removed all regulatory potential. The somewhat greater activity of D-mannose as compared to glucose was taken as improved positioning of the $-OH$ group on carbon atom 2. By the same trend of analysis, the $-OH$ group at the C-2 position was regarded as unnecessary since 2-deoxy-D-glucose and 2-amino-D-glucose showed powerful regulatory action with $-H$ and $-NH_2$, respectively, in that position. Quite significantly, the $-OH$ group at the C-2 position thus appears to be a promising site of substitution in the future development of synthetic invertase regulators.

When Glasziou and Waldron (585) published their findings with sugar derivatives and polyhydric alcohols, the data were not yet conclusive as to the precise structural requirements for invertase regulation. However, it was recognized that glucose, fructose, and sucrose were the only naturally-occurring sugars in sufficient abundance to account for invertase control, either directly via glucose, or indirectly through the interconversion of sucrose moieties. It was also apparent that the control mechanism must be highly selective for the various test compounds in order to give responses ranging from severe restriction to major stimulation of invertase. A scheme was presented (Fig. 10-1) to explain the apparent interrelationship of active test substances

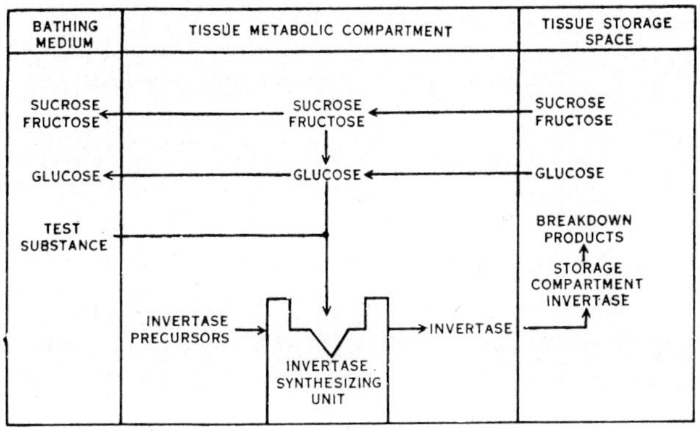

Fig. 10-1. Diagrammatic representation of a system developed by Glasziou and Waldron for measuring effects of test substances on invertase synthesis. A substance added to the bathing medium presumably competes with endogenous glucose for the repression site. Substances which fit well prevent invertase synthesis, while those which fit poorly may act to promote synthesis by denying glucose an access to the repressor site. [After Glasziou and Waldron (585).] Reproduced by permission of the *Australian Journal of Biological Sciences.*

with endogenous sugars and the enzyme-synthesizing mechanism. The synthesizing unit proper is depicted in the outer space metabolic compartment along with a precursor pool and the product invertase. A special structural requirement for repressor "fit" is also incorporated schematically in the shape of the invertase-forming unit. Inner space sucrose acts as the source of endogenous regulator. Hydrolysis of the storage sucrose is mediated with invertase formed by the outer space unit. Fructose is ultimately converted to glucose, which then must compete for the repressor site with test substances diffusing inward from the bathing medium.

Among the compounds tested, the first seven listed in Table 10-5 were believed to fit the structure of the repressor site and bear the correct configuration for invertase supression. Their effect would be additive with respect to endogenous glucose. Other substances would achieve less effective repression by virtue of poor fit or inadequate configuration for regulatory activity. Stimulatory action would occur when the additive compound blocks the active site from endogenous glucose without conferring a regulatory potential of its own.

D. *Mechanism of glucose and sugar-derivative action*

In 1967 Glasziou *et al.* (589) further advanced their understanding of the structural specifications and mode of action of invertase-regulating substances. Sugars tested in addition to those listed in Table 10-5 are shown in Table 10-6. Since specific steric

TABLE 10-6

EFFECTS OF SUGARS AND DERIVATIVES ON INVERTASE SYNTHESIS IN SUGARCANE STORAGE TISSUE

[After Glasziou *et al.* (589).] Reproduced by permission of *Phytochemistry*, Pergamon Press, Ltd., Oxford.

Class	Compound	Invertase content relative to controls		Classification*
		Glucose	Water	
Hexoses and derivatives	D-Mannose	0.43	0.15	R
	3-Deoxy-D-glucose	0.88	0.52	R
	4-Deoxy-D-glucose	0.95	0.32	R
	Phenyl β-D-glucopyranoside	1.1	0.63	R
	D-Fructose	1.2	0.42	R
	L-Sorbose	1.7	0.45	R
	Methyl α-D-mannopyranoside	3.1	1.1	N
	6-Deoxy-L-mannose	3.8	1.2	N
	6-Deoxy-D-galactose	4.5	2.8	I
	6-Deoxy-L-galactose	5.4	3.1	I
	D-Galactose	6.6	1.3	N
	L-Mannose	11.0	1.4	N
Pentoses and derivatives	D-Arabinose	1.9	0.82	N
	Methyl β-D-xylopyranoside	3.1	0.95	N
	2-Amino-D-lyxose	3.2	2.3	I
	2-Deoxy-D-ribose	3.6	2.4	I
	D-Xylose	3.7	0.9	N
	D-Ribose	5.3	0.7	N
	L-Xylose	8.4	1.6	I
	D-Lyxose	11.0	2.2	I
Tetroses	D-Erythrose	0.5	0.22	R

*R = repressor; I = inducer; N = no significant effect.

requirements were being sought, any substances possibly experiencing *in vivo* alteration, as indicated by abnormal respiration, tissue discoloration, or leakage of stored sugar, was not evaluated further. According to Glasziou and his co-workers, the rapid conversion of a test compound to the natural regulator is indicated by its ability to maintain endogenous sugar pools. Glucosamine was shown in these studies to have primary activity owing to its non-interference with respiration.

In addition to glucosamine, which has repressor activity nearly identical to glucose, particular attention was given to the effects of D-galactose, D- and L-mannose, and phenyl β-D-glucopyranoside, as compared with D-glucose and water, in determining structural requirements for active regulation. From earlier results and data shown in Table 10-6, several deductions were drawn with respect to structural specifications of the repressor: (a) The pyranose ring structure was taken as an active configuration by virtue of the repressor activity of β-D-glucopyranoside (a compound which has little respiratory effect and does not maintain the endogenous sugar pool); (b) only the β pyranose form is active because of the comparative inaction of methyl α-D-glucopyranoside and methyl α-D-mannopyranoside (Table 10-5); (c) an –OH group is not necessary at the C-4 position. The latter conclusion was based on the fact that D-mannose, a better repressor than D-glucose (Table 10-6), differs in orientation from D-glucose only at the C-2 position, while D-galactose, which does not show repressor activity, differs from D-glucose only at the C-4 position. The compound 4-deoxy-D-glucose, having no –OH group on carbon 4, showed regulatory activity, indicating that the –OH group was not needed, and that if one is present it must not be orientated as in D-galactose. (d) A fourth conclusion held that fructose and glucose are regulatory (585), but with variable response in time-course experiments of short duration (589). The latter condition renders sucrose either ineffective or stimulatory, presumably because of insufficient time for conversion to the glucose pool. Glasziou *et al.* (589) reported no consistent repressor differences between D-fructose and D-glucose supplied to immature storage tissue, although Hatch and Cillekens found fructose to be appreciably more effective than glucose in mature storage tissue (unpublished).

In order to formulate more meaningful hypotheses based on these interpretations, Glasziou *et al.* (589) proposed three possible configurations to explain the structural requirements for invertase regulators (Figs. 10-2a to 10-2c). Several alternatives were considered: (I) A single active site is involved and only pyranose sugar forms can have activity (with restrictions shown in Fig. 10-2a); (II) a single active site is fitted both by pyranose and furanose ring structures; (III) two active sites are fitted by pyranose and furanose ring forms. Each of the alternative hypotheses assumes that compounds configuratively incapable of repression or induction can accomplish *apparent* induction by competetively blocking the endogenous repressors from the active site.

The authors preferred the third alternative for several reasons. Of the compounds which should have given active repression in accordance with (I), *i.e.*, D-arabinose, D-lyxose, 2-deoxy-D-ribose, D-ribose, D-lyxosamine, and D-xylose, only D-ribose and D-arabinose actually did so (Table 10-5). In addition, repressor action by D-erythrose, a furanose, does not conform to (I), nor does the action of L-sorbose conform to (I) since the –OH group at C-4 has a D-galactose-like orientation. In relation to hypothesis (II), Glasziou *et al.* (589) constructed three-point fit models for pyranose and furanose ring forms (Figs. 10-2b and 10-2c) which account for the repressor activity by L-sorbose and D-erythrose. The atomic models are spatially equivalent. For pyranose a "boat" structure of the β-anomer is formed with points at C-4, the ring oxygen, and the –OH oxygen at C-1. Corresponding points of the furanose ring are at The C-1, C-3, and ring-oxygen positions. However, in spite of accounting for activity by L-sorbose and D-erythrose in the furanose forms, the 5-carbon sugars still posed questions with respect to the inaction of methyl β-D-xylopyranoside.

Hypothesis (III) was ultimately favored regardless of its additional complexity. The same structural requirements (Fig. 10-2a) would hold, with the added specification that a carbinol group at C-5 having D-aldohexose-like orientation is essential (accounting or inactivity of 6-deoxyl-L-galactose, Table 10-6). This eliminates ketohexoses, aldopentoses, and aldotetroses as potential repressors, although they might retain an apparent stimulatory effect by competing with endogenous glucose. Relative to invertase synthesis, pentoses would be potentially inhibitory in the furanose form and stimulatory in the pyranose form. Under these conditions the third hypothesis accounts for the discrete effects of glucose and fructose in mature tissue, the inactivity of methyl β-D-xylopyranoside, and the irregular behavior of pentoses (589).

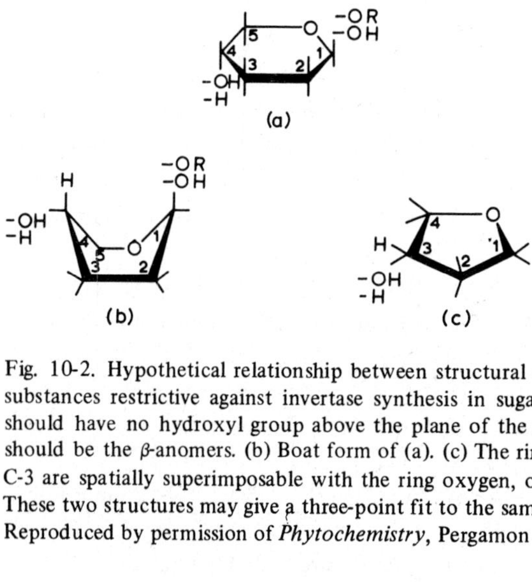

Fig. 10-2. Hypothetical relationship between structural conformation and repression potential of substances restrictive against invertase synthesis in sugarcane storage tissue. (a) Pyranose sugars should have no hydroxyl group above the plane of the ring at the C-4 position, and pyranosides should be the β-anomers. (b) Boat form of (a). (c) The ring oxygen, oxygen at C-1 and hydrogen at C-3 are spatially superimposable with the ring oxygen, oxygen at C-1 and hydrogen at C-4 of (b). These two structures may give a three-point fit to the same active site. [After Glasziou *et al.* (589).] Reproduced by permission of *Phytochemistry*, Pergamon Press, London.

E. *Glucose and fructose specificity*

It was mentioned briefly above that glucose and fructose showed comparable repression of invertase in immature storage tissues, but that differential results were obtained with mature tissues. Glasziou *et al.* (589) noted that the enzyme peroxidase behaves somewhat like invertase by increasing when tissues are bathed in water. However, the two enzymes responded differently to the inhibitor *p*-fluorophenylalanine, a fact attributed in part to the slower turnover rate of peroxidase (589). Invertase level was suppressed while peroxidase experienced no significant loss. In addition, peroxidase was unaffected by glucose concentrations repressive for invertase, while equimolar fructose suppressed peroxidase by about 50 percent. Another feature of peroxidase was a major increase in activity when storage tissues stood in water for 12 hours. This was taken as evidence of endogenous peroxidase repressors being lost by diffusion to the water (589). Glasziou *et al.* concluded that the continued peroxidase synthesis in the presence of glucose demonstrates a specificity of glucose for invertase mRNA, rather than a general specificity for substrates, ribosomes, or enzymes common to the general process of enzyme synthesis.

5. MECHANISM OF HORMONAL ACTION

A. *Stability vs. synthesis of mRNA* [Glasziou *et al.* (588, 591); Gayler and Glasziou (567, 566)]

Experiments with inhibitors of protein and RNA synthesis have shown that the rate of invertase synthesis must be limiting for a specific RNA fraction (presumably mRNA) in order for auxin and GA to give regulatory action (588, 591). These experiments were unable to distinguish between hormonal effects on *stability* of mRNA and on *synthesis* of mRNA. However, Gayler and Glasziou (566) were able to estimate the half-life for peroxidase mRNA decay by chemically blocking mRNA synthesis and measuring the rate of decline for enzyme-forming capacity. This method was subsequently adapted by Gayler and Glasziou (567) for studying the relationships of enzyme synthesis to mRNA stability.

B. *mRNA as a rate-limiting factor in auxin and GA enzyme regulation*

In 1967, at the 6th International Conference on Plant Growth Substances, Glasziou *et al.* (591) presented evidence that auxin and GA share a common mode of action in altering the synthesis of sugarcane invertase and peroxidase. Regardless of differential effects, the common site of action was a step in the transcription or stabilization of mRNA. This work paralleled earlier sugarcane studies with respect to tissue source, *i.e.*, basal tissues of elongating *Pindar* internodes.

Of some 16 enzymes studied for activity induction during 12 hours of tissue immersion in water, only invertase and peroxidase were significantly increased. The possibility that these two enzymes shared a common (polycistronic) message code was not accepted since Glasziou *et al.* (589) had shown that glucose is regulatory for invertase mRNA only. The variable responses of invertase synthesis rates when tissues were placed in water were traced in part to rate-limiting transcriptive steps (involved in mRNA synthesis and stabilization) or translative steps (involved in peptide synthesis). For peroxidase, which is rapidly synthesized in storage tissue after 4 to 6 hours incubation, transcription is at first rate limiting, with translative steps becoming rate limiting somewhat later. The effect of GA on incubating tissues was nil for invertase but repressive for peroxidase, the latter effect being confined to the transcription period. This was proven by pretreating tissues with glucose and glycine to disrupt the mRNA coding for invertase, and subsequently demonstrating increased invertase production by transfer to water and GA solution.

Estimates on rates of peroxidase and invertase synthesis between 3 and 6 hours after auxin or GA treatment revealed that only the transcriptive events of protein synthesis were affected. Glasziou *et al.* (591) concluded that hormones have a primary efect on mRNA synthesis or stabilization. Specifically, the hormones were thought to influence pool size of essential transcriptive intermediates (possibly ribonucleoside triphosphates). It was also pointed out that the hormonal regulation of invertase remained supplementary to a metabolite control system.

C. *Stability studies subsequent to chemical blockage of RNA synthesis*

Working with bathing tissues or dialyzed tissue extracts, Gayler and Glasziou (567) measured invertase and peroxidase synthesis rates after preventing further mRNA synthesis with actinomycin D or 6-methylpurine. By this method it was possible to determine whether GA or NAA affected reactions before or after the synthesis of essential mRNA fractions.

Gayler and Glasziou claim that stability of the respective invertase and peroxidase mRNA fractions as a hormonal effect can be measured if it is shown that the hormones do not affect peptide synthesis, incident to protein formation, or stability of the enzymes themselves. The key feature of such experiments, enzyme-forming capacity, is taken as the difference between enzyme level at an early time after RNA blockage and enzyme level at later times. In this respect peroxidase and invertase might seem to be difficult subjects since Glasziou *et al.* (589) have shown that peroxidase once formed is comparatively stable, while invertase, with a half-life of about 2 hours, is unstable and breaks down readily (588).

By preventing RNA synthesis with 6-methylpurine, Gayler and Glasziou (567) were able to demonstrate a positive NAA effect on invertase synthesis (Fig. 10-3). In other experiments increases approaching 50 percent were obtained with NAA after blocking RNA formation with actinomycin D. The inhibitor levels and conditions employed were known to exclude further invertase mRNA synthesis (566). It was concluded that NAA acts to stabilize mRNA after it is formed, and that this may be the only role of auxin in promoting invertase synthesis.

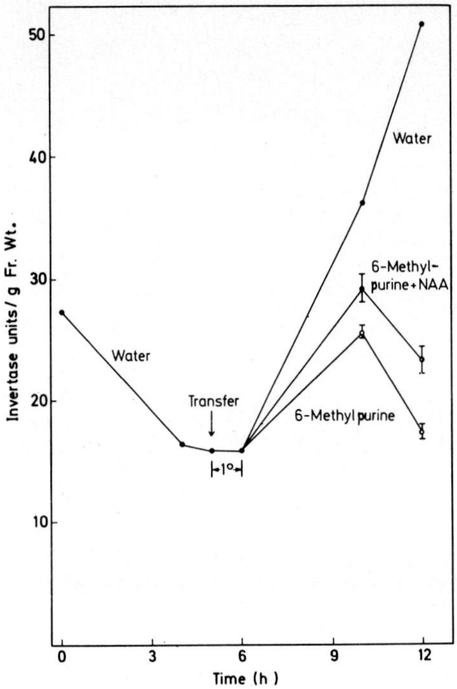

Fig. 10-3. Effect of NAA on invertase-forming capacity of sugarcane storage tissues with RNA synthesis blocked by 6-methylpurine. Tissue slices were incubated in water for 5 hours at 30 °C, then for 1 hour at 1 °C in water, 6-methylpurine, or 6-methylpurine plus NAA. Thereafter incubation proceeded at 30 °C in the same solutions. [After Gayler and Glasziou (567).] Reproduced by permission of *Planta (Berlin)*.

Analogous experiments under conditions of peptide-bond restriction by cycloheximide showed no effect of GA on invertase breakdown (Fig. 10-4). Earlier studies (591) had revealed an apparent stimulation of invertase by low GA (1×10^{-7} M) and inhibition at higher GA levels (5×10^{-3} M), although the reliability of the GA sample used has since been questioned (567). Inhibition of synthesis could not be repeated with another GA sample. It has also been shown that GA produced no effect when mRNA levels were nonlimiting (591). This was confirmed by the subsequent work of Gayler and Glasziou who concluded that GA has no direct bearing on either invertase breakdown or the peptide-bond-forming steps of invertase synthesis. Other experiments employed 6-methylpurine to block mRNA synthesis at a time when mRNA was limiting for both invertase and peroxidase formation. Addition of GA at this time led to increased yields of invertase, but not peroxidase, so that the GA-stabilizing effect appeared to be specific for invertase mRNA.

In addition to the NAA and GA experiments mentioned above, Gayler and Glasziou (567) studied the effects of abscisic acid (ABA) and kinetin under conditions such that

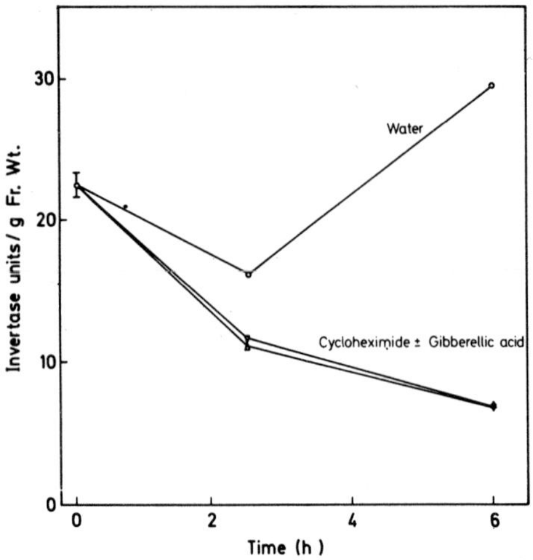

Fig. 10-4. Effects of GA on invertase synthesis in sugarcane storage tissue in the presence of cycloheximide. Tissue slices were incubated in water, cycloheximide, or cycloheximide plus GA at 1 °C for 2 hours. Subsequent incubations were performed at 30 °C. [After Gayler and Glasziou (567).] Reproduced by permission of *Planta (Berlin)*.

RNA synthesis was blocked with 6-methylpurine and peptide-bond synthesis was blocked with cycloheximide. When no inhibitor treatment was included, ABA was found to promote invertase synthesis without interaction with GA (Fig. 10-5). The

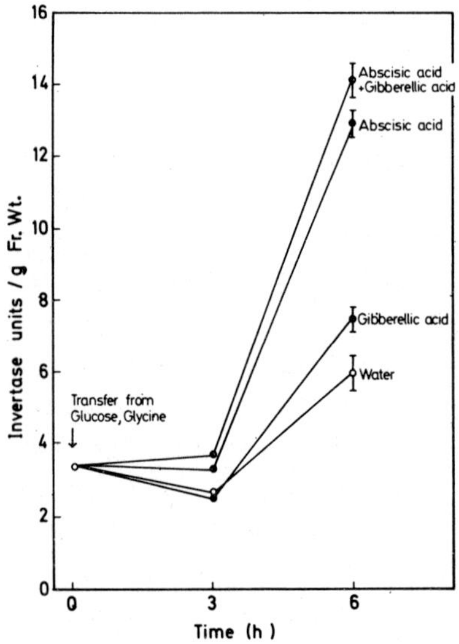

Fig. 10-5. Combined effects of ABA and GA on invertase synthesis in sugarcane storage tissue. Tissue slices were incubated in glucose–glycine solution for 12 hours prior to transfer to water, GA solution, ABA solution, or GA + ABA. [After Gayler and Glasziou (567).] Reproduced by permission of *Planta (Berlin)*.

cane invertase stimulation contrasted somewhat with the results of Chrispeels and Varner (324) who had worked with a different enzyme (α-amylase) under conditions of GA-induced stimulation. Saunders and Poulson (1303) found yeast invertase to be affected *in vitro* by ABA, but no such effect was obtained with ABA on dialyzed cane invertase preparations, nor with NAA, GA, or kinetin (567).

In general, Gayler and Glasziou were demonstrating that invertase regulation by auxin was applicable only to invertase, and from the work of Saunders and Poulson (1303) it was clear that not all invertases would respond as did cane invertase. In this respect it is interesting to note that sugarcane invertase and amylase have features in common not found between sugarcane and yeast invertases (43). Gayler and Glasziou (567) further observed that invertase synthesis was greatly increased by ABA, an effect still evident after RNA formation was blocked with 6-methylpurine (Fig. 10-6). From this they concluded that ABA is active subsequent to the formation of invertase

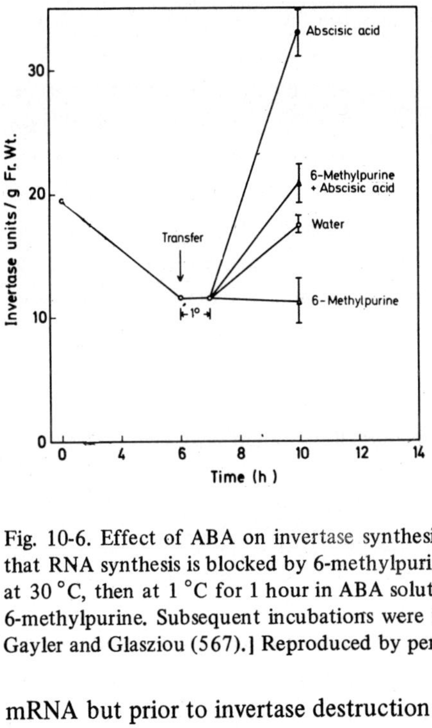

Fig. 10-6. Effect of ABA on invertase synthesis in sugarcane storage tissue under conditions such that RNA synthesis is blocked by 6-methylpurine. Tissue slices were incubated in water for 6 hours at 30 °C, then at 1 °C for 1 hour in ABA solution, water, 6-methylpurine solution, or in ABA plus 6-methylpurine. Subsequent incubations were for 3 hours at 30 °C in the same solutions. [After Gayler and Glasziou (567).] Reproduced by permission of *Planta (Berlin)*.

mRNA but prior to invertase destruction. Without additional evidence the effect could not be localized with respect either to mRNA stability or to peptide-bond synthesis.

Experiments with kinetin (6-furfuryladenine) revealed an inhibitory effect on invertase synthesis, but only during long-term experiments of more than 5 hours duration. The experiments were so designed that considerable increases in enzyme synthesis would have occurred within 3 hours if kinetin behaved as had auxin in earlier studies (588, 589). There was no short-term effect on mRNA synthesis, mRNA stabilization, or on peptide-bond formation. The long-term inhibition by kinetin was regarded as nonspecific in view of similar kinetin effects on peroxidase and a ribonuclease.

From these and prior results, Gayler and Glasziou (567) concluded that both auxin and GA act to stabilize the specific mRNA for invertase. Their evidence was consistent with the view that hormones regulate enzyme synthesis from mRNA after mRNA has been formed. This conclusion was opposed to the views of Jacob and Monod (783) who held that bacterial hormones increase mRNA synthesis as part of a control system governing enzyme synthesis.

6. SUCROSE INVERSION AND GROWTH

An underlying premise of this chapter holds that the regulation of vacuolar invertase is of decisive importance to sugarcane life processes. Dependent upon continual hexose metabolism, these processes cannot be accommodated solely by fresh photosynthate external to the storage compartment. On the other hand, and still fully within the realm of sugarcane physiology, invertase behavior is an equally appropriate topic when discussing growth as when discussing sugar storage. This thesis is substantiated by recent reports describing a close correlation between invertase activity and growth rate (590, 690, 567). Indeed, for many years an empirical relationship has been recognized between the tonnage of stalks produced and the sucrose therein contained, with one factor varying inversely with the other. Until recently, the precise relationship of invertase to slackening growth and increasing sucrose retention in storage has not been studied. At this point it is appropriate to examine the role played by invertase in governing growth potential.

A. *Invertase and growth responses to controlled environment*

In 1963 Hatch and Glasziou (690) described a series of controlled-environment experiments in which the rate of internode elongation was correlated with acid invertase activity. The correlation was shown to hold within variable water and temperature regimes, and for storage tissues of varying age.

For these experiments plants of the variety *Pindar* were grown by vermiculite-gravel culture and were transferred at 15 weeks to controlled environments consisting of five temperature and three water regimes in factorial combination. At harvest, tissue samples were taken of immature internodes (just below the apical meristem), of partially-mature internodes, and of fully-mature stalk tissue close to the base of the plant. Growth rate was estimated by making a series of 12 needle marks at 1-cm intervals on elongating internodes 3 days prior to harvest. The distance between needle marks was again measured at time of harvest when the leaf sheaths were removed. These marks were made with needles fixed in a holder which enabled the points to be pressed through the sheath without discernible damage to the plant. Acid and neutral invertases were assayed in dialyzed crude extracts. Moisture content, dry weight, and sugar content were also determined for the internode samples.

At zero time, when the controlled water and temperature variables were initiated, Hatch and Glasziou found that internode elongation and acid invertase were positively related as a function of tissue maturity (Fig. 10-7). In addition, neutral invertase was directly related to total sugar content. After 10 days in controlled environments, the acid invertase content and growth rate showed parallel increases of up to 10-fold (Fig. 10-8).

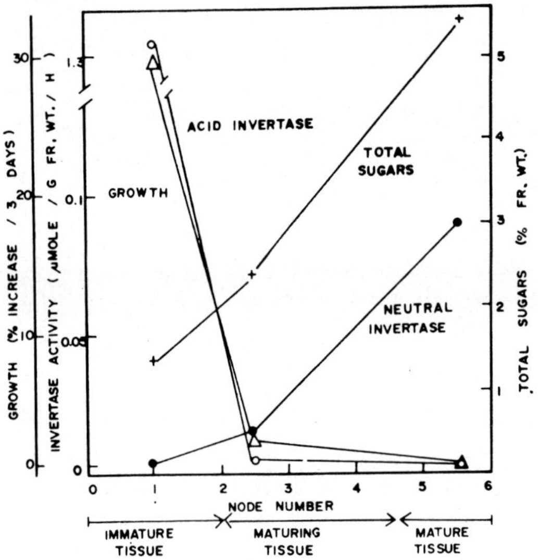

Fig. 10-7. Invertase activity, sugar content, and internode elongation of 15-week-old sugarcane at the time of entry into different controlled environments. At this time, internode elongation and acid invertase were positively related as a function of tissue maturity. [After Hatch and Glasziou (690).] Reproduced by permission of *Plant Physiology*.

Both water and temperature were powerful regulatory factors. With adequate water supply, increasing temperature from 18 to 34 °C produced much greater invertase activity; when water supply was restricted, the enzyme remained nearly unchanged regardless of temperature (Fig. 10-9). Similar relationships were observed with respect to elongation rate. In this instance, however, the most direct factor relative to growth is shown to be invertase rather than environment *per se*, as so frequently is the case with field experiments. Sugar content was directly related to acid invertase activity when water supply was adequate, but not when water was restricted. Similar trends were evident after 30 days. At this time the linear relationship between neutral invertase and total sugar content was still observed.

The close correlation between neutral invertase activity and sugar content of mature tissues (Fig. 10-7) was taken as evidence of a regulatory role for invertase in

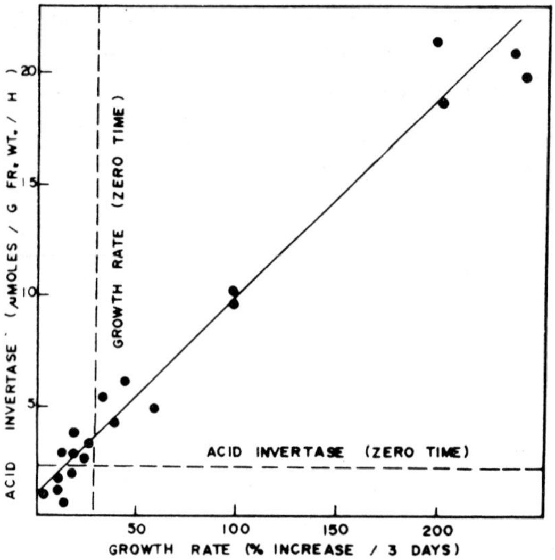

Fig. 10-8. Positive relationship between the rate of internode elongation and acid invertase activity of sugarcane plants grown for 10 days under variable water and temperature regimes. [After Hatch and Glasziou (690).] Reproduced by permission of *Plant Physiology*.

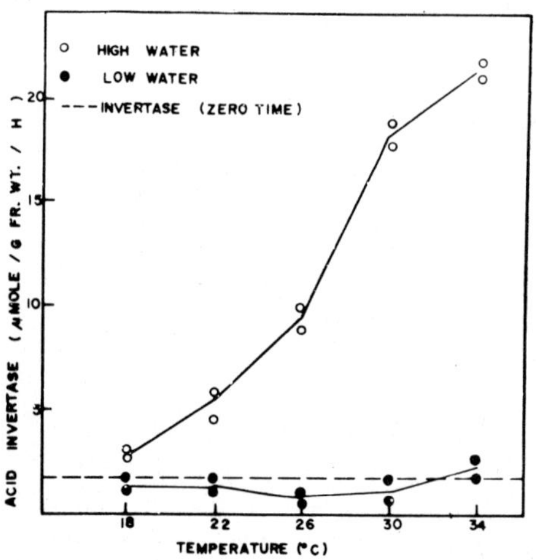

Fig. 10-9. Response of sugarcane acid invertase to high and low water regimes of 10 days duration. Invertase source = immature storage tissue. "High" and "low" water refer to water supplies given twice daily and twice weekly, respectively. [After Hatch and Glasziou (690).] Reproduced by permission of *Plant Physiology*.

sucrose movement from conducting to storage tissue in mature internodes (690). When factors of tissue age or temperature were independent variables, the neutral invertase activity was high during times of sugar storage and low when sugar was not being stored. Independent experiments including different species of *Saccharum* revealed only neutral invertase in mature stalks of S. *officinarum* hybrids having large storage potential; however, acid invertase was found in water shoots having low sugar content. *S. spontaneum* varieties with low storage potential contained both acid and neutral invertase in mature storage tissue. The authors noted that the relationship of neutral invertase to sugar content would not necessarily be apparent over a long period in which sugar efflux, related to sugar content, would be balanced against average influx.

In summarizing their findings relating invertase activity with growth, Hatch and Glasziou suggested that invertases help to disburse new photosynthate (sucrose) between the processes of growth and storage. However, their observations on sugar accumulation in response to cold temperatures were not interpreted in terms of more rapid translocation [as Went (1559) had interpreted similar findings], but rather in accordance with sugar being diverted to growth processes at higher temperatures.

Controlled-temperature studies in Puerto Rico (34) have also shown a relationship between acid invertase and growth, and between invertase and sucrose content of immature storage tissue. However, major sucrose accumulation was induced by cool temperature in only one of the two varieties tested. *P.R. 980*, a high tonnage variety of *S. officinarum*, *S. spontaneum,* and *S. sinense* parentage, and *P.R. 1059*, a variety with high sucrose storage capacity, each experienced severe growth restriction after 10 weeks of continual exposure to 55–60 °F temperatures, as compared with plants maintained at 80–85 °F. At the end of the treatment period *P.R. 980* contained about 25 percent less invertase and *P.R. 1059* about 88 percent less invertase as a function of low temperature. *P.R. 1059* correspondingly accumulated far more sucrose at low temperature than did *P.R. 980*. Some support for a highly-specific invertase regulatory system can be taken from the fact that of four hydrolytic enzymes assayed, only invertase was suppressed by low temperature in *P.R. 1059*, whereas each of the enzymes was suppressed in *P.R. 980*. Invertase was the only enzyme measured in either variety that was reduced to indiscernible levels by 10 weeks of cold treatment.

Additional evidence of a growth–invertase relationship was obtained by Alexander (44) from sugarcane treated with the growth inhibitor 6-azauracil. Fresh weights of plants harvested 6 weeks after foliar inhibitor applications revealed major growth restriction by the higher 6-azauracil levels (Fig. 10-10). Sucrose values for immature

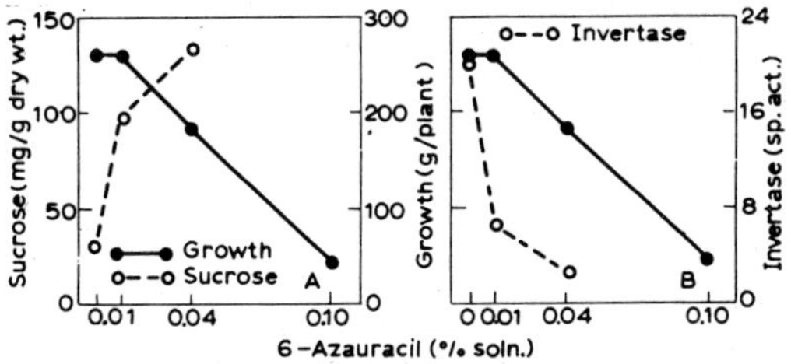

Fig. 10-10. Effects of 6-azauracil as a foliar treatment of immature sugarcane. (A) Growth decline and increased sucrose content of immature storage tissue. (B) Growth decline plus invertase decline in immature storage tissue. [After Alexander (44).]

storage tissue were inversely related, and invertase positively related, to growth. However, the invertase relationship was not linear. Perhaps more important was the observation that invertase was clearly sensitive to inhibitor levels too low to affect growth (below 0.01 percent). This and other evidence of growth-lag responses to chemicals affecting enzyme synthesis was interpreted as a possible means to alter sugar-storage reactions with low inhibitor levels without adversely affecting tonnage (44).

B. *Relationship between invertase and GA-induced growth*

Further evidence of a positive correlation between total acid invertase activity and the rate of internode elongation was presented by Glasziou and Bull (590) in 1965. Utilizing growth-promoting effects of GA, the properties and limitations of an essen-

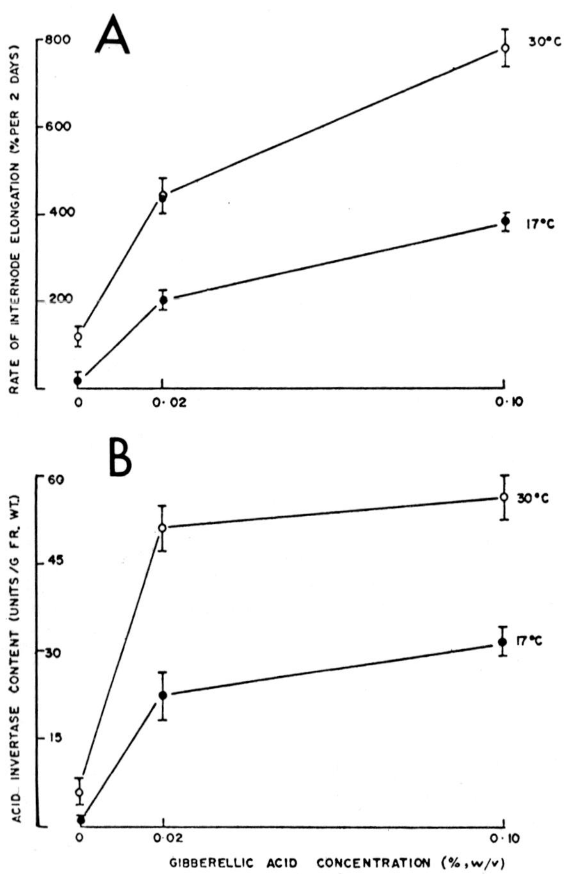

Fig. 10-11. Effect of gibberellic acid on (A) rate of internode elongation and (B) acid invertase content of sugarcane after 28 days of treatment. Two levels of GA were applied at weekly intervals at the rate of 0.5 ml/stalk. [After Glasziou and Bull (590).] Reproduced by permission of *I.S.S.C.T.*

tially linear relationship were examined and then defined in a schematic model. As in many earlier and subsequent reports the variety *Pindar* was used as the tissue source; elongation-rate measurements (690) and invertase assays (689) were as described previously. Two GA concentrations (0.02 and 0.10 percent, w/v) were applied at weekly intervals to 6-month-old plants maintained at 17 and 30 °C. A given stalk received 0.5 ml of GA solution applied to partially-inclosed spindle leaves.

Treatment with GA caused rapid stimulation of both elongation rate and acid invertase level in immature internodes (Fig. 10-11). The nearly perfect linear relationship described earlier (690) between elongation rate and invertase activity tended to break down at the higher GA level, and in a manner such that continued elongation was accompanied by lesser increases of invertase. This was attributed in part to the standard enzyme assay being conducted at a temperature other than that of the treated plant, and also to initial growth measurements which did not take into account the thinning effect of high GA on rapidly-elongating internodes (259). Correction for these two factors enabled the authors to plot this and analogous data as depicted in Fig. 10-12. A highly significant correlation coefficient (r = 0.92) was then obtained

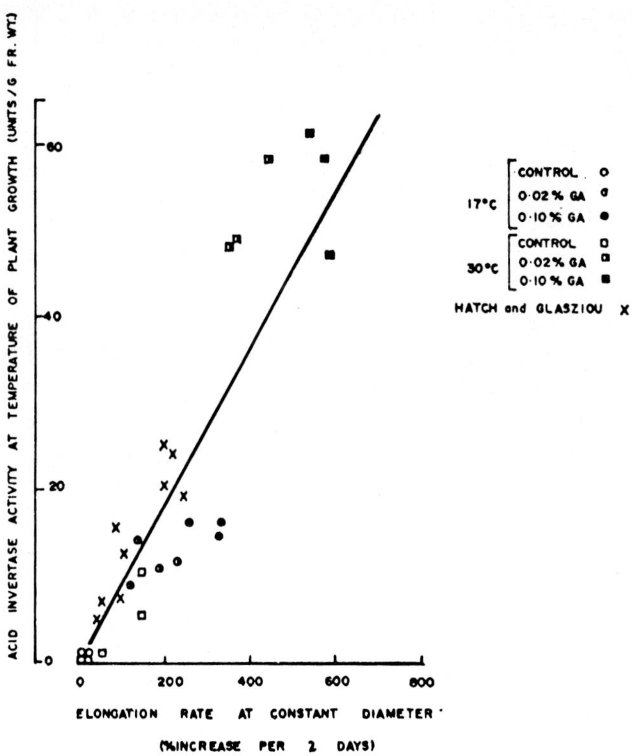

Fig. 10-12. Regression of rate of internode elongation at constant diameter on acid invertase activity at the temperature of plant growth. The regression line was calculated from these data and data supplied by Hatch and Glasziou on temperature and water stress treatments (r = 0.92). [After Glasziou and Bull (590).] Reproduced by permission of *I.S.S.C.T.*

between invertase activity and growth at constant internode diameter. These results describe a positive correlation which holds over a range of growth rates in considerable excess of ordinary field growth rates.

Taking note of the fact that it is the vacuolar or storage compartment invertase which predominates quantitatively in storage tissue, and which is subject to rapid control, Glasziou and Bull proceeded to construct a model which would explain the observed correlation between growth and invertase activity (Fig. 10-13). The scheme shown in Fig. 10-13 was based upon two hypotheses already supported by experi-

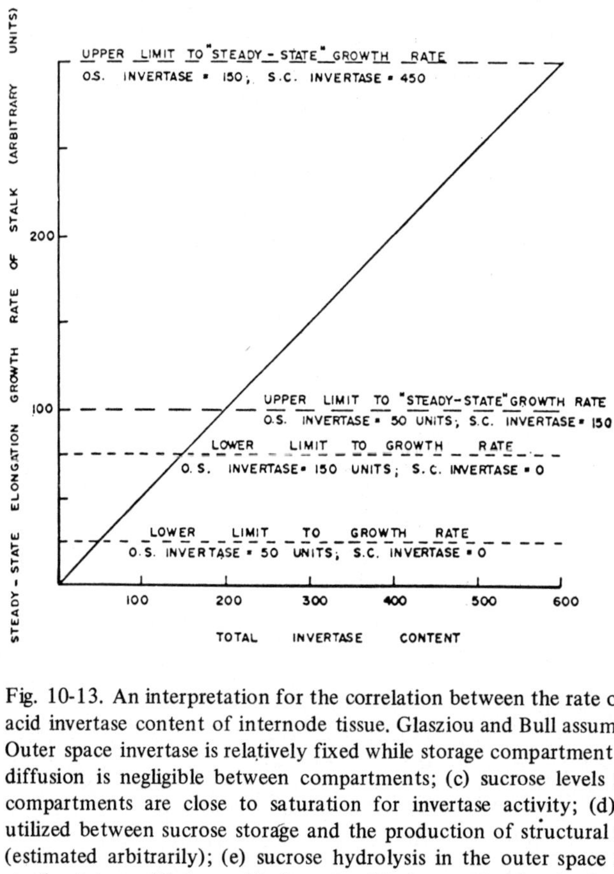

Fig. 10-13. An interpretation for the correlation between the rate of internode expansion and total acid invertase content of internode tissue. Glasziou and Bull assumed the following conditions: (a) Outer space invertase is relatively fixed while storage compartment invertase is variable; (b) sucrose diffusion is negligible between compartments; (c) sucrose levels in the outer space and storage compartments are close to saturation for invertase activity; (d) the hexose phosphate pool is utilized between sucrose storage and the production of structural materials in a ratio of about 3:1 (estimated arbitrarily); (e) sucrose hydrolysis in the outer space and storage compartments is in steady-state equilibrium with the rate of hexose utilization in the metabolic compartment; (f) the rate of hexose phosphate conversion to structural materials may be equated with internode expansion. [After Glasziou and Bull (590).] Reproduced by permission of *I.S.S.C.T.*

mental evidence (579, 1268): (a) Sugar utilization for growth structural purposes is irreversible; and (b) sucrose accumulation into the vacuole is a reversible process with sugar efflux reliant upon sucrose hydrolysis by vacuolar invertase. The model was constructed by plotting the sum of an arbitrarily constant outer space invertase and a variable inner space invertase against hexose irreversibly lost to growth. Ratios less than 3.0 for inner space invertase indicate that growth rate is proportional to total invertase. Ratio values greater than 3.0 indicate that vacuolar sucrose levels must fall, and a deviation from the linear relationship will occur when the sucrose level becomes limiting for the rate of hexose production.

The model thus constitutes a correlation between instantaneous growth rates and total invertase levels. However, measured values for a physiological system would consider growth over an appropriate period correlated with mean invertase levels during that period. The *in vivo* rate of vacuolar invertase formation is coupled to the level of hexose in the cytoplasm. Rapid turnover of this enzyme (585) facilitates automatic adjustment to stabilize the cytoplasmic hexose level, and therefore to stabilize growth rate. The authors further noted a 3-fold daily fluctuation of vacuolar invertase, while subsequent studies showed an acid invertase fluctuation close to 7-fold (1340, 54). Glasziou and Bull (590) explained these results in terms of an inevitable daily decline of photosynthate supply to a point no longer adequate to maintain the cytoplasmic hexose pool. Production of vacuolar invertase would then be depressed. The hexose pool is maintained via hydrolysis of stored sucrose with the result that stored sucrose is used to maintain growth. Under these circumstances a deviation must occur from the linear correlation of growth rate and total invertase level (590).

From this brief review it is seen that Glasziou and Bull have described a "cause–effect" relationship which accounts for observed experimental results relative to the invertase–growth relationship. This work was presented in 1965 when the auxin–carbohydrate mediated control system described earlier in this chapter was not yet fully developed. However, it was recognized even in 1965 that only part of the overall growth control system was accounted for in the cause–effect model. For example, the feature of substrate limitation as a means for explaining variable outer space invertase obviously is circumvented under low-temperature conditions which restrict growth, promote sucrose storage, and allow photosynthesis to continue as at normal temperatures[4]. It would now appear, more than 6 years after Glasziou and Bull presented their interpretation of the invertase–growth relationship, that the mechanism of environmental growth control remains relatively obscure, while details of invertase control have greatly advanced through understanding of the auxin–sugar relationships to stability and destruction of invertase mRNA.

---

[4]Waldron *et al.* (1518), in 1967, reported that sugarcane exposed to a prolonged 17 °C/10 °C day and night temperature regime experienced a reversible loss of photosynthetic efficiency. The change was subsequent to growth decline and increased sugar storage. Although their published data lacked several important figures, it appeared that, during the first 4 days of 17 °C/10 °C treatment, there was a 90-percent decline in growth rate, but only a 9-percent loss of photosynthetic efficiency.

PART III

SACCHARUM SINK PHYSIOLOGY

Chapter 11

Maturation and Natural Ripening

1. INTRODUCTION

During the early months of sugarcane growth and development, sugar storage processes operate in immature storage tissue and in the small number of fully elongated joints near the base of the stalk. Growth, as opposed to sugar storage, is the plant's primary concern at this time. Many authorities feel that sucrose will not accumulate to maximum levels until the plant encounters conditions highly restrictive against growth. Eventually the cane plant experiences *maturation*, that is, the rapid growth processes tend to slacken as water and nitrogen resources are depleted. The increasingly predominant bulk of the plant becomes a succession of fully elongated joints. Except in the region of expanding internodes still subtended by green leaves, the salient physiological feature will tend to be one of sugar storage rather than utilization. For the plant as a whole a potential has been created for massive sugar accumulations in the storage tissue previously laid down. The fulfillment of this potential is commonly described as *ripening*.

In physiological terms the processes of aging, maturation, and ripening are not synonymous even though they may seem to be to the casual observer. Maturity means different things to different persons involved with sugarcane. The most correct meaning pertains to the botanical completion of a stalk suitable for producing new plantlets from each node. The stalk will contain stored sugar to support reproduction, but its storage potential has not necessarily been realized. Maturity is not synonymous with age. If water and nitrogen are continually abundant the plant may never mature regardless of age. Nor is maturity synonymous with ripening. Sugarcane can easily be ripened within a few months after germination by withholding water, nutrients, or other factors needed for growth. But such plants are by no means mature. From a cultural point of view, however, maturity, particularly the second stage of maturity, is so closely allied with ripening that the ripening process is conveniently depicted as a culmination or perfection of maturity.

In general, a majority of modern commercial canes will tend to mature, and hence ripen, in the order of 2 to 4 months later than their growers would like. This explains in part the widespread interest in chemical "ripening agents", growth-controlling compounds, and various field practices such as topping, water regulation, and fertilizer programming – all of which encourage the plant to ripen a little earlier, or better, or more predictably than it would have done in its own good time. In this context the grower may inadvertently delay ripening as a consequence of earlier efforts to achieve maximum growth with fertilizers. Nickell and Tanimoto (1112) state that excess nitrogen available at harvest time is the "prime cause" of low sucrose content. Clements (334) depicts heavy nitrogen fertilization as permitting a smaller quantity of sugar to be stored even though the potential storage capacity has been increased. Samuels and Alers-Alers (1290) have shown that under Puerto Rico conditions the application of nitrogen to ratoons older than 15 weeks can significantly lower sucrose yield, and Bonnet (208) recommends that all of the nitrogen should be applied at planting or immediately after harvest. Climate is another factor having tremendous bearing on maturity. In temperate climates having short growing seasons sugarcane seldom achieves full maturity (1475, p. 311). Age of the cane at harvest has been shown to affect the maturation profile within the stalk (410). As a rule, each variety will tend to approach a ripening "peak" after which its sucrose content will decline if the cane remains unharvested.

In keeping with the central theme of this book, the present chapter emphasizes physiological aspects of ripening in the aging, maturing, source-to-sink system. This is done with full understanding that, to many plantation managers, the ripened status is less a physiological condition than a preharvest necessity which must be imposed upon the plant by whatever means are available. In essence, we are concerned here with ripening as a natural and parallel function of maturity.

The physiological information appertaining to ripening is conveniently compiled within the following categories: (a) Potential of *Saccharum* species to accumulate sucrose; (b) accumulation mechanisms alluding specifically to mature storage tissue; (c) ripening as a function of moisture, nitrogen, and potassium supply; and (d) ripening control.

2. THEORY OF SUGARCANE RIPENING

Clements (345) has described sugarcane ripening as a physiological senescence intermediate between rapid growth phases and the ultimate death of the plant. Agronomic concepts of ripening are usually based upon the appearance of internodes no longer subtended by green leaves, and a parallel accumulation of sucrose in each successive internode toward a common high value. Van Dillewijn (1475, p. 309) describes the ripened stalk as a succession of "joints" whose individual sucrose values can be plotted as the crest of a flat plateau (Fig. 11-1). Accordingly, only the immature or green-leaf internodes and the basal internodes (with typically high fiber content) do not retain appreciable sugar. Natural ripening is also a long-term process in which the older internodes assume an early lead and continue to store sucrose even while younger internodes are ripening above. It should be emphasized, however, that the detachment of an aged blade from a maturing internode does not mean that this internode cannot receive more sugar. If this were the case, grower efforts to ripen sugarcane would have no effect other than to reduce the number of internodes laid down (350).

The uppermost curve in Fig. 11-1 illustrates a fulfillment of storage capacity for receptive joints of a given variety under a given set of conditions. The shape and magnitude of such curves will presumably vary among different varieties grown in different regions. Nonetheless, the thesis that successive, fully-extended joints store sucrose until some characteristic level is reached remains sound. On the other hand, the statement that "ripening is storage of excess sucrose" is an oversimplification from both the practical and physiological viewpoints.

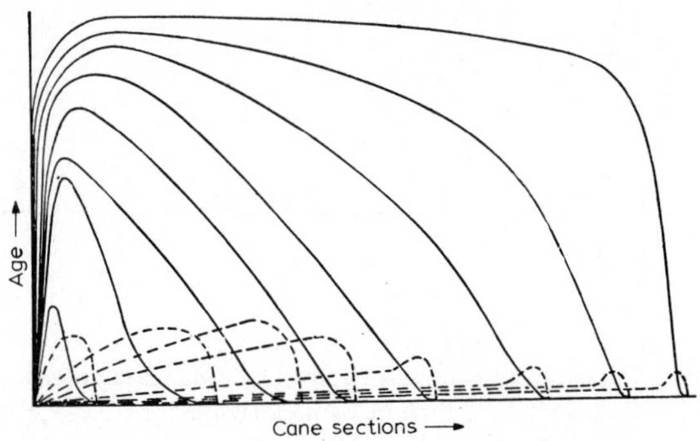

Fig. 11-1. Diagrammatic representation of the sucrose and glucose distribution in sugarcane stalks of increasing age. Sucrose is shown by solid lines, glucose by broken lines. The figure abscissa, from left to right, represents cane sections extending from the stalk base upwards. Increasing age is plotted along the figure ordinate from bottom to top. [After Van Dillewijn (1475, p. 309).] Reproduced by permission of the *Ronald Press Company*, New York. *Botany of Sugarcane.*

Between successive nodes each joint bears its own sugar profile. Sucrose values are highest toward the center and decline toward each end. These differences are accentuated in younger joints of the green-leaf area. In all probability this reflects a differential invertase distribution, as described by Sacher *et al.* (1269), in which the intercalary meristem bears much more invertase than the central internode tissues. Fig. 11-2 illustrates the Brix distribution of a partially-mature stalk in which individual joints of the millable portion contain less sugar at their respective nodes (1475, p. 314). The reverse is seen to be true within the non-millable section. In the latter tissues the elongating internodes are expected to contain acid invertases in nearly direct proportion to growth rate (590, 690). In this illustration the reversal of intranodal sugar distribution occurs at about the time that growth ceases, and sugar storage becomes the main feature.

Although Van Dillewijn's writing preceded the development of the sugar accumulation cycle, the illustrations he used can be taken as tacit evidence of vacuolar invertase decline, and hence of growth decline, as a motivating force toward sucrose retention over utilization. It should be pointed out that sucrose might accumulate more rapidly in the green-leaf storage tissues, but so long as growth and metabolic processes continue at high levels there is little expectation that sucrose will long remain in storage. It follows that a multitude of climatic and cultural factors known to alter the balance between sugar utilization and storage might logically do so by altering invertase con-

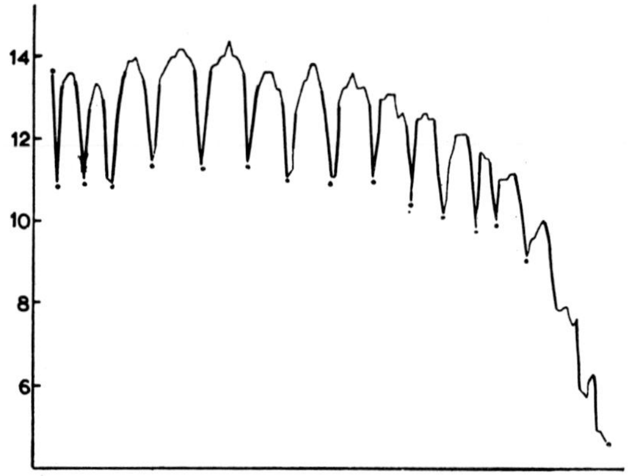

Fig. 11-2. Brix distribution in a sugarcane stalk. Shown in addition to the general trend of the stalk are the individual curves of specific internodes. The node positions are shown by dots. In the older portion of the stalk (left) the internode Brix values are higher than in the node, while the reverse is true in the younger portion (right). [From Van Dillewijn (1475), after Ramiah and Varahalu (1215).] Reproduced by permission of the *Ronald Press Company*, New York. *Botany of Sugarcane.*

trol systems. As discussed in the previous chapter, there is mounting evidence that water, nitrogen source, temperature, and the cane genotype bear a powerful influence over invertase-regulatory mechanisms.

The ultimate question dwarfing all others concerns the ripening control mechanism responsible to the intact source-to-sink system of sugarcane. All that is known today relating to growth and inversion control, and this is a very great amount, does not half explain the operation of a functional source-to-sink system in which a massive storage of sucrose is accomplished with consistency at levels far in excess of plant survival needs. The potential of this mechanism was established during the long evolution of *Saccharum* species. Its day-to-day operation must somehow program the photosynthetic activity of the green top, the storage processes of the oldest joint, and all intervening life processes.

3. MATURITY

For sugarcane the term *maturity* means different things to different people. The most correct meaning is that which pertains to the botanical entity itself, that is, to a highly complex living organism for which maturity is an inevitable sequel to earlier growth and development phases. Moreover, when the plant scientist considers the multitude of environmental factors, internal physiological factors, and the largely unknown biochemical mechanisms interplaying within this plant from the moment of germination, he can begin to appreciate the fact that a sugarcane plant matured to the limits of its potential is a work of art.

Clements (345) has depicted maturity as the culmination of diphasic physiological processes. The first phase ends at about the time when the aging leaf detaches from its subtending internode; the second phase includes all subsequent events relating to sugar accumulation in the fully-expanded internodes. At no time, however, is the maturation process ever fully divorced from the varietal, cultural, and ecological factors which had influenced earlier periods of the plant's life.

At about the time when the plant crop germinates, or during the early growth of ratoons, sugarcane is ordinarily supplied with ample water and fertilizer elements needed for abundant growth. Tissue analyses during these first weeks and months reveal high nitrogen and water contents, high enzyme levels for almost any system assayed, high levels of endogenous auxins in the meristem and adjoining immature storage tissue, much invert sugar and sugar derivatives, and numerous intermediates of photosynthesis, respiration, and nitrogen metabolism in varying amounts. Respiratory activity is high; there is rapid uptake and transpiration of water with parallel uptake and continual circulation of nutrient elements. Sucrose is rapidly synthesized and stored, and with equal rapidity is retracted from storage to be metabolized, or to be committed irreversibly to the structure of new plant tissue.

The storage parenchyma cells at this time are large, thin-walled and hydrated. New storage tissues, leaves, and roots are formed as if the plant's very life depended upon it – and indeed it does. The factory chemist analyzing these tissues finds them abounding in "impurities", that is, he finds little sucrose and an abundance of other substances having little apparent purpose in the mill but to complicate sucrose extraction and purification. For the plant, however, these are not impurities at all; to the contrary, they are valuable substances entirely necessary to maintain the plants's life processes.

With passage of time the meristem literally moves upward, leaving behind anatomically complete but immature internodes in the process of elongation. Each successive internode completes its own vegetative cycle which includes the thickening and strengthening of cell walls, marked increase of non-sugar dry matter, gradual dehydration, increased sucrose accumulation and retention, and decreased elongation rates. Eventually the internode ceases to elongate and its leaf detaches and drops away from the stalk. The first stage of maturation has now been achieved. Clements (345) points out that the internode may contain more sucrose at this time on a dry weight basis than it ever will again. However, a potential still exists for additional increases of up to 50 percent in what Clements describes as the "second phase" of maturity. The belief that maturation is complete at the time of leaf fall is quite erroneous, and it has been shown to be erroneous both by conventional sugar analyses and by radioactive carbon techniques.

The second maturation phase is regulated largely by varietal features subject to improvement by sugarcane breeders, and by soil and ecological factors. Of the latter, available nitrogen, potassium, and moisture appear to be far and away the most important. So long as moisture and nitrogen are readily available the plant will tend to perform continued growth activity and has but little chance to achieve maximum sugar storage. The grower who can manipulate both nitrogen and moisture is in excellent position to improve the second-phase maturity, and hence ripening, by judicious programming of their supply. In humid, non-irrigated regions having abundant rainfall the grower must give his utmost attention to wise fertilizer usage.

Certain guidelines are required to achieve both high tonnage and a high degree of ripening. Tissue and climate indices (indexes) have been developed for this purpose and incorporated into discrete programs of sugarcane culture. When combined and interpreted skillfully on the basis of accumulated data and experience, a *crop log* emerges which tells much about the plant's current status, its needs, and what can be done to meet these needs. Sugarcane indexes have also aided the physiologist. In their light the sugarcane plant is seen in one of its finest profiles, that of a highly sensitive and potentially successful integrator of ecological, physiological, and biochemical factors.

Age is not necessarily synonymous with maturity. After a number of months have passed the plant will tend to exhaust much of its available nitrogen. Water will become depleted in drier regions. But if water and nitrogen remain abundant the plant will not mature in the usual sense of the word regardless of its age. The planned exhaustion of nitrogen and water supplies has therefore become an important means of promoting maturity when aging *per se* will not achieve a comparable effect at the most opportune moment.

4. MECHANISM OF SUGAR STORAGE IN MATURE STALK TISSUE

A. *General*

More than 30 years ago Hartt (647, 649) described a positive correlation between invertase level and sucrose content in maturing cane internodes. The observed loss of invertase potential in tissues having completed most of their storage activity was taken as evidence of direct invertase involvement in sucrose synthesis. This interpretation has not been substantiated even though discrete roles of invertase in sugar storage processes are conclusively established. Sucrose hydrolysis is an essential and rate-limiting step for sugar uptake and storage by immature internodal tissue (579, 581, 1268). It is also known that an acid invertase largely responsible for sucrose hydrolysis in the cell wall or outer space is lost as storage tissues mature, while a neutral invertase is retained (690). However, the mechanism of sucrose storage in fully-elongated internodes and its relation to the processes operating in immature storage tissue has been somewhat more obscure.

Work by Hawker and Hatch (701) revealed that sucrose hydrolysis by invertases is a rate-limiting process for sugar storage in mature storage tissue. The properties and location of these enzymes differed to some extent from their counterparts in immature storage tissue. An acid invertase distinct from the outer space and vacuolar acid invertases was found firmly attached to the cell wall. A neutral invertase appeared to be situated in the cytoplasm. The storage mechanism developed by Hawker and Hatch involved active sucrose transport in a system similar to that proposed earlier by Bieleski (180) for sugar accumulation against a concentration gradient.

Hawker and Hatch used fully-developed internodal tissue, *i.e.*, stalk tissue taken below the oldest living leaf, from *Pindar* plants grown in controlled environments. Tissue discs cut from longitudinal "plugs" or slices were incubated in solutions of ^{14}C-labeled sugars. Parenchyma and conducting tissues were sectioned out and treated separately in some experiments. Sugars accumulated in alcohol-insoluble material were measured by determining the amount of $^{14}CO_2$ released by oxidation. The $^{14}CO_2$ was trapped in KOH contained in the center wells of Warburg manometric vessels and later released by addition of acid. The sum of labeled hexose released into the bathing medium plus the ^{14}C taken up by the tissue was used to estimate the hydrolysis of [^{14}C]sucrose supplied to incubating tissues. By this means distinction was drawn between invertase action in the cell wall (free space) and metabolic compartment (cytoplasm).

The results showed that several sucrose-splitting enzymes were active in mature storage tissue. In addition to the soluble pH 7.0 invertase described in earlier reports (581, 1268), Hawker and Hatch discovered an acid invertase tightly bound to the cell wall. Its pH optimum (3.8) and K_m value (3×10^{-4} M) distinguished it from both the outer space and vacuolar acid invertases operative in the sugar accumulation cycle. The enzyme retained stability and was not removed from cell wall preparations when washed in water, aqueous buffers, 1 M NaCl solution, and detergent, or when treated with diethyl ether or butanol followed by water. The enzyme resisted heating at 50 °C in water but not in acetone–ethanol. Another enzyme present in the mature stem tissue was identified as UDPG–fructose transglycosylase (sucrose synthetase). This catalyst was concentrated in vascular tissue, in contrast to neutral and acid invertases found predominately in the storage parenchyma (Table 11-1).

Uptake experiments with radioactive sucrose, fructose, and glucose revealed that, regardless of source, more than 50 percent of the label appeared in stored sucrose. Less than 5 percent was lost to respiratory reactions. The remaining ^{14}C was recovered from non-sugar components of the alcohol-soluble and alcohol-insoluble fractions. More than 98 percent of the stored sugar was sucrose. Also in keeping with the accumulation mechanism of immature storage tissue was a preference for glucose rather than fructose or sucrose as the most readily absorbed sugar. By calculation more

TABLE 11-1

LOCATION IN SUGARCANE STEM TISSUE OF ENZYMES OPERATIVE IN THE SUGAR ACCUMULATION PROCESS

[After Hawker and Hatch (701).] Reproduced by permission of *Physiologia Plantarum.*

Type of tissue	Enzyme activity (μmoles/g fresh wt./h)		
	Neutral invertase	Acid invertase (cell wall)	UDPG–fructose transglycosylase
Whole tissue	0.53	1.81	0.05
Longitudinal sections	0.42	0.85	0.07
Parenchyma	0.40	0.71	0.01
Sectioned conducting	0.09	0.51	0.18
Conducting, parenchyma free	0	0.21	0.45

than 86 percent of the supplied sucrose was shown to be hydrolyzed prior to uptake. It was also calculated that under no condition could less than 43 percent of the supplied sucrose have been hydrolyzed prior to storage, and the actual value might have approached 100 percent.

A close correlation was found between the level of cell wall acid invertase and sucrose hydrolysis at pH 4.5. As a function of pH the curves for sucrose storage and hydrolysis fitted closely with the acid invertase curve (Fig. 11-3). Moreover, whereas

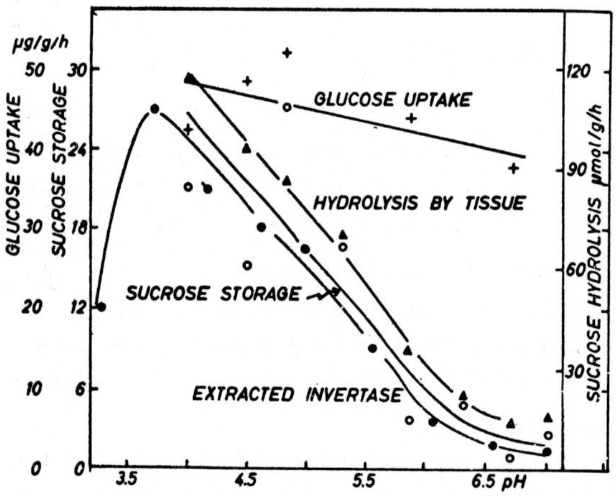

Fig. 11-3. Effects of pH on processes of sucrose storage and hydrolysis. Shown are acid invertase activity (•), sucrose hydrolysis by tissue discs (▲), sucrose stored from supplied [^{14}C]sucrose (○), and glucose uptake (+). [After Hawker and Hatch (701).] Reproduced by permission of *Physiologia Plantarum.*

glucose uptake was hardly affected by pH, sucrose storage increased about 10-fold between pH 7.0 and 4.0. Some indication of an invertase other than the acid cell wall enzyme was also found. The latter was evidenced by differing ratios of sucrose hydrolysis by tissue slices and isolated acid invertase when the level of neutral invertase varied.

B. *Relationships of invertase level to sucrose accumulation in mature storage tissue*

As discussed in Chapter 10, Hatch and Glasziou (690) discovered a relationship between neutral invertase and the rate of sucrose storage by mature stalk tissues of intact plants. The storage rate appeared to increase or decrease as a function of neutral invertase concentration. A similar relationship was reported by Hawker and Hatch for cell wall acid invertase of mature storage tissues from plants subjected to controlled environments. Changes in the acid invertase were of a lesser magnitude than those reported for neutral invertase. Acid invertase fluctuated between 0.1 and 3.0 μmoles/g of fresh tissue per hour, and neutral invertase between 0.05 and 7.0 μmoles/g of fresh weight per hour, in response to induced environmental changes.

Hawker and Hatch proposed that the contribution of neutral invertase toward sucrose hydrolysis remains essentially constant while that of acid invertase varies extensively with changing pH of the external medium. This concept is based on the assumption that cytoplasmic invertase is not affected by external pH changes. Thus, with some tissues bathed in a pH 7.0 medium the neutral invertase accounted for close to 70 percent of sucrose hydrolysis, while at pH 4.0 the same quantity of enzyme could not have hydrolyzed more than 10 percent. The authors pointed out that the *in vivo* pH value at the site of neutral invertase action may vary, and hence the level of neutral invertase extracted is not necessarily a measure of its work potential *in vivo*.

Hawker and Hatch concluded that sucrose storage in mature stalk tissue proceeds via steps analogous to those in immature storage tissue: (a) Sucrose hydrolysis occurring as a prerequisite and rate-limiting first step; (b) formation and interconversion of hexose phosphates; (c) formation of a sucrose derivative (presumably sucrose phosphate); and (d) movement of the sucrose moiety into the vacuole. The mechanism

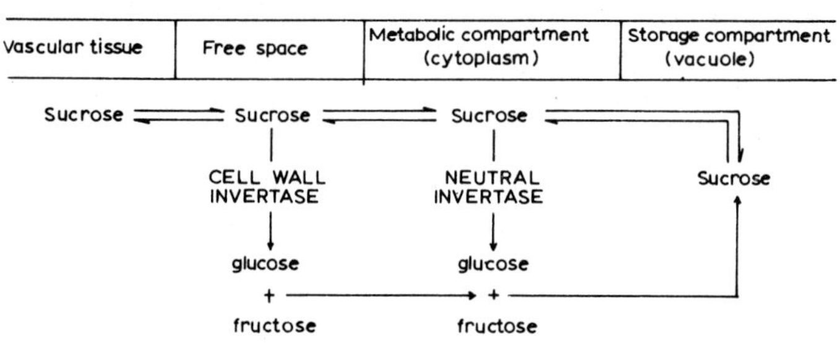

Fig. 11-4. The mechanism of sugar storage in mature storage tissue of sugarcane as depicted by Hawker and Hatch (701). [After Hawker and Hatch (701).] Reproduced by permission of *Physiologia Plantarum*.

differs from that of immature storage tissue in the nature and distribution of acid invertase. The sucrose storage processes envisioned by Hawker and Hatch for mature storage tissue are presented schematically in Fig. 11-4. All enzymes required to operate this system have been isolated from mature storage tissue (689, 691).

The assumed sucrose derivative is not shown in Fig. 11-4, but nonetheless an energy-dependent transport of sucrose was regarded as essential. Hawker and Hatch quite specifically defined active transport as "the unidirectional and energy-dependent movement of a compound across a membrane". They concluded that the storage processes of the mature stalk were consistent with the essential criteria of an active transport process as outlined by Collander (381). Although Hawker and Hatch differed from Bieleski in their interpretation of sucrose storage by mature stalk tissues, the authors did find the data published by Bieleski (180) to be generally consistent with their own concept of sucrose storage.

The paper by Hawker and Hatch (701) appears to have been the last report dealing strictly with sugar uptake and its essential enzymology in sugarcane. As such, certain conflicts over terminology and storage-process conception appeared imminent to the authors as new mechanistic detail emerged. Specifically, the point was made that active sugar transport does not require conditions of movement against a concentration gradient. The latter, of course, had been a key feature in prompting much of the earlier research relative to sugar storage. With respect to mature storage tissue (701) the measurement of net influx or efflux of sugar from sucrose solutions was viewed as being dependent upon endogenous vacuolar sucrose ("the diffusion gradient") without necessitating any change in the rate of active transport. For immature storage tissue, either sucrose, fructose, or glucose in the external solution were viewed as transiting inward by the same process, but accumulating in sucrose or hexose pools as a function of endogenous vacuolar invertase. According to Hawker and Hatch (701), Berliner (170) had predicted in 1959 that active transport and the analogous terminology relevant to the results of this process could be rendered inadequate as mechanistic detail is clarified.

Additional comments by Hawker and Hatch (701) implied an importance of sugar in the cell wall which had apparently been ignored during earlier studies. Hawker cited unpublished evidence showing free space sucrose levels at close to the concentrations found in the storage space. Since the latter may readily exceed 20 percent (w/v) in the intact mature stalk, the free space (cell wall) sucrose was thought to contribute to storage sugar values otherwise attributed to the inner space or storage volume. The concept of high levels of free space sucrose also implies differential influx–efflux rates. Hawker and Hatch (701) found that sucrose accumulation from a 1-percent (w/v) sucrose solution did not surpass the observed efflux from a 5-percent (w/v) storage sucrose concentration. Calculations based on the rate-limiting inversion steps for storage from a sucrose medium, and sucrose accumulation from glucose by tissues with invertase in nonlimiting supply, showed that sucrose influx may exceed efflux when steady-state conditions are established. The latter relationship was demonstrated for an endogenous sucrose level of 20 percent.

In summary, our present knowledge of the sugar storage mechanism at the site of sugar accumulation in mature storage tissue shows close agreement with storage processes active at the physiological sink, *i.e.* in actively-growing tissues. Relatively minor differences are noted with respect to the nature and positioning of essential invertases. In addition, there is foreseen a need for new conceptual developments in order to improve our understanding of sugar storage as it emerged during the 1960's.

5. STORAGE POTENTIAL OF *SACCHARUM* SPECIES

Phyllogeny of the genus *Saccharum* has been the object of widespread speculation and research. Morphological similarity, cross-fertility, extensive vegetative propagation, and high polyploidy within *Saccharum* species have complicated the work of systematic botanists as well as the sugarcane breeder in need of ancestral genetic material. The origin of species within the genus is depicted by Brandes (230) as paralleling the inundation of the Malaysian land mass during the late Cretaceous period. Assuming that *S. spontaneum* was the original type having general occurrence, Brandes suggests that *S. robustum* evolved by natural selection under differing environmental conditions, and that *S. officinarum* originated as New Guinea natives selected the sweetest and most succulent forms of *S. robustum*. *S. sinense* and *S. barberi* are regarded by Brandes as cultivated plants while Parthasarathy (1147) subscribes to their natural origin through crosses with local wild forms of *S. spontaneum* and cultivated *S. officinarum* in northern India. Some doubt exists as to whether certain species belong to *Saccharum* or *Erianthus*. The picture of species origin is further complicated by the probability that other *Saccharum* species once existed, and by the possibility that intergeneric crosses have occurred between *Saccharum* and other tropical grasses.

In this context it follows that differing sugar storage potentials logically exist among the *Saccharum* species. Moreover, significant studies by Bull and Glasziou (258) suggest that the varying potentials themselves could have formed the basis of strictly natural selection processes leading to the evolution of *S. officinarum*. Examination of sugar levels in various *Saccharum* species gave evidence of evolutionary sugar increases. Hypothetical ecological conditions were visualized in which selection for storage carbohydrate would favor the most readily-mobilized form, that is, sucrose. Those ratoons most rapidly mobilizing their stored sucrose would enjoy an evolutionary advantage. Additional studies based on sugar, moisture, and fiber contents placed the apparent limit of sugar accumulation in *Saccharum* species at about 27 percent of the fresh weight.

Bull and Glasziou (258) performed their experiments with *robustum*, *spontaneum*, *sinense*, and *officinarum* species of *Saccharum*, with *arundinaceus* and *maximus* species of *Erianthus*[1], and with local hybrid and commercial varieties. The plant clones were 12 months of age when sampled for sugar analyses. Tissue samples were taken from the basal three internodes, extracted with hot 70 percent ethanol, and assayed for total and reducing sugars. Fiber was determined by oven-drying samples to constant weight and subtracting total sugars.

Results compiled for eight species of the *Saccharum* complex are presented in Table 11-2. When total sugar content was plotted against the fiber content, the position of

TABLE 11-2

MEAN VALUES FOR SUGAR AND FIBER CONTENTS OF MEMBERS OF THE *SACCHARUM* COMPLEX

[After Bull and Glasziou (258).] Reproduced by permission of the *Australian Journal of Biological Sciences.*

Genus and species	No. of clones	Contents (% fresh wt. ± S.E.)		
		Sucrose	Reducing sugars	Fiber
Erianthus				
E. maximus	3	2.24 ± 0.44	0.73 ± 0.23	26.4 ± 0.9
E. arundinaceus	2	0.62 ± 0.16	0.61 ± 0.17	30.3 ± 0.3
Miscanthus				
M. floridulus	5	3.03 ± 0.56	0.79 ± 0.24	51.0 ± 2.0
Saccharum				
S. spontaneum	10	3.96 ± 0.46	0.44 ± 0.20	33.9 ± 2.1
S. spontaneum (Fiji)	30	5.35 ± 0.38	1.66 ± 0.06	31.8 ± 0.9
S. robustum	10	7.73 ± 0.83	0.27 ± 0.02	24.8 ± 1.6
S. sinense	2	13.45 ± 0.02	0.38 ± 0.08	12.8 ± 2.0
S. officinarum	25	17.47 ± 0.35	0.32 ± 0.02	9.8 ± 0.4

each species along a least squares regression line was consistent with theoretical evolutionary positions. *Miscanthus* contained the lowest sugar level and *S. officinarum* the highest. Intermediate positions were occupied by the wild *spontaneum* and *robustum* species of *Saccharum* (Table 11-2). These results were taken as evidence of natural selection for high sugar storage capability (258), in which the present high points are found in *S. officinarum* genotypes.

Additional supporting evidence for this thesis was taken from the characteristic

[1]The "*Saccharum* complex" described by Bull and Glasziou (258) includes at least four other genera closely related to *Saccharum: Erianthus, Miscanthus, Sclerostachya*, and *Narenga* [Mukherjee (1055)]. According to Celarier (309), the genus *Saccharum* might have evolved from *Erianthus*, with *Miscanthus* possibly acting as the common ancestor for the entire complex. On a morphological basis Hooker (746) was unable to distinguish *Erianthus* from *Saccharum* except for the "awned glume IV" of *Erianthus.*

weak flowering habit and loss of fertility of *S. officinarum*. The flowering vigor is restored, with concurrent loss of sucrose storage capacity, by hybridization of *S. officinarum* with *S. spontaneum*. The implication here is that natural selection favored sugar storage characteristics rather than flowering and seed-producing performance. Bull and Glasziou also noted the consistency between the evolutionary gain of storage capability and loss of flowering habit, on one hand, and the observation that unilateral selection for one character is usually correlated with adverse changes in other characters [Mather and Harrison (989)]. Obviously this is not a hard and fast rule since many varieties of *S. officinarum* accumulate high sucrose levels while producing abundant flowers.

The maximum sucrose potential for *Saccharum* was estimated on the assumption that at least 5 percent of the stalk must be fiber to meet structural requirements. A maximum sucrose value of about 27 percent of the fresh weight was obtained, within 99 percent confidence limits, under conditions such that the minimum moisture content would be 70 percent (Fig. 11-5). Although the data given in Fig. 11-5 is taken

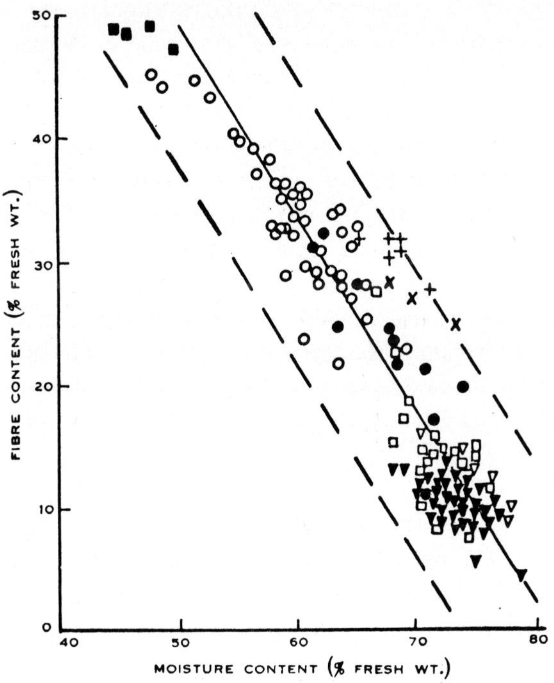

Fig. 11-5. Relationship between fiber and moisture content among members of the *Saccharum* complex, within 99% confidence limits ($r = -0.94$, significant at 0.1%). *S. spontaneum* (○); *S. robustum* (●); *S. officinarum* (▼); *S. sinense* (▽); *Saccharum* hybrids and commercial canes (□); *Erianthus maximus* (×); *E. arundinaceus* (+); *Miscanthus floridulus* (■). [After Bull and Glasziou (258).] Reproduced by permission of the *Australian Journal of Biological Sciences.*

from a limited number of clones, it appears highly unlikely that members of the *Saccharum* complex can exceed the indicated limits of sugar and moisture balance. Bull and Glasziou further noted that moisture was even more closely correlated with fiber than with sugar content. This is suggestive that high sugar levels do not produce an osmotic effect capable of limiting sugar accumulation.

From these results the authors concluded that *S. officinarum* need not have arisen solely by human selection, as Brandes (230) had suggested. Rather, a natural selection process in which new sucker growth was favored by large amounts of rapidly-mobilized sucrose was visualized as climaxing in *S. officinarum* genotypes.

6. MOISTURE

A vast amount of empirical data has been published relating moisture in one way or another with sucrose yield. The essentiality of water for maintaining turgor pressure and normal circulation is generally recognized along with its partial reactions in sugar synthesis and storage. However, our mechanistic knowledge of water roles in sucrose storage remains small in view of the fact that its presence is required by virtually every aspect of sugar production, transport, and storage. That fundamental knowledge of sugarcane water physiology can be gained but slowly is dictated by two hard facts: (a) The quantity of water actually taking part in biochemical reactions is extremely small; and (b) it is almost impossible to isolate water as the lone controlled variable.

It has been estimated that water constitutes more than 70 percent of the fresh weight of a sugarcane crop (1475, p. 270). Assuming that dry matter comprises about 30 percent, a somewhat misleading water/dry matter ratio is obtained close to 2.5:1. Van Dillewijn estimates a net water absorption in the order of 250 parts for each part of dry matter produced by the plant. By similar reasoning the "dry matter" itself must be regarded as roughly half water by virtue of the fact that water is utilized in the basic structure of carbohydrates.

Unlike mineral nutrients which are retained after absorption, only about 1 percent of the absorbed water is retained owing to transpirational losses. Earlier views holding that transpiration is a "necessary evil" (400) failed to recognize the possible significance of transpiration in maintaining turgor pressure, in regulating leaf temperature, and in facilitating nutrient uptake and translocation of assimilates. The term "evapotranspiration" has been used to denote the water loss in the atmosphere resulting from combined effects of plant transpiration and evaporation from the soil (258, 1427).

Much of the published data on sugarcane water requirements relate to water availability between field capacity and the permanent wilting point of the plant (1395, 1427, 316, 517, 330, 338). Wilkins and Ateshian (1572) found that ground water movement and salinity gradients in British Guiana appeared to conform to a direct relationship between the mean depth of the water table and cane quality. Some authors content that cane growth and sugar yield are not adversely affected by soil water variations until the wilting point is reached (1395). Clements (338), on the other hand, reported growth restrictions occurring before soil moisture had approached the wilting point. Mongelard (1031) observed differing responses of "drought-susceptible" and "drought-resistant" varieties to a given soil water potential. He suggested that more attention should be given to plant water potential and its relation to growth. In general terms, the plant water regime most effective in promoting cane ripening is that which gives the greatest restriction against growth while still maintaining a normal source-to-sink system for sugar synthesis, transport, and storage.

A. *Water and sugarcane ripening* [Hartt (648, 654–656)]

Early experiments by Hartt in Hawaii stressed the physiological importance of water to sugarcane when both maximum growth and maximum sugar storage are sought by the grower. Evidence from an initial study published in 1934 (648) suggested that photosynthesis may continue in wilting blades but at rates inferior to those of blades given adequate water supply. In this instance the test variety, *D. 1135*, was examined with an experimental design including dark treatments of up to 45 hours duration in addition to variable water supply. Hartt's findings included: (a) Increased reducing sugars in leaf blades and leaf sheaths, and less reducing sugars in stalks, of water-deficient plants; (b) sucrose and polysaccharide increases in blades of water-deficient plants; (c) appearance of polysaccharides other than starch in leaves, sheaths, and immature stalks. The polysaccharides fluctuated diurnally and in response to variable water supply. While Hartt considered several possible explanations for the sugar differentials, she tentatively concluded that water increases photosynthesis and sugar transport in addition to growth. Low water was taken to be conducive to polysaccharide synthesis in leaves exposed to light.

In a second study of water and cane ripening, Hartt (654) was perhaps the first physiologist to seriously consider whether withholding water improved quality by increasing sucrose content or by decreasing water content. She further considered whether increased sugar synthesis as a result of irrigation would offset the parallel increases in sugar utilization. Working with the variety *H. 109*, Hartt included enzyme analyses in one of the earliest efforts to define clearly the mechanism of water control over carbohydrate level. Her results showed that illuminated plants given adequate water contained more leaf sucrose and less storage sucrose than plants given inadequate water. Both green-leaf and dry-leaf stalks increased their sucrose content under low-water supply. However, low-water treatments adversely affected the expression of juice during subsequent milling operations.

Hartt recognized that dry-leaf cane had been formed before water variables were begun and therefore concluded that the increased sugar content was due to the transport and accumulation of sucrose not being used for growth and respiration. Many years later Hartt (342) observed a similar movement of [^{14}C]sucrose into the oldest internodes of the plant. Hartt envisioned the well-watered and illuminated plants as producing more photosynthate, but also as utilizing more in translocation, growth and respiration, ultimately causing a net decrease of sucrose in storage. High sucrose content of water-deficient cane was explained in terms of low utilization under the poor-growth conditions. The key feature here was that photosynthesis rate was not taken to be as important as utilization rate in determining juice quality. Various aspects of this concept are still being evaluated today.

Hartt (654) also observed decreasing invertase activity in leaf blades during 48 hours of total darkness, particularly in plants given normal water supply. In a recent study, Alexander and Montalvo-Zapata (51) reported an almost total depletion of meristem invertase during a comparable dark treatment; however, we have not detected appreciable invertase in sugarcane leaves.

The enzymes amylase, dextrinase, and maltase also showed sensitivity to the light and water variables in Hartt's study. Leaves containing the highest enzyme levels also contained the most sucrose and polysaccharide. Among cane tissues enzyme activity generally decreased in the order of leaf blade, leaf sheath, green-leaf internodes and dry-leaf internodes. In this study Hartt found little evidence of starch formation or starch–sucrose interconversion as reported by other workers (411, 434, 1307). However, results from later studies led Hartt and her co-workers to propose a night conversion of starch to sucrose (675) via reactions probably involving foliar amylase (670).

Subsequent studies (565) performed on ratoons of the *H. 109* crop substantiated Hartt's earlier tentative conclusions. It was shown that abundant water is essential for sucrose formation in the leaves, for sucrose translocation to the stalk, and for optimum juice expression during milling. Photosynthesis continued at a reduced rate in plants experiencing low-moisture stress (in soil at or below the wilting point). Although less sugar was produced, more sugar accumulated in the stalks by virtue of lowered utilization requirements. The increased sucrose was not considered to be of economic importance because of decreased extractability, and presumably because of reduced tonnage owing to growth restriction.

Years later, investigations by Ashton (116), by Hartt and Burr (674), and by Hartt (675) confirmed that low-water supply is restrictive against photosynthesis. However, Hartt (675) demonstrated that within certain limits water stress will impair photosynthesis less severely than sucrose transport. The slowing of translocation was viewed as an aid to storage processes by allowing more time for sugar accumulation. In addition, there appeared to be less sucrose hydrolyzed in transit under low-water stress, and a greater quantity of sucrose was available for storage because of curtailed growth. Hartt concluded that, unless water supply was so limiting as to prevent photosynthesis altogether, there was no physiological argument against withholding water for ripening purposes.

The validity of this thesis in agronomic terms can only be proven by field trials wherever sugar is grown. For example, Samuels *et al.* (1282) found that a highly-compacted Grumosol (Santo Isabel clay) responded to irrigation with increased tonnage of both stalks and sugar, but sucrose content of the stalks was lowered. The net increase of sucrose was closely related to increased efficiency of nitrogen fertilization, that is, 150 pounds of nitrogen per acre gave the highest stalk and sugar yields with irrigation, but without irrigation some 300 pounds of nitrogen per acre were needed to produce maximum yields. On a different soil type having different levels of available nitrogen an entirely different response to water might be obtained.

Irrigation studies by Vázquez (1481) in the Lajas Valley of Puerto Rico showed no appreciable increases in sugar yield for *P.R. 980* crops irrigated after the 5th month before harvest. So long as frequent irrigations were given during the early growth period, an estimated 10 inches of water consumption per crop would be saved by withholding water during the final 5 months. Moreover, under Lajas Valley conditions, there were no yield relationships evident between variable nitrogen levels (200 and 300 lbs/acre) and irrigation regime.

Withholding water to promote ripening remains an accepted practice to the present time (342, 1219, 763). This stems from the fact that it is one of the few practical means of ripening control available to the grower and not from a lack of physiological information relating to impaired growth and photosynthesis. In addition to possible growth and sugar losses resulting from water restriction there are other practical considerations with respect to mechanical harvesting and the accompanying need to remove as much of the green top and trash as possible. Continued supply of water up to harvest time with parallel continuation of luxuriant growth would constitute a further burden upon harvesting operations.

An example of good water management as a means of promoting cane ripening is shown by the programs of Humbert and his colleagues at Ingenio Los Mochis, Mexico. Humbert *et al.* (763) state that Los Mochis produced a record low factory sucrose recovery of 6.87 percent in 1959, largely as a result of field practices inducive to high tonnage but poor sucrose storage. At harvest the cane was generally green, immature, and growing. Consequently, subsequent irrigation and fertilizer programs were designed to promote growth only up to the latter part of the rainy season. At this time a water restriction was put into effect which extended through the early dry season. Fig. 11-6 illustrates the very considerable sugar increases obtained through the planned dehydration. As moisture declined from 80 to 70 percent in the 8 to 10 internodes, a drop of 1 percent gave an increase of 2.5 kg of sugar per ton of cane. These trends were consistent for both of the test varieties (*N.Co. 310* and *Co. 421*). Depending upon the stage of the grinding season, a maximum of 84 days and a minimum of 49 days elapsed between the final irrigation and the harvest date. The dehydration plan described by Humbert and his co-workers was designed to achieve an 8 to 10 moisture level of 73 percent at the time of harvest.

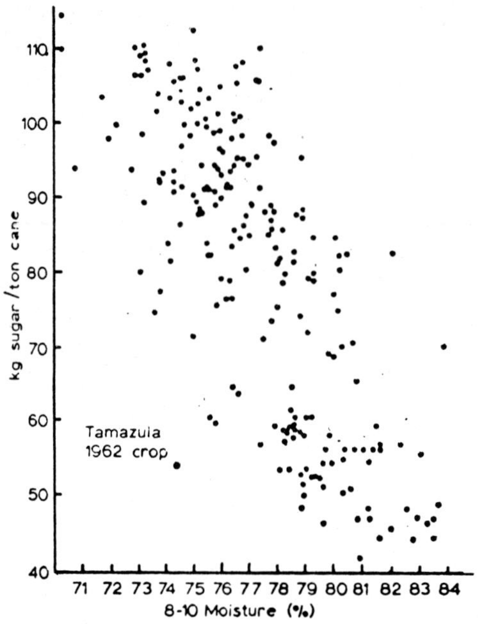

Fig. 11-6. Effects of planned dehydration, as reflected by moisture values for 8 to 10 stalk tissue, on sugar yield in kilograms of sucrose per ton of cane. [After Humbert *et al.* (763).] Reproduced by permission of *I.S.S.C.T.*

B. *Similar responses to deficient and excessive water supply*

Little attention has been given to excessive water supply even though temporary or localized inundation is a common occurrence throughout much of the sugar-producing world. Greenhouse experiments by Alexander *et al.* (55) revealed strikingly similar sugar and enzyme responses to deficient and excessive levels of water supply. Moreover, visual injury symptoms produced by the two water regimes were virtually indistinguishable.

Plants of the variety *P.R. 980* were grown in sand culture with adequate water supply until 14 weeks of age, at which time four variable water regimes were established: (a) No water; (b) normal water; (c) normal water plus night flooding; and (d) continuous flooding. Plants of one experiment were pretreated with 0.01 percent gibberellic acid (GA) given as an aqueous foliar spray 10 days before water variables were initiated to create a status of stimulated growth and water utilization. Results showed that over a 9-day period both the zero-water and continuous-flooding treatments produced wilting of leaf blades, drying of leaf sheaths, extensive yellowing of leaf tips, margins, and sheaths, and severe curling of spindle leaves. These symptoms were identical for both water regimes. Symptoms were delayed but not prevented by GA pretreatment.

Sugar changes were also comparable for zero-water and continuous-flooding treatments, with sucrose content declining in leaves and initially declining in immature internode tissue. Some level of continued photosynthesis and sugar transport was evidenced by a general recovery of storage sugar levels between the 5th and 9th day of water treatment. The GA-treated plants continued to increase green weight up to the 5th and 9th day in the low-water and continuously-flooded regimes, respectively. This was regarded as tacit evidence of a GA effect on water uptake or utilization efficiency.

Invertase, from immature storage tissue, declined in response to both high- and low-water regimes (Fig. 11-7). Pretreatment with GA gave the effect of invertase

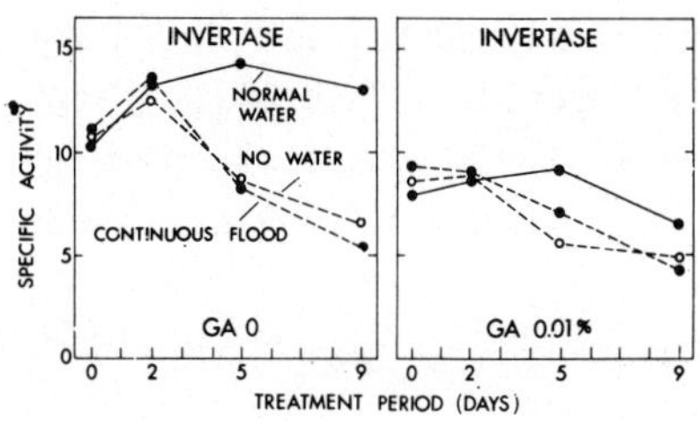

Fig. 11-7. Effect of gibberellic acid (GA) pretreatment on the response of sugarcane invertase to variable water regimes. Invertase differentials induced by moisture stress were nearly eliminated under conditions of rapid growth created by the gibberellic acid treatment. [After Alexander *et al.* (unpublished).]

suppression, particularly in the plants given adequate water, so that there was no longer a major invertase difference between plants given GA, excessive water, or insufficient water. Foliar amylase appeared to remain stable under conditions of low-water supply, but its response to continuous flooding was similar to that in the control of "normal" water regime. It was concluded that amylase synthesis proceeded by a mechanism distinct from invertase synthesis, one which resisted both the low-water and high-water repression observed against invertase.

Night flooding produced neither visual symptoms nor sugar responses characteristic of water deficiency or continuous flooding. Foliar ATPase was gradually repressed by night flooding, possibly as a perturbation of normal diurnal–nocturnal rhythms. Otherwise the plants observed in this study seemed remarkably tolerant to the temporary flood condition. It was tentatively concluded that distinct levels of external water supply did not produce discrete physiological regimes within the plant; rather, it seemed that common mechanisms of growth, sugar production, and sugar storage were minimally altered by water stress, at least as a short-term effect. Proof of this assumption will require a great deal of additional evidence.

7. NITROGEN AND POTASSIUM IN SUGARCANE RIPENING

Although many plant nutrients influence the processes of photosynthesis, sugar translocation and sugar storage, the benefits of abundant nutrient supplies are generally attributed to increased tonnage rather than sugar synthesis or storage effects. It has been stated that nitrogen fertilization will increase the area of actively-photosynthesizing leaves but will not increase the rate of photosynthesis itself (384). Only in the instance of potassium is there significant evidence that deficiency produces poor cane quality in addition to growth restriction. This may well be a reflection of low soil potassium rather than specific roles of the element in sugar storage. Samuels *et al.* (1282) have depicted both cane tonnage and sucrose content as major considerations in a fertilization program, but the effect of increased tonnage can be nullified and rendered unacceptable if accompanied by significant sugar losses. Traditionally, however, the predominant relationship of macronutrients to cane ripening has been viewed as the production of abundant storage tissue at a time when tissue growth will least interfere with maturation and ripening processes.

A. *Nitrogen*

Deleterious effects of nitrogen against the ripening of a 12-month crop can occur when: (a) Growth stimulation by residual nitrogen accompanies late irrigation; (b) nitrogen applications are either too heavy or are delayed too long into the growing season; and (c) when unfavorable rainfall patterns prevent nitrogen utilization early in the season and encourage nitrogen utilization late in the season. The picture is more complicated with 2-year crops, although Borden (216) has shown that under Hawaiian conditions both tonnage and quality are most affected by nitrogen during the first 9 months. Nitrogen source and residual soil nitrogen are contributing factors depending heavily on local soil properties and whether a plant crop or ratoon crop is being fertilized. According to Clements (350), excessive use of nitrogen tends to occur where growers receive a fixed sum per ton of cane regardless of sugar content; the other extreme is approached where mill operators control production, and emphasis is given not to sugar per acre but to sucrose percent cane in clean, straight, easily-harvested stalks.

Nitrogen in the form of ammonium sulfate has long been the most important nutritional factor for increasing sugar yields in Puerto Rico[2] (1282), although nitrogen fertilization is an accepted practice throughout all the sugarcane-growing regions of the world (1288). This is especially true in the areas responding to technical advances in

---

[2] Samuels, G., Landrau, Jr., P. and Capó, B.G., 1952. The response of sugarcane in Puerto Rico to various nitrogen sources, *J. Agric. Univ. P.R.* 36(3): 230–239.

foliar diagnoses, water management, fertilization by aircraft, and generally better understanding of sugarcane's growth and development requirements.

Nitrogen-source studies in Puerto Rico have failed to show consistent response differences between such compounds as cyanamide, sodium nitrate, ammonium nitrate, ammonium sulfate, Uramon, and ammonium superphosphate (1010, 521, 953). Similar results with differing nitrogen sources were reported from Hawaii (217). Experiments performed by Samuels *et al.*[2] (1282) revealed no appreciable differences in response to ammonium sulfate, ammonium nitrate, Uramon, calcium cyanamide, sodium nitrate and tankage on variable clay soils in Puerto Rico's humid and dry areas. Poorest results were obtained with liquid ammonium nitrate. Factors of production expense, transportation, ease of application and handling, and potential explosiveness (in the instance of ammonium nitrate) have therefore determined the practical nitrogen source for sugarcane rather than physiological considerations. Soil pH is of local importance relative to nitrogen source. Ammonium sulfate increases the hydrogen-ion level and can be detrimental on acid soils, or it can be beneficial in areas where the soil pH is 7.0 or higher[2].

In 1956 Samuels (1288) evaluated 16 years of nitrogen research on sugarcane in Puerto Rico, including 127 experiments with 12 varieties grown on nine soil types. He found that higher tonnage as a partial nitrogen response did not lower sucrose content; rather, within the limits of diminishing returns (about 200 pounds of nitrogen per acre), tonnage and sugar increased linearly on a tons per acre per month basis. Another study (1282) placed the upper nitrogen limit at about 250 pounds per acre for Puerto Rico. Efficiency of utilization declined in the order of fall planting, spring planting, and ratoons. Comparison of the Puerto Rico data with findings in Hawaii (215) revealed that maximum tonnage in the two regions required nearly equal amounts of nitrogen, and in Hawaii sugarcane utilized the nitrogen with moderately greater efficiency than in Puerto Rico. With respect to water supply, irrigated crops used nitrogen at about double the efficiency of those grown in Puerto Rico's humid areas (annual rainfall = 60 to 95 inches).

Samuels *et al.* (1282) also found evidence of cane quality improvement as a parallel feature of increased tonnage from nitrogen fertilization. A review of 152 field experiments with leading varieties showed a definite linear relationship between increased tonnage and sucrose percent cane in response to nitrogen fertilization (Fig. 11-8). It was also shown that neither the nitrogen source (ammonium sulfate, ammonium nitrate in one or two applications, or Uramon) nor method of application gave differences in response. In this study the regression equation was such that $Y = 0.10X - 2.69$, where Y is the percentage increase in sucrose percent cane and X is the percentage increase in tons of cane per acre. It should be noted that this equation specifies an increase in the quality factor only after the percentage increase in tons of cane reaches 27. For this reason the authors cautioned against nitrogen treatments on cane having little need of it, or of high-nitrogen application where only moderate quantities are required.

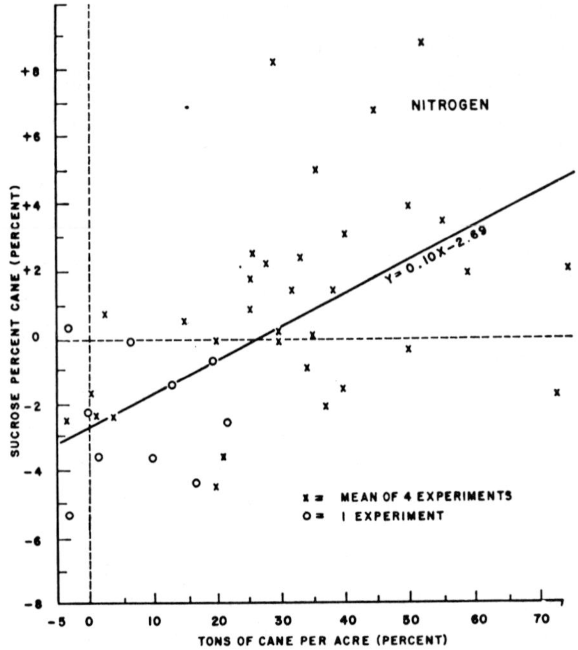

Fig. 11-8. Influence of nitrogen fertilization on the percentage increase or decrease in sugarcane yield (tons of cane per acre) and quality (sucrose percent cane). [After Samuels *et al.* (1282).] Reproduced by permission of the authors.

Bonnet *et al.* (207), working with the variety *M. 336* grown in sand culture, obtained significant weight responses to increasing nitrogen for stalks, roots, trash, and sugar for a 15-month crop. Grown in a greenhouse, these plants experienced neither the soil nor rainfall variables of field-grown material. Foliar-nitrogen and leaf-weight values were useful indicators of yield when given due consideration as to leaf rank and the age of cane at time of sampling. During the years just preceding this work the value of leaf nitrogen as an index for fertilizer programming was recognized by Clements (339, 343), Halais (627), Innes (773), and Capó *et al.* (297). Rouillard (1258) had proposed a vegetative index based on the weight of 20 leaves ($^{+}$3) taken from cane of specified age and season.

Under conditions of a 2-year crop the potential of nitrogen to depress cane quality is largely confined to the first 12 months. Borden (216) reported that during the first year nitrogen treatments given between 6 weeks and 11 months produced higher tonnages of green tops, higher contents of reducing sugars and moisture, and lower cane sucrose content than during the second year. By 15 months the heavily-fertilized cane (totaling up to 220 pounds of nitrogen per acre in two to four increments) usually contained higher sucrose except in those instances where treatments were delayed beyond 6 months. On the basis of time elapsed, the 6- to 15-month relationship described by Borden is consistent with the suggestion of Samuels *et al.* (1290) of a 2-month cutoff point for applied nitrogen on a 12-month crop.

In another study Samuels and Alers-Alers (1290) supplied variable combinations of nitrogen, phosphorus, and potassium to ratoons varying in age from 3 to 21 weeks. Working with the variety *P.R. 980* grown in a humid area on a silty-clay soil, it was found that nitrogen applications (equivalent to 125 pounds per acre) at 15 weeks or later significantly lowered sucrose content of the 12-month crop (Table 11-3). The nitrogen effect was also produced when phosphorus and potassium were present. Higher nitrogen applications (250 pounds per acre) significantly lowered sucrose when applied to a 3-week-old ratoon crop. Although this work was performed with only a single variety, the results are consistent with the view that excessive nitrogen available at harvest time is a major cause of poor sugarcane quality (1112).

TABLE 11-3

EFFECTS OF THE TIME OF NITROGEN APPLICATION ON THE YIELD AND QUALITY OF *P.R. 980* RATOONS

[After Samuels and Alers-Alers (1290).] Reproduced by permission of the authors.

Treatment No.	Fertilizer applied (lbs/acre)			Age (weeks)	Cane/acre (tons)	Sugar/acre (tons)	Sucrose % cane
	N	P_2O_5	K_2O				
1	125	0	0	3	61	7.6	12.33
2	125	0	0	9	65	7.9	12.03
3	125	0	0	15	63	7.3	11.46
4	125	0	0	21	57	6.4	11.31
5	250	0	0	3	68	8.0	11.70
6	63	0	0	3	56	7.0	12.32
7	125	50	25	3	73	9.0	12.29
8	125	50	25	21	65	7.3	11.14
9	250	100	50	3	76	9.0	11.81

Clements (345) maintains that cane growing on fields overly abundant in nitrogen, as well as with sulfur and moisture, can never achieve a highly-ripened status. Experiments in India (1028) and Venezuela (1127) indicate that nitrogen should be applied within the first 3 months of the 12-month crop for maximum sucrose production. Srivastava (1354) has stressed the importance of early nitrogen fertilization to obtain increased tillering, regardless of the fact that younger plants tend to have less extensive root systems and must therefore receive disproportionately higher nitrogen applications. In Puerto Rico, Bonnet (208) maintained that maturation is improved by applying all the nitrogen with the seed, at planting time, or as early as possible after harvest. Only sandy soils subject to severe leaching were regarded as justifying multiple nitrogen applications.

Little information has appeared regarding nitrogen effect upon sugar storage among different *Saccharum* species. However, workers in Australia (1269, 690) have demonstrated both nitrogen sensitivity of invertase-forming mechanisms and a *Saccharum* species differential for invertase content. Varietal differences within *S. officinarum* are widespread and the distinctions reported by Samuels *et al.* (1289) relevant to N, P, and K fertility are probably typical: (a) All varieties have a characteristic fertility potential giving maximum yield, but those responding best at high fertility will not necessarily do so at low fertility. (b) Varieties giving superior yields under poor fertility conditions may not do so under improved conditions. (c) Some varieties respond well to high fertility regardless of the region in which they are grown, while others respond poorly when removed from the site of their origin.

Landrau and Samuels (887) observed that each of four varieties grown at Isabela, Puerto Rico, on a limestone-derived Coto clay, responded more readily to the application and withholding of nitrogen than to phosphorus and potassium. Each variety retained its relative yielding power under varying conditions of fertilizer supply. Similar nitrogen responses were obtained with four varieties grown on a Coloso silt loam in the humid Arecibo area (1283). Under these conditions the withholding of potassium significantly lowered sucrose percent cane. Halais (628), in Mauritius, described differences in foliar nitrogen requirements between the varieties *Ebene 1-37* and *B. 37172*. The comparisons in this instance were based on optimum nitrogen values in relatively ideal environments.

B. *Potassium*

Potassium has been a difficult element for sugarcane physiologists and growers alike. In certain instances it has shown promise in improving cane tonnage and quality while in others little or no response of any kind has accrued from potassium fertilization. A suitable potassium index was developed with some difficulty after allowances were made for potassium interactions with moisture. In general, from the inconsistencies obtained with potassium in different regions, it appears that potassium is performing some highly-localized functions relative to sugar transport and storage which are essentially independent of the levels found in the leaf or leaf sheath.

An apparent relationship of potassium deficiency to low sucrose yields has been noted by numerous workers (651, 650, 1287, 1286, 1285, 161, 1289, 670). Samuels and Landrau (1283) obtained increased cane tonnage by potassium treatment of Coloso silty clay in the humid Arecibo area of Puerto Rico. Omission of potassium led to reduced sucrose content of the cane. In subsequent studies Samuels and Landrau (1286) obtained increased tonnage and quality with potassium fertilizers, but the response was confined largely to humid or semi-humid regions. Brix and percentage extractibility were not generally affected by potassium treatments. Humbert (762) has stressed a need to maintain adequate potassium in both sugarcane and the sugar beet to insure optimum quality. This task is made more difficult by inconsistencies between available soil potassium and the tissue potassium content as indicated by the foliar K index (935, 642).

Samuels and Landrau (1287) studied the components of available sucrose percent cane from a series of experiments which had responded to N, P, and K fertilization and found significant reductions in Brix, polarization, purity and available sugar in stalks and juice of potassium-deficient crops. Moreover, when potassium was available in adequate amounts, nitrogen applications significantly increased Brix and polarization values and improved the percent extraction. This might be taken as additional evidence of a specific K/N ratio needed for high juice quality, as suggested by Humbert (761) and Bonnet (208). In other studies with two varieties grown on Vega Baja silty clay in the humid to subhumid Río Piedras area, Landrau *et al.* (888) obtained only erratic responses to potassium fertilization which in turn were limited to the variety *B. 41227.* The same experiments gave significant yield increases with nitrogen applied up to 300 pounds per acre, but no response was obtained with applied phosphorus.

Acevedo-Ramos (2) offered several interesting but unsubstantiated explanations of potassium roles in sugarcane maturation based on changing foliar potassium content as a function of age. An early decrease was shown to be followed by later increases in potassium content of leaf blades. It was proposed that maturity might be hastened by late aerial potassium applications (assuming that a direct relationship of potassium content to maturity exists). Conversely, potassium increases at the late growth stages were also explained in terms of continued absorption as utilization declined, and transport of the element from old to young tissues within the plant.

The biochemical roles performed by potassium in sugarcane remain largely a matter of conjecture, although the possibility of direct potassium roles in hexose metabolism and sucrose transport cannot be dismissed. Hartt (650) established a relationship between potassium level and protein synthesis in blades and stalks. Other workers in Hawaii (77) observed a depression of photosynthesis rates in potassium-deficient plants. Borden (214) was unable to compensate for low sunlight intensity with applied potassium. Ordinarily, potassium fertilization will tend to increase both the nitrogen and moisture content of sugarcane (1293, p. 237).

Hartt (676) described both direct and indirect influences of potassium on sucrose transport in sugarcane. Indirectly, potassium deficiency might affect sugar movement owing to changes in growth, photosynthesis, or moisture content (271). Spanner's (1350) concept of potassium activity at the sieve plate offers a direct means by which insufficient potassium might drastically restrict sucrose translocation. Hartt (676) found that the movement of [^{14}C]sucrose from leaf to storage tissue in four Hawaiian clones was markedly decreased by potassium deficiency. This effect was detected in blades not yet showing visible deficiency symptoms or changes in photosynthetic activity. More severe potassium deficiency produced increases in foliar respiration rates, decreased photosynthesis, and decreased conversion of intermediate sugars to sucrose, in addition to the transport restrictions. Hartt concluded that repressed sucrose transport was a primary rather than secondary effect of low-potassium supply.

Various authors have noted an apparent essentiality of potassium for normal enzyme behavior in plant metabolic reactions (676, 1385, 510, 509, 11). Evans and Sorger (510) reviewed much of the background of this concept. Working with pea plants, Evans (509) found that pyruvate kinase activity seriously declined under conditions of potassium deficiency. Sugiyama *et al.* (1385) reported increased pyruvate kinase activity in leaves of wheat seedlings grown without adequate potassium. Abnormal chlorophyll and carbohydrate levels developed over the 14-day study period, but all parameters returned to normal within 3 days after addition of K_2SO_4 to the nutrient solution. With reference to sugarcane, Alexander (11) examined a number of metabolic enzymes in leaves of plants given gradually reduced potassium in nutrient solutions over a period of 18 weeks. Decreasing potassium supply increased hexokinase activity and repressed both phosphohexose isomerase and phosphoglyceryl kinase. Foliar glucose accumulation paralleled the decline of the latter two enzymes. As potassium supply approached deficiency proportions, *i.e.*, in the order of 1–2 meq/l, a severe loss of condensing enzyme activity was recorded.

8. RIPENING CONTROL THROUGH CROP LOGGING

In discussing individually the physiological factors related to sugarcane ripening, one risks giving the impression that any manipulation of these factors should be done on an individual basis, if and when it is convenient to the established production schedule. Fortunately, the essentially interacting nature of climate, moisture, and nutrition has long been recognized. Equally important is the understanding that sugarcane needs these factors in differing proportions during growth and development in order to achieve high tonnages of both cane and sugar. Striking progress has been made in adapting production programs to the physiological needs of sugarcane by use of various indexes. In essence, the practice involves periodic sampling of specific tissues, performance of mineral or moisture analyses on these tissues, evaluation of the data in the context of crop performance histories, and formulating appropriate cultural decisions relative to current parameter trends. The control of sugarcane culture based upon a continual influx of new growth information has culminated in the *crop logging* concept developed by Dr. Clements and his colleagues in Hawaii (348, 353, 334, 339, 343, 337, 336, 344, 346, 351)[3]. In discussing several of the indexes it will be seen that

[3]Clements *et al.* (342) has defined the crop log as "...the record of the progress a crop makes from its start until harvest". Owing to the continual influx of new information from carefully standardized analytical procedures, the system "...provides for a running picture of the crop's physiology which integrates climate and physiology in such a way that alterations in the management of a crop can be made while the crop is growing".

the crop log concept is potentially a self-improving system perfected by the data from each successive crop and the cumulative experience of the sugar grower.

A. *The primary index*

In abstract terms the thesis that all forms of life depend upon solar radiation is accepted the world over. The importance of sunlight to sugarcane was stressed years ago by Clements (334, 337) who observed enormous yield differences between the high-sunlight and shaded areas of Oahu. These differences were directly attributed to higher sunlight intensity and utilization on the leeward (Waipio) side as compared to the shaded windward side (Kailua). Soil moisture and nutritional factors were nearly equal for the two areas. Clements concluded that sunlight (heat and potential chemical energy) was the single overriding force determining sugarcane yield. After sunlight came a multitude of internal physiological factors and such external items as soil nutrients, moisture, and temperature. Clements proposed an internal index which was sufficiently responsive to soil and physiological factors to serve as a guide in planning the cultural programs most suited to local sunlight conditions. This was termed the *primary index*. It was defined as the total sugar level of the elongating cane sheaths expressed as percent of the dry matter (337). Putting this another way, sugar content of a specific intermediate storage tissue was taken as the most reliable indicator of how well the plant was integrating itself with its total environment.

In Clements' view the yield potential established by solar radiation would seldom be met owing to the operation of "deterring factors", both external and internal, ranging from insufficient moisture to man himself. An underlying assumption was that the plant is extremely sensitive to the deterrent factor, and that its responses to such factors will be reflected in the primary index. In practice Clements found that sheath sugar values close to 10 percent of the dry weight indicated a relative balance between sugar production and utilization; lower values meant that growth was outstripping photosynthesis, while higher values meant that storage predominated over utilization. A low primary index value was generally accompanied by high day and night temperatures, excessive tissue hydration, and low light intensity. High index values were associated with low temperatures, high light intensity, and low tissue hydration.

In the field, consistent interpretation of index values would border on the impossible were it not for supplemental indices. To establish these indices Clements made extensive measurements of sunlight (duration and intensity), temperature (24-hour day), moisture (percent of the green sheath weight), growth (elongation), nitrogen (percent of the dry weight of elongating blades), phosphorus (percent of the sugar-free dry weight of elongating sheaths), and potassium (percent of the sugar-free dry weight of elongating sheaths). When this information was compiled for some 16 crops over a 4-year period, Clements was able to specify sunlight, growth, and moisture as the most critical indices for the primary index. This does not mean that temperature and fertilizers played no part in establishing the index value, but rather the parts they did play tended to be incorporated within the three major indices. During the subsequent decades Clements and many others established moisture and nitrogen indexes as powerful tools in their own right. Moreover, it should be remembered that the primary index was developed under conditions such that sunlight was the salient variable, and soil factors such as macronutrients and moisture were relatively non-deterring.

In essence, the primary index defines the energy potential of a local area and indicates the limits within which efficient production can be attained. By this means the hazards of expending water and fertilizer resources toward high-energy yields, in areas having only low-energy potential, can be avoided. Such practices are uneconomical and frequently injurious to quality. The reasoning behind this principal is similar to that underlying the management of locally-productive varieties in areas where they have varying production potential (1289).

B. *The nitrogen index*

The commanding position of nitrogen in determining tons of cane per acre, tons of sugar per acre, and sucrose percent cane made it imperative to find a suitable nitrogen index. The ideal index would so integrate the plant's response to residual or applied nitrogen that a high level of correlation would exist between the index value and nitrogen content changes occurring throughout the plant. In 1942 Clements and Moriguchi (336) reported total nitrogen studies on plant and ratoon crops at Waipio and Kailua, Oahu, showing that elongating blades and green-leaf blades are the most reliable nitrogen indices. Leaf punches taken from the same leaves were also satisfactory. In some instances recoverable nitrogen exceeded the quantity of nitrogen applied, thereby indicating concurrent uptake of residual nitrogen. Evidence of a repression against nitrogen uptake by low soil temperature was also found. Of particular importance was Clements' demonstration that crop size in the two areas could relate inversely with respect to nitrogen content. In addition, on the basis of the N index, the best possible harvest time could be predicted for high-nitrogen crops which otherwise would have little chance to mature during periods of high temperature and rainfall.

Over the years, the N index was substantiated and perfected. Distinction was made between the nitrogen index (NI), which had referred to leaf nitrogen content as a percentage of the dry weight, and the *normal nitrogen index* (NN) which incorporates in its determining equation the values of sheath moisture (M) and age (A) for crops having outstanding yields over a period of years (344). Clements (341) and Clements *et al.* (342) further examined the effects of various ecological factors on leaf nitrogen content. From data presented in Table 11-4 it was evident that moisture, temperature, and age all affected foliar nitrogen levels. From this it was correctly concluded that, within normal ranges of nitrogen fertilization, there would be found differing con-

TABLE 11-4

PARTIAL REGRESSIONS FOR SEVERAL FACTORS AFFECTING LEAF NITROGEN (n = 1373)

Reproduced by permission of Dr. H.F. Clements (341).

Factor	Beta	"t" value
Sheath moisture	+0.6334	29.49*
Age	−0.2932	14.28*
Minimum temperature (°F)	−0.1262	7.06*
Maximum temperature (°F)	+0.0858	4.43*
Soil moisture	−0.0570	3.55*
Light	+0.0126	0.65
	R = 0.832	

*"t" values significant at the 5% level.

centrations of leaf nitrogen which varied on the basis of local ecological differences alone. However, since these differences appear not only in leaves but also reflect changes in the entire plant, this apparent shortcoming of nitrogen analysis became the basis for standardization as correction was made for characteristic nitrogen levels within each locality. Thus, in Puerto Rico, Samuels and Bangdiwala (1284) were able to "correct" differences in leaf nitrogen content among different plots on the basis of extenuating moisture and age data. This resulted in markedly increased precision of the nitrogen index.

In 1957 Clements (344) published findings with four varieties grown with and without irrigation at 15 locations on the islands of Oahu, Kauai, Maui, and Hawaii. Certain crop log data were submitted to multiple regression analyses. Partial regressions on leaf nitrogen were evaluated for solar radiation, temperature (maximum and minimum), the primary index, sheath moisture, and age. These studies revealed that the foliar nitrogen level is most consistently relevant to sheath moisture and age. Sunlight gave the least effect upon nitrogen content. Sheath moisture and age were the most critical factors regardless of whether the crops were irrigated or nonirrigated. However, it was shown that when data from the two moisture regimes were combined for the overall island ecology, it was necessary to include temperature data in order to obtain the most satisfactory coefficient of determination. Both the normal- and standard-nitrogen concepts were shown to be applicable under experimental conditions, with normal nitrogen being the most suitable to plantation conditions.

C. *The moisture index*

More than three decades ago Wadsworth (1515) proposed the use of hand refractometers, which measure changes in the refractive index of sampled cane juice, for measuring changes of water per unit mass of sugar. To the extent that the sugar stored within a specific internode is not subject to large diurnal variations, the refractometer was regarded as an adequate instrument for determining moisture in the sugarcane stalk.

Early in the 1940's Clements and Kubota (335) attempted to develop a moisture index to serve as a cultural guide wherever water control was possible through irrigation. By seeking a suitable index tissue they hoped to bypass the more elaborate transpirational measurements involving numerous soil, plant, and atmospheric factors. In effect, advantage was again being taken of the sugarcane plant's sensitivity to its environment. The moisture index approach was "...based on the simple hypothesis that the moisture level of a crop at any one time is the result of the interplay of all internal and external factors affecting the water relations of the plant as integrated by the plant itself. In this, all of the difficult and complicated calculations involved in the first (transpirational) approach are taken care of by the plant".

After examining data from eight crops at Waipo and Kailua (Oahu), Clements concluded that the most satisfactory tissue for a moisture index was the sheath from elongating leaves. Close correlations were found between the sheath moisture content on one hand, and moisture levels of the elongating internodes, the mature stalk, and the entire green top. By constructing appropriate graphs based upon sheath moisture values it was possible to predict with acceptable precision the actual moisture values of other plant parts. Clements had thus established the validity of "sheath percent moisture" as a parameter for ascertaining the practical irrigation requirements of a cane crop. The moisture index has also been useful in estimating the readiness of sugarcane for harvest.

Many examples could be given to show that the moisture index, as an integration of physiological activity, is not all that it was hoped to be. As a case in point, the author recently observed that sheath moisture decline was about identical for both flooded and water-deficient plants grown in sand culture (55). In this instance the moisture index offered a single explanation for two distinct kinds of physiological events, *i.e.*, senescence due to lack of water and senescence due to anaerobiosis. Moreover, the index is highly insensitive to forced chemical desiccation of the leaf blades (47). On the other hand, the practical usefulness of the moisture index in many regions over a period of many years is proof that Clements' view is empirically correct in theory and practice.

D. *The K and K–H_2O indexes*

The selection of a potassium index tissue posed a considerable problem because a number of tissues showed initial promise in this respect. Clements (343) regarded each of the following as being potentially suitable: Young leaf blades (leaves $^+3$ to $^+6$), young leaf sheaths (sheaths +3 to +6), mature leaf blades (leaf +7 and older), and mature leaf sheaths (sheath +7 and older). Potassium-content data were obtained for each of the four tissues from crops having a wide range of ages and growing conditions. Regression coefficients and statistical significance of the potassium values were determined. The tissue found to have the highest potassium correlation with the whole plant, green top, meristem, and mature stalks was the young sheath (Table 11-5).

TABLE 11-5

CORRELATIONS OF POTENTIAL POTASSIUM INDEX TISSUES WITH DIFFERENT PARTS OF THE SUGARCANE PLANT

[After Clements (343).] Reproduced by permission of *I.S.S.C.T.*

Possible index tissues	Different plant parts			
	Whole plant	Green top	Immature stalk	Mature stalk
Young blades	2.41*	8.52**	3.98**	3.41**
Old blades	2.06**	6.68**	3.87**	2.25*
Young sheaths	4.27**	8.39**	10.13**	5.35**
K index	5.12**	9.97**	9.47**	6.17**
Old sheaths	0.69	6.38**	4.43**	1.27

*"t" values significant at the 5% level.
**"t" values significant at the 1% level.

Clements also observed that the potassium correlations gained additional precision when based on sugar-free dry weight rather than total dry weight. The potassium index was therefore established as the potassium content of young sheaths expressed as a percentage of the sugar-free dry weight.

Since the potassium index varied from 0.17 to 5.10 percent among different plantations, field experiments were conducted with applied K_2O to ascertain the minimum level which would meet normal growth and development needs (343, 346). Initial experiments in which K_2O varied from 0 to 300 pounds per acre showed a marked sensitivity of the index to applied potassium, and that the minimum potassium index value corresponding to normal growth lies within the range of 1.84 to 2.92 percent (343). By use of factorial experiments in fields where both K and P were low, Clements tentatively concluded that the minimum potassium value needed by the plant was about 2.14. With similar experiments Clements (343) eventually arrived at a minimum potassium index value of 2.25[4]. In Puerto Rico, Samuels and Landrau (1283) obtained a slightly lower index value using elongating leaf blades. They recommended a flexible range in which a potassium value of 1.70 or less indicated a need for potassium, and 1.90 or more indicated no need.

[4]The minimum phosphorus index value established at this time was 0.080.

Clements (343) observed that applied potassium produced a rise in the moisture index (Table 11-6). Growth was increased by higher potassium applications, and this in

TABLE 11-6

POTASSIUM FERTILIZATION EFFECTS ON THE MOISTURE INDEX, PRIMARY INDEX, POTASSIUM INDEX, AND GROWTH OF SUGARCANE UNDER HAWAIIAN CONDITIONS

[After Clements (343).] Reproduced by permission of *I.S.S.C.T.*

Plots	K_2O (lbs/acre)	Moisture index	Primary index	K index	Growth
A*	55	81.8	13.3	1.87	5.59
B	100	82.8	10.8	2.92	6.02
C	200	83.0	10.8	3.02	5.97
D	300	83.2	10.1	3.28	6.08

*The "A" plot of each category is significantly different from all other plots within the category.

turn depressed the primary index while having no significant effect on the nitrogen index. Samuels and Landrau also noted that their indices were affected by rainfall, and possibly by light and temperature variations, during the growth period. Corrections were made for the additional moisture by use of rainfall records. It was found that for every 10 inches of rain falling between the time of leaf sampling and harvest, both nitrogen and potassium would increase by characteristic values. The latter were then used to adjust the indices along a common moisture basis. Samuels and his associates eventually abandoned the use of rainfall data and chose instead the moisture index which is easily obtained at the same time that tissues are sampled for other analyses.

Evans (508) has described a *potassium partition index* which is based upon two ratios: (A) The ratio of potassium content between leaf lamina and midrib, and (B) the ratio of total lamina dry matter to total midrib dry matter. This index takes into account the temporary potassium storage capacity of the midrib. A computed B/A ratio value (partition coefficient) greater than 1.0 indicates that the lamina is drawing preferentially upon potassium reserves, and if the value is less than 1.0 the midrib is preferentially retaining the element. Evans further stated that a partition coefficient higher than 1.0 (1.1 to 1.3) tends to appear in times of potassium deficiency, and values less than 1.0 (0.6 to 0.8) are common when potassium is abundant. It appears that the partitioning effect between midrib and lamina is unique with potassium among the major nutrients. In view of the midrib's central importance in sucrose transport (667, 692), and of suspected potassium roles in sugar movement (293), a relationship might possibly exist between the potassium localization and the translocation of freshly-formed photosynthate.

Samuels (1293, p. 202) has shown that sheath moisture changes can be correlated with leaf potassium and nitrogen contents. An increase in one is accompanied by an increase in the other. Clements (341) suggested that the nitrogen index is so closely related to the moisture index that nitrogen content can be estimated accurately on the basis of moisture levels.

With respect to the potassium–moisture relationship, Clements (346) took a novel approach by reporting sheath potassium as a K-percent sheath-tissue moisture index (the K–H_2O index). A need for the K–H_2O index stems from the fact that the potassium index proper is a reliable guide to potassium fertilization only when moisture regimes are relatively normal. During periods of drought or inadequate irrigation, or when excessively cloudy and wet conditions keep tissue moisture levels high, the potassium index may not be sufficiently consistent to serve as a reliable guide. In reporting sheath potassium on a tissue-moisture basis Clements was fully aware that potassium is soluble in the cell sap. The effect of moisture correction by the K–H_2O index was to reveal the truly high or low potassium levels at close to their actual values, rather than as near-normal values as the potassium index tends to do.

Evans (508), in Guyana, has used successfully a leaf K–H_2O index based upon the concentration of potassium in the leaf moisture. Thus, for a *top visible dewlap* leaf (T.V.D. leaf) having an adequate potassium content of 1.25 and a leaf moisture value of 72 percent, the leaf K–H_2O index value (required level of K aq.) would be 0.49 percent. Evans states that the leaf K–H_2O index is not an empirical correction for drought; rather, it is a relationship of an aqueous phase potassium concentration to the changes in leaf moisture content. The accuracy with which leaf moisture determinations are performed is particularly important since the final evaluation of potassium status rests heavily upon this parameter.

In 1970 Clements published crop logging studies relating to the nitrogen and potassium (K_2O) requirements of two varieties grown on the humid Hilo Coast (359). In essence the work substantiated nitrogen and potassium fertilization practices generally accepted for the Hawaiian 2-year crop, and in addition implied that even the highest fertilizer levels, more than adequate for quality, may have been insufficient for maximum yield. Up to 600 lbs/acre nitrogen and 750 lbs/acre potassium were used. Only small yield differences were obtained between varieties (*H. 53-263* and *H. 54-775*), and no proof was found that critical fertilizer ranges differ among varieties.

According to the crop log data, high values for the leaf nitrogen index were accompanied by low K–H_2O values, and an inverse relationship developed as nitrogen content diminished (359). Clements proposed correcting the low nitrogen–high potassium indexes by increased nitrogen supply, rather than withholding potassium, with a view toward maximum cane quality. Conversely, the proposed correction for high nitrogen–low potassium relationships was potassium fertilization, a treatment having the prospect of lowering foliar nitrogen. Among the secondary effects were nitrogen repression of K–H_2O values, increased tissue moisture by both macronutrients, a high sensitivity of the primary index to potassium, and significant tissue calcium responses to nitrogen (increased Ca) and to potassium (depressed Ca).

Clements further concluded that increased attention to crop fertilizer needs (by way of crop logging) and additional research on fertilization intensity for cane is warranted.

E. *Crop log ripening*

In 1948 Clements *et al.* (340) published a brief account of crop log techniques being used to guide ripening control in Hawaii. May and June are regarded in Hawaii as the best months for cane ripening (345), with early spring months giving somewhat less quality and fall months being the poorest of the year. Because Hawaiian sugarcane

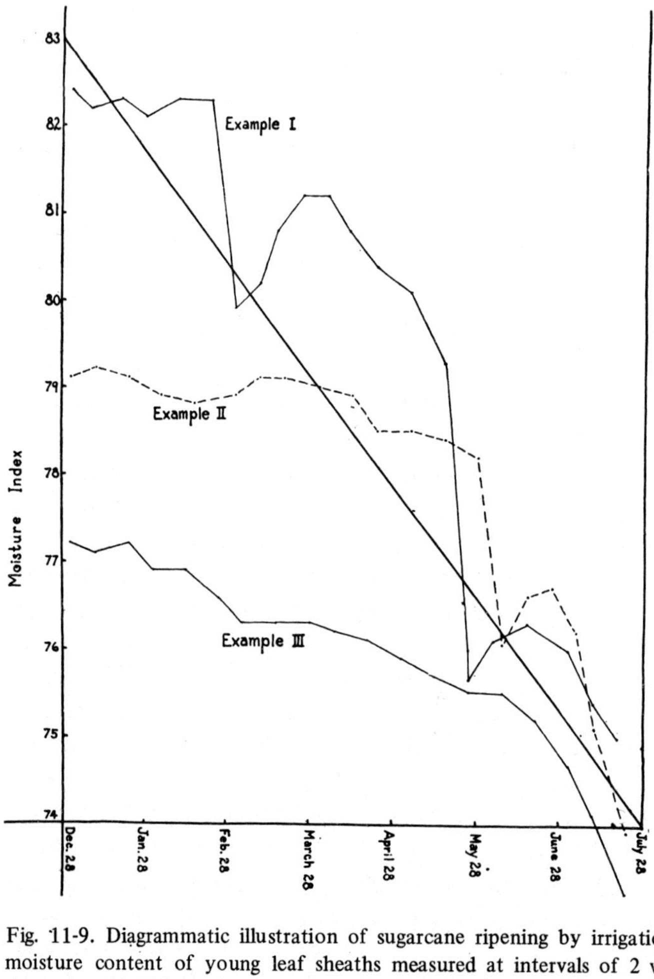

Fig. 11-9. Diagrammatic illustration of sugarcane ripening by irrigation control based upon the moisture content of young leaf sheaths measured at intervals of 2 weeks. Three examples are shown in which the moisture index is used to determine the time at which to begin ripening during the final 7-month period ending on the harvest date scheduled in the crop's cultural program. [After Clements *et al.* (340).] Reproduced by permission of the *Agricultural Experiment Station, University of Hawaii.*

is harvested throughout most of the year, ripening control can pose a definite problem for plantation managers. Clements studied a large amount of crop log data obtained from irrigated crops and drew three fundamental conclusions relating crop quality to moisture status: (a) Good quality is paralleled by final moisture index values in the order of 73 to 74 percent; (b) the final moisture index value in good quality crops is approached gradually over a period of several months; (c) quality of the harvested crop is affected by the moisture status extant throughout the growth of that crop. The third conclusion was based on the fact that sugarcane kept succulent between germination and ripening would not ripen as well as sugarcane grown partially dry.

The crop logging procedure adopted for ripening control began with inspection of the crop 7 months prior to the scheduled harvest, at which time initial sheath samples were taken for percent-moisture determination. Crop logging ordinarily involves sample harvests at 5-week intervals, but when the ripening log begins samples are taken 1 or 2 weeks apart. Clements estimated the time at which to begin ripening control by use of a moisture index scale plotted against time (the 7-month period ending at the scheduled harvest date) as shown in Fig. 11-9. In this illustration moisture logs are shown for three distinct situations, that is, for crops given high, low, and intermediate moisture supply during their growth history. The diagonal line between the highest moisture level (83 percent) and harvest date (July 28) was employed by Clements as an irrigation guide which established that no water would be applied until sheath moisture values dropped below the level shown by the line.

The first example given in Fig. 11-9 represented an unusually succulent crop whose high moisture values (over 82 percent) indicated that a long ripening period would be required. Irrigation was suspended until March 2 when the moisture index declined below 80 percent. Irrigation water was applied, the percent moisture values rose above the diagonal line, and they remained above this line until May 18. Irrigation was again performed and the crop went into its final ripening period before harvest. It should be noted that, upon irrigation, the moisture values rose but did not achieve their former levels.

Examples II and III represent crops having intermediate and low moisture values, respectively, at the initial index reading 7 months before harvest. These values reflect intermediate and dry conditions experienced by the crops during their growth histories. Each crop, but especially Example III, required much less ripening than the first crop. Normal irrigation was therefore maintained for both until their sheath moisture values intercepted the diagonal line. For Example II this occurred on April 2; water was then withheld, and irrigation was not again performed until June 8, when the final water application was made and the crop entered its closing phase.

For Example III the moisture index values never intercepted the diagonal line owing to the crop's dry environment. Since this cane had literally ripened while it was growing, the plantation manager stood to gain by promoting growth rather than ripening. Irrigation was therefore continued for as long as possible, being suspended only some

40 days before harvest. Clements made note of the fact that this crop remained under partial influence of its low-moisture history and continued to show moisture decline in spite of continued irrigation. Of course, had there been no crop log to serve as a guide, the grower stood to lose tonnage, and hence sugar, by withholding irrigation at an earlier date.

F. *Crop logging vs. analyses of 8–10 tissues and soils*

Cultural guides based on some kind of tissue-analysis program are gaining acceptance throughout most of the sugarcane-growing world. However, there has not been complete agreement as to the choice of tissue indices nor to the meaning of their changing values. Years after Clements formulated the crop log concept, Burr and his co-workers at the Experiment Station, H.S.P.A., Honolulu, developed the "stalk log" technique (157–159). Their method involved growing sugarcane with normal and deficient levels of each macronutrient, sectioning the plant at intervals, and analyzing each part in order to determine the most "sensitive" indicator tissue, *i.e.*, that tissue showing compositional differences of the greatest magnitude between the two nutritional regimes. They found that storage tissues which had recently completed their development were the most satisfactory; specifically, storage tissues centrally situated within those internodes subtended by leaves $^{+}8$, $^{+}9$, and $^{+}10$ were taken as the standard or "8–10" index tissue. These internodes have also proven to be good indicators of moisture status. On the other hand, Evans (508) maintains that mineral storage in stalks is a distinctly varietal feature, and that removal of central internode slices for analysis does not take into account the variable contents between node and internode (505).

As a source of indicative nutritional information, workers in Hawaii (157, 662, 273, 761) have implied a preference for 8–10 tissue analyses over foliar analyses. In particular, a more sensitive measure of the crop's nitrogen requirements has been claimed for 8–10 analyses when soil nitrogen is at near-sufficient levels (157). Data published by Humbert (761) indicates that 8–10 tissue analyses can reflect with sensitivity changing relationships among water, potassium, nitrogen, reducing sugar, and sucrose parameters. Hartt (662) has shown that, under Hawaiian conditions, an 8–10 phosphorus content exceeding 0.04 percent precludes further yield increases from phosphorus fertilization. Burr has described the 8–10 tissue as ". . .an excellent index to determine by analysis the stage of cane maturity" (273). In Puerto Rico, 8–10 stalk tissue has also been shown to be a suitable indicator for maturity studies (208). Moreover, the experiments by Bonnet have shown a considerable sensitivitv of K/N ratio values obtained from 8–10 stalk tissues.

Baver (157) has claimed a superiority of 8–10 tissue analyses over those of the earlier crop log tissues. He has also claimed that, in the instances of phosphorus and potassium, Truog's soil analyses were superior to tissue analyses. However, Clements

(351) took issue with these claims and defended both the sensitivity and reliability of the crop log as compared with 8–10 tissue analyses. Clements also presented evidence to show that soil analyses have not always given the grower a fair appraisal of crop needs, and in some instances ". . .have so blinded cane growers to the fertilizer needs of their crops that serious problems have existed of which they were not even aware".

Clements' work has always been characterized by a strong awareness of the sugarcane plant as a complex physiological entity. The tissue indexes, crop log theory, and successful crop log methodology are so orientated as to benefit the grower, but all of this is based upon fundamental physiological considerations. Nowhere in Clements' work is there any sign of his having abandoned the view that sugarcane is a remarkable product and integrator of its environment. Oddly enough, the historical literature of sugarcane reveals very few individuals who have possessed so clear a picture of the total plant, or who have retained this picture after they have become involved professionally with some aspect of sugarcane research or production.

G. *Growth and yield equations*

For more than a century various authors have attempted to explain the responses of plants to their ecology in terms of equations which accommodate the salient factors controlling plant growth. Clements *et al.* (342) describe two theories which underlie most of the historical work: (a) The *chemical* theory, postulating ". . .that the chemical composition of the substrate largely determines the species which will grow upon it"; and (b) the *physiographic* theory, holding that physiographic conditions rather than soil factors largely determine the behavior of a given species within a given region. The early theory of Liebig (941), which maintained that plant growth occurs in direct proportion to the supply of some minimum nutrient, retains much appeal to the present day, although its limitations have been pointed up by the studies of Mitscherlich (1027), Le Clerc (910), Shaw and Walters (1320), and others [reviewed by Clements *et al.* (342)].

Clements and his colleagues in Hawaii developed a number of growth formulas for sugarcane which recognize and try to accommodate interrelating features of cane morphology, physiology, and ecology. For example, the growth "prediction" equation

$$E = 1.2192\,X_1 - 0.0700\,X_2 + 6.0962\,X_3 + 1.0636\,X_4 - 2.2142\,X_5 + 2.3971\,X_6 + 3.4414\,X_7 + 0.0735\,X_8 - 1018.4475$$

essentially incorporates factors of crop age, sheath moisture, daily relative humidity, wind velocity, maximum and minimum temperatures, and daily solar radiation. Since all of this information is obtainable with the crop log, the grower using the crop log might view such equations as convenient means of integrating data; otherwise, this method would be prohibitively cumbersome for occasional application.

Another type of formula, the yield equation, attempts to define by mathematical means the most economic quantities of fertilizers needed to obtain a maximum yield response for a given set of conditions. An underlying thesis motivating the search for this equation is the recognition that soils cannot always supply adequate nutrients and the grower has only limited resources to expend toward supplementary fertilization. Capó (299) points out that the equation's usefulness is critically dependent upon its precision in estimating crop response to applied fertilizers, *i.e.*, "... the closeness with which the yield values estimated by the use of the formula approximate the yield values actually obtained with varying fertilizer levels". Many yield equations have been proposed [reviewed by Capó (299, 298)], of which the equation of the straight line and Law of Mass Action are probably the best known among plant physiologists. None appears to have retained sufficient precision when extended beyond the limited data available to the individual investigators (299).

Following many years of work relative to crop yield formulas (295, 296), Capó (299) proposed in 1965 a "new" fertilizer–yield equation developed with sugarcane growth data gathered in Puerto Rico. This equation has shown a high degree of precision in estimating sugarcane or corn response to nitrogen and potassium (299, 298), and to phosphorus, calcium, and magnesium (298). The equation is succinctly given as

$$Y = \frac{A}{1 + B(X - C)^2}$$

where Y is the crop yield, X is the quantity of fertilizer applied, and A, B, and C are parameters (A = maximum yield, C = a given nutrient in its best possible balance with all other growth factors). In fitting this equation to a set of data, Capó attempts to estimate in a simplified manner approximate parameter values and to correct the approximate values by multiple regression calculations. The obvious absence of ecological–physiological parameters (which in effect are incorporated within the value of Y) appears to lend added importance to the correction steps, and is best justified by the equation's ultimate precision. At least under Puerto Rico conditions, the applicability of this formula is increasingly substantiated (298).

9. MATURATION EFFECTS OF PHOTOPERIOD, DAILY TEMPERATURE, AND SEASONAL TEMPERATURE

Employing controlled-environment facilities at the David North Plant Research Centre, Brisbane, Glasziou and his co-workers (587) studied the main effects and interactions of 24-hour temperature, photoperiod duration, and thermoperiodicity on sugarcane. The salient features of their results included the following: (a) Additive effects of day and night temperatures were obtained for about 3 months, with complex interactions being evident at 6 months. (b) Maximum dry matter production, sugar production per plant, and sugar concentration in the stalk were all achieved at 30 °C. (c) Relatively low sugar production (up to 12 percent of the green weight) was obtained when temperature was held constant or when varied only on a daily basis. Relatively high sugar levels were produced (up to 17 percent of the green weight) when temperature was varied on a long-term basis by moving plants from high temperature to low temperature. (d) Sugar losses accrued when plants were moved from low temperature to high temperature.

This work was prompted by the fact that cane yield responses to temperature are not always consistent with the view that high average temperatures produce high cane tonnage but poor cane quality (1475). The minimum temperature needed for sugarcane growth has been placed at 15.6 °C by Verret and Das (1492) and at 12.2 °C by Ryker and Edgerton (1266). The question of average temperature *vs.* mean high and mean low temperatures is also of prime consideration. Among sugarcane-growing regions temperature extremes tend to increase with distance from the equator and to diminish as one approaches the equator. The same can be said of photoperiod in that longer days tend to have higher temperatures. In all instances rainfall must be reckoned as a complicating factor.

From the preceding sections on crop logging we have seen that sugarcane maturity, as a function of age, nitrogen status, and moisture status will complicate enormously the yield responses to light and temperature. Season, soil temperature, and air temperature all cause significant changes in the N index under field conditions[5] (118, 341). Sun and Chow (1388) in Taiwan, and Clements *et al.* (342) found positive relationships between growth rate and the monthly means for high and low temperatures. Borden (213) attributes to age the decreased response to ecological factors at later stages of development. Shaw (1321) interprets sucrose contents as a function of latitude and claims that peak values will be achieved at 18° north and 18° south latitude. By this view the primary factor is photoperiod rather than temperature.

On the other hand, sugarcane is readily grown on Iran's Khuzestan plain, some 30° to 33° north latitude, at high summer temperatures yielding greater tonnages than Louisiana and Florida (1389). Winter frosts are common and there are occasional severe freezes. Under these conditions sugarcane growth proceeds at an average temperature of 15.6 °C and ripening improves after mid-October so long as the minimum temperature remains above 2.5 °C. The limiting growth factor here is definitely temperature rather than sunlight (1389). In Puerto Rico, Lugo-López and Capó (963) found that cool night temperatures with relatively broad ranges between maximum and minimum values increased sucrose yields more than other climatic factors. Samuels (1291) describes cool temperature as a major factor in sugarcane ripening.

---

[5] Baver, L.D. and Humbert, R.P., 1956. Status of crop control in Hawaii, *Proc. Int. Soc. Sugar Cane Technol.* 9: 175–194.

Phytotron facilities such as those at Brisbane (587) and the controlled climate houses at the Experiment Station, H.S.P.A., Honolulu (245), constitute the primary means by which climatic factors have been studied as precisely-controlled variables in sugarcane growth and development. Even so, the sugarcane environment is greatly compromised by our best efforts to simulate natural field conditions. At constant temperature the interplay between climate, soil, and maturity can hardly be a natural one. Baver (159), for example, has shown that lowering temperature markedly restricts the uptake of nitrogen. Although data obtained by these means are perhaps applicable only to the theory of cane response to its natural environment, this is quite sufficient for a multitude of research purposes.

Glasziou *et al.* (587) performed their work under two broad sets of conditions: (a) Five day temperatures and five night temperatures, varied at 12-hour intervals, were provided in which the temperature treatments (18, 22, 26, 30 and 34 °C) were given in all combinations. Plants were grown in vermiculite with constant water and nutrient supplies. Treatments were effected by exchanging the plants among appropriate chambers. Harvests were made at 106 and 209 days. At 290 days a third harvest was made for plants maintained at constant temperature. (b) The second set of conditions included all combinations of three day temperatures and three night temperatures (22, 26, and 30 °C) with either 8- or 12-hour photoperiods given from 8:00 a.m. to 4:00 p.m., or from 6:00 a.m. to 6:00 p.m. Temperature changes were made on 8/16 or 12/12 hourly cycles with changes at 8:00 a.m. and 4:00 p.m., or 6:00 a.m. and 6:00 p.m., respectively. Plants were harvested after 200 days of treatment. There were four replicates of each treatment under both sets of conditions.

Results from these studies underscored four important concepts relating photoperiod and temperature to the fate of sucrose in sugarcane. First, under natural

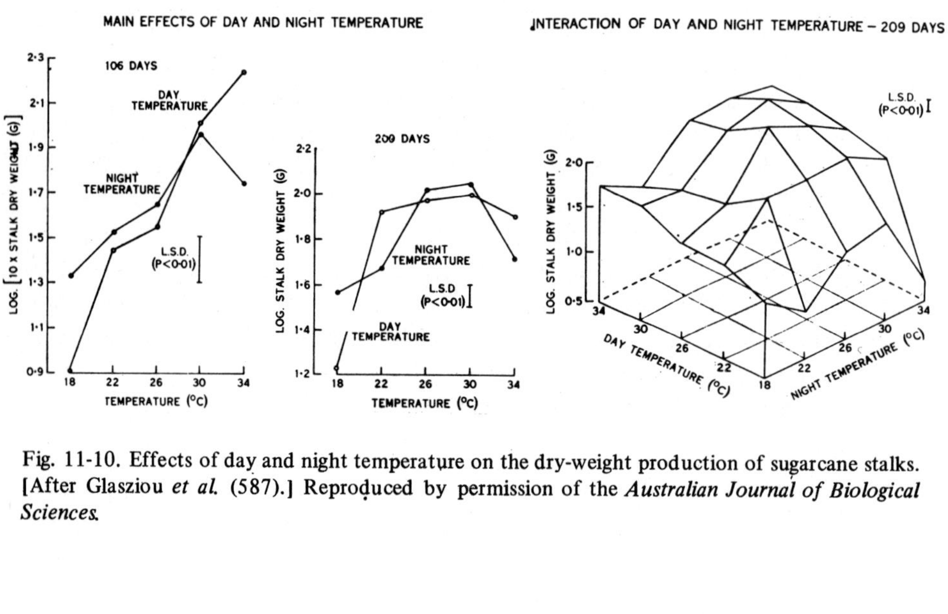

Fig. 11-10. Effects of day and night temperature on the dry-weight production of sugarcane stalks. [After Glasziou *et al.* (587).] Reproduced by permission of the *Australian Journal of Biological Sciences.*

photoperiod, sugarcane was shown to make its best growth under constant-temperature regimes rather than with changing day- and night-temperature regimes. Data for dry weight of stalks presented in Fig. 11-10 reveal no important interactions arising from 12-hour day- and night-temperature changes. After 3 months several interactions were obtained but these were related in part to positive responses gained from the constant-temperature regimes. Sugarcane appeared to lack the distinct photoperiodicity requirements noted by Went (1559) and others in many plant species. On the other hand, this is consistent with sugarcane's theoretical evolution on the coastal areas of New Guinea (230), where but slight seasonal temperature variations are found, temperatures rarely rise above 34 °C or fall below 22 °C, and day length is virtually constant throughout the year (587). Significantly, much of the constant-temperature effect was lost when photoperiod was shortened to 8 hours.

Second, during the "early adult" stage of growth, the rate of stalk development approached a constant value independent of temperature, but during the maturation or "late adult" stages the rate of stalk development declined. From Fig. 11-11 it can

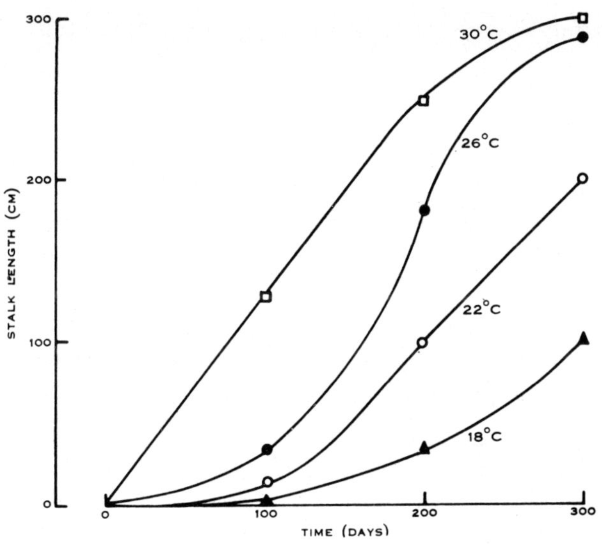

Fig. 11-11. Time course for growth of sugarcane stalks under conditions of constant temperature. [After Glasziou *et al.* (587).] Reproduced by permission of the *Australian Journal of Biological Sciences.*

be seen that, between 200 and 300 days, the growth rate of stalks was comparable at 22 and 30 °C; however, as the plants aged there was a shift downward in the temperature level needed for optimum growth (Figs. 11-10 and 11-11). In support of these trends the following stalk growth ratios between 18 and 30 °C were cited: 0.034 for the initial 106-day interval, 0.230 for the next 103 days, and 1.09 during the subsequent 81 days (587). It was concluded that the cane plant follows a chronological rather than physiological time scale in making the growth changes.

Third, under conditions of constant-temperature and photoperiod regimes throughout the growth period, environments producing the greatest dry matter production likewise gave the greatest quantity of sugar per plant and the highest sugar content on a dry-weight basis. Such a relationship between non-sugar dry weight and sucrose was perhaps recognized, if only intuitively, by earlier workers developing the tissue indices (337, 344, 346). This does not contribute to the theory that maximum sugar accumulation should occur in conjuction with a minimum of fiber production (258).

It was also observed that maximum sucrose content did not exceed about 12 percent of the fresh weight at a constant temperature of 30 °C, or at lower temperatures held constant, or with combinations of high day plus low night temperatures or low day plus high night temperatures. However, field-grown plants removed to a controlled 17 °C environment increased their sugar content from 10 to 17 percent of the green weight (Fig. 11-12). The increase required about 90 days. Removal of some

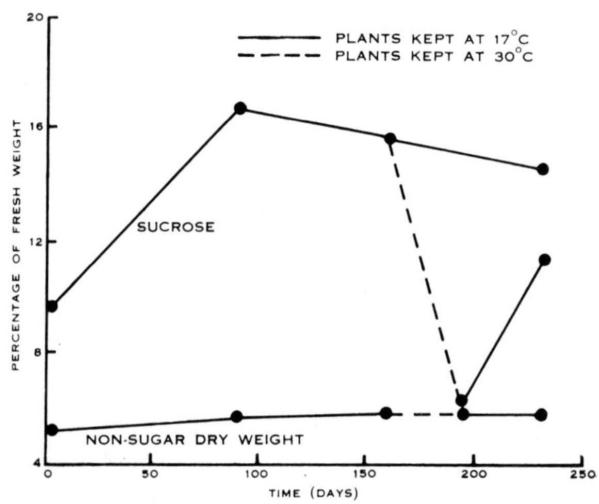

Fig. 11-12. Changes in the sugar contents of sugarcane stalks in response to long-term changes in temperature for growth. Four-month-old plants were transferred from the field to a constant-temperature greenhouse maintained at 17 °C. The latter temperature was held constant for 160 days, after which some plants were given 35 °C for 35 days and then returned to 17 °C. [After Glasziou *et al.* (587).] Reproduced by permission of the *Australian Journal of Biological Sciences.*

plants to a constant 30 °C environment led to relatively abrupt sugar losses over a 35-day period. This was paralleled by resumption of rapid stalk growth. Upon return once more to 17 °C the growth slackened and sugar accumulation resumed once again. Brodie *et al.* (245) also reported a positive cool temperature effect, with higher sucrose concentrations occurring at about 62 °F than at 72 °F of constant temperature.

On the basis of these results Glasziou *et al.* (587) discounted the belief that short-term or diurnal fluctuations in temperature are inducive to sugar storage "except that they be accompanied by an overall long-term change in average temperature akin to the seasonal variations experienced under field conditions". By this view, Shaw's (1321) designation of 18° north and south latitude for optimal sugar production relies upon a favorable combination of seasonal temperature and day-length variables. Temperature variations might be too small nearer the equator, and at greater distances the winter photoperiods might be too short. These interpretations by Glasziou and his colleagues do not support the belief that cool nights promote sugar storage in cane (963), whereas they lend indirect support to Clements' (334, 337) earlier conclusions at Oahu purporting that the long-term levels of solar radiation set the upper limits of sugar potential.

The picture will become clearer when controlled-environment data are contributed from other areas having different natural photoperiods. Queensland, after all, is one of the most productive areas in the world with respect to cane quality. As shown by the work of Brodie *et al.* (245), the varietal factor can also affect cane response to constant temperature. Innes and Shaw (774) reported that significant changes in the N index associated with time of cane planting were more clearly attributable to relative growth at the time of sampling than to mean temperature or photoperiod. In practical terms, the yield of a sugarcane crop may always be governed as much by the use made of varietal, moisture, and nutritional alternatives open to the grower as by the upper potential defined by ecological factors.

Chapter 12

Chemical Ripening and Sucrose Control

1. INTRODUCTION

In the previous chapter we saw that ripening follows naturally upon the depletion of soil moisture and nutrients – events which restrict further growth without appreciably restricting photosynthesis. In this context ripening closely parallels the process of aging and maturation without quite becoming synonymous with either. Where crop logging is practised the producer can manipulate ripening on the basis of current moisture and nutritional information. In these instances the sugar grower can improve upon natural ripening to the extent that he exercises a judicious control over water and nutrient supplies. However, because such control is not everywhere possible, and because much is left to be desired even where it is, a widespread interest has developed in the use of chemicals to induce ripening, to increase ripening, or to synchronize ripening in accordance with harvest schedules.

The search for chemical ripeners has continued for two decades with only limited success. "Promising" compounds appear in screening programs and a few receive extensive field evaluation, but not a single ripening agent has come into general use throughout the sugarcane world. Several reasons for this are readily apparent. Foremost is the fact that the sugarcane plant is a far more complex entity than anyone had imagined. When one considers that incubated tissue discs are not consistent in storing sugar, it is remarkable that intact field populations respond to chemical ripeners at all. A second reason is the failure to distinguish between the chemical's physiological potential on one hand and the producer's field technology on the other. Failure to produce ripening might as easily be blamed on inadequate application as upon inactivity of the chemical, but strangely enough it almost never is. A possible third factor has been the misuse or disuse of crop log information *at the screening level.* One must recognize that maturation is approached by degrees, by subtle shifting of many growth and storage processes. In this context it is clear that at times sugarcane may be highly responsive to chemical activity whereas at other times it is insensitive owing to an unfavorable physiological status. In essence, a given field of sugarcane may never respond to chemical ripeners unless treated under highly specific conditions of nitrogen and moisture supply.

Efforts to improve cane quality with chemicals have progressed along three general lines:. (a) Direct ripening by treatment of standing cane shortly before harvest; (b) removal of trash; and (c) sugar retention by postharvest deterioration control. The object in each case is to improve cane quality as quality is understood in the factory. In this sense the removal of trash can lead to improved sucrose recovery in the factory without materially affecting the sucrose content of the ripening stalk. This subject is treated at length in Chapter 13 (chemical desiccation). Scientists and growers have paid but little attention to the third category. Oddly enough, experiments designed to test a chemical's ripening potential seldom "follow through" to observe its quality-retaining capacity in cut cane. The problem of postharvest deterioration is in itself a matter of enormous importance and is treated separately in Chapter 15. The present chapter is concerned with quality improvement in the field via chemically-increased sucrose accumulation within the maturing stalk.

2. EARLY CONCEPTS OF ARTIFICIAL RIPENING

A. *Cultural ripening*

Recognizing that reduced growth was usually followed by increased sucrose, early workers tried to induce "artificial" ripening by restricting growth with various means at hand. Eckart (468), in 1913, attempted to increase maturity by cultivating between the rows of ripening cane. The objective was to restrict growth by root pruning, but his results were negative. Other workers advocated the stripping of cane to increase sucrose content by admitting air and light between rows. However, Das (409) and Eckart (467) claimed that stripping had but little effect on the cane, and Van Deventer (1474) reported that it lowered cane yield and quality.

Lodged or fallen cane has been looked upon as qualitatively inferior except in Hawaii where the plants are not expected to remain erect throughout the 2-year cultural period. According to Das (409, p.175), sugarcane in India was tied or supported by artificial barriers to prevent quality losses. As early as 1928 workers in Hawaii (1493) suggested that the addition of final molasses to the last irrigation treatment should promote ripening by withdrawal of nitrogen through microbial action. Das (409) proposed in 1931 that ripening might be increased by "stimulating" the enzymes involved. In this context he was not only taking a prophetic stand, but he was also proposing the much more difficult task of enzymatically increasing sucrose synthesis rather than simply retarding enzymes which degrade sucrose.

Until quite recently ripening has not been approached from the standpoint of chemical effects upon an intact source-to-sink system. Hence, little work is recorded relative to photosynthesis stimulation, more efficient loading of conducting tissue, more effective transport, more efficient accumulation and retention of sucrose at the sink areas, or control of the various invertases in storage tissues.

B. *Ripening with molasses*

In 1954, Sen (1314) reported that applications of 10-percent molasses solution to sugarcane foliage produced significant improvement in juice quality. The molasses was given in three increments equivalent to 10 pounds per acre during the rapid-growth phase of 3- to 5-month-old plants. This substantiated the work of Alvarer and Alaherlaha (64) who found that spray applications of final molasses given at the rate of 18 pounds per acre increased pol values by 2.0 percent. In a later study, Sen (1315) applied foliar molasses in concentrations ranging from 5 to 20 percent at five intervals between May and November. Leaf analyses revealed higher glucose and sucrose contents associated with molasses treatments but no significant differences were found between the molasses concentrations. The sucrose increase was about 1.0 percent over control values. Significant pol value increases were also obtained. The author concluded that foliar molasses applied repeatedly throughout the growing season might significantly improve cane quality.

In 1957 Yates and Bates (1601) summarized ripening experiments in British Guiana where final molasses was tested at rates of 1 to 8 tons per acre. One to three tons per acre in irrigation water produced no significant quality increases. In another experiment 4 tons of molasses per acre significantly improved quality at 18 days, while 2 and 8 tons gave lesser increases which were not statistically significant. Small sucrose increases were also obtained in a third experiment involving 2, 4, and 8 tons of molasses per acre applied in irrigation water. The largest increase was produced by the 8 tons per acre treatment which yielded a sucrose percent cane increase of 1.07. This was not statistically significant. Foliar molasses treatments also failed to increase sucrose.

Evans and Bates (506) reported in 1963 two large-scale experiments (24 replicates) in which small amounts of molasses were applied repeatedly by aircraft. The material was applied 2 or 3 times at the rate of 5 gallons per acre during an interval of 1 to 2 months before harvest. There were no effects of molasses whatever on Brix, pol or purity values. However, the quantity applied was extremely small.

3. THE "PROMISING" RIPENER; 1950–1970

A. *Ripening with 2,4-D*

In 1949 Beauchamp (162) presented a paper before the Cuban Sugar Technologists Association in which he outlined several highly-promising methods for improving cane quality with 2,4-D (2,4-dichlorophenoxyacetic acid). Using both liquid and powder forms applied to the plant or soil, 2,4-D was shown to increase sugar content independently of herbicidal effects upon weeds or of growth effects upon the cane itself.

The following year Beauchamp (163) elaborated upon a series of 2,4-D experiments in which timing of application and harvest, sampling methodology, and statistical treatment of data were described in detail. The varieties *Media Luna* and *P.O.J. 2878* were tested in commercial fields totaling about 30 acres. Aerial dust treatments were applied on February 23 at the rate of 26 pounds per acre on "late-irrigated" and "early-irrigated" fields. Data obtained during the first 14 days are presented in Table 12-1. Statistical analyses showed that for both varieties 2,4-D produced significant

TABLE 12-1

QUALITATIVE RESPONSE OF THE VARIETIES *P.O.J. 2878* AND *MEDIA LUNA 3-18* TO 2,4-D APPLIED AS A FOLIAR DUST AT THE RATE OF 10 POUNDS PER ACRE

Statistical analysis of variance showed significant differences relative to treatment and time of sampling. [After Beauchamp (163).] Reproduced by permission of the *Sugar Journal.*

Treatment	Days after treatment*	Brix	Pol	Purity	Calculated yield (96% sugar)
		Media luna 3-18			
Control	1	20.6	16.5	79.9	11.2
	8	19.9	17.3	86.7	12.3
	10	20.5	16.7	81.2	11.4
	12	18.6	16.2	87.1	11.6
	14	18.6	16.3	87.2	11.6
2,4-D	1	20.7	18.5	89.3	13.4
	8	20.5	18.7	91.0	13.7
	10	21.8	19.8	90.0	14.5
	12	19.9	17.3	86.7	12.3
	14	20.4	18.3	89.5	13.3
		P.O.J. 2878			
Control	1	20.4	16.4	80.2	11.2
	8	19.9	17.3	86.7	12.3
	10	20.6	16.5	79.7	11.1
	12	18.6	16.2	87.2	11.6
	14	18.6	16.2	87.1	11.6
2,4-D	1	20.5	16.7	81.2	11.4
	8	20.4	18.7	91.0	13.6
	10	20.7	18.5	89.3	13.4
	12	20.4	18.3	89.5	13.2
	14	19.9	17.3	86.7	12.3

*Stalk samples harvested 1 day after treatment were ground 4 days after harvest. All other samples were milled 1 day after harvest.

increases of Brix, polarization, purity, and yield values during the initial 10-day period following treatment. Somewhat greater increases were obtained during the second 10-day period, and thereafter the 2,4-D effect tended to decline. Ripening was most pronounced in the recently-irrigated fields. From this one could surmise that the 2,4-D action was not additive to natural ripening, but rather acted within the limits of natural ripening potential. Needless to say, Beauchamp's findings created considerable popular interest [see Editorial for the January, 1950 *Sugar Journal* (1174)].

Although Beauchamp's findings were substantiated by reports from India (311, 310), tests with 2,4-D in Louisiana (429), Puerto Rico (957, 961, 962), and British Guiana (1601, 506) were negative or inconclusive. Chacravarti *et al.* (311, 310) applied a 50-ppm solution of 2,4-D as a foliar spray at the rate of 60 gallons per acre. Sucrose content was increased by an average value of 0.55 percent. The effect was noted within 2 days and persisted up to 31 days. It was also obtained with relatively mature cane. Statistically significant improvement in sugar recovery, purity, and sucrose percent cane values was reported. Similarly, Chacravarti[1,2] obtained generally favorable results with foliar and soil 2,4-D treatments in subsequent trials.

However, De La Vega (429) achieved positive results in only about 50 percent of his trials in Louisiana, although weather conditions appear to have been unfavorable for ripening studies. Loustalot *et al.* (957) were unable to affect cane quality with foliar 2,4-D applied as an aqueous 0.2-percent solution in Puerto Rico. The variety *M. 336*, growing in the humid Mayaguez area, was treated on March 23, but no mention was made of the moisture and nitrogen status of the crop. *M. 336* is generally regarded as "sweeter" and of lower tonnage potential than either *P.O.J. 2878* or *Media Luna*.

Lugo-López and Grant (961) tested relatively large dosages of 2,4-D on ratoon crops of *P.O.J. 2878* in the humid Rio Piedras and Humacao areas of Puerto Rico. Aqueous solutions of the sodium salt were applied with knapsack sprayers equipped with hose extensions. Rates of 10, 20, and 30 pounds per acre were given 10, 20, and 30 days prior to harvest. At neither location was there a significant response for Brix, polarization, purity, available 96° sucrose percent cane, or tons of cane per acre. Lugo-López *et al.* (962) also evaluated 2,4-D as a ripening agent for *P.O.J. 2878* at several localities in Puerto Rico. The sodium salt was applied in aqueous spray solutions containing an equivalent of 2.5, 5.0, 7.5, 10.0, and 12.5 pounds per acre of 2,4-D (acid basis). In a second experiment 2,4-D solutions ranging from 0.025 to 0.20 percent were applied at the rate of 100 gallons per acre. Daily variations in Brix, polarization, purity and available 96° sucrose percent cane were recorded. No significant differences were obtained for any of the 2,4-D treatments, although the 0.20-percent solution gave moderately higher yields throughout the harvesting season. None of the reports from Puerto Rico included information relative to the crop's ripening status at time of treatment.

Yates and Bates (1601) likewise reported inconsistent results with 2,4-D as a ripening chemical. Soil applications equivalent to 2, 10, and 20 pounds per acre each increased sucrose percent cane at 10 and 20 days, but the increases were not statistically significant. An observational trial involving 2,4-D added to irrigation water at the

[1] Chacravarti, A.S., 1960. Foliar spray of 2,4-D (sodium salt) to increase sugar in cane. Report on large scale trials in Bihar, *Proc. Sugar Technol. Assoc. India* 28: 37–48.

[2] Chacravarti, A.S., 1962. Improvement of sugar recovery by application of 2,4-D (amine salt) to the root zone of sugarcane. Report on large scale trials in Bihar, *Indian J. Sugarcane Res. Dev.* 6: 80–91.

rate of 10 pounds per acre increased sucrose percent cane in the order of 1.7 percent at 20 days. However, in another experiment in which 2,4-D was added to irrigation water at rates of 5 and 10 pounds per acre, both treatments produced significant losses of sucrose percent cane at 18 days. Yates and Bates concluded that 2,4-D will not give consistent quality improvement under British Guiana conditions, but that in some varieties the chemical may help to prevent quality deterioration under adverse weather conditions.

In Queensland (1469), 2,4-D was tested as a foliar spray on 13-month-old cane at concentrations of 6 and 50 ppm in volumes equivalent to 60 gallons per acre. Boric acid (6.1 percent) was also included in some of the lower 2,4-D treatments. Samples harvested at 15 months revealed no significant changes in sucrose content. In another experiment 2,4-D concentrations of 5, 50, 500, and 5000 ppm were applied as foliar sprays. Stalk samples taken approximately 4 and 6 weeks later revealed no evidence of a sucrose effect in the top and basal internodes.

Coleman and Hebert (367) tested 2,4-D and 2, 4, 5-T (2,4, 5-trichlorophenoxyacetic acid) as foliar sprays on *C.P. 36-105* at rates of 200, 600, and 1000 ppm in 90 gallons of water per acre. There were no significant effects on cane quality 13 and 28 days after treatment. However, in another experiment 2,4-D at rates of 1 and 3 pounds per acre significantly improved sugar yield 8 days after treatment.

Relatively little attention has been given to the biochemical activity of 2,4-D in sugarcane although considerable information has accumulated from studies with other plants. In general, 2,4-D increases respiration and lowers carbohydrate level (820, 1313). Photosynthesis rate (7), hexose level (1218), and glucose catabolism (765)

TABLE 12-2

CHANGES IN LEAF SUGAR CONSTITUENTS OF IMMATURE SUGARCANE FOLLOWING FOLIAR SPRAY APPLICATION OF 2,4-D

An aqueous 0.20-percent solution was applied until runoff. In addition to 2,4-D, the herbicide solution contained 250 ppm boric acid, 550 ppm glucose, and 0.10 percent Tween 20. The control solution contained all additives except 2,4-D. [After Alexander (19).]

Sugar	Treatment	Days after treatment				
		1	3	9	27	Mean
		Sugar (mg/g dry wt.)				
Sucrose	Control	14.0	11.3	15.9	15.8	14.3
	2,4-D	10.7	15.0	29.1	11.6	16.6
Glucose	Control	8.2	1.3	1.7	4.1	3.8
	2,4-D	6.3	4.5	1.8	3.1	3.9
Fructose	Control	2.6	4.3	10.2	0.8	4.5
	2,4-D	3.7	2.3	10.0	2.4	4.6

appear to be affected. Wort (1588), as early as 1954, listed 18 important enzyme systems known to be affected by 2,4-D. Neely *et al.* (1076) found that invertase and phosphorylase were severely restricted in proliferating bean tissue induced by 2,4-D treatment.

Alexander (19) studied sugar and enzyme changes in greenhouse-grown sugarcane treated with 2,4-D at 10 weeks of age. A single foliar spray treatment of aqueous, 0.20-percent 2,4-D was applied once to the variety *P.R. 980*. Boron and glucose were included in the spray solution at rates of 250 ppm and 500 ppm, respectively, according to the method of Ballantyne (138), in an effort to improve herbicide absorption. Control plants were sprayed with aqueous boron and glucose without 2,4-D. All treatment solutions contained Tween 20 as wetting agent. Tissue samples were frozen for sugar and enzyme analyses at 1, 3, 9, and 27 days after treatment. It was found that leaf sucrose increased by the 3rd day and was significantly higher than control values at 9 days (Table 12-2). The sugar effect was no longer evident at 27 days.

Recognizing that at 9 days some unusual biochemical events must have been operative within the 2,4-D-treated leaves, one might suspect that increased photosynthesis,

TABLE 12-3

FOLIAR ENZYME RESPONSES TO SPRAY TREATMENT WITH 2,4-D

An aqueous 0.20-percent solution of 2,4-D was applied until runoff. Both control and 2,4-D solutions contained 250 ppm boric acid, 500 ppm glucose, and 0.10 percent Tween 20. [After Alexander (19).]

Enzyme	Treatment	Days after treatment				
		1	3	9	27	Mean
		Enzyme (specific activity)				
Acid phosphatase	Control	18.8	21.7	19.2	31.5	22.8
	2,4-D	21.8	20.6	11.3	48.2	25.5
ATPase	Control	16.5	24.3	26.3	40.7	27.0
	2,4-D	16.1	23.6	20.4	64.5	31.2
Glucose 6-phosphatase	Control	5.6	15.8	13.6	27.2	15.6
	2,4-D	5.9	18.2	4.2	30.9	14.8
Amylase	Control	227	117	162	180	172
	2,4-D	213	108	107	184	153
Phosphohexose isomerase	Control	34.6	20.9	25.7	41.6	30.7
	2,4-D	23.4	39.4	31.7	12.4	26.7
Glucose oxidase	Control	44.4	37.3	39.7	58.7	45.0
	2,4-D	114.0	29.4	64.3	27.5	58.8

increased sucrose biosynthesis, or decreased rates of transport could each account for the additional sugar. Several enzymes having significantly different levels at 9 days are listed in Table 12-3. The unusually low activity levels of acid phosphatase, and especially glucose 1-phosphatase, are suggestive of slower hydrolysis of phosphorylated sucrose precursors; hence, sucrose biosynthesis could have progresssed more rapidly. Abnormally low amylase activity at 9 days might indicate restricted sugar transport owing to greater starch accumulation. A necessity of amylase activity for sucrose transport from the leaves has been suggested by Hartt (665).

Foliar sucrose decline between 9 and 27 days after treatment was reflected in major activity increases for acid phosphatase, glucose 6-phosphatase, and amylase during the same period (Table 12-3). Also appearing as delayed 2,4-D effects were major losses of phosphohexose isomerase and glucose oxidase, in turn suggesting that hexose interconversion and glucose oxidation became restricted between 9 and 27 days as a result of 2,4-D treatment. Abnormally high ATPase at 27 days is taken as evidence of possible ATP shortages at that time. The point being made here is that a powerful herbicide such as 2,4-D can have major and long-term effects upon sugar-metabolizing enzymes which readily exceed normal enzyme changes. In this context it is quite natural that inconsistent sugar responses to 2,4-D will occur.

B. *Maleic hydrazide*

As a growth-inhibitory substance (or "anti-auxin") MH (maleic hydrazide; 1,2-dihydro-3,6-pyridazinedione) was first regarded as a possible ripening agent in the late 1940's. Naylor and Davis (1075) observed strikingly uniform growth effects, including loss of apical dominance, in 11 monocots and dicots treated with MH. In 1949 Naylor and Davis (1074) reported that corn plants exuded droplets of sucrose in response to spray application of the chemical. Tissue analyses revealed a 13-fold increase of total sugars. Currier *et al.* (398) treated barley, mustard, and bean plants with MH and found that starch accumulated in bean whereas barley produced an amber-colored sucrose exudate on both sides of the leaves. However, the principal carbohydrate increases were in fructosan polysaccharides. Growth and flowering was retarded in mustard. McIlrath (1002) found that cotton plants sprayed with MH (2400 ppm or 4800 ppm) ceased apical growth within 26 days, although renewed growth occurred in lateral shoots. The growth restriction was limited to younger plants approximately 35 days old. Sucrose and starch accumulations were also observed as an apparent consequence of restricted transport. Abnormally-thickened leaves were produced owing to cell enlargement. The elapsed time between planting and ball maturation was lengthened in response to the chemical treatment.

Growth and sucrose effects of MH have also been studied in sugar beet (1237, 1369, 1581). Stout (1369) and Peto (1166) obtained no significant sucrose increases from preharvest spray treatments, whereas Wittwer and Hansen (1581) reported that

MH significantly lowered sugar losses in storage when sugar beets were sprayed with an 0.25-percent solution. The treatment was effective when applied between 3 and 40 days prior to harvest.

As was true of 2,4-D, MH has not proven itself as a ripening agent on sugarcane. Positive effects are either inconsistent or they do not withstand statistical analyses. Yates and Bates (1601), applying 2.0 percent MH at the rate of 20 gallons per acre, found no significant differences in sucrose percent cane for samples taken 12 and 30 days after treatment. Trials in Queensland (1469) showed that MH applied to actively-growing cane in March produced C.C.S. (commercial cane sugar) increases amounting to about 4 units within a period of 7 weeks. Applications to mature cane shortly before harvest gave no effect. Subsequent studies with 4.0 percent MH applied to young cane yielded significant Brix increases in the top of the stalk, but a decreasing trend was found in the basal internodes. This is a relatively high MH level, and it caused marked growth restriction amounting to a loss of about 2 feet of millable stalk. Lower concentrations, 1.0 and 2.0 percent, did not affect juice quality. Another study comparing MH concentrations of 1.0, 2.0 and 4.0 percent revealed no qualitative improvement even though the two higher levels severely stunted growth.

In Puerto Rico, Lugo-López *et al.* (962) tested preharvest MH at Río Piedras and at Río Grande on ratoon crops of the variety *P.O.J. 2878*. Aqueous solutions were applied at the rate of 100 gallons per acre at levels of 0.025, 0.05, 0.10, 0.50, and 2.0 percent. Measurements for Brix, polarization, purity, and available 96° sucrose percent cane were taken up to 72 days after treatment but showed no significant sugar changes in response to the chemical.

In Trinidad (1509) MH was evaluated on 7-month-old plants of the variety *B. 41227*. Treatments were given at rates of 0.5, 1.0, and 2.0 gallons per acre and harvests were made at 5, 9, and 15 days after treatment. Small to moderate purity increases were obtained at 15 days for each chemical level. Brix values were increased by the 0.5- and 1.0-gallon treatments at 9 days. Some increases in polarization and extractable juice were also obtained; however, none of these changes were statistically significant. Coleman and Hebert (367) were unable to improve juice quality with MH applied as 2- and 6-percent solutions at the rate of 90 gallons per acre on *C.P. 34-120*.

Very little is known about the MH effects upon sugar-metabolizing enzymes in sugarcane. This compound was included in the sugar–enzyme evaluation studies discussed previously with respect to 2,4-D (19). The primary sugar effect of MH was a marked increase of reducing sugars, especially glucose, between 9 and 27 days after treatment. However, statistically significant enzyme changes were recorded at various posttreatment intervals for hexokinase, aldolase, phosphohexose isomerase, and condensing enzyme (Table 12-4). Hexokinase was generally more active in chemically-treated leaves than controls, and the effect was highly significant at 1 and 27 days. This enzyme (a glucokinase) catalyzes the synthesis of glucose 6-phosphate from free glucose plus ATP and performs an essential contribution toward the pathways of sugar formation and metabolism.

TABLE 12-4

FOLIAR ENZYME RESPONSES TO SPRAY APPLICATION OF MALEIC HYDRAZIDE (MH)

An aqueous 0.15-percent solution of MH was applied until runoff. Both control and MH solutions contained 250 ppm boric acid, 500 ppm glucose, and 0.10 percent Tween 20. [After Alexander (19).]

Enzyme	Treatment	Days after treatment				
		1	3	9	27	Mean
		Enzyme (specific activity)				
Hexokinase	Control	16.8	11.9	40.9	10.9	20.1
	MH	34.2	17.3	46.3	19.0	29.2
Aldolase	Control	39.4	19.8	31.6	21.6	28.1
	MH	35.8	24.9	22.0	7.2	22.5
Phosphohexose isomerase	Control	34.6	20.9	25.7	41.6	30.7
	MH	5.6	27.1	21.7	98.5	38.2
Condensing enzyme	Control	96.1	34.4	39.2	32.2	50.2
	MH	167.0	29.7	100.0	40.9	84.2

Aldolase was operating at subnormal levels at 9 and 27 days after MH treatment. The effect was significant at the 5-percent level on the 9th day and at the 1-percent level at 27 days. Catalyzing the interconversion of triose phosphate and fructose 1,6-diphosphate, aldolase is indispensable both in the latter stages of carbon assimilation and in the glycolytic breakdown of hexose. The enzyme phosphohexose isomerase was severely suppressed by MH at 1 day after treatment and was excessively active at 27 days. Both responses were significant at the 1-percent level. This enzyme catalyzes the reversible conversion of glucose 6-phosphate to fructose 6-phosphate. It is particularly important in sugarcane in that it offers the principal means for interconversion of the two sucrose moieties. Whether or not this catalyst is identical to its counterpart in immature storage tissue (579, 689), it does perform an analogous role in leaf sucrose metabolism.

Condensing enzyme fluctuated tremendously in leaves treated with MH. It was excessively active at 1 and 9 days after treatment. This enzyme participates in an acetyl-transferring sequence in which the acetyl group from coenzyme A is moved to oxaloacetate with the subsequent production of citrate (1397, 1079). It is therefore a highly-essential feature of the reaction sequence whereby sugar degradation products enter the Krebs or tricarboxylic acid cycle.

Taken together with the absence of significant sucrose accumulations in the leaf, the enzyme picture is suggestive of abnormally-fluctuating sugar metabolism in sugarcane leaves treated with MH. The enormous changes in work potential of each enzyme between 9 and 27 days helps to explain the lack of quality improvement noted by other workers during the 2- to 4-week interval after chemical treatment. Although the enzyme data is far too meager to draw firm conclusions, there is little doubt that MH can significantly alter the catalytic activity essential for sugar synthesis and metabolism in sugarcane leaves.

C. *Sucrol (Esso 59-G)*

Several petroleum products have been tested as ripening agents in Trinidad with varying degrees of success (1509). Prior to 1960 the highly refined oil "Sucrol" was depicted by its manufacturer as having ripening potential, although its mode of action was not specified. During initial large-scale trials involving some 50 acres of *B. 41227*, Sucrol was applied by aircraft at the rate of 1.5 gallons per acre. Samples taken at 7 and 14 days revealed significant loss of juice quality, but later samples taken at 22 and 28 days showed major quality improvement. Subsequent aerial trials with Sucrol produced no effect on 5-month-old *B. 37161* other than an early loss of sucrose at 2 weeks. Eleven-month-old *B.37172* and 6-month-old *B. 50112* failed to increase juice quality, although some evidence of improved TC/TS ratios (tons cane per tons sugar ratios) was obtained with *B. 37172*. In 1961 large-scale tests with 9-month-old *B. 41227* gave major improvement in TC/TS ratios. At 21 days after treatment the ratio improvement was from 14.33 to 11.88 (Table 12-5). A curious feature was the

TABLE 12-5

INFLUENCE OF SUCROL AERIAL APPLICATIONS ON TONS CANE PER TONS SUGAR RATIOS OF THE VARIETY *B. 41227*

[After Vlitos and Lawrie (1509).] Reproduced by permission of *I.S.S.C.T.*

Days after treatment	TC/TS ratios	
	Controls	Sucrol (1.5 U.S. gal/acre)
0	14.33	14.33
7	14.17	14.14
14	13.62	14.21
21	13.17	11.88
26	11.32	11.17
33	10.27	10.48

apparent lack of ripening prior to the 14- and 21-day period when rapid changes occurred in marked contrast to the gradual change in control plants.

New forms of Sucrol consisting of oil fractions having varying phytotoxicity were tested in 1961 on 1/200 acre plots. Of six formulations tested, one improved TC/TS ratios and two increased the rate of ripening.

Other petroleum products evaluated in Trinidad include albolineum oil and FS-40, the latter being diesel oil with pentachlorophenol and 2,4-D added in undisclosed amounts. This appears to have been one of the first efforts toward specific removal of the apical meristem. Foliar treatment with knapsack sprayers produced leaf damage within 4 days. Death of the meristem was "common", but no specific figures were reported (1509). However, no statistically significant differences were observed relative to ripening. In other experiments with FS-40, 10 and 20 gallons per acre produced faster ripening and improved TC/TS ratios within 14 days.

D. *TBA (Trysben), Pesco 1815, and Kuron*

In Hawaii (1112) one of the more promising compounds for artificial ripening has been TBA (2,3,6-trichlorobenzoic acid), commonly termed *Trysben*. It is a hormone-like herbicide whose biochemical effects upon plants remain largely obscure. Several disadvantages, including residual accumulation in the plant or soil and lack of clearance, have restricted its role to that of a reference compound in screening new ripening chemicals.

In Trinidad tests were conducted with a commercial mixture of 2-methyl-4-chlorophenoxyacetic acid and TBA, commonly termed *Pesco 1815*. Vlitos and Lawrie (1509) reported a series of trials in which certain treatments gave highly-promising results. One study involving Pesco 1815 at rates of 4, 8, and 12 pounds per acre gave no significant differences in TC/TS ratios but did produce an accelerated rate of ratio improvement. Another experiment with 1, 2, and 4 pounds per acre also failed to give ratios significantly different than controls; however, the rate of ripening was more rapid in chemical-treated plants. This is an important feature since having the cane ripened in accordance with harvest schedules is a matter of very real concern for the sugar grower.

A subsequent large-scale experiment with Pesco 1815 applied by helicopter at 4 pounds per acre gave clearly positive results (1509). Analyses obtained at 28 days with large samples constituting 7 to 9 tons of cane are summarized in Table 12-6. A highly significant lowering of the TC/TS ratio between treated and control fields appeared to verify similar but nonsignificant trends in smaller experiments. Ripening was accelerated by the aerial treatment between 20 and 28 days. As shown by Table 12-6, purity and pol values were most affected by Pesco 1815 while total weight of cane was least affected.

Pesco 1815 was tested in Puerto Rico toward the close of the 1970 grinding season (1295). One-half pound of active ingredient per acre was applied in aqueous solution at Central Mercedita, and on P.R. Land Authority plots at Loíza. Positive results were obtained at Mercedita with Brix and sucrose percent cane values increasing in the order

TABLE 12-6

QUALITATIVE RESPONSES OF THE VARIETY *B. 41227* TO PESCO 1815 APPLIED BY HELICOPTER 28 DAYS PRIOR TO HARVEST

[After Vlitos and Lawrie (1509).] Reproduced by permission of *I.S.S.C.T.*

Treatment	Replicate*	Brix	Pol	Purity	TC/TS
Control	1	19.0	65.0	80.4	9.42
	2	18.9	64.1	80.4	9.48
	3	19.0	64.3	82.1	9.37
	4	19.0	63.6	80.8	9.60
	5	19.0	63.6	80.8	9.60
	6	19.0	64.5	82.1	9.37
	7	19.0	63.7	80.8	9.60
	8	19.1	65.8	83.3	9.16
				TC/TS mean	9.40
Pesco 1815 (4 lbs/acre)	1	19.5	68.0	84.1	8.80
	2	19.2	67.5	85.9	8.75
	3	19.1	65.9	84.0	9.05
	4	19.3	67.2	82.9	8.99
	5	19.1	65.3	83.3	9.16
	6	19.0	66.0	84.0	9.05
	7	19.3	67.1	82.9	8.99
	8	19.5	68.0	84.1	8.80
				TC/TS mean	8.95

*Entire fields, totalling 40 acres, were treated. Each replicate represents a sample size in the order of 7 to 9 tons of stalks.

of 10 and 26 percent, respectively, in the variety *C.P. 5243*. There were no significant quality changes in the variety *P.R. 980* at Loíza. Pesco 1815 produced no significant sugar changes in greenhouse tests with *P.R. 980* in Puerto Rico (unpublished).

Tests with *Kuron* [2-(2,4,5-trichlorophenoxy)propionic acid] in Trinidad and British Guiana have also given favorable but inconsistent ripening responses. Vlitos and Lawrie (1509) summarized four experiments in which the chemical was applied at rates of 3 to 8 pounds per acre on the varieties *B. 41227* and *B. 49119*. Kuron was inactive in trials with 7- and 8-month-old plants. However, tests with 8-month-old first ratoons showed improved juice quality and TC/TS ratios within 26 days. Yates and Bates (1601) regarded Kuron as one of the more promising chemicals for cane ripening under British Guiana conditions. Preliminary tests in that country were highly encouraging. However, of two subsequent experiments, one produced only limited ripening and the other was negative.

E. *Boron*

An essentiality of boron for sugarcane growth has been established by Evans (504) who described characteristic boron deficiency symptoms. During the mid-1950's Gauch and Duggar found evidence that boron may perform fundamental roles in sugar transport across cell membranes (562). However, efforts to improve sugarcane quality with applied boron in British Guiana and Trinidad were negative (1601). In Puerto Rico, Alexander (20) sprayed immature *P.R. 980* plants with 50 and 500 ppm boric acid and failed to obtain significant sugar increases in leaf or immature storage tissue. Several significant but inconsistent effects of boron upon invertase and amylase were recorded.

Recent studies by Montalvo-Zapata[3] produced evidence of discrete boron roles in sugarcane growth and ripening processes. Over a period of 5 1/2 months, plants propagated in sand culture with only traces of boron experienced significant growth and quality losses without developing visual B-deficiency symptoms. Boron insufficiency lowered sucrose production in leaves and significantly altered the rates of sugar diffusion from bathing storage tissue slices. Growth decline was largely confined to lateral internode expansion. Prior work[4] had shown sugar diffusion rates from bathing storage tissue to be affected by borate additive. In Hawaii, Bowen[5] has examined physiological and biochemical effects of variable boron supply. Studies by Humbert *et al.*[6] in Peru have shown that excessive boron is restrictive against sugar and tonnage yields.

The possibility exists that boron may directly affect sucrose biosynthesis in sugarcane. Duggar and Humphreys (450) found that boron enhanced the formation of sucrose by sugarcane and pea-seedling homogenates. However, sucrose synthesis by partially-purified enzyme preparations was inhibited by added boron. Alexander (12) found that when sugarcane leaf homogenates were dialyzed to restrict their sucrose-synthesizing capacity, part of the activity was restored by adding traces of boron. The restoration of activity was accentuated when NAD and FAD were included with boron.

F. *Monopotassium phosphate*

Ripening activity by monopotassium phosphate has been reported from Trinidad (1509). Tested at rates of 12.5, 25, and 50 pounds per acre on 7-month-old *B. 41227*, statistically-significant increases in juice quality were recorded after 16 days with the

---

[3] Montalvo-Zapata, R., 1972. Studies on the roles of boron in growth and sugar-transport processes of sugarcane, *J. Agric. Univ. P.R.* 57(1): in press.

[4] Acín-Díaz, N. and Alexander, A.G., 1972. Studies on sugar diffusion from sugarcane storage tissue, *J. Agric. Univ. P.R.* 56(3): 253–266.

[5] Bowen, J.E., 1972. Biochemical and physiological effects of boron in sugarcane, *Proc. Int. Soc. Sugar Cane Technol.* 14: (in press).

[6] Humbert, R.P., Bahme, R.B., Fernández, E.D. and Thompson, L.I., 1970. Overcoming boron and salinity problems in growing sugarcane in the Tambo Valley of Peru, *Sugar y Azúcar* 65(9): 32–34.

highest treatment level. Subsequent trials showed that 50 pounds of monopotassium phosphate per acre significantly lowered TC/TS ratios. However, positive effects were not obtained with 12-month cane, with naturally-ripened cane, or when the chemical was applied at rates lower than 50 pounds per acre.

G. *Other early chemical trials*

Yates and Bates (1601) mention that TIBA (2,4,5-triiodobenzoic acid) failed to show ripening activity in its lone trial in British Guiana. As an "anti-auxin", TIBA is one of a group of substances which in theory should promote ripening by restricting growth. The growth inhibitor *Dowpon* (2,2-dichloropropionic acid) was regarded as highly promising in British Guiana at rates of 1 or 2 pounds per acre in 60 gallons of water.

Yates (1602) obtained ripening activity with *Dalapon* in British Guiana but was unable to repeat these results in Queensland. Dalapon improved quality in British Guiana at rates of 1 to 4 pounds per acre of 85 percent active material. This response was obtained only under conditions of moisture stress and low humidity. Under similar conditions in Queensland Dalapon failed to show ripening activity. Yates suggested that low night temperatures had reduced growth rate in excess of the chemical's potential to do so. Coleman and Hebert (367) reported that Dalapon failed to affect sucrose below the rate of 10 pounds per acre, and at 15 to 40 pounds per acre there were significant sucrose losses.

H. *Recent evaluations of D.A.-5, C.P. 41845, and Cycocel*

During 1969 and 1970 the products *D.A.-5* (DuPont) and *C.P. 41845* (Monsanto) were tested for ripening activity with some success by Bieske (183) in Queensland. Applied in aqueous solution at rates of 1 to 5 pounds per acre, singularly or as split applications, each compound retarded growth, induced side-shoots, and increased C.C.S. values. The effects were intensified with passage of time and increasing chemical levels. Possible commercial usage was suggested as a means of arresting the normal C.C.S. decline late in the season. At this period growth losses and foliar injury were not taken to be serious. However, some evidence was found of chemical injury on ratoon plants.

In 1970 Samuels *et al.* (1295), testing eight chemicals in 13 field experiments in Puerto Rico, found *C.P. 41845* to be highly promising as a ripening agent in both humid and dry regions[7]. Applied to *P.R. 980* under rainy conditions at Loíza, the compound prevented the usual decline in sucrose percent cane and purity values when given at the rate of 2 pounds active ingredient per acre. The compound Pesco 1815

---

[7] Similarly positive activity of *C.P. 41845* in Hawaii was recently described by L.G. Nickell and D.T. Takahashi [*Proc. Hawaiian Sugar Technol. Assoc.* (1971), pp. 73–82].

had failed to improve quality in *P.R. 980* under similar humid conditions. However, under drier conditions at Central Mercedita, *Pesco 1815* significantly increased sucrose percent cane values in *P.R. 641791* between 2 and 6 weeks after application. At Central Aguirre, on *P.R. 62258*, identical treatments produced significant sucrose percent cane increases from 2 to 4 weeks after application.

Tianco and Escober (1432) tested *C.P. 41845* in the Philippines at the rate of 4.0 kg/ha in 150 gallons of water. Results from three field trials with three varieties showed rendement increases in the order of 10 to 30 percent. These were paralleled by increased sugar yields without appreciable tonnage losses. The most favorable application period was about 6 weeks before harvest, the exact time being determined by rainfall and other conditions.

Greenhouse experiments in Puerto Rico have shown that *C.P. 41845* applied to immature *P.R. 980* plants as an 0.3-percent aqueous foliar spray produces significant increases in Brix, pol, and purity values within 11 days, with additional increases accruing within 33 days after treatment (Table 12-7). Sucrose yield was approximately tripled at 11 days and nearly quadrupled at 33 days relative to control yields. C.P. 41845 was severely restrictive against the number and growth rate of secondary shoots in the stool (52).

TABLE 12-7

EFFECTS OF C.P. 41845 (MONSANTO) ON SUGARCANE GROWTH, QUALITY, AND INVERTASE ACTIVITY 33 DAYS AFTER FOLIAR TREATMENT

Variety *P.R. 980.* Plants grown in sand culture with adequate water and nutrient supplies were sprayed once with aqueous C.P. 41845 solution at 15 weeks of age. [After Alexander and Montalvo (52).]

Treatment	Sucrose (mg/g)		Brix	Pol	Purity	Stalk wt. (g/stalk)	Shoot wt. (g/shoot)	Invertase (sp. act.)
	Leaf	Storage						
Control	57	168	9.8	24	62	175	21.2	14.1
C.P. 41845	93	361	15.4	53	84	104	6.3	0.8

Another compound showing ripening potential at the greenhouse level was the American Cyanamid product *Cycocel* (Fig. 12-1). Applied as an aqueous foliar spray to the variety *C.P. 52-43*, 0.3 percent active Cycocel progressively increased sucrose content up to the final harvest at 33 days after treatment. Lesser amounts (0.07 percent) increased sucrose up to 11 days. Cycocel significantly lowered the acid invertase levels of immature storage tissue. In subsequent greenhouse tests the compound promoted sucrose accumulation when applied singularly but failed to do so when combined with 0.005 percent active GA (gibberellic acid). However, Samuels *et al.* (1295) were unable to induce ripening with Cycocel in field-plot trials. During the same studies GA given singularly and in combination with Dalapon and silicon also failed to produce ripening.

In Hawaii, Nickell and Maretzki (1116) obtained positive ripening responses with both D.A.-5 and Cycocel. The chemicals were applied to the spindle of stalks 18 months of age or older. Both compounds compared favorably with Trysben (an effective but unreleased ripener) with respect to juice purity and pol percent cane values. Other chemicals showing recent promise as ripening agents in Hawaii include *GS-241, Hydrothol-191, Actidione*, and *Anisomycin* (1116). Owing to the diverse nature of these compounds Nickell and Maretzki felt that several modes of action might be operative in addition to growth suppression in the spindle area. It was proposed that optimum ripening, *i.e.*, the highest possible quality maintained for the longest possible time, might require combinations of chemical ripeners.

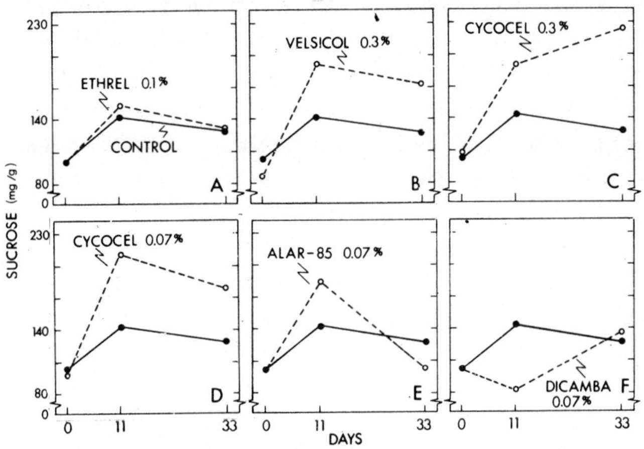

Fig. 12-1. Effects of potential sugarcane ripeners upon sucrose content of immature storage tissue. Greenhouse-grown plants of the variety *P.R. 980* were sprayed once with the indicated solutions at 12 weeks of age. Cycocel (C and D), and possibly the Velsicol compound (B), showed sufficient activity to warrant further testing at the greenhouse stage. [After Alexander *et al.* (unpublished).]

4. RIPENING WITH GIBBERELLIC ACID

A. *Historical*

Hori (752), in 1898, was probably the first to describe growth induction by gibberellin in plants. More than half a century was to pass before the growth and ripening potential of gibberellic acid in sugarcane was recognized. The commercial use of gibberellic acid or analogous compounds for cane ripening still belongs to the future.

The term gibberellic acid (GA, also "gibberellin A_3", and "gibberellin X") stems from the fungus *Gibberella fujikuroi* whose infection of rice seedlings produces phenomenal bursts of growth. A major effect of the growth stimulus is a rapid elongation of young leaf and stem cells still capable of extension. Because plants thus afflicted rise presumptuously above their healthy neighbors, the condition earned an early title of "bakanae" or "foolish seedling disease". The Japanese pathologist Kurosawa (864) was the first to recognize that a product of the infection was responsible for the increased growth. In 1935 Yabuta[8] crystallized the active compound and named it *gibberellin*. By the mid-1950's the unusual potential of GA in plant research and agriculture was recognized (399, 1024, 1367)[9].

B. *GA effects on sugarcane*

Studies of applied GA effects upon sugarcane were begun during the late 1950's by Coleman and his co-workers (368, 372) and by scientists in Australia[10] (259), British Guiana (154), and Puerto Rico (317). Early GA treatments included seedpiece soaking, foliar sprays, and lanolin paste applications to various tissues. Coleman *et al.* (372) studied GA effects upon germination, growth, flowering, and maturation. Germination was retarded and growth (elongation) was markedly increased. There was no significant effect on flowering. Other trials by Coleman and his co-workers revealed increased stem elongation but lower net weight. There were no appreciable effects of GA on extraction, Brix, sucrose, or purity.

Villareal and Santos (1501) reported that foliar GA applications failed to improve sugarcane yield or quality. In a preliminary field experiment Bates (154) obtained slight increases in stalk length for cane treated with GA 6 weeks before harvest, but no appreciable differences were obtained for stalk weight or juice quality. Similarly, Coleman *et al.* (370) obtained no significant growth or sugar responses from presoaking seedpièces in GA solution. Chardón (317) reported that soaking seedpieces in 20 and 100 ppm GA increased shoot growth after germination. This effect was augmented by adding urea to the GA solution. Urea also enabled the plants to resist a foliar yellowing which reportedly accompanied GA-induced growth (982, 1396).

Coleman (368) went to the unusual lengths of treating field cane at 10-day intervals over a 6-month period with GA levels beginning at 10 ppm and increasing to 100 ppm. Aqueous solutions in the order of 100 gallons per acre were applied to the variety *C.P. 44-101*. At harvest the treated plants averaged 30 additional inches in height. However, millable stalks were lengthened by only 10 inches and these were fewer in number. There was no significant GA effect upon tons of cane per acre, stalk weight, internode number, sucrose, or juice purity. This work dampened some of the growing enthusiasm

---

[8] Yabuta, T., 1935. Biochemistry of the "bakanae" fungus in rice, *Agric. Hortic. (Tokyo)* 10: 17–22.

[9] In addition, see reviews by Stowe and Yamaki (1370), Merck and Co., Inc. (74), Velsicol Chemical Corp. (73), Brian (143), Stuart and Cathey (1380), and Gould (573).

[10] Anon., 1964. *Rept. David North Plant Res. Cent.* (1964): 48–55.

for GA. However, Coleman did recognize that GA response was greatly dependent upon temperature and rainfall, with cool temperature and low moisture providing relatively favorable conditions.

Working with controlled-climate facilities, Bull (259) obtained favorable growth and sugar responses to applied GA with four varieties. Temperature regimes were controlled at 35, 29, 23, and 17 °C over an 8-week period. Aqueous GA solutions, 0.02 and 0.10 percent, were applied weekly to the leaf spindle. These treatments increased stalk length, fresh weight, fiber, and sugar content. Leaf area and leaf weight were decreased by GA. There was no GA effect on node number. The magnitude of GA response varied with variety, age, and temperature. GA produced relatively greater responses in young plants at low temperatures and in older plants at higher temperatures. Bull's findings substantiated the consensus that GA is relatively more effective in plants experiencing growth stress (243, 1380).

Research with GA in Hawaii slackened for several years owing to high costs of the refined product and to inconsistent or unfavorable earlier responses (70). With the advent of lower-priced material plus enormous advances in fundamental cane research, GA was reevaluated during the mid- and late-1960's (1108, 1109, 1406, 1408). In 1966 (1406) aerial applications of unrefined GA gave positive results in nine out of twelve trials conducted on two varieties. Both the *pol ratio* and *mill run* analysis methods used in Hawaii showed positive GA effects in 66 to 75 percent of the total number of trials. Plot test (1108) performed under carefully controlled conditions showed that it was possible to gain up to 5 tons of cane per acre and about 0.4 ton of sugar per acre from applied GA in the order of 2 to 4 ounces per acre. The crude GA proved to be about equal to the refined product on an activity basis (1108). However, subsequent paired plot trials (1408) on a large scale (150 replicates) were apparently inconclusive with respect to commercial usage of the available GA formulations.

Workers in Queensland (1130) obtained initially encouraging results with GA in field trials, but thereafter (1249) failed to achieve anything like the responses shown by experiments under controlled-climate conditions. A report by Robinson and Arvier (1249) in 1968 indicates that ecological factors are so variable that success in the commercial use of GA would be highly problematical. Turner (1161) suggests that inadequate tissue penetration may be an important limiting factor. This view is supported by aerial GA experiments at Central Aguirre in Puerto Rico (unpublished) which failed to affect cane tonnage or quality.

C. *GA effects upon sugar production and utilization*

In theory the expected effect of GA on sugareane should be an increased tonnage of stalks. That sugar effects are also possible is implied by the numerous field trials showing improved quality as a GA response. More direct evidence of a GA–sucrose relationship comes from the work of Glasziou and co-workers (591, 567) relating supplied GA to the stability of invertase mRNA. Recent laboratory and greenhouse evidence (37, 39, 53, 49, 50, 48) is suggestive of GA effects upon photosynthesis, sucrose biosynthesis; and utilization of stored sucrose.

Initial GA studies with immature plants in Puerto Rico implied that GA increased sugar synthesis by virtue of the fact that higher sucrose levels were found in GA-treated leaves (37, 39). Restricted transport was regarded as unlikely since sucrose also tended to increase in immature storage tissue and all plants contained abundant moisture. Sucrose biosynthesis experiments (44) with leaf homogenates showed that sucrose formation was increased up to 50 percent when GA was added at the rate of 0.001 μmole per ml of digest. A depressing GA effect was observed in the range of 0.01 to 0.10 μmole/ml. The small amount of GA needed for stimulation is suggestive of a GA–enzyme relationship, possibly an enzyme–GA union which confers on the catalyst an increased efficiency of action as proposed by Van Overbeek (1476).

The GA–sucrose relationship is strongly affected by the plant's nitrogen status. Working with immature *P.R. 980* plants grown with controlled nutrient supply in sand culture, Alexander (37) initiated nitrate regimes of 0, 5 and 50 meq/l at 12 weeks of age, and simultaneously applied foliar GA in aqueous solution at rates of 0, 0.01, and 0.10 percent. The nitrogen and GA treatments were combined in a 3 x 3 factorial design. Plants were harvested at 17 weeks for growth, sugar, and enzyme analyses. Sucrose values for immature storage tissue (Table 12-8) indicate that both the lowering

TABLE 12-8

EFFECTS OF FOLIAR GA ON SUCROSE STORAGE UNDER CONDITIONS OF VARIABLE NITROGEN REGIME

All plants were grown in sand culture with adequate water and nitrogen (10 meq/l nitrate) until 12 weeks of age. At that time variable nitrate supplies were initiated and GA solutions were applied once as foliar sprays. Immature storage tissues were harvested for sucrose analysis 5 weeks later. [After Alexander (37).]

Nitrogen (meq/l NO_3)	GA (% soln.)			
	0	0.01	0.10	Mean
	Sucrose (mg/g dry wt.)			
0	127	172	113	137
5	91	132	89	104
50	71	81	77	76

of nitrogen supply and application of 0.01 percent GA increased sucrose as main effects, but that the most pronounced GA activity occurred when nitrogen supply was limited. When nitrogen was low GA produced sucrose increases in excess of that which could be attributed to slackened growth, *i.e.*, in excess of the low nitrate x low GA sucrose value. It was believed that the higher sucrose values represented increased sucrose synthesis rather than improved translocation.

Additional evidence that GA affects the rate of sucrose synthesis, and that the GA effect is itself subject to chemical regulation, was obtained in recent greenhouse studies (39) with applied GA and silicon (Si). Using 12-week-old plants of the variety *P.R. 980*, three levels of GA (0, 0.01, and 0.10 percent) were combined factorially with four levels of Si (0, 100, 1000, and 10 000 ppm). The chemicals were applied as aqueous foliar sprays. There were four replicates in a completely randomized greenhouse design. Leaf and immature storage tissue samples harvested at 17 weeks revealed that GA caused moderate to large sucrose increases in both tissues (Table 12-9).

TABLE 12-9

SUCROSE RESPONSES IN IMMATURE SUGARCANE TREATED WITH FOLIAR COMBINATIONS OF GA AND SODIUM METASILICATE

Aqueous GA and Si solutions were applied in factorial combinations to *P.R. 980* plants at 14 weeks of age. Harvests were performed 5 weeks after treatment. [After Alexander (39).]

Tissue	GA (% soln.)	Si (ppm)				
		0	100	1000	10 000	Mean
		Sucrose (mg/g dry wt.)				
Leaf	0	52	62	81	29	56
	0.01	63	84	51	51	62
	0.10	64	90	46	22	56
Immature storage	0	48	58	125	58	72
	0.01	70	155	56	49	82
	0.10	32	130	62	18	61

However, GA was more effective when combined with 100 ppm Si and less effective at higher Si levels. It is evident that each chemical was somewhat more effective when combined with an intermediate level of the other chemical. Similarly, Si was found to enhance GA activity when supplied through the roots as a daily nutrient-solution supplement (39).

Indirect evidence of a GA effect upon sugarcane photosynthesis was obtained during a subsequent variable-illumination study (48). By holding sugarcane plants in darkness for 96 hours, and then reexposing them to sunlight, those plants which had been pretreated with GA recovered sucrose far more readily than darkroom controls (Fig. 12-2A). The sugar-forming capacity of GA-treated plants was superior even to the greenhouse control plants (Fig. 12-2B). At 96 hours (9:00 a.m.) all leaves were relatively free of sucrose, hence, the new values achieved at 102 hours are believed to reflect sugar-forming potential under conditions of unrestricted transport. Leaf analyses also showed that fructose and glucose were produced far more readily in GA-treated leaves.

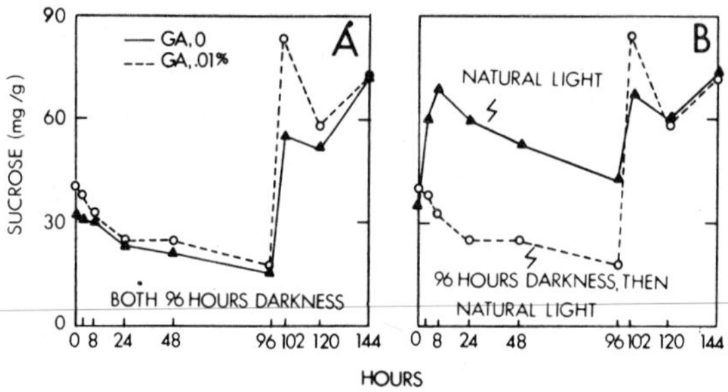

Fig. 12-2. Effects of variable light and GA pretreatment on sucrose content of sugarcane leaves: (A) Sucrose decline during 96 hours of darkness, followed by superior recovery in GA-treated plants after reillumination. (B) Sucrose content of darkened, GA-treated plants as compared with non-treated cane given natural illumination. The rate of sucrose increase between 96 and 102 hours was vastly superior for plants sprayed with GA. [After Alexander *et al.* (48).]

A paper chromatogram illustrating the higher reducing sugar levels in GA-treated leaves is presented in Fig. 12-3. The added quantities of hexose indicates that photosynthesis and not simply sucrose biosynthesis was increased by GA. This does not substantiate the $^{14}CO_2$ work of Haber and Tolbert (623) and of Hayashi (707), which suggested that GA has no effect on photosynthetic activity per unit of leaf area.

Improved sugar-forming potential would be of no more than academic interest if this potential was not reflected in improved stalk quality. Evidence that GA enhances ripening as a delayed effect after initial growth stimulation is presented in Figs. 12-4 and 12-5. In this study, Alexander *et al.* (49) initiated foliar GA treatments of variable number and frequency on greenhouse-grown *P.R. 980* plants at 10 weeks of age. At this time internodes 3 and 4 were just becoming visible (numbering from the base upward). Four months later, stalk samples were segmented into individual joints and sucrose analyses were conducted with clarified juice from each internode. It can be seen from Fig. 12-4 that all of the internodes laid down prior to the GA treatment lost sucrose by comparison with control plants. These losses continued from the subsequent two or three internodes. Apparently, the GA growth stimulation created a need for sugar which was met with stored sucrose from the first mature joints. However, after some 3 to 5 weeks had passed, the GA-treated plants began to accumulate more sucrose than control plants (Fig. 12-4). This storage continued long after the growth stimulation had ceased.

The delayed ripening effect thus envisioned is illustrated chromatographically in Fig. 12-5. It can be seen that the sucrose losses from stalks of GA-treated plants were not paralleled by increased reducing sugars – these being utilized for growth and respiratory processes. However, there was a greater predominance of reducing sugars at a lower level in control stalks than in GA-treated stalks, which is another way of saying that ripening was more advanced in the plants given GA. Alexander *et al.* (49) concluded that sucrose was lost only so long as the newly-stimulated growth was depen-

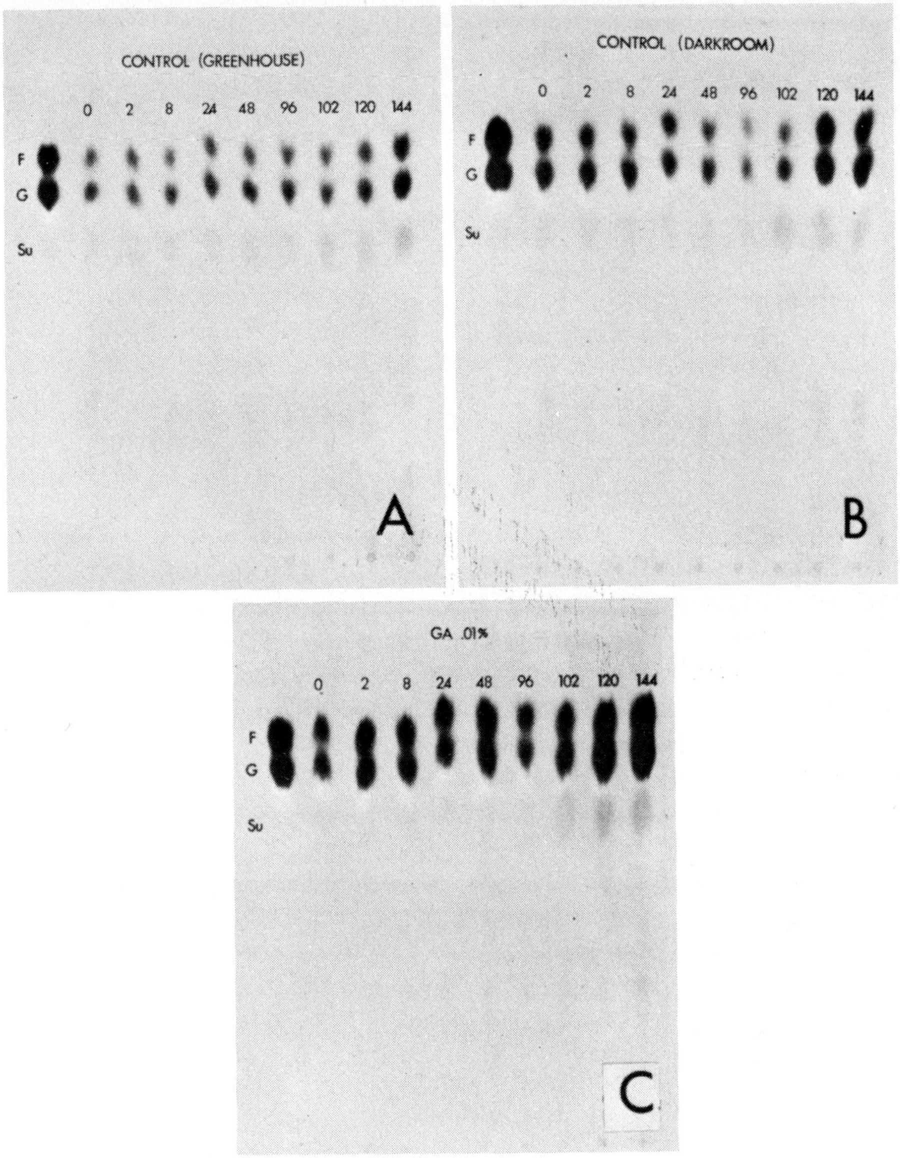

Fig. 12-3. Paper chromatograms illustrating leaf fructose, glucose, and sucrose in three groups of sugarcane plants given variable illumination and GA pretreatment. (A) General continuity of the three sugars among control plants retained in the greenhouse under natural illumination. (B) Darkroom control plants experiencing gradual decline of each sugar followed by rapid recovery upon reillumination at 96 hours. (C) Darkroom plants pretreated with GA showing exceptionally high hexose levels and accelerated recovery of all sugars following reillumination. The letters F, G, and Su appearing at the left-hand margins identify authentic fructose, glucose, and sucrose, respectively. [After Alexander *et al.* (48).]

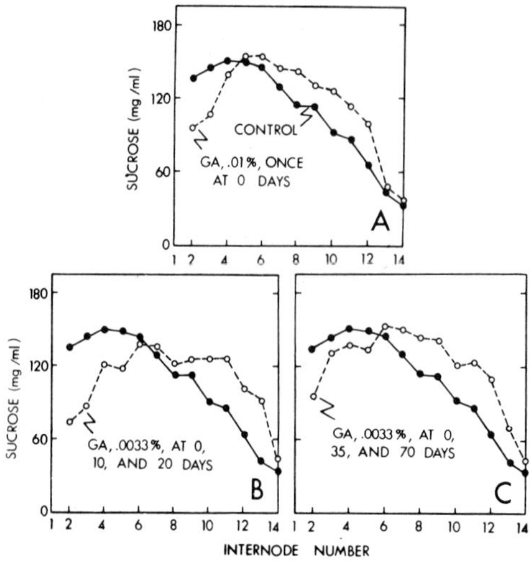

Fig. 12-4. Sucrose content of milled juice from individual internodes of GA-treated sugarcane. Internodes are numbered from the base upward. [After Alexander *et al.* (49).]

dent upon stored reserves; thereafter the GA-treated plants were able to satisfy growth needs and to increase storage levels as well. Quite possibly this was facilitated by the increased hexose levels produced by GA-treated leaves (Fig. 12-3). Added proof of this was taken from the fact that when part of the GA treatment was delayed until 35 or 70 days there was no loss of storage sucrose (Fig. 12-4).

D. *Delayed GA growth effects: The post-growth stimulatory phase*

Sugarcane properly treated with GA will accelerate internode expansion over a

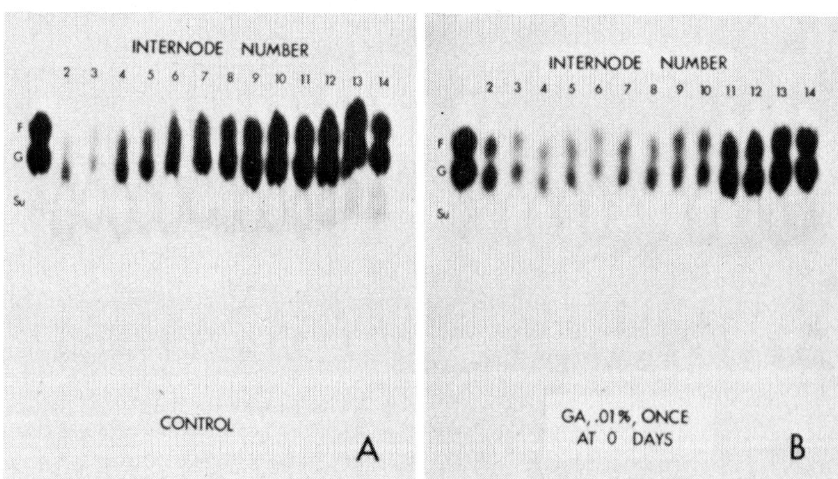

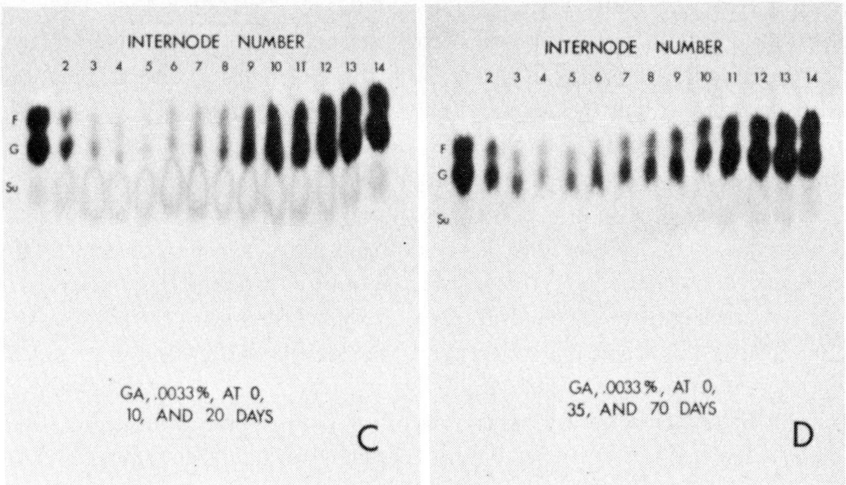

Fig. 12-5. Paper chromatograms of clarified milled juice from individual internodes of GA-treated sugarcane. Numerals refer to internodes, which were numbered from the base upward. The letters F, G, and Su appearing at the left-hand margins identify authentic fructose, glucose, and sucrose, respectively. Note the relative absence of fructose and glucose from internodes 3 to 10 of GA-treated stalks (B, C, D) as compared to stalks of control plants (A). [After Alexander *et al.* (49).]

length of 3 to 5 joints. This growth activity is followed within 4 to 6 weeks by severe growth decline[11], so severe in fact that even less growth is produced than by untreated controls. The post-stimulatory phase appears to reflect a new physiological regime

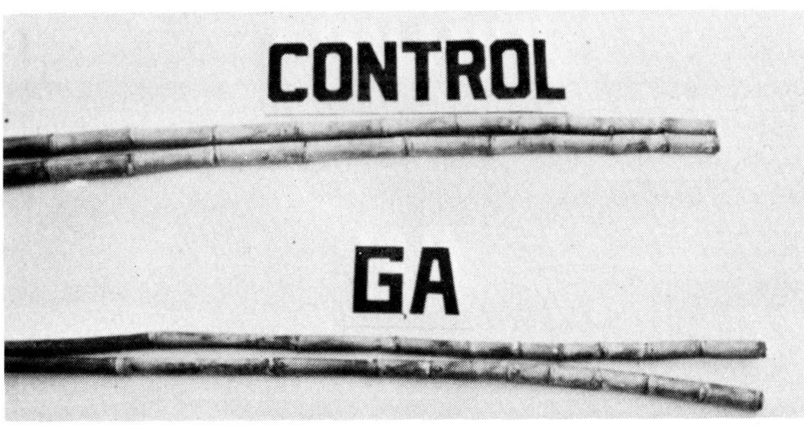

Fig. 12-6. Typical internode elongation followed by growth reversion to subnormal levels after foliar application of a 0.01-percent solution of GA. [Photographed by the author.]

---

[11]Tanimoto and Nickell (1408) state that the *Badilla* variety responds to GA with accelerated growth for several months.

distinct both from the pretreatment period and the rapid-growth period. There is evidence of distinctly different enzyme behavior patterns in leaf and immature storage tissues at this time (50). Typical stalks showing the temporary growth acceleration followed by shortening and thickening of the joints are illustrated in Fig. 12-6. Although not specifically mentioned, the early work by Coleman *et al.* (370) implied that growth reversion to subnormal levels could have taken place. Data presented by Bull (259) are also suggestive of possible growth reversion, although the experiments did not extend long enough for this to be shown clearly. Failure to recognize this growth decline as something more than a "wearing off" or a return to normalcy, *i.e.*, rather than as a new growth regime distinct from controls, pretreatment and growth-stimulatory phases, could account for many of the discrepancies in field results with GA.

Two approaches are open for improvement of GA growth performance. One approach is to increase GA efficiency during the limited period when rapid growth is possible; the second method seeks to limit the extent and duration of subnormal growth. Applying GA in multiple increments over an extended interval appears to give superior results by comparison with single large doses (1408, 1109, 1406). Alexander *et al.* (49) attempted to improve on this by giving all of the increments during a short interval (30 days) as compared with a long interval (70 days). The objective was to incorporate all of the GA while the plant was still physiologically "geared" to increase growth rather than to slacken growth. In each instance the total amount of GA applied was identical. As shown by Fig. 12-7, the attempt to increase GA effectiveness by

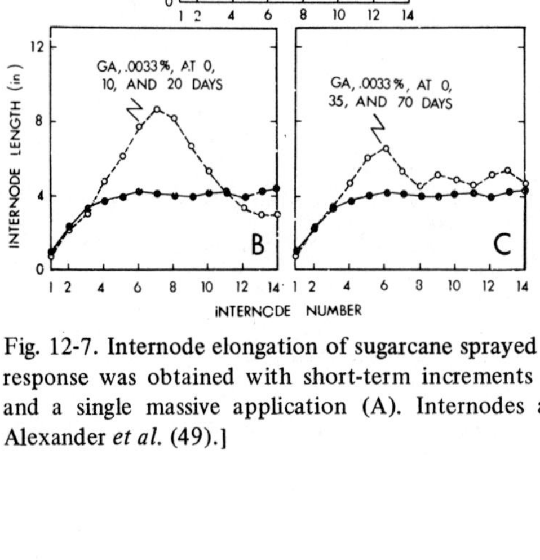

Fig. 12-7. Internode elongation of sugarcane sprayed with aqueous GA solutions. A superior growth response was obtained with short-term increments (B) as compared to long-term increments (C) and a single massive application (A). Internodes are numbered from the base upward. [After Alexander *et al.* (49).]

closely spacing its increments was highly successful under the prevailing greenhouse conditions. Based upon internode-length values, calculations of growth areas above the control line showed that short-term GA increments (Fig. 12-7B) more than doubled the growth increase from a single large dose (Fig. 12-7A), and markedly improved upon long-term increments (Fig. 12-7C). This effect was verified by internode-diameter values. Furthermore, while widely-spaced increments prevented growth from reverting to subnormal levels, they failed to even approach the growth stimulus attained by the first increment. This supports the theory that delayed increments are relatively inefficient because the plants will have entered a period of reduced growth capacity.

Recent findings offer hope that growth reversion itself can be controlled by chemical supplements added to the GA solution. Silicon has shown promise in this respect by acting as a "buffer" against desiccant-induced changes in photosynthesis and enzyme activity (46). Clements (354) suggests a protective role of silicon in photosynthesis by virtue of its ability to prevent high-manganese necrosis. In one field experiment in Puerto Rico (53), addition of silicon ($Na_2SiO_3 \cdot 9H_2O$) to the GA solution leveled off both the growth-stimulatory and reversion phases. By carefully timing treatment with silicon or other suitable "buffering" agents, it might be possible to prevent reversion after growth stimulation has been achieved. Workers at the Tate and Lyle, Ltd., Research Centre (1163) have also attempted to control the growth reversion phase. One such treatment includes the addition of *Dalapon* to the original GA solution.

5. CHEMICAL CONTROL OF SUCROSE

In today's sugarcane industry the use of chemicals is usually centered around production problems. Each year there is increased interest in the chemical control of germination, growth, flower induction, flower prevention, ripening, desiccation, defoliation, and postharvest deterioration. This emphasis is entirely correct and logical since ultimate sugar yield is the keystone of the sugar industry. Within this context the sugarcane physiologist has played a supporting role.

However, in strictly physiological and biochemical terms, sugarcane is beset with its own "problems" inherited through the ages as it evolved as a distinct botanical entity. These are also relevant to sucrose production and encompass the whole range of source-to-sink events which comprise the theme of this book. The inherent limitations of the sugarcane source-to-sink system are only beginning to be identified and their precise control clearly belongs to the future. Nonetheless, the alleviation of physiological "weak" spots based upon understanding of the plant's needs and biochemical adaptability will one day be attained. This is a matter of certainty if only because physiologists are by nature curious and growers by nature strive to produce more sugar. In the following sections some of the recent studies pertaining to chemical regulation of sucrose synthesis and retention are reviewed. It will be shown that both production problems and physiological limitations of the sugarcane plant can be alleviated by judicious use of chemicals.

A. *Increased synthesis with phosphatase inhibitors*

During the past two decades scientists have identified a series of sugar and acid phosphates serving as essential intermediates of sugar synthesis and metabolism. Virtually all of these have been found in sugarcane. In addition to the Calvin-cycle and C_4 pathway intermediates, the uridine phosphates allied to reactions of sucrose biosynthesis (450, 12, 303, 689, 920, 1462) assume tremendous importance in determining the rates of sugar formation and degradation. Numerous acid phosphatases are found in sugarcane leaves which are capable of depleting the pools of intermediate phosphates (11, 17). In Puerto Rico it has been observed that, under greenhouse conditions, physiological treatments which produce a high leaf sucrose content also bring about a suppression of the acid phosphatase (11, 19, 20, 15). This is especially true of low nitrogen regimes but is also characteristic of nearly all treatments producing physiological stress.

It was postulated (21) that the phosphatases could at times deplete the pools of sucrose precursors or energy reserves to levels rate limiting for sucrose formation. By catalyzing the type reaction

$$R{-}O{-}PO_3H_2 + H_2O \longrightarrow ROH + H_3PO_4$$

in which R represents a transferable sugar, sugar acid, or adenosine group, these enzymes would facilitate the hydrolysis of organic phosphates and the concurrent liberation of inorganic phosphate. It was thought that, by entering traces of suitable phosphatase inhibitor into the plant, one might suppress the enzymes and thereby increase sucrose synthesis without producing the growth curtailment characteristic of more severe chemical treatments.

A search was conducted in the laboratory for chemicals which would be absorbed by the plant and inhibit phosphatases at levels too low to cause tissue injury. Fluoride, an inhibitor of bone phosphatase, was only partially effective against the sugarcane enzymes. The element molybdenum (Mo), already a proven inhibitor of tomato (1352) and cauliflower (10) phosphatases, was highly effective *in vitro* against its sugarcane counterparts (17). Similarly, the element tungsten (W), having chemical properties very similar to Mo, proved to be an excellent inhibitor in the test tube.

Greenhouse studies designed to determine whether phosphatase inhibitors would perform *in vivo* gave generally positive results (21, 14, 20). In one study, immature plants of the variety *M. 336* were grown by sand culture with controlled water and nutrient supplies. Treatments consisting of foliar sprays or daily nutrient-solution supplements were begun at 14 weeks, and tissue samples were frozen periodically for several weeks thereafter. The moderate but continual suppression of ATPase and glucose 6-phosphatase, as shown in Table 12-10, was typical of the Mo effect for each

TABLE 12-10

FOLIAR ATPase AND GLUCOSE 6-PHOSPHATASE RESPONSES TO SPRAY APPLICATIONS OF THE PHOSPHATASE INHIBITOR MOLYBDENUM

Aqueous sodium molybdate solution (20 ppm Mo) with Tween 20 additive was applied once to 14-week-old plants of the variety *M. 336.* [After Alexander (21).]

Enzyme	Treatment	Days after treatment					
		0	3	9	18	27	Mean
		Enzyme (specific activity)					
ATPase	Control	13.8	31.4	25.0	17.5	31.8	24.0
	Mo	14.3	23.1	20.4	10.4	24.0	18.4
Glucose	Control	4.1	7.8	5.9	4.8	8.2	6.2
6-phosphatase	Mo	4.2	4.7	4.7	3.4	6.2	4.6

of the organic phosphates employed as substrate (21). Higher Mo (200 ppm) failed to produce greater suppression.

It should be emphasized that the *in vivo* Mo activity was not regarded as a direct inhibition such as that observed *in vitro*. Apparently, a long-term effect on enzyme-synthesizing capability was now operative, indicating that the living cane plant has a capability to resist or to recover from inhibitor activity. The plant must do so in order to prevent the irreparable injury to tissues which certainly would follow upon total enzyme inhibition. A partial but consistent inhibitory effect is therefore preferable to a highly-damaging effect or one of brief duration.

Sugar increases paralleling the phosphatase decline suggest that sucrose synthesis was increased under the prevailing conditions of enzyme restriction (Table 12-11). Sucrose was increased in the Mo-treated plants within 3 days and remained higher than in control plants at 9, 18, and 27 days regardless of rather large fluctuations occurring during this period.

Essentially comparable sugar and phosphatase effects were obtained with Mo as a nutrient-solution supplement (21, 20), and with W applied as a foliar spray (14). When supplied through the roots, Mo at 1.0 ppm was rendered ineffective by high calcium (9.0 meq/1) and by high iron (6.0 ppm). In general, phosphatase suppression is more difficult to accomplish in the greenhouse under conditions favorable for rapid growth, *i.e.*, with high nitrogen, abundant water or GA growth stimulation. Phosphatase level also varies among varieties (24, 28).

TABLE 12-11

SUCROSE CONTENT OF SUGARCANE LEAVES SPRAYED WITH THE PHOSPHATASE INHIBITOR MOLYBDENUM

Variety *M. 336*, 14 weeks of age. [After Alexander (21).]

Treatment	Days after treatment					
	0	3	9	18	27	Mean
	Sucrose (mg/g dry wt.)					
Control	25.2	20.4	29.2	19.7	25.0	23.9
Mo (20 ppm)	26.3	28.3	37.1	29.4	31.4	30.5

B. *The enzyme index*

The use of chemicals for phosphatase control would be most helpful within those varietal, cultural, or ecological regimes that favor excessive enzyme production. It would not be helpful to increase a phosphate pool size if it were already adequately large (under conditions of naturally low phosphatase activity). Thus, the effective use of phosphatase control at the field level can be visualized as requiring two kinds of information: (a) Current trends in moisture and nutritional status analogous to the crop log indexes; and (b) a phosphatase index indicating the current enzyme status relative to the varietal potential and cultural needs of the crop at a given period in its development.

Obviously the information needed to compile an enzyme index does not exist. On the other hand, it is possible to specify from greenhouse data that certain tissues will be more useful than others and that distinct enzyme trends based on changing moisture and nitrogen regimes will certainly be found. Once the necessary information is at hand, the chemical control of specific enzymes will best be performed as a supplementary cultural practice, preferably lending added effectiveness or precision to standard moisture and fertilizer programs. By this means, all events during the growth and ripening phases which rely upon large pools of sugar and acid phosphates could benefit by phosphatase control.

The features of phosphatase regulation outlined above are generally applicable to other enzymes and need not be taken up again. The lamina tissue of leaf $^{+}2$ is admirably suited for indexing photosynthetic enzymes and amylase. For an acid invertase index the elongating internode subtending leaf $^{+}2$ would be adequate and convenient. Neutral invertase should be sought in internode No. 8 or older. In creating a polyphenol oxidase index one would develop a standardized sample of the apical meristem.

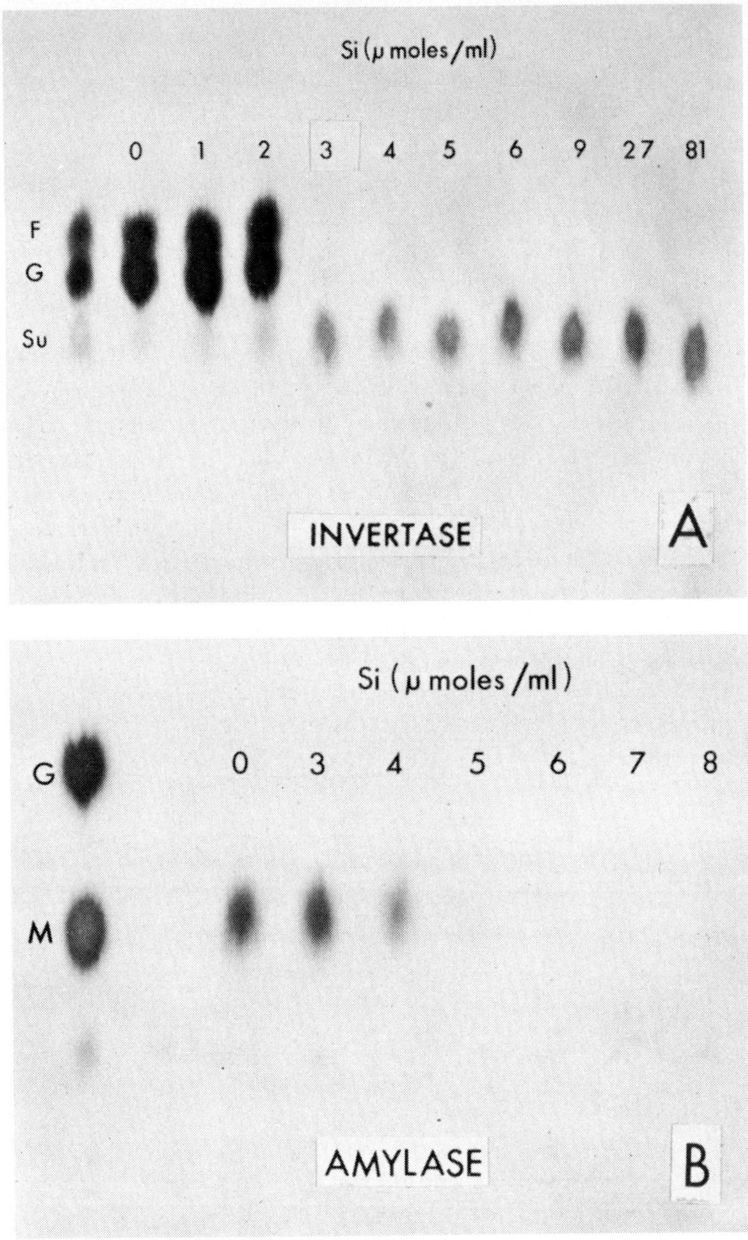

Fig. 12-8. (A) Paper chromatogram illustrating the *in vitro* inhibition of sugarcane acid invertase by sodium metasilicate. Activity against sucrose abruptly ceases when inhibitor levels exceed 2 μmoles per ml of reaction digest. (B) Similar inhibition of sugarcane amylase as evidenced by the decline of maltose (M) in starch–amylase reaction mixtures. [After Alexander (42).]

C. *Invertase and amylase control*

Although invertase and amylase rank among the most ancient of all known enzymes (1087, 1387), little effort has been made to control their behavior in living plants. It is increasingly clear that invertase control offers a means of regulating sugarcane growth as well as sucrose level (*cf.* Chapter 10, pp. 390–393). Similarly, recent evidence associating amylase with sugar content (34, 31, 11, 24, 15) and sucrose transport (670, 1155, 665) implies that amylase control is a potential means of sugar regulation. Efforts to alter the behavior of invertase and amylase in sugarcane with specific inhibitors have been partially successful (25, 1294, 30, 20).

Lead (Pb), mercury (Hg), and iodide have each shown promise as *in vitro* inhibitors of sugarcane invertase (16). Amylase is similarly affected (18). Cyanide is inhibitory for both enzymes. Manganese is possibly stimulatory for invertase and amylase under certain conditions (16, 18), and Si is an effective *in vitro* inhibitor of both catalysts (Fig. 12-8) (42). In a series of greenhouse experiments with immature sugarcane each element was tested by the author as a potential *in vivo* regulator when supplied through the leaves or roots. The reader is reminded that these initial experiments with highly-toxic materials were totally divorced from practical ripening studies. We were solely intent upon learning whether *in vivo* enzyme responses to chemicals would in any way corroborate their known *in vitro* effects.

Mercury ($HgCl_2$), provided as an aqueous foliar spray, effectively retarded amylase in the leaves of 10-week-old *M. 336* plants grown in sand culture (25). As shown by Fig. 12-9, 50 ppm and 1000 ppm elemental Hg produced moderate and severe amylase

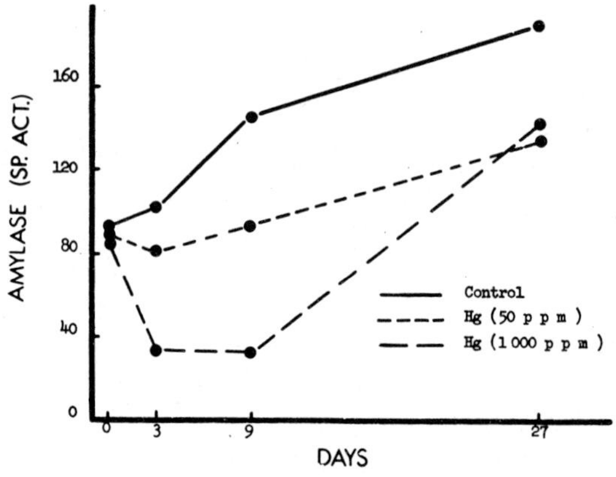

Fig. 12-9. Amylase suppression in sugarcane leaves following treatment with the inhibitor mercury (Hg). Aqueous mercuric chloride solutions were applied as foliar sprays to 12-week-old plants of the variety *M. 336*. [After Alexander (25.)]

suppression, respectively, as a short-term effect (within 9 days). As a long-term effect (at 27 days) both levels gave a moderate suppression. Because each treatment lowered invertase at 9 days it was thought that some fraction of the applied Hg had been translocated to the immature storage tissue used as invertase source. However, 1000 ppm Hg caused heavy sucrose losses in the leaves (Table 12-12) with no corresponding

TABLE 12-12

SUCROSE CONTENT OF SUGARCANE LEAVES SPRAYED WITH AQUEOUS MERCURY SOLUTIONS

Variety *M. 336*, 14 weeks of age. [After Alexander (25).]

Treatment	Days after treatment				
	0	3	9	27	Mean
	Sucrose (mg/g dry wt.)				
Control	83	113	128	128	113
Hg (50 ppm)	78	97	125	132	108
Hg (1000 ppm)	88	60	80	62	73

gain in storage sucrose. This illustrates vividly that the low amylase–high sucrose relationship obtained by physiological treatments (11, 15, 24, 31, 34) does not necessarily follow when amylase is lowered by chemical means. In addition, the fact that 50 ppm Hg also caused amylase suppression with no appreciable effect on sucrose indicates that the high Hg effect on sucrose was not mediated directly through amylase.

In a subsequent study (30), cyanide applied to cane foliage increased sucrose by 40 percent in leaves and by 69 percent in immature storage tissue within 3 days. Twelve-week-old plants were sprayed once with aqueous KCN solution containing 0.10 percent Tween 20. Leaf amylase content was markedly reduced by the cyanide treatment, as was both amylase and invertase in immature storage tissue. In another experiment, 20 ppm of cyanide supplied daily as a nutrient-solution supplement significantly lowered the foliar amylase and phosphatase levels over a period of 9 weeks.

The possibility that Si may alter invertase levels was implied by the early work of Ayres (125) in Hawaii and of D'Hotman De Villiers (435) in Mauritius who found that silicate-containing soil amendments increased sugarcane yields. More recent work by Clements (354) and Ayeres (126) has shown that calcium silicate improves cane quality as well as tonnage. In the instance of crushed basalt, Halais and Parish (629) showed that a soluble silica constituent was specifically responsible for the increased cane tonnage. Clements (356, 354) suggests that silicate precipitates solutes that are injurious to the cane roots and tops. Ayres (126) credits calcium silicate with raising the soil pH and decreasing the excessive uptake of manganese and aluminum. Quite significantly, Ayres proposed that some minimal level of "available" soil Si exists which is essential for normal sugarcane growth.

In vitro experiments with sodium metasilicate ($Na_2SiO_3 \cdot 9H_2O$) have shown that Si totally inhibits cane invertase within an extremely narrow concentration range of 2.0 to 3.0 μmoles/ml (Fig. 12-8A). At slightly higher Si concentrations cane amylase and yeast invertase are also inhibited. The first direct evidence that Si affects sugarcane enzymes *in vivo* was reported in 1966 (30) when Si added to nutrient solutions at rates of 20 and 200 ppm lowered invertase levels by 21 and 52 percent, respectively.

Samuels and Alexander (1294) studied Si interactions with Mn under sand culture conditions and observed that Si at levels of 50 and 500 ppm lowered invertase content as a main effect (Table 12-13). Manganese also tended to restrict invertase,

TABLE 12-13

INVERTASE AND AMYLASE RESPONSES TO SILICON AND MANGANESE GIVEN AS NUTRIENT-SOLUTION SUPPLEMENTS IN SAND CULTURE

Variety *M. 336*, treated from 5 to 14 weeks of age. Silicon source, $Na_2SiO_3 \cdot 9H_2O$; Mn source, EDTA-Na_2 Mn. [After Samuels and Alexander (1294).]

Enzyme	Si (ppm)	Mn (ppm)			
		0	10	100	Mean
		Enzyme (specific activity)			
Invertase	0	7.7	4.9	3.9	5.5
(immature	50	3.6	3.5	2.6	3.2
storage tissue)	500	2.0	2.8	1.2	2.0
	Mean	4.4	3.7	2.6	
Amylase	0	804	1205	1253	1087
(leaf)	50	956	1298	759	1016
	500	776	819	570	722
	Mean	845	1107	873	

and a combination of high Si (500 ppm) with high Mn (100 ppm) lowered invertase to about 16 percent of the control level (zero Si x zero Mn). This suppression, about 6-fold, produced a major sucrose rise in immature storage tissue, *i.e.*, from 1.1. to 6.5 percent on a dry-weight basis, which was also about 6-fold. Foliar amylase was increased by intermediate and high Mn levels (Table 12-13) but only when Si was not included in the nutrient solution. High Mn (100 ppm) was clearly repressive against the enzyme when combined with 50 or 500 ppm Si. Silicon also tended to lower the phosphatase and ATPase levels. By this means Si might benefit sucrose synthesis in a manner analogous to the Mo or W suppression of acid phosphatases (21).

Because of its ability to alter enzyme levels, Si appears to act in a protective or "buffer" capacity against extreme metabolic changes. This view was supported by observed Si stabilizing effects on enzymes during the post-growth stimulatory phase of GA action (50). Added evidence was found in the Si restriction of both growth-stimulatory and growth-reversion phases of GA activity (53), and in the Si prevention of desiccant activity against photosynthesis (46). It is also known from the work of Clements that Si prevents the uptake of excessive Mn from high-Mn soils (354). Samuels and Alexander (1294) demonstrated a similar Si–Mn absorption relationship in sand culture.

It is possible that photosynthetic mechanisms are protected by Si from extreme changes. The severe disruption of carbon assimilatory reactions produced by *Paraquat* and *Diquat* (45, 47) is significantly alleviated when leaves are pretreated with aqueous Si solutions (46). In the latter instance, plants pretreated with Si retained green foliage and normal sucrose content in the presence of desiccant levels highly destructive of tissues given no pretreatment.

6. CHEMICAL CONTROL OF THE APICAL MERISTEM

A. *Theoretical considerations*

Chemical restriction of growth requires the suppression or death of the meristematic region actively renewing the green-leaf and immature storage tissues. Successful treatment would enable the producer to terminate growth and initiate ripening in accordance with planned cultural and harvest schedules. This is an extremely important feature. In order to program an extended growth phase with water and nitrogen, or with growth-stimulatory chemicals, the grower must accept a shorter ripening period and less favorable conditions for natural ripening. Chemical growth control must therefore *accomplish quickly and directly the same degree of growth stress that nature would accomplish slowly and indirectly*. The ideal regulatory agent would be highly selective against some growth reaction utterly fundamental to all sugarcane plants irrespective of genetic composition, ecological environment, and local agronomic practices. As a theoretical example, this chemical might be one that would reduce to a minimal level the formation of mRNA for invertase, and would do so without disordering the physiological events operating in the normal source-to-sink system.

No substance has yet been discovered that will meet these specifications. However, there is evidence that compounds such as the purine and pyrimidine analogs can approximate the strictly physiological–biochemical requirements. When this is accomplished the problem of growth control will be reduced to the very practical proportions of economics and of agronomic technique.

B. *6-Azauracil*

In Chapter 10 (*cf.* p. 371) the pyrimidine analog 6-azauracil was discussed relative to its suppression of invertase and its consequent support of Glasziou and co-workers (690, 590) in depicting invertase as a key feature in governing growth. In another context, 6-azauracil is an excellent example of intensive and highly-localized enzyme suppression culminating in the death of a specific tissue – in this instance the apical meristem. In Table 12-14, growth, sugar, and enzyme responses to 6-azauracil

TABLE 12-14

SUGARCANE GROWTH, SUGAR, AND ENZYME RESPONSES TO FOLIAR TREATMENT WITH 6-AZAURACIL

Aqueous inhibitor solutions containing 0.10 percent Tween 20 were applied once to 14-week-old plants of the variety *P.R. 980.* [After Alexander (36).]

Criteria	6-Azauracil (% soln.)						
	0	0.001	0.005	0.01	0.04	0.10	0.40
	Total green weight (g/plant)						
Growth	254	249	236	254	180	42	–*
	Leaf sucrose (mg/g dry wt.)						
Sugar	60	68	59	57	62	106	–
	Immature storage tissue sucrose (mg/g dry wt.)						
	34	46	45	99	130	–	–
	Enzyme (specific activity)						
Enzymes							
Invertase	19.9	18.3	22.1	6.5	2.9	–	–
Amylase	51	36	54	30	24	–	–
Phosphatase	17.8	16.9	17.7	10.7	5.8	–	–
ATPase	16.8	17.0	18.3	12.1	6.9	–	–
Tyrosinase	18.1	17.6	18.9	10.8	6.2	–	–

*Blank spaces indicate that tissues were killed by 6-azauracil and no analyses were performed.

are summarized for immature sugarcane grown with controlled moisture and nutrient supplies (36). In essence there were three ranges of response: (a) Initial enzyme decline and sucrose increase between 0.005 and 0.10 percent 6-azauracil; (b) intensified enzyme decline and sucrose increase between 0.01 and 0.04 percent, accompanied by initial growth decline; and (c) reduction of enzymes to nil levels between 0.04 and 0.10 percent 6-azauracil, accompanied by high sucrose and severe growth restriction. The highest level (0.40 percent) caused death of the plants before the experiment was completed.

An extremely important point here is the fact that sugar increases accompanied enzyme suppression at inhibitor concentrations too low to affect growth. The level of each enzyme measured was lowered markedly between 0.005 and 0.01 percent, and in this range the storage sucrose level more than doubled while growth remained unaffected.

Invertase was particularly sensitive to 6-azauracil. Loss of this enzyme (pH 5.5) probably accounted for most of the increased sucrose at low inhibitor levels and for much of the growth changes at higher levels. Comparable enzyme–sugar changes occurring in anticipation of growth change has been observed in other sugarcane studies (11, 31, 23). The implication here is that sucrose accumulation (and hence ripening) is in fact a highly sensitive response to discrete enzyme behavior. As such, the field practice of ripening by growth restriction appears to be but a heavy-handed means of approaching enzyme control.

It is evident that, as the supplied inhibitor level exceeded 0.04 percent, the meristem's catalytic potential dropped below the minimal level needed to maintain life processes (Table 12-14). Already lowered to some 15 percent of control levels, invertase was probably too low to support new growth at 0.04 percent 6-azauracil[12].

In theoretical terms, the possibility that enzyme and sugar levels can be altered chemically without impairing growth has enormous implication for the sugar grower of the distant future. This would permit a significant degree of sucrose control during the growth phase, in effect constituting a pre-maturation ripening treatment. The two key prerequisites appear to exist in sugarcane. They are: (a) An abundance of sugar which exceeds normal growth needs, and (b) a discrepancy between actual enzyme level (or potential to synthesize enzyme) and the level at which growth restriction will occur, thus creating a working range within which enzyme behavior can be manipulated in favor of sugar storage without jeopardizing growth.

Another important feature of 6-azauracil is its rapid translocation to the apical meristem and the subsequent confinement of phytotoxicity to the meristematic area (Fig. 12-10). There was no permanent damage to leaf tissues below the 0.10-percent level, and the 0.04-percent treatment which caused moderate damage to the receiving foliage did not affect the leaves produced thereafter. Similarly, none of the inhibitor concentrations below 0.10 percent appreciably affected leaf enzymes, and no evidence of photosynthetic disruption was found. Fig. 12-10A, illustrating excised meristematic regions from typical control and 6-azauracil-treated plants, shows that the effect of

---

[12] The lower invertase level needed to maintain minimal growth without restricting sugar accumulation has been estimated at 35 to 40 percent of the normal content (40).

Fig. 12-10. Localized action of the growth inhibitor 6-azauracil against the meristematic region of sugarcane. (A) Excised meristematic tissue of a treated plant showing terminal effects precluding further growth activity. (B) Similarly treated plants showing normal leaf tissues but dead spindles. [Photographed by the author.]

0.04 percent 6-azauracil was terminal; there is no possibility of renewed growth from a meristem thus affected. Fig. 12-10B illustrates the outward appearance of similar plants 4 weeks after treatment. Although the green top appears to be quite normal, in each instance the spindle tissue is dead.

C. *6-Azauracil* x *GA*

Additional greenhouse experiments were performed to evaluate 6-azauracil as a growth retardant under conditions of accelerated growth (44, 36). Surmising that GA stimulation of the apical meristem might counter 6-azauracil activity, three levels of GA (0, 0.01, and 0.10 percent) were applied as foliar sprays in factorial combination with three levels of 6-azauracil (0, 0.005, and 0.05 percent). Fourteen-week-old plants of the variety *P.R. 980* were employed and a single harvest was made 6 weeks after treatment. Green-weight values showed that high 6-azauracil (0.05 percent) restricted growth regardless of GA level. In addition, the inhibitor produced general enzyme suppression and increased the sugar content of immature storage tissue and millable stalks (Table 12-15). Increasing GA modified somewhat the inhibitor action and high GA succeeded in keeping the meristem alive, although severely damaged. Similarly, phosphatase and invertase suppression was not quite so pronounced at the medium and high GA levels (Table 12-15). Nonetheless, GA clearly failed to prevent the inhibitor from suppressing growth.

In the preceding discussion considerable importance is attached to the enzyme and sugar changes produced by inhibitor levels too low to affect growth. The present factorial experiment (6-azauracil x GA), although not designed to do so, gave additional evidence that such changes can be brought about by subphytotoxic inhibitor levels. From growth data in Table 12-15 it is evident that the 0.005-percent 6-azauracil treatment increased "growth", *i.e.*, weight of millable stalks, in the presence of 0.10 percent GA. Without GA there was the usual growth suppression. From enzyme data in Table 12-15 it can be seen that the same treatment (medium 6-azauracil x high GA) produced enzyme suppression for each of the five systems assayed. This included a 25-percent reduction of invertase which was paralleled by a 12-percent increase in sucrose. Thus, under the greenhouse conditions employed, it was possible to lower enzyme levels, to increase sucrose, and to increase growth with a combination of selective growth inhibitor (6-azauracil) and growth stimulant (GA).

Further to this, millable "stalks" comprising 6 or 7 joints were ground with a small laboratory mill for Brix and pol analyses (Table 12-15). A moderate but positive ripening trend was found in response to both GA and 6-azauracil. As main effects GA was most active at 0.01 percent and 6-azauracil at 0.05 percent. A combination of intermediate GA and high 6-azauracil produced the maximum Brix and pol values.

Workers at the Tate and Lyle, Ltd., Research Centre (85) have also reported ripening activity by 6-azauracil and GA. The inhibitor effectively retarded growth with

TABLE 12-15

GROWTH, SUGAR, AND ENZYME RESPONSES TO FOLIAR COMBINATIONS OF 6-AZAURACIL AND GIBBERELLIC ACID

Aqueous solutions of GA plus inhibitor were applied once as foliar sprays on 14-week-old plants of the variety *P.R. 980.* [After Alexander (36).]

GA (% soln.)	6-Azauracil (% soln.)			6-Azauracil (% soln.)		
	0	0.005	0.05	0	0.005	0.05
	Stalk wt. (g/stalk)			Internode length (inches)		
0	121	96	51	4.6	4.6	2.5
0.01	100	109	58	6.0	6.3	3.7
0.10	119	147	79	7.8	8.3	4.7
	Storage sucrose (mg/g)			Brix		
0	144	159	–*	10.0	10.4	11.1
0.01	161	173	–	12.5	12.1	15.0
0.10	181	202	233	11.6	12.1	10.9
	Polarization			Invertase (sp. act.)		
0	17.4	19.2	30.1	10.8	7.7	–
0.01	29.8	29.2	41.3	6.9	5.9	–
0.10	22.9	25.3	25.1	5.8	4.3	2.1
	Amylase (sp. act.)			Phosphatase (sp. act.)		
0	176	131	–	17.7	4.4	–
0.01	115	89	–	14.3	13.2	–
0.10	115	87	65	13.3	9.0	4.1
	ATPase (sp. act.)			Tyrosinase (sp. act.)		
0	21.1	15.1	–	11.2	8.5	–
0.01	15.2	11.9	–	7.4	7.5	–
0.10	14.4	10.9	6.1	7.4	4.4	3.6

*Blank spaces signify that tissues were killed by 6-azauracil and no analyses were performed.

little phytotoxicity at the rate of 400 ppm. However, mixtures of the two compounds produced less ripening action than 6-azauracil given alone. It was also noted that GA reduced the growth-inhibitory action of 6-azauracil.

D. *6-Azauracil* x *nitrogen*

Although the results obtained with 6-azauracil on GA-treated plants were encouraging, it was felt that the ultimate test of a growth inhibitor should be performed on plants having preestablished moisture and nitrogen regimes heavily favorable to growth. Again employing the greenhouse-sand culture technique with abundant water supply, 10-week-old plants of the variety *P.R. 980* were given three nitrogen levels amounting to 0.5, 5.0, and 50 meq/l nitrate. In effect, this constituted a simulation of field conditions having insufficient, normal, and excessive available nitrogen under conditions of high moisture. In biochemical terms the inhibitor was probably absorbed into tissues containing extreme ranges of nitrogen metabolite pools. Moreover, extreme levels of the nitrate-inducible enzyme *nitrate reductase*[13] must also have been present. At 12 weeks, three levels of 6-azauracil were given as foliar sprays (0, 0.01, and 0.05 percent), and a single harvest was made 46 days thereafter.

Growth, sugar, and enzyme values showed that 6-azauracil remained active within a high-nitrogen regime (Table 12-16). However, each of the parameters reflected a strong "buffering" effect of high nitrogen against the inhibitor. For example, high 6-azauracil (0.05 percent) restricted stalk weight by 63 percent when the nitrate supply was limiting, but only by 31 percent when abundant nitrate was supplied. Similarly, high 6-azauracil increased sucrose in immature storage tissue by 100 percent at the intermediate nitrogen level, but only by 50 percent under a high-nitrogen regime. With respect to enzymes, invertase content was lowered some 50 percent by 0.05 percent 6-azauracil within the high-nitrogen regime, while only 0.01 percent 6-azauracil produced 56 percent inhibition when nitrogen was low (Table 12-16). ATPase is another good example of enzyme "resistance" to inhibitor action as a function of nitrogen regime[14]. This enzyme was highly sensitive to 0.01 percent 6-azauracil at the low nitrogen level, but it was unaffected by even 0.05 percent 6-azauracil when nitrogen was abundant.

In terms of growth inhibition the 6-azauracil treatments were regarded as a qualified success. A high nitrogen status is obviously more difficult to overcome by chemical means than is a status of hormonal stimulation. The impression we gained from this study is that 6-azauracil will make a strong bid to induce ripening under any nitrogen status, but its chances of success are not good unless some degree of nitrogen depletion has already occurred by natural means. The principal criticism of the chemical inhibitor in this instance is that it failed to shift the sugar equilibrium completely in favor of ripening when nitrogen was excessive. Brix and pol values indicate that sucrose was not being retained in the mature joints. The probable reason for this was the insufficient

---

[13]Maretzki, A. and Dela Cruz, A., 1967. Nitrate reductase in sugarcane tissues, *Plant Cell Physiol.* 8: 605–611.

[14]More recent evidence (48) shows that both "light" and "dark" ATPases are present in sugarcane tissues and that only the light-dependent enzyme is sensitive to variable nitrate supply (56). In terms of 6-azauracil action, it appears that only the nitrate-insensitive (or dark) ATPase was affected, and that the inhibitor activity was masked by high nitrogen induction of the light-dependent ATPase.

TABLE 12-16

EFFECTS OF VARIABLE NITROGEN REGIME ON SUGARCANE GROWTH, SUGAR, AND ENZYME RESPONSES TO FOLIAR TREATMENT WITH 6-AZAURACIL

P.R. 980 seedlings were grown in sand culture with a complete nutrient solution containing 10.0 meq/l nitrate. At 10 weeks the sand was flushed with tap water and variable nitrogen regimes were initiated. Foliar application of aqueous 6-azauracil solutions containing 0.10 percent Tween 20 was performed at 12 weeks. There were three replicates of each treatment. A single harvest was taken 46 days after the 6-azauracil application. [After Alexander (41).]

Nitrate (meq/l)	6-Azauracil (% soln.)			6-Azauracil (% soln.)		
	0	0.01	0.05	0	0.01	0.05
	Total green wt. (g/plant)			Stalk wt. (g/stalk)		
0.5	280	233	117	133	109	49
5.0	380	488	292	173	236	147
50.0	488	462	359	229	189	159
	Storage sucrose (mg/g)			Brix		
0.5	77	104	–*	12.3	13.3	14.2
5.0	47	88	94	11.9	10.0	9.2
50.0	51	66	76	10.9	9.0	8.3
	Polarization			Invertase (sp. act.)		
0.5	36.0	38.6	50.2	11.6	5.1	–
5.0	28.1	21.2	21.4	13.0	10.6	5.9
50.0	23.3	12.9	11.9	14.0	13.4	7.0
	Amylase (sp. act.)			Phosphatase (sp. act.)		
0.5	28.3	19.1	–	15.7	5.9	–
5.0	51.1	50.4	37.7	21.1	14.6	11.9
50.0	69.7	70.8	54.7	20.3	19.1	13.1
	ATPase (sp. act.)			Tyrosinase (sp. act.)		
0.5	19.3	8.4	–	20.6	10.6	–
5.0	23.8	18.2	17.2	24.9	22.1	18.4
50.0	17.8	18.9	16.2	35.0	22.8	16.3

*Blank spaces indicate that tissues were killed by 6-azauracil and no analyses were performed.

suppression of invertase, *i.e.*, to but 50 percent of the "control" level (Table 12-16). By our own estimate (40) a suppression to 35 to 40 percent of normal is needed to encourage ripening.

The partial invertase suppression is a useful case in point against strictly empirical evaluations of ripening compounds. Obviously, ripening did not occur if we accept the

Brix and pol data at face value, and in a screening trial 6-azauracil would have received a poor rating as a potential "ripener". But it is quite probable that further invertase suppression in the order of 10 to 15 percent would have produced ripening. Assuming this to be true, the compound would have accomplished about 4/5 of its assigned task without receiving credit for having accomplished anything, when in fact the cultural conditions were such as to preclude any reasonable chance of chemical ripening. In this instance the nitrogen supply was known to be too high for ready chemical ripening. Under field conditions similar information would have required continual updating of the plants' N index and moisture status as an integral part of the ripener-trial plan. It is very possible that the virtues of fairness and consistency will continue to elude the field-level ripener trial until such studies are habitually conducted in accordance with an overall culture plan based upon crop log information.

7. CHEMICAL SCREENING

A. *Limitations of the chemical ripener trial*

To the list of compounds already mentioned as having shown ripening potential, there could be added dozens more whose evaluation has neither proven nor disproven their worth as ripening agents. The most striking feature of chemical ripening studies to date is the fact that no totally satisfactory ripening compound has yet been discovered. A major reason for this has been reiterated many times: Sugarcane is a highly complex living organism whose precise control, difficult under the best of conditions, is vastly complicated by its varietal and ecological variables and by its cultural requirements. There is no real answer to this difficulty other than continued research at all levels.

Yet in all fairness, the methods used for chemical selection and testing have to bear some of the blame for past "failures". An underlying weakness of earlier ripening trials has been a gross overestimation of a single chemical's ability to quickly control an intact physiological system. In sugarcane the chemical has had to alter the system appreciably within a few days time. Not even such profound agents of growth as nitrogen and water, with all that their control implies in terms of life processes, can bring about much change in sugarcane without adequate allowance of time. Perhaps the only means by which any chemical could induce quick ripening is by action against a single reactive step so fundamental to growth that all growth processes are subservient to it. Such a step might be found, for example, in the control mechanism governing the extensive invertase fluctuations occurring daily in the meristematic area (1340, 54).

A second weakness of chemical ripening trials has been the failure to distinguish between a chemical's physiological capability on one hand and agronomic methodology on the other. Consequently, when a compound shows "promise", but only sporadically, there is no way of knowing whether the inconsistency stems from faulty timing or treatment technique, or whether the physiological task was simply too much for the compound to handle. To draw such distinctions one must obtain some idea of the physiological task to be performed. He must evaluate the current maturation status with respect to varietal behavior, moisture, and nitrogen. To this should be added the best possible information relative to the ripener's mode of action *as determined with sugarcane grown under greenhouse conditions or in controlled-climate facilities.*

There are few instances in the literature where an investigator has stated clearly the physiological task to be accomplished and the expected mode of action of the test chemical. There are a few exceptions to this statement. In 1957 Yates and Bates (1601) summarized the then current theory of action underlying each class of their trial compounds. Beauchamp (163), having no detailed knowledge of the 2,4-D mode of action, nonetheless specified very clearly the local cultural conditions needed for 2,4-D to be active – much more clearly, by the way, than most of the later workers who failed to obtain ripening with 2,4-D. This particular deficiency should be lessened over the years as more fundamental knowledge accumulates relative to cane physiology, particularly in connection with the specific chemical configurations acceptable to sugarcane control mechanisms.

A third shortcoming, if it can be so-called, has been the sugar industry's slowness in recognizing that cane quality improvement involves the improvement of an entire source-to-sink system rather than mere growth restriction. Tremendous advances have been made toward understanding photosynthesis, sucrose biosynthesis, sucrose translocation, and the sugar accumulation processes within the sugarcane plant. Taken together as a whole these processes form the intact system which makes ripening possible. Although the sugar grower, knowingly or otherwise, must deal with the whole system as he attempts to ripen sugarcane, until recently it was growth suppression which guided the thinking behind chemical ripener trials. Exceptions to this include the work of Yates and Bates (1601), and more recent work at the Tate and Lyle, Ltd., Research Centre (85) which examined the possibility of photosynthetic involvement in chemical-induced ripening.

Another questionable feature of the ripener trial has been its reliance upon stalk quality as the measure of ripening activity. Numerous authorities subscribe to the belief that *the best measure of any sugar-promoting factor is the tons of sucrose harvested per acre*. In physiological terms this is not necessarily true. As a measure of ripening activity it may be even less true insofar as the plant's ripening status remains undefined, *i.e.*, insofar as the magnitude of the ripener's task is unknown. The point being taken here is that ripening must be viewed in terms of changes by degrees, as subtle shifts in the balances of many growth-affecting processes. Within this context a test chemical might do much or little toward ripening induction without producing measurable changes in sucrose levels.

B. *The screening program*

Although very few compounds have been discovered with consistent ripening activity, interest continues to mount in chemical usage throughout the sugar-growing world. Even in areas where natural ripening excels there is continuing interest in chemical ripening agents. In heavy-rainfall areas such as Guyana there may always be a little magic in the thought that perhaps chemicals can succeed where nature fails, or at least lend nature a helping hand.

In general terms there are at least three current approaches to the screening of ripening compounds. Each method has its own advantages and disadvantages. Perhaps the most popular approach is that used at the Experiment Station, H.S.P.A., Honolulu. Virtually all of the work is conducted with mature, field-grown plants in two distinct stages following a preliminary screening phase (1112): (a) Small-scale plot trials to determine which compounds are active; and (b) large-scale field trials by aerial application. Field development has generally been stressed more heavily in Hawaii than in other regions. Nickell and Tanimoto (1112) considered it probable that numerous compounds can act in equally numerous ways to produce a ripened stalk. On this basis materials having widely distinct chemical properties and biological effects have been tested singularly and in combinations.

Screening tests in Hawaii have also employed large numbers of compounds. In 1965 Nickell and Tanimoto (1107) stated that more than 200 chemicals had been screened and that 46 had shown some level of activity on the basis of increased pol percent cane for the youngest 15 joints. These compounds were obtained commercially or provided by some 18 chemical companies. Twelve different classes of chemicals were screened. In addition there were 24 unidentified materials of unspecified composition.

In 1970 Nickell and Maretzki (1116) summarized recent ripening studies in Hawaii which incorporated chemical, biochemical, and biological properties in constructing a several-dimensional picture of ripener activity. Significantly, growth repression was depicted as only one of a series of active ripening features. Chemical evaluations included the study of growth effects in duckweed and cell suspension cultures, effects upon [^{14}C]leucine incorporation into cell-suspension protein, effects on three representative types of enzymes, and chemical effects on cell respiration. Although not all parameters showed a relationship to quality improvement, this appears to be the most far-sighted approach to ripener screening that has yet appeared in the literature.

The Hawaiian approach toward evaluating potential chemical ripeners constitutes a vigorous and well-balanced program designed to assist the sugar grower. Added to the fact that the Hawaiian sugar industry is receptive to new ideas, the sympathy for both fundamental and applied research prevalent at the Experiment Station, H.S.P.A. provides an ideal climate for advancing this most important aspect of sugarcane research.

In certain respects the ripening program of Tate and Lyle, Ltd. has been similar to that developed by Nickell and Tanimoto. Prior to 1965 there was strong emphasis on field trials with decidedly less attention given to fundamental aspects of chemical activity. More recently, very significant advances have been made toward understanding the endogenous growth substances which help control natural ripening (1046, 1047). Vlitos has eloquently stated the need for new fundamental knowledge (1508), and since 1967 increasing emphasis has been directed toward basic research at the Tate and Lyle, Ltd., Research Centre near London.

In 1968 (83) initial reports appeared from the Tate and Lyle group describing ripener trials with heated-greenhouse and controlled-climate chambers at the C.N.R.S. facilities, Gif-sur-Yvette, France. Principal features included the use of single-stemmed, highly uniform plants in the "young adult" stage, *i.e.*, having at least one mature joint, and the thorough wetting of both sides of the leaf by aqueous chemical solutions containing Tween 20. A similar methodology has been used in Puerto Rico since 1962. Quite significantly, growth restriction was taken as the main indicator of ripening activity rather than juice quality. Photosynthesis rate measurements were also initiated for some of the chemically-treated plants.

The further development of fundamental screening phases in support of field trials was reported from Tate and Lyle, Ltd. in 1969 (85). Using greenhouse facilities at Keston, Kent (England), uniformity selection and sampling technique was refined so that statistically significant differences could be shown with as few as two replicates. Factors of variety, moisture, temperature, and day length were relatively standardized. Criteria for ripening activity included measurements for growth, phytotoxicity, storage sugars, and photosynthesis. In addition, a new theory relative to hormonal activity in cane ripening was forwarded on the basis of data from inhibitor and water-stress experiments. Natural growth inhibitors from *Ceratonia siliqua* were also studied with possible reference to sugarcane ripening. This program encourages major advances in basic sugarcane knowledge while bringing a new level of precision to the measurement of ripening activity.

Chemical ripening trials at the David North Plant Research Centre, Brisbane, have led all others in the emphasis on fundamental ripening action. This work was facilitated by the fundamental backgrounds of a highly-competent and thoroughly dedicated staff. Added to this was the ready availability of controlled-climate and laboratory facilities. It was now feasible to grow plants having precisely-controlled conditions of light and temperature in addition to controlled nutrient and moisture supplies. By this means variable growth and ripening regimes could be established at will among test plant populations. As a result of this control, workers could begin to define both the optimum conditions for ripening activity and the outer environmental limits within which an active compound could perform.

However, in terms of ripening trials, one should not overrate the value of controlled climate facilities *per se*, since these in turn are totally dependent upon the imagination and persistence of the research personnel. In this context a great deal of new information can still be gained with conventional greenhouse facilities if these are used resourcefully by properly-motivated workers.

Chemical ripening studies by the author in Puerto Rico have been largely confined to the greenhouse and laboratory. This was not entirely a matter of choice since there has not been a sufficient staff here to evaluate more than a few compounds at the field level. No attempt was made to screen a large number of compounds; rather, we have explored in depth certain features of a few substances such as GA, metasilicate, and 6-azauracil. Emphasis in Puerto Rico has been directed toward chemical enzyme control, particularly invertase control, under various simulated growth regimes. Under such conditions it is possible for one or two individuals to develop in detail a particular physiological theory of ripening control. By thus concentrating limited resources, an appreciable quantity of new information can be gathered. The sugar industry at large may even find a practical use for some of it. However, without a complementary effort at the field level, an essentially unbalanced program can do but little in direct service to a local sugar industry.

Chapter 13

Chemical Desiccation

1. INTRODUCTION

Preharvest burning or "detrashing" is a common practice designed to lower the percentage of extraneous material[1] shipped to the factory and to facilitate harvesting procedure. Arceneaux and Davidson (91) state that when leaves accompany stalks during milling operations the sugar recovery is lessened in the order of 1 pound sugar for every 30 pounds of leaves per ton of cane. Similarly, the milling of fresh unburned cane would produce a minimum loss of 5 pounds of sugar per ton of stalks. Arceneaux[2] estimates that trash deliveries to the factory in Puerto Rico reduced sugar recovery in the order of 22 pounds per ton of cane. Birkett (185) lists four kinds of losses caused by trash in harvested sugarcane:

(1) Harvesting and transportation costs accrue for trash just as though it were millable cane.

(2) Trash contributes fiber without contributing sugar; hence, there is an increase of bagasse which contains an unextractable sugar residue.

(3) Extractable fluids in the trash contain impurities which in turn lower the purity of cane juice.

(4) Trash and extra fiber increase milling time and add to the wear on factory machinery.

Additional problems associated with trash include greater insect infestations, larger rat populations and reduced effectiveness of pre-emergence herbicide treatments.

Although the need to eliminate trash before milling is widely recognized, this is seldom accomplished to the satisfaction of growers and factory managers. Under humid conditions the preharvest burn is frequently rendered ineffective with the result that the TC/TS ratio and trash/cane ratio is increased significantly. Even with ideal weather there is no assurance of uniform burn, and Bates (155) concluded from aerial observations that fires tend to "channel" even within an apparently uniform field. In Puerto Rico preharvest burning has been practised since the late 1940's, generally with more success in the dry areas than in the humid and semi-humid regions. More recently there has been an added problem of cane held over from the previous season owing to a diminishing labor force and insufficiency of harvest machines. In such instances there are masses of fallen stalks sheltered by a younger green canopy which resists alike the penetration of sunlight and artificial drying agents.

[1] "Extraneous material" herein refers to immature tops (including all green leaves and their subtending internodes), attached dead leaves, fallen dead leaves, and water shoots.

[2] Arceneaux, G., 1963. Decline of sugar recoveries in Puerto Rico, *Commonwealth of Puerto Rico Dept. Agric. Tech. Bull.* No. 1.

In Louisiana (416), where winter freezes limit the growing season to about 10 months, the cane is generally too green to burn while standing. Leaves are burned after the cane has been cut, topped, and piled across the row. When the foliage is relatively green early in the harvest season the cut cane is frequently left in the field at least 2 days to assure leaf burn, and in the event of rain it must remain longer, with the risk of sucrose inversion, or be sent to the factory with leaves attached. The latter alternative is sometimes accepted in order to avoid sucrose losses introduced by waiting for favorable weather (1217). Postharvest burning to remove surface residues is standard practice in Hawaii and Guyana (155) despite certain objections. Studies in Puerto Rico have shown no yield effects by various trash disposal methods (886), although soil losses can sometimes occur when trash is not retained as a mulch (206).

There is a definite need for a safe and inexpensive compound that will consistently produce favorable burning conditions just prior to harvest. A theoretical means of accomplishing this is by chemical defoliation. Defoliants are used successfully on a number of crops including cotton, potatoes and certain legumes. In these instances burning is not an objective, and the defoliation process is helped immensely by a sensitive abscission layer localized at the base of the petiole. No such structure exists in sugarcane where leaf fall is usually prompted by mechanical disturbance after the death and partial decomposition of a leaf sheath which clings tenaciously to the stalk.

A more practical means of leaf removal from sugarcane is by desiccating the attached leaf and disposing of it by fire immediately before or after cutting the stalk. In order for any chemical to appreciably aid this process it must produce an enormous amount of drying, and it must do so cheaply and without harming cane quality. Bates (155) lists three requirements of a chemical desiccant suitable for use on sugarcane:

(1) It should be inexpensive, safe to handle, and readily dispersed with low-volume aerial equipment.

(2) It should have a rapid systemic action, essentially independent of post-application weather conditions, and it should leave no undesirable residues.

(3) It should not affect the quality of the current crop nor the growth of ratoon crops.

In the present chapter we shall see that the quest for chemical desiccants was largely unsuccessful until two quaternary ammonium compounds, *Paraquat* and *Diquat*, became available to the sugar industry. In certain respects these chemicals fill the desiccant role quite admirably. Robson and Procter (1250), of Plant Protection Ltd., generously depict Paraquat in the following terms:

"Paraquat treatment ensures an almost perfect burn of the green tops and sets in motion a long chain of economic savings, terminating in less trash going to the factory and a significant increase in sugar recovery."

Unfortunately, neither Paraquat nor its sister compound Diquat have performed this well for the majority of workers testing them. A frequent complaint has been quality deterioration within a few days after treatment, *i.e.*, the third requirement listed by Bates (155) has not been met. Other investigators find that outward symptoms of "scorch" or desiccation do not necessarily lead to better burns, apparently owing to unaffected leaf tissue more or less protected within or beneath the green canopy. Systemic desiccative action has not been conclusively established in sugarcane although a systemic effect has been suggested by several workers. Nonetheless, Diquat and Paraquat represent current high points in the chemical desiccation of sugarcane, and, as such, they deserve the primary attention of this chapter.

2. THE SEARCH FOR SUGARCANE DESICCANTS

Early desiccant studies generally centered around oils, applied either singularly or "fortified" with another chemical, and inorganic salts such as chlorates, borates, nitrates and phosphates. Characteristic of such compounds was a localized non-systemic action requiring large solution volumes in order to contact a maximum leaf area. A third group consisted of organic desiccants having systemic action and low-gallonage requirements that could be approached by aerial application. It should be noted that, regardless of the material being tested, early investigators were mainly interested in practical results, that is, the extent of desiccation, time required to produce desiccation, and chemical effects on juice quality.

According to Young (1603), the first desiccant trials in Hawaii were established by R.K. Conant at the Olau Sugar Company early in 1944. Test materials included straight diesel oil, a diesel oil emulsion, and sodium chlorate, each applied by a road-side spray truck. Sodium chlorate produced better drying and more effective burns than did the oils. It also appeared to improve juice quality while straight diesel oil caused sugar losses. On the other hand, Yates and Bates (1601) severely lowered juice quality with sodium chlorate tested as a sugarcane defoliant. Conant did observe that sodium chlorate damaged ratoons, and this feature was obviously unacceptable. Other early compounds tested in Hawaii were "Chile Potash Nitrate" and trisodium phosphate, applied singularly and in combinations with "2-7-R". Chile Potash Nitrate produced highly favorable drying but lowered juice quality.

Subsequent trials (1603) included sodium monochloroacetate (MCA, also termed "Dow Defoliant") applied by ground and aerial equipment. Good drying was obtained but at the expense of juice quality. The cotton defoliant "Shed-A-Leaf" was tested and gave more rapid drying than MCA, but it also lowered juice quality. The compounds "De-Fol-Ate" (magnesium chlorate) and S-4069 gave superior drying and improved burns without appreciably affecting cane quality. Other materials tested included a second formulation of magnesium chlorate ("Magron"), "Dinitro" (dinitro-*o*-*sec*-butylphenol) applied alone and in combination with oils, "OSA" in oil, "WSA" in water, diesel oil alone, ocean water, and aqueous ammonium sulfate (1603).

In 1951 Coleman and Hebert (367) tested Shed-A-Leaf (Chipman Chemical Co.) with sodium chlorate and sodium pentaborate at the rate of 30 pounds per acre on the variety *C.P. 36-105*. A definite loss of cane quality was recorded at 18, 25, and 39 days after application. Additional trials with pentachlorophenol, Endothal, and Shed-A-Leaf were performed during the autumn of 1951. Only Shed-A-Leaf at the rate of 30 pounds per acre effectively desiccated the leaves, but this treatment also lowered sucrose yield. In 1953 Dalapon, tested as a desiccant at rates of 1 to 10 pounds per acre, failed to produce foliar drying or significant sucrose effects. Later trials showed that 15, 20, and 40 pounds of Dalapon per acre caused foliar injury with small parallel losses in juice quality.

According to Davidson (416), Coleman conducted additional desiccant studies (unpublished) at the Houma Station between 1957 and 1959. Results showed that sodium and magnesium chlorate, polychlorobenzoic acid, and Ammate at 100 to 400 pounds per acre were slow acting and required 6 or 7 days to reach a desiccation level suitable for burning. Each chemical seriously lowered juice quality. The compounds "Golden Harvest" (pentachlorophenol) and C-56 (hexachlorocyclopentadiene) were effective within 2 days when applied in diesel oil. Also tested during this period were sodium pentachlorophenate, which was unsatisfactory as a cane desiccant, and Diquat (1,1′-ethylene-2,2′-dipyridylium dibromide), which proved to be the most promising chemical of the series.

In 1960 Bates (155) summarized a series of desiccation trials in British Guiana with 12 chemicals, most of which had proven to be useful on cotton or other crops. The majority of these gave negative or inconclusive results when applied to 8- to 12-month-old cane, varieties *B. 41227* and *B. 37161*, at rates 12.5 to 25 gallons per acre. Butynediol, an unsaturated glycol used as a defoliant of cotton, castor bean, soya bean, and fruit trees at 2 to 6 pounds per acre, failed to desiccate sugarcane at less than 7.5 pounds per acre, and then only after 96 hours had elapsed. Combination of Butynediol with aminotriazole and chelated copper failed to produce a synergistic effect as had been reported for other crops. An organic arsenic compound, Cacodylic acid (dimethylarsinic acid), used experimentally as a cotton desiccant (1334), did not appreciably desiccate sugarcane within 10 days when applied at 2, 4 and 8 pounds per acre. Sodium monochloroacetate produced "mediocre" results when tested on cane at 15 to 40 pounds per acre. This compound is effective on forage legumes but appeared to be of little value for sugarcane even at 40 pounds per acre.

Additional compounds mentioned by Bates (155) include diesel oil, Folex, Endothal, Borochlor (sodium chlorate plus sodium borate), Magron (magnesium chlorate hexahydrate), and Monuron [CMU= 3-(*p*-chlorophenyl)-1, 1-dimethylurea]. Aerial application of diesel oil at 5 gallons per acre or less produced phytotoxic symptoms but no generalized desiccation. When fortified with pentachlorophenol or dinitro-*o*-*sec*-butylphenol, there was good desiccation within 24 hours; however, the additives' extreme toxicity was considered prohibitive against general use. Folex also has a high degree of mammalian toxicity which precludes safe testing with hand equipment. Curiously, 4 and 6 pints per acre of Folex failed to lower spindle and sheath moisture as effectively as 3 pints. The latter amount lowered the sheath moisture percentage to 74.5, as compared with the control value of 79.8 percent. Endothal at 1 gallon per acre produced comparable desiccation, while Borochlor lowered sheath moisture values less than 1 percent at the "high" rate of 40 pounds per acre. Magron produced no appreciable drying.

Although CMU was reported to be an effective cane desiccant in Hawaii at 2 to 5 pounds per acre (72), Bates was unable to obtain appreciable desiccation in Guyana with 2.5 and 5 pounds per acre over a 2-week interval. Since the compound is also relatively insoluble and is absorbed only slowly by the leaves, its value as a sugarcane desiccant was regarded as questionable. Of the chemicals tested, Bates observed no deleterious sugar effect within 4 days after burning. He did observe a quality reduction after 7 days in plots burned while standing as compared with plots burned after cutting, but the deterioration was no more severe in chemically-treated cane than in controls. None of the chemicals appeared to damage ratoons.

In 1945 Arceneaux and Davidson (92) tested cyanamid as an aerial dust at rates of 30, 60, and 90 pounds per acre on the variety *C.P. 29-320*. Results were "disappointing" in that only the fully-exposed leaves were desiccated while the bulk of the green top remained unaffected. Desiccation improved with increasing cyanamid level, but no appreciable improvement in burning was obtained even at 90 pounds per acre. Furthermore, treated cane failed to accumulate sugar after receiving the chemical, although control cane continued to accumulate sugar at the rate of some 22 pounds per ton of cane over a 27-day period. It was calculated that cyanamid levels sufficient to improve burning would lead to serious losses of recoverable sugar. Arceneaux and Davidson concluded: "It would seem important, therefore, to examine critically any new scheme which might be employed in killing foliage to facilitate preharvest burning."

Bates (155) reported that initial Diquat evaluations were highly promising even when spray applications were followed shortly by moderate rainfall. Applied at rates of 1, 2, 3, and 4 pounds per acre, each treatment revealed clear phytotoxic action in the leaf lamina within 48 hours and pronounced desiccation within 72 hours. Midribs were also desiccated by the 3- and 4-pounds treatments. Virtually all leaves reportedly developed a distinct straw color, including those not contacted by the spray, and the treated plots produced a "dry trash" odor. Leaf sheaths assumed a "reddish-mauve coloration suggestive of *Cercospora vaginae*". The mean leaf moisture reduction for all Diquat plots was 17.6 percent. New, undamaged spindle leaves began appearing within about 7 days. Subsequent Diquat tests verified these findings and placed the optimum rate at 1 to 2 pounds of technical material per acre.

Bates tested a second quaternary ammonium compound, Paraquat (then identified only as P.P.910), in direct small-scale comparisons with Diquat (Table 13-1). A claim that P.P.910 was more active than Diquat in grasses appeared to be verified, although both compounds produced excellent desiccation. Bates was aware of reports (232, 743) indicating that Diquat was less active in the absence of high light intensity, but he minimized this aspect insofar as practical usage in the tropics was concerned. A definite light requirement for the typical phytotoxic action of both Diquat and Paraquat was later to assume great importance in determining their biochemical mode of action.

TABLE 13-1

COMPARISON OF DIQUAT (REGLONE) AND PARAQUAT (P.P. 910) DESICCATIVE ACTIVITY ON SUGARCANE SPINDLE AND T.V.D. LEAVES* 96 HOURS AFTER TREATMENT

[After Bates (155).] Reproduced by permission of *W. Heffer and Sons, Ltd.*, Cambridge.

Treatment		Desiccation parameter	
		Spindle tissue % moisture content	T.V.D. leaf % moisture content
P.P. 910	1 lb/acre	63.1	58.3
	2 lbs/acre	62.5	58.2
Reglone	1 lb/acre	65.9	60.9
	2 lbs/acre	63.5	62.3
Control		75.0	71.3

*T.V.D. leaves = top visible dewlap leaves.

Davidson (416) obtained similarly favorable desiccation with Diquat. One to 2 pounds per acre applied with knapsack sprayers in 125 gallons of water produced major drying within 2 to 3 days in clear weather, but lesser drying in cloudy weather. There was no destruction of meristem tissue. Sucrose levels reportedly remained constant for several weeks and subsequently increased as new green leaves were produced.

In Queensland, Vallance (1471) obtained comparable desiccation with Diquat treatments ranging from 2.5 to 10 pounds per acre. Excellent drying had been accomplished in the two varieties tested (*Pindar* and *Q. 57*) within 7 days. An important feature was the time allowed for desiccation; *Pindar* was held for 16 days and *Q. 57* for 11 days before burning. When milled, both varieties were found to have lost sugar. Vallance appears to have been the first investigator to recognize a danger in delaying harvest after treating sugarcane with this compound. In a later report (1472), Vallance mentioned that Diquat applied as foliar spray for weed control severely damaged the cane and lowered C.C.S. values (commercial cane sugar values) at rates of 2 and 4 pints per acre.

In general, the first workers to test Diquat and Paraquat found these chemicals to be superior to earlier desiccants. More recently they have been used with success in flower control (764, 1405). In fundamental research they have proven useful in studies of photosynthetic reactions and mechanisms of enzyme control. Among their desirable properties are low mammalian toxicity, solubility in water, rapid absorption, and inactivation upon contact with the soil. In many respects the quaternary ammonium compounds have become almost synonymous with the term "dessicant" in sugarcane-growing regions.

3. DIQUAT AND PARAQUAT: PROPERTIES AND MODE OF ACTION

A. *Chemical configuration and phytotoxicity*

Herbicidal properties of Diquat (6,7-dihydrodipyrido [1,2-a:2′,1′-c] pyrazidinium salt) and Paraquat (1,1′-dimethyl-4,4′-dipyridinium salt), were first discovered by Brian *et al.* (241) in 1955, although certain quaternary ammonium compounds had been used as redox indicators under the name of "viologens" since 1933 (1016, 1017). During the evaluation of several quaternary ammonium compounds at Jealott's Hill Research Station, one chemical showed outstanding herbicidal activity. It was originally prepared by R.J. Fielden at Blackley by quaternizing 2,2′-dipyridyl with ethylene dibromide, a reaction which produces the single crystalline product 1,1′-ethylene-2,2′-dipyridylium dibromide (Fig. 13-1).

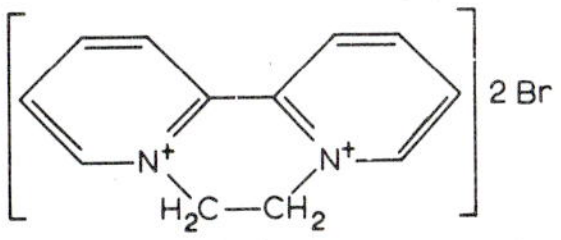

(X)

Fig. 13-1. The crystalline product 1,1′-ethylene-2,2′-dipyridylium dibromide originally prepared by R.J. Fields who quaternized 2,2′-dipyridyl with ethylene dibromide. The compound, originally designated simply as "X" by Brian *et al.* (241), was found to have exceptional phytotoxic activity when applied to plants in aqeuous solution. [After Brian *et al.* (241).] Reproduced by permission of *Nature*, London.

Elementary analyses of the product gave the empirical formula $C_{12}H_{12}N_2Br_2$, with all the bromine ionic. Possible dimeric or polymeric structures were eliminated when hydrogenation gave a fully saturated base, $C_{12}H_{22}N_2$, with a molecular weight of 186 [$C_{12}H_{22}N_2$ requires 194 (see 241)]. The compound forms a pale yellow monohydrate from water, m.p. > 320 °C. It is highly soluble in water (70 g in 100 ml at 20 °C) and is stable in acid or neutral solution. In alkaline solution colored products of considerable complexity are formed, apparently by the opening of a pyridine ring accompanied by uptake of one alkali molecule. Since this chemical is usually formulated in water and used in aqueous solution, the monohydrate is the form normally obtained and this form was given the common name Diquat (393).

Early work by Michaelis and Hill (1016, 1017) showed that, unlike the majority of organic compounds reduced in a two-electron process, the reduction of 4,4′-bipyridyl salts involved a delay in the addition of the second electron, so that there existed an intermediate reduction product having free-radical properties. The free radical shows exceptional stability in the 4,4′-bipyridyl series which Boon (209) attributes to resonance. It is also water-soluble and intensely colored. Homer *et al.* (743, 742) have shown that both Diquat and Paraquat behave in a similar manner.

Greenhouse tests revealed that the new herbicide (Diquat) was highly toxic for many plant species at low concentrations (241). It produced rapid wilting and desiccation but none of the abnormal growth responses characteristic of hormone-type herbicides. Aqueous Diquat solutions applied as a foliar spray in quantities equal to 0.5 pound per acre (in 100 gallons) were totally lethal for wheat, sugar beet, white mustard, marigold, red clover, and other species. At 0.125 pound per acre there was severe damage to nearly all plants tested. Similar effects were obtained without wetting agent and with a lower volume of material (20 gallons per acre). The degree of toxicity, rapidity of action, and independence of solution volume led Brian *et al.* (241) to suspect that the action was systemic. It was soon shown that uptake by intact bean leaves occurred within 5 minutes, and foliar uptake and translocation was demonstrated in broad bean and oat plants. Although readily absorbed through roots in culture solution, Diquat was not taken up from treated soil. Calderbank (282) states that Diquat is absorbed on soils by base exchange reactions and is so tenaciously held that more than ten times the lethal foliar concentration can be irrigated on to the soil without affecting the plant.

Subsequent greenhouse tests (241) showed that Diquat was active against several common weeds at rates of 0.125 to 0.5 pound per acre, including weeds resistant to 2,4-D and MCPA (2-methyl-4-chlorophenoxyacetic acid), such as chickweed (*Stellaria media*), groundsel (*Senecio vulgaris*), mayweed (*Matricaria* spp.) and speedwell (*Veronica* spp.). As little as 0.25 pound per acre was toxic for Russian thistle (*Salsola pestifer*). Other weeds killed by Diquat were red shank (*Polygonum persicaria*), annual nettle (*Urtica urens*), and black nightshade (*Solanum nigrum*).

Calderbank (282) reports that foliar injury symptoms of Diquat are at times visible within an hour and that rapid subsequent desiccation may limit the rate of transport. In this context Diquat was described as a contact herbicide whose unusually rapid desiccation is restricted to aerial tissues. The compound is extremely effective as a potato haulm killer (282). It has been used as a desiccant on Irish potatoes (283, 393) and cotton (282), as an arboricide (620), and as a crabgrass killer in tomatoes (365). Both Diquat and Paraquat have given postemergence weed control under fruit trees (65) and have controlled aquatic weeds (907, 908). Owing to its ease of handling and low mammalian toxicity, Calderbank (282) described Diquat as "a very pleasant alternative" to compounds such as sulfuric acid, arsenite, pentachlorophenol, and dinitrobutylphenol.

B. *Mode af action*

Studies by Homer *et al.* (742–744) suggested that phytotoxicity was related to reduction in a number of the quaternary salts. These included the diquaternary salts of 2,2′-, 2,4′-, and 4,4′-dipyridyl (743) already mentioned above. Requirements for free radical stability, on the basis of work by Michaelis and Hill (1017), were taken to include coplanar configuration of the pyridine rings and relative positioning of the nitrogen atoms such that the single electron can occupy any ring position. Herbicidal action would then depend upon the compounds' ability to form stable free radicals by the uptake of one electron. The hypothesis was tested by predicting and then demonstrating the phytotoxicity of 2,4′-dipyridyl dimethiodide. The relatively low phytotoxicity of this compound was explained by its difficulty in achieving coplanar configuration owing to hindrance by the nitrogen-attached methyl group in the 2-linked ring. The reduction concept also received support when Diquat and Paraquat were shown to have redox potentials of –349 and –446 mV, respectively.

Prior to 1954 free radicals had not been conclusively demonstrated in living tissues, although their presence had been postulated, with far-reaching biological implications, in oxidation–reduction reactions (1019, 1018), radiation of biological systems (1552), and chemical carcinogenesis (828). Commoner *et al.* (385), in 1954, described free radical analyses in plant and animal tissues by paramagnetic resonance absorption methods capable of detecting trace amounts of free radicals in the presence of natural diamagnetic substances. These chemical configurations were believed to participate in metabolic and photochemical reactions. Calvin (288) has shown that free radicals are normally formed during photosynthesis. Müller and Zimmer (1056) claim that free radicals are most likely to arise from irradiation, and demonstrated that their concentration increased with increasing irradiation dosages.

Boon (209) suggested several means by which a Diquat or Paraquat free radical might act within the plant. One possibility is the "short-circuiting" of electron flow during the energy-conversion phase of photosynthesis. Rather than $NADP^+$ being reduced to NADPH (*cf.* Chapter 2, pp. 72–78), the herbicide itself could be reduced and subsequently reoxidized. As discussed later in this chapter, the behavior of ATPases in Paraquat-treated sugarcane seems to support this theory. Another possibility is that toxic peroxide radicals, or hydrogen peroxide, might form subsequent to the reoxidation of the free radical by molecular oxygen (414).

Homer *et al.* (743) further suggested that the free radical *per se* need not be toxic for the observed herbicidal effects to occur. Alternative possibilities include a toxic mechanism by which the radical is produced from the quaternary salt, or the formation of toxic reaction products (peroxides) arising by oxidation of the reductant. Whatever the mechanism, it seems quite certain that the level of toxicant formed (and hence the amount of process disruption) is proportional to the level of free radical produced.

C. *Relationship of phytotoxicity to light*

As noted earlier, Davidson (416) mentions the lessened effectiveness of Diquat under cloudy conditions, and most persons working with Diquat or Paraquat on sugarcane note a preference for bright sunlight in accomplishing rapid desiccation. A relationship of light to the desiccants' effectiveness repeatedly appears in the literature dealing with their mode of action.

Mees (1008) has shown that chlorophyll is essential for the typically rapid action of Diquat against green plant tissues. The extreme sensitivity of green tissues to Diquat and Paraquat is illustrated by the work of Funderburk and Lawrence (546) who developed a bioassay, based on foliar bleaching of *Lemna minor* (duckweed), having sensitivity of 0.0005 ppm and 0.00075 ppm, respectively. An excellent analytical procedure described by Calderbank *et al.* (283) has a maximum sensitivity of only 0.01 ppm. Funderburk and Lawrence (547) reported that both dipyridyl compounds inhibited the Hill reaction in *Lemna minor* by reactions directly related to their redox potentials. Alexander and Montalvo-Zapata (51) observed that Paraquat-treated sugarcane held in total darkness for 72 hours failed to show injury symptoms or desiccation, but quite severe desiccation occurred within 6 hours after reexposure to sunlight.

Calderbank (282) reported that leaves can be immersed in Diquat solutions without ill effect so long as the leaf is darkened. That Diquat is nonetheless absorbed and translocated in darkness is shown by the rapid wilting and "general collapse" of these plants shortly after exposure to sunlight. Calderbank also observed that rapid phytotoxicity is confined to green tissues and that etiolated shoots are much more slowly affected. ATP production via photosynthetic phosphorylation is reportedly catalyzed by Paraquat in isolated spinach chloroplasts (735, 786). Mees (1008) has further shown that oxygen, as well as light and chlorophyll, is needed for Diquat and Paraquat to bring about the rapid destruction of green tissues. On the other hand, *Vicia faba* will eventually die even in total darkness following treatment with Diquat (209).

An important conclusion drawn by Mees (1008) was that light is not strictly essential for phytotoxic action. He observed light-increased phytotoxicity of Diquat in *Vicia faba*, but this effect was confined to green tissues. To Mees, the reduction of the herbicide to its free radical was the most essential step in a sequence of toxic reactions. Presumably, the energy required for reducing the herbicide to its free radical was obtained from photolysis of water in light and from respiration in the dark. Mees also noted that Diquat appeared to stimulate respiration as a transitory effect which was dependent upon a continuous supply of herbicide, while at other times respiration was inhibited.

D. *Theory of dipyridyl action*

By 1960 the observed effects of Diquat and Paraquat on plants could be incorporated into a general theory depicting their mode of action (282). In essence, the theory is based upon a "short-circuiting" of normal plant redox systems. Its principal weakness lies in its failure to account for the extremely rapid and spectacular destruction of green tissues, and its failure to give an entirely plausible explanation of the herbicides' sensitivity to light.

It was generally conceded that the rate of herbicidal action paralleled the intensity of the incident light, while less substantial evidence was suggestive of an oxygen requirement for phytotoxicity (743). Ordinarily, chlorophyll-bearing tissues conduct photosynthetic energy conversion as a natural prelude to CO_2 fixation, and in so doing generate reducing power which is subsequently utilized in carbon reduction. The vital processes of $NADP^+$ reduction and synthesis of ATP are dependent upon this reducing power. Since the reduction potential for $NADP^+$ is approximately –320 mV, sufficient reducing power is normally generated in chlorophyll-bearing tissues to reduce the quaternary pyridylium herbicides. It follows that in the presence of Diquat and Paraquat the available reducing power is channelled into the herbicide-reduction reactions. An extremely important feature of these reactions is their catalytic nature. The reduced herbicide, *i.e.*, the free radical form, is reoxidized by molecular oxygen and is thereby regenerated for continual diversion of reducing power.

Similarly, phytotoxicity in darkness [which has not been demonstrated with darkened sugarcane (51)] is thought to stem from a disruption of the respiratory chain of electron transport. It is clearly a much slower process (743, 1008). Electrons arising from substrate oxidation would be diverted from respiratory production of ATP, and again the reversibility of free radical reduction mediated by molecular oxygen would ensure a catalytic effect by minimal quantities of herbicide.

The theory of disrupted redox systems does not appear to tell the complete story of dipyridyl action. Failure to seriously damage darkened plants (other than *Vicia faba*) is not consistent with concepts of a malfunctioning respiratory system. On the other hand, the very rapid desiccation and death of illuminated green tissues would hardly be expected as an immediate response to disrupted photosynthesis. With respect to sugarcane, several pronounced enzyme changes have been recorded in desiccating plants with far-reaching importance in altering sugar levels (45, 47, 51). But again, these effects would not explain the characteristically rapid phytotoxic action.

Calderbank (282) and Boon (209) have suggested that toxic peroxide radicals might form during the reoxidation of Diquat and Paraquat free radicals. This is the most plausible explanation for their rapid and intense phytotoxicity. Workers at the Long Ashton Research Station (78) substantiated this concept with studies of Diquat effects on photochemical reactions of isolated chloroplasts. Results showed that Diquat does not affect the photochemical reduction of numerous artificial hydrogen acceptors, including ferricyanide, but that $NADP^+$ reduction is totally curtailed by small amounts (10^{-4} M) of the herbicide. The inhibition was competitive, with Diquat being reduced preferentially. In addition, it was shown that the reoxidation of Diquat is paralleled by a synthesis of hydrogen peroxide. The latter product was detected spectroscopically as a complex with metmyoglobin. It was concluded that Diquat can function as a catalyst of oxygen reduction by illuminated chloroplasts.

It was further shown that oxygen reduction was stimulated by the presence of a phosphate acceptor system comprised of ADP, orthophosphate, and Mg^{2+}, under conditions such that ATP is produced in quantities stoichiometric with the oxygen taken up (78). This was demonstrated by trapping the hydrogen peroxide in the presence of catalase and ethanol, and measuring oxygen reduction manometrically as an oxygen uptake. These results were interpreted as evidence of a Diquat-catalyzed cyclic photophosphorylation coupled to oxygen reduction. The redox indicators methyl and benzyl viologens (structurally related to Diquat) were shown to catalyze the reduction of oxygen analogously to vitamin K and FMN, with hydrogen peroxide being produced. However, since oxygen does not normally serve as a hydrogen acceptor in photosynthesis, it was considered possible that cyclic phosphorylation might not be a natural process (78).

From the evidence available it appears that some important aspects of the dipyridyl mode of action continue to elude definitive analysis. But it is also apparent that, aside from the herbicide–desiccant roles of Diquat and Paraquat, these materials should serve as excellent tools in the study of photosynthetic and other light-sensitive reactions in plants for years to come.

4. YIELD EFFECTS OF DIQUAT AND PARAQUAT

The dipyridyl herbicides appear to have proven themselves as useful desiccants and herbicides in sugarcane culture. However, inconsistencies have been reported relative to their effects on sugarcane tonnage and quality, and in some instances they have not performed according to expectations even as desiccants. In general terms it appears that the problems of adequate application and absorption have not been solved with respect to regional variables. In a strictly physiological context the problem of having a large portion of sugar-synthezing tissue destroyed, albeit only temporarily, has not been reconciled with the minimal sugar needs for maximum growth and ripening.

A. *Growth and yield responses in Natal*

Highly favorable weed control has been obtained with Paraquat and Diquat in Natal (1426, 1425, 602) where normally reliable herbicides such as CMU and DCMU have given relatively unfavorable results. Thompson and Gosnell (1426) found that Paraquat was more effective than other herbicides in controlling two of the most serious weeds, *Cyperus esculentus* and *Panicum maximum*, as well as numerous other weed species. Although Paraquat at 4 pints per acre produced a typical leaf injury or "scorch", the treated cane recovered a normal green top within a month after treatment (1425). Diquat caused less damage to the cane but likewise gave less effective weed control than Paraquat. In another experiment (1426), Paraquat at 4 pints per acre and Diquat at 2 pints per acre seemed to produce increases in cane "vigor" within a 3-month period. The initial injury or foliar "burn" quickly disappeared.

In subsequent trials (1426), Paraquat was shown to be the most effective postemergence herbicide tested – its effectiveness being further enhanced by combination within 2,4-D (1 1/3 pint Paraquat plus 1 pint 2,4-D), and by application to the row only. It was again found that Paraquat "set back" the sugarcane as a temporary effect. Regional trials with variable soils and weed populations throughout the Natal cane belt generally reaffirmed the superiority of Paraquat over the herbicides, and over Diquat in the instance of grass control. In none of the experiments was any permanent growth or qualitative change recorded; to the contrary, Paraquat- and Diquat-treated plants generally appeared to be more vigorous following a rapid recovery from initial chemical injury.

Experiments conducted at Mt. Edgecombe (602) showed that Paraquat caused no reduction of yield in trials carried through to harvest. Yields were reportedly increased as greater quantities of the herbicide were applied. Moreover, the herbicidal effect was extended more than 12 weeks by combination with *Bromacil.* Oddly enough, the only sunlight effect observed was a greater apparent efficiency culminating from application in the afternoon or on cloudy days.

Subsequent studies by Gosnell and Thompson (603) with five varieties at differing stages of growth did not bear out their earlier observations of increased vigor in response to Paraquat. It should be noted that the later report was based on a more complete set of data while the earlier interpretations of increased vigor were apparently based upon visual rankings. Paraquat applied at the rate of 0.75 pound per acre in 20 gallons of water caused an immediate reduction of the sugarcane population; in one instance a loss of about 50 percent (from 57 000 stalks to 29 000 stalks per acre) was recorded. Recovery was rapid and the trend was toward higher plant populations in treated areas by harvest time. However, there was a reduction of the length, diameter, and weight of stalks which was not reversed with time. The net effect was a 5 to 12 percent reduction in yield, the reduction being more pronounced when applications were delayed. Paraquat caused no apparent effect on sucrose percent cane. There was no significant interaction between variety and time for any of the parameters measured, although the variety *N. 51-168* resisted yield reduction as a Paraquat response. Gosnell and Thompson concluded that, in spite of reduced yields on most varieties, the use of Paraquat on young cane was justified by virtue of the excellent weed control obtained.

B. *Desiccation experiments showing quality losses*

As sugarcane desiccants, the dipyridyl herbicides have been less than satisfactory even though most workers are genuinely impressed with their swift action. Unpublished work by Coleman (416) with Diquat revealed only poor drying activity in cloudy weather, and in bright sunlight sugar ceased to accumulate for about 3 weeks after treatment. Other studies by Coleman, also unpublished (416), suggested that sucrose accumulation is restricted up to 70 days after Diquat treatment.

Vallance (1471), in Queensland, obtained trash reductions of approximately 5 percent in the varieties *Pindar* and *Q. 57* treated with 2.5 to 10 pounds of Diquat per acre. Excellent drying was obtained within 7 days of treatment. However, sugar losses occurred in the order of 1.5 C.C.S. units for *Q. 57* and 0.7 unit for *Pindar*. Furthermore, Vallance noted, "...Diquat was not translocated in the cane foliage and ... therefore a fairly complete coverage by the spray is necessary." This observation contrasts sharply with the highly systemic action of Diquat noted by Bates (155) under humid conditions in Guyana.

The limited systemic action of dipyridyl compounds in sugarcane, observed also by other workers, appears to constitute a major shortcoming since it is virtually impossible to contact more than a fraction of the green tops under field conditions by aircraft application. This possibly reflects a much more complex transport system in sugarcane as compared with most weed species, and it is perhaps instructive that even sucrose is not translocated efficiently in cane unless a host of physiological and ecological conditions are satisfactory. Very little work appears to have been done with respect to increasing dipyridyl effectiveness with wetting agents, although McWhorter (1006, 1005) and others (802) have shown that surfactants increase the toxicity of herbicides applied as foliar sprays. Gosnell and Thompson (603) used a surfactant with Paraquat applied for weed control but did not consider this to be essential for the control of *Cyperus* species.

Davidson (416) used Diquat to improve the postharvest burn of the variety *N. Co. 310* in Louisiana, but lost sugar as a result. Knapsack applications equivalent to 1 and 3 pounds per acre were given as morning and afternoon treatments 3 days before harvesting initial samples. The cane was cut in the morning, laid across the rows, and burned in the afternoon. Trash remaining after the burn amounted to 10.0 percent for the control cane, and 6.5 and 4.7 percent for the respective Diquat treatments. Sugar data presented in Table 13-2 indicate that sucrose declined in all Diquat-treated cane within 4 days after treatment. Subsequent samples showed that the cane also failed to accumulate sucrose at normal rates during the 23-day period following treatment. The smallest loss of sucrose at 4 days was approximately 6 pounds of sugar per ton of cane, an event which Davidson estimates is roughly equivalent to milling fresh, unburned material. The sugar loss was accentuated by delay of grinding to 11 and 23 days.

Chen and Liu (319), studying the effects of Paraquat as a foliar desiccant in Peru,

TABLE 13-2

QUALITATIVE EFFECTS OF DIQUAT ON SUGARCANE OVER A TIME COURSE OF 23 DAYS

Variety *N.Co. 310*, first ratoon, Houma, Louisiana. [After Davidson (416).] Reproduced by permission of *I.S.S.C.T.*

Treatment	Days	Crusher-juice analysis		Difference from control	
		Brix	Sucrose (%)	Brix	Sucrose (%)
Control	0	14.42	10.96	–	–
	4	14.78	11.20	–	–
	11	15.88	12.52	–	–
	23	16.69	13.74	–	–
Diquat					
1 lb/acre	0	14.42	10.96	–	–
(a.m. application)	4	14.02	10.44	–0.76	–0.76
	11	14.42	10.90	–1.46	–1.62
	23	14.77	11.47	–1.92	–2.27
3 lbs/acre	0	14.42	10.96	–	–
(a.m. application)	4	14.42	10.85	–0.36	–0.35
	11	14.22	10.71	–1.66	–1.81
	23	15.42	12.24	–1.27	–1.50
1 lb/acre	0	14.42	10.96	–	–
(p.m. application)	4	14.05	10.33	–0.73	–0.87
	11	14.32	10.76	–1.56	–1.76
	23	14.99	11.82	–1.70	–1.92
3 lbs/acre	0	14.42	10.96	–	–
(p.m. application)	4	13.85	10.05	–0.93	–1.15
	11	13.97	10.44	–1.91	–2.08
	23	14.12	10.85	–2.57	–2.89

found that juice quality declined concurrently with leaf desiccation. The sugar losses were most pronounced in the upper half of the stalk. In this instance the authors stressed the importance of time of harvest, since cutting the cane too early gave insufficient time for desiccation and cutting too late allowed excessive time for juice deterioration. It was felt that no net gain of sugar could be obtained by trash reduction unless juice quality was retained. According to Gumbs (619), Arvier (114) obtained similar results with Paraquat in Queensland. Arvier concluded that sucrose losses occur too rapidly to be offset by improved burning efficiency.

Recent Paraquat trials in Puerto Rico (308) have shown a marked visible desiccation while actual trash reduction has been so small as to preclude economic use of the chemical. This information came at a time when the P.R. sugar industry was urgently in need of a suitable desiccant owing to inclement weather, a shortage of labor, and large acreages of held-over cane. In a series of five experiments in 1968 and 1969, 2 pints of Paraquat per acre in 16 gallons of water produced good desiccation of all tissues contacted by the spray. Little additional desiccation was produced with 4 pints per acre. An average sucrose loss of 5.6 percent was obtained. It was concluded that use of more than 2 pints of desiccant per acre, or delay of more than 6 days before harvest, would produce significant sucrose losses. It was also estimated that a minimal trash reduction of 5 percent was needed to cover treatment costs amounting to about $ 12.00 per acre. Since the average reduction of extraneous material was only 3.9 percent, it was felt that Paraquat does not guarantee an acceptable trash reduction. It was noted, however, that this amount of desiccation markedly eased the work of the harvest machine operator and increased harvest efficiency.

The less than satisfactory performance of Paraquat in Puerto Rico tended to verify earlier results obtained by Gumbs (619) in Guyana. Among other observations Gumbs noted that Paraquat increased the stalk moisture content, apparently as a result of restricted transpiration at a time when water uptake from the soil continues unabated. Sugar losses were therefore adjusted for moisture increases and a maximum value of about 0.4 percent was obtained. The volume of spray solution was also found to affect sucrose losses. In one trial using three pints of Paraquat in 10, 25, 50 and 100 gallons of water, corrected sucrose percent cane reductions of 0.9, 0.1, 0.15 and 1.6 percent were obtained.

Gumbs performed Paraquat trials in both the wet and dry seasons at rates of 1, 2, and 3 pints per acre, each in 25, 50, and 100 gallons of water per acre (a 10-gallon treatment was also included during the wet season). In general, Paraquat increased the water content of millable cane in the order of 1.0 to 1.5 percent while at the same time reducing the trash by about 80 percent. The immature tops gained more water than the lower millable stalks[3].

It was concluded, however, that the savings made on trash reduction did not compensate for sucrose losses (619): "...The reduction in the absolute sucrose percent cane is found to be between 0.5 and 1.0 percent. This represents a loss of 4.5 to 9.0 percent of the total sugar even after correction is made for the increase in moisture content of the stalk. It is therefore concluded that the use of Gramoxone (Paraquat) as a desiccant prior to harvest is entirely ruled out on economic grounds."

5. FUNDAMENTAL DIPYRIDYL EFFECTS IN SUGARCANE

Greenhouse studies were performed in Puerto Rico in 1968 and 1969 to clarify

[3]R. Montalvo-Zapata and A. Alexander [*J. Agric. Univ. P.R.* 56(2): 134–153 (1972)] could not verify this effect in immature cane propagated with variable moisture regimes in sand culture. To the contrary, stalk weights increased as a function of moisture supply rather than Paraquat desiccation of leaves.

some of the dipyridyl-induced changes in sugarcane enzymology, and to determine whether such changes could be controlled (45, 47, 51, 46). It was shown that Paraquat and Diquat do not stimulate inversion in the stalks, but that sugar production is severely restricted while metabolism of sucrose appears to proceed at near-normal rates. In addition to ultimate photosynthetic restrictions caused by loss of leaf moisture and chlorophyll, a rather discrete inhibition appears to occur in the regenerative phase of CO_2 assimilation. At the greenhouse level some of the restrictions submit to partial control by chemical pretreatment of the foliage.

By use of small greenhouse plants ranging between 10 and 16 weeks of age, it was possible to apply treatments and to conduct examinations with precision unattainable at the field-plot level. In general, it was found that factors of time, chemical concentration, and light intensity have tremendous bearing on the desiccants' activity and ultimate effects. Other factors such as daily water supply, nitrogen supply, ambient temperature, and growth rate at the time of treatment appeared to have little influence. Under all conditions the characteristic dipyridyl effects on cane included severe foliar drying, loss of sucrose-forming capacity, and gradual recovery of the plant by production of new green leaves.

A. *Visual effects of Paraquat and Diquat*

In the greenhouse it was possible to distinguish about four distinct levels of dipyridyl injury relating either to the concentration applied or to the time elapsed after application. The symptoms are indistinguishable between Paraquat and Diquat. During these experiments the factors of solution volume and chemical translocation were inconsequential since all above-sand tissues were sprayed until visibly wet.

An example of the lowest injury level is illustrated in Fig. 13-2A. A very small quantity of Paraquat produced a typical reddish discoloration appearing as an isolated "blotch" on the leaf lamina. In the field these are frequently seen in adjacent or control plots owing to drift of minute spray droplets. Fully developed after about 3 days, such spots are permanent and remain visible long after the leaf has died and detached from the stalk. The surrounding lamina tissue is unaffected. There is no wilting or loss of photosynthetic activity external to the spot, although within the damaged area there is little or no sucrose being formed.

A second-level symptom is the visual wilting and curling of foliage until the leaves assume a rod-like appearance (Fig. 13-2B). The leaves are now losing moisture; however, they do retain an olive-green color and continue to produce some sugar. The restricted production is nonetheless important since it is only at this level of desiccation that drying can be accomplished with a minimum disruption of the ratio of sugar formed to sugar utilized. The second-level symptoms are terminal for low desiccant concentrations, but for higher levels they are transitory.

The third desiccation level involves the death and subsequent yellowing of most of the green top (Fig. 13-2C). Young spindle leaves not contacted by the spray solution

Fig. 13-2. Phytotoxicity symptoms produced by Diquat in sugarcane following contact with green foliar tissue in bright sunlight. Descriptions and interpretations for A, B, C, and D are presented in the text. [Photographed by the author.]

usually survive, and their emergence signals the beginning of general recovery. On the other hand, the fourth injury level is purely herbicidal (Fig. 13-2D). All foliar tissues are killed within 24 to 48 hours, desiccation extends to the leaf sheaths, to immature storage tissue, and eventually even to the mature internodes.

B. *Curtailed sucrose production*

Under greenhouse conditions ideal for thorough spray coverage of each plant, both Paraquat and Diquat caused rapid losses of sucrose-forming potential (45, 47). A relationship between time and chemical concentration was observed whereby relatively high levels, in the order of 0.05 to 0.50 percent, produced a given restriction within about 2 days, while lower concentrations produced similar effects within 3 to 6 days. For example, in one experiment 0.5 percent Paraquat produced a marked loss of leaf sucrose within 24 hours (Table 13-3), and the effect became increasingly severe with time. The slackened sucrose production was reflected in lowered juice quality between

TABLE 13-3

SUGAR RESPONSES OF IMMATURE SUGARCANE SPRAYED WITH AQUEOUS PARAQUAT SOLUTION

Sixteen-week-old plants of the variety *P.R. 980* were sprayed once with an aqueous 0.5-percent Paraquat solution containing 0.1 percent Tween 20. All plants were grown by sand culture in the greenhouse with abundant water and a complete nutrient supply. Leaf and immature storage tissues were quick-frozen periodically in dry ice and acetone for subsequent sugar and enzyme analyses. "Mature storage tissue" consisted of the basal 4 or 5 internodes fully expanded and free of leaves at the time of harvest. [After Alexander and Montalvo-Zapata (45).]

Tissue	Paraquat (% soln.)	Hours after treatment				
		0	24	48	72	168
		Sucrose (mg/g dry wt.)				
Leaf $^{+}1$–$^{+}4$	0	49	44	42	36	39
	0.5	47	33	20	16	7
Immature storage	0	62	41	31	25	54
	0.5	46	53	56	46	50
		Brix				
Mature storage	0	4.6	4.2	6.3	7.6	5.9
	0.5	5.5	5.2	7.5	4.7	2.1
		Polarization				
	0	8.1	9.9	15.5	18.2	13.3
	0.5	9.1	11.9	12.8	9.1	7.8

48 and 72 hours. Another experiment with 0.5 percent Diquat produced similar results (Table 13-4). Leaf sucrose was curtailed within 24 hours and juice quality declined after 72 hours.

TABLE 13-4

SUGAR RESPONSES OF SUGARCANE SPRAYED WITH AQUEOUS DIQUAT SOLUTION

Six-month-old plants of the variety *P.R. 980* were sprayed once with an aqueous 0.5-percent Diquat solution containing 0.10 percent Tween 20. Spray solutions were applied until all aerial tissues were thoroughly wet. All plants were grown by sand culture in the greenhouse with abundant water and a complete nutrient supply. Mature storage tissue consisted of the basal 10 to 12 internodes. [After Alexander and Montalvo-Zapata (47).]

Tissue	Diquat (% soln.)	Hours after treatment						
		0	24	48	72	96	120	144
		Sucrose (mg/g dry wt.)						
Leaf $^{+}1$–$^{+}4$	0	42	43	48	48	56	58	53
	0.5	47	29	28	29	23	27	27
Immature storage	0	69	73	71	72	77	84	72
	0.5	68	84	81	97	82	68	68
		Brix						
Mature storage	0	19.0	15.7	13.9	15.3	16.5	15.2	13.9
	0.5	18.0	13.1	13.5	14.8	12.8	11.5	9.5
		Polarization						
	0	70.2	54.8	47.2	51.9	56.9	54.6	48.9
	0.5	63.8	45.3	45.1	50.6	41.8	37.2	22.5

In neither of these experiments did sucrose decline appreciably in immature storage tissue. On the contrary, moderate sucrose increases were found up to 72 hours (Tables 13-3 and 13-4). This is explained in part by the desiccants' suppression of invertase within these tissues. It is also possible that under severe stress the plants maintained a sucrose flow toward the physiological sink, *i.e.*, toward the apical meristem, long after sucrose had ceased to be stored in the mature joints.

The essential conclusion drawn from these and other experiments was that loss of storage sucrose is the price to be paid for severely disrupting the balance between sugar production and utilization. More specifically, to suppress reactions of sugar synthesis while reactions of sugar utilization continue must inevitably place a burden upon sucrose accumulated in the stalk. The antidote of such losses is desiccation without damage to photosynthetic processes, accompanied by suppression of sugar-utilizing processes to balance the reduced rates of sugar formation.

Fig. 13-3 presents clear evidence that the loss of sugar-forming potential can be

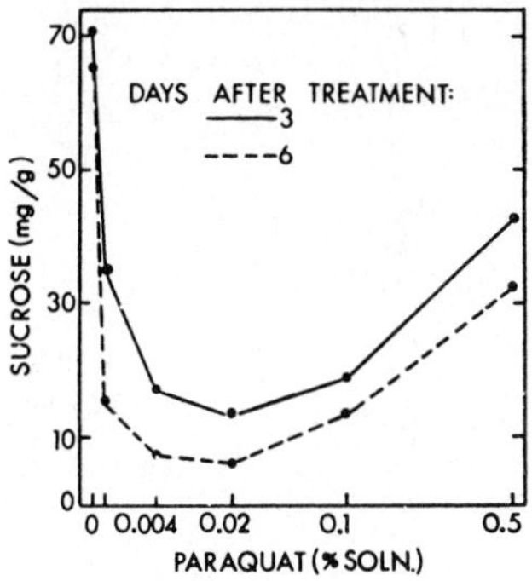

Fig. 13-3. Sucrose decline in sugarcane leaves sprayed with low concentrations of Paraquat, and partial retention of sucrose in leaves receiving greater amounts of the desiccant. [After Alexander and Montalvo-Zapata (47).]

balanced at least in part by even more severe chemical treatment (47). In this experiment the plants were sprayed with Paraquat levels ranging more than 600-fold, from 0.0008 to 0.5 percent. Considerably more sucrose was lost at the 0.004-percent level, where translocation and utilization processes continued, but not sugar production, than at the 0.5-percent level where presumably *all* life processes were slowed to subminimal rates. One practical implication here is that in the field more effective chemical desiccation might be achieved without quality losses by doubling or tripling standard chemical rates followed by burn and harvest operations within 1 to 2 days.

C. *Dipyridyl blockage of regenerative CO_2 assimilation reactions*

Paper chromatography of leaf extracts from desiccant-treated sugarcane revealed the presence of a sugar not normally found in readily-detectable quantities. Tentatively identified as ribose, a 5-carbon sugar intimately involved in the Calvin-cycle regeneration of CO_2 acceptor, it appeared in detectable amounts between 24 and 48 hours after treatment with 0.5 percent Paraquat (Fig. 13-4). In another study (47), the same sugar appeared in response to Paraquat within 3 days, the lowest level to produce ribose being 0.004 percent (Fig. 13-5). This sugar has also been found in sugarcane leaves treated with Diquat (47).

The appearance of ribose in response both to Paraquat and Diquat suggests that dipyridyl herbicides can block the photosynthetic conversion of ribose 5-phosphate to ribulose 5-phosphate during regeneration of the CO_2 acceptor, ribulose 1,5-diphosphate. This is a significant effect whether the Calvin cycle or C_4 pathway is operative

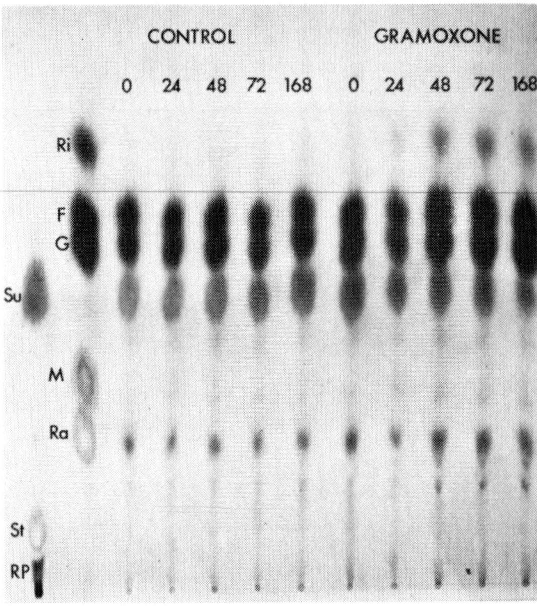

Fig. 13-4. Paper chromatography of leaf extracts from sugarcane treated with Paraquat (Gramoxone). An atypical sugar constituent believed to be ribose is shown in Paraquat preparations from 48 to 72 hours. Letters appearing adjacent to authentic sugars along the left-hand side signify the following (from top to bottom): Ri, ribose; F, fructose; G, glucose; Su, sucrose; M, melezitose; Ra, raffinose; St, stachyose; RP, ribose 5-phosphate. Numbers refer to harvest periods in hours from the time of desiccant application. [After Alexander and Montalvo-Zapata (45).]

because both systems use ribulose diphosphate, the former to receive CO_2 from the atmosphere (285, 287), the latter to receive carboxyl groups from C_4 acids (700, 699).

The reactions by which pentose phosphate is derived from triose phosphate have been examined previously (*cf.* Chapter 2, pp. 89, 90) and need not be reviewed here. The dipyridyl effect in sugarcane is believed to occur after ribose 5-phosphate is formed, *i.e.*, via the transketolase-catalyzed conversion of sedoheptulose plus thiamine pyrophosphate to thiamine pyrophosphate glycoaldehyde plus ribose 5-phosphate:

$$\begin{matrix}\text{Sedoheptulose} \\ + \\ \text{thiamine pyrophosphate}\end{matrix} \xrightarrow{\text{Transketolase}} \begin{matrix}\text{thiamine pyrophosphate glycoaldehyde} \\ + \\ \text{ribose 5-phosphate}\end{matrix}$$

The enzyme phosphoribose isomerase converts ribose 5-phosphate to ribulose 5-phosphate, involving a shift of the keto position from carbon atom 1 to carbon atom 2:

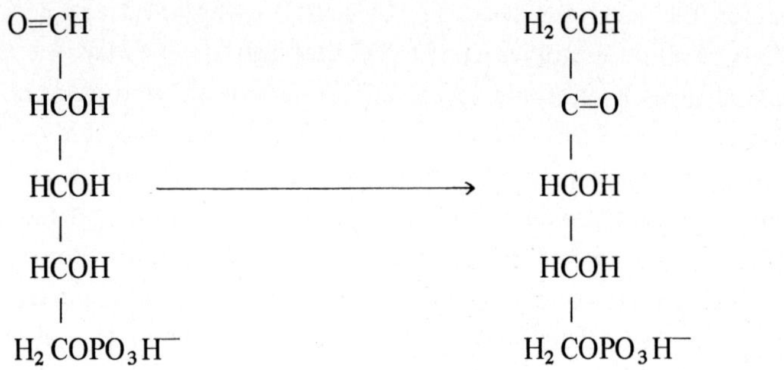

Ribose 5-phosphate   Ribulose 5-phosphate

It has been suggested (45) that Paraquat and Diquat suppress the phosphoribose isomerase enzyme and in doing so enable ribose 5-phosphate to accumulate. The accumulated pentose phosphate would then be hydrolyzed by ribose 5-phosphatase to produce free ribose in quantities detectable by conventional paper chromatography. Both enzymes, phosphoribose isomerase (861) and ribose 5-phosphatase (862), have been isolated from sugarcane leaves.

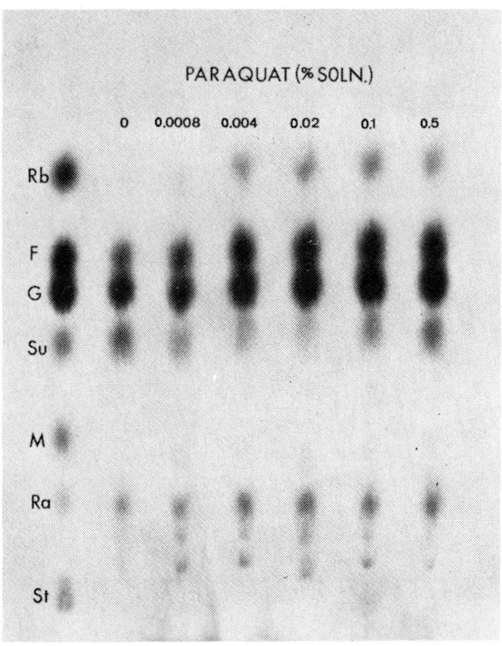

Fig. 13-5. Paper chromatogram illustrating the formation of ribose in sugarcane leaves sprayed with increasing levels of Paraquat. Letters shown along the left-hand margin refer to authentic sugars as identified in Fig. 13-4. Rb = ribose. [After Alexander and Montalvo-Zapata (47).]

Earlier in this chapter the apparent necessity of light for dipyridyl action was discussed (*cf.* p. 498). Greenhouse studies confirmed that light is essential for the desiccant-induced sugar changes herein described, and for certain enzyme changes to be discussed in the next section. For example, a controlled-illumination study (51) showed that Paraquat-treated sugarcane held in darkness did not experience a photosynthetic "short circuit" as would be evidenced by the appearance of ribose. Although leaf sucrose declined, this was a natural response to darkness which also occurred in control plants (Fig. 13-6A). However, reexposure of control plants to sunlight led to rapid sugar recovery (Fig. 13-6A), indicating that photosynthetic potential was retained, and only light was needed to produce sugar. Reexposure of Paraquat-treated plants to sunlight led to the production of ribose rather than sucrose (Fig. 13-6B), indicating that photosynthetic potential was tacitly restricted even in darkness and only light was needed for the absorbed Paraquat to become actively restrictive against normal CO_2 assimilation.

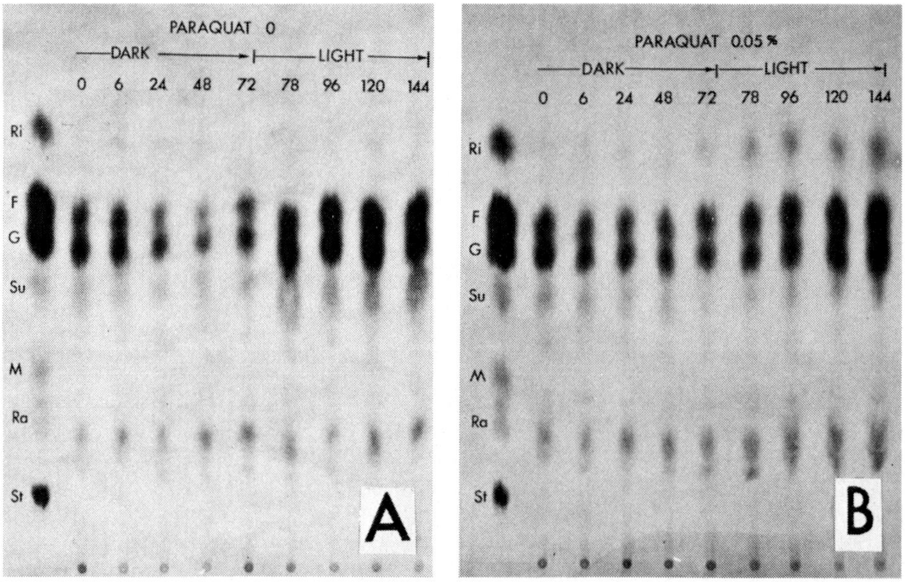

Fig. 13-6. Changes in the sugar constituents of sugarcane leaves treated with Paraquat and thereafter exposed to variable illumination. (A) Sucrose and reducing sugar decline in Paraquat-free plants darkened for 72 hours, and recovery of the three sugars after reillumination at 72 hours. (B) Failure of ribose to appear in Paraquat-treated plants kept in darkness, and the appearance of ribose upon reillumination. Also illustrated is the recovery of fructose and glucose, but not sucrose, after reexposure of plants to sunlight. [After Alexander and Montalvo-Zapata (51).]

The chromatogram illustrated in Fig. 13-6B shows that, after reillumination, the Paraquat-treated leaves did recover some fructose and glucose even though sucrose production was nil. Several implications were thus put forward: (a) Some level of photosynthetic activity was revived regardless of Paraquat inhibition, possibly via a "bypass" mechanism, and (b) Paraquat must also restrict some step in sucrose biosynthesis proper, *i.e.*, incident to the union of fructose with the glucose of UDPG or glucose 1-phosphate. A suitable bypass of the phosphoribose isomerase reaction appears to exist in chloroplasts via the synthesis of xylulose 5-phosphate from thiamine pyrophosphate glycoaldehyde plus glyceraldehyde phosphate, as described by Bassham (152, pp. 888 and 889). The production of ribulose 5-phosphate would follow by the action of ribulose phosphate–xyulose phosphate isomerase. Further clarification of the dipyridyl effect in sucrose biosynthesis, demonstration of the xylulose phosphate bypass in sugarcane, and clarification of the proposed differential effects upon the two pentose isomerase systems are all areas requiring further examination to increase our understanding of sugarcane photosynthesis and its antagonism by Paraquat and Diquat.

D. *Dipyridyl induction of abnormal enzyme behavior*

In the greenhouse, spray applications of Paraquat or Diquat were invariably followed by foliar enzyme changes – usually enzyme suppression – within a few hours. Abnormal enzyme behavior also occurred in immature storage tissue, a fact explained only by translocation of the absorbed chemicals through a considerable portion of the sugercane circulatory system. Several examples of the dipyridyl enzyme effects are currently presented with reference to amylase, invertase, peroxidase, and ATPase.

The usual amylase response was an activity increase such as that depicted in Fig. 13-7. In this instance the leaf amylase level increased substantially within 24 hours

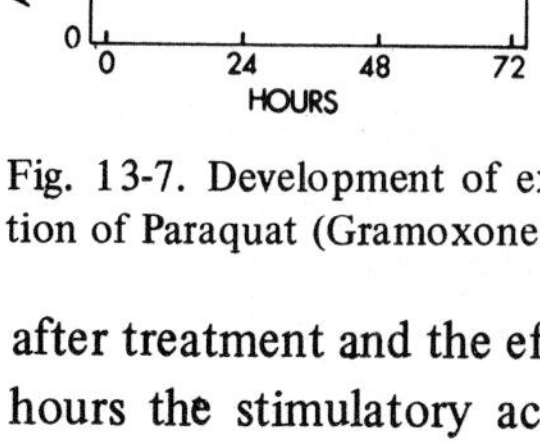

Fig. 13-7. Development of excessive amylase activity in sugarcane leaves following spray application of Paraquat (Gramoxone). [After Alexander and Montalvo-Zapata (45).]

after treatment and the effect persisted through a 72-hour period. Between 72 and 178 hours the stimulatory action completely subsided. In sugarcane several β-types make up the bulk of foliar amylase[4] (18, 11). The amylase group has long interested this

[4]Alexander, A.G. and Lebrón, J., 1969. Isolation and purification of amylase from sugarcane leaves, *Proc. Int. Soc. Sugar Cane Technol.* 13: 514–521.

author since the overall amylase level is frequently found in inverse proportion to sucrose-forming activity (11, 24, 15, 34, 44). In one instance (31), low amylase was shown to be a "common denominator" of sucrose accumulations induced by low levels of N, P, K and Ca. In sugarcane leaves the natural substrates are believed to be insoluble polysaccharides or glucans (667, 693) appearing as terminal photosynthetic products. Hartt (675) suggests that conversion of these residues to sucrose, a process for which amylase might be rate limiting, is an important feature of nocturnal sugar transport. The concept of direct polysaccharide–sucrose interconversion (1059, 1583) is not accepted at this laboratory.

Invertase is strongly suppressed *in vivo* by Paraquat and Diquat. Fig. 13-8 illustrates

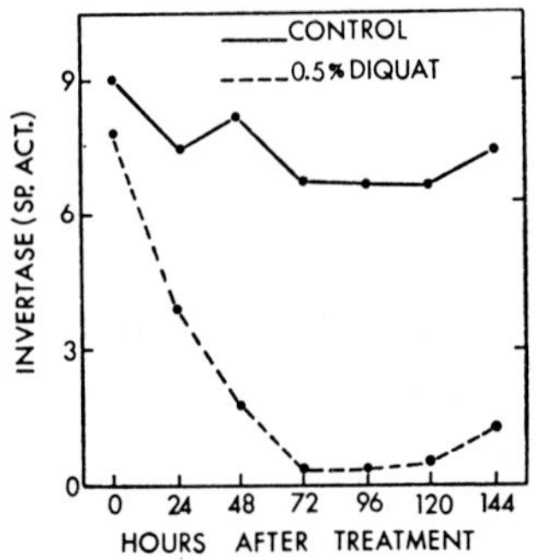

Fig. 13-8. Invertase decline in immature storage tissue of sugarcane sprayed with aqueous Diquat solution. [After Alexander and Montalvo-Zapata (47).]

a typical invertase response to 0.5 percent Diquat, including a loss of some 50 percent within 24 hours, 80 percent by 48 hours, and 95 percent by 72 hours. Since the invertase source was immature storage tissue it is clear that some fraction of the applied Diquat was absorbed and rapidly translocated toward the physiological sink. The invertase effect probably accounts for the temporary sucrose increases in immature storage tissue following Paraquat and Diquat treatments (Tables 13-3 and 13-4).

Controlled-illumination experiments have shown that invertase levels decline markedly during several days of continual darkness (51, 48). Paraquat produces a very similar effect. In one experiment, Paraquat-treated and control plants were held in darkness for 72 hours and invertase experienced a virtually identical decline within each group (Fig. 13-9). Upon reexposure to sunlight the untreated plants quickly recovered their invertase while the Paraquat-treated group failed to respond. In addition to suggesting a necessity of light for invertase synthesis, this response has shown that Paraquat irreversibly blocked the light-sensitive mechanism. It can thus be said that both sucrose production and invertase synthesis are affected by Paraquat much as if the plant was exposed to a continuous night of several weeks duration. In the instance of chemical injury, however, recovery does not begin at sunrise, but rather awaits the formation of a new green top.

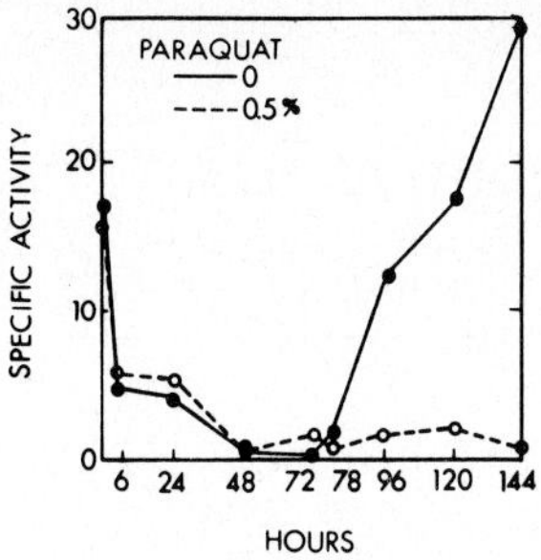

Fig. 13-9. Effects of Paraquat on invertase from immature storage tissue of sugarcane given variable light exposure. Illustrated is an invertase decline in common response to Paraquat and darkness. After reillumination at 72 hours there was complete recovery of invertase in Paraquat-free plants, but the enzyme failed to recover in plants sprayed with the herbicide. [After Alexander and Montalvo-Zapata (51).]

The rapid lowering of invertase level by small amounts of Paraquat and Diquat is a much desired property of the ideal ripening agent; in fact, some authors have tested Paraquat as a potential ripening agent. However, it appears that the indiscriminate destruction of photosynthetic processes more than offsets any sugar gains made possible by inversion control.

Peroxidase is another enzyme of interest relative to dipyridyl activity, although in sugarcane the enzyme is less sensitive to these chemicals than amylase or invertase, and its responses are less consistent. If peroxides are formed during the reoxidation of reduced free radicals, it is reasonable to suspect that peroxidase levels should be increased as one means available to the plant to rid itself of the toxic compounds. Fig. 13-10, depicting a major peroxidase increase in response to 0.5 percent Diquat, seems to support this contention, although the increase is so delayed as to cast doubt on direct peroxide induction of the enzyme.

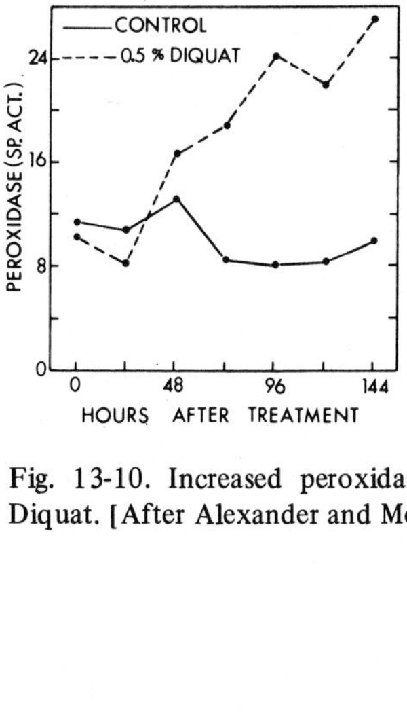

Fig. 13-10. Increased peroxidase activity in immature storage tissue of sugarcane treated with Diquat. [After Alexander and Montalvo-Zapata (47).]

ATPase level in sugarcane leaves has shown particular sensitivity to the dipyridyl desiccants. Table 13-5 summarizes a typical Diquat suppression of foliar ATPase over a

TABLE 13-5

DECLINE OF FOLIAR ATPase IN SUGARCANE SPRAYED WITH DIQUAT SOLUTION

[After Alexander and Montalvo-Zapata (47).]

Diquat (% soln.)	Hours after treatment							
	0	24	48	72	96	120	144	Mean
	ATPase (specific activity)							
0	10.5	13.7	11.2	10.4	9.3	10.2	10.0	10.8
0.5	9.8	6.4	6.3	4.9	3.6	3.7	3.2	5.4

period of 144 hours. Although treated leaves contained less than half the normal enzyme complement at 24 hours, there was little additional loss during the final 2 days of the experiment, at which time ATPase remained essentially constant at approximately 1/3 of control levels. At the time this residual level was taken as possible evidence of a distinct type of ATPase which was not sensitive to light and was relatively insensitive to dipyridyl herbicides. Subsequent work (48, 56) is strongly suggestive that distinct light-sensitive and "dark" ATPases exist in sugarcane leaves.

E. *ATPase suppression and photosynthetic phosphorylation*

A relationship of ATPase to photosynthetic and oxidative phosphorylation is increasingly implicated in the literature. At least three types of ATPases were recognized in chloroplasts by 1965 (1297, 165, 166). One enzyme is active at low rates in the dark (1132, 1167, 1563), and another is triggered by light but thereafter is active in darkness (165, 738, 974). A third ATPase is dependent upon light for continued action (974, 165, 121). Petrack and Lipmann (1167) were the first to note similarities common to photohydrolysis and photophosphorylation. It has been suggested that ATPase activity in chloroplasts represents a partial reaction in the mechanism of photophosphorylation, possibly a reversal of ATP synthesis (1167, 166, 1168, 789). Bennum and Avron (166) proposed that light-requiring ATPases share part of the photophosphorylative energy-transport system. Participation of ATPase in oxidative phosphorylation by animal mitochondria was established by 1960 (165). Evidence of light and dark ATPases has been found in sugarcane (48, 56).

As was true of Diquat (Table 13-5), Paraquat has also shown a pronounced suppression of foliar ATPase, but only under normal illumination (Table 13-6). Treatment

TABLE 13-6

EFFECTS OF VARIABLE ILLUMINATION ON THE ATPase DECLINE OF SUGARCANE SPRAYED WITH PARAQUAT SOLUTION

[After Alexander and Montalvo-Zapata (56).]

Illumination	Hours after Paraquat treatment				
	0	18	42	66	Mean
	ATPase (specific activity)				
Natural	22.4	15.0	5.8	4.9	12.0
Dark	22.3	22.6	16.2	18.4	19.9

with 0.05 percent Paraquat failed to clearly suppress the enzyme so long as the plants were maintained in darkness. In another experiment plants were treated with 0.05 percent Paraquat, held in darkness for 72 hours, and then reexposed to sunlight. ATPase was little affected until the cane was reilluminated at 72 hours (Fig. 13-11),

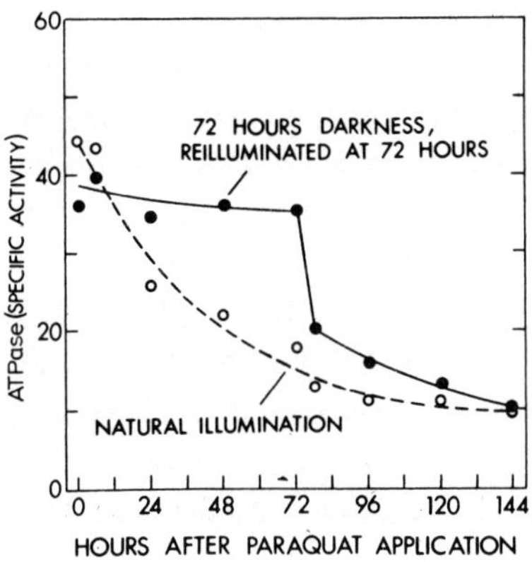

Fig. 13-11. Loss of ATPase in sugarcane leaf preparations following treatment of the plants with aqueous 0.05 percent Paraquat. An essentiality of light for the repressive action is indicated by failure of darkened plants to lose ATPase activity until they were reilluminated. [After Alexander *et al.* (56).]

but at this time a very abrupt loss of enzyme activity was recorded. This contrasted sharply with the much earlier but more gradual decline of ATPase in naturally-illuminated cane. A common essentiality of light for both the typical foliar desiccation and suppression of ATPase was thus demonstrated. In addition, the extremely rapid loss of ATPase upon reillumination suggests that the herbicide was absorbed in darkness and sufficiently translocated throughout the blade so that an intercellular conformation with the enzyme molecule was achieved. Presumably, only light was then needed for repressive action to begin, *i.e.*, following photoreduction of Paraquat to the toxic free radical.

As discussed earlier in this chapter, the photoreduced free radicals of Diquat and Paraquat appear to be effective electron carriers and are therefore able to participate in the movement of electrons during photosynthetic phosphorylation (209, 735, 343). Jagendorf and Avron (786), and Hill and Walker (735) reported that Paraquat increased photosynthetic phosphorylation, a result that is explained only by Paraquat acting as an electron carrier. Zweig *et al.* (1622), interpreting interactions with phenazine methosulfate plus inhibitors and cofactors of photophosphorylation, placed Diquat at the same site as phenazine methosulfate in the electron-transport pathway of chloroplasts. Literal extension of this hypothesis in interpreting the sugarcane data is suggestive that all of the light-dependent ATPase and part of the dark ATPase is controlled through photophosphorylative reactions.

F. *Chemical control of adverse dipyridyl activity*

Having worked with Paraquat and Diquat at the greenhouse level for more than a year, Alexander and Montalvo-Zapata were convinced that the favorable desiccative action was seriously compromised by parallel and unfavorable activity against sugar-metabolizing processes within the leaf. In 1969 (46) three greenhouse experiments were conducted in an effort to prevent or modify enzyme changes known to occur following dipyridyl treatments. Silicon (Si), given as the sodium metasilicate, was applied as aqueous foliar pretreatments at varying levels and intervals prior to application of Paraquat or Diquat. In each instance 10- to 12-week-old plants of the variety *P.R. 980* were used.

The results were generally more favorable than might have reasonably been expected. Visual inspection of desiccant-treated plants showed that those pretreated with Si (500 ppm, at minus 1 to minus 4 days) clearly retained a greener color and resisted the vigor decline characteristic of non-pretreated plants. A single Si pretreatment at minus 24 hours seemed to be as effective as several pretreatments. The silicate thereby incorporated appeared to have a "buffering" effect against sucrose changes and enzyme changes within the desiccant range of 0.0018 to 0.0162 percent. At higher concentrations the sugar and enzyme values deteriorated regardless of Si pretreatment. Although enzyme changes did not always repeat the trends of earlier studies, Si invariably suppressed changes toward either extreme. The buffering trend against enzyme extremes was noted for invertase, amylase, ATPase and peroxidase.

With respect to sugar, prior treatment with Si tended to preserve sucrose content to the extent that losses began at desiccant levels about nine times higher than in the absence of Si. Paper chromatograms of leaf extracts revealed that ribose was similarly delayed as a Si effect. This in turn suggests that, because of the buffering role of Si, photosynthesis was able to continue with little or no restriction in the presence of potentially repressive quantities of desiccant. On the other hand, sheath moisture values indicated that leaf drying *per se* was buffered over a 3-fold desiccant range, as compared with the 9-fold range noted for sucrose and ribose.

It should be stressed that the partial control of desiccant activity obtained under greenhouse conditions is primarily of academic interest and has not yet been performed at the field level. We had wished to learn, in strictly physiological–biochemical terms, whether or not such control was technically possible. Commercial feasibility of such treatments lies beyond the scope of a greenhouse study. Desiccant control will certainly be more difficult under conditions such that the precise treatment of the individual plant is no longer possible. Nonetheless, a distinction has to be drawn between physiological capability on the one hand and agronomic technique on the other if correct understanding and effective usage of desiccants is to be achieved. This principle is as true of chemical desiccation as it is of chemical ripening and sucrose control (*cf.* Chapter 12, pp. 483–485). In this context the control of desiccant activity has at least taken some encouraging first steps at the greenhouse and laboratory level.

6. SUGARCANE TOPPING

The mechanical removal of part or all of the green-leaf area has both physiological and economic implications relative to sugar yield. Nickell and Tanimoto (1107), for example, described a field study in Hawaii in which the growing point of mature canes was physically removed. This work followed upon the observation of Hartt and her co-workers (665, 670) that removal of the younger leaves led to increased sucrose transport out of mature leaves and to subsequent sucrose accumulation in the cane tip. In their field tests, Nickell and Tanimoto obtained no changes for about 8 days; thereafter sucrose gradually accumulated until the experiment was complete. An apparent need to eliminate the young green-leaf area was also suggested by leaf nitrogen data. Under Hawaiian cultural conditions it is impractical to top cane manually, but this information was a motivating force in subsequent searches for chemicals that would remove either the meristem or green-leaf spindle, or both.

In Puerto Rico, hand cutting remained the principal means of harvest until very recently. With a 12-month crop there was reasonable expectation that the stalks would remain straight and upright so that the top could be removed at any point with precision. Alers-Alers and Samuels (9) stated that the desired point of detachment varies with the producer, the variety, and system of payment. When payment is based solely upon tonnage the grower's tendency is to leave as much of the top as possible. When payment is based upon both tonnage and sucrose content some intermediate point of topping is sought. Certain varieties such as *P.R. 980* tend to drop all but a few leaves, while others, such as *B. 37161*, retain leaves along most of the stalk and thereby create a complicating factor.

Alers-Alers and Samuels (9) evaluated two topping methods on six varieties, basing their economic estimates on assigned values of $ 120 per ton of sugar produced and $ 2.00 per ton for cutting, loading, and transporting the cane to the mill. One method, "high topping", removed internodes 1 through 5 along with their subtending leaves (Fig. 13-12). "Low topping" removed internodes 1 through 10. The high

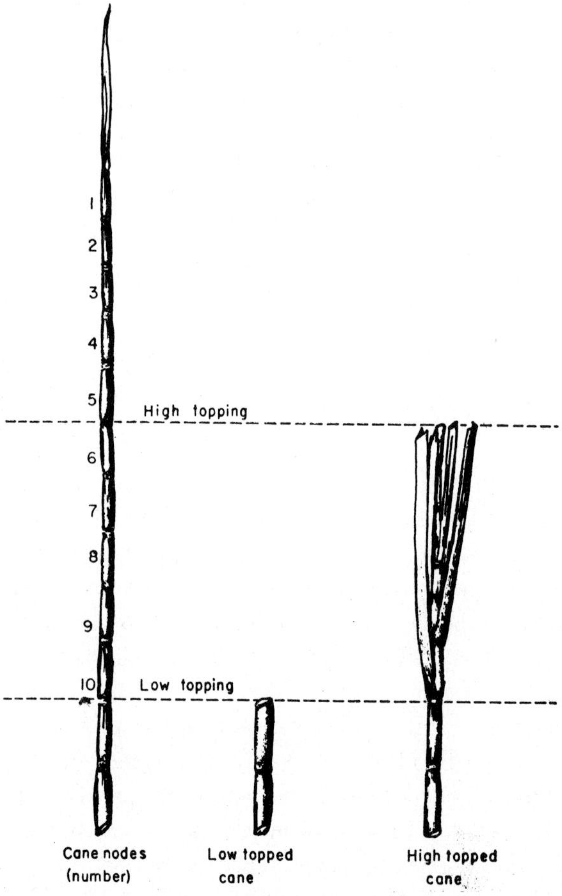

Fig. 13-12. Representation of low topping and high topping methods on the sugarcane stalk. [After Alers-Alers and Samuels (9).] Reproduced by permission of the authors.

topping method usually left part of the green top attached while low topping removed virtually all leaf, sheath, and immature stalk tissue. In general, the averages for all varieties showed that low topping was more profitable than high topping, although considerable differences were obtained among varietal and age factors. Under Puerto

Rico conditions the uppermost ten internodes at 12, 18, and 20 months seldom contained enough sugar to profitably warrant their handling and shipment to the factory. However, high topping has been commonly practised in Puerto Rico during recent years.

Studies by Ramp (1216, 1217) in Louisiana have shown that, in spite of the natural non-uniformity of sugarcane stands, detrashing by mechanical means, *i.e.*, by the detrashing harvester method, is superior to conventional hand cutting and burning operations, especially during inclement weather. In terms of clean cane, the machine selective topping method was superior to hand topping with respect to recoverable sucrose. Ramp (1217) also reviewed research with mechanical stripping rolls and stripping cylinders, the latter, when equipped with rubber strippers, being "...the most efficient and economical for the maximum removal of cane leaves".

At least one instance of natural topping followed by growth and sugar evaluations has been recorded (1469). A cyclone caused severe damage to experimental stands of *Pindar* at the Northern Sugar Experiment Station, Queensland, in March, 1956. Approximately 80 percent of the stalks were "decapitated". Comparison of Brix values between damaged and undamaged plants showed that topped cane lost sucrose from the basal internodes for about 7 weeks. This loss corresponded to new shoot growth from the upper eyes of broken canes. Some 2.5 months after injury the plants had recovered a little more than half of the normal leaf surface. From this time onward the plotted Brix values of damaged stalks began to converge upon those of undamaged stalks.

For observational purposes certain plots of the variety *Q. 57*, which had escaped cyclone damage, were topped mechanically and their subsequent Brix values were measured concurrently with the *Pindar* study. The two varieties gave essentially similar responses.

Although most sugar producers agree that some of the green top should be removed from sugarcane at harvest, the topping policy to be adopted is a very complex matter (436). Failure to mill some of the top can cause significant losses of sucrose even though a comparatively large amount of material may need to be ground. Molasses, contributing to rum manufacture, is also obtained from this material. In addition, the overhead costs can be reduced by grinding some of the top. In this context the top *per se* contrasts sharply with the associated dead leaves which constitute a total loss. Relative field tonnage might also be a decisive matter. Cane shortages incident to drought or otherwise poor growing conditions favor topping at the highest possible level, whereas good growing conditions resulting in no cane shortages at the factory tend to favor topping at a much lower level.

From an exhaustive study of varietal performance and topping response under the short-harvest conditions of Louisiana, Arceneaux (90) concluded that selective topping on a variety basis would minimize yield differences between high- and low-quality canes. He found wide differences in sugar content between upper and lower joints which in turn varied with time of harvest. Varieties which ripened late had poor-quality tops and would tend toward low sugar yield per ton of cane unless topping was much heavier than customary for Louisiana. Arceneaux claimed that by cutting away up to 30 percent of the total stalk weight, a low-quality variety would yield better than a high-quality variety, on the basis of sugar per ton of cane. Varieties still retaining low quality after severe topping were designated as unsuitable for early harvest. By delaying harvest, such cane was eventually but in a good state of maturity and sent to the mill with only a small portion of the top removed. It was also shown that "stubs" ordinarily left in the field constituted valuable weight losses in the order of 127 to 555 pounds per acre and sugar losses of 25 to 135 pounds per acre.

Coleman (371), in Hawaii, studied the effects of lower topping on machine-harvested cane of the variety *N.Co. 310.* He concluded that lower "average topping" would significantly increase cane quality at the mill without economical loss to the grower. In one experiment it was shown that removal of the upper 8 inches of each stalk reduced trash from 9.5 to 7.6 percent. This constituted a total trash reduction of 20 percent, and a 43.8-percent reduction of green trash. Analysis of the discarded portion revealed that it was of "inferior" quality (sucrose = 7.54 percent), and that the increased value of the topped stalks equaled the value of the discarded material.

Chapter 14

Flowering

1. INTRODUCTION

It is impossible to discuss sugarcane as a physiological source-to-sink system without treating an event of enormous importance which occurs at the physiological sink, or apical meristem, almost as a sidelight to the main events of this system, *i.e.*, to the synthesis, transport, and storage of sucrose. Under suitable conditions virtually all sugarcane plants will produce flowers. Some varieties flower profusely, others only reluctantly. A few profuse varieties are grown in regions where they have practically no inclination to flower at all. To the sugarcane breeder an abundance of tassels is highly desirable; to the grower heavy flowering represents production losses and hence is frowned upon. For the industry as a whole flowering has long offered an effective means of overcoming sugarcane's various shortcomings through the reconstitution of genetic material.

At a majority of sugarcane research institutions efforts have been made to control flowering. Breeders have made some progress toward achieving higher flower percentages and more uniform tasseling. To some extent this has been accomplished by regulating photoperiod and temperature. A few sugar-producing regions have relied heavily on imported varieties owing to the difficulty in obtaining sufficient tassels for domestic breeding. Many stations test imported material as part of their own improvement programs.

In a larger sense "flower control" usually refers to flower prevention. No matter how desirable the tassels might be in breeding plots, the sugar grower had little use for them in commercial plantings. Even today many a competent grower would willingly destroy part of the green canopy and accept limited sugar losses if by doing so he can prevent flowering and the attending quality decline. In this respect much interest has developed in chemicals which can be applied as foliar sprays with the expectation that they will prevent or restrict the production of a "flowering stimulus" which originates in the leaves.

The advent of floral initiation must be taken as a liability against the crop's tonnage and quality potential. Other conditions being favorable, the sugarcane plant may revert from the vegetative to the flowering state after as few as three joints have been laid down. In many regions those plants initiating floral primordia in August or September have not even approached their full tonnage potential. In essence, these canes will have exchanged a number of potential joints and the sugar they would have contained for a relatively worthless flower stalk. Some workers feel that even the limited amount of storage tissue produced prior to floral initiation cannot be made to ripen or to retain its sucrose as effectively as canes having no flower stalk to support. Added to this is the fact that many otherwise desirable varieties will commonly produce tassels on 80 percent or more of their millable stalks. In this context the extreme measures sometimes taken to prevent flowering are readily explained, if not excused, since significant yield losses must surely follow.

The mechanism of floral induction is not yet understood in its entirety. However, thanks to the extensive work by Coleman, James, Chu, and numerous other investigators, the outlines of this process are gradually emerging from obscurity. In the present chapter we shall see that light and its reception in the green canopy relates to important flowering reactions in the leaf blades quite aside from the processes of sucrose synthesis and transport so laboriously outlined in previous chapters. Regardless of the view one takes of the flowering phenomenon, it certainly encompasses both ends of the sugarcane source-to-sink system.

Of the many factors influencing the flowering process in sugarcane, photoperiod emerges as the most predominant. Temperature appears to follow as a close second. Neither of these can be controlled on an appreciable scale in a field of sugarcane. Because they cannot be controlled, and because they cannot yet be replaced by chemical treatments, the cane growers and breeders alike will have to wait many years before a complete story of sugarcane flowering can be rendered. All this is complicated by numerous environmental and cultural factors which influence flowering, and by the needs of a sugar industry which calls for more flowering on the one hand and prevention of flowering on the other.

In 1961 Salisbury (1278) attempted the unenviable task of summarizing plant flowering process in a few generalizations. Among those dealing with photoperiod were the following:

(1) On a 24-hour cycle of light and darkness, *short-day* plants will flower *if the day length is less than some critical amount*. When the 24-hour cycle is exceeded or shortened, the typical short-day plant will flower more in response to a dark period exceeding a minimum critical length than to the day length.

(2) *Long-day* plants flower in response to day lengths exceeding a certain minimum value. Again there is a response to dark periods of less than a maximum value which is more critical than the response to the day length. In both long-day and short-day plants there appear to be interactions between the light and dark periods.

(3) Flowering in short-day plants is inhibited when the dark period is interrupted by light. Similar treatments promote flowering in long-day plants.

(4) Within a given species many flowering responses may occur owing to intervention of another factor. Instances are cited in which a plant may be day-neutral at one temperature and day-sensitive at another. Some plants respond more to light quality than duration; others require a combination of day lengths arranged in a particular order.

These generalizations could have been applied to sugarcane alone. Its multitude of varieties from several species, grown as they are at a range of latitudes and with all imaginable cultural methods, seems to favor the short-day classification more than any other. However, so many exceptions can be cited that any effort at precise classification is highly arbitrary.

2. THE FLOWERING STAGES

Many workers treat sugarcane flowering as a single phenomenon, in general taking floral initiation as the critical step whereupon all else must follow. Paliatseas and Chilton (1135) suggest that much of the flower control research performed prior to 1956 was in effect aimed at *induction* control. These authors point out that flowering is a sequence of distinct physiological processes, and that environmental factors have different effects upon the various stages of flowering. Four distinct stages were recognized: (a) Initation of primordia, (b) floral organization, (c) floral maturation, and (d) tassel emergence. Floral initiation is generally taken as the most important stage[1].

In Louisiana, Chilton and Paliatseas (323) and Paliatseas *et al.* (1134) developed a technique to increase seed production based on protecting the final three stages from the Louisiana environment. Stalks which have initiated primordia are moved into a greenhouse where tassel maturation continues and a greater level of pollen is obtained than was otherwise possible. This method removes three of the four stages from the immediate control of nature. The initial step remains under natural control, and, in Louisiana, is notably affected by low temperature. Paliatseas and Chilton (1135) have also shown that the last stage of flowering, tassel emergence, is enhanced by high light intensities. Flower emergence is further aided by physical removal of the top of the restricting sheath or by slitting the sheath.

Some workers have stressed floral initiation and tassel emergence while giving scant attention to flower organization and maturation. The intermediate stages can be examined only with difficulty and are perhaps no more than incidental to most flowering studies. However, some controversy has developed over the time at which distinct varieties initiate flowers, and the subsequent lapse of time until tassels emerge. Vijayasaradhy and Narasimhan (1499) recognized the different stages of inflorescence and concluded that both early- and late-flowering varieties initiate primordia at essentially the same time. Burr *et al.* (271) and Coleman (366) claim that early- and late-flowering varieties initiate primordia on the same date, and that the time of tassel emergence bears little or no relation to the time of flower initation[2]. By this reasoning

[1]Moore (1162), in Hawaii, suggests that as many as seven stages may be involved in sugarcane flowering.

[2]The conception of commercial canes having a common flower induction period was based largely on findings with *H. 37-1933* (380). This view is no longer widely held.

the variety, along with a multitude of environmental and cultural factors, would determine the date of tassel emergence.

Other authors have not accepted the view that floral initiation is more or less simultaneous among all clones (1140, 352, 1362, 327). Panje and Srinivasan (1140) studied the flowering constancy of some 200 clones of *S. spontaneum* gathered from the Indian subcontinent, and found that, although the flowering season extended through 7 or 8 months, nearly all clones tasseled from year to year within a few days of the same date. A sample of 72 clones showed that primordia initiation was closely correlated with the time of flowering. Panje and Srinivasan concluded: "...The differences between clones in the time of flowering were mostly due to differences in the time of formation of primordia themselves and not so much due to the differences in the time of development and elongation of the inflorescence." Among clones forming primordia in June the tassel emergence occurred during any of the 5 subsequent months.

Clements and Awada (352) state that when a variety blooms over a period of several months not all of the primordia could have initiated on the same date. This conclusion was based on the fact that once the meristem has changed from a vegetative to reproductive state no new leaves are formed: "To suppose that a blossom which appears in January was also begun on September 9, assumes then that the top has stopped growing for a period of about 3 months. There is no evidence of this in the field."

Chu and Serapión (327) studied the time of floral initiation and tassel emergence in 78 varieties grown at Gurabo, Puerto Rico (18° 16′ north latitude) and concluded that flower primordia are definitely not formed on the same date. Data were collected over a 2-year period from 1967 to 1969. The earliest and latest dates of floral induction were September 3 to 5 and October 1 to 6, respectively. Thus, the time of flower initiation extended over a period of about 1 month. A close correlation was found between the time elapsed from floral induction to tassel emergence in early and late varieties. Little consistency was evident among intermediate varieties. It was also found that the date of floral initiation was quite constant from year to year. More than 50 percent of the varieties initiated primordia within 2 days of the same date in 1967 and 1969. On the basis of these results Chu and Serapión suggested that Puerto Rico has an inductive photoperiod ranging from September 3 to 30.

Because a majority of the varieties initiated flowers between September 13 (12 hours 17 minutes day length) and September 22 (12 hours 7 minutes day length), the optimum light period was shown to be about 12 hours 12 minutes. This contrasts with the optimum day length of 12 hours 30 minutes reported in Hawaii (271). The interpretation of nyctiperiod and latitude effects drawn by Clements and Awada (352) provides for decreasing periods of suitable night length as one moves farther from the equator. The study by Chu and Serapión indicates that Puerto Rico has an overall inductive period about 7 days longer than Hawaii and extending about 10 days later.

Chu and Serapión also underscored the fact that distinct time intervals are needed for flower development and tassel emergence by different varieties. Some 90 percent of the varieties studied required 7 to 10 weeks to produce a visible flower. The least time, 6 weeks, was recorded for the variety *Tuc. 2683* and the greatest time, almost 15 weeks, was recorded for *P.R. 1085*.

A. *Measurement of distinct flowering stages*

Since the first two flowering stages (reception of the stimulus and morphological organization of the flower) give no external evidence of their occurence, workers have had to rely upon visible bolting as the first certain evidence that flowering is in progress. However, two systems have been devised to measure the exact time of meristematic changeover from a vegetative to reproductive structure. These are the *leaf index* and the *stage* methods. The leaf index method, first used by Purvis (1198) in rye, was modified by Clements and Awada (352) for sugarcane. It is based on the fact that a sugarcane leaf takes about a week to form, and that once the second flowering stage has occurred there can be no new leaves produced. In practice this method is quite precise but the result is not known until after the tassel has emerged. At the beginning of the inductive photoperiod a label is attached loosely beneath leaf $^+5$ (counting the spindle leaf as $^+1$), and it is later replaced with a tight wire as the stalk matures. Clements and Awada assume that the number of leaves situated between the spindle leaf and youngest embryonic leaf is a constant, and therefore the number of leaves produced after treatments begin can be determined by counting the total number of leaves from the labeled $^+5$ to the flag leaf. The approximate dates corresponding to each stage in the flowering process can be estimated in this manner.

The stage method, developed by Salisbury (1278) and by Lincoln *et al.* (943) in *Xanthium*, is based upon microscopic examination of the apical meristem. Chu and Serapión (327) recently modified the stage system so that it was specifically adapted for examining floral initiation in sugarcane. By this technique, with much practice, the authors distinguished four discrete stages of the initiation process. The initial or "zero" stage is first indicated by a flattening of the vegetative growing point which at this time is slightly smaller than ordinary. The first stage includes visible swelling, basal constriction of the growing point, and hardening of the surrounding mantel of meristematic cells. A few individual primordia or bracts are visible. The second stage is characterized by a lengthening of the inflorescence primordia accompanied by increased basal constriction. Additional bracts appear during the third stage. In the final stage a "milk white" inflorescence covered entirely with bracts and much lengthened is observed.

A somewhat similar description of flower primordia induction and development is given by James (1160). Chu and Serapión point out that differences in the time of floral initiation by distinct varieties can be determined accurately with this method.

Fig. 14-1 illustrates the region of the apical meristem before and after development of the flower primordia.

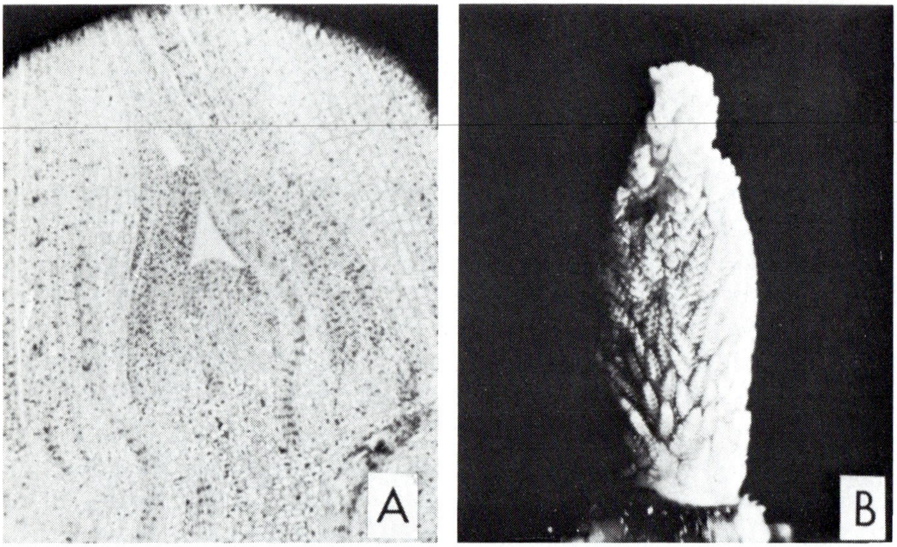

Fig. 14-1. Flower primordia induced at the sugarcane apical meristem. (A) Photomicrograph of a normal vegetative meristem. (B) Apical meristem region changed over to a complete but immature inflorescence. [After Clements and Awada (347).] Reproduced by permission of *Hawaiian Farm Science*. Agricultural Experiment Station, University of Hawaii, Honolulu.

Clements and Awada, and also Chu and Serapión, indicate that with practice the various flowering stages can be distinguished using their respective methods. Paliatseas and Chilton (1135) stress the fact that environmental factors, particularly low temperature, can interrupt the stepwise progression of flowering and thereby separate the stages in time. This is also a varietal feature. Specifically listed are the varieties *Co. 290, F. 36-819, Q. 28, C.P. 29-320,* and *C.P. 29-103*, whose formed primordia remain dormant during the Lousiana fall and winter. These develop to a length of 5 to 10 inches starting in late January or February and later emerge or remain depressed inside the spindle.

In Louisiana, fall and winter temperatures are low enough to prevent tasseling regardless of whether the variety is naturally reluctant to do so. Because of this, air-layering techniques were developed so that selected stalks could be transferred to greenhouses having warmer temperatures more conducive to flower development (1135). The technique was later refined because of excessive flower losses caused by the transfer process. It was then recognized that, in addition to temperature, such factors as the stage of floral development, inclusion of roots, light intensity, light quality, and direction of exposure in the greenhouse all affected the inclination to flower. Dissection of the upper spindle tissue and exposure to sunlight hastened tassel emergence.

B. *Abnormal development of the flowering stages*

A curious aspect of sugarcane flowering is that the process not only occurs in stages, but the progression of stages is not always normal after the initiation of viable primordia. Clements and Awada (347) cite one instance in which some 70 percent of the plants in Hawaiian fields initiated normal flowers in early autumn but only about 20 percent produced tassels. Although some authors (1135) point out that a partially-developed inflorescence may remain dormant through the winter months owing to low temperature, and later emerge as a normal tassel, in other instances completely abnormal structures appear which show that the flowering process has gone awry. These have been variously described as *multiple top, spindle top, witches' broom,* and *grassy top* (347).

According to Clements and Awada (347), the first description of abnormal flowers as a tassel-reversion phenomenon was presented by C.J. Engard, at the University of Hawaii, during the mid-1940's. This was explained in terms of a conflict in the hormonal control of the flowering and vegetative stimuli. By this theory a normal

A B

Fig. 14-2. Multiple top in sugarcane. (A) The condition shown with mature leaves removed. Small, weak shoots proliferate rather than a single strong shoot. (B) Close-up of (A) showing the absence of a central shoot for continuing normal stalk development. [After Clements and Awada (347).] Reproduced by permission of *Hawaiian Farm Science*. Agricultural Experiment Station, University of Hawaii, Honolulu.

changeover from vegetative to reproductive growth may occur, followed in turn by reestablishment of vegetative control. This reversion may terminate the flowering process at any point up to actual emergence of tassels (1160). The subsequent "monstrosities" which appear in place of normal tassels will vary with the stage at which reversion occurred. In some instances early reversion to the vegetative state will enable a strong new shoot to reestablish normal growth. In other cases a mass of small weak shoots predominate at the top (Fig. 14-2), or the top may die, and the growth processes are resumed from branches or lalas originating from the stalk below. Where normal vegetative growth has been reestablished, the eventual growth record of abnormal flowering will consist of a short section of small, misshapen internodes midway in an otherwise normal stalk.

3. FLOWERING AS A FUNCTION OF PHOTOPERIOD

By 1920 the classic studies of Garner and Allard (559) had shown that numerous plants bear a special sensitivity to light and produce flowers only in response to specific day or night lengths. Among the factors which influence flowering in sugarcane the photoperiodic requirements for floral induction have been examined more than any other. Even without precise knowledge of the inductive mechanism, which admittedly has never been very clear, it has long been recognized that photoperiod is the principial decisive factor. Burr (268) observed in 1950 that for Hawaiian sugarcane "...Day length is such a dominant influence that ... visible flower buds appear at almost the same time in all localities, approximately September 20."

However, because sugarcane possesses an extremely narrow range of day and night lengths suitable for flower production, it has been difficult to classify this plant on a photoperiod basis. Thus, various workers have classified the *Saccharum* species as short (1498, 1500, 268), intermediate (357, 1300, 352, 349, 1134), long–short (1273), and "stenophotoperiodic" (988). Allard (62), Allard and Evans (61), and Sartoris (1300), classified the variety *N.G. 492* as an intermediate, *i.e.*, neither long-day nor short-day, requiring a day length of 11 to 14 hours for flowering. Allard (62), working with a *S. spontaneum* variety near Washington, D.C., obtained floral initiation only with day lengths between 12 and 14 hours. Sartoris (1300) confirmed this observation with the same variety, obtaining initiation with 13 hours of daylight. On this basis the *spontaneum* species was thought to be intermediate in its response to photoperiod.

Clements (357), describing sugarcane as an intermediate day plant, observes that flowering occurs readily in response to a fixed dark treatment of 11 hours 30 minutes regardless of whether the plants go into treatment from 8-hour days, 13-hour days, 22-hour days, or from continuous light. Clements and Awada have also shown that the Hawaiian variety *H. 37-1933* flowers profusely with 11 hours 32 minutes of dark period, but produces few or no flowers when the dark period is lengthened by as little as 26 minutes or shortened by 34 minutes (352, 355). Burr (268) described sugarcane as a short-day plant after observing flower inhibition by dark period interruption. This interpretation was based on the inference of *short day* being *synonymous* with *long night*, and short-day plants requiring a long uninterrupted dark period in order to flower.

A. *Day length as one of several controlling factors*

That natural change in day length is not the lone guiding factor in sugarcane's propensity to flower has long been recognized on the basis of field observations. In 1938 Sartoris (1300) wrote: ". . .These changes (in day length) are constant from year to year, while the flowering of sugarcane is not constant. There are varieties that flower almost every year, some that seldom flower, and many that are irregular in their flowering. Even with varieties that flower profusely not all the stalks flower, although flowering and non-flowering stalks may be the same size and age. Furthermore, some stools have flowering stalks while others in the same plot do not have any. It is also a general observation that large stalks flower first and slender stalks later in the season." Sartoris drew the conclusion that most *S. officinarum* varieties could be expected to differentiate flower primordia in response to about 12 hours of light, while *S. spontaneum* varieties would require a longer photoperiod as suggested by their tendency to flower earlier (913). He noted that in the region near Palmira, Colombia, situated almost on the equator and having day lengths nearly constant at 12 hours, sugarcane commonly tassels throughout the year. Hansford (637) has also reported year-round flowering at the equator. The fact that this is not true of all sugarcane situated near the equator was taken by Sartoris as evidence of regulatory factors other than day length.

Clements and Awada (352) emphasized that varieties respond differently in their relation to the equator. They observed that varieties normally situated far from the equator tend to flower more readily as they are transplanted closer to the equator. Varieties normally grown close to the equator may experience greater difficulty in flowering when moved farther away. A specific example was cited whereby flower percentages were increased in Canal Point varieties at Baton Rouge (where flowering is uncertain) by subjecting plants to Hawaiian day lengths. This was equivalent to moving the plants toward the equator. On the other hand, Coimbatore varieties which blossom profusely in southern India do not flower so well farther north in Bihar State (352).

The flower response to photoperiod is materially affected by both internal and external factors. Burr (268) noted in 1950 that the "florigen" theory remained unproven, but indirect evidence for the existence of chemicals regulating floral initiation was mounting: "Light does something to a leaf, and the effect is transmitted through conducting tissue to the bud. This material will pass through a graft from the leaf of a sensitive variety to the bud of an insensitive one."

Coleman (379) reviewed the theories of hormonal activity in primordia induction and noted a requirement by sugarcane for 12.5 hours of high-intensity light prior to the dark period. Low nitrogen status, low soil moisture stress, high light intensity, and adequate plant size were cited as contributing factors by Clements and Awada (352, 355). Burr discussed the importance of correct physiological age (268) and "ripeness-to-flower". Within a given stool only the largest stalks may flower and this usually occurs only after two or three mature joints have been laid down (271). A general relationship between temperature and flowering has also been reported by many workers (1485, 240, 601, 94). Coleman (374) stressed the importance of night temperatures during the critical period of floral initiation.

Panje and Srinivasan (1139) studied the flowering behavior of some 340 *S. spontaneum* clones collected from 5° to 35° north latitude in India and concluded that the tendency to flower is inversely related to the latitude of origin. Other workers suggest that the position of cane plants within the field and direction of light exposure may affect the tendency to flower (1594). Burr (268) observed that the level and timing of nitrogen fertilization clearly affects flowering in Hawaii. Among four varieties tested, two flowered heavily in response to high potash fertilization while the remaining varieties were relatively unaffected.

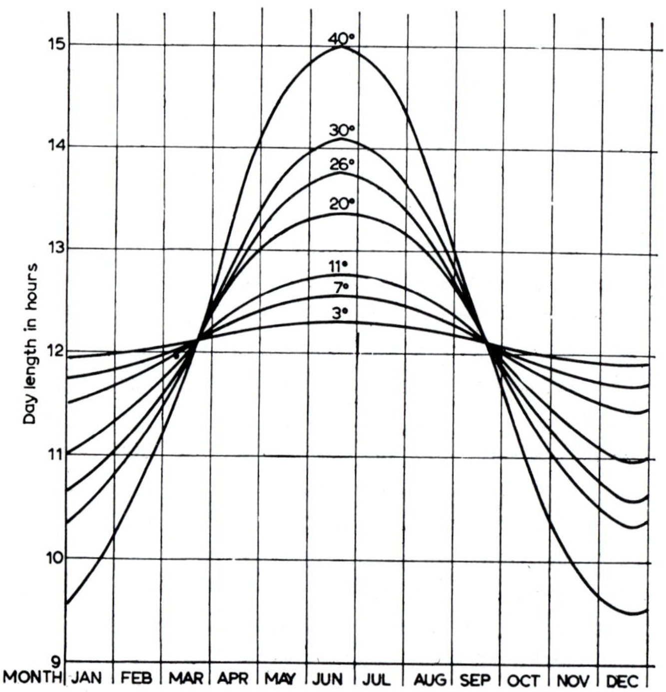

Fig. 14-3. Monthly variations in day length at specific latitudes north of the equator. In the southern hemisphere the shortest day occurs in June so that the curves are displaced 6 months on the abscissa. [After Paliatseas (1136).] Reproduced by permission of *I.S.S.C.T.*

B. *Flowering in relation to latitude and length of day*

In addition to the studies of Panje and Srinivasan (1139) relating flowering behavior to latitude, a number of workers have mentioned the year-round flowering of sugarcane at the equator (352, 1300, 637) where day length is nearly constant at about 12 hours (Fig. 14-3). However, flowering will sometimes fail to occur under these conditions or tassels may be extremely sparse. Burr *et al.* (271) point out that as distance from the equator is increased the period of floral initiation becomes more definite owing to greater yearly changes in day length. Brett (240) proposed a general flowering scale based on latitude. Accordingly, regions within 10° of the equator would have flowering before or during the month of the autumn equinox; for those lying between 10° and 15° flowering would begin during the first month after the autumn equinox, during the second month for areas between 20° and 25°, and during the third month for those between 25° and 30°. Brett recognized the limitations of a latitude scale as applied to the sugarcane world in general, but he emphasized that latitude strongly affects both the time and intensity of flowering in most regions.

Vijayasaradhy and Narasimhan (1499), working with four varieties at Coimbatore (11° north latitude), consistently obtained flower primordia near the end of August following a 12-hour 30-minute day which falls about August 9. In Hawaii, some 8° to 11° of latitude farther north, the 12.5-hour day falls around September 2, and flower buds become visible between September 20 and 24 (271). In Taiwan, about 23° north latitude, flower primordia become visible rather consistently on September 23 to 25 in *P.O.J. 2725* (271).

Juang (812) studied the flowering behavior of both prolific- and poor-tasseling varieties at different localities in Vietnam and Taiwan. A positive correlation was found between low latitude and earliness of flower-bud formation. In the Saigon area, flower-bud initiation occurred on August 20, some 15 days earlier than in Quang-Ngai province in Vietnam, and 35 days earlier than in Tainan, Taiwan (Table 14-1). Time required for arrowing and flowering was notably less at the lower latitudes. Varieties having characteristicly, poor flowering proficiency varied markedly with latitude whereas freely-flowering clones produced abundant tassels at all localities.

Since sugarcane flowers during the shortened days of fall and winter, the question inevitably arose as to whether flower embryos are formed in response to a specific or fixed day length, or to a series of shortening days (or lengthening nights). Lee and Lin (913) failed to induce flowering in *S. spontaneum* with a fixed day length of 6 hours, and day lengths of 9 and 15 hours delayed the time of flowering. Nevertheless, control plants and those given a 12-hour day completed a normal flowering sequence. The *S. spontaneum* variety employed was indigenous to Taiwan.

Sartoris (1300), working with the *S. spontaneum* variety *28 N.G. 292* (New Guinea), failed to induce flowering with 12-hour days, but he obtained abundant flowering with a 13-hour day length. Studies by Dutt and Yusuf (456) also indicated a

TABLE 14-1

DATES OF FLOWER-BUD FORMATION FOR SUGARCANE IN VIETNAM, HAWAII, AND TAIWAN

[After Juang (812).] Reproduced by permission of *I.S.S.C.T.*

Country	Area	Latitude (°N)	Appearance of buds	
			Date	Days delay after Saigon
Vietnam	Saigon	10.82	Aug. 20	0
	Banmethuot	12.68	Aug. 28	9
	Tuy-Hoa	13.08	Sept. 1	13
	Quang-Ngai	15.13	Sept. 5	17
U.S.A.	Hawaii	20.00	Sept. 20	32
Taiwan	Hungchuin	21.75	Sept. 21	33
	Wantan	22.60	Sept. 23	35
	Tainan	22.97	Sept. 25	37
	Taichung	24.13	Sept. 25	37

positive flowering response of *S. spontaneum* to fixed day lengths. Hu and Lee (755) induced flowering in four varieties with day length held constant at 12 hours. More recently, Lee *et al.* (914) found that in Taiwan flowering response to the 12-hour day varied greatly under different experimental conditions. Lee *et al.* (915) obtained flowering with both 12-hour days and 12-hour 30-minute days. A majority of the tested varieties produced flowers earlier when given the 12-hour treatment.

James and Smith (793) recently evaluated the effects of photoperiod, photoperiod duration, and light intensity on the flowering of eight sugarcane clones at Canal Point, Florida. Photoperiod results were in general agreement with the findings of Coleman (373) and of Paliatseas (1136) in that a photoperiod longer than 12.5 hours (14 hours), and several shorter than 12.5 hours (11 and 9 hours) appreciably reduced the number of emerged panicles. There was also a tendency for the 9-, 11-, and 14-hour photoperiods to delay tassel emergence. Light intensity, evaluated at a photoperiod of 12.5 hours, delayed flowering at levels of 86 and 1399 lux. The flowering delays produced by high light intensity and 14-hour days were essentially comparable.

James and Smith found that with a photoperiod of 12.5 hours an increased duration of the treatment from 0 to 12 weeks further delayed flower emergence. The greatest effect was obtained with 4 weeks of treatment given during the early stages of inflorescence formation, *i.e.*, with treatments starting September 27 or October 11. Artificial light (1399 lux) given for 2 weeks did not affect flowering if the plants were treated during normal daylight hours. No evidence was found in these studies of clone interactions with photoperiod or light intensity.

Noting that natural floral initiation occurs widely in response to a photoperiod of

12 hours 25 minutes, Coleman (369) examined the possibility of inducing flowering with a similar but fixed photoperiod. Varieties having profuse, intermediate, and reluctant flowering habits (*H. 37-1933, H. 44-3098*, and *H. 39-7028*, respectively) were tested. Potted plants 6 months of age were maintained in a dark chamber equipped with lights and controlled-temperature facilities. Similarly potted plants were maintained outside the dark chamber as the control. It was found that only *H. 37-1933*, the profuse flowering variety, could be readily induced to flower in response to a fixed day length of 12 hours 25 minutes. This photoperiod corresponds to the average day length for Hawaii between September 10 and 20. Some floral initiation was also accomplished with *H. 44-3098*, while none of the *H. 39-7028* plants produced flowers.

However, *S. officinarum* varieties do not appear to flower normally in response to fixed photoperiods. Chilton and Moreland (322) suggest that it is the *gradual* shortening of day length which ultimately induces flowering. They cite as evidence the tendency for primordia to appear on the descending curve of shortening autumn days rather than on the ascending curve ocurring in winter and spring. If a fixed day length alone was responsible for flowering there should be a flowering period in the spring as well as in the fall. One obviously missing factor here is temperature, particularly night temperature, which will be somewhat lower during the inductive spring photoperiod (374).

Coleman (373) describes experiments in Hawaii in which efforts to induce spring flowering included raising spring soil temperatures to the level of fall soil temperatures in a region where spring and fall air temperatures are alike. Soil moisture and age of cane was also comparable between spring and fall. No spring flowering occurred. Coleman therefore concluded that sugarcane perceives the difference between going from long days to short days, and from short to long days.

Panje and Srinivasan (1139) carefully examined the flowering dates of *S. spontaneum* clones and concluded that survival of individual canes in a given region is determined by the date on which the annual rainy season ends, while the flowering mechanism itself is controlled by photoperiod. Daniels (405) carried this interpretation a step further and speculated that, in the "Burma–China" region of *Saccharum*'s origin, there is such intense dryness that natural selection must have been incompatible with spring flowering.

4. ADDITIONAL FACTORS INFLUENCING FLORAL INITIATION AND RATE OF TASSEL DEVELOPMENT

A. *Temperature*

Although sugarcane growers have long recognized a temperature influence on flowering, there has been a shortage of specific temperature records and hence a failure to recognize the critical period in which temperature is most decisive (374). Moreover, the effects of temperature on flower initiation are frequently confused with its effects on flower development. Nonetheless, the existence of a temperature role remains obvious. Photoperiod is, of course, extremely important, but it does not change from year to year or from field to field, whereas temperature and flowering do vary immensely on this basis. Burr (383) suggests that temperature becomes proportionately more effective as a flowering-control factor at latitudes farther removed from the equator. It is probable that temperature is the most important of all modifying factors once the correct maturity and light requirements for primordia induction have been met.

Gard (558) listed six factors considered to be limiting for the breeding programs at Macknade, Queensland (18° 35′ south latitude). These included insufficient arrowing, low temperature preventing fertile pollen production, continual rainfall suppressing dehiscence, drought (inducing abortive tasseling), and strong winds which damage tassels and disperse pollen. Although situated within the tropics, the low-temperature effect was regarded as the most serious limiting factor at the C.S.R.Co. Station. The importance of temperature was substantiated by Glasziou (583) who reported that with controlled-temperature facilities in Queensland it was possible to induce flowering in some 20 *S. spontaneum* varieties.

Sartoris and Belcher (1302), who attached "cardinal importance" to the temperature factor in cane flowering, felt that temperature changes might account for abnormal flowering behavior after the unusual circumstance of 3 months flooding by water up to 6 feet deep at Canal Point, Florida. It was observed that such late-flowering varieties as *C.P. 34-79* and *F. 31-962* flowered earlier and more profusely following severe floods produced by tropical storms during the fall of 1947.

Paliatseas and Chilton (1135) used the example of irregular tassel emergence in Louisiana to emphasize the influence of temperature on different flowering stages. Floral initiation takes place nearly every year in Louisiana much as it does in tropical areas having favorable climates for flowering, yet tassels emerge only infrequently owing to the fall and winter climate being subject to periodic cold waves. Tassels usually appear only during those years having above-average fall and winter temperatures with no freezes. Another example of temperature effects upon flowering stages was given for Grand Isle, off the Louisiana coast, where both flower initiation and emergence occur regularly. In this instance abnormally low temperatures interrupt inflorescence development so that tassels do not appear on schedule in November, but growth may resume later with the result that tassels can appear from March to May.

Brett (240) observed that in Natal pollen fertility sometimes increased a season advanced from July to October, in this region October having warmer temperatures and longer days. Neither increasing day length nor higher humidity was found to be essential for producing the higher fertility levels (238, 239), and it was concluded that temperature alone must be responsible (240). Brett (239) also reported that in Natal low temperatures adversely affect the rate of inflorescence development as well as pollen fertility. In the instance of variety *Co. 290*, tassels may fail to emerge at all. Venkatraman (1485) cites a statement by F.A. López-Domínguez indicating that in Peru pollen fertility declines late in the season in response to low temperature. High humidity and cloudy weather were believed to prevent the normal opening of anthers.

Field observations published by Brett (240) in 1950 appear to have been the first to reveal night temperature as a critical factor in sugarcane flowering. Workers at the Mt. Edgecombe Station recognized a greater flowering proficiency when sugarcane was planted on a relatively high ridge. Comparing temperatures taken at two sites in a high field and a low field, Brett found that in March the lower field's average maximum temperatures were 89.0 and 87.9 °F, and its average minimum temperatures were 66.6 and 66.5 °F. Corresponding figures for the high field were 83.3, 82.1, and 68.9, 69.3 °F. Quite significantly, 65 percent of the varieties planted on the higher ground flowered readily at the lower level. Brett (240) concluded that if temperature differences did in fact account for the variations in flowering, then it was the minimum or night temperatures which were responsible.

Clements and Awada (352) state that at Kohala there is little tendency for cane to flower above 1300 feet elevation. On the island of Hawaii, cane grown on the south slopes between 1000 and 3300 feet tends to flower only lightly at the lower elevation and not at all higher up. These responses are best explained by the parallel differences in temperature.

Coleman (374) has stressed the importance of night temperature during the critical period of floral initiation in Hawaii. According to Burr *et al.* (271), the critical photoperiod for primordia induction extends from September 1 to 20. Studies by Coleman (369, 373) with a controlled photoperiod house had shown that night temperatures must be maintained between 70 and 80 °F for successful floral initiation in a number of clones. In one study (373) unsuccessful attempts were made to induce flowering on spring photoperiods by raising soil temperatures during March, April, and May to the level of fall soil temperatures. In another experiment it was shown that subnormal soil and root temperatures, *i.e.*, held at 60 °F beginning August 1, failed to alter flower initiation and tassel emergence. Coleman (369) also felt that night temperature, along with photoperiod and rainfall, was one of the factors capable of explaining the different flowering inclinations of *H. 37-1933* between the Kailua and Waipio stations. Data collected on January 6, 1955 for the 1954 flowering season showed a 92-percent floral initiation at Kailua and only 49 percent at Waipio.

By 1963 the importance of night temperature, or temperature of the dark period, was widely recognized in short-day plants (377). Lockhart (947) suggested that two temperature-sensitive processes occur consecutively during the dark period, the later process possibly involving the synthesis of flowering stimulus. On this basis and on the basis of his own findings with sugarcane, Coleman (374) emphasized the need to examine carefully the effects of night temperatures during the night phase of sugarcane's critical inductive photoperiod. In one study with mature *N.Co. 310* and *H. 37-1933* plants, temperatures were held at 65 °F from September 1 to 21. Although an inductive photoperiod was maintained, no flowers were produced by *H. 37-1933* and more than half of the *N. Co. 310* plants remained vegetative. Only 42 percent of the latter showed even a weak flowering stimulus. Along with field observations in Hawaii and Louisiana, this was taken as evidence of minimum night temperatures (65 °F and below) preventing floral initiation. Further to this, Paliatseas (1136) reports that in Louisiana a night temperature of 65 °F or lower for 10 days depresses floral induction, whereas similar temperatures for more than 10 days prevents initiation completely.

By 1959 Coleman (369) had shown that within two distinct climatological areas in Hawaii, environmental conditions affected floral induction only during September. Subsequent data gathered in Hawaii and Louisiana and published in 1963 (374) led Coleman to conclude that night temperatures during the induction period control floral initiation. From this perspective non-inductive nights produced by low temperature and by interruption with light were regarded as similar. As shown by Fig. 14-4,

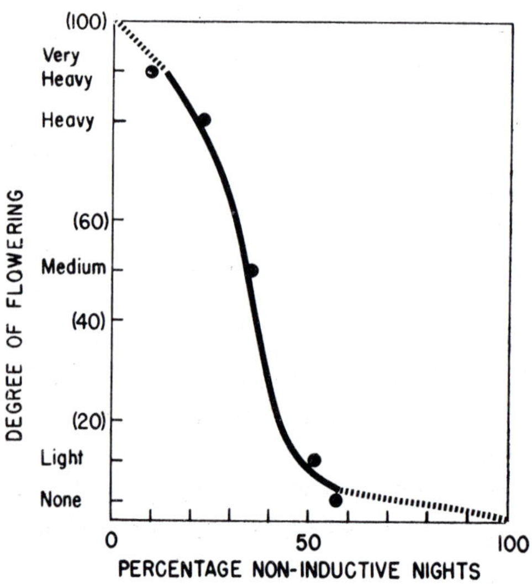

Fig. 14-4. Effect of the number of non-inductive nights on the degree of flowering of sugarcane. Actual values are shown by solid line, theoretical values by broken lines. [After Coleman (347).] Reproduced by permission of the *International Sugar Journal.*

the number of non-inductive nights produced by temperatures of 65 °F or below has an enormous bearing on the degree of flowering in Hawaii, particularly when the number of non-inductive nights exceeds about 20 percent. Specific data for the period September 1 to 20 revealed no flowering when the total number of non-inductive nights exceeded 10; with 10 there was light flowering, with 7 moderate flowering, and with 4 non-inductive nights heavy flowering occurred. In a later report Coleman (377) demonstrated a similar relationship between the degree of flowering and the number of non-inductive nights produced by interruption of the darkness by light. The possibility that different clones may have distinct "threshold" temperatures for inhibition, or that temperature might influence the critical length of dark period, was also pointed out by Coleman (374).

Studies by Clements and his colleagues have taken into account the importance of night temperature while placing somewhat more emphasis on night length. Clements and Awada (349) noted that darkroom temperature should preferably be held above 72 °F in order to induce flowering in varieties *Co. 312, N.Co. 310* and *H. 37-1933*, but the most critical factor was regarded as a night length of 11 hours 35 minutes. In all experiments efforts were made to keep the night temperature at 70 °F or higher. Temperatures were maintained between 72 and 76 °F with electric heaters during later trials.

With respect to day temperature, Clements and Awada (349) stressed the importance of maximum and minimum values and the range between them. The temperature range relationship to flowering is apparently recognized by most sugarcane workers. Evidence cited by Clements and Awada was obtained from du Toit in South Africa and Chilton in Louisiana. Vijayasaradhy, in India, supplied data to the authors indicating that minimum temperature may be more important than a narrow temperature range. Generally speaking, the temperature range tends to be narrow, in the order of 9 to 12 °F (349) in regions of heavy flowering. In Hawaii the minimum temperature from late August to mid-September is about 70 °F.

Clements and Awada also point out that tasseling can be profuse with minimum temperatures around 60 °F if high temperatures do not exceed about 87 °F. In other areas heavy flowering can occur when the high temperatures have exceeded 90 °F, but in these instances the minimum levels must also be higher, in the order of 70 to 73 °F. Again, flowering may not be heavy even with narrow temperature ranges if the minimum level is around 62 °F or less and the maximum is in the low 70's. Clements and Awada further stressed the fact that temperature ranges, and hence flower percentages, can vary greatly between two closely-situated areas or within a given area from one year to the next.

Clements (357) has examined in detail the effects of temperature on the flowering response to both lengthening and shortening dark periods. Darkrooms were employed in which night temperatures could be kept comparable to those out-of-doors. Three clones were used: *Co. 312* (Coimbatore, heavy tasseling under Hawaiian conditions), *N.Co. 310* (heavy tasseling but not easily forced), and *H. 37-1933* (ranging from profuse to poor tasseling). Effects of both cool and warm cycles were investigated with each series including potted plants left out-of-doors as well as the treated cane. Minimum outdoor temperatures for three cycles are shown in Fig. 14-5. A single warm

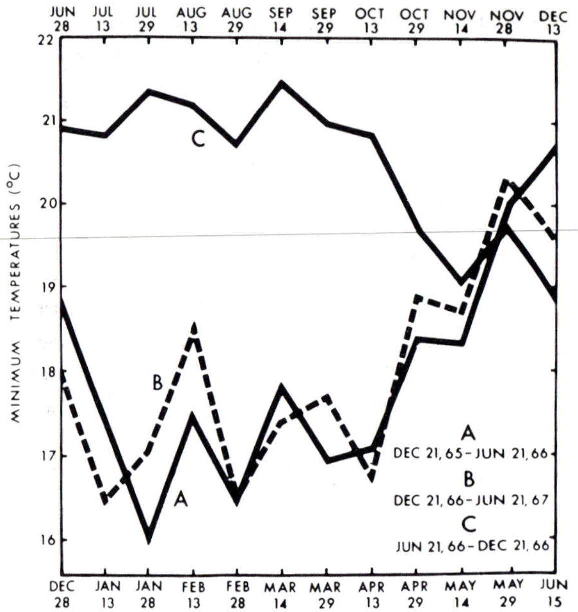

Fig. 14-5. Minimum out-of-door temperatures in two cool cycles (beginning in December) and one warm cycle (beginning in June) used to demonstrate the requirement of warm lenthening nights for normal flower production in Hawaii. [After Clements (357).] Reproduced by permission of *Plant Physiology*.

cycle (summer–autumn) remained near 21 °C until October, and flowering occurred in all clones. Two cool cycles (winter–spring) begun in December retained minimum temperatures in the range 16 to 18 °C. In contrast to warm lengthening nights, the cool lengthening nights produced complete but much less profuse flowering in all three clones. For *Co. 312* (heavy flowering) the effective night length remained the same with cooler temperature, whereas the remaining clones required 20 to 50 minutes additional time. Under cool conditions, shortening nights prohibited flowering in both cycles for *H. 37-1933* and at least partially restricted flowering in *N.Co. 310*. The same conditions partially restricted flowering in only one cycle for the profuse *Co. 312*. Of the plants kept outside, flowering occurred only under conditions of warm, lengthening nights. There was no flower production in response to the cool, shortening nights of spring.

Clements found that in all clones the warm cycle begun in June produced flowers some 10 to 14 days earlier than out-of-doors. This discrepancy was explained in terms of twilight effects experienced by out-of-doors plants but not by plants in the dark-room. Tropical twilights are short but rich in red and far-red light. Clements also noted that natural nights are never so totally dark as a dark chamber owing to moonlight and various building lights.

Some evidence suggests that, aside from absolute minimum night temperature, unnatural changing of night temperature will prevent flowering. In Hawaii (69), efforts to induce flowering in varieties *H. 37-1933* and *H. 32-8560* by use of "dark boxes" to shorten day length led to inhibition of all flowering. The plants received abnormal temperatures for about 2 hours each evening beginning August 1. Other studies with controlled climate houses showed that heavy-flowering varieties totally failed to produce flowers when temperatures were raised or lowered during the night or during the entire 24-hour period.

It appears that low flowering percentages and low pollen fertility associated with increasing elevation are related to low temperature. Burr *et al.* (271) state that in Hawaii flowering is rare at 2000 feet. According to De Surnay (431), a high correlation was found between anther fertility and elevations in Mauritius. The percentages of open anthers declined to zero at 700 feet for *M. 63-69*, and similarly declined at 1000 to 1200 feet for *Ebene 1-37*. Anther opening was not affected by rainfall. Brett (240) specifically attributes to temperature the elevation effects on flowering observed in Natal.

B. *Night length (nyctiperiod) and latitude*

Sugarcane is among the most sensitive of plants to light. According to Burr (268), Allard, in 1938, gave sugarcane its first specific classification as an intermediate type requiring neither exceptionally long nor short days to flower but rather a day length between 11 and 14 hours. In the autumn of 1946 Burr demonstrated that sugarcane would not flower if its lengthening night was interrupted by light. As little as "50 foot-candle minutes of light" served to interrupt the dark period. Burr concluded that "sugarcane behaves like a short-day plant", *i.e.* like those plants which must have an uninterrupted dark period in order to flower. Coleman (379), however, found that certain clones of *S. spontaneum* and *S. robustum* are not inhibited by night interruption.

Clements and Awada (352) emphasized the importance of very specific night lengths in sugarcane flowering. Beginning January 5 and extending to April 2, the varieties *Co. 312* and *N.Co. 310* were given night lengths of 11 hours, 11 hours 35 minutes, and 13 hours 30 minutes. The shortest night length prevented flowering, the intermediate treatment produced profuse blossoming, and the long night delayed flowering. Additional experiments led the authors to conclude that a night period of about 11 hours 32 minutes is very nearly the most conducive to flowering. Quite significantly, a shortening of nyctiperiod by as a little as 32 minutes (to 11 hours) eliminated flowering, and a 12-hour night was less conducive than one a mere 28 minutes shorter.

Clements and Awada (349) also speculated upon the significance of night length as a function of latitude. It was pointed out that the equatorial night length from the summer solstice to the winter solstice, about 11 hours 52 minutes, is not entirely suited to flowering but is close enough to promote a scattering of flowering throughout the year. James (1160) views the equatorial photoperiod as being neither highly conductive to flowering nor inhibitory against flowering, with the result that the normal complement of tassels may emerge thinly but as a continual event. Year-round blooming at the equator has been mentioned by other workers (637, 352, 1300).

While some tasseling is expected throughout the year at the equator, some point at either side of the equator should produce heavier flowering, that is, where the nyctiperiod is closer to 11 hours 30 minutes. Clements and Awada (349) place this at about 10° north or south latitude: "At 10° away from the equator, the 11:30 nyctiperiod is reached on about July 22 and the 12:00 period not until September 9 – giving a term of some 49 days when cane is exposed to the proper period for flowering. Thus, it is not surprising that tasseling a short distance away from the equator is heavier than either closer or still farther away."

Assuming that there is a single ideal dark period for all sugarcane plants, and that this period is close to 11 hours 30 minutes, Clements and Awada explained the differential flowering behavior of cane varieties in the following manner: "At 30° latitude away, the same period extends from about September 4 to about September 28, a term of only 24 days. Any reluctant tasseler would likely not have time enough to receive the full complement of stimuli needed for tasseling."

By this reasoning a variety which flowers heavily at 10° to 20° latitude may be reluctant to flower at 30° and may not flower at all at 35° latitude. This strongly implies that controlled night length should be a valuable tool for cane breeders situated along the northern and southern fringes of the sugarcane world. James (792, 295) has vividly illustrated this point in Florida. Working with three early-flowering varieties at Canal Point, he succeeded in delaying flowering (tassel emergence) up to 11 weeks by maintaining the plants on 11.5-hour dark periods from 1 to 6 weeks. Unlike Clements and Awada (349), who were mainly concerned with flower induction, James used the critical inductive night period as a means to delay the development of inflorescences that had already initiated. Therefore, whereas Clements and Awada stressed the importance of a specific night length in flower induction, and the duration of this night length in explaining varietal flowering behavior, James demonstrated for the first time that day length and its duration affects floral development independently of, and following, the inductive process.

Clements and Awada further observed that the duration of light treatment prior to dark treatment had no apparent importance with reference to nyctiperiod. Prior light treatments of several months duration had been tested, including continuous light, 22 hours, 13 hours 21 minutes, 9 hours 50 minutes, and 9 hours.

C. *Physiological maturity vs. age*

Before the cane plant can initiate flower primordia it must first pass through a stage of physiological immaturity, the "juvenile" phase. Until this is accomplished the plant will remain vegetative even though all other factors favor flower induction. The juvenile state is usually ascertained by the number of visible nodes or by the number of leaves. As a rule of thumb, stalks having three or four visible nodes are mature enough to flower. In Hawaii, cane planted after June 1 or ratooned after July 1 will not perceive the inductive photoperiod in September (271). Within a given stool there may be only one or two stalks mature enough to induce flowers by September. Since the physiologically immature stalks may trail their flowering neighbors by only an internode or two, it sometimes develops that the population and tassel counts taken at harvest will erroneously include stalks that could not have flowered regardless of the flowering treatment given. This is avoided by labeling with tags all stalks having reached "ripeness-to-flower" at the time of treatment. Subsequent flowering percentages will then be based on the tagged population only.

Coleman (379) points out that the exact physiological conditions which distinguish a potential flowering cane from a juvenile cane have not been determined. The capacity to synthesize the inductive hormone or other substances is probably a major factor. It has been suggested that juvenile plants may not be able to produce the flowering hormone, or the meristem may not be able to respond to the hormone. Transport of flowering substances is not logically a problem here. However, the overriding task of the juvenile cane is to establish a large root system, a large green canopy, and generally to get on with the business of growth. At this time there is probably an imbalance of hormones which heavily favors growth rather than flowering. The antiflowering effect of high N (*cf.* this chapter, pp. 555, 561) presumably acts via hormone balance, or via growth hormone efficiency, in maintaining a succulent growth regime.

Parentage is also a factor in determining "ripeness-to-flower". *S. spontaneum* clones tend to mature and flower sooner than *S. robustum*. Those belonging to *S. officinarum*, including a predominance of the world's commercial cane, mature and flower even later than *S. robustum* varieties. The resultant tasseling "gap" has been a serious problem for cane breeders seeking to bring wild genetic material (from *S. spontaneum*) together with *S. officinarum* material (*cf.* this chapter, pp. 547, 548).

5. FLOWERING CONTROL: THE BREEDER'S VIEWPOINT

Controlled flowering, that is, the ability to assure a reasonable percentage of normal tassels every year, has long been desired by breeders confronted with "reluctant" clones and clones which flowered profusely one year and sparsely the next. In cooler regions such as Louisiana and South Africa the problem has been much more severe since poor flowering or the absence of any flowering at all is commonplace. Clements and Awada (355) cited additional motives for flower control, including flower requirements for classification purposes, and induced flowering among non-flowering varieties for the development of commercial non-flowering clones.

In 1956 Chilton and Paliatseas (323) recommended that sugarcane breeding programs for Louisiana should be based on controlled flowering to avoid the traditional difficulties in obtaining seed. Some success has been attained in this direction. Coleman (373) reports that in 1961 some 6000 seedlings were produced in Hawaii as a result of crosses in which the flowering of one or both parents had been controlled. Important advances in flower development control have been accomplished by James (792, 795) in Florida. However, even in its limited scope success in flowering control has not come easily.

For many years sugarcane growers did not realize that their crops could be improved by controlled reconstitution of genetic material. Prior to the 1880's sugarcane was regarded as a sterile plant (985). According to Venkatraman (1485), fertile seeds were first discovered by Harrison and Bovell in Barbados in 1889. Prior to this all varieties were propagated from cuttings.

Although a number of early workers attempted to induce flowering in plants by regulating photoperiod (62, 1300, 913, 455, 453, 457, 61, 1605), no appreciable success was obtained with sugarcane prior to the early 1950's. The *S. officinarum* varieties and interspecific hybrids apparently resisted induced flowering even more than non-flowering wild types (323). According to Clements and Awada (352) little progress had been made toward induced flowering prior to 1958. In that year Dr. Clements paid an extended visit to the Sugarcane Breeding Institute, Coimbatore, India, where outstanding work had been performed relative to artificial flowering induction. He later wrote: "Placards at the Station proclaiming 'Sugarcane can be either forced to remain vegetative or induced to flower at any time', and 'Flowering in sugarcane is no longer seasonal at Coimbatore' at the time seemed very bold claims, indeed, but these turned out to be rather simple statements of fact. The methods used when taken back to Hawaii led to success there too, where until then essentially no progress had been made" (352).

In 1962 Clements and Awada (349) reported that, in the varieties *Co. 312*, *N.Co. 310* and *H. 37-1933*, flowering could be induced almost at will if suitable conditions were met. These included use of plants at least 5 months old, exposure to a night length of 11 hours 35 minutes (while simultaneously holding the temperature above 73 °F), exposure to high light intensities during the day (10 000 to 12 000 foot candles), and holding day temperature below 85 °F. A low soil moisture tension was also regarded as desirable, as indicated by Brett (240), by Clements and Awada (352), and by Burr *et al.* (271). In a subsequent report, Clements and Awada (355) stated that even very reluctant tasselers could be forced to flower if given a suitable night length for extended durations. A few flowers were obtained even with a minimum temperature of 58 °F when the correct night length was provided up to 24 weeks. One variety, *H. 51-4336*, resisted all attempts to force flowering.

Progress in flowering synchronization was also advanced during the 1960's. In 1962 George and Lalouette[3] published the results of photoperiod experiments with *C.P. 36-13* in Mauritius in which dark period interruption delayed flowering in addition to reducing flower percentage. Coleman (373) observed a similar delaying effect of night period interruption. By 1965 Skinner (1333) had succeeded in delaying flowering in early-blooming varieties by breaking the dark period during the time of flower initiation. Whether treatments affected flower initiation or development was not at this time clear. In 1968 James (795) reported evidence indicating that maintenance of the inductive night period (11.5 hours) for atypically long durations encouraged large-scale delays in tassel emergence for early-flowering varieties in Florida. This treatment also suppressed male sterility in the variety *L. 60-25*. By this means flowers were made available for crossing purposes throughout the entire flowering period at Canal Point (795).

A. *Flowering induction by controlled photoperiod*

Substantial success in the control of sugarcane tasseling followed upon the discovery of photoperiodism in plants and the application of this concept to sugarcane under experimental conditions. As early as 1938 Sartoris (1300) recognized that the *S. spontaneum* variety *28 N.G. 292* flowered only in response to day lengths in the order of 12 to 14 hours. Lee and Lin (913) made similar observations. They found that 6-hour "days" inhibited flowering and 9- or 15-hour days delayed flowering in *S. spontaneum.* Yusuf (1605) was probably the first to gain some success by photoperiod control as a means of inducing tassels in reluctant varieties and for controlling the time of flowering in early and late varieties. Although photoperiod, along with manuring treatments and water supply, was investigated in both wild and cultivated forms, no consistent control of flowering appears to have been attained. As recently as 1953 Warner (1534) noted that in Hawaii efforts to induce flowering by altering day length tended to suppress tasseling rather than increase it.

Continuation of the photoperiod, irrigation, and manuring studies by Vijayasaradhy and Narasimhan (1499) at Coimbatore underscored the photoperiod role and indicated that a natural day length of about 12 hours was critical. Deviations of 1 or 2 hours in either direction suppressed flowering. This was taken as evidence that sugarcane is an intermediate-type plant, a view expressed earlier by Allard and Evans (61) and more recently by Clements (357). Timing of the photoperiod treatment was found to be of major importance.

Vijayasaradhy and Narasimhan found that flowering was inhibited when treatments were given in the vegetative stage prior to floral induction. Given at the induction stage they delayed flowering, and during postinduction stages they produced no appreciable effect. It was also recorded that long dark periods given during the growth of both

[3] George, E.E. and Lalouette, J.A., 1962. Photoperiodic experiments on the sugarcane variety *C.P. 36-13*, *Proc. Int. Soc. Sugar Cane Technol.* 11: 516–527.

early- and late-blooming varieties delayed tassel emergence. Irrigation tended to accelerate flowering. With respect to the stages of flower development, it was concluded that both early- and late-flowering varieties initiate flower primordia at essentially the same time. This is definitely not true of early- and late-flowering canes in Puerto Rico (327). Although Vijayasaradhy and Narashimhan succeeded in forcing two non--flowering *S. spontaneum* canes to bloom (*Burma* and *Assam 301*), induced flowering remained a highly uncertain process at this time. Nonetheless, these authors had delved into most of the physiological concepts which needed exploring in order for authentic flower control to be attained.

Chilton and Moreland (322), in Louisiana, noted that prior efforts to induce flowering by adjusting photoperiod were based on fixed day lengths. They proceeded to test the theory that it is the gradual shortening of day length which causes flowering in sugarcane. In two experiments six varieties having *S. officinarum, S. barberi,* and *S. spontaneum* parentage were given gradually-diminishing photoperiods. Flowering was induced in all varieties. From this they concluded: "It is difficult to believe that flowers produced in the two experiments were due to chance."

Subsequent work by Chilton and Paliatseas (323) employed 81 varieties from Florida, Australia, Java, and Barbados. Photoperiod treatments were begun with a day length of 12 hours 44 minutes plus evening twilight. Day lengths were reduced by 1 minute per day for 80 to 85 days. Some 34 varieties flowered in response to the treatment, including one whose parentage was believed to include *S. officinarum, S. spontaneum,* and *Sorghum durra*. An additional 32 varieties initiated flower primordia. Chilton and Paliatseas concluded that flowering is a photoperiodic response and can be induced in sugarcane by gradually shortening the day length. The photoperiod effect was itself regarded as "conditioned" by environmental and physiological factors, ". . .with the concept that if the necessary environmental and physiological factors are satisfied and the sugarcane stalk will not respond to changing day length, then the problem of controlling the flowering of sugarcane resolves itself into a knowledge of these factors". This interpretation has subsequently become the basis for developing controlled flower-induction technology.

By 1957 Vijayasaradhy and his colleagues at Coimbatore (1498, 1500) had greatly advanced the understanding of photoperiod in sugarcane flowering and its potential use in flower induction where natural flowering seldom occurs. A Burma *S. spontaneum* was forced to tassel when plants with marcotted tops were given a 22-hour day length for a period of 39 days, followed by 16-hour nights for 9 days, and finally by natural photoperiod. This in itself might suggest classification as a long–short day plant (352), but other experiments showed that it would flower in response to 22 hours darkness given daily for 2 months (September 10 to November 10). Thereafter, Vijayasaradhy and his co-workers successfully forced into bloom nearly every variety tested by extending the natural dark period by 2 to 4 hours. In some cases the dark treatment was preceded by a 4-hour extension of the light period.

In general terms, fertility response to controlled photoperiod is perhaps best regarded as a varietal factor. Dutt (453, 455), who was among the first to induce earlier flowering with controlled photoperiod, observed significantly lower pollen fertility among treated tassels. Lee and Lin (913) failed to detect reduced pollen viability following similar treatments. Daniels (404), in Fiji, found no female sterility or abnormality of any sort in photoperiod-induced tassels. At Canal Point, James achieved a reduction of male sterility in *L. 60-25* with prolonged 11.5-hour dark periods. Rao and Kumari (1220) reported "abnormalities" in sugarcane treated with a 4-hour photoperiod after being converted to the vegetative state by long-day treatment. It was thought that an induced hormonal imbalance was responsible.

On the other hand, James (794) quite successfully used a controlled-photoperiod technique to improve flowering synchronization and pollen production in six clones at Canal Point. Early- to mid-season clones of *S. officinarum* x *S. sinense* x *S. spontaneum* parentage having a high degree of male sterility were subjected to 15.5-hour photoperiods between September 13 and October 25. Treatment duration varied from 2 to 6 weeks. Flowering was generally delayed among all treatments, with durations given later in the treatment period being most effective. With maximum flowering delay varying from 10 to 72 days, it was now possible to cross all mid-season flowering clones with the earliest clone, and to cross most of the late-flowering clones with the mid-season clones. All varieties produced pollen and were effective pollen parents when flowering was delayed by controlled photoperiod.

James (796) also employed a controlled-photoperiod technique to induce flowering in sparsely- or non-flowering varieties. In addition to six *C.P.* varieties, test clones included *H. 37-1933, Pindar, Badilla, U.S. 59-16-1, Cl. 47-83, Cl. 54-334*, and *Rakhra (S. sinense)*. Treatments consisted of supplementing natural photoperiod after July 1 and maintaining night temperatures above 71 °F. Plants grown in soil contained in large metal cans were transferred daily to air-conditioned darkrooms at 5:00 p.m. and removed at 8:00 a.m. Four photoperiod schedules were used. Each schedule included about 9 hours light (8:00 a.m. to 5:00 p.m.) plus variable supplemental light to give from 13 to 12.5 hours total photoperiod. Results showed that marked differences existed in the photoperiod requirements among clones. Earliest flowering was obtained by gradually decreasing the treatment from 13 to 12.5 hours over an interval of 35 days. *H. 37-1933* and *Pindar* flowered only when photoperiod was held constant at 12.5 hours. By use of several photoperiod schedules it was possible to make one or more crosses in all except two clones, underscoring the value of photoperiodically-induced flowering in a sugarcane breeding program. These and earlier (794) studies at Canal Point further stressed the need to determine precisely the time of floral initiation during a photoinduction treatment.

B. *Controlled flowering in S. spontaneum*

A very practical example of controlled flowering by regulation of photoperiod and temperature is found in the instance of wild canes of the *S. spontaneum* group. Several early investigators (62, 1300) had achieved flower control with a few reluctant *S. spontaneum* varieties and in so doing underscored the importance of photoperiod in flowering. By 1960 many breeders had come to recognize a need for "wild blood" in the genetic make-up of modern varieties in order to increase the vigor, yield, and hardiness of the "noble" or *S. officinarum* canes. *S. spontaneum* was the logical wild parent and potentially the most valuable source of wild genetic material. Unfortunately, most *S. spontaneum* varieties flower too early to be crossed with their *S. officinarum* counterparts, and for this reason breeders have had to use a small number of hybrids obtained by controlled crosses where the climate permitted a synchronization of tasseling.

The alternative for breeders not favored with a suitable climate was to attempt crossing *S. spontaneum* and *S. officinarum* canes with the aid of controlled-climate facilities. According to Daniels (405), early efforts included air shipment of viable pollen from places where it was available to places where needed. Brandes and Matz (226), by 1939, had flown *S. spontaneum* pollen from Florida to Columbia where crosses were made between *S. spontaneum* and *S. officinarum*, and between *S. spontaneum* and *S. officinarum* derivatives. Others (405, 281) effectively advanced the flowering in *S. officinarum* with adjusted photoperiod so that the earliest of the *S. officinarum* flowers coincided in time with the last of the *S. spontaneum* flowers. This method is restricted by lack of free-flowering noble canes and by the limited number of plants that can be treated with controlled-climate facilities (405). Another approach used with some success by Moriya (1037) in Taiwan was to lengthen the *S. spontaneum* vegetative period by interrupting the inductive dark period with incandescent lights. However, the delayed *S. spontaneum* plants had difficulty emerging their tassels owing to prevailing cooler temperatures.

Daniels (405) reports having achieved "near-noble" varieties using the adjusted photoperiod method of Chilton and Moreland (322), *i.e.*, by gradually shortening the photoperiod from 12 hours 44 minutes at the rate of 1 minute per day. He proceeded to test the same principle as a means of inducing *S. spontaneum* to flower after having been kept vegetative by breaking the inductive dark period with lights. Eight *S. spontaneum* varieties were induced to flower by reducing day length from 13 hours 15 minutes at the rate of 15 minutes per week. The treatment was most successful with night temperature constant at 72 to 74 °F, and relative humidity constant at 95 percent.

Glasziou (583) states that by use of phytotron facilities at Brisbane some 20 varieties of *S. spontaneum* were induced to flower with controlled night temperatures varying from 22 to 28 °C. In one study with the *S. spontaneum* variety *Mandalay*, day temperatures of 18, 22, or 26 °C produced flowering when the day length was 12.5 hours, and the night temperature was 26 °C. Day temperatures of 30 and 34 °C failed to produce flowers under these conditions. Glasziou surmised that for different night temperatures there should be different ranges of day temperatures optimal for floral induction. Burr (383) depicts temperature as a controlling factor over primordia initiation, flower development, and fertility, exceeding even day length, nyctiperiod and duration of the 11.5-hour night at latitudes far from the equator.

6. FLOWERING CONTROL: THE GROWER'S VIEWPOINT

From the grower's point of view flowering is undesirable because of its adverse effects on sugarcane yield and quality. Clements and Awada (352) report that in Hawaii flowering is especially harmful during the first year of the 2-year cycle. In one experiment at Ewa, heavy flowering the first year lowered yields by about 20 percent. The authors estimate that when tasseling approaches 75 to 80 percent, yield losses will approach 25 percent. They conclude: "It has been our considered judgment that for those areas, where a 2-year crop can be grown, first season tassel constitutes one of the major hazards for the producer and problems for the crop control superintendent."

As an effective source-to-sink system the flowered cane no longer compares favorably with a vegetative cane. Vegetative growth ceases and hence the volume of stalk tissue available for sucrose becomes limited. The top portion of the stalk may become pithy. Apical dominance is lost, side shoots tend to develop (at the expense of stored sucrose), leaf blades tend to become shortened and soon cease to be replaced by newer blades. Non-flowering stalks continue to push their green canopy upward and increasingly shade the photosynthesizing area remaining on the flowered canes. In essence both the tasseled stalks and those producing aberrations such as "multiple top" or "witches' broom" have lost much of their ability to manufacture and store sugar.

However, many varieties which tend to flower heavily are quite desirable in other respects. On the south coast of Puerto Rico, for example, the heavy-flowering variety *C.P. 5243*, with its upright growth habit, high stalk quality, lack of sheath spines and absence of cerrated leaf edges, ranks it high in the growers' and laborers' esteem. In such cases there may be a greater desire to prevent flowering by one means or another than to change varieties. On the other hand, the tendency among sugarcane breeders in Puerto Rico has been to set aside new selections which flower heavily regardless of their sugar-producing qualities (1164). To the extent that flowering can be prevented by cultural means this practice constitutes a serious error.

Numerous methods have been tried in attempts to prevent flowering. These include the use of flares or other light sources to interrupt the critical dark period, temperature control, mechanical defoliation, withholding water, and use of chemical sprays. In 1950, from preliminary observations in Hawaii, Burr (268) concluded that any treatment that arrests normal development, whether by water control, metabolic inhibition, defoliation, or chemical "burning", will tend to suppress flowering if applied during the critical period of floral induction.

Water control and chemical treatments presently hold the greatest promise. Defoliation and night interruption have not proven to be feasible on a commercial basis. It also appears that, regardless of the methods used, the treatments will always be attended with certain irregularities and frustrations. Owing to variable temperature (*cf.* this chapter, pp. 535–540) or other environmental factors, fields blooming heavily one year may not bloom at all another year, or only so lightly that one may never know whether his control efforts were effective.

A. *Effects of flowering on cane quality*

For years sugarcane growers suspected that flowering lowered sugar yields and experimental evidence clearly supports this view. As pointed out above, the flowered stalk is generally a less effective structure for sugar synthesis and storage than its vegetative counterpart. Whereas juice quality may temporarily increase as an immediate response to flowering (1164), the subsequent growth of new shoots triggers significant losses in stored sucrose. The stalk itself becomes "pithy" and there is an increase of fiber which further complicates the recovery of sugar in the factory. Moreover, in those regions where heavy flowering is followed by many months of growth time, major losses in tonnage will commonly follow. In addition to direct qualitative effects, as pointed out by Humbert *et al.* (764), flowering reduces the effectiveness of numerous cultural practices. Where tasseling is heavy the reduction or elimination of this problem is a prerequisite for continued improvement of water management, fertilization, weed control, and ripening practices.

Martin-Leake (985) states that the economic importance of cane flowering relates to its effect on tonnage and juice quality. Measurable weight loss begins a few weeks after floral induction, and, where moisture is plentiful, may continue to the point where close to 50 percent of the potential tonnage is lost. Both tonnage and quality decline is lessened under dry conditions. Additional changes that are more pronounced in flowering cane include a lower percentage of reducing sugars, higher ash content, and temporary increases in juice purity followed by loss of purity. Martin-Leake also claims that stalks infected with mosaic and other diseases have a greater tendency to flower.

That flowering lowers cane quality is perhaps best shown by the increased sucrose obtained when flowering has been prevented by one means or another. Thus, higher sugar yields have been recorded following tassel control by dark-period interruption (268), defoliation (1141), withholding moisture (349, 764), and by chemical sprays (1405, 764).

In 1963, a year of heavy flowering in Argentina, López Hernández (954) performed extensive quality studies relative both to specific quality factors and the rate at which their differences developed in flowering and non-flowering stalks. His parameters included fiber percent cane, "juice extraction percent cane", percent sucrose in the juice, sugar yield, and weight of cane. Samples from both flowering and non-flowering stalks were taken from the same variety. Differences between flowered and vegetative samples were found to be slight during the early flowering stages. There were practically no differences between samples at the elongation stage. But extensive differences had appeared by the time the flowers were 3 months old. With respect to fiber, much greater quantities were found in flowered canes, particularly in an upward gradient in the six uppermost internodes. From the 7th internode down both flowered and non-flowered stalks showed essentially equal fiber levels whose gradients increased toward the base of the stalk.

The fiber date strongly implied a need for topping the tasseled stalks before shipment to the factory. This was verified by juice extractibility and sucrose content of the juice. Owing to the greater percentage of fiber, the juice extraction percent cane values were some 17 percent lower in the flowered samples. However, below the 7th internode, extraction was essentially constant in both sets of samples. The sugar analyses likewise showed nearly constant sucrose values for flowered and non-flowered cane below the 7th internode.

Somewhat more sucrose (both apparent and actual) was found in the tops of flowered stalks. It was calculated that, were it not for the additional fiber, the flowered cane would yield close to 1 percent more sugar than the vegetative cane. Because of the higher fiber content, the extracted sucrose was about 5 percent lower in flowered samples, so that the final yield of flowered cane was about 4 percent lower than the yield of cane which had not bloomed. López Hernández (954) did not specifically mention the costs of delivering relatively useless tops to the factory, nor the added wear that high-fiber materials impose on factory machinery. His findings do agree quite closely with those obtained with flowering cane in Mexico (1164).

B. *Flowering control by moisture stress*

Many authors agree that controlled water supply during the critical period of flower induction is the most effective means of flower control available to the cane grower. Clements (357) wrote in 1968: "Sugarcane is very sensitive to draught and will not blossom if under stress; in fact, the imposition of a mild draught is one means used to prevent flowering in commercial fields." Clements and Awada (349) regarded low soil moisture tension as one of the factors which will assure flowering in varieties *Co. 312*, *N.Co. 310*, and *H. 37-1933*. In Puerto Rico, moisture stress delayed flowering in the majority of some 78 varieties studied by Chu and Serapión (327). Vijayasaradhy and Narasimhan (1499) employed irrigation as a means to accelerate flowering in India, and Brett (240) describes low soil moisture tension as a factor conducive to flowering in Natal.

Humbert *et al.* (764) found the withholding of irrigation from August 10 to September 20 to be an effective means of tassel prevention at Los Mochis, Mexico.

Fig. 14-6 illustrates the reduction of tassels obtained in *N.Co. 310* and *Co. 421* at Los Mochis by interrupting the normal water supply. Plants irrigated according to the normal 14-day intervals produced far more tassels than those watered at intervals greater than 25 days. Humbert *et al.* depict the plants' water stress response in terms of a physiological reprogramming aimed at survival of the cane rather than reproduction. When water is again supplied, the plants resume vegetative growth with the critical inductive photoperiod safely behind them for another year. However, the rainy season which coincides with flower induction renders this method impractical in most regions of Mexico.

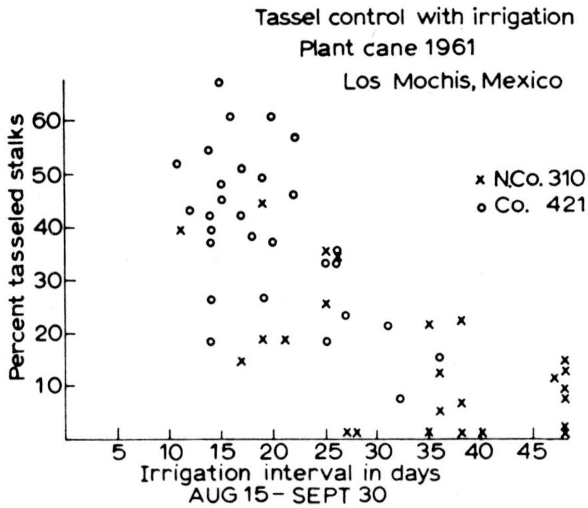

Fig. 14-6. Effect of withholding irrigation on sugarcane tasseling at Los Mochis, Mexico. Plants irrigated at normal 14-day intervals flowered heavily, but flowering was progressively restricted as the watering interval was lengthened. [After Humbert *et al.* (764).] Reproduced by permission of *I.S.S.C.T.*

At best, flower prevention by water management appears to be a difficult course of action. An obvious prerequisite is a very sparse rainfall during the summer months and early autumn, and only in limited areas can this be counted upon. Moreover, there is much involved beside simply withholding irrigation. There are problems of correct water resumption as well as correct timing of the stress if the treatment is to be successful without causing undue tonnage losses. Thus, fairly exact information is needed relative to the flowering habits of each variety, the soil physical properties, the degree of moisture stress required by a given date, the variety's ability to withstand the stress, its water requirements for normal growth resumption, and the plantation's ability to meet the new water requirements.

Tanimoto and Nickell (1405) emphasized that thorough knowledge of the soils and the timing of the last preflowering irrigation are essential features of successful water management at this period. They also stressed the importance of quickly satisfying water needs within the entire area under stress in order to prevent over-drying during the time of water resumption. Tanimoto (71) developed a moisture index designed to achieve 85.5 percent moisture in joints 4 to 5 by early September to insure proper conditioning of the plant for flower prevention.

Clements and Awada (352) attribute much of the "spotty" response to moisture-stress treatments to incorrect selection of the treatment period. During the late 1950's the recommendation given to Hawaiian growers called for completion of the pretreatment irrigation by August 10 and a resumption of irrigation after September 21. According to Clements and Awada, "these dates had the advantage of firmness even though it developed that they were not completely correct". Two shortcomings appeared in this recommendation: (a) Sugarcane thus treated tended to flower anyway, although somewhat later, and (b) much of the cane never fully recovered from the imposed drought. The latter difficulty was worsened by severe soil cracking and a resultant slowing down of the irrigation rounds. In effect, excessive water was required at a time when the days were very hot and water reserves were very low.

Clements and Awada subsequently devised a new flower-control program in which the final predrought irrigation round is completed by August 4, and, in the absence of intervening rainfall, irrigation is resumed after the first Monday in September (352). If there has been 1 or more inches of rainfall the irrigation is not resumed until after the next scheduled irrigation round. Table 14-2 summarizes the positive effects of this

TABLE 14-2

EFFECT OF WITHHOLDING IRRIGATION ON SUBSEQUENT FLOWERING OF SUGARCANE AT OLOKELE, 1961

[After Clements and Awada (352).] Reproduced by permission of the *Indian Journal of Sugarcane Research and Development.*

Field	Tassel control (% tassels)	Check (% tassels)
190 (a)	2	60
(b)	23	60
(c)	27	70
(d)	50	72
(e)	50	78
230	None	No check
330	Trace	15–30

program in a study conducted at Olokele in 1961 with variety *H. 37-1933*. Similar results were obtained at the Wailuku Sugar Company. Because at both plantations there is a shortage of water at this period, Clements and Awada recommended that drought be imposed on the first-year fields most likely to flower. This program eliminates one irrigation cycle, or two where rainfall has been adequate, and has not generally caused undue stress on the crop's vegetative phase (352).

Clements and Awada (352) describe temperature as a most important factor affecting the outcome of flowering control by water stress. Where night temperatures have been below normal during the inductive period, there may be few or no flowers regardless of water treatment: "In such areas where blossoming may be very heavy one year and very light another, it is sometimes frustrating to the crop control superintendent to apply treatments only to discover that particular year was a light year anyway." The authors proposed a solution based on temperature records for August and early September. Accordingly, having completed the last predrought round of irrigation by August 4, temperature records for the period August 1 to 15 should be examined in relation to the normal temperature–flowering pattern of the next 3 weeks. When it appears that the temperature trend has been favorable for induction, and hence flowering is likely, the drought treatment should be continued. If the temperature pattern indicates a strong possibility of natural flower repression, *i.e.*, a trend of subnormal night temperatures or unfavorable temperature ranges, irrigation can be continued. Quite obviously much will depend upon the experience and judgment of the crop manager, and upon the patient compiling of climate data at each plantation as a matter of management policy.

C. *Flowering control with chemicals*

Chemical flowering control is based on the understanding that a flowering stimulus or stimuli is produced in the leaves, and that if this production can be suppressed, even briefly during the critical inductive phase, the entire flowering process will be bypassed and normal vegetative growth can continue after a short suspension. Obviously, the destruction of part of the photosynthesizing green canopy must also be attended by some loss of growth and sugar production. It follows that chemical flower control by foliar destruction requires a chemical treatment whose ultimate yield effect is significantly less damaging than that of the flowers.

Experiments performed by Panje *et al.* (1141) at Lucknow, India, have shown that young blades situated at the spindle area are highly sensitive "for the perception of the photoperiodic stimulus". Removal of these leaves at the appropriate time will encourage the cane to remain vegetative. Evidence indicates that the treatment must be performed during a critical interval of some 2 weeks duration, with the exact dates being determined by latitude. The authors specify the third and fourth weeks of September at 26° 45′ north latitude, and about the fourth week of August at 17° north latitude. When successful such treatments increased both the yield and quality of cane (1141).

Raja Rao and Srivastava (1213) recently tested the compounds maleic hydrazide, α-naphthalene acetic acid (NAA), cobaltus nitrate, *p*-phenylenediamine, catechol, hydroquinone, versene, and pentachlorophenol for anti-flowering activity in India. Each was applied as a foliar spray aimed primarily at the spindle cluster during the last week of September. Pentachlorophenol significantly lowered the flower percentages for the two varieties treated (*Co. 1171* and *Co. 1345*). This chemical was regarded as having commercial possibilities in India. Other chemicals inhibited flowering from 30 to 60 percent. Split or multiple applications were generally more effective than single doses; however, insufficient contact of spray materials with the foliage remained a major limitation along with high costs of materials. Juice quality was generally improved by treatments giving significant tassel reduction.

As early as 1957 Burr *et al.* (271) described pentachlorophenol as one of the more effective chemicals producing flower inhibition in Hawaii. Other compounds tested in Hawaii with some success included CMU [3-(*p*-chlorophenyl)-1,1-dimethylurea], versene, maleic hydrazide, and NAA. Apparently, whatever compounds destroyed leaf tissue by phytotoxic action also reduced flowering, a response regarded as comparable to mechanical defoliation. Maleic hydrazide is generally active as a growth retardant. Attempts by Burr *et al.* to induce flowering with chemicals were negative.

Heavy N fertilizer applications have inhibited flowering in Hawaii, especially in younger plants just mature enough to flower (271). High N supplied in culture solutions did not prevent flowering in mature cane. The positive N effect in younger plants was attributed to extensive immaturity associated with N-induced succulence. Burr (268), in 1950, cited a study on Maui which showed an N relationship to flowering in *H. 37-1933.* The response varied with N level and the number of applications. When all of the N was applied at planting there was heavy flowering in the autumn. When half was applied late in August there were fewer flowers, and when 1/3 was applied at planting, 1/3 in late August, and the final 1/3 early in October, only a few tassels were produced. In another instance flowering in four varieties was found to vary with K fertilization. High-K treatments increased flowering in *H. 32-8560*, decreased flowering in *H. 38-2915*, and produced little effect on flowering in *H. 32-1063* and *H. 37-1933*.

In general, chemicals active in growth regulation have not gained wide acceptance in sugarcane flower control. Early tests in Hawaii (268) showed NAA to be less effective than either "activators" or maleic hydrazide. The latter compound was thought to be effective because of its growth-arresting properties. According to Humbert *et al.* (764), maleic hydrazide combined with gibberellic acid (GA) gave total flower inhibition in Australia. Neither compound was inhibitory when applied alone.

In Puerto Rico, GA proved to be highly effective in preventing *C.P. 52-43* from blooming when applied in late August shortly before the critical induction period[4]. Applied in large volumes with knapsack sprayers, GA treatments gave nearly 100 percent inhibition while improving both tonnage and quality. In the same study, ***Paraquat*** applied by aircraft at commercial rates was somewhat less effective in con-

[4] Alexander, A.G., Montalvo-Zapata, R., Spain, G.L. and Kumar, A., 1972. Sugarcane flower control studies with Paraquat, gibberellic acid, and sodium metasilicate, *J. Agric. Univ. P.R.* 56(3): 201–218.

trolling flowers and it significantly lowered tonnage. However, GA applied by aircraft the following year (1969) gave only a slight reduction of tassels and only small growth and sugar responses.

Following early tests with maleic hydrazide, which at best gave only about 60 percent control of flowering, workers in Hawaii (1405) developed more satisfactory chemical treatments using *Monuron* (3-*p*-chlorophenyl-1,1-dimethylurea), and subsequently *Diuron* [3-(3,4-dichlorophenyl)-1,1-dimethylurea]. Almost complete flower prevention was achieved in *H. 37-1933* when the chemicals were carefully applied. A recommendation was issued specifying that Monuron or Diuron should be given at the rate of 4 pounds of active material per acre between September 6 and 24. Although the substituted urea herbicides marked a high point in chemical flower control, research continued in efforts to discover a better chemical, that is, a compound having more activity, more leeway with respect to time of application, less cane toxicity, and a lower cost.

In 1960 the dipyridyl herbicide *Diquat* was tested in Hawaii and early results pointed to a highly effective anti-flowering action (1405). Initial dosages in the order of 2 pounds per acre were too high and were sometimes lethal to the cane. Further tests showed that as little as 0.125 pound per acre of the ionic form could be effective, and that the interval of time suitable for Diquat application was longer than that of prior materials. Use of Diquat in these early experiments led to improved sugar yields in the heavy-tasseling variety *H. 37-1933* and a significant reduction in the cost of chemical flowering control. Tanimoto and Nickell (1405) also pointed out the importance of application date relative to the time of floral induction for the variety in question. In addition to the time and rate of application, the varieties' inclination to flower, its age, condition of the crop, and geographical location of the field are all factors to be considered in designing effective chemical treatments.

Under humid conditions in Guyana, Evans and Bates (507) obtained little response from Diquat applied to three varieties during the period of floral induction. On the other hand, Clements (358) states that in Puerto Rico Diquat produced a 40-percent loss in the crop when applied under conditions of moisture stress. Most workers seem to overlook the close relationship between incident light intensity and the herbicidal mode of Diquat's action (*cf.* Chapter 13, pp. 498, 499). Hence, if applied during cloudy weather, especially if cool and rainy, much of the chemical's potential may be lost, conversely, if applied during a period of clear, hot days an unexpectedly rapid or severe action might develop. By the same reasoning the time of day should also be a factor, with early-morning treatments having greater activity than those applied in the afternoon or evening.

Humbert *et al.* (764) reported very favorable results with Diquat as an anti-flowering agent in Mexico. At Ingenio Xicotencatl tassel percentages were significantly lowered in varieties *N.Co. 310* and *Co. 421* by about 1 liter of Diquat per acre applied in 70 liters of water. As little as 0.25 liter of Diquat in 15 liters of water gave positive results. It was observed that cane harvested early (in January) experienced some quality decline, and Humbert *et al.* surmised that the chemical should not be applied to fields scheduled for early harvest in December or January. It was also noted that tasseling caused little tonnage losses for cane harvested early, but for cane harvested from February to June there was a progressive loss of tonnage owing to several months of lost growing time. While most of the Diquat applications at Xicotencatl were made during the first half of September, applications given as late as the third week in September also produced flower control. Earlier applications appeared to be necessary for best results in the more tropical regions of Mexico. According to Humbert *et al.*, Diquat has also given promising results for flower prevention in the Philippines (827).

Arvier (115) recently described flower-control experiments with Diquat in Queensland. Rates greater than 1.5 oz per acre of the ionic form adversely affected yield and quality. Flowering is not particularly troublesome in Queensland with the exception of the *N.Co. 310* variety in the southern districts.

D. *Defoliation and spindle removal*

It is widely accepted that leaves are the plant organs which perceive critical day lengths and respond by producing a stimulus which is essential for floral induction at the apical meristem. It was quite logical, therefore, that a number of workers should attempt to control cane flowering by removing the spindle leaves most active in producing this stimulus (71, 75, 378, 1141). The method has proven highly effective. It has also served as a useful tool for examining fundamental aspects of flowering physiology. Spindle removal is not generally used on a commercial scale except in a few regions having an abundance of inexpensive labor (1141).

By 1956 workers in Hawaii (71) had identified the very young spindle leaves (completely furled) as the most active in producing the "signal" for floral induction. As early as 1950 Burr (268) had concluded that this stimulus was a chemical, or a group of chemicals, which was translocated from the leaf to the inductive site: "Light does something to a leaf, and the effect is transmitted through the conducting tissue to the bud. This material will pass through a graft from the leaf of a sensitive variety to the bud of an insensitive one." By 1959 additional work in Hawaii had shown that severing the leaf spindle at the level of the uppermost dewlap totally prevented flowering. Time of spindle removal was critical. Removal of the blades on September 5 nearly eliminated induction, and similar treatments performed at three successive weeks before September 5 completely prevented it.

Subsequent studies by Coleman (378) from 1961 to 1963 were suggestive of separate roles for the spindle and mature leaves in producing the flowering stimulus. Beginning August 5, either the leaf spindle (spindle trimming) or all leaves except the leaf spindle (leaf trimming) were removed from ten different plants at weekly intervals until October 10. Another treatment consisted of removing both foliar parts from the same plants after various starting dates. Newly-emerging leaf tissue was cut away at weekly intervals. In compiling the flowering data, floral initiation was taken as all instances of primordia formation or some stage of expressed flower development, including abnormal flowering responses such as "bunchy top".

As shown in Fig. 14-7, the plants were far more sensitive to spindle removal than to

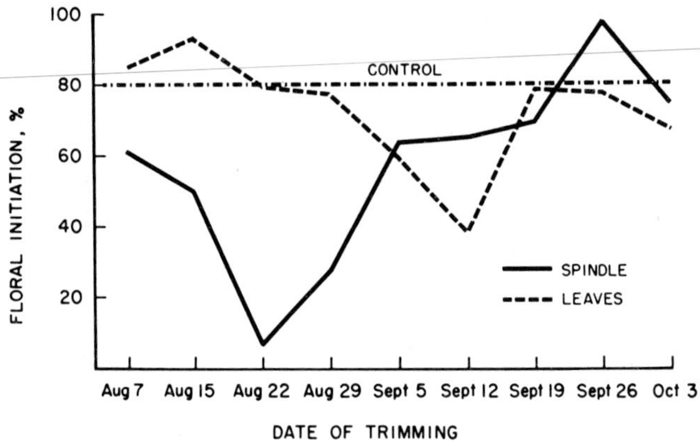

Fig. 14-7. Effects of spindle trimming and leaf trimming on the extent of flower initiation in sugarcane. The results suggest separate roles of the spindle and of all leaves except the spindle in producing a flowering stimulus. [After Coleman (378).] Reproduced by permission of *I.S.S.C.T.*

leaf removal. Loss of the spindle on August 15, 22, and 29 was highly prohibitive against floral initiation, whereas leaf trimming was effective only on September 12. Essentially comparable results were obtained recently by Chu and Serapión (1158) in Puerto Rico. With regard to actual tassel emergence it was again observed that spindle trimming was more effective than leaf trimming, in this case the treatment being effective as late as the September 19 removal date. It was also shown that spindle trimming at any time during the inductive period tended to increase the percentage of abnormal flowers, whereas leaf trimming prior to September 5 produced the opposite effect.

Coleman (378) interpreted his data in terms of separate but interdependent roles for spindle and leaf tissues in cane flowering. The period of essentiality for spindles begins as early as August 15[5]. Leaves were regarded as essential only around September 12. The critical leaf activity thus coincided with the photoperiodically-sensitive interval from September 1 to September 20 (271). Coleman did not take this to mean that leaves were not important prior to September 5; rather, he concluded that tissue regrowth compensated sufficiently for the leaf material lost in August. On the other hand, the role performed by leaves in August was considered to be distinct from the

[5]Chu and Serapión (1158) have moved this period up to August 1 for three test varieties at Gurabo, Puerto Rico.

leaf role in September. Coleman's work was the first to show that the differentiation process required a stage prior to photoinduction, a stage essentially complete by August 29, and that this activity was localized in the spindle.

Defoliation studies by Panje *et al.* (1141) at Lucknow essentially verified Coleman's concepts of stimulus perception and showed that sugarcane can be kept vegetative by this means under Indian conditions. Two types of defoliation were employed: (a) Removal of the spindle cluster, including the blade adjacent to the uppermost dewlap, and (b) removal of the spindle cluster in a similar manner while in addition removing the next three blades at their respective dewlaps. Treatments were given at 6-day intervals from August 21 to October 8. It was found that defoliation on any date between September 14 and 26 gave nearly total inhibition of flowering. The results were further consistent with those of Coleman (378) in that the young expanding blades of the spindle cluster were found to be the principal perceptive tissues for the photoperiodic stimulus. Subsequent experiments with six varieties showed that each variety was most sensitive to defoliation during the third week of September. Progressively later treatments were increasingly less effective. In tropical India, an experiment performed during 1965–1966 showed that August 21 and September 1 were effective defoliation dates.

Juice quality analyses were performed by Panje and his co-workers in conjuction with defoliation treatments between 1961 and 1963, and again in 1965–1966 (1141). The quality of treated plants, *i.e.*, defoliated non-flowered canes, was generally higher than that of non-defoliated flowered canes. Defoliation appeared to shorten the subtending internodes of leaves which had been removed; however, yields were generally higher for the defoliation treatments. It was further noted that flowered canes developed lateral shoots from the top three to four nodes. Pithiness also developed in the flowered canes. Neither feature was evident in non-flowered material.

Panje *et al.* (1141) concluded that defoliation should be a suitable means of flower prevention in India, particularly in areas having major growth periods after the time of floral induction. Temporary growth losses produced by defoliation were deemed less severe than losses produced by flowering. The authors suggested that, in tropical India, the growth of cane on small holdings with an abundance of labor would give the defoliation method certain advantages over chemical flowering control, the latter being quite costly in India. Moreover, the removed leaves could be used as fodder for the grower's cattle.

Julien (813), in Mauritius, verified the importance attached by earlier workers to spindle leaves in primordia induction, but in addition his results suggested the presence of a flowering inhibitor in mature leaves. Working with the variety *U.S. 48-34*, the removal of leaves $^+3$ and $^+4$ produced earlier flowering by comparison with undefoliated controls. Removal of the spindle (all leaves younger than that showing a visible dewlap), or of leaves $^+1$ or $^+2$, delayed flowering and reduced its intensity. Julien explained the repressive effect of lower leaves in terms of inhibitor synthesis and weakened perception of the flowering stimulus within these leaves. In addition, he is one of the few flowering researchers to describe the older leaves in their correct context as competing channels of photosynthate flow in a source-to-sink system: "It thus appears that the lower leaves, +3 and +4, are inhibitory not only because they may be less sensitive in perceiving the flowering stimulus, but also because they may either produce a solute stream which may dilute or prevent the flowering stimulus from reaching the apex, or they may act as sinks for the flowering stimulus or they may produce a transmissible flowering inhibitor."

E. *Relative effectiveness of defoliation and chemical treatments*

In 1959 workers in Hawaii (75) reported direct comparisons between the defoliation method and chemical treatments as means of flower prevention. The compounds maleic hydrazide (MH) and CMU, then at the forefront of potential flower-control agents, were evaluated against spindle trimming for 1 and 3 weeks (Fig. 14-8). It was

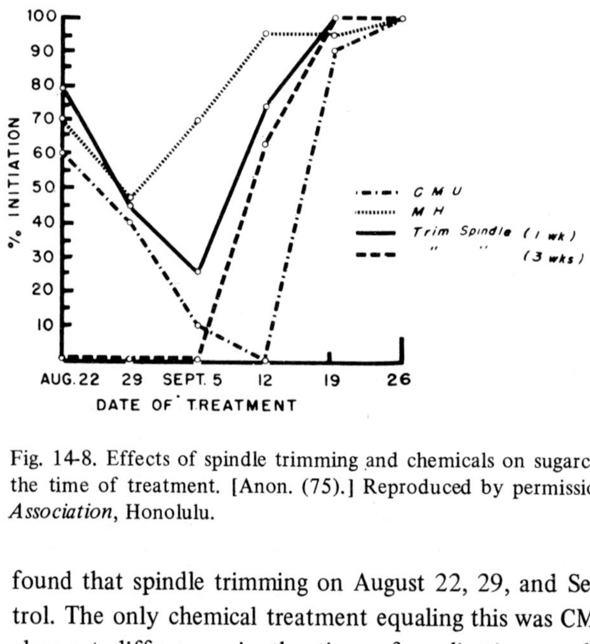

Fig. 14-8. Effects of spindle trimming and chemicals on sugarcane flower initiation in relation to the time of treatment. [Anon. (75).] Reproduced by permission of the *Hawaiian Sugar Planters' Association*, Honolulu.

found that spindle trimming on August 22, 29, and September 5 gave complete control. The only chemical treatment equaling this was CMU given on September 12. The clear-cut differences in the time of application producing maximum results is an apparent confirmation that separate processes are active in the leaves (damaged by CMU) and in the spindle. In addition, the fact that maleic hydrazide had to be applied earlier than CMU to be effective is further evidence of its growth-suppressing activity, *i.e.*, of its action against the apical meristem rather than leaf-destroying activity as in the case of CMU.

During the subsequent decade both CMU and maleic hydrazide slipped into the background as DCMU, Diquat, and Paraquat were in turn proven to be more effective in flower control. Defoliation never gained acceptance in Hawaii on a commercial scale. However, leaf and spindle trimming have been extremely useful tools in the study of flowering mechanisms.

F. *Flower control with nitrogen*

Effects of N and K on flowering were mentioned briefly in a prior section (*cf.* this chapter, p. 555). In general, heavy N fertilization will give some degree of flower control, but the grower must expect a lower quality of cane when such treatments represent either an extension of the fertilization period or use of more N at ratooning than is normally prudent. It is not unlikely that future generations, having recourse to better growth-regulating chemicals, or better ripening methodology in general, will be able to extend the safe N fertilization time. Under certain conditions it may become possible to program N fertilization so as to accomplish flower control as well.

A clear example of controlled N and water supply having flower-prevention potential was presented by workers in Hawaii (Makiki) in 1956 (71). Although the high-N treatment, totaling 200 lbs/acre, is not excessive, one-half of this amount was given a full 6 months after ratooning (Table 14-3). In this study high N alone pro-

TABLE 14-3

EFFECT OF NITROGEN LEVEL AND TIME OF DROUGHT ON SUGARCANE FLOWERING IN HAWAII

[Anon. (71).] Reproduced by permission of the *Hawaiian Sugar Planters' Association,* Honolulu.

Treatments*	Flowering (%)
Check, low N	90
Check, high N	80
Low N without water July 15–Aug. 31	65
High N without water July 15–Aug. 31	30
Low N without water Aug. 9–Sept. 23	5
High N without water Aug. 9–Sept. 23	0
Low N without water Sept. 2–Oct. 19	95
High N without water Sept. 2–Oct. 19	30

*All plots received 100 lbs N/acre at ratooning on Jan. 24. High-N plots received an additional 100 lbs N/acre on Aug. 1.

duced only a 10-percent reduction in tasseling, but high N combined with "drying off" before or after the critical induction period was far more effective. When high N was combined with a water-stress period encompassing both the preinductive flowering stage in August and the photoperiodically-critical inductive stage in September (drought between August 9 and September 23), a complete prevention of tasseling was attained. It was suggested (71) that high N combined with water stress should give optimum flower control. Under these conditions a period of rapid vegetative growth must be expected following resumption of water supply.

7. MECHANISM OF SUGARCANE FLOWERING

Defoliation studies relating to the critical photoperiodic and prephotoperiodic stages of floral induction have placed in focus the physiological mechanism by which primordia initiation occurs. The key actor in this mechanism is a stimulatory substance produced in the leaves in response to a highly critical photoperiod. No attempt is made here to review flowering mechanisms as they are generally understood in higher plants, a number of excellent reviews being readily available (437, 1278, 889, 947). It can safely be said that an entire branch of the plant sciences has grown up around the topic of floral induction alone. Coleman and his colleagues in Hawaii have led the exploration of basic flowering physiology in sugarcane, and a thorough analysis of this subject was presented by Coleman in Taiwan (379).

There is general agreement among plant scientists that flowering physiology, to be meaningful, must be studied on a plant-by-plant basis. This is especially appropriate for sugarcane. Plants native to the tropics are particularly sensitive to small changes in photoperiod (1606), and we have seen that sugarcane is no exception. Such plants are frequently more sensitive to the dark period than to day length. After all has been said, one might still depict sugarcane as a "long-night" plant, and certainly many of its varieties behave as such.

Perhaps sugarcane has been selected too exclusively for its growth and sugar properties, and perhaps its vegetative reproductive system is so effective that flowering is not very important as a means of survival. In any event sugarcane has long defied classification on a photoperiodic basis (*cf.* this chapter, p. 530), and its genetic make-up has enormously complicated efforts to unravel its flowering mechanism. In 1962 Coleman (373) wrote: ". . .With sugarcane, the problem is complicated by the genetic complexity of the plant which results in exceptions to nearly every generalization one attempts to make." Because of this there may be greater mechanistic differences among distinct cane varieties ("intermediate, short, and long–short") than there are among long-day or short-day species having critical inductive photoperiods and predictable responses to these photoperiods. The present review lends support to the belief that there need not be one universal theory of flowering (1556), or one flowering hormone (307).

A. *The inductive stimulus*

Most investigators assume that the stimulus causing floral initiation in a previously vegetative meristem consists of one or more substances having hormone-like qualities. Workers have long sought a specific flowering hormone and even coined the name "florigen" (312), but a single flowering substance, if it exists at all, has eluded all efforts toward its isolation. Zeevaart (1606) states categorically that a flowering hormone exists, and that its extraction and structural elucidation ranks among the most urgent problems in flowering physiology.

Additional questions concern the mechanism of flowering-hormone synthesis, the means of photoperiod control over the mechanism, the sequence of biochemical events leading to the hormone's production, and hormonal transport to the inductive site. In the interests of sugarcane flower control it is important to discover the limiting step (or steps) in hormonal synthesis and transport. It is here that the breeder or grower would attain his maximum influence in producing the desired flowering response. Toward this end, sugarcane scientists must still surmount the problem of extracting the "stimulus" and designing a reliable bioassay for its activity measurement.

Translocation of the flowering stimulus in sugarcane almost certainly constitutes added problems for the investigator if the pathways are identical to those of assimilated $^{14}CO_2$. This appears to be the case in *Perilla* (313) and other plants (947, pp. 408–409), where close correlations are reported between ^{14}C transport and movement of the flowering stimulus. In sugarcane this would presumably involve diurnal fluctuations in stimulus exit from the blades, temporary accumulation in the leaf sheath, movement through a long and highly-complicated vascular system, and a downward flow toward the stalk base prior to an upward diversion toward the apical meristem. Julien (813) has taken into account the theoretical dilution or preventative effects of solute movement on the passage of a flowering stimulus between the sugarcane leaf and meristem.

That a flowering material of some sort is synthesized in cane leaves and translocated to the meristem has been demonstrated by Burr (268). In this instance a method frequently used in short-day plants, the grafting of an induced leaf (donor) to a non-induced plant (receptor), was performed successfully and flowering proceeded in the non-induced plant. Another method sometimes used to demonstrate a stimulus synthesis and movement is the exposure of only one or a few leaves to an inductive photoperiod, followed by flower production in the remaining unexposed parts of the plant. In a few instances this technique has been used in sugarcane to demonstrate the leaf rank most perceptive to the inductive photoperiod.

A third method illustrating the synthesis and transport of a flowering factor involves the removal of leaves after the critical photoperiod has been perceived, and subsequently obtaining flowers from the apical meristem. This method was demonstrated by a leaf-trimming study reported in Hawaii in 1959 (75). The experiments included late treatments (leaf removal on September 12 and 19) which had little or no preventative action against flowering, and earlier treatments (August 22 to September 5) which were highly preventative (Fig. 14-8).

In general, sugarcane is a plant not particularly conducive to experiments of this type. If sugarcane behaved unequivocally as a short-day or a long-day plant, much might be learned about its production of flowering hormone by studying a simpler plant from the same category. It may well be that, for purposes of studying the inductive mechanism, sugarcane clones behaving as short-day plants should be used exclusively, with research being concentrated on the partial reactions characteristic of short-day plants. The underlying assumption here is that the biochemistry of actual primordia formation is identical among short-day, intermediate, and long-day clones.

B. *Gibberellin effects*

Considerable evidence has been published to show that gibberellins applied to a vegetative plant can affect the changeover to a flowering status (1371, 891, 890, 1221). The hormones apparently stimulate the inductive mechanism of long-day plants and of various species requiring a cold period to flower (138, 892). Stowe and Yamaki (1371) point out that neither the gibberellins nor other hormones will induce flowering when the photoperiod is clearly non-inductive. Flowering can be induced in some species having little sensitivity to day length; in these instances the gibberellin effect may relate to increased physical size or changes in physiological maturity (1221). According to Stowe and Yamaki (1371), a number of workers have reported flowering inhibition by gibberellin in short-day plants. Lincoln and Hamner (944), working with the short-day plant *Xanthium*, found that gibberellic acid (GA) increased the degree of flowering without directly affecting floral initiation. They suggested that GA may act to increase storage capability for the stimulus in immature *Xanthium* tissues. Storage of the flowering stimulus in sugarcane leaves has been discounted by Julien (813). Gibberellin has also been found to induce male sterility in hybrid maize (1086).

Alexander *et al.*[4] employed GA in efforts to prevent flowering in *C.P. 52-43*, a variety which usually blooms heavily on the south coast of Puerto Rico. In 1968 aqueous 0.01 percent solutions of active GA were applied with knapsack sprayers at the rate of 100 gallons per acre. The treatments were given to 6-month-old ratoon plants on August 22 and repeated on August 29. Nearly 100 percent inhibition was obtained with GA given in this manner. Twenty-six percent of the control plants and 0.02 percent of GA-treated plants produced tassels by December 27.

In 1969 GA tests were again conducted wit *C.P. 52-43* in plots staked out in the same field (unpublished). Treatments consisted of 0.01 percent aqueous GA applied once to different plots at 7-day intervals from August 19 to September 16. Although flowering was not particularly heavy in control plots, the tendency of GA to prevent flowering rather than to stimulate flowering was again evident (Table 14-4). Applications given

TABLE 14-4

TASSELING RESPONSE OF SUGARCANE SPRAYED WITH GIBBERELLIC ACID AT 7-DAY INTERVALS FROM AUGUST 19 TO SEPTEMBER 16

Central Mercedita, Ponce. Variety *C.P. 52-43*. Aqueous GA solutions, 0.01%, 100 gal/acre. [After Alexander and Montalvo-Zapata (unpublished.)]

Date of GA application (1969)	Percent tassels on counting date		
	Dec. 5	Dec. 12	Dec. 29
Control (no GA)	8	18	24
August 19	0	0	9
August 26	0	1	7
September 2	0	0	2
September 9	0	1	5
September 16	0	1	3

on August 19 and 26 were less effective than those of September 2 and 9, but all treatments (even as late as September 16) suppressed flowering. A delaying effect of GA on tassel emergence was also evident among those GA plants that bloomed. Whereas in control plots about 3/4 of the tassels had emerged by December 12, only traces of tasseling had occurred in GA-treated plots by this date.

Although admittedly the heavy and repeated dosages of GA used to prevent flowering in Puerto Rico exceeds the economic limits of commercial application, the results weigh heavily against a direct gibberellin role in floral induction or development in sugarcane. A more likely prospect is that endogenous gibberellins are either quantitatively reduced or their growth-stimulatory effects are countered by the flowering substance produced at this time. This interpretation is consistent with the view of Clements and Awada (347) who depict the "decision" to flower or not to flower in terms of changing hormonal balances in the apical meristem. By this reasoning, the flowering substances produced in the leaves and newly-arrived at the growing point can induce flowering only by achieving a sustained quantitative superiority over the hormones which regulate vegetative growth.

C. *Importance of red and far-red light*

Clements (357) has cautioned against direct comparisons of darkroom "nights" with natural nights owing to the absence in fluorescent light sources of the red and far-red energy which is present in the natural morning and evening twilights. James (796) notes the discrepancy in photoperiod values when determined as the hours from sunrise on the one hand, and as the hours from "sunrise to sunset plus civil twilight" on the other hand. Very little is known about the red, far-red reactions in sugarcane leaves although considerable progress has been made in other plant species (218). In particular, the synthesis of phytochrome and its dark conversion to the red-absorbing form should be investigated further in relation to the dark-period requirements for floral induction.

Coleman (379) indicates that the dark phase of floral induction probably involves the phytochrome conversion mechanism. Significantly, studies by Burr in Hawaii (268) showed that far-red light failed to produce a dark-period interruption, whereas both incandescent and fluorescent light effectively did so. Following earlier studies in which *H. 37-1933* was apparently prevented from flowering by far-red irradiation, Coleman (373) found that plants exposed to an inductive day length (12.5 hours) were not prevented from flowering when given 1 hour of far-red irradiation during the dark period. Similar plants exposed to 30 minutes of red light during the dark period failed to flower. Other plants given an 11.5-hour dark period (inductive) followed by 4.5 hours of far-red irradiation plus 8 hours of sunlight failed to initiate flowers. From this Coleman concluded that red light, but not far-red light, will inhibit flowering when supplied during the inductive dark period. It was further shown that far-red light will not reverse the inhibitory action of red light in sugarcane as it does for certain short-day plants (445).

In general, both short- and long-day plants show an action spectrum for light interruption of the dark period which peaks in the orange-red region between 620 and 655 nm (1278). Inhibitory effects of the orange-red light are usually reversed by far-red light between 710 and 740 nm. Salisbury (1278) points out that the action spectrum for light interruption of the dark period does not exclude possible effects of other light phenomena, including those involving blue light.

D. *Enzyme behavior during flowering*

The study of metabolic activity *per se* has not generally been fruitful in clarifying the flowering mechanism in plants (1606). In sugarcane certain metabolic changes are to be expected at the apical meristem as a normal diurnal response and as a logical response to almost any factor which promotes or retards growth. It is therefore difficult to distinguish between the causes of flowering and the effects of flowering on a metabolic basis.

Much progress has been made with the short-day *Xanthium pennsylvanicum* and *Pharbitis nil* in subdividing floral induction into "partial reactions" (1606). One approach is the use of antimetabolites and metabolic inhibitors aimed at preventing hormone synthesis. The cobaltous ion appears to extend the critical dark period, an effect which is reversed by glutathione (1278). Moreover, application of 2,4-dinitrophenol during the dark period strongly inhibits flowering. Zeevaart (1606) interprets this to mean that high-energy phosphates are required for specific reactions although the nature of these reactions remains obscure. The antimetabolites ethionine and 5-fluorouracil, when given during the dark period, produce strong inhibitory responses, the latter compound being specifically active in the apical meristem. The ethionine effect can be reversed with methionine which suggests that transfer of methyl groups may be involved (1278).

Another growth analog, 6-azauracil, also highly active against the apical meristem in sugarcane, was tested by Alexander and Montalvo-Zapata for anti-flowering activity in 1968 (unpublished). An aqueous 0.005-percent solution of the inhibitor was applied as a foliar spray on August 29 to four varieties having moderate- to heavy-flowering records in the Río Piedras area. The solutions were applied until runoff with knapsack sprayers. No tassels were produced in any of the plots. Normal vegetative growth ceased for all plants contacted by the material, although lalas had sprouted from the uppermost joints by the time of harvest in February. The high cost of 6-azauracil and its severe growth effects are presently prohibitive for its general use in flower control.

Greenhouse tests have shown a powerful inhibitory action of 6-azauracil against meristematic enzymes which does not extend to the green canopy in general (*cf.* Chapter 12, pp. 476–478). Invertase, ATPase, and other enzymes have been shown to decline to a small fraction of control levels shortly before the death of the growing point. Possibly the inhibitor acts to prevent the formation of specific mRNA or another factor critical for normal enzyme synthesis. In any event, excessively low levels of cane invertase alone might upset the meristematic physiology, which normally requires a high rate of inversion at the growing point and adjacent immature storage tissue. The key role of the meristem in flowering and its dependence upon invertase for normal growth activity certainly offers a promising means of flower prevention by enzyme control, *i.e.*, by invertase suppression. However, initial efforts in Puerto Rico to control flowering with sodium metasilicate, an invertase inhibitor much less costly than 6-azauracil, have been negative[4].

Additional efforts have been made to establish an enzyme basis for biochemical changes occurring in sugarcane leaves from the preinductive stage through the tassel development stage (Alexander and Montalvo-Zapata, unpublished). Two heavy-flowering varieties (*P.R. 1028* and *M. 336*) and two light- or non-flowering varieties (*B. 42-231* and *P.R. 980*) were planted at Río Piedras during April 1968, in concrete soil benches. From August 17 to November 5 leaves of varying rank were quick-frozen and later assayed for β-amylase and ATPase. β-Amylase is regarded as a critical factor in the diurnal conversion of starch to sucrose, and hence in the movement of assimilates from leaf to growing point. ATPase is regarded as an indicator of photosynthetic energy-conversion activity which might also affect the transport of solutes from leaves to the apical meristem (*cf.* Chapter 13, pp. 516, 517).

By January, 1969, heavy tasseling had occurred in *P.R. 1038* and *M. 336* while the weak-flowering varieties produced no tassels. Although the enzyme analyses were only exploratory, several important differences were observed in their behavior patterns upon examination of activity data (Table 14-5): (a) Absolute activity was

TABLE 14-5

ENZYME BEHAVIOR IN FLOWERING AND NON-FLOWERING SUGARCANE VARIETIES DURING THE PREINDUCTIVE, INDUCTIVE, AND POSTINDUCTIVE PERIODS (AUGUST 17–NOVEMBER 5, 1968)

[After Alexander and Montalvo-Zapata (unpublished).]

Enzyme	Leaf rank	Variety*	Specific activity at sampling date (1968)									
			8/17	8/27	9/6	9/16	9/26	10/6	10/16	10/26	11/5	Mean
β-Amylase	−1	*P.R. 1028*	259	271	384	370	230	280	126	248	215	265
		M. 336	243	428	348	250	220	318	117	239	248	279
		B. 42-231	156	190	166	197	352	256	134	205	186	205
		P.R. 980	115	237	118	60	74	79	63	119	84	105
	+1	*P.R. 1028*	148	118	340	309	190	249	175	250	168	216
		M. 336	138	144	385	229	153	93	121	81	158	167
		B. 42-231	365	90	214	112	115	55	126	116	69	140
		P.R. 980	191	120	63	134	76	101	86	80	80	104
	+4	*P.R. 1028*	35	39	71	47	32	32	32	53	40	42
		M. 336	30	48	53	56	35	46	38	28	28	40
		B. 42-231	29	65	38	26	61	98	26	24	26	44
		P.R. 980	25	30	42	42	37	33	28	27	48	35
ATPase	−1	*P.R. 1028*	180	136	112	168	98	122	75	91	88	119
		M. 336	143	174	177	129	112	139	110	110	114	134
		B. 42-231	70	84	118	98	82	79	54	32	42	73
		P.R. 980	69	47	64	122	72	115	83	79	69	80
	+1	*P.R. 1028*	88	79	91	128	81	52	77	77	53	81
		M. 336	37	76	69	76	84	67	57	55	52	64
		B. 42-231	85	58	39	72	45	22	35	22	20	44
		P.R. 980	53	67	25	74	68	31	39	30	18	45
	+4	*P.R. 1028*	26	31	49	43	12	53	44	28	30	35
		M. 336	23	24	28	47	33	30	23	29	18	28
		B. 42-231	18	39	14	22	31	36	21	11	15	29
		P.R. 980	33	15	55	19	23	17	12	14	10	22

*At Río Piedras heavy-flowering varieties include *P.R. 1028* and *M. 336*; Light- or non-flowering varieties include *B. 42-231* and *P.R. 980.*

higher for both catalysts in the younger or spindle leaf (−1) as compared with mature leaves (+1 and +4); (b) activity was higher for both catalysts in the flowering varieties than in the non-flowering varieties; (c) both enzymes tended to be more active during the critical inductive period, from August 27 to September 16, than during the tassel development period, from October 6 to November 5; and (d) the latter trend was more pronounced in flowering varieties than in non-flowering varieties.

In the instance of spindle-leaf amylase the discrepancy between flowering and non-flowering varieties was both pronounced and consistent (Fig. 14-9). The enzyme

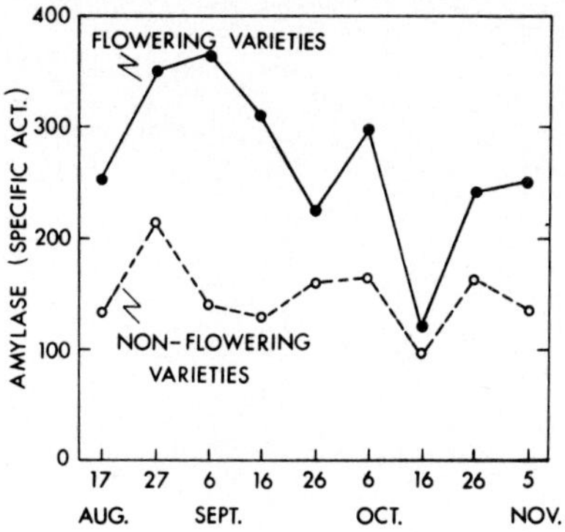

Fig. 14-9. Divergent amylase action in spindle leaves of flowering and non-flowering sugarcane varieties during preinductive, inductive, and postinductive stages. Plants were grown at Río Piedras, Puerto Rico (18° 16′ north latitude), 1968. [After Alexander and Montalvo-Zapata (unpublished).]

action was particularly high during the period August 27 to September 16 in flowering canes – a trend which the non-flowering plants clearly did not show. Amylase values for the two groups converged only once during the experimental period, around October 16, by which time flower induction is complete in Puerto Rico. These patterns may reflect an amylase role in the transit of a flowering factor from cane leaves to the apical meristem.

The results thus substantiate findings of other workers which are suggestive of higher levels of physiological activity in spindle leaves during the inductive photoperiod. Although the enzyme activity patterns may reflect only the symptomatology surrounding photoinductive reactions, our expectations are that they reflect specific patterns of translocation capacity. This can be taken to include transport of flowering substances along with photosynthate. In any event, much additional work is needed before firm conclusions can be drawn.

E. *Stability of the flowering stimulus*

An extremely important step in the flowering process is the production and accumulation of a "stabilized stimulus". As related previously, this stimulus is believed to be a hormone having the property of forcing the growth of floral tissue rather than vegetative tissue. It is produced in the leaf and transported to the apical meristem where, presumably, its stability permits accumulation to a critical inductive level. The existence of a highly-stable, hormone-like material in sugarcane stem tips was reported by Coleman and Nickell (376) in 1964. Their findings were obtained with stem tips isolated under aseptic conditions and kept alive by tissue culture techniques adapted specifically for growth studies with isolated primordia.

Flower primordia isolated about 3 months after initiation (376) were observed to produce new inflorescence tissue in several plates (Fig. 14-10). Since the isolated tissue

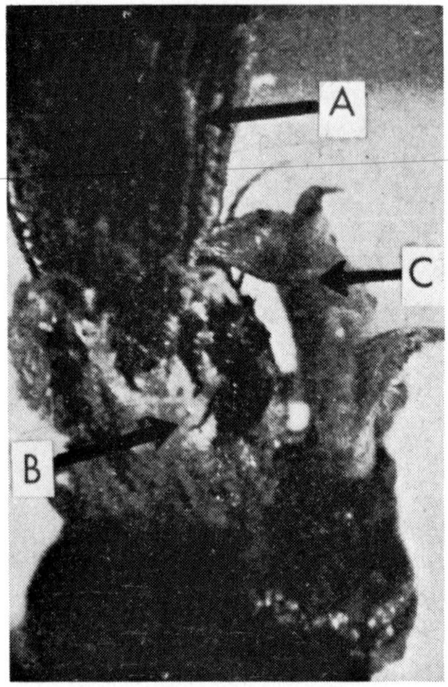

Fig. 14-10. Exised tip of a flowering sugarcane stalk maintained for 6 months on an artificial growth medium. (A) Old unextended inflorescence tissue; (B) newly-developed inflorescence tissue; (C) developing vegetative shoot. [After Coleman and Nickell (376).] Reproduced by permission of *Nature*, London.

had been cultured under continuous light, it was considered improbable that the stimulus was produced after isolation. This would mean that the flowering substance produced more than 3 months earlier had survived the isolation process and the conditions of artificial culture. Nickell and Coleman proposed that this stability was aided in part by the absence of a normal dilution factor incident to the growth and translocation activity of the natural stem tip. The stability obtained in the tissue cultures was apparently greater than that of the normal stem tip where the stimulus is presumably destroyed by light interruption of the dark period and by low temperatures or adverse temperature ranges.

F. *Summary of the cane flowering mechanism*

Precise knowledge of the flowering hormone, that is, its synthesis, properties, and mode of action, still eludes plant physiologists even in relatively simple short-day and long-day plants. Relatively few scientists have even approached this subject in sugarcane. It is therefore hardly surprising that our present understanding of the cane flowering mechanism is drawn more by deduction than by direct examination of its partial reactions. On the other hand, the vast amount of empirical flowering information has established some firm outlines of the flower inductive and developmental processes. Moreover, as pointed out by Coleman (379), the scheme which emerges for sugarcane recapitulates the strongest features of the flowering theories advanced for other plants.

In 1969 Coleman (379) summarized schematically the cane flowering process in the light of our best available evidence (Fig. 14-11). In essence, this scheme describes the production of several critical substances which are translocated and together bring about the flowering stimulus in a stepwise manner:

(1) The cane plant first achieves sufficient maturity to flower and is then exposed to an *inductive photoperiod* at *inductive temperatures*. The process specifically begins upon the perception by the leaves of day lengths at least 12 hours long. This step continues in the leaves, which now "recognize" the correct day length, with the result that several substances accumulate to a critical minimum level required for success of the subsequent dark reactions.

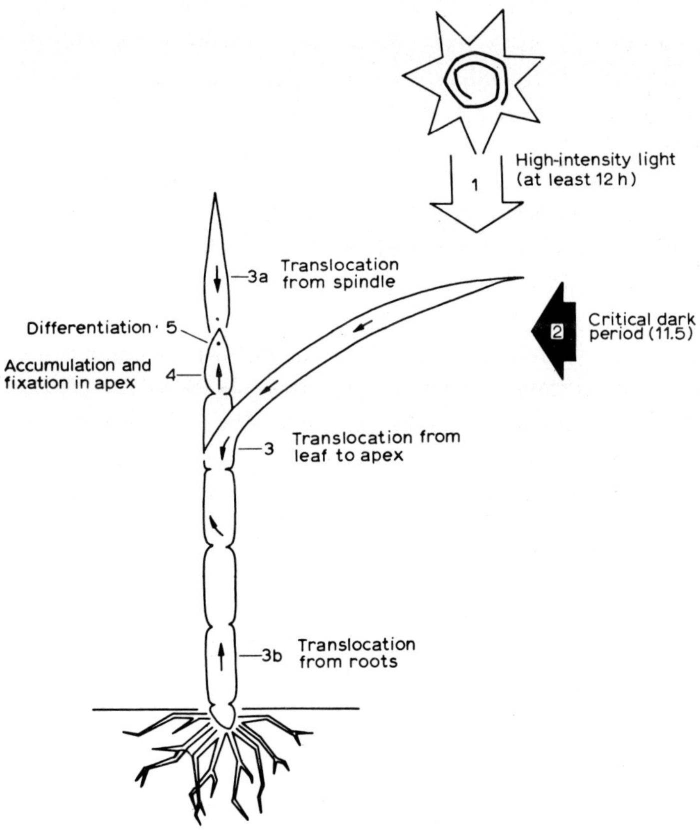

Fig. 14-11. Schematic representation of the partial processes of flowering in sugarcane. [After Coleman (379).] Reproduced by permission of R.E. Coleman.

(2) The second step also proceeds in the leaves but specifically requires an *inductive night length of at least 11 hours 30 minutes*. This dark process accomplishes the conversion of a pigment (phytochrome) from an active to an inactive form, and the production of still another substance which can be transported to the apical meristem. Coleman describes the latter substance as a "stabilized stimulus".

(3) The third step involves translocation of the stabilized stimulus to the apical meristem via the pathway used for sucrose transport (*cf.* Chapter 7, pp. 276–284). This translocation apparently proceeds in both light and darkness but it probably requires light for maximum rates of movement.

(4) The fourth step is critical but only vaguely understood. Over a period of days there is either an accumulation of the stabilized substance in the apical meristem, or a synthesis of yet another substance in the apical meristem, until a critical flowering "threshold" level is reached. At this point Coleman interprets the essentiality for both physiological maturity and an attached spindle to mean that a biochemical preconditioning is required for reception of the stabilized stimulus. The specific reactions of this process are unknown. There is tacit evidence that these may include abnormally high invertase levels and generally high activity of hydrolytic enzymes (Alexander and Montalvo-Zapata, unpublished). The stabilized stimulus received from the leaf plus the substance produced in the meristem are believed to accumulate in a stable form which quantitatively determines the extent of floral induction once the critical minimum level is surpassed. In this connection, Coleman (380) proposes that an additional stimulus critical for flower induction is received from the roots.

(5) The fifth step involves the actual differentiation of the flower primordium. This is the first point at which a scientist can visually examine the flowering process in its progress.

Coleman (379) aptly described flowering as an "intricate" process and wisely attributes to its biochemical reactions some of the differences in flowering behavior recorded among the *Saccharum* species. If one reflects upon the complexity of other sugarcane processes whose biochemistry is partially known, for example, the C_4-dicarboxylic acid pathway or the sugar accumulation cycle, then by analogy we must conclude that we know very little about the total induction process. However, with increased knowledge and better understanding of the flowering mechanism, better flowering control must surely follow. Future cane breeders could conceivably employ flowering hormones or their precursors as partial substitutes for the present photoperiod and temperature requirements. Undoubtedly the grower will have new control measures less drastic than the present chemical-defoliation or drought treatments.

Chapter 15

Postharvest Physiology

1. INTRODUCTION

Some irony may be found in the knowledge that a well-ripened sugarcane crop, the culmination of many months or years of cultural programing, may lose its sugar within a few days after harvest operations begin. One should never underestimate the capacity of sugarcane to lose very quickly the sugar gained so slowly at no small expense. In simplest terms this is the final proof that accumulated sugar represents a balance between sugar synthesis and utilization. Once it is cut the sugarcane plant can do little to manufacture new sugar, but it can still do much in the nature of sugar utilization. To this is added in the last days of the crop new losses relating to harvest and shipment injuries, to postharvest microbial deterioration, burning, washing, and a final inversion process which accompanies the moisture losses from severed stalks. All this occurs at a time when the cane stalk is no longer replenished with new photosynthate.

In essence, there are two areas of postharvest quality decline: (a) Inversion processes accompanying harvest operations and subsequent delays in delivery of cane to the factory; (b) factory losses incident to inefficient processing which may be heightened by sugar inversion and conversion reactions within the milled juice. Losses can and do reach substantial proportions within each area. Studies such as those by Guilbeau *et al.* (618) in Louisiana suggest that field losses borne by the grower considerably exceed the factory losses borne by the processor. Other workers underscore quality depreciations in the factory (759, 1457) where sugar changes can be measured with greater accuracy.

The present chapter is principally concerned with sucrose transformations which occur in the "field", that is, from the time that stalks are subjected to preharvest burning until they are finally ground at the mill, at which time the sugarcane plant loses its last semblance of a physiological source-to-sink system. From the sugar grower's standpoint this is a most critical period since he is paid on the basis of estimated recoverable sugar determined from cane samples delivered to the factory. He receives no credit whatever for the more exemplary quality which may have existed 10, 5, or even 3 days previously.

Postharvest sugar changes have not always been viewed in terms of sucrose losses. Some workers believe that harvested cane kept in the field for a week or more will have a higher sugar content than it did at the time of cutting. Others envisioned sugar losses for several days after cutting followed by a net increase. Exactly where this sugar would come from has never been made clear. The magnitude of so-called "after-ripening" appears to be far less pronounced when full account is given to moisture or weight losses and purity changes relative to recoverable sucrose. There is general agreement that, by the second week after harvest, the accumulated sugar experiences unfavorable changes such that the sucrose not already inverted will be exceedingly difficult to recover from the low-quality juice.

The microbiological deterioration of sugarcane stalks, milled juice, and raw sugar has attracted widespread attention in recent years [reviewed by Tilbury (1437, 1434)]. Although biodeterioration subsequent to milling operations lies beyond the scope of this book, the reactions in harvested stalks leading to cane "souring", produced largely by the lactic acid bacterium *Leuconostoc mesenteroides*, are seen to parallel endogenous physiology in the sense that accumulated sucrose is seriously depleted through inversion. During the interval between cutting and grinding the biodeterioration processes probably encompass both physiological and pathological events of enormous proportions.

The terms *sour cane* and *stale cane* which frequently appear in postharvest literature are herein taken to have a common basis in the metabolism of storage sucrose which otherwise would have been recovered in the factory. The former term stems from the odor of acidity arising from partial degradation of hexoses by *L. mesenteroides*; the latter term most appropriately describes the aging cut stalks which have depleted their sucrose via continuing inversion and respiratory reactions. Whether there is common usage of endogenous cane invertases in releasing hexose for sugarcane metabolism and bacterical growth processes, or whether the bacterium produces its own invertases (hence degrading sucrose as a function of microbial population size), remains a matter of speculation at this writing.

2. NATURE AND MAGNITUDE OF POSTHARVEST DETERIORATION

A. *Historical*

Irrespective of the fact that a severed cane stalk will evidence little outward change for several weeks, it is probable that most sugar planters were aware of postharvest quality decline throughout the history of sugarcane agriculture. What effect this may have had on primitive operations having little yield incentive is debatable, but published reports indicating genuine concern began to appear toward the end of the 19th century (395). The deterioration picture was somewhat complicated by the fact that in certain regions, and not without justification, growers purposely retained their harvested cane in the field for a week or more in the belief that quality was thereby improved.

Stubbs (1381), in 1895, attributed cane deterioration in Louisiana to "ferments" active at high temperatures, ". . .with an abundance of moist air. . .", and thereupon advised against windrowing cut cane except as a measure to prevent freezing injury.

According to Cross and Belile (395), Went and Geerligs (1560) reported cane quality decline in 1894 and observed that wet stalks deteriorated less rapidly than dry ones. The existence but incongruity of the moisture–inversion relationship still challenges investigators today.

Early workers also recognized the importance of time (or milling delay) and storage-environment factors. Müller von Czernicki (401) in Java, reported cane stored indoors for 5 days experienced a purity loss of 12 percent, and that a loss of 20 percent was obtained with cane stored 5 days indoors after lying for 1 day in the field. De Savorin Lohman (951) observed that stored cane deteriorated less rapidly under shelter than in the field. Other workers found very little cane deterioration in Egypt (28) during the coldest month, while in Louisiana it was shown that cut stalks covered with trash had experienced only a 6.9-percent drop in purity after 42 days in the field (1381).

Apparently the earliest specific reference to a cane invertase role in postharvest deterioration was made in 1907 by Browne and Blouin (252) in Louisiana. Believing that invertase was confined to the green top, they attributed the postharvest sucrose losses "...very largely to the diffusion of the inverting enzyme from the green tops into the stalk". The fact that topping of cane reduced the extent of deterioration was taken as evidence of the enzyme movement. Hall (631), in 1913, used the term "inversion" in describing postharvest deterioration without specifically assigning an invertase role. He appears to have been the first investigator to publish on the marked differences in deterioration rate as a varietal feature. He found that the native Argentine varieties were much less susceptible to inversion than cane from Java. In a subsequent report (632) Hall dispelled some prior theories relating inversion susceptibility of Java canes to their physical properties. It had been proposed that since the Java varieties were relatively long and thin the resultant increased absorption and radiation of heat affected inversion rates. This view was not supported by Hall's evidence. It was also shown that borer infestation was not a primary cause of inversion since the soft native and imported canes which were severely attacked by the insect deteriorated less readily than the hard Java varieties which were seldom attacked.

Concluding from Hall's work that "...the inverting power must be a function of the cane itself", Cross and Belile performed studies which established the presence of an inverting enzyme in the millable stalks and the subsequent retention of a viable catalyst in the milled juice (395). Moreover, the possibility of more than one enzyme was recognized, and the changing rates of sucrose loss with time were correctly attributed to enzyme level or activity: "...The work carried out points to the fact that the inversion is caused by one or more enzymes, which are present to a small extent in the freshly-cut cane, and which are built up in greater quantity or rendered more active by the cane during storage". The authors continued: "...It appeared to us possible that the inversion in the stored canes might also be due to the ferment invertase, and we therefore stored some of the juice of one of these canes with chloroform and toluene, and analyzed it after a certain time. It was found that considerable inversion had taken place. As bacteria were excluded by the antiseptics added, the inversion must have been due to a ferment, probably invertase, present in the deteriorated canes".

It is interesting that Cross and Belile were not content with having established the enzyme nature of postharvest deterioration, but in addition made serious attempts to establish the plant's *need* for inversion and to devise methods to prevent it. They tentatively concluded that the stalk was busily preparing for new shoot production for which sucrose would be needed in a more assimilable form. Evidence was also presented which tentatively linked sucrose inversion to proteolytic hydrolysis, presumably a parallel increase in the availability of amino acids. Among the methods tested for preventing deterioration it was found that burying cane in the ground was quite effective. In one experiment stalks buried for 29 days showed few ill effects. More practical but increasingly less effective means included: (a) Storage of cane in a trash-covered "heap", the whole pile being kept constantly moist by frequent drenchings with water; (b) storage of cane in a heap covered with trash; and (c) storage in a shaded place. None of the treatments were suitable substitutes for rapid transport and milling of the cane to prevent losses. "If they (the factory and field managements) will make such arrangements as will ensure the cane reaching the factory within a few hours after cutting, the great saving of losses will far more than compensate for the trouble and cost of perfecting such arrangements." To give Cross and Belile their full due it must be recorded that no better suggestion has come forth during the ensuing 55 years. However, with the possible exception of Queensland (82), "such arrangements" have nowhere been perfected.

B. *After-ripening*

Under certain conditions the moisture losses from harvested cane are paralleled by improved juice quality. Barnes (145) described sugarcane in the cool Gurdaspur district of India in which the increased concentration of sucrose owing to water loss more than offset the parallel sugar losses caused by decreased milling efficiency. Growers in this area commonly allowed the stripped cane to remain in the field to improve quality. Barnes proposed that a limited amount of drying can produce ripening, assuming that ripening is a "water starvation phenomenon", and that the benefits should be greater if the cane is of relatively low quality when cut. This interpretation was partially substantiated with postharvest experiments, but the positive effect was confined to the initial 24 to 48 hours and relatively low temperatures. Barnes also observed a positive correlation between the moisture–sucrose relationship and variety. He surmised that similar after-ripening might not occur in areas having higher temperatures. On the other hand, Weinburg (1551) studied cane deterioration under both warm and cool conditions in Java and India and found no significant differences in rate of quality decline. Somewhat similar effects were observed by Alexander working with *P.R. 980* in Puerto Rico (unpublished). Small Brix and pol increases over a 7-day period were accompanied by moderate weight losses and decreased extractibility. There was no significant increase of recoverable sucrose as a delayed-grinding response.

In Louisiana, prior to 1955, the opinion was widely held that increased sugar yields and profits could be gained by holding cane in heap rows for a week or longer after cutting (617). It was thought that sucrose declined for 3 or 4 days and then increased before ultimately deteriorating. This view developed less from experimental evidence than from observations of promptly-delivered cane yielding less sugar than comparable material which was delayed for a week or more. Guilbeau *et al.* performed a series of six postharvest experiments with *N.Co. 310* and found that under certain conditions higher sugar content was obtained from cane held in heap rows for 9 days. This was attributed to weight losses by the cane. However, a more general effect was the loss of both sugar and tonnage. The greatest depreciations resulted from lowered purity of the normal juice which led to significant reductions in the estimated quantities of recoverable sugar.

C. *The role of environment*

Although the enzymatic basis of postharvest quality decline was long recognized in principle, the main research effort has stressed empirical factors having more or less practical implications for the sugar grower and manufacturer. By the early 1930's an enormous amount of postharvest work had been published in relation to environment, varieties, condition of the harvested cane, manner of its handling and storage, and time–deterioration relationships [reviewed by Lauritzen and Balch[1]]. The most salient feature of all this effort was the predominance of environment over every other factor, including variety, thereby reducing the final major problem of the crop's culture to a regional level.

Numerous early workers recognized and attempted to evaluate a role of environmental conditions in cane deterioration without having recourse to precise environment control (145, 1604, 630, 912, 1298, 1582). In at least one instance the surmised temperature–moisture relationship to deterioration rate was the opposite of that actually operative. There was general agreement that cane stored in the shade deteriorated less rapidly than if stored in the sun (401, 745, 1298, 912, 951). Yet in no instance could a precise evaluation be given of air movement, humidity, and temperature. On the other hand, environmental interactions of some sort must have been suspected by most trained scientists approaching cane deterioration in the field.

Successful attempts were made to evaluate ambient temperature (145, 1298), although again the results were compromised by failure to take humidity into account.

[1] Lauritzen, J.I. and Balch, R.T., 1934. Storage of mill cane, *U.S. Dept. Agric. Tech. Bull.* No. 449: 30 pp.

Lauritzen and Balch[1] note that the variety factor affected deterioration rate in a number of reports (132, 197, 394, 633, 745, 877), but in each instance the tendency was to rely solely on local varieties. This in turn confined the deterioration data to regional interpretation. Retaining stalks in a moist condition proved highly beneficial for some workers (68, 394, 396, 401, 1560), while others, including Müller von Czernicki (401) in Java and Sanyal (1298) in India, did not recognize a relationship of moisture to deterioration rate. In Hawaii, Wold (1582) found deterioration more nearly related to moisture and original condition of cane than to storage methods, *i.e.*,

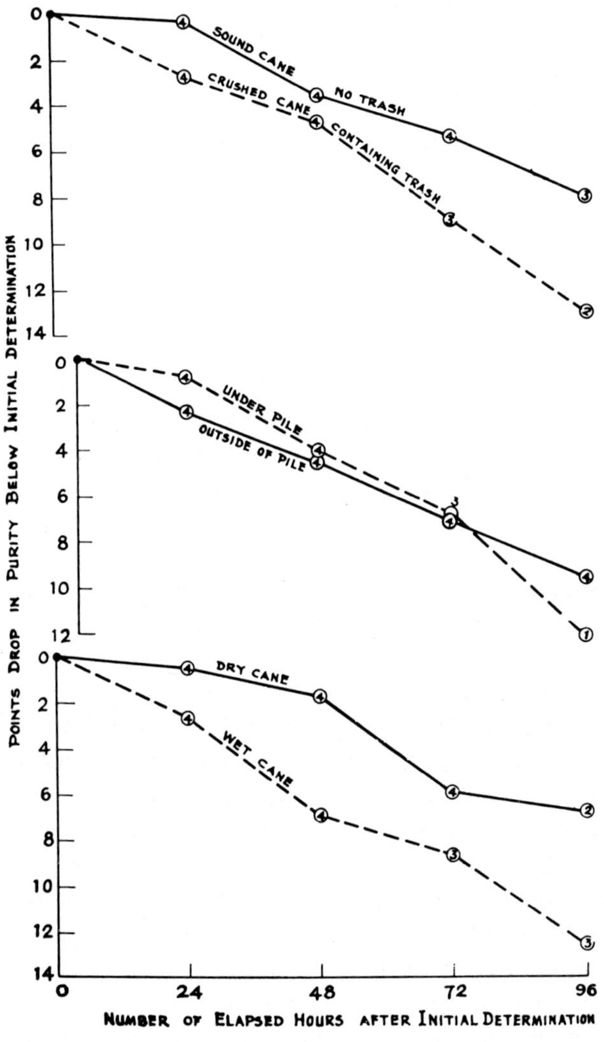

Fig. 15-1. Juice purity decline in sugarcane stalks in relation to moisture, condition of cane, and method of cane storage. [After Wold (1582).] Reproduced by permission of the *Hawaiian Sugar Planters' Association*, Honolulu.

piles *vs.* open storage (Fig. 15-1). Moreover, "... sound, clean, dry cane deteriorates much slower than cane which is damaged, dirty, and wet, as, of course, we would expect to be the case". Wold found that wetness was especially detrimental in mechanically-harvested material and recommended that, if possible, harvesting operations should be suspended during rainy weather. In retrospect it would appear that only by use of controlled-environment facilities will precise information become available relative to the main effects and interactions of environmental factors in cane deterioration. In limited measure such information had begun to appear during the 1960's. However, practical benefits from fundamental climate–physiology relations will rely almost exclusively on the experience and skill of the agronomist.

D. *Burned cut vs. burned standing cane*

Young (1604), in Queensland, evaluated sugar and weight changes occurring in cut and standing burned cane during a 5-day period. The burned cane left standing gained weight during the 1st day and either gained or maintained additional weight during the ensuing 4 days. Cut burned cane rapidly lost weight. By the 5th day there was an apparent loss of sucrose in standing cane and increase in cut cane. The sucrose decline was accountable to the increased moisture uptake by the burned stalks whose evapotranspiration rates were now less than normal. Conversely, the sucrose gain of some 3 percent, when balanced against a weight loss of 6 percent, suggested that a net loss had occurred in the cut cane. Commercial cane sugar values (C.C.S.values) supported this interpretation. It was further shown that no appreciable loss of sugar had occurred in standing cane prior to the 4th day, whereas cut cane lost some 3 percent of the original sugar within 2 days. Studies by Calma (284) in the Philippines showed greater sugar losses for burned standing cane than for cut cane.

In Mexico, Turner and Rojas (1457) found deterioration rates of unburned cane (*Co. 213*) unaffected by age, but distinct daily losses in weight and recoverable sugar were recorded along with increased fiber. Sugar and fiber changes were much more severe in burned cane (variety *Pepecuca*) than in unburned cane[2]. Turner (1456) had reported earlier that age of cane directly affected the weight loss of cut stalks left in the field. There was increased weight loss with advancing age. The age–weight relationship did not hold for factory rendement.

Samuels and Cayere (1292), in Puerto Rico, evaluated over a 5-day period the sucrose changes in burned cane harvested immediately and ground at 1-day intervals, and cane left standing and ground at 1-day intervals. Of the two varieties studied, *P.R. 1028* (a "sweet" variety) lost a greater percentage of sucrose than *P.R. 980* (a high-

[2]Following the presentation by Dr. Rojas (1457), Dr. Clements (Hawaii) stressed the role of prevailing temperature in determining postburning deterioration rates. Dr. Evans (Guyana) stated that standing burned cane deteriorates more rapidly than cut cane and attributed this to the increased moisture content.

tonnage variety). Most of the sugar loss occurred after the 3rd day. Burned standing cane showed slightly greater quality decline than burned cut cane. It was also observed that delayed grinding in wet weather produced greater losses than in dry weather.

E. *Deterioration of frozen cane*

Frozen cane and frost-induced deterioration can be a serious matter in Louisiana, Florida, Argentina, and other regions situated on the northern or southern periphery of the sugarcane world. Cross (397) states that frozen cane suffers two types of decomposition: (a) Increased inversion and alcoholic fermentation by endogenous enzymes, and (b) bacterial decomposition leading to acid fermentation and production of gums. In addition, the stalk structure appears to deteriorate or soften to the extent that a newly-soluble "gummy" material passes into the juice which otherwise would have remained in the bagasse. Thus from a factory standpoint ". . .the juice of frozen cane is in a state of incipient fermentation, whose sugar content has suffered a greater or less diminution, and which contains more impurities than usual, especially certain substances which make the extraction of the sugar more difficult". Lauden (900) estimates that the Louisiana sugar industry lost 200 000 tons of cane in 1962 and 100 000 tons in 1963 owing to quality decline following freezing injury. The intensity and duration of the freeze, postfreeze temperatures, presence of microbes, and the degree of new microbial accesses to the stalk interior all contribute to the ultimate freezing effect upon quality.

F. *Magnitude of postharvest sugar losses*

Hughes (759), in describing sugar losses recorded at the Hawaiian Commercial and Sugar Company, Ltd., Puunene, Maui, during the period 1929 to 1953, cites a vivid discrepancy between the sugar produced by the cane plant and that actually recovered in the factory. Depicted in Fig. 15-2 are the yield increases on a tons per acre basis accompanied by processing losses which had increased by 350 percent in 25 years. These statistics were based on processing data which could be measured with relative accuracy. Burning and field inversion losses were assumed to be constant during the quarter-century period. While the latter cannot be substantiated, the point was made that the sugar industry can needlessly lose enormous quantities of sugar during postharvest operations. Fig. 15-2 also underscores the futility of increasing sugar production at the field level if the sugar is not proportionately recovered in the factory. Indeed, if such losses were typical of all sugar-growing regions there would be little point in improving sugar yields per acre. Turner and Rojas (1457) expressed a similar view in Mexico: ". . .We demand of the geneticists sweeter canes, of agronomy the best use of fertilizers, cultivation and irrigation, all for more sugar production in the fields, then we lose part of that sugar and continue our demands for better canes."

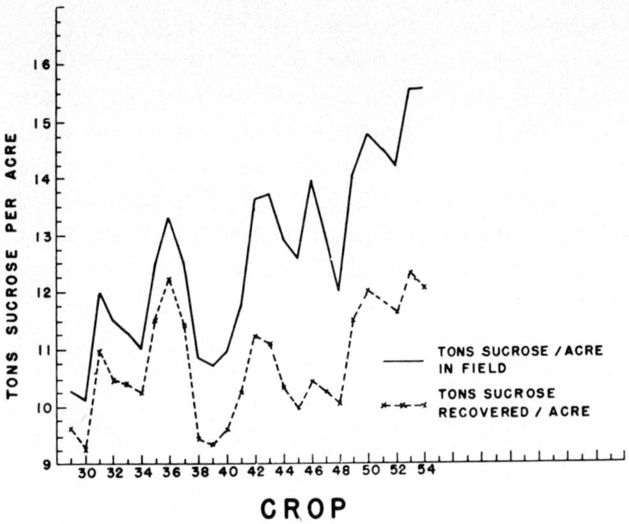

Fig. 15-2. Discrepancy between sucrose production in the field and sucrose recovery in the factory during a 24-year period at Puunene, Maui (Hawaii). [After Hughes (759).] Reproduced by permission of the *Hawaiian Sugar Planters' Association*, Honolulu.

About a year after Hughes published the Maui data, Guilbeau *et al.* (617, 618) in Louisiana reported quality losses from delayed grinding which exceeded those occurring in the factory. Sugar decline varied from a minimum of about 12 percent to nearly 50 percent of the recoverable sugar from fresh cane after it has been held for 14 days. Holding the stalks for only 9 days produced a maximum loss of 37 percent. Mean values from six experiments showed that, of the recoverable sugar present in cane cut for 1 day, 11 percent was lost by the 9th day and 23 percent after 13 days. This attrition stemmed from combined losses in weight, sucrose, and purity, with purity decline being the largest contributing factor. On a yield basis of 25 tons per acre (at 1 day after cutting), it was estimated that more than 2 tons of this weight would have vanished by the 9th day.

Under conditions appertaining to factory operations in Louisiana in 1955, it was anticipated that the greatest increase in factory expenditures would arise from increased overhead operating costs per 100 pounds of sugar when sugar recoveries fell below 160 pounds of raw sugar per ton of stalks (617). Efferson and Cobb (474) had shown that factories obtaining less than 150 pounds of raw sugar per ton of cane operated at a significant loss since the cost per 100 pounds was $ 7.99 (U.S.). Increased operating costs since that time [1949] would make the differences even greater. Guilbeau *et al.* estimated that processing 1-day-old cane would be profitable, whereas processing after 9 or 14 days would be highly unprofitable. Moreover, since most of the loss in recoverable sugar occurs before the cane is purchased, losses to the sugar grower are substantially larger than those in the factory (617).

In Puerto Rico, Boneta-García and Lugo-López measured the sucrose decline in whole stalks of six varieties stored in the shade or sun for a 15-day period (203). A daily sucrose decline of statistically-significant magnitude was obtained for each variety, although the rate and extent of deterioration varied considerably among varieties. *M. 336* was least affected while *P.R. 1000* was most sensitive to quality decline. There was a general trend toward slightly higher sucrose retention in shaded cane, but this effect did not attain statistical significance. The mean daily sucrose loss for all varieties was 0.211 percent. Variety means ranged from 0.127 to 0.373 percent for *M. 336* and *P.R. 1000*, respectively.

3. INVERTASES AND POSTHARVEST INVERSION

A. *Invertases present in harvested cane*

On the basis of the sucrose storage processes elaborated by workers in Australia, an accurate picture exists of the invertases present in sugarcane (*cf.* Chapter 9, pp. 349–353). Essentially there are two invertase types based upon pH preference (acid or neutral), which in turn have distinct spatial distribution within the cell (inner space and outer space), and within the stalk (immature storage tissue and mature storage tissue). Even within the elongating joint there are distinct acid invertase gradients between the central storage areas and intercalary meristem (1269). The invertases are probably most abundant in the immature storage tissue where they perform roles in growth processes as well as sugar storage, but they are also present in the fully-mature stalks. To the extent that immature storage tissues accompany stalks to the mill, *i.e.*, under a policy of "high topping", an abundance of acid invertase must be added to the systems ordinarily released from the mature stalks which thereafter participates in sucrose inversion within the crude juice.

The acid invertase of immature storage tissue was first described by Glasziou (582). This enzyme is intimately involved in sucrose inversion in the outer space just prior to its movement into the storage vacuole (1268). The neutral enzyme (pH 7.0) was at first recognized only in mature storage tissues (690). The level of acid invertase varies seasonally (689) and diurnally (1340, 54). Significant correlations have been reported between acid invertase content and expansion rate in immature internodes (690, 590), suggesting that, within certain limits, invertase may function as a growth-regulatory factor. Acid invertase virtually disappears from internodal tissue after expansion has ceased (690).

Studies by Hawker and Hatch (701) with mature stalk tissue have shown that sucrose accumulation is mediated by invertases having somewhat different properties and cellular distribution than their counterparts in immature storage tissue. Earlier work by Hatch and Glasziou (690) had demonstrated a relationship between neutral invertase activity and rate of sugar storage by mature stalk tissues, with storage rate increasing or decreasing as a function of neutral invertase level. This appears to be the same neutral invertase which is active in immature storage tissue, having survived the maturation processes in which acid invertase declines and ultimately disappears. However, Hawker and Hatch (701) discovered another acid invertase bound firmly to the cell wall of mature stalk tissue. The optimum pH (3.8) and K_m value (3×10^{-4}M) distinguish this enzyme from both the outer space and inner space acid invertases functional in the sugar accumulation cycle. It resists heating and is highly stable when treated with aqueous buffers, sodium chloride solution, detergents, diethyl ether and butanol. Although the low pH preference of the acid invertase does not suggest a high level of action in the stalk, the *in vivo* activity may be considerably greater than suggested by its properties in the laboratory. However, Hawker and Hatch reported about 80 percent of the sucrose hydrolysis in bathing tissue slices was accountable to the neutral invertase (701).

In summarizing the inversion potential of sugarcane stalks, it is safe to assume that at least one acid invertase and one neutral invertase are present and viable in cane stalks awaiting shipment to the factory. Toward the upper end of each stalk there will be found at least one additional acid invertase which will increase quantitatively as greater amounts of immature stalk tissue are retained for milling. It must be emphasized that all invertases will lose their tissue specificity and become contaminants once the stalks are ground and the enzymes are released into the milled juice.

B. *Distribution of invertases within the sugarcane stalk*

In general, early descriptions of cane deterioration were consistent with our present understanding of discrete functional and spatial separation of cane invertases. Coates found that stalks of *P.O.J.* varieties inverted sucrose more rapidly in the top third than in the bottom third when sectioned and stored in shade (361). Earlier studies by Cross and Harris in Argentina showed that in four *P.O.J.* varieties, plus *Kavangire* and *Criolla*, the upper half of the stalk contained less sucrose than the lower half (396). In each instance (except *Criolla*) the postharvest inversion rate over a 10-day period was higher in the top half. Each of the varieties also experienced a greater weight loss in the upper half. Cross and Harris attributed the sucrose losses specifically to an endogenous invertase which they believed to be more highly concentrated in the upper stalk tissues. Lauritzen and Balch (902) describe an ascending sucrose gradient from the top to the bottom of millable stalks in which the middle third and bottom third are more nearly equal than the middle and top portions. The low sucrose of the top was empirically related to the fact that it was "... greener, softer, and more active physiologically than the other two sections".

Lauritzen and Balch (902) critically examined the relative sugar and invertase distributions in Louisiana cane. Data collected in five experiments relative to sucrose inversion, moisture loss, and Brix values in the top, center, and bottom third of stalks sectioned before storage and after storage are shown in Fig. 15-3. The treatments

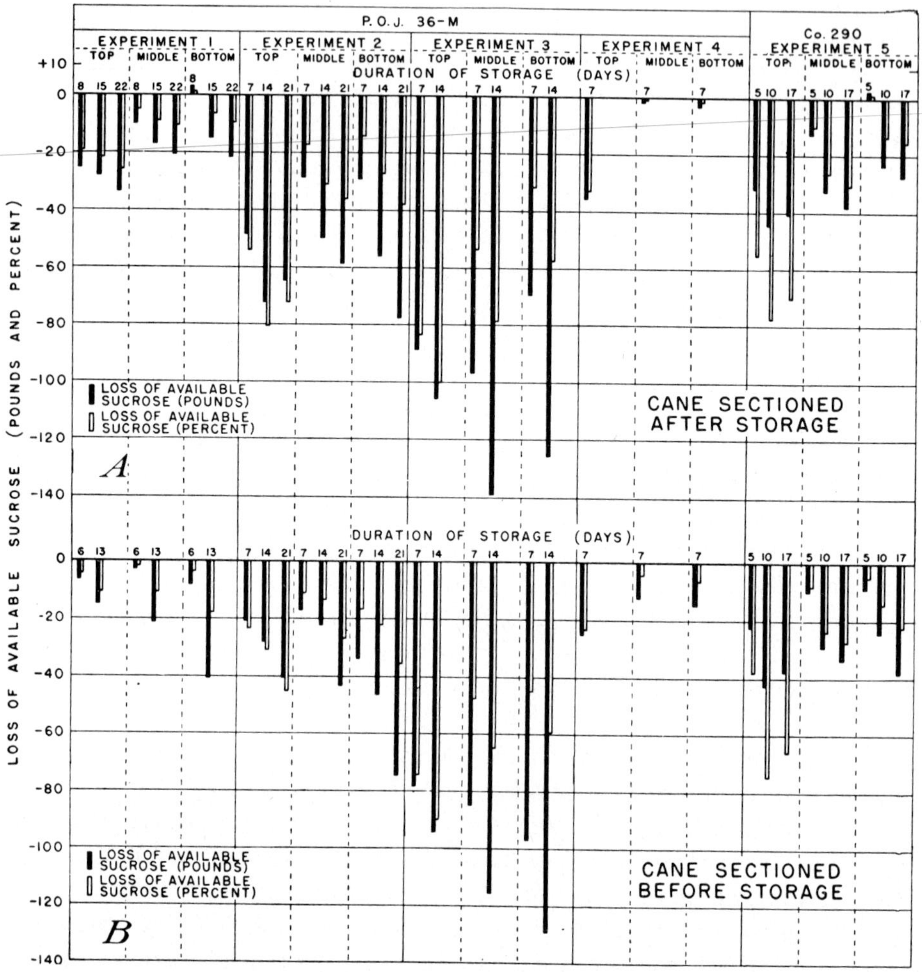

Fig. 15-3. (A) Sucrose losses from different portions of the sugarcane stalk as related to the whole stalk during various periods of storage. Stalks were sectioned into one-third lengths and analyzed after storage. (B) Results of similar analyses performed with different stalk portions sectioned before storage. [After Lauritzen and Balch (902).] Reproduced by permission of the *Journal of Agriculture Research,* U.S. Gov. Printing Office, Washington, D.C.

included cane stored under dry and shaded conditions, and cane stored with controlled temperature and humidity. The most striking results were related to moisture. Regardless of the stalk portion sampled there was less inversion when humidity was high. The rate of sucrose inversion was positively correlated with the rate of moisture loss.

Moreover, the moisture and inversion changes were greatest in stalks sectioned before storage.

Within the intact stalks, declining gradients for purity, moisture loss, and percentage sucrose loss were established from the top to the bottom (902). The cutting of stalks into sections rearranged these gradients so that changes were greatest in the top and bottom sections and least in the center. In addition to the sectioning effect, the variety and length of time elapsed after harvest strongly affected each of the measured gradients. The sugar, moisture, and inversion trends were more pronounced in the upper portions of intact stalks in storage than in the sectioned upper portions in storage. At the opposite end there were greater moisture losses and Brix increases in severed bottom sections than in intact bottom sections. The authors concluded that, owing to sucrose variations among the different stalk sections, there may be no direct relationship between rate of sugar loss and actual loss. Specifically, the low-sucrose portions would have to produce a much greater inversion rate to show the greatest loss of sucrose. Such interpretations are interesting, but it should be remembered that sugar accumulation in mature and immature storage tissues involves essentially different mechanisms, and the utilization demands upon stored sucrose vary enormously with the maturity of storage tissue.

Rizk and Normand (1239) studied the relationship of invertase types to sugar content among three Louisiana varieties with special reference to different portions of the stalk. Their data showed that the level of both acid and neutral invertase hinged upon the variety being studied, and certain relationships did exist between sugar components and each of the invertase types. Of the three varieties tested invertase content was highest in *C.P. 42-10*, the variety having the lowest purity and percentage of sucrose. Similarly, both invertases were most active in the top third which was lowest in purity and sucrose content (Table 15-1). The sugar and enzyme values were

TABLE 15-1

SUGAR CONTENTS AND INVERTASE ACTIVITY IN THREE DIFFERENT PORTIONS OF THE SUGARCANE STALK

[After Rizk and Normand (1243).] Reproduced by permission of the *Sugar Journal.*

Third of stalk	Purity	Sugars			Invertase**		A/N ratio
		Sucrose (%)	Reducing*	Total*	Acid	Neutral	
Bottom	79.28	14.36	61.25	324	30.63	23.54	1.37
Center	74.00	12.77	65.86	300	30.18	20.96	1.64
Top	59.70	8.31	72.45	232	43.50	29.33	1.69
L.S.D. at 5%:	1.55	0.35	1.10	22.9	3.49	4.98	0.265

*Expressed as mg/ml of juice.

**Expressed as μg of glucose produced by inversion in 4 hours by 0.1 ml of dialyzed juice.

relatively equal between middle and bottom portions of the stalk. This is further evidence that the potential for ripening and enzyme control is considerably greater in the top of the stalk where both primary and secondary ripening stages have yet to be completed. Rizk and Normand also noted that conditions of high invertase level, high reducing sugars, and low sucrose were characteristic of lower-yielding varieties as well as of the least mature areas of the stalk. A rather close relationship between invertase level and both sugar and tonnage potential has been noted in Puerto Rico varieties (28). The latter work was performed exclusively with acid invertases situated in the apical meristem.

While studying sugarcane invertases in Puerto Rico, the author has given preference to the group of acid invertases concentrated in meristematic and extremely immature internodal tissues. This choice has been vindicated at least in part by the sugar gradient studies of Lauritzen and Balch (902), and the sugar–invertase experiments of Rizk and Normand (1239), as well as by virtually all physiological studies in which the author included invertase level as a parameter relating to growth or sugar production. In general, the high acid invertase and low sucrose values were found in tissues still actively involved in growth processes, in high-tonnage varieties as opposed to "sweet" varieties, and in growth-promoting treatments as opposed to growth-restrictive treatments. This is not to say that acid invertases have no bearing on sugar recovery, for certainly they will act upon sucrose in the milled juice, nor does this detract in any way from the need for a practical method to control the acid and neutral invertases retained as stable entities in the mature joints.

It is also appropriate to mention that the acid invertase values for mature storage tissue which appear in several of the Rizk and Normand reports far exceed the apparent acid invertase potential found in similar tissues by workers in Australia and Puerto Rico. Quite possibly the acid invertases may vary as a regional response in addition to the maturity and varietal factors already documented.

C. *Relationships of invertase type and distribution to burning and storage factors*

Recent postharvest inversion studies by Rizk and Normand (1240–1242) in Louisiana showed that the behavior of acid and neutral invertases was strongly affected by variety, preharvest burning, and storage duration. Some evidence was found of sucrose concentration differentially affecting the invertase types, and of complex interactions operating between each of these factors.

Initial experiments (1241) with *C.P. 42-10, C.P. 36-105*, and *C.P. 48-103* revealed that burned stalks were significantly lower in purity than unburned stalks in all varieties as an average of all storage periods (1, 3, 8, 15, and 21 days). Significantly lower juice volumes were obtained from burned material. Juice volume also varied appreciably on the basis of variety and position of stalk analyzed, *i.e.*, top, center and bottom. Burning produced initial sucrose increases in the top third of the stalk, while the remainder was unaffected. Consequently, for the first 2 weeks the burned cane as a whole tended to give higher sucrose-content values than the unburned controls. This effect disappeared after 15 days. The authors emphasized that entire stalks of all

TABLE 15-2

INVERTASE ACTIVITY IN BURNED AND UNBURNED STALKS OF THREE SUGARCANE VARIETIES GIVEN VARIABLE STORAGE PERIODS

[After Rizk and Normand (1241).] Reproduced by permission of the *International Sugar Journal.*

Treatment	Variety	Days in storage					Treatment varieties
		1	3	8	15	21	
		Acid invertase activity*					
Burned	*C.P. 42-10*	23.7	33.5	26.7	24.0	0	21.6
	C.P. 36-105	38.2	34.7	24.0	27.2	0	24.8
	C.P. 48-103	37.8	35.7	28.3	36.3	0	27.6
	Burned × periods	33.2	34.6	26.3	29.2	0	
Unburned	*C.P. 42-10*	52.2	66.8	60.2	40.8	44.2	52.8
	C.P. 36-105	49.8	51.8	38.5	30.8	30.5	40.3
	C.P. 48-103	52.8	59.3	57.8	29.7	27.7	45.5
	Unburned × periods	51.6	59.3	52.2	33.8	34.1	
		Neutral invertase activity*					
Burned	*C.P. 42-10*	16.7	27.3	22.8	26.0	0	18.6
	C.P. 36-105	20.7	30.3	20.5	23.3	0	19.0
	C.P. 48-103	15.3	24.3	25.3	31.0	0	19.2
	Burned × periods	17.6	27.3	22.9	26.8	0	
Unburned	*C.P. 42-10*	24.5	33.0	26.2	23.7	24.3	26.3
	C.P. 36-105	24.7	35.7	19.0	17.8	21.0	23.6
	C.P. 48-103	33.0	36.5	30.3	21.8	13.8	27.1
	Unburned × periods	27.4	35.1	25.2	21.1	19.7	
L.S.D. at 5% for invertase:					Acid	Neutral	
Treatments × varieties × periods					5.2	3.5	
Treatments × periods					3.2	2.0	
Treatments × varieties					2.5	1.5	

*Expressed as μg of glucose produced by hydrolysis in 4 hours by 0.1 ml of dialyzed juice.

varieties may behave similarly and somewhat predictably, but different portions of stalks from different varieties will vary markedly in response to burning and storage period. These variations were attributed to the action of endogenous invertases.

The levels of both acid and neutral invertases were reduced by burning in all varieties (Table 15-2). For both enzyme types there was a tendency to increase for about 3 days followed by a gradual decline. The effect of burning was to accelerate the decline phase after minimizing the extent of initial rise. As can be seen from Table 15-2, there was a total loss of invertases in burned cane between 15 and 21 days, an event quite at odds with our present concepts of invertase synthesis, regulation, and inhibition. With respect to invertase distribution, both types tended to decline in the cane tops in response to burning and storage. The pH 7.0 enzyme was a relatively constant factor in all parts of unburned cane. In general, differences found between the acid and neutral invertases were confined to varietal rather than harvest and storage factors.

Acid invertase tended to vary more than the neutral invertase in relation to burning, variety, stalk distribution and storage period. On this Rizk and Normand (1241)

TABLE 15-3

THE RATIO OF ACID INVERTASE ACTIVITY TO NEUTRAL INVERTASE ACTIVITY IN BURNED AND UNBURNED STALKS OF THREE SUGARCANE VARIETIES GIVEN VARIABLE STORAGE PERIODS

[After Rizk and Normand (1241).] Reproduced by permission of the *International Sugar Journal.*

Treatment	Variety	Acid/neutral (A/N) invertase ratio* at different storage time (days)					Treatment × varieties
		1	3	8	15	21	
Burned	*C.P. 42-10*	1.44	1.22	1.16	0.94	0	0.95
	C.P. 36-105	1.91	1.17	1.17	1.11	0	1.07
	C.P. 48-103	2.37	1.48	1.12	1.20	0	1.23
	Burned × periods	1.90	1.28	1.15	1.08	0	
Unburned	*C.P. 42-10*	2.13	2.04	2.30	1.73	1.84	2.00
	C.P. 36-105	2.02	1.44	2.02	1.81	1.44	1.74
	C.P. 48-103	1.67	1.66	1.95	1.41	2.03	1.74
	Unburned × periods	1.94	1.71	2.09	1.65	1.77	
L.S.D. at 5% for A/N ratio:							
Treatments × varieties × periods			0.19				
Treatments × periods			0.11				
Treatments × varieties			0.08				

*Invertase expressed as μg of glucose produced by hydrolysis in 4 hours by 0.1 ml of dialyzed juice.

elected to express the enzyme responses in terms of a ratio of acid to neutral invertase [the "A/N ratio" (1239, 1243)]. In the present study the A/N ratio differed with respect to variety and burning, decreasing with storage time in both burned and control cane, and particularly so in the burned material (Table 15-3). Owing to the greater stability of neutral invertase, the A/N ratio was claimed to be less subject to environmental factors than acid invertase alone, while retaining the same general trends of the more sensitive acid enzyme. In this connection it has been suggested that the A/N ratio might serve as an aid to maturity evaluation (1243).

Rizk and Normand (1242) further elaborated the quantitative relationships between total sugar components and sucrose on the one hand and invertase on the other. Certain of these relationships are summarized in Tables 15-4 and 15-5 for both burned and

TABLE 15-4

INTERACTIONS FOR SUGAR CONTENTS AND INVERTASE ACTIVITY OF BURNED AND UNBURNED SUGARCANE STALKS SECTIONED INTO ONE-THIRD PORTIONS

[After Rizk and Normand (1242).] Reproduced by permission of the *International Sugar Journal.*

Treatment	Stalk portion	Sugars			Invertase**		A/N ratio
		Sucrose (%)	Reducing*	Total*	Acid	Neutral	
Burned	Bottom	15.49	81.01	361	27.00	19.23	1.15
	Center	14.17	89.61	352	25.93	18.86	1.14
	Top	10.86	97.21	325	21.06	18.63	0.96
Unburned	Bottom	15.10	85.96	357	42.60	25.93	1.64
	Center	14.39	92.07	351	46.03	25.56	1.84
	Top	10.34	104.17	310	49.96	25.56	2.01
	L.S.D. at 5%:	0.43	1.43	3.18	2.48	N.S.***	0.08

*Expressed as mg/ml of juice.
**Expressed as μg of glucose produced by hydrolysis in 4 hours by 0.1 ml of dialyzed juice.
***N.S., not significant.

unburned cane. Variations among different stalk portions and varieties were generally less pronounced in the cane that had been burned. In unburned cane the acid invertase level, and hence the A/N ratio, was highest in immature tissues and lowest in mature tissues, in inverse proportion to sucrose content and total sugar content. This was essentially an extension of the invertase–sugar relationship already recognized in uncut sugarcane (701, 1243) which apparently was not affected by cutting *per se.* Burning tended to reduce invertase levels, particularly acid invertase situated in the topmost portions of the stalk, so that a relative activity trend was established in reverse of that found with unburned stalks. Moreover, the changes in absolute sugar levels produced by burning did not alter the trend of relative sugar concentrations with respect either to stalk portion or variety.

Activity of the neutral invertase did not vary appreciably among different stalk portions whether the cane was burned or not. This is consistent with findings in Australia (690, 1268, 584) attributing marked stability to the neutral enzyme in contrast to the changing levels of acid invertase. Consequently, the A/N ratio was again closely correlated with acid invertase level, increasing from the bottom to top in unburned cane and increasing from top to bottom in burned cane. Quite possibly the preference of fire for the acid invertase relates to the less toughened condition of the top joints where greater amounts of acid invertase are situated. It should be recalled that at least one acid invertase is located in mature storage tissues (701), and, according to the data in Table 15-4, the acid invertase level was less affected by fire in the mature or "bottom" stalk portion.

TABLE 15-5

COMPARISONS BETWEEN SUGAR CONTENTS AND INVERTASE ACTIVITY OF BURNED AND UNBURNED SUGARCANE STALKS FOR THE INTERACTION TREATMENTS × VARIETIES

[After Rizk and Normand (1242).] Reproduced by permission of the *International Sugar Journal.*

Treatment	Variety	Sugars			Invertase**		A/N ratio
		Sucrose (%)	Reducing*	Total*	Acid	Neutral	
Burned	*C.P. 42-10*	10.51	96.38	319.40	21.56	18.56	0.95
	C.P. 36-105	14.13	90.88	357.72	24.80	18.96	1.07
	C.P. 48-103	15.89	80.57	360.02	27.63	19.20	1.23
Unburned	*C.P. 42-10*	10.57	92.24	301.46	52.83	26.33	2.00
	C.P. 36-105	13.36	105.72	356.54	40.30	23.63	1.74
	C.P. 48-103	15.90	84.20	361.50	45.46	27.10	1.74
	L.S.D. at 5%:	0.43	1.43	3.18	2.48	1.51	0.08

*Expressed as mg/ml of juice.
**Expressed as μg of glucose produced by hydrolysis in 4 hours by 0.1 ml of dialyzed juice.

Another effect of burning was an apparent reversal of the A/N ratio relationship to reducing sugar concentration (Table 15-5). The expected relationship in standing or unburned cane is a direct one, *i.e.*, higher invertase levels should produce greater quantities of reducing sugar, and this was in fact the response obtained (1242). The reversal of this trend by burning is perhaps tacit evidence of a differential heat effect upon the invertases of the upper stalk and those of the mature tissue, the latter presumably more heat resistant. It might also be said that fire is an appropriate means to rid the plant of unwanted invertase, but this is conjecture. Rizk and Normand proposed that a fire-induced change in the A/N–reducing sugar relationship helped to explain the differing deterioration characteristics between burned and unburned cane as described by Balch *et al.* (133).

Rizk and Normand (1242) also noted that the varietal response differences in A/N ratio (Table 15-5) could have practical implications for variety-selection programs. The fact that *C.P. 42-10* contained the highest acid invertase level before burning and the lowest level afterward reflects a striking enzyme sensitivity which might be harnessed in evaluating maturity, postharvest sugar retention, and other factors. Alexander (28) presented evidence in 1967 showing invertase analyses to be useful in evaluating both tonnage and sugar potentials of extremely young plants. The latter study was designed to aid the local breeding program which was experiencing difficulty in producing suitable varieties for Puerto Rico's changing sugar industry.

D. *Inversion as a function of variety, temperature, moisture, and condition of cane*

Although few studies have been performed relating to invertase activity within harvested stalks, most of the available evidence shows little or no relation between the field behavior and laboratory behavior of sugarcane invertases. Thorough studies by Lauritzen and Balch (901, 902, 905) have shown that under Louisiana conditions the divergent changes stem from complex interplay of variety, temperature, loss of moisture, and maturity factors.

Hall (632) appears to have been the first to describe deterioration rate as a varietal feature. Similar observations were reported by Haldane (630) and by Cross and Belile (395). Differing "susceptibility" to inversion among discrete varieties has been dealt with at length by Lauritzen and his co-workers in Louisiana (901, 905). Lauritzen and Balch (905) studied ten varieties under postharvest conditions of controlled temperature and humidity during storage periods of 6 to 7 days, 13 to 15 days, and 20 to 24 days. All cane was cut and stripped by hand and was neither frozen nor burned. In general, the varietal resistance or susceptibility factors were independent of storage conditions, a matter of considerable importance to sugar growers. Only under extremely moist storage conditions were the differing varietal tendencies toward inversion obscured. The practical lesson here is that the inversion-inclined varieties must be milled even more quickly than other varieties, and that, wherever possible, stored cane should be kept moist.

Lauritzen and Balch (901) observed no definite relationship between sucrose content and inversion as a varietal factor. Varieties highly "resistant" to inversion could as well contain characteristically low sucrose levels, and high sucrose varieties might readily be prone to inversion. Moisture, on the other hand strongly affected the inversion rate under Louisiana conditions (905). In this context it was implied that the rate of moisture loss affects inversion by virtue of the differing protection offered against evaporation by the waxy stem coating. The latter differs as a varietal feature (903). Moisture losses through the cut ends of the stalk have been reduced by treatment with paraffin (905, 1299).

It is common knowledge that invertases are hydrolytic enzymes, that is, they utilize elements of water in their hydrolysis of sugar linkages. Abundant rainfall descending upon a ripened stand of cane will usually increase invertase as an integral part of renewed growth. It is therefore surprising that, in experiments by Lauritzen and Balch (905), postharvest inversion was increased by the loss of moisture in all but a few "resistant" varieties. The principal exception was the variety *Badilla.* It was concluded that a physiological condition develops ". . .in certain varieties under certain field conditions that practically prevents inversion of sucrose under a rather wide range of conditions that are normally favorable to inversion". No theory was advanced to explain the physiological basis of these "conditions". Quite possibly there was no real reduction in available water at the cellular sites of the specific acid and neutral invertase reactions, whereas the general loss of water may have increased the effective substrate concentration. The varietal factor again appeared to be operating since the degree of inversion rose with increased susceptibility. Moisture loss *per se* was not a varietal factor although certain physical features that affect moisture loss may be varietal characteristics. In this connection maturity may also be an important factor relating to postharvest inversion. Dymond (463), working with the *Uba* variety in South Africa, found that immature or low-quality cane deteriorated more rapidly than mature cane having a high sucrose content.

Among the factors influencing the rate of moisture loss from harvested stalks, Lauritzen and Balch (905) stressed the differences between vapor pressure at the stalk surface and the ambient air. The vapor pressure of the cane results from a series of vapor pressures. Working with *P.O.J. 213*, Sartoris (1299) observed that about half the moisture lost from three-node sections passed through the cut ends. More water was lost through the root rings than through internodes. Early experiments in Louisiana showed that holding relative humidity at 98 percent severely restricted moisture loss. Lowering relative humidity to about 70 percent led to 6-fold increases in lost moisture; however, coating the cut ends with paraffin lowered the outward movement of water, and coating the entire stalk with paraffin produced further reductions in moisture loss. It was also shown that vapor pressure is higher at cut ends and root bands than at the internodes. Sartoris (1299) claimed that water was lost more readily from bundles of cane than from individual stalks, but Lauritzen and Balch (905) observed greater moisture losses from spread stalks than from bundles. In the storage rooms, stalks of a given variety held at a given temperature lost moisture mainly as a function of decreasing relative humidity.

Haldane (630), in upper India, attributed moisture losses to the unusual temperature and humidity conditions accompanying "hot" westerly winds typical of the period from early March to the end of June. Moreover, large differences in drying rate were recorded between varieties. Among the varietal factors contributing to moisture loss or retention were the occurrence of longitudinal splitting, inability to form a sufficient waxy covering, and preference of certain varieties for low or almost swampy habitats. Rapid moisture loss from the varieties *Barkh, Co. 205*, and *Pansahi* seemed to be related to increased fiber content.

Lauritzen (904), in Louisiana, employed purity losses as an index of sucrose inversion. In Puerto Rico, Samuels and Cayere (1292), observing marked purity decline in harvested wet cane and only small purity decline in harvested dry cane, interpreted this as evidence of greater inversion under rainy conditions added to weight losses by postharvest drying.

Lauritzen and Balch (905) stressed the practical importance of increased inversion being associated with the drying of cane. Obviously it is a simpler matter to keep piles of harvested cane moist than to enter the stalk (by means not yet known) with chemical inhibitors or regulators (also not yet known) and control the endogenous invertases (themselves but partially known). During earlier studies in Louisiana, Lauritzen and Balch had shown that inversion could be kept to minimal levels for 7 to 10 days by sprinkling cane stored in piles. More recent findings supported this (905); irrespective of variety and temperature (up to 75 °F), the harvested stalk experienced little inversion so long as it was kept moist. With a few varieties high moisture tended to mask completely the effects of temperature on inversion.

The somewhat peculiar relationship between moisture and temperature described in Louisiana (905) has the effect of placing in a secondary perspective one of the most fundamental of all enzyme parameters, that is, the relationship of reaction velocity to ambient temperature. Thus, instead of finding a pronounced increase of inversion as temperature increased from 37 to 75 °F, only small changes in inversion rate were obtained so long as high-moisture conditions were maintained. Moreover, it has been shown that temperatures toward the center of storage piles are generally lower than the mean of day and night temperatures[1]. This is particularly evident with increasingly large piles. Samples taken from the center of dry piles showed less inversion than samples taken from the exterior. Piles as large as 2000 tons did not accumulate respiratory heat if sprinkled once or twice daily. As the piles of cut cane became drier the rising temperatures increasingly stimulated inversion, although drying rate *per se* was not a varietal factor[1]. This relationship likewise holds under long-term field conditions with the result that escaping moisture is generally more important than temperature in determining inversion losses throughout the harvest season. In Louisiana, the cane harvested early under low rainfall, low relative humidity, and high "susceptibility" (relatively poor maturation) will tend to lose more sucrose by inversion than cane harvested late in the season. Consequently, the sugar losses from delayed milling will tend to be greater during the early part of the season.

The temperature response reported by Lauritzen and Balch (905) was not in close agreement with earlier reports (912, 1255, 145) which seem to have been based upon empirical evidence. Lee (912), in the Philippines, observed that cane stored in the shade experienced less inversion than cane exposed to the sun, and therefore concluded that higher temperature was responsible. Barnes (145) considered it probable that the after-ripening effects observed in the cool regions of northern India would not be found in warmer climates. Studies by Rosenfeld (1255) in Egypt attributed increased inversion to high temperatures, although a possible moisture gradient role was not taken into consideration as has been done by Lauritzen and Balch (902, 905). Sanyal (1298) actually recorded greater moisture losses accompanying increased inversion at high temperatures but specified temperature as the principal factor rather than the loss of moisture. With respect to moisture–inversion relationships, the majority of early workers concluded that inversion is retarded as a function of moisture loss [see reviews by Kuyper (877), Lauritzen and Balch[1], Rocha de Almeida and Frota de Souza (1251), and Rosenfeld (1255)].

Lauritzen and Balch (905) also observed the development of an inversion "gradient" under high-moisture conditions that was inversely related to increasing temperature, but under low-moisture conditions showed a positive relationship with prolonged storage intervals. Thus, between 46 and 66 °F, there was a decrease of inversion in moist cane; however, under low-moisture conditions in which drying progressed at equal rates irrespective of temperature, there was an infrequent gradient at 6 to 7 days, a more general gradient at 13 to 15 days, and a universal gradient in all lots of cane at 20 to 24 days. Initial inversion rates were generally consistent among varieties whereas the mid- and late-period analyses showed marked varietal differences with the most pronounced inversion occurring at lower temperatures.

It was surmised from the temperature and moisture-decline data that ". . .a substance is formed (or a condition is developed) during the early part of the storage period that retards and finally arrests inversion" (905). Such a substance or condition would agree especially well with the higher temperature suppression of invertase and the assumed high metabolic activity retained under high-moisture conditions. Varietal differences are also consistent with the formation of specific inhibitory substances. On the other hand, this view is not particularly consistent with the carbohydrate- and auxin-mediated control system elaborated in Australia (1267, 1269, 586, 585, 589, 567), nor with the protein-like invertase inhibitors described in other plants (1180, 1181, 1182). Each of the latter mechanisms subscribe to conventional temperature–growth activity relations favorable to increased invertase content. Possibly the weakest point of the Lauritzen and Balch concept is the fact that in more than two decades since this proposal was published no invertase-inhibiting substance has been isolated from cane stalks. This may in part reflect insufficient research, but recent attempts in Puerto Rico to isolate a proteinaceous invertase inhibitor from sugarcane stem tissue proved negative[3]. Maretzki and Alexander[4] found tacit evidence of invertase inhibitors during gel-filtration studies of cane apical meristem extracts. In any case the possibility of an

---

[3] Acín Díaz, N.M. and Alexander, A.G., 1972. Absence of a proteinaceous invertase-regulatory system in sugarcane stem tissue, *J. Agric. Univ. P.R.* 56(1): 85–87.

[4] Maretzki, A. and Alexander, A.G., 1967. Gel-fitration studies of invertase from sugarcane meristem, *Enzymologia* 33(5): 299–307.

endogenous inhibitor being produced after harvest cannot be discounted, nor is the likelihood of an inhibitory microbial by-product excluded at this time.

E. *Inversion as a function of enzyme and substrate level*

From the limited information available there appears to be no direct relationship between inversion rates and the sucrose or invertase contents of harvested cane. Lauritzen and Balch (905) found no connection between inversion resistance and the invertase content of the millable stalk. In an earlier study [1939] it had been shown that the variety *C.P. 29-99*, definitely not prone to inversion, contained more invertase than other varieties in which postharvest inversion was common (901). Similarly, the variety *C.P. 29-136* was found to be the most inversion-prone of all varieties tested but it contained less invertase than *C.P. 29-99.* Lauritzen *et al.* (901) concluded that any relationship of invertase content to inversion rate must be operative at localized sites within the cell rather than throughout the stalks as a whole. This view is strongly substantiated by our present knowledge of invertase types, distribution, and functional specialization. In retrospect it seems odd that Lauritzen and Balch did not apply similar reasoning to explain invertase stimulation by moisture losses which occurred in the stalk as a whole.

Lauritzen and Balch correctly stated that sucrose content is not necessarily a measure of maturity (905), but nonetheless their data showed a generally positive correlation between high sucrose and maturity on the one hand and increased resistance to inversion on the other. This was specifically an intravarietal feature and no such correlation was found between varieties. In accordance with our present understanding of cane invertases this is best explained by the loss of acid invertase during the physiological aging of internodal tissue. The parallel ripening or "maturation" would be incidental to invertase content. The interpretation given by Lauritzen and Balch (905) contends that an "equilibrium substance" capable of resisting inversion is either formed during storage, or it increases in cane as a function of age.

F. *Inversion control in stored cane*

Sugar growers and scientists have long recognized the need to control quality losses in harvested cane, but no totally suitable method has been devised. More than 75 years ago Stubbs (1381) thought topping the stalks would help under Louisiana conditions: "...Topping frequently prevents rapid decomposition and after a bud killing frost, should be practised, provided windrowing is deemed expedient."

In order to insure continuous mill operation it is necessary to store some cane at the sugar factory. Cane may also be stored in the field to avoid congestion at the mill yard. As already noted, numerous early workers observed that if such cane remained wet in the piles there was a marked reduction in quality decline. Various aspects of moistening stored cane were examined in studies by Lauritzen and Balch[1] working under Louisiana conditions. Among the parameters studied were pile sizes (less than 1 ton, 7 to 70 tons, and 260 tons). In addition, temperature–pile size relationships were studied in stacks ranging from less than a ton to 800 tons. Different varieties were included along with variable shade and sprinkling treatments. Inversion and various qualitative analyses were performed.

The results showed that sprinkling of small piles prevented major sucrose losses in all varieties[1], and that failure to maintain a moist condition led to heavy sucrose losses by inversion. It was found that inversion was closely related to moisture losses and increased as drying progressed. When sprinkling was not performed as a treatment the occurrence of natural rainfall tended to reduce inversion. The sprinkling effect held for 6 to 10 days in piles ranging from 7 to 260 tons. Little evidence of microbial development, increased acidity, or of non-sugar organic compounds was found during storage whether the stalks were moistened or not. Shading offered some additional protection.

Many earlier workers felt that shading harvested cane was a sure means of reducing deterioration (401, 745, 1298, 912, 951). The practice has not been widely adopted, however, possibly because the large piles required tend to promote deterioration over extended periods (1582). Boneta-García and Lugo-López in Puerto Rico (203) obtained consistent small reductions in quality loss by storing cane in the shade as opposed to full sun; however, the trend was not statistically significant.

Although sprinkling tended to lower the temperature of piled stalks, Lauritzen and Balch[1] did not feel that the temperature difference between sprinkled and unsprinkled cane was sufficient to account for the observed inversion differences. The positive moistening effect was instead attributed to the maintenance of stalk turgidity. The temperature changes at the center of large piles lagged somewhat behind the changes in external air temperature, but the fact that internal temperatures did fluctuate along with ambient temperature indicated that there was no progressive heat accumulation from respiratory and microbial processes. Similar conclusions were drawn by Wold (1582) in Hawaii who found little heat generated in storage piles unless they were left standing for long periods of time.

Maturity was a major factor in the rate of inversion in stored cane[1]. As maturation level increased the extent of deterioration slackened. The authors suggested that observed varietal differences in deterioration rate were explained in part by distinct maturity differences among the test varieties. These views are consistent with the findings of Foster (536) in Queensland.

4. INVERSION CONTROL IN MILLED JUICE

At the moment when the stalk is crushed in the factory it ceases to exist as an intact living entity capable of growth and reproduction. The invertases formerly contained therein are totally divorced from the discrete spatial and functional roles they had performed since germination. However, these enzymes do remain active in the juice where, given sufficient time, there is little to prevent massive hydrolysis of sucrose. In essence, the enzymes are given *in vitro* access to unlimited substrate with none of the *in vivo* control mechanisms operating to govern their action.

Although lying beyond the technical scope of this book, the final behavior of the sugarcane invertases is not without interest to the cane physiologist and the factory manager alike. It is perhaps appropriate to mention that invertases "running free" in the crude milled juice are nearly as susceptible to chemical inhibition as they are in a conventional enzyme extract. The milled extract is an enormous preparation but an *in virtro* one nonetheless, totally lacking the complexity and inaccessibility of the living cell. In relative terms the sugar manufacturer has a much simpler task in controlling invertase than does the physiologist working with an *in vivo* system.

Nonetheless, factory operators do not appear to have solved the problem of newly-liberated invertases *per se*. Use of antiseptics effective against bacteria probably do not affect the cane enzymes[5]. Although normal operations stressing speed and cleanliness should help to restrict invertase damage, a major challenge lies in the discovery of an inhibitor which will prevent invertase activity within the juice from the moment of expression until the milling processes themselves prohibit further enzyme action. Such an inhibitor might be incorporated into standing cane just prior to harvest, or possibly could be applied as a spray over the stalks immediately before grinding to effect instant mixing with the juice.

A. *Inversion control with sodium metasilicate*

Studies in Puerto Rico have supported the feasibility of inhibiting cane invertases and microbial development with an appropriate invertase inhibitor added to milled juice (474, 57). In these experiments unfiltered juice samples from freshly-milled stalks of *P.R. 980* were added to stoppered flasks containing suitable amounts of sodium metasilicate (Si). The Si solutions were incubated at 84 °F and samples were drawn daily for sugar analyses and pH measurements. The *in vivo* inhibitory properties of Si for several cane enzymes have been discussed at length (42). With purified cane invertase preparations the inhibition occurs rather abruptly at Si levels between 2 and 3 μmoles/ml of juice. In raw juice the inhibition occurred at higher Si levels and over a broad concentration range, *i.e.*, between 20 and 60 μmoles/ml. The higher Si requirement was apparently related to debris and suspended matter in the crude juice. A single passage of the juice through filter paper lowered the effective Si level and range to the order of 10 to 12 μmoles/ml.

---

[5] In the instance of the antiseptic *Busane 881*, the author obtained no effect upon semi-purified cane or yeast invertase preparations by additive levels ranging up to 500 ppm (unpublished).

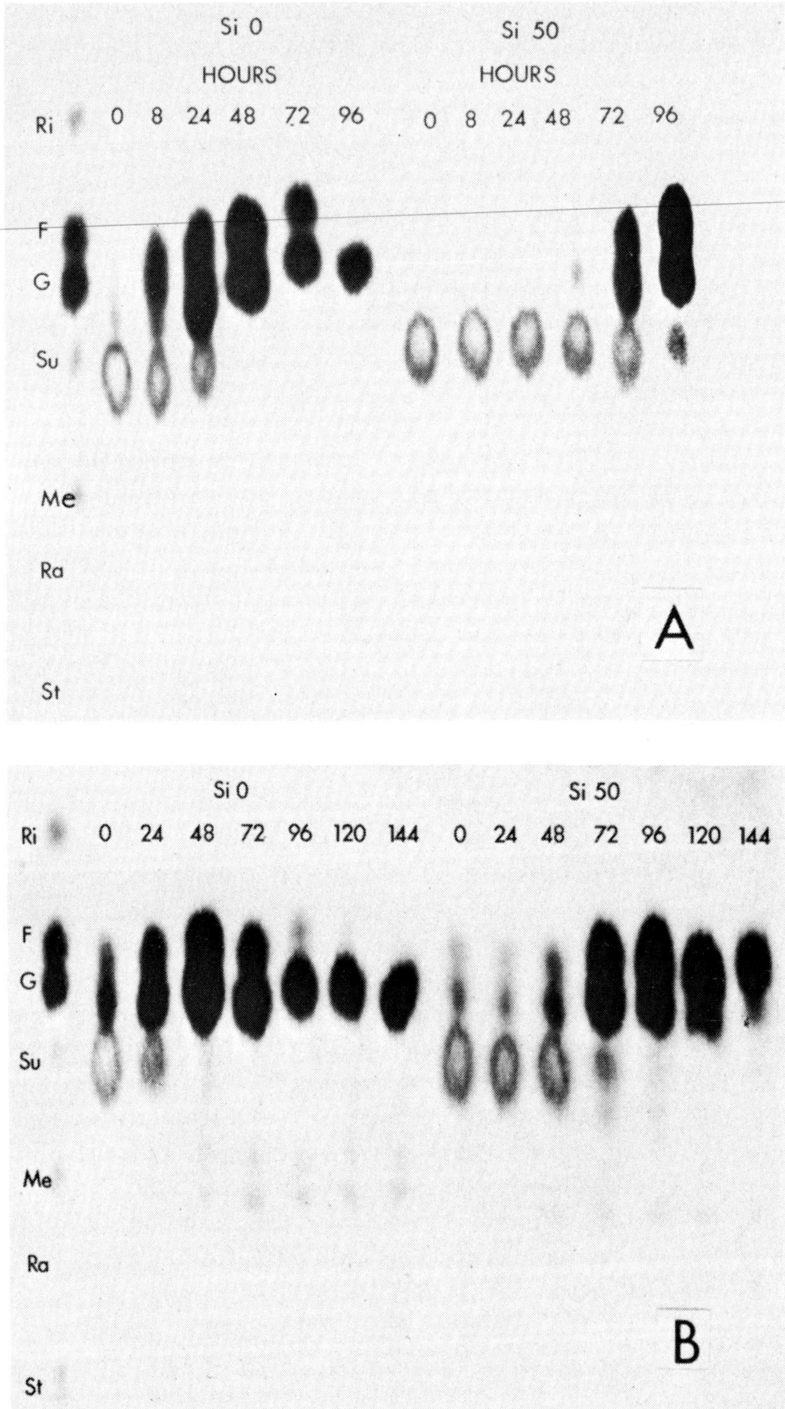
Si 0
HOURS
Si 50
HOURS
Ri
0 8 24 48 72 96
0 8 24 48 72 96
F
G
Su
Me
Ra
St
A
Si 0
Si 50
Ri
0 24 48 72 96 120 144
0 24 48 72 96 120 144
F
G
Su
Me
Ra
St
B

When treated with Si, the crude juice became slightly darker in color and flocculation of suspended matter occurred immediately. This appearance was retained for several days in samples incubated at 84 °F. The metasilicate produced a strongly basic pH [50 μmoles gave pH 11.1 at zero hours (57)] whose duration was a function of Si level. Fifty μmoles of Si maintained the pH above 7.0 for about 36 hours. Some evidence of microbe growth in the Si solution appeared between 48 and 60 hours; however, by this time the Si-free control samples had greatly deteriorated with respect to color, acidity, and sucrose content.

The suppression of bacterial development was not anticipated but can be explained in part by the medium's high pH and by the absence of a suitable carbon source (fructose or glucose). This suggests that bacterial growth is dependent upon cane invertase products or bacterial invertase products. The *in vivo* inhibition of bacterial invertase seems plausible since the absorption of Si in inhibitory quantities would be a relatively simple matter in unicellular organisms.

The paper chromatograms in Fig. 15-4 illustrate sucrose inversion and subsequent hexose changes in typical deterioration experiments with Si-treated juice from mature *P.R. 980* stalks. In these instances 50 μmoles/ml Si had been added to one quantity of juice while a similar quantity, designated as the control or "Si 0", was allowed to deteriorate at 84 °F. Juice samples taken at 8- or 24-hour intervals were chromatographed on Whatman No. 1 filter paper and the sugar spots developed with silver nitrate. It can be seen that, at zero hours, sucrose (Su) was the predominate sugar in both treated and untreated juice (Fig. 15-4A). In the absence of Si the invertase products fructose and glucose appeared within 8 hours, and these in turn were utilized between 48 and 96 hours. The bacterial preference was clearly for fructose (F) rather than glucose (G) in the untreated juice. Virtually all sucrose was gone by 48 hours and nearly all fructose had disappeared by 96 hours. However, the Si-treated juice did not begin to show appreciable inversion until after 48 hours. At 72 hours inversion had progressed to about the same extent noted at 8 hours in the control series but some sucrose was retained even at 96 hours.

Fig. 15-4. Paper chromatograms illustrating sucrose, fructose, and glucose changes in sugarcane juice incubated with and without sodium metasiliciate (Si). (A) During a 4-day period, in the absence of Si, sucrose inversion was complete by 48 hours and virtually all fructose had been utilized by 96 hours. Silicate-treated juice was still undergoing sucrose inversion at 96 hours. (B) During a 6-day period, in the absence of Si, only fructose appears to have been utilized following sucrose inversion. In silicate-treated juice, glucose rather than fructose was utilized after sucrose inversion. Dark spots represent the invertase products fructose and glucose. Grey spots, corresponding to "Su", represent sucrose. Authentic sugars are identified as follows: Ri, ribose; F, fructose; G, glucose; Su, sucrose; Me, melezitose; Ra, raffinose; St, stachyose. [After Alexander *et al.* (57).]

B. *Silicate mode of action*

It has been proposed that the Si action is essentially physical, that is, silicic acid gel might entrap the enzyme–substrate complex or the water involved in the hydrolytic reaction (38, 42). Similarly, hexose moieties freed by the enzyme might also be trapped within the gel. This thesis, which has never been proved, rests on the following evidence: (a) Silicate becomes inhibitory over an extremely narrow concentration range, in the order of 2.4 to 2.9 μmoles/ml for both yeast and cane invertases. This implies a rather abrupt physical change within the Si solution, most probably a shift of the silicic acid from a sol to gel form, rather than random encounter of enzyme and inhibitor molecules. (b) Silicic acid gels are known to develop in aqueous solutions as a function of pH and temperature (1507, 1050, 1411). Protein–silicate complexes have been described in rice (127). Evidence of organic linkages with soluble silica has been found in *Equisetum* and certain grasses (959), and in several forages (1477). (c) The enzyme inhibitory action of metasilicate has shown a particular affinity for hydrolytic enzymes, *i.e.*, cane amylase, phosphatase, ATPase, and yeast and cane invertases (42).

Tacit evidence of a Si union with the fructose portion of sucrose has been found and is illustrated chromatographically in Fig. 15-4B (57). Recalling the microbe preference for fructose in Si-free juice (Fig. 15-4A), even to the extent that fructose was nearly exhausted without apparent use of glucose, it was surprising to find that glucose was the sugar eventually utilized in the Si-treated juice. In these experiments it was necessary to extend the deterioration time to 144 hours in order for the preferential hexose utilization to become clear. Throughout this period the fructose seemed to remain unaffected. As a tentative explanation it might be said that some configuration of Si had attached to the substrate at the fructose end and in so doing rendered the β-fructosidic linkage inaccessible to enzymic hydrolysis. Evidence for silicate–sugar complexes formed with sucrose and fructose, but not with glucose, was obtained by gas–liquid chromatography analyses (57). Under conditions of enzyme inaccessibility to the fructose end of sucrose, hydrolysis would have to occur at the glucose end through the mediation of an α-glucosidase. An invertase of this type ("taka invertase") is known in immature storage tissues in small amounts (16), and it is probable that traces of the enzyme are present in the milled juice. This might explain the slow but eventual inversion in Si-treated samples. The hydrolysis, having once occurred, would leave the Si–fructose configuration intact so that the bacteria could not metabolize its preferred hexose.

Presumably, the proposed Si–fructose configuration effectively blocks carbon atom No. 6 so that phosphorylation to fructose 6-phosphate cannot occur. In effect it would be fructose which is preserved by Si even more effectively than sucrose. Microbes would now be forced to metabolize glucose. Phosphorylation of glucose to glucose 6-phosphate (via hexokinase) and subsequent conversion to fructose

6-phosphate (via phosphohexose isomerase) might also be a slow process if either of the essential enzymes is present in rate-limiting supply, which could very well be the case. The combined delays in initial inversion plus slow glucose conversion to fructose might thus explain the Si-induced delay in sucrose breakdown.

An interesting feature of the inversion experiments with *P.R. 980* juice was an apparent effect of the cane maturity. The majority of juice samples was from very mature canes, as were those of the experiments depicted in Fig. 15-4. At zero time sucrose was about the only sugar present in the crude juice. For these samples about 24 hours were needed for major inversion to occur, another 24 hours passed before the process was complete, and the use of Si further delayed the process by about 48 to 60 hours. On the other hand, use of less mature cane whose juice already contained large quantities of hexose at zero time led to far more rapid inversion and less effective inversion control by Si. Since other workers[1] (1239, 902, 1241, 463) have observed more rapid postharvest deterioration in immature portions of the stalk than in mature cane, it appears that the amount of reducing sugar present may be a common denominator of potential inversion rates. Aside from the use of hexose for microbe development, and hence the production of microbial invertase, the specific relationship of hexoses to cane enzymes in milled juice is quite obscure. Workers in Australia developed an *in vivo* invertase control mechanism operating with inversion products (585, 586, 588). Alexander (16) found that *in vitro* invertase preparations inactivated by prolonged dialysis were reactivated by hexose additives.

C. *Possible "sucrase"-type reactions in milled juice*

A growing body of evidence indicates that certain bacterial enzymes (dextransucrase, levansucrase, amylosucrase) catalyze the synthesis of dextrins, levans, and starch–glycogen polysaccharides from sucrose (708, 709, 724). A new disaccharide, leucrose, has been synthesized from sucrose through the action of dextransucrase, an enzyme isolated from the bacterium *Leuconostoc mesenteroides* (1368). A levansucrase from *Aerobacter levanicum* has been shown to produce a branched polysaccharide, or levan, from sucrose and other substrates having a terminal β-fructofuranosidic group linked to the anomeric carbon of an aldose (724).

During the present investigations with sugarcane juice, paper chromatograms have frequently shown evidence of sucrose derivatives other than fructose and glucose which appear to signify unidentified oligosaccharides, polysaccharides, and lower molecular weight products of hexose metabolism. Indications of chemical-type polymerization were also found in the presence of metasilicate levels exceeding 50 μmoles/ml. However, there has been no evidence of sucrose derivatives having formed prior to the enzymic inversion of sucrose. This observation is consistent with the view that invertase control is the key to sucrose preservation in milled sugarcane juice.

5. BIODETERIORATION IN MECHANICALLY-HARVESTED CANE

Virtually all of the postharvest studies cited to this point have dealt with hand-cut and hand-trimmed cane that had been sent to the mill or stored as whole stalks in a relatively undamaged condition. So long as this material was ground within 2 or 3 days the deterioration processes could be held to a reasonable minimum. With the advent of mechanical harvesters, particularly the chopper harvester, the deterioration problem worsened owing to the increased ease and rate of bacterial infection of the injured stalks. The chopped cane problem had reached serious proportions in Queensland by the early 1960's. Egan and Rehbein (475) found that microbe entry into the stalks was aided tremendously by machine operations, particularly when the blades were dull or improperly aligned. Subsequent reports suggest that increased deterioration is a necessary evil of the mechanical harvester with which the sugarcane scientist has not yet been able to cope.

Although rapid processing of chopped cane has not in itself solved the deterioration problem, it is still the most practical control method available. In Australia, as in other regions, it has long been recognized that burned cane must be milled with all possible speed to avoid quality decline (1360). Waddell, in 1952 (1511) and 1954 (1512), reemphasized the need to avoid delays between burning and milling. New circumstances arising from the introduction of chopper harvesters were studied by Vallance and Young (1470) who concluded that "...taking a broad view there was no difference between the rate of deterioration of cut-up cane and that of whole stalk when both were milled within 2 days of harvesting..." Keniry *et al.* (826) and Foster (536) reported processing operations being affected by as little as 18 hours delay in grinding. Waddell and Price (1513) state that so long as the volume of chopped cane remained low it was possible to meet the 2-day limit. However, with increasing use of the chopper harvester the influx of deteriorating material began to exceed mill capacities. This problem was accentuated by the 5-day week in Queensland which causes some cane to stand about 2.5 days over the weekend[6].

By 1962 the deterioration of chopped cane had reached such serious proportions in Queensland that Egan and his colleagues undertook to clarify its cause and to determine means of control (480). In 1963 Egan and Rehbein (475) surmised that chopped cane deterioration was essentially a form of "storage rot" caused by microorganisms having extremely rapid growth rates. The work of Pederson and Hucker (1154) showed that the leaves and stalks of growing plants invariably support bacteria. This was also true of cane stalks and exudates from the stalks being shipped to the factory. The number of possible bacterial types is countless. One of the most common is the

---

[6] According to Egan (484), sufficient cane is held over the weekend to allow the mill to operate until noon on Monday. This cane would have been burned on Thursday evening or early Friday morning. It would be cut on Friday morning if harvested manually, or Friday afternoon if by chopper harvesters. Storage time would therefore vary from 56 to 72 hours.

slime-forming *Leuconostoc* which is found on most deteriorating vegetables. Nearly all bacteria, including *Leuconostoc*, are sensitive to heat and are destroyed during the factory heating operations which precede liming and evaporation processes.

Within the sugar factory bacteria can lower yields by sucrose hydrolysis and subsequent fermentation to acids, alcohol and carbon dioxide, and by producing "slime" which retards the flow of sugar solutions (1154). In 1964 Egan (476) attempted unsuccessfully to control the deterioration ("souring") by spraying chopped cane with bactericide. He concluded that more effective antiseptics were required to justify additional research. Egan confirmed the results of Stephenson and Doolan (1360) showing delays in harvesting burned cane to seriously diminish quality. He also confirmed that chopped cane deteriorates faster than whole cane.

Foster (536), in reviewing studies of weekend storage losses in chopped cane, noted evidence that sugar diminishes less in green cane than in burned cane. Development of dextran-like substances was particularly serious in the burned material. About 18 to 20 hours in storage sufficed for dextrins to cause crystal elongation in addition to the sucrose decline.

Waddell and Price (1513) proposed operational changes designed to minimize microbial deterioration. Certain Queensland mills controlled the problem by processing chopped cane toward the end of the week which ensured that no rapidly-deteriorating material stood over the weekend. This procedure is less satisfactory in mills receiving a large percentage of their cane in chopped form. Extending the weekly grinding period and altering the mill roster system have also been considered. At the field level growers were advised to wash down the harvest machines after use and to keep the blades sharp and properly adjusted. The importance of frequent burning and weekend storage of only freshly-burned cane was also stressed.

A. *Cause of "sour cane"; Leuconostoc mesenteroides*

In 1965 Egan (480) reported that the bacterium *Leuconostoc mesenteroides* is the principal cause of "souring" in chopped cane. Among the characteristics of this organism are its rapid growth in sucrose solutions, simultaneous production of a thick cell wall or capsule surrounding the bacterial cells, and the subsequent union of capsules to form conglomerates (1156). The microbe infects cane wherever the stalk is cut or broken. It rapidly colonizes the injured tissue and produces large populations within 24 hours. In addition to lowering the sucrose content, juice purity is lowered, pH decreases, and titratable acidity increases markedly within 2 days after infection. Egan found that whole stalks harvested manually were little affected under similar conditions. In a subsequent paper presented at Taipei in 1968 (484), Egan reported that weekend storage losses in Queensland during 1962, 1963 and 1966 amounted to apparent C.C.S. losses of 0.64, 0.91 and 1.31 units. When corrected for weight losses these values came to 6.0, 8.8, and 11.0 percent of the original C.C.S. present, while whole stalks lost only 1 to 2 percent in storage.

The bacteria which produce "gum" or "slime" in sugar solutions and are found in large numbers in milled cane juice were assigned to the genus *Leuconostoc* Van Tieghem by Hucker and Pederson (756) in 1930. In 1939 Bergey *et al.* (169) adopted the Hucker and Pederson characterization designating *Leuconostoc mesenteroides* as the species commonly occurring in milled cane juice. Egan (477) found small populations of *Leuconostoc* on the surface of burned and unburned standing cane but none inside the stalk. Mayeaux (993), in Louisiana, found the organism only on harvested cane. Both workers isolated *Leuconostoc* species from cane soils.

McCleskey *et al.* (998) isolated four distinct colonial types of *L. mesenteroides* from cane juice. The four types also varied with respect to certain fermentative reactions, in the amount of gum, acid, and carbon dioxide produced, and in relation to the pH and temperature requirements for growth. In addition to *Leuconostoc*, Pederson and Hucker found the bacterial genera *Bacillus, Micrococcus, Flavobacterium, Achromobacterium* and *Escherichia* in raw sugar mills (1154). Species of *Leuconostoc* found in sucrose solutions in addition to *mesenteroides* include *L. dextranicum* and *L. citrovorum* (1335). Alford and McCleskey (60) distinguished between the three *Leuconostoc* species on the basis of fermentation tests, *i.e., L. mesenteroides* ferments both sucrose and pentose, *L. dextranicum* ferments sucrose but not pentoses, and *L. citrovorum* ferments neither sucrose nor pentoses.

For several decades *Leuconostoc* species have been credited with dextran formation in deteriorating sugarcane. McCalip and Hall (997), in 1938, attributed the "slow filtering muds and poor crystallizing sirups and molasses" of frozen cane to "viscous fermentation" by this organism. Infection was facilitated by ". . .frost-killed eye passages, borer holes and freeze splits". Dextran was only partially removed by ordinary clarifying operations.

Alford and McCleskey (60) emphasized the heterogeneity of *Leuconostoc* species and claimed that *L. dextranicum* rather than *L. mesenteroides* was the most effective gum producer in sugar solutions. Pederson and Hucker (1154) described *L. mesenteroides* as one of the principal microbes producing enzymes capable of hydrolyzing raw sugar in storage as well as in the crude juice. The same authors (757) describe several *Leuconostoc* species historically associated with both beet and cane sugar processing[7]. McCleskey *et al.* (998) depict *L. mesenteroides* as the organism most commonly found in sugar solutions, although both the serological and biochemical heterogeneity of *Leuconostoc* species was noted. Skole *et al.* (1335), in 1968, stated that of the three major *Leuconostoc* species, ". . .*L. mesenteroides* is probably most often encountered in sucrose solutions, and by virtue of its ability to produce a slime or viscous fermentation, it is of most concern to the sugar industry."

---

[7] Perquin (1156) reported that gelatinous grains occurring in raw sugar beet juice were synonymous with the "froschlaich" usually associated with sucrose fermentation by *L. mesenteroides*. In this instance, the lactic acid bacterium *Betabacterium vermiforme* was depicted as the responsible organism.

Tilbury (1437) isolated more than 200 types of microorganisms from deteriorating cane in the West Indies and United Kingdom. Among 80 lactobacilli the most predominant species was *L. mesenteroides*, although the homofermentative organisms *Lactobacillus plantarum* and *Lactobacillus casei* appeared in equal abundance after 10 days of storage. Tilbury (1433, 1436) also states that *L. mesenteroides* is probably the principial deterioration organism on Jamaica cane air freighted to England.

B. *Dextrans; their nature and effects on sucrose solutions*

In addition to sucrose losses the production of polysaccharides by bacteria constitutes a major postharvest deterioration problem. Bacterial polysaccharides were recognized nearly a century ago as "slime masses" in sugar refineries (1335). Hucker and Pederson (757) state that Kircher, in 1839, was probably the first to observe organisms accompanying the formation of slime in beet juice. According to Skole *et al.* (1335), Pasteur had recognized in 1861 that the slime formation associated with "viscous fermentation" in sugar solutions was a result of contamination with certain microorganisms.

Broadly speaking, there are two types of hydrophilic polysaccharide gels produced by bacteria: (a) Glucosans (dextrans), and (b) fructosans (levans). Usually appearing as slimes or gums, these substances frustrate normal refining operations in sugar factories by blocking pipelines and hindering filtration processes. According to Scarr (1304), such masses are termed "froschlaich" or "frog's spawn" in Europe. Scarr also mentions the work of Schiebler, who, in 1874, first equated the gum deposits in sugar refineries with dextran formation from sucrose.

Dextrans have probably existed within standing cane in small quantities throughout the history of sugarcane agriculture, and certainly they have been present to varying degree in the milled juice. According to Tantaoui (1410), since 1935 the Nag Hamadi sugar factory in Egypt has been "...an unwilling host for the most undesirable dextran forming microorganisms...", which annually created problems relative to increased juice acidity, increased viscosity of the juice, and abnormal crystal shapes. However, prior to 1960, the occurrence of dextrans in cane juice was generally associated with epidemics (1092, 419). Concern over dextrans in the sugar mills increased rapidly when, in the early 1960's, mechanically-harvested cane was found wanting in processing quality, particularly chopped cane, and most particularly chopped cane that had stood in bins for longer than 2 days.

As pointed out by Keniry *et al.* (825), it became necessary to discover a reliable indicator of processing quality. It has been shown that chopped cane might have exceedingly poor processing quality while still retaining high purity and most of its original sucrose. Bruijn (253), searching for an analytical method for quality control, investigated volatile acids, ethanol, succinic acid, starch, and soluble polysaccharides in juice samples obtained at factories or from a small laboratory mill. All except the soluble polysaccharides were found to be unsuitable. The latter were reasonably constant in freshly-cut cane, they increased during deterioration, and they readily precipitated upon addition of alcohol to the juice. Bruijn did not at first associate the polysaccharide formation with *Leuconostoc* since he did not detect lactic acid, a normal by-product of *L. mesenteroides* cultures, and because the polysaccharide increased more rapidly during dry storage than during humid storage. Moreover, Nicholson and Lilienthal (1092) had shown in 1959 that *Leuconostoc* was not needed for polysaccharide to be produced in stored cane stalks.

Bruijn subsequently isolated the principal polysaccharide from 6-week-old stalks and examined its structure by periodate oxidation, gas–liquid chromatography, and infrared spectra analyses (254). It was shown to be a relatively low molecular weight polymer (8000 to 34 000) which yielded only glucose residues upon acid hydrolysis. The structure was depicted as a straight chain, α-glucoside having 25 percent $1 \rightarrow 6$ and 75 percent $1 \rightarrow 4$ α-glucoside linkages. Nicholson and Lilienthal (1092) maintained that the polysaccharide formed in whole stored stalks constitued approximately 60 percent $1 \rightarrow 4$ and 30 percent $1 \rightarrow 6$ linkages. Commenting on these and Bruijn's findings, Egan (481) surmised that non-dextran polysaccharides were produced in whole cane, but that substantial amounts of dextran should appear in chopped cane having large *Leuconostoc* populations.

In 1959 Nicholson and Horsley developed an analytical method believed to be specific for dextrins (1093). The method provides for enzymic removal of starch, protein removal by trichloroacetic acid precipitation, and the separation of insoluble material by filtration. Dextrin is measured as a "haze" developed in 50 percent alcohol. Foster (536) recently questioned whether the carbohydrate responsible for the "haze" is a true dextran. Analyses of freshly-cut cane from the Mulgrave area of Queensland gave high values by the haze method, but not all of the cane samples were infected.

Keniry *et al.* (825) evaluated lactic acid, gums, and dextran as indicators of processing quality for chopped cane. They obtained a positive correlation between dextran level and processing performance in certain mill materials, as determined by final molasses purity and crystal elongation, the latter being an important qualitative factor of raw sugar. Dextrin was analyzed by the techniques of Nicholson and Horsley (1093).

In a second article Keniry *et al.* (826) reported on the rate of dextran formation in freshly-burned chopped and whole cane during the 1966 grinding season in northern Queensland. Dextran was not present in freshly-harvested material but appeared within 9 or 10 hours. For freshly-burned chopped cane a grinding delay of only 20 hours lowered processing performance. High temperature and wet weather accelerated deterioration as indicated by dextran content. The maximum acceptable delay in grinding chopped cane was set at 18 hours for cool and dry weather, and at 14 hours for hot and humid weather. Vickers (1494) reported later that in the Tully area of

Queensland even the 14 hours limit has proven excessive for chopped cane.

In 1966 Egan (479) examined the effect of "sour storage rot" on pH, titratable acidity, gum content, C.C.S. values, purity, and reducing sugars of initial juice. He considered the most important deterioration factor to be increased gum content, and a parallel was drawn between deterioration of chopped cane in Queensland and frozen cane in Louisiana. In a later paper (482) Egan correlated the major gum increases in storage with prior chopping of the stalks.

Egan's concept of gum content appears to include more than strictly dextran, but nonetheless his data showed a strong correlation between polysaccharide formation and deterioration of chopped cane. Using the alcohol precipitation method of Roberts and Friloux (1247), Egan removed gums from fresh juice by bringing the final alcohol content to 75 percent (484). The gums were described as "...alcohol-precipitable, water-soluble polysaccharides of high molecular weight...", and included certain "...gum constituents of sugarcane as well as such deterioration products as dextran". Natural starches having much higher molecular weights were removed by centrifugation.

Data for weekend storage gathered during the 1965 and 1966 grinding seasons are shown in Table 15-6. Gum content increased moderately in stored whole cane, but

TABLE 15-6

GUM CONTENT OF FRESHLY-MILLED JUICE FROM WHOLE AND CHOPPED CANE, INCLUDING WATER-SOLUBLE POLYSACCHARIDES AND DEXTRAN, FOLLOWING REMOVAL OF STARCH AND HIGHER MOLECULAR WEIGHT POLYSACCHARIDES BY CENTRIFUGATION

[After Egan (484).] Reproduced by permission of *I.S.S.C.T.*

Year	Gum content*			
	Whole-stalk cane		Mechanically-chopped cane	
	Fresh	Stored	Fresh	Stored
1965	6.9	10.0**	10.3	47.1**
1966	6.8	9.0**	6.4	23.1**

*Expressed as mg of gum/10 ml of juice.
**Differences between fresh and stored values significant at the 1% level.

nearly 8 times more gum was formed in chopped stalks during storage. Chopped cane increased gum content by about 50 percent during overnight storage. Egan reiterated his own earlier conclusions and those of other workers: "...Storage periods that seemed safe for whole stalks are quite unacceptable for chopper harvested cane, which must be crushed as rapidly as possibly" (484).

C. *Control of biodeterioration*

Efforts to measure the extent of biodeterioration and to control its progress at the field and factory have met with only partial success. Tilbury (1437) found that juice viscosity was a promising indicator of deterioration for routine quality control. Dextran content *per se* has also been suggested as a quality control parameter for cane arriving at the factory (1438, 1494). Irvine and Friloux (779) compared titratable acidity (TA) and gum content (GC) as indicators of juice quality. Gum content was found to be more sensitive and accurate than titratable acidity, although considerable variation was obtained relative to burning operations and freezing. Egan (484) similarly concluded that titratable acidity involved too much variation to be useful as a deterioration indicator.

Attempts to control deterioration by dipping stalks in formaldehyde were not successful (1438). Efforts to inhibit bacterial growth inside the stalk with alternating electromagnetic wave energy were also negative (1435). Tilbury (1439) explored the possibility of inhibiting bacterial growth by reducing water availability with molasses. *In vitro* tests had shown that the minimum molasses level inhibitory for *Leuconostoc* was 30° Brix. However, application of up to 60° Brix molasses to severed ends of infected stalks failed to restrict bacterial growth.

Egan (478) was not successful in preventing stalk infection by continual spraying of chopper harvester blades with bactericide. The outer edge of each stalk effectively removed the antiseptic. Treatment of the soil with bactericides was discounted for technical and economic reasons. Dipping stalks in bactericides was not effective. Partial control was obtained by fumigating chopped cane in the harvester bins with formaldehyde (483); however, this treatment was not economically feasible. Egan regarded speed as the principal answer to deterioration: ". . .The moral of the story is clear – if chopper harvesters are used, the cane must be crushed as quickly as possible." Tilbury (1438) and Vickers (1494) also point to minimal delay between cutting and grinding as the most practical means of deterioration control.

However, Tilbury has developed an enzyme approach to the polysaccharide problem which is highly encouraging. It involves the hydrolysis of dextran by incorporating the enzyme dextranase into bacteria-containing juice. Studies in Jamaica (1438) showed that dextranase removed an average of 72 percent of the dextrin present in milled juice. Variation among samples was explained in part by presence of both $1 \rightarrow 6$ and $1 \rightarrow 4$ α-glucosidic linkages, the enzyme apparently being specific for the $1 \rightarrow 6$ linkage. Much of the juice examined in Jamaica contained high dextran levels which in turn were positively correlated with high rainfall and excessive maturity. In Puerto Rico, where cultural and climatic conditions are somewhat similar to those of Jamaica, Tilbury obtained an average dextran hydrolysis of 94.6 percent with dextranase added to juice samples from three randomly-selected mills (1440).

The dextranase method appears to offer the best avenue for removing massive quantities of dextran already formed and hence of improving sugar recovery from juice heavily infected with *Leuconostoc.* This would not recover the sucrose already metabolized in the dextran-forming processes, nor would the dextranase reaction prevent continued growth and sugar utilization by the bacterial populations. One possible means of *Leuconostoc* control which does not appear to have been explored is the chemical control of cane and bacterial invertases in freshly-milled juice. It is reasonable to assume that bacterial growth is based upon a continued supply of fructose and glucose as carbon source, and that growth requires sucrose inversion, whether by cane or bacterial invertases. Control might therefore be achieved with an invertase inhibitor effective *in vitro* and absorbed by unicellular organisms. The metasilicate studies by workers in Puerto Rico offer some support for this premise (38, 57).

Chapter 16

Cell and Tissue Physiology

1. INTRODUCTION

Regardless of the tremendous advances in our knowledge of sugar manufacture, its movement, and its accumulation in the cane storage compartments, much less would be known about the growth and physiological behavior of storage parenchyma cells were it not for a new "botanical frontier" loosely described as *tissue culture*. Largely an end in itself during early microbial studies, the technique whereby an organism is grown on artificial media in glass vehicles has evolved into higher animal and plant tissue studies where each year new fundamental and practical applications become apparent. Within the new sphere of study the sugarcane plant has once more been blessed. But again the plant is favored less by its natural adaptability to tissue culture than by the hard work of a few dedicated scientists. Indeed, as herein recounted, the monocotyledonous group of which sugarcane is a member was long regarded as unsuitable for the morphogenesis studies presently holding the spotlight of tissue culture research.

What is meant by "tissue culture"? Partanen (1146) defines this term as "the maintenance and growth of plant cells *in vitro* under aseptic conditions". Regardless of its tissue origin the most characteristic cell type *in vitro* is very similar to the parenchyma cell of an intact plant. Growth of free cells in an agitated liquid medium is perhaps more correctly termed "cell culture" or "cell suspension culture". A larger aggregation of similar cells may be described correctly as a "tissue culture", but the term is still somewhat loose in that the tissue is a simple one rather than a complex composition of diversified cell types.

In addition to simple and complex tissues we find that organized systems of tissues are also grown *in vitro*; hence, such terms "organ culture", and "endosperm culture" appear frequently in the literature. Some types of tissue culture studies deal specifically with root, shoot, or leaf organs. Other studies dealing with morphogenesis begin with a single cell or isolate and proceed to simple tissue (callus), organs (roots, shoots, and leaves) and finally to complete plants or plantlets. No attempt will be made here even to summarize the various branches of plant research in the tissue culture category. Excellent books (1150, 1568, 1567) and review articles (1146, 1145, 1234, 1374) are available for this purpose.

As observed by Partanen (1146), "plant tissue culture was put into its proper perspective long before it was achieved". He notes that about 25 years were required to solve technological problems *after* the culture of plant tissues was demonstrated. Indeed, the transcendence of technological barriers was at times so involved that even professional plant scientists find it difficult to trace the development toward its original goals. The present chapter attempts to sketch some of the advances that led to plant tissue culture as we know it today – especially to the morphogenesis and "ploidy"-variant studies now possible in monocot-derived tissues.

Collectively, an enormous effort was made to discover appropriate media for *in vitro* growth of plant tissues. Even while various nutrient, hormone, and carbon-source combinations were being evaluated, many workers recognized that the attribute of cell *totipotency* – the capacity to initiate and develop such organized cell growth as constitutes a functional new plant – was being lost as a feature of culturing time. It was found that manipulation of the medium's composition was one means of inducing totipotency expression. It was further recognized that, in spite of the need for chemically-defined media, such compositions seldom supported growth quite so well as a medium supplemented with coconut milk or yeast extract. More effective "chemically-defined" media are still being sought.

Considerable attention is given herein to tissue culture advances achieved with virus-induced tumor tissues in tobacco, and subsequently to advances in monocot tissue culture. Much was learned, for example, about maize and rice tissue requirements before scientists could be certain that totipotency was possible in artificial growth media. We shall see that organized growth potential was eventually established in cultured sugarcane cells. The significance of this accomplishment is stressed, (a) in terms of new "ploidy" levels, (b) in terms of new genetic constitutions among new sugarcane plants, and (c) in terms of genetic reconstitution by purely vegetative means as opposed to conventional "crossing over" methods.

Throughout this book an international focus upon sugarcane has been retained, but it must be admitted that cane tissue culture as it is known today is a Hawaiian phenomenon. Thanks largely to L.G. Nickell's sympathy for fundamental research in general, and perhaps for tissue culture in particular, workers in Hawaii have made enormous strides in developing the tissue culture technique. In only 8 years sugarcane has become a major contributor to this "new frontier" of botanical knowledge. In a more mundane sense a fine measure of tissue culture applicability to agronomic, physiological, and biochemical problems in a complex agricultural plant has been taken in Hawaii. It is unlikely that a better example of potential industrial gain from purely basic research will be found in tropical agriculture.

Finally, it is well to add here a note of caution if only to counterbalance the almost excessive praise for tissue culture which has appeared in the literature. It is quite true that most students of tissue culture are impressed with its diverse potential as an instrument of research, but this potential very largely remains to be realized. Tissue culture is not an easy tool, and some of its desirable features are perhaps not so desirable upon closer examination. Muir *et al.* (1051), for example, depict the same morphological and physiological variability which attracts some workers as being so troublesome in analytical studies that the development of single cultured cells becomes a desirable alternative. In sugarcane, tissue culture research requires a greater investment of experience, trained personnel and specialized facilities than many, if not most, research stations can afford. Moreover, such very critical physiological concepts as growth and maturation control in the intact plant, still accomplished in the standing crop only by empirical means, can scarcely be approached by study of isolated cells, tissues, organs, or plantlets absolved from all the realities of the sugarcane field.

2. FUNDAMENTALS OF TISSUE CULTURE WITH VIRUS-INDUCED TUMORS

A. *Tissue culture development with isolated Rumex tumors*

Nutrition studies of cultured sugarcane cells were preceded by more than a decade of relevant research in other plant species. Much of this work centered around atypical growth in host plants afflicted by virus (191, 262, 1096, 1095, 1094).

In 1949 Burkholder and Nickell (262) described the *in vitro* culture of virus wound tumors of *Rumex acetosa*. The virus itself, *Aureogenus magnivena*, was established by Black (189, 191) about 6 years earlier in the roots of sorrel (*Rumex*). Suscept plants included 43 species in 20 families, and Black surmized that many others remained to be discovered. In 1946 (190) and 1947 (191) Black published on the successful isolation and growth in pure culture of the *Rumex* root tumors. After extensive subculture in chemically-defined media the tumors were still capable of transmitting the virus through tissue grafts to healthy plants.

Burkholder and Nickell originally obtained the tumor tissue from Black who had grown it on White's (1567) medium. New tissue cultures were grown on Ricker's (1233) modification of White's medium which was well suited to examining variable nitrogen sources and concentrations. Preliminary experiments showed that nitrogen and phosphorus levels employed by Ricker were less satisfactory for growing the virus tumor tissue. New experiments based on the triangle system were designed to produce a more favorable nutrient formula. This method bears a major obstacle in that when one ion is varied the remaining ions in the triangle are also varied. Eventually a suitable combination of nitrate, phosphate, and sulfate was obtained which produced rapid growth of light green tissue (indicating healthy tissue in this instance). Both nitrogen and phosphorus levels were notably higher than those used by other workers. Sucrose, agar, and various B vitamins were included in the standard medium. The pH was adjusted to about 5.2. In addition to producing rapid growth, stability was increased by relatively simple changes in the basal medium. At this time [1949] the induction of discrete plant organs from the otherwise disordered mass of cultured cells had not yet been accomplished.

During the following year Nickell (1095) published on the hormonal and colchicine responses of *Rumex* tumor tissue. In these studies 3-year-old stock cultures were maintained on the same high-nitrogen and high-phosphorus media developed by Burkholder and Nickell (262). In this instance the pH was adjusted to 4.5. Growth values were measured after 3 weeks incubation by dividing the final wet weights by the original wet weights. Respiration was also measured. For the latter experiments a Warburg manometric apparatus was employed in which chlorophyll-free tissues were incubated in darkness or near-darkness for 6 hours at 30 °C. Estimates of oxygen-uptake changes were made at 30-minute intervals.

A generally positive correlation was obtained between the growth effects and oxygen-uptake effects of hormones. With the exception of TIBA (2,4,5-triiodobenzoic acid), whose action was growth-inhibitory, each compound stimulated growth and respiration below the 1.0-ppm level and inhibited at higher concentrations. TIBA also stimulated respiration. The relationship between growth and respiration was unique at the time for culture tissue, and very few papers had been published on the subject with conventional tissue sources. The relationship was also unusual in the sense that growth measurements referred to a 3-week interval by contrast to the 3-hour interval for respiration. Moreover, tissue samples were situated in a liquid medium during respiration measurements and in a solid medium for the growth studies. For each compound tested the uptake of oxygen was increased far more than was growth. Using the growth response to IAA (indole-3-acetic acid) as an arbitrary scale of 100 percent, the maximum stimulation attained was 20 to 30 percent. In general, inhibition of oxygen uptake required higher chemical levels in respiration experiments than in growth experiments, the latter having more time to accumulate the test compound.

Another early study by Nickell with *Rumex* virus tumor tissue dealt with the substitution of aspartic acid for the usual carbon and nitrogen sources (1096). To a limited extent aspartic acid served in place of sucrose as a carbon source, but it was very nearly as effective as nitrate in supplying nitrogen. Because the use of aspartic acid resulted in much greener tissue than was produced with the usual nitrogen sources, it was suggested that the organic acid promotes chlorophyll formation in addition to acting as a supply of carbon and nitrogen. Nickell further concluded that aspartic acid is assimilated intact by the tumor cells.

The possibility that aspartic acid may perform other roles in addition to carbon and nitrogen supply was strongly implied by its stimulatory effect on tissue growth even when large amounts of sucrose and nitrate were present. This supports similar interpretations drawn by White and Munns (1566) who found that the growth of yeast cells was much greater when hexoses were replaced with aspartic acid in the culture medium.

B. *Analysis of variable factors in tumor tissue culture*

In 1954 Nickell (1101) summarized the work with *Rumex* tumor tissue induced by the virus *Aureogenus magnivena* Black. Because in a large measure the conditions for tissue growth in crop plants such as sugarcane must be similarly defined, this work deserves analysis here in some detail. Nickell described the tumor growth as "...numerous zones of proliferating cells located generally at the periphery of the nodular masses. Differentiation of vascular elements occurs eventually in each of these zones, but there is *ordinarily* a definite lack of cell and tissue organization of any normal type." The fact that on occasion the tumor tissue would form organs such as leaves and roots was suggestive of differentiation potential controlled both by the medium's composition and by the culture's environment. Among the regulatory factors involved Nickell made note of the following:

(1) *Light*. Growth of sorrel tissue in darkness rather than light appeared to increase the likelihood of organ induction. On 12 occasions fewer than 1000 subcultures produced roots in darkness, whereas some 70 000 subcultures produced roots only 4 times when grown in light.

(2) *Inorganic nutrition*. An abnormally high amount of phosphorus was needed in the growth medium (0.008 M), some 10 to 100 times greater for the tumor tissue than was generally used in culture media at that time. The nitrogen requirement was also high with nitrate being the most suitable nitrogen source (1094). Sulfur, as sulfate, sulfite, or cysteine was needed only in trace amounts. Nickell (1101) speculated that the excessive phosphorus and nitrogen requirements were in some way related to nucleic acid synthesis, or that more phosphorus and nitrogen entered storage in tumor tissue than is ordinarily the case with normal tissue metabolism.

(3) *Carbon source*. Sucrose served as the most convenient carbon source, although glucose, fructose, and raffinose were also suitable. Contrary to reports by other workers, soluble starch also acted as a good carbon source. Studies by Brakke and Nickell (221, 222) dealt specifically with α-amylase secretion by the *Rumex* virus tumors.

(4) *Basal medium*. The most suitable basal medium for culturing virus tumor tissue was determined on the basis of growth data from many types of experiments. The medium ultimately selected was comprised of the usual macro- and micronutrients plus sucrose and agar. Thiamine, pyridoxine, and niacinamide were also included. Although the vitamins B_1, B_6, and nicotinamide were long assumed to be needed (1101), subsequent work (1097) showed that vitamin B_1 alone was required. After the essentiality of vitamin B_1 was established, Nickell found that addition of a suitable antibiotic to the basal medium would prevent the death of tissues which otherwise occurs in the absence of vitamin B_1 (following the second transfer). Effective antibiotics included penicillin, terramycin, streptomycin, thiolutin, and bacitracin (1098).

(5) *Organic acids as carbon and nitrogen sources*. Many organic acids were tested as carbon sources but only aspartic acid was utilized appreciably by the growing tumor cells. As sources of nitrogen, the amino acids arginine, aspartic acid, glycine, proline, and threonine showed some promise, but only aspartic acid approached nitrate in its effectiveness as the nitrogen source (1094). That aspartic acid may perform yet another function was shown by its stimulatory effect on cell growth even when sucrose and nitrate were already present in abundance (1096). Nickell (1101) sug-

gested a rate-limiting role of aspartic acid in protein synthesis.

(6) *Plant hormones and colchicine.* Colchicine plus several plant hormones stimulated respiration in tumor cultures. IAA was more effective than NOA (β-naphthoxyacetic acid), 2,4-D, TIBA, and colchicine. With the exception of TIBA, which inhibited growth at levels higher than 0.0001 ppm, each of the compounds stimulated growth at concentrations ranging from 0.001 to 0.1 ppm. It is interesting that colchicine, famous for its ability to induce polyploidy, closely paralleled the plant hormones in its effects on respiration and growth.

The growth inhibitor maleic hydrazide, soon to receive attention as a sugarcane growth repressor and hence as a ripening agent, was also found to inhibit tumor growth. At less than 1.0 ppm maleic hydrazide restricted tumor growth by nearly 50 percent (1099). The chemical's effect was that of an anti-auxin, similar to TIBA, and no formative effects or stimulatory action at lower levels were detected.

(7) *Nucleic acids and related compounds.* A number of additive tests were performed with nucleic acids, purines, and pyrimidines in relation to growth of the cultured tumors. This work was motivated by the tissue's high phosphorus requirement and the attending theory that this requirement reflected the presence of a virus in the tissue. Of the two nucleic acid types, RNA was growth-stimulatory up to 0.8 mg/ml while DNA was slightly inhibitory at all levels (1101). A hypothesis was advanced, and partially substantiated, which held that a constituent common to both RNA and DNA was inhibitory, but that uracil overcomes the inhibition while thymine does not. A second hypothesis, suggesting that the different effects of RNA and DNA relate to the differing pyrimidine base (uracil in RNA and thymine in DNA), was discarded when uracil was found to be growth-stimulatory while thymine had little effect. The prior hypothesis gained support when adenine was shown to inhibit tumor growth; however, initial efforts to overcome adenine inhibition with uracil were inconclusive.

Purines of the hypoxanthine–xanthine–uric acid series all stimulated tumor tissue growth at low concentrations (1101). The growth effect was apparently related to the number of keto groups present. As the purine concentration was increased, uric acid (having three keto groups) was the first to become inhibitory, while hypoxanthine (one keto group) was the last to inhibit.

(8) *Temperature, light, and pH requirements.* Variable-temperature experiments established the optimum temperature for virus tumor growth at about 23 °C (1101). An additional 2 °C led to severe growth decline and death of the tissues. Tissue growth was arrested below 20 °C, but the effect was neither lethal nor permanent. Tissues held as low as 5 °C for more than 3 months produced normal growth upon their return to 23 °C (1094). Tumor tissues cultured in darkness grew equally well as in the light. Absence of chlorophyll owing to the darkness had no effect on tissue growth, and the dark treatment appeared to favor tissue differentiation. An extremely broad pH range was found to be suitable, *i.e.*, between pH 3.5 and 6.2. The growth response showed individual peaks at pH 4.2, 5.2, and 6.2 (1094).

3. MORPHOGENESIS IN MONOCOT TISSUE CULTURES

A. *General background*

There is probably no greater challenge to plant scientists than the unraveling of tissue differentiation mechanisms and the control of these mechanisms in the production of new plants for scientific and agricultural purposes. Toward this end cell and tissue culture techniques have become important new avenues of approach in sugarcane (714, 1110, 1106, 715) and various other plant species (1225, 1102, 1146, 190).

An initial prerequisite for meaningful morphogenetic research *in vitro* was the demonstration that totipotency does in fact exist at the cell level. For many years scientists questioned whether freely-suspended cells must always grow as an uncontrolled mass, or whether such cells retain the potential for organized growth leading to roots, shoots, and complete plants. A series of papers published by Steward and his colleagues (1363–1365) in 1958 clearly established the totipotency of carrot cells. The phenomenon has since been reported in cells of tobacco (1479), sugarcane (714), and other species. In sugarcane tissue cultures the development of "ploidy" variants (715)[1] and completely new plants (714) was recently accomplished by Heinz and his co-workers.

Steward *et al.* (1363) initially studied the growth and multiplication of dicotyledonous cells in multicellular but unorganized masses. A second report (1364) dealt with carrot cell cultures grown on a basal medium supplemented with coconut milk, 2,4-D, and kinetin. It was shown that the inability of primary explants to differentiate roots gradually disappeared after continual subculturing of minute cell aggregates. The appearance of root initials thus coincided with the loss of an unknown repression factor, and with the growth of cell aggregates to such size that the inner cells behaved differently than the outer cells. Having initiated roots in liquid suspension, shoot formation initiated upon transfer of the cultures to a semisolid agar medium. "Plantlets", complete with xylem, cambium, and secondary-thickening tissues, developed in orderly stages. A third report (1365) treated at length the behavior of cells relieved of physical and physiological growth restraints, *i.e.*, in suspension culture, and emphasized that "...orderly development begins when cells become organized into nodules or growth centers". In addition to the constraint by surrounding cells, organized growth was highly sensitive to the medium's nutrient composition. In the instance of carrot tissues coconut milk was required for the growing cells to "...recapitulate events which normally stem from the development of the fertilized egg".

The establishment of totipotency in plant cells was followed by numerous studies of plant tissue morphogenesis *in vitro*. For nearly a decade this work focused on

[1] Heinz, D.J. and Mee, G.W.P., 1970. Colchicine-induced polyploids from cell suspension cultures of sugarcane, *Crop Sci.* 10: 696–699.

dicotyledonous plants. Success with monocots hinged upon new media development and isolation techniques which permitted the induction of callus tissue on one medium followed by culture transfer to another medium where differentiation sometimes occurred. Survival of the newly-differentiated plants depended on further transfers to a growth medium, or, in the instance of sugarcane (714), to water culture and transplantation in vermiculite or soil.

One of the few reports of plant development from cultured monocot tissue was published by Wilmar and Hellendoorn (1577) in 1968. Callus tissues, derived from sterile seedlings of *Asparagus officinalis* L., were grown on a modified Linsmaier–Skoog medium with 2,4-D and kinetin added. Growth experiments on solid agar medium showed that the callus ceased to proliferate when 2,4-D and kinetin were omitted, but that numerous shoots and a few roots were then initiated. Each of the growth substances was repressive against organ formation without affecting callus growth. Later experiments performed with cell suspensions showed that callus continued to grow for only a limited time with 2,4-D and kinetin present, and that growth subsequently declined and the cells tended to aggregate. Aggregation was paralleled by the formation of small nodules resembling young "embryoids". Withholding 2,4-D led to reduced cell size, increased aggregation to the point of "clumping", and the formation of true embryoids. Optimal embryoid growth was achieved in the absence of 2,4-D. Kinetin was benefical for embryo generation and subsequent growth but only at low concentrations in the order of 0.1 mg/ml.

The asparagus embryoids developed in a pattern identical to embryos formed *in vivo*, with certain morphological differences possibly relating to the medium's osmotic concentration. Young embryoids achieved geotropic orientation and developed into normal plantlets after being transferred to solid media. When the embryoids were left for prolonged periods in suspension culture, and when plantlets were left on a solid medium, the tendency was toward "dedifferentiation" with the apex becoming abnormal. This was prevented in plantlets by transfer to a simpler medium after growing about 1 week on the solid agar. Successful plant development was thus found to require a series of precisely-timed transfers to a succession of media, at the end of which the young plants could be established in vermiculite or soil. Wilmar and Hellendoorn wrote: ". . .With this succession of media we were able to grow completely healthy normal plants from undifferentiated callus cells. Among these plantlets were normal diploids as well as some tetraploids." These findings were verified with tissue of the wild carrot, *Daucus carota*. The authors concluded that differentiation in monocots, as in dicots, is a natural potential of cells which cannot find expression in callus growth.

B. *Morphogenesis in maize*

The *in vitro* examination of morphogenesis in tropical grasses began with the studies of maize endosperm cultures by La Rue during the late 1940's (896, 897). In

1949 he was the first to isolate maize endosperm as a continuous culture. In a note published 2 years earlier, La Rue (896) described infrequent regenerative tissue originating from corn endosperm. Neither very young nor moderately-aged endosperms would grow, but intermediate tissues survived for a time on various media. Exposed surfaces produced thin layers of callus tissue having many "folds, knobs and bud-like protrusions". Only about one growth in a thousand developed roots and only a single specimen formed miniature leaves. At that time, describing visible annular and reticulate elements, La Rue noted: "This is the first instance of the development in culture of an embryo-like structure from the endosperm of an angiosperm." He further observed that, while the corn tissue's regeneration resembled the gymnosperms *Zamia* and *Cycas*, the corn endosperm is neither gametophytic nor sporophytic, but a triploid tissue[2] which produced in this instance a sporophyte-like structure.

La Rue continued his work with maize endosperm and reported in 1949 the tissue's successful subculture for more than one year (897). In addition to White's (1567) medium the tobacco and sunflower media of Riker and Gutsche (1233), endosperm tissue was maintained with some success on "extracts of yeast, prune, grape, *Radicula aquatica*, green corn grains, and with cow's milk". In each instance sucrose was the lone source of carbon. Endosperms were cultured from 23 maize strains. The normal chromosome number, 30, was observed as were numbers of 20 and 10.

Maize endosperm morphogenesis was further examined by Straus and La Rue (1373) and by Straus (1374). Oddly enough, La Rue's (896) observation of vascular tissue in differentiated roots and shoots received little or no verification for a number of years. Maize endosperm generally remained homogenous *in vitro*. What differentiation did occur was regarded as an infrequent spontaneous property rather than a controllable potential residing within the cell. In 1954 Straus and La Rue (1373) summarized extensive studies in which the conditions required for optimal growth were defined. This work was based on the belief that organ differentiation is due to changes in the tissue environment rather than to "a purely fortuitous phenomenon". This thesis has proven to be valid. Much of the subsequent progress toward organized growth control *in vitro* has been based on control of the supporting medium's composition.

Among the features of endosperm growth discussed by Straus and La Rue, the following observations are instructive for growth studies with cultured monocot tissues: (a) A lag phase of about 8 days passed before tissue growth entered an exponential phase. Maximum growth was achieved in about 20 days. (b) Neither the rate nor uniformity of growth was very satisfactory on White's medium alone or on White's medium supplemented with tomato juice. This was largely overcome by adding yeast extract to the basal medium. Filtered yeast preparation was more effective than

---

[2] Maize endosperm is normally a triploid tissue containing two sets of maternal and one set of paternal chromosomes (1374).

the autoclaved material. (c) Certain carbon sources, *i.e.*, lactose, galactose, arabinose, rhamnose, and glycerol, permitted no growth at all. Starch was surprisingly effective in this capacity. Similar results had recently been reported for virus tumor tissue (1094) and pawpaw endosperm (885)[3]. Sucrose, fructose, and glucose proved to be excellent carbon sources for cultured maize endosperm. (d) Excessively high sugar concentrations (about 12 percent sucrose) appeared to limit growth, possibly by virtue of increased osmotic concentration or abnormal water uptake. Below about 2.0 percent the sugar level may again become limiting for growth. (e) Optimum growth temperature lay in a rather narrow range while pH was found to be suitable over a broad range. The most favorable temperature was about 25 °C; an increase to 28 °C lowered the growth rate by about 50 percent, and lowering temperature to 20 °C reduced growth to less than a quarter of that at 25 °C. The pH range was not critical for endosperm cultures. Good growth was obtained between pH 4.5 and 8.2; optimum growth required a pH value of 6.1 to 7.0. Most media fall within this range (the pH of yeast extract is about 5.0).

Straus and La Rue (1373) also examined the factors responsible for growth promotion. Their experiments suggested that the stimulatory factor or factors may be replaced in part by high levels of casein hydrolysate or amino acid mixture. Endosperm growth seldom exceeded a third of that produced on the basal medium plus yeast extract. Thus it was apparent at an early date that yeast extract contained undefined but essential "metabolites or nutrilites other than amino acids. . .". This difficulty in obtaining a completely satisfactory artificial medium was later experienced by Nickell and Maretzki (1113) working with sugarcane cells. In the latter instance sufficient growth was attained (about 60 percent of the usual growth on basal medium plus yeast extract) so that various physiological and metabolic studies could proceed on the support of chemically-defined media. Acceptance of a less-than-optimum medium is based on the knowledge that the "limiting" unknown factors are not limiting in the strictest sense, *i.e.*, that they must be added at a certain level or no growth of any sort will be possible. Rather, the essential substances are presumably synthesized in the tissue at slow but nonetheless adequate rates.

In explaining an observed preference by maize endosperm for sucrose rather than glucose or fructose, Straus and La Rue considered such factors as relative tissue penetration rates, biosynthesis of sugars within the cell from infiltrated sugar substrates, phosphorylation reactions at the cell surface, and correct enzyme complements for sustaining these reactions at the required rates. Very little work had been performed with ^{14}C-labeled sugars at that time [1954], yet the authors' thinking has been vindicated by events.

---

[3]Years later workers observed starch utilization by sugarcane cell suspensions. In this case the phenomenon was traced to secretion of an α-amylase from the cultured cells to the external medium (*cf.* this chapter, pp. 628, 629).

During the 1960's a "sugar accumulation cycle" for sugarcane parenchyma cells was developed in which the cellular membranes are viewed as highly selective for the passage of different sugars (*cf.* Chapter 9, pp. 348–356). Consequently, sucrose is not taken up so readily as fructose or glucose, inversion occurs in an outer space prior to entry into a discrete metabolic compartment, and reassembly of sucrose takes place in an inner space. To accomplish all this, various types of invertases and other enzymes relative to hexose phosphorylation and interconversion are precisely situated in the cell membranes and compartments. At the present time this aspect of carbohydrate movement into cultured parenchyma cells has not been assigned much importance; however, future studies may need to take these processes into consideration, particularly if the efficiency of carbon supply becomes a growth-limiting factor under some future set of conditions. In addition, the process of carbohydrate storage and remobilization must eventually contribute to any final explanation of differential growth behavior among ploidy variants at the cell level, or among newly-formed plants at the organ-differentiation level.

C. *Morphological changes in cultured monocot cells*

In 1954 Straus (1374) published a second paper relating to maize tissue growth *in vitro*.This report dealt specifically with the ontogeny, morphology, and cytology of the endosperm. Much of the information unveiled at that time has helped to lay the foundations of present morphogenesis research in higher plants, not the least of which are the *Saccharum* species monocots. In essence, Straus mapped the tissue transition from normal endosperm to the derived tissue culture. A cytological approach was taken. New tissue was found to arise largely from the outermost layer of normal endosperm cells and the cell layer immediately beneath the marginal layer. On rare occasions new tissue was found to originate deep within the cultured endosperm.

It was shown that whereas relatively immature endosperm tissue is required for explantation, the tissue may proceed to develop cells of a type characteristic of mature endosperm. This appeared to be a transitory process – it was not again encountered after the transition from normal endosperm tissue to culture tissue was complete. In effect, this represented a loss of totipotency, *i.e.*, a loss of the cell's capacity to differentiate new tissues and organs under *in vitro* conditions. A decade later, Heinz *et al.* (714) showed that sugarcane cells retain a high degree of totipotency *in vitro*, but a rather exacting manipulation of the cultural environment is required for this potential to find expression.

D. *Cytological and chromosomal aberrations*

An important finding by Straus (1374) was the appearance of atypical chromosome complements in the maize cells soon after being established on a cultural medium. The occurrence of polyploid, hypoploid, or aneuploid numbers became almost as common as the normal count ($3n = 30$). As many as 105 chromosomes were counted with accuracy. A number of chromosomes appeared to be double, possibly representing nonseparated sister chromatids. The general appearance was similar to the c-mitosis described by Levan (934) in 1938, an effect commonly induced by colchicine in mitosis stages subsequent to metaphase. Some cell division figures showing 41 and 48 chromosomes were found incident to irregular polyploidy and aneuploidy. Hypoploid figures were less common in the endosperm-derived tissue than polyploids.

Additional changes found in the cultured cells included cell-plate initiation in the telophase, the appearance of "giant cells", and partial evidence of polyteny occurrence. It was thought that two or more divisions sometimes occurred in the same cell, a premise which could not be confirmed by chromosome counts but one tacitly substantiated by the existence of exceptionally large chromosomes. Polyteny was also offered as an explanation for the giant cells. There was no evidence of true endomitosis in the maize tissue cultures.

Chromosomal aberrations were observed by Straus in about 30 percent of the anaphase figures. Both sectioned and smeared preparations revealed bridges. No specific reference was made to fragments but the author mentioned frequent observations of "lagging chromosomes". Some of the bridges failed to break, resulting in atypical ("dumbbell-shaped") nuclei upon formation of the nuclear membrane. Other atypical nuclei having numerous lobes were found in aging culture cells.

Straus suggested that the frequent occurrence of bridges, and indeed of polyploidy, aneuploidy, and hypoploidy, may be traced to the supporting medium. Reference was made to the abundance of nucleic acids present in the yeast extract and to the probability that these may induce both increases and decreases in chromosome number. The condition of "stickiness" accompanying bridge formation has been associated with nucleic acid content (842). Earlier work by McClintock (999) and by Clark and Copeland (329) associated bridge formation with the condition of the original endosperm. Tissues derived from variegated or mosaic maize endosperms frequently produced aberrations of this type. It is interesting to note that Straus retained an open mind with respect to the cause of ploidy and atypical chromosome configurations. He suggested that, although yeast extract may seem a likely source of a change-inducing factor, such changes might also be the normal course of events in cell and tissue culture. This view is strengthened by the fact that varying ploidy levels have been obtained in sugarcane cells supported entirely by chemically-defined media (1113).

E. *Hypothetical means of ploidy change*

Straus (1374) attached major importance to the fact that changes in chromosome number were a frequent occurrence in cultured maize cells. Possible explanations for the phenomenon were reviewed. The changing of chromosome complements *in vitro* is an enormously important concept for sugarcane and other crop plants wherein genetic exchange by convential breeding methods is restricted inherently, or by technical problems such as the non-synchronization of flowering among wild and cultivated species. Straus considered first the possibility that specific substances induce atypical ploidy levels. He cited the roles of cell "organizers" or "disorganizers" as depicted by Spemann (1351) in 1938, as well as frequent references to unknown factors contained in the added yeast extract. As early as 1936 La Rue (895) described the importance of age in regenerative growth induction in embryos. The non-specificity of inductive substances was also noted at that time. Straus cites a number of workers who obtained colchicine-like effects with organic and inorganic substances chemically unrelated to the alkaloid. He concluded: "It would appear that there is no specific mechanism whereby spindle formation and subsequent chromosome separation are effected, judging from the diverse substances capable of disturbing these activities."

A number of authors are cited (1374) who approached the question of induced polyploidy from the standpoint of polysomaticism or endoreduplication, in which case the chromosomes would be duplicated within the "energic" nucleus. Polyteny, wherein the chromosomal strand numbers are increased within the energic nucleus, was also submitted as a possible cause of polyploidy. In these circumstances it is frequently difficult or impossible to count the chromosomes, and such parameters as relative nuclei volumes or relative numbers of "heterochromatin bodies" may be measured instead. In general, polysomaty and endoreduplication are most common in mature plant tissues [early literature reviewed by D'Amato (403)].

F. *"Loss" of totipotency*

In discussing his work with the maize endosperm-derived tissues, Straus (1374) discounted any appreciable chance that totipotency might be expressed under the cultural conditions employed: "The few isolated examples of regeneration of complete plantlets [reported by La Rue (896)] occurred in endosperms which had been in culture for only a short time. Since then the tissue has passed through approximately 95 transfers and has produced an estimated 15 kg of tissue. Not a single example of complex differentiation was observed during that period. Unfortunately, only conjectures may be raised in explanation for the lack of regenerative powers." On the other hand, Straus did not abandon the possibility that totipotentiality was still retained by the cultured cells. With reference to the age factor Straus felt that totipotency might be expressed if tissue could be isolated at a more favorable period: "If it were possible to get endosperm to grow in culture some time before 12 days postpollination, it might be possible to escape the effects on the postulated (age) influences, and then the tissue might be able to demonstrate its inherent totipotency."

Loss of totipotency has been observed in tissue cultures isolated from numerous plant species (1061, 1445, 565, 1479, 819). Murashige and Nakano (1061), for example described growth decline and loss of organ-forming capability in continuously-cultured tobacco callus. Shoot formation was reduced to nil between 1.5 and 3 years after explanting, whereas root-forming ability was lost completely within about 18 months. Callus itself lost most of its initial growth rate. Growth and differentiation capacity varied with the individual pith cell originally isolated. Both totipotent and non-totipotent cell lines were obtained. Repeated subculturing invariably produced a depressed morphogenetic capacity which proved to be irreversible. Totipotent lines were characteristically unstable. Murashige and Nakano explained the loss of totipotency in terms of somatic mutations resulting in senescene: "It is suggested that an accumulation of somatic mutations, *i.e.*, genetic alterations resulting in reductions in the morphogenetic potential of cells, is a basis underlying senescence." Selection during the progressive subculture of cells was viewed as favoring those cells having growth and reproduction requirements most in harmony with the cultural environment.

Norstog (1123) published in 1956 the results of endosperm studies in *Lolium perenne* L. (English rye grass) grown on several cultural media. Over an interval of 2.5 years there was no evidence of tissue differentiation or organization in the cultured tissue. However, microscopic examination showed that some differentiation of starch-storage cells had taken place, and chromosomal aberrations were observed in about half of the anaphase figures.

Yatazawa *et al.* (1600) reported somewhat similar results with cultured tissues from *Oryza sativa* L. (rice). Callus tissues induced on rice seedling roots were grown more than 2 years on a modified Heller medium with yeast extract and 2,4-D added. No sign of organ formation was detected, although some tissue differentiation was observed at the histological level.

4. NUTRITIONAL AND METABOLIC ASPECTS OF SUGARCANE CELL CULTURE

A. *General*

With the rapid development of plant cell and tissue culture technology it was inevitable that this concept should be adopted in approaching various physiological, biochemical, and genetic problems in crop plants. The special emphasis received by sugarcane is explained in part by the plant's refusal to yield fast and final answers to its physiological problems during decades of conventional research. This emphasis is further explained by the fact that L.G. Nickell, having become well versed in tissue culture theory and technology, applied this background to a series of traditional sugarcane problems having need of a new basic approach.

In 1964 Nickell (1106) reported the initial isolation of sugarcane cells and tissues from pith parenchyma. Over a 2-year period, successful isolations were made from 22 varieties and it was shown that these cultures could be maintained almost indefinitely. Nickell's first objectives were to determine: (a) Whether sugarcane clones could be isolated and established; (b) whether sugarcane presented special technical difficulties to be overcome; (c) the optimum cultural conditions for growing the tissue isolates; and (d) whether physiological and morphological characteristics of the isolates differed among varieties. In 1965, at the 12th Congress, I.S.S.C.T., Nickell (1110) listed 12 major areas of fundamental sugarcane research in which organ, tissue, and cell culture had already shown promise as useful tools. In 1968 Nickell and Maretzki (1114) listed five specific areas in which tissue and cell culture had assumed particular importance for sugarcane scientists:

(1) As a general tool for approaching sugarcane nutritional and chemical responses.
(2) For specific study of sugar metabolism and storage.
(3) For specific study of amino acid metabolism.
(4) For the study of photosynthesis.
(5) As a tool for performing chemical transformations of diploid cells.

B. *Development of a suitable medium*

The original sugarcane isolates had been prepared with a modification of White's (1567) nutrient medium to which coconut milk and 2,4-D were added (1106). Coconut milk was widely used with monocots to provide unknown growth factors. It was soon recognized, however, that sugarcane isolates gave a better performance on a medium supplemented with yeast extract. Efforts continued toward development of more suitable media for specific purposes. The striking importance of arginine at both the tissue and cellular levels (1110, 975) prompted the search for a chemically-defined medium with which the full potential of tissue culture technology could be brought to bear in biochemical research. Nickell and Maretzki (1113) largely succeeded in developing such a medium by 1968.

Although the induction and isolation of callus tissues in dicotyledonous plants had become common by the late 1960's, relatively little progress had been made with monocots. Moreover, the culture of monocot tissue on chemically-defined media met with little success prior to the work by Nickell and Maretzki (1113). According to these authors only a single relevant report had appeared, dealing with rice callus tissue grown on a solid synthetic medium (1590), and studies of monocot cell suspension cultures were essentially confined to corn endosperm grown on a modified Straus medium (604). During this period most cell suspension cultures were grown on "complex nutrients", that is, with media additives such as coconut milk, yeast extract, or malt extract. Since the contents of the latter were not precisely known their presence imposed major restrictions on the interpretation of subsequent metabolic and biochemical data.

Nickell and Maretzki developed their medium in a stepwise manner proceeding with individually-prepared stocks of the component parts. They were combined in the desired amounts just prior to autoclaving. These included: White's inorganic salts, mixed vitamins, mixed amino acids, single amino acids, and labile components (sterilized by vacuum filtration through sintered-glass filters). The test culture, obtained from variety *H. 50-7209*, was isolated from parenchyma tissue of internode No. 6. The callus culture was maintained on a prior medium with subcultures being prepared at monthly intervals.

The earliest experiments aimed at developing a new medium included direct comparisons of combined yeast and malt extracts with coconut water. These were based on the knowledge that coconut water was somewhat inferior to yeast extract in supporting tissue growth (1226). A later experiment showed that only yeast extract supported growth; malt extract failed to do so. The inclusion or deletion of malt extract had no effect on the growth-supporting activity of yeast extract. Nickell and Maretzki did note, however, that malt extract contained very little total nitrogen, and that only 7 percent of the total nitrogen existed in amino form.

This information, taken together with the newly-recognized importance of arginine, prompted further experiments evaluating the performance of amino acids as media constituents. Toward this end a mixture of amino acids (M-1) was at first substituted for the yeast extract; later experiments tested individual amino acids. In addition, the original vitamin mixture (B_1, B_6, and nicotinamide) was replaced by a five-vitamin mixture which included biotin and riboflavin for the first time. Initial experiments with the now-defined medium showed that it supported some growth but considerably less than that obtained with yeast extract. Nickell and Maretzki felt that the new medium still lacked an essential component other than amino acids and vitamins. Other explanations included improper levels or balance of the amino acids, and inhibitor–activator relationships among the amino acids. Rossini[4] found that leaf parenchyma tissue of *Calystegia sepium* L., cultured on a chemically-defined medium, produced maximum growth in the presence of auxin and cytokinin additives.

A new amino acid mixture (M-2) was prepared by adjusting levels of individual acids and by addition or removal of others from the M-1 mixture. In subsequent "single-omission" experiments, each of the 14 amino acids given in M-1 was removed one at a time. It soon became apparent that removal of lysine, phenylalanine, or valine produced no effect whatever on culture growth. However, the removal of arginine, aspartic acid, and glutamic acid produced very poor growth responses (Fig. 16-1). Total protein (precipitated with trichloroacetic acid from aqueous extracts of dried cells) was found to be very low where histidine, tyrosine, arginine, and the acids aspartic and glutamic had been removed from the media. Arginine appeared to be the

---

[4] Rossini, L., 1969. Histophysiologie végétale. Une nouvelle méthode de culture *in vitro* de cellules parenchymateuses séparées des feuilles de *Calystegia sepium* L., *C. R. Acad. Sci. (Paris)* 268: 683–685.

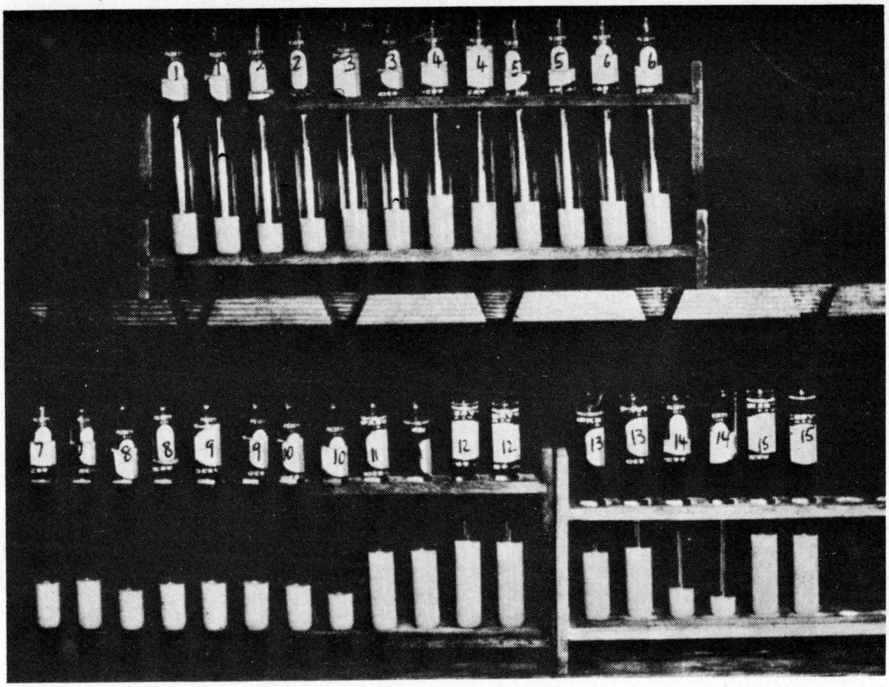

Fig. 16-1. Response of sugarcane cell suspension cultures to the removal of individual amino acids from the growth medium. Demonstrated by settled cells in duplicate cultures. [After Nickell and Maretzki (1113).] Reproduced by permission of *Physiologia Plantarum*.

most critical factor relative both to growth and protein content of the cells. In general, protein content was also low in cells grown without isoleucine or cysteine. In the absence of threonine more protein was produced than in control cells.

Nickell and Maretzki continued with numerous amino acid experiments in which the individual acids were added to a basal medium adequate in all other constituents known to be essential. These experiments always included a "negative control", *i.e.*, basal medium without amino acids, and a "positive control" or basal medium plus a complete amino acid mixture (M-2). Cultural conditions were maintained as in earlier studies. Table 16-1 summarizes the results of nine or more experiments in this series. From this information the authors concluded that four amino acids – leucine, lysine, tryptophan, and valine – were not needed, and hence a new mixture (M-3) was adopted for future cell-suspension studies. With M-3 added to the basal synthetic medium, Nickell and Maretzki obtained growth at a level around 60 percent of that obtained with White's basal medium plus yeast extract and arginine. The reader should note, however, that these workers now possessed exact information as to their medium's composition and could proceed accordingly with nutritional and metabolic studies.

TABLE 16-1

GROWTH OF SUGARCANE CELL SUSPENSION CULTURES AS A FUNCTION OF SPECIFIC AMINO ACID ADDITIVES

[After Nickel and Maretzki (1113).] Reproduced by permission of *Physiologia Plantarum.*

Normal growth on the basal medium without added amino acids was assigned the value 100. All additive growth responses were computed as percentages of this value.

Amino acid additive	Growth (as % of 100)	Amino acid additive	Growth (as % of 100)
Control (basal medium only)	100	Histidine	43
Complete (mixture M-2)	201	Isoleucine	65
Complete minus arginine	107	Leucine	28
Arginine	116	Lysine	39
Alanine	120	Methionine	82
α-Aminobutyric acid	77	Phenylalanine	61
Asparagine	155	Proline	94
Aspartic acid	172	Serine	100
Cysteine	89	Threonine	63
Cystine	84	Tryptophan	39
Glutamic acid	187	Tyrosine	85
Glutamine	75	Valine	30
Glycine	117		

Seperate investigations to determine the substance or substances in yeast extract which accounted for the additional growth over that produced with a defined medium remained inconclusive (1113). A number of compounds having known growth-stimulatory effects on intact plants, cultured tissues, and cultured cells gave negative results when tested on sugarcane cell suspensions (variety *H. 50-7209*). These compounds included adenine (5.0 to 10.0 mg/l), gibberellic acid (0.01 to 10.0 mg/l), kinetin (0.01 to 10.0 mg/l), combinations of kinetin and gibberellic acid, *myo*-inositol (1.0 to 100 mg/l), and D-sorbitol (1.0 to 100 mg/l).

C. *Carbohydrate sources; starch*

In 1969 Nickell and Maretzki (1114) reported that glucose, fructose, and sucrose each serves as an excellent source of carbon for sugarcane tissue cultures (Table 16-2). Galactose was quite suitable although somewhat less effective. The fact that starch also acts as an excellent carbon source is not generally typical of tissue cultures (563, 564), but an explanation for this is found in the tissue's secretion of a non-inducible amylase (1114), possibly identical to an α-amylase discovered by Brakke and Nickell (221) in *Rumex*[5]. For this reason cultured sugarcane cells can make equally good use of starch.

[5] An α-amylase secreted by sugarcane cell suspension cultures was described in 1971 [Maretzki, A., Dela Cruz, A. and Nickell, L.G., 1971. Extracellular hydrolysis of starch in sugarcane cell suspensions, *Plant Physiol.* 48: 521–525]. The enzyme appeared when starch was substituted for sucrose as the carbon source, and secretion was enhanced by supplied gibberellic acid.

TABLE 16-2

RELATIVE PROFICIENCY OF DIFFERENT CARBOHYDRATES IN SUPPORTING THE GROWTH OF SUGARCANE CELL SUSPENSION CULTURES

Variety *H. 50-7209.* [After Nickell and Maretzki (1114).] Reprinted by permission of *Academia*, Publishing House of the Czechoslovac Academy of Sciences, Prague.

Carbon source	Growth as dry cell weights (mg)	Growth as % of growth on sucrose
Sucrose	203	100
Glucose	179	88
Fructose	167	82
Mannitol	42	21
Sorbitol	52	25
Mannose	46	22
Sorbose	19	9
Galactose	116	57
Xylose	11	5
Starch	191	94

Since the cells continually secrete this enzyme, it has been suggested that starch may be utilized for growth regardless of the other energy sources present (1114). Taking this point a step further, Nickell and Maretzki proposed that the amylase presence may explain the very low starch levels found in most of the highly-productive Hawaiian varieties. The breeder's selection of the low-starch character might in fact be an unknowing selection for high amylase. Similar and other trends of thought relative to the foliar amylase role in cane have been discussed elsewhere (*cf.* Chapter 5, pp. 198–202; Chapter 6, pp. 256–261).

Before leaving the subject of carbon source for sugarcane cell suspensions, another concept suggested by Nickell and Maretzki deserves attention, that is, the commercial-scale production of sucrose by cell suspensions utilizing starch as an inexpensive carbon source. As shown in Table 16-2, starch is very nearly as good a carbon source as sucrose at the basic research level. It was suggested that appropriate sugarcane (or sugar beet) clones might be used to produce sugar from starch, providing that the chosen clones secrete large amounts of amylase: ". . .There are of course, many technical hurdles in this proposed method of producing sucrose, but the presence of amylase in sugarcane cell cultures suggests that one of the scientific hurdles has already been cleared." It might be added that the provision of a cheap external source of starch encompasses another hurdle already passed. Under *in vivo* conditions such that the polysaccharide source is an endogenous one, a competitive situation would exist in which the respective biosynthetic mechanisms deplete common pools of sucrose and starch precursors. In this case starch would hardly be a cheap carbon source since its very presence means that the sucrose-producing system has been deprived of part of its precursor supply.

D. *Importance of arginine in the growth medium*

Although arginine metabolism and its biochemical activity in tissue growth is examined in detail elsewhere (*cf.* this chapter, pp. 643–651), the nutritional–biochemical context of arginine is appropriately outlined at this time. In 1964 Nickell and Kortschak (1105) reported a marked growth-stimulatory effect of arginine on intact sugarcane plants. An essential role of the amino acid in sugarcane growth was considered. This view was substantiated by tissue culture experiments in which arginine stimulated the growth of excised parenchyma cells. Employing a cell suspension culture from the variety *H. 50-7209*, Maretzki and Nickell (975) demonstrated an apparent requirement for this amino acid in cell growth. A fully-defined medium containing yeast extract plus only small amounts of arginine remained growth-limiting for the amino acid.

Radiotracer studies with arginine labeled uniformly in the carbon structure showed that arginine uptake was initially rapid – more so than the uptake of labeled threonine or labeled valine. The radioactivity ratio of protein to non-protein was high for several hours of incubation with [^{14}C]arginine, but within 24 hours an equilibrium was reached similar to that obtained with threonine and valine. There was no competition between arginine and lysine, or between arginine and canavanine, for a site of entry into the cell, although competition of this nature appears to occur in arginine-transporting systems of *Saccharomyces* species (614). Further to this, the protein-synthesis inhibitor cycloheximide had no effect on the rate of arginine accumulation in sugarcane cells. Protein synthesis continued in the absence of externally-supplied arginine. Moreover, ethanol extraction of the labeled cell constituents showed that most of the ^{14}C remained in arginine during the period of cell exposure to labeled arginine. Taken together, this evidence implicates arginine as a significant factor in sugarcane growth processes (975). The amino acid would not appear to be actively transported; rather, a biosynthetic pathway for arginine production must ordinarily function within the cell (1114).

5. TOTIPOTENCY CONTROL AND POLYPLOIDY IN SUGARCANE CELLS

A. *General*

In 1969 Nickell and Torrey (1115) summarized the proceedings of an international conference held under sponsorship of the Rockefeller Foundation for the purpose of evaluating cell- and tissue-culture technology as a new means for crop improvement. Three aspects of cell and tissue culture were examined: (a) Meristem culture emphasizing rapid clonal multiplication; (b) haploid culture from anthers for greater speed and precision in recombining genetic material; and (c) use of protoplasmic fusion to achieve cell hybridization. The latter aspect, although highly theoretical, shows particular promise in achieving interspecific hybrids or even intergeneric hybrids where barriers to such hybridization currently exist in food or fiber crops. A problem of this nature had plagued sugarcane breeders for years (*cf.* Chapter 14, pp. 547–549). The first two aspects, clonal multiplication and haploid culture, were deemed immediately applicable.

Torrey stressed two objectives of the conference which reflect the relative novelty of plant cell and tissue technology and its rapid advance into botanical and agricultural areas of research: (a) To determine the lagging facets of tissue culture and the means for their correction, and (b) to attain better utilization of the new technology with a view toward reducing world-wide hunger. The point was made that, although the culturing of plant cells, tissues, and even organs now appears to be feasible with virtually all species, very little has been done with most of the major plant crops. Maize, sorghum, and manihot, and succulent plant crops in general, were cited[6].

Exceptions to this point include rice, sugarcane and various cereals. The consensus of opinion at the conference was that success with monocotyledons were less the result of "breakthroughs" than of concentrated effort with these plants during the decade of the 1960's. Among other developments, this concerted effort with monocots underscored the advantages of artificial growth media in preference to coconut milk. The higher contents of auxin and inorganic constituents of the synthetic media were apparently decisive in producing greater growth than had been possible with dicots growing on the natural medium.

A second point, having special reference to sugarcane, related to the appearance of "mosaic" plants regenerated from cell cultures. Because the somatic tissues of certain plants contain cells with varying chromosome numbers, it follows that some of the new plants obtained from their cultures should have chromosome numbers distinct from that of the parent material. Such plants have been obtained with sugarcane and grown successfully in the field for comparison with commercial varieties (715, 714).

Other important points discussed, having definite applicability to the future of sugarcane cell and tissue culture, included genetic instability and synchrony of cell division. Instability of cell and tissue cultures, apparently stemming from genetic instability, is widely recognized and was a much-discussed point at the congress. A persistent question was whether or not the instability arises because the "pressures" characteristic of a multicellular environment have been removed. Nickell and Torrey mention that auxins increase the chromosome number stability, as does frequent subculture of diploid cells. It was further noted that synchrony of cell division, occurring in only about 10 percent of the cells in rapidly-growing cultures, can be increased to about 40 percent with hydroxyurea. Synchrony of cell division was

---

[6] Apparently the work in maize by La Rue (896, 897), Straus and La Rue (1373) and Straus (1374) was overlooked.

reportedly increased by application and release of osmotic pressure shock, low temperature, low water supply, removal of a required compound, limited supply of carbon and nitrogen in the growth medium, and irradiation with blue light followed by red light.

B. *Totipotency control*

In 1966 Murashige and Nakano (1062) described the successful production of tetraploid *Nicotiana tabacum* L. plants from the diploid variety *Wisconsin 38* by use of tissue culture technology. In essence, tissues and plants were reconstituted *in vitro* from single cells isolated from pith tissue. Plants of this variety contain cells with distinct levels of polyploidy concentrated in the pith region (or central parenchyma) some 3.5 to 10.5 cm from the stem apex. The culture technique used to proliferate cells and later to reconstitute tissues was published by Muir and his associates (1052) in 1958. By adapting the "filter-paper raft-nurse callus method" to tobacco, Murashige and Nakano obtained new tissue from which shoots were induced and carefully rooted. When brought to maturity in the greenhouse the newly-rooted plants were found to be morphologically and cytogenetically similar to polyploids obtained by conventional methods. Thus, the potential to produce genetic variants in plants by tissue culture was demonstrated, in this instance the tetraploid plants being established "...with as much ease as diploid plants". Also working with *N. tabacum* L., Nitsch and his colleagues[7] developed new plants to the adult stage beginning with cultured tissue. In this instance the work was initiated with cultured anther tissue. The haploid adult plants were vigorous and morphologically similar to normal diploids, but the inflorescences were infertile.

At this time [1966] the expression of totipotency *in vitro* had not been conclusively established with other species. In order to do so Murashige and Nakano questioned whether totipotency control could be achieved with general success among species. As pointed out by Nickell (1103), no appreciable success had been obtained in culturing individual cells as recently as 1954 when White (1568) published his book updating animal and plant cell culture. However, the value of *in vitro* "cultivation" of plant tissues was thoroughly recognized and successes soon followed in tissue production from single isolated cells (1051, 1479). By 1966 Murashige and Nakano no longer regarded cell growth *in vitro* as a major obstacle. Development of incubation methods, including 10 days in darkness at 26.7 °C on "high-salt nutrient agar", with supplemental IAA or kinetin, had greatly eased the problem of separating discrete cells. Nonetheless the controlled growth of organs still seemed beyond the realm of general application.

In 1968 Reinert and Backs (1227) reported that a large degree of totipotency

---

[7] Nitsch, J.P., 1970. Personal communication with the author.

control, that is, the regulation and maintenance of regenerative capacity *in vitro*, had been achieved with carrot cells. The key factor was the media composition. Callus explants cultured on White's (1568) medium, containing sucrose and 2,4-D, grew slowly, producing roots but no embryos while losing their morphogenic capability in varying degree over a period of 116 weeks. Identical explants cultured similarly on the formula of Murashige and Skoog (1060) produced roughly 4 to 6 times more growth, including embryos as well as roots. Both media contained equal amounts of sucrose and 2,4-D, but the formula of Murashige and Skoog included subtle variations in macro- and micronutrient content.

As early as 1959 Reinert (1226) had shown that high nitrogen and low auxin levels were necessary for embryo development from carrot cells. During the previous year (1225) he had reported that bud and root formation by carrot tissue was enhanced when auxins were deleted from the medium. During the subsequent studies with carrot tissue Reinert and Backs (1227) observed that embryo-forming ability was sometimes lost when 2,4-D was present in the medium, but that transfer of the cultures to a medium lacking 2,4-D led to further embryo formation. Moreover, the omission of auxin from 2,4-D-free media served to induce embryo formation. In each instance totipotency gradually declined after its recovery or induction.

Three important conclusions were drawn from the carrot-tissue studies: (a) Totipotency can be regulated and maintained over long periods by slight changes in the medium's composition; (b) changes in cell behavior are positively correlated with rate of cell growth; and (c) loss of totipotency or "morphogenetic capacity" of the tissue cultures ". . .is probably caused by the decrease of some stable information or substance which is present in the freshly isolated explants and which slowly diminishes during growth *in vitro*" (1227). Reinert and Backs further concluded that a critical balance exists between nitrogen and auxin levels for the production of embryos. The ability of some cultures to form embryos without 2,4-D was explained in terms of a "minimal" medium for *in vitro* embryogenesis.

By 1966 refined methods in plating procedure (1479) and microchamber technique (465) had made possible the complete regeneration of shoot and root systems in such species as *Cichorium endiva, Nicotiana tabacum*, and *Daucus carota*. The expression of regeneration potential could now be controlled by manipulating nutritional constituents of the media. Murashige and Nakano had shown that by appropriately balancing the auxin and cytokinin levels, controlled shoot and root growth had been accomplished with *Convolvulus arvensis, Cyclamen persicum, Daucus carota, Isatis tinctora*, and *Nicotiana tabacum*.

C. *Polyploidy by tissue culture*

Although the induction of polyploid cells from diploid cells is of major importance in many plant species, many other species are by nature polysomatic (1062, 403,

1145). In this case there may be no inductive phase with colchicine or other treatment to obtain polyploid cells; rather, the isolation of such cells and the reconstitution of tissues and plants from them comprises the main problem. In the genus *Saccharum*, polyploidy is characteristic and extensively developed. The series n = 24, 27, 28, 30, 32, 36, 40, 48, 50, 56, 60, and 64 has been developed by a number of authors (1118, 235, 454, 1148, 1210). The basic genome number in *Saccharum* is placed at 10 by Nishiyama (1118), but this remains a controversial point. Apparently no diploid plant is extant. The study of polyploidy in *Saccharum* is, of course, of academic interest in tracing the evolution of its different species. It is equally important with respect to breeding future varieties, and toward this end new information is being contributed through tissue-culture technology.

In 1963 Nickell (1103) reviewed the rapidly-developing field of plant cell growth by submerged on suspension culture. Although at this time tissue culture with sugarcane was still in its infancy, Nickell outlined the main features of ploidy control and emphasized the non-homogenous nature even of callus tissues with respect to chromosome number. The paper by Partanen (1145) was cited in which tissue culture was depicted as a major new avenue toward cellular differentiation control, *i.e.*, polyploidy control by refined regulation of the tissue's environment and nutrition. Nickell further noted the work of Torrey (1444) who succeeded in controlling the chromosome numbers of pea callus tissue by manipulating the culture medium. Torrey regarded tissue culture as possibly the first satisfactory tool for close examination of mixed polyploid and diploid cells. Emphasis was again laid on nutritional requirements for cell growth and the importance of the physical–chemical environment, as well as the stimulatory effects of chemicals on tetraploid mitosis. The work by Partanen and by Torrey appears to have influenced the subsequent development of tissue-culture research with sugarcane in Hawaii.

More recently, Heinz and his co-workers (715) successfully identified sugarcane cell suspension cultures with stable chromosome levels. For this purpose a number of commercial varieties were maintained in a single medium under constant conditions for 6 years. Parenchyma tissue from internodes 4 to 10 was taken from *H. 39-7028, H. 49-3533, H. 49-5, H. 50-7209,* and *N.Co. 310*. All tissue samples were explanted on White's basal medium. Supplementary coconut water and 2,4-D were given in accordance with Nickell (1106) to induce callus tissue. These tissues were transferred to a liquid yeast medium, also containing 2,4-D, where they were maintained at 21.7 °C for six years, and from which subcultures were prepared at monthly intervals. Chromosome counts based on whole cells were made with cell samples fixed in Farmer's solution. Chromosome numbers from leaf tissue were also determined for *H. 50-7209* and *N.Co. 310*.

Considerable variation in chromosome number was found among the five clones and their derived suspension cultures. After six years each clone had developed new chromosome population patterns based in part on a natural screening for *in vitro* survival. The original variability among clones was attributed to multiform germplasm and its interactions with the sugarcane environment. In general, leaf-smear or pollen-mother cell preparations gave chromosome counts in the order of $2n$ = 112–114. Counts for *N.Co. 310, H. 39-7028*, and *H. 49-5* were in agreement with reports from other workers; however, *H. 50-7209* varied from $2n$ = 108 to $2n$ = 128 with the bivalent number being highest at 57 ($2n$ = 114).

Greater differences in chromosome number were obtained with cell suspension cultures from the various clones. For example, each of three isolates from *H. 50-7209* revealed different numbers in addition to divergent cell growth form, texture, color, and shape on the solid medium. Fig. 16-2 illustrates the chromosome variability range for *H. 50-7209* grown in liquid culture. Variability in cell size (Fig. 16-3), which was

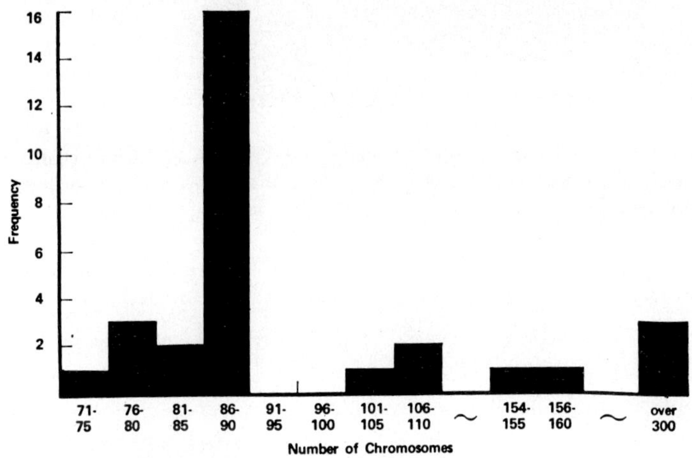

Fig. 16-2. Distribution of sugarcane chromosome numbers in cell suspension cultures of *H. 50-7209* stock culture. [After Heinz *et al.* (715).] Reproduced by permission of the *American Journal of Botany.*

quite common in all the cultures, was paralleled by varying levels of ploidy. With specific reference to isolate No. 9643 (from *H. 50-7209*) the authors wrote: "The chromosomes in cells of this culture were very sticky and hard to spread. In addition to the cells observed in the range $2n$ = 111–140, many polyploid cells were evident, but counts could not be obtained because of the stickiness of the chromosomes." This was the only isolate from *H. 50-7209* that even approached the chromosome count of the parent clone. Another isolate showed $2n$ = 71–90. A third isolate contained two races in the same culture, one race having $2n$ = 51–90 and the other $2n$ = 151–185. Further to this, the observation of chromosomal instability in microsporocytes supported the contention that *H. 50-7209* is a "chromosomal mosaic".

The occurrence of high polyploidy was most pronounced in suspension cultures of

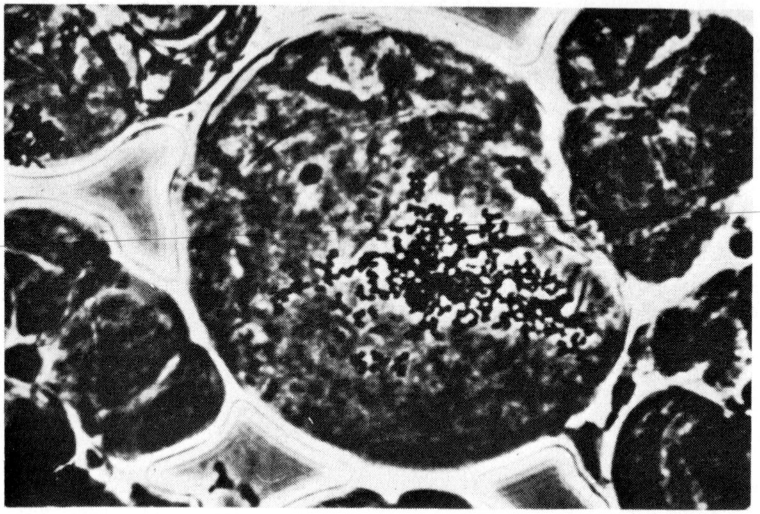

Fig. 16-3. Cells from stock culture of *H. 50-7209* illustrating typical variation in cell size characteristic of sugarcane cultures. The center cell is a polyploid, the cell at upper left is a haploid. [After Heinz *et al.* (715).] Reproduced by permission of the *American Journal of Botany*.

H. 39-7028 (Fig. 16-4A). Chromosomes showed a marked "stickiness" similar to those of *H. 50-7209*. High polyploidy was further indicated by the presence of multinucleate cells (Fig. 16-4B). Although precise counting was not possible it was estimated that polyploidy was usually in excess of $2n = 250$. Since the multinucleate condition was also found in leaf cells this was regarded as a parental characteristic rather than an aberration of *in vitro* cell growth. By contrast, leaf cells of the *N.Co. 310* plants contained the expected chromosome count ($2n = 112$) whereas suspension cultures of *N.Co. 310* produced variable growth of cells and tissue. Only cells of a "polyploid aneuploid" nature were observed whose frequency distribution was $2n$ = 151–196.

Heinz *et al.* (715) discussed the important implication of sugarcane cell culture based on the chromosomal losses and their effects upon cell genetic make-up. If a selective survival process is operative, the loss of certain chromosomes may not affect survival of suspension cultures of single cells or pieces of tissue; on the other hand, the loss of chromosomes has been advanced as a partial explanation for totipotency decline (1104, 1111): "Cell populations are naturally screened for survival under *in vitro* culture, while genetic systems necessary for totipotency have no selective advantage under these conditions and could be lost from the population" (715).

A number of possibilities for chromosome change in suspension culture were brought forward by the 6-year study. These include: (a) Initial occurrence of haploidy followed by doubling of the chromosome number resulting in a partial polyploid–aneuploid series (determined from relative haploid–polyploid ratios in *H. 50-7209*,

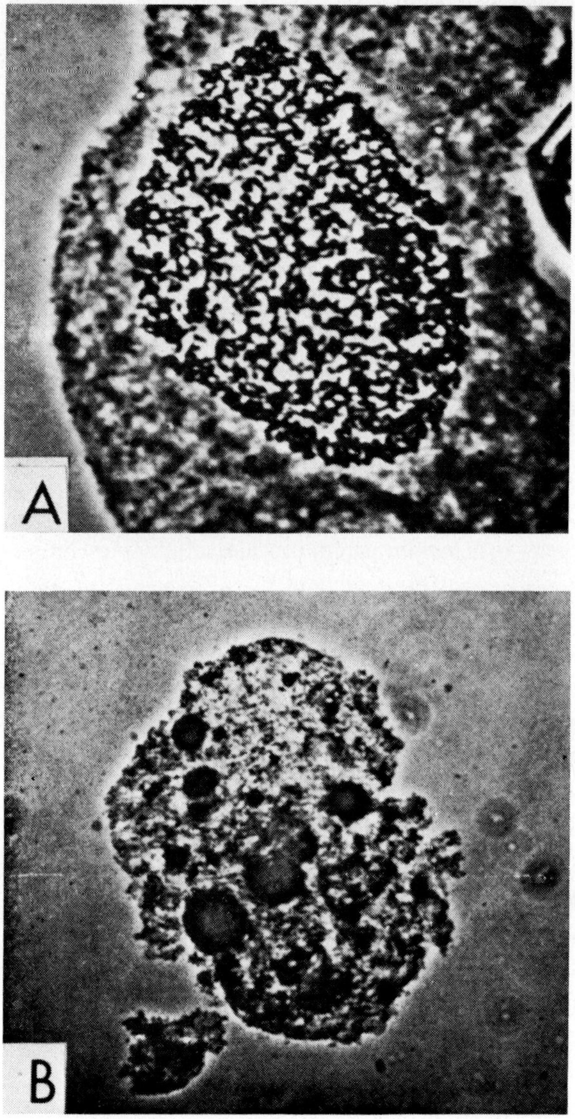

Fig. 16-4. Chromosomes of sugarcane clones from cell suspension cultures. (A) Metaphase in a cell from a culture of *H. 39-7028* showing high polyploidy. (B) Multinucleate cell from a culture of the same clone. [After Heinz *et al.* (715).] Reproduced by permission of the *American Journal of Botany*.

H. 49-5, and *H. 49-3533*); (b) doubling of chromosome number with subsequent loss of some chromosomes having poor selective advantage [based on culture stabilization for *N.Co. 310* at less than full polyploidy ($2n = 224$)]; (c) loss of the normal somatic level by increased chromosome number followed by decrease, or by loss of chromosomes followed by "polyploidization"; (d) production of chromosal mosaics following crosses in which widely different or intergeneric parent material was used. Heinz and his co-workers concluded that research data relative to biochemistry, physiology, pathology, and genetics might be examined with increased understanding by virtue of the genetic variations obtained in cell suspension culture, that is, by chromosomal losses in cell cultures.

An interesting parallel may be seen in the somatic instability found in suspended cultures of *H. 50-7209* (715), and the conclusion by Price (1188) that little or no genetic exchange occurs between the chromosomes of *S. spontaneum* and *S. officinarum* species. Price points out that as many as four species contribute genetic material to a modern cane variety. Chromosal increases paralleling the crosses and backcrosses account for high aneuploid chromosome numbers and the characteristically complex genetics. The fact that *S. spontaneum* readily "nobilizes" when backcrossed to *S. officinarum* is explained in terms of an unusual increase of *S. officinarum* chromosomes. *S. spontaneum* chromosomes apparently do not recombine with those of *S. officinarum*; rather, the use of a male *S. spontaneum* parent with *S. officinarum* leads to progeny of $2n + n$, that is, the *S. officinarum* parent provides a full set of chromosomes. However, the relative prevalence of bivalents and the infrequency of multivalents evidence a poor rate of chromosal exchange between "wild" and "noble" material. Price (1188), in 1963, suggested the use of irradiation as a means to break linkages between desirable and undesirable *S. spontaneum* genes which are not ordinarily severed during the crossing over processes. Otherwise, he cautioned breeders not to become impatient when interspecific crosses are not accompanied by increased chromosome numbers.

A more recent report by Price (1190) confirms the general chromosomal consistency in noble canes (mainly $2n = 80$) having but few aneuploids. He has also shown that atypical chromosome number is not necessarily reflected in the cane's morphology (clone *Khajuria*). One member of twin seedlings, *P.B. 54-2-2,* was reported to have survived. Walker (1521), following the oral presentation of this paper, commented that chromosome loss ". . .has a profoundly lowering effect on the appearance of progeny", while Heinz (716) noted that there was little relation between a variety's chromosome number and its performance.

6. ORGAN DIFFERENTIATION FROM CALLUS TISSUE

A. *General*

In 1969 Barba and Nickell (140) reported several effects of culture age and nutrition on organ differentiation and development (organogenesis) in interspecific *Saccharum* hybrids. At about the same time Heinz and Mee (714) published on sugarcane tissue organogenesis in numerous varieties grown on a single medium. Since dicots rather than monocots have been the prime object of organ differentiation studies, the recent publications on sugarcane help to fill an important gap in our knowledge of the *in vitro* growth of monocotyledons.

Initially, Barba and Nickell employed callus tissue isolated from four varieties (*H. 109, Badilla, H. 37-1933,* and *H. 50-7209*) and subcultured for 5 years. Two media were used, that of White (1567) published in 1943, and a medium used by Murashige and Skoog (1060) for research on tobacco tissue morphogenesis. Variable levels of NAA (α-naphthalene acetic acid), 2,4-D, kinetin, and coconut water were added to the media singularly and in combinations. No shoot formation was induced in any of the tissue cultures by any treatment. This was in general agreement with other authors who reported a gradual decline in the ability of cultured tissues to differentiate shoots (1061, 1479, 1480, 1445).

New isolates from the same four varieties receiving the same chemical treatments gave positive results with 2,4-D (0.05 mg/l added to Murashige and Skoog medium). Shoots were induced by 2,4-D in *Badilla, H. 37-1933*, and *H. 50-7209*. There was no response by *H. 109* to any level of 2,4-D. Roots were also induced by 2,4-D but only in the variety *H. 109*. Similar results were obtained when NAA was added. Low levels of kinetin (0.05 and 0.5 mg/l) and coconut water (10 percent) failed to aid growth and differentiation, either alone or when added with NAA; however, high kinetin (5.0 mg/ml) was inhibitory for culture growth and for differentiation of new tissues. In this connection, Nitsch and Strain[8] observed intense darkening of sugarcane explants (*Badilla, B.-49119* and *B.-50112*) cultured with purine cytokinins, whereas those of the substituted urea category did not produce this effect.

Significantly, the media employed by Barba and Nickell (140) played a major role in determining whether tissue initiation was to occur. With regard to growth of callus tissue, White's medium was superior to that of Murashige and Skoog, but White's medium was inferior in its support of shoot or root induction in the newly-isolated cultures. Moreover, tissue cultures isolated on White's medium and subcultured more than once on this medium appeared to lose permanently their ability to differentiate shoots. This was also true of the Murashige and Skoog medium when subcultured more than once.

In addition to the medium's effects on tissue growth, factors of auxin concentration and variety markedly affected callus growth and organ differentiation (140). Whereas *H. 109* callus tissue increased growth and produced roots with 2,4-D added up to 0.5 mg/l, a higher auxin level suppressed growth. In *Badilla* and *H. 50-7209* tissue shoots were produced even in the absence of 2,4-D, but the clones varied in their response to different 2,4-D levels. Tissue from the variety *H. 37-1933* produced shoots at the level of 0.05 mg/l of 2,4-D but failed to do so either at higher or lower concentrations. Nickell and Barba underscored the fact that *H. 109* tissues failed to produce shoots without 2,4-D, or with any treatment or combination of treatments,

[8] Nitsch, J.P. and Strain, G.C., 1969. Histophysiologie végétale. Effet de diverses cytokinines sur le brunissement d'explantats de canne à sucre, *C.R. Acad. Sci. (Paris)* 268: 806–809.

and that all varieties were unable to differentiate tissues when supplied with high 2,4-D (5.0 mg/l).

These studies also pointed out an apparent difference between tissue differentiation and tissue development. Since prior work (1110) had shown that Dalapon (2,2-dichloropropionic acid) was effective in inducing root formation, this chemical was also evaluated by Barba and Nickell (140) during the organogenesis experiments with aged and newly-isolated cultures. At concentrations as high as 50 mg/l Dalapon did not interfere with shoot initiation, but it did prevent the growth of developing shoots. Interesting enough, Dalapon at 50 mg/l enhanced root initiation in *H. 109*, the variety whose callus tissue could not be induced to differentiate shoots under any condition.

B. *New plant induction from callus tissue cultures*

In 1969 Heinz and Mee (714) reported the successful differentiation of plants from cultured callus tissues isolated from distinct *Saccharum* species. This work was prompted by the recent findings of Heinz *et al.* (715) suggesting that aneuploid chromosomal series might be developed via cell culture. In essence, it was now within the realm of possibility to obtain new clonal types originating at the level of simple cells through manipulation of cell suspension cultures. By this means the separation of mutant tissue from normal tissue would be bypassed entirely. In furthering this work Heinz and Mee (714) successfully induced differentiation in shoot parenchyma, leaf tissue and inflorescence tissue from a wide range of *Saccharum* species. The implications of such work for the future of sugarcane can hardly be overestimated.

The plant differentiation work was planned with four objectives: (a) Improved technology for induction of callus tissue from distinct sugarcane tissues; (b) differentiation of plants from the callus tissue; (c) improved "rearing" technology for survival of the newly-induced plants; and (d) increased knowledge of the variability in differentiated plants. Heinz and Mee approached the problem by isolating shoot apices, young leaves, and inflorescences (pre-microsporocyte to mature pollen stages) from a range of *S. officinarum* and interspecific hybrid clones. Sterilized tissues were cultured on a modified Murashige and Skoog (1060) medium to which 2,4-D, thiamine, *myo*-inositol, coconut water, and sucrose were added. In addition to their studies of callus and differentiated tissue, the authors compared enzyme behavior within abnormal and normal clones – specifically the systems peroxidase, esterase, and polyphenol oxidase.

Callus tissue was induced successfully on explanted apices (Fig. 16-5A), leaf tissue (Fig. 16-5B), and inflorescences. Callus formed most rapidly when the basal medium contained 2,4-D (3.0 ppm) and coconut water. Explanted shoot apices produced callus on the exposed cells of immature internodal tissue; leaf callus formed first on the cut edge and later spread over the leaf surface. Reproductive tissue formed callus initially on cut surfaces and later on branches, rachis, and glumes. No callus growth was

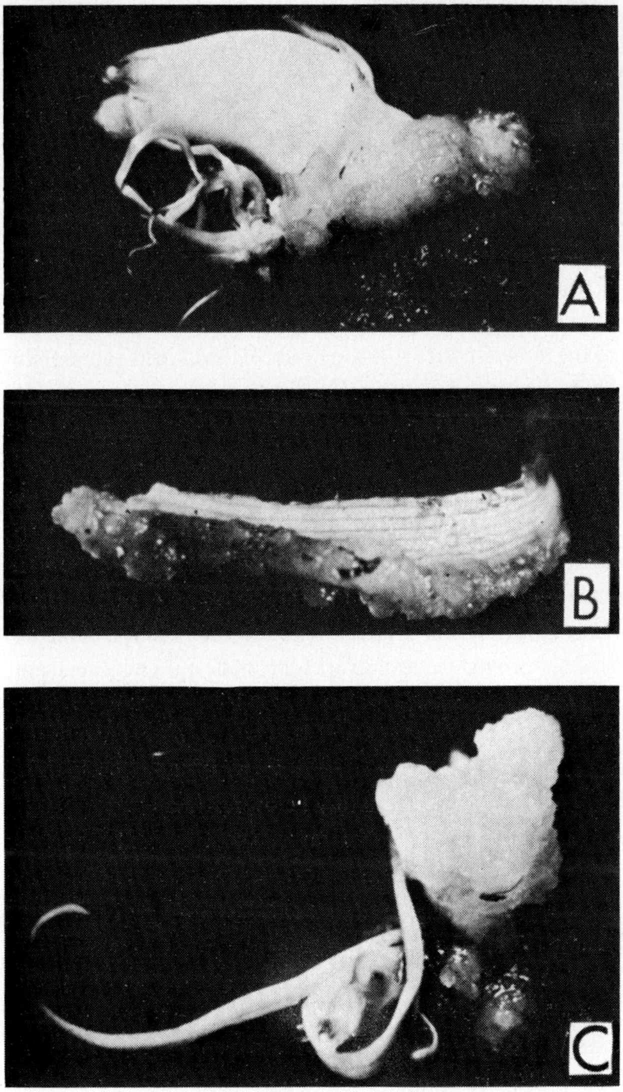

Fig. 16-5. Organ and plantlet development from cultured sugarcane tissues. (A) Shoot apex showing callus tissue originating from exposed parenchyma tissue. (B) Leaf section with callus formed on the cut surface. (C) Plantlets developing after differentiation from callus tissue. [After Heinz and Mee (714).] Reproduced by permission of *Crop Science*.

detected on anthers or ovaries. About 2 to 4 weeks were required for callus tissue to form.

Plant differentiation was accomplished by transferring callus tissue to a basal medium lacking 2,4-D. This procedure was most effective with callus which had been transferred at least several times previously to a 2,4-D-treated medium. Greater numbers of plants were obtained thereafter upon removal of the callus to a 2,4-D-free basal medium. Fig. 16-5C illustrates organ formation from callus tissue which typically appeared about 1 month after callus transfer. Having once differentiated, the new organs exercised a dominance effect which prevented further plant differentiation from the callus tissue. This dominance was verified when undifferentiated callus isolated from the new plants accomplished organ differentiation on a fresh medium. Development of new plants and roots was consistent with the characteristic patterns of the original clones (*H. 37-1933* and *H. 50-7209*).

The newly-differentiated plants were transferred to water culture to promote root development and were later potted in vermiculite. Many plants were lost in water culture, particularly those making slow growth or having poorly-developed roots. Subsequently the survival rate was improved by first transferring the differentiated plants to a 2,4-D-free medium for 2 to 3 weeks prior to water culture. Curiously, individual plants developed from callus tissue retained their morphological identity, while considerable variation was observed between plants arising from the same callus tissue. This may be further evidence of cell heterogeneity within the callus tissue. Variety *H.50-7209*, a known chromosomal "mosaic", produced more than 150 plants from callus tissue. Some 25 plants were obtained from *H. 37-1933* (714). All of the newly-differentiated plants revealed morphological variations relating to the parental clone. A single plant from *H. 37-1933* callus proved to be a dwarf with stiff, upright leaves and high silicate deposits on the leaf surface (Fig. 16-6). A higher chromosome number (2*n*

Fig. 16-6. Left: Normal development of *H. 37-1933* from a vegetative cutting. Right: Abnormal *H. 37-1933 #5* differentiated from callus tissue. [After Heinz and Mee (714).] Reproduced by permission of *Crop Science.*

= 117–124) further distinguished this plant from *H. 37-1933* ($2n$ = 106–107). Electrophoresis patterns for esterases also deviated from the parental enzyme patterns.

Whereas chromosome counts were not made for *H. 50-7209* variants, a number of morphological differences were recorded. These included heavier tillering, slower growth, and greater erectness than the parental clone. Single variants from *H. 38-7208, H. 44-3098*, and *Yellow Caledonia* showed comparable electrophoretic patterns for the esterase, peroxidase, and polyphenol oxidase systems examined. In general, the plants differentiated from callus retained individual uniformity throughout the subsequent propagation.

The work by Heinz and Mee greatly strengthened the thesis that new sugarcane plants can be induced at the cell level, quite aside from conventional crossing methods and all that these entail. The authors conclude: "The formation of callus tissue and the subsequent differentiation of plants offer the breeder of asexually reproduced plants the opportunity to change the chromosome complement and make-up without crossing." This technique, developed to its full potential, may enable cane breeders to transcend the enormous climatic and interspecific limitations imposed upon the conventional breeding program.

7. ARGININE BIOCHEMISTRY IN SUGARCANE CELL CULTURES

During the period 1966–1969, Maretzki and his co-workers (975, 976, 977, 978) performed tissue culture studies on the role of arginine in sugarcane growth. Sufficient information was gathered relative to arginine nutrition, its biosynthesis, and its role in protein synthesis to suggest a decisive position in determining sugarcane yield and quality.

In 1964 Nickell and Kortschak (1105) observed a growth-stimulatory effect of arginine as it was being tested among a number of organic nitrogen sources supplied in nutrient solution. As little as 50 ppm added to the nutrient solution produced significant growth increases. Other higher plants have shown positive growth response to arginine since the late 1940's [reviewed by Maretzki *et al.* (978)]. The sugarcane growth response to arginine was verified in sugarcane cell cultures by Maretzki and Nickell (975). In some instances arginine was highly effective as the lone source of nitrogen for excised tissues (644, 1331). According to Maretzki *et al.* (978), arginine was one of a number of amino acids shown to have a regulatory effect on nitrate reductase in cultured tobacco (524). The amino acid has also been shown to overcome growth inhibition by glycine in groundsel roots (1331).

The increasing implication of arginine in various aspects of nitrogen metabolism by higher plants prompted Maretzki and his colleagues to investigate its activity in cultured sugarcane cells. This approach was facilitated by a newly-developed and fully-defined tissue culture medium (*cf.* this chapter, pp. 625–628). In most of the subsequent experiments, cell suspensions were prepared by transferring cells from a stock medium to a modified White's medium in which a known mixture of amino acids (M-2) was incorporated along with vitamins, 2,4-D, and a carbon source (sucrose). Cell suspensions were maintained for 3-week intervals during which growth increases in the order of 25 to 50 mg were obtained. Test incubations employed third- or fourth-generation cells from the chemically-defined medium, which were then treated with ^{14}C-labeled amino acids following transfer to a similar but amino acid-deficient medium.

A. *Cell growth response to arginine*

Growth experiments with ^{14}C-labeled amino acids (978) verified earlier observations of an arginine growth-stimulatory effect on sugarcane plants (1105) and cultured cells (1113). On a dry-weight basis, slow-growing cultures from the varieties *H. 49-5* and *H. 50-7209* approximately doubled their dry weight during a 3-week period. Variety *H. 39-7028* cultures nearly quadrupled in dry weight. The optimum arginine concentration was about 6.0 μmoles per 100 ml of medium, with 12.0 μmoles being somewhat inhibitory. Samples taken at 2-day intervals indicated that the growth stimulation was not immediate, but began after about 7 days, approximately at the completion of one cell division cycle. Arginine-treated cells most rapidly surpassed control cells between 19 and 21 days of growth. Little difference in cell size was recorded between treatments but arginine-free cultures tended to aggregate more than controls. Typically, all cultures contained a few "giant" cells having no relation to amino acid treatment.

The arginine requirement for cell growth was further substantiated by growth decline upon withdrawal of arginine from the medium. In each of the three clones a withdrawal of arginine resulted in lower contents of total free amino acids. This was sometimes accompanied by increased total protein content.

Noting that other authors had implicated *N*-acetylglutamic acid and α-*N*-acetyl-L-ornithine as arginine precursors in plant tissue cultures (444), Maretzki *et al.* (978) studied the growth effects of these compounds on sugarcane cells when substituted for arginine (Table 16-3). The relatively poor response obtained was possibly a function of inadequate uptake. Argininosuccinic acid, another precursor of arginine, was even less suitable as a replacement for arginine in the culture medium. Nonetheless, the authors did not feel that this reflected a metabolic block in the arginine synthesis pathway, and proposed instead that an arginine biosynthesis pathway must proceed normally in the cultured cane cells.

Penetration studies of labeled arginine and arginine precursors showed that only small amounts of potential arginine precursors were recovered in soluble form. Both [^{14}C]citrulline and [^{14}C]ornithine contributed a large part of their label to the protein fraction. Maretzki *et al.* (978) surmised that, in order to enter protein, both amino

TABLE 16-3

RESPONSE OF SUGARCANE CELL SUSPENSION CULTURES TO ARGININE SUBSTITUTES SUPPLIED TO AN ARGININE-FREE GROWTH MEDIUM

Variety *H. 50-7209.* A synthetic medium was employed using the amino acid mixture M-2 with or without arginine. [After Maretzki *et al.* (978).] Reproduced by permission of *Physiologia Plantarum.*

Arginine substitute	Growth as % of control cultures given arginine
None	2
N-Acetylglutamic acid	52
N-Acetyl-L-ornithine	49
Ornithine	68
Citrulline	93
Argininosuccinic acid	29

acids must first convert to arginine, and hence the arginine produced within the cell must be used largely for protein synthesis.

B. *Comparative uptake and assimilation of arginine by cane, duckweed, and carrot cells*

From the beginning the arginine experiments by Maretzki and his co-workers had shown a very high rate of uptake by cane cells. Even before a chemically-defined medium was available it appeared that arginine uptake might exceed that of other amino acids. Fig. 16-7 illustrates comparative uptake rates for uniformly-labeled arginine, valine, and threonine by cells cultured on a basal medium to which yeast extract had been added. Under these conditions, *i.e.*, unlimiting exogenous supply, a simulation of the natural cell state is attained such that differences in amino acid uptake rate may be a measure of preference for a specific amino acid. Within about 5 hours arginine uptake quite clearly exceeded that of valine and threonine, or even the combined uptake of valine and threonine. A steady-state incorporation of amino acids was achieved in about 24 hours.

Further study showed that amino acid uptake by sugarcane cells differed from the uptake by cells of other species. Again using labeled arginine, valine, and threonine, it was found that carrot parenchyma cells and floating duckweed tissue absorbed the isotopes at different rates and proportions than the sugarcane cell suspensions. Duckweed incorporated arginine at only a fraction of the sugarcane rate, and at less than half the rates for valine and threonine. The latter amino acids were taken up in comparable amounts in both sugarcane and duckweed. Carrot parenchyma cells also differed from cane cells with respect to arginine and threonine uptake. Moreover, the

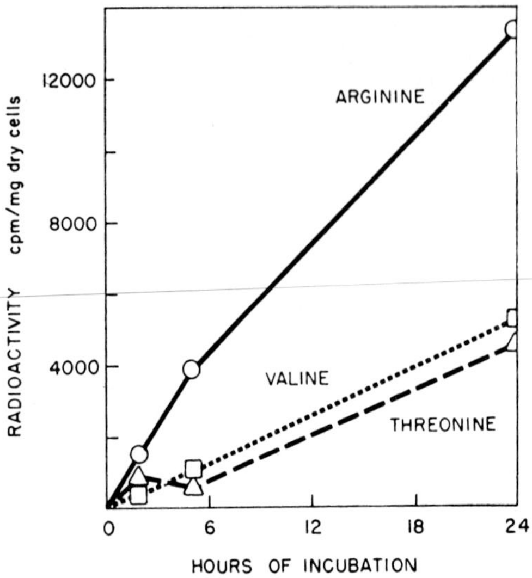

Fig. 16-7. Uptake of ^{14}C-labeled arginine, valine, and threonine by cell cultures of *H. 39-7028* incubated in a yeast–malt growth medium. Each amino acid was uniformly labeled. The rate of arginine uptake clearly exceeded that of valine and threonine. cpm = counts/minute. [After Maretzki *et al.* (977).] Reproduced by permission of *Physiologia Plantarum.*

sugarcane cell cultures appeared to exhaust their arginine supply in the supporting medium within a few hours, even when relatively large amounts were present. Carrot cells assimilated arginine at increasing rates for at least 24 hours. The authors interpreted this as further evidence that sugarcane cells grown in a synthetic medium were highly dependent upon arginine.

C. *Arginine incorporation into cell proteins*

Purified protein preparations free of non-incorporated labeled amino acids were examined by Maretzki *et al.* (978). It was found that, in addition to penetrating the cell more rapidly, arginine was incorporated into cellular proteins at a faster rate than valine or threonine. Protein constituents obtained by acid hydrolysis revealed more than 80 percent of the protein label still residing in arginine after 24 hours incubation. The remainder was largely confined to aspartic and glutamic acids and proline.

Maretzki and his co-workers also considered the significance of arginine incorporation into specific protein fractions. This presents a particularly difficult problem and many aspects have to be considered. The quantities of amino acids externally supplied, their relative balance, their replenishment, internal biosynthesis and interconversion, and imbalance caused by exogenous provision of amino acids are among the factors that come into play (168, 978). Nonetheless the fact remained that sugarcane cell proteins incorporated radioactivity faster after exposure to labeled arginine than after exposure to other amino acids (threonine and valine). Fractionation of the cell proteins into five range groups was accomplished by variable saturation with ammonium sulfate. Specific activity determinations for each of the five groups failed to show a preference for arginine by any particular fraction. It was suggested that related proteins (such as the high-arginine histones reported by other workers) may exist in sugarcane cells.

It might also be added that similar studies based upon catalytic protein fractions could be highly instructive. For example, relative arginine incorporation into amylase and invertase, or into the several cane invertases, or into other sensitive enzymes in cell cultures given simulated diurnal photoperiods could contribute a new dimension to our present understanding of enzyme control in the intact plant. At the present time the possibilities for advancing our enzyme knowledge via labeled amino acid incorporation into cell cultures appear significant indeed.

Maretzki *et al.* (978) hypothesized that an insufficient exogenous arginine supply might limit cell growth by preventing adequate protein formation. This was investigated by first depleting arginine levels in the cell culture and then adding unlabeled arginine plus a labeled amino acid. Specifically, arginine-deficient cells of *H. 50-7209* were transferred to a basal medium which included a known amino acid mixture (M-2) plus ^{14}C-labeled leucine or tyrosine. Arginine was also added in some tests and withheld in others. It was found that the presence of arginine in the medium had no effect on the uptake of other amino acids or their utilization in protein synthesis. These results are not necessarily conclusive.

In discussing their data relating arginine to cell growth, the authors found no support for the thesis that arginine performs solely as a source of nitrogen. They did conclude that arginine fulfils a role distinct from that of other amino acids. This was viewed as an indirect but growth-regulatory function. In general, their findings did not point to a rate-limiting role for arginine in protein synthesis. On the other hand, the high requirement for arginine, its rapid uptake, and its unknown intercellular synthetic capability point to a program of abundant arginine utilization which may falter when either external or endogenous sources are limited. Under such conditions the observed stimulatory effect of added arginine is readily explained.

D. *Arginine catabolism products*

Maretzki *et al.* published a second report in 1969 dealing further with arginine biochemistry in sugarcane çell culture (977). Attention was focused on the products of arginine catabolism, particularly on the conversion of arginine to *N*-carbamylputrescine.

Other workers have reported the production of *N*-carbamylputrescine (NCP), along with agmatine and putrescine, in higher plants experiencing both normal and abnormal growth [reviewed by Maretzki *et al.* (977)]. No clear picture of this compound's function in plants seems to exist, although its appearance as an intermediate of putrescine formation in barley seedlings was mentioned. In tobacco, putrescine may reflect an alternate route for the synthesis of nicotine's pyrrolidine ring.

Discovery of NCP in cane cells occurred while Maretzki and his co-workers were examining arginine metabolism in cultured cells of *H. 50-7209* grown under partial arginine stress. Arginine was depleted in the cultures by 6 days incubation on an arginine-free mixture of amino acids (M-2). Transfer of the cultures to a complete M-2 medium, *i.e.*, with uniformly-labeled arginine included, was followed by rapid uptake of the label. Small amounts of $^{14}CO_2$ were produced, an event undetected when [^{14}C]valine or [^{14}C]leucine were supplied. During the first 2 hours of incubation some 8 percent of the radioactive arginine appeared in newly-formed proteins; within 12 hours this value increased to 15 percent.

Cell cultures were incubated with [^{14}C]arginine for periods ranging from 5 minutes to 2 hours; thereafter they were lyophilized and extracted for autoradiography. Chromatographed extracts were found to contain three predominant radioactive products: Free arginine, *N*-carbamylputrescine, and a third product which co-chromatographed with guanidine. Table 16-4 summarizes the relative concentra-

TABLE 16-4

RELATIVE CONCENTRATIONS OF ARGININE AND *N*-CARBAMYLPUTRESCINE IN ETHANOL-SOLUBLE EXTRACTS OF SUGARCANE CELL CULTURES GROWN FOR 3 WEEKS IN THE PRESENCE OR ABSENCE OF EXOGENOUS ARGININE

[After Maretzki *et al.* (977).] Reproduced by permission of *Phytochemistry*.

White's medium plus 2,4-D, sucrose, and amino acid mixture M-2	Dry cells (mg)	Concentration (μmoles/mg dry cells)	
		Arginine	*N*-Carbamylputrescine
Minus arginine	62.6	0.0077	0.0130
Plus arginine (33 μmoles/ml)	124.8	0.0123	0.0290

tions of arginine and NCP obtained from the cells after 3-weeks incubation. The ratio of arginine to NCP remained unaffected by an excess supply of arginine, or by the fact that major growth differences were recorded. Under the specified conditions NCP was regarded as a normal product of arginine metabolism in *H. 50-7209*.

Experiments designed to measure the cellular increases in radioactive arginine and NCP were performed using the ethanol-soluble pool. This approach was validated by the lack of any evidence for arginine conversion prior to its entry into this pool, or of evidence for extracellular enzymes capable of producing NCP from arginine. Arginine-deficient cells were incubated with [^{14}C]arginine and samples were withdrawn for analysis at 15-minute intervals. Total ^{14}C uptake and the relative proportions of radioactivity in arginine and NCP were determined. The results showed that labeled

NCP began to appear in cells within a few minutes after penetration by [^{14}C]arginine (Fig. 16-8). The conversion to NCP proceeded rapidly and continued throughout the 2nd hour of incubation when further arginine uptake had nearly ceased.

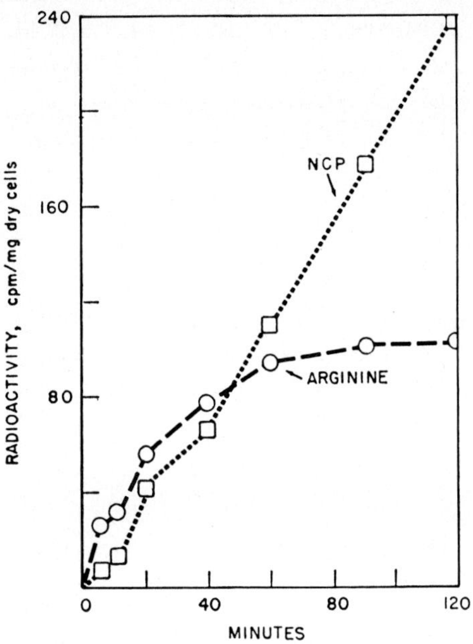

Fig. 16-8. Specific activity increase (in terms of dry cell weight) of arginine and *N*-carbamylputrescine (NCP) in sugarcane cells of *H. 50-7209* incubated in a medium containing [^{14}C]arginine over a time course of 120 minutes. [After Maretzki *et al.* (977).] Reproduced by permission of *Phytochemistry*.

Other cell cultures were preincubated in unlabeled arginine and transferred to the normal defined medium without [^{14}C]arginine. This step was designed to clarify subsequent cell growth and changing distribution patterns of ^{14}C in NCP, guanidine, and arginine during the post-labeling period. During 96 hours of incubation, the cell growth doubled (dry weight basis), arginine markedly declined, NCP increased slightly, and guanidine made large increases, apparently at the expense of arginine. The authors noted that arginine derived from hydrolyzed protein might also enter such reactions, and some arginine may have been incorporated into protein.

Additional information was gathered relative to the NCP position in the paths of ^{14}C movement. Cell suspensions were incubated with either guanido-labeled arginine or ureido-labeled citrulline, and subsequent comparisons were made of the radioactivity in free arginine and NCP. Although under equimolar conditions nearly 20 percent more of the labeled arginine was taken up than labeled citrulline during a 24-hour period, more NCP was produced from citrulline than from arginine. This was suggestive that NCP synthesis can proceed via citrulline rather than arginine.

The possibility of alternate paths of NCP synthesis is illustrated in Fig. 16-9. By one route the decarboxylation of arginine would give rise to agmatine; in the second, citrulline produced through the mediation of arginine desimidase would be decarboxylated to yield NCP. The existence of the second route in sugarcane cells is favored by the data of Maretzki and his colleagues. The essential enzyme, arginine desimidase, has been isolated from *Chlorella* by Shafer and Thompson (1317). Neither arginine desimidase nor arginine carboxylase has yet been reported in sugarcane.

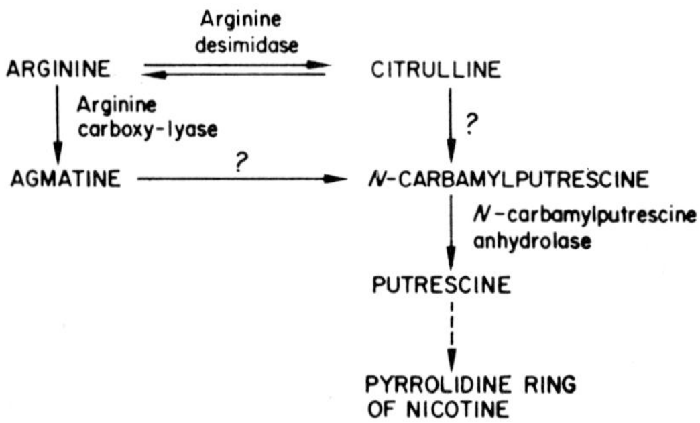

Fig. 16-9. Metabolic relationship of arginine and putrescine. [After Maretzki *et al.* (977).] Reproduced by permission of *Phytochemistry*.

In discussing their results, Maretzki *et al.* (977) point out that the known catabolic pathways for arginine in pine, bacteria, and fungi have not been discovered in sugarcane cell cultures. Moreover, the production of free guanidine incident to arginine metabolism, as observed in the sugarcane cells, has not been reported in other higher plants. Direct cleavage of the arginine molecule to yield guanidine does not appear to occur in sugarcane cells since a necessary intermediate, α-aminovaleric acid, has not been detected chromatographically. Nor have the required intermediates been found for guanidine synthesis via glutamic semialdehyde, or by urea reduction following arginase activity against arginine.

Another feature of NCP behavior in sugarcane cell cultures is its slow metabolism following production from arginine. It continues to accumulate in the alcohol-soluble pool long after appreciable increase in arginine has stopped (Fig. 16-8). In addition, NCP is not excreted from the cells to the surrounding medium. On the other hand, Maretzki *et al.* report that NCP is mobile in the sap of fresh leaf tissue. Detached cane leaves placed in a labeled arginine solution for 3 hours convert 2 to 3 percent of the total incorporated radioactivity into NCP. The conversion proceeds with or without illumination. Recovery of labeled NCP in the solution indicates basipetal transport through the leaf lamina.

Although the study of arginine metabolism, and in particular its conversion to NCP, has distinct advantages when performed in tissue culture, similar work might also be advanced with intact or detached leaf blades where suitable facilities for tissue culture are lacking. Moreover, arginine metabolism might also be examined in connection with the synthesis of arginine or other amino acids incident to photosynthetic CO_2 assimilation in cane leaf tissues or isolated chloroplasts.

It appears that much additional work remains before the arginine role in sugarcane growth is entirely clear. Maretzki *et al.* (977) wrote: "Neither *N*-carbamylputrescine nor guanidine appear to provide sugarcane cells with the growth stimulus which led to our investigation of arginine metabolism in this plant. The cause for the arginine effect on growth is believed to lie elsewhere and remains to be determined."

8. CHEMICAL EFFECTS ON SUGARCANE CELL CULTURES

Most agronomists and physiologists working with sugarcane will attest to the increasing influx of chemicals into sugar-growing programs. There exists an enormous potential for chemicals to promote ripening (*cf.* Chapter 12, pp. 443–457), to produce desiccation (*cf.* Chapter 13, pp. 491–495), and to control flowering (*cf.* Chapter 14, pp. 554–557), in addition to their long-established roles as "pesticides". It must also be recognized that, except for mostly empirical effects on growth and sugar yield, very little information accompanies the commercial compound relative to its mode of action, the limits of its growth- and sugar-regulating potential, or even with respect to the kinds of changes that can be induced. For example, it is improbable that the manufacturers of Diquat foresaw its potential as a sugarcane desiccant and flower-controlling agent. Nor is it likely that the dipyridyl group and other current compounds have given all that they might have contributed to sugarcane culture. From this point of view one can appreciate the need for new technological tools with which the biochemical potential of a commercial product can be examined quickly, precisely, and unencumbered by the cultural or agronomic environment of the intact crop plant. It is therefore important that researchers in Hawaii have begun to utilize cell and tissue cultures in exploring chemical effects on the sugarcane cell at a totally fundamental level.

In 1967 Nickell (1110) evaluated the effects of Diquat, Paraquat, and Endothal on cultured sugarcane tissues isolated from eight varieties. Tissues were grown on White's basal medium containing supplemental coconut water, 2,4-D, and arginine. The work was prompted in part by differing varietal responses to Diquat as a flower-controlling agent. Preliminary results indicated that Diquat was a powerful growth inhibitor in *H. 50-7209* tissues but was much less active on tissues derived from *H. 37-1933*.

Additional experiments were performed with tissues from eight varieties being treated with nine compounds (Table 16-5). Growth effects and differential variety responses were again the central points of interest. It was found that, when added at the level of 50 ppm, the compounds 2,4-D, 2,4,5-T, TBA (2,3,6-trichlorobenzoic

TABLE 16-5

EFFECTS OF VARIOUS HERBICIDES ON THE GROWTH OF TISSUES CULTURED FROM EIGHT SUGARCANE VARIETIES

Growth values are given in numerical rankings based on the following scale: 0=no detectable growth; 1=slight growth; 2=less growth than the control culture; 3=control; 4=growth exceeding that of the control culture. [After Nickell (1110).] Reproduced by permission of *I.S.S.C.T.*

Variety	Treatment									
	Control	2,4-D	2,4,5-T	TBA	Tordon	Diquat	Paraquat	Endothal	Dalapon	Amitrole
H. 39-7028	3	4	4	2	4	Dead	0	0	2	Dead
H. 37-1933	3	4	3	3	3	Dead	1	1	3	2
H. 39-5803	3	3	3	3	3	Dead	Dead	1	3	3
H. 49-5	3	2	4	4	3	0	1	1	3	2
Badilla	3	3	3	3	3	Dead	0	0	3	3
H. 62-9824	3	3	4	3	4	Dead	0	1	3	3
N. Co. 310	3	3	2	2	3	0	1	1	3	3
H. 49-3533	3	2	3	2	3	0	1	1	2	3

acid), and Tordon were non-toxic by comparison with other test chemicals. To the contrary, Diquat, Paraquat, and Endothal were relatively toxic to the test varieties.

Possibly the most important finding was a consistent induction by Dalapon of organ-like structure differentiation (Table 16-5). This occurred in all varieties in response to 50 ppm Dalapon. In varieties *N.Co. 310* and *Badilla* (Fig. 16-10), definite shoot and root tissues were recognized. In another report Nickell (1104) observed that the Dalapon effect was relatively unique among herbicides tested in tissue culture. He stressed the importance of an organ-inducing characteristic in the overall production of new plants originating from a single cell.

In 1967 Nickell (1111) reported further on the Dalapon effect with special reference to organ induction in the Hawaiian varieties *H. 39-7208, H. 49-5*, and *H. 50-7209*. An improved technique was described wherein the tissue cultures were first transferred from a 2,4-D-containing basal medium to the same medium without 2,4-D. After 3 weeks the cultures were transferred to another 2,4-D-free medium to which Dalapon had been added. Two of the cultures (from *H. 50-7209* and *H. 49-5*) showed increased tendency toward morphological change, apparently at the expense of lessened growth potential. Color changes and increased differential growth rates were also recorded. Cultures from *H. 39-7028* showed a tendency to increase growth. This work generally substantiated the differential *in vitro* response of varieties to chemicals and stressed the importance of Dalapon (or other chemicals) as a manipulative tool in approaching the unsolved mechanisms of tissue differentiation.

In 1970 Nickell and Maretzki (1116) described a several-dimensional approach in

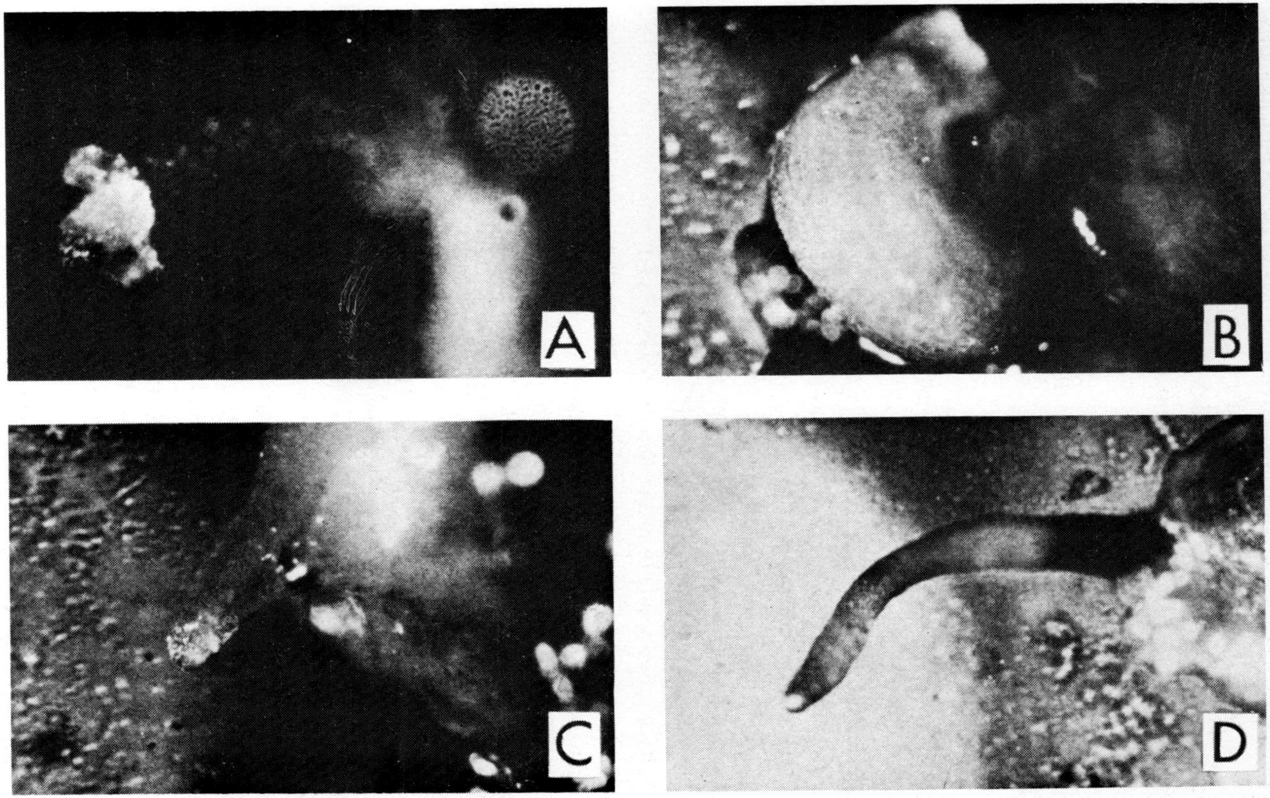

Fig. 16-10. Organ-like structures differentiated from sugarcane cultures after addition of 50 ppm of Dalapon to the growth medium. (A) Root in *N.Co. 310.* (B) Shoot in *Badilla*. (C) Root in *Badilla*. (D) Root in *Badilla*. [After Nickel (1110, 1104).] Reproduced by permission of *I.S.S.C.T.* and the *Hawaiian Sugar Planters' Association*.

evaluating chemical ripeners at a fundamental level. Included in the examination of a given compound were its effects on duckweed growth, growth of cell suspension cultures, uptake and incorporation of amino acids by cell suspension cultures, and effects on relevant enzyme levels. Conventional ripening data were also recorded along with oral toxicity (in rats) and chemical effects on the respiration of cell suspension cultures. In certain instances (with anisomycin and actidione, for example) the ripener activity indicated by cell culture data was in close agreement with juice quality responses in cane of 18 months or older.

9. AMYLASE SECRETION BY TISSUE CULTURES

In 1969 Nickell and Maretzki (1114) reported an effective utilization of starch as a carbon source by sugarcane tissue cultures. It was proposed that an amylase secreted by the cells could account for the small quantities of starch found in most Hawaiian cane varieties, and that breeder selection might unintentionally favor high amylase. Further to this, it was proposed that commercial-scale tissue cultures might be used to produce sucrose from an inexpensive polysaccharide through utilization of the amylase factor. It is therefore appropriate to record here that starch is not a universal source of carbon for *in vitro* growth of plant tissues, and to explore briefly the rather unique production of amylase which makes this utilization possible in sugarcane cells.

In establishing media for specific tissue culture purposes, early workers found that starch was either utilized but poorly (728, 729, 730) or not at all (563, 564). An exception to this was the work of Nickell and Burkholder (1094) who reported in 1950 that starch was quite suitable as a carbon source for tissue cultures of *Rumex acetosa*. The following year Brakke and Nickell (221) reported starch hydrolysis by an α-amylase secreted from intact *Rumex* cells into the starch-containing medium. In the presence of abundant maltase this was similar, in effect, to supplying the tissue cultures with glucose.

An important feature of the enzyme was its extracellular nature. Endogenous amylase is commonly released upon rupture of cells or wounding of intact tissues. The wounding process itself, *i.e.*, the destruction of the enzyme's normal configuration within the cell, was formerly thought to be a prerequisite for activating plant enzymes (221, 829). Black (189) attached great importance to the act of wounding in tumor induction: "...Although the writer is not certain that all tumors arise at the site of a wound it is certain from preliminary experiments that some of them do." Black made a point of including the term "wound" in the names coined for both the disease and virus.

More recent studies have shown that peroxidase, acid phosphatase, and IAA oxidase, in addition to amylase, are secreted by tissue cultures of six different species (1376). Corn roots have been shown to secrete invertase, RNAase, and DNAase into bathing solutions (315). Noting these and other reports, Varner (1478, p. 20) concluded that "...many – perhaps all – plant cells have a limited capacity for modifying their environment through the secretion of hydrolytic enzymes."

Straus (1375) found invertase in cell wall fractions of cultural tissues from rose, pear, tobacco, corn, and other species. Invertase release was obtained by prolonged incubation or treatment with papain. Unlike a sugarcane invertase whose activity closely parallels growth rate in elongating internodes (690, 590), Straus found no relationship between the activity of cell wall invertase and growth rate.

Brakke and Nickell (221) concluded from their studies of *Rumex* virus tumor tissue, growing on a starch-containing medium, "...that large protein molecules comprising the enzyme pass outward through the plasma membrane and the cell wall". They had no way of knowing at that time whether the α-amylase was localized in the cell wall or lightly bound on the cell surface. However, these workers did recognize the unique concept of having large, catalytic protein molecules secreted from the cell to its external environment where it would bring about chemical changes important to continued cell growth.

Brakke and Nickell (221) quite understandably set about to determine whether amylase secretion was a normal function of the *Rumex* root or a unique property of the virus-induced tumor. Following development of a microassay suitable for quantitative study of the secreted α-amylase, Brakke and Nickell evaluated the enzyme's physical–chemical properties (221) and later studied its behavior when treated with variable levels of plant hormones (222). The latter included 2,4-D, IAA, and β-naphthoxyacetic acid supplied to the enzyme preparation (inoculated liquid medium) at levels ranging up to 100 ppm. Even at the highest hormone level there was no effect produced on the enzyme that exceeded the limits of experimental error. The greatest effect recorded was a 10-percent activity decrease produced by 100 ppm of β-naphthoxyacetic acid.

In a subsequent paper Nickell and Brakke (1100) examined biological factors relating to the amylase secretion, including rate of production and conditions governing the enzyme's secretion and activity. Included at this time were experiments with various crown-gall tissues. The failure of these tissues to grow rapidly with starch as their carbon source was correlated with inadequate secretion of a starch-hydrolyzing enzyme.

The studies by Maretzki *et al.*[5] on α-amylase help to explain the adaptation of sugarcane cell suspensions to a starch energy source. They do suggest certain inconsistencies in the carbohydrate–growth relationships of cultured cells and intact tissues. Maretzki *et al.* do not claim starch induction of amylolytic activity, but induction *per se* becomes a mute point in view of the accelerated release of enzymes to the external medium. However, even if one assumes an adequate enzyme complement to bring the large α-amylase products to the level of sugar phosphates, the meaning of these reactions in the context of sugarcane growth remains hazy. The increased starch hydrolytic potential showed no consistent relationships to cell growth, whereas the hydrolysis of sucrose has been positively correlated with expansion rates of intact stem tissue (*cf.* Chapter 10, pp. 386–393). Treatment with gibberellic acid (GA) did not increase cell growth even though amylase activity was increased. Moreover, the GA effect, coming more than 48 hours after hormone treatment, is inconsistent with the GA role of invertase mRNA stabilization in intact tissues or tissue extracts (*cf.* Chapter 10, pp. 381–386). This picture is further complicated by the metabolic sink nature of expanding sugarcane tissues. The latter are subject to a regulated and varying input of photosynthate and may perform in a feedback control system for source reactions (*cf.* Chapter 4, pp. 175, 176, 185–187)[9, 10]. Hence, the question remains as to whether or not the growth of cell suspension cultures offers an authentic model of growth processes operating in the physiological source-to-sink system.

---

[9]Beevers, H., 1969. Metabolic sinks. Chapter 8 in *Physiological Aspects of Crop Yield*, Am. Soc. Agron., Madison, Wisc.

[10]Neales, T.F. and Incoll, L.D., 1968. The control of leaf photosynthesis rate by level of assimilate concentration in the leaf. A review of the hypothesis, *Bot. Rev.* 34: 107–125.

BIBLIOGRAPHY

A

1 Abbot, E.V., 1961. A new strain of sugarcane mosaic virus, *Phytopathology* 51: 643.
2 Acevedo-Ramos, G., 1962. Analysis of probable relationships between leaf potassium percentage and sucrose content and maturity of sugarcane, *J. Agric. Univ. P.R.* 46(1): 15–22.
3 Adams, M. and Hudson, C.S., 1943. New methods for the purification of invertase and some properties of the resulting products, *J. Am. Chem. Soc.* 65: 1359–1368.
4 Ahrens, W., 1924. Weitere Untersuchungen über die Anhängigkeit des gegenseitigen Mengenverhältnisses der Kohlenhydrate in Laubblatt vom Wassergehalt. *Bot. Arch.* 5: 234–259 [*Bot. Abstr.* 14: 1012 (1925)].
5 Akazawa, T., Minamikawa, T. and Murata, T., 1964. Enzymatic mechanisms of starch synthesis in ripening rice grains, *Plant Physiol.* 39: 371–378.
6 Akazawa, T., 1965. Starch, inulin, and other reserve polysaccharides. Chapter 12 in *Plant Biochemistry* (Bonner, J.F. and Varner, J.E., eds.), Academic Press, New York, N.Y.
7 Akers, J.J. and Fang, S.C., 1956. Studies on plant metabolism. VI. Effect of 2,4-D on the metabolism of aspartic acid and glutamic acid in the bean plant, *Plant Physiol.* 31: 34–37.
8 Aldrich, S.R. and Leng, E.R., 1966. *Modern Corn Production*, F and W Publishing Corp., Cincinnati, Ohio.
9 Alers-Alers, S. and Samuels, G., 1963. The topping of sugarcane, *J. Agric. Univ. P.R.* 47(4): 257–264.
10 Alexander, A.G., 1960. *Effects of Varying Nutrient Levels on Growth and Enzyme Activity of Cauliflower*, Thesis submitted to the Faculty of the Graduate School, University of Maryland, College Park, Md., in partial fulfillment of requirements for the degree of Doctor of Philosophy, 1960.
11 Alexander, A.G., 1964. Sucrose–enzyme relationships in immature sugarcane as affected by variable nitrate and potassium supplied in sand culture, *J. Agric. Univ. P.R.* 48(3): 165–231.
12 Alexander, A.G., 1964. The biosynthesis of sucrose in sugarcane, *J. Agric. Univ. P.R.* 48(4): 265–283.
13 Alexander, A.G. and González-Ibañez, J., 1964. Residual effects of Diuron [3-(3,4-dichlorophenyl)-1,1-dimenthylurea] on the sugar content and sugar-metabolizing enzymes of ratoon sugarcane 25 months following variable soil treatment, *J. Agric. Univ. P.R.* 48(4): 284–303.
14. Alexander, A.G., 1965. Effects of tungsten and molybdenum on sucrose content and hydrolytic enzymes of immature sugarcane, *J. Agric. Univ. P.R.* 49(4): 429–442.
15. Alexander, A.G., 1965. Physiological studies of enzymes catalyzing the synthesis and hydrolysis of sucrose, starch, and phosphorylated hexose in sugarcane, *J. Agric. Univ. P.R.* 49(1): 60–75.
16 Alexander, A.G., 1965. Hydrolytic proteins of sugarcane: The acid invertases, *J. Agric. Univ. P.R.* 49(3): 287–307.
17 Alexander, A.G., 1965. The hydrolytic proteins of sugarcane: The acid phosphatases, *J. Agric. Univ. P.R.* 49(2): 204–228.
18 Alexander, A.G., 1965. Hydrolytic proteins of sugarcane: Amylase, *J. Agric. Univ. P.R.* 49(3): 308–324.
19 Alexander, A.G., 1965. Changes in leaf sugar content and enzyme activity of immature sugarcane following foliar application of indole-3-acetic acid, 2,4-dichlorophenoxyacetic acid, and maleic hydrazide, *J. Agric. Univ. P.R.* 49(1): 1–34.
20 Alexander, A.G., 1965. Sucrose–enzyme relationships in immature sugarcane treated with variable molybdenum, calcium, iron, boron, lead, trichloroacetic acid, β-glycerophosphate, and starch, *J. Agric. Univ. P.R.* 49(4): 443–461.
21 Alexander, A.G., 1965. Induction of varying sugar levels in leaves of immature sugarcane by use of acid phosphatase inhibitors, *J. Agric. Univ. P.R.* 49(1): 35–39.
22 Alexander, A.G., 1965. Hydrolytic proteins of sugarcane: The Q enzyme, *J. Agric. Univ. P.R.* 49(2): 176–203.
23 Alexander, A.G., 1965. Abnormal enzyme activity as an early indicator of nutrient deficiencies in plants, *Proc. Caribb. Food Crops Soc.* 3: 23–28.

24 Alexander, A.G., 1965. Behavior of enzymes governing starch- and sucrose-forming pathways in two sugarcane varieties supplied with variable nitrate and phosphate in sand culture, *J. Agric. Univ. P.R.* 49(2): 153–175.
25 Alexander, A.G., 1966. Effects of amylase and invertase regulators upon sugar content, protein content, and enzyme activity of immature sugarcane, *J. Agric. Univ. P.R.* 50(1): 18–35.
26 Alexander, A.G., 1966. Oxidizing enzymes of sugarcane: Cytochrome *c* oxidase, *J. Agric. Univ. P.R.* 50(2): 131–145.
27 Alexander, A.G., 1966. The oxidizing enzymes of sugarcane: Polyphenol oxidase (tyrosinase), *J. Agric. Univ. P.R.* 50(2): 113–130.
28 Alexander, A.G., 1967. Evaluation of sugar–enzyme relationships among twelve Puerto Rico sugarcane varieties, *J. Agric. Univ. P.R.* 51(1): 29–38.
29 Alexander, A.G., 1967. *In vitro* effects of Diuron [3-(3,4-dichlorophenyl)-1,1-dimethylurea] upon enzymes catalyzing the synthesis and hydrolysis of sucrose, starch, and phosphorylated hexose in sugarcane, *Proc. Int. Soc. Sugar Cane Technol.* 12: 582–589.
30 Alexander, A.G., 1967. Enzyme–sugar relationships in immature sugarcane treated with ascorbic acid, cysteine, hydroxylamine, cyanide, silicon, and iron, *J. Agric. Univ. P.R.* 51(1): 46–54.
31 Alexander, A.G., 1967. High sucrose and abnormal enzyme activity as a function of nutritional stress in sugarcane, *J. Agric Univ. P.R.* 51(4): 325–333.
32 Alexander, A.G., 1967. The biosynthesis of starch in sugarcane, *Proc. Int. Soc. Sugar Cane Technol.* 12: 625–638.
33 Alexander, A.G., 1967. Purification and electrophoretic behavior of sugarcane invertases, *J. Agric. Univ. P.R.* 51(1): 39–45.
34 Alexander, A.G. and Samuels, G., 1968. Controlled-temperature studies of growth, enzymology, and sucrose production by two sugarcane varieties in Puerto Rico, *J. Agric. Univ. P.R.* 52(3): 204–217.
35 Alexander, A.G., 1968. *In vitro* effects of silicon on the action patterns of sugarcane acid invertase, *J. Agric. Univ. P.R.* 52(4): 311–322.
36 Alexander, A.G., 1968. Growth, enzyme, and sugar responses of immature sugarcane to foliar treatments with 6-azauracil and gibberellic acid, *J. Agric. Univ. P.R.* 52(4): 295–310.
37 Alexander, A.G., 1968. Interrelationships of gibberellic acid and nitrate in sugar production and enzyme activity of sugarcane, *J. Agric. Univ. P.R.* 52(1): 19–28.
38 Alexander, A.G., 1968. Conservación de la sacarosa en el jugo de la caña de azúcar con meta-silicato de sodio (with English translation), *Informe Técnico* Núm. 26, Estación Experimental Agrícola, U.P.R., Río Piedras, P.R.
39 Alexander, A.G., 1969. Effects of combined silicon and gibberellic acid on enzyme behavior and sucrose content of immature sugarcane, *Proc. Int. Soc. Sugar Cane Technol.* 13: 522–531.
40 Alexander, A.G., 1969. The use of chemicals for sucrose control in sugarcane. *Sugar y Azúcar* 1969(2): 21–25.
41 Alexander, A.G., 1969. Interrelationships of nitrate and 6-azauracil in the growth, enzymology, and sucrose production of immature sugarcane, *J. Agric. Univ. P.R.* 53(2): 81–92.
42 Alexander, A.G., 1969. *In vitro* effects of silicon on hydrolytic and oxidative enzymes of sugarcane, *13th Congr. Int. Soc. Sugar Cane Technol., Taiwan, 1968*, Preprint No. A-03; Summary, 13: 532.
43 Alexander, A.G., 1969. Comparative studies of yeast and sugarcane invertases, *J. Agric. Univ. P.R.* 53(1): 41–56.
44 Alexander, A.G., 1969. The potential of sugarcane to produce sucrose, *Proc. Int. Soc. Sugar Cane Technol.* 13: 1–24.
45 Alexander, A.G. and Montalvo-Zapata, R., 1969. Enzyme studies of sucrose decline in sugarcane desiccated with Paraquat, *J. Agric. Univ. P.R.* 53(4): 230–250.
46 Alexander, A.G. and Montalvo-Zapata, R., 1970. The use of silicon to preserve sucrose in sugarcane desiccated with Paraquat and Diquat *J. Agric. Univ. P.R.* 54(2): 247–263.
47 Alexander, A.G. and Montalvo-Zapata, R., 1970. Enzymatic factors in the sucrose decline of

sugarcane desiccated with Paraquat, Diquat, and Dinitrobutylphenol, *J. Agric. Univ. P.R.* 54(1): 28–49.

48 Alexander, A.G., Kumar, A., Montalvo-Zapata, R. and Spain, G.L., 1970. Response of sugarcane enzymes to variable light: Variable illumination studies of invertase, ATPase, and amylase in plants experiencing nitrate- and gibberellic acid-induced stress, *J. Agric. Univ. P.R.* 54(3): 448–476.

49 Alexander, A.G., Montalvo-Zapata, R. and Kumar, A., 1970. Gibberellic acid activity in sugarcane as a function of the number and frequency of applications, *J. Agric. Univ. P.R.* 54(3): 477–503.

50 Alexander, A.G., Montalvo-Zapata, R. and Kumar, A., 1970. Enzyme–silicon studies of gibberellic acid-treated sugarcane during the post-growth stimulatory phase, *J. Agric. Univ. P.R.* 54(1): 82–95.

51 Alexander, A.G. and Montalvo-Zapata, R., 1970. Relationships of light to enzyme and sucrose transformations in sugarcane treated with Paraquat, *J. Agric. Univ. P.R.* 54(2): 264–296.

52 Alexander, A.G. and Montalvo-Zapata, R., 1971. Progress in chemical sucrose control, *Proc. P.R. Sugar Technol Annu. Meet., November, 1970.*

53 Alexander, A.G., Montalvo-Zapata, R. and Spain, G.L., 1972. Prevention of sugarcane flower production with Paraquat, gibberellic acid, and silicon: Chemical effects on growth, sucrose production, and enzyme activity, *J. Agric. Univ. P.R.* (in press).

54 Alexander, A.G., Montalvo-Zapata, R. and Justiniano, M., 1972. Diurnal behavior of sugarcane acid invertase, *J. Agric. Univ. P.R.* (in press).

55 Alexander, A.G., Samuels, G. and Spain, G.L., 1972. Physiology of sugarcane under water stress: Invertase, ATPase and amylase behavior in plants experiencing water deficiency, night flooding, and continuous flooding, *J. Agric. Univ. P.R.* 56(2): 115–133.

56 Alexander, A.G., Montalvo-Zapata, R. and Kumar, A., 1972. Light- and nitrogen-sensitive adenosine triphosphatases in sugarcane leaves, *Proc. Int. Soc. Sugar Cane Technol.* 14: (in press).

57 Alexander, A.G., Acín-Díaz, N. and Montalvo-Zapata, R., 1971. Inversion control in sugarcane juice with sodium metasilicate, *Proc. Int. Soc. Sugar Cane Technol.* 14: (in press).

58 Alers-Alers, S. and Samuels, G., 1970. Sugarcane topping in Puerto Rico (personal communications with the author, March, 1970).

59 Alfaro, J. 1928. Some experiments with the *Uba* cane, *Proc. Annu. Conf. Cuban·Sugar Technol. Assoc.* 2: 36–45.

60 Alford, J.A. and McCleskey, C.S., 1942. Some observations on bacteria causing slime in cane juice, *La. Acad. Sci.* 1(1): 36–41.

61 Allard, H.A. and Evans, H., 1941. Growth and flowering of some tame and wild grasses in response to different photoperiods, *J. Agric. Res.* 62: 193–228.

62 Allard, H.A., 1938. Complete or partial inhibition of flowering in certain plants when days are too short or too long, *J. Agric. Res.* 57: 775–789.

63 Allen, M.B., Arnon, D.I., Capindale, J.B., Whatley, F.R. and Durham, L.J., 1955. Photosynthesis by isolated chloroplasts. III. Evidence for complete photosynthesis, *J. Am. Chem. Soc.* 77: 4149–4155.

64 Alvarer, F.G. and Alaherlaha, P., 1954. Increasing the sugar content of growing cane by spraying it with molasses, *Caña Azúcar* 2(2): 23–24,26 [Abstr., *S. Afr. Sugar J.* 38: 125 (1954)].

65 Amling, H.J., Turner, J.L. and Taylor, T.D., 1963. Preliminary evaluation of two dipyridyl quaternary salts for post-emergent weed control in apple, peach, and pecan plantings, *Proc. Southern Weed Conf.* 16: 164–167.

66 Anderson, I.C. and Fuller, R.C., 1958. Photophosphorylation by isolated chromatophores of the purple sulfur bacteria, *Arch. Biochem. Biophys.* 76: 168–179.

67 Andrews, T.J. and Hatch, M.D., 1969. Properties and mechanism of action of pyruvate, phosphate dikinase from leaves, *Biochem. J.* 114: 117–123.

68 Anon., 1914. Barbados Dept. Agric. The deterioration of cut cane, *Barbados Dept. Agric. Work*, 1910– 1912 (Part III): 42–46.
69 Anon., 1952. *Annu. Rept. Exp. Sta. Hawaiian Sugar Plant. Assoc.*, pp. 48–49.
70 Anon., 1956. Wonder chemical gibberellic acid increases growth rate of sugarcane, *Annu. Rept. Exp. Sta. Hawaiian Sugar Plant. Assoc.*, pp.11–12.
71 Anon., 1956. Cane flowering reaches practical stage, *Annu. Rept. Exp. Sta. Hawaiian Sugar Plant. Assoc.*, pp. 49–50.
72 Anon., 1956. *Annu. Rept. Exp. Sta. Hawaiian Sugar Plant. Assoc.*, pp. 57–58.
73 Anon., 1957. Abstracts of current research on the effects of gibberellic acid on plants, *Velsicol Chem. Corp. Bull.* No. 512.
74 Anon., 1957. Gibrel prepared by Merck and Co., Inc., 44 pp.
75 Anon., 1959. Flowering of sugarcane, *Annu. Rept. Exp. Sta. Hawaiian Sugar Plant. Assoc.*, pp. 61–63.
76 Anon., 1960. Photosynthesis rate decreased by nutritional deficiencies, *Annu. Rept. Exp. Sta. Hawaiian Sugar Plant. Assoc.*, pp. 19–20.
77 Anon., 1961. Cultural practices. Potassium deficiency. *Annu. Rept. Exp. Sta. Hawaiian Sugar Plant. Assoc.*, pp. 12–13.
78 Anon., 1962. *Long Ashton Agric. Hortic. Res. Sta. Annu. Rept.* (1960–1962): 32.
79 Anon., 1964. Chemical control of growth and ripening, *Rept. David North Plant Res. Cent.* (1964): 48–55.
80 Anon., 1967. Investigations into the polysaccharides of sugarcane, *Sugar Milling Res. Inst. Annu. Rept.* (1967): 15–17.
81 Anon., 1968. Photosynthesis in sugarcane, *Annu. Rept. Tate Lyle Ltd. Res. Cent.*, pp. 57–60.
82 Anon., 1968. Deterioration no longer major problem, *Annu. Rept. Queensland Soc. Sugar Cane Technol.* 41: 29–30.
83 Anon., 1968. Chemical ripening. *Annu. Rept. Tate Lyle Ltd. Res. Cent.* (1968): 21–26.
84 Anon., 1968. Investigation into the polysaccharides of sugarcane, *Sugar Milling Res. Inst. Annu. Rept.* (1968): 8.
85 Anon., 1969. Chemical ripening. *Annu. Rept. Tate Lyle Ltd. Res. Cent.* (1969): 31–32.
86 Anon., 1969. Sugarcane research goals and problem areas. B. Production–Goal. III. In *A National Program of Research for Sugar*, Rept. of Joint Task Force, U.S.D.A., State Universities, and Land Grant Colleges.
87 Anon., 1969. Sugar cane is different, *Nature* 22(4): 847.
88 Anon., 1969. Photosynthesis in sugarcane, *Annu. Rept. Tate Lyle Ltd. Res. Cent.* (1969): 43–48.
89 Anon., 1970. Photosynthesis in sugarcane, *Annu. Rept. Tate Lyle Ltd. Res. Cent.* (1970): 35–37.
90 Arceneaux, G., 1935. Studies of ripening of sugarcane in Louisiana and of effect of topping upon yields of cane and sugar per acre, *U.S.Dept.Agric. Circ.* No. 368, 32 pp.
91 Arceneaux, G. and Davidson, L.G., 1944. Some effects of trash in cane on milling results, *Sugar Bull.* 22(18): 151–158.
92 Arceneaux, G. and Davidson, L.G., 1948. Test of cyanamid for killing sugarcane foliage in advance of harvest, *Sugar Bull.* 26(15): 230–231, 238.
93 Arceneaux, G., Coleman, R.E. and Hebert, L.P., 1950. Evidence of inheritance to freezing injury in sugarcane seedlings produced at Canal Point, Florida, *Proc. Int. Soc. Sugar Cane Technol.* 7: 116–127.
94 Arceneaux, G. and Kassem, E.S., 1963. A plan for the improvement of sugarcane varieties in Egypt, *Sugar J.* 25: 10–36.
95 Arceneaux, G., 1967. Cultivated sugarcanes of the world and their botanical derivation, *Proc. Int. Soc. Sugar Cane Technol.* 12: 844–854.
96 Arceneaux, G., 1969. Breeding sugarcane varieties for the northern Caribbean, *Proc. Int. Soc. Sugar Cane Technol.* 13: 1034–1046.
97 Arnon,, D.I., Allen, M.B. and Whatley, F.R., 1954. Photosynthesis by isolated chloroplasts, *Nature* 174: 394–396.

98 Arnon, D.I., 1955. The chloroplast as a complete photosynthetic unit, *Science* 122: 9–16.

99 Arnon, D.I., Allen, M.B. and Whatley, F.R., 1956. Photosynthesis by isolated chloroplasts. IV. General concept and comparison of three photochemical reactions, *Biochim. Biophys. Acta* 20: 449–461.

100 Arnon, D.I., Whatley, F.R. and Allen, M.B., 1957. Triphosphopyridine nucleotide as a catalyst of photosynthetic phosphorylation, *Nature* 180: 182–185.

101 Arnon, D.I., Whatley, F.R. and Allen, M.B., 1958. Assimilatory power in photosynthesis, *Science* 127: 1026–1034.

102 Arnon, D.I., 1959. Conversion of light into chemical energy in photosynthesis, *Nature* 184: 10–21.

103 Arnon, D.I., Whatley, F.R. and Allen, M.B., 1959. Photosynthesis by isolated chloroplasts. VIII. Photosynthetic phosphorylation and the generation of assimilatory power, *Biochim. Biophys. Acta* 32: 47–57.

104 Arnon, D.I., 1961. Cell-free photosynthesis and the energy-conversion process. In *Light and Life* (McElroy, W.D. and Glass, B., eds.), pp. 489–566, Johns Hopkins Press, Baltimore, Md.

105 Arnon, D.I., 1965. Ferredoxin and photosynthesis, *Science* 149: 1460–1470.

106 Arnon, D.I. Tsujimoto, H.Y. and McSwain, B.D., 1965. Photosynthetic phosphorylation and electron transport, *Nature* 207: 1367–1372.

107 Arnon, D.I., 1967. Photosynthetic activity of isolated chloroplasts, *Physiol. Rev.* 47(3): 317–358.

108 Arnon, D.I., Tsujimoto, H.Y. and McSwain, B.D., 1967. Ferredoxin and photosynthetic phosphorylation, *Nature* 214: 562–566.

109 Aronoff, S. and Bacon, J.S.D., 1952. The action of invertase preparations. II, *Arch. Biochem. Biophys.* 41: 476–478.

110 Arreguin-Lozano, B. and Bonner, J., 1949. Experiments on sucrose formation by potato tubers as influenced by temperature, *Plant Physiol.* 24: 720–738.

111 Artschwager, E., 1925. Anatomy of the vegetative organs of sugarcane, *J. Agric. Res.* 30: 197–242.

112 Artschwager, E., 1954. A taxonomic study of *Saccharum sinense* Roxb. and *S. barberi* Jeswiet, *U.S.Dept. Agric. Tech. Bull.* No. 1098, 87 pp.

113 Artschwager, E. and Brandes, E.W., 1958. *Sugarcane*, Agriculture Handbook No. 122, U.S. Gov. Printing Office, Washington, D.C.

114 Arvier, A.C., 1965. The pre-harvest application of desiccants to sugarcane foliage, *Proc. 32nd Conf. Queensland Soc. Sugar Cane Technol.* 32: 125–132.

115 Arvier, A.C., 1969. Further studies of chemical control of arrowing, *Proc. 36th Conf. Queensland Soc. Sugar Cane Technol.* 36: 143–145.

116 Ashton, F.M., 1956. Effects of a series of cycles of alternating low and high soil water contents on the rate of apparent photosynthesis in sugarcane, *Plant Physiol.* 31: 266–273.

117 Aubert, J.P., Milhaud, G. and Millet, J., 1957. L'assimilation de l'anhydride carbonique par de bactéries chimioautotrophes, *Ann. Inst. Pasteur* 92: 515–528.

118 Aughtry, J.D., 1958. The responses of ratoon cane to nitrogen as influenced by climate and age of cane, *J. Jamaican Assoc. Sugar Technol.* 21: 8-15.

119 Avigad, G., 1964. Sucrose–uridine disphosphate glucosyltransferase from Jerusalem artichoke tubers, *J. Biol. Chem.* 239: 3613–3618.

120 Avron, M., Krogmann, D.W. and Jagendorf, A.T., 1958. The relation of photosynthetic phosphorylation to the Hill reaction, *Biochim Biophys. Acta* 30: 144–153.

121 Avron, M., 1962. Light-dependent adenosine triphosphatase in chloroplasts, *J. Biol. Chem.* 237(6): 2011–2017.

122 Axelrod, B. and Bandurski, R.S., 1953. Phosphoglyceryl kinase in higher plants, *J. Biol. Chem.* 204: 939–948.

123 Axelrod, B., 1965. Mono- and oligosaccharides. Chapter 11 in *Plant Biochemistry* (Bonner, J. and Varner, E.J., eds.), p.231, Academic Press, New York, N.Y.

124 Axelrod, B. and Jang, R., 1954. Purification and properties of phosphoriboisomerase from alfalfa, *J. Biol. Chem.* 209: 847–855.

125 Ayers, A., 1930. Cane growth studies at the Waipo Station. Experiment E, *Hawaiian Plant. Rec.* 34: 445–460.

126 Ayers, A., 1966. Calcium silicate slag as a growth stimulant for sugarcane on low-silicon soils, *Soil Sci.* 101: 216–217.

B

127 Baba, K. and Baba, A., 1959. A relation between protein and silicate in rice plants, *Nippon Nogei Kagaku Kaishi* 33(8): 710–714.

128 Babu, C.N., 1967. Genetical studies in *Saccharum spontaneum* L. Inheritance of habit and occurrence of sprawlers, *Proc. Int. Soc. Sugar Cane Technol.* 12: 1014–1020.

129 Bacon, J.S.D., 1961. The development of invertase activity in washed slices of root tissue, *Biochem. J.* 79: 20–21.

130 Baeyer, A., 1870. Uber die Wasserentziehung und ihre Bedeutung für das Pflanzenleben und die Gahrung, *Ber. Dtsch. Chem. Ges.* 3: 63–75. Reviewed in *Photosynthesis and Related Processes* (Rabinowitch, E.I., ed.), Vol. I, 1945, p. 246, Interscience Publishers, New York, N.Y.

131 Bailey, K. and Webb, E.C., 1948. Purification of yeast hexokinase and its reaction with β,β'-dichlorodiethyl sulphide, *Biochem. J.* 42: 60–68.

132 Balch, R.T. and Lauritzen, J.I., 1933. Windrowing qualities of *Co. 281* and other varieties of sugarcane under Louisiana conditions, *U.S. Dept. Agric. Circ.* No. 304, 15 pp.

133 Balch, R.T., 1950. Effect of burning on the deterioration of sugarcane under Louisiana conditions, *U.S. Dept. Agric. Tech. Bull.* No. 1021, 23 pp.

134 Balch, R.T., 1953. Further notes on starch in Louisiana canes, juices and raw sugars, *Sugar J.* 14(8): 11–15.

135 Baldry, C.W., Bucke, C. and Coombs, J., 1969. Light/phosphoenol pyruvate dependent carbon dioxide fixation by isolated sugarcane chloroplasts, *Biochem. Biophys. Res. Commun.* 37: 828–832.

136 Baldry, C.W., Bucke, C., Coombs, J. and Gross, D., 1970. Phenols, phenol-oxidase and photosynthetic activity of chloroplasts isolated from sugarcane and spinach, *Planta* 94: 107–123.

137 Baldry, C.W., Bucke, C. and Coombs, J., 1970. Effects of some phenol-oxidase inhibitors on chloroplasts and carboxylating enzymes of sugarcane and spinach, *Planta* 94: 124–133.

138 Ballantyne, D.J., 1961. Growth regulators and the flowering of evergreen azaleas (*Rhododendron* cv.), *Proc. Am. Soc. Hortic. Sci.* 78: 521–531.

139 Baltscheffsky, H. and De Kiewiet, D.Y., 1964. Existence and localization of two phosphorylation sites in photophosphorylation of isolated spinach chloroplasts, *Acta Chem. Scand.* 18: 2406–2408.

140 Barba, R. and Nickell, L.G., 1969. Nutrition and organ differentiation in tissue cultures of sugarcane, a monocotyledon, *Planta* 89: 299–302.

141 Barber, C.A., 1916. Studies in Indian sugarcanes. II, *Mem. Dept. Agric. India, Bot. Ser.* 8: 103–199.

142 Barber, C.A., 1916. The classification of indigenous Indian canes, *Agric. J. India* 11: 371–376.

143 Barber, C.A., 1920. The origin of sugarcane, *Int. Sugar J.* 22: 249–251.

144 Barker, S.A., Bourne, E.J. and Peat, S., 1959. The enzymatic synthesis and degradation of starch. IV. The purification and storage of the Q enzyme of the potato, *J. Chem. Soc.* 3: 1705–1717.

145 Barnes, J.H., 1916. The after-ripening of sugarcane. Chemical changes which take place after cutting, *Agric. J. India* 12: 200–215.

146 Barnett, N.M. and Naylor, A.W., 1966. Amino acid and protein metabolism in Bermuda grass during water stress, *Plant Physiol.* 41: 1222–1230.

147 Barrier, G.E. and Loomis, W.E., 1957. Absorption and translocation of 2,4-dichlorophenoxyacetic acid and ^{32}P in leaves, *Plant Physiol.* 32: 225–231.

148 Bassham, J.A., Benson, A.A. and Calvin, M., 1950. The role of malic acid, *J. Biol. Chem.* 185: 781–787.

149 Bassham, J.A. and Calvin, M., 1957. *The Path of Carbon in Photosynthesis*, p.7, Prentice-Hall, Englewood Cliffs, N.J.

150 Bassham, J.A., Benson, A.A., Kay, L.D., Harris, A.Z., Wilson, A.T. and Calvin, M., 1954. The path of carbon in photosynthesis. XXI. The cyclic regeneration of carbon dioxide acceptor, *J. Am. Chem. Soc.* 76: 1760–1770.

151 Bassham, J.A., 1964. Kinetic studies of the photosynthetic carbon reduction cycle, *Annu. Rev. Plant Physiol.* 15: 101–120.

152 Bassham, J.A., 1965. Photosynthesis: The path of carbon. Chapter 34 in *Plant Biochemistry* (Bonner, J. and Varner, J.E. eds.), pp. 887–888, Academic Press, New York, N.Y.

153 Bassham, J.A. and Kirk, M., 1968. *Comparative Biochemistry and Biophysics of Photosynthesis*, pp. 365–378, Univ. Tokyo Press, Tokyo.

154 Bates, J.F., 1957. Preliminary experiments on the effects of gibberellic acid on germination, growth, and flowering of sugarcane, *Proc. Br. W. Indies Sugar Technol.* (1957): 165–173.

155 Bates, J.F., 1960. Preliminary trials with desiccants in sugarcane, *Proc. Br. W. Indies Sugar Technol.* (1960): 43–48.

156 Bauer, L., 1953. Zur Frage Stoffbewegungen in der Pflanze mit besonder Berücksichtigung der Wanderung von Fluorochromen, *Planta* 42: 367–451.

157 Baver, L.D., 1960. Plant and soil composition relationships as applied to cane fertilization, *Hawaiian Plant. Rec.* 56(1): 1–53.

158 Baver, L.D., 1962. *Annu. Rept. Exp. Sta. Hawaiian Sugar Plant. Assoc.*, p. 1.

159 Baver, L.D., 1963. A decade of research progress, 1950–59, *Hawaiian Plant. Rec.* 57(1): 1–18.

160 Bean, R.C. and Hassid, W.Z., 1955. Synthesis of disaccharides with pea preparations, *J. Am. Chem. Soc.* 77: 5737–5738.

161 Beauchamp, C.E., 1939. The composition of the crude chlorophyll of cane leaves and its relationships with cane growth, *Proc. Int. Soc. Sugar Technol.* 6: 811–832.

162 Beauchamp, C.E., 1949. A new method of increasing the sugar content of sugarcane, *Proc. Cuba Sugar Cane Technol. Assoc.* 23: 55–87.

163 Beauchamp, C.E., 1950. Effects of 2,4-D on sugar content of sugarcane, *Sugar J.* 13(5): 57–70; 13(6): 20–30.

164 Beevers, L. and Hageman, R.H., 1963. The mechanism of induction of nitrate reductase in higher plants, *Plant Physiol.* 38: xxxii (Suppl.).

165 Bennun, A. and Avron, M., 1964. Light-dependent and light-triggered adenosine triphosphatases in chloroplasts, *Biochim. Biophys. Acta* 79: 646–648.

166 Bennun, A. and Avron, M., 1965. The relation of light-dependent and light-triggered adenosine triphosphatases to photophosphorylation, *Biochim. Biophys. Acta* 109: 117–127.

167 Benson, A.A. and Calvin, M. 1950. Carbon dioxide fixation by green plants, *Annu. Rev. Plant Physiol.* 1: 25–42.

168 Berg, W.E., 1968. Kinetics of uptake and incorporation of valine in the sea urchin embryo, *Exp. Cell Res.* 49: 379–395.

169 Bergey, D.H., Breed, R.S., Murray, E.G.D. and Hitchens, A.P., 1939. *Bergey's Manual of Determinative Bacteriology*, Williams and Wilkins Co., Baltimore, Md.

171 Bergman, N. and Rettger, L.F., 1918. The influence of carbohydrate on the nitrogen metabolism of bacteria, *J. Bacteriol* 3: 389–402.

170 Berliner, R.W., 1959. Membrane transport. In *Biophysical Science – A Study Program* (Oncley, J.L., ed.), p. 342, John Wiley and Sons, New York, N.Y.

172 Berry, J.A., Downton, W.J.S. and Tregunna, E.B., 1970. The photosynthetic carbon metabolism of *Zea mays* and *Gomphrena globosa*: The location of the CO_2 fixation and the carboxyl transfer reactions, *Can. J. Bot.* 48(4): 777–786.

173 Bews, J.W., 1929. *The World's Grasses*, 408 pp., Longmans, Green and Co., London.

174 Biddulph, O., 1941. Diurnal migration of injected radiophosphorus from bean leaves, *Am. J. Bot.* 28: 348–352.

175 Biddulph, O., Cory, R. and Biddulph, S., 1956. The absorption and translocation of sulfur in the red kidney bean, *Plant Physiol.* 31: 28–33.
176 Biddulph, O. and Cory, R., 1957. An anylysis of translocation in the phloem of the bean plant using THO, ^{32}P, and $^{14}CO_2$, *Plant Physiol.* 32: 608–619.
177 Biddulph, O., Biddulph, S., Cory, R. and Koontz, H., 1958. Circulation patterns for phosphorus, sulfur, and calcium in the bean plant, *Plant Physiol.* 33: 293–300.
178 Bieleski, R.L., 1960. The physiology of sugarcane. III. Characteristics of sugar uptake in slices of mature and immature storage tissue, *Aust. J. Biol. Sci.* 13: 203–221.
179 Bieleski, R.L., 1960. The physiology of sugarcane. IV. Effects of inhibitors on sugar accumulation in storage tissue slices, *Aust. J. Biol. Sci.* 13: 221–231.
180 Bieleski, R.L., 1962. The physiology of sugarcane. V. Kinetics of sugar accumulation, *Aust. J. Biol. Sci.* 15: 429–444.
181 Bieleski, R.L., 1966. Sites of accumulation in excised phloem and vascular tissues, *Plant Physiol.* 41: 455–466.
182 Bieleski, R.L., 1968. The physiology of sugarcane. II. The respiration of harvested sugarcane, *Aust. J. Biol. Sci.* 11: 315–328.
183 Bieske, G.C., 1970. Chemical ripening of sugarcane, *Proc. Queensland Soc. Sugar Cane Technol.*, pp. 117–124.
184 Bird, I.F., Porter, H.K. and Stocking, C.R., 1965. Intracellular localization of enzymes associated with sucrose synthesis in leaves, *Biochem. Biophys. Acta* 100: 366–375.
185 Birkett, L.S., 1962. The influence of tops and trash on the economics of sugar production (Private Report, Brookers Sugar Estates, Guyana).
186 Birt, L.M. and Hird, J.R., 1956. The uptake of amino acids by carrot slices, *Biochem. J.* 64: 305–311.
187 Bjorkman, O., 1966. The effects of oxygen concentration on photosynthesis in higher plants, *Physiol. Plant.* 19: 618–633.
188 Bjorkman, O. and Gauhl, E., 1969. Carboxydismutase activity in plants with and without β-carboxylation photosynthesis, *Planta* 88: 197–203.
189 Black, L.M.A., 1945. A virus tumor disease of plants, *Am. J. Bot.* 32: 408–415.
190 Black, L.M.A., 1946. Plant tumors induced by the combined action of wounds and virus, *Nature* 158: 56–57.
191 Black, L.M., 1947. Virus tumors in plants. *Growth* (Suppl.), *6th Growth Symp.*, pp. 79–84.
192 Black, C.C., 1970. The photosynthetic unit in plants which reduce CO_2 via the C_4-dicarboxylic acid cycle, *Int. Conf. on the Photosynthetic Unit, Gatlinburg, Tenn., May 19–21, 1970.*
193 Blackman, F.F., 1905. Optima and limiting factors, *Ann. Bot.* 19: 281–295.
194 Blackman, F.F. and Matthaei, G.L.G., 1905. Experimental researches in vegetable assimilation and respiration. IV. A quantitative study of carbon-dioxide assimilation and leaf temperature in natural illumination, *Proc. R. Soc. (London), Ser.* B. 76: 402–445. Reviewed in *Photosynthesis and Related Processes* (Rabinowitch, E.I., ed.), 1945, Vol. I, p. 172, Interscience Publishers, New York, N.Y.
195 Blackman, F.F. and Smith, A.M., 1911. Experimental researches in vegetable assimilation and respiration. IX. On assimilation in submerged water plants, concentration of carbon dioxide and other factors, *Proc. R. Soc. (London), Ser. B.* 83: 389–412.
196 Blinks, L.R., 1960. Chromatic transients in the photosynthesis of green, brown, and red algae. In *Comparative Biochemistry of Photoreactive Systems* (Allen, M.B., ed.), pp. 367–368, Academic Press, New York, N.Y.
197 Blouin, R.E., 1913. Una comparación de los resultados de los ensayos con las cañas de Java con los de las cañas "kavangire", zwinga, y morada y rayada del país, *Rev. Ind. Agric. Tucumán* 4: 141–150.
198 Bodnár, J., 1925. Biochemistry of the phosphorus metabolism of higher plants. I. The enzymic conversion of inorganic phosphoric acid into organic form, *Biochem. Z.* 165: 1–15 [*Chem. Abstr.* 20: 2518 (1926)].
199 Boehm, J., 1883. Uber Starkebildung aus Zucker, *Bot. Z,* 41: 49 (not seen).

200 Böhning, R.H., 1949. Time course of photosynthesis in apple leaves exposed to continuous illumination, *Plant Physiol.* 24: 222–240.
201 Böhning, R.H. and Burnside, C.A., 1956. The effect of light intensity on rate of apparent photosynthesis in leaves of sun and shade plants, *Am. J. Bot.* 43: 557–561.
202 Bonde, E.K., 1952. The influence of carbon dioxide concentration upon the rate of photosynthesis in *Sinapsis alba*, *Physiol. Plant.* 5: 298–304.
203 Boneta-García, E. and Lugo-López, M.A., 1962. Losses of sucrose in cut cane kept under shade or sun for different periods, *J. Agric. Univ. P.R.* 46(3): 189–194.
204 Bonner, J., 1950. *Plant Biochemistry*, Academic Press, New York, N.Y.
205 Bonner, J. and Varner, J.E., 1965. *Plant Biochemistry*, Academic Press, New York, N.Y.
206 Bonnet, J.A., Abruña, F. and Lugo-López, M.A., 1950. Trash disposal and its relation to cane yield, soil and water losses, *J. Agric. Univ. P.R.* 34(3): 286–293.
207 Bonnet, J.A., Riera, A.R. and Roldán, J., 1956. Correlation at different ages between nitrogen, green- and dry-matter contents of leaves, and yield of sugarcane grown in sand culture, *J. Agric. Univ. P.R.* 40(2): 101–109.
208 Bonnet, J.A., 1962. Chemical concept of sucrose formation and maturity status of harvested sugarcane in Puerto Rico, *Sugar J.* 25: 45–54.
209 Boon, W.R., 1968. The chemistry and mode of action of the bipyridylium herbicides Diquat and Paraquat, *Focus* (Plant Protection Information Service), Plant Protection Ltd., Fernhurst, Haslemere, Surrey, England.
210 Bor, N.L. 1940. Three new genera of Indian grasses, *Indian Forester* 66: 267–272.
211 Bor, N.L., 1940. *Flora of Assam*, Vol. 5, Calcutta, India (not seen).
212 Bor, N.L., 1960. *Grasses of Burma, Ceylon, India and Pakistan*, Pergamon Press, London.
213 Borden, R.J., 1937. Cane growth studies. The effect of sunlight on the utilization of nitrogen and potash by *H. 109* cane, *Hawaiian Plant. Rec.* 41: 3–5.
214 Borden, R.J., 1940. Nitrogen–potash–sunlight relationships, *Hawaiian Plant. Rec.* 44: 237–242.
215 Borden, R.J., 1944. Crop relations with special reference to nitrogen efficiency, *Hawaiian Plant. Rec.* 48: 65–72.
216 Borden, R.J., 1948. Nitrogen effects upon the yield and composition of sugarcane, *Hawaiian Plant. Rec.* 52(1): 1–51.
217 Borden, R.J., 1949. Recent developments in sources of nitrogen for fertilizing crops, *Hawaiian Plant. Rec.* 53: 78–88.
218 Borthwick, H.A., Hendricks, S.B. and Parker, M.W., 1952. The reaction controlling floral initiation, *Proc. Natl. Acad. Sci. (U.S.)* 38: 929–934.
219 Boysen Jensen, P., 1933. Uber die Bestimmung der Assimilationsintensität, *Planta* 21: 368–380.
220 Brachet, J., 1960. *The Biological Role of Ribonucleic Acid*, Elsevier Publishing Co., Amsterdam.
221 Brakke, M.K. and Nickell, L.G., 1951. Secretion of α-amylase by *Rumex* virus tumors *in vitro*. Properties and assay, *Arch. Biochem. Biophys.* 32: 28–41.
222 Brakke, M.K. and Nickell, L.G., 1952. Lack of effect of plant growth-regulators on the action of α-amylase secreted by virus tumor tissue, *Bot. Gaz.* 113: 482–484.
223 Brandes, E.W. and Klaphaak, P.J., 1925. Breeding of disease resisting sugar plants for America, *The Reference Book of Sugar Industry of the World*, pp.50–57 (not seen).
224 Brandes, E.W., 1929. Into primeval Papua by seaplane, *Natl. Geogr. Mag.* 56: 253–332.
225 Brandes, E.W. and Sartoris, G.B., 1936. Sugarcane: Its origin and improvement, *U.S.D.A. Yearbook of Agriculture* (1936): 561–611.
226 Brandes, E.W. and Matz, J., 1939. Problems and progress in breeding temperate zone sugarcane, *Sugar J.* 2: 3–6.
227 Brandes, E.W., Sartoris, G.B. and Grassl, C.O., 1947. Assembling and evaluating wild forms of sugarcane and closely related plants, *Proc. Int. Soc. Sugar Cane Technol.* 6: 128–154.
228 Brandes, E.W., 1951. Changes in seasonal growth gradients in geographically displaced sugarcane, *Proc. Int. Soc. Sugar Cane Technol.* 7: 1–32.

229 Brandes, E.W., 1956. Origin, dispersal and use in breeding of the Melanesian garden sugarcanes and their derivatives, *Saccharum officinarum* L., *Proc. Int. Soc. Sugar Cane Technol.* 9: 709–750.
230 Brandes, E.W., 1958. *Sugarcane*, U.S.D.A. Agriculture Handbook No. 122, U.S. Gov. Printing Office, Washington, D.C.
231 Breaux, R.D. and Dunkelman, P.H., 1969. Breeding for resistance to sugarcane mosaic with interspecific hybrids, *Proc. Int. Soc. Sugar Cane Technol.* 13: 927–932.
232 Breese, T.C. (I.C.I., Ltd.), 1959. Personal communication with Dr. J.F. Bates.
233 Bremer, G., 1922. Een cytologisch onderzoek van eenige soorten en soortbastaarden van het geslacht *Saccharum, Arch. Suikerind. Ned. Indië*, Mededel. Proefsta. Java Suikerind. (1922): 1–112 (not seen).
234 Bremer, G., 1924. De cytologie van het suikerriet. III. De chromosomen van primitieve vormen van het geslacht *Saccharum*, *Arch. Suikerind. Ned. Indië* (1924): 477–508 (not seen).
235 Bremer, G., 1925. The cytology of the sugarcane. III. The chromosomes of primitive forms of the genus *Saccharum, Genetica* 7: 293–322.
236 Bremer, G., 1932. On the somatic number of sugarcane forms and the chromosome numbers of indigenous Indian canes, *Proc. Int. Soc. Sugar Cane Technol.* 4: Bull. No. 20.
237 Bremer, G., 1949. Increase of chromosome numbers in species hybrids of *Saccharum, Proc. 8th Int. Congr. Genet., Stockholm, 1948. Hereditas*(Suppl.) (1949): 541–542.
238 Brett, P.G.C., 1949. Further report on sugarcane breeding in South Africa, *Proc. S. Afr. Sugar Technol. Assoc.* 23: 108–114.
239 Brett, P.G.C., 1950. Investigations on sugarcane breeding in Natal during 1949, *Proc. S. Afr. Sugar Technol. Assoc.* 24: 99–105.
240 Brett, P.G.C., 1950. Flowering and pollen fertility in relation to sugarcane breeding in Natal, *Proc. Int. Soc. Sugar Cane Technol.* 7: 43–56.
241 Brian, R.C., Homer, R.F., Stubbs, J. and Jones, R.L., 1958. A new herbicide; 1,1′-ethylene-2,2′-dipyridylium dibromide, *Nature* 181: 446–447.
242 Brian, P.W., Petty, J.H.P. and Richmond, P.T., 1959. Effect of gibberellic acid on development of autumn colour and leaf fall of deciduous woody plants, *Nature* 183: 58.
243 Brian, P.W., 1959. Effects of gibberellins on plant growth and development, *Biol. Rev.* 34: 37–84.
244 Brix, H.B., 1962. The effect of water stress on the rates of photosynthesis and respiration in tomato plants and Loblolly pine seedlings, *Physiol. Plant.* 15: 10–20.
245 Brodie, H.W., Yoshida, R. and Nickell, L.G., 1969. Effect of air and root temperatures on growth of four sugarcane clones, *Hawaiian Plant. Rec.* 58(3): 21–52.
246 Brown, A.H. and Franck, J., 1948. On the participation of carbon dioxide in the photosynthetic activity of illuminated chloroplast suspensions, *Arch. Biochem.* 16: 55–60.
247 Brown, A.H. and Frenkel, A.W., 1953. Photosynthesis, *Annu. Rev. Plant Physiol.* 4: 23–58.
248 Brown, A.H. and Weis, D., 1959. Relation between respiration and photosynthesis in the green algae, *Ankistrodesmus braunii, Plant Physiol.* 34(3): 224–234.
249 Brown, H.T. and Morris, G.H., 1893. A contribution to the chemistry and physiology of foliage leaves, *J. Chem. Soc.* 63: 604–677.
250 Brown, H.T. and Escombe, F., 1902. The influence of varying amounts of carbon dioxide in the air on the photosynthetic process of leaves and on the mode of growth of plants, *Proc. R. Soc. (London), Ser. B.* 70: 397–405.
251 Brown, R. and Danielli, J.F. (eds.), 1954. Active transport and secretion, *Symp. Soc. Exp. Biol.* 8: 1–502.
252 Browne, C.A. and Blouin, R.F., 1907. The chemistry of the sugar cane and its products in Louisiana, *La. Agric. Exp. Sta. Bull.* No. 91.
253 Bruijn, J., 1966. Deterioration of sugar cane after harvesting. Part I. Changes in juice composition, *Int. Sugar J.* 68: 331–334.
254 Bruijn, J., 1966. Deterioration of sugar cane after harvesting. Part II. Investigation of the polysaccharide formed, *Int. Sugar J.* 68: 356–358.

255 Buchanan, J.G., Bassham, J.A., Benson, A.A., Bradley, D.F., Calvin, M., Daus, L.L., Goodman, M., Hayes, P.M., Lynch, V.H., Norris, L.T. and Wilson, A.T., 1952. The role of phosphate in the metabolism of photosynthetic and chemoautotrophic organisms. Part 5 in *Phosphorus Metabolism* (McElroy, W.D. and Glass, B., eds.), Vol. 2, pp. 440–466, Johns Hopkins Press, Baltimore, Md.

256 Buchanan, J.G., 1953. The path of carbon in photosynthesis. XIX. The identification of sucrose phosphate in sugar beet leaves, *Arch. Biochem. Biophys.* 44: 140–149.

257 Buchanan, J.G., Lynch, V.H., Benson, A.A., Bradley, D.F. and Calvin, M., 1953. The path of carbon in photosynthesis. XVIII. The identification of nucleotide coenzymes, *J. Biol. Chem.* 203: 935–945.

258 Bull, T.A. and Glasziou, K.T., 1963. The evolutionary significance of sugar accumulation in *Saccharum, Aust. J. Biol. Sci.* 16: 737–742.

259 Bull, T.A., 1964. The effects of temperature, variety, and age on the response of *Saccharum* spp. to applied gibberellic acid, *Aust. J. Agric. Res.* 15: 77–84.

260 Bull, T.A., 1971. The C_4 pathway related to growth rates in sugarcane. Personal communication, February, 1971.

261 Burkard, J. and Neuberg, C., 1934. The origin of sucrose, *Biochem. Z.* 270: 229–234 [*Chem. Abstr.* 28: 5099 (1934)].

262 Burkholder, P.R. and Nickell, L.G., 1949. Atypical growth of plants. I. Cultivation of virus tumors of *Rumex* on nutrient agar, *Bot. Gaz.* 110: 426–437.

263 Burley, J.W.A., 1961. Carbohydrate translocation in raspberry and soybean, *Plant Physiol.* 36: 820–824.

264 Burma, D.P. and Mortimer, D.C., 1956. The biosynthesis of uridine disphosphate glucose and sucrose in sugar beet leaf, *Arch. Biochem. Biophys.* 62: 16–28.

265 Burr, G.O., 1936. Carbonic anhydrase and photosynthesis, *Proc. R. Soc. (London), Ser. B* 120: 42–46.

266 Burr, G.O. and Tanimoto, T., 1949. An improved micro-method for the determination of reducing sugars, *Proc. Hawaiian Acad. Sci.* 24: 7.

267 Burr, G.O. and Tanimoto, T., 1950. An improved micro-method for sugars using direct colorimetry of ferricyanide, *Fed. Proc.* 9: 157–158.

268 Burr, G.O., 1950. The flowering of sugarcane, *Rept. Hawaiian Sugar Technol.*, pp. 47–49.

269 Burr, G.O. and Tanimoto, T., 1955. Absorption and distribution of nutrients in sugarcane. Part II. Potassium, *Hawaiian Plant. Rec.* 59(1): 11–13.

270 Burr, G.O., Hartt, C.E., Tanimoto, T., Takahashi, D. and Brodie, H.W., 1957. The circulatory system of the sugarcane plant. *Radioisotopes in Scientific Research*, Pergamon Press, New York. *Proc. 1st (UNESCO) Int. Conf.* 4: 351–368.

271 Burr, G.O., Hartt, C.E., Brodie, H.W., Tanimoto, T., Kortschak, H.P., Takahashi, D., Ashton, F.M. and Coleman, R.E., 1957. The sugarcane plant, *Annu. Rev. Plant Physiol.* 8: 275–308.

272 Burr, G.O., 1960. *Rept. Hawaiian Sugar Plant. Assoc., Exp. Sta. Commun.*, pp. 14–15.

273 Burr, G.O., 1961. Personal communication with Dr. J.A. Bonnet, Estación Experimental, Río Piedras, P.R.

274 Burr, G.O., 1969. A note on the efficiency of sugarcane, *Taiwan Sugar Exp. Sta. Res. Rept.* No. 3.

275 Burr, G.O., 1970. Photosynthesis via the PGA and malic acid pathways, *Taiwan Sugar Exp. Sta. Res. Rept.* No. 6.

276 Burt, R.L., 1964. Carbohydrate utilization as a factor in plant growth, *Aust. J. Biol. Sci.* 17: 867–877.

277 Burt, R.L., 1966. Some effects of temperature on carbohydrate utilization and plant growth, *Aust. J. Biol. Sci.* 19: 711–714.

278 Burton, K. and Krebs, H.A., 1953. The free energy changes associated with the individual steps of the tricarboxylic acid cycle, glycolysis and alcoholic fermentation and with the hydrolysis of the pyrophosphate groups of adenosine triphosphate, *Biochem. J.* 54: 94–107.

279 Burton, W.G., 1965. The sugar balance in some British potato varieties during storage. I. Preliminary observations, *Eur. Potato J.* 8: 80–91.

280 Butler, G.W., 1963. Ion uptake by young wheat plants. II. The "apparent free space" of wheat roots, *Physiol. Plant.* 6: 617–635.
281 Buzacott, J.H., 1956. Photoperiodic control of the flowering of sugarcane, *Sugar Bull.* 32: 165–169.

C

282 Calderbank, A., 1960. Diquat: A new herbicide and desiccant, *J. Agric. Vet. Chem.* 1: 197–200.
283 Calderbank, A., Morgan, C.B. and Yuen, S.H., 1961. Determination of Diquat residues in potato tubers, *Analyst* 86: 569–579.
284 Calma, V.C., 1941. Studies on the deterioration of burnt sugarcane, *Philipp. Agric.* 29: 660–671.
285 Calvin, M. and Benson, A.A., 1949. The path of carbon in photosynthesis. IV. The identity and sequence of the intermediates in sucrose synthesis, *Science* 109: 140–142.
286 Calvin, M., Bassham, J.A. and Benson, A.A., 1950. Chemical transformations of carbon in photosynthesis, *Fed. Proc.* 9: 524–534.
287 Calvin, M., 1956. The photosynthetic carbon cycle, *Proc. 3rd Int. Congr. Biochem., Brussels*, pp. 211–225, Academic Press, New York, N.Y.
288 Calvin, M., 1959. Free radicals in photosynthetic systems, *Rev. Mod. Phys.* 31: 157–161.
289 Calvin, M. and Bassham, J.A., 1962. *The Photosynthesis of Carbon Compounds*, p. 10, W.A. Benjamin, Inc., New York, N.Y.
290 Canny, M.J., 1960. The breakdown of sucrose during translocation, *Ann. Bot. (London)* [N.S.] 24: 330–344.
291 Canny, M.J., 1960. The rate of translocation, *Biol. Rev.* 35: 507–532.
292 Canny, M.J., 1961. Measurements of the velocity of translocation, *Ann. Bot. (London)* [N.S.] 25: 152–167.
293 Canny, M.J., 1962. The mechanism of translocation, *Ann. Bot. (London)* [N.S.] 26: 603–617.
294 Canny, M.J., 1962. The translocation profile: Sucrose and carbon dioxide, *Ann. Bot. (London)* [N.S.] 26: 181–196.
295 Capó, B.G., 1934. Fertilizers and crop yields, *Sugar Manual for Puerto Rico and Hispaniola*, pp. 63–72.
296 Capó, B.G., 1938. A modification of Mitscherlich's method for the determination of the nutrient contents of a soil, *J. Agric. Univ. P.R.* 22(2): 137–170.
297 Capó, B.G., Samuels, G., Landrau, P., Jr., Alers-Alers, S. and Riera, A., 1955. The method of foliar diagnosis as applied to sugarcane, *Univ. P.R. Agric. Exp. Sta. Bull.* No. 123.
298 Capó, B.G., 1967. Additional evidence on the applicability of the new fertilizer–yield equation, *J. Agric Univ. P.R.* 51(2): 97–120.
299 Capó, B.G., 1967. A new fertilizer–yield equation, *Proc. Int. Soc. Sugar Cane Technol.* 12: 380–389.
300 Caputto, R., Leloir, L.F., Trucco, R.E., Cardini, C.E. and Paladini, A.C., 1940. The enzymatic transformation of galactose into glucose derivatives, *J. Biol. Chem.* 179: 497–498.
301 Caputto, R., Leloir, L.F., Cardini, C.E. and Paladini, A.C., 1950. Isolation of the coenzyme of the galactose phosphate–glucose phosphate transformation, *J. Biol. Chem.* 184: 333–350.
302 Cardini, C.E., Paladini, A.C., Caputto, R. and Leloir, L.F., 1950. Uridine diphosphate glucose: The coenzyme of the galactose–glucose phosphate isomerization, *Nature* 165: 191–192.
303 Cardini, C.E., Leloir, L.F. and Chiriboga, J., 1955. The biosynthesis of sucrose, *J. Biol. Chem.* 214: 149–155.
304 Cardini, C.E. and Leloir, L.F., 1957. Biosynthesis of sucrose, *Ciencia Invest. (Buenos Aires)* 13: 514. Biosynthesis of glucosides [*Chem. Abstr.* 58: 8248 (1958)].
305 Cardini, C.E. and Recondo, E., 1962. Specificity of nucleotide diphosphate sugars in sucrose biosynthesis, *Plant Cell Physiol.* 3: 313–318.

306 Carlson, M.C., 1929. Microchemical studies of rooting and non-rooting rose cuttings, *Bot. Gaz.* 87: 64–79.
307 Carr, D.J., 1966. Some aspects of the physiology of flowering, *Adv. Sci.* 23: 186–192.
308 Cayeré-Echavarría, A., 1969. Pruebas con desecantes en caña de azúcar (Autoridad de Tierras de Puerto Rico, 1968 y 1969), *Proc. P.R. Sugar Technol. Assoc.* (1969).
309 Celarier, R.P., 1956. Cytotaxonomy of the Andropogoneae. 1. Subtribes Dimeriinae and Saccharinae, *Cytologia* 21: 272–291.
310 Chacravarti, A.S., Srivastava, D.P. and Khanna, K.L., 1955. Use of synthetic hormones to step up sugar in cane, *Curr. Sci.* 24(9): 316–317.
311 Chacravarti, A.S., Srivastava, D.P. and Khanna, K.L., 1955. Foliar application of 2,4-D to increase sugar in cane, *Sugar J.* 18(6): 23–25.
312 Chaĭlakhyan, M.K., 1936. Facts in support of a hormonal theory of plant development, *C.R. Acad. Sci. U.S.S.R.* [N.S.] 4: 79–83 [*Chem. Abstr.* 31: 1464 (1937)]. *C.R. Acad. Sci. U.S.S.R.* [N.S.] 3: 443–447 [*Chem. Abstr.* 31: 5837 (1937)].
313 Chaĭlakhyan, M.K. and Butenko, R.G., 1957. *Plant Physiol. (U.S.S.R.)* 4: 426 (not seen).
314 Chamberlin, T.C. and Salisbury, R.D., 1907. *Geology* 3: 173 [quoted from Merrill (1012)].
315 Chang, C.W. and Bandurski, R.S., 1964. Exocellular enzymes of corn roots, *Plant Physiol.* 39: 60–64.
316 Chang, Jen-Hu, Cambell, R.B., Brodie, H.W. and Baver, L.D., 1967. Evapotranspiration research at the H.S.P.A. Experiment Station, *Proc. Int. Soc. Sugar Cane Technol.* 12: 10–24.
317 Chardón, C.E., 1956. Gibberellic acid, a new plant growth-promoting substance, *Proc. P.R. Sugar Technol. Assoc.* (1956).
318 Chen, D., Kessler, B. and Monselise, S.P., 1964. Studies on water regime and nitrogen metabolism of citrus seedlings grown under water stress, *Plant Physiol.* 39: 379–386.
319 Chen, J.C.P. and Liu, P.P.D., 1965. Evaluation of cane leaf desiccant Gramoxone, *Sugar J.* 27: 22–23, 32.
320 Cheniae, G.M. and Martin, I.F., 1968. Site of manganese function in photosynthesis, *Biochim. Biophys. Acta* 153: 819–837.
321 Childers, N.F. and Cowart, F.F., 1935. The photosynthesis, transpiration, and stomata of apple leaves as affected by certain nutrient deficiencies, *Proc. Am. Soc. Hortic. Sci.* 33: 160–163.
322 Chilton, S.J.P. and Moreland, C.F., 1954. Experiments on the flowering of sugarcane, *Sugar Bull.* 32: 165–169.
323 Chilton, S.J.P. and Paliatseas, E.D., 1956. Studies on the flowering of sugarcane, *Proc. Int. Soc. Sugar Cane Technol.* 9: 652–656.
324 Chrispeels, M.J. and Varner, J.E., 1967. Hormonal control of enzyme synthesis: On the mode of action of gibberellic acid and abscisin in aleurone layers of barley, *Plant Physiol.* 42: 1008–1016.
325 Chu, C.C. 1970. Solar radiation and photosynthesis of sugarcane in the field, *Taiwan Sugar* 17(3): 14–21.
326 Chu, T.L., 1962. The wild cane (*S. spontaneum* L.) in Taiwan, *Rept. Taiwan Sugar Exp. Sta.* No. 28.
327 Chu, T.L. and Serapión, J.L., 1971. Flower initiation and tassel emergence in sugarcane, *J. Agric. Univ. P.R.* 55(1): 101–115.
328 Clark, H., 1936. Effect of ammonium and nitrate nitrogen on the composition of the tomato plant, *Plant Physiol.* 11: 5–24.
329 Clark, F.J. and Copeland, F.C., 1940. Chromosome aberrations in the endosperm of maize, *Am. J. Bot.* 27: 247–251.
330 Cleasby, T.G. and Hill, J.N.S., 1967. The overhead irrigation of sugarcane in Natal, *Proc. Int. Soc. Sugar Cane Technol.* 12: 25–33.
331 Clements, H.F., 1928. Plant nutrition studies in relation to the triangular system of water cultures, *Plant Physiol.* 3: 441–458.
332 Clements, H.F., 1930. Hourly variations in carbohydrate content of leaves and petioles, *Bot. Gaz.* 89: 241–272.

333 Clements, H.F., 1932. Mannose and the first sugar of photosynthesis, *Plant Physiol.* 7: 547–550.

334 Clements, H.F., 1940. Integration of physiologic and climatic factors with reference to production of sugarcane, *Hawaiian Plant. Rec.* 44: 210–233.

335 Clements, H.F. and Kubota, T., 1942. Internal moisture relations of sugarcane. The selection of a moisture index, *Hawaiian Plant. Rec.* 46(1): 17–35.

336 Clements, H.F. and Moriguchi, S., 1942. Nitrogen and sugarcane. The nitrogen index and certain quantitative field aspects, *Hawaiian Plant. Rec.* 46(4): 163–190.

337 Clements, H.F., 1943. The primary index, its meaning and application to crop management with special reference to sugarcane, *Hawaiian Plant. Rec.* 47(4): 257–297.

338 Clements, H.F., 1948. Managing the production of sugarcane, *Rept. Hawaiian Sugar Technol. Assoc., 6th Annu. Meet.*, pp. 1–15.

339 Clements, H.F., 1948. Crop logging sugarcane in Hawaii, *Better Crops with Plant Food* 32(9): 11–18, 45–48.

340 Clements, H.F., Shigeura, G. and Akamine, E.K., 1948. Ripening sugarcane, *Biennal Rept. Agric. Exp. Sta. Univ. Hawaii* (1946–1948): 120–124.

341 Clements, H.F., 1951. Environmental influences on the growth of sugarcane. In *Mineral Nutrition of Plants* (Truog, E., ed.), pp. 451–469, Univ. Wisconsin Press, Madison, Wisc.

342 Clements, H.F., Shigeura, G. and Akamine, E.F., 1952. Factors affecting the growth of sugarcane, *Univ. Hawaii Agric. Exp. Sta. Tech. Bull.* No. 18.

343 Clements, H.F., 1954. Crop logging of sugarcane, principles and practices, *Proc. Int. Soc. Sugar Cane Technol.* 8: 79–97.

344 Clements, H.F., 1957. Crop logging of sugarcane: The standard nitrogen index and the normal nitrogen index, *Univ. Hawaii Agric. Exp. Sta. Tech. Bull.* No. 35.

345 Clements, H.F., 1959. Quality in sugar production–field aspects, *Rept. Hawaiian Sugar Technol Assoc., 18th Annu. Meet.*, pp. 17–24.

346 Clements, H.F., 1959. Recent developments in the crop logging of sugarcane, *Proc. Int. Soc. Sugar Cane Technol.* 10: 522–528.

347 Clements, H.F. and Awada, M., 1960. Multiple top in sugarcane, *Hawaiian Farm Sci.* 9(1): 1–3.

348 Clements, H.F., 1961. Crop logging of sugarcane in Hawaii, *Plant Analysis and Fertilizer Problems*, Am. Inst. Biol. Sci., pp. 131–147.

349 Clements, H.F. and Awada, M., 1962. The flowering of sugarcane, *Rept. Hawaiian Acad. Sci.* (Abstr., April, 1962).

350 Clements, H.F., 1962. The ripening of sugarcane, *Sugar y Azúcar*, March issue, 1962.

351 Clements, H.F., 1962. Crop logging *vs.* 8–10 and soil analysis, *Int. Sugar J.* 64: 129–130, 159–162.

352 Clements, H.F. and Awada, M., 1964. Factors affecting the flowering of sugarcane, *Indian J. Sugar Cane Res. Dev.* 8: 140–159.

353 Clements, H.F., 1964. Interaction of factors affecting yield, *Annu. Rev. Plant Physiol.* 15: 409–442.

354 Clements, H.F., 1965. The roles of calcium silicate slags in sugarcane growth, *Rept. Hawaiian Sugar Technol. Assoc.* (1965): 103–125.

355 Clements, H.F. and Awada, M., 1967. Experiments in the artificial induction of flowering in sugarcane, *Proc. Int. Soc. Sugar Cane Technol.* 12: 795–812.

356 Clements, H.F., 1967. Effects of silicate on the growth and leaf freckle of sugarcane in Hawaii, *Proc. Int. Soc. Sugar Cane Technol.* 12: 197–215.

357 Clements, H.F., 1968. Lengthening versus shortening dark periods and blossoming in sugarcane as affected by temperature, *Plant Physiol.* 43: 57–60.

358 Clements, H.F., 1969. Commentary following presentation of paper by Humbert *et al.*, *Proc. Int. Soc. Sugar Cane Technol.* 13: 467.

359 Clements, H.F., 1970. Crop logging of the sugarcane: Nitrogen and potassium requirements and interactions using two varieties, *Hawaiian Agric. Exp. Sta. Tech. Bull.* No. 81.

360 Click, R.E. and Hackett, D.P., 1963. The role of protein and nucleic acid synthesis in the development of respiration in potato tuber slices, *Proc. Natl. Acad. Sci. (U.S.)* 50: 243–250.
361 Coates, C.E., 1931. Keeping qualities of P.O.J. canes, *Sugar Bull.* 9(1): 5–6.
362 Cohen, C.N. and Monod, J., 1957. Bacterial permeases, *Bacteriol. Rev.* 21: 169–194.
363 Cohn, M. and Cori, G.T., 1948. On the mechanism of action of muscle and potato phosphorylase, *J. Biol. Chem.* 175: 89–93.
364 Cohn, M., 1949. Mechanism of cleavage of glucose 1-phosphate, *J. Biol. Chem.* 180: 771–781.
365 Colby, S.R. and Warren, G.F., 1963. Herbicides: Combination enhances selectivity, *Science* 141: 362.
366 Coleman, R.E., 1959. *Factors Involved in the Flowering of Sugarcane (Saccharum* spp.*)*, Thesis, University of Hawaii Library (not seen).
367 Coleman, R.E. and Hebert, L.P., 1957. Effects of certain defoliants and growth regulators upon sugarcane, *Sugar Bull.* 35(24): 389–391.
368 Coleman, R.E., 1958. Effect of gibberellic acid on the growth of sugarcane, *Sugar J.* 20: 23–26 (April issue).
369 Coleman, R.E., 1959. Factors involved in the flowering of sugarcane (*Saccharum* spp.), *Proc. Int. Soc. Sugar Cane Technol.* 10: 805–814.
370 Coleman, R.E., Todd, E.H., Stokes, I.E. and Coleman, O.H., 1959. The effects of gibberellic acid on sugarcane, *Proc. Int. Soc. Sugar Cane Technol.* 10: 588–603.
371 Coleman, R.E., 1959. Quality of harvested cane affected by trash and topping, *Sugar J.* 21(12): 9–11.
372 Coleman, R.E., Todd, E.H., Stokes, I.E. and Coleman, O.H., 1960. Some responses of sugarcane to gibberellic acid, *Sugar J.* 23: 11–21.
373 Coleman, R.E., 1962. Control of flowering and the use of pollen storage as techniques in a sugarcane breeding programme, *Proc. Int. Soc. Sugar Cane Technol.* 11: 533–540.
374 Coleman, R.E., 1963. Effect of temperature on flowering in sugarcane, *Int. Sugar J.* 6: 351–353.
375 Coleman, R.E., 1963. Physiology of flowering, *Rept. Hawaiian Sugar Technol. Assoc.* (1963): 108–109.
376 Coleman, R.E. and Nickell, L.G., 1964. Stability of the flowering stimulus in isolated stem tips of sugarcane *Nature* 201: 941–942.
377 Coleman, R.E., 1965. Effect of intercalated noninductive nights on floral initiation in sugarcane, *Phyton* 22: 15–18.
378 Coleman, R.E., 1967. Some aspects of the flowering stimulus production in sugarcane, *Proc. Int. Soc. Sugar Cane Technol.* 12: 813–818.
379 Coleman, R.E., 1969. Physiology of flowering in sugarcane, *Proc. Int. Soc. Sugar Cane Technol.* 13: 992–1000.
380 Coleman, R.E., 1971. Personal communication with the author, April, 1971.
381 Collander, R., 1959. Cell membranes. In *Plant Physiology* (Steward, F.C., ed.), Vol. 2, pp. 11–16, Academic Press, New York, N.Y.
382 Colombo, B., Felicetti, L. and Baglioni, C., 1965. Inhibition of protein synthesis by cycloheximide in rabbit reticulocytes, *Biochem. Biophys. Res. Commun.* 18: 389–395.
383 Commentary by Dr. George Burr following presentation of a paper by Dr. N. I. James, 1969, *Proc. Int. Soc. Sugar Cane Technol.* 13: 991.
384 Commentary by Dr. L.G. Nickell following presentation of a paper by Hartt *et al.*, 1967, *Proc. Int. Soc. Sugar Cane Technol.* 12: 609.
385 Commoner, B., Townsend, J. and Pake, G., 1954. Free radicals in biological materials, *Nature* 174: 689–691.
386 Conchie, J., Moreno, A. and Cardini, C.E., 1961. A trisaccharide glycoside from wheat germ, *Arch. Biochem. Biophys.* 94: 342–343.
387 Cooper, R.A. and Kornberg, H.L., 1965. Net formation of phosphoenolpyruvate from pyruvate by *Escherichia coli*, *Biochim. Biophys. Acta* 104: 618–620.

388 Cori, C.F., Colowick, S.P. and Cori, G.T., 1937. The isolation and synthesis of glucose 1-phosphoric acid, *J. Biol. Chem.* 121: 465–477.
389 Cori, C.F. and Green, A.A., 1943. Crystalline muscle phosphorylase. II. Prosthetic group, *J. Biol. Chem.* 151: 31–38.
390 Cori, C.F. and Illingworth, B., 1957. The prosthetic group of phosphorylase, *Proc. Natl. Acad. Sci. (U.S.)* 43: 547–552.
391 Cori, G.T. and Cori, C.F., 1940. The kinetics of the enzymatic synthesis of glycogen from glucose 1-phosphate, *J. Biol. Chem.* 135: 733–756.
392 Crafts, A.S., 1933. Sieve-tube structure and translocation in the potato, *Plant Physiol.* 8: 81–104.
393 Cronshey, J.F.H., 1961. A review of experimental work with Diquat and related compounds, *Weed Res.* 1: 68–77.
394 Cross, W.E. and Belile, J.A., 1914. La deterioración de cañas cortadas, *Rev. Ind. Agric. Tucumán* 5: 272–290.
395 Cross, W.E. and Belile, J.A., 1915. The deterioration of cut canes, *Int. Sugar J.* 17: 218–225.
396 Cross, W.E. and Harris, W.G., 1916. Deterioración de las cañas de semillero de Java después de cortadas, *Rev. Ind. Agric. Tucumán* 7: 219–250.
397 Cross, W.E., 1966. The problem of frozen cane in the Argentine, *Sugar J.* (March issue): 9–12.
398 Currier, H.B., Day, B.E. and Crafts, A.S., 1951. Some effects of maleic hydrazide on plants, *Bot. Gaz.* 112(3) 272–280.
399 Curtis, P.J. and Cross, B.E., 1954. Gibberellic acid. A new metabolite from the culture filtrates of *Gibberella fujikuroi*, *Chem. Ind.* (1954): 1066.
400 Curtiss, O.F., 1926. What is the significance of transpiration? *Science* 62: 267–271.
401 Czernicki, Müller, von, O.F., 1900. Oorspronkelijke verhandelingen. Het laboratorium ten dienste der rieten suikerproductie, *Arch. Java-Suikerind.* Jaarg. 8: 597–657.

D

402 Dainty, J. and Hope, A.B., 1959. Ionic relations of cells of *Chara australis.* I. Ion exchange in the cell wall, *Aust. J. Biol. Sci.* 12: 395–411.
403 D'Amato, F., 1952. Polyploidy in the differentiation and function of tissues and cells in plants, *Caryologia* 4: 311–358.
404 Daniels, J., 2959. Personal commentary following paper by Panje and Srinivasan, *Proc. Int. Soc. Sugar Cane Technol.* 10: 823.
405 Daniels, J., 1962. Experimental control of flowering in *Saccharum spontaneum* L., *Proc. Int. Soc. Sugar Cane Technol.* 11: 527–533.
406 Daniels, J., 1967. Sugarcanes and related plants of the Fiji Islands, *Proc. Int. Soc. Sugar Cane Technol.* 12: 1004–1013.
407 Daniels, J., Glasziou, K.T. and Bull, T.A., 1967. Flowering in *Saccharum*, *Proc. Int. Soc. Sugar Cane Technol.* 12: 1027–1032.
408 Darlington, C.D. and Janaki-Ammal, E.K., 1945. *Chromosome Atlas of Cultivated Plants*, pp. 1–397, Allen and Unwin, Ltd., London.
409 Das, U.K., 1931. The problem of juice quality, *Hawaiian Plant. Rec.* 35: 163–200.
410 Das, U.K., 1934. The sugarcane plant. A study of millable cane and sucrose formation, *Hawaiian Plant Rec.* 38: 33–94.
411 Das, U.K., 1936. Nitrogen nutrition of sugarcane, *Plant Physiol.* 11: 251–317.
412 Davenport, H.E., Hill, R. and Whatley, F.R., 1952. A natural factor catalyzing reduction of methaemoglobin by isolated chloroplasts, *Proc. R. Soc. (London), Ser. B.* 139: 346–358.
413 Davenport, H.E. and Hill, R., 1960. A protein from leaves catalyzing the reduction of haem–protein compounds by illuminated chloroplasts, *Biochem. J.* 74: 493–501.
414 Davenport, H.E., 1960. Summary of research. Plant Biochemistry, *Annu. Rept. Long Ashton Res. Sta.* (1960): 32.

415 Davenport, H.E., 1960. A protein from leaves catalyzing the reduction of metmyoglobin and triphosphopyridine nucleotide by illuminated chloroplasts, *Biochem. J.* 77: 471–477.

416 Davidson, L.G., 1962. Effects of desiccants on sugarcane, *Proc. Int. Soc. Sugar Cane Technol.* 11: 319–323.

417 Davis, W.A., Daish, A.J. and Sawyer, G.C., 1916. Studies on the formation and translocation of carbohydrates in plants. I. The carbohydrates of the mangold leaf, *J. Agric. Sci.* 7: 255–326 [*Chem. Abstr.* 10: 2473–2474].

418 Davis, W.A. and Sawyer, G.C., 1916. Studies on the formation and translocation of carbohydrates in plants. III. Carbohydrates of the leaf and the leaf-stalks of the potato. Mechanism of the degradation of starch in the leaf, *J. Agric. Sci.* 7: 255–326 [*Chem. Abstr.* 10: 2474 (1917)].

419 Davis, C.W., 1959. Filtrability of raw sugar. A review of recent work done by the Colonial Sugar Refining Co. Ltd., *Int. Sugar J.* 61: 300–302.

420 Decker, J.P., 1955. The uncommon denominator in photosynthesis as related to tolerance, *Forest Sci.* 1: 88–89.

421 Decker, J.P., 1955. A rapid, post-illumination deceleration of respiration in green leaves, *Plant Physiol.* 39(1): 82–84.

422 Decker, J.P., 1957. Further evidence of increased carbon dioxide production accompanying photosynthesis, *J. Solar Energy Sci. Eng.* 1: 30–33.

423 Decker, J.P. and Wien, J.D., 1958. Carbon dioxide surges in green leaves, *J. Solar Energy Sci. Eng.* 2(1): 39–41.

424 Decker, J.P., 1959. Some effects of temperature and carbon dioxide concentration on photosynthesis of *Mimulus*, *Plant Physiol.* 34: 103–106.

425 Dedonder, R.A., 1961. Glycosidases and transglycosidation, *Annu. Rev. Biochem.* 30: 347–382.

426 Deerr, N., 1911. *Cane Sugar*, Norman Rodger (publisher), Manchester, England.

427 De Fekete, M.A.R., Leloir, L.F. and Cardini, C.E., 1960. Mechanism of starch biosynthesis, *Nature* 187: 918–919.

428 De Fekete, M.A.R. and Cardini, C.E., 1964. Mechanism of glucose transfer from sucrose into the starch granule of sweet corn, *Arch. Biochem. Biophys.* 104: 173–184.

429 De La Vega, G.A.K., 1952. Aplicación de hormonas en la caña de azúcar, *La. Ind. Azúcar* No. 710: 298–304 [Circular No. 147 de la Estación Experimental Agrícola de Tucumán].

430 De Saussure, N., 1804. Recherches chimiques sur la végétation, Paris Nyon. Reviewed in *Photosynthesis and Related Processes* (Rabinowitch, E.I., ed.), 1945, Vol. I, p. 23, Interscience Publishers, New York, N.Y.

431 De Surnay, A., 1955. Cane breeding in 1955, *Rept. Mauritius Sugar Ind. Res Inst.*, pp. 25–27.

432 De Vries, H., 1878. *Neue Z. Rübenzuckerind.* (cited by Colin, M.H., 1916. Le saccharose dans la betterave. Formation et disparition, *Rev. Gén. Bot.* 28: 321–328).

433 De Wit, C.T., 1959. Potential photosynthesis of crop surfaces, *Neth. J. Agric. Sci.* 7: 141–149 [*Chem. Abstr.* 54: 3605 (1960)].

434 De Wolf, C.J., 1926. Die Saccharosebildung in Kartoffeln während des Trocknens, *Biochem. Z.* 176: 225–245; 178: 36–59.

435 D'Hotman De Villiers, O., 1961. Soil rejuvenation with crushed basalt in Mauritius. I. Consistent results of world-wide interests, *Int. Sugar J.* 63: 363–364.

436 Discussion comments by Mr. L.S. Birkett and Dr. H. Evans following presentation of paper by F.A. Gumbs (619), *Proc. Br. W. Indies Sugar Technol.* 2: 249–265 (1966).

437 Doorenbos, J. and Wellensiek, S.J., 1959. Photoperiodic control of floral induction, *Annu. Rev. Plant Physiol.* 10: 147–184.

438 Dormer, K.J. and Street, H.E., 1949. The carbohydrate nutrition of tomato roots, *Ann. Bot. (London)* [N.S.] 13: 199–217.

439 Doudoroff, M., Kaplan, N. and Hassid, W.Z., 1943. Phosphorolysis and synthesis of sucrose with a bacterial preparation, *J. Biol. Chem.* 148: 67–75.

440 Doudoroff, M., 1943. Studies on the phosphorolysis of sucrose, *J. Biol. Chem.* 151: 351–361.

441 Doudoroff, M., Barker, H.A. and Hassid, W.Z., 1947. Studies with bacterial sucrose phosphorylase. I. The mechanism of action of sucrose phosphorylase as a glucose-transferring enzyme (transglucosidase), *J. Biol. Chem.* 168: 725–732.

442 Doudoroff, M., Wiame, J.M. and Wolochow, H., 1949. Phosphorolysis of sucrose by *Pseudomonas putrefaciens, J. Bacteriol.* 57: 423–427.

443 Doudoroff, M., 1950. *Enzymologia* 9: 59 (not seen).

444 Dougall, D.K., 1965. The biosynthesis of protein amino acids in plant tissue culture. I. Isotope competition experiments using glucose $U^{14}C$ and the protein amino acids, *Plant Physiol.* 40: 891–897.

445 Downes, R.W. and Hesketh, J.D., 1968. Enhanced photosynthesis at low oxygen concentrations. Differential response of temperate and tropical grasses, *Planta* 78: 79–84.

446 Downes, R.W., 1969. Differences in transpiration rates between tropical and temperate grasses under controlled conditions, *Planta* 88: 261–273.

447 Downs, R.J., 1956. Photoreversibility of flower initiation, *Plant Physiol.* 31: 279–284.

448 Downton, W.J.A. and Treguna, E.B., 1967. Carbon dioxide compensation – its relation to photosynthetic carboxylation reactions, systematics of the Gramineae, and leaf anatomy, *Can. J. Bot.* 46: 207–215.

449 Dugger, Jr., W.M., Humphreys, T.E. and Calhoun, B., 1957. The influence of boron on starch phosphorylase and its significance in translocation of sugars in plants, *Plant Physiol.* 32: 364–370.

450 Dugger, Jr., W.M. and Humphreys, T.E., 1960. Influence of boron on enzymatic reactions associated with biosynthesis of sucrose, *Plant Physiol.* 35: 523–530.

451 Duloy, M., Mercer, F.V. and Rathgeber, N., 1962. Studies in translocation. III. The cytophysiology of the phloem of *Cucurbita pepo, Aust. J. Biol. Sci.* 15: 459–467.

452 Dunckelman, P.H. and Breaux, R.D., 1969. Evaluation of germplasm in the U.S.D.A. sugarcane program at Houma, Louisiana, *Proc. Int. Soc. Sugar Cane Technol.* 13: 888–892.

453 Dutt, N.L., 1932. Scientific reports of the Imperial Agricultural Research Institute, Pusa, 1932–1933.

454 Dutt, N.L. and Rao, K.S.S., 1933. Observations on the cytology of the sugarcane, *Indian J. Agric. Sci.* 3: 37–56.

455 Dutt, N.L., 1943. Control of flowering in sugarcane, *Indian Farming* 4: 1.

456 Dutt, N.L. and Yusuf, N.D., 1945. Control of cane arrowing, *Curr. Sci.* 14: 304–306.

457 Dutt, N.L. and Yusuf, N.D., 1945. Photoperiod in relation to flowering in sugarcane, *Curr. Sci.* 14(11): 304–309.

458 Dutt, N.L. and Narasimhan, R., 1949. The occurrence of starch and its importance as a specific character in *Saccharum*, *Curr. Sci.* 18: 346–347.

459 Dutt, N.L. and Rao, J.T., 1950. The present taxonomic position of *Saccharum* and its congeners, *Proc. Int. Soc. Sugar Cane Technol.* 7: 286–293.

460 Duysens, L.N.M., 1961. Cytochrome oxidation by a second photochemical system in the red alga *Porphyridium cruentum*. In *Progress in Photobiology* (Christensen, B.C. and Buckmann, B., eds.), pp. 135–142, Elsevier Publishing Co., Amsterdam.

461 Duysens, L.N.M., Amesz, J. and Kamp, B.M., 1961. Two photochemical systems in photosynthesis, *Nature* 190: 510–511.

462 Duysens, L.N.M. and Amesz, J., 1962. Function and identification of two photochemical systems in photosynthesis, *Biochim. Biophys. Acta* 64: 243–260.

463 Dymond, G.C., 1924. Deterioration of cut *Uba* cane, *S. Afr. Sugar J.* (1924): 99–104.

E

464 Earle, F.S., 1928. *Sugar Cane and its Culture*, John Wiley and Sons, New York, N.Y.

465 Earle, E.D. and Torrey, J.G., 1965. Colony formation by isolated *Convolvulus* cells plated on defined media, *Plant Physiol.* 40: 520–528.

466 Eaton, F.M. and Ergle, D.R., 1948. Carbohydrate accumulation in the cotton plant at low moisture levels, *Plant Physiol.* 23: 167–187.
467 Eckart, C.F., 1909. The question of stripping, *Hawaiian Plant. Rec.* 1: 64–85.
468 Eckart, C.F., 1913. Project File No. 381, Exp. Sta. Hawaiian Sugar Plant. Assoc. Library, Honolulu (not seen).
469 Eckstein, O., 1939. Effect of potash manuring on the production of organic matter, *Plant Physiol.* 14: 113–128.
470 Edelman, J., 1954. Transfer reactions catalyzed by some sucrose preparations, *Biochem. J.* 57: 22–33.
471 Edelman, J., Ginsburg, V. and Hassid, W.Z., 1955. Conversion of monosaccharides to sucrose and cellulose in wheat seedlings, *J. Biol. Chem.* 213: 843–854.
472 Edelman, J., Shibko, S.I. and Keys, A.J., 1959. The role of the scutellum of cereal seedlings in the synthesis and transport of sucrose, *J. Exp. Bot.* 10: 178–189.
473 Edelman, J. and Hall, M.A., 1963. Synthesis of invertase in washed tissue slices of *Helianthus tuberosus* L., *Biochem. J.* 88: 36 p.
474 Efferson, J.N. and Cobb, M., 1951. Final results of the operation of raw sugar mills in Louisiana, 1937 to 1949, *La. Agric. Exp. Sta. Bull.* No. 457, 34 pp.
475 Egan, B.T. and Rehbein, C.A., 1963. Bacterial deterioration of mechanically harvested cut up sugarcane during storage over weekends, *Proc. Queensland Soc. Sugar Cane Technol.* 30: 11–19.
476 Egan, B.T., 1964. Investigations into the sour storage rot problem, *Proc. Queensland Soc. Sugar Cane Technol.* 31: 15–26.
477 Egan, B.T., 1965. The infection process in sour storage rot, *Proc. Queensland Soc. Sugar Cane Technol.* 32: 21–24.
478 Egan, B.T., 1965. Investigations on the chemical control of sour storage rot, *Proc. Queensland Soc. Sugar Cane Technol.* 32: 25–30.
479 Egan, B.T., 1966. Some effects of sour storage rot on cane juice quality, *Proc. Queensland Soc. Sugar Cane Technol.* 33: 11–20.
480 Egan, B.T., 1967. A sour storage rot of mechanically harvested chopped-up sugarcane, *Proc. Int. Soc. Sugar Cane Technol.* 12: 1199–1204.
481 Egan, B.T., 1967. Post-harvest cane deterioration, *Int. Sugar J.* 69: 111.
482 Egan, B.T., 1967. Gum content and pH as measures of the losses due to sour storage rot, *Proc. Queensland Soc. Sugar Cane Technol.* 34: 257–262.
483 Egan, B.T., 1968. Investigations on the chemical control of sour storage rot. II. Formalin fumigation, *Proc. Queensland Soc. Sugar Cane Technol.* 35: 31–37.
484 Egan, B.T., 1969. Post-harvest deterioration losses in sugarcane in Queensland, *Proc. Int. Soc. Sugar Cane Technol.* 13: 1729–1735.
485 Ehara, K. and Sekioka, H., 1962. Effect of atmospheric humidity and soil moisture on the translocation of sucrose-^{14}C in the sweet potato plant, *Proc. Crop Sci. Soc. Japan* 31: 41–44 (English summary).
486 El Sharkawy, M. and Hesketh, J., 1965. Photosynthesis among species in relation to characteristics of leaf anatomy and CO_2 diffusion resistances, *Crop Sci.* 5: 517–521.
487 Emerson, R., 1929. The relation between maximum rate of photosynthesis and concentration of chlorophyll, *J. Gen. Physiol.* 12: 609–622.
488 Emerson, R., 1929. Photosynthesis as a function of light intensity and of temperature with different concentrations of chlorophyll, *J. Gen. Physiol.* 12: 623–639.
489 Emerson, R. and Arnold, A., 1932. A separation of the reactions in photosynthesis by means of intermittent light, *J. Gen. Physiol.* 15: 391–420.
490 Emerson, R., and Green, L., 1938. Effect of hydrogen-ion concentration on *Chlorella* photosynthesis, *Plant Physiol.* 13: 157–168.
491 Emerson, R. and Lewis, C.M., 1941. Carbon dioxide exchange and the measurement of the quantum yield of photosynthesis. *Am. J. Bot.* 28: 789–804.
492 Emerson, R. and Lewis, C.M., 1943. The dependence of the quantum yield of *Chlorella* photosynthesis on wave length of light, *Am. J. Bot.* 30: 165–178.

493 Emerson, R., Chalmers, R. and Cederstrand, C., 1957. Some factors influencing the long-wave limit of photosynthesis, *Proc. Natl. Acad. Sci. (U.S.)* 43: 133–143.

494 Emerson, R. and Chalmers, R.V., 1958. Speculations concerning the function and phylogenetic significance of the accessory pigments of algae, *Phycol. Soc. Am. Bull.* 11: 51–56.

495 Engard, C.J. and Nakata, A.H., 1947. A growth inhibitor and a growth promotor in sugarcane, *Science* 105: 577–580.

496 Epps, H.M.R. and Gale, E.F., 1942. The influence of the presence of glucose during growth on the enzymic activities of *Escherichia coli*: Comparison of the effect with that produced by fermentation acids, *Biochem. J.* 36: 619–623.

497 Epstein, E., 1955. Passive permeation and active transport of ions in plant roots, *Plant Physiol.* 30: 529–535.

498 Esau, K., Cheadle, V.I. and Gifford, E.M., 1953. Comparative structure and possible trends of specialization of the phloem, *Am. J. Bot.* 40: 9–19.

499 Esau, K., Currier, H.B. and Cheadle, V.I., 1957. Physiology of phloem, *Annu. Rev. Plant Physiol.* 8: 349–374.

500 Esau, K., 1966. Exploration of the food conducting system in plants, *Am. Sci.* 54: 141–157.

501 Espada, J., 1962. Enzymic synthesis of adenosine diphosphate glucose from glucose 1-phosphate and adenosine triphosphate, *J. Biol. Chem.* 237: 3577–3581.

502 Euler, H. Von and Josephson, K., 1923. Experiments with invertase, *Ber.* 56B: 446–452; The preparation of a highly active invertase and a note on its sulfur content, *Ber.* 56: 453–455; *Ber.* 56: 1749–1751.

503 Evans, W.C., Handley, W.R.C. and Happold, F.C., 1941. Some observations on the production of tryptophanase by *Escherichia coli*; in particular the effect of the presence of glucose and amino acids on the formation of tryptophanase, *Biochem. J.* 35: 207–212.

504 Evans, H., 1959. Elements other than nitrogen, potassium, and phosphorus in the mineral nutrition of sugarcane, *Proc. Int. Soc. Sugar Cane Technol.* 10: 473–508.

505 Evans, H., 1961. A guide to the interpretation of nutritional diagnostic analysis of sugarcane in British Guiana, *Sugar J.* 23: 8–16 (February issue).

506 Evans, H. and Bates, J.F., 1963. A summary of investigations on the possibility of artificially ripening sugarcane with various chemicals, *Proc. Int. Soc. Sugar Cane Technol.* 11: 298–307.

507 Evans, H. and Bates, J.F., 1966. Some observations on the incidence and prevention of flowering of sugarcane in Guyana, *Proc. Br. W. Indies Sugar Technol.* 1-2: 279–290.

508 Evans, H., 1967. Tissue diagnostic analyses and their interpretation on sugarcane, *Proc. Int. Soc. Sugar Cane Technol.* 12: 156–180.

509 Evans, H.J., 1963. Effect of potassium and other univalent cations on activity of pyruvate kinase in *Pisum sativum*, *Plant Physiol.* 38: 397–402.

510 Evans, H.J. and Sorger, G.J., 1966. Role of mineral elements with emphasis on the univalent cations, *Annu. Rev. Plant Physiol.* 17: 47–76.

511 Everson, R.G., Cockburn, W. and Gibbs, M., 1967. Sucrose as a product of photosynthesis in isolated spinach chloroplasts, *Plant Physiol.* 42: 840–844.

512 Everson, R.G. and Slack, C.R., 1968. Distribution of carbonic anhydrase in relation to the C_4 pathway of photosynthesis, *Phytochemistry* 7: 581–584.

513 Everson, R.G., 1969. Bicarbonate equilibrium and the apparent $K_m(CHCO_3^-)$ of isolated chloroplasts, *Nature* 222: 876.

514 Everson, R.G., 1970. Carbonic anhydrase and CO_2 fixation in isolated chloroplasts, *Phytochemistry* 9: 25–32.

515 Ewart, A.J., 1897. *Ann. Bot.* 11: 439; 12: 363 (not seen).

516 Ewart, M.H., Simovitch, D. and Briggs, D.R., 1954. Studies on the chemistry of the living bark of the black locust in relation to its frost hardiness. VIII. Possible enzymatic processes involved in starch–sucrose interconversions, *Plant Physiol.* 29: 407–413.

517 Ewart, G.Y., 1967. Consumptive use and replenishment standards in irrigation, *Proc. Int. Soc. Sugar Cane Technol.* 12: 34–51.

F

518 Feingold, D.S., Avigad, G. and Hestrin, S., 1957. Enzymatic synthesis and reactions of a sucrose isomer α-D-galactopyranosyl β-D-fructofuranoside, *J. Biol. Chem.* 224: 295–307.

519 Fenson, D.S., 1957. The bio-electric potentials of plants and their functional significance, *Can. J. Bot.* 35: 573–582.

520 Fenson, D.S., 1959. The bio-electric potentials of plants and their functional significance. III. The production of continuous potentials across membranes in plant tissue by the circulation of the hydrogen ion, *Can. J. Bot.* 37: 1003–1026.

521 Fernández-García, R., 1928. *Annu. Rept. Insular Exp. Sta., Puerto Rico* (1927–1928): 84–85.

522 Feuilherade, L., 1929. Starch in *Uba* juices, *S. Afr. Sugar J.* 13(5): 305–309.

523 Fildes, P., 1938. The production of indole by suspensions of *Bact. coli* ccvii, *Biochem. J.* 32: 1600–1606.

524 Filner, P., 1966. Regulation of nitrate reductase in cultured tobacco cells, *Biochim. Biophys. Acta* 118: 299–310.

525 Fischer, E., 1890. *Ber.* 23: 3687; 1895. *Ber.* 28: 3024 (not seen).

526 Fischer, J. and Hodges, T.K., 1969. Monovalent ion stimulated adenosine triphosphatase from oat roots, *Plant Physiol.* 44: 385–395.

527 Fletcher, R.A. and Osborne, D.J., 1965. Regulation of protein and nucleic acid synthesis by gibberellin during leaf senescence, *Nature* 207: 1176–1177.

528 Fletcher, R.A. and Osborne, D.J., 1966. Gibberellin, as a regulator of protein and ribonucleic acid synthesis during senescence in leaf cells of *Taraxacum officinale*, *Can. J. Bot.* 44: 739–745.

529 Fleury, P. and Courtois, J., 1943. Oxidation of sucrose by periodic acid, *Bull. Soc. Chim. France* 10: 245–251 [*Chem. Abstr.* 37: 3740 (1943)]. Constitution du tétracide dérivé du saccharose par oxydation au moyen de l'acide periodique, puis du brome, *C. R. Acad. Sci. (Paris)* 216: 65–67.

530 Flowers, T.J., 1967. *The Effect of Water Deficit on the Metabolism of Potato Tuber Discs*, Ph. D. Thesis, University of Nottingham, School of Agriculture, Nottingham (not seen).

531 Flowers, T.J. and Hanson, J.B., 1969. The effect of reduced water potential on soybean mitochondria, *Plant Physiol.* 44: 939–945.

532 Fogg, G.E., 1968. *Photosynthesis*, American Elsevier Publishing Co., New York, N.Y.

533 Forrester, M.L., Krotkov, G. and Nelson, C.D., 1966. Effect of oxygen on photosynthesis in detached leaves. I. Soybean, *Plant Physiol.* 41: 422–427.

534 Forrester, M.L., Krotkov, G. and Nelson, C.D., 1966. Effect of oxygen on photosynthesis, photorespiration, and respiration in detached leaves. II. Corn and other monocotyledons, *Plant Physiol.* 41: 428–531.

535 Forster, G., 1786. Da Planta Esculentis Indularum Oceani Australis Commentio Botanica. Berolini Opud Hank et Spener, p. 77 [cited from Brandes *et al.* (227)].

536 Foster, D.H., 1969. Deterioration of chopped cane, *Proc. Queensland Soc. Sugar Cane Technol.* 36: 21–28.

537 Franck, J., 1949. The relation of the fluorescence of chlorophyll to photosynthesis. Chapter 16 in *Photosynthesis in Plants* (Franck, J. and Loomis, W.E., eds.), pp. 318–323, Iowa State College Press, Ames, Iowa.

538 Frenkel, A.W., 1954. Light induced phosphorylation by cell-free preparations of photosynthetic bacteria, *J. Am. Chem. Soc.* 76: 5568–5569.

539 Fridhandler, L. and Quastel, J.H., 1955. Absorption of amino acids from isolated surviving intestine, *Arch. Biochem. Biophys.* 56: 424–440.

540 Fruton, J.S. and Simmonds, S.W., 1963. *General Biochemistry*, 2nd edn., John Wiley and Sons, New York, N.Y.

541 Frydman, R.B. anu Hassid, W.Z., 1963. Biosynthesis of sucrose with sugarcane leaf preparations, *Nature* 199: 382–383.

542 Frydman, R.B., 1963. Starch synthetase of potatoes and waxy maize, *Arch. Biochem. Biophys.* 102: 242–248.
543 Frydman, R.B. and Cardini, C.E., 1964. Biosynthesis of phytoglycogen from adenosine diphosphate D-glucose in sweet corn, *Biochem. Biophys. Res. Commun.* 14: 353–357.
544 Fuente, G. and Sols, A., 1962. Transport of sugars in yeast. Mechanism of utilization of the disaccharides and related glycosides, *Biochim. Biophys. Acta* 56: 49–62.
545 Fuller, R.C. and Gibbs, M. 1959. Intercellular and phytogenetic distribution of ribulose 1,5-diphosphate carboxylase and D-glyceraldehyde 3-phosphate dehydrogenase, *Plant Physiol.* 34: 324–329.
546 Funderburk, H.H. and Lawrence, J.M., 1963. A sensitive method for determination of low concentrations of Diquat and Paraquat, *Nature* 199: 1011–1012.
547 Funderburk, H.H. and Lawrence, J.M., 1964. Mode of action and metabolism of Diquat and Paraquat, *Weeds* 12: 259–264.

G

548 Gaastra, P., 1959. Photosynthesis of crop plants as influenced by light, carbon dioxide, temperature, and stomatal diffusion resistance, *Meded. Landbouwhogesch. Wageningen* 59: 1–68.
549 Gaff, D.F. and Carr, D.J., 1961. The quantity of water in the cell wall and its significance, *Aust. J. Biol. Sci.* 14: 299–311.
550 Gaff, D.F., Chambers, T.C. and Markus, K., 1964. Studies of extrafasicular movement of water in the leaf, *Aust. J. Biol. Sci.* 17: 581–586.
551 Gale, E.F., 1938. Factors influencing bacterial deamination. III. Aspartase II: Its occurrence in and extraction from *Bacterium coli* and its activation by adenosine and related compounds, *Biochem. J.* 32: 1583–1599.
552 Gale, E.F., 1940. The production of amines by bacteria. I. The decarboxylation of amino acids by strains of *Bacterium coli*, *Biochem. J.* 34: 392–413.
553 Gale, E.F. and Epps, H.M., 1942. The effects of the pH of the medium during growth on the enzymic activities of bacteria and the biological significance of the changes produced, *Biochem. J.* 36: 600–618.
554 Gale, J. and Hagen, R.M., 1966. Plant antitranspirants, *Annu. Rev. Plant Physiol.* 17: 269–282.
555 Galmiche, H.M., 1968. Photosynthetic incorporation of carbon from CO_2 into malic acid and phosphoglyceric acid in *Zea mays.* In *Photosynthesis in Sugarcane*, Proc. Int. Symp. held June 12 and 13, 1968, at the Royal Lancaster Hotel, London, pp. 36–39.
556 Ganguli, N.C., 1958. Enzymatic formation of uridine diphosphate glucose with preparations from *Impatiens holstii*, *J. Biol. Chem.* 232: 337–345.
557 Garb, S., 1961. Differential growth-inhibitors produced by plants, *Bot. Rev.* 28: 422–443.
558 Gard, K.R., 1956. The apparent influence of temperature during the cane breeding season on the fertility of the fuzz period, *Proc. Int. Soc. Sugar Cane Technol.* 9: 665–668.
559 Garner, W.W. and Allard, H.A., 1920. Effect of the relative length of day and night and other factors of the environment on growth and reproduction in plants, *J. Agric. Res.* 18: 553–606.
560 Gassner, G. and Goeze, G., 1932. The influence of potash nutrition on the rate of assimilation of wheat leaves, *Bot. Ges.* 50(a): 412–482 [*Chem. Abstr.* 26: 5607 (1932)].
561 Gates, C.T. and Bonner, J., 1959. The response of the tomato plant to a period of water shortage. IV. Effects of water stress on the ribonucleic acid metabolism of tomato leaves, *Plant Physiol.* 34: 49–55.
562 Gauch, H.G. and Dugger, Jr., W.M., 1953. The role of boron in the translocation of sucrose, *Plant Physiol.* 28: 457–466.
563 Gautheret, R.J., 1939. Sur la possibilité de réaliser la culture indéfinie des tissus de tubercules de carotte, *C. R. Acad. Sci. (Paris)* 208: 118–120.

564 Gautheret, R.J., 1945. *La Culture des Tissues*, Gallimard, Lagny-sur-Marne, France.
565 Gautheret, R.J., 1948. Sur la culture de trois types de tissue de scorsonère: Tissus normaux, tissus de crown-gall et tissus accoutumé á l'hétéro-auxine, *C.R. Acad. Sci. (Paris)* 226: 270–271.
566 Gayler, K.R. and Glasziou, K.T., 1968. Plant enzyme synthesis. Decay of messenger RNA for peroxidase in sugarcane stem tissue, *Phytochemistry* 7: 1247.
567 Gayler, K.R. and Glasziou, K.T., 1969. Plant enzyme synthesis: Hormonal regulation of invertase and peroxidase synthesis in sugar cane, *Planta* 84: 185–194.
568 Geiger, D.R., 1966. Effect of sink region cooling on translocation, *Plant Physiol.* 41: 1667–1672.
569 Geiger, D.R. and Batey, J.W., 1967. Translocation of ^{14}C sucrose in sugar beet during darkness, *Plant Physiol.* 42: 1743–1749.
570 Geller, D. and Gregory, J.S., 1956. Light-induced oxidation–reduction changes in *Rhodosporillum rubrum* extracts, *Fed. Proc.* 15: 260.
571 *Genetics in Plant Breeding, Brookhaven Symp. Biol.* No. 9, 1956.
572 Gewitz, H.S. and Voelker, W., 1962. Uber die Atmungsfermente der *Chlorella, Z. Physiol. Chem.* 330: 124–131.
573 Gibberellins. *Advances in Chemistry Series* (Gould, R.F., ed.), American Chemical Society, Washington, D.C., 1961.
574 Gibbs, M. and Cynkin, M.A., 1958. Conversion of carbon-14 dioxide to starch and glucose during photosynthesis by spinach chloroplasts, *Nature* 182: 1241–1242.
575 Gibbs, M., 1959. Metabolism of carbon compounds, *Annu. Rev. Plant Physiol.* 10: 329–378.
576 Gilbert, G.A. and Swallow, A.J. 1949. The influence of ions on the activity of Q enzyme, *J. Chem. Soc.* 4: 2849–2852.
577 Gilbert, G.A. and Patrick, A.D., 1952. Enzymes of the potato concerned in the synthesis of starch. I. The separation and crystallization of Q enzyme, *Biochem. J.* 51: 181–186.
578 Ginsburg, V., 1964. Sugar nucleotides and the synthesis of carbohydrates, *Adv. Enzymol.* 26: 35–88.
579 Glasziou, K.T., 1960. Accumulation and transformation of sugars in sugarcane stalks, *Plant Physiol.* 35(6): 895–901.
580 Glasziou, K.T., Sacher, J.A. and McCalla, D.R., 1960. On the effects of auxins on membrance permeability and pectic substances in bean endocarp, *Am. J. Bot.* 47: 743–752.
581 Glasziou, K.T., 1961. Accumulation and transformation of sugars in stalks of sugarcane. Origin of glucose and fructose in the inner space, *Plant Physiol.* 36(2): 175–179.
582 Glasziou, K.T., 1962. Accumulation and transformation of sugars in sugarcane stalks: Mechanism of inversion of sucrose in the inner space, *Nature* 193: 1100.
583 Glasziou, K.T., 1962. Commentary following presentation of paper by J. Daniels, *Proc. Int. Soc. Sugar Cane Technol.* 11: 532.
584 Glasziou, K.T., Hatch, M.D. and Sacher, J.A., 1963. Accumulation and transformation of sugars in sugarcane storage tissue, *Proc. Int. Soc. Sugar Cane Technol.* 11: 334–338.
585 Glasziou, K.T. and Waldron, J.C., 1964. The regulation of invertase synthesis in sugarcane: Effects of sugars, sugar derivatives, and polyhydric alcohols, *Aust. J. Biol. Sci.* 17(3): 609–618.
586 Glasziou, K.T. and Waldron, J.C., 1964. Regulation of acid invertase levels in sugarcane stalks by auxin- and metabolite-mediated control systems, *Nature* 203: 541–542.
587 Glasziou, K.T., Bull, T.A., Hatch, M.D. and Whiteman, P.C., 1965. Physiology of sugarcane. VII. Effects of temperature, photoperiod duration, and diurnal and seasonal temperature changes on growth and ripening, *Aust. J. Biol. Sci.* 18(1): 53–66.
588 Glasziou, K.T., Waldron, J.C. and Bull, T.A., 1966. Control of invertase synthesis in sugarcane. Loci of auxin and glucose effects, *Plant Physiol.* 41: 282–288.
589 Glasziou, K.T., Waldron, J.C. and Most, B.H., 1967. Glucose regulation of enzyme synthesis in sugar cane stem tissue, *Phytochemistry* 6: 769–775.
590 Glasziou, K.T. and Bull, T.A., 1967. The relation between total invertase activity and internode expansion in sugarcane stalks, *Proc. Int. Soc. Sugar Cane Technol.* 12: 575–581.

591 Glasziou, K.T., Gayler, K.R. and Waldron, J.C., 1968. Effects of auxin and gibberellic acid on the regulation of enzyme synthesis in sugarcane stem tissue. In *Biochemistry and Physiology of Plant Growth Substances* (Proc. 6th Int. Conf. on Plant Growth Substances) (Wightman, F. and Setterfield, C., eds.), Runge Press, Ottawa.

592 Glasziou, K.T. and Gayler, K.R., 1969. Sugar transport: Occurrence of trehalase activity in sugar cane, *Planta* 85: 299–302.

593 Glasziou, K.T., 1970. Personal communication, September, 1970.

594 Glasziou, K.T. and Bull, T.A., 1972. Feedback control of photosynthesis in sugarcane (in press). Personal communication with Dr. T.A. Bull, February, 1971.

595 Goldsworthy, A., 1966. Experiments on the origin of CO_2 released by tobacco leaf segments in the light, *Phytochemistry* 5: 1013–1019.

596 Goldsworthy, A., 1968. Comparison of the kinetics of photosynthetic carbon dioxide fixation in maize, sugarcane and tobacco, and its relation to photorespiration, *Nature* 217: 62.

597 Gomori, G., 1943. Hexose diphosphatase, *J. Biol. Chem.* 148: 139–149.

598 González-Ríos, P., 1966. Estudio sobre las variedades de caña de azúcar en Puerto Rico, Boletín No. 199, Estación Experimental Agrícola, U.P.R., Río Piedras, P.R.

599 Good, N.E., 1965. Interpretations of the CO_2 dependence of the Hill reaction, *Can. J. Bot.* 43: 119–127.

600 Gooding, E.G.B., 1942. Some observations on the daily march of photosynthesis in the leaves of sugarcane, *Trop. Agric. (Trinidad)* 19: 45–47.

601 Gordon, J., 1961. Flowering of cane, *S. Afr. Sugar J.* 45: 715.

602 Gosnell, J.M. and Thompson, G.D., 1964. The results of herbicide trials, 1963–1964, *Proc. S. Afr. Sugar Technol. Assoc.* (1964): 166–175.

603 Gosnell, J.M. and Thompson, G.D., 1967. The effects of Paraquat on the growth and yield of sugarcane, *Proc. Int. Soc. Sugar Cane Technol.* 12: 493–500.

604 Graebe, J.E. and Novelli, G.D., 1966. A practical method for large scale plant tissue culture, *Exp. Cell Res.* 41: 509–520.

605 Graham, D. and Walker, D.A., 1962. Some effects of light on the interconversion of metabolites in green leaves, *Biochem. J.* 82: 554–560.

606 Grassl, C.O., 1946. *Saccharum robustum* and other wild relatives of "noble" sugarcanes, *J. Arnold Arboretum* 27: 234–252.

607 Grassl, C.O., 1959. Introgression between *Saccharum* and *Miscanthus* in New Guinea, *Abstr. 9th Int. Bot. Congr., Montreal.*

608 Grassl, C.O., 1967. Introgression between *Saccharum* and *Miscanthus* in New Guinea and the Pacific area, *Proc. Int. Soc. Sugar Cane Technol.* 12: 995–1003.

609 Grassl, C.O., 1969. Saccharum names and their interpretation, *Proc. Int. Soc. Sugar Cane Technol.* 13: 868–875.

610 Green, D.E. and Stumpf, P.K., 1942. Starch phosphorylase of potato, *J. Biol. Chem.* 142: 355–366.

611 Green, A.A. and Cori, G.T., 1943. Crystalline muscle phosphorylases. I. Preparation, properties, and molecular weight, *J. Biol. Chem.* 151: 21–30.

612 Greenway, H., 1963. Plant responses to saline substrates. III. Effect of nutrient concentration on the growth and ion uptake of *Hordeum vulgare* during a sodium chloride stress, *Aust. J. Biol. Sci.* 16: 616–628.

613 Gregory, F.G. and Richards, F.J., 1929. Physiological studies in plant nutrition. I. The effect of manurial deficiency on the respiration and assimilation rate in barley, *Ann. Bot. (London)* 43: 119–161.

614 Grenson, M., Mousset, M., Wiame, J.M. and Bechet, J., 1966. Multiplicity of the amino acid permeases in *Saccharomyces cerevisiae.* I. Evidence for a specific arginine-transporting system. *Biochim. Biophys. Acta* 127: 325.

615 Gromet-Elhanan, Z. and Arnon, D.I., 1965. Effect of desaspidin on photosynthetic phosphorylation, *Plant Physiol.* 40: 1060–1065.

616 Grossman, I.W. and Sacktor, B., 1968. Histochemical localization of renal trehalase: Demonstration of a tubular site, *Science* 161: 571–572.

617 Guilbeau, W.F., Coll, E.E. and Martin, L.F., 1955. Effects of delay in grinding on value and processing quality of sugarcane juice, *Sugar J.* 18: 30–31 (July).
618 Guilbeau, W.F., Coll, E.E. and Martin, L.F., 1956. Losses from delay in delivering harvested cane, *Sugar Bull.* 34: 28–30.
619 Gumbs, F.A., 1966. Further work on Gramoxone as a desiccant, *Proc. Br. W. Indies Sugar Technol.* 2: 249–265.
620 Gunn, J.S. and Tatham, P.B., 1961. Diquat as an arboricide, *Nature* 189: 808–809.
621 Gunning, B.E.S. and Barkley, W.K., 1963. Kinin-induced transport and senescence in detached oat leaves, *Nature* 199: 262–265.
622 Gunning, B.E.S., Pate, J.S. and Briarty, L.G., 1968. Specialized "transfer cells" in minor veins of leaves and their possible significance in phloem translocation, *J. Cell Biol.* 37: C7–C12.

H

623 Haber, A.H. and Tolbert, N.E., 1957. Photosyntnesis in gibberellin-treated leaves, *Plant Physiol.* 32: 152–153.
624 Haddon, E., 1927. Starch in sugar cane, *Rev. Agric. Maurice* 4: 61–62.
625 Haddon, E., 1926. A problem for the factory working *Uba* juice, *S. Afr. Sugar J.* 10: 629–631.
626 Hagerman, R.H. and Arnon, D.I., 1955. Changes in glyceraldehyde phosphate dehydrogenase during the life cycle of a green plant, *Arch. Biochem. Biophys.* 57: 421–436.
627 Halais, P., 1959. The determination of nitrogenous fertilizer requirement of sugarcane crops by foliar diagnoses, *Proc. Int. Soc. Sugar Cane Technol.* 10: 515–537.
628 Halais, P., 1962. The detection of N, P, K deficiency trends in sugarcane crops by means of foliar diagnosis run from year to year on a follow-up basis, *Proc. Int. Soc. Sugar Cane Technol.* 11: 214–221.
629 Halais, P. and Parish, D.H., 1963. Silica and manganese content of cane sheaths in relation to soil and nutrition, *Mauritius Sugar Ind. Res. Inst. Annu. Rept.* (1963): 74–76.
630 Haldane, J.H., 1933. Dyrage and deterioration of cane varieties in upper India, *Int. Sugar. J.* 35: 140–143.
631 Hall, J.A., 1913. Inversión del azúcar en las variedades, *Rev. Ind. Agric. Tucumán*, Año 4(4): 148–150.
632 Hall, J.A., 1914. Rate of inversion in cut cane, *Int. Sugar J.* 16: 235.
633 Hall, J.A., 1914. Inversion in cut sugar cane, *Louisiana Planter and Sugar Manufacturer* 52: 233–234.
634 Hanes, C.S., 1940. The breakdown and synthesis of starch by an enzyme system from pea seeds, *Proc. R. Soc. (London), Ser. B* 128: 421–450.
635 Hanes, C.S., 1940. Reversible formation of starch from glucose 1-phosphate catalyzed by potato phosphorylase, *Proc. R. Soc. (London), Ser. B* 129: 174–208.
636 Hanes, C.S. and Maskell, E.J., 1942. The influence of hydrogen-ion concentration upon the equilibrium state in phosphorylase reactions, *Biochem. J.* 36: 76–79.
637 Hansford, C.G., 1935. The introduction of sugarcane varieties into Uganda (1926–1934). *E. Afr. Agric. J.* 1: 20–24.
638 Happold, F.C. and Hoyle, L., 1935. The *coli*–tryptophan–indole reaction. I. Enzyme preparations and their action on tryptophan and some indole derivatives, *Biochem. J.* 29: 1918–1926.
639 Happold, F.C. and Hoyle, L., 1936. The *coli*–tryptophan–indole reaction. II. The non-induction of tryptophanase in media containing glucose, *Br. J. Exp. Pathol.* 17: 136–143.
640 Haq, S. and Hassid, W.Z., 1965. Biosynthesis of sucrose phosphate with sugarcane leaf chloroplasts, *Plant Physiol.* 40(4): 591–594.
641 Harden, A. and Young, W.J., 1908. The alcoholic fermentation of yeast juice. III. The function of phosphates in the fermentation of glucose by yeast-juice, *Proc. R. Soc. (London), Ser. B* 80: 299–311.

642 Hare, C.J., 1963. The effect of soil physical properties on the growth of sugarcane with special reference to the availability of moisture and potassium, *Proc. Int. Soc. Sugar Cane Technol.* 11: 130–139.

643 Harel, S. and Reinhold, L., 1966. Effect of DNP on translocation in the phloem, *Physiol. Plant.* 19: 634–643.

644 Harris, G.P., 1956. Amino acids as sources of nitrogen for the growth of isolated growth embryos, *New Phytol.* 55: 253–268.

645 Hartley, W., 1950. The global distribution of tribes of the Gramineae in relation to historical and environmental factors, *Aust. J. Agric. Res.* 1: 355–373.

646 Hartt, C.E., 1929. Potassium deficiency in sugarcane, *Bot. Gaz.* 88: 229–261,

647 Hartt, C.E., 1933. Studies on the invertase of sugarcane, *Hawaiian Plant. Rec.* 37: 13–14.

648 Hartt, C.E., 1934. Water and cane ripening, *Hawaiian Plant. Rec.* 38: 193–206.

649 Hartt, C.E., 1934. The synthesis of sucrose by invertase in sugarcane. Paper presented at the *11th Annu. Meet. Am. Soc. Plant Physiol.*, 1934.

650 Hartt, C.E., 1934. Some effects of potassium upon the amounts of protein and amino forms of nitrogen, sugars, and enzyme activity of sugarcane, *Plant Physiol.* 9: 453–490.

651 Hartt, C.E., 1934. Some effects of potassium upon the growth of sugarcane and upon the absorption and migration of ash constituents, *Plant Physiol.* 9: 399–452.

652 Hartt, C.E., 1936. The fluctuations of sugars in the leaf blades of the sugar cane plant during the day and the night, *Hawaiian Plant. Rec.* 39: 298–326.

653 Hartt, C.E., 1936. The fluctuations of sugars in the leaf sheaths of the sugar cane plant during the day and the night, *Hawaiian Plant. Rec.* 40: 329–354.

654 Hartt, C.E., 1936. Further notes on water and cane ripening, *Hawaiian Plant. Rec.* 40: 355–381.

655 Hartt, C.E., 1937. Water and cane ripening. Report of committee in charge of the Experiment Station, *Proc. Hawaiian Sugar Plant. Assoc.* pp. 112–114.

656 Hartt, C.E., 1939. The third study of water and cane ripening, *Hawaiian Plant. Rec.* 43: 145–158.

657 Hartt, C.E., 1943. The synthesis of sucrose in the sugarcane plant. I, *Hawaiian Plant. Rec.* 47: 113–132.

658 Hartt, C.E., 1943. The synthesis of sucrose in the sugarcane plant. II, *Hawaiian Plant. Rec.* 47: 155–170.

659 Hartt, C.E., 1943. The synthesis of sucrose in the sugarcane plant. III, *Hawaiian Plant. Rec.* 47: 223–255.

660 Hartt, C.E., 1944. The synthesis of sucrose in the sugarcane plant. IV. Concerning the mechanism of sucrose synthesis in the sugarcane plant, *Hawaiian Plant. Rec.* 48: 31–42.

661 Hartt, C.E. and Burr, G.O., 1951. Translocation by sugarcane fed radioactive carbon dioxide, *Proc. 7th Int. Bot. Congr.*, pp. 748–749.

662 Hartt, C.E., 1959. The growth of sugarcane as influenced by phosphorus. The critical range of plant phosphorus, *Proc. Int. Soc. Sugar Cane Technol.* 10: 467–473.

663 Hartt, C.E., 1963. Tracing sugar in the cane plant, *Proc. Hawaiian Acad. Sci.*, 37th Annu. Meeting.

664 Hartt, C.E. and Kortschak, H.P., 1963. Tracing sugar in the cane plant, *Proc. Int. Soc. Sugar Cane Technol.* 11: 323–334.

665 Hartt, C.E., 1963. Translocation of sugar in the cane plant, *Rept. Hawaiian Sugar Technol.* (1963): 151–167.

666 Hartt, C.E., 1963. Translocation as a factor in photosynthesis, *Naturwissenschaften* 21: 666–667.

667 Hartt, C.E., Kortschak, H.P., Forbes, A.J. and Burr, G.O., 1963. Translocation of ^{14}C in sugarcane, *Plant Physiol.* 38: 305–318.

668 Hartt, C.E., 1963. Rate of photosynthesis–wind injury and age effects, *Annu. Rept. Exp. Sta. Hawaiian Sugar Plant. Assoc.* (1963): 4.

669 Hartt, C.E. and Kortschak, H.P., 1964. Sugar gradients and translocation of sucrose in detached blades of sugarcane, *Plant Physiol.* 39(3): 460–474.

670 Hartt, C.E., Kortschak, H.P. and Burr, G.O., 1964. Effects of defoliation, deradication, and darkening the blade upon translocation of ^{14}C in sugarcane, *Plant Physiol.* 39(1): 15–22.

671 Hartt, C.E., 1965. The effect of temperature upon translocation of ^{14}C in sugarcane, *Plant Physiol.* 40: 74–81.

672 Hartt, C.E., 1966. Translocation in colored light, *Plant Physiol.* 41: 369–372.

673 Hartt, C.E., 1965. Light and translocation of ^{14}C in detached blades of sugarcane, *Plant Physiol.* 40: 718–724.

674 Hartt, C.E. and Burr, G.O., 1967. Factors affecting photosynthesis in sugarcane, *Proc. Int. Soc. Sugar Cane Technol.* 12: 590–609.

675 Hartt, C.E., 1967. Effects of moisture supply upon translocation and storage of ^{14}C in sugarcane, *Plant Physiol.* 42: 338–346.

676 Hartt, C.E., 1969. Effect of potassium deficiency upon translocation of ^{14}C in attached blades and entire plants of sugarcane, *Plant Physiol.* 44(10): 1461–1469.

677 Hartt, C.E., 1970. Effect of potassium deficiency upon translocation of ^{14}C in detached blades of sugarcane, *Plant Physiol.* 45: 183–187.

678 Hassid, W.Z., 1938. Isolation of a hexose monophosphate from pea leaves, *Plant Physiol.* 13: 641–647.

679 Hassid, W.Z., Doudoroff, M. and Barker, H.A., 1944. Enzymatically synthesized crystalline sucrose, *J. Am. Chem. Soc.* 66: 1416–1419.

680 Hassid, W.Z., Doudoroff, M., Barker, H.A. and Dore, W.H., 1946. Isolation and structure of an enzymatically synthesized crystalline disaccharide D-glucosido-D-ketoxyloside, *J. Am. Chem. Soc.* 68: 1465–1467.

681 Hassid, W.Z. and Doudoroff, M., 1950. Synthesis of disaccharides with bacterial enzymes, *Adv. Enzymol.* 10: 123–143.

682 Hassid, W.Z. and Putman, E.W., 1950. Transformation of sugars in plants, *Annu. Rev. Plant Physiol.* 1: 109–124.

683 Hassid, W.Z. and Bean, R.S., 1955. Synthesis of disaccharides with pea preparations, *Proc. 3rd Int. Congr. Biochem., Brussels*, pp. 163–165.

684 Hassid, W.Z. and Putman, E.W., 1952. Sugar transformations in leaves of *Canna indica, Fed. Proc.* 11: 226–227.

685 Hassid, W.Z., 1958. The synthesis and transformation of the oligosaccharides in plants, including their hydrolysis. In *Encyclopedia of Plant Physiology* 6: 125–136.

686 Hassid, W.Z., 1967. Transformation of sugars in plants, *Annu. Rev. Plant Physiol.* 17: 253–280.

687 Hatch, M.D. and Turner, J.F., 1958. Glycolysis by an extract from pea seeds, *Biochem. J.* 69: 495–501.

688 Hatch, M.D., 1963. A uridine diphosphatase from sugarcane, *Biochem. J.* 88: 423–427.

689 Hatch, M.D., Sacher, J.A. and Glasziou, K.T., 1964. Sugar accumulation cycle in sugarcane. I. Studies on enzymes of the cycle, *Plant Physiol.* 38(3): 338–343.

690 Hatch, M.D. and Glasziou, K.T., 1963. Sugar accumulation cycle in sugarcane. II. Relationship of invertase activity to sugar content and growth rate in storage tissue of plants grown in controlled environments, *Plant Physiol.* 38: 344–348.

691 Hatch, M.D., 1964. Sugar accumulation by sugarcane storage tissue. The role of sucrose phosphate, *Biochem. J.* 93: 521–526.

692 Hatch, M.D. and Glasziou, K.T., 1964. Direct evidence for translocation of sucrose in sugarcane leaves and stems, *Plant Physiol.* 39(2): 180–184.

693 Hatch, M.D. and Slack, C.R., 1966. Photosynthesis by sugarcane leaves. A new carboxylation reaction and the pathway of sugar formation, *Biochem. J.* 101: 103–111.

694 Hatch, M.D. and Slack, C.R., 1967. The participation of phosphoenolpyruvate synthetase in photosynthetic CO_2 fixation of tropical grasses, *Arch. Biochem. Biophys.* 120: 224–225.

695 Hatch, M.D., Slack, C.R. and Johnson, H.S., 1967. Further studies on a new pathway of photosynthetic carbon fixation in sugarcane and its occurrence in other plant species, *Biochem. J.* 102: 417–422.

696 Hatch, M.D. and Slack, C.R., 1968. A new enzyme for the interconversion of pyruvate and phosphopyruvate and its role in the C_4-dicarboxylic acid pathway of photosynthesis, *Biochem. J.* 106: 141–146.
697 Hatch, M.D. and Slack, C.R., 1969. *Biochem. J.* 112: 549–558.
698 Hatch, M.D., Slack, C.R. and Bull, T.A., 1969. Light-induced changes in the content of some enzymes of the C_4-dicarboxylic acid pathway of photosynthesis and its effect on other characteristics of photosynthesis, *Phytochemistry* 8: 697–706.
699 Hatch, M.D. and Slack, C.R., 1969. NADP-specific malate dehydrogenase and glycerate kinase in leaves and evidence for their location in chloroplasts, *Biochem. Biophys. Res. Commun.* 34(5): 589.
700 Hatch, M.D. and Slack, C.R., 1970. *Progress in Photochemistry*, Vol. 2, Interscience Publishers, London (not seen).
701 Hawker, J.S. and Hatch, M.D., 1965. Mechanism of sugar storage by mature stem tissue of sugarcane, *Physiol Plant.* 18: 444–453.
702 Hawker, J.S., 1965. The sugar content of cell walls and intercellular spaces in sugarcane stems and its relation to sugar transport, *Aust. J. Biol. Sci.* 18: 959–969.
703 Hawker, J.S. and Hatch, M.D., 1966. A specific sucrose phosphatase from plant tissues, *Biochem. J.* 99: 102–107.
704 Hawker, J.S., 1967. Inhibition of sucrose phosphatase by sucrose, *Biochem. J.* 102: 401–406.
705 Hawker, J.S., 1967. The activity of uridine diphosphate glucose–D-fructose 6-phosphate 2-glucosyltransferase in leaves, *Biochem. J.* 105: 943–946.
706 Haworth, W.N. and Law, J., 1916. Constitution of the disaccharides. I. Structure of sucrose, *J. Chem. Soc.* 109: 1314–1325.
707 Hayashi, T., 1961. The effect of gibberellin treatment on the photosynthetic activity of plants, *4th Int. Conf. on Growth Regulation*, pp. 579–588, Iowa State University Press, Ames, Iowa.
708 Hehre, E.J., 1949. Synthesis of a polysaccharide of the starch–glycogen class from sucrose by a cell-free, bacterial enzyme system (amylosucrase), *J. Biol. Chem.* 177: 267–279.
709 Hehre, E.J., 1951. Enzymic synthesis of polysaccharides: A biological type of polymerization, *Adv. Enzymol.* 11: 297–337.
710 Hehre, E.J., 1951. Synthesis of polysaccharides without the intermediation of phosphate. In *Phosphorus Metabolism* (McElroy, W.D. and Glass, B., eds.), Vol. 1, pp. 48–52, Johns Hopkins Press, Baltimore, Md.
711 Heinicke, A.J., 1934. Photosynthesis in apple leaves during late fall and its significance in annual bearing, *Proc. Am. Soc. Hortic. Sci.* 32: 77–80.
712 Heinicke, A.J. and Childers, N.F., 1935. The influence of water deficiency on photosynthesis and transpiration in apple leaves, *Proc. Am. Soc. Hortic. Sci.* 33: 155–159.
713 Heinz, D.J., 1967. Wild *Saccharum* species for breeding in Hawaii, *Proc. Int. Soc. Sugar Cane Technol.* 12: 1037–1043.
714 Heinz, D.J. and Mee, G.W.P., 1969. Plant differentiation from callus tissue of *Saccharum* species, *Crop Sci.* 9: 346–348.
715 Heinz, D.J., Mee, G.W.P. and Nickell, L.G., 1969. Chromosome number of some *Saccharum* species hybrids and their cell suspension cultures, *Am. J. Bot.* 56(4): 450–456.
716 Heinz, D.J., 1969. Personal commentary following presentation of paper by Dr. S. Price, *Proc. Int. Soc. Sugar Cane Technol.* 13: 926.
717 Heinz, D.J., 1971. Personal communication with the author, March, 1971.
718 Hellebust, J.A. and Forward, D.F., 1962. The invertase of the corn radicle and its activity in successive stages of growth, *Can. J. Bot.* 40: 113–126.
719 Henderson, I.F. and Henderson, W.D., 1963. *A Dictionary of Biological Terms*, 8th edn., D. Van Nostrand Co., New York, N.Y.
720 Hesketh, J.D. and Musgrave, R.B., 1962. Photosynthesis under field conditions. IV. Light studies with individual corn leaves, *Crop Sci.* 2: 311–315.
721 Hesketh, J.D. and Moss, D.N., 1963. Variation of response of photosynthesis to light, *Crop Sci.* 3: 107–110.

722 Hesketh, J.D., 1963. Limitations to photosynthesis responsible for differences among species, *Crop Sci.* 3: 493–496.
723 Hesketh, J.D. and Baker, D., 1967. Light and carbon assimilation by plant communities, *Crop Sci.* 7: 285–293.
724 Hestrin, S., Feingold, D.S. and Avigad, G., 1956. The mechanism of polysaccharide production from sucrose. 3. Donor–acceptor specificity of levansucrase from *Aerobacter levanicum*, *Biochem. J.* 64: 340–352.
725 Hew, C.S., Nelson, C.D. and Krotkov, G., 1967. Hormonal control of translocation of photosynthetically assimilated ^{14}C in young soybean plants, *Am. J. Bot.* 54: 252–256.
726 Hew, C.S. and Krotkov, G., 1968. Effect of oxygen on the rates of CO_2 evolution in light and darkness by photosynthesizing and non-photosynthesizing leaves, *Plant Physiol.* 43: 464–466.
727 Hew, C.S. and Gibbs, M., 1969. A study of corn and sugarcane chloroplasts, *Abstr. 11th Int. Bot. Congr.*, p. 90.
728 Hildebrandt, A.C. and Riker, A.J., 1949. The influence of various carbon compounds on the growth of marigold, Paris-daisy, periwinkle, sunflower and tobacco tissue *in vitro, Am. J. Bot.* 36: 74–85.
729 Hildebrandt, A.C. and Riker, A.J., 1950. Growth of plant tissue *in vitro* influenced by the concentration of sugars and polysaccharides, *Am. J. Bot. (Abstr.)* 37: 678–679.
730 Hildebrandt, A.C. and Riker, A.J., 1953. Influence of concentrations of sugars and polysaccharides on callus tissue grown *in vitro, Am. J. Bot.* 40: 66–76.
731 Hill, R., 1937. Oxygen evolved by isolated chloroplasts, *Nature* 139: 881–882.
732 Hill, R., 1939. Oxygen produced by isolated chloroplasts, *Proc. R. Soc. (London), Ser. B* 127: 192–210.
733 Hill, R., 1951. Reduction by chloroplasts, *Symp. Soc. Exp. Biol.* 5: 222–231.
734 Hill, R., 1955. The cytochrome components and chlorophyll in relation to the carbon cycle, *Proc. Int. Congr. Biochem., Brussels*, pp. 225–227.
735 Hill, R. and Walker, D.A., 1959. Pyocyanine and phosphorylation with chloroplasts, *Plant Physiol.* 34: 240–245.
736 Höber, R., 1947. *Physical Chemistry of Cells and Tissues*, Churchill, London.
737 Hoch, G., Owens, O.H. and Kok, B., 1963. Photosynthesis and respiration, *Arch. Biochem. Biophys.* 101: 171–180.
738 Hoch, G. and Martin, I., 1963. Photo-potentiation of adenosine triphosphate hydrolysis, *Biochem. Biophys. Res. Commun.* 12(3): 223–228.
739 Hodgkinson, K.C. and Veale, J.A., 1966. The distribution of photosynthate within lucerne as influenced by illumination, *Aust. J. Biol. Sci.* 19: 15–21.
740 Hogarth, D.M., 1969. The genetic basis for starch content in sugarcane, *Proc. Int. Soc. Sugar Cane Technol.* 13: 933–938.
741 Homann, P.H. and Schmid, G.H., 1967. Photosynthetic reactions of chloroplasts with unusual structure, *Plant Physiol.* 42: 1619–1622.
742 Homer, R.F. and Tomlinson, T.E., 1959. Redox properties of some dipyridyl quaternary salts, *Nature* 184: 2012–2013.
743 Homer, R.F., Mees, G.C. and Tomlinson, T.E., 1960. Mode of action of dipyridyl quaternary salts as herbicides, *J. Sci. Food Agric.* 11(6): 309–315.
744 Homer, R.F. and Tomlinson, T.E., 1960. The stereochemistry of the bridged quaternary salts of 2,2′-bipyridyl, *J. Am. Chem. Soc.* 504: 2498–2503.
745 Hommes, F., 1926. Achteruitgang van riet op het emplacement, *Arch. Suikerind. Ned. Indië* 34: 545–551.
746 Hooker, J.D., 1896. Gramineae. In *Flora British India*, Vol. 7 (not seen).
747 Hooker, J.D., 1897. *Flora British India*, Vol. 7 [cited from Dutt and Rao (459)].
748 Hoover, W.H., Johnston, E.S. and Brackett, F.S., 1933. *Smithsonian Misc. Collect.* 87: 1–19 (not seen).

749 Horecker, B.L., Smyrniotis, P.Z. and Seegmiller, J.E., 1951. The enzymatic conversion of 6-phosphogluconate to ribulose 5-phosphate and ribose 5-phosphate, *J. Biol. Chem.* 193: 383–396.

750 Horecker, B.L. and Smyrniotis, P.Z., 1953. Transaldolase: The formation of fructose 6-phosphate from sedoheptulose 7-phosphate, *J. Am. Chem. Soc.* 75: 2021–2022.

751 Horecker, B.L., Smyrniotis, P.Z. and Klenow, H., 1953. The formation of sedoheptulose phosphate from pentose phosphate, *J. Biol. Chem.* 205: 661–682.

752 Hori, S., 1898. Some observations on "bakanae" disease of the rice plant (in Japanese), *Mem. Agric. Res. Sta. (Tokyo)* 12(1): 110–119.

753 Hough, L. and Jones, J.K.N., 1953. The synthesis of sugars from simpler substances. Part V. Enzymic synthesis of sedoheptulose, *J. Chem. Soc.* 342–345.

754 Hrishi, N., Marimuthammal, S. and Selvanathan, S.J., 1969. The use of chemical mutagens in sugarcane, *Proc. Int. Soc. Sugar Cane Technol.* 13: 1024–1032.

755 Hu, T.H. and Lee, S., 1957. Photoperiodic experiments for inducing flowering of sugarcane, *Rept. Taiwan Sugar Exp. Sta.* 16: 22–36.

756 Hucker, G.J. and Pederson, C.S., 1930. Studies on the *Coccacceae. XVI.* The genus *Leuconostoc, N.Y. (Geneva) Agric. Exp. Sta.Tech. Bull.* No. 167.

757 Hucker, G.J. and Pederson, C.S., 1942. A review of the microbiology of commercial sugar and related sweetening agents, *N.Y. Agric. Exp. Sta. J. Paper* No. 495, 22 pp.

758 Hudson, C.S. and Brauns, D.H., 1915. Crystalline *d*-fructose pentaacetate, *J. Am. Chem. Soc.* 37: 1283–1285; 2736–2745.

759 Hughes, R.H., 1956. Sugar losses – field and factory, *Hawaiian Plant. Rec.* 55: 167–175.

760 Hülsmann, W.C., 1962. On the relationship between the oxidation of malate and isocitrate and the synthesis of long-chain fatty acids, *Biochim. Biophys. Acta* 62: 620–622.

761 Humbert, R.P., 1958. Potash fertilization in the Hawaiian sugar industry. *Potassium Symp.,* Editors Int. Potash Institute, Berne, pp. 319–344.

762 Humbert, R.P., 1963. Potash and sugarcane quality, *Proc. Int. Soc. Sugar Cane Technol.* 11: 115–123.

763 Humbert, R.P., Zamora, M. and Fraser, T.B., 1967. Ripening and maturity control progress at Ingenio Los Mochis, *Proc. Int. Soc. Sugar Cane Technol.* 12: 446–452.

764 Humbert, R.P., Lima, L.G. and Goveas, J., 1969. Tassel control progress with Reglone in the Mexican sugar industry, *Proc. Int. Soc. Sugar Cane Technol.* 13: 462–467.

765 Humphreys, T.B. and Duggar, W.M., 1957. The effect of 2,4-dichlorophenoxyacetic acid on pathways of glucose catabolism in higher plants, *Plant Physiol.* 32: 136–140.

766 Humphries, E.C., 1951. The absorption of ions by excised root systems. II. Observations on roots of barley grown in solutions deficient in phosphorus, nitrogen, or potassium, *J. Exp. Bot.* 2: 344–379.

767 Humphries, E.C., 1963. Dependence of net assimilation rate on root growth of isolated leaves, *Ann. Bot. (London)* [N.S.] 27: 175–184.

768 Humphries, E.C. and Thorne, G.N., 1964. The effect of root formation on photosynthesis of detached leaves, *Ann. Bot. (London)* [N.S.] 28: 391–400.

769 Hurwitz, J., Weissbach, A., Horecker, B.L. and Smyrniotis, P.Z., 1956. Spinach phosphoribulokinase, *J. Biol. Chem.* 218: 769–783.

I

770 Ikemori, M. and Nishida, K., 1968. Carbonic anhydrase in the marine alga *Ulva pertusa, Physiol. Plant.* 21: 292–297.

771 Iljin, W.S., 1929. Standortsfeuchtigkeit und der Zuckergehalt in den Pflanzen, *Planta* 7: 59–71.

772 Ingen-Housz, J., 1796. Essay on the food of plants and the renovation of soils (Appendix to Chapter 15, General Report from the Board of Agriculture, London). Reviewed in *Photosyn-*

thesis and Related Processes (Rabinowitch, E.I., ed.), 1945, Vol. I, p. 17, Interscience Publishers, New York, N.Y.

773 Innes, R.F., 1948. Plant analysis in relation to the nutrition of sugarcane in Jamaica, *Proc. Br. W. Indies Sugar Technol.* (1947–51): 92–114.

774 Innes, R.F. and Shaw, M.E.A., 1967. The influence of seasons, irrigation, varieties, and level of nitrogen dressings on the nitrogen index of sugarcane on three soil types, *Proc. Int. Soc. Sugar Cane Technol.* 12: 390–400.

775 *International Conference on the Peaceful Uses of Atomic Energy, 1955*, United Nations, New York, N.Y.

776 Irvine, J.C. and Robertson, G., 1916. Evidence indicating the existence of a new form of fructose. A reactive form of methyl fructoside, *J. Chem. Soc.* 109: 1305–1314.

777 Irvine, J.C., Oldham, J.W.H. and Skinner, A.F., 1929. Condensation of glucose and fructose. Synthesis of an isosucrose, *J. Am. Chem. Soc.*. 51: 1279–1293.

778 Irvine, J.C. and Oldham, J.W.H., 1929. The coupling of glucose and γ-fructose. Conversion of sucrose into isosucrose, *J. Am. Chem. Soc.* 51: 3609–3612.

779 Irvine, J.E. and Friloux, J.J., 1965. Juice acidity and gum content as measures of cane deterioration, *Sugar Azúcar* 60: 58.

780 Irvine, J.E., 1967. Photosynthesis in sugarcane varieties under field conditions, *Crop Sci.* 7: 297–300.

781 Izawa, S. and Good, N.E., 1967. Inhibition and uncoupling of phosphorylation in chloroplasts, *Brookhaven Symp. Biol.* 19: 169–187.

J

782 Jackson, W.A. and Volk, R.J., 1970. Photorespiration, *Annu. Rev. Plant Physiol.* 21: 385–432.

783 Jacob, F. and Monod, J., 1961. Genetic regulatory mechanisms in the synthesis of proteins, *J. Mol. Biol.* 3: 318–356.

784 Jacobsen, L., Overstreet, R. and Carlson, R.M., 1957. The effect of pH and temperature on the absorption of potassium and bromide by barley roots, *Plant Physiol.* 32: 658–662.

785 Jagathesan, D. and Sreenivasan, T.V., 1969. Cytogenetical studies in *Narenga porphyrocoma.* Study of self-incompatibility, *Proc. Int. Soc. Sugar Cane Technol.* 13: 963–967.

786 Jagendorf, A.T. and Avron, M., 1958. Cofactors and rates of photosynthetic phosphorylation by spinach chloroplasts, *J. Biol. Chem.* 231: 277–290.

787 Jagendorf, A.T. and Margulies, M., 1960. Inhibition of spinach chloroplast photosynthetic reactions by *para*-chlorophenyl-1,1-dimethylurea, *Arch. Biochem. Biophys.* 90: 184–195.

788 Jagendorf, A.T. and Uribe, E.C., 1966. ATP formation caused by acid–base transition of spinach chloroplasts, *Proc. Natl. Acad. Sci. (U.S.)* 55: 170–177.

789 Jagendorf, A.T. and Uribe, E.G., 1967. Photophosphorylation and the chemiosmotic hypothesis, *Brookhaven Symp. Biol.* 19: 215–245.

790 Jagendorf, A.T., 1967. The chemiosmotic hypothesis of photophosphorylation. In *Harvesting the Sun* (San Pietro, A., Greer, F.A. and Army, T.R., eds.), pp. 69–77, Academic Press, New York, N.Y.

791 Jakoby, W.G., Brummond, D.P. and Ochoa, S., 1956. Formation of 3-phosphoglyceric acid by carbon dioxide fixation with spinach leaf enzymes, *J. Biol. Chem.* 218: 811–822.

792 James, N.I., 1966. Photoperiod research at Canal Point, Florida, *I.S.S.C.T. Sugarcane Breeders' Newsletter* No. 18, September, 1966.

793 James, N.I. and Smith, G.A., 1969. Effect of photoperiod and light intensity on flowering in sugarcane, *Crop Sci.* 9: 794–796.

794 James, N.I., 1969. Delayed flowering and pollen production in male-sterile sugarcane subjected to extended day length, *Crop Sci.* 9: 279–282.

795 James, N.I., 1969. Graduated delay of flowering in sugarcane with 11.5-hour dark periods, *Proc. Int. Soc. Sugar Cane Technol.* 13: 984–991.

796 James, N.I., 1970. Photoperiodic control of flowering in the Florida sugarcane program, *Sugar Azúcar* (January issue).
797 James, W.O. and Das, V.S.R., 1957. The organization of respiration in chlorophyllus cells, *New Phytologist* 56: 325–343.
798 Janaki-Ammal, E.K. and Singh, T.S.N., 1936. A preliminary note on a new *Saccharum* x *Sorghum* hybrid, *Indian J. Agric. Sci.* 6: 1105–1106.
799 Janaki-Ammal, E.K., 1937. Report of sugarcane geneticist, 1937 [cited from Raghavan (1210)].
800 Janaki-Ammal, E.K., 1941. Intergeneric hybrids of *Saccharum*. I–III, *J. Genet.* 41: 217–253.
801 Janaki-Ammal, E.K., 1942. Intergeneric hybrids of *Saccharum*. IV. *Saccharum–Narenga*, *J. Genet.* 44: 23–32.
802 Jansen, L.L., Gentner, W.A. and Shaw, W.C., 1961. Effects of surfactants on the herbicidal activity of several herbicides in aqueous spray solutions, *Weeds* 9: 381–405.
803 Jensen, R.G. and Bassham, J.A., 1966. Photosynthesis by isolated chloroplasts, *Proc. Natl. Acad. Sci. (U.S.)* 56: 1095–1101.
804 Jenson, R.D. and Taylor, S.A., 1961. Effects of temperature on water transport through plants, *Plant Physiol.* 36: 639–642.
805 Jervis, E.L., Johnson, F.R., Sheff, M.F. and Smyth, D.H., 1956. The effect of phlorhizin on intestinal absorption and intestinal phosphatase, *J. Physiol. (London)* 134: 675–688.
806 Jeswiet, J., 1925. Beschrijving der soorten van het suikerriet. XI. Bijdrage tot de systematiek van het geslacht *Saccharum, Arch. Suikerind. Ned. Indië*, Meded. Proefsta. Java Suikerind. (1925): 391–404 [cited from Price (1188)].
807 Jeswiet, J., 1929. The development of selection and breeding of the sugarcane in Java, *Proc. Int. Soc. Sugar Cane Technol.* 3: 44–57.
808 Johnson, H.S. and Hatch, M.D., 1968. Distribution of the C_4-dicarboxylic acid pathway of photosynthesis and its occurrence in dicotyledonous plants, *Phytochemistry* 7: 375–380.
809 Johnson, H.S. and Hatch, M.D., 1969. The C_4-dicarboxylic acid pathway of photosynthesis. Identification of intermediates and products and quantitative evidence for the rate of carbon flow, *Biochem. J.* 114: 127–134.
810 Johnson, H.S. and Hatch, M.D., 1970. Properties and regulation of leaf nicotinamide–adenine dinucleotide phosphate–malate dehydrogenase and 'malic' enzyme in plants with the C_4-dicarboxylic acid pathway of photosynthesis, *Biochem. J.* 119: 273–280.
811 Jones, H., Martin, R.V. and Porter, H.K., 1959. Translocation of ^{14}carbon in tobacco following assimilation of ^{14}carbon dioxide by a single leaf, *Ann. Bot. (London)* 23: 493–508.
812 Juang, P.Y., 1969. A study of flowering behavior of sugarcane in different geographic conditions, *Proc. Int. Soc. Sugar Cane Technol.* 13: 840–848.
813 Julien, R., 1969. The role of leaves in the perception and inhibition of the flowering stimulus in sugarcane, *Proc. Int. Soc. Sugar Cane Technol.* 13: 976–983.

K

814 Kagan, B.O., Latker, S.N. and Zfasman, E.M., 1942. Phosphorolysis of sucrose by the cultures of *Leuconostoc mesenteroides*, *Biokhimiya 7: 92–108* [*Chem. Abstr. 37: 4760 (1943)*].
815 Kamen, M. and Newton, J.W., 1957. Photophosphorylation by subcellular particles from *Chromatium*, *Biochim. Biophys. Acta* 25: 462–474.
816 Kandasami, P.A., 1961. Interspecific and intergeneric hybrids of *Saccharum spontaneum* L. I. Functioning of gametes, *Cytologia* 26: 117–121.
817 Kandler, O. and Senser, M., 1968. Differences in the pattern of products of photosynthesis after short term photosynthesis, in $^{14}CO_2$, of *Oryza* and *Sorghum*. In *Photosynthesis in Sugarcane*, Proc. Int. Symp. held June 12 and 13, 1968, at the Royal Lancaster Hotel, London, pp. 30–32.
818 Kandler, O. and Gibbs, M., 1956. Asymmetric distribution of ^{14}C in the glucose phosphates formed during photosynthesis, *Plant Physiol.* 31: 411–412.

819 Kehr, A.E. and Smith, H.H., 1954. Genetic tumors in *Nicotiana* hybrids. In *Abnormal and Pathological Plant Growth, Brookhaven Symp. Biol.* 6: 55–78.

820 Kelly, S. and Avery, G.S., 1949. The effect of 2,4-dichlorophenoxyacetic acid and other physiologically-active substances on respiration, *Am. J. Bot.* 36: 421–426.

821 Kemble, A.R. and Macpherson, H.T., 1954. Liberation of amino acids in perennial ryegrass during wilting, *Biochem.J.* 58: 46–50.

822 Kendall, A.I. and Farmer, C.J., 1912. Studies in bacterial metabolism. I, *J. Biol. Chem.* 12: 13–17.

823 Kendall, A.I. and Farmer, C.J., 1913. Studies in bacterial metabolism. VII, *J. Biol. Chem.* 13: 63–70.

824 Kendall, A.I., 1922. Studies in bacterial metabolism. LVII, *J. Infect. Dis.* 30: 211–224.

825 Keniry, J.S., Lee, J.B. and Davis, C.W., 1967. Deterioration of mechanically harvested chopped-up cane. Part I. Dextran – A promising quantitative indicator of the processing quality of chopped-up cane, *Int. Sugar J.* 69: 330–333.

826 Keniry, J.S., Lee, J.B. and Davis, C.W., 1967. Deterioration of mechanically harvested chopped-up cane. Part II. The rate of dextran formation, *Int. Sugar J.* 69: 357–360.

827 Kennett, R.D., 1967. Personal communication between Dr. R.P. Humbert and the author.

828 Kensler, C.J., Dexter, S.O. and Rhoads, C.P., 1942. *Cancer Res.* 2: 1 (not seen); Fitzhugh, A.F., 1953. Malignant tumors and high polymers, *Science* 118: 783.

829 Kertesz, Z.I., 1937. On the determination of plant enzymes, *Plant Physiol.* 12: 845–851.

830 Kessler, E., 1955. On the role of manganese in the oxygen-evolving system of photosynthesis, *Arch. Biochem. Biophys.* 59: 527–529.

831 Kessler, E., 1957. Stoffwechselphysiologische Untersuchungen an Hydrogenase enthaltenden Grunalgen. I. Uber die Rolle des Mangans bei Photoreduktion und Photosynthese, *Planta* 49: 435–454.

832 Ketellapper, H.J., 1963. Stomatal physiology, *Am. Rev. Plant Physiol.* 14: 249–270.

833 Key, J.L., 1964. Ribonucleic acid and protein synthesis as essential processes for cell elongation, *Plant Physiol.* 39: 365–370.

834 Key, J.L. and Shannon, J.C., 1964. Enhancement of ribonucleic acid synthesis in excised soybean hypocotyl tissue, *Plant Physiol.* 39: 360–364.

835 Key, J.L. and Ingle, J., 1964. Requirement for the synthesis of DNA-like RNA for growth of the excised plant tissue, *Proc. Natl. Acad. Sci. (U.S.)* 52: 1382–1387.

836 Key, J.L., 1966. Effect of purine and pyrimidine analogs on growth and RNA metabolism in the soybean hypocotyl. The selective action of 5-fluorouracil, *Plant Physiol.* 41: 1257–1264.

837 Kiessling, W., 1939. The glycogen–phosphorylating enzyme complex and a reversible enzyme glycogen synthesis, *Biochem. Z.* 302: 50–72 [*Chem. Abstr.* 34: 4749 (1940)].

838 King, N.J., Mungomery, R.W. and Hughes, C.G., 1965. *Manual of Cane Growing*, American Elsevier Publishing Co., New York, N.Y.

839 Kiyasu, J.Y. and Chaikoff, I.L., 1957. On the manner of transport of absorbed fructose, *J. Biol. Chem.* 224: 935–939.

840 Kliewer, W.M., 1965. Changes in concentration of glucose, fructose, and total soluble solids in flowers and berries of *Vitis vinifera*, *Am. J. Enol. Viticult.* 16: 101–110.

841 Klimek, M., 1965. Thymidine incorporation into mammalian strain L cells after the action of 5-fluorodeoxyuridine and the effect of uracil, *Neoplasma* 12(5): 465–468.

842 Kodani, M.A., 1948. Sodium ribose nucleate and mitosis. Induction of morphological changes in the chromosomes and of abnormalities in mitotic divisions in the root meristem, *J. Hered.* 39: 327–335.

843 Kok, B., 1948. A critical consideration of the quantum yield of *Chlorella* photosynthesis, *Enzymologia* 13: 1–56.

844 Kok, B., 1949. On the interrelation of respiration and photosynthesis in green plants, *Biochim. Biophys. Acta* 3: 625–631.

845 Kok, B., 1956. On the reversible absorption change at 705 mμ in photosynthetic organisms, *Biochim. Biophys. Acta* 22: 399–401.

846 Kok, B., 1965. Photosynthesis: The path of energy. Chapter 35 in *Plant Biochemistry*

(Bonner, J. and Varner, J.E., eds.), pp. 903–960, Academic Press, New York, N.Y.
847 Komatsu, S., Ozawa, S. and Makino, Y., 1933. Biochemical studies on the maturity of sugarcane, *Mem. Coll. Sci. Kyoto Imp. Univ., Ser. A* 16: 1–125.
848 Koningsberger, V.J., 1942. De algemeen-biologische beteekenis van vitaminen en hormonen, *Natuurkd. Voordr. 'Diligentia', Nieuwe Reeks* 20: 13–25 (not seen).
849 Koningsberger, V.J., 1947. Over de primaire werking van groeistoffen van het auxine-type, *Meded. Koninkl. Vlaam. Acad. Wet. Belg., Kl. Wet.* 13: 5–33 (not seen).
850 Konzak, C.F., Nilan, R.A., Wagner, J. and Foster, R.J., 1964. Efficient chemical mutagenesis. The use of induced mutations in plant breeding, *Radiat. Bot.* 5: 49–70 (Suppl.).
851 Kortschak, H.P., Hartt, C.E. and Burr, G.O., 1957. PGA and photosynthesis in sugarcane, *Proc. Hawaiian Acad. Sci.*, p. 21.
852 Kortschak, H.P., Hartt, C.E. and Burr, G.O., 1965. Carbon dioxide fixation in sugarcane leaves, *Plant Physiol.* 40(2): 209–213.
853 Kortschak, H.P. and Hartt, C.E., 1966. The effects of varied conditions on carbon dioxide fixation in sugarcane leaves, *Naturwissenschaften* 52: 253.
854 Kortschak, H.P., 1968. Photosynthesis in sugarcane and related species. In *Photosynthesis in Sugarcane*, Proc. Int. Symp. held June 12 and 13, 1968, at the Royal Lancaster Hotel, London, pp. 18–29.
855 Kortschak, H.P. and Forbes, A., 1969. The effects of shade and age on the photosynthesis rate of sugarcane, *Prog. Photosynth. Res.* 1: 383–387.
856 Kortschak, H.P. and Nickell, L.G., 1970. Calvin-type carbon dioxide fixation in sugarcane stalk parenchyma tissue, *Plant Physiol.* 45: 515–516.
857 Koukol, J., Dugger, Jr., W.M. and Palmer, R.L., 1967. Inhibitory effect of peroxyacetyl nitrate on cyclic photophosphorylation by chloroplasts from black valentine bean leaves, *Plant Physiol.* 42: 1419–1422.
858 Kramer, P.J. and Decker, J.P., 1944. Relation between light intensity and rate of photosynthesis of loblolly pine and certain hardwoods, *Plant Physiol.* 19: 350–357.
859 Kriedemann, P.E., 1968. An effect of kinetin on the translocation of ^{14}C-labeled photosynthate in citrus, *Aust. J. Biol. Sci.* 21: 569–571.
860 Kryukova, N., 1940. Synthesis and hydrolysis of sucrose in the tissues of higher plants under the conditions of inhibited phosphorylation, *Biokhimiya* 5: 574–583 [*Chem. Abstr.* 35: 4805 (1941)].
861 Kumar, A. and Alexander, A.G., 1970. Phosphoribose isomerase from sugarcane leaves (research note), *J. Agric. Univ. P.R.* 54(4): 691–692.
862 Kumar, A. and Alexander, A.G., 1971. Studies on the ribose-5-*P* phosphatase of sugarcane, *J. Agric. Univ. P.R.* 55(1): 1–11.
863 Kumar, A., Acín, N.M. and Alexander, A.G., 1972. Relationships of chlorophyll and enzyme gradients to sucrose content of sugarcane leaves, *Annu. Rept. Agric. Exp. Sta. Univ. P.R.* (1970–1971).
864 Kurosawa, E., 1926. Experimental studies on the secretion of *Fusarium heterosporum* on rice plants (in Japanese), *Trans. Natl. Hist. Soc. Formosa* 16: 213–227.
865 Kursanov, A.L., 1934. Photosynthesis of green fruits and its dependence on the normal activity of the leaves, *Planta* 22: 240–250 [Chem. Abstr. 28: 5499 (1934)].
866 Kursanov, A.L., 1936. The use of the vacuum infiltration method for the determination of the synthetic and hydrolytic actions of invertase in living plant tissues, *Biokhimiya* 1: 269–294 [*Chem. Abstr.* 31: 1456–1457 (1937)].
867 Kursanov, A.L., 1936. Reversible action of invertase in plant cells, and the role of structural protoplasmic elements, *Biokhimiya* 1: 411–423 [*Chem. Abstr.* 31: 7466 (1937)].
868 Kursanov, A.L., and Kryukova, N.N., 1939. Participation of a phosphatase in the synthesis of sucrose, *Biokhimiya* 4: 229–240 [*Chem. Abstr.* 34: 1710–1711 (1940)].
869 Kursanov, A.L., 1940. Reversible action of enzymes in living plant cells, *Biochem. Inst. Acad. Sci. U.S.S.R. Moscow)*, pp. 1–232.
870 Kursanov, A.L., Brovchenko, M.I. and Pariiskaya, A.N., 1950. Flow of assimilates to the

conducting tissue in rhubarb (*Rheum rhaponticum* L.) leaves, *Fiziol. Rast.* 6: 527–536 (A.I.B.S. Translation 6: 544–552).
871 Kursanov, A.L., 1956. The utilization of radioactive isotopes in biology and agriculture in the U.S.S.R., *Peaceful Uses At. Energy* 12: 3–9.
872 Kursanov, A.L., 1960. The physiology of the whole plant, *Occas. Publ. Wye Collect.* 12 (not seen).
873 Kursanov, A.L. and Brovchenko, M.I., 1961. Effect of adenosine triphosphate (ATP) on the uptake of assimilates by the vascular system of the sugar beet plant, *Fiziol. Rast.* 8: 270–278 [*Chem. Abstr.* 56: 9126 (1963)].
874 Kursanov, A.L., 1961. The transport of organic substances in plants, *Endeavour* 20: 19–25.
875 Kursanov, A.L. and Brovchenko, M.I., 1961. Effect of ATP on the entry of assimilate into the conducting systems of sugar beets, *Fiziol. Rast.* (Engl. transl.) 8: 211–217.
876 Kursanov, A.L., 1963. Metabolism and the transport of organic substances in the phloem, *Adv. Bot. Res.* 1: 209–278.
877 Kuyper, J., 1924. Achteruitgang van riet tusschen het oogenblik van snijden en van vermalen, *Arch. Suikerind. Ned. Indië*, Meded. Proefsta. Java Suikerind. 32(3e): 25–54 (not seen).

L

878 Labat, J.B., 1922–24. Nouveau voyage aux isles de l'Amerique. Avec une description exacte et curieuse de toute ces isles . . . 6 v. La Haye and Paris [cited from Brandes and Sartoris (225)].
879 Laetsch, W.M., Stetler, D. and Vlitos, A.J., 1965. A preliminary definition of the ultrastructure of sugarcane chloroplasts, *Annu. Rept. Tate Lyle Cent. Agric. Res. Sta., Trinidad* (1965): 475–481.
880 Laetsch, W.M., 1968. Chloroplast specialization in dicotyledons possessing the C_4-dicarboxylic acid pathway of CO_2 fixation, *Am. J. Bot.* 55: 875–883.
881 Lake, J.V., 1967. Respiration of leaves during photosynthesis. I. Estimates from an electrical analogue, *Aust. J. Biol. Sci.* 20: 487–493.
882 Lake, J.V., 1967. Respiration of leaves during photosynthesis. II. Effects on the estimation of mesophyll resistance, *Aust. J. Biol. Sci.* 20: 495–499.
883 Lal, K.N. and De, R., 1953. Studies in crop physiology. Photosynthesis, respiration and pigment content of sugarcane leaves in relation to age of plant, leaf development and nitrogen deficiency, *J. Indian Bot. Soc.* 32: 199–207.
884 Lalouette, J.A., 1969. Breeding of sugarcane varieties in Mauritius, *Proc. Int. Soc. Sugar Cane Technol.* 13: 1062–1067.
885 Lampton, R.K., 1952. *Developmental and Experimental Morphology of the Ovule and Seed of Asimina triloba Dunal*, Thesis, Univ. of Michigan, Ann Arbor, Mich. (not seen).
886 Landrau, Jr., P., Lugo-López, M.A., Samuels, G. and Silva, S., 1954. Leaving sugarcane trash undisturbed on a lateric soil compares favorably with currently used trash disposal methods, *J. Agric. Univ. P.R.* 38(1): 1–8.
887 Landrau, Jr., P. and Samuels, G., 1954. Response of four sugarcane varieties to fertilizers during the first Isabela cycle, 1946–1951, *J. Agric. Univ. P.R.* 38(2): 73–95.
888 Landrau, Jr., P., Samuels, G. and Alers-Alers, S., 1959. The response of two sugarcane varieties to fertilizers at Río Piedras, 1954–1957, *J. Agric. Univ. P.R.* 43(2): 73–88.
889 Lang, A., 1952. Physiology of flowering, *Annu. Rev. Plant Physiol.* 3: 265–306.
890 Lang, A., 1956. Induction of flower formation in biennial *Hyoscyamus* by treatment with gibberellin, *Naturwissenschaften* 43: 284–285.
891 Lang, A., 1956. Bolting and flowering in biennial *Hyoscyamus niger* induced by gibberellin, *Plant Physiol.* 31 (Suppl.): 35.
892 Lang, A., 1957. The effect of gibberellin upon flower formation, *Proc. Natl. Acad. Sci. (U.S.)* 43: 709–717.
893 Lang, A., 1965. Physiology of flower initiation, *Encyclopedia Plant Physiol.* 15: 1380–1536.

894 Larner, J. and Villar-Palasi, C., 1959. Enzymes in a glycogen-storage myopathy, *Proc. Natl. Acad. Sci. (U.S.)* 45: 1234–1235.

895 La Rue, C.D., 1936. The growth of plant embryos in culture, *Bull. Torrey Bot. Club* 63: 365–382.

896 La Rue, C.D., 1947. Growth and regeneration of the endosperm of maize in culture, *Am. J. Bot.* (Abstr.) 34: 585–586.

897 La Rue, C.D., 1949. Cultures of the endosperm of maize, *Am. J. Bot.* (Abstr.) 36: 798.

898 Lasnitski, I., Mathews, R.E.F. and Smith, J.D., 1954. Incorporation of 8-azaguanine into nucleic acids, *Nature* 173: 346–348.

899 Latzko, E. and Gibbs, M., 1969. Enzyme activities of the carbon reduction cycle in some photosynthetic organisms, *Plant Physiol.* 44: 295–300.

900 Lauden, L.L., 1963. In the field with Lloyd Lauden, *Sugar Bull.* 41: 80.

901 Lauritzen, J.I., Balch, R.T. and Fort, C.A., 1939. Resistance to inversion of sucrose in harvested sugarcane in Louisiana, *Proc. Int. Soc. Sugar Cane Technol.* 6: 809–818.

902 Lauritzen, J.I. and Balch, R.T., 1940. Inversion of sucrose in the different parts of the sugarcane stalk, *J. Agric. Res.* 61: 1–16.

903 Lauritzen, J.I., 1942. Relationship of waxy covering of stalk of sugarcane to loss of moisture and inversion of sucrose in mill cane, *Sugar Bull.* 21(4): 25–31.

904 Lauritzen, J.I., 1942. Testing varieties of sugarcane for resistance to inversion of sucrose and for windrowing qualities in Louisiana, *Sugar Bull.* (1942): 210–215.

905 Lauritzen, J.I. and Balch, R.T., 1948. Inversion of sucrose and other physiological changes in harvested sugarcane in Louisiana, *U.S. Dept. Agric. Tech. Bull.* No. 939.

906 Lavintman, N. and Cardini, C.E., 1968. Changes in sucrose synthetase activities in aging potato tuber slices, *Plant Physiol.* 43: 434–436.

907 Lawrence, J.M., Funderburk, H.H., Blackburn, R.D. and Beasley, P.G., 1962. The status of Diquat and Paraquat as aquatic herbicides, *Proc. 16th Southeastern Assoc. Game and Fish Commun.* (1962).

908 Lawrence, P.G., Beasley, P.G., and Funderburk, H.H., 1963. Water quality in plastic pools, containing aquatic plants, before and after treatments with bipyridylium compounds (Abstr.) *Proc. Southern Weed Conf.* 16: 366–367.

909 Lebedev, A. and Dikanova, A., 1935. Enzymic synthesis of sucrose, *Z. Physiol. Chem.* 231: 271–272. [*Chem. Abstr.* 29: 2978 (1935)].

910 Le Clerc, J.A., 1910. Tri-local experiments on the influence of environment on the composition of wheat, *U.S. Agric. Bur. Chem. Bull.* 128: 1–18.

911 Ledon, A.C. and Gonzales, F.A.Z., 1950. Industrialization of photosynthesis through the use of sugarcane, *Proc. Cuban Sugar Technol.* 24: 563–572.

912 Lee, H.A., 1923. The deterioration of cut cane in Pampanga, *Sugar Cent. Plant. News* 4: 7–15.

913 Lee, S. and Lin, K.S., 1951. Studies of the photoperiodic effect on sugarcane, *Proc. Int. Soc. Sugar Cane Technol.* 7: 33–43.

914 Lee, S., Hu, T.H., Pan, Y.L. and Chung, C.H., 1967. Photoperiodic experiments for inducing flowering of sugarcane. Effect of different irradiation conditions of 12-hour day on sugarcane flowering, *Rept. Taiwan Sugar Exp. Sta.* 44: 7–20.

915 Lee, S., Hu, T.H. and Tu, T.T., 1969. Photoperiodic induction of flowering in sugarcane, *Proc. Int. Soc. Sugar Cane Technol.* 13: 1001–1005.

916 Lee, Y.P., 1960. Potato phosphorylase. I. Purification, physicochemical properties and catalytic activity, *Biochim. Biophys. Acta* 43: 18–30.

917 Leloir, L.F., 1951. The metabolism of hexosephosphates. Chapter 2 in *Phosphorus Metabolism* (McElroy, W.D. and Glass, B., eds.), Vol. 1, pp. 67–93, Johns Hopkins Press, Baltimore, Md.

918 Leloir, L.F. and Cabib, E., 1953. The enzymic synthesis of trehalose phosphate, *J. Am. Chem. Soc.* 75: 5445–5446.

919 Leloir, L.F., 1953. The biosynthesis of sucrose, *J. Am. Chem. Soc.* 75: 6084.

920 Leloir, L.F. and Cardini, C.E., 1955. The biosynthesis of sucrose phosphate, *J. Biol. Chem.* 214: 157–165.

921 Leloir, L.F. and Cardini, C.E., 1957. Biosynthesis of glycogen from uridine diphosphate glucose, *J. Am. Chem. Soc.* 79: 6340–6341.
922 Leloir, L.F., Olavarria, J.M., Goldemberg, S.H. and Carminatti, H., 1959. Biosynthesis of glycogen from uridine diphosphate glucose, *Arch. Biochem. Biophys.* 81: 508–520.
923 Leloir, L.F. and Goldemberg, S.H., 1960. Synthesis of glycogen from uridine diphosphate glucose in liver, *J. Biol. Chem.* 235: 919–923.
924 Leloir, L.F., De Fekete, M.A.R. and Cardini, C.E., 1961. Starch and oligosaccharide synthesis from UDP-glucose, *J. Biol. Chem.* 236: 636–641.
925 Lemieux, R.U. and Huber, G., 1953. A chemical synthesis of sucrose, *J. Am. Chem. Soc.* 75: 4118.
926 Lemieux, R.U. and Huber, G., 1956. A chemical synthesis of sucrose. A conformational analysis of the reactions of 1,2-anhydro-α-D-glucopyranose triacetate, *J. Am. Chem. Soc.* 78: 4117–4119.
927 Lemieux, R.U., 1953. A chemical synthesis of octa-*O*-acetyl-β-D-maltose, *Can. J. Chem.* 31: 949–951.
928 Lennox, C.G., 1947. Sugar cane collection in New Guinea during 1937, *Proc. Int. Soc. Sugar Cane Technol.* 6: 171–182.
929 Leonard, O.A., 1938. Transformation of sugars in sugar beet and corn leaves and invertase activity, *Am. J. Bot.* 25: 78–83.
930 Leonard, O.A., 1939. Carbohydrate transformations in leaf blades with special reference to sucrose synthesis, *Am. J. Bot.* 26: 475–484.
931 Leonard, O.A., 1939. Translocation of carbohydrates in the sugar beet, *Plant Physiol.* 14: 55–74.
932 Leonard, O.A. and King, D.L., 1938. Vein loading and transport in detached leaves, *Plant Physiol.* 43: 460–463.
933 Leopold, A.C., 1964. Auxins. In *Plant Growth and Development*, p. 81, McGraw-Hill Book Company, New York, N.Y.
934 Levan, A., 1938. The effect of colchicine on root mitoses in *Allium*, *Hereditas* 24: 471–486.
935 Leverington, K.C., Sedl, J.M. and Burge, J.R., 1963. Some problems in predicting potassium requirements of sugarcane, *Proc. Int. Soc. Sugar Cane Technol.* 11: 123–130.
936 Levitt, J., 1957. The significance of 'apparent free space' (AFS) in ion absorption, *Physiol. Plant.* 10: 882–888.
937 Li, H.W., Loh, C.S. and Lee, C.L., 1948. Cytological studies of sugarcane and its relatives. I. Hybrids between *S. officinarum, M. japonicus* and *S. spontaneum*, *Bot. Bull. Acad. Sin.* 2: 147–160.
938 Li, H.W. and Shang, K.C., 1951. Genetical studies of the interspecific cross,.cane varieties and *Saccharum robustum*, *Rept. Taiwan Sugar Exp. Sta.* 7: 25–36.
939 Li, H.W., Ma, T.H. and Shang, K.C., 1951. Cytological studies of sugarcane and its relatives, *Rept. Taiwan Sugar Exp. Sta.* 7: 1–14.
940 Liddle, A.M., Manners, D.J. and Wright, A., 1961. Studies on carbohydrate-metabolizing enzymes. 6. The action of potato phosphorylase (P-enzyme) on starch-type polysaccharides, *Biochem. J.* 80: 304–309.
941 Liebig, J., 1840. *Organic Chemistry in its Application to Agriculture and Physiology*, 409 pp., Taylor and Walton, London.
942 Liebig, J., 1843. Die Wechselwirtschaft, *Ann. Chem.* 46: 58–97. Reviewed in *Photosynthesis and Related Processes* (Rabinowitch, E.I., ed.), 1945, Vol. I, p. 246, Interscience Publishers, New York, N.Y.
943 Lincoln, R.G., Raven, K.A. and Hamner, K.C., 1956. Certain factors influencing expression of the flowering stimulus, *Bot. Gaz.* 117: 193–206.
944 Lincoln, R.G. and Hamner, K.C., 1958. An effect of gibberellic acid on the flowering of *Xanthium*, a short day plant, *Plant Physiol.* 33: 101–104.
945 Lineweaver, H. and Burk, D., 1934. The determination of enzyme dissociation constants, *J. Am. Chem. Soc.* 56: 658–666.

946 Lo, C.C. and Shong Sun, 1969. Collecting wild canes in Taiwan, *Proc. Int. Soc. Sugar Cane Technol.* 13: 1047–1055.

947 Lockhart, J.A., 1961. Mechanism of the photoperiodic process in higher plants, *Encyclopedia Plant Physiol.* 16: 390–438.

948 Loh, C.S., 1947. The *Saccharum* x *Miscanthus* hybrids, *J. Sugarcane Res.* 1(2): 1–9 (Chinese with English summary).

949 Loh, C.S. and Tseng, P.M., 1950. Notes of sugar cane nobilisation methods, *Proc. Int. Soc. Sugar Cane Technol.* 7: 254–265.

950 Loh, C.S., 1969. Sugarcane breeding in Taiwan, *Proc. Int. Soc. Sugar Cane Technol.* 13: 1068; Sugarcane breeding – Retrospect and prospect, *Proc. Int. Soc. Sugar Cane Technol.* 13: 1069–1086.

951 Lohman, de Savornin, C., 1900. *Arch. Java Suikerind.*, p. 1175 (not seen).

952 Loomis, W.E., 1949. Photosynthesis – an introduction. Chapter 1 in *Photosynthesis in Plants* (Franck, J. and Loomis, W.E., eds.), pp. 12 and 13, Iowa State College Press, Ames, Iowa.

953 López-Domínguez, F.A., 1923. Fertilizer experiments on sugarcane, *Insular Exp. Sta. Bull.* No. 29.

954 López Hernández, J.A., 1965. The quality of flowering cane, *Sugar Azúcar* 60: 41–42.

955 Losada, M., Trebst, A.V. and Arnon, D.I., 1960. Photosynthesis by isolated chloroplasts, *J. Biol. Chem.* 235(3): 832–839.

956 Losada, M., Whatley, F.R. and Arnon, D.I., 1961. Separation of two light reactions in noncyclic photophosphorylation of green plants, *Nature* 190: 606–610.

957 Loustalot, A.J., Cruzado, H.J. and Muzik, T.J., 1950. The effect of 2,4-D on sugar content of sugarcane, *Sugar J.* 13(5): 78.

958 Loustalot, A.J., Gilberts, S.G. and Drosdoff, M., 1950. The effect of nitrogen and potassium levels in tung seedlings on growth, apparent photosynthesis and carbohydrate composition, *Plant Physiol.* 25: 394–412.

959 Lovering, T.S. and Engel, C., 1967. Translocation of silica and other elements from rock into *Equisetum* and three grasses. *Geological Survey Professional Paper 594-B*, U.S. Gov. Printing Office, Washington, D.C.

960 Lozano, B.A. and Bonner, J., 1949. Experiments on sucrose formation by potato tubers as influenced by temperature, *Plant Physiol.* 24: 720–729.

961 Lugo-López, M.A. and Grant, R., 1952. Preharvest foliage sprays of sugarcane with 2,4-D, *J. Agric. Univ. P.R.* 36(3): 187–193.

962 Lugo-López, M.A., Samuels, G. and Grant, R., 1953. Failure of preharvest foliage sprays with 2,4-D and maleic hydrazide to affect the sucrose content of sugarcane, *J. Agric. Univ. P.R.* 37(1): 44–51.

963 Lugo-López, M.A. and Capó, B.G., 1954. The effect of weather and climate on the sucrose content of sugarcane, *J. Agric. Univ. P.R.* 38(4): 149–169.

964 Lumry, R., Spikes, J.D. and Eyring, H., 1954. Photysynthesis, *Annu. Rev. Plant Physiol.* 5: 271–340.

965 Lundegardh, H., 1955. Mechanisms of absorption, transport, accumulation, and secretion of ions, *Annu. Rev. Plant Physiol.* 6: 1–24.

966 Lundegardh, H., 1961. Response of chloroplast cytochrome to light and substrates, *Nature* 192: 243–248.

967 Lundquist, A., 1964. The nature of two loci incompatibility system in grasses, *Hereditas* 52: 189–196.

M

968 Magasanik, B., 1961. Catabolite repression, *Cold Spring Harbor Symp. Quant. Biol.* 26: 249–254.

969 Mandel, H.G., Carlo, P.E. and Smith, P.K., 1954. The incorporation of 8-azaguanine into nucleic acids of tumor-bearing mice, *J. Biol. Chem.* 206: 181–189.

970 Mandel, H.G., 1957. Incorporation of 8-azaguanine and growth inhibition in *Bacillus cereus*, *J. Biol. Chem.* 225: 137–150.
971 Mandelstram, J., 1957. Turnover of protein in starved bacteria and its relationship to the induced synthesis of enzyme, *Nature* 179: 1179–1181.
972 Mangelsdorf, P.C. and Reeves, R.G., 1939. The origin of Indian corn and its relatives, *Texas Agric. Exp. Sta. Bull.* No. 574.
973 Mangelsdorf, A.J., 1953. Sugarcane breeding in Hawaii. II. 1921 to 1952, *Hawaiian Plant. Rec.* 54: 101–137.
974 Marchant, R.H. and Packer, L., 1963. Light and dark stages in the hydrolysis of adenosine triphosphate by chloroplasts, *Biochim. Biophys. Acta* 75: 458–460.
975 Maretzki, A. and Nickell, L.G., 1967. Dependence on arginine of sugar cane cells in submerged culture, *Abstr. 7th Int. Congr. Biochem., Tokyo* J-207.
976 Maretzki, A., Nickell, L.G. and Thom, M., 1968. *N*-Carbamylputrescine: A major product of arginine metabolism in cultured sugarcane cells, *Plant Physiol.* 43 (Suppl.): S–8.
977 Maretzki, A., Thom, M. and Nickell, L.G., 1969. Products of arginine catabolism in growing cells of sugarcane, *Phytochemistry* 8: 811–818.
978 Maretzki, A., Nickell, L.G. and Thom, M., 1969. Arginine in growing cells of sugarcane. Nutritional effects, uptake and incorporation into proteins, *Physiol. Plant.* 22: 827–839.
979 Maretzki, A., Thom, M. and Nickell, L.G., 1969. The effect of osmotic pressure stress on cell cultures of sugarcane, *Abstr. 11th Int. Bot. Congr.*, p.140.
980 Marks, P.A., Burka, E.R., Rifkind, R. and Danon, D., 1963. Polyribosomes active in reticulocyte protein synthesis, *Cold Spring Harbor Symp. Quant. Biol.* 28: 223–226.
981 Marsh, H.V., Galmiche, J.M. and Gibbs, M., 1963. Effect of light on the citric acid cycle in *Scenedesmus*, *Plant Physiol.* (Suppl.) 38: iv.
982 Marth, P.C., Audia, W.W. and Mitchell, J.W., 1956. Effects of gibberellic acid on growth and development of plants of various genera and species, *Bot. Gaz.* 118: 106–111.
983 Martin, J.P., 1938. *Sugarcane Diseases in Hawaii*, pp. 43 and 46, Advertiser Publishing Company, Honolulu.
984 Martin, J.P., 1938. Sugarcane diseases in Hawaii, *Rept. Exp. Sta. Hawaiian Sugar Plant. Assoc.* p. 295.
985 Martin-Leake, H., 1946. The flowering of the sugar cane, *Int. Sugar J.* 48: 174–176.
986 Masuda, Y., 1959. Role of cellular RNA in the growth response of *Avena* coleoptile to auxin, *Physiol. Plant.* 12: 324–335.
987 Mateus Ventura, M., 1954. Action of enzymatic inhibitors on transpiration and the behavior of stomata. II. Action of sodium arsenite, 2,4-dinitrophenol, and janus green on isolated leaves of *Stizolobium alterrimum*, *Rev. Bras. Biol.* 14: 153–161.
988 Mathan, C.C., Gaillochet, J., Stroun, M., Luciani, F., Gandrieu, A., Dionnet, S. and Gaston, M., 1966. Variations in the types of photoperiodic reactions in plants according to modification of light intensity and quality. Stenophotoperiodism and ambiphotoperiodism, *Proc. Symp. Praha-Nitra Acad. (Praha)*, pp. 313–322 (not seen).
989 Mather, K. and Harrison, B.H., 1949. The manifold effect of selection. I, *Heredity* 3: 1–52; II, *Heredity* 3: 131–162.
990 Matherne, R.J., 1969. A history of major Louisiana sugarcane varieties, *Proc. Int. Soc. Sugar Cane Technol.* 13: 1056–1061.
991 Mathieson, M.J. and Catheside, D.G., 1955. Inhibition of histidine uptake in *Neurospora crassa*, *J. Gen. Microbiol.* 13: 72–83.
992 Mayaudon, J., Benson, A.A. and Calvin, M., 1957. Ribulose 1,5-diphosphate and CO_2 fixation from *Tetragonia expansa* leaves extract, *Biochim. Biophys. Acta* 23: 342–351.
993 Mayeaux, P.A., 1960. *Some Studies on the Microbial Flora of Sugarcane*, M.S. Thesis, Louisiana State University, New Orleans, La. (not seen).
994 Mayer, J.R., 1848. Die organische Bewegung in ihrem Zusammenhang mit dem Stoffwechsel, Heilbronn. Reprinted in *Die Mechanik der Warme*; Gesammelte Schriften, Stuttgart. Reviewed in *Photosynthesis and Related Processes* (Rabinowitch, E.I., ed.), 1945, Vol. I, p. 26, Interscience Publishers, New York, N.Y.

995 Mayer, A. and Porter, H.K., 1960. Translocation from leaves of rye, *Nature* 188: 921–922.

996 McAlister, E.D. and Myers, J., 1940. The time course of photosynthesis and fluorescence observed simultaneously, *Smithson. Inst. Misc. Collect.* 99: 6–26.

997 McCalip, M.A. and Hall, H.H., 1938. Effect on factory cane juices and sirups of *Leuconostoc mesenteroides* isolated from frost damanged Louisiana sugarcane of the 1937 crop, *Proc. Int. Soc. Sugar Cane Technol.* 6: 986–1004.

998 McCleskey, C.S., Faville, L.W. and Barnett, R.O., 1947. Characteristics of *Leuconostoc mesenteroides* from cane juice, *J. Bacteriol.* 54(6): 697–708.

999 McClintock, B., 1939. The behavior in successive nuclear divisions of a chromosome broken at meiosis, *Proc. Natl. Acad. Sci. (U.S.)* 25: 405–416.

1000 McCready, R.M. and Hassid, W.Z., 1941. Transformation of sugars in excised barley shoots, *Plant Physiol.* 16: 599–610.

1001 McCune, D.L., 1958. *Effect of Moisture Tension on the Production and Movement of Carbohydrate in Plants*, Ph.D. Thesis, Purdue University, Lafayette, Ind.

1002 McIlrath, W.J., 1950. Response of the cotton plant to maleic hydrazide, *Am. J. Bot.* 37: 816–819.

1003 McLean, F.T., 1920. *Ann. Bot. (London)* 34: 367–389 (not seen).

1004 McMahon, D. and Bogorad, L., 1967. Inhibition of the formation of photosynthetic enzymes by inhibitors of photosynthesis, *Plant Physiol.* 43: 188–192.

1005 McWhorter, C.G., 1961. The effectiveness of five phenylureas as foliar sprays and the influence of surfactants on their activity, *Proc. Southern Weed Conf.* 14: 54–59.

1006 McWhorter, C.G., 1963. Effects of surfactants on the herbicidal activity of foliar sprays of Diuron, *Weeds* 11: 265–269.

1007 Meagher, W.R., and Hassid, W.Z., 1946. Synthesis of maltose 1-phosphate and D-xylose-1-phosphate, *J. Am. Chem. Soc.* 68: 2135–2137.

1008 Mees, G.C., 1960. Experiments on the herbicidal action of 1,1′-ethylene-2,2′-dipyridylium dibromide, *Ann. Appl. Biol.* 48: 601–612.

1009 Mendelssohn, K., 1958. Superfluids. *Science* 127: 215–221.

1010 Méndez, F. and Chardón, F., 1940. *Annu. Rept. Univ. P.R. Agric. Exp. Sta.* (1939–1940): 27–28.

1011 Mendicino, J., 1960. Sucrose phosphate synthesis in wheat germ and green leaves, *J. Biol. Chem.* 235: 3347–3352.

1012 Merrill, E.D., 1946. Correlations of the indicated biologic alliances of the Philippines with the geologic history of Malaysia, *Chron. Bot.* 10: 216–236.

1013 Meyer, A., 1886. Bildung der Stärkekörner in den laubblättern aus zuckerarten Mannit und Glycerin, *Bot. Z.* 44: 105 (not seen).

1014 Meyer, B.S. and Anderson, D.B., 1952. *Plant Physiology*, 2nd edn., p. 356, D. Van Nostrand Co., New York, N.Y.

1015 Meyer, K., 1943. The chemistry of glycogen, *Adv. Enzymol.* 3: 109–135.

1016 Michaelis, L. and Hill, E.S., 1933. The viologen indicators, *J. Am. Chem. Soc.* 55: 1481–1494.

1017 Michaelis, L. and Hill, E.S., 1933. The viologen indicators, *J. Gen. Physiol.* 16: 859–873.

1018 Michalis, L. and Schubert, M.P., 1938. The theory of reversible two-step oxidation involving free radicals, *Chem. Rev.* 22: 437–470; Haas, E., 1937. Wirkungsweise des Proteins des gelben Ferments. Kurze Mitteilung, *Biochem. Z.* 290: 291; Waters, W.A., 1948, *Chemistry of Free Radicals*, Oxford Publishers, Toronto, Canada.

1019 Michaelis L., 1951. Chapter 44 in *The Enzymes* (Sumner, J.B. and Myrbäck, K., eds.), Vol. 2, Part I, Academic Press, New York, N.Y.

1020 Michaux, A., 1803. *Flora Boreali Americana* 1: 54 (not seen).

1021 Miller, E.S. and Burr, G.O., 1935. Carbon dioxide balance at high light intensities, *Plant Physiol.* 10: 93–114.

1022 Miller, E.C., 1938. *Plant Physiology*, 2nd edn., pp. 598–599, McGraw-Hill Book Co., New York, N.Y.

1023 Milner, Y. and Avigad, G., 1964. Thymidine diphosphate nucleotides as substrates in the sucrose synthetase reaction, *Nature* 206: 4986. The UDP-glucose:D-fructose glucosyltransferase system from sugar beet roots, *Israel J. Chem.* 2: 316.

1024 Mitchell, J.E. and Angel, C.R., 1950. Plant-growth-regulating substances obtained from cultures of *Fusarium moniliforme*, *Phytopathology* 40: 872–873.

1025 Mitchell, J.W., Dugger,Jr., W.M. and Gauch, H.G., 1953. Increased translocation of plant-growth modifying substances due to application of boron, *Science* 118: 354–355.

1026 Mitchell, P., 1966. Chemiosmotic coupling in oxidative and photosynthetic phosphorylation, *Biol. Rev. Cambridge Phil. Soc.* 41: 445–592.

1027 Mitscherlich, E.A., 1909. Das Gesetz des Minimums und das Gesetz des abrehmenden Bodentrages, *Landwirtsch. Jahrb.* 38: 537–552.

1028 Mohan-Roa, N.V. and Narasemhan, R.L., 1956. Some aspects of nitrogen nutrition in Andhara, *Proc. Int. Soc. Sugar Cane Technol.* 9: 74–93.

1029 Molengraaff, G.A.F., 1921. Modern deep-sea research in the East Indian Archipelago, *Geogr. J.* 57: 95–121.

1030 Mommaerts, W.F.H.M., Illingworth, B., Pearson, C.M., Guillory, R.J. and Seraydarian, K., 1959. A functional disorder of muscle associated with the absence of phosphorylase, *Proc. Natl. Acad. Sci. (U.S.)* 35: 791–797.

1031 Mongelard, J.C., 1969. The effect of different water regimes on the growth of two sugarcane varieties, *Proc. Int. Soc. Sugar Cane Technol.* 13: 643–651.

1032 Monod, J., 1947. The phenomenon of enzymatic adaption, *Growth* 11: 223–289.

1033 Monod, J., Changeux, J.P. and Jacob, F., 1963. Allosteric proteins and cellular control systems, *J. Mol. Biol.* 6: 306–329.

1034 Monod, J., 1956. Remarks on the mechanism of enzyme induction. In *Enzymes: Units of Biological Structure and Function* (Gaebler, O.H., ed.), p. 7, Academic Press, New York, N.Y.

1035 Moriya, A., 1938. Cytological studies on sugarcane–sorghum hybrids. A preliminary note, *Jap. J. Gen.* 12: 146–150 (not seen).

1036 Moriya, A., 1940. Contributions to the cytology of genus *Saccharum*. I. Observations on the F_1 progeny of sugarcane–sorghum hybrids, *Cytologia* 11: 117–135.

1037 Moriya, A., 1959. Cytological basis of sugarcane breeding in the Far East, especially in Taiwan, *Coll. Agric. Utsunomiya Univ., Spec. Bull.* 6: 50 (not seen).

1038 Mortenson, L.E., Valentine, R.C. and Carnahan, J.E., 1962. An electron-transport factor from *Clostridium pasteurianum*, *Biochem. Biophys. Res. Commun.* 7: 448–452.

1039 Moss, D.N., Musgrave, R.B. and Lemon, E.R., 1961. Photosynthesis under field conditions. III. Some effects of light, carbon dioxide, temperature, and soil moisture on photosynthesis, repspiration, and transpiration of corn, *Crop Sci.* 1: 83–87.

1040 Moss, D.N., 1962. The limiting carbon dioxide concentration for photosynthesis, *Nature* 193: 587.

1041 Moss, D.N., 1963. The effect of environment on gas exchange of leaves, *Conn. Exp. Sta. Bull.* No. 664: 86–101.

1042 Moss, D.N., 1966. Respiration in light and darkness, *Crop Sci.* 6: 351–354.

1043 Moss, D.N., 1967. Nutrient deficiencies reduce photosynthesis, *Plant Food Rev.* 13 (2): 15–16.

1044 Moss, D.N., 1967. High activity of the glycolic acid oxidase system in tobacco leaves, *Plant Physiol.* 42: 1463–1464.

1045 Moss, D.N., 1968. Photorespiration and glycolate metabolism in tobacco leaves, *Crop Sci.* 8: 71–76.

1046 Most, B.H. and Vlitos, A.J., 1963. Preliminary studies of gibberellin-like substances in sugarcane. *Regulateurs Naturels de la Croissance Végétale*, pp. 287–302, Editions du Centre National de la Recherche Scientifique, Paris.

1047 Most, B.H. and Vlitos, A.J., 1967. Studies on endogenous gibberellin-like substances in sugarcane, *Proc. Int. Soc. Sugar Cane Technol.* 12: 610–624.

1048 Mothes, K., 1960. Uber das Altern der Blätter und die Möglichkeit ihrer Wiederverjungung, *Naturwissenschaften* 47: 337–350.
1049 Mothes, K., 1966. Der Einfluss des Wasserzustandes auf Fermentprozesse und Stoffumsatz, *Encyclopaedia of Plant Physiology* 3: 656–664.
1050 Moulik, S.P. and Ghosh, B.N., 1963. Effects of temperature and pH on the gelation of silicic acid, *J. Indian Chem. Soc.* 40 (11): 907–910.
1051 Muir, W.H., Hildebrandt, A.C. and Riker, A.J., 1954. Plant tissue cultures produced from single isolated cells, *Science* 119: 877–878.
1052 Muir, W.H., Hildebrandt, A.C. and Riker, A.J., 1958. The preparation, isolation, and growth in culture of single cells from higher plants, *Am. J. Bot.* 45: 589–597.
1053 Mukherjee, S.K., 1949. Studies in *Saccharum spontaneum* and allied grasses. I. Preliminary report on collection, *Indian J. Genet. Plant Breed.* 9: 47–58.
1054 Mukherjee, S.K., 1954. Revision of the genus *Saccharum* Linn., *Bull. Bot. Soc. Bengal* 8: 143–148.
1055 Mukherjee, S.K., 1957. Origin and distribution of *Saccharum, Bot. Gaz.* 119: 55–61.
1056 Müller, A. and Zimmer, K.G., 1961. Studies on radiation-produced free radicals in biological systems. In *Free Radicals in Biological Systems*, pp. 325–335, Academic Press, New York, N.Y.
1057 Muller, H.J., 1927. Artificial transmutation of the gene, *Science* 66: 84–87.
1058 Muller, K. and Leopold, A.C., 1965. The mechanism of kinetin-induced transport in corn leaves, *Planta* 68: 186–205.
1059 Müller-Thurgau, H., 1822. Uber Zuckeranhäufung in Pflanzenteilen in Folge niederer Temperatur, *Landwirtsch. Jahrb.* 11: 751–828.
1060 Murashige, T. and Skoog, F., 1962. A revised medium for rapid growth and bioassays with tobacco tissue cultures, *Physiol. Plant.* 15: 473–497.
1061 Murashige, T. and Nakano, R., 1965. Morphogenetic behavior of tobacco tissue cultures and implication of plant senescence, *Am. J. Bot.* 52(8): 819–827.
1062 Murashige, T. and Nakano, R., 1966. Tissue culture as a potential tool in obtaining polyploid plants, *J. Hered.* 57: 114–118.
1063 Murata, T., 1961. Studies on the photosynthesis of rice plants and its culture significance, *Bull. Natl. Inst. Agric. Sci. Tokyo, Ser. D* (9): 1–170.
1064 Murata, T., Minamikawa, T. and Akazawa, T., 1963. Adenosine diphosphate glucose in rice and its role in starch synthesis, *Biochem. Biophys. Res. Commun.* 13: 439–443.
1065 Murata, T., Minamikawa, T., Akazawa, T. and Sugiyama, T., 1964. Isolation of adenosine diphosphate glucose from ripening rice grains and its enzymic synthesis, *Arch. Biochem. Biophys.* 106: 371–378.
1066 Murata, T., Sugiyama, T. and Akazawa, T., 1964. Enzymic mechanism of starch synthesis in ripening rice grains, *Arch. Biochem. Biophys.* 107: 92–101.
1067 Murata, T., Sugiyama, T. and Akazawa, T., 1965. Enzymic mechanism of starch synthesis in ripening rice grains. II. ADPG pathway, *Arch. Biochem. Biophys.* 107: 92–97.
1068 Myers, J. and French, C.S., 1960. Relationship between time course, chromatic transient and enhancement phenomena of photosynthesis, *Plant Physiol.* 35: 963–969.
1069 Myers, J. and French, C.S., 1960. Evidences from action spectra for a specific participation of chlorophyll *b* in photosynthesing systems, *J. Gen. Physiol.* 43: 723–736.
1070 Myrbäck, K., 1960. Invertase. In *The Enzymes* 4: 379–396.

N

1071 Nakamura, M., 1959. The sucrose-synthesizing enzyme in beans, *Bull. Agric. Chem. Soc. Japan* 23: 398–405.
1072 Nakata, S. and Leopold, A.C., 1967. Radioautographic study of translocation in bean leaves, *Am. J. Bot.* 54 (6) 769–772.

1073 Narayanawsami, S., 1940. Megasporogenesis and the origin of triploids in *Saccharum*, *Indian J. Agric. Sci.* 10: 534–551.

1074 Naylor, A.W. and Davis, E.A., 1949. Some effects of maleic hydrazide on growth and respiration of representative monocots and dicots, *Proc. Am. Soc. Plant Physiol. (24th Meet.)*, Abstr., p. 13.

1075 Naylor, A.W. and Davis, E.A., 1950. Maleic hydrazide as a plant growth inhibitor, *Bot. Gaz.* 112(1): 112–126.

1076 Neely, W.B., Ball, C.D., Hamner, C.L. and Sell, H.M., 1950. Effect of 2,4-dichlorophenoxyacetic acid on the invertase, phosphorylase and pectin methoxylase activity in the stems and leaves of the red kidney bean plant, *Plant Physiol.* 25: 525–528.

1077 Neidhardt, F.C. and Magasanik, B., 1956. Inhibitory effect of glucose on enzyme formation, *Nature* 178: 801–802.

1078 Neidhardt, F.C. and Magasanik, B., 1957. Reversal of the glucose inhibition of histidase biosynthesis in *Aerobacter aerogenes*, *J. Bacteriol.* 73: 253–259.

1079 Neilands, J.B. and Stumpf, P.K., 1964. *Outlines of Enzyme Chemistry*, pp. 334–336, John Wiley and Sons, New York, N.Y.

1080 Nelson, C.D., Perkins, H.J. and Gorham, P.R., 1058. Note on a rapid translocation of photosynthetically assimilated ^{14}C out of the primary leaf of the young soybean plant, *Can. J. Biochem. Physiol.* 36: 1277–1278.

1081 Nelson, C.D., Perkins, H.J. and Gorham, P.R., 1959. Evidence for different kinds of concurrent translocation of photosynthetically assimilated ^{14}C in the soybean, *Can. J. Bot.* 37: 1181–1189.

1082 Nelson, C.D., Clauss, H., Mortimer, D.C. and Gorham, P.R., 1961. Selective translocation of products of photosynthesis in soybean, *Plant Physiol.* 36: 581–588.

1083 Nelson, C.D., 1962. The translocation of organic compounds in plants, *Can. J. Bot.* 40: 757–770.

1084 Nelson, J.M. and Auchincloss, R., 1933. The effects of glucose and fructose on the sucrose content in potato slices, *J. Am. Chem. Soc.* 55: 3769–3772.

1085 Nelson, O.E. and Rines, H.W., 1962. The enzymatic deficiency in the waxy mutant of maize, *Biochem. Biophys. Res. Commun.* 9: 297.

1086 Nelson, P.M. and Rossman, E.C., 1958. Chemical induction of male sterility in inbred maize by use of gibberellins, *Science* 127: 1500–1501.

1087 Neuburg, C. and Mandl, I., 1950. Chapter 14 in *The Enzymes* (Sumner, J.B. and Myrbäck, K., eds.), Academic Press, New York, N.Y.

1088 Neufeld, E.F., Ginsburg, V., Putman, E.W., Fanshire, D. and Hassid, W.Z., 1957. Formation and interconversion of sugar nucleotides by plant extracts, *Arch. Biochem. Biophys.* 69: 602–616.

1089 Neufeld, E.F. and Hassid, W.Z., 1963. Biosynthesis of saccharides from glycopyranosyl esters of nucleotides ("sugar nucleotides"), *Adv. Carbohydr. Chem.* 18: 309–356.

1090 Neumann, J. and Jagendorf, A.T., 1965. Uncoupling photophosphorylation by detergents, *Biochim. Biophys. Acta* 109: 382–389.

1091 Newmann, J. and Drechsler, Z., 1967. Inhibition of photo-induced electron transport and related reactions in isolated chloroplasts by phenol, *Plant Physiol.* 42: 573–577.

1092 Nicholson, R.I. and Lilienthal, B., 1959. Formation of a polysaccharide in sugarcane, *Aust. J. Biol. Sci.* 12: 192–203.

1093 Nicholson, R.I. and Horsley, M., 1959. Determination of dextran and starch in cane juices and sugar products, *J. Agric. Food Chem.* 7: 640–643.

1094 Nickell, L.G. and Burkholder, P.R., 1950. Atypical growth of plants. II. Growth *in vitro* of virus tumors of *Rumex* in relation to temperature, pH, and various sources of nitrogen, carbon, and sulfur, *Am. J. Bot.* 37: 538–547.

1095 Nickell, L.G., 1950. Effect of certain plant hormones and colchicine on the growth and respiration of virus tumor tissue from *Rumex acetosa*, *Am. J. Bot.* 37: 829–835.

1096 Nickell, L.G., 1950. Effect of aspartic acid on growth of plant-virus tumor tissue, *Nature* 166: 351–352.

1097 Nickell, L.G., 1952. Vitamin B_1 requirement of *Rumex* virus tumor tissue, *Bull. Torrey Bot. Club* 79: 427–430.

1098 Nickell, L.G., 1952. Stimulation of plant growth by antibiotics, *Proc. Soc. Exp. Biol. Med.* 80: 615–617.

1099 Nickell, L.G., 1953. Effect of maleic hydrazide on normal and atypical growth of *Rumex acetosa*, *Am. J. Bot.* 40: 1–3.

1100 Nickell, L.G. and Brakke, M.K., 1954. Secretion of α-amylase by *Rumex* virus tumors *in vitro.* Biological studies, *Am. J. Bot.* 41: 390–394.

1101 Nickell, L.G., 1954. Nutritional aspects of virus-tumor growth, *Brookhaven Symp. Biol.* 6: 174–186.

1102 Nickell, L.G., 1956. The continuous submerged cultivation of plant tissue as single cells, *Proc. Natl. Acad. Sci. (U.S.)* 42: 848–850.

1103 Nickell, L.G., 1963. Submerged growth of plant cells, *Adv. Appl. Microbiol.* 4: 213–234.

1104 Nickell, L.G., 1964. Unusual effect of Dalapon on cane tissue cultures, *Rept. Exp. Sta. Hawaiian Sugar Plant. Assoc.*, p. 2.

1105 Nickell, L.G. and Kortschak, H.P., 1964. Arginine: Its role in sugarcane growth, *Hawaiian Plant Rec.* 57: 230–235.

1106 Nickell, L.G., 1964. Tissue and cell cultures of sugarcane – another research tool, *Hawaiian Plant. Rec.* 57: 223–229.

1107 Nickell, L.G. and Tanimoto, T., 1965. Effects of chemicals on ripening of sugarcane, *Rept. Hawaiian Sugar Technol.* (1965): 152–166.

1108 Nickell, L.G. and Tanimoto, T., 1965. Gibberellins ready for commercial evaluation, *Rept. Exp. Sta. Hawaiian Sugar Plant. Assoc.*, p. 12.

1109 Nickell, L.G. and Tanimoto, T., 1966. Field studies with gibberellic acid, *Rept. Exp. Sta. Hawaiian Sugar Plant. Assoc.*, p. 2.

1110 Nickell, L.G., 1967. Tissue and cell culture for sugarcane research, *Proc. Int. Soc. Sugar Cane Technol.* 12: 887–892.

1111 Nickell, L.G., 1967. Another look at effects of Dalapon, *Rept. Exp. Sta. Hawaiian Sugar Plant. Assoc.*, p. 3.

1112 Nickell, L.G. and Tanimoto, T., 1968. Sugarcane ripening with chemicals, *Rept. Hawaiian Sugar Technol.* (1967): 104–109.

1113 Nickell, L.G. and Maretzki, A., 1969. Growth of suspension cultures of sugarcane cells in chemically defined media, *Physiol. Plant.* 22: 117–125.

1114 Nickell, L.G. and Maretzki, A., 1969. Nutritional and metabolic studies with sugarcane cell suspensions. In *Continuous Cultivation of Microorganisms, Proc. 4th Symp.*, pp. 373–382.

1115 Nickell, L.G. and Torrey, J.G., 1969. Crop improvement through plant cell and tissue culture, *Science* 166: 1068–1070.

1116 Nickell, L.G. and Maretzki, A., 1970. Sugarcane ripening compounds: Comparison of chemical, biochemical, and biological properties, *Hawaiian Plant. Rec.* 58(5): 71–79.

1117 Nielsen, K.F., Halstead, R.L. and MacLean, A.J., 1960. Effects of soil temperature on the growth and chemical constitution of lucerne, *Proc. 8th Grass Congr.*, pp. 287–292.

1118 Nishiyama, I., 1956. Basic numbers in the polyploidy of *Saccharum, J. Hered.* 47: 91–99.

1119 Nitsan, J. and Lang, A., 1966. DNA synthesis in the elongating non-dividing cells of the lentil epicotyl and its promotion by gibberellin, *Plant Physiol.* 41: 965–970.

1120 Noddack, W. and Kopp, C., 1940. Untersuchungen über die Assimilation der Kohlensäure durch die grünen Pflanzen. IV. Assimilation und Temperatur, *Z. Phys. Chem.* A187: 79–102.

1121 Nomura, T., Kono, Y. and Akazawa, T., 1969. Enzymic mechanism of starch breakdown in germinating rice seeds. II. Scutellum as the site of sucrose synthesis, *Plant Physiol.* 44: 765–769.

1122 Nooden, L.D. and Thimann, K.V., 1963. Evidence for a requirement for protein synthesis for auxin-induced cell enlargement, *Proc. Natl. Acad. Sci. (U.S.)* 50: 194–200.

1123 Norstog, K.J., 1956. Growth of rye-grass endosperm *in vitro*, *Bot. Gaz.* 117: 253–259.

1124 Nurmia, M., 1935. Transformation of sugars in plants, *Ann. Acad. Sci. Fenn., Ser. A* 44: 1–105.

O

1125 Oparin, A. and Kursanov, A., 1931. Enzymic synthesis of sucrose, *Biochem. Z.* 239: 1–17 [*Chem. Abstr.* 25: 590 (1931)].

1126 Ordin, L. and Hall, M.A., 1968. Cellulose synthesis in higher plants from UDP glucose, *Plant Physiol.* 43: 473–476.

1127 Ortega, D. and Segura, G., 1962. Epoca de aplicación de nitrógeno en caña de azúcar, *Jornadas Agronómicas* III, Cagua, Univ. Central de Venezuela, Facultad de S. Agronómicas, Maracay, Venezuela.

1128 Osborne, D.J. and Hallaway, H.M., 1964. The auxin, 2,4-dichlorophenoxyacetic acid as a regulator of protein synthesis and senescence in detached leaves of *Prunus*, *New Phytol.* 63: 334–347.

1129 Osborne, D.J., 1965. Interactions of hormonal substances in the growth and development of plants, *J. Sci. Food Agric.* 16: 1–13.

1130 Osterlind, S., 1948. The retarding effect of high concentrations of carbon dioxide and carbonate ions on the growth of a green algae, *Physiol. Plant.* 1(2): 170–175.

1131 Ozbun, J.L., Volk, R.J. and Jackson, W.A., 1964. Effects of light and darkness on gaseous exchange of bean leaves, *Plant Physiol.* 39: 523–527.

P

1132 Packer, L. and Marchant, R.H., 1964. Action of adenosine triphosphate on chloroplast structure, *J. Biol. Chem.* 239: 2061–2069.

1133 Paladini, A.C. and Leloir, L.F., 1952. Studies on uridine diphosphate glucose, *Biochem. J.* 51: 426–430.

1134 Paliatseas, E.D., Steib, R.J., Dunckelman, P.H. and Chilton, S.J.P., 1954. The production of true seed of sugarcane in Louisiana, *Proc. Int. Soc. Sugar Cane Technol.* 8: 361–364.

1135 Paliatseas, E.D. and Chilton, S.J.P., 1956. The induction of the emergence of the inflorescence of sugarcane, *Proc. Int. Soc. Sugar Cane Technol.* 9(1): 657–664.

1136 Paliatseas, E.D., 1962. Further studies on flowering of sugarcane in Louisiana, *Proc. Int. Soc. Sugar Cane Technol.* 11: 504–515.

1137 Pandya, K.P. and Ramakrishnan, C.V., 1956. Biosynthesis of sucrose in sugarcane leaves, *Naturwissenschaften* 43: 85–87.

1138 Panje, R.R. and Prasad, J.P.R., 1959. Effect of ionizing radiations on sugarcane buds, *Proc. Int. Soc. Sugar Cane Technol.* 10: 775–782.

1139 Panje, R.R. and Srinivasan, K., 1959. Studies in *Saccharum spontaneum.* The flowering behavior of latitudinally displaced populations, *Bot. Gaz.* 120: 193-202.

1140 Panje, R.R. and Srinivasan, K., 1959. Studies in *Saccharum spontaneum.* A note on the flowering sequence of *Saccharum spontaneum* clones, *Proc. Int. Soc. Sugar Cane Technol.* 10: 819–824.

1141 Panje, R.R., Raja Rao, T. and Srivastava, K.K., 1969. Studies on the prevention of flowering in sugarcane. 1. Effect of suppression of flowering by defoliation on the yield and juice-quality of cane, *Proc. Int. Soc. Sugar Cane Technol.* 13: 468–475.

1142 Park, J.T. and Johnson, M.J., 1949. Accumulation of labile phosphate in *Staphylococcus aureus* grown in the presence of penicillin, *J. Biol. Chem.* 179: 585–592.

1143 Parkin, J., 1899. Contributions to our knowledge of the formation, storage and depletion of carbohydrates in monocotyledons, *Phil. Trans. R. Soc. (London), Ser. B* 191: 35.

1144 Parkin, J., 1912. The carbohydrates of the foliage leaf of the snowdrop (*Galanthus nivalis*) and their bearing on the first sugar of synthesis, *Biochem. J.* 6: 1–47.

1145 Partanen, C.R., 1959. Quantitative chromosomal changes and differentiation in plants. In *Developmental Cytology* (Rudnick, D. ed.), Ronald Press, New York, N.Y.

1146 Partanen, C.R., 1963. Plant tissue culture in relation to developmental cytology, *Int. Rev. Cytol.* 15: 215–243.

1147 Parthasarathy, N., 1946. The probable origin of north Indian sugar canes, *J. Indian Bot. Soc.* (M.O.P. Iyenger Commun. Vol.): 133–150.

1148 Parthasarathy, N., 1948. Origin of noble canes (*Saccharum officinarum* L.), *Nature* 161: 608.

1149 Parthasarathy, N., 1951. Chromosome elimination in *Saccharum*, *Nature* 168: 383–384.

1150 Paul, J.R., 1961. *Cell and Tissue Culture*, Williams and Wilkins Co., Baltimore, Md.

1151 Payne, J.H., 1969. Cane diffusion – the displacement process in principle and practice, *Proc. Int. Soc. Sugar Cane Technol.* 13: 103–121.

1152 Peaslee, D.E. and Moss, D.N., 1966. Photosynthesis in K- and Mg-deficient maize (*Zea mays* L.) leaves, *Proc. Soil Sci. Soc. Am.* 30: 220–223.

1153 Peat, S., 1951. The biological transformations of starch, *Adv. Enzymol.* 2: 339–375.

1154 Pederson, C.S. and Hucker, G.J., 1946. The significance of bacteria in sugar mills, *Proc. Cuba Sugar Technol. Assoc., 20th Meet.*, pp. 225–230.

1155 Penot, M., 1962. Physiologie végétale. Actions exercées a distance sur l'activité amylolytique de la feuille, *C. R. Acad. Sci. (Paris)* 255: 159–161.

1156 Perquin, L.H.C., 1940. On the incidental occurrence of rod-shaped, dextran producing bacteria in a beet-sugar factory, *Antonie van Leeuwenhoek* 6: 227–249.

1157 Personal commentary by J.N. Warner following presentation of paper by Vijayasaradhy and Narasimhan, *Proc. Int. Soc. Sugar Cane Technol.* 8: 401 (1953).

1158 Personal communication with Dr. T.L. Chu, Gurabo Substation, Gurabo, Puerto Rico.

1159 Personal communication with Dr. K.T. Glasziou, January, 1971.

1160 Personal communication with Dr. N. James, October, 1971.

1161 Personal communication with Dr. J.N. Turner, Plant Protection Ltd., Fernhurst, Haslemere, Surrey, England.

1162 Personal communication with Dr. P.H. Moore, September, 1970.

1163 Personal communication with Dr. R.A. Yates, Tate and Lyle Ltd. Research Centre, Westerham Road, Keston, Kent, England.

1164 Personal communication with Dr. R.P. Humbert, Consultant, Puerto Rico Sugar Rehabilitation Program, San Juan, Puerto Rico.

1165 Petinov, N.S., 1962. *The Physiology of Irrigated Agricultural Plants*, U.S.S.R. Acad. Sci., Moscow (not seen).

1166 Peto, F.H., 1952. Effects of preharvest sprays of maleic hydrazide on sugar beets, *Abstr. Am. Soc. Sugar Beet Technol.*, Salt Lake City, p. 4.

1167 Petrack, B. and Lipmann, F., 1961. Photophosphorylation and photohydrolysis in cell-free preparations of blue-green algae. In *Light and Life* (McElroy, W.D. and Glass, B., eds.), pp. 621–630, Johns Hopkins Press, Baltimore, Md.

1168 Petrack, B., Craston, A., Sheppy, F. and Farron, F., 1965. Studies on the hydrolysis of adenosine triphosphate by spinach chloroplasts, *J. Biol. Chem.* 240(2): 906–914.

1169 Petrie, A.H.K. and Wood, J.G., 1938. Studies on the nitrogen metabolism of plants. III. On the effect of water content on the relationship between proteins and amino acids, *Ann. Bot. (London)* [N.S.] 2: 887–898.

1170 Pfeffer, W., 1900. *Physiology of Plants*, Clarendon Press, London.

1171 Phillis, E. and Mason, T.G., 1937. On the effects of light and of oxygen on the uptake of sugar by the foliage leaf, *Ann. Bot (London)* [N.S.] 1(2): 231–237.

1172 Pictet, A. and Vogel, H., 1928. Synthesis of sucrose, *Helv. Chim. Acta* 11: 436–442 [*Chem. Abstr.* 22: 2743 (1928)].

1173 Pictet, A. and Vogel, H., 1928. Saccharose C and D, *Helv. Chim. Acta* 11: 905–909 [*Chem. Abstr.* 23: 376 (1929)].

1174 Piper, F., 1950. Hormones to increase yield (Editorial), *Sugar J.* 12(8): 3.

1175 Pitman, M.G., 1965. Transpiration and the selective uptake of potassium by barley seedlings (*Hordeum vulgare* cv. Bolivia), *Aust. J. Biol. Sci.* 18: 987–998.

1176 Porter, H.K. and May, L.H., 1955. Metabolism of radioactive sugars by tobacco leaf discs, *J. Exp. Bot.* 6: 43–63.

1177 Posthumus, O., 1931. Survey of cane varieties indigenous to Java and imported original varieties, *Arch. Suikerind. Ned. Indië*, Deel II, Afl. Nr. 32, pp. 901–911 [cited from Brandes (229)].

1178 Pottinger, P.K. and Oliver, I.T., 1962. The intracellular distribution of UDP-glucose–starch synthetase in potato tubers, *Biochim. Biophys. Acta* 58: 303–306.

1179 Prat, H., 1936. La systématique des graminées, *Ann. Sci. Nat., Sér. 10 (Bot.)* 18: 167–254.

1180 Pressey, R., 1966. Separation and properties of potato invertase and invertase inhibitor, *Arch. Biochem. Biophys.* 113: 667–674.

1181 Pressey, R., 1967. Invertase inhibitor from potatoes: Purification, characterization, and reactivity with plant invertases, *Plant Physiol.* 42: 1780–1786.

1182 Pressey, R., 1968. Invertase inhibitors from red beet, sugar beet, and sweet potato roots, *Plant Physiol.* 43: 1430–1434.

1183 Pressey, R., 1969. Potato sucrose synthetase: Purification, properties, and changes in activity associated with maturation, *Plant Physiol.* 44: 759–764.

1184 Pressey, R., 1970. Changes in sucrose synthetase and sucrose phosphate synthetase activities during storage of potatoes, *Am. Potato J.* 47(7): 245–251.

1185 Price, S., 1957. Cytological studies in *Saccharum* and allied genera. III. Chromosome numbers in interspecific hybrids, *Bot. Gaz.* 118: 146–159.

1186 Price, S. and Warner, J.N., 1959. The possible use of induced mutations for sugarcane improvement, *Proc. Int. Soc. Sugar Cane Technol.* 10: 782–791.

1187 Price, S., 1961. Cytological studies in *Saccharum* and allied genera. VII. Maternal chromosome transmission by *S. officinarum* in intra- and interspecific crosses, *Bot. Gaz.* 122: 298–305.

1188 Price, S., 1963. Cytogenetics of modern sugar canes, *Econ. Bot.* 17: 97–106.

1189 Price, S., 1967. Interspecific hybridization in sugarcane breeding, *Proc. Int. Soc. Sugar Cane Technol.* 12: 1021–1026.

1190 Price, S., 1969. Chromosome numbers in miscellaneous clones of *Saccharum* and allied genera, *Proc. Int. Soc. Sugar Cane Technol.* 13: 921–926.

1191 Priestley, J.H., 1924. The first sugar of photosynthesis and the role of cane sugar in the plant, *New Phytol.* 23: 255–265.

1192 *Principles of Sugar Technology* (Honig, P., ed.), 1953, Elsevier Publishing Co., Amsterdam.

1193 Pristupa, N.A., 1959. The transport form of carbohydrates in pumpkin plants, *Fiziol. Rast.* (English translation) 6: 26–32.

1194 Pucher, G.W., Leavenworth, C.S., Ginter, W. and Vickery, H.B., 1947. Studies in the metabolism of *Grassulacean* plants; the effect upon the composition of *Bryophyllum calycinum* of the form in which nitrogen is supplied, *Plant Physiol.* 22: 205–227.

1195 Purdie, T. and Irvine, J.C., 1903. *J. Chem. Soc.* 83: 1036 (not seen).

1196 Purdie, T. and Irvine, J.C., 1905. *J. Chem. Soc.* 87: 1028 (not seen).

1197 Purdie, T. and Paul, D.M., 1907. The alkylation of D-fructose. *J. Chem. Soc.* 91: 289–299.

1198 Purvis, O.N., 1934. An analysis of the influence of temperature during germination on the subsequent development of certain winter cereals and its relation to length of day, *Ann. Bot.* 48: 919–954.

1199 Putman, E.W. and Hassid, W.Z., 1954. Sugar transformation in leaves of *Canna indica.* I. Synthesis and inversion of sucrose, *J. Biol. Chem.* 207: 885–902.

Q

1200 Quastel, J.H. and Yates, E.D., 1936. The action of dyestuffs on invertase. The nature of the union between yeast invertase and sucrose, *Enzymologia* 1: 60–80.

1201 Quayle, J.R., Fuller, R.C., Benson, A.A. and Calvin, M., 1954. Enzymatic carboxylation of ribulose diphosphate, *J. Am. Chem. Soc.* 76: 3610–3611.
1202 Quayle, J.R., 1961. Metabolism of C_1 compounds in autotrophic and heterotrophic micro-organisms, *Annu. Rev. Microbiol.* 15: 119–152.

R

1203 Rabinowitch, E.I., 1945. *Photosynthesis and Related Processes*, Vol. I, Interscience Publishers, New York, N.Y.
1204 Rabinowitch, E.I., 1951. *Photosynthesis and Related Processes*, Vol. II, Part I, Interscience Publishers, New York, N.Y.
1205 Rabinowitch, E.I., 1952. Phososynthesis, *Annu. Rev. Plant Physiol.* 3: 229–264.
1206 Rabinowitch, E.I., 1953. Progress in photosynthesis, *Sci. Am.* (November): 80.
1207 Racker, E., De la Haba, G. and Leder, I.G., 1953. Thiamine pyrophosphate, a coenzyme of transketolase, *J. Am. Chem. Soc.* 75: 1010–1011.
1208 Racker, E., 1955. Synthesis of carbohydrate from carbon dioxide and hydrogen in a cell-free system, *Nature* 175: 249–251.
1209 Racker, E., 1957. The reductive pentose phosphate cycle. I. Phosphoribulokinase and ribulose diphosphate carboxylase, *Arch. Biochem. Biophys.* 69: 300–310.
1210 Raghavan, T.S., 1951. The sugarcanes of India. Some cytogenetic considerations, *J. Hered.* 42: 199–206.
1211 Raghavan, V., 1965. Action of purine and pyrimidine analogs on the growth and differentiation of the gametophytes of the fern *Asplenium nidus*, *Am. J. Bot.* 52(9): 900–910.
1212 Raistrick, H. and Clark, A.B., 1921. Studies on the cycloclastic power of bacteria. II. A quantitative study of the aerobic decomposition of tryptophan and tyrosine by bacteria, *Biochem. J.* 15: 76–82.
1213 Raja Rao, T. and Srivastava, K.K., 1969. Studies on the prevention of flowering in sugarcane. II. The effects of some chemical sprays, *Proc. Int. Soc. Sugar Cane Technol.* 13: 476–483.
1214 Ramakrishnan, C.V., 1958. Sucrose and starch synthesis in sugarcane plants, *Experientia* 14: 91–92.
1215 Ramiah, P.V. and Varahalu, T., 1938. Variations in the concentration of juice in sugarcane, *Madras Agric. J.* 26: 458–464 (not seen).
1216 Ramp, R.M., 1962. Development of a cutter–cleaner–loader sugarcane harvester for use in Louisiana. A Progress Report (U.S.D.A.–A.R.S.), pp. 42–66.
1217 Ramp, R.M., 1967. Progress in the development of a successful Louisiana sugarcane detrasher, *Proc. Int. Soc. Sugar Cane Technol.* 12: 327–346.
1218 Ramussen, L.W., 1947. The physiological action of 2,4-dichlorophenoxyacetic acid on dandelion, *Taraxacum officinale*, *Plant Physiol.* 22: 377–392.
1219 Ranganathan, V., 1959. A note on the hydration of cane sheaths as an indicator of maturity, *Indian J. Sugar Cane Res. Dev.* 4(1): 50–51.
1220 Rao, J.T. and Kumari, R.K., 1959. Preliminary observations on the fertility of essential organs in arrows of certain parental sugarcane varieties subjected to photoperiodic treatment, *Proc. Int. Soc. Sugar Cane Technol.* 10: 814–819.
1221 Rappaport, L., 1957. Effect of gibberellin on growth, flowering, and fruiting of the earlypak tomato, *Lycopersicum esculentum*, *Plant Physiol.* 32: 440–444.
1222 Recondo, E. and Leloir, L.F., 1961. Adenosine diphosphate glucose and starch synthesis, *Biochem. Biophys. Res. Commun.* 6: 85–88.
1223 Recondo, E., Dankert, M. and Leloir, L.F., 1963. Isolation of adenosine diphosphate D-glucose from corn grains, *Biochem. Biophys. Res. Commun.* 12: 204–207.
1224 Reeves, R.G. and Mangelsdorf, P.C., 1942. A proposed taxonomic change in the tribe Maydeae, *Am. J. Bot.* 29: 815–817.

1225 Reinert, J., 1958. Morphogenesis and its control on tissue cultures of carrots, *Naturwissenschaften* 45: 344–345.

1226 Reinert, J., 1959. *Planta* 53: 318 (cited from Street, H.E. and Henshaw, G.G., 1963. *Symp. Soc. Exp. Biol.* 17: 234–256).

1227 Reinert, J. and Backs, D., 1968. Control of tipotency in plant cells growing *in vitro*, *Nature* 220: 1340–1341.

1228 Reinhold, L. and Powell, R.G., 1956. A stimulatory action of indole-3-acetic acid on the uptake of amino acids by plant cells, *Nature* 177: 658–670.

1229 Reinke, J., 1883. *Bot. Z.* 41: 697, 713, 732 (not seen).

1230 Report on gibberellic acid field trials on sugarcane 1963–1964. Personal communication with Dr. P.R. Robinson, David North Plant Research Center, Colonial Sugar Refining Co. Ltd., Indooroopilly, Queensland, Australia.

1231 Rhoads, C.P., 1955. *Antimetabolites and Cancer*, Am. Assoc. Adv. Sci., Washington, D.C.

1232 Rickenberg, H.V., Cohen, G.N., Buttin, G. and Monod, J., 1956. La galactoside-perméase d'*Escherichia coli*, *Ann. Inst. Pasteur* 91: 829 (not seen).

1233 Riker, A.J. and Gutsche, A.E., 1948. The growth of sunflower tissue *in vitro* on synthetic media with various organic and inorganic sources of nitrogen, *Am. J. Bot.* 35: 227–238.

1234 Riker, A.J. and Hildebrandt, A.C., 1958. Plant tissue cultures open a botanical frontier, *Annu. Rev. Microbiol.* 12: 469–480.

1235 Riklis, E. and Quastel, J.H., 1958. Effects of metabolic inhibitors on potassium-stimulated glucose absorption by isolated surviving guinea pig intestine, *Can. J. Biochem. Physiol.* 36: 363–371.

1236 Riklis, E. and Quastel, J.H., 1958. Effects of cations on sugar absorption by isolated surviving guinea pig intestine, *Can. J. Biochem. Biophys.* 36: 347–362.

1237 Ririe, D. and Mikkelson, D.S., 1952. The effect of maleic hydrazide on sugar beet growth and sucrose content in certain field experiments, *Abstr. Am. Soc. Sugar Beet Technol.*, Salt Lake City, p. 3.

1238 Rizk, T.Y. and Normand, C.W., 1968. Enzyme activity and sucrose inversion, *Proc. 63rd Meet. Assoc. Southern Agric. Workers*, p. 301.

1239 Rizk, T.Y. and Normand, C.W., 1968. Enzyme activity and sucrose inversion, *Sugar J.* 31(3): 12–13.

1240 Rizk, T.Y. and Normand, C.W., 1969. Effect of burning and storage on cane deterioration. Part I. On cane quality, *Int. Sugar J.* 71: 7–9.

1241 Rizk, T.Y. and Normand, C.W., 1969. Effect of burning and storage on cane deterioration. Part II. On invertase activities, *Int. Sugar J.* 71: 35–37.

1242 Rizk, T.Y. and Normand, C.W., 1969. Effect of burning and storage on cane deterioration. Part III. On sugar–invertase relationships, *Int. Sugar J.* 71: 75–76.

1243 Rizk, T.Y. and Normand, C.W., 1968. Effect of sugarcane maturity on invertase activity, *Sugar J.* 31(3): 11–12.

1244 Roach, B.T., 1969. Quantitative effects of hybridization in *Saccharum officinarum* x *Saccharum spontaneum* crosses, *Proc. Int. Soc. Sugar Cane Technol.* 13: 939–954.

1245 Roach, B.T., 1969. Cytological studies in *Saccharum*. Chromosome transmission in interspecific and intergeneric crosses, *Proc. Int. Soc. Sugar Cane Technol.* 13: 901–920.

1246 Roberts, B.R., 1964. Effects of water stress on the translocation of photosynthetically assimilated carbon-14 in yellow poplar. In *The Formation of Wood in Forest Trees* (Zimmerman, M.H., ed.), pp. 273–288, Academic Press, New York, N.Y.

1247 Roberts, E.J. and Friloux, J.J., 1965. Determination of the soluble polysaccharides in sugarcane products, *Sugar Azúcar* 60(11): 66–67.

1248 Robinson, E. and Brown, R., 1952. The development of the enzyme complement in growing root cells, *J. Exp. Bot.* 3: 356–374.

1249 Robinson, P.R. and Arvier, A.C., 1969. Field trials with gibberellic acid on sugarcane in Australia in 1968. Personal communication.

1250 Robson, J.W. and Procter, G.C., 1963. Paraquat as a herbicide and desiccant in tropical agriculture, *World Crops* 15: 264–268.

1251 Rocha de Almeida, J. and Frota de Souza, A., 1937. A deterioracáo das cannas cortadas, *Rev. Agric. (Piracicaba)* 11: 89–121.

1252 Roe, J.H., 1934. A colorimetric method for the determination of fructose in blood and urine, *J. Biol. Chem.* 107: 15–22.

1253 Rorem, E.S., Walker, Jr., H.G. and McCready, R.M., 1960. Biosynthesis of sucrose and sucrose phosphate by sugar beet leaf extracts, *Plant Physiol.* 35: 269–272.

1254 Rosado-Alberio, J., Weier, T.E. and Stocking, C.R., 1968. Continuity of the chloroplast membrane systems in *Zea mays* L., *Plant Physiol.* 43: 1325–1336.

1255 Rosenfeld, A.H., 1935. Evaporation and deterioration of cut cane in Egypt, *Egypt Minist. Agric. Technol. Sci. Serv. Bull.* No. 155: 22 pp.

1256 Rosenfeld, A.H., 1956. *Sugarcane around the World*, University of Chicago Press, Chicago, Ill.

1257 Rothstein, A., 1954. The Enzymology of the Cell Surface. *Protoplasmatologia* 2: E4, Springer-Verlag, Vienna.

1258 Rouillard, G., 1953. Relation between vegetative index and weight of sugar per acre, *Proc. Int. Soc. Sugar Cane Technol.* 8: 317–320.

1259 Rowan, K.S. and Turner, D.H., 1957. Physiology of pea fruits. V. Phosphate compounds in the developing seed, *Aust. J. Biol. Sci.* 10: 414–425.

1260 Roxburgh, W., 1876. *Flora Indica* [cited from Dutt and Rao (459)].

1261 Roychoudhury, R. and Sen, S.P., 1964. Studies on the mechanism of auxin action: Auxin regulation of nucleic acid metabolism in pea internodes and coconut milk nuclei, *Physiol. Plant.* 17: 352–362.

1262 Ruben, S., Randall, M., Kamen, M. and Hyde, J.L., 1941. Heavy oxygen (^{18}O) as a tracer in the study of photosynthesis, *J. Am. Chem. Soc.* 63: 877–879.

1263 Rubin, B.A., 1936. Ratio of synthetic to hydrolytic action of invertase as a characteristic value for different varieties of onions, *Biokhimiya* 1: 467–477 [*Chem. Abstr.* 31: 7466–7467 (1937)].

1264 Ruhland, J., 1911. Untersuchungen über den Kohlendydratstoffwechsel von *Beta vulgaris* (Zuck.), *Jahrb. Wiss. Bot.* 50: 200–373.

1265 Ruttner, F., 1953. *Fundamentals of Limnology*, Univ. Toronto Press.

1266 Ryker, T.C. and Edgerton, C.S., 1931. Studies on sugarcane roots, *La. Agric. Exp. Sta. Bull.* No. 223.

S

1267 Sacher, J.A. and Glasziou, K.T., 1962. Regulation of invertase levels in sugarcane by an auxin–carbohydrate mediated control system, *Biochem. Biophys. Res. Commun.* 8(4): 280–282.

1268 Sacher, J.A., Hatch, M.D. and Glasziou, K.T., 1963. Sugar accumulation cycle in sugarcane. III. Physical and metabolic aspects of cycle in immature storage tissues, *Plant Physiol.* 38(3): 384–454.

1269 Sacher, J.A., Hatch, M.D. and Glasziou, K.T., 1963. Regulation of invertase synthesis in sugarcane by an auxin- and sugar-mediated control system, *Physiol. Plant.* 16: 836–842.

1270 Sachs, J., 1862. Ueber den Einfluss des Lichtes auf die Bildung des Amylums in den Chlorophyllkornern, *Bot. Z.* 20: 365–373.

1271 Sachs, J., 1864. Ueber die Auflösung und Wiederbildung des Amylums in den Chlorophyllkornern bei wechselnder Beleuchtung, *Bot. Z.* 22: 289–294.

1272 Sachs, J., 1887. *Lectures on the Physiology of Plants*, Clarendon Press, London.

1273 Sachs, R.M., 1956. Floral initiation in *Cestrum nocturnum* L., a long–short day plant, *Plant Physiol.* 31: 185–191.

1274 Sachs, R.M. and Weaver, R.J., 1968. Gibberellin- and auxin-induced berry enlargement in *Vitis vinifera* L., *J. Hortic. Sci.* 43: 185–195.

1275 Sacktor, B., 1968. Trehalase and the transport of glucose in the mammalian kidney and intestine, *Proc. Natl. Acad. Sci. (U.S.)* 60: 1007–1014.

1276 Saeki, T., 1960. Interrelationships between leaf amount, light distribution and total photosynthesis in a plant community, *Bot. Mag. (Tokyo)* 73: 55–63.

1277 Saïd, H. and Nada, I.A.A., 1949. Sugar metabolism of successive barley leaves from fully manured and phosphorus-deficient plants in relation to feeding with sucrose and sodium phosphate either alone or in mixture, *Proc. Egypt. Acad. Sci.* 5: 78–85.

1278 Salisbury, F.B., 1961. Photoperiodism and the flowering process, *Annu. Rev. Plant Physiol.* 12: 293–236.

1279 Salyaev, R.K., 1963. The problem of the mechanism of water absorption by plant roots, *Dokl. Akad. Nauk S.S.S.R.* 152: 1253–1255 [*Chem. Abstr.* 60: 3274 (1964)].

1280 Salyaev, R.K., 1964. Electron-microscopic examination of the "apparent free space" of root cells, and the role it plays in water absorption, *Dokl. Akad. Nauk S.S.S.R.* 158: 737–738 [*Chem. Abstr.* 65: 7636 (1966)].

1281 Sankaranarayanan, P., Krishnamurthy, T.N. and Satish Rao, C., 1969. Germplasm evaluation in sugarcane foreign hybrid varieties (Barbados, Queensland, and U.S.A.), *Proc. Int. Soc. Sugar Cane Technol.* 13: 893–900.

1282 Samuels, G., Lugo-López, M.A. and Landrau, Jr., P., 1952. Factors affecting the sucrose content of sugarcane: Fertilizers, *J. Agric. Univ. P.R.* 36 (3): 194–202.

1283 Samuels, G., and Landrau, Jr., P., 1952. The response of sugarcane to fertilizers. I. The Arecibo cycle, 1944–1950, *J. Agric. Univ. P.R.* 36(3): 203–229.

1284 Samuels, G., Capó, B.G. and Bangdiwala, I.S., 1953. The nitrogen content of sugarcane as influenced by moisture and age, *J. Agric. Univ. P.R.* 37(1): 1–12.

1285 Samuels, G. and Cibes, H., 1953. Influence of mineral deficiencies on the growth and yield of sugarcane, *J. Agric. Univ. P.R.* 47(2): 61–75.

1286 Samuels, G. and Landrau, Jr., P., 1954. the influence of potassium on the yield and sucrose content of sugarcane, *J. Agric. Univ. P.R.* 38(4): 170–178.

1287 Samuels, G. and Landrau, Jr., P., Influence of fertilizers on the components of available sucrose-percent-cane, *J. Agric. Univ. P.R.* 39(2): 84–91.

1288 Samuels, G., 1956. The efficiency of sugarcane in its use of nitrogen fertilizer applications, *J. Agric. Univ. P.R.* 40(4): 209–217.

1289 Samuels, G., Landrau, Jr., P. and Capó, B.G., 1956. Influence of fertility levels on the varietal response of sugarcane, *J. Agric. Univ. P.R.* 49(3): 129–143.

1290 Samuels, G. and Alers-Alers, S., 1964. Effect of time of nitrogen application on the sucrose content of sugarcane ratoons, *J. Agric. Univ. P.R.* 48(4): 304–307.

1291 Samuels, G., 1965. Sugarcane ripening and maturity: Theoretical background, *Proc. Annu. Congr. P.R. Sugar Technol. Assoc.* (1965).

1292 Samuels, G. and Cayere, A., 1967. The influence on sucrose of delay in grinding of sugarcane varieties burnt before harvesting, *Proc. Annu. Congr. P.R. Sugar Technol. Assoc.* 45: 92–101.

1293 Samuels, G., 1969. *Foliar Diagnosis for Sugarcane*, 1st edn., Agricultural Research Publications, Río Piedras, Puerto Rico.

1294 Samuels, G. and Alexander, A.G., 1969. Influence of variable manganese and silicon on the nutrition, sugar production, and enzyme activity of immature sugarcane, *J. Agric. Univ. P.R.* 53(1): 14–27; *Proc. Int. Soc. Sugar Cane Technol.* 13: 544–555.

1295 Samuels, G., Vélez, A., Riera, A., Yates, A. and Walker, B., 1970. Evaluation of chemical ripeners for sugarcane. A final report relating to chemical ripener studies conducted jointly by personnel from the Agricultural Experiment Station, Univ. P.R., and from Tate and Lyle, Ltd., London, in cooperation with the Department of Agriculture, Commonwealth of Puerto Rico.

1296 San Pietro, A. and Lang, H.M., 1958. Photosynthetic pyridine nucleotide reductase. I, *J. Biol. Chem.* 231: 211–229.

1297 San Pietro, A. and Black, C.C., 1965. Enzymology of energy conversion in photosynthesis, *Annu. Rev. Plant Physiol.* 16: 155–174.

1298 Sanyal, P.B., 1925. Deterioration of sugarcane during its storage by windrowing, *Indian Dept. Agric. Mem., Chem. Ser.* 8: 105–126.

1299 Sartoris, G.B., 1929. Rate of deterioration of sucrose content of some *P.O.J.* sugarcane varieties in Louisiana, *U.S. Dept. Agric. Circ.* No. 97: 27 pp.

1300 Sartoris, G.B., 1938. The behavior of sugarcane in relation to length of day, *Proc. Int. Soc. Sugar Cane Technol.* 6: 796–801.

1301 Sartoris, G.B., 1947. New kinds of sugarcane. *U.S.D.A. Yearbook of Agriculture* (1943–4947): 353–356.

1302 Sartoris, G.B. and Belcher, B.A., 1949. The effect of flooding on flowering and survival of sugarcane, *Sugar* 44: 36–39.

1303 Saunders, P.F. and Poulson, R.H., 1968. Biochemical studies on the possible mode of action of abscisin II (dormin). In *Biochemistry and Physiology of Plant Growth Substances* (Proc. 6th Int. Conf. on Plant Growth Substances) (Wightman, F. and Setterfield, G., eds.), Runge Press, Ottawa.

1304 Scarr, M.P., 1949. Production of polysaccharides by rod-shaped bacteria in sugar factory and refinery processes, *Proc. Soc. Appl. Biol.* (1949): 100–104.

1305 Schmid, R., Robbins, P.W. and Traut, R.R., 1959. Glycogen synthesis in muscle lacking phosphorylase, *Proc. Natl. Acad. Sci. (U.S.)* 45: 1236–1240.

1306 Scholander, P.F., Hammel, H.T., Bradstreet, E.D. and Hemmingsen, E.A., 1965. Sap pressure in vascular plants, *Science* 148: 339–346.

1307 Schroeder, H. and Herrmann, F., 1931. The carbohydrates and carbohydrate metabolism in foliage. 1. The increase in sucrose content during drying, *Biochem. Z.* 235: 407–424 [*Chem. Abstr.* 25: 4913 (1931)].

1308 Schumacher, W. and Hülsbruch, M., 1955. The movement of fluorescent dyes through the structures of plants, *Planta* 45: 118–124.

1309 Schwabe, W.W., 1953. Physiological studies in plant nutrition. XVI. The mineral nutrition of Bracken, *Ann. Bot. (London)* [N.S.]17: 225–262.

1310 Schwartz, M. and Ebert, G.A., 1968. Electron transport, proton movement and phosphorylation, *R.I.A.S.* (1968): 50–53.

1311 Schwimmer, S. and Rorem, E.S., 1960. Biosynthesis of sucrose by preparations from potatoes stored in the cold and at room temperature, *Nature* 187: 1113–1114.

1312 Sekioka, H., 1963. The effect of some environmental factors on the translocation and storage of carbohydrate in the sweet potato, potato and sugar beet. V. Relationships between the translocation of carbohydrate, and atmospheric humidity and soil moisture, *Sci. Bull. Fac. Agric. Kuyshu Univ.* 20: 293–299 (English summary).

1313 Sell, H.M., Luecke, R.W., Taylor, B.M. and Hamner, C.L., 1949. Changes in chemical composition of the stems of red kidney bean plants treated with 2,4-dichlorophenoxyacetic acid, *Plant Physiol.* 24: 295–299.

1314 Sen, S.C. and Bhattacharya, H.C., 1954. Effect of foliar fertilization on the growth and quality of sugarcane crops, *Proc. Sugar Technol. Assoc. India* 23(II): 99–103.

1315 Sen, S.C., 1959. Studies on the effect of the application of molasses solution through foliage on the quality of sugarcane crop, *Indian J. Sugar Cane Res. Dev.* 3(1): 29–32.

1316 Seward, A.C., 1959. *Plant Life through the Ages*, Hafner Publishing Co., New York, N.Y.

1317 Shafer, J. and Thompson, J.F., 1968. Arginine desimidase in *Chlorella, Phytochemistry* 7: 391–400.

1318 Shang, K.C., Juang, P.Y., Chu, T.L. and Huang, S.T., 1969. A study on the transmission of some important characteristics of Taiwan originated wild cane (*Saccharum spontaneum* L.), *Proc. Int. Soc. Sugar Cane Technol.* 13: 968–974.

1319 Shannon, J.C., 1968. Carbon-14 distribution in carbohydrates of immature *Zea mays* kernels following $^{14}CO_2$ treatment of intact plants, *Plant Physiol.* 43: 1215–1220.

1320 Shaw, G.W. and Walters, E.H., 1911. A progress report upon soil and climatic factors influencing the composition of wheat, *Calif. Exp. Sta. Bull.* 216: 549–574.

1321 Shaw, H.R., 1953. An international glance at sucrose content of cane, *Proc. Int. Soc. Sugar Cane Technol.* 8: 283–289.

1322 Shen, G.M., 1960. Translocation and distribution of assimilates from the leaves of rice plant during its various developing periods. Experiments with radioactive carbon (^{14}C), *Agric. Sin.* 11(1): 30–40 (in Chinese with English summary).
1323 Shin, M. and Arnon, D.I., 1965. Enzymic mechanisms of pyridine nucleotide reduction in chloroplasts, *J. Biol. Chem.* 240: 1405–1411.
1324 Shindy, W. and Weaver, R.J., 1967. Plant regulators alter translocation of photosynthetic products, *Nature* 214: 1024–1025.
1325 Singh, B.N. and Lal, K.N., 1935. Limitations of Blackman's law of limiting factors and Harder's concept of relative minimum as applied to photosynthesis, *Plant Physiol.* 10: 245–268.
1326 Singh, B.N. and Kumar, K., 1935. The reactions of the assimilatory system to alterations of light intensity, *Proc. Indian Acad. Sci.* 1B: 754–762.
1327 Singh, B.N. and Lal, K.N., 1935. Investigation of the effect of age on assimilation of leaves, *Ann. Bot.* 49: 291–307.
1328 Singh, B.N., 1941. Growth of the sugarcane plant in India. I. Age–fertilizer effects on the physiology and chemistry of the sugarcane, *Proc. Indian Acad. Sci.* 14B: 201–234.
1329 Singh, B.N., 1941. The growth of the sugarcane plant in India. II. Physiological effects of deficiency or excess of added fertilizers upon growth characters, carbohydrate metabolism, yield and juice quality of sugarcane, *Proc. Indian Acad. Sci.* 14B: 359–383.
1330 Sisler, R.M., Dugger, Jr., W.M. and Gauch, H.C., 1956. The role of boron in the translocation of organic compounds in plants, *Plant Physiol.* 31: 11–17.
1331 Skinner, J.C. and Street, H.E., 1954. Studies on the growth of excised roots. II. Observations on the growth of excised groundsel roots, *New Phytol.* 53: 44–67.
1332 Skinner, J.C., 1956. The inheritance of hariness in sugarcane, *Proc. Int. Soc. Sugar Cane Technol.* 9: 668–677.
1333 Skinner, J.C., 1966. Using wild species to breed better canes, *Cane Growers Bull., Bur. Sugar Exp. Sta.* 29(4): 112–116.
1334 Skogley, R.E. and Ahlgren, G.H., 1955. *Proc. Northeastern Weed Control Conf.* 9: 401.
1335 Skole, R.D., Newman, H. and Barnwell, J.L., 1968. Occurrence and metabolic activity of the polysaccharide producing bacteria (genus *Bacillus*) in sugar refining, *Proc. Annu. Meet. Indian Sugar Technol.* 27(1): 69–79.
1336 Skou, J.C., 1965. Enzymatic basis for active transport of Na^+ and K^+ across cell membrane, *Physiol. Rev.* 45: 596–617.
1337 Skukla, J.P. and Prabhu, K.A., 1959. Biosynthesis of sucrose, *Naturwissenschaften* 46: 325.
1338 Skukla, J.P. and Prabhu, K.A., 1959. Studies on biosynthesis of sucrose, *Experientia* 16: 202–203.
1339 Slabnik, E., Frydman, R.B. and Cardini, C.E., 1968. Some properties of potato tuber UDPG: D-fructose 2-glucosyltransferase (EC 2.4.1.14) and UDPG:D-fructose 6-phosphate 2-glucosyltransferase (EC 2.4.1.13), *Plant Physiol.* 43: 1063–1068.
1340 Slack, C.R., 1965. The physiology of sugarcane. VIII. Diurnal fluctuations in the activity of soluble invertase in elongating internodes, *Aust. J. Biol. Sci.* 18: 781–788.
1341 Slack, C.R., 1966. Inhibition of UDP-glucose:D-fructose 2-glucosyltransferase from sugar cane stem tissue by phenol oxidation products, *Phytochemistry* 5: 397–403.
1342 Slack, C.R. and Hatch, M.D., 1967. Comparative studies on the activity of carboxylation and other enzymes in relation to the new pathway of photosynthetic carbon dioxide fixation in tropical grasses, *Biochem. J.* 103: 660–665.
1343 Slack, C.R., 1968. The photoactivation of a phosphopyruvate synthetase in leaves of *Amaranthus palmeri, Biochem. Biophys. Res. Commun.* 30: 483–488.
1344 Slack, C.R., Hatch, M.D. and Goodchild, D.J., 1969. Distribution of enzymes in mesophyll and parenchyma-sheath chloroplasts of maize leaves in relation to the C_4-dicarboxylic acid pathway of photosynthesis, *Biochem. J.* 114: 489–498.
1345 Slack, C.R., 1969. Localization of certain photosynthetic enzymes in mesophyll and parenchyma-sheath chloroplasts of maize and *Amaranthus palmeri, Phytochemistry* 8: 1387–1391.

1346 Slack, C.R., 1970. Personal communication, February, 1970.

1347 Slatyer, R.O., 1970. Comparative photosynthesis, growth, and transpiration in two species of *Atriplex, Planta* 93: 175–189.

1348 Small, J., 1939. Technique for the observation of protoplasmic streaming in sieve tubes, *New Phytol.* 38: 176–177.

1349 *Sorghum Production and Utilization* (Wall, J.S. and Ross, W.M., eds.), 1970, Avi Publishing Company, Westport, Conn.

1350 Spanner, D.C., 1958. The translocation of sugar in sieve tubes, *J. Exp. Bot.* 9: 332–342.

1351 Spemann, H., 1938. *Embryonic Development and Induction*, Yale University Press, New Haven, Conn.

1352 Spencer, D., 1954. The effect of molybdate on the activity of tomato acid phosphatases, *Aust. J. Biol. Sci.* 7: 151–160.

1353 Srere, P.A., Cooper, J.R., Klybas, V. and Racker, E., 1955. Xylulose 5-phosphate, a new intermediate in the pentose phosphate cycle, *Arch. Biochem. Biophys.* 59: 535–538.

1354 Srivastava, S.C., 1969. On the rationale of the time of nitrogen fertilization for sugarcane, *Proc. Int. Soc. Sugar Cane Technol.* 13: 794–799.

1355 Stadler, L.J., 1928. Mutations in barley induced by X-rays and radium, *Science* 68: 186–187.

1356 Stanescu, P.P., 1926. Les variations quantitatives des substances hydrocarbonées dans les feuilles des plantes vertes au cours d'une journée, *C. R. Acad. Sci. (Paris)* 182: 154–156 [*Chem. Abstr.* 20: 1649 (1926)].

1357 Stebbins, G.L., 1956. Taxonomy and the evolutions of genera with special reference to the family Gramineae, *Evolution* 10: 235–245.

1358 Steemann Nielsen, E., 1952. Experimental carbon dioxide curves in photosynthesis, *Physiol. Plant.* 5: 145–159.

1359 Stephenson, M. and Gale, E.F., 1937. Factors influencing bacterial deamination. I. The deamination of glycine, *dl*-alanine and *l*-glutamic acid by *Bacterium coli, Biochem. J.* 31: 1316–1322.

1360 Stephenson, R. and Doolan, A., 1947. An investigation into the effects of delay upon burnt cane, *Proc. Queensland Soc. Sugar Cane Technol.* (1947): 197.

1361 Stevenson, G.C., 1959. Commentary following presentation of paper by S. Price and J.N. Warner, *Proc. Int. Soc. Sugar Cane Technol.* 10: 791.

1362 Stevenson, G.C., 1965. *Genetics and Breeding of Sugar Cane*, p. 81, Longmans, Green and Co., London.

1363 Steward, F.C., Mapes, M.O. and Smith, J., 1958. Growth and organized development of cultured cells. I. Growth and division of freely suspended cells. *Am. J. Bot.* 45: 693–703.

1364 Steward, F.C., Mapes, M.O. and Means, K., 1958. Growth and organized development of cultured cells. II. Organization in cultures grown from freely suspended cells, *Am. J. Bot.* 45: 705–708.

1365 Steward, F.C., 1958. Growth and organized development of cultured cells. III. Interpretations of the growth from free cell to carrot plant, *Am. J. Bot.* 45: 709–713.

1366 Stiller, M., 1962. The path of carbon in photosynthesis, *Annu. Rev. Plant Physiol.* 13: 151–170.

1367 Stodola, F.H., Raper, K.B., Fennel, D.I., Conway, H.F., Sohns, V.E., Langford, C.T. and Jackson, R.W., 1955. The microbiological production of gibberellins A and X, *Arch. Biochem. Biophys.* 54: 240–245.

1368 Stodola, F.H., Sharpe, E.S. and Koepsell, H.J., 1955. The preparation, properties and structure of the disaccharide leucose, *J. Am. Chem. Soc.* 78: 2514–2518.

1369 Stout, M., 1952. Two years results evaluating effect of preharvest sprays of maleic hydrazide on respiration and spoilage of sugar beets, *Abstr. Am. Soc. Sugar Beet Technol.*, Salt Lake City, p. 4.

1370 Stowe, B.B. and Yamaki, T., 1957. The history and physiological action of the gibberellins, *Annu. Rev. Plant Physiol.* 8: 181–216.

1371 Stowe, B.B. and Yamaki, T., 1959. Gibberellins: Stimulants of plant growth, *Science* 129: 807–816.
1372 Strakosch, S., 1907. On the carbohydrate metabolism of the sugar beet, *Z. Ver. Zuckerind.* 57: 1057–1068 [*Chem. Abstr.* 11: 1054 (1908)].
1373 Straus, J. and La Rue, C.D., 1954. Maize endosperm tissue grown *in vitro*. I. Culture requirements, *Am. J. Bot.* 41: 687–694.
1374 Straus, J., 1954. Maize endosperm tissue grown *in vitro*. II. Morphology and cytology, *Am. J. Bot.* 41: 833–839.
1375 Straus, J., 1962. Invertase in cell walls of plant tissue cultures, *Plant Physiol.* 37: 342–348.
1376 Straus, J. and Campbell, W.A., 1963. Release of enzymes by plant tissue cultures, *Life Sci.* 2: 50–62.
1377 Street, H.E. and Lowe, J.S., 1950. The carbohydrate nutrition of tomato roots. II. The mechanism of sucrose absorption by excised roots, *Ann. Bot. (London)* [N.S.] 14: 307–329.
1378 Strugger, S., 1949. *Praktikum der Zell- und Gewebephysiologie der Pflanze*, Springer-Verlag, Berlin.
1379 Strugger, S. and Peveling, E., 1961. Die elektronenmikroskopische Analyse der extrafaszikulären Komponente der Transpirationsstromes mit Hilfe von Edelmetallsuspensoiden adäquater Disparsität, *Ber. Dtsch. Bot. Ges.* 74: 300–304 (not seen).
1380 Stuart, N.W. and Cathey, H.M., 1961. Applied aspects of the gibberellins, *Annu. Rev. Plant Physiol.* 12: 369–394.
1381 Stubbs, W.C., 1895. Windrowed *versus* standing canes, *La. Exp. Sta. Bull.* No. 37.
1382 Stumpf, P.K., 1948. Carbohydrate metabolism in higher plants. I. Pea aldolase. *J. Biol. Chem.* 176: 233–241.
1383 Stumpf, P.K., 1950. Carbohydrate metabolism in higher plants. III. Breakdown of fructose diphosphate by pea extracts, *J. Biol. Chem.* 182: 261–272.
1384 Stumpf, P.K. and Horecker, B.L., 1956. The role of xylulose 5-phosphate in xylulose metabolism of *Lactobacillus pentosus*, *J. Biol. Chem.* 218: 753–768.
1385 Sugiyama, T., Goto, Y. and Akazawa, T., 1968. Pyruvate kinase activity in wheat plants grown under potassium deficient conditions, *Plant Physiol.* 43: 730–734.
1386 Sumner, J.B. and O'Kane, D.J., 1948. The chemical nature of yeast saccharase, *Enzymologia* 12: 251–253.
1387 Sumner, J.B. and Somers, G., 1953. *Chemistry and Methods of Enzymes*, p. 349, Academic Press, New York, N.Y.
1388 Sun, V.G. and Chow, N.P., 1949. The effect of climatic factors on the yield of sugarcane in Taiwan. Multiple factors investigation, *Rept. Taiwan Sugar Exp. Sta.* 2: 44–98.
1389 Sund, K.A., 1969. The influence of cold weather on the cultivation and harvest of sugarcane at Haft Tappeh, Iran, *Proc. Int. Soc. Sugar Cane Technol.* 13: 609–614.
1390 Sutherland, G.K., 1960. Polysaccharides and the viscosity of mill syrups, *Int. Sugar J.* 62: 185–186.
1391 Sutherland, G.K., 1960. An investigation of the polysaccharides present in sugar mill syrups, *Aust. J. Biol. Sci.* 13(3): 300–306.
1392 Swanson, C.A. and El-Shishiny, E.D.H., 1958. Translocation of sugars in the concord grape, *Plant Physiol.* 33: 33–37.
1393 Swanson, C.A., 1959. Translocation of organic solutes. In *Plant Physiology, a Treatise* (Steward, F.C., ed.), Vol. 2, pp. 481–551, Academic Press, New York, N.Y.
1394 Swanson, C.A. and Geiger, D.R., 1967. Time course of low temperature inhibition of sucrose translocation in sugar beets, *Plant Physiol.* 42: 751–756.
1395 Swezey, J.A. and Wadsworth, H.A., 1940. Irrigation interval control as an aid in lowering production costs, *Hawaiian Plant. Rec.* 44: 49–69.
1396 Szalai, I., 1969. Relation between the chlorophyll content and paleness of gibberellic acid-treated leaves, *Physiol. Plant.* 22: 587–593.
1397 Szent-Györgyi, A., 1956. Bioenergetics, *Science* 124: 873–875.
1398 Szilard, L., 1960. The control of the formation of specific proteins in bacteria and in animal cells, *Proc. Natl. Acad. Sci. (U.S.)* 46: 277–292.

T

1399 Tagawa, K. and Arnon, D.I., 1962. Ferredoxins as electron carriers in photosynthesis and in the biological production and consumption of hydrogen gas, *Nature* 195: 537–543.

1400 Tagawa, K., Tsujimoto, H.Y. and Arnon, D.I., 1962. The role of chloroplast ferredoxin in the energy conversion process of photosynthesis, *Proc. Natl. Acad. Sci. (U.S.)* 49: 567–572.

1401 Tagawa, K., Tsujimoto, H.Y. and Arnon, D.I., 1963. Separation by monochromatic light of photosynthetic phosphorylation from oxygen evolution, *Proc. Natl. Acad. Sci. (U.S.)* 50: 544–549.

1402 Tagawa, K., Tsujimoto, H.Y. and Arnon, D.I. 1965. Analysis of photosynthetic reactions by the use of monochromatic light, *Nature* 199: 1247–1520.

1403 Tamaoki, L. and Mueller, G.C., 1962. Synthesis of nuclear and cytoplasmic RNA of Hela cells and the effects of actinomycin D, *Biochem. Biophys. Res. Commun.* 9: 451–454.

1404 Tamiya, H., Miyachi, S. and Hirokawa, T., 1957. Some new pre-illumination experiments with ^{14}C. In *Research in Photosynthesis* (Gaffron, H. *et al.*, eds.), Interscience Publishers, New York, N.Y.

1405 Tanimoto, T. and Nickell, L.G., 1967. Field control of sugarcane flowering in Hawaii with Diquat, *Proc. Int. Soc. Sugar Cane Technol.* 12: 113–117.

1406 Tanimoto, T. and Nickell, L.G., 1967. Re-evaluation of gibberellin for field use in Hawaii, *Annu. Rept. Hawaiian Sugar Technol. Assoc.* (1966): 185–190.

1407 Tanimoto, T. and Nickell, L.G., 1967. Estimation of drought resistance of sugarcane varieties, *Proc. Int. Soc. Sugar Cane Technol.* 12: 893–896.

1408 Tanimoto, T. and Nickell, L.G., 1968. Effect of gibberellin on sugarcane growth and sugar production, *Annu. Rept. Hawaiian Sugar Technol. Assoc.* (1967): 137–146.

1409 Tanner, W., Loffler, M. and Kandler, O., 1969. Cyclic photophosphorylation *in vivo* and its relation to photosynthetic CO_2-fixation, *Plant Physiol.* 44: 422–428.

1410 Tantaoui, M., 1952. Dextran – its effect on polarization and true sucrose determination in sugar juice, *Sugar J.* 15: 36–38 (Nov. issue).

1411 Tarutani, T., 1970. Chromatographic behavior of silicic acid on Sephadex columns, *J. Chromatogr.* 50: 523–526.

1412 Teoh, T.S., Aylmore, L.A.G. and Quirk, J.P., 1967. Retention of water by plant cell walls and implications for drought resistance, *Aust. J. Biol. Sci.* 20: 41–50.

1413 Tewfic, S. and Stumpf, P.K., 1949. Carbohydrate metabolism in higher plants. II. The distribution of aldolase in plants, *Am. J. Bot.* 36: 567–571.

1414 Tewfic, S. and Stumpf, P.K., 1949. Carbohydrate metabolism in higher plants. IV. Observations on triose phosphate dehydrogenase, *J. Biol. Chem.* 192: 519–526.

1415 Thaine, R , Ovenden, S.L. and Turner, J.S., 1959. Translocation of labelled assimilates in the soybean, *Aust. J. Biol. Sci.* 12: 349–372.

1416 Thaine, R., 1961. Transcellular strands and particle movement in mature sieve tubes, *Nature* 192: 772–773.

1417 Thaine, R., 1962. A translocation hypothesis based on the structure of plant cytoplasm, *J. Exp. Bot.* 13: 152–160.

1418 Thimann, K.V. and Marre, E., 1954. Studies on the growth and inhibition of isolated plant parts. IV. The action of hexose phosphates on *Avena* coleoptile sections, *Am. J. Bot.* 41: 556–560.

1419 Thimann, K.V. and Leopold, A.C., 1955. In *The Hormones* (Pincus, G. and Thimann, K.V., eds.), Vol. 3, Academic Press, New York, N.Y.

1420 Thom, M. and Maretzki, A., 1970. Peroxidase and esterase isozymes in Hawaiian sugarcane, *Hawaiian Plant Rec.* 58(6): 81–91.

1421 Thomas, J.B. and Haans, A.J.M., 1955. Photosynthetic activity of fragments of *Spirogyra* chloroplast, *Biochim. Biophys. Acta* 18: 286–288.

1422 Thomas, M.D. and Hill, G.R., 1949. Chapter 2 in *Photosynthesis in Green Plants* (Frank, J. and Loomis, W.E., eds.), Iowa State College Press, Ames, Iowa.

1423 Thomas, M.D., 1955. Effect of ecological factors on photosynthesis, *Annu. Rev. Plant Physiol.* 6: 135–156.

1424 Thomas, R. and Venkatraman, T.S., 1930. Sugarcane–sorghum hybrids, *Agric. J. India* 25: 164.

1425 Thompson, G.D., 1962. Developments in chemical weed control, *S. Afr. Sugar J.* (1962): 313, 315.

1426 Thompson, G.D. and Gosnell, J.M., 1963. The results of herbicide trials conducted in the cane belt of Natal, 1962–1963, *Proc. S. Afr. Sugar Technol. Assoc.* (1963): 143–152.

1427 Thompson, G.D., 1967. The relationship of potential evapotranspiration of sugarcane to environmental factors, *Proc. Int. Soc. Sugar Cane Technol.* 12: 3–9.

1428 Thorne, G.N. and Evans, E.A., 1964. Influence of tops and roots on net assimilation rate of sugar beet and spinach beet and grafts between them, *Ann. Bot. (London)* [N.S.] 28: 499–508.

1429 Thuljaram Rao, J., Srinivasan, K.V. and Alexander, K.C., 1966. A red rot resistant mutant of sugarcane induced by gamma irradiation, *Proc. Indian Acad. Sci.* 64B: 224–230.

1430 Thuljaram Rao, J., Alexander, M.P. and Kandaswami, P.A., 1967. Intergeneric hybridization between *Saccharum* and *Bambusa, J. Indian. Bot. Soc.* 46: 199–208.

1431 Thuljaram Rao, J., Alexander, M.P. and Kandaswami, P.A., 1969. *Saccharum* × *Bambusa* hybridization. Studies on the development of the hybrid embryo, *Proc. Int. Soc. Sugar Cane Technol.* 13: 955–962.

1432 Tianco, A.P. and Escober, T.R., 1970. Chemical ripening of sugarcane with C.P. 41845, *Sugar News* (Nov., 1970): 508–531.

1433 Tilbury, R.H., 1967. "Sour cane", *Annu. Rept. Tate Lyle Ltd., Res. Cent.* (1967): 318–358.

1434 Tilbury, R.H., 1967. Microbiological deterioration of raw cane sugar in the tropics, *Soc. Chem. Ind.* (Monograph No. 23): 63–79.

1435 Tilbury, R.H., 1968. Sour cane, *2nd Q. Rept., Tate Lyle Ltd., Res. Cent.* pp. 84–96 (private circulation).

1436 Tilbury, R.H., 1968. "Sour cane", *Annu. Rept. Tate Lyle Ltd., Res. Cent.* (1968): 32–35.

1437 Tilbury, R.H., 1968. Biodeterioration of harvested sugarcane. In *Biodeterioration of Materials, Proc. 1st Int. Symp. Biodeterioration, Southampton*, pp. 717–730.

1438 Tilbury, R.H., 1969. The ecology of *Leuconostoc mesenteroides* and control of post-harvest biodeterioration of sugarcane in Jamaica, *Proc. W. Indies Sugar Technol. Assoc., Annu. Meet.* (private communication).

1439 Tilbury, R.H., 1969. Sour cane, *1st Q. Rept., Tate Lyle Ltd., Res. Cent.*, pp. 88–102 (private circulation).

1440 Tilbury, R.H., 1970. Report on dextrin and dextranase tests in Puerto Rico, March 16–20, 1970 (personal communication).

1441 Tishel, M. and Mazelis, M., 1966. The accumulation of sugars in potato tubers at low temperature and some associated enzymatic activities, *Phytochemistry* 5: 895–902.

1442 Tolbert, N.E., 1958. Secretion of glycolic acid by chloroplasts, *Brookhaven Symp. Biol.* 11: 271–275.

1443 Tolbert, N.E., 1963. In *Photosynthesis Mechanisms in Green Plants*, Publication No. 1145, Natl. Acad. Sci., Natl. Res. Council, Washington, D.C., p. 648.

1444 Torrey, J.G., 1959. In *Cell, Organism and Milieu* (Rudnick, D., ed.), pp. 189–222, Ronald Press, New York, N.Y.

1445 Torrey, J.G., 1967. Morphogenesis in relation to chromosomal constitution in long-term plant tissue cultures, *Physiol. Plant.* 20: 265–275.

1446 Tottingham, W.E., Lepkovsky, S., Schulz, E.R. and Link, K.P., 1926. Climatic effects in the metabolism of the sugar beet, *J. Agric. Res.* 33: 59–76.

1447 Trebst, A.V., Tsujimoto, H.Y. and Arnon, D.I., 1958. Separation of light and dark phases in the photosynthesis of isolated chloroplasts, *Nature* 182: 351–355.

1448 Trebst, A.V., Losada, M. and Arnon, D.I., 1960. Photosynthesis by isolated chloroplasts. XII. Inhibitors of CO_2 assimilation in a reconstituted chloroplast system, *J. Biol. Chem.* 235: 840–844.

1449 Tregunna, E.B., Krotkov, G. and Nelson, C.D., 1961. Evolution of carbon dioxide by tobacco leaves during the dark period following illumination, *Can. J. Bot.* 39: 1045–1056.

1450 Tregunna, E.B., Krotkov, G. and Nelson, C.D., 1964. Further evidence on the effects of light on respiration during photosynthesis, *Can. J. Bot.* 42: 989–997.

1451 Tregunna, B., 1966. Flavin mononucleotide control of glycolic acid oxidase and photorespiration in corn leaves, *Science* 151: 1239–1241.

1452 Trivelloni, J.C., Recondo, E. and Cardini, C.E., 1962. Adenosine diphosphate glucose and glucoside biosynthesis, *Nature* 195: 1202.

1453 Trudinger, P.A., 1956. Fixation of carbon dixode by the strict autotroph *Thiobacillus denitrificans, Biochem. J.* 64: 274–286.

1454 Tsuno, Y. and Shimizo, T., 1962. Studies on yield forecasting in main crops. VI. On the relation between nitrogen content in the leaves and photosynthetic ability of the rice plant at the ripening stage, *Proc. Crop Sci. Soc. Japan* 30: 325–329.

1455 Tsuno, Y. and Fujise, K., 1965. Studies on the dry matter production in sweet potato. IX. The effect of potassium on dry matter production of sweet potato, *Proc. Crop Sci. Soc. Japan* 33: 236–241.

1456 Turner, A.W., 1960. Deterioration of cane quality with time after cutting at San Cristobal, Veracruz, Mexico, *Proc. Int. Soc. Sugar Cane Technol.* 10: 606–613.

1457 Turner, A.W. and Rojas, B.A., 1963. Deterioration of sugarcane after cutting, *Proc. Int. Soc. Sugar Cane Technol.* 11: 312–318.

1458 Turner, D.H. and Turner, J.F., 1958. Uridine diphosphoglucose pyrophosphorylase of pea seads, *Biochem. J.* 69: 448–452.

1459 Turner, J.F., 1953. Synthesis of sucrose by a plant enzyme extract, *Nature* 172: 1149–1159.

1460 Turner, J.F., 1954. Synthesis of sucrose by a partially purified plant tissue extract, *Nature* 174: 692–693.

1461 Turner, J.F., 1957. The biosynthesis of sucrose, *Biochem. J.* 67: 450–456.

1462 Turner, J.F., 1958. Biosynthesis of sucrose [*Chem. Abstr.* 52: 5498a (1958)].

1463 Turner, J.S., Turner, J.F., Shortman, K.D. and King, J.E., 1958. The inhibition of photosynthesis by oxygen. II. The effect of oxygen on glyceraldehyde phosphate dehydrogenase from chloroplasts, *Aust. J. Biol. Sci.* 11: 336–342.

1464 Turner, J.S. and Brittain, E.G., 1962. Oxygen as a factor in photosynthesis, *Biol. Rev.* 37: 130–170.

1465 Tysdal, H.M., 1956. Promising new procedures in sugarcane breeding, *Proc. Int. Soc. Sugar Cane Technol.* 9(1): 618–631.

U

1466 Uribe, E.G. and Jagendorf, A.T., 1967. On the localization of organic acids in acid-induced ATP synthesis, *Plant Physiol.* 42: 697–705.

1467 Uribe, E.G. and Jagendorf, A.T., 1967. Organic acid specificity for acid-induced ATP synthesis by isolated chloroplasts, *Plant Physiol.* 42: 706–711.

V

1468 Valentine, R.C., Jackson, R.L. and Wolf, R.S., 1962. Role of ferredoxin in hydrogen metabolism of *Micrococcus lactilyticus, Biochem. Biophys. Res. Commun.* 7: 453–456.

1469 Vallance, L.G., 1956. Sugar and cane quality studies, *Rept. Bur. Sugar Exp. Sta. (Queensland)* 56: 24–25.

1470 Vallance, L.G. and Young, H.E., 1959. Deterioration of cut-up cane with reference to mechanical harvesting, *Proc. Queensland Soc. Sugar Cane Technol.* 26: 9.

1471 Vallance, L.G., 1960. Leaf desiccation, *Rept. Bur. Sugar Exp. Sta. (Queensland)* 60: 25–26.
1472 Vallance, L.G., 1961. Cane deterioration, *Rept. Bur. Sugar Exp. Sta. (Queensland)* 61: 25.
1473 Van Der Veen, R., 1949. Induction phenomena in photosynthesis. I, *Physiol. Plant.* 2: 217–234.
1474 Van Deventer, W., 1927. The cultivation of sugarcane in Java. Translated copy in files, *Exp. Sta. Hawaiian Sugar Plant. Assoc.*, p. 1 (not seen).
1475 Van Dillewijn, C., 1952. *Botany of Sugarcane*, Chronica Botanica Co., Waltham, Mass.
1476 Van Overbeek, J., 1966. Plant hormones and regulators (gibberellin and enzymes), *Science* 152(2): 727–743.
1477 Van Soest, P.J. and Jones, L.H.P., 1969. Effect of silica in forages upon digestibility, *J. Dairy Sci.* 51(10): 1644–1648.
1478 Varner, J.E., 1965. Enzymes. Chapter 2 in *Plant Biochemistry* (Bonner, J. and Varner, J.E., eds.), Academic Press, New York, N.Y.
1479 Vasil, V. and Hildebrandt, A.C., 1965. Growth and tissue formation from single, isolated tobacco cells in microculture, *Science* 147: 1454–1455.
1480 Vasil, V. and Hildebrandt, A.C., 1965. Differentiation of tobacco plants from single, isolated cells in microcultures, *Science* 150: 889–892.
1481 Vázquez, R., 1970. Water requirements of sugarcane under irrigation in Lajas Valley, Puerto Rico, *Univ. P.R. Agric. Exp. Sta. Bull.* No. 224: 36 pp.
1482 Veldstra, H., 1944. Researches on plant growth substances. V. Relation between structure and activity. II. Contemplation on place and mechanism of the action of the growth substances, *Enzymologia* 11: 137–163.
1483 Venis, M.A., 1964. Induction of enzymatic activity by indolyl-3-acetic acid and its dependence on synthesis of ribonucleic acid, *Nature* 202: 900–901.
1484 Venkatraman, T.S. and Thomas, R., 1932. Sugarcane–sorghum hybrids. Part I. General outline and early characters, *Indian J. Agric. Sci.* 2: 19–27.
1485 Venkatraman, T.S., 1932. Sugarcane breeding in different countries, *Proc. Int. Soc. Sugar Cane Technol.* 4: (Bull. No. 44).
1486 Venkatraman, T.S., 1936. Scientific Reports of the Imperial Institute of Agriculture Research, Pusa. Report of the sugarcane expert, p. 102.
1487 Venkatraman, T.S., 1937. Sugarcane–bamboo hybrids, *Indian J. Agric. Sci.* 7: 513–514.
1488 Venkatraman, T.S., 1938. Hybridization in and with the genus *Saccharum* (its scientific and economic aspects), Presidential Address, *25th Indian Sci. Congr., Calcutta*, pp. 1–18.
1489 Venkoba Rao, B., 1954. A brief review of the work on the use of X-rays in sugarcane breeding in Mysore, *Proc. Biennial Conf. Sugar Res. Dev. Workers, Jullundur.* 2(2): 120–127.
1490 Verduin, J. and Loomis, W.E., 1944. Absorption of carbon dioxide by maize, *Plant Physiol.* 19: 278–293.
1491 Verduin, J., 1953. A table of photosynthesis rates under optimal, near-natural conditions, *Am. J. Bot.* 40: 675–679.
1492 Verret, J.A. and Das, U.K., 1927. Rate of cane growth at various ages, *Hawaiian Plant Rec.* 31: 314–360.
1493 Verret, J.A. and Mangelsdorf, A.J., 1928. *Rept. Exp. Sta. Hawaiian Sugar Plant. Assoc.* (1928): 42.
1494 Vickers, R.P., 1968. The Tully area cane deterioration investigation, *Proc. Queensland Soc. Sugar Cane Technol.* 35: 19–29.
1495 Vickery, H.B., Pucher, G.W., Wakeman, A.J. and Leavenworth, C.S., 1940. Chemical investigations of the tobacco plant. VIII. The effect upon the composition of the tobacco plant of the form in which nitrogen is supplied, *Conn. Agric. Exp. Sta. Bull.* No. 442: 65–119.
1496 Vickery, R.S. and Mercer, F.V., 1963. The uptake of sucrose by bean leaf tissue. I. The general nature of the uptake, *Aust. J. Biol. Sci.* 17: 338–347.
1497 Vijayalakshmi, U. and Rao, J.T., 1960. Effects of gamma rays on germination and growth in some species and hybrids of *Saccharum, Curr. Sci.* 29: 397–398.
1498 Vijayasaradhy, N. and Nathan, S.J.S., 1957. Experimental studies of the factors controlling flowering in sugarcane. I, *Indian J. Sugarcane Res. Dev.* 1: 151–163.

1499 Vijayasaradhy, N. and Narasimhan, R., 1954. Control of flowering of sugarcane, *Proc. Int. Soc. Sugar Cane Technol.* 8: 371–401.

1500 Vijayasaradhy, N. and Vanithamony, P., 1957. Experimental studies of the factors controlling flowering in sugarcane. II, *Indian J. Sugarcane Res. Dev.* 1: 210–219.

1501 Villareal, E.P. and Santos, O., 1958. *Proc. Philipp. Sugar Technol., 6th Annu. Meet.* (1958): 87–91.

1502 Virtanen, A.I. and Nordlund, M., 1934. Synthesis of sucrose in plant tissue, *Biochem. J.* 28: 1729–1732.

1503 Vishniac, W. and Ochoa, S., 1952. Phosphorylation coupled to photochemical reduction of pyridine nucleotides by chloroplast preparations, *J. Biol. Chem.* 198: 501–506.

1504 Vishniac, W., Horecker, B.L. and Ochoa, S., 1957. Enzymic aspects of photosynthesis, *Adv. Enzymol.* 19: 1–77.

1505 Viswa Nath, B., Ramasubrahmarrya Ayyar, T.S. and Varahala, T., 1934. First year (1932–1933) ripening tests with sugarcane x sorghum crosses, *Indian J. Agric. Sci.* 4: 210–227.

1506 Vittorio, P.V., Krotkov, G. and Reed, G.B., 1954. Synthesis of radioactive sucrose by tobacco leaves from ^{14}C uniformly labelled glucose and glucose 1-phosphate, *Can. J. Bot.* 32: 369–377.

1507 Vlasov, N.A. and Morgen, E.A., 1964. The state of silicic acid in aqueous solutions, *Izv. Fiz.-Khim. Nauchn.-Issled. Inst. Irkutskom Gos. Univ.* 6(1): 192–199 [*Chem. Abstr.* 63: 14125 (1965)].

1508 Vlitos, A.J., 1967. Fundamental research on the physiology and biochemistry of sugarcane – is it really necessary? *Agronomie Tropicale* 6–7: 663–666.

1509 Vlitos, A.J. and Lawrie, I.D., 1967. Chemical ripening of sugarcane. A review of field studies carried out in Trinidad over a five-year period, *Proc. Int. Soc. Sugar Cane Technol.* 12: 429–445.

1510 Von Stieglitz, C.R., 1932. The starch contents of some sugarcane in Queensland, *Proc. Queensland Soc. Sugar Cane Technol.* 3: 63–68.

W

1511 Waddell, C.W., 1952. Stale cane losses, *Proc. Queensland Soc. Sugar Cane Technol.* 19: 39.

1512 Waddell, C.W., 1954. Stale cane losses, *Proc. Queensland Soc. Sugar Cane Technol.* 21: 9.

1513 Waddell, C.W. and Price, R.A., 1967. Mechanical harvesting in Australia and its effect on the sugar content of cane, *Proc. Int. Soc. Sugar Cane Technol.* 12: 304–312.

1514 Wadleigh, C.H. and Shine, J.W., 1939. Organic acid content of corn plants as influenced by pH of substrate and form of nitrogen supplied, *Am. J. Bot.* 26: 244–248.

1515 Wadsworth, H.A., 1936. Some aspects of the internal water economy of the sugarcane plant, *Hawaiian Plant Rec.* 40: 21–33.

1516 Waggoner, P.E. and Simmonds, N.W., 1966. Stomata and transpiration of droopy potatoes, *Plant Physiol.* 41: 1268–1271.

1517 Waggoner, P.E., 1966. Decreasing transpiration and the effect upon growth. In *Plant Environment and Efficient Water Use* (Pierre, W.D., Kirkham, D., Pesek, J. and Shaw, R., eds.), Am. Soc. Agron., Madison, Wisc.

1518 Waldron, J.C., Glasziou, K.T. and Bull, T.A., 1967. The physiology of sugarcane. IX. Factors affecting photosynthesis and sugar storage, *Aust. J. Biol. Sci.* 20: 1043–1052.

1519 Walker, D.A. and Zelitch, I., 1963. Some effects of metabolic inhibitors, temperature, and anaerobic conditions on stomatal movement, *Plant Physiol.* 38: 390–396.

1520 Walker, D.A., 1964. Improved rates of carbon dioxide fixation by illuminated chloroplasts, *Biochem. J.* 92: 226–236.

1521 Walker, D.T.I., 1969. Personal commentary following presentation of paper by S. Price, *Proc. Int. Soc. Sugar Cane Technol.* 13: 926.

1522 Walker, G.J. and Hope, P.M., 1963. The action of some α-amylases on starch granules, *Biochem. J.* 86: 452–462.
1523 Wang, T.S.C., 1964. Soil fatigue *versus* root excretion, *Taiwan Sugar* 11: 17–21.
1524 Wanner, H., 1952. Phosphataseverteilung und Kohlenhydrattransport in der Pflanze, *Planta* 41: 190–194.
1525 Warburg, O., 1920. The velocity of the photochemical decomposition of carbon dioxide in living cells. II, *Biochem. Z.* 188–217 [*Chem. Abstr.* 14: 2652 (1920)].
1526 Warburg, O., 1925. The assimilation of carbon dioxide, *Biochem. J.* 166: 386–406.
1527 Warburg, O., Krippahl, G. and Schroder, W., 1955. Wirkungsspektrum eines Photosynthese-Ferments, *Z. Naturforsch.* 10(b): 631–639.
1528 Warburg, O., Krippahl, G., Gewitz, H. and Volker, W., 1959. Uber den chemischen Mechanismus der Photosynthese, *Z. Naturforsch.* 14(b): 712–724.
1529 Warburg, O. and Krippahl, G., 1963. Die chemischen Gleichungen der Photosynthese, *Z. Physiol. Chem.* 332: 225–243.
1530 Warburg, O., 1963. Remarks in discussion of a paper by D.I. Arnon. In *La Photosynthèse, Colloq. Int. Cent. Natl. Rech. Sci. (Paris)* 119: 540 (not seen).
1531 Warburg, O. and Ostendorf, P.Z., 1963. Quatenbedarf der Photosynthese in Blattern, *Z. Naturforsch.* 18(b): 933–936.
1532 Wardlaw, I.F., 1968. The control and pattern of movement of carbohydrates in plants, *Bot. Rev.* 34: 79–105.
1533 Wardlaw, I.F., 1969. The effect of water stress on translocation in relation to photosynthesis and growth. II. Effect during leaf development in *Lolium temulentum* L., *Aust. J. Biol. Sci.* 22: 1–16.
1534 Warner, J.N., 1953. The evolution of a philosophy on sugarcane breeding in Hawaii, *Hawaiian Plant. Rec.* 54: 139–162.
1535 Warner, J.N. and Grassl, C.O., 1959. The New Guinea expedition for collecting of sugarcane, *Proc. Int. Soc. Sugar Cane Technol.* 10: 792–794.
1536 Warren Wilson, J., 1967. Effects of seasonal variation in radiation and temperature on net assimilation and growth rates in an arid climate, *Ann. Bot. (London)* 31: 41–57.
1537 Wassink, E.C., Vermeulen, D., Reman, G.H. and Katz, E., 1938. On the relation between fluorescence and assimilation in photosynthesizing cells, *Enzymologia* 5: 100–109.
1538 Wassink, E.C., 1946. Experiments on photosynthesis of horticultural plants, with the aid of the Warburg method, *Enzymologia* 12: 33–55.
1539 Watson, D.J., 1958. The dependence of net assimilation rate on leaf-area index, *Ann. Bot. (London)* [N.S.] 22: 37–54.
1540 Weatherley, P.E., 1953. On the uptake and hydrolysis of sucrose by leaf tissues, *New Phytol.* 52: 76–79.
1541 Weatherley, P.E., 1954. Preliminary investigations into the uptake of sugars by floating leaf disks, *New Phytol.* 53: 204–213.
1542 Weatherley, P.E., 1955. On the uptake of sucrose and water by floating leaf discs under aerobic and anaerobic conditions, *New Phytol.* 54: 13–28.
1543 Weatherley, P.E., Peel, A.J. and Hill, G.P., 1959. The physiology of the sieve tube. Preliminary experiments using aphid mouth parts, *J. Exp. Bot.* 10: 1–16.
1544 Weaver, R.J., 1952. Response of Black Corinth grapes to applications of 4-chlorophenoxyacetic acid, *Bot. Gaz.* 114: 107–113.
1545 Weaver, R.J. and McCune, S.B., 1959. Effect of gibberellin on seedless *Vitis vinifera*, *Hilgardia* 29: 247–275.
1546 Weaver, R.J., Van Overbeek, J. and Pool, R.M., 1966. Effect of kinins on fruit set and development in *Vitis vinifera*, *Hilgardia* 37: 181–201.
1547 Webb, J.A. and Gorham, P.R., 1965. Radial movement of ^{14}C translocates from squash phloem, *Can. J. Bot.* 43: 97–103.
1548 Webb, K.L. and Burley, J.W.A., 1962. Sorbitol translocation in apple, *Science* 137: 766.
1549 Webster, G., 1954. Incorporation of radioactive glutamic acid into the proteins of higher plants, *Plant Physiol.* 29: 382–385.

1550 Webster, G., Whitman, S. and Heintz, R., 1962. Cytoplasmic formation of ribosomes, *Plant Physiol. (Suppl.)* 37: xx.

1551 Weinburg, J., 1903. The deterioration of cut sugarcane, *Int. Sugar J.* 5 (not seen).

1552 Weiss, J., 1946. Biological action of radiations, *Nature* 157: 584; Evenari, M. and Stein, G., 1953. The influence of light upon germination, *Experientia* 9: 94–95.

1553 Weissbach, A., Smyrniotis, P.Z. and Horecker, B.L., 1954. Pentose phosphate and CO_2 fixation with spinach extracts, *J. Am. Chem. Soc.* 76: 3611–3612.

1554 Weissbach, A. and Horecker, B.L., 1955. Enzymatic formation of phosphoglyceric acid from ribulose diphosphate and carbon dioxide, *J. Biol. Chem.* 218: 795–810.

1555 Weissbach, A., Horecker, B.L. and Hurwitz, J., 1956. The enzymic formation of phosphoglyceric acid from ribulose diphosphate and carbon dioxide, [*Chem. Abstr.* 50: 7184 (1956)].

1556 Wellensiek, S.J., 1962. The control of flowering, *Neth. J. Agric. Sci.* 10: 390–397.

1557 Weller, D.M., 1930. Accumulations of starch in the stalks of *Natal Uba* cane grown on acid soil, *Hawaiian Plant. Rec.* 33: 294–299.

1558 Went, F.W. and Hull, H.M., 1949. The effects of temperature upon translocation in the tomato plant, *Plant Physiol.* 24: 505–526.

1559 Went, F.W., 1961. In *Encyclopedia of Plant Physiology* (Ruhland, W., ed.), 16: 1–23, Springer-Verlag, Berlin.

1560 Went, F.A.F.C. and Geerligs, H.C.P., 1894. Over den achteruitgang van het saccharosegehalte van gesneden suikerriet, *Arch. Java Suikerind.* Jaarg. 2: 249–253 (not seen).

1561 Went, J.S. and Thimann, K.V., 1937. *Phytohormones*, Macmillan and Co., New York, N.Y.

1562 Wessels, J.S.C. and van der Veen, R., 1956. The action of some derivatives of phenylurethan and of 3-phenyl-1,1-dimethylurea on the Hill reaction, *Biochim. Biophys. Acta* 19: 548–549.

1563 Wessels, J.S.C. and Baltscheffsky, H., 1960. Adenosine triphosphatase activity in chloroplasts, *Acta Chem. Scand.* 14: 233–246.

1564 Whelan, W.J. and Bailey, J.M., 1954. The action pattern of potato phosphorylase, *Biochem. J.* 58: 560–569.

1565 Whelan, W.J., 1961. Recent advances in the biochemistry of glycogen and starch, *Nature* 190: 954–957.

1566 White, J. and Munns, D.J., 1950. Utilization of aspartic acid and asparagine by yeast, *Nature* 165: 111.

1567 White, P.R., 1943. *A Handbook of Plant Tissue Culture,* Catell Press, Lancaster, Pa.

1568 White, P.R., 1954. *The Cultivation of Animal and Plant Cells*, 239 pp., Ronald Press, New York, N.Y.

1569 Whittingham, C.P., 1968. Photometabolism of maize leaves. In *Photosynthesis in Sugarcane,* Proc. Int. Symp. held June 12 and 13, 1968, at the Royal Lancaster Hotel, London, pp. 33–34.

1570 Wieb, H.H. and Wihrheim, S.E., 1962. The influence of internal moisture deficit on translocation, *Plant Physiol.* 37: (Proc. Annu. Meet., 1–1i).

1571 Wieb, H.H. and Wihrheim, S.E., 1962. The influence of internal moisture stress on translocation. In *Radioisotopes in Soil–Plant Nutrition Studies*, pp. 279–288. Int. Publ., Inc., New York, N.Y.

1572 Wilkins, R.A. and Ateshian, K.H., 1967. Relationship between ground water, salinity and sugarcane at Rose Hall Estate, *Proc. Int. Soc. Sugar Cane Technol.* 12: 54–81.

1573 Willenbrink, I., 1957. Uber die Hemmung des Stofftransports in den Siebröhren durch lokale Inaktivierung verschiedener Atmungenzyme, *Planta* 48: 269–342.

1574 Williams, A.M., 1956. Light induced uptake of inorganic phosphate in cell-free extracts of obligately anaerobic photosynthetic bacteria, *Biochim. Biophys. Acta* 19: 570.

1575 Williamson, A.R. and Schweet, R., 1964. Role of the genetic message in initiation and release of the polypeptide chain, *Nature* 202: 435–437.

1576 Willstätter, R. and Stoll, A., 1918. *Untersuchungen über die Assimilation der Kohlensäure*, Springer-Verlag, Berlin.

1577 Wilmar, C. and Hellendoorn, M., 1968. Growth and morphogenesis of asparagus cells cultured *in vitro, Nature* 217: 369–370.

1578 Wilson, J.W., 1967. The components of leaf water potential. I. Osmotic and matric potentials, *Aust. J. Biol. Sci.* 20: 329–347.

1579 Wilson, J.W., 1967. The components of leaf water potential. II. Pressure potential and water potential, *Aust. J. Biol. Sci.* 20: 349–357.

1580 Wilson, J.W., 1967. The components of leaf water potential. III. Effects of tissue characteristics and relative water content on water potential, *Aust. J. Biol. Sci.* 20: 359–367.

1581 Wittwer, S.H. and Hansen, C.M., 1951. Progress report on the effects of preharvest foliage sprays of maleic hydrazide on storage losses of sugar beets, *Proc. Am. Soc. Sugar Beet Technol. (Detroit).*

1582 Wold, R.L., 1946. Cane deterioration in a storage pile, *Hawaiian Plant. Rec.* 50(1): 5–10.

1583 Wolff, C.J. de, 1926. Die Saccharose-Bildung in Kartoffeln während des Trocknens, *Biochem. Z.* 176: 225–245.

1584 Wolfrom, M.L., Georges, L.W. and Miller, I.L., 1949. Crystalline derivatives of isomaltose, *J. Am. Chem. Soc.* 71: 125–127.

1585 Woo, K.C., Anderson, J.M., Boardman, N.K., Downton, W.J.S., Osmond, C.B. and Thorne, S.W., 1970. Deficient photosystem II in agranal bundle sheath chloroplasts of C_4 plants, *Proc. Natl. Acad. Sci. (U.S.)* 67(1): 18–25.

1586 Wood, H.G. and Stjernholm, R.L., 1961. Transcarboxylase. II. Purification and properties of methylmalonyl-oxaloacetic transcarboxylase, *Proc. Natl. Acad. Sci.(U.S.)* 47: 289–294.

1587 Wood, G.H., 1962. Some factors influencing starch in sugarcane, *Proc. S. Afr. Sugar Technol. Assoc.* 36: 123–135.

1588 Wort, D.J., 1954. Influence of 2,4-D on enzyme systems, *Weeds* 3(2): 131–135.

Y

1589 Yamada, N., Murata, Y. and Iyama, I., 1953. Study of the respiration of crop plants, *Proc. Crop Sci. Soc. Japan* 21: 195–198.

1590 Yamada, Y., Tanaka, K. and Takahashi, Ė., 1967. Callus induction in rice, *Oryza sativa* L., *Proc. Japan Acad.* 43: 156–160 (not seen).

1591 Yamaha, T. and Cardini, C.E., 1960. The biosynthesis of plant glycosides. I. Monoglucosides, *Arch. Biochem. Biophys.* 86: 127–132.

1592 Yamaha, T. and Leloir, L.F., 1960. The biosynthesis of plant glycosides. II. Gentiobiosides, *Arch. Biochem. Biophys.* 86: 133–137.

1593 Yamasaki, M. and Arikado, H., 1937. Effect of defoliation on sugar accumulation in successive joints of sugarcane, *Rept. Gov. Exp. Sta., Tainan, Formosa* 4: 1–32 [*Chem. Abstr.* 31: 7943 (1937)].

1594 Yamasaki, M. and Oda, H., 1938. On the arrowing tendency of sugarcanes along the edges of the fields, *Proc. Int. Soc. Sugar Cane Technol.* 6: 793–795.

1595 Yamasaki, M. and Arikado, H., 1946. *Proc. Crop Sci. Soc. Japan* 13: 313–315 (not seen).

1596 Yamashita, T. and Butler, W.L., 1968. Photoreduction and photophosphorylation with Tris-washed chloroplasts, *Plant Physiol.* 43: 1978–1986.

1597 Yang, T.T., 1961. A study of translocation of photosynthate in sugarcane plants with ^{14}C and ^{32}P, *Rept. Taiwan Sugar Exp. Sta.* 23: 47–64.

1598 Yap, G.G., 1920. A study of the photosynthesis of sugarcane, *Philipp. Agric.* 8: 269–276.

1599 Yarwood, C.E., 1946. Detached leaf culture, *Bot. Rev.* 12: 1–56.

1600 Yatazawa, M., Furuhashi, K. and Shimizu, M., 1967. Growth of callus tissue from rice-root *in vitro, Plant Cell Physiol.* 8: 363–373.

1601 Yates, R.A. and Bates, J.F., 1957. Preliminary experiments on the effects of chemicals on the ripening of sugarcane, *Proc. Br. W. Indies Sugar Technol.* (1957): 174–189.

1602 Yates, R.A., 1964. Artificial ripening of sugarcane with Dalapon, *Trop. Agric. (Trinidad)* 41: 225–230.

1603 Young, D.P., 1955. Review of foliage desiccant experiments for sugar cane in Hawaii, *Rept. Hawaiian Sugar Technol.* 14: 96.

1604 Young, H.E., 1963. The deterioration of burnt standing cane and burnt cut cane, *Proc. Int. Soc. Sugar Cane Technol.* 11: 307–311.

1605 Yusuf, N.D., 1948. Consolidated report on the scheme for research on sugarcane physiology, Coimbatore, for the years 1942–1947 (not seen).

Z

1606 Zeevaart, J.A.D., 1962. Physiology of flowering, *Science* 137: 723–731.

1607 Zelitch, I., 1958. The role of glycolic acid oxidase in the respiration of leaves, *J. Biol. Chem.* 233: 1299–1303.

1608 Zelitch, I., 1961. Biochemical control of stomatal opening in leaves, *Proc. Natl. Acad. Sci. (U.S.)* 47: 1423–1433.

1609 Zelitch, I. and Waggoner, P.E., 1962. Effect of chemical control of stomata on transpiration and photosynthesis, *Proc. Natl. Acad. Sci. (U.S.)* 48: 1101–1108.

1610 Zelitch, I. and Waggoner, P.E., 1962. Effect of chemical control of stomata on transpiration of intact plants, *Proc. Natl. Acad. Sci. (U.S.)* 48: 1297–1299.

1611 Zelitch, I., 1964. Organic acid and respiration in photosynthetic tissue, *Annu. Rev. Plant Physiol.* 15: 121–142.

1612 Zelitch, I., 1967. Water and CO_2 transport in the photosynthetic process. In *Harvesting the Sun* (San Pietro, A., Greer, F.A. and Army, T.R., eds.), pp. 231–248, Academic Press, New York, N.Y.

1613 Zemplén, G. and Gerecs, A., 1929. Synthesis of sucrose, *Ber.* 62B: 984 [*Chem. Abstr.* 23: 4195 (1929)].

1614 Zholkevitch, V.N., 1954. Use of labelled carbon under field conditions for observations on transport of assimilates, *Dokl. Akad. Nauk S.S.S.R.* 96: 653–656 (English translation).

1615 Zholkevitch, V.N. and Koretskaya, T.F., 1959. Metabolism of pumpkin roots during soil drought, *Fiziol. Rast.* 6: 690–700.

1616 Ziegler, H., 1956. Untersuchungen über die Leitung und Sekretion der Assimilate, *Planta* 47: 447–500.

1617 Ziegler, H., 1958. Uber die Atmung und die Stofftransport in den isolierten Leitbündeln der Blattstiele von *Heracleum mantegazzianum, Planta* 51: 186–200.

1618 Zimmermann, M.H., 1957. Translocation of organic substances in trees. II. On the translocation mechanisms in phloem of white Ash (*Fraxinus americana* L.), *Plant Physiol.* 32: 399–404.

1619 Zimmermann, M.H., 1958. Translocation of organic substances in the phloem of trees. In *The Physiology of Forest Trees* (Thimann, K.V., ed.), Ronald Press Co., New York, N.Y.

1620 Zimmermann, M.H., 1960. Transport in the phloem, *Annu. Rev. Plant Physiol.* 11: 167–190.

1621 Zittle, C.A., 1951. Reactions of borate with substances of biological interest, *Adv. Enzymol.* 12: 493–527.

1622 Zweig, G., Shavit, N. and Avron, M., 1965. Diquat in photoreactions of isolated chloroplasts, *Biochim. Biophys. Acta* 109(2): 332–346.

Author Index

Acevedo-Ramos, G., 319, 421
Acín-Díaz, N., 454, 594
Ahrens, W., 200
Akazawa, T., 201, 207, 209, 214, 216
Alaherlaha, P., 443
Alers-Alers, S., 398, 419, 519, 520
Alexander, A.G., 96, 104, 107–109, 112, 170, 202, 211–215, 218–220, 305, 312, 313, 317, 319, 320, 325, 349, 350, 364, 367, 371, 412, 414, 415, 422, 446, 447, 454, 456, 457, 460–466, 469–478, 480, 482, 496, 498, 504, 507, 510–514, 516–519, 555, 564, 565, 567–569, 591, 594, 599, 601
Alfaro, J., 196
Alford, J.A., 604
Allard, H.A., 530, 545
Allen, M.B., 204
Alvarer, F.G., 443
Andrews, T.J., 103
Anon. 165, 166
Arceneaux, G., 28, 47, 53, 58–60, 489, 493, 521
Arikado, H., 183
Arnold, A., 70
Arnon, D.I., 75–79, 81, 86, 91, 304
Aronoff, S., 233
Arreguin-Lozano, B., 200, 211
Artschwager, E., 3, 10–12, 21, 23, 28
Arvier, A.C., 459, 503, 557
Ashton, F.M., 168, 169, 171, 412
Ateshian, K.H., 410
Auchincloss, R., 230
Avigad, G., 248, 249
Avron, M., 516, 518
Awada, M., 526–532, 537, 539, 541–543, 549, 551, 565
Axelrod, B., 249
Ayers, A., 473

Babu, C.N., 50
Backs, D., 632, 633
Bacon, J.S.D., 233
Baeyer, A., 84
Balch, R.T., 197, 200, 205, 206, 208, 213–218
Baldry, C.W., 125
Ballantyne, D.J., 447
Bangdiwala, I.S., 425
Barba, R., 638–640
Barber, C.A., 13, 21, 33, 35
Barker, S.A., 218
Barnes, J.H., 576, 593
Barnett, N.M., 304
Barrier, G.E., 297
Bassham, J.A., 70, 84, 85, 88, 90–92, 97, 245, 513
Bates, J.F., 443, 445, 449, 453–455, 458, 484, 489–494, 502, 556
Batey, J.W., 289, 320
Baver, L.D., 432, 436
Bean, R.C., 243, 244
Beauchamp, C.E., 443–445, 484
Beevers, H., 187, 340
Belcher, B.A., 536
Belile, J.A., 575, 591
Bennun, A., 516
Benson, A.A., 70
Bergey, D.H., 604
Bergman, N., 360
Berliner, R.W., 406
Biddulph, O., 232, 276, 278, 296, 344
Bieleski, R.L., 297, 332–338, 340–342, 403, 406
Bieske, G.C., 455
Bjorkman, O., 119, 178
Black, C.C., 93, 94
Black, L.M.A., 613, 654
Blackman, F.F., 70, 84, 130, 147, 152
Blinks, L.R., 79, 142
Blouin, R.F., 195, 199, 202, 575
Bodnár, J., 231
Boehm, J., 328
Bogorad, L., 87
Böhning, R.H., 133, 136, 137
Bonde, E.K., 147
Boneta-García, E., 582, 596
Bonner, J., 73, 75, 200, 206, 211, 217, 230, 236
Bonnet, J.A., 96, 398, 418, 421
Boon, W.R., 496, 497, 499
Bor, N.L., 14, 16, 18
Borden, R.J., 416, 418, 421, 435
Bowen, J.E., 454
Brachet, J., 364

Brakke, M.K., 615, 628, 654, 655
Brandes, E.W., 3, 5, 10–15, 19–22, 28, 52, 54, 407, 410, 548
Brauns, D.H., 229
Bremer, G., 5, 41, 45, 46
Brett, P.G.C., 533, 536, 537, 541, 551
Brian, P.W., 458, 495, 496
Brittain, E.G., 178
Brodie, H.W., 439
Brown, A.H., 199
Brown, R., 329
Browne, C.A., 195, 199, 202, 575
Bruijn, J., 605
Buchanan, J.G., 238–240, 243, 245, 249
Bull, T.A., 63, 64, 103, 196, 360, 369, 390–393, 407–409, 459, 466
Burk, D., 338
Burkard, J., 231
Burkholder, P.R., 613, 614, 654
Burley, J.W.A., 284
Burma, D.P., 240, 249
Burnside, C.A., 136, 137
Burr, G.O., 89, 101, 134, 163, 164, 166, 167, 189, 192, 193, 325, 327, 412, 432, 525, 531–533, 536–539, 541, 544, 549, 555, 557, 566
Burt, R.L., 314

Calderbank, A., 496, 498, 499
Calma, V.C., 579
Calvin, M., 70, 84, 85, 91, 92, 97, 99, 245, 497
Canny, M.J., 285, 296, 297, 300, 301, 312, 315, 324
Capó, B.G., 317, 416, 418, 434, 435
Caputto, R., 238, 241, 242, 248, 249, 355
Cardini, C.E., 238
Carlson, M.C., 198
Carr, D.J., 303
Cathey, H.M., 458
Cayere, A., 579
Celarier, R.P., 3, 15, 40, 196, 408
Chacravarti, A.S., 445
Chalmers, R.V., 79
Chardón, C.E., 458
Chen, J.C.P., 502
Childers, N.F., 160
Chilton, S.J.P., 525, 528, 534, 536, 544, 546, 548
Chow, N.P., 435
Chrispeels, M.J., 365, 385
Chu, C.C., 124
Chu, T.L., 526–528, 551, 558
Clark, F.J., 622
Clements, H.F., 227, 228, 231, 398, 401, 411, 416, 418, 419, 422–433, 435, 467, 473, 526, 532, 537, 539–545, 549, 551, 553, 554, 565, 579
Cobb, M., 581
Cohen, C.N., 340
Cohn, M., 237
Coleman, R.E., 446, 449, 455, 458, 459, 466, 491, 502, 522, 525, 532, 534, 537–539, 541, 543–545, 557–559, 562, 566, 569–572
Collander, R., 415
Colombo, B., 375
Commoner, B., 497
Conchie, J., 247
Copeland, F.C., 622
Cori, C.F., 206, 207, 213, 218, 226, 231
Cowart, F.F., 160
Crafts, A.S., 295, 298, 299, 304
Cross, W.E., 574, 575, 580, 591
Currier, H.B., 448
Czernicki, Müller, von, O.F., 575, 578

D'Amato, F., 623
Danielli, J.F., 329
Daniels, J., 7, 23, 535, 547, 548
Darlington, C.D., 41
Das, U.K., 435, 442
Davidson, L.G., 489, 492–494, 498, 503
Davis, E.A., 448
Davis, W.A., 227
De, R., 162
Decker, J.P., 133, 142
Dedonder, R.A., 233
Deerr, N., 5, 25, 45
De Fekete, M.A.R., 248
Dela Cruz, A., 481, 628, 655
De La Vega, G.A.K., 445
De Saussure, N., 69
De Surnay, A., 541
De Vries, H., 199
De Wit, C.T., 136, 139
D'Hotman De Villiers, O., 473
Dikanova, A., 232, 234
Dormer, K.J., 329
Doudoroff, M., 235, 237
Downton, W.J.A., 112, 114
Dugger, Jr., W.M., 217, 246, 330–332, 454
Dutt, N.L., 16, 37, 41, 196–198, 202, 533, 547
Duysens, L.M.V., 80
Dymond, G.C., 592

Ebert, G.A., 83
Eckart, C.F., 442
Eckstein, O., 159
Edelman, J., 244, 350
Efferson, J.N., 581
Egan, B.T., 602–604, 606–608
El Sharkawy, M., 114
Emerson, R., 70, 79, 124, 131, 144, 148, 159
Epps, H.M.R., 360, 361
Epstein, E., 331
Esau, K., 344
Escober, T.R., 456
Evans, H., 443, 453, 454, 530, 545, 556, 579
Evans, H.J., 422, 428, 429, 432
Evans, W.C., 360
Everson, R.G., 146, 205
Ewart, A.J., 130

Fenson, D.S., 311
Fischer, E., 228
Flowers, T.J., 304
Fogg, G.E., 88
Forbes, A., 134, 183–185
Forrester, M.L., 172, 173, 179
Foster, D.H., 596, 602, 603, 606
Franck, J., 175
French, C.S., 79
Frenkel, A.W., 72
Friloux, J.J., 607, 608
Frota de Souza, A., 594
Fruton, J.S., 207, 213, 236, 237, 243, 362
Funderburk, H.H., 498

Gaastra, P., 136
Gaff, D.F., 303
Gale, E.F., 360, 361
Galmiche, H.M., 100, 142, 146
Ganguli, N.C., 241
Gard, K.R., 536
Garner, W.W., 530
Gassner, G., 159
Gauch, H.G., 330, 344, 454
Gauhl, E., 119
Gayler, K.R., 352, 353, 363, 365, 382, 383, 385, 386
Geerligs, H.C.P., 575
Geiger, D.R., 277, 289, 293, 320
George, E.E., 545
Gerecs, A., 230
Gibbs, M., 91
Gilbert, G.A., 208
Ginsburg, V., 249
Glasziou, K.T., 63, 65, 177, 196, 233, 249, 275, 278, 284, 285, 299, 327, 339–350, 352–354, 360, 363, 365–367, 369–387, 390–393, 405, 407–409, 436–438, 459, 476, 536, 548, 582
Goeze, G., 159
Goldsworthy, A., 114, 173
Gosnell, J.M., 501, 502
Gould, R.F., 458
Grant, R., 445
Grassl, C.O., 5, 6, 7, 13, 14, 18, 19, 23, 24, 38, 56
Green, A.A., 207, 213
Green, L., 148
Greenway, H., 305
Guilbeau, W.F., 573, 581
Gumbs, F.A., 503, 504
Gutsche, A.E., 619

Haber, A.H., 462
Haddon, E., 196
Halais, P., 418, 420, 473
Haldane, J.H., 591, 592
Hall, J.A., 575, 591
Hamner, K.C., 564
Hanes, C.S., 200, 207, 213, 218, 222, 226, 231
Hansen, C.M., 448
Hansford, C.G., 531
Hanson, J.B., 304
Harden, A., 231
Harrison, B.H., 409
Hartley, W., 14, 15
Hartt, C.E., 61, 112, 134, 137, 144, 161, 163, 164, 166–168, 171, 175, 176, 181, 186, 188, 189, 192, 193, 195, 199, 200, 202, 204, 205, 209, 231–233, 235, 273–277, 279–293, 296, 305–312, 314–316, 318, 320–322, 324, 402, 411, 412, 421, 432, 448, 514, 519
Hassid, W.Z., 232, 234, 235, 243–245, 249, 351, 352
Hatch, M.D., 94, 98, 100–108, 111, 112, 115, 205, 246, 275, 278, 282, 285, 299, 320, 348–350, 354, 355, 360, 367, 378, 386, 387, 403–406, 582, 583
Hawker, J.S., 176, 281, 353, 354, 403–406, 582, 583
Haworth, W.N., 229
Hayashi, T., 462
Hebert, L.P., 446, 449, 455, 491
Hehre, E.J., 198
Heinicke, A.J., 160
Heinz, D.J., 56–58, 617, 621, 634–638, 640–642

Hellendoorn, M., 618
Henderson, I.F., 332, 362
Henderson, W.D., 332, 362
Herrmann, F., 168, 200
Hesketh, J.D., 112, 114, 137, 138, 140, 141, 144, 148, 149, 152, 154, 155
Hew, C.S., 143
Hill, E.S., 495, 497
Hill, G.R., 148, 159
Hill, R., 71, 76, 470
Höber, R., 328
Hodgkinson, K.C., 205
Hogarth, D.M., 37
Homer, R.F., 496, 497
Hooker, J.D., 16, 18, 408
Hoover, W.H., 148
Horecker, B.L., 88
Hori, S., 457
Horsley, M., 606
Hrishi, N., 44, 45
Hu, T.H., 534
Huber, G., 230
Hucker, G.J., 602, 604, 605
Hudson, C.S., 229
Hughes, R.H., 580, 581
Hülsbruch, M., 289
Humbert, R.P., 413, 414, 420, 421, 454, 542, 550, 551, 556, 557
Humphreys, T.E., 217, 246, 454
Humphries, E.C., 314

Iljin, W.S., 168
Incoll, L.D., 175
Ingen-Housz, J., 69
Innes, R.F., 418, 439
Irvine, J.C., 228–230
Irvine, J.E., 133, 190, 191, 608

Jackson, W.A., 113, 114
Jacob, F., 362, 386
Jagathesan, D., 35
Jagendorf, A.T., 83, 518
James, N.I., 527, 534, 542, 544, 545, 547, 565
Janaki-Ammal, E.K., 30, 32, 33, 35, 37, 41, 42
Jenson, R.D., 316
Jeswiet, J., 13, 14, 18, 21, 27
Johnson, H.S., 98, 102, 104, 106, 108
Johnson, M.J., 238
Jones, H., 288, 324
Juang, P.Y., 533, 534
Julien, R., 559

Kagan, B.O., 235
Kandasami, P.A., 16, 19
Kandler, O., 102
Kendall, A.I., 360
Keniry, J.S., 602, 605, 606
Kiessling, W., 226
King, D.L., 297
Kirk, M., 88
Klaphaak, P.J., 54
Kok, B., 72–75
Komatsu, S., 123, 195
Koretskaya, T.F., 304
Kortschak, H.P., 94, 96, 97, 99, 103, 105, 106, 113, 114, 129, 134, 137, 176, 182–188, 205, 289–293, 310, 311, 630, 643
Kramer, P.J., 133
Krotkov, G., 143
Kryukova, N., 232, 233, 235
Kubota, T., 426
Kumar, A., 107, 127, 135, 144, 555
Kumari, R.K., 547
Kurosawa, E., 458
Kursanov, A.L., 147, 232, 233, 235, 277, 284, 304, 311, 325, 344
Kuyper, J., 594

Laetsch, W.M., 202, 206
Lake, J.V., 113
Lal, K.N., 134, 144, 162, 164, 180, 182
Lalouette, J.A., 51, 463
Landrau, Jr., P., 319, 416, 420, 421, 427, 428
La Rue, C.D., 618, 620, 623, 631
Latzko, E., 91
Lauden, L.L., 580
Lauritzen, J.I., 577, 578, 584, 586, 591–596
Law, J., 229
Lawrence, J.M., 498
Lawrie, I.D., 451–453
Lebedev, A., 232, 234
Lebrón, J., 513
Le Clerc, J.A., 433
Lee, H.A., 593
Lee, S., 533, 534, 545, 547
Leloir, L.F., 208, 216, 218, 240–242, 246, 247, 249
Lemieux, R.U., 230
Lennox, C.G., 19, 23
Leonard, O.A., 234, 289, 297
Leopold, A.C., 297
Levan, A., 622
Lewis, C.M., 131
Li, H.W., 31, 32, 38, 46, 49
Liebig, J., 84, 433

Lilienthal, B., 606
Lin, K.S., 533, 545, 547
Lineweaver, H., 338
Lipmann, F., 516
Liu, P.P.D., 502
Lockhart, J.A., 537
Loh, C.S., 37, 38, 41, 50, 52, 61, 62
Loomis, W.E., 137, 140, 147, 148, 150, 174, 297
López Hernández, J.A., 550, 551
Losada, M., 77, 80
Loustalot, A.J., 159, 170, 445
Lowe, J.S., 329
Lugo-López, M.A., 317, 435, 445, 582, 596
Lundegardh, H., 328
Lundquist, A., 35

Magasanik, B., 361
Mandelstram, J., 362
Mangelsdorf, P.C., 15
Maretzki, A., 65, 109, 304, 457, 481, 485, 594, 620, 625–632, 643–654, 655
Marks, P.A., 364, 375
Martin, J.P., 124, 330
Martin-Leake, H., 550
Mason, T.G., 329
Mather, K., 409
Matherne, R.J., 55
Matz, J., 548
May, L.H., 244, 340
Mayeaux, P.A., 604
Mayer, J.R., 69
McAlister, E.D., 178
McCleskey, C.S., 604
McClintock, B., 622
McCready, R.M., 232
McIlrath, W.J., 448
McMahon, D., 87
McWhorther, C.G., 502
Mee, G.W.P., 617, 638, 640–642
Mees, G.C., 498
Meidner, H., 157
Mendelssohn, K., 298
Mercer, F.V., 277
Merrill, E.D., 8–10
Meyer, A., 328
Meyer, K., 218
Michaelis, L., 495, 497
Michaux, A., 16
Miller, E.C., 168, 227
Milner, Y., 248, 249
Mitchell, J.W., 331
Mitchell, P., 83
Mitscherlich, E.A., 433
Molengraaff, G.A.F., 7, 8, 10
Mongelard, J.C., 411
Monod, J., 339, 340, 361, 362, 364, 386
Montalvo-Zapata, R., 107, 108, 112, 412, 454, 456, 494, 498, 504, 507–518, 555, 567–569
Moore, P.H., 525
Moreland, C.F., 535, 546, 548
Moriguchi, S., 424
Moriya, A., 30, 31, 548
Morris, G.H., 199
Mortenson, L.E., 77
Mortimer, D.C., 240, 249
Moss, D.N., 112, 138, 140–142, 149–152, 155, 157, 160–162, 173, 175, 180–182
Muir, W.H., 612
Mukherjee, S.K., 13, 16, 17, 408
Müller, A., 497
Muller, H.J., 43
Munns, D.J., 614
Murashige, T., 624, 632, 633, 639, 640
Murata, T., 248
Musgrave, R.B., 137, 138, 148
Myers, J., 79, 178
Myrbäck, K., 233

Nakano, R., 624, 632
Nakata, S., 297
Narasimhan, R., 37, 196–198, 202, 525, 533, 545, 546, 551
Narayanawsami, S., 46
Naylor, A.W., 304, 448
Neales, T.F., 175
Neely, W.B., 447
Neilands, J.B., 364
Nelson, C.D., 284, 298, 319
Nelson, J.M., 230
Nelson, O.E., 214
Neuberg, C., 231
Neufeld, E.F., 249
Nicholson, R.I., 196, 606
Nickell, L.G., 115, 305, 397, 455–457, 465, 485, 519, 542, 556, 569, 570, 613–616, 620, 625–630, 632, 634, 638–640, 643, 651–655
Nishiyama, I., 40, 41, 45
Nitsch, J.P., 632, 639
Nooden, L.D., 363
Nordlund, M., 230, 231
Normand, C.W., 585–591
Norstog, K.J., 624
Nurmia, M., 231, 234

Oldham, J.W.H., 230
Oliver, I.T., 214
Oparin, A., 232, 233
Osterlind, S., 145

Paliatseas, E.D., 525, 528, 532, 534, 536, 538, 544, 546
Panje, R.R., 526, 532, 533, 535, 554
Parish, D.H., 473
Park, J.T., 238
Parkin, J., 329
Partanen, C.R., 611, 634
Parthasarathy, N., 12, 13, 18, 34, 40, 41, 46, 407
Paul, D.M., 229
Payne, J.H., 330
Peaslee, D.E., 160, 162
Peat, S., 218
Pederson, C.S., 602, 604
Perquin, L.H.C., 604
Petinov, N.S., 304
Peto, F.H., 448
Petrack, B., 516
Peveling, E., 303
Phillis, E., 329
Pictet, A., 229, 230
Pitman, M.G., 305
Porter, H.K., 244, 340
Posthumus, O., 6
Pottinger, P.K., 214
Poulson, R.H., 385
Price, R.A., 602, 603
Price, S., 6, 27, 28, 39, 40, 42, 43, 46, 47, 49, 51, 638
Priestley, J.H., 228
Procter, G.C., 490
Purdie, T., 228, 229
Purvis, O.N., 527
Putman, E.W., 234, 244, 245, 351, 352

Quastel, J.H., 328

Rabinowitch, E.I., 113, 129–133, 138, 141, 144, 145, 152
Racker, E., 88
Raghavan, T.S., 31, 34, 35, 37, 41
Raja Rao, T., 554
Ramiah, P.V., 400
Ramp, R.M., 521
Rao, J.T., 16, 31, 41, 44, 547
Recondo, E., 208, 246–259
Reeves, R.G., 15
Rehbein, C.A., 602
Reinert, J., 632, 633, 643
Reinke, J., 130, 132
Rettger, L.F., 360
Rickenberg, H.V., 339
Riker, A.J., 619
Riklis, E., 328
Rines, H.W., 214
Rizk, T.Y., 585–591
Roach, B.T., 39, 47, 50
Roberts, E.J., 607
Robertson, G., 229
Robertson, R.N., 329
Robinson, P.R., 459
Robson, J.W., 490
Rocha de Almeida, J., 594
Rojas, B.A., 579, 580
Rosado-Alberio, J., 120
Rosenfeld, A.H., 593
Rossini, L., 626
Rothstein, A., 339
Roughan, P.G., 65
Rouillard, G., 418
Roxburgh, W., 18
Roychoudhury, R., 364
Ruben, S., 71, 85, 233
Ruhland, J., 227
Ruttner, F., 144
Ryker, T.C., 435

Sacher, J.A., 348, 351–353, 366, 368–370, 372, 375, 399
Sachs, J., 199
Saeki, T., 136, 139
Salisbury, F.B., 524, 527, 566
Samuels, G., 317, 319, 398, 413, 416–421, 425, 427, 428, 435, 455, 456, 474, 475, 519, 520, 579, 593
Santos, O., 458
Sanyal, P.B., 578, 594
Sartoris, G.B., 12, 20, 530, 531, 533, 536, 545, 592
Sawyer, G.C., 227
Scarr, M.P., 605
Scholander, P.F., 303
Schroeder, H., 200, 562
Schumacher, W., 289
Schwartz, M., 83
Schweet, R., 364
Sen, S.C., 442, 443
Sen, S.P., 364
Senser, M., 102
Serapión, J.L., 526–528, 551, 558
Seward, A.C., 9

Shafer, J., 650
Shang, K.C., 49
Shaw, G.W., 433
Shaw, H.R., 435, 439
Shen, G.M., 323
Simmonds, N.W., 156
Simmonds, S., 207, 213, 236, 237, 243, 362
Singh, B.N., 134, 144, 161, 164, 165, 181, 182
Singh, T.S.N., 30
Sisler, R.M., 331
Skinner, J.C., 49, 545
Skole, R.D., 604, 605
Skoog, F., 633, 639, 640
Slabnik, E., 248
Slack, C.R., 93, 94, 98, 100–103, 105–107, 109, 112, 115–122, 127, 205, 282, 283, 313, 320, 349, 368
Slatyer, R.O., 64
Small, J., 296
Smith, A.M., 70
Smith, G.A., 534
Sorger, G.J., 422
Spain, G.L., 555
Spanner, D.C., 299, 421
Spemann, H., 623
Sreenivasan, T.V., 35
Srere, P.A., 91
Srinivasan, K., 526, 532, 533, 535
Srivastava, K.K., 554
Srivastava, S.C., 419
Stadler, L.J., 43
Stanescu, P.P., 227
Steemann Nielsen, E., 145, 155
Stephenson, M., 160, 603
Stevenson, G.C., 18, 50, 61, 63
Steward, F.C., 617
Stoll, A., 143, 159
Stout, M., 448
Stowe, B.B., 457, 458, 564
Strain, G.C., 639
Strakosch, S., 228
Straus, J., 619–623, 631, 655
Street, H.E., 329
Strugger, S., 303
Stuart, N.W., 457, 458
Stubbs, W.C., 574, 595
Stumpf, P.K., 364
Sugiyama, T., 422
Sun, V.G., 435
Sutherland, G.K., 197, 198
Swanson, C.A., 277, 285, 293, 314
Szilard, L., 362
Tagawa, K., 77
Takahashi, D.T., 455
Tanimoto, T., 305, 397, 465, 485, 519, 552, 553, 556
Tanner, W., 83
Tantaoui, M., 605
Taylor, S.A., 316
Teoh, T.S., 303, 304
Thaine, R., 289, 296, 324
Thimann, K.V., 363
Thom, M., 65
Thomas, M.D., 136, 148, 159
Thomas, R., 30
Thompson, G.D., 501, 502
Thompson, J.F., 650
Tianco, A.P., 456
Tilbury, R.H., 574, 605, 608
Tió-Lladó, M., 134, 135
Tolbert, N.E., 107, 462
Torrey, J.G., 630, 634
Tottingham, W.E., 227
Trebst, A.V., 92,
Tregunna, E.B., 112, 114, 143, 172, 174, 179
Trivelloni, J.C., 247
Tseng, P.M., 37, 50
Turner, A.W., 579, 580
Turner, D.H., 246
Turner, J.F., 245, 246
Turner, J.N., 459
Turner, J.S., 178

Vallance, L.G., 494, 502, 602
Van Deventer, W., 442
Van Dillewijn, C., 123, 124, 196, 398–400
Van Overbeek, J., 460
Varahalu, T., 400
Varner, J.E., 73, 75, 209, 217, 364, 365, 385, 655
Vázquez, R., 413
Veale, J.A., 205
Venis, M.A., 365
Venkatraman, T.S., 17, 30, 537, 544
Verduin, J., 137, 140, 143, 144, 146, 147, 150, 174
Verret, J.A., 435
Vickers, R.P., 606, 608
Vickery, R.S., 277
Vijayasaradhy, N., 525, 533, 545, 551
Villareal, E.P., 458
Virtanen, A.I., 230, 231
Viswa Nath, B., 30
Vittorio, P.V., 244
Vlitos, A.J., 202, 217, 451–453, 480

Vogel, H., 229, 230
Volk, R.J., 113, 114
Von Stieglitz, C.R., 196

Waddell, C.W., 602, 603
Wadsworth, H.A., 425
Waggoner, P.E., 153, 156
Waldron, J.C., 65, 177, 180–183, 186, 315, 316, 372–374, 376, 377, 393
Walker, D.A., 518
Walters, E.H., 433
Warburg, O., 70, 79, 84
Wardlaw, I.F., 302, 322
Warner, J.N., 7, 19, 43, 56, 545
Warren Wilson, J., 64
Wassink, E.C., 131, 133, 134
Watson, D.J., 61
Weatherley, P.E., 299
Webb, K.L., 284
Weinburg, J., 576
Weller, D.M., 196
Went, F.A.F.C., 575
Went, F.W., 389, 437
Whelan, W.J., 214
White, P.R., 613, 619, 625, 632, 633, 639
Whittingham, C.P., 114
Wilkins, R.A., 410
Willenbrink, J., 299
Williamson, A.R., 364
Willstätter, R., 143, 159
Wilmar, C., 618
Wilson, J.W., 302
Wittwer, S.H., 448
Wold, R.L., 578, 596
Wolfrom, M.L., 228
Woo, K.C., 94, 125–127
Wort, D.J., 447

Yabuta, T., 458
Yamaha, T., 249
Yamaki, T., 457, 458, 564
Yamasaki, M., 183
Yang, T.T., 323
Yarwood, C.E., 328
Yatazawa, M., 624
Yates, R.A., 443, 445, 449, 453–455, 484, 491
Young, D.P., 491
Young, H.E., 579, 602
Young, W.J., 231
Yusuf, N.D., 533, 545

Zeevaart, J.A.D., 563, 566
Zelitch, I., 143, 153, 156, 157, 172
Zemplén, G., 230
Zholkevitch, V.N., 304
Ziegler, H., 299
Zimmer, K.G., 497
Zimmermann, M.H., 299
Zittle, C.A., 331
Zweig, G., 518

Subject Index

Abscisic acid (ABA), effects on invertase synthesis (illustrated) 384, 385
N-Acetylglutamic acid, in cell culture (tabulated) 644, 645
α-*N*-Acetyl-L-ornithine, in cell culture (tabulated) 644, 645
Acid invertase, bound to cell walls 403; in bound form 350; correlation with growth rate 350; discovery of in storage tissue 349; diurnal fluctuation of 393; diurnal–nocturnal variations of 313; in immature storage tissue 582, 583; *vs.* internode expansion (illustrated) 388; localization of in parenchyma tissue 266; response to variable moisture regime 388; retention of in *S. spontaneum* storage tissue 369; seasonal variation of (illustrated) 350; in *S. spontaneum* stalks 389; and sugar accumulation, as function of pH (illustrated) 352; as a transferase 350
Acid–neutral invertase relationships 587, 588
Acid/neutral invertase ratio (A/N ratio) 585–591; in burned and unburned stalks (tabulated) 588, 589; relationship to reducing sugars 590, 591; and varietal responses 591
Acid phosphatases, low-nitrogen effects 96; non-specific 96
Acropetal transport, in morning-harvested *vs.* afternoon-harvested blades 311; reduced by darkening leaf base (illustrated) 291; of sucrose 291
Actidione 654
"Activated" sucrose, in sugar accumulation process 339
Active absorption, by animal tissues 328
Active accumulation, decline with age 336, 337
Active metabolism, required for sugar storage processes 336, 337
Active sucrose transport, dependence upon light 292
Active sugar absorption, cane storage tissue 329; historical 329
Active vein loading 276, 277
Additive chromosome behavior 46
Adenosine diphosphate glucose (ADPG), structure 209
Adenosine diphosphate glucose pyrophosphorylase (ADPG pyrophosphorylase) 209
Adenosine triphosphate (ATP), formation coupled with light-driven electron transfer 76; formation by "dehydration" 83; formation in mitochondria 76; light regeneration for dark CO_2 assimilation 71; probable participation in sucrose transport 127; product of energy conversion reactions 71; production of, collaboration of chloroplasts and mitochondria 72
Adenylate kinase 105, 109; localization of in C_4 species 112
ADPG, *see* Adenosine diphosphate glucose
Aerial contamination, effects on sugarcane 134, 135
"After-ripening" 573, 574, 576
Age, *vs.* maturity 402
Air turbulence, effects on CO_2 supply 181; effects on leaf geometry and shading 181
Aldolase, effects of maleic hydrazide on 450
Alkaline pyrophosphatase 105, 109
Allied genera, historical groupings 16; the *Saccharum* complex 15, 16; use in Hawaiian cane breeding 57, 58
Allosteric transition hypothesis 364, 365
Amino acids, as photosynthesis products 109
Ammonium sulfate, as a major N source 416, 417
Amylase, chemical control of 472–475; increased activity with chemical desiccants 513; inhibition of by $HgCl_2$ (illustrated) 472; inhibition of by silicate (illustrated) 471
α-Amylase, in cane leaves 209; secretion by cell suspension cultures 654–656
β-Amylase, in cane leaves 209; gradients in detached blades 127; response to variable water regimes 415; theoretical role in assimilate transport 127
Amylopectin, structure of 217
Amylose, structure of 217
"Amylosucrase" 256, 257
Andropogoneae 14, 15
Aneuploids, in *S. officinarum* cell suspensions 638

Anisomycin 654
Apical meristem, chemical control of 475–483; as a metabolic sink 325
Apparent free space (A.F.S.) 327; effects on cell wall mass flow 303, 304
Arbutin, formation from UDPG and ADPG 247
Arginine, biochemistry of 643–651; catabolism products in cell suspension cultures 647–651; conversion to *N*-carbamyl-putrescine 647–651; growth-limiting role in cell cultures (theoretical) 647–651; incorporation into cultured cell proteins 646; metabolic relationships to putrescine (schematic) 650; uptake and conversion to *N*-carbamylputrescine (illustrated) 649
Arginine carboxylase 650
Arginine desimidase 650
Arginosuccinic acid, in cell culture (tabulated) 644, 645
Artificial ripening, early concepts of 442, 443
Asiatic bank 8
Asparagus officinalis L., tissue culture of 618
Aspartase 360
Aspartate aminotransferase 105
Aspartic acid, discovery as initial C_4 pathway product 95
Assimilate movement, theories of 295–302
ATP, *see* Adenosine triphosphate
ATPase(s), effects of night flooding on 415; gradients in detached blades 127; light and dark types in cane leaves 516–518; repression of by night flooding 325; suppression by desiccants, light requirement for 517; suppression by Diquat 516; suppression by Paraquat (illustrated) 516–518
Aureogenus magnivena 613–615
Australia shelf 3, 8
Australian bank 8
Autosyndesis, as a function of high polyploidy 31; in interspecific crosses 42
Auxin(s), biochemical action of 363, 364; relation to N source in invertase synthesis 369–371
– –carbohydrate control mechanisms, for invertase 372
– –carbohydrate control system, loci of 374–376
– -controlled induction system, for invertase 353, 354
6-Azauracil, as a chemical ripener 476–483; in control of apical meristem (illustrated) 476–478; destruction of apical meristem (illustrated) 478; effects on growth and acid invertase (illustrated) 389; × gibberellic acid 479, 480; growth *vs.* enzyme effects 477; growth and sugar effects (tabulated) 476, 482; invertase effects 371; × nitrogen 480–483; rapid transport of 477

"Back reactions", in photosynthesis 178
Backcross methods, development of 28
Barrier membrane, impermeable to sucrose 329, 330; selectively permeable 329, 330
Basic *Saccharum* chromosome number 34, 35
Basipetal transport, increased by darkening leaf base (illustrated) 291; origin of driving force in leaf apex 127
Basipetal sucrose transport, energy source for 292, 293; possible role of ATP 293
Bicarbonate, possible substrate for ribulose diphosphate carboxylase 146
– utilization, by aquatic plants 145
– buffering, of CO_2 concentration in photosynthesis 144, 145
Bidirectional flow, in sieve tubes 296
Biodeterioration 574; increase with chopper harvesters 602, 603; of mechanically-harvested cane 602–609; operational changes to minimize 603; role of *L. mesenteroides* 602–605
– control 608, 609; by dextranase 608, 609; failure of antiseptics 603; failure of molasses, formaldehyde, bactericide 608; by invertase inhibition 609
Bipyridyl free radicals 495, 496
Borate, relationship with starch phosphorylase 332
– carrier role, for sugars across impermeable membranes 331
– (ion)–sugar complexes 454; theoretical (illustrated) 331
Boron, affecting cane growth and quality 454; enzyme relationships 454; roles of in sugar transport (theoretical) 454
Bourbon cane, origin of 5
Brix, distribution profile in a cane stalk (illustrated) 400
Bud mutations 45
Burning, preharvest 489, 490; quality effects in cut and standing cane 579

C_4-dicarboxylic acids, photosynthesis conditions, effects on initial yield of (tabulated) 187–189

C_4 pathway, biochemistry *vs.* morphology 113; decarboxylation *vs.* transcarboxylation 99, 100; discovery 93–95; discovery by Kortschak and co-workers 94–98; discovery of oxaloacetic acid as an early product 98; effects of CO_2 concentration 97; enzymology of 102–112; essential requirements for operation of 101; essentiality of light 99; establishing essential steps 98–102; evidence against decarboxylation reaction 100; failure of PGA to predominate 94; labeling of the C-1 atom of 3-PGA 98; labeling of the C-4 atom 98; light regulation of key enzymes 109; measurement in intact systems 98, 99; operation of in isolated chloroplasts 121; origin of 4; possible operation in Calvin-cycle plants 101; production of glycine and serine 109; relation to cane growth 63, 64; schematic representation 100; side reactions 108, 109; size of photosynthetic unit 93, 94; species utilizing 102; steady-state measurements 97, 98; summary reactions 100; synthesis of CO_2 acceptor 102, 103; theory of carbon movement from malate to acetyl-CoA 101; theory of cytoplasmic exchange reactions 100; as two linked cycles 101, 102

– enzymes, subcellular localization of 121

– species, characteristics of 112, 113; leaf extraction methods 95, 99; methods of exposure to $^{14}CO_2$ 95; more efficient photosynthetic reactions 113

– products, lowered equally by macronutrient deficiencies 165

Calcium deficiency, effects on foliar amylase (illustrated) 320; effects on photosynthesis rate (illustrated) 164; and foliar sucrose accumulation 175; increased foliar sucrose content (tabulated) 319

Calvin cycle, in sugarcane 188; in sugarcane stalk tissue 115

Cane fertility, discovery of 544

Cane ripening, by water management (illustrated) 413, 414

Canna indica, synthesis of sucrose-*P* in leaves of 244

N-Carbamylputrescine, formation from arginine 647–651; slow metabolism of 650

N-Carbamylputrescine anhydrolase 650

Carbohydrate "residues" (glucans), in leaf, stem, and root tissues 205

Carbon-14 (^{14}C), flow in sugarcane under normal conditions 274–289; non-randomization of in transient sucrose 283; randomization of in storage sucrose 283; tracing methods in translocation studies 274–276; transport of, increasing percentage entering sucrose 284

Carbon dioxide,

– absorption, diurnal changes in sugarcane leaves (illustrated) 191; temperature and moisture effects 142

– assimilation, Calvin cycle 83–91; essential enzymes 92; function of light intensity (illustrated) 137; indirect nutritional effects 159, 160; K effects on leaf permeability 160, 161; K effects during sugarcane life cycle 161, 163; K, Mg and Ca deficiency effects on 160–164; N, P, and K effects on 159, 160; nutritional effects 159, 160; related to leaf-area index 124; relationships with leaf water loss 149; seasonal effects 136; *vs.* water deficit 167–169

– availability, importance of diffusion path 146, 158

– compensation point 113; definition 157; diurnal variation of 124; effects of ambient O_2 on 172; effects of moisture and temperature on 157; linked with photorespiration 173, 174; in maize and sorghum 157; and photorespiration 157; in sugarcane 157

– diffusion, concentration effects 142; delay by "cytoplasmic exchange reaction" 142; light and stomata effects 142; physical barriers in leaves 149, 158; physical and biochemical resistances to 157, 158; related to differential light saturation among species 149; resistances, illustrated 158

– reduction, *activated CO_2* theory (Warburg) 84, 85; formaldehyde theory 84

Carbon reduction enzymes, low activity of *in vitro* 91, 92

Carbonic anhydrase, in Calvin-cycle chloroplasts 145, 146; inhibition of 146; role in bicarbonate formation from water 146; role in bicarbonate utilization in photosynthesis 145, 146

Carrier complexes, sugar–borate 330–332

Catabolite repression 360–362; theory of 361

Cell culture, nutritional and metabolic aspects 624–630

Cell suspension culture(s), amino acid assimilation by 645, 646; amino acid uptake by 644–646; amino acid uptake (illustrated) 646; α-amylase secretion by 654–656; asexual production of new genotypes in 643; authenticity of as growth models 656; chemical effects on 651–656; in chemical ripener screening 652–654; effects of arginine and arginine precursors 644–646; high polyploidy in (illustrated) 637; importance of chromosome losses in 636; mechanisms of chromosome change in 636–638; multinucleate cells (illustrated) 637; Murashige and Skoog medium 639, 640; organ differentiation in (illustrated) 653; plantlet induction from callus tissue 640–643; plantlet rearing in 642; preferential uptake of arginine by (illustrated) 646; requirement for arginine 644–646; somatic instability in 638; study of arginine biochemistry in 643–651; totipotency decline in 636; variable cell sizes (illustrated) 636
Cell wall acid invertase 403
Cell wall transport, as extension of xylem flow 303
Cell wall water, as a buffer against moisture deficit 303; role in species drought resistance 303, 304
Chemical desiccants, disruption of sugar synthesis–utilization balance 508; historical research 491–493; induction of abnormal enzyme behavior 513–516; need of 489, 490; requirements of 490; search for 491–495
Chemical desiccation, and improvement of harvest conditions 504; and increased water uptake 504
Chemical flowering control, differential perceptivity of leaf ranks 554; theory of 554
Chemical growth control, theory of 475, 483, 484
Chemical ripener(s), failure of 441; lack of fundamental knowledge 483, 484; physiology *vs.* field technique 441; screening of 483–487; screening program for 485–487; search for (1950–1970) 443–457
– trials, limitations of 483, 484; in Puerto Rico 487
Chemical ripening, categories of 441; with C.P. 41845 455, 456; with Cycocel 455–457; with 2,4-D 443–448; with D.A.-5 455; with Dalapon 455; early concepts of 442, 443; with gibberellic acid 457–467; with Kuron 453; with maleic hydrazide 448–451; with monopotassium phosphate 454, 455; with Pesco 1815 452, 554; with Sucrol (Esso 59-G) 451, 452; with TBA (Trysben) 452; with TIBA 455
Chemiosmotic hypothesis 83
Cheribon canes, origin of 5
Chewing canes 6
3-(*p*-Chlorophenyl)-1,1-dimethylurea (CMU, Monuron), as a cane desiccant 492, 493
Chlorophyll,
– concentration, in detached blades 127
– concentration gradients, factors affecting 127
– content, gradients within and among leaf ranks 144
– gradients, in cane leaves 323; relation to basipetal transport 127
– stability 143, 144
Chlorophyll *a* 71; excitation of 72, 73
Chlorophyll *a*/*b* ratios 144
Chlorophylls *b* and *c*, in Photosystem II 74
Chloroplast(s), bundle-sheath type in parenchyma cells (illustrated) 204; cooperation of discrete types 115–119; isolated, CO_2 assimilation by 121; isolation difficulties 121; parenchyma sheath and mesophyll (illustrated) 116; scheme for cooperative function 118; as site of photosynthetic reactions 71; as site of sugar synthesis 71; sucrose synthesis by 121
– cooperation, effects of physical structures 119, 120
– grana, and water-soluble constituents 92
– membranes 122
– permeability 122
Chromosome mutations 43, 44
Chromosome number, methods of analysis 41
Chromosome transmission and inheritance 45–51
Cichorium endiva, tissue regeneration in 633
Citrulline, in cell culture (tabulated) 645
CMU, *see* 3-(*p*-Chlorophenyl)-1,1-dimethylurea
Companion cells, metabolically active 297
Concentration gradients, role of in assimilate transport 300
Condensing enzyme, effects of maleic hydrazide on 450
Configuration models, the "fit" concept (illustrated) 377; for invertase regulators 376, 377

Constant temperatures, effects on enzymes (tabulated) 317; effects on sucrose levels 317
Controlled cross, development in Java 27, 28
Cool nights, increase of sucrose yield in Puerto Rico 317
C.P. 41845 (Monsanto), effects on sugarcane growth and quality (tabulated) 455, 456; invertase repression by 456
Creole, in Louisiana industry 54, 55; selection as the *Saccharum* type cane 18
Cretaceous epoch 3, 9
Crop log, definition of 422
Crop logging, in cane ripening control 422–434
Cultivated canes, probable ancestry 12–14
Cultural ripening 442
Cyclic photophosphorylation 75, 76, 78; operation of 75
Cytogenetics, of cultivated canes 39–45

2,4-D, *see* 2,4-Dichlorophenoxyacetic acid
Dalapon, effects on cell suspension cultures 652; organ induction by in cell cultures 652
Dark reactions, in CO_2 assimilation 70
Dark respiration 142; suppressed in light 179
Dark translocation, of sucrose 292
David North Plant Research Centre, cane growth and ripening 486
Day length, as a function of distance from equator (illustrated) 532
DCMU, *see* 3-(3,4-Dichlorophenyl)-1,1-dimethylurea
Deaminase 360
Defoliation, effects on sucrose transport (illustrated) 321; and loss of photosynthetic potential 322
De novo enzyme synthesis 364
Density-gradient centrifugation, for chloroplast isolation 124
Desiccant–light relationships 512, 514, 515
Detached blades, darkened portions become artificial sinks 290; failure to act as a sink in light 290; reduced translocation rates in 290; use in sugar transport studies 289–293
Detrashing, mechanical 521
Dextran(s) 195; in burned chopped and whole cane 606, 607; glucosans 605, 606; "haze" assay for 606; increase of in standing (harvested) cane 607; nature of and effects on sucrose solutions 605–607; in standing cane 605; tests for in milled juice 605–607
Dextranase, method for dextran removal from milled juice 608, 609
"Dextransucrase" 256, 257
Dicarboxylic acids, *see* C_4-dicarboxylic acids
2,4-Dichlorophenoxyacetic acid (2,4-D), as a chemical ripener 443–448; effects on leaf enzymes (tabulated) 447; effects on leaf sugars (tabulated) 446
3-(3,4-Dichlorophenyl)-1,1-dimethylurea (DCMU), Photosystem II inhibitor 74
Differential enzyme retention, by leaves 120
Diphasic maturation processes 401, 402
Dipyridyl action, greenhouse studies of 504–519; theory of 498–500
Diquat, and appearance of ribose in cane leaves 509–513; and curtailed sucrose-forming potential 507–509; effects on cane quality (tabulated) 503; effects on cell suspension cultures 651; lack of mobility 496; light requirement for phytotoxic action 498; phytotoxic action of 497; properties and mode of action 495–500; quality decline with desiccation 502–504; and quality deterioration 490, 491; structure of 495; as a sugarcane desiccant (tabulated) 493–495; theory of desiccative action 498–500; visual effects of on sugarcane (illustrated) 506; yield effects of 500–504
Diurnal invertase fluctuation, illustrated 313
Diurnal sugar gradients (leaf), effect on dark translocation 292
Driving force, light regulation of in detached blades 293

Electron carriers, Photosystem II 74
Electroosmosis, theory (Spanner) for passage of sieve plates 299
Endosperm culture 617–621
Endothal, effects on cell suspension cultures 651
Energy capture, from solar radiation 71–83
Energy conversion, in sugarcane 122–127; in sugarcane, empirical 122, 123
– efficiency 71, 72
– potential 79
Enzyme(s), localization of sugar-storing processes 404; temperature × variety effects (tabulated) 317
– index 470
– induction 361
– regulation, mRNA as a rate-limiting factor 381, 382; theories of 360–365
– synthesis, *de novo* 364; *transcriptive vs. translative* steps 382

Equations, for estimating plant yield 433, 434
Erianthus, introgression with *Saccharum* species 22; starch in 196; sugar storage potential of 408
Erianthus maximus, contribution to cultivated canes 25; features and growth habit 24
Escherichia coli 360, 361
Evolution of *Saccharum*, general 3, 4
Extinct *Saccharum* species 12
Extrafascicular movement, in cell walls 303

FAD, *see* Flavin adenine dinucleotide
Female transmission, of somatic chromosome number 36
Ferredoxin, discovery and roles 77–79
Ferredoxin–$NADP^+$ reductase 78
Ferricyanide 73, 76
Fertilizer–yield equation 434
Fiber–moisture relationship, among *Saccharum* species (illustrated) 409
Flavin adenine dinucleotide (FAD), effects on starch synthetase reaction 217; glucose oxidase cofactor 217
Flora, in Cretaceous and Pleistocene epochs 9, 10; evolution of in Malaysia 9
Floral induction, by controlled photoperiod 545–547; by controlled photoperiod in sparsely- or non-flowering clones 547; effects of warm and cool cycles (illustrated) 540; fixed *vs.* shortening day length 546, 548
Floral initiation 525; and floral development, temperature effects 535; night temperature effects 536–541; *vs.* tassel emergence 526; temperature effects 535–541; twilight effects 540
Floral maturation 525
Floral organization 525
"Florigen" 363, 563
Flower development, time needed for 527
Flower induction mechanism 524
Flower primordia, contrasted with vegetative meristem (illustrated) 528
Flowering, adverse effects of 523, 524; adverse effects on quality, yield 549; atypical stage development 529, 530; closing gap between *S. officinarum* and *S. spontaneum* 7; in controlled climate facilities 548; critical role of night temperature 536–541; day length as one of multiple controlling factors 531; day length requirement, modifying factors 532; effects of latitude and length of day 533–535; effects of rainy season termination 535; essential conditions for 544; failure to flower with spring photoperiod 7; fixed (constant) *vs.* shortening day length 533, 535; GA effects on tassel emergence 565; hormone balances in juvenile cane 543; inconsistency of 543, 544; and increased fiber 550, 551; inductive *vs.* non-inductive nights (illustrated) 538; juvenile (pre-flowering) phase 543; lack of spring floral induction 535; optimal dark period for 530; photoperiod effects 524; photoperiod *vs.* light intensity 534; physiological maturity *vs.* age 542, 543; pre-photoinductive phase 558, 559; quality effects of 550, 551; relation to equator 531; relation of night length (nyctiperiod) to latitude 541, 542; reversion to vegetative growth 530; role of lengthening *vs.* shortening dark periods 539–541; role of night length (nyctiperiod) 539, 541, 542; *S. officinarum* synchronously with *S. spontaneum* 7; in *S. spontaneum* 533, 534; separate roles for spindle and mature leaves 557–559; *vs.* sugar storage, differential selection pressure for (theory) 409; summation of processes in higher plants 524; synchronization of among varieties 545; tassel emergence *vs.* day length 534; year-round at the equator 533, 542
control 523; with 6-azauracil 567; the breeder's viewpoint 543–549; with chemicals 554–557; with CMU 555, 560; at Coimbatore 544; critical timing of irrigation cycles 553, 554; with DCMU 556, 561; defoliation *vs.* chemical treatments (illustrated) 560, 561; by defoliation and spindle removal 557–560; difficulties of control by water management 552, 553; with Diquat 556, 557; with GA 555, 564, 565; the grower's viewpoint 549–562; with maleic hydrazide 560; with NAA 555; by nitrogen fertilization 555; by nitrogen, importance of moisture (tabulated) 561, 562; by nitrogen management 561, 562; quality improvement 559; red light interruption of dark period 566; in *S. spontaneum* 547–549; by spindle removal and leaf trimming (illustrated) 558; synchronization of *S. spontaneum* with *S. officinarum* 548; temperature as a factor in water management 554; by water management 551–554

– hormone, transport past a tissue graft 531
– inhibitor, in mature leaves 559
– mechanism 562–572; amylase behavior in flowering *vs.* non-flowering clones (illustrated), preinductive to postinductive 569; ATPase and amylase changes from preinductive to postinductive periods (tabulated) 568; enzyme activity *vs.* hormonal transport (theory) 567, 568; enzyme behavior (preinductive to post-inductive) 566–569; enzyme changes *vs.* leaf rank and variety (tabulated) 568; foliar *vs.* meristematic stimuli (theory) 572; GA effects 564, 565; GA effects on hypothetical hormone balance 564, 565; hormonal synthesis and transport 563; inductive "stimulus" 563; phytochrome conversion 566; role of red and far-red light 565, 566; stability of flowering stimulus 569, 570; stem tip culture in artificial medium (illustrated) 570; summary of flowering sequence 571, 572; summary of, with illustration 570–572
– prevention, by low temperature 528, 536
– scale (latitude) 533
– stages 525–530; measurement of 527–529
– stage methods, *stage vs. index* 527

Fluorescence, escape form of excess energy quanta 73
– intensity, relation to O_2 concentration 179

Foliar analyses, *vs.* 8–10 tissue and soil analyses 432, 433

Foliar canopy, light reception by 135; radiation received by individual leaves (tabulated) 183

Foliar nitrogen, content, related to CO_2 assimilation rate (illustrated) 166, 167; factors affecting 425

Foliar starch, amylolytic degradation of 209, 210; possible restrictions upon photosynthesis 209

Foliar sucrose accumulation, and deficiencies of N, P, K and Ca 175

Free radicals, in living tissues 495, 497

Frozen cane, deterioration of 580

Fructose, believed first sugar product of photosynthesis 227, 231; tetraacetyl forms of 229, 230; tetramethyl forms of 229

Fructose 1-phosphate, structure 243

Fructose 6-phosphate, structure 243

Fumarase 105

Functional reduced gametes 34

GA, *see* Gibberellic acid

β-Galactosidase 362

Galactowaldenase 238, 240

Gamete behavior, in intergeneric and interspecific crosses 20

Gamete ploidy levels 36, 37

Garden canes, dependence upon early man 11

Gene loci, for high sucrose 63

Gene mutations 44, 45

Gene transmission and character inheritance 49–51

Germplasm pool, in Hawaiian cane breeding 56, 57

Gibberellic acid (GA) 363; combined with Cycocel 456, 457; combined with variable silicate treatments 461; effects at controlled temperatures 459; effects on internode elongation and acid invertase (illustrated) 390; effects on internode expansion (illustrated) 466; effects on invertase synthesis (illustrated) 384; effects on sucrose 460–464; effects on sucrose biosynthesis 460; effects on sugar production and utilization 459–464; effects on sugar synthesis (illustrated) 461–465; effects on sugarcane 458, 459; effects with variable nitrogen regimes (tabulated) 460; efficiency of multiple *vs.* single applications (illustrated) 464–466; post-growth stimulatory phase (illustrated) 464–466; in variable-illumination studies 461–464

Glucan(s) 195, 205; foliar 199

α-Glucan, accumulations of physiological importance 206; daily conversion of 206; insoluble cane photosynthate 204–206

Glucosamine, invertase suppression by 373, 374, 379

Glucose, absorption preference for 403; accumulation of by alternate pathway 346, 347; believed first sugar product of photosynthesis 227, 231; transfer from sucrose to starch (equations) 258; uptake of, exceeding fructose in storage tissue 351, 352

"Glucose effect" 360–362; (on invertase), localized on invertase synthesis 374

Glucose oxidase, effects of 2,4-D on 447, 448

Glucose 1-phosphate, not absorbed by cane storage tissue 335; structure 236; temporary accumulation of 97, 98

Glucose 6-phosphate isomerase, in cane storage tissue 264

Glyceraldehyde 3-phosphate dehydrogenase 109

Glycerate kinase, in C_4 pathway- and Calvin-cycle species 107
Glycolate, as source of photosynthetically-produced CO_2 143, 144
Glycolic acid oxidase, and photorespiration 173, 174
Gradients, in source–sink translocation 296–299
Growth, and sucrose inversion 386–393
– control, theory of in chemical ripening 475
– -lag response, to chemical enzyme control 390
– rate, correlation with total acid invertase content (illustrated interpretation of) 392
– –yield equations 433, 434
Guanidine, in arginine metabolism 650

H. 37-1933, use in developing translocation pathways 275
Hawaiian cane breeding 56–58
Hexokinase, effects of maleic hydrazide on 450; and potassium deficiency 422; in sugarcane leaves 314
Hexose, methylation studies of 228, 229
– phosphorylation, effects of P deficiency on 232; in sugarcane 232
– interconversion, enzymes for in cane storage tissue 349; requirement of ATP and Mg^{2+} for 349
Hexose phosphates, recognition of in plant tissues 231, 232
Hill reaction 76; associated with grana 126
Hormonal enzyme regulation 362–364
Hydroxypyruvate, as 3-PGA precursor 106

IAA, *see* Indole-3-acetic acid
Illumination, effects on desiccant–enzyme relationships 514, 515
Indexes, as cultural guidelines 402; enzyme 470; moisture 425, 426; potassium 420, 426–430; potassium–H_2O 426–430; primary 423, 424; vegetative 418
Indole-3-acetic acid (IAA), invertase effects of 367–369
Induced mutations 43–45
Infertility belief 26
Inhibition, of Photosystem II 74
Inner space 327
Insular conditions, affecting *Saccharum* evolution 10
Intergeneric chromosomal homology 32
Intergeneric crosses 28–35
"Intermediate day plant", interpretation of sugarcane 530
International variety movement 59
Internode elongation, *vs.* acid invertase activity, rate regression of 391
Interspecific chromosome homology 36
Interspecific cross(es) 35–37; at Coimbatore 35; *vs.* intergeneric cross 4
Introgression theory (*S. officinarum* × *Miscanthus*) 37–39
Inversion, as function of postharvest enzyme and substrate level 595; increased with drying of cane 592, 593; postharvest, as function of variety, moisture, temperature and condition of cane 591–595; in stored cane as a varietal feature 591
– control 359, 360; feedback repression 366; mechanisms of 365–372; metasilicate mode of action 600, 601; with sodium metasilicate (illustrated) 597–599; in stored cane 595, 596
Invertase(s), dialysis effects 366; distribution within the stalk 583–586; glucose repression of 366; and growth rate 386–393; in mature storage tissue 403; mode of action (illustrated) 234; performance of in sugar storage 404, 405; and postharvest inversion 582–596; in potato tubers 260, 261; present in harvested stalks 582, 583; proteinaceous inhibitors of 594; response of and growth response to controlled environment 386; response to variable water regimes 415; silicate inhibition of (illustrated) 471; sucrose synthesis by 402; species distribution of acid and neutral 63; sugarcane *vs.* bacterial in milled juice 596, 597; suppression by Paraquat and Diquat (illustrated) 514, 515; as a transferase 233, 234; unproven role in sucrose synthesis 233, 234
– activity, *vs.* internode expansion (illustrated) 387
– control, with chemicals 472–475; in milled juice 596–601; *vs.* total protein synthesis 374
– destruction rate, unaffected by invertase inhibitors 375
– –growth relationship, with constant high and low temperatures 389; water and temperature effects 387
– –moisture relationship, affected by GA 415
– mRNA, hormonal stabilization of 365
– precursors, in rate-limiting supply 370, 371

– regulation, by glucose 360; glucose and fructose specificity 380, 381; by glucose and glucose derivatives 372–381; hormonal action mechanism 381–386; mechanism of glucose and sugar-derivative action 378–380; repressor potential *vs.* structural conformation (illustrated) 380; of spatially-distinct forms 371, 372
– regulators, configuration models 376, 377
– synthesis, NAA effects on 375; rate limiting for mRNA 375
– type–distribution relationships, affected by burning and storage factors 586–591

Iodine reaction, for starch 219; in starch phosphorylase assay 210
Isoenzyme(s), sensitivity to nitrogen and light supplies 65, 66
– analysis, esterase and peroxidase 65, 66; in genotype evaluation 65, 66
Isomaltose, synthesis of 228
Isosucrose, chemical synthesis of 228–230; synthesis by hexose condensation 229, 230

Kinetin, effects on invertase synthesis 385, 386

Leaf angle, incident to solar radiation 61
Leaf area, rate of production *vs.* photosynthesis rate 65
Leaf-area index 61
Leaf competition, effects on sucrose transport (illustrated) 321
Leaf rank, differential contribution of sucrose to growth and storage processes 324
Leaf variability, importance of in photosynthesis 139; importance of in sun *vs.* shade conditions 139
Leaf water potential, components of 302
"Levansucrase" 234, 256, 257
Leuconostoc, species of 604
Leuconostoc mesenteroides 574; cause of "sour cane" 603; colonial types of 604, 605; in dextran formation 604, 605, 608; effects on milled juice 603, 604; in milled juice 195, 196; production of "gum" or "slime" in milled juice 604
Light, activating role in sucrose transport 310; effects on sucrose transport 309–314; reception by leaves as a function of leaf geometry 193; required for desiccant action 498; required for desiccant action (illustrated) 512; transport effects in morning *vs.* afternoon 310, 311
– adaptability 133
– compensation point 130–135, 139; definition 131; relation to cell density 131, 132; relation to chlorophyll density 131–133; relation to respiration 131, 132; relation to temperature and CO_2 supply (illustrated) 132; "sun" *vs.* "shade" species 136
– intensity, diurnal changes for sugarcane leaves (illustrated) 191; *vs.* respiration 142, 143
– quality, effects on sucrose transport 310
– regulation, of C_4 pathway enzymes 109
– response curves, convergent in weak light 140; equation for 139
– saturation, age effects on 133, 134; not attained in sugarcane, maize 140, 141; linear phase 131; over a range of light intensities 131; in shade *vs.* sun species 132, 133; sigmoid light curves 131; "sun" *vs.* "shade" species 136; upper limits of intensity 138
– saturation (of photosynthesis) 129; discovery of 130; lack of in sugarcane 181; as a varietal feature 181

Limit dextrin 200, 207
Limiting factors concept, of photosynthesis rate (Blackman) 147, 148
Long-day plants 524
Louisiana canes 54–56

Magnesium deficiency, effects on chlorophyll content 162; effects on CO_2 assimilation 162
Malate, flow of between chloroplast types 119
Malate dehydrogenase 105
Malaysia, geologic transition of 7–9
Maleic hydrazide, as a chemical ripener 448–451; effects on cane enzymes 449–451
Malic acid, as a dark reaction product 96; discovery as initial C_4 pathway product 95; oxidative decarboxylation of 119
Malic enzyme 105, 106, 120, 121; CO_2 generation from malate 119; in CO_2 "shuttle" 105; role in C_4 pathway 106
Malonic acid, effect on 3-PGA formation 97
Manganese, role in Photosystem II 74
Mannitol, in sugar accumulation studies 335
Mass flow, *vs.* active transport 297; development of theory 297–302; along hydrostatic pressure gradient 297
– concept, lack of explanation for sieve plate permeability 298

Maternal (*S. officinarum*) transmission, of somatic chromosome numbers 45–48
Maturation, effects of photoperiod and temperature 434–439; general considerations 397, 398; role of temperature 434–439
Mature storage tissue, sugar storage processes in 405, 406
Maturity, botanical context of 400–402; delay of 397, 398; as a diphasic phenomenon 401, 402; indexes of 402; nitrogen effects 397, 398; as opposed to age and ripening 397
Mechanism of sugar storage, mature stem tissue (illustrated) 405
Meiotic chromosome configurations 45
"Melting pot" concept, in Hawaiian cane breeding 58
Mesophyll chloroplasts 112; complete photosynthetic enzyme complement 117; site of malate, aspartate, 3-PGA appearance 117
Messenger RNA (mRNA), hormonal control of 362, 363; hormonal regulation *vs.* metabolite control 382; stability *vs.* synthesis of in invertase regulation 381; stabilization of by NAA 382
– synthesis, auxin effects on 375, 382
Metasilicate, *see also* Silicate; action on invertase (illustrated) 598, 599; configuration with sucrose, fructose 600, 601; use in "buffering" desiccant action 518, 519
6-Methylpurine, blockage of mRNA synthesis by 382, 383
Michaelis–Menten criteria, in sugar storage process 346
Milled juice, inversion control in 596–601
Miscanthus, chromosome number 40; sugar storage potential of 408
Miscanthus floridulus, in Fiji 24
Moisture–fiber relationship, among *Saccharum* species (illustrated) 409
Moisture index 425, 426; as integrator of internal and external factors 426; limitations of 426
Molasses, ripening with 442, 443
Molybdenum, inhibitor of acid phosphatase 468, 469
Monuron (CMU), as a cane desiccant 492, 493
Morphogenesis, in maize cell cultures 618–621
Mosaic disease, in Louisiana 54, 55
Mosaic resistance, in Louisiana 52
Mountain sugarcane nurseries 53
Movement of ^{14}C, in inner space (stored) sugars (illustrated) 346
Multiple top, illustrated 529

NADP, *see* Nicotinamide adenine dinucleotide phosphate
α-Naphthalene acetic acid (NAA), effects on invertase synthesis (illustrated) 383; invertase stimulation by 366–369
"Narcotic acting substances", theoretical effects on chlorophyll 175
Narenga, chromosome number 40; generic *vs.* specific classification 18
Natal Uba, low amylase activity in 202; starch in 196
Natural hybrids 28
Net CO_2 assimilation, differential species response to light 111; light effects on 109, 111
Net photosynthesis (*P*), equation for estimating 139; single leaf 137; ultimate value for 140; variation among species 140
Neutral invertase 582, 583; inhibition of by kestose 350; inhibition of by Tris 350; localization of in mature storage tissue 349; localization of in parenchyma tissue 266; in mature stalks (*S. officinarum*) 388, 389; role in sugar storage 387, 388; stability of in stored cane 590
Nicotiana tabacum, sucrose synthetase and sucrose-*P* synthetase in 254, 255
Nicotinamide adenine dinucleotide phosphate,
oxidized – ($NADP^+$), electron acceptor in photosynthetic energy conversion 73; reduction by ferredoxin 76, 77
reduced – (NADPH), product of energy conversion reactions 71
– -specific malate dehydrogenase 106, 107
Night flooding, effects on foliar ATPase 415
Nitrate N, in invertase synthesis 370; variable regimes of 371
Nitrogen, deleterious effects on ripening 416; effects of differing sources 417; excessive use of 416; importance of application timing 419; optimal season for application 417; quality repression by 419; ripening effects in *Saccharum* species 420; in sugarcane ripening 416–420; tonnage *vs.* quality effects of increasing 417
– deficiency, CO_2 assimilation effects 164; effects on foliar amylase (illustrated) 320; effects on growth, chlorophylls *a* and *b* 164; effects on sucrose transport 318–320; and foliar sucrose accumulation 175; increased

foliar sucrose content (tabulated) 319; loss of chlorophyll 164; and phosphorus deficiency, effects on photosynthesis rate 164–167; repression of transport rate and velocity (tabulated) 318
– fertilization, effects on cane tonnage and quality (illustrated) 418
– index (NI) 424, 425; relation to moisture and age 425
– metabolism, effects of water deficit on 304
– –quality relationships, in a 2-year crop 418, 419
– regime, effects on sucrose and starch phosphorylase 222, 223
– requirement, as a function of water regime 413
– utilization efficiency, effects of irrigation on 417
Nobilization process 4
"Noble" cane, origin of term 5, 6
Noble canes, origin of 3; properties of 6
Noncyclic photophosphorylation 76, 77; dependence upon water 81; equations 78
Nonpolar transport, of phosphorus in xylem 291
Normal nitrogen index (NN) 424, 425
Northern Caribbean canes, improvement of 52
North Indian canes, classification 18; origin of 12, 13
Nutrient deficiencies, effect on foliar amylase (illustrated) 320; effect on foliar sucrose content (tabulated) 319

Organ culture 611
Organ differentiation, in cell suspension cultures (illustrated) 653; from cultured callus tissue 638–640; role of 2,4-D in 639–642; role of growth media in 639, 640
Organogenesis 638–640; organ and plantlet development (illustrated) 641
Origin of commercial cane hybrids 25–27
Original canes 4, 5
"Original" clones, 25-year performance 59
Ornithine, in cell culture (tabulated) 645
Oryza sativa L., in tissue culture 624
Osmotic *vs.* matrix potentials 302, 303
Outer space 327; acid invertase localized in 351
Oxaloacetic acid, identification of in C_4 pathway 99; possible carboxyl donor 101
Oxidation, of water 74
Oxidative decarboxylation, of malate, as source of reducing power 127
Oxygen, effects on CO_2 compensation point 179; effects on photorespiration and dark respiration 179
– evolution, from H_2O in photochemical reduction process 73; from leaf discs not inhibited by sucrose 177; in Photosystem II 74
– inhibition, of photosynthesis, in Photosystems I and II 179

P700, in Photosystem I 73
Paraquat, apparent *vs.* actual desiccation 503, 504; and appearance of ribose in cane leaves 509–513; and curtailed sucrose-forming potential 507–509; differential effects on foliar hexose–sucrose levels 512; effects on cell suspension cultures 651; effects on sugarcane stand 501; light requirement for phytotoxic action 498; phytotoxic action of 497; properties and mode of action 495–500; quality decline with desiccation 502–504; and quality deterioration 490, 491; as a sugarcane desiccant (tabulated) 493–495; theory of desiccative action 498–500; visual effects of on sugarcane 505–507; yield effects of 500–504
Parenchyma-sheath chloroplasts 112, 113; light-induced absorbance changes (illustrated) with cytochrome *f* 126, 127; partial photosynthetic enzyme complement 117; site of fructose phosphates and ribulose phosphate 117
Passive *vs.* active uptake, of non-electrolytes 328
Passive sugar absorption, cane storage tissue 329, 330
Pedigree, Hawaiian cane varieties 58
– complexity, *H. 49-5* as example 28, 29
Pentose phosphate, replenishment of 88
Performance history, of improved canes 58–60
Permanent wilting point 169
Permeability, of sieve plates 298
Permease, in sugar accumulation 339, 340
Peroxidase, hormonal regulation of 381, 382; increased activity with Diquat 515; mRNA for 382, 383
Peroxisomes, sparcity of in C_4 species 113
3-PGA, *see* 3-Phosphoglyceric acid
pH, effects on sugar storage processes (illustrated) 404
– gradient, a form of potential energy 83
Phenol oxidase, chemical regulation of 125

Phenolic compounds, interference with photosynthetic enzymes 120; release from leaf tissues 120
Phloem, sharing of by discrete compounds 298
Phloem elements, difficulties in study of 296
Phloem exudation, *superfluidity* theory 298
Phloem "loading" 297, 298
Phloem transport, turgor pressure as driving force 299
Phosphatases 96
Phosphoenolpyruvate carboxylase (PEP-carboxylase), higher levels in C_4 plants 121; progressive release of 120; rate of action 104, 109
3-Phosphoglyceric acid (3-PGA), mistaken for phosphomalic acid 95; phosphatase action on 96; reception of ^{14}C from labeled malate and aspartate 98; utilized in two chloroplast types 118–120
Phosphoglyceryl kinase, and potassium deficiency 422
Phosphoglucomutase, in cane storage tissue 264
Phosphohexose isomerase, effects of 2,4-D on 447, 448; effects on maleic hydrazide on 450; and potassium deficiency 422; in potato tubers 260, 261
Phosphohydroxypyruvate, as 3-PGA precursor 106
Phosphoribose isomerase 89, 510, 511; in sugarcane leaves 107
Phosphoribulokinase 107; localization of in C_4 species 112
Phosphorolysis 207
Phosphorus deficiency, effects on foliar amylase (illustrated) 320; effects on starch and total carbohydrates 165; effects on sugar phosphate pools 165; and foliar sucrose accumulation 175; increased foliar sucrose content (tabulated) 319; photosynthesis effects in young *vs.* old plants 167; repression of transport rate and velocity (tabulated) 318
Phosphorylase(s), features of plant and animal types 208; muscle 207, 208; in polyglucoside degradation 208
Phosphorylation, first evidence of in higher plants 231, 232; of hexoses in sugarcane 232; of leaf sugars prior to vein loading 325
Photochemical reduction, scheme for 73
Photon 73
Photoperiod, role in sugarcane flowering 530–535
Photoperiodic classification, of sugarcane 530
Photoperiodicity, lack of in cane ripening 437
"Photoperoxides", theoretical role in photosynthetic enzyme inhibition 175
Photophosphorylation, differential chemical inhibition 79; differential red and far-red effects 79; discrete cyclic and noncyclic reactions 78–83; lack of in isolated cane chloroplasts 124; multiple light reactions 80–82
Photorespiration 93, 113–115, 142, 172–174; apparent lack of in C_4 pathway species 113; CO_2 "burst" in initial postillumination darkness 172, 173; CO_2 postillumination "burst" affected by O_2 179; CO_2 "surge" in darkness 142; complicating effects on CO_2 measurement 172; differences related to divergent enzyme potentials 113; distinct from "dark" respiration 173; greater carbon assimilation in absence of 173; linked with glycolate metabolism 173, 174; low rates of in C_4 species 113; O_2 effects on 172, 173, 179; and O_2 supply 172–173; prior illumination effects 142; theories for lack of 113; theories for lack of in C_4 species 172
Photosynthate, contribution to growth and storage processes 324; sucrose as the principal transient form 284, 285
^{14}C-labeled –, atypical movement in boron-deficient plants 331, 332; differential gradients of in immature leaves 323
Photosynthesis, bipyridylium herbicide effects on 107, 108; comparison of light- and CO_2 assimilation phases 111, 112; diurnal course of with adequate *vs.* inadequate water supply 171; history of summary reaction 69; inhibition by *o*-phenols 125; in isolated chloroplasts 72; light and dark reactions 70; mechanism of light control 112; minimal quantum requirements 84; single-leaf models 137, 138; standardization of conditions 136; in sugarcane, general 93, 94; summary of electron flow pathway 78; summary reaction 69; below wilting point 168
– constituents, release of by differential grinding 120
– control, age and seasonal effects 183–185; CO_2 supply and 180, 181; construction of model for sugarcane 180; in context of growth and development needs 179, 180; feedback *vs.* biochemical models 187; as function of leaf rank 183; irreversible

product repression 187; leaf geometry (shading) effects on 180, 181; light intensity and 180, 181; operation of stomatal aperature 177; product repression in irreversible rate changes 187; removal of shading effects (illustrated) 181; role of sinks 185, 186; in sugarcane 179–193; temperature effects 182; by young leaves 183
– efficiency 124; air temperature effects on (illustrated) 182
– inhibitors, in cane chloroplasts 125
– rate, adjustments of and stomatal resistance 186; atmospheric CO_2 *vs.* bicarbonate CO_2 144–146; Blackman's concept of *limiting factors* 147, 148; cloud effects (in maize) 151; CO_2 absorption as a theoretical function of its atmospheric concentration 149; CO_2 assimilation as a function of the leaf's history 148; CO_2 compensation point 156, 157; CO_2 concentration *vs.* light intensity (illustrated) 151; CO_2 concentration responses as a varietal feature 190; CO_2 conductivity as a species response factor 153; CO_2 diffusion as affected by leaf moisture 155–156; CO_2 diffusion resistance effects 142; CO_2 "fertilization" 151, 152; CO_2 as a limiting factor among species 152–155; CO_2 saturation 148; CO_2 saturation as a function of light intensity 148; CO_2 "tensions" in aqueous solution 145; correlation with leaf thickness and porosity 191; cumulative increase with alternating soil moisture 170; daily course of (illustrated) 169; decline in nutrient-deficient plants 158–167; depressed by high osmotic concentration 192; differential response of leaves as a canopy position effect 150, 151; diurnal changes in 185; divergent varietal responses to light intensity (illustrated) 189; effects of average CO_2 concentration 147; effects of blade portion on 192; effects of CO_2 concentration 146–151; effects of leaf moisture content (tabulated) 193; effects of leaf sucrose on (illustrated) 186; effects of light intensity 130; effect of low light intensity 111; effects of stomatal arrangement and area 153; effects of water supply 167–172; equation describing CO_2 diffusion factors 149; "factor intensities" effect 143; as function of chlorophyll content 143, 144; as function of CO_2 supply 144–158; as function of plant age (illustrated) 184; as function of *Saccharum* species 190, 191; general consideration 129, 130; general effects of nutrient deficiencies 158, 159; history of CO_2 concentration studies 147; importance of dark reaction kinetics 153; insufficiency of normal CO_2 supply 147; interspecific and intraspecific light effects 138; leaf character relationships 190; *vs.* leaf moisture 192; leaf position effect on 150; light saturation of as a varietal feature 190; midday depression and partial recovery with moisture stress 171; midday plateau with adequate water 171; N nutrition effects on 160; N, P, and K deficiency effects in water culture 165; need for continued assimilate translocation 192; need for greater leaf area and improved leaf geometry 193; nocturnal recovery of under water stress 170; O_2 inhibition of 178, 179; optimal temperature for 182; product repression 153, 155, 174–179; product repression with adequate moisture 171, 172; product repression linked with K deficiency 175; product repression of photosynthetic enzymes 175; raising of by clouds and midday shade 170; respiration effects on 129; seasonal effects 64; slowed by water deficit 412; soil moisture effects 169–172; solarization effects 192; and stomata number and length 191; stomatal resistance estimated by measuring moisture loss 149; sucrose repression of 175–178; summer depression of 184, 185; summer depression of (illustrated) 185; temperature effects on 129; theoretical maximum 141; time lag between irrigation and increase 169, 170; varietal effects 189–192
– rate changes, reversibility of in mature leaves 186
– repression, and stomatal resistance 186, 187
Photosynthetic carbon reduction, theories of 84
Photosynthetic efficiency loss, in response to controlled temperature 393
Photosynthetic light reactions (3), schematic representation of 82
Photosynthetic light response, of individual leaves 135–142; for predicting crop yields 139
Photosynthetic light saturation, of maize 148

Photosynthetic phosphorylation, in cell-free preparations, 72; theoretical relation to sucrose transport 159
Photosystem I (Photoact I) 72–74; active in mesophyll and parenchyma-sheath chloroplast types 125; thermogradient 74
Photosystem II (Photoact II) 74, 75; absence of in C_4 species parenchyma-sheath chloroplasts 125; lack of in C_4 species 94; sensitivity to heat, age and light 74
Photosystems I and II, diagram 75
Physiological efficiency concepts 61
Physiological maturity 397
Phytogeologic history, of *Saccharum* 4–15
Plant classification, by CO_2 assimilation system 93
Plantlet initiation, in cultured tissue (illustrated) 641
Plastoquinone, role in chemiosmotic hypothesis 83
Ploidy variants 612
P.O.J. 2878, origin of in Java 28
Polar transport, of sucrose in phloem 291
Polarity, as means of distinguishing between phloem and xylem solutes 292
Pollen fertility, and temperature 536, 537, 541, 543
Polyglucoside branching 217, 218
Polyhydric alcohols, effects on acid invertase 373
Polynesian canes 23, 24
Polysaccharide(s), in milled juice 195, 196; pullulan in *S. officinarum* 197, 198; types in sugarcane 195, 196; in water-deficient plants 411; water soluble 198
– breakdown, diurnal and nocturnal 221
– formation and degradation, schematic representation of 220
– synthesis, effects of N, P, and K treatments 221; effects of water, N, P, and K supply 221–223; theory of competition with sucrose-forming reactions 221
Polyteny 623
Porosity, of sugarcane leaves, diurnal changes (illustrated) 191
Postharvest deterioration, after-ripening 575, 576; burned cut *vs.* burned standing cane 579; control of by sprinkling 595, 596; "ferments" 574; of frozen cane 580; historical 574–576; inversion conception of 575, 576; inversion control methods 575, 576; inversion control in milled juice with metasilicate 599; inversion as a function of variety, moisture, temperature, condition of cane 591–595; inversion gradients 594; and invertase inhibitor substance 594; magnitude of sugar losses 580; and maturity 595; of milled juice 596–601; and milling delay 575; and moisture 574, 575; and moisture loss 592, 593; moisture–temperature relationship 593, 594; nature and magnitude of 574–582; purity, moisture, and sucrose gradients in harvested stalks 585; role of environment 577–579; role of invertases 582–596; stability of neutral invertase 590; sucrose production *vs.* sucrose recovery (illustrated) 581; sun *vs.* shade storage 582; in top, center, and bottom of stalks (illustrated) 584; wet *vs.* dry storage (illustrated) 578
Postharvest inversion, possible mechanism of 346
Postharvest quality decline, two types 573
Postmeiotic endomitosis 46
Potassium, biochemical roles of 421, 422; role in sugar transport 421; in sugarcane ripening 420–422
– deficiency, effect on basipetal sucrose transport 161, 162; effects on foliar amylase (illustrated) 320; effect on invertase 233; effect on photosynthesis rate 161; and foliar sucrose accumulation 175; increased foliar sucrose content (tabulated) 319; and loss of cane quality 318, 319; and poor cane quality 416, 419, 420; producing reversible changes in photosynthesis rate 186; repression of transport rate and velocity (tabulated) 318
– fertilization, effects on tissue moisture content 427
– index 420, 426–430; definition of 427; relation to sheath moisture 428, 429
– $-H_2O$ index 426–430
– /nitrogen ratio, and cane quality 318, 319
– partition index 427
Potato tubers, sucrose synthetase and sucrose-*P* synthetase in 253, 254
P.R. 980, development and pedigree 53, 54
Primary index 423, 424; definition 423; plant production and local sunlight potential 424
Primula obconica 296
Product repression 174–179, 316; end-product accumulation and utilization 174, 175; feedback reactions 174, 175; as function of xylem sugar contents 177, 178; general aspects of 174, 175; and moisture stress 187;

by O_2 178; O_2 effects unrelated to light intensity, CO_2 supply 178; by O_2 in higher land plants 178; O_2 repression of photosynthesis 172; of photosynthetic enzymes 175; sucrose effects on photosynthesis 175–178

Pseudomonas saccharophila 226

Pullulanase 197

Pulse-chase experiments, with C_4 pathway 107

Putrescine, metabolic relationships to arginine (schematic) 650

Pyranose ring configuration, role of in invertase regulation 379, 380

Pyrophosphorylase, in synthesis of UDPG from UTP and glucose-1-*P* 241

Pyruvate, theoretical non-diversion of in C_4 species 113

Pyruvate kinase, increased by potassium deficiency 422

Pyruvate, P_i dikinase, light sensitivity of 103, 109; localization of in C_4 species 112; properties of 102; role in C_4 species 102, 103

Pyruvic carboxylase 104, 105

Q enzyme, in cane leaf preparations 211, 212, 218; distribution of in cane tissues (illustrated) 219; mode of action 218; from potato 218; preparation methods 218, 219; properties of 218, 219

Qualitative character improvement 51, 52

Quality inheritance, genetic *vs.* environmental and physiological factors 62

Quantitative inheritance 49, 50

Quaternary ammonium herbicides, historical 495, 496

Radiation flux density, measurement among species 138, 139

Raffinose, possible transient form of sucrose 284

Reducing sugar(s), content, variable illumination effects (illustrated) 313; diurnal–nocturnal fluctuations of (illustrated) 313; transport of to roots 227

Reductive pentose phosphate cycle 85–91; carboxylation phase 86, 87; history of 70; reductive phase 87, 88; regenerative phase 88–91; similarities between reductive phase and glycolysis 87, 88

Regional sugarcane improvement 51–60

Regional variety classifications 26, 27

Respiration, in conducting phloem 299; effects of water deficit 304, 305

Ribose, appearance of in desiccated leaf tissue (illustrated) 516–512

Ribose 5-phosphatase 107, 511

Ribose 5-phosphate, conversion to ribulose 5-phosphate 89

Ribulose diphosphate 510; as C-4 carboxyl group acceptor 107, 108

Ribulose diphosphate carboxylase (RuDP-carboxylase), extraction difficulty 119; higher levels in Calvin-cycle plants 121; intensitivity to light 109, 111; localization of in C_4 species 112; possible localization in one chloroplast type 119; rate of action 104

Ripener activity, empirical *vs.* physiological measures of 484

Ripener screening, regional methods of 485–487

"Ripeness-to-flower", in *Saccharum* spp. 543

Ripening, artificial 442–448; early cultural 442; endogenous control mechanism 400; general considerations 397, 398; of green-leaf and leafless joints 401; increased by long-term moisture stress 309; moisture roles in 410–415; as a physiological senescence 398; phytotron studies in Queensland 435–439; quality improvement with chemicals 441; role of temperature 434–439; theory of 398–400; by with-holding moisture 305

– control, crop logging 422–434; by crop logging (illustrated) 430; example of crop log in practice 430–432

Root chilling, effects on ^{32}P uptake and transport 316, 317

Saccharininae 14, 15; evolution pathway 41

Saccharophiles, *vs.* amylophiles 227

"Saccharose D" 229

Saccharum, basic chromosome number(s) 40, 634; distinction from *Erianthus* 18

– complex 408; distinguishing features 16; distribution 17

– crosses, × *Bambusa* 30, 31; with *Erianthus*, *Imperata*, and *Zea* 32, 33; lack of Mendelian segregation 31; lack of synapsis 31; × *Narenga* 33; × *Sorghum* 29, 30

– evolution, in discrete centers 10; role of primitive man 10

– fertility, discovery of 4

– genome, lack of wild germplasm 42

– genome analysis 41, 42

– improvement, new methods of 42

– migrations 10–12
– movement, to western hemisphere 11
– speciation 18–20
– species, barriers between 6, 7; common gene pool 14; conditions preventing distinction 7; difficulty in systematizing 14; male *vs.* female gametic contribution 19, 20; sugar storage potential of 407–410
Saccharum barberi, origin of 13, 14, 18
Saccharum edule, features and classification 19; possible backcross form 38; use in Fiji 24
Saccharum officinarum, backcross with *Sclerostachya* 40; chromosome exchange with *S. spontaneum* 49; cross with *Erianthus procerus* 48; cytogenetic origin 40; hybridization of 6; as a "horticultural" species 5; as intensively selected strains rather than a species 369; introgression with *Miscanthus* 6
Saccharum robustum, distinguishing features 13; distribution 13; features contributed to *S. officinarum* 24; in *H. 37-1933* genotype 47; habitat 22; in Hawaiian cane breeding 56, 57; hybridization of 19; features and growth habit 22; × *Miscanthus* crosses 38, 39; use in breeding programs 46; as wild ancestor of *S. officinarum* 19
Saccharum sinense, origin of 13, 14
Saccharum spontaneum, centers of diversity 22, 23; features and growth habit 23; pausity of in modern genotypes 59, 60; mobilization of 46
Saturating light intensity 130–135; as a varietal feature 192
Sclerostachya, chromosome number 40
Second maturation phase, N, K, and moisture effects 402
Sedoheptulose 7-phosphate 88
"Seedling canes" 27
Selection pressure, concept, for *S. officinarum* evolution 407–409; for sucrose in *Saccharum* evolution 63
Self-defoliation, breeding for 322
"Short-day plants" 524; interpretation of sugarcane 531
Sieve plate resistances, calculation of 298
Sieve tube(s), hypothetical structure and internal movement (illustrated) 301; turgor pressure of 296
Silicate, *see also* Metasilicate; "buffering" effects against chemical desiccation 475; "buffering" effects against metabolic changes 474, 475; effects on cane quality 473; in invertase and amylase control 473–475
Sink(s), failure of aged leaves to act as 322; sugar content effects on photosynthesis 185, 186
Soil moisture, effects on photosynthesis rate 169–171
Solar energy, conversion to chemical energy, summary reactions 71; illustrated use of in growth processes *vs.* dry matter production 123; inefficient use of 122–124
Solarization 136; relation to CO_2 supply, lack of assimilate transport 192
Somatic metaphase, illustrated (*S. officinarum* × *Erianthus procerus*) 48
Somatic mutations, in cultured cell senescence 624
Sour cane 574
"Sour storage rot" 607
Source and sink conceptions, in cane breeding 62, 63
Source-to-sink system, *Saccharum* evolution of 60
"Sport" sugarcanes 26
Stale cane 574
Stalk log 433
Starch(es), believed primary photosynthate 195; conception of transitory *vs.* storage forms 214; distribution among *Saccharum* species 196; diurnal variation of in leaves (illustrated) 199; evidence of foliar starch in *S. officinarum* 202; foliar, confined to grana-free (bundle-sheath) chloroplasts 202; foliar, temporary hexose storage 199; fractional precipitation of 197; insoluble photosynthate 320; iodine test for in chloroplasts 202; lack of in cane storage tissue 336; localized in parenchyma-sheath cells 196; in perspective 196–206; physiological role of 198; predominance in "wild" *Saccharum* species 196, 197; removal from crude juice 196, 197; role in germination 198; role in storage tissue 198; in *S. barberi* 196; in *S. sinense* 196; in *S. spontaneum* 196; in sugarcane leaves 198–202; theory of condensation from hexose 200; theory of instantaneous hydrolysis 202; transmission as a discrete inheritable factor 37
conversion, nocturnal, to sucrose 204, 205; to sucrose in wilting leaves 230; theory of

to "cane sugar" 200, 201
– degradation, essential enzymology 209, 210
– grains, in bundle-sheath chloroplasts (illustrated) 203; from *Saccharum* species storage tissue (illustrated) 197
– –sucrose interconversion 320, 321, 514; correct spatial distribution of essential enzymes for 204; enzymology of 201; present conceptions (illustrated) 201; thermodynamic balance of 201
– synthesis, from carbonic acid and water 195; competition with sucrose synthesis 202; effects of FAD additive 217; mechanisms of synthesis 206–210; mediation of synthesis by amylase 206; relative effectiveness of UDPG and ADPG in (illustrated) 247; with UDPG as substrate 215; with UTP, with UDP + ATP 216; *in vivo vs. in vitro* considerations 216, 217

Starch phosphorylase 206–208, 257; activation of 213, assay for 210; in cane leaves 210; dialysis inhibition 212; distribution of 213; effects of inorganic phosphorus 222; evidence of two enzymes 211; fractional precipitation of (illustrated) 211; negative correlation with sucrose production 221, 222; from pea and potato 207; preparation of 210; reaction, illustrated 207; reaction, theoretical equilibrium in cane leaves 207; *vs.* sucrose, in *Uba Marot, M. 336* 222, 223; time course of reaction (illustrated) 212

Starch synthetase (UDPG–, ADPG–starch transglucosylase) 208–210; evidence of in cane leaves 214–217; reaction, equation for 208; utilization of UDPG *vs.* ADPG 208, 209

Steady-state photosynthesis 91

Stomata, as "hydrostats" 156

Stomatal opening, control, use of chemical inhibitors 156; effects of CO_2 concentration 150; light and water relationships 149, 150

Stomatal resistance 142; and low-temperature shock 187

Stomatal width, of sugarcane leaves, diurnal changes (illustrated) 191

Storage sucrose, asymmetric labeling of 343; maintained by active storage processes 329; multiple pools of 342

Storage sugar, leakage of 334

Storage tissue slices, as model of *in vivo* storage sink 333

"Sucrase", as a transferase 234

Sucrose, as a by-product of aging (theory of) 228; cleavage by sucrose synthetase 270; diffusive movement along cell walls 353; diurnal variation of in leaves (illustrated) 199; importance of 225; metabolism of in transit 296; octamethyl form of 229; as a primary photosynthate 225, 227, 228; principal transient carbohydrate 200; as principal transient sugar 225; production *vs.* recovery in the factory (illustrated) 581; relationship with starch phosphorylase 200; repression of photosynthesis 175, 176; role of in water phase of cell walls 353; as a secondary photosynthate 227; *vs.* starch, sucrose having higher priority in cane 221, 222; in storage cell walls, role of 282; temperature × variety effects 317; and vigor, inheritance of 50
– absorption, direct absorption of sucrose 328, 329; lack of direct absorption system 329, 330
– accumulation, efflux rate, unaffected by sucrose 342; evidence for alternate pathway 346, 347; profile (illustrated) 399; rate-limiting step 346, 347; role of cell wall sugar 406, 407; role of in *Saccharum* evolution 63; schematic representation for cane storage tissue 270; sucrose rapidly remobilized for growth 342; theory of via sucrose-*P*, without prior hydrolysis 355
– ascension, in the cane stalk, via xylem tissue 282; through stalk to spindle and meristem 281
– biosynthesis, context of 225, 226; with detached blades in glucose solution 231; effects of P deficiency on 232; empirical demonstration of 230, 231; historical aspects 225–233; by invertase in presence of H_3PO_4 232; mediation by invertase 233, 234; nucleoside specificity for 246–249; phosphorylation of precursors in cane 232
– control, with chemicals 467–475; with phosphatase inhibitors 468–470
– –starch interconversion 200, 256–261; effects of temperature, glucose-6-*P* 257; historical aspects 256, 257; operation of invertase 201; roles of UDPG and ADPG in 248; in storage organs 257
– –starch interrelationships, schematic representation of 220
– storage, against concentration gradient 327; effects of constantly high and low temperatures 317; process, summary of

356, 357; role of sucrose-*P* 354, 355
– structure 236; confirmed by periodic acid oxidation 229
– synthesis, believed favored by water deficit 168; biological synthesis 230, 231; in cane storage tissue 264–270; by chemical means 228–230; by condensation 228, 229; effects of constantly high and low temperatures 317; enzymic synthesis 241–245; equal labeling of hexose moieties 245; *vs.* hydrolysis, in potato tuber 259, 260; lack of in inner space 344; low synthesis in isolated chloroplasts 205; scheme for synthesis from phosphorylated intermediates 239; in sugarcane leaves 261–264; in sugarcane leaves, historical 261–263; UDPG-transglycosylase mechanisms in 238–249
– synthesis reactions, in germinating rice seeds 255, 256; differential inhibition by ADP 254; localization of in plant tissues 254–256; sugar nucleotide effects on (illustrated) 253; temperature effects 254
– transport, acropetal 291; affected by lalas, suckers 324; basal accumulation in detached blades 289, 290; basipetal 289–291; in the cane stalk, via cell walls 282; in the cane stalk, via plasmodesmata 282; competing streams effect on older leaves 278; in darkness, related to diurnal sampling period 292; in detached leaves 289–293; difficulty in exiting from leaf 322; dilution effects on labeled photosynthate 283; distribution after 5 hours 283; distribution after 6 weeks 283; distribution within the plant (tabulated) 282; diurnal–nocturnal content of leaf and storage tissue (illustrated) 312; downward flow and partial ascension (illustrated) 281; effects of ATP on 311; effects of dark treatments (illustrated) 291; effects of light on 309–314; effects of nitrogen deficiency on 284; effects of stool complex on 323, 324; effect of veinal spreading on 279, 280; effects of water stress on 302–309, 305–307; effects of wind and mechanical injury 322, 323; as a function of leaf age 277, 278; in germinating rice seeds 255, 256; hexose conversion to sucrose in transit 278, 279; increased time requirement with increasing age 289; independence from leaf geometry, stalk attachment 291; initial accumulation in nodes 281; initial descent within the stalk 281; initial movement of ^{14}C in leaf tissue 276–279; integrity of transient molecule 278; intercellular leakage 290; interconversion of ^{14}C-labeled hexoses 278; lack of common ^{14}C carrier molecule in sugarcane 279; to lalas and suckers 288; lateral (between leaf veins) 277; lateral movement within the stalk 281, 282; leaf competition effects 321, 322; light saturation of 311; as the limiting factor in cane photosynthesis 323; under low light intensity 325; mass flow in sugarcane 325; mechanisms for downward *vs.* upward 315, 316; mechanism of driving force 293; mechanism of nutrient deficiency action on 319, 320; to metabolic sink 282, 283; movement in lamina *vs.* midrib 279, 280; movement in leaf lamina tissue (illustrated) 277; movement from leaf sheath to stalk 279, 280; movement within the stalk 280–284; movement toward stalk center 280; multiple gradients in 300; nutrient deficiency effects on 318–321; nocturnal transport 209; to oldest joints 287; pathway in leaf blade and sheath (illustrated) 279; photochemical control of (theory) 311; photosynthetic ATP a major source of driving force 324, 325; photosynthetic ATP as source of driving force (theory) 311, 312; polarity of 291, 292; position effect within the blade 277; profile, temperature effects on (illustrated) 315; Q_{10} values for 315; rate of 285–288; related to growth status 283; in relation to site of ^{14}C incorporation 279; repression by cool air and root temperatures (illustrated) 316; role of blade apex in creating driving force 290; root- and air-temperature effects on 314, 315; to roots and external medium 281; specialized source and sink areas in cane 324, 325; among stalks of a single stool 288, 289; in suckers, using phloem tissue 288; sucrose transported annually, empirical estimates for 1970 273; in sugarcane leaf midrib (illustrated) 278; studies in Australia 278, 279; temperature effects 314–317; temperature × light intensity effects 316; theories of active and passive movement 276; theory of a sucrose derivative 284; unaffected by transpiration of surrounding leaves 322; unilateral flow of ^{14}C 280; value of detached blades in the study of 289; veinal loading 276, 277; water requirements 168; young

stalk and sucker contribution to sugar-utilizing areas 288
– transport mechanism, additional research requirements 325, 326; sieve plate resistance an unsolved problem 326; in sugarcane 324–326
– transport pathways, general considerations 273; outline of in sugarcane 273, 274; segmentation of conducting tissues 275
– transport *velocity 277*, 285–288; velocity of movement through entire stool 323; measured in Hawaii and Australia 285; relation to $^{14}CO_2$ exposure time, dosage 285
– -type reactions, in milled juice 601
– uptake, inversion of in the outer space 352; paralleling outer space invertase activity 352
Sucrose kinase, absence of in cane tissue 270
Sucrose octaacetate 229, 230
Sucrose phosphatase 96, 252; inhibition of by sucrose 176, 177
Sucrose phosphate 240; enzymic synthesis of 241–245; evidence for participation in sucrose accumulation 354, 355; hydrolysis of 242; as an intermediate in sugar accumulation 354; in mature storage tissue reactions 405; position of phosphate group 243; restricted movement into metabolic compartment 354, 355; role in sucrose storage without invertase mediation 270; role in sugar accumulation (illustrated) 355; synthesis of 242; synthesis and role of 269, 270; synthesis, significant role of in sugar accumulation 269, 270; synthesis of by storage tissue preparations 348, 349; traces of in sugarcane reaction media 264
Sucrose phosphate phosphatase 264; inhibition of by EDTA 354
Sucrose phosphate synthetase 248–256; discovery of 242; evidence of in cane storage tissue 264; evidence of in storage tissue 348, 349; extraction, purification, properties 253–254; extraction from sugarcane leaf and storage tissues 269, 270; in isolated sugarcane chloroplasts 263, 264; isolation problems, properties of 252, 253; in leaf preparations, improved assay 354; in pea, bean and broad bean 251; preparation of, from sugarcane chloroplasts 263, 264; properties and reaction conditions 242, 243; purification of 251, 252; in storage tissue 354
Sucrose phosphorylase 225, 226, 234–238; absence of in cane leaf and storage tissue 264; absence of in sugar accumulation cycle 348; in cane leaves 261, 262; discovery of in *Pseudomonas* 235; equilibrium constant 236; equilibrium constant in cane leaves 261; mode of action (illustrated) 236; properties and mode of action 236–238; reaction, distinct from starch phosphorylase 237, 238; reaction equation 235, 261; reaction, role of phosphate 237; in sucrose absorption 329
Sucrose synthetase (UDPG–fructose transglycosylase) 249–256; absence in *S. spontaneum* var. *Mandalay* 265, 266; apparent absence in cane leaves 242; in cane storage tissue 264–266; in cane storage tissue, properties of 264, 266; discovery of 241, 242; discovery in sugarcane 263, 264; distribution in *Saccharum* forms 265, 266; early evidence of 250; effects of borate on 246; effects of Mn^{2+} and mercaptoethanol 259; effects of nucleoside diphosphate sugars 248; effects of phenols and *p*-benzoquinone 267–269; effects of protein inhibitors on 259; evidence of in sugarcane leaf preparations 262, 263; extraction, purification and properties 253, 254; inhibition by intermediate quinones 268; inhibition of, mode of inhibitor action 269; inhibition of, partial reversal with 2-mercaptoethanol 269; inhibition by phenol oxidation products 267–269, 349; inhibition by pyrophosphate 266; in isolated sugarcane chloroplasts 263, 264; *K* values for 242; label distribution in product moieties 266; localized in vascular strands 349; localized in vascular tissue 266, 267; low-temperature induction of 259; loss of by action of phenol oxidation products 267; Mg^{2+} requirement for 266; in pea, bean and broad bean 251; plant tissue sources 242; possible function in sieve tubes 267; reactions illustrated 241, 242; specificity for UDPG as glucose donor 241; stabilization by cysteine or DIECA in extracting media 267; and starch formation 257, 258; stimulated by Mg^{2+} 244; in storage tissue 348; substitution of D-fructose with D-xylulose, D-rhamnulose, and L-sorbose 243; in sugarcane leaves, borate effects on 262; in sugarcane leaves, FAD effects on 262, 263; in sugarcane, properties

and distribution 263, 264; sulfhydryl enzyme 349; suppression by thio inhibitors 268, 269; temperature, variety, maturity effects 258–261
Sugar(s), effects on acid invertase 373; enzyme regulation by and hormones 360–365
– absorption, active entry into inner space 333, 334; anaerobic inhibition shown reversible 334; anaerobic restriction of 329, 334; anaerobic restriction of second (active) stage 334; hexoses more rapid than sucrose 335; lack of starch accumulation 336; by mature and immature storage tissue 333, 334; movement and fate of sugars in immature storage tissue 335, 336; passive entry into outer space 333; relative rates for sucrose, glucose (illustrated) 335; sucrose repression of glucose 335; in two stages (illustrated) 334; two-stage process 333, 334
– accumulation, "activation" of sucrose (sucrose–X) 343; active, evidence of sucrose derivative 341, 342; bathing tissue technique 332, 333; against concentration gradient 332–340; against concentration gradient, free energy change involved 344; concept, elaboration by Glasziou 341–347; for 404; evidence of cyclic reactions 341; evidence against a rate-limiting carrier 344; evolutionary selection pressure for (hypothetical) 407–409; four-stage sequence (illustrated) 344; fructose and glucose in the inner space 344–347; greater rate of in young storage tissue 341; hexose interconversion in cytoplasm 343; inhibitor effects 336, 337; initial work with tissue slices 332, 333; inner space hexoses as inversion products 345; inner space sugars in steady-state condition 345; insensitive to phloridzin 337; label movement from sucrose (inner space) pool 345; maturity effects 336; mechanism, in mature storage tissue 402–407; mechanism for storage of "activated" sucrose 339; membrane permeability unaffected by inhibitors 337; multiple enzyme-like reactions 339; multiple outer space pools for sucrose 342; net concentration changes in the inner space 342; permease step hypothesized 339, 340; respiration increases 336; steady-state sequence for loss of sucrose (illustrated) 345; storage sugar loss via respiration 336; sucrose-*P* 343; sucrose principal stored sugar 345; sucrose as source of glucose and fructose 342; sucrose storage in vacuole 343; theoretical maximum 408, 409; theorized storage of hexose 345
– accumulation cycle 327, 348–355, 621; enzymology of 264–267, 348–350; inner space 351; metabolic compartment 351; origin of 4; outer space 351; role of invertase 351–354; role of sucrose phosphate 354, 355; schematic representation of 353; summary of 356, 357
– accumulation kinetics 337–340; catalytic nature of receptor 338, 339; diffusion phase not rate limiting 338; evidence for enzyme-like reaction governing absorption rate 339; hyperbolic relationship of external concentration to rate of accumulation 337, 338; initial lack of sugar interconversion 337; K_m for sucrose, glucose, fructose 338; rate variation as a function of sugar concentration (Lineweaver–Burk plot of) 338; sugar interconversion following rate-limiting step 337; transitory sugar–receptor complex 338
– accumulation potential, in *Saccharum* species 407–410
– accumulation process, as developed by Bieleski (illustrated) 339
– derivatives, effects on acid invertase 373
– efflux, governed by vacuolar invertase 392, 393; from outer space, as a diffusion process (illustrated) 347; from storage vacuole, as a diffusion process (illustrated) 347
– interconversion and sugar accumulation pathway (illustrated) 347
– storage, general considerations 327; mechanism of in mature stalk tissue (illustrated) 405; and sugar transformation, criteria of 343, 344
Sugar phosphates, first evidence of in sugar synthesis 232; in sugar interconversion reactions 231–233
"Sugarcane", *vs.* "canebrake" 21
Sugarcane,
– chloroplasts, electron transport in 124
– growth, role of extended growing season 64, 65
– leaves, reflection of solar radiation by 123; chlorophyll content in, gradients 134
– photosynthesis, in detached blades 137; response to artificial light (illustrated) 141; seasonal effects on 134; temperature effects on 134

– ripening, and nitrogen management 416–420; and potassium management 420–422
– storage tissue, cross-section and 3-dimensional view of stalk (illustrated) 330
– topping 519–522
"Sun" *vs.* "shade" plants 136
Superfluidity, theory of ordered molecular state 298

Tassel emergence 525; prevented by low temperature 536, 537
Tasseling control, by withholding irrigation (illustrated) 552
Taxonomy, of chromosome transmission 47
Temperature, constant, and cane growth (illustrated) 437; cool night temperature and cane quality 435; daily *vs.* seasonal in cane ripening 435, 436; day and night effects on ripening (illustrated) 436; effects on sucrose transport profile (illustrated) 315; high- and low-temperature effects on sucrose 317; lack of diurnal or short-term effects on ripening 439; long-term effects on sucrose content (illustrated) 438
Theories,
– of assimilate movement 295–302
– of solute uptake 328–332
– of sugar and hormonal enzyme regulation 360–365
Thiobacillus denitrificans, reductive pentose phosphate cycle in 70
Tissue culture, amino acid requirements 626–628; areas of importance for sugarcane scientists 625; arginine in 630; atypical polyploidy levels 622; carbohydrate sources for 628, 629; cell "organizers" and "disorganizers" 623; "chemically-defined" media 620; cytological and chromosomal aberrations 621, 622; definition 611; development of a suitable medium 625–628; fundamentals developed with virus-induced tumors 613–616; "giant cells" 622; limitations of 612, 613; means of ploidy change (hypothetical) 622, 623; as means of sugar production from starch 629; morphogenesis in monocot cultures 617–624; morphological changes in maize tissue 621; "mosaic plants" in 631, 642; N and P requirements of growth media 613, 614; organ differentiation in 638–643; plantlet initiation 617; polyploidy in cane cell suspensions 633–638; regulatory factors 613–616; role of Hawaiian workers 612; search for artificial growth media 612; shoot and root regeneration 633; starch as a sugar substitute 628, 629; studies with *Rumex* tumors 613, 614; totipotency control 632, 633; totipotency control and polyploidy in 630–638; variable chromosome numbers in cell suspension cultures (illustrated) 635, 636; White's medium 613, 619, 625, 639
Tissue indexes 402; as integrators of climate, moisture, and nutritional factors 422
Tissue slices, accurate model of intact storage conditions 336
Top visible dewlap (T.V.D.) 429
Topping, early *vs.* late varieties 522; "high" *vs.* "low" systems (illustrated) 520; to minimize varietal yield differences 521, 522
Totipotency, definition 612; demonstration of in cell cultures 617, 618; loss of 623, 624
Traces, effect on sucrose transport 280, 281
Transaminase, in sugarcane leaves 109
Transcarboxylase activity, search for 106, 107
Transcellular strands, illustrated 301
Transcellular streaming 296, 297; velocity of 297
Transcription, of enzyme structural codes 365
Transient sucrose, hydrolysis of upon entering storage parenchyma 284
Transient sugars (stachyose, raffinose, verbascose) 284
Transketolase 89, 510
Translocation, age effects 298; assimilate forms in 298; Canny's theory of 300–302; carbohydrate gradient as a fluid hydrostatic gradient 298; carbohydrate gradients, seasonal effects on 299; energy expenditure in 299; low-temperature effects on 314; multiple sucrose gradients in 300; nitrogen deficiency effects 298; requirement of sink 298; Spanner's theory of 299; summary of key features 296; Thaine's theory of 296, 297
– gradient(s), role of sink in 300–302; slope of as a function of sucrose utilization 302
– driving force, along entire length of detached blade 293
– profile 286–288, 296; illustrated 287
– system, summary of operational theory 300–302
Transpiration rate, affected by CO_2 concentration 150

Transpirational water, pathway of, from xylem to leaf surface 303
Transport pathways, features of in tropical grasses 273
Transport rate, from $^{14}CO_2$-exposed leaf segment 285; estimates of for sugarcane source–sink pathway 286; relation to leaf rank, climate, edaphic factors 285; schematic illustration of 286
Transport polarity, reversal of in darkness 292, 293
Trash, losses accruing from 489
Trehalase, possible role in hexose movement from storage vacuole 353; in sugarcane storage tissue 352, 353
Trehalose phosphate 241
Tris–HCl buffer, inhibition of invertase by 266
Troboeg, name for *S. edule* 19
Tryptophanase 360
Tubular strands, across sieve plates 296, 297
Tungsten, inhibitor of acid phosphatase 468, 469
Turgor pressure, as transport driving force 299

Uridine diphosphate galactose (UDP-galactose) 239, 240
Uridine diphosphate glucose (UDPG), *vs.* ADPG as starch synthetase substrates 258; appearance of on photosynthetic product radiograms 239; compounds analogous to 239; discovery of 238; as an enzyme cofactor 238; enzymic synthesis of 245, 246; formation from glucose-1-*P* plus UDP and ATP 240; formation from glucose-1-*P* plus UTP 240; in galactowaldenase reaction 238; implication of in sucrose biosynthesis 238–241; in sucrose-*P* synthesis 245; synthesis of in sugar beet leaves 240
Uridine diphosphate glucose pyrophosphorylase (UDPG pyrophosphorylase), effects of borate on 246; in cane storage tissue 264, 349
Uridine diphosphate phosphatase (UDP phosphatase) 270

Vacuolar invertase, diurnal fluctuation of 393
Variety(ies), effects on sugar and enzyme responses to temperature 317; *H. 37-1933*, soil moisture effects on photosynthesis 169
– differences, sucrose *vs.* starch, enzyme basis of 223
– nomenclature, historical 25, 26
Vegetative index 418
Veinal loading, of ^{32}P 297
Vellai, history of (*Otaheite*, *Bourbon*, *Caña Blanca*) 35

Wallace's Line 5, 9
"Warburg effect" 178
Water, and cane ripening 168, 169; roles of in cane ripening 410–415
– deficiency, effects on juice expression 411; growth restriction *vs.* photosynthesis restriction 411, 412
– deficit, effects on cell cultures 304; effects on life processes 302; effects on respiration 304, 305; effects on transport rate 412; as a means to ripen cane 305
– movement, via cell walls 303
– –nitrogen relationships 413
– stress, biochemical aspects of 304, 305; context of in higher plants 302–304; effects on internode expansion 307; effects on sucrose translocation 305–307; effects on sucrose transport (illustrated) 306; effects on sucrose transport profile (illustrated) 308; effects on transport velocity 307; growth restriction greater than sucrose synthesis restriction 309; initial effects on photosynthate movement 306, 307; lack of parameters for 302; long-term effects on sucrose storage 309; producing atypical sucrose accumulations 307; short-term effects on sucrose storage 307–309; slower transport theoretically increases time for sugar storage 309
– stress–time relationships, as affecting sucrose transport (illustrated) 308
– supply, similar symptoms for excessive and deficient 414, 415
– tension, effects on water absorption rate 307
Whole chromosome retention and elimination 49
Wild sugarcanes, centers of diversity 21, 22; early expeditions for 20, 21; geographic distribution 21–23; in western hemisphere 21
Wind injury, and loss of transport driving force 323; simulated on cane leaves 322, 323

Xylem transport, of ^{32}P, nonpolar 292
Xylulose 5-phosphate 513; conversion to ribulose 5-phosphate 90